THE THEORY AND PRACTICE
OF COMPILER WRITING

McGraw-Hill Computer Science Series

Ahuja: *Design and Analysis of Computer Communication Networks*

Barbacci and Siewiorek: *The Design and Analysis of Instruction Set Processors*

Ceri and Pelagatti: *Distributed Databases: Principles and Systems*

Debry: *Communicating with Display Terminals*

Donovan: *Systems Programming*

Filman and Friedman: *Coordinated Computing: Tools and Techniques for Distributed Software*

Givone: *Introduction to Switching Circuit Theory*

Goodman and Hedetniemi: *Introduction to the Design and Analysis of Algorithms*

Katzan: *Microprogramming Primer*

Keller: *A First Course in Computer Programming Using Pascal*

Kohavi: *Switching and Finite Automata Theory*

Liu: *Elements of Discrete Mathematics*

Liu: *Introduction to Combinatorial Mathematics*

MacEwen: *Introduction to Computer Systems: Using the PDP-11 and Pascal*

Madnick and Donovan: *Operating Systems*

Manna: *Mathematical Theory of Computation*

Newman and Sproull: *Principles of Interactive Computer Graphics*

Payne: *Introduction to Simulation: Programming Techniques and Methods of Analysis*

Révész: *Introduction to Formal Languages*

Rice: *Matrix Computations and Mathematical Software*

Salton and McGill: *Introduction to Modern Information Retrieval*

Shooman: *Software Engineering: Design, Reliability, and Management*

Tremblay and Bunt: *An Introduction to Computer Science: An Algorithmic Approach*

Tremblay and Bunt: *An Introduction to Computer Science: An Algorithmic Approach, Short Edition*

Tremblay and Manohar: *Discrete Mathematical Structures with Applications to Computer Science*

Tremblay and Sorenson: *An Introduction to Data Structures with Applications*

Tremblay and Sorenson: *The Theory and Practice of Compiler Writing*

Tucker: *Programming Languages*

Wiederhold: *Database Design*

Wulf, Levin, and Harbison: *Hydra/C. mmp: An Experimental Computer System*

McGraw-Hill Series in Computer Organization and Architecture

Bell and Newell: *Computer Structures: Readings and Examples*
Cavanagh: *Digital Computer Arithmetic: Design and Implementation*
Gear: *Computer Organization and Programming: With an Emphasis on Personal Computers*
Hamacher, Vranesic, and Zaky: *Computer Organization*
Hayes: *Computer Architecture and Organization*
Hayes: *Digital System Design and Microprocessors*
Hwang and Briggs: *Computer Architecture and Parallel Processing*
Kogge: *The Architecture of Pipelined Computers*
Siewiorek, Bell, and Newell: *Computer Structures: Principles and Examples*
Stone: *Introduction to Computer Organization and Data Structures*
Stone and Siewiorek: *Introduction to Computer Organization and Data Structures: PDP-11 Edition*

THE THEORY AND PRACTICE OF COMPILER WRITING

Jean-Paul Tremblay
Paul G. Sorenson

Department of Computational Science
University of Saskatchewan, Saskatoon
Canada

McGraw-Hill Book Company

New York   St. Louis   San Francisco   Auckland   Bogotá   Hamburg
Johannesburg   London   Madrid   Mexico   Montreal   New Delhi
Panama   Paris   São Paulo   Singapore   Sydney   Tokyo   Toronto

This book was set in Times Roman by Science Typographers, Inc.
The editors were Eric M. Munson, Kaye Pace, Ellen W. MacElree, and Jo Satloff;
the production supervisor was Joe Campanella.
The drawings were done by Volt Information Sciences, Inc.
R.R. Donnelley & Sons Company was printer and binder.

THE THEORY AND PRACTICE OF COMPILER WRITING

1234567890DOCDOC898765

ISBN 0-07-065161-2

Library of Congress Cataloging in Publication Data

Tremblay, Jean-Paul, date
    The theory and practice of compiler writing.

    (McGraw-Hill computer science series)
    Includes bibliographies and index.
    1. Electronic digital computers—Programming. 2. Compiling (Electronic computers) I. Sorenson, P. G.
II. Title. III. Series.
QA76.6.T734 1985   001.64′2   84-25096
ISBN 0-07-065161-2

Dédié—Dedicated

À la mémoire de mon père
Philippe Tremblay

To my father, Chester,
and
in memory of my mother,
Josephine Sorenson

CONTENTS

Preface   xvii

Chapter 1 Introduction   1
   1-1   Programming Languages   1
   1-2   Translators   4
   1-3   Model of a Compiler   5
        Bibliography   11

Chapter 2 Notation and Concepts for Languages and
Grammars   13
   2-1   Sets and Strings   14
        2-1.1 Basic Concepts of Set Theory   14
        Exercises 2-1.1   18
        2-1.2 Relations   19
        Exercises 2-1.2   27
        2-1.3 Strings   29
   2-2   Discussion of Grammars   30
        Exercises 2-2   37
   2-3   Classification of Grammars   37
        Exercises 2-3   42
   2-4   Context-Free Grammars and Parsing   42
        2-4.1 Syntax Terminology   43
        Exercises 2-4.1   50
        2-4.2 A View of Parsing   52
        Exercises 2-4.2   56
        2-4.3 Reduced Grammars and Grammars with ε-Rules   57
        Exercises 2-4.3   63
        2-4.4 Extended BNF Notation   64
        Exercises 2-4.4   66
        Bibliography   67

Chapter 3 Programming-Language Design 68

3-1 Overview of the Problem 69
3-2 Preliminary Considerations 70
3-3 Sources of Ideas 72
3-4 Goals and Design Philosophies of Programming Languages 74
    3-4.1 Human Communication 74
    3-4.2 Prevention and Detection of Errors 75
    3-4.3 Usability 78
    3-4.4 Programming Effectiveness 78
    3-4.5 Compilability 80
    3-4.6 Efficiency 81
    3-4.7 Machine Independence 83
    3-4.8 Simplicity 84
    3-4.9 Uniformity 84
    3-4.10 Orthogonality 85
    3-4.11 Generalization and Specialization 86
    3-4.12 Other Design Philosophies 86
3-5 Detailed Design 88
    3-5.1 Microstructure 88
    3-5.2 Expression Structure 92
    3-5.3 Data Structure 93
    3-5.4 Control Structure 102
    3-5.5 Compile Structure 113
    3-5.6 I/O Structure 114
3-6 Reduction of Size 116
3-7 Pragmatics 116
3-8 Comments on the Design of Ada 120
    3-8.1 Evaluation of Ada from a Language Design Viewpoint 122
        Usability and Program Effectiveness 122
        Machine Independence and Portability 129
        Efficiency 129
        Modularity and Maintainability 129
        Compilability and Compile Structure 130
        Simplicity 130
    3-8.2 Ada Programming Support Environment 131
    3-8.3 Software Technology for Adaptable Reliable Systems
        (STARS) 132
    Chapter Exercises 134
    Bibliography 135

Chapter 4 Scanners 138

4-1 The Scanning Process 139
4-2 An Elementary Scanner Design and Its Implementation 141
    Exercises 4-2 150
4-3 Regular Grammars and Regular Expressions 151
    Exercises 4-3 155
4-4 Finite-State Acceptors 156
    4-4.1 Deterministic Finite-State Acceptors 156
    4-4.2 Nondeterministic Finite-State Acceptors 157

	4-4.3	Nondeterministic Finite-State Acceptors with ε-Transitions	162
		Exercises 4-4	165
4-5		Equivalence of Regular Grammars and Finite-State Acceptors	166
		Exercises 4-5	169
4-6		Equivalence of Regular Expressions and Finite-State Acceptors	170
		Exercises 4-6	176
4-7		A Scanner Generator	177
		Exercises 4-7	181
		Bibliography	181

Chapter 5 Compile-Time Error Handling

			182
5-1		Overview of Error Handling	182
5-2		Error Detection	185
	5-2.1	The Nature of Syntax Errors	185
	5-2.2	How Errors Are Detected	187
	5-2.3	Where Errors Are Detected	189
5-3		Error Reporting	190
5-4		Error Recovery	195
	5-4.1	Ad Hoc Recovery Mechanisms	195
	5-4.2	Syntax-Directed Recovery	197
	5-4.3	Secondary Error Recovery	199
	5-4.4	Context-Sensitive Recovery	200
5-5		Error Repair	200
	5-5.1	Ad Hoc Repair	201
	5-5.2	Syntax-Directed Repair	201
	5-5.3	Context-Sensitive Repair	202
	5-5.4	Spelling Repair	203
		Chapter Exercises	205
		Bibliography	206

Chapter 6 Top-Down Parsing

			208
6-1		General Top-Down Parsing Strategies	208
	6-1.1	Brute-Force Approach	209
		Exercises 6-1.1	219
	6-1.2	Recursive-Descent Parsers	219
		Recursive-Descent Parsing Algorithm	219
		Error Detection in Recursive-Descent Parsers	224
		Exercises 6-1.2	228
	6-1.3	Notions of Top-Down Parsing with Limited Backup	228
	6-1.4	Top-Down Parsing with Limited Backup	229
		Exercises 6-1.4	234
6-2		Top-Down Parsing with No Backup	235
	6-2.1	Notions of Parsing with No Backup	235
	6-2.2	Simple $LL(1)$ Grammars	236
		Exercises 6-2.2	241
	6-2.3	$LL(1)$ Grammars without ε-Rules	242
		Exercises 6-2.3	248
	6-2.4	$LL(1)$ Grammars with ε-Rules	249

Exercises 6-2.4   258
6-2.5   Error Handling for $LL(1)$ Parsers   260
Exercises 6-2.5   272
Chapter Exercises   272
Bibliography   273

Chapter 7   Bottom-Up Parsing   274

7-1   Polish Expressions and Their Compilation   275
   7-1.1   Polish Notation   276
   7-1.2   Conversion of Infix Expressions to Polish Notation   278
   7-1.3   Error Detection for Infix Expressions   283
   Exercises 7-1   285
7-2   Operator Precedence Grammars   286
   7-2.1   Notions and Use of Operator Precedence Relations   287
   7-2.2   Formal Definition of Operator Precedence Relations   293
   7-2.3   Operator Precedence Parsing Algorithm   294
   7-2.4   Precedence Functions in Operator Precedence Parsers   298
   7-2.5   Error Detection in Operator Precedence Parsers   300
   Exercises 7-2   301
7-3   Simple Precedence Grammars   302
   7-3.1   Notions and Use of Precedence Relations   302
   7-3.2   Formal Definition of Precedence Relations   306
   7-3.3   Parsing Algorithm for Simple Precedence Grammars   309
   7-3.4   Precedence Functions for Simple Precedence Grammars   311
   7-3.5   Error Recovery for Simple Precedence Parsers 320
   7-3.6   Notions of Extended Precedence   332
   Exercises 7-3   339
7-4 LR Grammars   341
   7-4.1   Concepts and Terminology   341
   Exercises 7-4.1   346
   7-4.2 $LR(0)$ Parsers   346
   Exercises 7-4.2   352
   7-4.3 $SLR(1)$ Parsers   353
   Exercises 7-4.3   361
   7-4.4   Canonical $LR(1)$ Parsers   362
   Exercises 7-4.4   369
   7-4.5 $LALR(1)$ Parsers   370
   Exercises 7-4.5   375
   7-4.6   Efficient Generation of Lookahead Sets for $LALR(1)$
       Parsers   375
   Exercises 7-4.6   383
   7-4.7   Representation and Optimization of LR Parsers   383
       Sparse-Matrix Representations   384
       Optimization Transformations   386
   7-4.8   Error Detection and Recovery in LR Parsers 389
       Early Methods of Error Recovery   389
       Application of Graham-Rhodes Method to LR *Parsers*   392
       Other LR *Error-Recovery Methods*   410

7-5   Comparison of Parsing Methods   410
       Bibliography   415

Chapter 8   Symbol-Table-Handling Techniques   418

8-1   Perspective and Motivation   418
8-2   When to Construct and Interact with the Symbol Table   419
8-3   Symbol-Table Contents   422
8-4   Operations on Symbol Tables   426
8-5   Symbol-Table Organizations for Non-Block-Structured
       Languages   428
       8-5.1   Unordered Symbol Tables   428
       8-5.2   Ordered Symbol Tables   429
       8-5.3   Tree-Structured Symbol Tables   433
       8-5.4   Hash Symbol Tables   450
8-6   Symbol-Table Organizations for Block-Structured Languages   464
       8-6.1   Block-Structured Language Concepts   465
       8-6.2   Stack Symbol Tables   467
       8-6.3   Stack-Implemented Tree-Structured Symbol Tables   468
       8-6.4   Stack-Implemented Hash-Structured Symbol Tables   471
       Chapter Exercises   474
       Bibliography   476

Chapter 9   Run-Time Storage Organization and
Management   477

9-1   Static Storage Allocation   477
       Exercises 9-1   480
9-2   Dynamic Storage Allocation   480
       9-2.1   Activation Records   482
       9-2.2   Parameter Area   483
       9-2.3   Display Area   484
       9-2.4   Run-Time Address Calculation   487
       9-2.5   Handling Recursive Procedures   488
       Exercises 9-2   491
9-3   Heap Storage Allocation   492
       9-3.1   Implicit Storage Requests   493
       9-3.2   Explicit Storage Requests   493
       9-3.3   Management of Fixed-Length Blocks   495
       9-3.4   Management of Variable-Length Blocks   496
               First-Fit Heap Storage-Management Strategy   497
               Boundary-Tag Heap Storage-Management Strategy   501
               Buddy-System Heap Storage-Management Strategy   506
       9-3.5   Free-as-You-Go Storage Release   512
       9-3.6   Garbage Collection   513
       9-3.7   Compaction   517
       Exercises 9-3   519
       Bibliography   520

Chapter 10 Intermediate Forms of Source Programs 521

10-1 Polish Notation 522
10-2 N-tuple Notation 523
10-3 Abstract Syntax Trees 525
10-4 Threaded Code 527
10-5 Abstract Machine Code 531
    10-5.1 Portability and Abstract Machine 531
    10-5.2 The P-Code Abstract Machine for PASCAL 532
    Chapter Exercises 534
    Bibliography 535

Chapter 11 Semantic Analysis and Code Generation 536

11-1 What Is Meant by Semantic Analysis 537
11-2 Implicit Stacking in Recursive-Descent Compilation 540
11-3 Semantic Stacks in Bottom-Up Compilation 548
11-4 Action Symbols in Top-Down Compilation 554
11-5 Attributed Translation 559
    11-5.1 Attributed Translation Grammar 560
    11-5.2 *L*-Attributed Translation Grammar 563
11-6 Example Language Constructs 568
    11-6.1 Declarations 568
        Constant Type 570
        Variable Declarations 571
        Procedure Declarations 578
    11-6.2 Expressions 579
    11-6.3 Assignment Statements 591
    11-6.4 Control Statements 592
        Case-Selection Statement 593
        Repeat-While Statement 595
        For Loop Statement 596
    11-6.5 Procedure Calls and Returns 598
        Procedure Calls 598
        Return Statements and Procedure Termination 603
    11-6.6 Input and Output Statements 603
        Input Statements 603
        Output Statements 607
    11-6.7 Compiler Aids 607
    Chapter Exercises 609
    Bibliography 609

Chapter 12 Code Optimization 610

12-1 Introduction 610
12-2 Basic Blocks 611
12-3 Folding 612
12-4 Redundant-Subexpression Elimination 620
12-5 Optimization within Iterative Loops 631
    12-5.1 Loop Unrolling 635
    12-5.2 Frequency Reduction 637

	12-5.3 Strength Reduction	646
	12-5.4 Combining Loop-Optimization Techniques	651
12-6	Global Optimization through Flowgraph Analysis	655
	12-6.1 Flowgraph Construction	655
	12-6.2 Flowgraph Analysis	660
	Flowgraph-Analysis Problems	661
	Flow-Analysis Algorithms	667
	12-6.3 Applications to Program Optimization	678
	12-6.4 Implementation and Further Considerations	680
	Chapter Exercises	681
	Bibliography	683

Chapter 13 Machine-Dependent Optimization 684

13-1	Introduction to Machine-Dependent Optimization	684
13-2	Register-Allocation Optimization	686
	13-2.1 Register Allocation in Single-Register Machines	686
	13-2.2 Register Allocation in Multiregister Machines	694
13-3	Machine Architecture and the Generation of Real Code	702
	13-3.1 The PDP-11	703
	13-3.2 The VAX-11	710
	13-3.3 The MC68000	716
	Chapter Exercises	720
	Bibliography	721

Chapter 14 Compiler-Compilers 722

14-1	Introduction to Compiler-Compilers	723
14-2	Examples of Parser Generators	726
	14-2.1 YACC: A *LALR*(1) Parser Generator	727
	14-2.2 An Attributed *LL*(1) Parser Generator	735
14-3	Machine-Independent Code Generation	742
	14-3.1 The Production-Quality Compiler-Compiler System	743
	Introduction	743
	The Formalization of Instruction-Set Processors and TCOL	745
	The Code-Generation Process: Its Phases and Organization	749
	14-3.2 The Table-Driven Generator of Graham and Glanville	755
	Introduction	756
	The Target-Machine Description	757
	The Code-Generation Process	758
	Results and Extensions	760
	14-3.3 Other Code-Generation Systems	761
	Fraser's Knowledge-Based Code-Generator Generator	761
	The Finite-State Approach of Donegan	763
	Bibliography	764

Appendix Algorithmic Notation 767

A-1	Format Conventions	768
	A-1.1 Name of Algorithm	768
	A-1.2 Introductory Comment	768

A-1.3   Steps   768
A-1.4   Comments   768
A-2   Statements and Control Structures   768
A-2.1   Assignment Statement   769
A-2.2   If Statement   769
A-2.3   Case Statement   770
A-2.4   Repeat Statement   770
A-2.5   Go To and Exitloop Statements   772
A-2.6   Exit Statement   772
A-2.7   Variable Names   773
A-3   Data Structures   773
A-3.1   Arrays   773
A-3.2   Dynamic Storage   774
A-4   Arithmetic Operations and Expressions   774
A-5   Strings and String Operations   775
A-6   Relations and Relational Operators   775
A-7   Logical Operations and Expressions   776
A-8   Input and Output   776
A-9   Subalgorithms   777
A-9.1   Functions   777
A-9.2   Procedures   778
A-9.3   Parameters   778

Indexes   781

Name Index   781
Subject Index   785

PREFACE

This book is intended as a text for a one- or two-semester course in compiler design at the senior undergraduate or introductory graduate level. It can also be used as a self-study and reference book in compiler design. The purpose of this text is to cover the underlying concepts and techniques used in compiler design. Some of these techniques can be used in software engineering or software design.

The reader should have at least one year of experience in programming a high-level language and an assembly language. In addition, a familiarity with elementary data structures and discrete mathematics is a definite asset. The text, however, is reasonably self-contained.

Chapter 1 contains an overview of compiler design and gives a model for a compiler.

Chapter 2 covers the basic notations and concepts of discrete mathematics, grammars, and languages. This material is used in the remainder of the book. Students who are familiar with this material can quickly peruse it or ignore it. They need not have a complete mastery of the concepts on their first reading. They can, however, refer to the material when it is used in subsequent chapters.

In Chapter 3 we introduce the elements of programming language design. We attempt to give a unified treatment of the topics in sufficient depth to be useful to persons actually designing a programming language. Much of this material is appearing in a compiler book for the first time.

Chapter 4 details the informal and the formal approaches to lexical analyzers (i.e., scanners).

Chapter 5 gives an overview of error handling. Although it doesn't contain many detailed algorithms on error recovery and repair strategies, it discusses important factors and considerations of error recovery and repair in general. Detailed algorithms for particular strategies are given in Chapters 6 and 7.

Chapter 6 is the first of two chapters on parsing. The chapter deals with top-down parsing. In the first section we examine a number of ad hoc methods. The second section gives a detailed description of syntax-directed translation using $LL(1)$ grammars.

Chapter 7 discusses several syntax-directed bottom-up parsing techniques. The discussion includes several precedence and *LR* parsers along with associated error detection and recovery strategies.

In Chapter 8, first we outline the important functions of a symbol table in the translation process and then give the details of several symbol-table organizations for block-structured and non-block-structured languages.

Chapter 9 provides a description of the static, dynamic, explicit, and implicit storage-allocation strategies that are frequently adopted when compiling programs for a wide variety of existing languages.

In Chapter 10 we discuss the advantages of using intermediate source forms. Five types of intermediate source forms are examined in detail.

Chapter 11 deals with semantic analysis and code generation. This chapter presents four types of syntax-directed processing techniques, which include translation grammars and attribute translation.

Chapter 12 presents several machine-independent optimization strategies, including folding, redundant subexpression elimination, optimization within iterative loops, and global optimization through flow analysis.

Chapter 13 covers several machine-dependent optimization techniques such as register allocation and peephole optimization

Chapter 14 gives a brief overview of compiler-compiler systems. The main focus is on the PQCC and Graham-Glanville systems. Much of this material appears in a compiler book for the first time.

As we mentioned earlier, the book can be used in a two-semester course. Depending on the level of such a course, the instructor may wish to supplement the text with reading assignments from the references. Several one-semester courses are possible. For example, the following selection of topics constitutes such a course:

Chapters 1 and 2
Chapter 3 (can be omitted if students don't do their own language design)
Sections 4-1 and 4-2
Chapter 5
Sections 6-1.2 and 6-2 (except Sec. 6-2.5)
Sections 7-4.1, 7-4.2, 7-4.3, and 7-4.6
Sections 8-5.3 and 8-5.4 and parts of Sec. 8-6
Chapter 9 (select one or two methods)
Chapter 10
Chapter 11 (select a few methods of code generation)

An important aspect of teaching a course in compiler writing is to illustrate the key theoretical concepts. A frequently used strategy for achieving this goal is to have a student design a simple programming language and implement a compiler for this language. Many texts in compiler writing do not, because of size considerations and level of presentation, adequately present details that illustrate the implementation of a compiler. In a separate volume, entitled *An Implementation Guide to Compiler Writing* (published with McGraw-Hill in 1982), we present, in a case study manner, the development of a small compiler typical of those developed in a first compiler course. Instructors can use this book as a guide to illustrate difficulties that commonly arise when implementing a compiler. It can also be used as a sample document that is similar to what students should produce for their own compilers. It is often necessary for instructors teaching a course in compiler writing to set up their own "toy" compiler as a vehicle for illustrating techniques for implementing a compiler. Also, many of the problems that are encountered in writing a compiler for a newly designed language must be illustrated. In this guide we attempt to fulfill this role.

The guide begins with a documented description of a simple program language, GAUSS, which serves as an example for the student. GAUSS is a block-structured language whose design was influenced by ALGOL, PASCAL, PL/I, and FORTRAN. It also contains string-manipulation facilities capable of manipulating variable-length strings. It then illustrates the topics of scanner generation, $LL(1)$ parsing, symbol-table construction, code generation, semantic analysis, error detection, and repair for the GAUSS language. Finally, the guide describes an interpreter for the code generated by the GAUSS compiler and discusses the run-time environment in which the machine code is executed. The code generated by the compiler executes on a hypothetical machine which is stack oriented.

ACKNOWLEDGMENTS

We would like to thank the many people who assisted us in the preparation of this manuscript. Brent Clark assisted in the preparation of some parts of Chapters 12 and 13. Jack Copeck contributed to earlier drafts of Chapters 6 and 12. Howard Hamilton assisted in program flow analysis techniques. Rod Nickel contributed to the part of Chapter 7 that deals with error detection and recovery in precedence parsers. Lyle Opseth assisted in error detection and recovery in Chapter 7 and a preliminary version of Chapter 14. Darwyn Peachey assisted in the preparation of Chapter 5 and some error detection and recovery techniques in Chapters 6 and 7. Henry Spencer contributed to Chapter 3, and Joe Wald contributed to the attributed translation part of Chapter 11. Special thanks is due to John DeDourek, who class-tested the manuscript and proofread the entire galley form of the book. We also wish to thank the reviewers of the manuscript: Michael Bauer, James Harp, John Lowther, and Tom Pennello. A thanks to Chris Fraser for his comments on Chapter 14. We are grateful to Sue Wotton, who did such an excellent job of typing the manuscript, and to Gail Walker for her typing support. Finally, we are very grateful for the comments of our students in the Department of Computational Science at the University of Saskatchewan, who have class-tested preliminary versions of the book during the last seven years.

Jean-Paul Tremblay
Paul G. Sorenson

INTRODUCTION

1-1 PROGRAMMING LANGUAGES

Interactions involving humans are most effectively carried out through the medium of language. Language permits the expression of thoughts and ideas, and without it, communication as we know it would be very difficult indeed.

In computer programming, a programming language serves as a means of communication between the person with a problem and the computer used to help solve it. An effective programming language enhances both the development and the expression of computer programs. It must bridge the gap between the often unstructured nature of human thought and the precision required for computer execution.

A program solution to a given problem will be easier and more natural to obtain if the programming language used is close to the problem. That is, the language should contain constructs which reflect the terminology and elements used in describing the problem and are independent of the computer used. Such a programming language is usually high-level. Digital computers, on the other hand, accept and understand only their own special low-level language, consisting typically of long sequences of zeros and ones. These sequences are generally unintelligible to humans. This type of low-level language is quite different from the high-level language used to describe a problem in a given area.

A hierarchy of programming languages based on increasing machine independence includes the following:

1. Machine-level languages
2. Assembly languages
3. Higher-level or user-oriented languages
4. Problem-oriented languages

A *machine-level language* is the lowest form of computer language. Each instruction in a program is represented by a numeric code, and numerical addresses are used throughout the program to refer to memory locations in the computer's memory. All bookkeeping aspects of the program are the sole responsibility of the machine-language programmer. Finally, all diagnostics and programming aids must be supplied by the programmer. Also included as machine-level programs are programs written in microcode (i.e., microprograms). Microcode allows for the expression of some of the more powerful machine-level instructions in terms of a set of basic machine instructions.

Assembly language is essentially a symbolic version of a machine-level language. Each operation code is given a symbolic code such as ADD for addition and MUL for multiplication. Moreover, memory locations are given symbolic names such as PAY and RATE. Some assembly languages contain macroinstructions which are at a higher level than assembly-languages instructions. Assembly-language systems offer certain diagnostic and debugging assistance that is normally not available at the machine level.

A *high-level language* such as FORTRAN, PASCAL, or PL/I offers most of the features of an assembly language. While some facilities for accessing system-level features may not be provided, a high-level language offers a more enriched set of language features such as structured control constructs, nested statements, blocks, and procedures.

A *problem-oriented language* provides for the expression of problems in a specific application or problem area. Examples of such languages are SEQUEL for database retrieval applications and COGO for civil engineering applications.

In this book we concern ourselves exclusively with the development of translators for high-level algebraic languages such as ALGOL, PASCAL, and FORTRAN. Although the class of high-level languages includes both procedural and nonprocedural languages, this book concentrates on procedural languages. Unlike procedural programs, the position of a particular statement in a nonprocedural program has no bearing on its execution; that is, the interchange of any two statements in a nonprocedural program will not affect the results obtained though its execution. Examples of nonprocedural languages are PSL, a requirements statement language, and CSMP, a simulation and modeling language.

Advantages of high-level languages over low-level languages such as machine and assembly languages include the following:

1. High-level languages are easier to learn than their lower-level counterparts. The learning of many high-level languages requires little or no computer hardware background because such languages are relatively machine-independent. Furthermore, these languages are closer to their problem areas than lower-level languages.
2. The programmer does not have to be concerned with clerical tasks involving numerical or symbolic references to instructions, memory locations, constants, etc. Such tasks are handled by a system which translates the high-level language program into machine language.

3. A programmer is not required to know how to convert data from external forms to various internal forms within the memory of a computer. The ability of a programmer to convert, say, numeric data into internal forms such as floating-point numbers and packed-decimal numbers should be irrelevant.

4. Most high-level languages offer a programmer a variety of control structures which are not available in low-level languages. High-level languages offer several of the following language constructs:

Conditional statements (such as IF-THEN-ELSE and CASE statements)
Looping statements (for both counted and conditional loops)
Nested statements
Block structures

These control structures improve programming style and facilitate certain programming approaches such as structured programming. Resulting programs are easier to read, understand, and alter. This results in reduced programming costs because programs are less complicated.

5. Programs written in a high-level language are usually more easily debugged than their machine- or assembly-language equivalents. High-level languages offer constructs that eliminate or reduce certain kinds of programming errors that occur in low-level languages. For example, the declaration of variables in a program adds a certain degree of redundancy which is useful in detecting errors in the improper use of variables. Languages often enforce a disciplined use of pointers. Moreover, a structured program is much more easily debugged than its unstructured counterpart.

6. Since most high-level languages offer more powerful control and data-structuring capabilities than low-level languages, the former class of languages facilitates the expression of a solution to a particular problem.

7. Because of the availability of certain language features such as procedures, high-level languages permit a modular and hierarchical description of programming tasks. These tasks can then be assigned to a team of programmers, thus facilitating a division of labor with a minimum of disruption and effort. Such an approach permits better documentation of a problem. Also, increased compatibility among programs and programmers can be realized.

8. Finally, high-level languages are relatively machine-independent. Consequently, certain programs such as FORTRAN and COBOL programs are portable. These programs can be executed on different computers with little, if any, change even though these computers have different internal architectures and machine-language instruction sets. Program portability reduces costs and, in general, protects an installation against computer obsolescence. Often when a computer is replaced, all associated assembly- and machine-language programs become obsolete.

Points 1 through 5 have been stressed in the past and found to be very important. Today, points 6 through 8 are receiving considerable attention and promise to be dominant considerations in the immediate future.

High-level language programs, of course, must be translated automatically to equivalent machine-language programs. The notions of such translators are examined in the next section.

1-2 TRANSLATORS

A *translator* inputs and then converts a *source program* into an *object* or *target program*. The source program is written in a *source language* and the object program belongs to an *object language*.

If the source language being translated is assembly language and the object program is machine language, the translator is called an *assembler*. Assembly language resembles closely machine language. In an *elementary* assembly language, most of its instructions are symbolic representations of corresponding machine-language instructions. Each assembly instruction contains an ordered set of fields. For example, the first field might represent a label which is followed immediately by an operation field. This field in turn might be followed by one or more operand fields. More sophisticated assembly languages, however, support *macroinstructions*. A macroinstruction can be expanded to a sequence of simple machine-language instructions. High-level language constructs such as case statements, nested statements, and blocks are not usually contained in assembly languages.

A translator which transforms a high-level language such as FORTRAN, PASCAL, or COBOL into a particular computer's machine or assembly language is called a *compiler*. The time at which the conversion of a source program to an object program occurs is called *compile time*. The object program is executed at *run time*. Figure 1-1 illustrates the compilation process. Note that the source program and data are processed at different times, namely, compile time and run time, respectively.

Another kind of translator, called an *interpreter*, processes an internal form of the source program and data at the same time. That is, interpretation of the

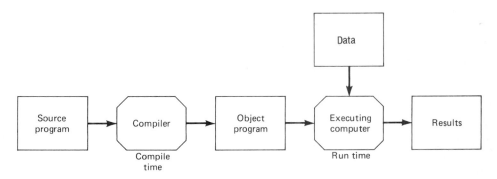

Figure 1-1 Compilation process.

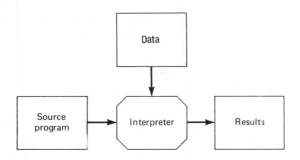

Figure 1-2 Interpretive process.

internal source form occurs at run time and no object program is generated. Figure 1-2 illustrates this interpretive process. Some interpreters analyze each source statement every time it is to be executed. Such an approach is very time-consuming and is seldom used. A more efficient approach involves applying compilation techniques to the translation of the source program to an intermediate source form. This intermediate source form is then interpreted by the interpreter program.

Interpreters have become increasingly popular lately, particularly in microcomputer environments where the overhead of interpretation seems to be significantly less for the user. For example, a main reason why languages such as BASIC, APL, LISP, and SMALLTALK-80 have become very popular is because they have been implemented in an interpretive environment.

In this book, we concentrate on compiler construction techniques. Although a complete compiler will not be found in this text, the reader is referred to the accompanying text, *An Implementation Guide to Compiler Writing*, where a compiler for the high-level programming language GAUSS is described in detail.

A compiler can be described in a modular fashion. The next section gives an overview of such an approach.

1-3 MODEL OF A COMPILER

The task of constructing a compiler for a particular source language is complex. The complexity and nature of the compilation process depend, to a large extent, on the source language. Compiler complexity can often be reduced if a programming-language designer takes various design factors into consideration. Several of these programming-language design factors are discussed in Chap. 3. Since we are dealing with high-level source languages such as ALGOL and PASCAL, however, a basic model of a compiler can be formulated. Such a model is given in Fig. 1-3. Although this model may vary for the compilation of different high-level languages, it is nevertheless representative of the compilation process.

A compiler must perform two major tasks: the analysis of a source program and the synthesis of its corresponding object program. The analysis task deals with the decomposition of the source program into its basic parts. Using these

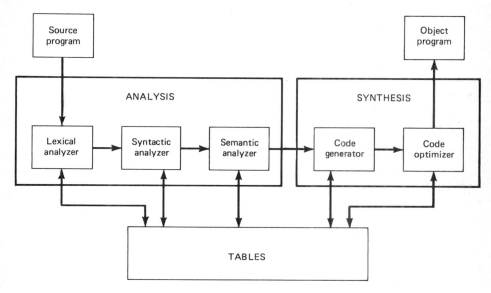

Figure 1-3 Components of a compiler.

parts, the synthesis task builds their equivalent object program modules. The performance of these tasks is realized more easily by building and maintaining several tables. More will be said about the contents of these tables shortly.

A source program is a string of symbols each of which is generally a letter, a digit, or certain special symbols such as +, −, and (,). A source program contains elementary language constructs such as variable names, labels, constants, keywords, and operators. It is therefore desirable for the compiler to identify these various types as classes. These language constructs are given in the definition of the language.

The source program (see Fig. 1-3) is input to a *lexical analyzer* or *scanner* whose purpose is to separate the incoming text into pieces or *tokens* such as constants, variable names, keywords (such as DO, IF, and THEN in PL/I), and operators. In essence, the lexical analyzer performs low-level syntax analysis. For efficiency reasons, each class of tokens is given a unique internal representation number. For example, a variable name may be given a representation number of 1, a constant a value of 2, a label the number 3, the addition operator (+) a value of 4, etc. For example, the PL/I statement

TEST: IF A > B THEN X = Y;

would be translated by the lexical analyzer into the following sequence of tokens (and associated representation numbers):

TEST   3
:   26
IF   20

A	1
>	15
B	1
THEN	21
X	1
=	10
Y	1
;	27

Note that in scanning the source statement and generating the representation number of each token we have ignored spaces (or blanks) in the statement. The lexical analyzer must, in general, process blanks and comments. Both of these classes of items typically do not represent executable parts of a program and are ignored, for example, in PL/I.

Certain programming languages allow the continuation of statements over multiple lines. Lexical analyzers must then handle the input processing of such multiple-line statements. Also, some scanners place constants, labels, and variable names in appropriate tables. A table entry for a variable, for example, may contain its name, type (e.g., REAL, INTEGER, or BOOLEAN), object program address, value, and line in which it is declared.

The lexical analyzer supplies tokens to the syntax analyzer. These tokens may take the form of a pair of items. The first item gives the address or location of the token in some symbol table. The second item is the representation number of the token. Such an approach offers a distinct advantage to the syntax analyzer; namely, all tokens are represented by fixed-length information: an address (or pointer) and an integer. Chapter 4 describes the scanning process in more detail.

The syntax analyzer is much more complex than the lexical analyzer. Its function is to take the source program (in the form of tokens) from the lexical analyzer and determine the manner in which it is to be decomposed into its constituent parts. That is, the syntax analyzer determines the overall structure of the source program. This process is analogous to determining the structure of a sentence in the English language. In such an instance we are interested in identifying certain classes such as "subject," "predicate," "verb," "noun," and "adjective."

In syntax analysis we are concerned with grouping tokens into larger syntactic classes such as *expression*, *statement*, and *procedure*. The syntax analyzer (or *parser*) outputs a *syntax tree* (or its equivalent) in which its leaves are the tokens and every nonleaf node represents a syntactic class type. For example, an analysis of the source statement

$$(A + B)*(C + D)$$

can produce the syntactic classes ⟨factor⟩, ⟨term⟩, and ⟨expression⟩ as exhibited in the syntax tree given in Fig. 1-4. The syntax-tree approach is described in Chap. 2, where a set of rules known as a *grammar* is used to define precisely the source language. A grammar can be used by the syntax analyzer to determine the

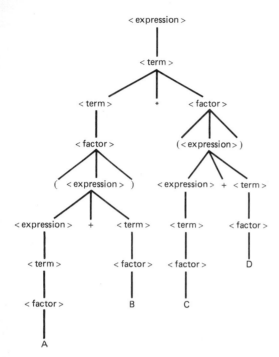

Figure 1-4 A syntax tree for the expression $(A + B)*(C + D)$.

structure of the source program. This recognition process is called *parsing*, and consequently we often refer to syntax analyzers as *parsers*. Several classes of parsers are discussed in detail in Chaps. 6 and 7.

The syntax tree produced by the syntax analyzer is used by the semantic analyzer. The function of the semantic analyzer is to determine the *meaning* (or *semantics*) of the source program. Although it is conceptually desirable to separate the syntax of a source program from its semantics, the syntax and semantic analyzers work in close cooperation. Nevertheless, the semantic-analysis process is a different and unique process in a compiler. For an expression such as $(A + B)*(C + D)$, for example, the semantic analyzer must determine what actions are specified by the arithmetic operators of addition and multiplication. When the parser recognizes an operator such as "+" or "*," it invokes a *semantic routine* which specifies the action to be performed. This routine may check that the two operands to be added have been declared, that they have the same type (if not, the routine would probably make them the same), and that both operands have values. The semantic analyzer often interacts with the various tables of the compiler in performing its task.

The semantic-analyzer actions may involve the generation of an intermediate form of source code. For the expression $(A + B)*(C + D)$, the intermediate source code might be the following set of quadruples:

$(+, A, B, T1)$
$(+, C, D, T2)$
$(*, T1, T2, T3)$

where $(+, A, B, T1)$ is interpreted to mean "add A and B and place the result in temporary T1," $(+, C, D, T2)$ is interpreted to mean "add C and D and place this result in T2," and $(*, T1, T2, T3)$ is interpreted to mean "multiply T1 and T2 and place the result in T3." The exact form of the intermediate source language used depends, to a large extent, on how it is to be processed during the synthesis task. An infix expression may be converted to an intermediate form called Polish notation. Using this approach, the infix expression $(A + B)*(C + D)$ would be converted to the equivalent suffix–Polish expression AB + CD + *. The latter expression contains the arithmetic operators in the order in which they are to be executed. Another type of intermediate form of source language can be a syntax tree which represents the parse of the source program. (See Chap. 10.)

The output of the semantic analyzer is passed on to the code generator. At this point the intermediate form of the source-language program is usually translated to either assembly language or machine language. As an example, the translation of the three quadruples for the previous expression can yield the following sequence of single-address, single-accumulator assembly-language instructions:

LDA A Load the contents of A into the accumulator.
ADD B Add the contents of B to that of the accumulator.
STO T1 Store the accumulator contents in temporary storage T1.
LDA C Load the contents of C into the accumulator.
ADD D Add the contents of D to that of the accumulator.
STO T2 Store the accumulator contents in temporary storage T2.
LDA T1 Load the contents of T1 into the accumulator.
MUL T2 Multiply the contents of T2 by that of the accumulator.
STO T3 Store accumulator contents in temporary storage T3.

The topic of code generation is presented in Chap. 11. The output of the code generator is passed on to a *code optimizer*. This process is present in more sophisticated compilers. Its purpose is to produce a more efficient object program. Certain optimizations that are possible at a local level include the evaluation of constant expressions, the use of certain operator properties such as associativity, commutativity, and distributivity, and the detection of common subexpressions. Because of the commutativity of the multiplication operator, the previous assembly code can be reduced to the following:

LDA A
ADD B
STO T1
LDA C
ADD D
MUL T1
STO T2

Note that the expression evaluated by this code is $(C + D)*(A + B)$.

More global optimizations can also be performed. These include the single evaluation of multiple occurrences of identical subexpressions and removing statements that are invariant inside a loop and placing them outside of that loop. These kinds of optimizations are machine-independent. There are, however, certain machine-dependent optimizations which can also be performed. Optimal register allocation is an example of this kind of optimization. A good code optimizer can produce as good or even better code than an experienced assembly-language programmer. Optimization techniques are the topic of Chaps. 12 and 13.

The model of a compiler given in Fig. 1-3 makes distinctions between its successive phases. In certain compilers, however, some of these phases are combined. In our discussion of this model the details are omitted on how the five processes interact with each other. Let us examine some possible interactions between the lexical and syntax analyzers. One possibility is that the scanner generates a token for the syntax analyzer for processing. The syntax analyzer then "calls" the scanner when the next token is required. Another possibility is for the scanner to produce all the tokens corresponding to the source program before passing control to the syntax analyzer. In this case the scanner has examined the entire source program—this is called a *separate pass*. Some compilers make as little as one pass while other compilers have been known to make more than 30 passes (e.g., some of IBM's first PL/I compilers). Factors which influence the number of passes to be used in a particular compiler include the following:

1. Available memory
2. Speed and size of compiler
3. Speed and size of object program
4. Debugging features required
5. Error-detection and -recovery techniques desired
6. Number of people and time required to accomplish the compiler writing project

Several educationally oriented or student compilers such as WATFIV and PL/C are essentially one-pass compilers. In these compilers very little (if any) code optimization is performed. The reason for this is the belief that programs will be compiled more times than executed. Such programs are often executed once and discarded. Also the semantic-analyzer and code-generation phases are invariably combined into one phase. Great emphasis is placed on debugging, error detection, error recovery, and diagnostic capabilities.

Certain source languages, however, cannot be compiled in a single pass. Compilers for PL/I and FORTRAN often contain many passes. In particular, the optimization phase may require that several passes of the source program (or its intermediate form) be made. In addition, the optimization phase is often spread throughout the other passes of the compilation process (e.g., certain constant folding, as described in Chap. 12, has been incorporated in the lexical analyzer of some compilers).

Other combinations are possible. Sometimes the syntax-analyzer, semantic-analyzer, and code-generation phases can be combined into a single phase.

An aspect of compiler construction which was omitted in Fig. 1-3 deals with the area of error detection and error recovery. *Error recovery* is most closely associated with the syntax-analysis phase. The aim of error recovery is to prolong the compilation life of the program as long as possible before the compiler "gives up" on the source program. A strategy that is often adopted is that if at all possible, the object program is executed. This approach can reduce the number of times a source program has to be compiled before becoming error-free. Some error-recovery approaches insert and/or discard tokens in attempting to correct the portion of the source program which is syntactically incorrect. We attach significant importance to this topic in this book. In particular, Chap. 5 introduces the general notions of error detection and error recovery. Also, particular strategies for different parsing techniques are illustrated in Chaps. 6 and 7.

Another aspect of compiling which has been ignored in the current discussion deals with the various symbol tables that must be created and maintained during the executions of the required object program. The topic of symbol tables is presented in Chap. 8. Also, certain language constructs in the source language imply that several data structures must be stored and maintained in the memory of the computer. The design and implementation of these structures is called *run-time organization and implementation or storage management*. For block-structured languages, string-oriented languages such as SNOBOL, and languages which permit the declaration and manipulation of programmer-defined data structures, the run-time considerations are very significant and complex. Details of these problems are dealt with in Chap. 9.

In closing, a comment on the relative difficulty of implementing each of the phases in Fig. 1-3 is in order. The lexical-analysis phase is perhaps the most straightforward. Next in difficulty comes the syntactic-analysis or parsing phase. A lot of research, based on formal language theory, has been done on these two phases. As a result, the scanning and parsing phases can be largely automated. The theory of scanning is developed in Chap. 4. Chapters 6 and 7, on the other hand, describe the theory of parsing. The real difficulties in compiler construction are in the semantic-analysis, code-generation, and code-optimization phases. Another problem area is the portability of programs. These difficulties, which are often language- and machine-dependent, are examined in Chaps. 10, 11, 12, and 13.

Several attempts have been made at automating compiler construction. Some of these efforts have enjoyed limited success. These *translator-writing* or *compiler-compiler* systems are briefly discussed in Chap. 14.

BIBLIOGRAPHY

Aho, A. V., and J. D. Ullman: *Principles of Compiler Design*, Reading. Mass.: Addison-Wesley, 1977.
Barrett, W. A., and J. D. Couch: *Compiler Construction, Theory and Practice*, Chicago: Science Research Associates, Inc., 1979.

Calingaert, P.: *Assemblers, Compilers and Program Translators*, Rockville, Md.: Computer Science Press, Inc., 1979.

Cocke, J., and J. T. Schwartz: *Programming Languages and Their Compilers*, Courant Institute of Mathematical Sciences, New York University, April 1970.

Gries, D.: *Compiler Construction for Digital Computers*, New York: John Wiley & Sons, 1971.

Knuth, D. E.: "A History of Writing Compilers," *Computers and Automation*, Vol. 11, No. 12, December 1962, pp. 8–14.

Lewis, P. M. II, D. J. Rosenkrantz, and R. E. Stearns: *Compiler Design Theory*, Reading, Mass.: Addison-Wesley, 1976.

Pollack, B. W. (ed.): *Compiler Techniques*, Princeton, N.J.: Auerbach, 1972.

Rosen, S., *Programming Systems and Languages*, New York: McGraw-Hill, 1967.

Tremblay, J. P., and P. G. Sorenson: *An Implementation Guide To Compiler Writing*, New York: McGraw-Hill, 1982.

TWO

NOTATION AND CONCEPTS
FOR LANGUAGES AND GRAMMARS

This chapter covers basic material which we will use extensively throughout the remainder of this book. Rather than spreading this material in various chapters of the text, therefore forcing the reader to read at least those parts of each chapter where the notions are introduced, we felt that a better alternative would be to put in this chapter *basic fundamental material* which is common to most of the remaining chapters. In this way the text can be read in a modular manner, thus allowing the reader to select certain chapters without loss of continuity.

The first section deals with basic material concerning sets and strings. Section 2-2 introduces the notion of a grammar and its use in describing the syntax of a language. In the third section, a classification of grammars is given and the classification is shown to form a hierarchy. The material dealing with context-free grammars of Sec. 2-4 introduces basic notions such as parsing, syntax tree, and ambiguity. The problem of specifying the syntax of a programming language by the use of a metalanguage is discussed at some length. The material in Secs. 2-1, 2-2, 2-4.1, and 2-4.2 is drawn primarily from Tremblay and Manohar (1975).

Readers who are familiar with the notions of sets, relations, and strings can proceed to Sec. 2-2. Readers who have been exposed to grammars can begin at Sec. 2-4.

2-1 SETS AND STRINGS

A programming language consists of a set of programs (or strings). As we will see shortly, it is convenient to use a grammar as a formal vehicle for generating these programs. Several relations can be defined on the rules of a grammar, and these relations can lead to efficient compilation algorithms for the language associated with that grammar. Consequently, the purpose of this section is to give a brief introduction to the basic elements of sets and strings. In particular, the concepts of sets and operations on sets are given in Sec. 2-1.1. The notion of a relation is introduced in Sec. 2-1.2. Other important aspects about relations which are introduced in this subsection include the graph and transitive closure of a relation. The section ends with an elementary treatment of strings.

2-1.1 Basic Concepts of Set Theory

By a *set* we mean a collection of objects of any sort. The word "object" is used here in a very broad sense to include even abstract objects. A fundamental concept of set theory is that of membership or belonging to a set. Any object belonging to a set is called a *member* or an *element* of that set.

If an element p belongs to a set A, we write $p \in A$, which is read as "p is an element of the set A" or "p belongs to the set A." If there exists an object q which does not belong to the set A, we express this fact as $q \notin A$.

There are many ways of specifying a set. For example, a set consisting of the decimal digits is generally written as

$$\{0, 1, 2, 3, 4, 5, 6, 7, 8, 9\}$$

The names of the elements are enclosed in braces and separated by commas. If we wish to denote this set as D, we write

$$D = \{0, 1, 2, 3, 4, 5, 6, 7, 8, 9\}$$

where the equality sign indicates that D is the set $\{0, 1, 2, 3, 4, 5, 6, 7, 8, 9\}$.

This method of specifying a set is not always convenient. For example, the set D can be more easily described by using a *predicate* as follows:

$$D = \{x | x \text{ is a decimal digit}\}$$

where the symbol | is read as "such that." In this case, the predicate is " is a decimal digit." If we let $P(x)$ denote any predicate, then $\{x | P(x)\}$ defines a set and is read "the set of all x such that $P(x)$ is true." An element a belongs to this set if $P(a)$ is true; otherwise a does not belong to the set. If we denote the set $\{x | P(x)\}$ by B, then $B = \{x | P(x)\}$.

Sets which are specified by listing their elements can also be characterized by means of a predicate. For example, the set $\{a, b, 1, 9\}$ can be defined as

$$\{x | (x = a) \vee (x = b) \vee (x = 1) \vee (x = 9)\}$$

where the symbol $\vee$ denotes a logical disjunction (or). A predicate can also contain the logical connectives $\wedge$ (logical conjunction or and), $\neg$ (logical nega-tion), $\rightarrow$ (if then), $\Leftrightarrow$ (if and only if), and the relational operators $<$, $\leq$, $=$, $\neq$, $\geq$, and $>$. Furthermore, a predicate can also contain the *existential quantifier* ($\exists$, meaning "there exists") and the *universal quantifier* ($\forall$, representing "for every").

Although it is possible to characterize any set by a predicate, it is sometimes convenient to specify sets by another method, such as

$$C = \{1, 3, 5, \dots\}$$

$$S = \{a, a^2, a^3, \dots\}$$

In this representation the missing elements can be determined from the elements present and from the context.

The number of distinct elements present in a set may be finite or infinite. We call a set *finite* if it contains a finite number of distinguishable elements; otherwise a set is *infinite*.

Note that no restriction has been placed on the objects that can be members of a set. It is not unusual to have sets whose members are themselves sets, such as $A = \{0, \{a, b\}, 1, \{p\}\}$. It is important, however, to distinguish between the set $\{p\}$, which is an element of A, and the element p, which is a member of $\{p\}$ but not a member of A.

For any two sets A and B, if every element of A is an element of B, then A is called a *subset* of B, or A is said to be *included* in B, or B includes A. Symbolically, this relation is denoted by $A \subseteq B$, or equivalently by $B \supseteq A$. For any two sets A and B, note that $A \subseteq B$ does not necessarily imply that $B \subseteq A$ except for the following case. Two sets A and B are said to be *equal* iff (if and only if) $A \subseteq B$ and $B \subseteq A$ so that $A = B$. The set A is called a *proper subset* of a set B if $A \subseteq B$ and $A \neq B$. This relation is represented by $A \subset B$.

We now introduce two special sets; the first includes every set under discussion while the second is included in every set under discussion. A set is called a *universal set* (E) if it includes every set under discussion. For example, the universal set for natural numbers may be $E = \{0, 1, 2, \dots\}$. A set which does not contain any element is called an *empty set* or a *null set*. An empty set will be denoted by ϕ.

Given any set A, we know that the null set ϕ and the set A are both subsets of A. Also for any element $p \in A$, the set $\{p\}$ is a subset of A. Similarly, we can consider other subsets of A. Rather than finding individual subsets of A, we would like to say something about the set of all subsets of A. For any set A, a collection or family of all subsets of A is called the *power set* of A. The power set of A is denoted by $\rho(A)$ or 2^A, so that $\rho(A) = 2^A = \{x \mid x \subseteq A\}$.

We now introduce the concept of an indexed set. Let $J = \{s_1, s_2, s_3, \dots\}$ and A be a family of sets $A = \{A_{s_1}, A_{s_2}, A_{s_3}, \dots\}$ such that for any $s_i \in J$ there corresponds a set $A_{s_i} \in A$, and also $A_{s_i} = A_{s_j}$ iff $s_i = s_j$. A is then called an *indexed set*, J the *index set*, and any subscript such as the s_i in A_{s_i} is called an *index*.

An indexed family of sets can also be written as $A = \{A_i\}_{i \in J}$. In particular, if $J = \{1, 2, 3, \ldots\}$, then $A = \{A_1, A_2, A_3, \ldots\}$. Also, if $J = \{1, 2, 3, \ldots, n\}$, then $A = \{A_1, A_2, A_3, \ldots, A_n\} = \{A_i\}_{i \in I_n}$ where $I_n = \{1, 2, \ldots, n\}$. For a set S containing n elements, the power set $\rho(S)$ is written as the indexed set $\rho(S) = \{B_i\}_{i \in J}$ where $J = \{0, 1, 2, \ldots, 2^n - 1\}$.

Let us now consider some operations on sets. In particular, we emphasize the set operations of intersection, union, and complement. Using these operations, one can construct new sets by combining the elements of given sets. The *intersection* of any two sets A and B, written as $A \cap B$, is the set consisting of all elements which belong to both A and B. Symbolically,

$$A \cap B = \{x \mid x \in A \land x \in B\}$$

For any indexed set $A = \{A_i\}_{i \in J}$,

$$\bigcap_{i \in J} A_i = \{x \mid x \in A_i \text{ for every } i \in J\}$$

For $J = I_n = \{1, 2, \ldots, n\}$, we can write

$$\bigcap_{i=1}^{n} A_i = \bigcap_{i \in I_n} A_i = A_1 \cap A_2 \cap \cdots \cap A_n$$

Two sets A and B are called *disjoint* iff $A \cap B = \phi$. A collection of sets is called a *disjoint collection* if, for every possible pair of sets in the collection, the two sets are disjoint. The elements of a disjoint collection are said to be *mutually disjoint*.

Let A be an indexed set $A = \{A_i\}_{i \in J}$. The set A is a disjoint collection iff $A_i \cap A_j = \phi$ for all $i, j \in J, i \neq j$.

For any two sets A and B, the *union* of A and B, written as $A \cup B$, is the set of all elements which are members of the set A or the set B or both. Symbolically, it is written as $A \cup B = \{x \mid x \in A \lor x \in B\}$.

For any indexed set $A = \{A_i\}_{i \in J}$,

$$\bigcup_{i \in J} A_i = \{x \mid x \in A_i \text{ for at least one } i \in J\}$$

For $J = I_n = \{1, 2, 3, \ldots, n\}$, we may write

$$\bigcup_{i=1}^{n} A_i = A_1 \cup A_2 \cup \cdots \cup A_n$$

The *relative complement* of B in A (or of B with respect to A), written as $A - B$, is the set consisting of all elements of A which are not elements of B, that is,

$$A - B = \{x \mid x \in A \land x \notin B\}$$

The relative complement of B in A is also called the *difference* of A and B. The relative complement of A with respect to the universal set E, that is, $E - A$, is called the *absolute complement* of A.

So far we have been concerned with sets, their equality, and operations on sets to form new sets. We now introduce the notion of an ordered pair.

An *ordered pair* consists of two objects in a given fixed order. Note that an ordered pair is not a set consisting of two elements. The ordering of the two objects is important. We denote an ordered pair by (x, y).

The equality of two ordered pairs (x, y) and (u, v) is defined by

$$(x, y) = (u, v) \Leftrightarrow ((x = u) \wedge (y = v))$$

where the symbol "$\Leftrightarrow$" denotes *logical equivalence*; that is, $A \Leftrightarrow B$ means that A is equivalent to B. At this point we want to also define the term "imply." A is said to *imply* B written $A \Rightarrow B$, if and only if $A \to B$ is always *true*. In mathematics, the notations $A \to B$ and $A \Rightarrow B$ are often used interchangeably.

The idea of an ordered pair can be extended to define an ordered triple and, more generally, an *n*-tuple. We write an *n*-tuple as $(x_1, x_2, \ldots, x_n)$.

An important idea in set theory is the notion of a cartesian product. Given two sets A and B, the set of all ordered pairs such that the first member of the ordered pair is an element of A and the second member is an element of B is called the *cartesian product* of A and B and is written as $A \times B$. Accordingly

$$A \times B = \{(x, y) | (x \in A) \wedge (y \in B)\}$$

This notion of cartesian product can be extended to any finite number of sets. Let $A = \{A_i\}_{i \in I_n}$ be an indexed set and $I_n = \{1, 2, \ldots, n\}$. We denote the cartesian product of the sets $A_1, A_2, \ldots, A_n$ by

$$\underset{i \in I_n}{\times} A_i = A_1 \times A_2 \times \cdots \times A_n$$

which is defined recursively as

$$\underset{i \in I_1}{\times} A_i = A_1 \quad \text{and} \quad \underset{i \in I_m}{\times} A_i = \left(\underset{i \in I_{m-1}}{\times} A_i \right) \times A_m \quad \text{for } m = 2, 3, \ldots, n$$

Our definition of cartesian product of n sets is related to the definition of n-tuples in the sense that

$$A_1 \times A_2 \times \cdots \times A_n$$

$$= \{(x_1, x_2, \ldots, x_n) | (x_1 \in A_1) \wedge (x_2 \in A_2) \wedge \cdots \wedge (x_n \in A_n)\}$$

As an example, consider the following sets:

$$A_1 = \{1, 3\}, \qquad A_2 = \{3, 4\}, \qquad A_3 = \{1, 3, 4, 6\}$$

Several set operations are exhibited in the following:

$$A_1 \cup A_2 = \{1, 3, 4\}$$

$$A_1 \cap A_3 = \{1, 3\}$$

$$\bigcup_{i=1}^{3} A_i = \{1, 3, 4, 6\}$$

$$\bigcap_{i=1}^{3} A_i = \{3\}$$

$$A_3 - A_1 = \{4, 6\}$$

$$\rho(A_1) = \{\phi, \{1\}, \{3\}, \{1, 3\}\}$$

$$A_1 \times A_2 = \{(1, 3), (1, 4), (3, 3), (3, 4)\}$$

In this section we have introduced the basic concepts of set theory. We now turn our attention to the notions of relations and orderings.

EXERCISES 2-1.1

1 Give another description of the following sets and indicate those which are infinite sets.
(a) $\{x | x$ is an integer and $5 \leq x \leq 12\}$
(b) $\{2, 4, 8, \dots\}$
(c) All the countries of the world

2 Given $S = \{2, a, \{3\}, 4\}$ and $R = \{\{a\}, 3, 4, 1\}$, indicate whether the following are *true* or *false*.
(a) $\{a\} \in S$
(b) $\{a\} \in R$
(c) $\{a, 4, \{3\}\} \subseteq S$
(d) $\{\{a\}, 1, 3, 4\} \subset R$
(e) $R = S$
(f) $\{a\} \subseteq S$
(g) $\{a\} \subseteq R$
(h) $\phi \subset R$
(i) $\phi \subseteq \{\{a\}\} \subseteq R \subseteq E$
(j) $\{\phi\} \subseteq S$
(k) $\phi \in R$
(l) $\phi \subseteq \{\{3\}, 4\}$

3 Show that $(R \subseteq S) \wedge (S \subset Q) \rightarrow R \subset Q$ is always true. Is it correct to replace $R \subset Q$ by $R \subseteq Q$? Explain your answer.

4 Give the power sets of the following.
(a) $\{a, \{b\}\}$
(b) $\{1, \phi\}$
(c) $\{X, Y, Z\}$

5 Given $A = \{x | x$ is an integer and $1 \leq x \leq 5\}$, $B = \{3, 4, 5, 17\}$, and $C = \{1, 2, 3, \dots\}$, find $A \cap B$, $A \cap C$, $A \cup B$, and $A \cup C$.

6 Show that $A \subseteq A \cup B$ and $A \cap B \subseteq A$.

7 Show that $A \subseteq B \Leftrightarrow A \cup B = B$.

8 If $S = \{a, b, c\}$, find nonempty disjoint sets A_1 and A_2 such that $A_1 \cup A_2 = S$. Find other solutions to this problem.

9 The *symmetric difference* of two sets A and B is the set $A + B$ defined by $A + B = (A - B) \cup (B - A)$. Given $A = \{2, 3, 4\}$, $B = \{1, 2\}$, and $C = \{4, 5, 6\}$, find $A + B$, $B + C$, $A + B + C$, and $(A + B) + (B + C)$. Show that $A + B + C$ is associative.

10 Give examples of sets A, B, C such that $A \cup B = A \cup C$, but $B \neq C$.

11 Write the members of $\{a, b\} \times \{1, 2, 3\}$.

12 Write $A \times B \times C$, B^2, A^3, $B^2 \times A$, and $A \times B$ where $A = \{1\}$, $B = \{a, b\}$, and $C = \{2, 3\}$.

13 Show by means of an example that $A \times B \neq B \times A$ and $(A \times B) \times C \neq A \times (B \times C)$.

14 Show that for any two sets A and B

$$\rho(A) \cup \rho(B) \subseteq \rho(A \cup B)$$

$$\rho(A) \cap \rho(B) = \rho(A \cap B)$$

Show by means of an example that

$$\rho(A) \cup \rho(B) \neq \rho(A \cup B)$$

15 Prove the identities

$$A \cap A = A \qquad A \cap \phi = \phi \qquad A \cap E = A \qquad \text{and} \qquad A \cup E = E$$

16 Show that $A \times (B \cap C) = (A \times B) \cap (A \times C)$.

17 Show that $A \times B = B \times A \Leftrightarrow (A = \phi) \vee (B = \phi) \vee (A = B)$

18 Show that $(A \cap B) \cup C = A \cap (B \cup C)$ iff $C \subseteq A$

19 Show that $(A - B) - C = (A - C) - (B - C)$

20 Prove that $(A \cap B) \times (C \cap D) = (A \times C) \cap (B \times D)$

2-1.2 Relations

The concept of a relation is a basic concept in mathematics as well as in everyday life. Associated with a relation is the act of comparing objects which are related to one another. The ability of a computer to perform different tasks based upon the result of a comparison is an important attribute used several times during the execution of a typical program. In this subsection we first formalize the concept of a relation and then discuss methods of representing a relation by using a matrix or its graph. The relation matrix is useful in determining the properties of a relation and also in representing a relation on a computer. Various basic properties of a relation are given, and certain important classes of relations are introduced.

The word "relation" suggests some familiar examples of relations such as the relation of father to son, sister to brother, or uncle to nephew. Familiar examples in arithmetic are relations such as less than, greater than, or that of equality between two real numbers. We also know the relation between the area of an equilateral triangle and the length of one of its sides and the area of a square and the length of a side. These examples suggest relationships between two objects.

Throughout the discussion we consider relations, called binary relations, between a pair of objects. Any set of ordered pairs defines a *binary relation*. We call a binary relation simply a relation. It is sometimes convenient to express a particular ordered pair, say, $(x, y) \in R$, where R is a relation, as xRy.

In mathematics, relations are often denoted by special symbols rather than by capital letters. A familiar example is the relation "less than" for real numbers. This relation is denoted by $<$. In fact, $<$ should be considered as the name of a set whose elements are ordered pairs. More precisely the relation $<$ is

$$< = \{(x, y) \mid x, y \text{ are real numbers and } x \text{ is less than } y\}$$

Let S be a binary relation. The set $D(S)$ of all objects x such that for some y, $(x, y) \in S$ is called the *domain* of S, that is,

$$D(S) = \{x \mid (\exists y)((x, y) \in S)\}$$

where the symbol $\exists$ denotes existential quantification. Similarly, the set $R(S)$ of all objects y such that for some x, $(x, y) \in S$ is called the *range* of S, that is,

$$R(S) = \{y \mid (\exists x)((x, y) \in S)\}$$

Since a relation has been defined as a set of ordered pairs, it is therefore possible to apply the usual operations of sets to relations as well. The resulting sets will also be ordered pairs and will define some relations. If R and S denote two relations, then $R \cap S$ defines a relation such that

$$x(R \cap S)y \Leftrightarrow xRy \wedge xSy$$

Similarly, $R \cup S$ is a relation such that

$$x(R \cup S)y \Leftrightarrow xRy \vee xSy$$

Also

$$x(R - S)y \Leftrightarrow xRy \wedge x\$y$$

where $x\$y$ denotes that x is not related to y in relation S.

A binary relation R in a set X is *reflexive* if, for every $x \in X$, xRx, that is, $(x, x) \in R$. The relation R is *symmetric* if, for every x and y in X, whenever xRy, then yRx. R is said to be *transitive* if, for every x, y, and z in X, whenever xRy and yRz, then xRz. R is *irreflexive* if, for every $x \in X$, $(x, x) \notin R$. Finally, R is said to be *antisymmetric* if, for every x and y in X, whenever xRy and yRx, then $x = y$.

Several important classes of relations having one or more of the properties given here will be discussed later in this subsection.

A relation R from a finite set X to a finite set Y can also be represented by a matrix called the *relation matrix* of R.

Let $X = \{x_1, x_2, \ldots, x_m\}$, $Y = \{y_1, y_2, \ldots, y_n\}$, and R be a relation from X to Y. The relation matrix can be obtained by first constructing a table whose rows are labeled by successive elements of X and whose columns are labeled by successive elements of Y. If x_iRy_j, then we enter a 1 in the ith row and jth column. If x_pRy_q, then we enter a zero in the pth row and the qth column. As a special case, consider $m = 2$, $n = 3$, and R given by

$$R = \{(x_1, y_1), (x_2, y_1), (x_2, y_3)\}$$

The required table for R is Table 2-1.

If we assume that the elements of X and Y appear in a certain order, then the relation R can be represented by a matrix whose elements are 1s and 0s. This matrix can be written down from the table constructed or can be defined in the

Table 2-1

	y_1	y_2	y_3
x_1	1	0	0
x_2	1	0	1

following manner:

$$r_{ij} = \begin{cases} 1, & \text{if } x_i R y_j \\ 0, & \text{if } x_i \not{R} y_j \end{cases}$$

where r_{ij} is the element in the ith row and the jth column. The matrix obtained this way is the relation matrix. If X and Y have m and n elements, respectively, then the matrix is an $m \times n$ matrix. For the relation R just given, the relation matrix is

$$\begin{bmatrix} 1 & 0 & 0 \\ 1 & 0 & 1 \end{bmatrix}$$

One not only can write a relation matrix when a relation R is given but also obtain the relation if the relation matrix is given.

Throughout the remainder of this subsection, unless otherwise stated, we will assume $X = Y$; that is, the relations are defined in a set X. Thus the relation matrices are square. A relation matrix reflects some of the properties of a relation in a set. If a relation is reflexive, all the diagonal entries must be 1. If a relation is symmetric, the relation matrix is symmetric. If a relation is antisymmetric, its matrix is such that if $r_{ij} = 1$, then $r_{ji} = 0$ for $i \neq j$.

A relation can also be represented pictorially by drawing its *graph*. Although we shall introduce some of the concepts of graph theory which are discussed in later chapters, here we shall use graphs only as a tool to represent relations. Let R be a relation in a set $X = \{x_1, x_2, \ldots, x_n\}$. The elements of X are represented by points or circles called *nodes*. The nodes corresponding to x_i and x_j are labeled x_i and x_j, respectively. These nodes may also be called vertices. If $x_i R x_j$, that is, if $(x_i, x_j) \in R$, then we connect nodes x_i and x_j by means of an arc and put an arrow on this arc in the direction from x_i to x_j. When all the nodes corresponding to the ordered pairs in R are connected by arcs with proper arrows, we get a *directed graph* of the relation R. If $x_i R x_j$ and $x_j R x_i$, then we draw two arcs between x_i and x_j. For the sake of simplicity, we may replace the two arcs by one arc with arrows pointing in both directions. If $x_i R x_i$, we get an arc which starts from node x_i and returns to x_i. Such an arc is called a *sling*.

From the graph of a relation it is possible to observe some of its properties. Several examples are given in Fig. 2-1.

Another very important notion which is used in later chapters is that of a partition. Let S be a given set and $A = \{A_1, A_2, \ldots, A_n\}$ where each A_i, $i = 1, 2, \ldots, n$, is a subset of S and $\bigcup_{i=1}^{n} A_i = S$, then the set A is called a *covering* of S, and the sets $A_1, A_2, \ldots, A_n$ are said to *cover* S. If, in addition, the elements of A, which are subsets of S, are mutually disjoint, then A is called a *partition* of S, and the sets $A_1, A_2, \ldots, A_n$ are called the *blocks* of the partition.

We now proceed to define an important class of relations which partitions a set. A relation R in a set X is called an *equivalence relation* if it is reflexive, symmetric, and transitive. If R is an equivalence relation in a set X, then $D(R)$, the domain of R, is X itself. Therefore, R will be called a relation on X. Some

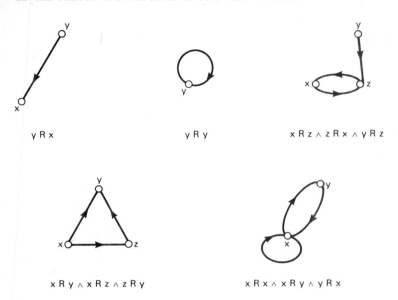

yRx
            yRy
                        x R z ∧ z R x ∧ y R z

x R y ∧ x R z ∧ z R y
                        x R x ∧ x R y ∧ y R x

Figure 2-1 Graphs of relations.

examples of equivalence relations are equality of numbers on a set of real numbers, similarity of triangles on a set of triangles, and the relation of lines being parallel on a set of lines in a plane. Another example of an equivalence relation which will be used in the discussion on hashing functions (see Chap. 8) is that of equality in a modular number system. Let I denote the set of all positive integers, and let n be a positive integer. For $x \in I$ and $y \in I$, we define R as

$$R = \{(x, y)|x - y \text{ is divisible by } n\}$$

Note that "$x - y$ is divisible by n" is equivalent to the statement that both x and y have the same remainder when each is divided by n.

Perhaps the most important idea about relations that is used in formal parsing techniques involves taking the "transitive closure" of a relation. We now develop this idea.

Since a binary relation is a set of ordered pairs, the usual operations such as union and intersection on these sets produce other relations. We now consider another operation on relations—relations which are formed in two or more stages. Familiar examples of such relations are the relation of being a nephew or a brother's or sister's son, the relation of an uncle or a father's or mother's brother, and the relation of being a grandfather or a father's or mother's father. These relations can be produced in the following manner.

Let R be a relation from X to Y and S be a relation from Y to Z. Then a relation written as $R \circ S$ is called a *composite relation* of R and S where

$$R \circ S = \{(x, z)|x \in X \wedge z \in Z \wedge (\exists y)(y \in Y \wedge (x, y) \in R \wedge (y, z) \in S)\}$$

The operation of obtaining $R \circ S$ from R and S is called *composition* of relations.

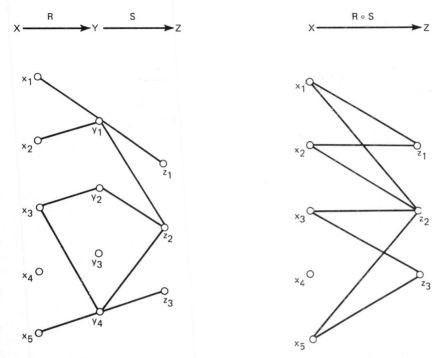

Figure 2-2 Relations R, S, and $R \circ S$.

Note that $R \circ S$ is empty if the intersection of the range of R and the domain of S is empty. $R \circ S$ is nonempty if there is at least one ordered pair $(x, y) \in R$ such that the second member $y \in Y$ of the ordered pair is a first member in an ordered pair in S. For the relation $R \circ S$, the domain is a subset of X and the range is a subset of Z. In fact, the domain is a subset of the domain of R, and its range is a subset of the range of S. From the graphs of R and S one can easily construct the graph of $R \circ S$. As an example, see Fig. 2-2.

The operation of composition is a binary operation on relations, and it produces a relation from two relations. The same operations can be applied again to produce other relations. For example, let R be a relation from X to Y, S a relation from Y to Z, and P a relation from Z to W. Then $R \circ S$ is a relation from X to Z. We can form $(R \circ S) \circ P$, which is a relation from X to W. Similarly, we can also form $R \circ (S \circ P)$, which again is a relation from X to W.

Let us assume that $(R \circ S) \circ P$ is nonempty, and let $(x, y) \in R$, $(y, z) \in S$, and $(z, w) \in P$. This assumption means $(x, z) \in R \circ S$ and $(x, w) \in (R \circ S) \circ P$. Of course, $(y, w) \in S \circ P$ and $(x, w) \in R \circ (S \circ P)$, which shows that

$$(R \circ S) \circ P = R \circ (S \circ P)$$

This result states that the operation of composition on relations is associative. We may delete the parentheses in writing $(R \circ S) \circ P$, so that

$$(R \circ S) \circ P = R \circ (S \circ P) = R \circ S \circ P$$

We know that the relation matrix of a relation R from a set $X = \{x_1, x_2, \ldots, x_m\}$ to a set $Y = \{y_1, y_2, \ldots, y_n\}$ is given by a matrix having m rows and n columns. We shall denote the relation matrix of R by M_R. M_R has entries which are 1s and 0s. Similarly the relation matrix M_S of a relation S from the set Y to a set $Z = \{z_1, z_2, \ldots, z_p\}$ is an $n \times p$ matrix. The relation matrix of $R \circ S$ can be obtained from the matrices M_R and M_S in the following manner.

From the definition it is clear that $(x_i, z_k) \in R \circ S$ if there is at least one element of Y, say, y_j, such that $(x_i, y_j) \in R$ and $(y_j, z_k) \in S$. There may be more than one element of Y which has properties similar to those of y_j, for example, $(x_i, y_r) \in R$ and $(y_r, z_k) \in S$. In all such cases, $(x_i, z_k) \in R \circ S$. Thus when we scan the ith row of M_R and kth column of M_S, and we come across at least one j, such that the entries in the jth location of the row as well as the column under consideration are 1s, then in this instance, the entry in the ith row and kth column of $M_{R \circ S}$ is also 1; otherwise it is 0. Scanning a row of M_R along with every column of M_S gives one row of $M_{R \circ S}$. In this way, we can obtain all the rows of $M_{R \circ S}$.

In general, let the relations A and B be represented by $n \times m$ and $m \times r$ matrices, respectively. Then the composition $A \circ B$ which we denote by the relation matrix C is expressed as

$$c_{ij} = \bigvee_{k=1}^{m} a_{ik} \wedge b_{kj} \qquad i = 1, 2, \ldots, n; \qquad j = 1, 2, \ldots, r$$

where $a_{ik} \wedge b_{kj}$ and $\bigvee_{k=1}^{m}$ indicate bit-ANDing (i.e., $1 \wedge 0 = 0 \wedge 1 = 0 \wedge 0 = 0, 1 \wedge 1 = 1$) and bit-ORing (i.e., $1 \vee 1 = 1 \vee 0 = 0 \vee 1 = 1, 0 \vee 0 = 0$), respectively.

Let us now consider some distinct relations R_1, R_2, R_3, R_4 in a set $X = \{a, b, c\}$ given by

$$R_1 = \{(a, b), (a, c), (c, b)\}$$
$$R_2 = \{(a, b), (b, c), (c, a)\}$$
$$R_3 = \{(a, b), (b, c), (c, c)\}$$
$$R_4 = \{(a, b), (b, a), (c, c)\}$$

Denoting the composition of a relation by itself as

$$R \circ R = R^2 \qquad R \circ R \circ R = R \circ R^2 = R^3 \qquad \cdots \qquad R \circ R^{m-1} = R^m \qquad \cdots$$

let us write the powers of the given relations. Clearly

$$R_1^2 = \{(a, b)\} \qquad R_1^3 = \phi \qquad R_1^4 = \phi \qquad \cdots$$
$$R_2^2 = \{(a, c), (b, a), (c, b)\} \qquad R_2^3 = \{(a, a), (b, b), (c, c)\}$$
$$R_2^4 = R_2 \qquad R_2^5 = R_2^2 \qquad R_2^6 = R_2^3 \qquad \cdots$$
$$R_3^2 = \{(a, c), (b, c), (c, c)\} = R_3^3 = R_3^4 = R_3^5 \qquad \cdots$$
$$R_4^2 = \{(a, a), (b, b), (c, c)\} \qquad R_4^3 = R_4 \qquad R_4^5 = R_4^2 \qquad \cdots$$

Given a finite set X, containing n elements, and a relation R in X, we can interpret R^m ($m = 1, 2, \ldots$) in terms of its graph. This interpretation is done for a number of applications throughout the text. With the help of such an interpretation or from the examples given here, it is possible to say that there are at most n distinct powers of R, for R^m, $m > n$, that can be expressed in terms of $R, R^2, \ldots, R^n$. Our next step is to construct the relation in X given by

$$R^+ = R \cup R^2 \cup R^3 \cup \cdots$$

Naturally, this construction will require only a finite number of powers of R to be calculated, and these calculations can easily be performed by using the matrix representation of the relation R and the Boolean multiplication of these matrices. Let us now see what the corresponding relations R_1^+, R_2^+, R_3^+, and R_4^+ are

$$R_1^+ = R_1 \cup R_1^2 \cup R_1^3 \cdots = R_1$$
$$R_2^+ = R_2 \cup R_2^2 \cup R_2^3 \cdots = R_2 \cup R_2^2 \cup R_2^3$$
$$= \{(a,b), (b,c), (c,a), (a,c), (b,a), (c,b), (a,a), (b,b), (c,c)\}$$
$$R_3^+ = \{(a,b), (b,c), (c,c), (a,c)\}$$
$$R_4^+ = \{(a,b), (b,a), (c,c), (a,a), (b,b)\}$$

Observe that the relations $R_1^+, R_2^+, \ldots, R_4^-$ are all transitive and that $R_1 \subseteq R_1^+$, $R_2 \subseteq R_2^+, \ldots, R_4 \subseteq R_4^+$. From the graphs of these relations one can easily see that R_i^+ is obtained from R_i ($i = 1, 2, 3, 4$) by adding only those ordered pairs to R_i such that R_i^+ is transitive. We now define R^+ in general.

Definition 2-1 Let X be any finite set and R be a relation in X. The relation $R^+ = R \cup R^2 \cup R^3 \cup \cdots$ in X is called the *transitive closure* of R in X.

Theorem 2-1 The transitive closure R^+ of a relation R in a finite set X is transitive. Also for any other transitive relation P in X such that $R \subseteq P$, we have $R^+ \subseteq P$. In this sense, R^+ is the smallest transitive relation containing R.

Based on this theorem, the transitive closure of the relation matrix for some relation A can easily be computed by using the following algorithm due to Warshall.

Procedure WARSHALL (A, n, P). Given the relation matrix A with n rows, the following steps produce the transitive closure of A, which is denoted by P. The variables i, j, and k are local integer variables.

1. [Initialize]
     P ← A
2. [Perform a pass]
     Repeat through step 4 for k = 1, 2,...,n
3. [Process rows]
     Repeat step 4 for i = 1, 2,...,n

4. [Process columns]
    Repeat for j = 1, 2,...,n
        $p_{ij} \leftarrow p_{ij} \lor (p_{ik} \land p_{kj})$.
5. [Finished]
    Exit ☐

To show that this algorithm produces the required matrix, note that step 1 produces a matrix in which $p_{ij} = 1$ if there is a path of length 1 from v_i to v_j. Assume that for a fixed k, the intermediate matrix P produced by steps 3 and 4 of the algorithm is such that the element in the ith row and jth column in this matrix is 1 if and only if there is a path from v_i to v_j which includes only nodes from $v_1, v_2,...,v_k$ as intermediate nodes. Now with an updated value of k, we find that $p_{ij} = 1$ either if $p_{ij} = 1$ in an earlier step or if there is a path from v_i to v_j which traverses through v_{k+1}. This means that $p_{ij} = 1$ if and only if there is a path from v_i to v_j which includes only nodes from $v_1, v_2,...,v_{k+1}$ as intermediate nodes.

Instances of transitive closures of relations will be given in Chaps. 6 and 7, where such relations are derived from a grammar and used in the parsing phase. Also, the transitive closure of a graph of a program can be used to perform certain optimizations in that program. This aspect of compiler writing is the topic of Chaps. 12 and 13.

In terminating this subsection we introduce the notion of the converse of a relation. Given a relation R from X to Y, a relation $\tilde{R}$ from Y to X is called the *converse* of R, where the ordered pairs of $\tilde{R}$ are obtained by interchanging the members in each of the ordered pairs of R. This means, for $x \in X$ and $y \in Y$, that $xRy \Leftrightarrow y\tilde{R}x$.

From the definition of $\tilde{R}$ it follows that $\tilde{\tilde{R}} = R$. The relation matrix $M_{\tilde{R}}$ of $\tilde{R}$ can be obtained by simply interchanging the rows and columns of M_R. Such a matrix is called the *transpose* of M_R. Therefore,

$$M_{\tilde{R}} = \text{transpose of } M_R$$

The graph of $\tilde{R}$ is also obtained from that of R by simply reversing the arrows on each arc.

We now consider the converse of a composite relation. For this purpose, let R be a relation from X to Y and S be a relation from Y to Z. Obviously, $\tilde{R}$ is a relation from Y to X, $\tilde{S}$ from Z to Y; $R \circ S$ is a relation from X to Z, and $R \tilde{\circ} S$ is a relation from Z to X. Also the relation $\tilde{S} \circ \tilde{R}$ is from Z to X. We now show that

$$R \tilde{\circ} S = \tilde{S} \circ \tilde{R}$$

If xRy and ySz, then $x(R \circ S)z$ and $z(R \tilde{\circ} S)x$. But $z\tilde{S}y$ and $y\tilde{R}x$, so that $z(\tilde{S} \circ \tilde{R})x$. This is true for any $x \in X$ and $z \in Z$; hence the required result.

The same rule can be expressed in terms of the relation matrices by saying that the transpose of $M_{R \circ S}$ is the same as the matrix $M_{\tilde{S} \circ \tilde{R}}$. The matrix $M_{\tilde{S} \circ \tilde{R}}$ can be obtained from the matrices $M_{\tilde{S}}$ and $M_{\tilde{R}}$, which in turn can be obtained from the matrices M_S and M_R.

Later in the text, the concept of a relation will be applied to a grammar. In fact there are several interesting relations which can be obtained from a grammar. Many of the operations which are to be performed on these relations have been discussed in this subsection.

EXERCISES 2-1.2

1 Give an example of a relation which is neither reflexive nor irreflexive.

2 Give an example of a relation which is both symmetric and antisymmetric.

3 If relations R and S are both reflexive, show that $R \cup S$ and $R \cap S$ are also reflexive.

4 If relations R and S are reflexive, symmetric, and transitive, show that $R \cap S$ is also reflexive, symmetric, and transitive.

5 Determine whether the following relations are transitive:

$$R_1 = \{(1,1)\} \qquad R_2 = \{(1,2),(2,2)\}$$
$$R_3 = \{(1,2),(2,3),(1,3),(2,1)\}$$

6 Given $S = \{1,2,3,4\}$ and a relation R on S defined by

$$R = \{(1,2),(4,3),(2,2),(2,1),(3,1)\}$$

show that R is not transitive. Find a relation $R_1 \supseteq R$ such that R_1 is transitive. Can you find another relation $R_2 \supseteq R$ which is also transitive?

7 Given $S = \{1,2,\ldots,10\}$ and a relation R on S where

$$R = \{(x,y) \mid x + y = 10\}$$

what are the properties of the relation?

8 Let R be a relation on the set of positive real numbers so that its graphical representation consists of points in the first quadrant of the cartesian plane. What can we expect if R is (a) reflexive, (b) symmetric, and (c) transitive?

9 Let L denote the relation "less than or equal to" and D denote the relation "divides," where xDy means "x divides y." Both L and D are defined on the set $\{1,2,3,6\}$. Write L and D as sets, and find $L \cap D$.

10 Show that the relations L and D given in Exercise 9 are both reflexive, antisymmetric, and transitive. Give another example of such a relation. Draw the graphs of these relations.

11 Let R denote a relation on the set of ordered pairs of positive integers such that $(x,y)R(u,v)$ iff $xv = yu$. Show that R is an equivalence relation.

12 Given a set $S = \{1,2,3,4,5\}$, find the equivalence relation on S which generates the partition whose equivalence classes are the sets $\{1,2\}$, $\{3\}$, and $\{4,5\}$. Draw the graph of the relation.

13 Prove that the relation "congruence modulo m" given by

$$\equiv = \{(x,y) \mid x - y \text{ is divisible by } m\}$$

over the set of positive integers is an equivalence relation. Show also that if $x_1 \equiv y_1$ and $x_2 \equiv y_2$, then $(x_1 + x_2) \equiv (y_1 + y_2)$.

14 Prove the following equivalences and equalities:

(a) $\tilde{\tilde{R}} = R$

(b) $R = S \Leftrightarrow \tilde{R} = \tilde{S}$

(c) $R \subseteq S \Leftrightarrow \tilde{R} \subseteq \tilde{S}$

(d) $R \tilde{\cup} S = \tilde{R} \cup \tilde{S}$

(e) $R \tilde{\cap} S = \tilde{R} \cap \tilde{S}$

15 Show that if a relation R is reflexive, then $\tilde{R}$ is also reflexive. Show also that similar remarks hold if R is transitive, irreflexive, symmetric, or antisymmetric.

16 What nonzero entries are there in the relation matrix of $R \cap \tilde{R}$ if R is an antisymmetric relation in a set X?

17 Given the relation matrix M_R of a relation R on the set $\{a, b, c\}$, find the relation matrices of $\tilde{R}$, $R^2 = R \circ R$, $R^3 = R \circ R \circ R$, and $R \circ \tilde{R}$.

$$M_R = \begin{bmatrix} 1 & 0 & 1 \\ 1 & 1 & 0 \\ 1 & 1 & 1 \end{bmatrix}$$

18 Two equivalence relations R and S are given by their relation matrices M_R and M_S. Show that $R \circ S$ is not an equivalence relation.

$$M_R = \begin{bmatrix} 1 & 1 & 0 \\ 1 & 1 & 0 \\ 0 & 0 & 1 \end{bmatrix} \qquad M_S = \begin{bmatrix} 1 & 0 & 0 \\ 0 & 1 & 1 \\ 0 & 1 & 1 \end{bmatrix}$$

Obtain equivalence relations R_1 and R_2 on $\{1, 2, 3\}$ such that $R_1 \circ R_2$ is also an equivalence relation.

19 Using Warshall's algorithm, obtain the transitive closure of the relation whose graph is given in Fig. 2-3.

20 For the graph of the relation R given in Fig. 2-4, determine $M_{\tilde{R}}$, $M_R \wedge M_{\tilde{R}}$, and $M_{\tilde{R}} \wedge M_R$.

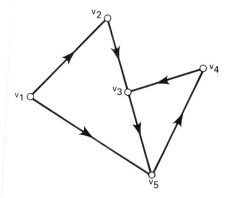

Figure 2-3

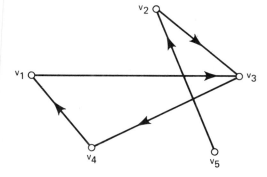

Figure 2-4

2-1.3 Strings

In this subsection we are concerned with some elementary properties of strings. There are many interesting properties exhibited by string operations, just as there are interesting properties for arithmetic operations over the natural numbers. To refamiliarize ourselves with some of the properties associated with operations, let us consider the operation of addition on the natural numbers. This operation can be represented, in general, by a functional system in two variables:

$$f(x, y) = x + y$$

where x and y are natural numbers. This system exhibits certain interesting properties. First, the sum of any two natural numbers is a natural number. This property is called *closure*. Closure is a necessary property for a system (i.e., a set and an operation on that set) to be classified as an algebraic system. Second, $(x + y) + z = x + (y + z) = x + y + z$ when x, y, and z are natural numbers; accordingly the operation of addition is said to be *associative*. Third, there exists a number i such that for every natural number x, $x + i = x$. This number is zero and is called the unit element or *identity* of the additive system. Many other important properties, such as distributivity and commutativity, exist when arithmetic operations such as addition and multiplication are applied to the set of natural numbers.

We begin a discussion of strings by formally defining a string. To do so, we must introduce the notion of an alphabet and the operation of concatenation. Simply stated, an alphabet V is a finite nonempty set of symbols. The set $V = \{a, b, c, \ldots, z\}$ is a familiar example of an alphabet and $\{\alpha, \beta, \gamma, \varepsilon\}$ is a four-character alphabet (which is a subalphabet of the Greek alphabet).

The *concatenation* of two alphabetic characters, say $'a'$ and $'b'$, is said to form a sequence of characters, namely, $'ab'$. (Note that henceforth when we refer to a character from an alphabet or a sequence of such characters, they are enclosed in single quote marks.) The operation of concatenation also applies to sequences of characters. For example, $'ab'$ concatenated with $'ab'$ is $'abab'$. We denote the concatenation operator by the special symbol $\circ$. This allows us to write expressions such as $'ab' \circ 'a'$, which is identical in value to $'aba'$.

A *string* (or *sentence*) over an alphabet V is either a letter from the alphabet V or a sequence of letters derived from the concatenation of zero or more characters from the alphabet V. Examples of strings over an alphabet $V = \{a, b, c\}$ are $'a'$, $'ca'$, $'ccba'$, and $'bbb'$.

Let $V \circ V = V^2$ designate all strings of length 2 on V, $V \circ V \circ V = V^2 \circ V = V^3$ designate all strings of length 3 on V, and in general, $V \circ V \circ \cdots \circ V = V^n$ designate all strings of length n on V. Then the closure of V, denoted as V^+, is defined as

$$V^+ = V \cup V^2 \cup V^3 \cup \cdots$$

For completeness, a special string ε called the empty (or null) string is often combined with V^+ to form the closure set V^* of V. That is, $V^* = \{\varepsilon\} \cup V \cup V^2 \cup V^3 \cup \cdots = \{\varepsilon\} \cup V^+$. The string ε has the identity property (i.e., $x \circ \varepsilon =$

$\varepsilon \circ x = x$ for any string x which is an element of V^*), and it is called the identity element in the system formed by the set V^* and the operation of concatenation. Associativity is another property of this system (that is, $(x \circ y) \circ z = x \circ (y \circ z) = x \circ y \circ z$ for $x, y, z \in V^*$).

As an example, consider the set of strings V^* that can be generated from an alphabet $V = \{x, y\}$. Some subsets of V^* are

$$V^2 = \{ \text{'}xx\text{'}, \text{'}xy\text{'}, \text{'}yx\text{'}, \text{'}yy\text{'} \}$$

$$V^3 = \{ \text{'}xxx\text{'}, \text{'}xxy\text{'}, \text{'}xyx\text{'}, \text{'}xyy\text{'}, \text{'}yxx\text{'}, \text{'}yxy\text{'}, \text{'}yyx\text{'}, \text{'}yyy\text{'} \}$$

$$V^4 = \{ \text{'}xxxx\text{'}, \text{'}xxxy\text{'}, \text{'}xxyx\text{'}, \text{'}xxyy\text{'}, \text{'}xyxx\text{'}, \text{'}xyxy\text{'}, \text{'}xyyx\text{'}, \text{'}xyyy\text{'},$$
$$\text{'}yxxx\text{'}, \text{'}yxxy\text{'}, \text{'}yxyx\text{'}, \text{'}yxyy\text{'}, \text{'}yyxx\text{'}, \text{'}yyxy\text{'}, \text{'}yyyx\text{'}, \text{'}yyyy\text{'} \}$$

$$\vdots$$

We will, on many occasions, refer to the closure set V^* of an alphabet.

As another example of a string, let us examine FORTRAN. The FORTRAN alphabet consists of 26 letters, 10 digits, and a set of special characters, such as '(', ')', ',', '=', and '+'. It is only these characters that are used in writing a FORTRAN program. Hence a program can be viewed as the concatenation of characters over an alphabet to yield an arbitrarily long string. In Chap. 4, we see that the problem of ensuring that only the proper set of characters appears in a program is handled by the scanning phase of a compiler.

Let x, y, and z be strings over an alphabet where $z = xy$. The string x is called a *prefix* or *head* of z. If $y \neq \varepsilon$, then x is called a *proper prefix* or *proper head*. Similarly, y is called a *suffix* or *tail* of z, and if $x \neq \varepsilon$, then y is called a *proper suffix* or *proper tail*.

Some of the concepts introduced here are used in the next section, where the notions of grammars and languages are introduced.

2-2 DISCUSSION OF GRAMMARS

Programming languages must be precisely defined. Unfortunately, for some of the earlier programming languages the existence of a particular compiler finally provided the precise definition of such a language. The proper specification of a programming language involves the definition of the following:

1. The set of symbols (or alphabet) that can be used to construct correct programs
2. The set of all syntactically correct programs
3. The "meaning" of all syntactically correct programs

In this section we shall be concerned with the first two items in the specification of programming languages.

A language L can be considered a subset of the closure (including the empty string) of an alphabet. The language consisting of this closure set is not particularly interesting, since it is too large. Our definition of a language L is a set of strings or sentences over some finite alphabet V_T, so that $L \subseteq V_T^*$.

How can a language be represented? A language consists of a finite or an infinite set of sentences. Finite languages can be specified by exhaustively enumerating all their sentences. However, for infinite languages, such an enumeration is not possible. On the other hand, any means of specifying a language should be finite. One method of specification which satisfies this requirement uses a generative device called a *grammar*. A grammar consists of a finite nonempty set of rules or *productions* which specify the syntax of the language. As well, a grammar imposes structure on the sentences of a language. Many grammars may generate the same language but impose different structures on the sentences of that language. The study of grammars constitutes an important subarea of computer science called *formal language theory*. This area emerged in the mid-1950s as a result of the efforts of Noam Chomsky (1959), who gave a mathematical model of a grammar in connection with his study of natural languages. In 1960, the concept of a grammar became important to programmers because the syntax of ALGOL 60 was described by a grammar.

A second method of language specification is to have a machine, called an *acceptor*, determine whether a given sentence belongs to the language. This approach is discussed further in Chaps. 4, 6, and 7 along with some very interesting and important relationships that exist between grammars and acceptors.

In this section we are concerned with a grammar as a mathematical system for defining languages and as a device for giving some useful structure to sentences in a language. It was mentioned earlier that a grammar imposes a structure on the sentences of a language. For a sentence in English such a structure is described in terms of subject, predicate, phrase, noun, and so on. On the other hand, for a program, the structure is given in terms of procedures, statements, expressions, etc. In any case, it may be desirable to describe all such structures and to obtain a set of all the correct or admissible sentences in a language. For example, we may have a set of correct sentences in English or a set of valid ALGOL programs. The grammatical structure of a language helps us determine whether a particular sentence does or does not belong to the set of correct sentences. The grammatical structure of a sentence is generally studied by analyzing the various parts of a sentence and their relationships to one another.

Consider the sentence "the cat ate a mouse." Its structure (or *parse*) is shown in Fig. 2-5. This diagram of a parse displays the syntax of a sentence in a manner similar to a tree and is therefore called a *syntax tree*. Each node in the diagram represents a phrase of the syntax. The words such as "the" and "cat" are the basic symbols, or primitives, of the language.

The syntax of a small subset of the English language can be described by using the symbols

S: sentence   V: verb   O: object   A: article   N: noun

SP: subject phrase   VP: verb phrase   NP: noun phrase

in the following rules:

S → SP VP	N → 'mouse'
SP → A N	N → 'tree'
A → 'a'	VP → V O
A → 'the'	V → 'ate'
N → 'monkey'	V → 'climbs'
N → 'banana'	O → NP
N → 'cat'	NP → A N

These rules state that a sentence is composed of a "subject phrase" followed by a "verb phrase"; the "subject phrase" is composed of an "article" followed by a "noun"; a verb phrase is composed of a "verb" followed by an "object"; and so on.

The structure of a language is discussed by using symbols such as "sentence," "verb," "subject phrase," and "verb phrase," which represent *syntactic classes* of elements. Each syntactic class consists of a number of alternative structures, and each structure consists of an ordered set of items which are either primitives (of the language) or syntactic classes. These alternative structures are called *productions* or *rules of syntax*, or *replacement rules*. For example, the production, S → SP VP defines a "sentence" to be composed of a "subject phrase" followed by a "verb phrase." The symbol → separates the syntactic class "sentence" from its definition. The syntactic class and the arrow symbol along with the interpretation of a production enable us to describe a language.

A system or language which describes another language is known as a *metalanguage*. The metalanguage used to teach German at most universities is

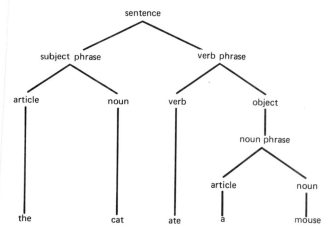

Figure 2-5 Syntax tree for an English sentence.

English, while the metalanguage used to teach English is English. The diagram of the parse of a sentence describes its syntax but not its meaning or *semantics*. At this time, we are mainly concerned with the syntax of a language, and the device which we have just defined to give the syntactic definition of the language is called a *grammar*.

Using the grammatical rules for our example, we can either produce (generate) or derive a sentence in the language. A computer programmer is concerned with producing programs which adhere to the productions (grammatical rules) of the language. The compiler of a language, on the other hand, is faced with the problem of determining whether a given sentence (source program) is syntactically correct based upon the given grammatical rules. If the syntax is correct, the compiler produces object code.

Consider the problem of trying to generate or produce the sentence "the cat ate the mouse" from the set of productions given. It is accomplished by starting first with the syntactic class symbol S and looking for a production which has S to the left of the arrow. There is only one such production, namely,

S → SP VP

We have replaced the class S by its only possible composition. We then take the string

SP VP

and look for a production whose left-hand side is SP and then replace it with the right-hand side of that production. The application of the only production possible produces the string

A N VP

We next look for a production whose left part is A, and two such productions are found. By selecting the production A → 'the' and upon substituting its right-hand side in the string A N VP, we obtain the string

the N VP

This enumerative process is continued until we arrive at the correct sentence. At this point, the sentence contains only primitive or terminal elements of the language (no classes). A complete derivation or generation of the sentence "the cat ate a mouse" is as follows:

S ⇒ SP VP
  ⇒ A N VP
  ⇒ the N VP
  ⇒ the cat VP
  ⇒ the cat V O
  ⇒ the cat ate O
  ⇒ the cat ate NP
  ⇒ the cat ate A N
  ⇒ the cat ate a N
  ⇒ the cat ate a mouse

Here the symbol ⇒ denotes that the string on the right-hand side of the symbol can be obtained by applying one replacement rule to the previous string.

The rules for the example language can produce a number of sentences. Examples of such sentences are

The cat ate a banana.
The monkey climbs a tree.
The monkey climbs the tree.
The banana ate a cat.

The last of these sentences, although grammatically correct, does not make sense because of its semantics. This situation is often allowed in the specification of languages. There are many valid FORTRAN and PASCAL programs that do not make sense. It is easier to define languages if certain sentences of questionable validity are allowed by the replacement rules.

There is another important thing to note concerning the generation of strings (i.e., sentences) from a grammar. We have neglected (for legibility reasons) to put into the terminal symbols of the grammar the blank characters which normally appear between the words in the sentences. Throughout the book, we assume, unless it is obvious from context of the text, that a blank delimits all terminal symbols.

The set of sentences that can be generated by the rules of the previous example is finite. Any interesting language usually consists of an infinite set of sentences. As a matter of fact, the importance of a finite device such as a grammar is that it permits the study of the structure of a language consisting of an infinite set of sentences.

Let the symbols L, D, and I denote the classes L: letter, D: digit, and I: identifier. The productions which follow are recursive and produce an infinite set of names because the syntactic class I is present on both the left and the right sides of certain productions.

$$I \rightarrow L \qquad D \rightarrow 0$$
$$I \rightarrow ID \qquad D \rightarrow 1$$
$$I \rightarrow IL \qquad \cdots$$
$$L \rightarrow a \qquad D \rightarrow 9$$
$$L \rightarrow b$$
$$\cdots$$
$$L \rightarrow z$$

It is easily seen that the class I defines an infinite set of strings or names in which each name consists of a letter followed by any number of letters or digits. This set is a consequence of using recursion in the definition of the productions

$I \to ID$ and $I \to IL$. In fact, recursion is fundamental to the definition of an infinite language by the use of a grammar

Let us now formalize the idea of a grammar and how it is used. For this purpose, let V_T be a finite nonempty set of symbols called the *terminal alphabet*. The symbols in V_T are called *terminal symbols*. The *metalanguage* which is used to generate strings in the language is assumed to contain a set of syntactic classes or variables called *nonterminal symbols*. The set of nonterminal symbols is denoted by V_N, and the elements of V_N are used to define the syntax (structure) of the language. Furthermore, the sets V_N and V_T are assumed to be disjoint. The set $V_N \cup V_T$ consisting of nonterminal and terminal symbols is called the *vocabulary* of the language. In much of the discussion in this section we use capital letters such as $A, B, C, \ldots, X, Y, Z$ to denote nonterminal symbols, and $S_1, S_2, \ldots$ to represent the elements of the vocabulary. The strings of terminal symbols are denoted by lowercase letters $x, y, z, \ldots$ while strings of symbols over the vocabulary are given by $\alpha, \beta, \gamma, \ldots$. The length of a string α will be denoted by $|\alpha|$.

Definition 2-2 A *grammar* is defined by a 4-tuple $G = (V_N, V_T, S, \Phi)$ where V_T and V_N are sets of terminal and nonterminal (syntactic class) symbols, respectively. S, a distinguished element of V_N and therefore of the vocabulary, is called the starting symbol. Φ is a finite nonempty subset of the relation from $(V_T \cup V_N)^* V_N (V_T \cup V_N)^*$ to $(V_T \cup V_N)^*$. In general, an element (α, β) is written as $\alpha \to \beta$ and is called a *production rule* or a *rewriting rule*.

For our example defining an identifier, we may write the grammar as $G_1 = (V_N, V_T, S, \Phi)$ in which

$V_N = \{ I, L, D \}$

$V_T = \{ a, b, c, d, e, f, g, h, i, j, k, l, m, n, o, p, q, r,$

$\qquad s, t, u, v, w, x, y, z, 0, 1, 2, 3, 4, 5, 6, 7, 8, 9 \}$

$S = I$

$\Phi = \{ I \to L, I \to IL, I \to ID, L \to a, L \to b, \ldots, L \to z,$

$\qquad D \to 0, D \to 1, \ldots, D \to 9 \}$

Definition 2-3 Let $G = (V_N, V_T, S, \Phi)$ be a grammar. For $\sigma, \psi \in V^*$, σ is said to be a *direct derivative* of ψ, written as $\psi \Rightarrow \sigma$, if there are strings ϕ_1 and ϕ_2 (including possibly empty strings) such that $\psi = \phi_1 \alpha \phi_2$ and $\sigma = \phi_1 \beta \phi_2$ and $\alpha \to \beta$ is a production of G.

If $\psi \Rightarrow \sigma$, we may also say that ψ directly produces σ or σ directly reduces to ψ. For grammar G_1 of our example, we have listed in Table 2-2 some illustrations of direct derivations.

The concepts can now be extended to produce a string σ not necessarily directly but in a number of steps from a string ψ.

Table 2-2

ψ	σ	Rule used	ϕ_1	ϕ_2
I	L	$I \rightarrow L$	ε	ε
LL	Lx	$L \rightarrow x$	L	ε
LDL	$L1L$	$D \rightarrow 1$	L	L
$LDDL$	$L2DL$	$D \rightarrow 2$	L	DL

Definition 2-4 Let $G = (V_N, V_T, S, \Phi)$ be a grammar. The string ψ *produces σ* (σ reduces to ψ, or σ is the derivative of ψ), written as $\psi \stackrel{+}{\Rightarrow} \sigma$, if there are strings $\phi_0, \phi_1, \ldots, \phi_n$ ($n > 0$) such that $\psi = \phi_0 \Rightarrow \phi_1, \phi_1 \Rightarrow \phi_2, \ldots, \phi_{n-1} \Rightarrow \phi_n = \sigma$. The relation $\stackrel{+}{\Rightarrow}$ is the transitive closure of the relation $\Rightarrow$. If we let $n = 0$, we can define the reflexive transitive closure of $\Rightarrow$ as

$$\psi \stackrel{*}{\Rightarrow} \sigma \qquad \Leftrightarrow \qquad \psi \stackrel{+}{\Rightarrow} \sigma \quad \text{or} \quad \psi = \sigma$$

Returning to grammar G_1, we show that the string $a13$ is derived from I by following the derivation sequence:

$$I \Rightarrow ID \Rightarrow IDD \Rightarrow LDD \Rightarrow aDD \Rightarrow a1D \Rightarrow a13$$

Note that as long as we have a nonterminal symbol in the string, we can produce a new string from it (assuming no rules of the form $A \rightarrow A$). On the other hand, if a string contains only terminal symbols, then the derivation is complete, and we cannot produce any further strings from it.

Definition 2-5 A *sentential form* is any derivative of the unique nonterminal symbol S. The language L generated by a grammar G is the set of all sentential forms whose symbols are terminal, i.e.,

$$L(G) = \{\sigma | S \stackrel{*}{\Rightarrow} \sigma \text{ and } \sigma \in V_T^*\}$$

Therefore, the language is merely a subset of the set of all terminal strings (sentences) over V_T.

We conclude this section by introducing the Backus Naur form (BNF) of metalanguage, which is slightly different from the metalanguage which was previously used. The metavariables or syntactic classes will be enclosed by the symbols $\langle$ and $\rangle$. Using this terminology, the symbol $\langle$sentence$\rangle$ is a symbol of V_N and the symbol "sentence" is an element of V_T. In this way, no confusion or ambiguity arises when we attempt to distinguish the two symbols.

BNF has been used extensively in the formal definition of many programming languages. A popular language described using BNF is ALGOL. For example, the definition of an identifier in BNF is given as

$\langle$identifier$\rangle ::= \langle$letter$\rangle | \langle$identifier$\rangle\langle$letter$\rangle | \langle$identifier$\rangle\langle$digit$\rangle$

$\langle$letter$\rangle ::= a|b|c| \cdots |y|z$

$\langle$digit$\rangle ::= 0|1|2| \cdots |8|9$

Note that the symbol ::= replaces the symbol → in the grammar notation, and |
is used to separate different right-hand sides of productions corresponding to the
same left-hand side. The symbols ::= and | are interpreted as "is defined as" and
"or," respectively. In Sec. 2-4.4 we examine an extended version of BNF.

In this section we have formally introduced the concept of a grammar. There
are a number of restrictions that can be placed on the rewriting rules of a
grammar. The result of imposing these restrictions is to classify grammars into
four distinct classes. The next section looks at this classification of grammars.

EXERCISES 2-2

1 Using the example grammar in the text which described a small subset of the English language, give
derivations for the following sentences:

the monkey ate a banana
the cat climbs a tree
the cat ate the monkey

2 Consider the following grammar with the set of terminal symbols $\{a, b\}$:

$$S \rightarrow a \qquad S \rightarrow Sa \qquad S \rightarrow b \qquad S \rightarrow bS$$

Describe the set of strings generated by the grammar.

3 Write grammars for the following languages:
   (a) The set of nonnegative odd integers
   (b) The set of nonnegative even integers with no leading zeros permitted

4 The following grammar generates simple arithmetic expressions involving addition ($+$), subtraction
($-$), multiplication ($*$), and division ($/$). The symbol i represents a variable name.

$$V_N = \{E, T, F\}, \qquad V_T = \{i, *, /, +, -, (,)\}, \qquad S = E$$

$$F \rightarrow i \qquad\qquad T \rightarrow T/F$$

$$F \rightarrow (E) \qquad\quad E \rightarrow T$$

$$T \rightarrow F \qquad\qquad E \rightarrow E + T$$

$$T \rightarrow T * F \qquad E \rightarrow E - T$$

Give the derivations for the following expressions:

$$i + i, \quad i - i/i, \quad i * (i + i), \quad i * i + i$$

5 Write grammars for the following languages.
   (a) The set of FORTRAN names. Remember that FORTRAN names must have no more than six
characters.
   (b) The set of PL/I comments. The set of terminal symbols for the grammar is assumed to be
$\{A, B, C, \ldots, Z, 0, 1, \ldots, 9, \#, !, *, -, +, /, \Box\}$, where the symbol $\Box$ denotes a blank.

2-3 CLASSIFICATION OF GRAMMARS

In this section the grammar classification of Chomsky is presented and some
comments are made about the hierarchy that is formed by this classification.
Chomsky classified grammars into four classes by imposing different sets of

restrictions on the productions. The first class is a grammar whose rules are unrestricted and is therefore called an *unrestricted grammar*. In the second class there is a restriction on the productions as given in the following definition.

Definition 2-6 A *context-sensitive grammar* contains only productions of the form $\alpha \rightarrow \beta$, where $|\alpha| \le |\beta|$, where $|\alpha|$ denotes the length of α.

This form of restriction on a production prevents β from being empty. The production form of a context-sensitive grammar can be stated in another manner. This second form involves letting α and β in the production $\alpha \rightarrow \beta$ be expressed as $\alpha = \phi_1 A \phi_2$ and $\beta = \phi_1 \psi \phi_2$ (ϕ_1 and/or ϕ_2 are possibly empty) where ψ must be nonempty. Then the meaning of "context-sensitive" becomes clearer with the following reformulation. The application of a production $\phi_1 A \phi_2 \rightarrow \phi_1 \psi \phi_2$ to a sequential form means that A is rewritten as ψ in the context between ϕ_1 and ϕ_2. These two forms of rules are equivalent in the sense that a language definable by a grammar having rules of the first form is always definable by some (often different) grammar having rules of the second form. Context-sensitive grammars are said to generate context-sensitive languages.

The language $L(G_2) = \{a^n b^n c^n | n \ge 1\}$ is generated by the following context-sensitive grammar:

$$G_2 = (\{S, B, C\}, \{a, b, c\}, S, \Phi)$$

where Φ consists of the productions

1. $S \rightarrow aSBC$
2. $S \rightarrow abC$
3. $bB \rightarrow bb$

4. $bC \rightarrow bc$
5. $CB \rightarrow BC$
6. $cC \rightarrow cc$

The following is a derivation for the string $a^2 b^2 c^2$:

$S \Rightarrow aSBC$	by production 1
$\Rightarrow aabCBC$	by production 2
$\Rightarrow aabBCC$	by production 5
$\Rightarrow aabbCC$	by production 3
$\Rightarrow aabbcC$	by production 4
$\Rightarrow aabbcc$	by production 6

We now impose a further restriction on the type of production allowable for a context-sensitive grammar to obtain a context-free grammar.

Definition 2-7 A *context-free grammar* contains only productions of the form $\alpha \rightarrow \beta$, where $|\alpha| \le |\beta|$ and $\alpha \in V_N$.

With such grammars, the rewriting variable in a sentential form is rewritten regardless of the other symbols in its vicinity or context. This has led to the term "context-free" for grammars consisting of productions whose left-hand side consists of a single class symbol. Context-free grammars do not have the power to represent even significant parts of the English language, since context dependency is often required in order to analyze properly the structure of a sentence. Context-free grammars are not capable of specifying (or determining) that a certain variable was declared when it is used in some expression in a subsequent statement of a source program. However, these grammars can specify most of the syntax for computer languages, since these languages are, by and large, simple in structure. Context-free grammars are said to generate context-free languages. Grammar G_1 of Sec. 2-2 is an example of a context-free grammar. Another example of a context-free grammar is the one used to generate the language $L(G_3) = \{a^n b a^n | n \geq 1\}$, where $G_3 = (\{S, C\}, \{a, b\}, S, \Phi)$ and Φ is the set of productions

$$S \rightarrow aCa$$
$$C \rightarrow aCa$$
$$C \rightarrow b$$

A derivation for $a^3 b a^3$ consists of the following steps:

$$S \Rightarrow aCa$$
$$\Rightarrow aaCaa$$
$$\Rightarrow aaaCaaa$$
$$\Rightarrow aaabaaa$$

A final restriction leads to the definition of regular grammars.

Definition 2-8 A *regular grammar* contains only productions of the form $\alpha \rightarrow \beta$, where $|\alpha| \leq |\beta|$, $\alpha \in V_N$, and β has the form aB or a, where $a \in V_T$ and $B \in V_N$.

The languages generated by such grammars are said to be regular. An example of a regular grammar is the following, which generates the language $L(G_4) = \{a^n b a^m | n, m \geq 1\}$, where $G_4 = (\{S, A, B, C\}, \{a, b\}, S, \Phi)$ and the set of productions is

$$S \rightarrow aS$$
$$S \rightarrow aB$$
$$B \rightarrow bC$$
$$C \rightarrow aC$$
$$C \rightarrow a$$

The sentence $a^3 b a^2$ has the following derivation:

$$S \Rightarrow aS$$
$$\Rightarrow aaS$$
$$\Rightarrow aaaB$$
$$\Rightarrow aaabC$$
$$\Rightarrow aaabaC$$
$$\Rightarrow aaabaa$$

Let the unrestricted, context-sensitive, context-free, and regular grammars be denoted by the class symbols T_0, T_1, T_2, and T_3, respectively. If $L(T_i)$ represents the class of languages that can be generated by the class of T_i grammars, it can be shown that

$$L(T_3) \subset L(T_2) \subset L(T_1) \subset L(T_0)$$

and therefore the four classes of grammars form a hierarchy. Corresponding to each class of grammars there is a class of machines (acceptors) that will accept the class of languages generated by the former. We discuss models of some of these acceptors in Chaps. 4, 6, and 7.

To show that $L(T_1) \subset L(T_0)$ involves introducing the notion of a decision problem associated with a language.

Given a language L and some element (or string) x, the decision problem associated with this set (the set of sentences of L) is to determine whether or not x belongs to L. The decision problem associated with a language is said to be *fully decidable* if there exists an algorithm which will answer this question in a finite time. A language whose decision problem is fully decidable is said to be *recursive*. The decision problem is said to be *semidecidable* if there exists an algorithm which can say yes in a finite time when $x \in L$ but may say no when $x \notin L$. A language whose decision problem is semidecidable is said to be *recursively enumerable*.

Clearly this is not a mathematical definition of recursive and recursively enumerable languages. For an adequate definition, the intuitive notion of algorithm would have to be replaced by a formal notion such as a Turing machine (see Davis, 1958).

Now let us return to the problem of what is involved in showing that $L(T_1) \subset L(T_0)$. It can be shown (see Davis, 1958) that "A set is recursively enumerable if it is a T_0 language." In other words, an unrestricted grammar has the generative power of a Turing machine. Recall that the decision problem associated with any recursively enumerable set is semidecidable. To show that $L(T_1) \subset L(T_0)$ involves formulating a fully decidable algorithm for any T_1 language, that is, formulating an algorithm which will determine whether or not a given string x belongs to $L(G)$ for a context-sensitive grammar G. Such an algorithm can be found in Hopcroft and Ullman (1969).

To show that $L(T_2) \subset L(T_1)$ involves choosing a particular context-sensitive language which is not context-free. Consider the language $L = \{ \#a^n b^m a^n b^m ccc\# \mid n, m \geq 1\}$. This language, which was initially formulated by Chomsky (1959), is context-sensitive, since he obtained a context-sensitive grammar for this grammar. He also proved that no context-free grammar can generate the above language.

In terminating this section we show that $L(T_3) \subset L(T_2)$. Since both regular and context-free grammars are discussed extensively throughout the remaining chapters, it is instructive to prove that the class of regular languages is a proper subset of the context-free languages. Consider the languages $L_1 = \{a^n ba^n \mid n \geq 1\}$ and $L_2 = \{a^n ba^m \mid n, m \geq 1\}$. A context-free grammar for L_1 consists of the rules

$$S \rightarrow aAa$$
$$A \rightarrow aAa$$
$$A \rightarrow b$$

A regular grammar for L_2 is easily constructed, and a possible set of rules are

$$S \rightarrow aS$$
$$S \rightarrow aB$$
$$B \rightarrow bC$$
$$C \rightarrow aC$$
$$C \rightarrow a$$

It can be shown that L_1 is context-free but not regular. This is done in the following theorem.

Theorem 2-2 There are context-free languages which are not regular languages.

PROOF Let us assume that there exists a regular grammar which generates the previously introduced language L_1. A derivation in a regular grammar has a number of characteristics. First, each sentential form in a derivation contains at most one nonterminal which occurs at the right end of the sentential form. Second, the length of each successive sentential form (except the last) increases by 1. Assume that we have a derivation for the string $a^n b a^n$. Such a terminal string must be directly produced by the sentential form $a^n b a^{n-1} Y$. Let q denote the number of nonterminals in the grammar and choose $n > q$. Since only one terminal character can be added to each sentential form at each step (except the first), the derivation contains $2n + 1$ lines. Also, since exactly one nonterminal occurs on each line (except for the last), there must be some nonterminal symbol which is repeated in the derivation. This phenomenon must happen because $n > q$. The result of this is a derivation which looks like

$$\vdots$$
$$a^n b \ldots X$$
$$\vdots$$
$$a^n b \ldots X$$
$$\vdots$$
$$a^n b a^n$$

where the nonterminal X has been repeated in some sentential form. Note that a portion of the derivation can be deleted or duplicated at will. Consequently, after the generation of $a^n b$ on the left, the grammar is unable to generate exactly a^n on the right. The resulting language is L_2. Therefore, L_1 is not regular and $L(T_3) \subset L(T_2)$.

We have informally discussed the Chomsky classification. In the remainder of this book, however, we will restrict ourselves primarily to the classes of context-free and regular grammars. The class of context-free grammars has been studied in great depth and has been adequate for specifying most of the language constructs in current programming languages. In the next section we examine context-free grammars more closely.

EXERCISES 2-3

1 Obtain a context-sensitive grammar which will generate the language $L = \{ xx$ where $x = x_1 x_2 \cdots x_n$ and $x_i \in \{a, b\}$ for all $1 \le i \le n\}$. For example, if $x = ab$, then $abab$ is in the language.

2 Obtain a context-sensitive grammar for the language $\{a^{m^2} | m \ge 1\}$.

3 Construct a context-sensitive grammar for the language $\{w | w \in \{a, b, c\}^* - \{\varepsilon\}\}$, where w contains the same number of a's, b's, and c's.

4 Two equivalent definitions of a context-sensitive grammar are given in the text. Productions such as $BC \to CB$ satisfy one definition but not the other. Show that both definitions are equivalent.

5 Give a grammar which generates $L = \{w | w$ consists of an equal number of a's and b's$\}$.

6 Give a context-free grammar which generates $L = \{w | w$ contains twice as many 0s as 1s$\}$.

7 Construct a regular grammar which will generate all strings of 0s and 1s having both an odd number of 0s and an odd number of 1s.

8 Obtain a grammar for the language $L = \{0^i 1^j | i \ne j$ and $i, j > 0\}$.

9 Obtain a context-sensitive grammar which generates the language $\{a^p | p$ is a prime$\}$.

2-4 CONTEXT-FREE GRAMMARS AND PARSING

The syntax of common programming languages like ALGOL 60, FORTRAN, and PASCAL cannot be completely described by context-free grammars. Powerful formalisms, such as context-sensitive grammars or the "W-grammars" of the ALGOL 68 Report (Van Wijngaarden, 1975), are necessary. Unfortunately, there are no truly successful parsing algorithms for these techniques. Because of this, the definition of the syntax of a programming language is usually given in two parts. Most of the syntax is specified in the form of a context-free grammar which can be parsed efficiently. The context-free grammar describes the overall structure of a program but allows certain statements which are not allowed in the programming language. The remainder of the specification consists of context-sensitive restrictions placed on the context-free syntax. Such restrictions include type-matching rules for identifiers and the requirement that a call of a procedure contain exactly as many arguments as there are parameters in the definition of the procedure.

The two-part syntax descriptions discussed in the preceding paragraph are often clearer, though less precise, than descriptions using the more sophisticated formalisms. Moreover, the two-part description parallels the structure of practical compiler algorithms. The context-free part of the syntax is usually described formally by some variant of the BNF notation introduced in Sec. 2-2. This part of the syntax is analyzed by one of the parsing algorithms discussed in Chaps. 6 and 7. The context-sensitive restrictions are usually stated informally in some natural language. These restrictions are checked during compilation by means of a set of tables in the compiler. For example, information is saved from one occurrence of an identifier and is used in processing later occurrences of that identifier.

Both the semantics of the programming language (that is, the meaning of each construct and program in the language) and the context-sensitive syntax of the language are commonly specified by a narrative description. In the compiler it is often convenient to check the context-sensitive syntax of a statement or expression during its translation, that is, its semantic processing. Because semantics and context-sensitive syntax have been so closely associated in both the description and the translation of a language, it has become common to use the terms "semantics" and "semantic processing" to apply to both the actual semantics and the context-sensitive syntax of the programming language. In recent years this usage of the term semantics seems to be decreasing, because of the slow development of formal definitional methods for semantics and context-sensitive syntax. In this book we use the term semantics to refer to the meaning of constructs or programs in a programming language, and not to refer to any restrictions on the class of valid programs.

Context-free grammars are clearly very important in the description and translation of programming languages, because they are the most powerful formalisms for which we have effective and efficient parsing algorithms. Consequently, in this section and throughout the rest of the book we concentrate on context-free grammars. The first subsection is concerned with additional grammatical terminology which applies to context-free grammars. In Sec. 2-4.2 the discussion of parsing, which was first introduced in Sec. 2-2, is continued. The syntax-tree representation of a parse is emphasized. Fundamental notions of grammars and parsing such as ambiguity are examined. Section 2-4.3 looks at the problem of eliminating useless rules and symbols in a given grammar, thus producing a reduced equivalent form. Also, the significance of allowing rules whose right parts are the empty string is investigated. Finally, Sec. 2-4.4 deals with the extension of the basic BNF notation which was introduced in Sec. 2-2. Throughout the remainder of this chapter, we equate the term grammar with context-free grammar.

2-4.1 Syntax Terminology

A number of terms such as production rule (or production), terminal symbol, nonterminal symbol, grammar, and sentential form were introduced in Sec. 2-2. We now introduce additional terms that will facilitate the discussion of syntactic analysis.

Definition 2-9 Let $G = (V_N, V_T, S, \Phi)$ be a grammar, and let $\sigma = \phi_1 \beta \phi_2$ be a sentential form. Then β is called a *phrase* of the sentential form σ for some nonterminal A if

$$S \overset{*}{\Rightarrow} \phi_1 A \phi_2 \quad \text{and} \quad A \overset{+}{\Rightarrow} \beta$$

Furthermore, β is called a *simple phrase* if $S \overset{*}{\Rightarrow} \phi_1 A \phi_2$ and $A \Rightarrow \beta$.

Care must be exercised when applying this definition. $A \overset{+}{\Rightarrow} \beta$ does not necessarily imply that β is a phrase of $\phi_1 \beta \phi_2$; one must also have $S \overset{*}{\Rightarrow} \phi_1 A \phi_2$. For example, consider the sentential form $\langle\text{letter}\rangle\langle\text{digit}\rangle\langle\text{letter}\rangle$ in relation to the following grammar:

$$G_5 = (\{\langle\text{identifier}\rangle, \langle\text{letter}\rangle, \langle\text{digit}\rangle\}, \{a, b, \ldots, z, 0, 1, \ldots, 9\}, \langle\text{identifier}\rangle, \Phi)$$

where Φ is

$\langle\text{identifier}\rangle ::= \langle\text{letter}\rangle \mid \langle\text{identifier}\rangle\langle\text{letter}\rangle \mid \langle\text{identifier}\rangle\langle\text{digit}\rangle$

$\langle\text{letter}\rangle ::= a \mid b \mid \ldots \mid y \mid z$

$\langle\text{digit}\rangle ::= 0 \mid 1 \mid \ldots \mid 8 \mid 9$

Note that $\langle\text{digit}\rangle$ is not a phrase of this sentential form. What are the phrases of $\langle\text{letter}\rangle$ b? A derivation for this sentential form is

$$\langle\text{identifier}\rangle \Rightarrow \langle\text{identifier}\rangle\langle\text{letter}\rangle \Rightarrow \langle\text{letter}\rangle\langle\text{letter}\rangle \Rightarrow \langle\text{letter}\rangle \, b$$

Therefore

$$\langle\text{identifier}\rangle \overset{*}{\Rightarrow} \langle\text{letter}\rangle\langle\text{letter}\rangle \quad \text{and} \quad \langle\text{letter}\rangle \Rightarrow b$$

Consequently, b is a simple phrase. Another derivation for the given sentential form is

$$\langle\text{identifier}\rangle \Rightarrow \langle\text{identifier}\rangle\langle\text{letter}\rangle \Rightarrow \langle\text{identifier}\rangle b \Rightarrow \langle\text{letter}\rangle b$$

where

$$\langle\text{identifier}\rangle \overset{*}{\Rightarrow} \langle\text{identifier}\rangle b \quad \text{and} \quad \langle\text{identifier}\rangle \Rightarrow \langle\text{letter}\rangle$$

Again, the only phrase which is also a simple phrase is $\langle\text{letter}\rangle$. Also, $\langle\text{letter}\rangle$ b is a phrase (but not simple).

In the subsequent discussion the leftmost simple phrase of a sentential form will be required. We therefore give the following definition.

Definition 2-10 The *handle* of a sentential form is its leftmost simple phrase.

In the current example, we have two possible simple phrases, namely, $\langle\text{letter}\rangle$, and b, and since $\langle\text{letter}\rangle$ is the leftmost simple phrase, it is also the handle.

In the following pages we briefly discuss the problem of syntax analysis or parsing. Recall that the parse of a sentence is the construction of a syntax tree for that sentence. As indicated in Sec. 2-2, a syntax tree is an important aid to

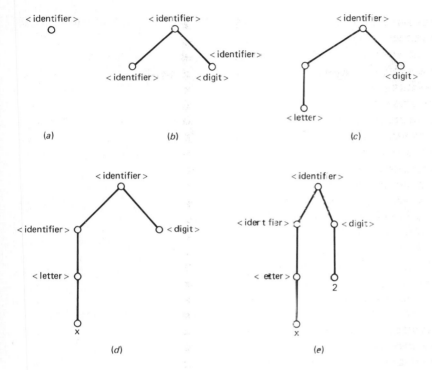

Figure 2-6 Syntax tree for identifier x2.

understanding the syntax of a sentence. The structural relationships between the parts of a sentence are easily seen from its syntax tree. Consider the grammar described earlier for the set of valid identifiers or variable names. A derivation of the identifier x2 is $\langle\text{identifier}\rangle \Rightarrow \langle\text{identifier}\rangle\langle\text{digit}\rangle \Rightarrow \langle\text{letter}\rangle\langle\text{digit}\rangle \Rightarrow x\langle\text{digit}\rangle \Rightarrow x2$. Let us now illustrate how to construct a syntax tree corresponding to this derivation. This process is shown as a sequence of diagrams in Fig. 2-6, where each diagram corresponds to a sentential form in the derivation of the sentence. The syntax tree has a distinguished node called its *root*, which is labeled by the starting symbol $\langle\text{identifier}\rangle$ of the grammar. From the root we draw two downward branches (see Fig. 2-6b) corresponding to the rewriting of $\langle\text{identifier}\rangle$ by $\langle\text{identifier}\rangle\langle\text{digit}\rangle$. The symbol $\langle\text{identifier}\rangle$ in the sentential form $\langle\text{identifier}\rangle$ $\langle\text{digit}\rangle$ is then rewritten as $\langle\text{letter}\rangle$ by using the production $\langle\text{identifier}\rangle ::= \langle\text{letter}\rangle$ (see Fig. 2-6c). This process continues for each production applied until a complete syntax tree for x2 is obtained in Fig. 2-6e.

A syntax tree for a sentence of some language always has a root node which is labeled by the starting symbol of the grammar. The leaf nodes of the syntax tree represent the terminal symbols in the sentence being parsed. All nonleaf nodes correspond to nonterminal symbols. Each nonterminal node has a number of branches emanating downward, each of which represents a symbol in the right side of the production being applied at that point in the syntax tree.

The syntax tree corresponding to the following derivation of the identifier b11 of the example grammar is given in Fig. 2-7.

$$\langle identifier\rangle \Rightarrow \langle identifier\rangle\langle digit\rangle \Rightarrow \langle identifier\rangle\langle digit\rangle\langle digit\rangle$$
$$\Rightarrow \langle letter\rangle\langle digit\rangle\langle digit\rangle \Rightarrow b\langle digit\rangle\langle digit\rangle$$
$$\Rightarrow b1\langle digit\rangle \Rightarrow b11$$

Note that another possible derivation for the same identifier is

$$\langle identifier\rangle \Rightarrow \langle identifier\rangle\langle digit\rangle \Rightarrow \langle identifier\rangle\langle digit\rangle\langle digit\rangle$$
$$\Rightarrow \langle identifier\rangle\langle digit\rangle1 = \langle identifier\rangle11$$
$$\Rightarrow \langle letter\rangle11 \Rightarrow b11$$

and this derivation has the same syntax tree as that given in Fig. 2-7. Therefore, for each syntax tree there exists one or more derivations.

More generally, any sentential form can have a syntax tree. The leaf nodes in such a tree can designate terminal and nonterminal symbols. Let A be the root of a subtree for a sentential form $\sigma = \phi_1\beta\phi_2$, where β forms the string of leaf nodes emanating from that subtree. Then β is the phrase for A of the sentential form σ. β is a simple phrase if the subtree whose root is A consists of the application of the single production $A \rightarrow \beta$.

Consider the example grammar

$$G_6 = (\{\langle expression\rangle, \langle factor\rangle, \langle term\rangle\}, \{i, +, *, (,)\}, \langle expression\rangle, \Phi)$$

where Φ consists of the productions

$$\langle factor\rangle ::= i|(\langle expression\rangle)$$
$$\langle term\rangle ::= \langle factor\rangle|\langle term\rangle * \langle factor\rangle$$
$$\langle expression\rangle ::= \langle term\rangle|\langle expression\rangle + \langle term\rangle$$

and i stands for an identifier or variable name. The syntax tree for the sentential form $\langle expression\rangle + \langle term\rangle * \langle factor\rangle$ is given in Fig. 2-8, where $\langle expression\rangle + \langle term\rangle * \langle factor\rangle$ and $\langle term\rangle * \langle factor\rangle$ are its phrases while $\langle term\rangle * \langle factor\rangle$ is a simple phrase.

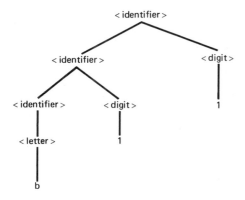

Figure 2-7 Syntax tree for the identifier b11.

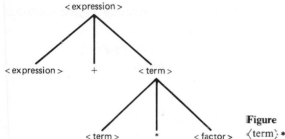

Figure 2-8 Syntax tree for $\langle$expression$\rangle$ + $\langle$term$\rangle$ * $\langle$factor$\rangle$ in G_6.

An important question which arises in formal languages is whether a sentential form has a unique syntax tree. Consider the simple grammar G_7, which has the following productions:

$$S \rightarrow S * S$$
$$S \rightarrow a$$

where a is a terminal symbol. Let us find a derivation for the sentence $a * a * a$. One such derivation is

$$S \Rightarrow S * S \Rightarrow S * S * S \Rightarrow a * S * S \Rightarrow a * a * S \Rightarrow a * a * a$$

where the leftmost S in the second step has been rewritten as $S * S$. Another possibility, of course, is that the rightmost S in the same step is rewritten as $S * S$. Both possibilities are diagramed in Fig. 2-9. It is clear that the two syntax trees are different. That is, we have two different parses for the same sentence. The existence of more than one *parse* for some sentence in a language can cause a compiler to generate a different set of instructions (object code) for different parses. Usually, this phenomenon is intolerable. If a compiler is to perform valid translations of sentences in a language, that language must be unambiguously defined. This concept leads us to the following definition.

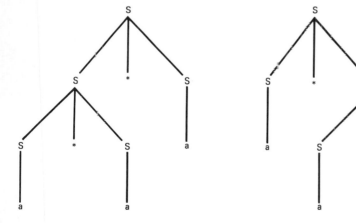

Figure 2-9 Two distinct syntax trees for the sentence $a * a * a$ in G_7.

> **Definition 2-11** A sentence generated by a grammar is *ambiguous* if there exists more than one syntax tree for it. A grammar is ambiguous if it generates at least one ambiguous sentence; otherwise it is *unambiguous*.

It should be noted that we called the grammar ambiguous and not the language which it generates. There are many grammars which can generate the same language; some are ambiguous and some are not. There are certain languages, however, for which no unambiguous grammars can be found. Such languages are said to be *inherently ambiguous*. For example, the language $\{x^i y^j z^k | i = j \text{ or } j = k\}$ is an inherently ambiguous context-free language.

The question which naturally arises at this point is: Does there exist an algorithm which can accept any context-free grammar and determine, in some finite time, whether it is ambiguous? The answer is no! A simple set of sufficient conditions can be developed such that when they are applied to a grammar and are found to hold, then the grammar is guaranteed to be unambiguous. We wish to point out that these conditions are sufficient but not necessary. In other words, even if a grammar does not satisfy the conditions, it may still be unambiguous. We will formulate such a set of conditions for subclasses of the context-free grammars in Chaps. 6 and 7.

Let us examine another example of an ambiguous grammar. In particular, consider the grammar G_8 for unparenthesized arithmetic expressions consisting of the operators + and * with single-letter identifiers:

$$\langle\text{expression}\rangle ::= i | \langle\text{expression}\rangle + \langle\text{expression}\rangle | \langle\text{expression}\rangle * \langle\text{expression}\rangle$$

Assume that the sentence $i * i + i$ is to be parsed. Two possible derivations are as follows:

$$
\begin{aligned}
\langle\text{expression}\rangle &\Rightarrow \langle\text{expression}\rangle * \langle\text{expression}\rangle \\
&\Rightarrow \langle\text{expression}\rangle * \langle\text{expression}\rangle + \langle\text{expression}\rangle \\
&\Rightarrow i * \langle\text{expression}\rangle + \langle\text{expression}\rangle \\
&\Rightarrow i * i + \langle\text{expression}\rangle \\
&\rightarrow i * i + i \\
\langle\text{expression}\rangle &\Rightarrow \langle\text{expression}\rangle + \langle\text{expression}\rangle \\
&\Rightarrow \langle\text{expression}\rangle * \langle\text{expression}\rangle + \langle\text{expression}\rangle \\
&\Rightarrow i * \langle\text{expression}\rangle + \langle\text{expression}\rangle \\
&\Rightarrow i * i + \langle\text{expression}\rangle \\
&\Rightarrow i * i + i
\end{aligned}
$$

Their corresponding syntax trees are given in Fig. 2-10. Since there exist two distinct syntax trees for the sentence $i * i + i$, the grammar is ambiguous. Intuitively, this grammar is ambiguous because it is not known whether to evaluate * before + or conversely. The grammar can be rewritten in such a manner that the multiplication will have precedence over addition. This revision is accomplished

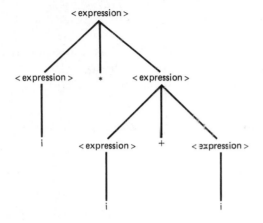

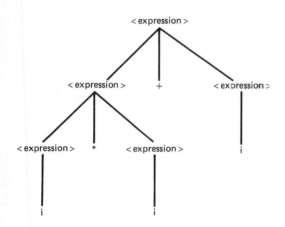

Figure 2-10 Ambiguous syntax trees for $i * i + i$ in G_8.

using the following set of productions:

$\langle \text{expression} \rangle ::= \langle \text{term} \rangle \,|\, \langle \text{expression} \rangle + \langle \text{term} \rangle$

$\langle \text{term} \rangle ::= \langle \text{factor} \rangle \,|\, \langle \text{term} \rangle * \langle \text{factor} \rangle$

$\langle \text{factor} \rangle ::= i$

Note that in this grammar an $\langle \text{expression} \rangle$ is defined to include a $\langle \text{term} \rangle$. A $\langle \text{term} \rangle$ can involve a multiplication but not an addition operator. Since in an $\langle \text{expression} \rangle$ all $\langle \text{term} \rangle$s must be resolved before $\langle \text{expression} \rangle$s, multiplication must have precedence over addition.

In this subsection we have shown that the syntax tree is a very important tool in the representation of the derivation of a sentence. A question that may arise at this point is: Given a grammar and a sentence of a language, how do we go about constructing the parse tree? We shall briefly look at this problem in the next subsection.

EXERCISES 2-4.1

1 Given the following derivation, what are some of the phrases, simple phrases, and handle of the sentential form *abdbcefg*?

$$S \Rightarrow BC \Rightarrow abC \Rightarrow abDCFG \Rightarrow abdCFG$$
$$\Rightarrow abdbcFG \Rightarrow abdbceG \Rightarrow abdbcefg$$

2 Using grammar G_6 in the text, what are the phrases, simple phrases, and handle for each of the following sentential forms:

(*a*) $i + i * i$
(*b*) $i * (i + i)$
(*c*) $i + (\langle \text{term} \rangle + \langle \text{factor} \rangle)$
(*d*) $\langle \text{term} \rangle * (\langle \text{factor} \rangle + i)$

3 Write a context-free grammar for a number in FORTRAN. Give a derivation and its syntax tree for each of the following:

(*a*) 251
(*b*) −61
(*c*) −72.25
(*d*) 1.73
(*e*) 14.25E+02
(*f*) −72.3E−05

4 Formulate a context-free grammar for the language of parenthesized logical expressions consisting of the logical variable b and the logical operators ¬(not), ∨(or), and ∧(and) such that ¬ has higher priority than ∧, which in turn has higher priority than ∨. Give a derivation and associated syntax trees for each of the following sentences:

(*a*) ¬b ∨ b
(*b*) ¬(b ∧ b) ∨ b
(*c*) (b ∧ ¬b) ∨ (b ∨ b)

5 Rewrite the grammar of Exercise 4 so as to incorporate the logical operators → (if then) and ↔ (if and only if). The priority of the augmented set of logical operators is given from highest to lowest priority as:

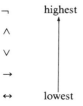

¬	highest
∧	
∨	
→	
↔	lowest

Give a derivation and its associated syntax tree for each of the following sentences:

(*a*) (b ∨ b) → b
(*b*) ¬b → b ∨ b
(*c*) (¬b ∨ b) ↔ ¬(b ∧ b)

6 Obtain a context-free grammar for a FORMAT statement in FORTRAN. Assume that the FORMAT statement does not contain any Hollerith constants. Give a derivation and its associated syntax tree for each of the following sentences:

(*a*) 10 FORMAT(I5, F6.3)
(*b*) 20 FORMAT(E12.5)
(*c*) 30 FORMAT(I5/F5.2)
(*d*) 40 FORMAT(I4, 3X, 16)
(*e*) 50 FORMAT(I3, 2(F7.2))

7 Formulate a context-free grammar for a picture clause in COBOL. Give a derivation and its associated syntax tree for each of the following sentences:

   (*a*) 999
   (*b*) − ZZ99.99
   (*c*) 99V99
   (*d*) \$,\$\$\$.99
   (*e*) *, * * *.99CR

8 Formulate a context-free grammar for a declaration statement in PL/I. Ignore the precision and initial attributes. Also ignore level numbers. Give a derivation and its associated syntax tree for each of the following:

   (*a*) DECLARE A FIXED BINARY, B FLOAT
   (*b*) DECLARE (A, B) FIXED;
   (*c*) DECLARE CHARACTER(6);
   (*d*) DECLARE (A(10), B(−1 : 2), C) FLOAT;

9 Show that the following grammar segment is ambiguous.

   ⟨statement⟩::= IF ⟨Boolean⟩ THEN ⟨statement⟩ ELSE ⟨statement⟩

   ⟨statement⟩::= IF ⟨Boolean⟩ THEN ⟨statement⟩

Rewrite this grammar so as to remove the ambiguity.

10 Suppose we want to implement a DDC (decimal digit calculator) compiler for the DDC language which performs arithmetic operations on integer arguments. The BNF grammar description below was written to describe the DDC language syntactically. Unfortunately, the grammar is ambiguous.

   ⟨DDC expr⟩::= ⟨DDC term⟩

         |⟨DDC expr⟩ ⟨op1⟩ ⟨DDC expr⟩

   ⟨DDC term⟩::= ⟨decimal arg⟩

         |⟨DDC term⟩ ⟨op2⟩ ⟨decimal arg⟩

   ⟨decimal arg⟩::= ⟨digit⟩

         |⟨decimal arg⟩ ⟨digit⟩

   ⟨digit⟩::= 0|1|2|3|4|5|6|7|8|9

   ⟨op1⟩::= + | −

   ⟨op2⟩::= * | /

   (*a*) Demonstrate that the grammar is, indeed, ambiguous.
   (*b*) Correct the grammar so that it is unambiguous
   (*c*) According to your grammar, what is the value of 7 + 6*3/2?
   (*d*) If we change the BNF description of ⟨op1⟩ and ⟨op2⟩ to read

   ⟨op1⟩::= * | /

   ⟨op2⟩::= + | −

what is the value of the expression 7 + 6*3/2 in the language described by your corrected grammar?

11 Write a BNF description for a PL/I ⟨procedure head⟩ statement. An example of a procedure head is

   EXAMPLE: PROCEDURE (X, Y, Z) RECURSIVE

      RETURNS (CHARACTER (*) VARYING);

Assume that only one of FIXED, FLOAT, BIT(*) VARYING, or CHARACTER(*) VARYING can appear as a RETURNS argument. You may assume ⟨identifier⟩ to be a terminal in the grammar.

12 Give an example (other than the one given in the text) of an inherently ambiguous language.

2-4.2 A View of Parsing

Given a sentence in the language, the construction of a parse can be illustrated pictorially in Fig. 2-11, where the root and leaves (which represent the terminal symbols in the sentence) of the tree are known and the rest of the syntax tree must be found. There are a number of ways by which this construction can be accomplished. First, an attempt to construct the tree can be initiated by starting at the root and proceeding downward toward the leaves. This method is called a *top-down parse*. Alternatively, the completion of the tree can be attempted by starting at the leaves and moving upward toward the root. This method is called a *bottom-up parse*. The top-down and bottom-up approaches can be combined to yield other possibilities. Such possibilities, however, will not be explored in this book.

Let us briefly discuss top-down parsing. Consider the identifier x2 generated by the BNF grammar of G_5 of the previous subsection. The first step is to construct the direct derivation $\langle$identifier$\rangle \Rightarrow \langle$identifier$\rangle \langle$digit$\rangle$. At each successive step, the leftmost nonterminal A of the current sentential form $\phi_1 A \phi_2$ is replaced by the right part of a production $A ::= \psi$ to obtain the next sentential form. This process is shown for the identifier x2 by the five trees of Fig. 2-12.

We have very conveniently chosen the rules which generate the given identifier. If the first step had been the construction of the direct derivation $\langle$identifier$\rangle \Rightarrow \langle$identifier$\rangle \langle$letter$\rangle$, then we would have eventually produced the sentential form x $\langle$letter$\rangle$ where it would have been impossible to obtain x2. At this point, a new alternative would have to be tried by restarting the procedure and choosing the rule $\langle$identifier$\rangle ::= \langle$identifier$\rangle\langle$digit$\rangle$. We shall discuss top-down parsing in much more detail in Chap. 6.

A bottom-up parsing technique begins with a given string and tries to reduce it to the starting symbol of the grammar. The first step in parsing the identifier x2 is to reduce x to $\langle$letter$\rangle$, resulting in the sentential form $\langle$letter$\rangle$ 2. The direct derivation $\langle$letter$\rangle$ 2 $\Rightarrow$ x2 has now been constructed, as shown in Fig. 2-13b. The

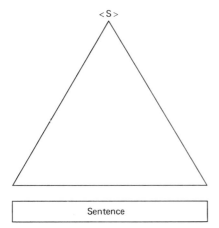

Figure 2-11

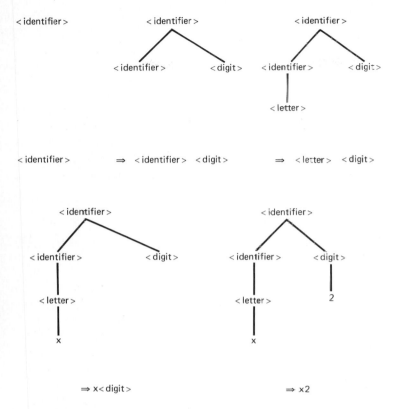

Figure 2-12 Trace of a top-down parse.

next step is to reduce ⟨letter⟩ to ⟨identifier⟩, as represented by Fig. 2-13c. The process continues until the entire syntax tree of Fig. 2-13e is constructed. Note that it is possible to construct other derivations, but the resulting syntax tree is the same. We will return to the very important problem of bottom-up parsing in Chap. 7.

In addition to the relation ⇒, which was defined in connection with a grammar in Sec. 2-2, we can also define the following *leftmost canonical* direct derivation:

$$\phi_1 A \phi_2 \underset{L}{\Rightarrow} \phi_1 \beta \phi_2$$

if $A \to \beta$ is a rule of the grammar and $\phi \in V_T^*$. This relation can be easily extended as before to $\underset{L}{\overset{+}{\Rightarrow}}$ and $\underset{L}{\overset{*}{\Rightarrow}}$, where the relation $\psi \underset{L}{\overset{+}{\Rightarrow}} \sigma$ may be read "ψ left-produces σ."

There are, in general, many sequences of strings $\phi_1, \phi_2, \ldots, \phi_n$ such that

$$S \Rightarrow \phi_1 \Rightarrow \phi_2 \Rightarrow \cdots \Rightarrow \phi_n \Rightarrow \sigma$$

is a derivation of a sentence σ in the language. Whenever ϕ_i contains at least two

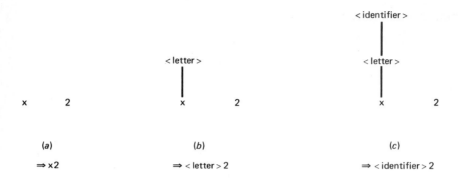

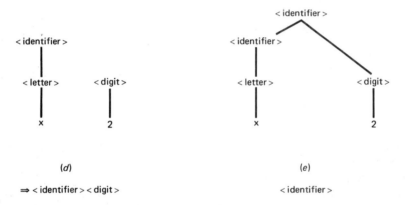

Figure 2-13 Trace of a bottom-up parse.

nonterminal symbols, we have a choice as to which nonterminal will be replaced first. The relation $\underset{L}{\overset{+}{\Rightarrow}}$ specifies that there is exactly one $\underset{L}{\Rightarrow}$ derivation. Note that this statement holds only for unambiguous grammars.

Similarly, we can define a *rightmost canonical* direct derivation

$$\phi_1 A \phi_2 \underset{R}{\Rightarrow} \phi_1 \beta \phi_2$$

if $A \rightarrow \beta$ is a rule of the grammar and $\phi_2 \in V_T^*$. Again the relation is easily extended to $\underset{R}{\overset{+}{\Rightarrow}}$ and $\underset{R}{\overset{*}{\Rightarrow}}$ where the relation $\psi \underset{R}{\overset{+}{\Rightarrow}} \sigma$ may be read as "ψ right-produces σ." The relation $\underset{R}{\overset{+}{\Rightarrow}}$ specifies that there is exactly one $\underset{R}{\Rightarrow}$ derivation. For example, the leftmost and rightmost derivations for $i + i * i$ in the revised grammar G_8 discussed earlier are

$$\langle expression \rangle \underset{L}{\Rightarrow} \langle expression \rangle + \langle term \rangle \underset{L}{\Rightarrow} \langle term \rangle + \langle term \rangle$$

$$\underset{L}{\Rightarrow} \langle factor \rangle + \langle term \rangle \underset{L}{\Rightarrow} i + \langle term \rangle$$

$$\underset{L}{\Rightarrow} i + \langle term \rangle * \langle factor \rangle \underset{L}{\Rightarrow} i + \langle factor \rangle * \langle factor \rangle$$

$$\underset{L}{\Rightarrow} i + i * \langle factor \rangle \underset{L}{\Rightarrow} i + i * i$$

and

$$\langle expression \rangle \underset{R}{\Rightarrow} \langle expression \rangle + \langle term \rangle$$

$$\underset{R}{\Rightarrow} \langle expression \rangle + \langle term \rangle * \langle factor \rangle$$

$$\underset{R}{\Rightarrow} \langle expression \rangle + \langle term \rangle * i$$

$$\underset{R}{\Rightarrow} \langle expression \rangle + \langle factor \rangle * i$$

$$\underset{R}{\Rightarrow} \langle expression \rangle + i * i \underset{R}{\Rightarrow} \langle term \rangle + i * i$$

$$\underset{R}{\Rightarrow} \langle factor \rangle + i * i \underset{R}{\Rightarrow} i + i * i$$

respectively. The leftmost and the rightmost derivations correspond to a left-to-right and right-to-left top-down parse, respectively.

The general problem of parsing is to start with a string σ of terminal symbols, for example, $i + i * i$, and to find a sequence of productions such that $\langle expression \rangle \overset{*}{\Rightarrow} \sigma$. The bottom-up method (proceeding from left to right) attacks the problem by first "reducing" the above string to

$$\langle factor \rangle + i * i$$

then reducing this string to

$$\langle term \rangle + i * i$$

and then

$$\langle expression \rangle + i * i$$

and

$$\langle expression \rangle + \langle factor \rangle * i$$

etc., where a reduction is the opposite of a production. This process continues until everything is reduced to $\langle expression \rangle$ or until it is shown that it cannot be done. Note that the sequence of reductions is the reverse of the right canonical derivation. In general, bottom-up parsing from left to right proceeds by right reductions.

In a left-to-right bottom-up parse, the handle is to be reduced at each step in the parse. The questions which arise are: how do we find the handle of a sentential form and to what do we reduce it?

One obvious approach is merely to select one of the possible alternatives. If a mistake is subsequently detected, we must retrace our steps to the location of the error and try some other alternative. This process is called "backup," and it can be very time-consuming.

A more efficient solution involves looking at the context around the substring which is currently being considered as a potential handle. This evaluation is done automatically by humans when they evaluate an expression like $i + i * i$. The question of whether to evaluate $i + i$ first is answered by looking ahead at the symbol $*$, which indicates that we should not. In Chaps. 6 and 7 we will formulate strategies which will guarantee that we can parse any sentence in a given language without backup if certain conditions are imposed on the grammar.

EXERCISES 2-4.2

1 Given the grammar

⟨number⟩ ::= ⟨integer⟩|⟨real number⟩

⟨integer⟩ ::= ⟨digit⟩|⟨integer⟩⟨digit⟩

⟨real number⟩ ::= ⟨integer⟩ · ⟨integer⟩|

⟨integer⟩ · ⟨integer⟩ E ⟨scale factor⟩|

⟨integer⟩ E ⟨scale factor⟩

⟨scale factor⟩ ::= ⟨integer⟩|⟨sign⟩⟨integer⟩

⟨sign⟩ ::= +|−

⟨digit⟩ ::= 0|1|2| ⋯ |9

where ⟨number⟩ is the starting symbol of the grammar, give leftmost and rightmost canonical derivations for the following sentences:

(*a*) 100

(*b*) 0.2

(*c*) 6E−3

(*d*) 87.25E+7

2 For the grammar

⟨factor⟩ ::= i|(⟨expression⟩)

⟨term⟩ ::= ⟨factor⟩|⟨term⟩ * ⟨factor⟩|

⟨term⟩/⟨factor⟩|⟨term⟩ ↑ ⟨factor⟩

⟨expression⟩ ::= ⟨term⟩|⟨expression⟩ + ⟨term⟩|

⟨expression⟩ − ⟨term⟩

where ↑ denotes the exponentiation operator and is *meant* to have the highest priority. Give leftmost canonical derivations for the sentences:

(*a*) $i * i \uparrow i$

(*b*) $i + i \uparrow i$

(*c*) $(i + i) \uparrow (i * i)$

Rewrite the grammar so that the exponentiation operator does have the highest operator priority. Give the leftmost canonical derivations for the sentences just given.

3 Construct top-down and bottom-up traces (as in Figs. 2-12 and 2-13) of parse trees for the grammar and sentences given in Exercise 1.

4 Construct top-down and bottom-up traces (as in Figs. 2-12 and 2-13) of parse trees for the grammars and sentences given in Exercise 2.

2-4.3 Reduced Grammars and Grammars with ε-Rules

Given a context-free grammar, there are a number of questions concerning its simplicity which can be asked. Some of the questions are the following:

1. Are rules of the form $A \rightarrow A$ absent from the grammar?
2. Does each nonterminal produce some part of a terminal sentence?
3. Beginning with the starting symbol of the grammar, does each symbol of the grammar occur in some sentential form?

If the answer to each of these questions is yes, then a grammar is said to be *reduced*. Note that other definitions of reduced grammars have been used in the literature. The first part of this subsection is concerned with obtaining from a grammar its reduced equivalent. By equivalent we mean that both grammars generate the same language.

The remainder of this subsection examines the ramifications of allowing empty productions or ε-rules in a context-free grammar. An *ε-rule* is a rule whose right part is the empty string. Such a rule will be denoted by $A \rightarrow \varepsilon$ or $A \rightarrow$. In Sec. 2-3 such rules were disallowed initially for the classes of context-sensitive, context-free, and regular grammars. If context-sensitive grammars had contained ε-rules, the associated decision problem would have no longer been fully decidable. Furthermore, if we had allowed ε-rules in context-free grammars but not in context-sensitive grammars, a context-free grammar with ε-rules would not have been context-sensitive. Since in the remainder of this book we are concerned almost exclusively with context-free and regular grammars, these problems are not important.

The use of ε-rules in context-free grammars has certain advantages. The most important advantage is that their use permits a more compact and perhaps a more natural description of the language. We shall see that the generative power of a context-free grammar with ε-rules is (except for the empty string) exactly the same as that of a grammar without ε-rules.

Let us now consider the problem of obtaining the reduced equivalent of a given context-free grammar. Rules of the form $A \rightarrow A$ can be removed from the grammar. Such productions are not only useless but they make the grammar ambiguous. Since such a rule can be applied any number of times, there are many possible distinct syntax trees for some sentence in the language.

Consider the following grammar:

$S \rightarrow aAa$ $B \rightarrow abb$

$A \rightarrow Sb$ $B \rightarrow aC$

$A \rightarrow bBB$ $C \rightarrow aCA$

On examining this grammar, we find that it is impossible to produce any terminal sentences from the nonterminal C. That is, $\{x|C \overset{*}{\Rightarrow} x$ and $x \in \{a, b\}^+\}$ is empty. Consequently any rule which contains C can be deleted. Making these deletions yields the following grammar:

$S \rightarrow aAa$ $A \rightarrow bBB$

$A \rightarrow Sb$ $B \rightarrow abb$

If a nonterminal symbol generates at least one terminal string, such a symbol is said to be an *active nonterminal.*Given a context-free grammar, we would like to formulate an algorithm which will determine the set of active symbols. Initially, each symbol in the set $\{A|A \rightarrow \alpha$ and $\alpha \in V_T^*\}$ is active. We can obtain, in a recursive manner, other active symbols from the following observation: If all nonterminal symbols in the right part of a rule are active, then the symbol in its left part is also active. Observe that all terminal symbols are considered to be active.

For the grammar just given, the initial set of active symbols is $\{B\}$. Since the symbol B is active, so is A. S then becomes active because the symbols a and A are. At this point no additional symbols (such as C) are found to be active; so the process halts. The set $\{A, B, S\}$ represents the active symbols of the sample grammar. This computational process is incorporated in the following algorithm.

Algorithm ACTIVE Given a context-free grammar $G = (V_N, V_T, S, \Phi)$, this algorithm determines the active set of nonterminals, V'_N, in G. The rules of the grammar are then scanned for selection. A rule is selected if all its nonterminals are active. The resulting set of rules is denoted by Φ'. The number of nonterminals in G is denoted by m. The sets W_k for $1 \le k \le m$ represent a family of sets.

1. [Compute initial set of active nonterminals]
   $W_1 \leftarrow \{A|A \rightarrow \alpha \in \Phi$ and $\alpha \in V_T^*\}$
2. [Calculate successive sets of active nonterminals]
   Repeat for k = 2, 3,...,m
   $W_k \leftarrow W_{k-1} \cup \{A|A \rightarrow \alpha \in \Phi$ and $\alpha \in (V_T \cup W_{k-1})^+\}$
   If $W_k = W_{k-1}$ or k = m
   then $V'_N \leftarrow W_k$
   $\Phi' \leftarrow \{A \rightarrow \alpha \in \Phi|A, \alpha \in (V_T \cup V'_N)^*\}$
   Exit   □

Note that $W_k \supseteq W_{k-1}$ for all k. Also, since the grammar contains m nonterminals there is no need to compute any set beyond W_m. When the equality of two successive W sets is detected, the desired set of active nonterminals has been obtained, and the sets V'_N and Φ' can then be generated. The reader should verify that $L(G) = L(G')$, where $G' = (V'_N, V_T, S, \Phi')$. That is, both grammars generate exactly the same language.

For the sample grammar given earlier. the sequence of active nonterminal sets is $W_1 = \{B\}$, $W_2 = \{B, A\}$, $W_3 = \{B, A. S\}$, and $W_4 = W_3$.

Another subclass of undesirable symbols are those that cannot occur in any sentential form derivable from the starting symbol of the grammar. Alternatively, we are only interested in those symbols which belong to the set $\{A \mid S \overset{*}{\Rightarrow} \phi_1 A \phi_2$ where $A \in V_T \cup V_N\}$. A symbol which occurs in some sentential form derivable from the starting symbol is called a *reachable symbol*; otherwise it is called an *unreachable symbol*.

The set of reachable symbols can be easily obtained by first noting that the starting symbol of the grammar is reachable. Second, if the nonterminal in the left part of a production is reachable, then so are all the symbols in its right part. This fact can be used repeatedly until all reachable symbols are found. As an example, consider the grammar:

$$S \rightarrow aSb \qquad A \rightarrow aAc$$
$$S \rightarrow bAB \qquad C \rightarrow aSbS$$
$$S \rightarrow a \qquad C \rightarrow aba$$
$$B \rightarrow d$$

The initial set of reachable symbols is $\{S\}$. Since S is reachable, then from productions $S \rightarrow a$, $S \rightarrow aSb$, and $S \rightarrow bAB$. it directly follows that the new set of reachable symbols is $\{S, A, B, a, b\}$. Now that A and B are reachable, it follows from productions $B \rightarrow d$ and $A \rightarrow aAc$ that c and d are reachable. Note that C is unreachable. Consequently the set of reachable symbols is $\{S, A, B, a, b, c, d\}$. The rules with C as their left part can therefore be deleted from the grammar. The reduced grammar then becomes

$$S \rightarrow aSb \qquad A \rightarrow aAc$$
$$S \rightarrow bAB \qquad B \rightarrow d$$
$$S \rightarrow d$$

A more formal algorithm which is similar in structure to Algorithm **ACTIVE** follows.

Algorithm REACHABLE Given a context-free grammar $G' = (V'_N, V'_T, S, \Phi')$, this algorithm determines the set of reachable symbols in the vocabulary $V'_N \cup V'_T$ according to the informal method just described. The sets W_k for $0 \le k \le m$, where m denotes the number of symbols in V'_N, represent a family of sets. The new reachable sets of terminal and nonterminal symbols are represented by V_T'' and V_N'', respectively. The set of remaining productions is denoted by Φ''.

1. [Compute initial set of reachable symbols]
   $$W_0 \leftarrow \{S\}$$
2. [Calculate successive sets of reachable symbols]
   Repeat for $k = 1, 2, ..., m$
   $$W_k \leftarrow W_{k-1} \cup \{A \in V_N' \cup V_T' | B \rightarrow \phi_1 A \phi_2 \in \Phi' \text{ where } B \in W_{k-1}\}$$
   If $W_k = W_{k-1}$ or $k = m$
   then $V_N'' \leftarrow W_k \cap V_N'$
   $$V_T'' \leftarrow W_k \cap V_T'$$
   $$\Phi'' \leftarrow \{A \rightarrow \alpha \in \Phi' | A, \alpha \in W_k^+\}$$
   Exit   □

This algorithm is similar to Algorithm **ACTIVE** in the sense that $W_k \supseteq W_{k-1}$ and the stopping criterion is the same as that used in the previous algorithm. Note that $L(G') = L(G'')$ where $G'' = (V_N'', V_T'', S, \Phi'')$.

A nonterminal is called *useful* if it is both active and reachable. Otherwise, a nonterminal is said to be *useless*.

A grammar is *reduced* if all *useless* symbols and associated rules have been eliminated, and all rules of the form $A \rightarrow A$ have been removed.

A reduced grammar is obtained by applying Algorithms **ACTIVE** and **REACHABLE** to its unreduced equivalent and removing rules of the form $A \rightarrow A$. It should be noted, however, that the order of application of these algorithms is important. First, we should eliminate from the original grammar those nonterminals (and associated rules) which are inactive. Second, the resulting grammar from the first step can then be used as input to Algorithm **REACHABLE**. With this order of application, some symbols may become unreachable only after an inactive nonterminal and its associated rules have been removed, but not conversely. As an example of this phenomenon, consider the following grammar which is meant to generate the language $\{a^m b^n a^m b^k ccc \cup ccc | m, n, k, \geq 1\}$:

$S \rightarrow ccc$	$B \rightarrow aBa$
$S \rightarrow Abccc$	$B \rightarrow AC$
$A \rightarrow Ab$	$C \rightarrow Cb$
$A \rightarrow aBa$	$C \rightarrow b$

By first applying Algorithm **ACTIVE** we find that the set of inactive nonterminals is $\{A, B\}$. Upon removing those productions involving these inactive symbols we obtain the grammar

$$S \rightarrow ccc, C \rightarrow Cb, C \rightarrow b$$

With the application of Algorithm **REACHABLE**, the symbol C has now become unreachable. The resulting reduced grammar contains the single rule $S \rightarrow ccc$. It should be emphasized that before the application of Algorithm ACTIVE C was reachable, but it then became unreachable after it was determined that A and B were inactive. Had we applied the two algorithms in the reverse order, a different grammar would have been obtained. This grammar obviously would not have been truly reduced.

In the remainder of this book, it is assumed, unless otherwise specified, that all grammars are reduced. The remainder of this subsection introduces the notion of an empty production in context-free grammars. We show that allowing such productions does not alter the generative power capability of a context-free grammar. That is, context-free grammars with or without empty productions generate exactly (to within the empty string) the same family of languages.

Consider the following grammar which generates the language $\{a^n b a^m | n, m \geq 0\}$:

$$S \rightarrow AS \qquad C \rightarrow aC$$

$$A \rightarrow a \qquad C \rightarrow a$$

$$A \rightarrow \varepsilon \qquad C \rightarrow \varepsilon$$

$$S \rightarrow bC$$

This grammar contains two empty productions. A derivation for the string $a^2 b$ is

$$S \Rightarrow AS$$
$$\Rightarrow AAS$$
$$\Rightarrow aAS$$
$$\Rightarrow aaS$$
$$\Rightarrow aabC$$
$$\Rightarrow aab$$

In attempting to show that context-free grammars with and without ε-rules are equivalent, it is first desirable to obtain those nonterminals that can generate the empty string. The following algorithm, which is very similar to Algorithms ACTIVE and REACHABLE computes this set of nonterminals.

Procedure EMPTY $(V_N, V_T, S, \Phi, V_{N_\varepsilon})$ Given a context-free grammar $G = (V_N, V_T, S, \Phi)$ with m nonterminals, this algorithm computes the set $V_{N_\varepsilon} = \{A \in V_N | A \overset{*}{\Rightarrow} \varepsilon\}$. The sets W_k for $1 \leq k \leq m$ denote a family of sets.

1. [Compute initial set of empty productions]
    $$W_1 \leftarrow \{A | A \rightarrow \varepsilon \in \Phi\}$$
2. [Compute each successive set of nonterminals which can produce ε]
    Repeat for k = 2, 3,...,m
        $W_k \leftarrow W_{k-1} \cup \{A | A \rightarrow \alpha \text{ where } \alpha \in W_{k-1}^*\}$
        If $W_k = W_{k-1}$ or k = m
        then $V_{N_\varepsilon} \leftarrow W_k$
            Exit   □

This algorithm can then be used in the next algorithm, which, when given a grammar containing ε-rules, attempts to construct an equivalent grammar without ε-rules.

Algorithm ε-RULE-FREE Given a context-free grammar with ε-rules and m nonterminals, this algorithm obtains an equivalent grammar $G' = (V_N, V_T, S', \Phi')$ such that Φ' does not contain ε-rules. Algorithm EMPTY is used to generate the set of nonterminals which can generate the empty string. This set of nonterminals is denoted, as before, by V_{N_ε}, and $\Phi_{\varepsilon\text{-free}}$ represents the rules of Φ which are not ε-rules. Φ_1 is used to represent the expansion of those nonempty rules.

1. [Select the rules of G which are not ε-rules]
   $$\Phi_{\varepsilon\text{-free}} \leftarrow \{A \rightarrow \alpha \mid \alpha \neq \varepsilon \text{ and } A \rightarrow \alpha \in \Phi\}$$
2. [Determine the nonterminal symbols of G which can generate the empty string]
   Call EMPTY $(V_N, V_T, S, \Phi, V_{N_\varepsilon})$ (This algorithm returns the set V_{N_ε})
3. [Expand certain nonempty rules of G to compensate for the removal of ε-rules]
   $\Phi_1 \leftarrow \phi$ (ϕ is the empty set)
   Repeat for each rule in $\Phi_{\varepsilon\text{-free}}$ of the form $A \rightarrow \alpha$ where there is at least one B_i, $1 \leq i \leq n$, such that
   $\alpha = \phi_1 B_1 \phi_2 B_2 \phi_3 ... \phi_n B_n \phi_{n+1}$ and $B_1, B_2, ..., E_n \in V_{N_\varepsilon}$

   Add as many rules $A \rightarrow \beta$ to the set Φ_1 as can be obtained as follows: β is obtained from α by omitting some combination of $B_1, B_2, ..., B_n$. However, do not add $A \rightarrow \varepsilon$ to Φ_1
   Add rule $S' \rightarrow S$ to Φ_1
4. [Obtain the set of rules for the equivalent grammar]
   $\Phi' \leftarrow \Phi_{\varepsilon\text{-free}} \cup \Phi_1$
   Exit   □

Using the previous grammar as an example, step 1 yields the set $\Phi_{\varepsilon\text{-free}} = \{S \rightarrow AS, A \rightarrow a, S \rightarrow bC, C \rightarrow aC, C \rightarrow a\}$. From the invocation of Algorithm EMPTY in step 2, we obtain $V_{N_\varepsilon} = \{A, C\}$. In step 3, the rules $S \rightarrow AS$, $S \rightarrow bC$, and $C \rightarrow aC$ generate the rules $S \rightarrow S$, $S \rightarrow b$, and $C \rightarrow a$, respectively. Thus Φ_1 becomes the set $\{S \rightarrow S, S \rightarrow b, C \rightarrow a\}$. Step 4 yields the set $\Phi' = \{S \rightarrow AS, A \rightarrow a, S \rightarrow bC, C \rightarrow aC, C \rightarrow a, S \rightarrow S, S \rightarrow b\}$. Note that the rule $S \rightarrow S$ would be removed eventually, since such rules were ruled out in a reduced grammar. This task would be accomplished by a grammar reducer, as was described earlier in this section.

As another example, consider the simple grammar
$S \rightarrow A$
$A \rightarrow a$
$A \rightarrow \varepsilon$

Our algorithm transforms this grammar into the equivalent grammar containing the rules $S \rightarrow A$ and $A \rightarrow a$. Note, however, the original grammar generates the language $\{a, \varepsilon\}$ while the equivalent ε-free grammar generates the language $\{a\}$! This example illustrates that our algorithm has overlooked a special case, namely, if $S \in V_{N_\varepsilon}$, then a new starting symbol S' should be introduced and the rule $S' \rightarrow S$ should be added to the set of productions. furthermore, the rule $S' \rightarrow \varepsilon$ should also be added to Φ_1. Therefore, in order to preserve true language equivalence when $S \in V_{N_\varepsilon}$, we have been forced to add a new starting symbol S' to the new grammar and allow one ε-rule of the form $S' \rightarrow \varepsilon$. It should also be noted that since S' occurs only in the left part of one rule, the special ε-rule, $S' \rightarrow \varepsilon$, can be used only in the derivation of a single sentence—the empty string. This special case can be incorporated in a revision of step 3 as follows:

3'. [Expand certain nonempty rules of G to compensate for the removal of ε-rules]

$\Phi_1 \leftarrow \phi$
Repeat for each rule in $\Phi_{\varepsilon\text{-free}}$ of the form $A \rightarrow \alpha$ where there is at least one B_i, $1 \le i \le n$, such that
$\alpha = \phi_1 B_1 \phi_2 B_2 \phi_3 ... \phi_n B_n \phi_{n+1}$ and $B_1, B_2, ..., B_n \in V_{N_\varepsilon}$
Add as many rules $A \rightarrow \beta$ to the set Φ_1 as can be obtained as follows: β is obtained from α by omitting some combination of $B_1, B_2, ..., B_n$. However, do not add $A \rightarrow \varepsilon$ to Φ_1.
If $S \in V_{N_\varepsilon}$
then add rule $S' \rightarrow S$ and $S' \rightarrow \varepsilon$ to Φ_1
else add rule $S' \rightarrow S$ to Φ_1 □

As was mentioned earlier, the use of ε-rules permits a more compact and natural description of a programming language. Some of the parsing methods to be discussed in Chaps. 6 and 7 permit their use and others do not. In the methods that do, however, we will see that the use of ε-rules is at times severely restricted by other conditions which are imposed on the grammar.

EXERCISES 2-4.3

1 Show that Algorithm ACTIVE does compute the active set of nonterminals in a given grammar.

2 Give a trace of Algorithm ACTIVE for the following input grammar:

$S \rightarrow aAbA$ $A \rightarrow bBC$

$S \rightarrow aba$ $A \rightarrow a$

$A \rightarrow aAb$ $B \rightarrow aBc$

3 In Algorithm ACTIVE show for each integer $n > 1$ that there exists a grammar with n variables such that $W_k \ne W_{k+1}$ for $1 \le k \le n - 1$.

4 Trace through Algorithm REACHABLE using as input each of the following grammars:

(a) $S \rightarrow aAa$ $B \rightarrow abb$
      $A \rightarrow Sb$ $C \rightarrow aCB$
      $A \rightarrow bBB$

(b) $S \rightarrow bS$ $B \rightarrow C$
      $S \rightarrow ba$ $B \rightarrow ba$
      $S \rightarrow A$ $B \rightarrow aCC$
      $A \rightarrow a$ $C \rightarrow CCa$
      $A \rightarrow Bb$ $C \rightarrow b$

5 In Algorithm REACHABLE show that for each integer $n > 1$ there exists a grammar with n variables such that $W_k \neq W_{k+1}$ for $1 \leq k \leq n - 1$.

6 Write a computer program which when given a grammar will return a reduced grammar which is equivalent to the original grammar. Note that an important aspect of this task is to choose a suitable representation for the productions of the grammar. The chosen representation should facilitate the operations which are to be performed in Algorithms ACTIVE and REACHABLE.

7 Using Algorithm EMPTY, compute the set of nonterminals which produce the empty string in the following grammar:

$S \rightarrow AB$ $D \rightarrow AAE|b|\varepsilon$

$A \rightarrow CC|a$ $E \rightarrow SS$

$B \rightarrow DD|\varepsilon$ $C \rightarrow c$

8 Repeat Exercise 7 for the sample grammar

$S \rightarrow AB|ab|C$

$A \rightarrow C|D|ab$

$B \rightarrow S|ba$

$C \rightarrow b|DS|AB|\varepsilon$

$D \rightarrow a|AbC|\varepsilon$

9 Write a computer program based on Algorithm ε-RULE-FREE which transforms a grammar with ε-rules to an equivalent grammar without ε-rules.

2-4.4 Extended BNF Notation

At the end of Sec. 2-2 we introduced BNF notation. Although the specification of programming languages is possible with this basic notation, it is desirable to extend the notation. It should be stressed, however, that from a specifications point of view both notations are equivalent; but the extended notation permits a more readable and compact specification of a language than does basic BNF. The first part of this subsection describes several such extensions.

Consider the following BNF description of the syntax for a term in an arithmetic expression:

$\langle \text{term} \rangle ::= \langle \text{factor} \rangle | \langle \text{term} \rangle * \langle \text{factor} \rangle$

Since $\langle \text{term} \rangle$ can contain an arbitrary number of $\langle \text{factor} \rangle$s, the use of recursion is required.

Let the braces {and} be additions to the metasymbol set of the basic BNF metalanguage. We define $\{z\}$ to mean zero or more occurrences of z. Using this notation, the previous BNF description can be equivalently written as

$\langle \text{term} \rangle ::= \langle \text{factor} \rangle \{ * \langle \text{factor} \rangle \}$

Frequently, in the description of a language, it is useful to specify a minimum and/or maximum number of times a particular element within the braces can be repeated. For example, an external name in PL/I can contain a maximum of seven characters the first of which must be an alphabetic character. This name can be specified with the use of braces as

$\langle \text{PL/I external name} \rangle ::= \langle \text{alphabetic} \rangle \{ \langle \text{alphanumeric} \rangle \}_0^6$

$\langle \text{alphanumeric} \rangle ::= \langle \text{alphabetic} \rangle | \langle \text{digit} \rangle | \_$

$\langle \text{alphabetic} \rangle ::= a|b| \ldots y|z|\$| \# |@$

Clearly, basic BNF could be used here, but such a description would be more lengthy and is left as an exercise to the reader. In the absence of a minimum replication factor, it is assumed to be zero. The previous external name definition can also be written as

$\langle \text{PL/I external name} \rangle ::= \langle \text{alphabetic} \rangle \{ \langle \text{alphanumeric} \rangle \}^6$

The element within the braces, in general, can contain a string of symbols, one of which can be the metasymbol |. For example, by $\{ \langle \text{letter} \rangle | \langle \text{digit} \rangle \}$ we mean a pattern of zero or more symbols each of which is either a $\langle \text{letter} \rangle$ or a $\langle \text{digit} \rangle$. The external name definition just given can be rewritten as

$\langle \text{PL/I external name} \rangle ::= \langle \text{alphabetic} \rangle \{ \langle \text{alphabetic} \rangle | \langle \text{digit} \rangle | \_ \}^6$

Another optional feature which can also be specified with braces is the use of the brackets [and]. By the term [x], we mean zero or one occurrence of x. Clearly [x] is equivalent to $\{x\}^1$. As an example, the DO loop statement in PL/I with the optional BY clause would look like this:

DO $\langle \text{variable} \rangle = \langle \text{expression} \rangle$ TO $\langle \text{expression} \rangle$ [BY $\langle \text{expression} \rangle$]

Recall from Section 2-2 that the implied concatenation operator has priority over the alternation operator (|). For example, in the rule $\langle A \rangle ::= \langle B \rangle \langle C \rangle | \langle D \rangle$ the nonterminal $\langle A \rangle$ can be either the string $\langle B \rangle \langle C \rangle$ or $\langle D \rangle$. In order to change the usual order of evaluation, parentheses must be used. The rule $\langle A \rangle ::= \langle B \rangle (\langle C \rangle | \langle D \rangle)$ would define $\langle A \rangle$ to be either $\langle B \rangle \langle C \rangle$ or $\langle B \rangle \langle D \rangle$. Such a parenthesizing technique can be used to rewrite a BNF description of the form

$\langle \text{term} \rangle ::= \langle \text{factor} \rangle | \langle \text{term} \rangle * \langle \text{factor} \rangle | \langle \text{term} \rangle / \langle \text{factor} \rangle$

into the form

$\langle \text{term} \rangle ::= \langle \text{factor} \rangle \{ (* | /) \langle \text{factor} \rangle \}$

A problem which arises when a metalanguage is used to describe a certain language is the ability to distinguish between a symbol used in the metalanguage and that same symbol being a terminal symbol of the language being described.

For example, in the description

1. ⟨subscript variable⟩::= ⟨identifier⟩ (⟨subscript list⟩)
2. ⟨subscript list⟩::= ⟨subscript exp⟩{ , ⟨subscript exp⟩}
3. ⟨subscript exp⟩::= ⟨term⟩{(+ | −)⟨term⟩}
4. ⟨term⟩::= ⟨factor⟩{(*|/)⟨factor⟩}
5. ⟨factor⟩::= ⟨identifier⟩|(⟨subscript exp⟩)

there is an ambiguity in the use of parentheses [(,)]. In production groups 1 and 5 the parentheses are part of the language which is being described, while in groups 3 and 4 the parentheses are part of the metalanguage. When confusion of this kind arises, the terminal symbols of the target language should be enclosed in quotes (or some other convenient symbol). In the current example productions 1 and 5 should be rewritten as

1'. ⟨subscript variable⟩::= ⟨identifier⟩ '(' ⟨subscript list⟩ ')'
5'. ⟨factor⟩::= ⟨identifier⟩| '(' ⟨subscript exp⟩ ')'

As another example, consider the description of a portion of a basic BNF rule. The sequence of rules

⟨BNF rule⟩::= ⟨left part⟩ '::= ' ⟨right part⟩

⟨right part⟩::= ⟨right part element⟩{ '|' ⟨right part element⟩}

is such a description where the symbols '::= ' and '|' denote terminal symbols in the target language. Now that we have made the quote symbol a metasymbol, a question which arises is: How do we represent a quote when it is a terminal symbol of the target language? This problem can be handled in a manner similar to that used in many programming languages; namely, the quote symbol can be represented by two consecutive quotes. Using this approach, the description

⟨quote⟩::= ''''

specifies a single quote symbol.

The extensions to basic BNF introduced in this section will be used to advantage in several of the later chapters. In particular, this extended notation will be used extensively in Chap. 6 in conjunction with top-down parsing.

EXERCISES 2-4.4

1 Using extended BNF notation, describe a FORMAT statement in FORTRAN which does not contain any Hollerith constants.

2 Give an extended BNF description of SNOBOL 4.

3 Give an extended BNF description of ALGOL 60.

4 Give an extended BNF description of a PICTURE clause in COBOL.

5 Give an extended BNF description of a RECORD description in COBOL.

6 Formulate an algorithm which will convert extended BNF rotation into pure or basic BNF form.

BIBLIOGRAPHY

Aho, A. V., and J. D. Ullman: *Principles of Compiler Design*, Reading, Mass.: Addison-Wesley, 1977.

Aho, A. V., and J. D. Ullman: *The Theory of Parsing, Translation, and Compiling*, Vol. 1, *Parsing*, Englewood Cliffs, N.J.: Prentice-Hall, 1972.

Bar-Hillel, Y.: *Language and Information-Selected Essays on Their Theory and Application*, Reading, Mass.: Addison-Wesley, 1964.

Barnard, D. T.: "Automatic Generation of Syntax-Repairing and Paragraphing Parsers," Computer Systems Research Group Report No. 52, University of Toronto, Toronto, 1975.

Chomsky, N.: "On Certain Formal Properties of Grammars," *Information and Control*, Vol. 2, No. 2, 1959, pp. 137–167.

Davis, M.: *Computability and Unsolvability*, New York: McGraw-Hill, 1958.

Ginsberg, S.: *The Mathematical Theory of Context-Free Languages*, New York: McGraw-Hill, 1966.

Gries, D. E.: *Compiler Construction for Digital Computers*, New York: John Wiley & Sons, 1971.

Harrison, M. A.: *Introduction to Formal Language Theory*, Reading, Mass.: Addison-Wesley, 1978.

Hopcroft, J. E., and J. D. Ullman: *Formal Languages and Their Relation to Automata*, Reading, Mass.: Addison-Wesley, 1969.

Hopcroft, J. E., and J. D. Ullman: *Introduction to Automata Theory, Languages and Computation*, Reading, Mass.: Addison-Wesley, 1979.

Lewis, P. M., D. J. Rosenkrantz, and R. E. Stearns: *Compiler Design Theory*, Reading, Mass.: Addison-Wesley, 1976.

Nelson, Raymond J.: *Introduction to Automata*, New York: John Wiley & Sons, 1968.

Salomaa, A.: *Formal Languages*, New York: Academic Press, 1973.

Tremblay, J. P., and R. P. Manohar: *Discrete Mathematical Structures with Applications to Computer Science*, New York: McGraw-Hill, 1975.

Weingarten, F. W.: *Translation of Computer Languages*, San Francisco: Holden-Day, 1973.

van Wijngaarden, A., et al.: "Revised Report on the Algorithmic Language ALGOL 68," *Acta Informatica*, Vol. 5, 1975, pp. 1–236.

Wirth, N.: "The Programming Language PASCAL (Revised Report)," Technical Report No. 5, Eidgenossische Technische Hochschule, Zurich, July 1973.

THREE

PROGRAMMING-LANGUAGE DESIGN

A significant factor in the process of programming is the programming language being used. The language shapes the very thought processes of the programmer, and the quality of the language can greatly influence the quality of the programs produced. The importance of good language design cannot be understated.

It is regrettable that many existing programming languages were, in one way or another, poorly designed. The main cause of this is that too often unsystematic, "seat-of-the-pants" techniques were used to design these languages.

In the last few years, however, some basic principles underlying the design of good programming languages have begun to emerge. Although much has been learned, the existing material is fragmented and often hard to find. This chapter attempts to give a unified treatment of the topic, in sufficient depth to be useful to persons actually designing a programming language.

This chapter consists of eight sections. Section 3-1 gives a general overview of the problem and places some limits on the scope of the discussion. Section 3-2 introduces some considerations which must enter the design process at the very beginning. Since most programming-language constructs are derived from already existing sources, some consideration is then given to the sources and evaluation of ideas. Section 3-4 discusses, in detail, the goals of programming languages as well as the overall design principles that guide the construction of a language. Section 3-5 is an in-depth discussion of design details; it attempts to survey current ideas on a variety of topics. Section 3-6 discusses how to reduce language size. Section

3-7 completes the coverage of language design by identifying a number of pragmatic issues in designing a language. Section 3-8 comments on the design of the programming language Ada.

3-1 OVERVIEW OF THE PROBLEM

In recent years, one of the most prevalent art forms in the programming world has been the design of programming languages. The number of programming languages proposed and designed is extremely large. Even the number of languages for which a translator has been implemented is immense. Sammet (1976) notes 167 such languages in her 1974–1975 roster. Although the first primitive programming languages came into existence over 25 years ago, until recently there was little order in the process of designing new languages.

The early languages were pioneering efforts, exploring a new field. It is not surprising that they were poorly designed. No criticism should be leveled against the designers of FORTRAN; they had quite enough trouble designing and implementing one of the first high-level languages. No one could reasonably expect them to anticipate the requirements and standards applying 25 years later. If there is any criticism to be awarded in connection with FORTRAN, its targets should be the users who have clung so tenaciously to certain obsolete language features during reviews by standards committees, and certain language designers who have so enthusiastically perpetuated FORTRAN's flaws.

It should be noted that our references to FORTRAN in the preceding paragraph and throughout this chapter refer to FORTRAN IV rather than FORTRAN 77.

After the initial development of high-level languages and the implementation of the first few compilers, there ensued a fairly lengthy period in which conscious attempts were made to design new languages without the flaws of the old. Most of these attempts were failures, not so much from a lack of ideas on how to design better languages as from a surplus of ideas. A good example of this process is the notion that "if it could mean something, it should" (Radin and Rogoway, 1965), which led to PL/I.

More recently, the experience from previous mistakes has led to real knowledge about how to build good programming languages. Basic ideas and principles are becoming sufficiently well established that it is practical to state explicit guidelines for language design. Those areas that are not yet understood are being systematically investigated.

This discussion will accordingly attempt to emphasize a systematic, ordered approach to language design. It should be remembered, however, that to do proper justice to many topics it is often necessary to discuss particulars as well as generalities. The field of language design is by no means fully developed, and many areas are not yet very well unified. Also, many areas interrelate so strongly that it is difficult to discuss them separately.

By necessity, this discussion will, however, restrict its coverage. Elaborate descriptions of possible language features will be limited. It is assumed that the potential language designer has sufficient background in programming languages to be aware of the major ideas. Specific features will be discussed for specific reasons, but no attempt will be made to give a general catalog. There are already several such catalogs (Elson, 1973; Pratt, 1975; Nicholls, 1975). A basic proposition of this entire chapter is that a good language is not just a haphazard collection of features but a unified whole.

It will be assumed that the languages under discussion are "high-level" languages. The discussion will also be restricted largely to procedural languages for writing software ("software" is used here in its most general sense to mean "programs to be used by someone else"). Much of what is said will be applicable to other classes of languages. The designer of a nonprocedural language will omit consideration of some topics (e.g., control structures), but many general principles will remain applicable. Languages intended for nonsoftware purposes (e.g., for use as a glorified calculator or for investigation of algorithms) will sacrifice some considerations to improve others (a calculator language will sacrifice readability and structure for conciseness and convenience; an algorithm-testing language will sacrifice efficiency for convenience and natural notation), but this will change only the priority of the various considerations.

On-line command systems and query languages are to some extent a separate issue. Some of the same principles apply, but many specialized considerations intervene. Martin (1973) gives a good treatment of such matters.

One further restriction of the discussion will be made. It is assumed that languages are designed with the intent to implement a translator for them, even if the implementation is a purely hypothetical prospect. Languages for other purposes (e.g., to serve as a basis for discussion) are not obliged to follow the rules.

3-2 PRELIMINARY CONSIDERATIONS

In the design of a new language, certain matters require thought well before any consideration is given to the details of the design. Proper attention to these in advance can avoid trouble later.

The first and most important question that must be asked is:

Is it necessary to design a new language?

Almost any alternative approach will be simpler and faster than attempting the difficult and time-consuming task of designing a completely new language.

Is there an existing language that can be used to fill the requirement? Even if it requires a new implementation, implementing an existing language is easier and faster than designing and then implementing a new language.

Can an existing language be extended? It is easier to design a clean extension to an existing language, even if the extension implies a new compiler, than to design an entire new language. If this approach is taken, however, care should be taken not to make the extension so large and complex that it becomes, in effect, a new language. In such cases, the necessity of retaining some interface to the old language will probably seriously compromise the design of the extension. Also, if one is extending an existing language, it is necessary to select the base language carefully so that the work of extension will be minimized and the extension will fit gracefully into the language. The objective should be to produce a language which is somewhat larger but equally well constructed.

Would it be possible to modify an existing language, possibly using a macroprocessor or something similar? Even a facility for parameterless macros (simply substituting a specified text for each occurrence of a defined identifier) can produce major alterations in the syntax of a language, if skillfully used (e.g., RATFOR as defined by Kernighan and Plauger, 1976). However, the power of this approach for more complex tasks, such as introducing new data structures, is limited.

Serious consideration should be given to these techniques as alternatives to a new language, simply on the grounds of minimizing the work and time involved. There is perhaps no other computer-related problem which looks so temptingly easy and is so terribly hard as doing a good job of language design. Dispense with the notion that it is possible to whip up a design over the weekend and start implementing a translator for it on Monday. A month later, there will still be minor points of language design to settle, and the implementation will have gotten almost nowhere.

Assuming that the decision has been made that none of the preceding approaches will suffice, the next point of interest is:

What is the purpose of the language?

A language is often designed specifically for an area of application. The more attention that is given to restricting the area of application of the language, the better the language will be for problems in that area. In fact, it is not advisable to attempt to design a general-purpose language suitable for any problem. All such attempts to date have been disappointing (notably PL/I and ALGOL 68). Presently, all evidence indicates that no one knows how to do a proper job of designing a language that will be "good for everything."

Finally, the relation of the new language to existing languages must be considered. Weinberg (1971) discusses the psychological phenomenon of "inhibition," which occurs when an old language and a new language are similar but not identical. The user is subject to serious confusion owing to uncertainty about how much of the old language carries over into the new one. For example, FORTRAN programmers learning PL/I formatted I/O have great trouble with E- and F-type formats, which are similar but not identical to the equivalent FORTRAN constructs.

In summary, it is better to make the new language distinctly different from rather than closely similar to any existing language. If the new and old languages are so similar, perhaps the necessity of the new language has not been properly examined.

3-3 SOURCES OF IDEAS

Inspiration for programming language design has sprung from several sources in the past. Several of these important sources will be discussed in this section: natural languages, mathematics, existing programming languages, and proper usage and experiments.

We derive much of our current practice in programming languages from natural languages. Obviously, many of our constructs are phrased in a manner which is based on natural language. Less obviously, we also derive more subtle conventions such as the notion of the significant blank, the related idea that (except in strings) any number of blanks is equivalent to one blank, and the concept that the end of a line is usually no more significant than a blank.

Generally speaking, constructs derived from natural language are valuable for their obviousness and readability. They do (at least roughly) what they say. This is a major advantage even to experienced programmers and may be crucial for languages intended for novices and nonprogrammers. On the other hand, the problem of inhibition with regard to other programming languages may operate here. Languages which look too much like English may produce higher error rates as users attempt other English constructions only to discover that they do not work as expected. Using natural language as a model can also result in excessive wordiness, COBOL being an obvious example. Note also that natural languages often contain much ambiguity, which is undesirable in a programming language. Generally speaking, a good strategy is to use natural language as a guide when designing the detailed syntax of new constructs, while avoiding its influence elsewhere.

We next turn to mathematics as a source of ideas. Mathematics has been a significant source for conventions and devices used in programming languages (most obviously the arithmetic expression). It is entirely possible that new programming languages will incorporate other borrowings from mathematics.

It is important, however, to remember that programming is not mathematics. Generally, programmers and mathematicians use different methods and solve different problems while working toward different objectives. It should be noted in particular that, in order to achieve the brevity which is so important to complex formula manipulation, mathematicians often show a complete disregard for clarity and obviousness. This is exemplified in the awesome proliferation of character sets in mathematical notation. While mathematics is a useful source of ideas, particularly with regard to data types, the language designer should be very careful about adopting the mathematical notation for a given concept. Consider, for example, the language APL, which is heavily mathematically oriented. A real implementation problem which arises is the representation of some of the APL symbols on traditional I/O devices.

Existing programming languages can be the best single source of ideas for programming-language designers. Designers must be very careful about including such ideas in their own product, however, because designers in the past have made serious errors in design.

A few basic principles can be enunciated for distinguishing good ideas worthy of perpetuation from bad ideas worthy only of extinction. Perhaps the major principle is to ask "Why was it done that way?" Once you obtain an answer to this question, ask "Is that reason (still) valid?" Often the answer to this question will be no. For example, FORTRAN's strange restrictions on array subscripts date back to its first implementation: the implementors wished to make efficient use of the addressing features of their hardware and were afraid that this could not be done if any expression were allowed as a subscript. Although this can perhaps be considered reasonable (or at least understandable) in the circumstances, it certainly is not defensible today, considering the serious reduction in usability that results.

It is also worthwhile to remember that even if the overall verdict on a language is "a bad design," this does not mean that it does not conceal worthwhile features somewhere deep inside. For example, although APL can be criticized on many fronts, its powerful array-manipulation operators may well be worth copying.

Similarly, the fact that a feature is commonly available may not imply that it is a good idea. Many languages have followed ALGOL 60's lead in allowing the size of arrays to be decided at run time, a feature which introduces considerable implementation problems and interferes with compile-time error checking. This feature may be of only limited value in certain applications areas. The phenomenon of default declarations, inherited from FORTRAN, is another example of bad language design. This feature in particular illustrates the fact that some currently popular features are in fact strongly detrimental to program quality.

Another consideration is that a poorly designed feature may be the result of trying to meet two requirements at the same time, with the result that one of them (perhaps the more conspicuous one) is poorly served. An example of this is the pass-as-if-by-macro-substitution parameters of ALGOL 60 (also known as "pass-by-name"), which appear to have resulted from confusion of the two notions "procedure," a logical concept, and "macro," an implementation technique for procedure.

Some desirable features can be identified from observing the way programmers use the facilities of existing languages. In particular, it is possible to derive restrictions that can improve error checking or readability while not restricting the programmer, by observing what parts of a language are rarely used. For example, some of the motivation for the anti-GOTO forces comes from the observation that good programmers do not use the full power of the GOTO—they use the GOTO to simulate less general but more understandable structures.

Similarly, by observing established patterns of usage one can determine what features are desirable. For example, measurements of actual programs by Alexander (1972) have established that two-thirds of all IFs do not have an ELSE clause; so it would probably be unreasonable to require the ELSE in all IFs. The relatively recent notion of experimenting with design changes (Gannon, 1975) under controlled conditions offers basically the same types of conclusions. Undoubtedly research will continue in the areas of measuring programming-language use and experimenting in programming-language design.

3-4 GOALS AND DESIGN PHILOSOPHIES OF PROGRAMMING LANGUAGES

When a programming language is designed, particular attention must be given to the goals of the language. A number of important goals, such as human communication, the prevention and detection of errors, usability, program effectiveness, compilability, efficiency, machine independence, and simplicity, are described in turn.

This section is also concerned with design philosophies. Philosophies such as uniformity, orthogonality, generality, language modularity, minimality, and level of abstraction are discussed.

3-4.1 Human Communication

While it is important to communicate efficiently with the computer, detect errors well, and so on, the most basic goal of a programming language is communication between human beings. If a program cannot be understood by humans, it is difficult to verify and it cannot be maintained or modified. Even if the program is still clear to its author, this is a strictly temporary condition. It has been suggested by Kernighan and Plauger (1976) that readability is the best single index of good programming. Certainly, one of the crucial factors in achieving readable programs is an understandable programming language.

It is important to realize that the problems of human communication cannot be left entirely to comments or external documentation. Programmers dislike writing excessive comments and tend to avoid them. External documentation is all too often out-of-date and incomplete. Also, this can sometimes apply to internal documentation. A good and very reliable form of documentation is the program itself—if it is readable. Programming languages must be designed with constant attention to clarity and understandability.

It is vital to distinguish between readability and writability. It is important to be able to write programs easily. It is *necessary* to be able to read programs easily. The readability of programs is far more important in the long run than their writability (Hoare, 1973). This is of particular significance because many "powerful" and "convenient" features tend to produce monumentally obscure programs (e.g., APL "one-liners").

The most basic implication of the readability problem for the design of programming languages is that the syntax must reflect the semantics. If the syntax of the programming language does not accurately and completely reflect the manipulations being carried out, there is little hope for understanding the program. Making the syntax match the semantics implies several things. The syntax must clearly state what is happening in sufficient detail to be understandable but not in such unnecessary detail as to be overwhelming. Care should be taken to ensure that a construct performing a particular operation does not read as if it were doing something similar but not quite the same. Furthermore, it is most undesirable for significant actions to be undertaken without any indication in the syntax whatsoever. This rule may seem obvious, but a considerable number of languages violate it (notably PL/I with its conversions and ON-units, and ALGOL 68 with its coercions).

A most unfortunate choice of terminology in the field of computer science is the term syntactic sugar because it implies that making language constructs understandable is an unnecessary frill. It is vital that the syntax of a programming language should reflect human thought patterns, rather than the more "elegant" but much more obscure patterns of, for example, the lambda calculus (Church, 1941) (or, still worse, the peculiarities of a particular computer's instruction set).

A final facet that must be mentioned with regard to human communication through programming languages is that programmers are not computers. Just because a compiler can understand a given construct there is no guarantee that a programmer can. The limitations of the human mind make it quite easy for a complicated structure to become unmanageable, while the compiler has no problem. For example, a simple stack algorithm handles nested constructs for a compiler. Human beings, however, probably do not function in a stacklike manner, and deeply nested constructs can very easily become completely incomprehensible. Humans are ill-equipped to cope with situations where the effect of a construct depends in a complex way on context (as can arise through the use of PL/I ON units). It is also quite possible for a construct to be ambiguous to a human while it is clear and obvious to a compiler (Weinberg, 1971). A good example of this is the simple arithmetic expression "a/b/c". In general, a parser will not consider this ambiguous, but how many human programmers would write it without using parentheses? Although it may be more time consuming for a compiler to disallow such a construct, the protection can be worth it.

3-4.2 Prevention and Detection of Errors

It is a recognized fact that programmers make errors. Although much current work in the field of software engineering is directed toward stopping errors at the source (the programmer), there is no foreseeable chance that errors will be eliminated entirely. It is therefore necessary to assist the programmer in the task of not only preventing but also detecting, identifying, and correcting errors. A good programming language can be a major factor in this. In fact, the efforts of Lampson et al. (1977) in the design of EUCLID, a PASCAL-based language intended for the expression of system programs which are to be verified, indicates that a programming language can significantly affect the ease with which a program can be verified to be error-free. Undoubtedly, more research will be conducted in this important area.

One of the most fundamental services a high-level language performs is to make certain classes of errors impossible. A good example of this is the old assembly-language hazard of branching into the middle of the data. Given a properly functioning compiler, there is no chance whatsoever that an ALGOL programmer will ever commit this blunder. This is an excellent example of a point made by Wirth (1974) that high-level languages are not just clerical aids but are even more valuable in that the restrictions they impose on the programmer actually assist in producing error-free programs.

A similar benefit of high-level languages is that certain classes of errors are rendered unlikely, though not impossible. For example, the programmer is much less likely to make an error of control flow in a language such as PASCAL than in assembly language, because PASCAL provides constructs which organize control flow better than the conditional branches of assembly language (or FORTRAN!). This sort of error prevention is usually a question of providing the programmer with constructs which are convenient to use, are close to the programmer's thought processes, and impose reasonable restrictions on the program.

Even with all possible help in the prevention of errors, some errors will still be made. It is therefore desirable that the programming language should detect errors and render them as conspicuous as possible, so that they can be eliminated.

Error detection is based on useful redundancy. An error is detected by noticing that two portions of the program, carrying some of the same information, do not match each other.

The explicit declaration of variables exemplifies beneficial redundancy. When a variable is referenced, the compiler can check that the variable is of a type for which the particular operation is meaningful. If the type is inappropriate, an error has been made.

It should be noted that not all redundancy is useful redundancy. An excellent example of redundancy that is not only useless but can be actively harmful is the necessity in FORTRAN of repeating COMMON definitions in each program component using them. An error in one such repetition generally goes undetected and will usually have serious consequences.

Useful redundancy can easily be built into a language. The most significant sources of useful redundancy are mandatory declarations of all variables and strong type checking (of the type used in ALGOL and PASCAL). One side issue of strong type checking is the absence of automatic conversions or coercions which attempt to turn the data type supplied into the one which is "obviously" desired in the context. Such behind-the-scenes fudging defeats much of the value of type checking and can result in obscure code. For example, in ALGOL 68 (which has coercions), if x is a pointer-to-integer, the one variable which cannot be altered by the assignment

$$x := x + 1$$

is x itself! Dereferencing (ALGOL 68 terminology for pointer chasing), conversion, etc., should be present only if explicitly requested.

Default declarations, as in FORTRAN, are a good example of unnecessary loss of useful redundancy. Default declarations interfere seriously with type checking, encourage programming sloppiness, and often are so complex as to be confusing (how many human beings are aware of PL/I's exact defaults?).

Another area of useful redundancy which is not as well used as it should be is selection by name rather than by position. Everyone knows that it is much easier and clearer to say "x.size" rather than "x[5]" when you mean the "size" field of the "x" structure. It is generally acknowledged that a CASE statement which requires the programmer to label the alternatives with the values that cause them to be selected is much clearer and less error-prone than an unlabeled version.

Having discussed some of the more important aspects of error prevention, let us turn our attention to error detection. Error detection must be reliable. Unreliable error detection is worse than none at all, since programmers tend to rely on it when they should not. This can result in errors that are almost impossible to find. An example of this is the "union" type of ALGOL 68 (e.g., the value of a variable can be either real or integer), which cannot be checked at compile time. If one is combining separately compiled modules into a single program, it is almost impossible to provide completely reliable checking for unions without ruinous expense.

Error detection should also be accurate. The user should be told exactly where and how the error occurred, so that it can be analyzed and corrected. Although the biggest single factor in this is the compiler (see Chap. 5), language design also has a large impact. For example, a language with unrestricted pointer variables (e.g.., PL/I) will make the detection and analysis of runaway-pointer errors almost impossible.

An important aspect of error detection pertains to the question of compile-time versus run-time detection. Generally speaking, languages should be designed to permit error detection at compile time. This is generally much cheaper and usually makes the generation of intelligent error messages much easier. It is also easier (and much safer!) to continue a compilation to find further errors than to continue execution after an error. Whenever possible, language rules should be designed so that they can be easily enforced at compile time. For example, it is generally difficult and expensive to detect at run time that a pointer variable points to an object of the wrong type. If pointer variables are declared not as "POINTER" but as "POINTER TO type," such error detection can be done almost entirely at compile time.

Some classes of errors simply cannot be discovered at compile time—for example, the general problem of deciding whether an array subscript is in range. The run-time support routines should be set up so that run-time checks are simple and not excessively expensive. Ideally, it should be so simple and cheap to make the run-time checks that the checks could be left in for "production" runs, when error detection is even more vital. As Hoare states (Hoare, 1973), "What would we think of a sailing enthusiast who wears his life jacket when training on dry land, but takes it off as soon as he goes to sea?"

An example of how run-time checking can be made impractically expensive is the combination of circumstances in PL/I which makes it possible to get "dangling pointers" (pointers which point to now-deallocated objects). This sort of error cannot be found at compile time and is difficult and costly to check at run time.

3-4.3 Usability

We now turn to the topic of usability. It is obviously important that a language be easy to use. Certain aspects of this property deserve specific mention. The most important consideration, readability, has already been discussed and thus will not be covered here.

It is desirable that the constructs of a language be easy to learn and to remember. Once programmers are familiar with the language, it should not be necessary for them to consult manuals constantly. The language should be so simple and straightforward that the proper way to do something is reasonably apparent. On the other hand, there should not be many different ways to do the same thing, as the programmer will then flounder helplessly trying to decide which is best. The best example of general violation of this aspect of usability is ALGOL 68, which can do almost anything—if the programmer can only figure out how! PL/I is a good example of a language which provides many different ways to do something (most languages make do with one sort of integer; PL/I has three!).

Another important principle is "no surprises," also known as the "rule of least astonishment." A programmer who has made the effort to learn the language should be able to predict the behavior of a construct accurately if it can be predicted at all. PL/I is the major bad example here; it is strewn with constructs which do not do what the programmer thinks, as exemplified with FIXED division (see Hughes, 1973).

Some languages are much adored for their flexibility. Flexibility is like redundancy—it can be useful or useless. It is obviously necessary for languages to be able to meet demands that cannot be fully anticipated by their designers. However, useless flexibility can be a problem. An example of this is the feature of ALGOL 60 which allows a variable name to be redeclared in an inner BEGIN block: the compiler has to cope with several variables having the same name, unpleasant possibilities for programmer errors emerge, and the feature is seldom used (with the obvious exception of subprograms). Generally speaking, useless flexibility should be eliminated whenever possible.

If it does not interfere too seriously with other considerations, a language should be concise. Unfortunately, conciseness does tend to interfere strongly with readability (for example, in APL). There is also a conflict with useful redundancy in that repeating information (the essence of redundancy) often requires more writing (for example, declaring all variables). Conciseness should probably be given the lowest priority among the various design issues.

3-4.4 Programming Effectiveness

This topic is distinguished from the previous one, usability, by a rather fuzzy boundary. Roughly speaking, this subsection is concerned with the software-engineering aspects of language use rather than the convenience to the individual programmer.

A major concern in software engineering is the recording of the decisions made during program development. The program itself is the best place to record such decisions. The programming language should facilitate a clear statement of the programmer's intentions. This implies, in particular, that the decision should not be obscured beneath the mound of details required to implement it.

Whenever possible, the language should allow programmers to state their wants and have the compiler do the implementation. Most constructs of high-level languages do this to some extent. In the all-too-frequent cases where the complexity is too great for the compiler or where the question of how to implement the decision is itself a significant decision, the language should allow the implementation details to be cleanly separated from the statement of the original decision. A few languages, such as LIS (Ichbiah et al., 1973) and Ada, have separate specification and implementation sections in their programs. The procedure notion provides this separation for executable code. Ideas as to how to achieve separation for things such as data structures are much less well developed.

In addition to stating decisions clearly, it is also desirable to be able to localize the effect of decision changes. Such changes are inevitable; it should not be necessary to rewrite the entire program when a change is required. This idea leads directly to the notion of abstraction, which is the concept that a programmer may make use of a particular notion (e.g., the data type "list") without needing to know the details of its implementation. This greatly simplifies the use of such predefined program segments, and is a key factor in controlling the complexity of programs. If one adds the restriction that the user not only does not need to know the implementation details of the abstraction but in fact has no way to use such knowledge, the implementation of the abstraction can then be changed without any alterations to programs using it.

It is obviously desirable for a programming language to support abstraction. Existing languages support it to some extent; the procedure again is the basic tool. Unfortunately, more powerful tools are needed to support, say, a "list" abstraction properly. This has been an active area of research (Liskov and Zilles, 1974; Horning, 1976; Shaw, 1976; SIGPLAN, 1976), and developments in it can be expected to be important to language design.

The matter of support for abstraction leads also to the question of support for various techniques of program construction, such as top-down programming. There are some problems in providing such support. In particular, while there are many different methods, new ones are still evolving, and no one method is clearly superior to all others. If a language is to be used with a specific programming methodology, definite attention should be given to making the language assist in the use of the method; otherwise, the designer should try to avoid enforcing any particular technique.

The final aspect of programming effectiveness to be discussed is that languages should discourage trickery. Cute, clever programming tricks are highly detrimental to readability and are seldom justified. Although the language cannot make such things impossible, a language which is clear, readable, and straightforward will at least hinder such activities. In particular, the language designer should be aware that certain language features encourage trickery. Such features are generally characterized by having a legitimate purpose but being overly general for that purpose. This leaves the way open for "clever" programmers to try to squeeze as much activity into the feature as possible. The best-known example of this is the operator-priority structure and powerful, complex operators of APL, which lead to the infamous "one-liner" when their capabilities are abused. Another example of bad operator-precedence design is in C (Kernighan and Ritchie, 1978), which has approximately one dozen priority levels.

3-4.5 Compilability

A language must be compilable. Less obviously, it should be as simple as possible to compile subject to no major reduction in its communicative effectiveness and usability. Compiler writing is already a complex job, and any increase in its complexity may make the task unmanageable in the sense that the finished product will be bigger, more complex, and hence less reliable.

Complexity can be introduced in both the analysis and synthesis phases of the compilation process. Languages which demand a significant amount of context in order to be parsed successfully are difficult for compiler writers whether they are using an ad hoc parsing technique or a more formalized table-driven parsing method [e.g., a simple precedence (Wirth and Weber, 1966), extended precedence (McKeeman, 1966), LR(k) (Knuth, 1965; DeRemer, 1969), or LL(k) (Rosenkrantz and Stearns, 1970) method]. This type of complexity is commonly introduced in languages in which the comma and/or parenthesis are used to fulfill many different roles. For example, a parenthesis may be used to group subexpressions, enclose arguments in a procedure call, enclose parameters in a procedure definition, surround the subscripts of an array reference, and set off logical expressions, ON-unit arguments, and file names—all in one language called PL/I. A parser look-ahead of two or three may be required, thus slowing down the compiler tremendously and adding to the size of the parsing table.

The generation of code can also be made more difficult if overly complex language features are needlessly included—especially if they are rarely used and/or can be simulated by simpler constructs. The infamous ALGOL 60 call-by-name (or call-as-if-by-macro) parameter passing feature exemplifies such a difficult-to-compile construct. It necessitates the generation of a section of object code [often called a "thunk" (Ingerman, 1961)] for each argument. This code must be reevaluated at run time each time the corresponding formal parameter is referenced. Practice has shown that simpler schemes, such as call-by-reference and call-by-value, are sufficiently powerful parameter-passing methods.

In addition to problems in compilation, some thought should be given to debugging aids, measurement tools, and other aids to program testing. Such facilities are quite important to users of a language if programs are to be verified properly. These notions are elaborated on in Sec. 3-5.5, Compile Structure.

As much as possible, attempts should always be made to complete the language design before entering into a compiler implementation. Often, however, the compilability of a language is not entirely appreciated until the implementation stage. In this sense, compilability violates the ideal of having distinct design and implementation stages more than any other program-language design goal.

3-4.6 Efficiency

"More computing sins are committed in the name of efficiency (without necessarily achieving it) than for any other single reason—including blind stupidity." (Wulf, 1972a).

Efficiency has been the most excessively overemphasized topic in the history of programming-language development. Is there justification in producing a program that executes twenty times as fast as the competition—but fails in half the runs? Efficiency is important after, not before, reliability.

Efficiency must be considered in the context of the total environment, remembering that machines are getting cheaper and programmers are getting more expensive. For example, it is generally undesirable to spend a significant effort to improve a program's efficiency by 10 percent because the savings simply do not justify the investment.

It is also worth remembering that efficiency is not just speed—space, I/O access, and paging patterns are also involved in efficiency. Space inefficiency in particular can be just as important as time inefficiency, and it is becoming more important in light of recent developments in minicomputers and microcomputers.

While it has certainly been overemphasized, efficiency cannot be ignored entirely. The pronouncement "we don't need to worry about efficiency anymore because the hardware will be so cheap that we needn't bother' is partly true—but only partly. Differences in efficiency of 10 or 20 percent, or even 30 or 40 percent, can be tolerated. When the difference is a factor of 2 or a factor of 10, the situation is no longer tolerable, for the following reasons (Hoare, 1973):

1. However cheap and fast the hardware is, it is cheaper and faster when running an efficient program.
2. The speed and cost of peripherals are not improving anywhere near as quickly as those of CPUs.
3. Users should not have to sacrifice readability and reliability in order to get their money's worth out of the improved hardware.

This being the case, it is necessary to determine the main causes of inefficiency. The biggest single cause of inefficiency is a mismatch between the hardware and the language. Sometimes this indicates revisions to the language, usually to drop features that the hardware cannot support efficiently.

Trying to match a language *too* closely to the hardware can result in a rather bad language. The best example of this is the FORTRAN IV restrictions on array subscripts. These restrictions adapt FORTRAN admirably well to the addressing hardware of the IBM 709, but this no longer constitutes an advantage, and the subscript restrictions are certainly among the more irritating features of FORTRAN.

Another degradation of efficiency arises from "booby-trapped" constructs—innocent-looking constructs that execute incredibly inefficiently. This is really a special case of the mismatch problem mentioned earlier, but it deserves explicit discussion. The language designer should strive to avoid situations where a minor change to a program produces a massive change in efficiency. Such gross unpredictability will understandably upset users. The speed and space requirements of a construct should be roughly reflected in its size and complexity as the programmer sees it—more expensive operations should require more writing. To some extent, this is another application of the "no surprises" rule mentioned earlier.

Accepting that inefficiency can be a problem, what are the potential cures for it? The one that is invariably presented is extensive optimization in the compiler (see Chaps. 12 and 13). Optimizing compilers can be very helpful, particularly where the scarce resource is space. In addition, specific features can also help (e.g., a GOTO-less language will require much less compiler effort for analysis of the control flow paths).

The optimizing compiler, however, cannot be presented as the whole answer. A good optimizing compiler is difficult and time-consuming to write. Because of larger size and greater complexity, it will probably be less reliable than a nonoptimizing compiler. Great care must be taken that the semantics of the language are not changed by optimization. Finally, optimizers generally run much more slowly than simpler compilers, which can be a surprisingly significant factor even at installations which think they spend most of their time on production runs.

One much-neglected way of easing the efficiency problem is that of giving optimization advice to the compiler. Although it is not always clear exactly what form much of this advice should take, a few significant ideas are available which can make a great deal of difference. An order-of-magnitude speed improvement can result from being able to advise the compiler that certain variables will be heavily used and should receive special attention regarding access time (such attention might take the form of placing them in registers rather than main storage). Sizable space improvements can result from being able to advise the compiler that a large data structure should be packed as tightly as possible regardless of access time.

Finally, significant improvements in efficiency can be obtained by making the language simple enough that it is easy to generate reasonably efficient code. PASCAL (Jensen and Wirth, 1975) is a good example of this. PASCAL omits most of the less efficient constructs, and the constructs it does have are simple enough and few enough that a modest amount of effort can produce highly efficient code.

3-4.7 Machine Independence

Although one of the original hopes for high-level languages was that they would be machine-independent, this hope has not been fully realized. Most current languages remain strongly machine-dependent, and the transportability of programs suffers as a consequence.

Before machine independence is discussed, the definition of machine-independent must be clarified. A workable definition is as follows: a language is machine-independent if and only if a program which has been compiled and run correctly on machine X will, when transported to machine Y, run with exactly the same output given the same input.

Note that the fact that a language is not machine-independent does not necessarily rule out transportation of programs. Often a subset of the language will be machine-independent (for example, a subset not including floating-point arithmetic). Even in a language that is very machine-dependent (e.g., one that includes floating-point arithmetic or a "word" data type), it is often possible to avoid machine dependencies enough to make specific programs transportable.

Most machine dependencies result from specifying parameters in terms of a particular machine rather than in terms of the actual dimensions involved. The best example of this is the specification of integer variables. Most languages just say "integer," and there is no indication of what sort of precision is needed. COBOL and PL/I specify the number of digits required. The simplest approach is to specify the smallest and largest numbers that will be contained in a particular variable, as is done in PASCAL.

PASCAL, in fact, is certainly worth studying as an example of how to make a language nearly machine-independent without pain. Other significant languages that come close to PASCAL in machine independence are FORTRAN and COBOL; however, their machine independence has come about as a result of efforts in standardization rather than through original language design.

One area of extreme machine dependence is floating-point arithmetic. The fundamental cause of this is that there is, as yet, no sufficiently general way to define the precision of numbers and operations in a manner independent of the implementation. However, IEEE has proposed a standard for floating-point numbers and, hopefully, this will be incorporated in future language design efforts.

Similar troubles arise in connection with the character set. The exact bit patterns representing a given character are not usually relevant, but the collating sequence of the characters varies enough from machine to machine to make machine independence very difficult. It is usually safe to assume that

1. Digits are in order.
2. The uppercase alphabet is in order.
3. The lowercase alphabet is in order.
4. The blank precedes any printable character.

Note that "in order" means $'a' < 'b'$ but does not forbid the existence of x such that $'a' < x < 'b'$.

Nonprinting "control characters" also cause problems, especially for I/O. One aspect that is quite difficult to make machine-independent is the question of how the end of a line is marked in character I/O. Some machines use a "newline" character, while others rely on a fixed length or a length count. An approach that is often adopted is to include line-feed control as part of the I/O primitives even if the machine uses a "newline" character. Other I/O questions, such as direct-access files, are often so machine-dependent that any language incorporating special constructs for them is destined to sizable machine dependencies.

It should be pointed out that machine independence is not required for all languages. In particular, languages intended for writing operating systems or other specialized machine-dependent software will inevitably have a significant degree of machine dependence. For some application-oriented languages (e.g., real-time control languages), it is questionable whether it is necessary to remove all machine dependencies.

3-4.8 Simplicity

Simplicity is a major question in the design of any language. It is clear that most users prefer a simple language. In fact, a language which fails to be simple will generally fail in many other respects, as attested to by the lack of overwhelming support for PL/I and ALGOL 68. While the lack of simplicity can result in an unaccepted language, simplicity by itself does not imply a good language. BASIC is certainly a simple language, but it is not particularly well designed and should be avoided, if possible, for any type of serious software development.

On the basis of the history of programming languages, one or two statements can be made about the best way of achieving simplicity (Wirth, 1974). Simplicity is not achieved through lack of structure; the result of this is chaos. Simplicity is not achieved through limitless generality; the result of this is a language that is impossible either to truly master or to completely implement.

Simplicity is best achieved through restriction of objectives, great care as to readability and obviousness, and the basing of the language around a few well-defined, simple concepts.

3-4.9 Uniformity

Uniformity is defined as "doing the same thing the same way regardless of context." If adopted as a language-design principle, it can help in reducing the number of things programmers have to think about at one time, since they do not need to consider context to know how a feature will act.

Like several other aspects which have been considered before, uniformity can be useful or useless depending on how it is applied. An example of useful uniformity is the notion in ALGOL of the expression; anywhere you need an arithmetic value, you can use any expression. In general, useless uniformity is having a construct behave the same way in two contexts that are sufficiently different that the programmer does not expect identical behavior and has no use for it. A possible example of useless uniformity is the merging of the ideas of "expression" and "statement" in ALGOL 68. With the single and somewhat debatable exception of using an IF in an expression, this construct is of questionable use in most programs.

A subtopic of "uniformity" that deserves consideration is the matter of eliminating special cases. Doing something one way most of the time and then another way in one particular case (possibly for implementation reasons) should be avoided. A good example of this is the method used to assign a value to a label variable in PL/I—it is completely different from the method used in assigning a value to an element of a label array. Such special cases have three specific problems:

1. They complicate the language.
2. They lead to implementation differences, since some people will implement them faithfully and others will "improve" the obviously bad design by eliminating them.
3. They tend to become "hardened" and cannot be removed even after they have outlived their usefulness, since this would invalidate existing implementations.

Point 3 is illustrated by the fact that we are still living with the IBM 709, as hardened into FORTRAN.

3-4.10 Orthogonality

Orthogonality is another design philosophy, prominent largely because of its extensive use in ALGOL 68. The basic idea of orthogonality is to have several general concepts, each of which functions on its own without knowledge of the inner structure of the others. Good examples of this from ALGOL 68 are value accessing (e.g., simple variables, array accesses) and arithmetic operators (e.g., " + "). The value-accessing primitives yield a value; they do not care how it is used. The arithmetic operators combine two values; they do not care how the values are obtained.

Although orthogonality can result in considerable improvements in simplicity, the example of ALGOL 68 provides a warning: it is doubtful if orthogonality is useful as a substitute for simplicity. The additional fact that highly general orthogonality seems to be harder to achieve than simplicity supports the arguments against concentrating on orthogonality to the exclusion of all else.

The alternative to orthogonality (which has sometimes been characterized as "provide all features everywhere") is sometimes called "diagonality" ("provide features where needed or useful"). For example, the orthogonality of value access and arithmetic, mentioned above, is unquestionably valuable. However, it is not so clear that it is valuable to extend this orthogonality to not caring whether the values are simple values or arrays. The difficulty of a straightforward extension to arrays is that things like:

$$a := a/a[1]$$

have implementation-dependent results. Here is a case where a bit less orthogonality (i.e., a bit more "diagonality") seems called for. The operator structure that works so well for simple scaler operands simply does not extend cleanly to arrays. Note that this does not rule out all array operators; assignment and comparison are still useful and straightforward.

3-4.11 Generalization and Specialization

The basic philosophy of generality is "if we allow this, then let's allow everything similar as well." In a manner similar to orthogonality, this notion is an aid to simplicity but not a substitute for simplicity. If carried too far, generality can result in rarely used, error-prone features which can be difficult to implement. The implementation of strings in ALGOL 68 provides an example. A proper implementation of strings allows variable, unbounded length. The designers of ALGOL 68 decided to generalize this; ALGOL 68 allows the bounds of "flexible" arrays to change at any time and makes strings just a special case of this. As it turns out, flexible arrays are an implementer's nightmare and are of marginal use except to provide strings. An alternative approach is simply to define "string" as a primitive as some ALGOL 68 subset implementers have done.

One other special case of generality versus specialization is worth mentioning. Many languages have built-in functions which take any number of arguments, whereas it is very seldom that user functions can do this. Only I/O functions and a few special functions like MAX and MIN really need variable numbers of arguments. In most instances, users do not need variable-length argument lists for their own procedures if the language already provides these special cases.

3-4.12 Other Design Philosophies

Language modularity is the basic philosophy advanced in PL/I; the idea is that users learn a subset appropriate to their own needs so that no one needs to memorize the entire (immense) language. This notion fails as a substitute for simplicity in that it works well only if programmers never make a mistake. When they do make a mistake, they may well have to understand the entire language to decide what happened and why, because the mistake may very well cause activation of features unknown to them.

On a somewhat smaller scale, the use of defaults often achieves a kind of modularity in which users are effectively working in a sublanguage which is better suited to their needs. This is often a useful feature, provided that the user does understand both the whole language and the structure of the defaults. This normally requires that the defaults be used only in cases where they are absolutely self-evident.

Minimality is the notion that the language should contain the absolute minimum number of constructs with which it can possibly survive. This is generally a good philosophy, but it fails if carried too far. A Turing machine is very minimal, but you would not want to program one. It is important to distinguish between a minimal set of constructs, which is the smallest possible set, and a minimal usable set, which is the smallest set that still satisfies the basic requirement of usability reasonably well

An example of where the "minimal set of constructs" doctrine is applied most frequently is in connection with control structures, usually with reference to a set which does not contain the GOTO. It can be shown that sequential flow and the WHILE loop are sufficient to generate all other constructs (even the IF), but such a minimal set is far from usable.

Programming-language designers should generally attempt to have the constructs of their language come from more or less the same level of abstraction. The brief discussion to follow illustrates this idea under two headings: avoiding constructs which are too primitive to fit well into the language, and avoiding constructs which are too high-level to fit well.

A language which is reasonably well removed from the liabilities of the hardware should not contain one or two constructs that bring them back again. For example, to avoid reintroducing the hardware "branch" (i.e., the GOTO), provide a reasonably good set of high-level control primitives. To avoid reintroducing that troublesome construct, the unrestricted pointer, either put some restrictions on it like restricting it to point only to objects of a specific type or do away with it completely by implementing something like Hoare's recursive-data types (Hoare, Dahl, and Dijkstra, 1972). To avoid reintroducing the "word" in a situation where a word contains, say, a 12-bit count and then 4 flag bits, arrange the storage-allocation strategy of your compiler so that

```
PACKED RECORD[
                count : 0 to 4095;
                flag1,flag2,flag3,flag4 : BOOLEAN;
                ];
```

results in a desired storage assignment and full type checking is retained.

It is also generally undesirable to have constructs from a higher level of abstraction included. This is not so much because they clutter up the language as because it is hard to introduce a reasonably general set without defining essentially an entire new language. The users will want to know why when you included a primitive that sorts a file, you could not include a similar primitive to sort an array. Under special circumstances, it may be necessary to include a few such constructs. For example, even in a language that supports strings only as fixed-length vectors of characters, it is useful to have literal string constants such as "'a string'" available as a constant of type "array of character." Generally, however, such constructs only make the users more aware that they do not have an entire language at the higher level of abstraction.

3-5 DETAILED DESIGN

This section discusses, on various levels and from several viewpoints, some of the details which go into a language. Some areas of language design have been investigated well enough that it is possible to lay down fairly concrete guidelines; this is done whenever possible. However, many topics are not yet at such a stage, and an attempt is made only to give general discussion on such matters.

The language designer reading this section should recognize that most of this section presents consensus opinions rather than hard facts. Designers should, by all means, feel free to follow different advice or to strike out on their own (see, however, Sec. 3-3, and Hoare, 1973, on the dangers of too much inventiveness). This section is intended to provide a baseline for those who intend to strike out, and a foundation for those who just need to put a language together and do not wish to innovate extensively.

The section is organized on the basis of the various types of structures a program exhibits, and emphasis is placed on how these structures are influenced by the programming language in use. In this context the implications for language design are discussed. The structures are ordered essentially in a bottom-up sequence, working from lowest level to highest level.

3-5.1 Microstructure

What is here called microstructure basically covers those issues of language design which affect the appearance of the language but do not change its semantics. The most significant principle of language microstructure is that the meaning of a construct, such as an operator, should be obvious from its appearance. In other words, the tokens of the language should be easily recognized for what they are and what they do.

The most conspicuous and lowest-level aspect of microstructure is the character set used. Too large a character set can result in users puzzling over the meanings of the obscure hieroglyphics in a program. Too small a character set often results in rather strained syntax, as witness the overuse of parentheses in PL/I. The character set should be as standard as possible to avoid changing programs or the language itself when moving between machines.

In general, the best character set appears to be the 7-bit ASCII set. This is the English-language version of the ISO International Standard Character Set, and is the de facto standard for most of the industry. It is missing perhaps half a dozen useful characters, but in general it is suitable for most programming languages. The 8-bit EBCDIC character set generally has about the same assortment of available characters but suffers from the existence of several versions and heavy dependence on specific manufacturers.

It is likely that the 48-character set, which was used in earlier years of the computing industry, will be phased out. It is clearly difficult to attempt to implement the programming languages of today on this small character set.

To be readable to a compiler, a program must be entered into the machine in some manner. The punched card is no longer a heavily used input medium. The current trend is toward on-line entry, either onto magnetic storage media for later transfer to the computer or, increasingly, directly into the computer via time-sharing terminals or work stations. Quite often the programmer does the typing if time sharing or work stations are used; most other methods employ data-entry specialists. Whatever system is in use, programs should be easy to type.

Some general principles can be set down for easy typing. When using multicharacter nonalphanumeric symbols, try to avoid combinations which require the typist to press the shift key for one character and release it for the next; such sequences slow down typing dramatically. The best multicharacter symbols are those which repeat the same character twice, rather than using two different characters.

Keyboards differ, and hence if an installation has several different terminal types, they quite possibly all have different keyboards. This is significant if programmers do their own typing, since it is hard to become familiar with one keyboard if you have to take whichever terminal is free. The major result of this is that even programmers who can touch-type have to look at the keys for characters other than the letters, the digits, and the following special symbols: , . / ? ( ). Some of the other character placements are nearly standard, but that is not good enough. Try to use keywords or combinations of the above characters for frequently used symbols.

Ideally, it is easier to type short symbols rather than long ones (such as keywords). This is not, however, a valid reason for using one obscure character when a well-chosen keyword would be much clearer.

Another factor which affects the general choice of symbols is that the length of a given symbol should reflect certain semantic characteristics. For operator symbols, lower-priority operators should have longer symbols (it is surprising how much difference this makes to readability).

Generally, keywords are preferable to nonalphanumeric combinations. Use nonalphanumerics only where the meaning is absolutely obvious. When you are thinking about a remainder operator, "REM" or "MOD" is much more obvious than "//" or "%." Keywords can profitably be used as punctuation as well as operators; "MOVE x TO y" is much clearer than "MOVE x : y" or "MOVE(x, y)."

It is almost impossible to generate a good representation for some symbols given the current character sets. Examples of this are the assignment operator (left-pointing arrow), the not-equals operator (slashed equals sign), and the exponentiation operator (upward arrow). Assignment is particularly painful, since it is desirable to have a good left-arrow symbol to eliminate the FORTRAN practice of using " = " for assignment. The best that can be done in ASCII, " < − ", unfortunately is rather hard to type: " < " is shifted, "−" is not (on most keyboards). Not-equals is almost as bad, since ASCII is also lacking a good symbol for "not" (the tilde " ~ " is almost always placed very high on the line, making it unsuitable). If "#" is free, it is probably the best; otherwise " < > " or "/ = ." Exponentiation is a lesser problem, and the FORTRAN solution, " * *," is reasonably well accepted. It is often desirable to have several sorts of brackets; although ASCII provides three ("(···)", "[···]", "{ ··· }") more are sometimes needed. The French quotation marks " < < " ··· " > > "

can often be used; combinations of the existing brackets such as "[ )" $\cdots$ "( ]" are usable but may be hard to type and are not attractive.

It is generally a good idea to use a symbol for only one purpose, especially if it is an operator. It is regrettable, from the viewpoint of parsing and error checking, that most programming languages carry over from mathematics the convention of using " − " for both subtraction and unary negation. If the designer feels like experimenting, perhaps "NEG" could be used for negation.

When a suitable combination of nonalphanumeric characters is not self-evident, a keyword must be chosen for a symbol. Certain general principles can be laid down for the choice of such keywords.

Keywords should be pronounceable. It is easier to remember a syllable than a sequence of unrelated, unpronounceable letters.

Keywords generally should be chosen so that they are unlikely to duplicate user-defined identifiers. Even if there is some means of distinguishing the two, the potential for confusion is high. When choosing keywords, try to use verbs and prepositions; programmers tend to use nouns and adjectives as variable names.

Keywords should be spelled the way the user would expect them. If you must use "SIZE" as an operator, do not spell it "SIZ." Such peculiar spellings will cause more trouble than they save. If at all possible, do not have two keywords with very similar spellings (for example, "PROGEND" and "PROCEND").

Abbreviate keywords only when the abbreviation is absolutely self-evident. This saves considerable typing and is frequently used. Abbreviating "PROCE-DURE" to "PROC" or "PREDECESSOR" to "PRED" is certainly justified; abbreviating "EXTERNAL" to "EX" or "REAL" to "RE" is not. Abbreviating "INTEGER" to "INT" is probably justified.

Sometimes it will be necessary to have a pair of keywords bracketing something. A popular practice in recent years, notably by ALGOL 68 (Lindsey and van der Meulen, 1972; Van Wijngaarden et al., 1975), has been to reverse the spelling of the leading keyword to get the trailing keyword. This works some of the time, but many of the results are horrible. It is probably best to use only the following pairs, which are gaining wide acceptance:

IF	FI
CASE	ESAC
DO	OD

If you have to end a construct which starts with "SELECT," use "ENDSELECT," not "TCELES." Another alternative, which is harder to design, is to try to find a keyword which "fits" as a trailing keyword (example: "LOOP...REPEAT"). It is also possible to use a pair of keywords (example: "LOOP...ENDLOOP") instead of a single keyword, if no serious confusion is introduced elsewhere. Also, try to avoid overusing a keyword; the PL/I "END" is a gross violator of this.

One further matter that is important with respect to keywords is how to tell them apart from user-defined identifiers. There are three distinct approaches:

1. Keywords are "reserved" and may not be used as identifiers.
2. Keywords are distinguished from identifiers on the basis of context.
3. Keywords are preceded by some special character to mark them.

Generally, alternative 1 works best—it is simple and, given a careful choice of keywords, seldom causes trouble. Alternative 2, that used in PL/I, significantly complicates the parser. It probably was adopted in PL/I because the number of keywords in some implementations was so large that no user could reasonably be expected to avoid them all. Languages of a more realistic size do not have such problems. Alternative 3 is often used in ALGOL 60 and ALGOL 68 implementations. It involves extra typing and makes the program unreadable. The most successful single implementation of ALGOL 60 (the Burroughs one) uses alternative 1.

User-defined identifiers deserve some discussion. The usual basic set is letters plus digits, except that the first character must be a letter. If both uppercase and lowercase letters are available, they should be considered equivalent. There are few things more confusing than having "A" and "a" acting as separate variables. It has become customary to add a few extra characters to the list of "letters," for convenience. Probably the most important one is the underscore "_", which allows, in effect, the use of "blanks" inside identifiers. This provides a major improvement in readability.

With modern string-handling techniques there is no justification for limiting the length of identifiers, either explicitly ("maximum 6 characters") or implicitly ("only the first 6 are significant"). This approach does not require unlimited storage, as few identifiers will be longer than about 15 characters (Alexander, 1972). A "silent limit" of, say, 255 characters will never be exceeded or even approached, especially if identifiers cannot be split across line boundaries.

Another aspect of microstructure which deserves careful attention is the design of the comment convention. It must be brief (not "COMMENT"), and it must be easy to type (not "/*"). As Hoare points out (Hoare, 1973), probably the best type of comment convention is one that is fairly common in assemblers but uncommon in high-level languages: a particular symbol starts a comment, which then extends to the end of that line. This eliminates the "runaway" comments of PL/I, and this convention turns out to be surprisingly convenient to use. A significant question is the choice of a beginning symbol. While various symbols have been used for such comments, the requirement of easy typing may eliminate many of them. Also, such one-character symbols are often useful as operators. Ideally, such a symbol should:

1. Be a two-character symbol, preferably both the same character.
2. Be a symbol seldom, if ever, used as an operator, with no obvious meaning as such.
3. Be composed of characters located in the same place on all keyboards.

The symbol "//" is an example of a good choice.

On the matter of program appearance, most languages have followed ALGOL's lead in declaring that the blank is significant only in that (except within strings) it separates two symbols and may not occur within a symbol. If the system has a "tab" character, it is useful to treat it the same way. It is also reasonable to treat end-of-line the same way, except that it also may terminate comments. It is most undesirable to require constructs to start in certain columns.

One final matter concerning the appearance of the language: unless it is planned to use an automatic source-text formatter as part of the compiler, it is a good idea to have some means of causing a skip to the next page of printout. If the system has a form-feed character available, it is a simple matter to arrange for the compiler's scanner to ignore such characters as tokens. When the source is output, the form-feed character would generate the required skip to next page.

3-5.2 Expression Structure

The expression is often the fundamental unit of computation in a language. Its components, operators and value accesses, are too peculiar to specific languages to be given much treatment here, but some comments can be made on expressions in general.

One topic related to expressions is the question of order of evaluation. The normal method of determining order of evaluation is based on two levels: explicit bracketing and operator binding.

Explicit bracketing comprises both parentheses and the overall bracketing provided by the boundaries of the expression. In this connection, it is worth noting an idea a few languages (such as LISP) have: having two types of parenthesis constructs, "[ ]" and "( )", so that complex expressions become more readable.

Operator binding is the most familiar aspect of order of evaluation. Three basic systems of binding exist: left-to-right, right-to-left, and priority. Left-to-right cannot be recommended; the only reason it is used at all (quite frequently in assemblers) is that it is simple. Right-to-left is notable only because it is used in APL. It is used mainly because of the wide variety of operators, which makes it difficult to try to assign precedences to them all. An alternative approach for a language with lots of operators is to assign priorities to some of the simpler operators and require explicit bracketing of the rest. Experiments in language design (Gannon, 1975) have indicated that APL's "natural" right-to-left rule is in fact harder to understand than simple priority rules.

One thing that must be avoided is large numbers of priority levels, as in C, which can confuse rather than illuminate. Restriction to a small number of priority levels can best be done by considering which operators are, psychologically speaking, on different levels.

The desire to reduce the number of levels should not lead the designer into placing, on the same level, operators which are psychologically on different levels. For example, the decision in PASCAL to put "AND" on the same level as " * " and "OR" on the same level as " + " may have been a mistake: simple multiple comparisons such as "a = b AND c = d" are illegal; this must be written "(a = b) AND (c = d)".

A minor aspect of operator binding is the relationship of unary and binary operators. In many languages this is complicated considerably by the fact that not all unary operators have the same priority; NOT is often given a very low priority. While there is some justification for this (to put the logical operators all in the same range of priority), it is probably simpler to take the approach of ALGOL 68 (Van Wijngaarden et al., 1975): all unary operators have a priority higher than all binary operators.

A matter related to expression structure is the much-praised notion of the "expression language," the idea that every construct returns a value and may be used anywhere a value is required. At first sight, the concept looks appealing. The whole idea of the "statement" vanishes It becomes possible to use an IF or CASE to select which of several values should be used at a particular point in an expression. Unfortunately, a deeper examination shows that the loss of "statement" is more than counterbalanced by the additional complexity in the behavior of "expression." Furthermore, all but the simplest cases of using a complex construct inside, say, an arithmetic expression become unreadable. It is also very unclear just what value should be returned from, for example, a loop. If users are allowed to supply their own values, this makes things worse. The expression language is a novel idea, but in reality it appears to increase complexity, widens the field for trickery and cleverness at the expense of readability, and does not add any particularly useful capabilities.

The one possible exception to this is the conditional expression: a simple IF-expression which chooses one of two values. This is reasonably easy to understand and is sometimes useful; arguments against it are the infrequency of use and the difficulty of arriving at a concise yet readable syntax.

The alternative to an expression language is the statement language, where a distinction is made between statements and expressions. Control constructs are statements and are not valid expressions Expressions yield a value and generally, barring the misuse of function calls, do not have side effects. This type of organization corresponds well to the way programmers normally think about their programs: a "statement" performs an action, an "expression" yields a value.

3-5.3 Data Structure

Four aspects of data structure will be considered in this subsection. First, a discussion of the alternative forms for data declarations is presented. Next, an overview of the variety of data types that are available in programming languages today and that should be considered if a new-language design is undertaken. The effects of storage-allocation strategies on language-design aspects are then described. The final topic deals with a discussion of the scope of variables in a programming language.

The declarations of a language are the means by which nonprocedural information is conveyed to the compiler. While there exists a large number of specialized forms of declarations to meet specific needs, this discussion will focus on the three common requirements of most programming languages: declarations for constants, types, and variables.

It has recently become obvious that it is extremely useful to be able to give names to constants. This avoids the use of "magic numbers" in the body of the code. In this way program readability is greatly improved and it is much easier to change the value of, say, a table size. Some languages (see Clark and Horning, 1971) have even taken the position that, with the exception of 0, 1, and 2, all numeric constants occurring in the code must be given names by constant declarations. Consequently, "magic numbers" may not occur anywhere except in such declarations.

Another aspect of the declaration of constants is that it is useful to be able to write a constant for any data type in the program. For example, it should be possible to write an array constant. Such constants would largely eliminate the need to initialize arrays, as most initialized arrays are really array constants, and would prevent the programmer from accidentally destroying the contents of such a constant.

Similarly, it is useful, essentially as a form of abbreviation, to be able to give names to types and then use those names in the declaration of variables or in the construction of more complex types. Such type declarations can save a great deal of writing while also improving readability.

The syntax of constant and type declarations can be similar, as in the following:

CONST table_size = 437;
TYPE big_array = ARRAY [1 TO 1000, 1 TO 1000] OF integer;

The similarities between the two may bring up a tempting thought: Why not generalize both to a parameterless macrofacility?

The basic reason to avoid this is that constants and types are, by and large, the only things that would be declared. Consequently, such an overgeneralized construct would be an open invitation to "clever" tricky programming.

If the designer decides not to allow initialization of variables, the syntax of variable declarations becomes quite simple. A very readable syntax is that used by PASCAL:

VAR a, b, c : integer;

Note that this syntax is really suitable only when all information about, say, array bounds is localized in the type specification. Readability of this form diminishes rapidly if the list of variable names is cluttered up with other things such as initialization.

Let us now turn to a discussion of data types in programming languages. The basic reference for modern data types is Hoare's work (Hoare, Dahl, and Dijkstra 1972). Wirth's work on PASCAL (Jensen and Wirth, 1975) is worth looking at as a practical implementation of many of Hoare's ideas. Since the material on this topic is heavily based on these two documents, no further mention of these references is made. Hehner (1975) and Tennent (1975) also present some interesting ideas.

The basis of all notions of data structure is the data type. What is a data type? Although there has been considerable difference of opinion on this, the most prevalent view is that a data type is a set of values plus a set of operations operating on these values. For example, "integer" might be the set of values "..., $-2, -1, 0, 1, 2, ...$" and the set of operations "$+, -, *, /, \leftarrow$." Note that the presence of the operations as part of the definition also implies that the members of the set of values cannot be chosen arbitrarily; there must be some consistency among them so that the same operations will apply to all.

There are three distinct approaches to types in programming languages. The first is to have none at all, characteristic of assembly language and some "midlevel" languages. The desirability of types is well established; so no further attention will be given to their absence. The remaining two approaches are called "hard" and "soft" typing. In both approaches a value has a type associated with it. The basic distinction between the two approaches is that in a soft-typed language any variable may contain any value (as in SNOBOL and APL), whereas in a hard-typed language a specific type is associated with every variable and the variable may contain only values belonging to that type's set of values.

Generally speaking, it is now accepted that while soft typing renders a language slightly smaller and somewhat more concise, hard typing is vastly superior from the viewpoint of compile-time error checking (Wirth, 1974) and introduces no noticeable inconvenience. Further discussion will assume hard typing.

While no two language designers agree on exactly how the broad variety of data types should be subdivided, types can generally be grouped into three categories: simple, compound, and complex. These terms are relative and the boundaries between them are fuzzy.

The simple data types are on the comparatively primitive level of a language; they are used to build more complex types and are usually provided more or less directly by the machine upon which the compiler is implemented.

One matter of general interest in simple types is the question of ordering; that is, are the values of a type considered to be in a specific sequence? This basically determines whether comparisons such as " $<$ " are valid for all simple types, and it may also influence the counted loop of the language. In some cases, such as numbers, ordering is obviously required. For some other situations, the precise nature of the ordering is less obvious. Specific comments will be made on this point throughout the subsection.

The most elementary kind of simple type is what has been called the enumeration type, in which the programmer simply gives a list of identifiers as the set of values. Examples of this case are:

TYPE color = (red, green, blue)
TYPE job_status = (executing, waiting, terminated)

Note that these sample declarations constitute declarations of the values "red," "green," etc., as well as the identifiers "color" and "job_status." The valid operations on values of such types are equal and not-equal comparisons and assignment. The constants of this type are simply the names given. Obviously, within the machine the values of an enumeration type are represented as small integers, but this is not visible to the programmer; "red" is not a value of type "integer." It is not clear whether enumeration types should be ordered or not; perhaps the programmer should be able to ask for a specific enumeration type to be ordered. Without them, the programmer is frequently driven to simulate them using integers, a process which works but is error-prone. Any language intended for serious software work should have enumeration types.

Probably the most common form of a data type is the number. There is really very little that can be said about floating-point numbers, other than that they are, at this time, machine-dependent in almost all language implementation. The discussion will therefore be confined largely to integers. While the simple type "integer" is straightforward enough, there are two notable modifications that can be made.

The first modification involves the idea of the "subrange," a type which has, as its value set, a subset of the integers. Examples of this modification are as follows:

```
TYPE cents = 0 TO 99
TYPE day_of_month = 1 TO 31
TYPE inning = 1 TO 9
```

Subranges allow the compiler to optimize storage allocation, since it is easy to determine exactly how much space a subrange variable needs. Subrange types are a much more readable way of doing this than things like "short_integer." Subranges are also machine-independent, whereas "integer" is not. Finally, and most importantly, subranges provide very valuable redundancy; the compiler can easily generate code to check that the value being assigned into a subrange variable is within the subrange. A certain amount of this checking can even be done at compile time.

While subranges are definitely valuable, one respect in which they are somewhat weak is in formal definition. The close relationship between subranges and integers complicates the process of defining them because the programmer naturally expects them to be usable anywhere integers are. This means that a formal definition must consider subrange values to be automatically converted to integer values whenever necessary. Probably the best solution to this is to say that a subrange type is really "integer" in disguise, and that the only respect in which it is not identical to "integer" is that a subrange variable may store only a subset of the full "integer" value set. It may also be helpful to have subranges of other types than "integer" (e.g., subranges of "character"). It might be best to say that any ordered type may have subranges defined on it.

The other notable modification to "integer" is one that is also applicable to floating-point. The idea, which is originally due to Hoare (1973), is that one should be able to associate units (e.g., kilograms, clock ticks, meters per second) with numeric variables. This is essentially a way of providing more useful redundancy. The compiler could check to see that operations performed on numeric values were indeed valid. For example, adding kilograms to clock ticks is definitely somebody's error; a value obtained by multiplying meters per second by seconds should be assigned only into a variable containing meters. A full facility for specifying such things would be somewhat complex (consider, for example, conversions from feet to meters, the use of Newtons as a synonym for kilogram-meters per second-squared), but the idea is novel and is supported by Ada.

After the numeric data types, the "character" types are probably the most frequently used. It is unfortunate that current hardware does not support truly variable-length strings well. The result is a multiplicity of approaches to characters:

1. "Character" is a simple type, holding one character. Strings are implemented as arrays of characters.
2. Strings may vary in length but must have a specified maximum length for purposes of storage allocation.
3. Strings may vary arbitrarily in length (efficiency penalties are accepted for the sake of usability).

A fourth approach, the use of fixed-length strings, will not be considered.

The first approach essentially bypasses the problem. The properties of the array are now the key to the usefulness of strings. Unfortunately, arrays are quite ill-suited to the implementation of strings; one can either accept the poor string handling that results, as in PASCAL, or attempt to stretch the properties of the array and generally meet with undesirable results, as in ALGOL 68.

The second approach is possibly the best compromise; unfortunately, it has the usual properties of compromises. It is not as simple as alternative 1 or as usable as alternative 3. If the language must run without extensive run-time support (e.g., for writing an operating system) or must be very efficient, this is probably the method to use.

Environmental or efficiency constraints permitting, the third approach is the best one. The loss in efficiency can often be surprisingly small, and the gain in usability as exhibited in SNOBOL can be sizable.

The last of the simple types is "Boolean," which is infrequently used but quite essential when it does occur. The PL/I approach is to generalize the Boolean variable into a string of bits analogous to a string of characters. Since actual measurements (Alexander, 1972) show that the overwhelming majority of bit strings are actually one bit long, the generalization seems to have been unnecessary. For most languages, Boolean is sufficient.

Although Boolean could be defined as a separate data type, the simplest approach is simply to predefine it, as in PASCAL, by

TYPE boolean = (false, true)

If enumeration types are available, this approach satisfies all requirements and needs no further intricacies inside the compiler.

Now that we have finished with the simple types, the next subject of discussion is the compound types. These are types constructed in fairly simple ways from simpler types.

The most obvious variety of compound type is the array. Two aspects of it deserve comment. First, consideration should be given to extending subscripts to data types other than integers. While general floating-point numbers are obviously unsuitable as subscripts, enumeration types and single characters can quite often be usefully employed as subscripts. The approach taken in PASCAL in fact takes advantage of this. The dimensions of an array are given in terms of the types of its subscripts:

TYPE nonsense = ARRAY [color, 1 TO 99] OF integer

(see the definition of color earlier).

The second issue concerning arrays is the question of dynamic arrays, whose sizes are determined at block entry rather than at compile time. Dynamic arrays add to compile-time complexity and, for this reason, have been left out of some languages. However, they can be very useful in applications where array size is dependent on input data. The increase in complexity is often outweighed by the usefulness of dynamic arrays, and therefore in many cases dynamic arrays should be included in a language.

The other compound data type is the record, sometimes known, confusingly, as the "structure." For many applications it is just as fundamental as the array. The lack of records is probably a major factor in the rejection of ALGOL 60 by the data-processing community.

One fairly useful embellishment of the record is the tagged-variant record. This allows for the frequent situations where the structure of part of the record is dependent on the data in an earlier part of it:

```
TYPE name=
RECORD
            given_names : string;
            CASE sex : (male, female)
            OF
            female:
                    married_name : string;
                    maiden_name : string;
            OR
            male:
                    last_name : string;
            ESAC
    ENDRECORD
```

The record has some fixed fields (e.g., "given_names") followed by a tag field which selects which variant of the remainder of the record is in use. The tag field is named "sex" and is of the enumeration type "(male, female)." The tag field is followed by the variants, which in this case are either "married_name" and "maiden_name" or "last_name." With such an arrangement, the compiler can set up run-time checks to ensure that any reference, for example to "maiden_name," is referencing a record whose "sex" field is "female." PASCAL and Ada support such a facility.

COBOL has the interesting notion of being able to use "filler" as a field name in a record. This feature essentially gives the programmer an anonymous field of the given size. This can be useful if a file of records is being processed by several programs, some of which ignore certain fields.

One less than obvious compound data type is a simple form of set. While sets in general are part of a subject covered later under "complex" data types, one restricted form of set deserves mention, since it can be implemented simply and efficiently but is still fairly useful. If the number of possible elements of a set is quite small, it is possible to implement the set by simply allocating a field of bits. One bit is allocated for each possible element. The bit is 1 or 0, to indicate whether or not the element is currently in the set.

With this scheme, set manipulations are done easily by the machine's logical instructions. For example, a set over an enumeration type

TYPE colorset = SET OF color;

(see definition of "color" earlier) can be especially useful.

The final compound data type that will be considered is the pointer. The pointer is referred to as a compound type as opposed to a simple type because it is most wisely used in conjunction with and not independent of another data type. In fact, it is fairly widely agreed that undisciplined use of pointers is, if anything, even worse than undisciplined use of the GOTO. There are two major pro-gramming-language design solutions to this.

The first solution is Hoare's *recursive data types* (Hoare, Dahl, and Dijkstra, 1972), which eliminate the explicit use of a pointer altogether. The basic idea behind recursive data types is that instead of having, say, one field of a record point to another record, the second record is conceptually a field of the first. A recursive data type is one in which the name of the type being defined occurs in its own definition. Such a notion has been used in the definition of a list in LISP and in defining a recursive pattern in SNOBOL 4, in particular. Trees can also be defined in such a manner. In actual fact the implementation at the machine level is the same, via a pointer, but recursive data types hide this completely from the programmer. A recursive data type is a relatively new concept, and it is too early yet to tell whether it will prove to be decisively superior to the alternative, namely, retaining the pointer but placing restrictions on it.

The second solution basically depends on what restrictions should be placed on the pointer. There are two restrictions which appear to fill the requirements. The first is to require the pointer to point to an object of a specific type. In other words, one does not declare a variable to be of type "POINTER"; one declares it to be of type, say, "POINTER TO integer." This restriction alone eliminates most of the hazards of pointers.

The second restriction, which has been suggested by Wirth (1974), is that there should be no "address-of" operator; that is, it should be impossible to make a pointer point at a named variable. Pointers should point only into anonymous, dynamically allocated heap storage. This largely prevents the possibly serious confusion arising from referencing the same storage location under several different names.

The final variety of data type is the complex data type, which is one involving nontrivial implementation effort, nontrivial overhead, and a significant probability that a particular implementation will be far from optimal for some users. Examples of some such data types are lists, general sets, trees, stacks, and queues.

While such data types can be implemented using pointers or recursive data types, such implementations are very hard to change if it is discovered that they need tuning (e.g., if the implementation is very fast, it generally turns out that storage space is the real bottleneck). The long-range solution to this appears to be the idea of data abstraction.

The basic notion of data abstraction is that it should be possible to define a "user interface" for such a data type. This interface specifies what the various operations do to values of the type without mentioning how the values or the operations are implemented. The implementation itself then consists of specifying how the values are implemented (in terms of more primitive data types) and how the operations are implemented (a procedure for each operation). The user can then use the data type without knowing or caring about the details of the implementation, and the implementation can be changed without rewriting user programs.

Data abstractions are currently in the early experimental stages, and there is no agreement on the details. For those wishing to investigate further, Horning (1976) is a more detailed introduction to the ideas presented here, Liskov and Zilles (1974) gives an excellent demonstration of the use of data abstractions, and Shaw (1976) and the rest of the SIGPLAN (1976) issue constitute an excellent overview of the subject.

One feature of some languages is the provision for automatic conversions or coercions. An example of a conversion is converting the string "123" into the numeric value 123 if the string is added to a numeric variable. Coercions have been mentioned in Sec. 3-4.2. There are good reasons why such features should not be included in clean languages. They complicate the language excessively, hamper genuine extensibility (e.g., data abstraction), and severely impede readability because of frequent and excessive violation of the principle of least astonishment. This does not preclude the inclusion of data conversions and pointer chasing in new languages; it simply means that such things should always be explicitly requested and should not be supplied behind the programmer's back.

Explicit conversion facilities may take one of two forms. The simplest form is that of functions which take a value of one type and return a value of another type (e.g., a function "round" taking "real" and returning "integer"). The alternative is the ALGOL 68 approach, which has a special operator that takes an input value and a data type and converts the input value to the given type.

The allocation of storage for variables in a program is, in its details, the business of the compiler and the run-time system. Certain overall policies, however, are part of the language design. There are basically four forms of variable allocation; they will be discussed in turn, with comments on each.

The simplest and oldest form of allocation is static allocation, immortalized in FORTRAN and in ALGOL 60's OWN facility. It now appears that the major usefulness of static allocation is its use not within procedures but globally. Most cases where one would use ALGOL-60-style OWN can be better organized as a set of static variables with a set of procedures to operate on them. This makes static allocation relevant to data abstraction and modularity (see Sec. 3-5.5).

The most popular form of allocation, pioneered by ALGOL 60, is local, dynamic, or automatic allocation. The usefulness and implementation simplicity of local allocation make it the form of choice for normal variables within procedures.

The third form of allocation, retention, is one that has not been used extensively. This is different from both static and local allocation, in that storage is allocated on entry to a procedure or block, but it is not necessarily freed on exit —it remains allocated and may again become accessible via various mechanisms. It currently appears that the main usefulness of retention is in the implementation of backtracking algorithms, but broader applications may yet be found.

The final form of allocation is another familiar one, the allocation on explicit program request of anonymous storage ("heap" allocation is the ALGOL 68 term), with the program keeping track of it by a pointer. An exactly analogous process goes on, slightly less visibly, when recursive data types are in use. A heap form of allocation is a standard feature of many programming languages (e.g., ALGOL 68 and PL/I). One point relevant to implementation is that while programmers have the freedom to request allocation of heap storage at any time, they probably should not also have the freedom to do their own deallocation. This will most assuredly result in "dangling pointers." Recovering storage that is no longer accessible to the program should be the responsibility of the run-time system, not the programmer.

The final major issue regarding data structures is the scope of names. The original purpose of restricting the scope of names in ALGOL 60 was largely to facilitate storage allocation. Scope and storage allocation are no longer as strongly coupled as they once were. Nevertheless, restrictions on the scope of names are still present to assist in reducing the complexity of programs.

In order to maintain the complexity of programs and segments of programs within human grasp, it is necessary to restrict the interactions between different segments. Accessing a given variable is one of the most important interactions between the different parts of a program, and for this reason scope restrictions have continued in programming languages. Some comments must be made, however, concerning the nature of the scope rules that are used.

One of the most fundamental questions of the organization of scopes is, what is the basic area of scope restrictions? The most common answer is the one originated by ALGOL 60—the BEGIN-END block. This does appear, however, to be an excessively general structure. Multiple nested blocks with variables declared at each level begin to exceed the human mind's limited capability for handling nesting. The alternative basis for scope restrictions is the procedure. Instead of allocating variables and controlling their accessibility with arbitrary blocks, such controls can be accomplished at procedure entry and exit. This approach has been in use for a long time (having been introduced in FORTRAN) but nevertheless, when coupled with local rather than static allocation, is quite workable, as witnessed by its modern use in PASCAL. Since it is somewhat simpler than BEGIN-END scope control, it can be recommended.

One somewhat more restrictive aspect of scope control is one that has been mentioned several times elsewhere in this section, namely, ensuring that one variable is not accessible by two different names. It has been suggested (Tennent, 1975) that the compiler should, in fact, check for such situations and consider them errors. In general, this is an idea with some merit; in practice, it could become rather difficult when constructs involving pointers are considered. Even if pointers cannot point to named variables, one can still have two pointers pointing to the same piece of anonymous storage. Recursive data types might clear up some of these problems.

Another aspect of scope which is a restriction that many compilers enforce is the requirement that entities (procedures, variables, etc.) must be declared before they are used. For variables and constants this is not too unpleasant. It may be desirable to provide some extensions to permit, for example, recursive data types or data types with pointers that refer to each other.

The biggest problem with the declare-before-use rule is for procedures. It really is desirable to be able to call a procedure which occurs later in the program, even if one does not have the classic situation of mutually recursive procedures. It is a serious nuisance to have to reorder the procedures in a program to suit the compiler rather than the programmer. Some effort in the compiler is probably justified to avoid having to introduce this restriction.

A final point which is a question of scope but is sometimes not recognized as such is the matter of the field names within a record. In some languages, notably COBOL, these names are accessible from the outside without further qualification. In many modern languages (e.g., PASCAL), "a.x" must be written "a.x" even if there is no other "x" in the program.

The choice of approach here is not obvious; the COBOL approach certainly can involve much less writing, but the PASCAL approach probably improves readability and certainly simplifies both the compiler and the language semantics. Certainly, if the COBOL approach is taken, it is vital that the compiler check for possible ambiguity; it must not be possible to have two different interpretations of the same name at the same place by rearranging the declarations.

3-5.4 Control Structure

There has been a great deal of controversy regarding the best choice for control-structure primitives. Much of the discussion centers around the inclusion or exclusion of the GOTO. It is almost universally agreed that it is better to use high-level control constructs rather than the unrestricted GOTO. It is equally widely accepted that a suitable set of high-level constructs would eliminate both the necessity of and the desire for the GOTO. What is not so well agreed upon is what should comprise such a set. It is obviously necessary to be able to group several statements for execution in sequence. There is little dispute that the IF statement and some sort of loop terminating on a Boolean condition are desirable. Almost as indisputable are some form of CASE statement for multiway choices and some form of FOR loop controlling an index variable. The major area of dispute is centered around "escape" constructs and constructs for the handling of exceptional conditions which often, but not always, are one and the same.

Clearly, this discussion has some elements of the minimal versus minimal-useful issue mentioned in the consideration of design philosophy in Sec. 3-4. No one disputes that a program which uses escape constructs can also be written without them. The basic question is whether it is significantly easier to read and to write programs with such constructs available—more research is required in this area. The rest of this subsection will discuss various constructs in detail.

The simplest control structure is the combination of several statements into a single statement, as with ALGOL's BEGIN-END statement. Languages without such a construct (FORTRAN, BASIC) suffer badly from its absence. Given its desirability, there are three distinct methods for obtaining such a combination: explicit brackets, self-bracketing constructs, and bracketing by indentation.

Explicit brackets are best typified by the ALGOL 60 BEGIN-END pair (here considered without the possibility of including declarations within it). BEGIN...END is one choice; there are others. In particular, PL/I uses DO...END, which is possibly a weak choice because of the similarity to the loop construct, and C (Ritchie, 1974) uses { ... }.

All explicit-bracketing schemes unfortunately have one defect. They treat the cases "one statement" and "several statements" differently (a violation of "uniformity"). It is often necessary, for debugging or modification, to put several statements where before only one was present. Any explicit-bracketing scheme requires brackets to be inserted whenever this is done, which is a major annoyance.

This difficulty is solved by the self-bracketing-constructs approach, in which any control construct which may have to contain some statements is organized so as to have distinctive punctuation bracketing the point where the statements may occur. For example, one may add a terminating keyword to an IF to make it self-bracketing:

IF expression THEN statements FI

or

IF expression THEN statements ELSE statements FI

It is comparatively easy to make the full set of control constructs self-bracketing, thereby eliminating explicit bracketing. The different keywords terminating each self-bracketing construct also add valuable redundancy. Self-bracketing constructs have been used successfully in several languages (Van Wijngaarden et al., 1975; Clark, 1971; Wirth, 1982).

The final possibility, bracketing by indentation, uses the two-dimensional nature of the program to make the compiler aware that the ELSE in

```
IF x
THEN
      IF y
      THEN
            . . .
ELSE
      . . .
```

belongs to the outer IF rather than to the inner one. This approach, which has been around for quite some time, appears interesting but contains some possible pitfalls. The loss of the terminating keywords is a significant loss of redundancy. This may cause trouble if a new line with an incorrect indentation level is added or if revisions to a section of a program require widespread changes in indentation level. Also, indentation is not generally significant in natural languages; programmers are not accustomed to considering it as significant.

Whenever statements are grouped, it is obviously necessary to separate them from each other. The almost universally accepted convention is to use the semicolon ";". One minor issue of debate is whether the semicolon should separate statements ("BEGIN . . . ; . . . ; . . . END") or terminate them ("BEGIN . . . ; . . . ; . . . ; END"). Using it as a separator is perhaps more elegant, and can sometimes be easier to parse, but actual measurements (Gannon, 1975) show that the terminating-semicolon form is far less error-prone.

The next most fundamental control construct is the IF statement, which provides a two-way choice of action. In such a choice, it is quite possible that one of the two actions is in fact null, thus resulting in the familiar

```
IF boolean
THEN
      statements
FI
```

(the FI together with the THEN serves to bracket the statement sequence). However, the second action is not always null, which leads to the equally familiar

```
IF boolean
THEN
      statements
ELSE
      statements
FI
```

which provides for both actions. Measurements by Alexander (1972) on the relative frequency of these two forms reveals that roughly 35 percent of IFs have an ELSE. This number is too small to justify requiring the ELSE; so the IF should be accepted as having both forms.

One issue which is relevant to several constructs, including the IF, is the question "what is a Boolean expression?" To date, this question has been answered in at least three different ways:

1. "Boolean" is an independent data type, with constants "TRUE" and "FALSE." Certain operators, such as the comparison operators, yield Boolean results.
2. "Boolean" is the same as "integer." True and false are nonzero and zero, respectively. Comparison operators yield 1 or 0.
3. "Boolean" is the same as "integer." True and false are odd and even, respectively (i.e., distinguished by the low-order bit of the integer). Comparison operators yield 1 or 0.

Of these three, the first is preferable. The difficulty with the second is that "clever" programmers often make use of their knowledge of how the Boolean expression is evaluated to write "IF x" where they should write "IF x = 1." The resulting loss in readability is sizable. Similar objections apply to the third alternative. Another problem with the second and third methods is that the confusion of "Boolean" and "integer" interferes with error checking.

A natural generalization of the IF is from a two-way choice to an *n*-way choice. Often this choice is made on the basis of the value of an integer variable. Several forms of the CASE construct have been proposed, and several issues are of importance.

First, many older CASE constructs rely on the textual order of the alternatives in order to decide which case corresponds to which alternative:

```
CASE choice-expression
OF
        statements1 OR
        statements2 OR
    . . .
ESAC
```

(Note that "OR" is used as a delimiter, not as the "or" operator.) Textual order unfortunately opens up possibilities for error if one case is forgotten or misplaced. A much better scheme is one in which each case is labeled with the value(s) that cause it to be chosen:

```
    CASE choice-expression : 1 TO 10
    OF
            1: statements OR
          2,3: statements OR
  4 THRU 7: statements OR
        . . .
          10: statements
    ESAC
```

It is usually desirable to specify the range of possible choice values, partly for easier implementation and partly to provide valuable redundancy. It definitely is useful to be able to specify the same action for more than one value and to be able to give a range of values instead of writing them all out. For the sake of readability it is highly desirable that the values used in the labels be restricted to simple constants.

Note also that with this scheme there really is no reason to restrict the choice-expression type to be "integer"; it would be equally valid to make a choice on the basis of a value of "character" or enumeration type, for example. Efficient implementation should decide what limitations must be placed on the type of the choice expression.

Another issue which is relevant is the question of the precise implementation of such a CASE. At least two alternatives suggest themselves: either use the value of the choice expression to index into a table of action addresses, or evaluate the choice expression, store its value, and compare it successively with each value label. Each scheme has its advantages. Indexing is faster, whereas (if ranges are allowed as labels) sequential checking can reduce storage requirements noticeably. It may be worthwhile to give the programmer a choice or allow the compiler to choose based on an optimization formula.

A natural question that arises is

What if the value of the choice expression does not correspond
to any of the value labels?

This definitely should not cause a random jump to somewhere in the code! The usual strategy here is to include an ELSE clause which is executed if none of the alternatives are selected:

```
CASE ....
        ....
ELSE
        statements
ESAC
```

It has also been suggested (Weinberg et al., 1975), with some justification, that it would be useful to have a clause (perhaps an "ALSO" clause) containing statements that would be executed if any of the labeled alternatives was executed. For example, this would provide a simple way of handling matters such as setting an "action-taken" flag or disposing of a successfully processed data item.

It is sometimes suggested that the syntax for the IF should be merged with that of the CASE, since the IF is really just a special case of CASE. A solid counterargument, however, is that the overwhelming majority of the choice constructs used are IFs (Alexander, 1972), and that the popularity of the IF (particularly with no ELSE clause) justifies special syntax to improve readability.

A more generalized CASE construct that has been suggested by Dijkstra (1975) and Weinberg et al. (1975) is of the form

CASE
> Boolean: statements OR
> Boolean: statements OR
> . . .

ESAC

In this form, each of the "Booleans" is evaluated; when one of them is true, the corresponding "statements" section is executed. It is not clear what ought to happen should two or more of the "Booleans" both happen to be true; possibly the first one to be true should be used. This may provide a more generally useful form of the sequential checking mentioned earlier as a plausible implementation of the usual CASE. This form appears potentially quite useful, especially if equipped with an ELSE and an ALSO clause. The Weinberg paper also has some other interesting ideas on choice structures.

The other major control construct is the loop. A large majority of its uses are accounted for by the simple case in which termination occurs on the basis of a Boolean condition. One problem is where the termination condition should be checked: at the beginning of each iteration, at the end, or even in the middle. All three cases are useful. By far the best solution is that proposed by Dahl (in Knuth, 1974) in which the check is potentially in the middle:

LOOP
> statements

UNTIL Boolean:
> statements

REPEAT

Either group of statements may be null. This construct covers all three forms. It also, by and large, eliminates the necessity for having special constructs which terminate loop execution or restart the iteration (often written "EXIT" and "CYCLE," respectively).

One minor question in Boolean-condition loops is whether to terminate repetition on the Boolean condition becoming true ("UNTIL") or becoming false ("WHILE"). The traditional choice is WHILE. The WHILE school claims that the UNTIL focuses attention on the termination of the loop whereas the WHILE focuses attention where it belongs, namely, on the nature of the repetition. The UNTIL school claims that the WHILE focuses attention on the mechanics of the repetition while the UNTIL focuses attention where it belongs, namely, on the (Boolean) condition that the loop is working toward.

The other notable form of loop is the iterative FOR loop, which alters the value of an index variable in some predefined way on each iteration. Although the FOR loop could be constructed by the user from an ordinary Boolean-condition loop, this construction process is tricky and error-prone, and hence it is a good idea to have a built-in FOR loop.

In order to achieve reasonable readability and reliability, a FOR loop needs some rather extensive restrictions. Modification of the index variable should not be permitted inside the loop; the compiler should enforce this restriction. Any values used to set the parameters of the index-variable alteration should be evaluated on entry to the loop and should not be alterable thereafter. It is not clear just what the value of the index variable should be on exit from the loop; a simple solution is to say that the FOR itself constitutes the declaration of the index variable and that the index variable is accessible only within the loop. This also relieves the programmer of the nuisance of having to declare the index variable.

The remaining problem is the nature of the variation of the index variable. The traditional approach is to specify an initial value, final value, and increment. Many designers (Hoare, 1972) tend to consider this overgeneralized and detrimental to readability, especially when applied to floating-point numbers. The approach taken by PASCAL is to restrict the increment of the loop to be 1 or -1 by giving the bounds of the loop as "x TO y" or "x DOWNTO y," and to prohibit floating-point index variables. It has been observed by Alexander (1972) that this covers the vast majority of cases. Note that there is no particular reason why the index variable should not be, for example, of type "character" rather than "integer." Consider the example:

```
FOR i FROM 'a' TO 'x'
DO
            . . .
            . . .
    END
```

(Note the use of "FROM" where some forms use the assignment operator; "FROM" is probably clearer.) It is desirable to exclude floating-point numbers, however; the peculiarities of floating-point arithmetic complicate things too much and thereby interfere with readability.

In languages with the "set" as a basic data type, it may well be desirable to have a FOR which simply sequences through the members of a programmer-supplied set:

```
FOR x IN a_set
DO
            . . .
            . . .
    END
```

Here the index variable x simply assumes in turn the value of each member of the set. In what order should the index variable assume the various values? Perhaps the least offensive solution is to say that the order is implementation-defined and should not be depended upon in programs.

Although the PASCAL approach to the FOR loop can be recommended, designers wishing to experiment have several other options. The set-driven FOR loop previously discussed is useful in a language which handles sets well. Another proposal, which has been experimented with by Gannon (1975), is a FOR loop of the form:

```
FOR x IN arrayname
DO
        . . .
        . . .
END
```

where on each iteration, the index variable x refers to one element of the array (i.e., any reference to x refers to that element of the array). This FOR loop has the decided advantage that nested loops are not necessary for work with multidimensional arrays. Its limitation is that FOR loops are not always for array handling.

The procedure is another fundamental control construct. The procedure is one of the most important tools for breaking big problems up into little pieces, and this has implications for its design. In particular, the procedure-call interface must be efficient, and it must be possible to check types of parameters and results fully.

One of the least-standardized aspects of procedures is the matter of parameter passing, although it now appears that two types of parameters are used most often. The first is the pass-by-value parameter, where an expression is evaluated and the result is made available as the parameter. The other useful type of parameter is the pass-as-variable parameter (also called pass-by-reference), in which a variable is passed in to be modified. This may be implemented either by passing a pointer or by copying in the initial value and copying out the final value. A minor matter of note is that the syntax of pass-by-value and pass-as-variable should be distinct, so that the programmer knows what variables may be modified by a procedure. Perhaps one should say:

```
procedure_name(x, y, VAR z)
```

to pass x and y as values and z as a variable.

The utility of passing procedures themselves as parameters is debatable for some types of languages. If this feature is rarely used the language designer is probably justified in omitting it, since it can be simulated with not too much difficulty, is awkward to implement, and makes it hard to do complete run-time error checking. The same comments apply to ALGOL 60's pass-as-if-by-macro-substitution parameters.

The other side of the parameter-passing issue is the matter of returning a value from a procedure. Some languages make a distinction between functions, which return values, and procedures, which do not. Such a distinction is probably most appropriate when, as in an early version of PASCAL, functions are not allowed to have side effects (i.e., to alter parameters or global variables). It certainly corresponds well to the programmer's intuitive idea of "doing something" versus "yielding a value." It should be noted, however, that it is very hard to enforce a no-side-effects rule.

The actual method of returning a value from a value-returning procedure is a problem for which several solutions have been found:

1. An explicit RETURN construct is used with provisions for tacking on a value, e.g., "RETURN(x)."
2. A value is returned by assigning the value into the procedure's own name as if it were a variable.
3. In an expression language (see Sec. 3-5.2), the procedure's executable body as a whole has a value, which is the one returned.

The disadvantages of an expression language narrow this down to the first or the second alternative. The second alternative is less attractive because it involves the use of the procedure name in a rather strange way, but it has the advantage that it is not coupled to a return-of-control construct. A designer who does not wish to return from procedures except by "flowing off the end" will probably end up adopting alternative 2; most other designers will probably opt for the convenience and cleanliness of alternative 1.

As a final matter of syntax we should address the question of what a call to a procedure should look like. ALGOL and its descendants simply use the procedure name as a statement. This seems the simplest approach for situations involving a returned value. Unfortunately, it makes pure procedure calls look just like variable accesses, which is probably undesirable, since procedures do not return values. For this reason, some language designers have introduced a special keyword (e.g., CALL) to clearly delineate the two types of procedure invocations.

No consideration of procedures should ignore the question of whether they should be implemented as subroutines or macros. Although the subroutine implementation is usual, it has been suggested that the programmer should be able to decide which method to use, independently of the contents of the procedure itself. When designing a language for implementing system software, or other tasks where execution speed may become critical, such flexibility may be beneficial. It should be noted, however, that there are problems in ensuring that the procedure sees the same environment either way.

There have been some studies (Wulf, 1972b) of the more general question of specifying the interface to a procedure (i.e., calling conventions) in a language-independent manner. This would simplify linkage between different languages, allow optimized linkage sequences for critical situations, and simplify handling of such things as variable-length parameter lists. The issue is, however, rather complex because machine dependencies creep in; no excellent solution has yet appeared.

The most controversial control constructs currently are the "escape" constructs, which allow departures from the "single-entry, single-exit" concept of control structures. The RETURN mentioned earlier in connection with procedures is an escape construct, and some languages do not have it. Generally, the RETURN is sufficiently useful and its operation is sufficiently clear that few people object to it.

Another highly restricted but very valuable escape construct is the STOP statement, which is used to terminate execution of the program. STOP is invaluable for coping with error situations; it should be available in any language which runs under an operating system (i.e., which can associate a meaningful action with STOP).

Of the more controversial constructs, probably the best is Zahn's situation-driven escape, publicized by Knuth (1974). An example is roughly as follows (with some alterations to the original syntax):

```
SITUATIONS found, not_found
IN
      search for something
CAUSE
      found: report its location OR
      not_found: report failure
THEN END
```

where the body of the construct ("search for something") may contain any number of statements of the form
```
SIGNAL found
```
or
```
SIGNAL not_found
```

The execution of a SIGNAL statement causes immediate execution of the corresponding "statements" after the CAUSE, and then termination of the whole construct.

The use of situation names "found" and "not_found" in this example illustrates the major point of the construct. The search loop may terminate in one of two ways, each requiring a different action, and neither being truly "abnormal" compared with the other. The principal value of this particular construct lies in separating the cause of the exit (termination of the search) from the actions taken as a result, thereby rendering both the search code and the action code more readable.

Some work has been done, notably by Brinch Hansen (1973, 1974, 1975), on control structures for managing parallel processes. This area is maturing, and it is becoming increasingly important to have such features in a language, at least for some areas of work such as communications software.

An important area of control structures which has not been thoroughly investigated is the whole question of exception handling. How does one build control structures to cope with reporting and dealing with error conditions, whether detected by the hardware, the run-time checks, or the user's own program? A number of open questions exist, and undoubtedly more research will be undertaken in this area.

A minor aspect of control structures is the question:

Where does the program start execution?

A good, readable approach is that taken in PL/I in which execution begins with a call to a procedure named "main." This also provides an elegant means of passing parameters to a program as parameters to "main." C (Ritchie, 1974) provides a similar type of construct.

One useful structure which has not become widely accepted is the coroutine. Coroutines can be considered as either a generalization of procedures or a specialized, highly efficient simulation of parallel processes. The idea is that an active coroutine may pass control to another active coroutine. When control returns to a previously invoked coroutine, this coroutine carries on where it left off, resuming execution immediately after the exchange-control construct that resulted from the last transfer of control.

Coroutines are particularly useful for situations where one part of a program "feeds" another part a stream of data; many programs can be characterized in this way. An easy way to implement such a program is by using parallel processes; unfortunately, this is prohibitively inefficient in most systems. Coroutines can be made almost as efficient as procedure calls. It is not clear whether the number of active coroutines should be constant at run time (i.e., a coroutine is a special sort of procedure) or variable at run time (i.e., a coroutine is a special sort of procedure invocation). It appears that the first alternative handles most requirements.

Two very useful constructs, which may not strictly belong under "control structures" but which do not clearly belong anywhere else, are assertions and invariance relations. These constructs basically offer the programmer an opportunity to state (Boolean) conditions which should be true at a point in the program (assertions) or everywhere in the program (invariance relations). These notions have not been applied to languages used for production programming mainly because of the difficulty in proving large programs correct. Again, this may change as research proceeds in this area, and unquestionably the development of EUCLID (Lampson et al., 1977) is a step in this direction. For further information in this area it is worthwhile to read the report on EUCLID.

Even if assertions and invariance relations are treated simply as another form of comment, they are valuable. It is also possible (Clark, 1971) to have the compiler generate code to check at run time that the conditions are true. This feature can assist verification considerably. Finally, there is the possibility of being able to apply automated theorem-proving techniques to such assertions; this would greatly simplify writing correct programs. One problem with this approach is that current programming languages are seldom at a high enough level to express complex assertions easily.

A number of control constructs have been proposed for nondeterministic operations and "backtracking" (unraveling the effects of previous code to go back and try again), as discussed in Prenner et al. (1972) and Bobrow and Raphael (1974). These constructs are particularly applicable in artificial intelligence.

We have intentionally ignored the GOTO construct because current experience indicates that with a decent set of control constructs, the GOTO is simply unnecessary (Wulf, 1972a). A common thought among proponents of the GOTO is: "I just might need it; something might come up." The answer to this appears to be: "Nothing ever does." It cannot be too strongly emphasized that this statement applies only if a good set of non-GOTO constructs is provided. Many languages are somewhat deficient in this matter.

The following control constructs are clear failures or primitive attempts at doing what has been done better and more simply:

1. LABEL variables.
2. Dynamic instruction modification (e.g., COBOL's ALTER).
3. The overly restrictive FORTRAN DO-loop.

The designer is well advised to ignore these.

3-5.5 Compile Structure

"Compile structure" is the term used here to cover certain aspects of a language which tie in very strongly with the compilation process. The major topics of interest are directives to the compiler, operations within the language which are done at compile time rather than at run time, and the question of separate compilation of different "modules" of a program.

It is often desirable to give the compiler certain items of information which cannot easily be expressed in the language itself. The most prevalent approach to this is to have a special form of comment (the ALGOL 68 term "pragmat" seems to be the best word for it) which has no significance to the language itself but which contains directives to the compiler rather than normal comment text. One method of distinguishing pragmats from normal comments is to have them begin with the normal comment delimiter, which is then followed by a sequence of characters. This sequence should be exceedingly unlikely in comment text. For example:

    // This is a comment.
    //:: This is a pragmat.

The actual contents of a pragmat are, of course, compiler-dependent; a pragmat might contain settings of options, optimization advice, specifications of listing format, and so on. Another, perhaps better, way of handling pragmats is to define them in the phrase structure of the language so that the parser can parse them and build trees for them if necessary.

Languages vary greatly in the amount of manipulation possible at compile time. It is notable that most facilities for compile-time operations are rather seldom used; one or two specific constructs seem to fill most needs.

The most notable such facility is the ability to request that the compiler insert the contents of another source file at a specific point in its input stream (the PL/I "%INCLUDE" facility). A language should have this feature or some equivalent facility. A pragmat could be used to specify the inclusion.

The other major compile-time facility is conditional compilation—the ability to ignore selective parts of the input text on the basis of compile-time conditions. While there are several ways of doing this, the method used by ALGOL 68 (Van Wijngaarden et al., 1975) is very noteworthy, since it does not require the introduction of yet another construct into the language. The ALGOL 68 approach is simply to check the selection expressions of IFs and CASEs to see if they can be evaluated at compile time. If they can, only one of the alternative statement sequences need be compiled (note that it is still desirable to error-check the others). This approach is simple to implement and works well.

The issue of separate compilation has generated considerable debate. Its desirability is not in question, as anyone who has ever implemented a large software system will testify to its value. The fact that just about every systems-implementation language includes some sort of separate-compilation facility is additional evidence.

The main difficulty is the poor support for separate compilation in current systems. It is vital to a good separate-compilation system that there be some way to verify the correctness (e.g., matching data types) of calls to separately compiled modules. Unfortunately, most current linkage editors (the usual tools for putting modules together) do not include facilities for such checking. The result of this is that compiler writers usually must implement their own linkage system, which is not necessarily a separate program.

A major language-design question is:

What should the form of the separately compilable "module" be?

The traditional answer is "a procedure"; unfortunately, this does not fulfill the frequent requirements for having "static" or "own" data items associated with a procedure or with a group of several procedures.

The best approach is probably one in which a module contains both data items and procedures. It may be desirable to restrict the scope of the data items to the module itself, so that they may be accessed from outside only via the procedures. Such an arrangement provides a crude form of the data-abstraction facilities mentioned earlier. If the language contains one of the more complex data-abstraction techniques, that technique may be used as the basis for the definition of "module." Ada supports many of these ideas and a discussion of these features is given in Sec. 3-8.

It is desirable to specify the possible interactions between modules instead of adopting an "anything goes" policy; some work has been done on this (DeRemer, 1976), especially as these concepts relate to the implementation of data-abstraction facilities.

3-5.6 I/O Structure

A final important component in any programming language is the set of facilities for handling input and output. The language designer cannot choose to ignore this aspect—the bad experience resulting from the design of ALGOL 60 dictates that this is so. Undoubtedly, ALGOL 60 would be a much more popular language today had the ALGOL committee defined an input/output structure.

Input and output facilities can be provided at three levels of sophistication in the language. A first level is commonly called the "format-free" form of input/output. PL/I's data-directed and list-directed I/O and COBOL's DISPLAY and EXHIBIT statements are examples of this type of I/O. The main function of these statements is to provide a simple form of program/programmer communication to verify program correctness. The programmer should be allowed to display easily values of important variables and to check quickly the logic of a program on small, selected sets of input data.

At the second level is the formatted form of input/output. In this form the value of each variable in an input or output list is read or written according to predefined format controls. These controls usually indicate a field length and data type which are applied to the value of a particular variable in the format list. FORTRAN's formatted I/O and PL/I's edit-directed I/O provide examples of this type of structure. In COBOL, the format specification is tied to a record description which is physically separate from the I/O statement. Unfortunately, if a programmer wishes to handle a record for input/output differently from how it is stored, two record descriptions have to be created—one reflecting how the data are to be displayed or are organized for input and one dictating how the information is stored.

The C language presents an unusual and innovative variation for formatted I/O. The format control characters are included as part of a textual string used for annotation. For example:

```
printf(''the value of x is %d:\ n the value of st is %s'',x,st)
```

will print

```
    the value of x is 4:
    the value of st is string
```

if $x = 4$ and st = ''string.'' The format control characters d and s correspond to integer (base 10) and string formats, respectively, and the '' \ n '' indicates a new line.

A main consideration with formatted I/O is whether or not to allow format specifications to vary dynamically at execution as is accomplished, for example, in ALGOL 68's format statement. The following statement illustrates this concept:

```
outf(stand out;
    $c(''SUN'', ''MON'', ''TUES'', ''WEDNES'', ''THURS'', ''FRI'',
        ''SATUR'') ''DAY'' $, i);
```

The name of the appropriate day will be output based on the value of i.

Considerable overhead is incurred by allowing dynamic format specifications; however, for applications involving a significant amount of sophisticated I/O editing, the overhead may be warranted.

The final type of I/O really involves facilities for the storage and retrieval of information in files. It is generally agreed that there are three types of file organizations: sequential, indexed (or indexed sequential), and direct. Other organizations based on secondary keys are possible but are generally not provided in a high-level procedure-oriented language. Since the access facilities for each of the file organizations are usually provided through system routines, the types of files expressible in a language are somewhat machine-dependent. In addition, the types of facilities provided depend on the amount of data-processing activity expected to be completed using the language.

3-6 REDUCTION OF SIZE

Although "keeping it small" is important throughout the design of a language, it is useful to pay special attention to size reduction once the design has solidified.

The basic reasons for keeping a language small can be summed up simply: the smaller the language, the easier it is to read, the easier it is to write, the easier it is to produce a reliable, efficient compiler, and the easier it is to write clear, readable documentation describing it. The basic reason for increasing the size of the language is the so-called Turing tarpit: if the language is too simple, one may be able to do anything in it but it may be impossible in practice to do anything in particular.

The major mechanism for eliminating constructs from a language is reviewing them for usefulness. Will the construct be used? Does it duplicate the facilities of another construct? Is there a simpler subset of the construct which would account for almost all uses of it (i.e., is the construct overgeneralized)?

The removal of a construct must be considered carefully as its removal will require the user to simulate its effect. If the construct will never be used, obviously it should be removed. If the construct will be infrequently used but is difficult or impossible to simulate with the other constructs, it should probably be left in (the CASE statement is a good example). Assuming that the construct will be used with moderate frequency and that it is not overly difficult to simulate, the final consideration is that simulating it will inconvenience the user, increase the size and complexity of the program, and decrease the program's reliability because of the possibility of an erroneous simulation. The designer must weigh these considerations carefully.

3-7 PRAGMATICS

This section is concerned with certain aspects of the practice of programming-language design. In particular, we discuss a number of tools which can be used to specify a language, the problem of evaluating a language design, and language-implementation considerations.

In any discussion of language-design tools, a few words should be said about terminology. Good, well-thought-out terminology can help make language documentation easier to read and understand, even during the design process itself. If possible, new terms should not be coined; most of them are already available for your use. The ALGOL 68 documentation (Van Wijngaarden et al., 1975; Lindsey et al., 1972) is an excellent example of terminology which is different (seemingly) but not significantly different from a functional point of view. It is undesirable to force your users (or yourself) to learn another new language just to discuss your programming language.

The method you use to describe your language is a significant design tool. Currently, language description is split into three parts; context-independent syntax (what is normally thought of as syntax), context-dependent syntax (type checking, consistency, etc.), and semantics (what the constructs do).

Descriptive techniques for context-independent syntax have reached an adequate level of formalization while retaining simplicity. BNF has been around for quite a while, and with all of its simplicity, it is almost adequate. With the additions to BNF discussed in Sec. 2-4.4, it will serve well enough for just about any design process. For final documentation, the syntax charts (see Jensen and Wirth, 1975, or Barnard, 1975) are perhaps clearer (although Barnard's form is not as general as BNF). For the design process, however, syntax charts are rather unwieldly; extended BNF is considerably easier to write. There is no evidence that more complex methods than these are either necessary or desirable for describing reasonable languages.

Context-dependent syntax (this is a poor term, but there does not seem to be a better one) is a somewhat stickier problem. The attempts that have been made to produce a formal notation for it, notably the two-level grammars used to describe all the syntax of ALGOL 68, have resulted in notations that are cumbersome to use and obscure to read. Currently, narration is probably the best descriptive technique for context-dependent syntax.

Several methods are available for describing the semantics of a language. Some of the best methods for practical use are those developed by Hoare (1969) for control structures and Hoare, Dahl, and Dijkstra (1972) for data structures. Hoare's control-structures method has gained general acceptability; however, his data-structures method is less completely accepted, since data structures are still the subject of much dispute. Hoare and Wirth (1972) have used these methods to define most of the semantics of PASCAL in a document which is remarkably readable.

It is possible to describe a language either top-down (start with "program") or bottom-up (start with "number," "identifier," etc.). For reasonably sized languages, there is little to choose between them. The top-down approach is perhaps slightly clearer for situations where there is little nesting of definitions (e.g., the description of "statement"). The bottom-up approach seems definitely superior for cases involving much nesting (e.g., the description of "expression").

For descriptive purposes, it is often much clearer to use a slightly ambiguous definition rather than go through the complexities necessary to remove all ambiguity. Obviously, this point is applicable primarily to the user's manual, not to the formal definition.

It is worth pointing out that formal descriptions are not just methods of ensuring that all implementations do things the same way. They serve also as a method of uncovering weak spots in the design, by requiring the designer to put everything down on paper. An attempt should be made to formalize context-independent syntax (at least) as early as possible. It is a good way of discovering that you have not really thought about some parts of the language.

Formal descriptions should be as readable as possible. An all too common problem is the use of needlessly unreadable notation in descriptions (e.g., using single characters, often from strange alphabets, where mnemonic names should be used).

A language is of little worth unless it is properly documented. An informal presentation of the language for the user should be written before the design is finalized. Not only will this ensure that this vital task gets done, but trying to explain things simply is a fine way of finding problems and omissions.

Remember that at least four different kinds of documents are involved—the design working documents, cleaned-up formal presentations for reference (especially for implementers), informal presentations for regular users and experienced newcomers, and tutorial presentations for inexperienced newcomers. Tutorial presentations may be skipped if the new users will be experienced programmers, but both formal and informal presentations are probably essential.

Although Hehner (1975), for one, has experimented with top-down design of languages, and this idea certainly has some merits, the method invariably used today for language design is bottom-up. The approach usually used is to combine a number of features into a language, modifying the features as necessary to make the language fit together smoothly. Attention needs to be given to both the selection of features and their combination.

If it is vital that the language be implemented and running quickly (say, for a project which is waiting for it), then stick to old, proven features. Remember that if a feature is new and controversial, a better form of it may evolve overnight. Consequently, you will be left with the choice of either making your language conspicuously obsolete or falling prey to the "moving-target" problem. It is very difficult to implement a language which keeps changing.

It is important to watch out for unfavorable interaction if several features are combined into one. Such interactions can cause even greater problems than poor features. Often two features drawn from different languages will overlap somewhat when they are put together. For example, if you borrow PASCAL's data types but also include variable-length strings, there is little point in supplying PASCAL's single-character variables. In fact, there is potential built-in confusion: is 'x' a character or a character string?

We now turn to the important problem of evaluating a language design. After the first draft of the design is finished, it should be subjected to a variety of evaluation processes to determine what changes should be made (don't assume that there won't be any!). Except in an emergency, this phase of the design should be carried out in a very leisurely fashion to allow everybody to have second (third, fourth, etc.) thoughts about everything.

To avoid the problem of tunnel vision (you have worked on it so long that you have convinced yourself that it is good), see what other people think of it. Try it out on potential users, remembering that their complaints and suggestions should be examined carefully—what they want is not always what they say they want. If you have people on hand with experience in language design, try it out on them. Some of their criticisms may derive from differences in opinion rather than from real flaws, but they will usually make this clear. Remember that you do not have to accept other people's suggestions—but do not ignore them.

Try some nontrivial sample programs in the language. Set yourself a serious programming goal and then try to achieve it within your language. Do not deliberately avoid the unpleasant areas; in particular, try out your I/O on a real situation. It is probably a good idea to deliberately tackle at least one problem which will result in several hundred lines of program. The time invested will most likely be justified by the results.

When you are doing sample programs, there are a few distinctive signposts of trouble that should be watched for. GOTOs and "temporary" variables are often symptomatic of defects in either programming technique or language design. If you find yourself needing either one, ask yourself whether this is likely to be a frequent situation. If so, do something about it. Another, more generalized symptom of trouble is having to repeat yourself frequently. Such repetition is an error-prone nuisance; users do not like it, and they are justified in this.

Consider what sort of code the compiler will generate. Perhaps you might try hand compiling one or two of your sample programs. This is a good way of uncovering mismatches between the language and the machine.

Finally, let it stew a while. If you find yourself thinking "that really should be done better—but that way will do," drag your dissatisfaction out and look at it. It will be a lot easier to fix now than when the implementation is half complete. Make a list of things you think are flaws—no matter how trivial they seem. Think about them. If you think about them long enough, you may find yourself fixing them. Be careful to do this in advance of the actual implementation effort, as leaving it to a later date can lead to a severe case of the moving-target problem.

After the language design has been properly evaluated and the language is settled, the next step is to implement it. Once the implementation starts, your worries are almost over. Ideally, you will be implementing it yourself. If not, keep in close touch with the implementers; make sure they commit no heresies, but think seriously about any criticisms they offer. A more serious problem will be the inevitable requests from somebody (or everybody) else for changes.

The moving-target problem is the single worst obstacle a language implementation can face. There are two notable techniques for avoiding it. First, a useful way to deal with change requests which are clearly ridiculous but which cannot be ignored for "political" reasons is to reply "certainly, in the next version." The idea here is to get a working version up and then think about improvements. This method should be used only to forestall changes that are clearly ridiculous, because the secret of the method is that the "next" version recedes into the indefinite future. Changes which may be improvements must be handled differently.

The second method is more generally applicable, and was used by the SUE group at the University of Toronto (Clark, 1971). The idea here is to schedule "change points" at fairly wide intervals, say 3 months. Between change points, the language is frozen. Suggested changes are accumulated and thought about until the next change point and are then acted on if they seem justifiable. This method results in comparatively few changes, at regulated times, and tends to defuse the moving-target problem.

It is highly desirable that the whole language design be the responsibility of one person. Consultation with others is desirable, but one person should have complete and final say. Committee languages generally are "kitchen sink" languages; such a language seldom exhibits either unity or cleanliness (consider PL/I as an example). It is also desirable to have a single implementer if at all possible.

The basic scenario of language design is described in the following informal algorithm.

1. Ask questions: What is wanted? How will it be used?
2. Consider possible features.
3. Consider the overall design and the integration of the features into it. Watch feature interactions.
4. Consider details (syntactic carbohydrates, etc.). Consider parsing and error checking.
5. Write formal definitions. Write a user's manual. Write anything else that strikes you as useful.
6. Evaluate the design as discussed earlier. Make changes and begin step 3 again. Do not proceed to step 7 until you are completely satisfied.
7. Reduce the size. Iterate earlier steps if necessary. Do not proceed to step 8 until you have exhausted all possibilities.
8. Implement it.
9. Wait for the user reaction.
10. Admit that you may have made mistakes.
11. Start on a new version of the language considering possible extensions.

In closing, it should be remembered that research in the field of language design is ongoing, and it is highly likely that some of the more serious problems will be solved in the near future. We next consider certain design aspects of Ada.

3-8 COMMENTS ON THE DESIGN OF ADA

Ada is a general-purpose language for numeric computation, general systems programming, general applications programming, real-time industrial applications, and embedded computer applications. (Embedded systems are systems in which a computer is but a part of a large whole, for example, a computer is embedded in a ship, a cruise missile, or an aircraft.) Ada was named in honor of Ada Augusta, Countess of Lovelace and daughter of the poet Lord Byron. Ada Lovelace was a colleague of Charles Babbage. Babbage had created a difference engine that could be programmed in a manner similar to a Jacquard loom. Since Ada often programmed the difference engine, many consider her to be the first programmer. Ada was designed by a language team led by Jean Ichbiah.

The U.S. Department of Defense (DOD) sponsored the development of the language. The purpose of this sponsorship was to develop a programming language suited for embedded computer applications (i.e., military-related applications). The development effort began in 1975 with the formation of the DOD Higher-Order Language Working Group whose mandate was to establish a single high-level programming language for developing embedded computer applications.

Initially, a set of requirements for a common programming language was produced. These requirements were produced in a sequence of reports called Strawman, Woodman, Tinman, Ironman, and Steelman. Input to these documents came from industry, universities, and the DOD. The notion of designing a programming language based on a set of requirements (Steelman) was a new approach. These requirements specified characteristics in areas such as data types, modules, tasks, and control structures. Also included were requirements such as readability and simplicity.

By 1977 it became clear that no existing programming language met the Tinman requirements and that a new language should be designed and developed. It was recommended that PASCAL, PL/I, or Algol 68 be used as a starting point in the design of the new language.

Four of the sixteen language design proposals received were deemed to be acceptable and were funded for a six-month preliminary design phase. The four winning designs, all based on PASCAL, were submitted for evaluation. Because of their PASCAL base, the preliminary designs were produced in six months.

The four preliminary designs were evaluated by many (around 80) evaluators from industry, government, and universities. These evaluations resulted in two of the four languages being selected for one year of further development. The two completed designs were subsequently analyzed by some 50 analysis teams. Their findings were evaluated and the winning language proposed was named Ada. A preliminary reference manual for Ada (*SIGPLAN Notices*, 1979) and a rationale for its design (Ichbiah et al., 1979) were produced. A more recent version of the reference manual was published in 1983 (ANSI, 1983).

Although many computer scientists and users participated in the design of Ada, it was not designed by a committee. Jean Ichbiah assumed complete responsibility for all the design decisions. Ada appears to be a coherent, integrated whole rather than a collection of interesting but disjointed features.

This section first examines Ada with respect to the design criteria presented earlier. During the development of the Ada language, it became obvious that the language was only one component of a set of tools which would be required for the development of software throughout its life cycle.

The second subsection briefly examines the features of an Ada programming support environment (APSE). Ada is also a part of a larger Department of Defense effort to improve software technology. This effort is called the Software Technology for Adaptable Reliable Systems (STARS) program. We also outline the basic components of the STARS program.

3-8.1 Evaluation of Ada from a Language Design Viewpoint

Here we consider Ada from the programming language design criteria presented in Sec. 3-4. In certain instances Ada is discussed with respect to more than one criterion. For example, the criteria of usability and programming effectiveness are combined. In particular we discuss Ada with respect to the following issues in turn: usability and program effectiveness (including abstraction); machine independence and portability; efficiency; modularity and maintainability; compilability and compile structure; and simplicity. We also examine some drawbacks of the Ada language. The discussion contains some Ada program segments.

Recall that Ada is similar to PASCAL. Ada contains the following levels of program structure: characters, lexical units (or tokens), expressions, assignment statements, control structures, declarations, program units, and compilation units. A *program unit* associates declarations, which define the attributes of identifiers with statements, which use these declarations. A *compilation unit*, on the other hand, is a unit of structure for developing a program and separate compilation.

A compilation unit is either a subprogram or a module. As in PASCAL, an Ada subprogram is either a function or a procedure. A module, however, is a language construct that reflects a recent development in programming language design. A module can be either a *package* or a *task*. Figure 3-1 exhibits the composition of a compilation unit.

A package is used to specify a collection of logically related computational resources. For example, a stack package can provide a collection of resources for representing and manipulating stacks. Operations for pushing elements onto and popping elements from a stack would be included in such a package. A task is a modular program unit that is used in the specification of concurrency. Here we deal with both kinds of modules. Much greater emphasis, however, will be given to packages.

Usability and program effectiveness. The value of abstraction has been recognized by programmers in recent years. Most programming languages support abstraction. In Ada, however, the concept of abstraction has been elevated to a prominent position. Ada also directly supports the development of software by both bottom-up and top-down methodologies. First we discuss the support of abstraction in Ada by using packages, generics, and tasks. Second, a brief description of Ada's support of structured software development is given.

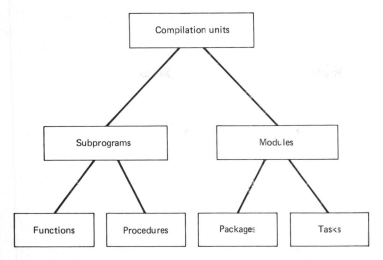

Figure 3-1 Classification of compilation units in Ada.

Packages The concept of a package in Ada is an important contribution to the theory of programming. A package, which is used to define logically related resources, consists of two components: a package specification and a package body. Each component is a unit that can be compiled separately. The package specification component describes the resources available in the package to a programmer. This component is usually written and compiled before use is made of the package. The package body specifies how the resources of the package are implemented.

The structure of a package is given in the following example:

```
package package_name is
: visible part
private
: private part
package body package_name
: package body
end package_name
```

The package specification part consists of a sequence of declarations for data types, data objects, subprograms, and so on. The declarations preceding the keyword "private" make up the visible part of the package specification. The remainder of the package specification, which is optional, is the private part of the specification. An example of a package that contains a private specification part is given later. The declared names identify the resources in the form of functions and procedures. Recall that names can also identify data types, data objects, and so on.

The package body describes how the resources or facilities mentioned in the package specification are realized. The body may include declarations of local variables, implementation of subprograms, initialization specification, and so on.

An example of a package that facilitates the manipulation of complex numbers will now be given. The operations on complex numbers are restricted to adding, subtracting, and multiplying complex numbers. The package specification in the example has a data type declaration (COMPLEX) that contains two elements—the first (R) represents the real part of the complex number and the second (I) is its imaginary part. Each complex operation has as input two complex numbers and produces as a result a complex number.

A package specification for the complex number application may take the following form:

```
package COMPLEX_SYSTEM is
     type COMPLEX is
          record
               R: FLOAT;
               I: FLOAT;
          end record;
     function '' + ''(A, B: COMPLEX) return COMPLEX;
     function '' − ''(A, B: COMPLEX) return COMPLEX;
     function '' * ''(A, B: COMPLEX) return COMPLEX;
end COMPLEX_SYSTEM
```

In this example three functions, denoted by "+", "−", and "*" are defined. In these instances, only the name, the type of returned value (e.g., COMPLEX), and the names and types of the formal parameters are given.

Ada permits names of subprograms to be *overloaded*. That is, more than one subprogram can have the same name provided the different cases are distinguishable by examining the types, number, and names of parameters and the type of the result (for a function). Conceptually, overloading supports abstraction since the same subprogram name can be used for equivalent operations on different data types. In the current example, the operators "+", "−", and "*" are all overloaded. Note that in these instances the predefined operations are overloaded.

The package specification for complex number manipulation can be separately compiled. All names in the specification part, such as COMPLEX and the record components R and I, are all accessible or visible to the user.

The following example illustrates this flexibility.

```
declare
     use COMPLEX_SYSTEM
     A, B, C: COMPLEX;
begin
     A.R:= 12.5;
     C.I:= −1.5;
end;
```

A package body for the previous body specification for complex number manipulation could be as follows:

```
package body COMPLEX_SYSTEM is
    function '' + '' (A, B: COMPLEX) return COMPLEX is
    begin
        return (A.R + B.R, A.I + B.I);
    end;
    function '' − '' (A, B: COMPLEX) return COMPLEX is
    begin
        return (A.R − B.R, A.I − B.I);
    end;
    function '' * '' (A, B: COMPLEX) return COMPLEX is
        RTEMP, ITEMP: COMPLEX;
    begin
        RTEMP:= A.R * B.R − A.I * B.I;
        ITEMP:= A.R * B.I + A.I * B.R;
        return (RTEMP, ITEMP);
    end;
end COMPLEX_SYSTEM;
```

Although the current complex number package treats complex numbers as abstract objects, it does permit the manipulations of their real and imaginary components. Such flexibility, however, should not always be made available to the user. The components of a complex number can be made unavailable to the user by declaring type COMPLEX to be a private data type. The following example exhibits such a private data type.

```
package COMPLEX_SYSTEM_P is
    type COMPLEX is private;
    function '' + '' (A, B: COMPLEX) return COMPLEX;
    function '' − '' (A, B: COMPLEX) return COMPLEX;
    function '' * '' (A, B: COMPLEX) return COMPLEX;
    function CREATE_COMPLEX (A, B: FLOAT) return COMPLEX;
private
    type COMPLEX is
        record
            R: FLOAT;
            I: FLOAT;
        end record;
end COMPLEX_SYSTEM_P;
```

In this example the user can declare complex variables. These variables can be manipulated by the operators defined in the package. The user, however, cannot refer to the individual components of complex numbers. Consequently, we include the function CREATE_COMPLEX, which creates a complex number from its real and imaginary components. The private data type COMPLEX is said to be hidden from the user.

In summary, packages support abstraction by allowing irrelevant implementation details to be hidden and make visible to the user only high-level resources.

Generics Generic program structures and generic packages are mechanisms for supporting abstraction. Generic program structures support abstraction by using a common program structure and parameters to capture the similarities among several program subprograms. We first discuss generic program structures and then extend these notions to packages.

The notion of using parameters to support abstraction has existed for a long time. Subprograms have been the main vehicle for this type of support. In Ada, subprogram parameters must be variables. Ada, however, allows generic program structures. These structures have parameters whose values can be variables, types, and subprogram names.

Generic subprograms can be viewed as a macrofacility in a macro-assembly language. As such, a generic subprogram cannot be called directly. Instead it must be referenced with generic parameter values and instantiated at compile time. This instantiated version can then be executed. The compile-time process of instantiating a generic subprogram yields *instances* of the parent generic subprogram.

The following subprogram is an example of a generic procedure that interchanges two data types.

```
generic (type T)
procedure INTERCHANGE(A, B: in out T) is
      TEMP: T;
begin
      TEMP := A;
      A:= B;
      B:= TEMP;
   end INTERCHANGE;
```

Observe that the program contains a generic clause with a parameter type T, which is the generic parameter of the procedure interchange. Three instantiations of the procedure INTERCHANGE, denoted by INTERCHANGE_I, INTERCHANGE_R, and INTERCHANGE_V, that interchange integers, reals, and vectors are:

```
procedure INTERCHANGE_I is new INTERCHANGE(INTEGER);
procedure INTERCHANGE_R is new INTERCHANGE(FLOAT);
procedure INTERCHANGE_V is new INTERCHANGE(VECTOR);
```

The interchange procedures generated for each of these instantiations at compile time will have different codes, especially, for the procedure that interchanges vectors.

The previous example has shown that the generic variable can be a type. Generic parameters can also denote subprogram names. For example, a generic subprogram could be written to obtain the definite integral of an arbitrary function. In this case the generic variable would denote a function name.

Ada also permits the writing of generic packages. There are, however, differences between generic subprograms and generic packages, which makes a generic facility for packages more useful than that for subprograms. First, subprograms have parameters while packages do not. Therefore, the generic parameter is an improvement of an already existing feature in subprograms, whereas it provides a new facility for packages. Second, subprogram declarations are essentially instantiated by a subprogram invocation. Package specifications, on the other hand, cannot be multiply instantiated. Consequently, a generic facility for subprograms provides a compile-time version of an already existing facility available at run time through subprogram invocations while a generic facility for packages provides a new facility.

As an example of a generic package, consider the design of a flexible package for storing symbol table values. A generic package specification for such an application might take the following form:

```
generic (type T; SIZE: INTEGER);
package TABLE is
        function SEARCH(KEY: T) return INTEGER;
        procedure ADD(KEY: T);
        procedure DELETE(KEY: T);
end TABLE;
```

Observe that the package specification contains two generic parameters—a type parameter and a variable parameter. By instantiating this generic package, several symbol tables of different value types and sizes can be created. For example, the following statements instantiate three separate symbol tables:

```
package INTEGER_TABLE is new TABLE(INTEGER, 50);
package FLOAT_TABLE is new TABLE(FLOAT, 75);
package NAME_TABLE is new TABLE(STRING, 100);
```

The first symbol table contains 50 elements of type integer. The second symbol table contains up to 75 real numbers. The third table can contain up to 100 strings.

Tasks Ada provides facilities in real-time applications for multitasking (i.e., concurrency). A task is a module that can be compiled independently. Like a package, a task is divided into a specification part and a body. The task specification part contains *entry* resource declarations that define the procedure-like calls, possibly to other tasks that can be used to communicate with the task. Entry calls, however, require synchronization between the calling and called tasks before they can be executed. The intertask communications are handled by a "rendezvous" in the form of an accept statement. During an accept statement only one path of execution is possible. After completing the executions of an accept statement, the rendezvous is said to be complete and the tasks then continue in an independent manner.

Support of software development Ada supports both bottom-up and top-down software development methodologies.

Bottom-up program development involves the implementation of higher-level program units in terms of already implemented lower-level program units. Most high-level programming languages support bottom-up program development because many of these languages have a subprogram facility that has a well-defined user interface that "hides" the details of implementation.

Top-down program development, on the other hand, begins from a high-level specification that is successively broken down into lower-level specifications until the specifications have been refined at the lowest level of the programming language being used. This approach is more in line with current software development methodologies since it corresponds more closely to the tasks that are performed by systems analysts. The top-down approach to program development, however, is more abstract than its bottom-up counterpart because program specifications are expressed in terms of lower-level specifications (e.g., modules) that are not yet implemented. Another advantage of top-down development is the early verification of the interfaces between program modules. In a bottom-up approach, the interfaces are the last (and more difficult and time consuming) things to be checked out.

Ada is well-suited to support both bottom-up and top-down methodologies because the module (package and task) facility permits the abstraction of the algorithm and data objects.

Ada directly supports top-down development through the aid of program units and subunits. A *stub* indicates the syntactic-interface information and the location where a separately compiled subunit will eventually be placed. For example, a programmer may write the following:

```
package body SAMPLE is
    . . .
    procedure P(A: TYPE_A) is separate;
    . . .
begin
    . . .
end SAMPLE;
```

where the keyword "separate" indicates to the compiler that the subunit containing the procedure P with the parameter A (of type TYPE_A) will be compiled later.

At a later time, a programmer may compile the following subunit:

```
separate(SAMPLE)
procedure P(A: TYPE_Z) is
    . . .
begin
    . . .
end P;
```

In this example, the keyword "separate" and its argument SAMPLE indicate to the compiler that the procedure P that follows is a subunit of SAMPLE and is to be compiled as though it were completely in the package SAMPLE outlined earlier. The compiler can recall the context surrounding the declaration of P in SAMPLE before proceeding to compile procedure P.

The previous examples illustrate that both Ada subprogram and package specifications can be treated as separate linguistic objects. Such specifications allow the programmer to specify the syntactic form of the interface with an indication that the semantic interface will follow separately. The compiler can also check the validity of the syntactic interface. This approach in Ada represents a novel programming language design direction which is a significant advance in the support of programming methodologies.

Machine independence and portability. Ada allows machine independent programs, even for floating-point numbers. Ada facilities program portability by segregating and controlling references to non-Ada environments.

Representation specifications allow a programmer to specify a straightforward mapping between a data object and its storage representation. Consequently, the structure of machine registers or hardware-defined data structures can be specified.

Second, special constructs called *pragmas* facilitate the specification of compiler directions that influence the compilation of a program without affecting its meaning. For example, the interface pragma indicates that a procedure has been written in some other language.

Third, there exist predefined set programs that enable an escape from the type system. For example, a programmer may view an object of one type as one of another type. A floating-point number can be viewed in terms of its hardware representation.

Portability is also one of the important issues in the Ada programming support environment. This environment is outlined in Sec. 3-8.2.

Efficiency. A potential drawback of using Ada is the size and complexity of the compilers required. These limits may restrict the types of computers on which Ada can be readily implemented. Another efficiency consideration involves the efficiency of object code produced. Since Ada was designed for the programming of embedded systems, which have severe time and space restrictions, this concern is understandable. These issues, however, are presently being examined by compiler writers.

Modularity and maintainability. Several kinds of inconsistencies that usually occur during the development of large systems will not occur in systems developed in Ada. A compilation data base allows modularization and separate compilation of components while still being able to perform type-checking on the entire program. The package and task facilities in Ada permit the writing of very modular programs. For example, the separation of the logical and physical interfaces by having a specification part and body in a package leads to the following maintainability advantages:

1. Any changes to a package body do not require any alterations to the source programs that reference the package. Furthermore, these programs need not be recompiled.
2. Any changes made to the private portion of the specification part of a package do not require changes in the source code of programs that reference the package. These changes, however, may require the recompilation of the source programs.
3. Any changes to the visible portion of the specification part of a package may require changes to the source program and, consequently, must be recompiled. For example, another procedure may be added to the visible part of a given package, or the number of parameters of a given procedure within a package may be altered.

Compilability and compile structure. Units of Ada programs are separately compilable. In many instances, separate compilation of programs has led to problems. For example, it is possible to invoke a procedure with several parameters defined in one module with the wrong number of arguments in the invocation which occurs in a different module.

The Ada approach is to allow the separate compilation of several units. However, information about other units may have to be present. A data base, which is managed by the Ada compiler, is used to keep track of the various compilations and their logical interdependences between units in the separate source programs. Also, it is intended that the Ada compiler provide a query capability for checking the recompilation status of the database.

As mentioned earlier, certain kinds of program changes will require the recompilation of other dependent units. The Ada database, however, contains information that assists in reducing the amount of recompilation required. Furthermore, the approach is meant to preserve the same degree of consistency, regardless of the number of separately compiled units.

Ada strongly supports compile structure. As mentioned earlier, Ada contains programs that give directions to the compiler. Also, Ada has the ability to request that the compiler insert another source file at a specific point in the input stream. Finally, Ada, through its package facility, supports separate compilation.

Simplicity. Although elegant, Ada is not a small language. Its size and complexity are a well-publicized complaint of the language. A recent paper (Wickmann, 1984) addresses the size of Ada. It appears that not too much can be pruned from the language without reducing its capabilities. Although the language is huge, it appears to be piecewise simple. There are ways to manage this complexity. The first is to improve the training of programmers. Another way to manage complexity is to require the use of techniques to control complexity. For example, packages and generics can be used for this purpose.

In summary, it appears that Ada is overall a well-designed language that promises to become prominent during the next decade. One of the attractive aspects of Ada is the environment in which it is to be used. The next subsection examines this environment.

3-8.2 Ada Programming Support Environment

The original goals that led to the definition of the Ada language included the following:

1. Handle software throughout its life cycle.
2. Improve program reliability.
3. Promote the development of portable software.
4. Promote the development of software development tools.

It became apparent from the beginning that these objectives could not be met by Ada alone. Ada was envisaged as just one component of a comprehensive, integrated programming environment.

A series of requirements documents for an Ada programming support environment (APSE) was produced culminating in a final document called Stoneman (Stoneman, 1980). This final document outlined tools that were considered to be necessary for handling the software throughout its life cycle in a cost-effective manner.

Here we examine the objectives of an APSE and then outline the mechanisms for meeting these objectives.

Objectives. In examining some of the primary objectives of an Ada environment, a host target configuration is assumed throughout the discussion. In this configuration, the software development for the target machine, which runs the software, is supported on a host machine.

An important objective of an Ada environment is to support an application throughout its life cycle, that is, from its initial requirements specification through to its maintenance. The support of this objective implies that the environment must be:

1. Initially designed to support an application through its life cycle.
2. Designed so that its database holds all relevant application information (e.g., source code and documentation) and provides configuration control.

Configuration control records and analyzes the ways in which database objects are created and used.

The Stoneman report firmly recommends that an open-ended environment be used. In such an environment, the user may develop individual support tools. This approach permits the upgrading of the tool kit to reflect recent developments in the disciplines, thereby avoiding obsolescence. A potential disadvantage of the open-ended environment approach is the potential lack of programmer portability, that is, a programmer may experience difficulty in moving from one environment to another. Another perhaps more serious disadvantage is the lack of the capability of recording a complete and accurate set of relationships among database objects.

A second important objective is the support for the Ada language as a vehicle for reducing software development and maintenance costs. Whenever possible, the environment should offer strong support for the language and support program libraries. The level of support provided by the environment makes Ada a prime candidate as the implementation language for the support tools in the Ada environment.

The Ada environment should provide project team support. All the relevant information about an application throughout its life cycle should be captured in an environment database. Such an approach would permit a project controller to assign development responsibilities, police interfaces, and merge results.

Portability is another very important consideration in the design of an Ada environment. Project portability, tool portability, retargetability, rehostability, etc., are all important issues.

The KAPSE / MAPSE / APSE approach. We now briefly describe the parts of an environment intended to meet the various objectives just outlined. Because of the portability objective, the Stoneman report recognized three distinct levels within the environment as shown in Fig. 3-2. An APSE consists of a kernel APSE (called KAPSE), a minimal APSE (called MAPSE), and additional tools specific to a particular APSE. The KAPSE is a system and tool portability level that interfaces with an existing operating system (if present) and provides run-time support and several other basic (i.e., low-level) functions. For example, a KAPSE may contain basic routines for input/output, data-base management, and program invocation and control.

The MAPSE contains minimal support tools for the Ada software of an application throughout its life cycle. A typical MAPSE would include an Ada compiler, a database management system, a linker/loader, an editor, a debugger, and other tools. It is likely that most (if not all) of the tools in an APSE would be written in Ada.

More details on Ada programming support environments can be found in a special issue of *IEEE Computer* (June 1981), and particular environments are proposed by Stenning (Stenning et al., 1981) and Wolfe (Wolfe et al., 1981).

3-8.3 Software Technology for Adaptable Reliable Systems (STARS)

Recall that an APSE provides automated support for the software life cycle. The STARS program broadens this support further to include the unautomated, and in many cases unautomatable, aspects of the environment. The goal of the

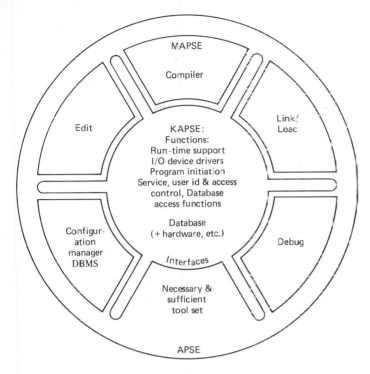

Figure 3-2 The Stoneman model.

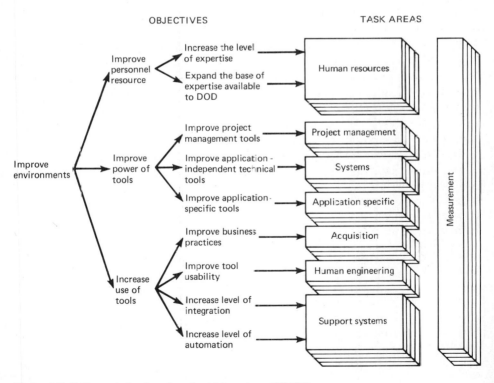

Figure 3-3 Software technology for adaptable systems (STARS).

STARS program is to improve productivity while achieving greater system reliability and adaptability.

The overall objective of the STARS effort, to improve software practice by improving the environment, consists of three objectives: improving the personnel, improving the tools, and encouraging more extensive use of the tools. Each of these three objectives can be subdivided into several subobjectives as shown in Fig. 3-3. More details on the STARS program can be found in a special issue of *IEEE Computer* (November 1983).

CHAPTER EXERCISES

1 To demonstrate that the minimal set of control constructs contains only sequencing and the WHILE loop, construct the IF-THEN-ELSE from the WHILE loop and Boolean variables.

2 Suggest an alternative to the use of "OR" as punctuation in the CASE statement (so that "OR" can be used as a Boolean operator).

3 Find three logical errors in Hoare's arguments against separate compilation in Hoare (1973).

4 The capabilities of FORTRAN and ALGOL are really not all that different. Justify ALGOL.

5 Three methods of avoiding the design of a new language were mentioned. Find one example of each.

6 To complement the discussion on features ambiguous to humans but not to compilers, find one aspect of PL/I which prevents a feature from being ambiguous to the COMPILER but not to HUMANS.

7 Find one common example of unreliable error checking.

8 With regard to compile-time versus run-time checking, describe one feature in which some run-time checking can be transferred to compile time.

9 Name one error check which cannot be done at compile time and is often expensive at run time.

10 Find another example (other than the redefine rule) of useless flexibility in ALGOL 60.

11 Find an example (outside FORTRAN) of a language feature which is a mistaken attempt to get close to the hardware in the interests of efficiency.

12 Find another example (other than those given) of useless uniformity.

13 Describe one place in PL/I where its defaults are actually justifiable and useful.

14 Find another case (other than FORTRAN default declarations) of a language feature causing a loss of useful redundancy.

15 Name three points where PL/I fails as a medium for human communication because of syntax not clearly reflecting semantics.

16 Under programming effectiveness, mention was made of bogging the programmer down under a mass of irrelevant detail. Find one case of this in PL/I.

17 Describe a method of supplying optimization advice in the situation where one finds a single expression (or a few expressions) occurring very frequently inside a FOR-loop.

18 A rhetorical suggestion made in the microstructure section was to ask your typists/keypunchers which they prefer, COBOL or SNOBOL. Do it; find out what languages your typists do prefer and which ones they dislike, and why.

19 Design a syntax for a conditional expression, that is, an IF-THEN-ELSE expression.

20 A rough definition of the type "integer" was given in the type-structure section. Draw up a more precise definition of "integer" in terms of the values and operators of which it consists. Do not forget the comparison operators.

BIBLIOGRAPHY

"The Ada Programming Language Standard," *ANSI*, MIL-STD-1815A-1983, stock no. 008-000-00394-7, U.S. Government Printing Office, Washington, D.C. February 1983.

Alexander, W. G.: "How a Programming Language Is Used," Report CSRG-10, Computer Systems Research Group, University of Toronto, Toronto, Canada, February 1972.

Barnard, D. T.: "Automatic Generation of Syntax-Repairing and Paragraphing Parsers," Report CSRG-52, Computer Systems Research Group, University of Toronto, Toronto, Canada, March 1975.

Berard, E. V.: "Ada Steps Out," *Datamation*, Vol. 29, No. 9, September 1983, pp. 114–123.

Bobrow, D. G., and B. Raphael: "New Programming Languages for Artificial Intelligence Research," *ACM Computing Surveys*, Vol. 6, No. 3, September 1974. pp. 153–174.

Booch, G.: *Software Engineering with Ada*, Benjamin/Cummings, 1983.

Brender, R. F., and I. R. Nassi: "What Is Ada?", *Computer*, Vol. 14, No. 6, June 1981, pp. 17–24.

Brinch Hansen, P.: "Concurrent Programming Constructs," *ACM Computing Surveys*, Vol. 5, No. 4, December 1973, pp. 223–245.

Brinch Hansen, P.: "A Programming Methodology for Operating System Design," IFIP Congress, 1974, Stockholm, Sweden, pp. 394–397.

Brinch Hansen, P.: "Concurrent PASCAL Introduction," Caltech Technical Report, July 1975.

Carlson, W. E.: "Ada: A Promising Beginning," *Computer*, Vol. 14, No. 6, June 1981. pp. 13–15.

Church, A.: *The Calculi of Lambda-Conversion*, *Annals of Mathematics Studies*, Vol. 6, Princeton, N. J.: Princeton Univ. Press, 1941.

Clark, B. L.: "The Design of a Systems Programming Language," M.Sc. Thesis, University of Toronto, Toronto, Canada, 1971.

Clark, B. L., and J. J. Horning: "The Systems Language for Project SUE," *SIGPLAN Notices*, Vol. 6, No. 9, October 1971, pp. 79–88.

Computer, Vol. 14, No. 6, June 1981, pp. 11–64 (special issue on Ada).

Computer, Vol. 16, No. 11, November 1983, pp. 9–104 (special issue on STARS).

DeRemer, F.: "Practical Translators for LR(k) Languages," Ph.D. Thesis, Massachusetts Institute of Technology, Cambridge, Mass. 1969.

DeRemer, F., and H. H. Kron: "Programming-in-the-Large versus Programming-in-the-Small," *IEEE Transactions on Software Engineering*, Vol. SE-2, No. 2, June 1976, pp. 80–86.

Dijkstra, E. W.: "Guarded Commands, Non-Determinacy, and a Calculus for the Derivation of Programs," *Proceedings of the International Conference on Reliable Software*, *SIGPLAN Notices*, Vol. 10, No. 6, June 1975, pp. 2.0–2.13.

Druffel, L. E., S. T. Redime, Jr., and W. E. Riddle: "The STARS Program: Overview and Rationale," *Computer*, Vol. 16, No. 11, November 1983, pp. 21–29.

Elson, M.: *Concepts of Programming Languages*, Palo Alto, Calif.: Science Research Associates, Inc., 1973.

Gannon, J. D.: "Language Design to Enhance Programming Reliability," Report CSRG-47, Computer Systems Research Group, University of Toronto, Toronto, Canada, January 1975.

Gries, D., and N. Gehani: "Some Ideas on Data Types in High Level Languages," Report TR 75-244, Cornell University, Ithaca, N.Y. May 1975.

Hehner, E. C. R.: "Merlin—Towards an Ideal Programming Language," Report CSRG-57, Computer Systems Research Group, University of Toronto, Toronto, Canada, July 1975.

Hoare, C. A. R.: "An Axiomatic Basis for Computer Programming," *Communications of the ACM*, Vol. 12, No. 10, October 1969, pp. 576–583.

Hoare, C. A. R.: "A Note on the FOR Statement," *BIT*, Vol. 12, No. 2, 1972, pp. 334–341.

Hoare, C. A. R.: "Hints on Programming Language Design," Report CS403, Stanford University, Stanford, Calif. October 1973.

Hoare, C. A. R., and N. Wirth: "An Axiomatic Definition of the Programming Language PASCAL," Eidgenossiche Technische Hochule (ETH), Report 6, Zurich, Switzerland, November 1972.

Hoare, C. A. R., O. J. Dahl, and E. W. Dijkstra: *Structured Programming, Notes on Data Structuring*, New York: Academic Press, 1972, pp. 83–155.

Horning, J. J.: "Some Desirable Properties of Data Abstraction Facilities," *SIGPLAN Notices*, 1976 Special Issue, Vol. 11, No. 3, March 1976, pp. 60–62.

Hughes, J. K.: *PL/I Programming*, New York: John Wiley & Sons, 1973.

Ichbiah, J. D., et al.: "Rationale for the Design of the Ada Programming Language," *SIGPLAN Notices*, Part B, Vol. 14, No. 6, June 1979.

Ichbiah, J. D., J. P. Rissen, and J. C. Heliard: *Machine Oriented Higher Level Languages, The Two-Level Approach to Data Independent Programming in the LIS System Implementation Language*, North-Holland Publishing Co., IFIP, 1973, pp. 161–174.

Ingerman, P. Z.: "Thunks," *Communications of the ACM*, Vol. 4, No. 1, 1961, pp. 55–58.

Jensen, K., and N. Wirth: *PASCAL User Manual and Report*, 2d ed., New York: Springer-Verlag, 1975.

Kernighan, B. W., and D. M. Ritchie: *The C Programming Language*, Englewood Cliffs, N. J.: Prentice-Hall, 1978.

Kernighan, B. W., and P. J. Plauger: *Software Tools*, Reading, Mass.: Addison-Wesley, 1976.

Knuth, D. E.: "On the Translation of Languages from Left to Right," *Information and Control*, Vol. 8, No. 6, 1965, pp. 607–639.

Knuth, D. E.: "Structured Programming with GOTO Statements," *ACM Computing Surveys*, Vol. 6, No. 4, December 1974, pp. 261–301.

Lampson, B. W., J. J. Horning, R. L. London, J. G. Mitchell, and G. L. Popek: "Report on the Programming Language Euclid," *SIGPLAN Notices*, Vol. 12, No. 2, February 1977.

Leavitt, R.: "Is Ada a Good Programming Language?", *Proceedings of CIPS Session '82*, May 1982, pp. 20–31.

Ledgard, H.: *Ada: An Introduction*, 2d ed., New York: Springer-Verlag, 1983.

Lindsey, C., and S. G. van der Meulen: *Informal Introduction to ALGOL 68*, New York: American Elsevier, 1972.

Liskov, B., and S. Zilles: "Programming with Abstract Data Types," *Proceedings of the Symposium on Very High Level Languages, SIGPLAN Notices*, Vol. 9, No. 4, April 1974, pp. 50–59.

Martin, E. W.: "The Context of STARS," *Computer*, Vol. 16, No. 11, November 1983, pp. 14–20.

Martin, J.: *Design of Man-Computer Dialogues*, Englewood Cliffs, N.J.: Prentice-Hall, 1973.

McKeeman, W. M.: "An Approach to Computer Language Design," CS 48, Computer Science Department, Stanford University, Stanford, Calif., 1966.

Nicholls, J. E.: *The Structure and Design of Programming Languages*, Reading, Mass.: Addison-Wesley, 1975.

Plauger, P. J.: "Signal and Noise in Programming Languages," ACM National Conference, 1975, p. 216.

Pratt, T. W.: *Design and Implementation of Programming Languages*, Englewood Cliffs, N.J.: Prentice-Hall, 1975.

Prenner, C. J., J. M. Spitze, and B. Wegbreit: "An Implementation of Backtracking for Programming Languages," *SIGPLAN Notices*, Vol. 7, No. 11, November 1972, pp. 36–44.

Pyle, I. C.: *The Ada Programming Language*, Englewood Cliffs, N. J.: Prentice-Hall, 1981.

Radin, C., and H. P. Rogoway: "Highlights of a New Programming Language," *Communications of the ACM*, Vol. 8, No. 1, January 1965, pp. 9–17. Also in S. Rosen: *Programming Systems and Languages*, New York: McGraw-Hill, 1967.

Ritchie, D. M., and K. Thompson: "The UNIX Time-Sharing System," *Proceedings of the 4th Symposium on Operating Systems Principles, SIGOPS*, October 1973. Also in *Communications of the ACM*, Vol. 17, No. 7, July 1974, pp. 365–375.

Ritchie, D. M.: C Reference Manual, in *Documents for Use with the UNIX Time-Sharing System*, Murray Hill, N.J.: Bell Laboratories, 1974.

Rosenkrantz, D. M., and P. M. Stearns: "Properties of Deterministic Top Down Grammars," *Information and Control*, Vol. 17, No. 3, 1970, pp. 226–256.

Sammet, J. E.: "Roster of Programming Languages for 1974–75," *Communications of the ACM*, Vol. 19, No. 12, 1976, pp. 655–669.

Shaw, M: "Research Directions in Abstract Data Structures," *SIGPLAN Notices*, 1976 Special Issue, Vol. 11, No. 3, March 1976, pp. 66–68.

SIGPLAN Notices, "Preliminary Ada Reference Manual," Vol. 14, No. 6, 1979.

SIGPLAN Notices, 1976 Special Issue, *Proceedings of Conference on Data: Abstraction, Definition, and Structure*, Vol. 11, No. 2, 1976.

Stenning, V., et al.: "The Ada Environment: A Perspective," *Computer*, Vol. 14, No. 6, June 1981, pp. 26–36.

Stoneman Requirements for Ada Programming Support, Department of Defense, February 1980.

Tennent, R. D.: "PASQUAL: A Proposed Generalization of PASCAL," Queen's University, Report 75-32, February 1975.

Van Wijngaarden, A., et al.: "Revised Report on the Algorithm Language ALGOL 68," *Acta Informatica*, Vol. 5, 1975, pp. 1–236.

Wegner, P.: *Programming with Ada: An Introduction by Means of Graduated Examples*, Englewood Cliffs: N. J.: Prentice-Hall, 1980.

Weinberg, G.: *The Psychology of Computer Programming*, New York: Van Nostrand Reinhold, 1971.

Weinberg, G., D. P. Geller, and T. W. S. Plum: "IF-THEN-ELSE Considered Harmful." *SIGPLAN Notices*, Vol. 10, No. 8, August 1975, pp. 34–44

Wickmann, B. A.: "Is Ada Too Big? A Designer Answers The Critics," *Communications of the ACM*, Vol. 27, No. 2, February 1984, pp. 98–103.

Wirth, N.: "On the Design of Programming Languages," *IFIP*, 1974, pp. 386–393.

Wirth, N.: *Programming in Modula-2*, New York: Springer-Verlag, 1982.

Wirth, N., and H. Weber: "A Generalization of ALGOL and Its Formal Definition: Parts 1 and 2," *Communications of the ACM*, Vol. 9, Nos. 1, 2, 1966, pp. 13–23, 89–99.

Wolfe, M. I., et al.: "The Ada Language System," *Computer*, Vol. 14, No. 6, June 1981, pp. 37–45.

Wulf, W. A.: "A Case against the GOTO," *SIGPLAN Notices*, Vol. 7, No. 11, November 1972a, pp. 63–69.

Wulf, W. A.: "The Problems of the Definition of Subroutine Calling," *SIGPLAN Notices*, Vol. 7, No. 12, December 1972b, pp. 3–8.

FOUR

SCANNERS

The analysis of a source program during compilation is often complex. The construction of a compiler can often be made easier if the analysis of the source program is separated into two parts, with one part identifying the low-level language constructs (tokens) such as variable names, keywords, labels, and operators, and the second part determining the syntactic organization of the program. This chapter discusses the first and easier of the two analyzers, the lexical analyzer or scanner, which was introduced in Chap. 1.

Two aspects of scanners concern us. First we describe what the tokens of the language are. The class of regular grammars, introduced in Chap. 2, is one vehicle which can be used to describe tokens. Another description approach which is briefly introduced involves the use of regular expressions. Both description methods are equivalent in the sense that both describe the set of regular languages.

The second aspect of scanners deals with the recognition of tokens. Finite-state acceptors are devices that are well suited to this recognition task primarily because they can be specified pictorially by using transition diagrams.

Section 4-1 describes the requirements of a scanner. Based on these requirements, Sec. 4-2 presents an elementary scanner design and its implementation. Regular expressions and regular grammars are dealt with in Sec. 4-3. Section 4-4 deals with deterministic and nondeterministic finite-state acceptors, including nondeterministic acceptors with ε-transitions. The equivalence of regular grammars and finite-state acceptors and the equivalence of regular expressions and finite-state acceptors are shown in the next two sections. Methods of converting from an acceptor to a regular grammar or a regular expression and vice versa are also examined. These notions, in addition to being useful in understanding scanner generators, are also useful in gaining insight into higher-level syntax analyzers such as LR(1) and LALR(1) parsers, which are discussed in Chap. 7. The chapter concludes with a presentation of a scanner generator.

Sections 4-1 and 4-2 contain an elementary, nonautomated approach to scanner generation. The reader who is not interested in scanner generators on first reading need not read the remainder of this chapter. A scanner generator is a system which automatically generates a scanner for a particular language, given the description of the tokens for that language. Readers who intend to study LR parsers in Chap. 7 are advised to study Sec. 4-4.

4-1 THE SCANNING PROCESS

The scanner was briefly introduced in Chap. 1. This section elaborates on the scanning process, that is, what the scanner does in relation to the entire compilation process.

The scanner represents an interface between the source program and the syntactic analyzer or parser. The scanner, through a character-by-character examination of the input text, separates the source program into pieces called *tokens* which represent the variable names, operators, labels, and so on that comprise the source program.

As was mentioned in Chap. 1, the parser usually generates a syntax tree of the source program as defined by a grammar. The leaves of the tree are the terminal symbols of the grammar. It is these terminal symbols or tokens which the scanner extracts from the source code and passes to the parser. It is possible for the parser to use the terminal character set of the language as the set of tokens, but since tokens can be defined in terms of simpler regular grammars rather than the more complex grammars used by parsers, it becomes desirable to use scanners. Using only parsers can become costly in terms of execution time and memory requirements, and complexity and execution time can be reduced by using a scanner.

The separation of lexical analysis (scanning) and syntactic analysis can also have other advantages. Scanning characters is typically slow in compilers, and by separating it from the parsing component of compilation, particular emphasis can be given to making the process efficient. Furthermore, more information can be made available to the parser when it is needed. For example, it is easier to parse tokens such as keywords, identifiers, and operators, rather than tokens which are the terminal character set (i.e., A, B, C, etc.). If the first token for a DO WHILE statement is DO rather than just 'D', the compiler can determine that a repetition loop is being parsed rather than other possibilities such as an assignment statement.

The scanner usually interacts with the parser in one of two ways. The scanner may process the source program in a separate pass before parsing begins. Thus the tokens are stored in a file or large table. The second way involves an interaction between the parser and the scanner. The scanner is called by the parser whenever the next token in the source program is required. The latter approach is the preferred method of operation, since an internal form of the complete source program does not need to be constructed and stored in memory before parsing can begin. Another advantage of this method is that multiple scanners can be written for the same language. These scanners vary depending on the input interfaces used in the language. Throughout this book, the scanner will be assumed to be implemented in this manner. In most cases, however, it makes little difference how the scanner is linked to the parser.

As mentioned earlier, the scanner breaks the source program into pieces called tokens. The type of token is usually represented in the form of a unique internal representation number or integer. For example, a variable name or identifier may be represented by the number 1, a constant by 2, a label by 3, and so on. The token, which is a string of characters (or a value in the case of a constant), is often stored in a table. Thus the values of constants are stored in a constant table while variable names are stored in a symbol table for variables. The scanner then returns the internal type of the token and sometimes the location in the table where the token was stored. Not all tokens may be associated with a symbol or constant table location. While variable names and constants are stored in a table, operators, for example, may *not* be. The scanner might return a unique token or internal representation number for each operator. Conversely, one internal representation number might represent the entire class of operators and the scanner would also return the particular operator by making reference to this operator in an operator table. Note that the strategy of assigning a unique representation number for each member of a class is not possible for classes such as identifiers because the number of identifiers is not known in advance. Furthermore, later syntactic and semantic processing often associates other information with these identifiers, and this information would be stored in the symbol table (see Chap. 8). Such information might involve a variable's type and address.

As an example of the values returned by a scanner, assume that the representation number of a variable name has a value of 1, a constant a value of 2, a label a value of 3, a keyword a value of 4, the addition operator a value of 5, the assignment operator a value of 6, and so on. Labels and variable names are appended to the identifier table and constants to the constant table. Assume that such insertions are done in sequential order. Also assume that if a token such as an operator is not associated with a table, then zero is returned for the location. Then the PL/I statements

```
SUM: A = A + B;
     GOTO DONE;
```

would have the following items returned by the scanner:

Token	Internal representation number	Location
SUM	3	1
:	11	0
A	1	2
=	6	0
A	1	2
+	5	0
B	1	3
;	12	0
GOTO	4	0
DONE	3	4
;	12	0

Notice in this example that blanks are suppressed by the scanner. More will be said about blank suppression shortly. The advantage of using this method for returning the representation number from the scanner is that all representation numbers returned are of a fixed size. Furthermore, it is more efficient for the parser to work with integer values representing the symbols rather than the actual variable-length strings.

Some features that are available in a language have no syntactic meaning yet are included to improve human readability. For example, blank characters are allowed anywhere in FORTRAN but are to be ignored by the compiler. The scanner should recognize these constructs and ignore them by passing the next token to the parser which is not one of these types.

Having examined the scanning process and some of its requirements, we now turn our attention to the design and implementation of a simple scanner.

4-2 AN ELEMENTARY SCANNER DESIGN AND ITS IMPLEMENTATION

As described in the previous section, the main purpose of the scanner is to return the next input token to the parser. To be able to return a token, the scanner must isolate the next sequence of characters in the source text which designates a valid token. To do this, the scanner must also edit the source program, removing information such as comments, blanks, line boundaries, and whatever else is not important to the parsing and code-generating phases of the compiler. The scanner must identify the complete token and sometimes differentiate between keywords and identifiers. Furthermore, the scanner may perform symbol-table maintenance, inserting identifiers, literals, and constants into the tables after they have been converted to an internal form. Note that such symbol-table operations are sometimes performed later in the compilation process, rather than at scanning time. This subsection is concerned with the design and implementation of a scanner to perform these tasks.

Tokens can be described in several ways. One way of describing tokens is by using a regular grammar (see Sec. 2-3). Using this method of specification, generative rules are given for producing the desired tokens. For example, the regular grammar

$$\langle\text{unsigned integer}\rangle ::= 0|1|2|\dots|9|$$
$$0\langle\text{unsigned integer}\rangle|1\langle\text{unsigned integer}\rangle|$$
$$\dots |9\langle\text{unsigned integer}\rangle$$

contains the rules for generating the set of natural numbers.

Recall, however, that a scanner must recognize tokens. With this in mind, we investigate the possibility of describing tokens in a recognitive rather than generative manner. Describing tokens by means of how they can be recognized (or accepted) is often done in terms of a mathematical model called a *finite-state acceptor*.

In the remainder of this section we shall describe a set of tokens by specifying an acceptor which will recognize that set. Although regular grammars can also be used for this purpose, their application to scanner writing is delayed until the next section.

We first introduce the concept of a finite-state acceptor as a machine. The discussion here will be rather informal. A more formal and detailed discussion of this machine is given in Sec. 4-4. A *finite-state acceptor* (FSA) or *finite automaton* may be thought of as a machine consisting of a read head and a finite state control box. The machine reads a tape one character at a time (from left to right), as shown in Fig. 4-1. There are a finite number of states that the FSA can be in. A change in state occurs in the machine whenever the next character is read.

Whenever an FSA begins reading a tape, it is always in a certain state designated as the *starting state*. Some of the states the acceptor may be in are called *final states*, and if the acceptor attempts to read beyond the end of the tape while in a final state, the string which was on the tape is said to be *accepted* by the FSA. In other words, the string belongs to the language which is accepted by the FSA.

Finite-state diagrams or *transition diagrams* are often used to pictorially represent an FSA. An example of such a diagram is illustrated in Fig. 4-2. The FSA which is represented in the diagram accepts decimal real numbers which have at least one digit after the decimal point. The nodes of the finite-state

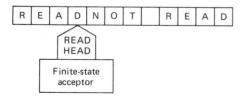

Figure 4-1 A finite-state acceptor.

diagram represent the states of the FSA, and in Fig. 4-2, the states are named S, A, and B. The arcs leading from one state to another indicate the state transitions, with the characters immediately above or beside the arcs denoting the input characters which cause this state transition. The arrow and the word "start" signify which state of the FSA is the starting state. In Fig. 4-2, the starting state is S. The nodes that consist of a pair of concentric circles are final states. In Fig. 4-2, only state B is a final state.

The behavior of the FSA in Fig. 4-2 is easily demonstrated. Assume that the tape the FSA is reading contains the string 12.75. The FSA begins in state S, the starting state, and it remains in this state as each digit in the string preceding the decimal point is read. When the decimal point is read, the FSA changes to state A, and then it changes to state B when the first digit (i.e., 7) following the decimal point is read. The FSA then reads the next digit (5) and remains in state B. As the end of the tape has now been reached, the FSA terminates in the final state B and accepts the given decimal number as being valid.

If the FSA had not been in state B after a string had been read, the string would have been rejected. The string 12. is such a case. Rejection may also occur if no transition is designated at a certain state for some character that has been read. In the FSA of Fig. 4-2, this would occur if the FSA was in state S, state A or state B and, say, an alphabetic character had been read. Examples of strings which would be rejected for this reason are A15.1 and 12.B75.

The FSA that was used in this example of a finite-state diagram is called a *deterministic finite-state acceptor*. A formal definition of this type of acceptor is the topic of Sec. 4-4.

As a second example of an acceptor, consider the transition diagram of Fig. 4-3 which accepts the set of PL/I variable names. The acceptor contains the two states S and A, with the first being the start state and the second the final state. Notice the label of the arc in state A. The acceptor remains in state A if it reads any letter or digit or a special character from the set $\{ \#, @, \$, \_ \}$.

As a final example, let us consider a more complex example of a scanner. Again the scanner will take the form of a finite-state diagram. It is useful to name

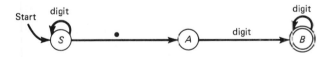

Figure 4-2 A finite-state diagram for a decimal number.

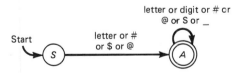

Figure 4-3 A finite-state diagram for PL/I variable name.

the tokens in the diagram once they are identified (which would be at a final state) and to include some processing information to improve the comprehensibility of the diagram. Figure 4-4 depicts the finite-state diagram for a language which consists of the tokens < , <= , = , >= , > , <> , (,), +, −, *, /, := (assignment), ;, identifiers, keywords, constants, and literals (which are enclosed in apostrophes). Comments, which begin with a /* and end with a */, and blanks are ignored by the scanner, in the sense that they are treated simply as token separators.

A few things should be pointed out about this finite-state diagram. An arc which is labeled with a "not" preceding a character indicates that all input characters other than the one listed can cause the indicated state transition. The arc labeled "error" indicates that an invalid character has been found in the source text and that it cannot appear in any token except inside comments and literals. Furthermore, the scanner uses the longest input string possible for determining the token. Thus the character sequence "<= " is considered one token rather then two.

How the finite-state acceptor of Fig. 4-4 identifies tokens deserves some comment. States 5, 6, and 7 are used to recognize the tokens < , <= , and < > from the input string. If neither of the characters = or > follows the character < , then the acceptor ends up in the final state 5, indicating that the token is < . Otherwise the token <= or <> is determined as the acceptor ends up in either state 6 or state 7, respectively. Similarly, states 2, 3, and 4 are used for finding comments and the token /. If an asterisk follows the slash, all characters following the /* and until the one following the next */ are considered to be a part of the comment. Because a comment is not to be returned as a token to the parser, the scanner returns to the starting state immediately after scanning the comment so that the next token can be identified.

States 19 and 22 are used to recognize identifiers and integer constants, respectively. Identifiers begin with a letter and consist of all alphanumeric characters which follow. Constants are comprised of all digits until the next nonnumeric character is read. States 20 and 21 identify string literals. Literals begin and end with an apostrophe (') with the final state 21 designating the end of the literal. Because two consecutive apostrophes are used to represent a single apostrophe as a character within the string, a transition from state 21 to 20 occurs when this is the case.

The scanner depicted in Fig. 4-4 ignores blanks and comments and returns to the starting state whenever one of these types has been read. Blanks and comments are still used as separators, however, because the end of some tokens occurs whenever a character which cannot be included as part of that token is read. This occurs for constants when a blank follows a series of digits. In order to determine the end of some tokens, it is necessary to read one character beyond the end of that token.

Notice also that in Fig. 4-4, keywords and identifiers are detected in the same manner; however, a search of the keyword table is necessary to determine whether

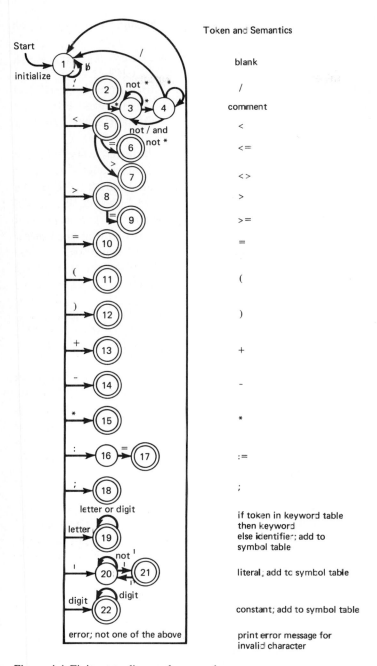

Token and Semantics

blank

/

comment

<

<=

<>

>

>=

=

(

)

+

-

*

:=

;

if token in keyword table
then keyword
else identifier; add to
symbol table

literal, add to symbol table

constant; add to symbol table

print error message for
invalid character

Figure 4-4 Finite-state diagram for example scanner.

the token is a keyword or an identifier. This is indicated in the semantic description given in the diagram.

There is a set of subprograms which many scanners employ to perform some of the more frequently required tasks. The function GET_CHAR, for example, returns the next input character from the source text. The function KEYWORD determines if its argument is a keyword and if so returns the internal representation number for this token. Other procedures may be used to add a new identifier to the symbol table.

By representing the scanner as a finite-state diagram, it can be easily implemented using a case statement or by simulating a case statement where each case represents one of the states attainable after a state transition from the starting state. The code for each case determines the token by using the longest sequence of input characters possible and performs any processing associated with this token. This may involve converting a constant to its internal numeric form or adding an identifier to the symbol table. Then the scanner returns the internal representation number of the token and possibly its location in some table. An algorithm based on the above observations follows.

Procedure SCAN(PROGRAM, LOOKAHEAD, CHAR, TOKEN, POS). This procedure is an implementation of the scanner specified by the finite-state machine in Fig. 4-4. Given the source string, PROGRAM, this algorithm returns the internal representation number of the next token, TOKEN, in that string. If this token represents an identifier, literal, or constant, then the procedure also returns its numeric table position, POS. CHAR represents the current character being scanned in the source string. LOOKAHEAD is a logical variable which designates whether or not the lookahead symbol in CHAR has been used in the previous call to SCAN. A value of "false" denotes that lookahead was not used. The following functions are used in the algorithm:

GET_CHAR(PROGRAM). Returns the next character in the source string.
INSERT(STRING, type). Inserts the given token, STRING (if necessary), and its
    type (i.e., a constant, literal, or variable name) into the symbol table.
KEYWORD(STRING). Returns the internal representation number of its argu-
    ment if it is a keyword and 0 otherwise.

The local variable STRING contains the actual token consisting of a variable name, literal, or constant. Finally, the variables DIVISION, LEQ, NEQ, LTN, GEQ, GTN, EQ, LEFT, RIGHT, ADDITION, SUBTRACTION, MULTIPLICA-TION, ASSIGNMENT, SEMICOLON, LITERAL, IDENTIFIER, and CONSTANT contain the internal representation numbers of the tokens /, <= , <> , < , >= , > , = , (,), +, −, *, := , ;, literals, identifiers, and constants, respectively.

1. [Initialize]
       POS ← 0
2. [Get first character]
       If not LOOKAHEAD
       then CHAR ← GET_CHAR(PROGRAM)
       LOOKAHEAD ← false
3. [Loop until a token is found]
       Repeat step 4 while true
4. [Case statement to determine next token]
       Select by (CHAR)
       Case '□':   (scan and ignore blanks)
           CHAR ← GET_CHAR(PROGRAM)
       Case '/':
           CHAR ← GET_CHAR(PROGRAM)
           If CHAR = '*'   (scan and ignore comments)
           then Repeat while true
               CHAR ← GET_CHAR(PROGRAM)
               If CHAR = '*'
               then Repeat while CHAR = '*'
                   CHAR ← GET_CHAR(PROGRAM)
                 If CHAR = '/'
                 then CHAR ← GET_CHAR(PROGRAM)
                   Exit loop
           else LOOKAHEAD ← true
               TOKEN ← DIVISION   (/)
               Return
       Case '<':
           CHAR ← GET_CHAR(PROGRAM)
           If CHAR = '='
           then TOKEN ← LEQ   (<=)
           else If CHAR = '>'
               then TOKEN ← NEQ   (<>)
               else LOOKAHEAD ← true
                 TOKEN ← LTN   (<)
           Return
       Case '>':
           CHAR ← GET_CHAR(PROGRAM)
           If CHAR = '='
           then TOKEN ← GEQ   (>=)
           else LOOKAHEAD ← true
               TOKEN ← GTN   (>)
           Return
       Case '=':   (=)
           TOKEN ← EQ
           Return

```
Case '(':                                  (()
     TOKEN ← LEFT
     Return
Case ')':                                  ())
     TOKEN ← RIGHT
     Return
Case '+':                                  (+)
     TOKEN ← ADDITION
     Return
Case '−':                                  (−)
     TOKEN ← SUBTRACTION
     Return
Case '*':                                  (*)
     TOKEN ← MULTIPLICATION
     Return
Case ':':
     CHAR ← GET_CHAR(PROGRAM)
     If CHAR = '='
     then TOKEN ← ASSIGNMENT      (:=)
          Return
     else
          CHAR ← GET_CHAR(PROGRAM)
          Write('UNKNOWN TOKEN ":"', CHAR,
          'IN SOURCE STRING')
Case ';':                                  (;)
     TOKEN ← SEMICOLON
     Return
Case '''':                                 (literal)
     STRING ← ''
     Repeat while true
        CHAR ← GET_CHAR(PROGRAM)
        If CHAR = ''''
        then CHAR ← GET_CHAR(PROGRAM)
             If CHAR ≠ ''''
             then LOOKAHEAD ← true
                  POS ← INSERT(STRING, LITERAL)
                  TOKEN ← LITERAL
                  Return
             STRING ← STRING ∘ CHAR
Default:
     If CHAR >= 'A' and CHAR <= 'Z'
     then STRING ← CHAR              (identifier)
          CHAR ← GET_CHAR(PROGRAM)
          Repeat while  (CHAR >= 'A' and CHAR <= 'Z')
                     or (CHAR >= '0' and CHAR <= '9')
```

```
            STRING ← STRING ∘ CHAR
            CHAR ← GET_CHAR(PROGRAM)
        LOOKAHEAD ← true
        If KEYWORD(STRING) > 0
        then TOKEN ← KEYWORD(STRING)
            Return
        POS ← INSERT(STRING, IDENTIFIER)
        TOKEN ← IDENTIFIER
        Return
    If CHAR >= '0' and CHAR <= '9'      (constant)
    then STRING ← CHAR
        CHAR ← GET_CHAR(PROGRAM)
        Repeat while CHAR >= '0' and CHAR <= '9'
            STRING ← STRING ∘ CHAR
            CHAR ← GET_CHAR(PROGRAM)
        LOOKAHEAD ← true
        POS ← INSERT(STRING, CONSTANT)
        TOKEN ← CONSTANT
        Return
    Write('ERROR--UNKNOWN CHARACTER', CHAR,
        'IN SOURCE STRING')
    CHAR ← GET_CHAR(PROGRAM)                               □
```

This procedure uses the parameters LOOKAHEAD and CHAR to describe what has happened in the scanning of the next input character in the previous invocation of the procedure. If LOOKAHEAD has the value of true, the next input character is already in CHAR. Step 1 initializes the value of POS to a default value of zero. POS is set to its appropriate table value for an identifier, constant, or literal in step 4. Step 2 obtains the current input symbol if lookahead was not used in the previous invocation of SCAN. Step 3 repeatedly performs step 4. Since comments and blanks are ignored in the scanning process, step 4 must be repeated in such cases. Step 4, although lengthy, is straightforward. The case statement selects, depending on the value of the current character scanned (given by CHAR), the particular algorithm segment to be performed and causes the appropriate transfer to a state that implements the finite-state acceptor described in Fig. 4-4. Note the placement of Return statements in this step. A trace of this procedure is left as an exercise.

The model of a scanner presented here returns to the parser both a token and its table location, if applicable. For certain block-structured languages, however, table operations would be done later in the compilation process. In such cases the scanner would only return a token to the parser.

In some languages, it is not always possible to determine what a token is at the point where it has been entirely read when using the model of a FSA. The classic example is illustrated by the following two FORTRAN examples:

    DO10I = 1, 20
    DO10I = 1 + 20

The first statement is the start of a loop, and DO10I consists of the three tokens, DO, 10, and I while in the second statement, DO10I is a valid FORTRAN identifier. It is impossible to tell after having read just DO whether or not DO is part of an identifier or the token starting a DO statement. The problem can be solved using lookahead. Thus, whenever a special case arises where it is unclear as to what the token is, the scanner must look ahead in the source text in order to resolve this uncertainty.

Lookahead can be implemented using an input buffer. For example, parts of the source text are read several characters at a time into a vector. Two pointers are used. One pointer indicates the position of the current character being read in the buffer and the other pointer, the lookahead pointer, scans further along the input buffer whenever a decision must be made about a token. A buffering scheme must take into account the situation in which lookahead is required beyond the end of the current buffer and must be able to manage the input buffer to handle this situation.

Language policies must be taken into consideration when designing a scanner. Languages such as PL/I ignore blanks except for separating keywords and identifiers while other languages, such as FORTRAN, completely ignore blanks. Furthermore, keywords may or may not be reserved. The scanner presented in this section was designed assuming that keywords are reserved, but such is not the case in a language like PL/I. In such cases the scanner would return a token and let the parser decide whether or not a token was a keyword. As discussed earlier, table operations could be done later in the compilation process.

It was mentioned earlier that scanners can use regular grammars for recognizing tokens. Regular expressions can also be used to define a scanner, and the next section encompasses these two notions. Showing how regular expressions are used to define scanners, however, will be delayed until Sec. 4-7.

EXERCISES 4-2

1 What is the problem with identifying reserved words efficiently? For example, should a scanner traverse a sequence of states, the sequence depending upon the input characters so that there is a final state for each keyword and one for an identifier?

2 Write a scanner similar to procedure SCAN that handles card or newline boundaries. Tokens cannot be broken over boundaries. If card boundaries are used, assume that a card image is 80 characters; otherwise assume a special character in the input stream that indicates a new line.

3 Write a scanner for FORTRAN that uses lookahead to determine the next token. Use an input buffer.

4 Trace procedure SCAN for the program segment:

```
IF ALPHA <= BETA
THEN /* perform * operation */
     ALPHA := BETA * -493 - COM38A;
```

Several calls to procedure SCAN are required to scan the entire program segment. Indicate what token is returned by each invocation of procedure SCAN.

5 Give a finite-state diagram for floating-point numbers. Floating-point numbers must have a decimal point and at least one digit. The characteristic is optional and begins with an E, followed by an optional sign and one or two digits.

6 As part of your term project, implement a scanner for the language you have designed. Do not worry about the symbol table handling subprograms at this point; only be ready to call them where necessary. The other subprograms should be implemented.

4-3 REGULAR GRAMMARS AND REGULAR EXPRESSIONS

In Sec. 2-3, the grammar classification of Chomsky was introduced. In this section, one class of these grammars, the T_3 or regular grammars, is discussed. Regular expressions are also described in this section, and an algorithm for converting a regular grammar to a regular expression is given. Both formalisms can be used to describe tokens.

Recall from Chap. 2 that a *regular grammar* is defined to consist only of productions of the form $\alpha \rightarrow \beta$, where $|\alpha| \leq |\beta|$, $\alpha \in V_N$, and β has the form aB or a where $a \in V_T$ and $B \in V_N$. Furthermore, the languages generated by such grammars are said to be *regular*. Examples of regular grammars and regular languages were presented in Chap. 2.

A more compact way of representing regular languages is with the use of regular expressions. The equivalence of regular grammars and regular expressions will be demonstrated in the next two sections when proofs of the equivalence of regular grammars and finite-state acceptors and of regular expressions and finite-state acceptors are given.

Regular expressions make use of three operators: concatenation, alternation, and closure. Assume that the two expressions e_1 and e_2 generate the languages L_1 and L_2, respectively. *Concatenation* is then defined as $e_1 e_2 = \{xy | x \in L_1$ and $y \in L_2\}$. *Alternation*, which is denoted by either $|$ or $+$, is the union of the languages denoted by two expressions. Hence, $e_1 | e_2 = \{x | x \in L_1$ or $x \in L_2\}$. Closure, which is represented by the braces $\{\ \}$, denotes the repetition of the expression zero or more times. Thus, $\{e_1\} = \{x | x \in L_1^*\}$ where $L_1^* = \bigcup_{i=0}^{\infty} L_1^i$. These operators are analogous to the BNF operators introduced in Chap. 2. For example, the expression 110 consists of the digits 1, 1, and 0 concatenated together and denotes the language $L = \{110\}$. The expression $0|1$ denotes the language $L = \{0, 1\}$ while the expression $\{1\}$ denotes the language $L = \{1^i | i = 0, 1, 2, \ldots\}$.

Other examples of regular expressions that specify familiar sets of tokens follow.

{identifier} = letter {letter|digit}
{PL/I name} = (letter | # |$|@) {letter|digit| # |@|_|$}
{number} = (ε| +| −)({digit} . digit {digit})

Note that the terms letter and digit represent the sets of alphabetic letters and decimal digits, respectively.

Using the definitions of the above operators, a formal definition of regular expressions is now given.

Definition 4-1 Regular expressions are those expressions that can be constructed from the following rules:

1. ϕ is a regular expression denoting the empty set.
2. ε is a regular expression denoting the language consisting of only the empty string, that is, $\{\varepsilon\}$.
3. a, where $a \in V_T$, is a regular expression denoting the language consisting of the single symbol a, that is, the language $\{a\}$.
4. If e_1 and e_2 are regular expressions denoting the languages L_1 and L_2, respectively, then:
   (a) $(e_1)|(e_2)$ is a regular expression denoting $L_1 \cup L_2$.
   (b) $(e_1)(e_2)$ is a regular expression denoting $L_1 L_2$.
   (c) $\{e_1\}$ is a regular expression denoting L_1^*.

If the precedence of the operators in regular expressions are defined with closure ({ }) having the highest precedence, concatenation with the next highest, and alternation (|) having the lowest precedence, the parentheses can be eliminated whenever possible. Thus, $((p)|((p)(q)))$ would have the same meaning if the parentheses were omitted. In the case of $(p|q)r$, the parentheses cannot be removed, as the language denoted by the expression would become different.

Some examples of regular expressions are now given. The expression $\{a\}\{b\}$ represents the language $\{a^m b^n|m \geq 0 \text{ and } n \geq 0\}$. This expression can be compared with the expression $\{ab\}$ which generates the language $\{(ab)^m|m \geq 0\}$ and the expression $\{a|b\}$ denoting the language $\{x|x \in \{a, b\}^*\}$. The expression $\{aa|ab|ba|bb\}$ denotes all strings over $V_T = \{a, b\}$ of even length. This can be seen by observing that the expression $aa|ab|ba|bb$ denotes all strings of length two with zero or more combinations of the strings generated by this expression producing strings all of an even length.

It is convenient to define the equality of regular expressions. Two regular expressions are *equal* (=) or *equivalent* if they denote the same language. Thus, $0\{0\} = 00\{0\}|0$ as each expression generates the language $\{0^i|i \geq 1\}$.

The tokens of a programming language can be defined in terms of regular grammars and regular expressions. For example, an identifier which consists of letters and digits and must begin with a letter can be described by the regular grammar

$$S \rightarrow aA|bA|cA|\ldots|zA|a|b|c|\ldots|z$$
$$A \rightarrow aA|bA|cA|\ldots|zA|0A|1A|\ldots 9A$$
$$|a|b|c|\ldots|z|0|1|\ldots|9$$

and by the regular expression

$$(a|b|c|\ldots|z)\{a|b|c|\ldots|z|0|1|\ldots|9\}$$

Using letter as a shorthand representation for $a|b|c|\ldots|z$ and digit for $0|1|\ldots|9$, the expression might be written as letter$\{$letter$|$digit$\}$ to improve readability. As we shall see in Sec. 4-7, regular expressions are often used to describe tokens for a scanner generator.

For the remainder of this section, a method for converting regular grammars to regular expressions is presented. At this point, however, it should be noted that the regular-expression operators obey some algebraic rules. For example, both alternation and concatenation are associative, with alternation also being commutative. Thus we can write $(ab)c = a(bc)$, $(a|b)|c = a|(b|c)$, and $a|b = b|a$. Distributivity also applies, with concatenation distributing over alternation; that is, $a(b|c) = ab|ac$. Proofs of these identities are left as exercises. Finally, regular expressions can be used in equations and therefore evaluated. For example, $A = \{aA\}$ is a valid regular-expression equation.

To present a method of converting a regular grammar to a regular expression, consider the following regular grammar from Chap. 2 which generates the language $\{a^m b a^n | n, m \geq 1\}$.

1. $S \rightarrow aS$ 4. $C \rightarrow aC$
2. $S \rightarrow aB$ 5. $C \rightarrow a$
3. $B \rightarrow bC$

Replacing the production operator ($\rightarrow$) with an equal sign and combining all possible productions from a given nonterminal into one expression by using the alternation operator, the grammar can be written as the set of equations

$$S = aS|aB$$
$$B = bC$$
$$C = aC|a$$

By solving this set of equations, a regular expression with only terminal symbols is derived which generates the same language as the original regular grammar. Solutions for equations which are defined only in terms of themselves should be done first. In this example, the equation for C has a solution of $C = \{a\}a$. This can be shown by substituting this solution into the equation for C, giving

$$\{a\}a = a\{a\}a|a$$

Factoring yields

$$\{a\}a = (\{a\}a|\varepsilon)a$$

Now, $\{a\}a|\varepsilon = \{a\}$, since ε is in both sides of the equation, a is in both sides, and any string a^i is in both sides. Thus we have

$$\{a\}a = \{a\}a$$

The solution for C can be substituted into the second equation, and the third equation can be dropped as it is no longer needed. This results in the set of equations

$$S = a(S|B)$$
$$B = b\{a\}a$$

We immediately have a solution for B which can be substituted into the first equation. This results in the equation

$$S = a(S|b\{a\}a)$$

It can easily be shown that a solution for S is $S = \{a\}ab\{a\}a$, which is a regular expression generating the same language as the original regular grammar.

An algorithm which generates an equivalent regular expression from a regular grammar is now given.

Algorithm REGULAR_EXPRESSION. Given a regular grammar with the set of productions of the form $X_i \rightarrow \psi$ and ψ is of the form aX_j or a where $a \in V_T$, this algorithm generates an equivalent regular expression. X_1 is the starting symbol of the grammar and there are n terminal symbols in the grammar.

1. [Convert the regular expression equations]
   Repeat for each production $X_i \rightarrow \psi$ of the regular grammar
   If the equation X_i has not been initialized
   then Define $X_i = \psi$
   else Change $X_i = \alpha$ to $X_i = \alpha|\psi$ where α is the
        previously defined part of the equation X_i
2. [Convert equations to required format]
   Repeat for $i = 1, 2,...,n - 1$
   Convert equation X_i into the form $X_i = \alpha_i X_i|\psi_i$ where
   ψ_i is of the form $\beta_{0,i}|\beta_{i+1,i}X_{i+1}|...|\beta_{n,i}X_n$ and
   α_i and each $\beta_{j,i}$ is a regular expression over V_T
   Repeat for $j = i + 1, i + 2,...,n$
       Substitute $\{\alpha_i\}\psi_i$ for X_i in the equation for X_j
3. [Solve for the solution]
   Repeat for $i = n, n - 1,...,1$
   Convert the equation for X_i into the form $\alpha_i X_i|\psi_i'$ where ψ_i' is a
   regular expression over $V_T\psi_i'$
   Repeat for $j = i - 1, i - 2,...,1$
       Substitute the solution $\{\alpha_i\}\psi_i'$ for X_i into the equation for X_j

4. [Print the solution]

Write('THE SOLUTION IS', $\{\alpha_1\}\psi_1'$)

Exit □

The first step of the algorithm converts the regular grammar to a set of equations, each one of the form

$$X_i = \delta_1|\delta_2|\ldots|\delta_m|\psi_j X_j|\psi_k X_k|\ldots|\psi_l X_l$$

where each $\psi_i, \delta_i \in V_T$. Step 2 then converts each equation to the form

$$X_i = \alpha_i X_i|\beta_{0,i}|\beta_{i+1,i}X_{i+1}|\ldots|\beta_{n,i}X_a$$

While some algebraic manipulation may be required, it is possible for each equation to be converted to this form. Step 3 uses back substitution to solve the set of equations. The solution for X_n is easily found as this equation has the form $X_n = \alpha_n X_n|\psi_n'$ and it is $\{\alpha_n\}\psi_n'$. This solution is then substituted into each preceding equation. Once a solution for equation X_i has been found and substituted into the preceding equations, the equation for X_{i-1} has only the unknown X_{i-1} in it, and the equation can be written in the form $\alpha_{i-1}X_{i-1}|\psi_i'$. Thus a solution for X_{i-1} is easily computed. At the completion of step 3, the regular expression for X_1 is the regular expression equivalent to the regular grammar which the algorithm started with. A trace of this algorithm is left for the exercises.

In the next section, finite-state acceptors are introduced. Finite-state acceptors are theoretical machines which can be used to determine whether a given string can be generated from a regular grammar or a regular expression. In closing, a scanner generator based on regular expressions is discussed in Sec. 4-7.

EXERCISES 4-3

1 Describe floating-point numbers using a regular grammar and a regular expression. Floating-point numbers require at least one digit and a decimal point. The characteristic is optional and begins with an E, followed by an optional sign and one or two digits.

2 Show that the operation of alternation is commutative.

3 Prove that concatenation and alternation are both associative. Also prove that concatenation distributes over alternation; that is, $a(b|c) = ab|ac$.

4 What sets of strings do the following regular expressions describe?

(a) $\{ab\}\{b|a\}$

(b) $(digit\{digit\}|\varepsilon)(0|2|4|6|8)$ where digit represents $0|1|\ldots$ 9

(c) $\{00|11\}\{(01|10)\{00|11\}(01|10)\{00|11\}\}$

5 Trace Algorithm REGULAR_EXPRESSION on the regular grammar

1. $S \to aA$	5. $A \to a$
2. $S \to a$	6. $B \to bB$
3. $A \to aA$	7. $B \to c$
4. $A \to bB$	

6 Convert the following regular grammar to a regular expression

1. $S \to aA$	4. $B \to bC$
2. $A \to aA$	5. $C \to cB$
3. $A \to aB$	6. $C \to c$

7 Outline an algorithm for converting a regular expression to a regular grammar.

4-4 FINITE-STATE ACCEPTORS

In this section we continue the discussion of finite-state acceptors introduced in Sec. 4-2. Scanner generators often create a scanner which simulates a finite-state acceptor, as it is not difficult to program an acceptor on a computer. Three types of finite-state acceptors are examined: deterministic, nondeterministic, and nondeterministic with ε-transitions. The equivalence of these types of acceptors is also demonstrated.

4-4.1 Deterministic Finite-State Acceptors

A *deterministic finite-state acceptor* (DFA), which is also known as a *deterministic finite automaton*, is an acceptor which for any state and input character has at most one transition state that the acceptor changes to. If no transition state is specified, the input string is rejected.

The following definition formally introduces a DFA.

Definition 4-2 A *deterministic finite-state acceptor* (DFA) is a 5-tuple (K, V_T, M, S, Z) where:

K is a finite, nonempty set of elements called *states*.
V_T is an alphabet called the *input alphabet*.
M is a mapping from $K \times V_T$ into K.
$S \in K$ is called the *initial state* or *starting state*.
$Z \subseteq K$ is a nonempty set of *final states*.

The DFA is initially in state S and reads an input string from left to right. The mapping function M of the DFA defines the state transitions and is denoted by $M(Q, T) = R$, where Q and R are states of K and T is a character from the input alphabet. The mapping function indicates that when the acceptor is in state Q and T is the next input character, the acceptor changes to state R. The following two definitions complete the specification of the mapping function:

$$M(Q, \varepsilon) = Q \qquad \text{for all } Q \in K$$
$$M(Q, Tt) = M(M(Q, T), t) \qquad \text{for all } T \in V_T \text{ and } t \in V_T^*$$

The first definition implies that a DFA cannot change state without reading a character from the input alphabet, while the second definition is a recursive definition showing that when the DFA is in state Q with some input string $x = Tt$, the mapping $M(Q, T)$ is applied first with the result $P = M(Q, T)$. Then the mapping $M(P, t)$ can be applied. This definition extends the applicability of the mapping function to strings over V_T^* rather than just elements of V_T.

A sentence t is said to be *accepted* by a DFA if $M(S, t) = P$ for some DFA $F = (K, V_T, M, S, Z)$ such that $t \in V_T^*$ and $P \in Z$. The string t is accepted by the DFA if, after reading the entire string, the DFA terminates in a final state. The set of all $t \in V_T^*$ which is accepted by the DFA F is specified by $L(F)$. Thus $L(F)$ is defined as

$$L(F) = \{t | M(S, t) \in Z \text{ and } t \in V_T^*\}$$

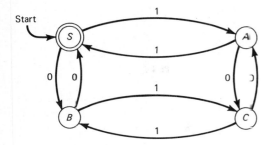

Start

Figure **4-5** An example of a deterministic finite-state acceptor.

The following DFA is an example of an acceptor which accepts strings consisting only of an even number of 0s and an even number of 1s.

$$F = (\{S, A, B, C\}, \{0,1\}, M, S, \{S\})$$

where M is defined as

$$M(S,0) = B \qquad M(S,1) = A$$
$$M(A,0) = C \qquad M(A,1) = S$$
$$M(B,0) = S \qquad M(B,1) = C$$
$$M(C,0) = A \qquad M(C,1) = B$$

The transition diagram for this acceptor is given in Fig. 4-5.

The mapping function for an acceptor is sometimes more conveniently illustrated with a transition table such as Table 4-1, which defines M in the previous example.

An example of a string which is accepted by this DFA is 110101, and a string not accepted is 11101. Traces of the DFA operating on these strings are given in Table 4-2.

In this subsection, deterministic finite-state acceptors were discussed. The next subsection examines finite-state acceptors which may have more than one transition for a given state and input character. Such an acceptor is shown to be no more powerful than its deterministic counterpart.

4-4.2 Nondeterministic Finite-State Acceptors

Nondeterministic finite-state acceptors (NFA), or *nondeterministic finite automata*, are similar to deterministic finite-state acceptors except that there may be more

Table 4-1

State	Input	
	0	1
S	B	A
A	C	S
B	S	C
C	A	B

Table 4-2 Traces of two strings using the DFA

Input string	
110101	11101
$M(S, 110101) = M(A, 10101)$	$M(S, 11101) = M(A, 1101)$
$= M(S, 0101)$	$= M(S, 101)$
$= M(B, 101)$	$= M(A, 01)$
$= M(C, 01)$	$= M(C, 1)$
$= M(A, 1)$	$= M(B, \varepsilon)$
$= M(S, \varepsilon)$	$= B$ (reject)
$= S$ (accept)	

than one possible state that is attainable from a given state for the same input character. Thus an ambiguity seems to arise because the acceptor has several possibilities to choose from. However, the acceptor is considered to explore all possibilities, one at a time, to determine if a string should be accepted. Consider the NFA given in Fig. 4-6 which accepts strings of the form $a^m b^n$ where $m, n \geq 1$. A string will be accepted by the NFA if at least one valid sequence of state transitions exists such that the acceptor is in a final state when the entire string has been read. From the finite-state diagram, it should be observed that in order for the acceptor to accept a string if possible, it stays in state A until the final character a is read. The acceptor then changes to state B. Similarly, the NFA stays in state B until the final character b is read, causing a transition to state C.

Definition 4-3 A *nondeterministic finite-state acceptor* is a 5-tuple (K, V_T, M, S, Z) where:

K is a finite, nonempty set of states.
V_T is an input alphabet.
M is a mapping of $K \times V_T$ into subsets of K (i.e., $K \times V_T \rightarrow 2^K$).
$S \in K$ is the starting state.
$Z \subseteq K$ is the set of final states.

Notice that the mapping function M is similar to that for a DFA except that M maps into a possibly empty set of states. Hence we write $M(Q, T) = \{P_1, P_2, \ldots, P_n\}$ where a transition from state Q to one of the states $P_1, P_2, \ldots, P_n$ occurs when a character T from V_T is read. The mapping function for an NFA is

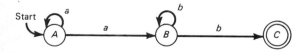

Start

Figure 4-6 An example of a nondeterministic finite-state acceptor.

extended with the following definitions:

$$M(Q, \varepsilon) = \{Q\} \qquad\qquad \text{where } Q \in K$$

$$M(Q, Tt) = \bigcup_{P \in M(Q,T)} M(P, t) \qquad\qquad \text{where } T \in V_T \text{ and } t \in V_T^*$$

$$M(\{Q_1, Q_2, \ldots, Q_n\}, x) = \bigcup_{i=1}^{n} M(Q_i, x) \quad \text{where } x \in V_T^*$$

The first definition implies that for the empty string, the acceptor must stay in the same state. The meaning of the second definition is less obvious. If $M(Q, T) = \{P_1, P_2, \ldots, P_n\}$, then the second definition can be written as $M(Q, Tt) = M(P_1, t) \cup M(P_2, t) \cup \cdots \cup M(P_n, t)$. Thus, $M(Q, Tt)$ is the set of all possible states that the acceptor may end up in after the string Tt has been read. The third definition extends the mapping function to $2^K \times V_T^*$ and defines the mapping to be the union of all the sets resulting from applying each individual state from the set of states to the string x.

A string x is said to be accepted by an NFA if at least one of the states attainable from the starting state by reading x is a final state; that is, x is accepted by the NFA $F = (K, V_T, M, S, Z)$ if for some state $A \in M(S, x)$, then $A \in Z$.

As an example of an NFA, consider a machine which accepts the set of strings in $\{a, b, c\}^*$ such that the last symbol in the input string also appears earlier in the string. For example, bab is accepted but $cbbca$ is not. The finite-state diagram for this acceptor is given in Fig. 4-7. For M as defined in Table 4-3, the acceptor is given as

$$F = (\{q_0, q_1, q_2, q_3, q_4\}, \{a, b, c\}, M, q_0, \{q_4\})$$

With the input string aca, the value of $M(q_0, aca)$ can be determined as follows:

$$M(q_0, a) = \{q_0, q_1\}$$

so

$$M(q_0, aca) = M(q_0, ca) \cup M(q_1, ca)$$

Table 4-3 Transition table for a nondeterministic finite-state acceptor

State	Input symbol		
	a	b	c
q_0	$\{q_0, q_1\}$	$\{q_0, q_2\}$	$\{q_0, q_3\}$
q_1	$\{q_1, q_4\}$	$\{q_1\}$	$\{q_1\}$
q_2	$\{q_2\}$	$\{q_2, q_4\}$	$\{q_2\}$
q_3	$\{q_3\}$	$\{q_3\}$	$\{q_3, q_4\}$
q_4	ϕ	ϕ	ϕ

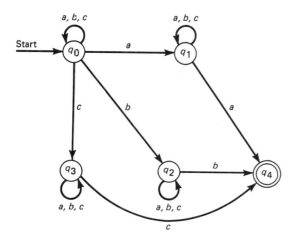

Figure 4-7 Transition diagram for a nondeterministic finite-state acceptor.

Now

$$M(q_0, c) = \{q_0, q_3\}$$
$$M(q_1, c) = \{q_1\}$$

so

$$M(q_0, ca) = M(q_0, a) \cup M(q_3, a)$$
$$= \{q_0, q_1\} \cup \{q_3\}$$
$$= \{q_0, q_1, q_3\}$$
$$M(q_1, ca) = M(q_1, a) = \{q_1, q_4\}$$

Hence

$$M(q_0, aca) = \{q_0, q_1, q_3\} \cup \{q_1, q_4\}$$
$$= \{q_0, q_1, q_3, q_4\}$$

and since $M(q_0, aca) \cap Z = \{q_4\}$, the string aca is accepted.

It should be emphasized that although a nondeterministic machine does not have unique moves, it does not contain a random device for choosing its move. Rather, the acceptor explores all possible move sequences, and if at least one of these sequences leads to a final state, then the input string is accepted.

While it might seem likely that nondeterministic finite-state acceptors are more powerful than deterministic acceptors, the following theorem proves that such is not the case. The theorem also provides a method for converting an NFA to a DFA.

Theorem 4-1 Let $F = (K, V_T, M, S, Z)$ be a nondeterministic finite-state acceptor accepting a set of strings L. Define a DFA $F' = (K', V_T, M', S', Z')$

as follows:

1. The alphabet of states consists of all the subsets of K. An element of K' is denoted as $[S_1, S_2, \ldots, S_i]$, where $S_1, S_2, \ldots, S_i$ are states of K. The states $S_1, S_2, \ldots, S_i$ are in the same canonical order, so that for some states in K, $\{S_1, S_2\}(= \{S_2, S_1\})$ is always $[S_1, S_2]$.
2. The set of input characters V_T is the same for F and F'.
3. The mapping M' is defined as
$$M'([S_1, S_2, \ldots, S_i], T) = [R_1, R_2, \ldots, R_j]$$
where
$$M(\{S_1, S_2, \ldots, S_i\}, T) = \{R_1, R_2, \ldots, R_j\}$$
4. If the starting state of F is S_i, then $S' = [S_i]$.
5. Z' is the set of all states in K' containing a final state in Z.

Then the set of strings accepted by F' is the same as that for F.

PROOF It must be shown that $L(F') = L(F)$ with the construction given in the theorem. Thus it is necessary to show that $M'(S', x) = [P_1, P_2, \ldots, P_i]$ is equivalent to $M(S, x) = \{P_1, P_2, \ldots, P_i\}$. This can be done by induction on the length of the string x. The result is trivial for $|x| = 0$, since $x = \varepsilon$ and $S' = [S]$ from the mapping $M(S, \varepsilon) = \{S\}$.

Assume that $M'(S', x)$ is equivalent to $M(S, x)$ for $|x| \leq m$. Then for $T \in V_T$
$$M'(S', xT) = M'(M'(S', x), T)$$
By the inductive hypothesis
$$M'(S', x) = [Q_1, Q_2, \ldots, Q_j]$$
is equivalent to
$$M(S, x) = \{Q_1, Q_2, \ldots, Q_j\}$$
By definition, we have
$$M'([Q_1, Q_2, \ldots, Q_j], T) = [R_1, R_2, \ldots, R_k]$$
is equivalent to
$$M(\{Q_1, Q_2, \ldots, Q_j\}, T) = \{R_1, R_2, \ldots, R_k\}$$
Thus the equivalence holds for $|x| \leq m + 1$ and
$$M'(S', xT) = [R_1, R_2, \ldots, R_k]$$
is equivalent to
$$M(S, xT) = \{R_1, R_2, \ldots, R_k\}$$
Thus
$$L(F) = L(F')$$

The construction given in the theorem may be applied to any NFA. For example, the NFA $F = (\{q_0, q_1, q_2\}, \{a, b\}, M, q_0, \{q_2\})$, where the mapping function is defined in Table 4-4, can be converted to a DFA as follows: Define $F' = (K', V_T, M', S', Z')$, where V_T is the same as for F and the starting state is $S' = [q_0]$. The states of K' are initially defined as $[q_0]$, $[q_1]$, and $[q_2]$, and the mapping M' is readily obtained from the transition table for F. The mapping of these states is

$$M'([q_0], a) = [q_0, q_1] \qquad M'([q_0], b) = [q_2]$$
$$M'([q_1], a) = [q_0] \qquad M'([q_1], b) = [q_1]$$
$$M'([q_2], a) = [q_1] \qquad M'([q_2], b) = [q_0, q_1]$$

A new state $[q_0, q_1]$ is created and from the mapping of F

$$M(\{q_0, q_1\}, a) = \{q_0, q_1\} \qquad M(\{q_0, q_1\}, b) = \{q_1, q_2\}$$

the mapping M' is defined as

$$M'([q_0, q_1], a) = [q_0, q_1] \qquad M'([q_0, q_1], b) = [q_1, q_2]$$

Similarly, the new state $[q_1, q_2]$ is added to K' and the mappings

$$M'([q_1, q_2], a) = [q_0, q_1] \qquad M'([q_1, q_2], b) = [q_0, q_1]$$

are defined. As no new states were created with the last mapping definitions, the creation of the DFA is nearly complete. The set of final states of F', which is all that is left to be defined, are those states of K' which contain an element of Z. In this example,

$$Z' = \{[q_2], [q_1, q_2]\}$$

The notion of a nondeterministic finite-state acceptor is extended to include state transitions with the empty string as input in the next subsection. The next subsection also shows that such an acceptor is no more powerful than an acceptor which cannot change state when reading the empty string.

4-4.3 Nondeterministic Finite-State Acceptors with ε-Transitions

In this subsection, nondeterministic finite-state acceptors are allowed to have state transitions with the empty string used as input. As might be expected, such an acceptor is no more powerful than the finite-state acceptors introduced in the

Table 4-4

State	Input	
	a	b
q_0	$\{q_0, q_1\}$	$\{q_2\}$
q_1	$\{q_0\}$	$\{q_1\}$
q_2	$\{q_1\}$	$\{q_0, q_1\}$

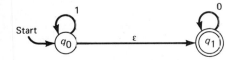

Start

Figure 4-8 A nondeterministic finite-state acceptor with ε-transitions.

previous subsections. Rather, it is a convenient construct for representing regular expressions.

The transition diagram for an NFA with ε-transitions is given in Fig. 4-8. This machine accepts strings of the form $1^m 0^n$ where $m, n \geq 0$. After reading a sequence of 1s from the input string, the acceptor changes to state q_1, before reading the 0s which follow. This is done by reading the empty string which is found between the last 1 and the first 0.

> **Definition 4-4** A *nondeterministic finite-state acceptor with ε-transitions* is a 5-tuple (K, V_T, M, S, Z), where K, V_T, S, and Z are the same as in Definition 4-3 and M is the mapping $K \times (V_T \cup \{\varepsilon\})$ into subsets of K.

Using this definition, the NFA depicted in Fig. 4-8 can be defined as $F = (\{q_0, q_1\}, \{0, 1\}, M, q_0, \{q_1\})$ with the mapping function defined by Table 4-5.

Before the equivalence of an NFA with ε-transitions and an NFA without ε-transitions can be proved, it is necessary to define ε-transitions and define the mapping function for $M(q, x)$ where $x \in V_T^*$.

> **Definition 4-5** ε-*CLOSURE* is a set of states of an NFA with ε-transitions, say F, such that ε-CLOSURE for some state of F, call it q, includes all states attainable from that state by making state transitions with ε-transitions. This is denoted by ε-CLOSURE(q).

In the example of Fig. 4-8, ε-CLOSURE(q_0) $= \{q_0, q_1\}$ and ε-CLOSURE(q_1) $= \{q_1\}$. Notice that ε-CLOSURE(q) for some state q invariably includes that state because a state can always be thought of as having an ε-transition to itself. Furthermore, ε-CLOSURE(P) $= \bigcup_{q \in P} \varepsilon$-CLOSURE($q$) for a set of states P. The definition of ε-CLOSURE allows the mapping function to

Table 4-5

	Input		
State	0	1	ε
q_0	ϕ	$\{q_0\}$	$\{q_1\}$
q_1	$\{q_1\}$	ϕ	ϕ

be extended with the definitions:

$$M(q, \varepsilon) = \varepsilon\text{-CLOSURE}(q)$$

$$M(q, Tt) = \varepsilon\text{-CLOSURE}(P) \text{ such that } T \in V_T, t \in V_T^*,$$

$$P = \{s | r \in M(q, T) \text{ and } s \in M(r, t)\}$$

The first definition states what the mapping of a state to a set of states is when the empty string is read. In the second case, the mapping $K \times V_T^+$ is defined, allowing the application of the mapping function to include strings.

It is now possible to show the equivalence of NFAs with ε-transitions to those without. The proof of the following theorem gives the method for constructing an NFA without ε-transitions.

Theorem 4-2 Define $F = (K, V_T, M, S, F)$ as an NFA with ε-transitions. Then there exists an NFA F' without ε-transitions such that $L(F) = L(F')$. In other words, the languages accepted by the two acceptors are the same.

PROOF Define an NFA F' without ε-transitions as (K, V_T, M', S, Z') where K, V_T, and S are the same as for F and

$$Z' = \begin{cases} Z \cup \{S\} & \text{if } \varepsilon\text{-CLOSURE}(S) \text{ contains a state of } Z \\ Z & \text{otherwise} \end{cases}$$

and $M'(q, a)$ is $M(q, a)$ for $q \in K$ and $a \in V_T$ where M is the mapping function M of F extended to strings. By induction on $|x|$ it is necessary to show that $M'(S, x) = M(S, x)$ if $|x| \geq 1$. Trivially if $x = \varepsilon$, then $M'(S, \varepsilon) = S$ and $M(S, \varepsilon) = \varepsilon\text{-CLOSURE}(S)$ and for F', $S \in Z$ if a final state is contained in $\varepsilon\text{-CLOSURE}(S)$ for F.

The inductive step is as follows. Assume $|x| \geq 1$ and $x = tT$ for $T \in V_T$ and $t \in V_T^*$. Then

$$M'(S, tT) = M'(M'(S, t), T)$$

$$= M'(M(S, t), T) \text{ by the inductive hypothesis}$$

Let $M(S, t) = P$. Then

$$M'(P, T) = \bigcup_{q \in P} M'(q, T) = \bigcup_{q \in P} M(q, T)$$

Thus,

$$\bigcup_{q \in P} M(q, T) = M(S, tT)$$

and

$$M'(S, tT) = M(S, tT)$$

We must show that $M'(S, x)$ contains a final state if and only if $M(S, x)$ contains a final state. It was previously shown that such is the case of $x = \varepsilon$. Consider $x = tT$ with $T \in V_T$ and $t \in V_T^*$. By the construction of F', if

Table 4-6

State	Input	
	0	1
q_0	$\{q_1\}$	$\{q_0, q_1\}$
q_1	$\{q_1\}$	ϕ

Figure 4-9

$M(S, x)$ contains a final state, then so does $M'(S, x)$. We must also show the converse; that is, $M(S, x)$ contains a final state if $M'(S, x)$ also does. Consider $M'(S, x)$ containing a state of Z' other than S. Then $M(S, x)$ must contain a corresponding final state, say, Z. This comes from the construction of F'. Furthermore, if $S \in M(S, x)$, then we have a state in ε-CLOSURE(S) and F also in $M(S, x)$ because $M(S, x) =$ ε-CLOSURE($M(M(S, t), T)$).

   Using the construction from the proof given above, an NFA without ε-transitions can be constructed from the NFA given near the beginning of this subsection. The acceptor $F' = (\{q_0, q_1\}, \{0,1\}, M', q_0, \{q_0, q_1\})$ has its mapping function as defined in Table 4-6. The transition diagram for F' is given in Fig. 4-9.
   This section has introduced three types of finite-state acceptors with each new acceptor appearing to be more powerful than the previous one. It was proven that the languages which can be accepted by each acceptor were the same, however. The next two sections demonstrate the equivalence of regular grammars and regular expressions to finite-state acceptors. Methods to convert from a regular grammar or a regular expression to a finite-state acceptor and vice versa are also described.

EXERCISES 4-4

1 Design a deterministic finite-state acceptor for sentences in $\{a, b\}$ such that every a has a b immediately to its right. Include the finite-state diagram for this acceptor.

2 Find a deterministic finite-state acceptor equivalent to the nondeterministic one given as

$$F = (\{q_0, q_1, q_2\}, \{a, b\}, M, q_0, \{q_2\})$$

where the mapping function M is defined in Table 4-7.

Table 4-7

State	Input	
	a	b
q_0	$\{q_0, q_1\}$	$\{q_2\}$
q_1	$\{q_0\}$	$\{q_1\}$
q_2	$\{q_1, q_2\}$	$\{q_0, q_1\}$

Table 4-8

State	Input		
	a	b	ε
q_0	$\{q_0, q_1\}$	$\{q_2\}$	ϕ
q_1	$\{q_0\}$	$\{q_1\}$	$\{q_0, q_2\}$
q_2	ϕ	$\{q_0, q_1\}$	$\{q_1\}$

3 Convert the nondeterministic finite-state acceptor with ε-transitions defined as

$$F = (\{q_0, q_1, q_2\}, \{a, b\}, M, q_0, \{q_2\})$$

to one without ε-transitions. The mapping function is given in Table 4-8.

4 Convert the nondeterministic finite-state acceptor of Exercise 3 to a deterministic finite-state acceptor.

5 Construct a nondeterministic finite-state acceptor which accepts all strings over $\{0, 1\}$ having at least one 1.

4-5 EQUIVALENCE OF REGULAR GRAMMARS AND FINITE-STATE ACCEPTORS

The equivalence of regular grammars and finite-state acceptors is shown in this section. First, a method for constructing an NFA from a regular grammar is given. Then a way of converting a DFA to a regular grammar is illustrated, completing the proof that the languages accepted by finite-state acceptors are the same as the languages which can be produced by regular grammars.

The following theorem and proof provide the procedure for converting a regular grammar to a nondeterministic finite-state acceptor.

Theorem 4-3 There exists a nondeterministic finite-state acceptor $F = (K, V_T, M, S, Z)$ which accepts the language generated by the regular grammar $G = (V_N, V_T, S, \Phi)$.

PROOF Define the NFA F with the states of F being $V_N \cup \{X\}$ where $X \notin V_N$. The initial state of the acceptor is S (the start symbol of the grammar), and its final state is X. For each production of the grammar, construct the mapping M from Φ in the following manner:

1. $A_j \in M(A_i, a)$ if there is a production $A_i \to aA_j$ in G.
2. $X \in M(A_i, a)$ if there is a production $A_i \to a$ in G.

The acceptor F, when processing sentence x, simulates a derivation of x in the grammar G. It is necessary to show that $L(F) = L(G)$. Let $x = a_1 a_2 \cdots a_m, m \geq 1$, be in the language $L(G)$. Then there exists some derivation in G such that

$$S \Rightarrow a_1 A_1 \Rightarrow a_1 a_2 A_2 \Rightarrow \cdots \Rightarrow a_1 a_2 \cdots a_{m-1} A_{m-1} \Rightarrow a_1 a_2 \cdots a_m$$

for a sequence of nonterminals $A_1, A_2, \ldots, A_{m-1}$. From the construction of M, it is clear that $M(S, a_1)$ contains A_1, $M(A_1, a_2)$ contains $A_2, \ldots,$ and $M(A_{m-1}, a_m)$ contains X. Therefore, $x \in L(F)$ since $M(S, x)$ contains X and $X \in Z$.

Conversely, if $x \in L(F)$, a derivation of G which simulates the acceptance of x in F can be easily obtained, thereby concluding that $x \in L(G)$.

To illustrate how an NFA is constructed from a regular grammar, consider the grammar $G = (V_N, V_T, S, \Phi)$ where $V_N = \{S, A, B\}$, $V_T = \{a, b\}$, the set of productions Φ are:

1. $S \to aS$ 4. $A \to aB$
2. $S \to bA$ 5. $B \to b$
3. $A \to aA$

and which generates strings of the form $a^m b a^n b$ where $m \geq 0$ and $n \geq 1$. Define an NFA $F = (K, V_T, M, S, Z)$ where $K = \{S, A, B, X\}$, $V_T = \{a, b\}$, $Z = \{X\}$, and M is given by

1. $M(S, a) = \{S\}$ from the production $S \to aS$.
2. $M(S, b) = \{A\}$ from the production $S \to bA$.
3. $M(A, a) = \{A, B\}$ from the productions $A \to aA$ and $A \to aB$.
4. $M(B, b) = \{X\}$ from the production $B \to b$.
5. $M(A, b) = M(B, a) = \phi$ since there are no productions corresponding to these mappings.

Then F is a nondeterministic finite-state acceptor which accepts the language represented by the regular grammar G.

Just as a nondeterministic finite-state acceptor can be constructed from a regular grammar in a straightforward manner, a regular grammar also can be derived from a deterministic finite-state acceptor in a simple way. The following theorem, like the previous theorem, furnishes the procedure needed to construct a regular grammar.

Theorem 4-4 There exists a regular grammar $G = (V_N, V_T, S, \Phi)$ which produces the language accepted by a given deterministic finite-state acceptor $F = (K, V_T, M, S, Z)$.

PROOF Define the regular grammar G with the states of K being the nonterminals of G. The starting symbol of G is S (the starting state of F), and the set of productions are defined as:

1. $A_i \rightarrow aA_j \in \Phi$ if $M(A_i, a) = A_j$.
2. $A_i \rightarrow a \in \Phi$ if $M(A_i, a) = A_j$ and $A_j \in Z$.

It must be shown that $S \overset{*}{\Rightarrow} x$ if and only if $M(S, x) \in Z$ for $|x| \geq 1$. In the case of $x = \varepsilon$ and $M(S, x) \in Z$, add the production $S \rightarrow \varepsilon$ to Φ.

Let $x = a_1 a_2 \cdots a_n \in L(F)$ and $n \geq 1$. Then there is the set of transitions:

$$M(S, a_1) = A_1, \ M(A_1, a_2) = A_2, \ldots, M(A_{n-1}, a_n) = A_n$$

where A_n is a final state of F. Thus G contains the productions

$$S \rightarrow a_1 A_1, \ A_1 \rightarrow a_2 A_2, \ldots, A_{n-1} \rightarrow a_n$$

and the grammar G can produce strings accepted by F.

Conversely, if $x \in L(G)$, then an acceptance of x in F which simulates a derivation in G can be easily obtained, thereby concluding that $x \in L(F)$.

To illustrate the conversion of a deterministic finite-state acceptor to a regular grammar, consider the acceptor $F = (\{S, A, B, C\}, \{0, 1\}, M, S, \{S\})$ where the mapping function is given in Table 4-9. This DFA accepts strings which have an even number of 0s and 1s. Using the method for constructing a regular grammar as given in Theorem 4-4, the grammar G is defined as $G = (\{S, A, B, C\}, \{0, 1\}$ $S, \Phi)$, where Φ is defined as

1. $S \rightarrow 0B$	7. $B \rightarrow 0S$
2. $S \rightarrow 1A$	8. $B \rightarrow 0$
3. $S \rightarrow \varepsilon$	9. $B \rightarrow 1C$
4. $A \rightarrow 0C$	10. $C \rightarrow 0A$
5. $A \rightarrow 1S$	11. $C \rightarrow 1B$
6. $A \rightarrow 1$	

Table 4-9

	Input	
State	0	1
S	B	A
A	C	S
B	S	C
C	A	B

Because S is a final state, wherever a production of the form $\alpha \to \beta S$ occurs, the production $\alpha \to \beta$ is also included in Φ. The production $S \to \varepsilon$ is also in Φ because $S \in Z$ in the DFA.

Because nondeterministic finite-state acceptors are equivalent to deterministic acceptors, the equivalence of finite-state acceptors to regular grammars has been established by Theorems 4-3 and 4-4. Thus regular grammars may be used to represent scanners which are implemented as finite-state acceptors. However, regular expressions are more easily used to depict scanners, and demonstrating the equivalence of regular expressions to finite-state acceptors is the topic of the next section.

EXERCISES 4-5

1 Convert the grammar G to a finite-state acceptor where $G = (\{A, B, C, D\}, \{0,1\}, A, \Phi)$ and Φ is defined as

  1. $A \to 0B$
  2. $A \to 1C$
  3. $B \to 1A$
  4. $C \to 0C$
  5. $C \to 0D$
  6. $C \to 1$
  7. $D \to 0$

2 Derive a regular grammar from the deterministic finite-state acceptor $F = (\{A, B, C\}, \{a, b\}, M, A, \{C\})$, where M is defined in Table 4-10.

3 This exercise illustrates the idea that because more than one finite-state acceptor can accept the same language, the results of converting an NFA to a DFA, the resulting DFA to a regular grammar,

Table 4-10

	Input	
State	a	b
A	A	B
B	A	C
C	C	B

Table 4-11

	Input		
State	0	1	2
A	$\{A, B\}$	$\{C\}$	$\{D\}$
B	$\{A\}$	$\{B, D\}$	ϕ
C	$\{B\}$	$\{A, B\}$	$\{E\}$
D	ϕ	$\{A, B, D\}$	$\{C\}$
E	$\{E\}$	ϕ	$\{C, E\}$

and finally the regular grammar back to an NFA, using the methods of the previous two sections, does not necessarily result in the same NFA. Perform these steps on the acceptor $(\{A, B, C, D, E\},$ $\{0, 1, 2\}, M, A, \{C, E\})$, where the mapping function is defined in Table 4-11.

4-6 EQUIVALENCE OF REGULAR EXPRESSIONS AND FINITE-STATE ACCEPTORS

Regular expressions, which were introduced in Sec. 4-3, are often used as a convenient way of describing scanners. The importance of this will become evident in the next section when a scanner generator which uses regular expressions as input is presented. This section details the methods for generating a finite-state acceptor from a regular expression or turning a finite-state acceptor into a regular expression. In so doing, it will be shown that regular expressions and finite-state acceptors are equivalent. After recalling the theories of the previous section, it then can be seen that the languages which can be derived from regular grammars and regular expressions are the same.

It is conceptually easier to understand how a regular expression can be converted to a finite-state acceptor by using a transition diagram. Before proceeding, however, it is useful to show how the three regular expressions ε, ϕ, and ρ, where $\rho \in V_T$, are represented in a transition diagram. Figure 4-10 illustrates the finite-state diagrams associated with each of these expressions. The expression ε is drawn in Fig. 4-10a and indicates that no state transition occurs on empty input (ε-transitions will be included later). Figure 4-10b indicates that the regular expression ϕ does not accept any input string, including ε, and the transition that occurs with the regular expression ρ is exhibited in Fig. 4-10c.

With the transition diagrams of Fig. 4-10 representing the most simple regular expressions, more complex regular expressions can be developed using the

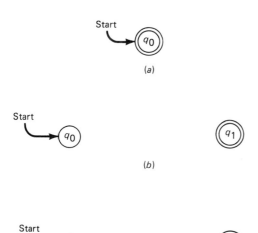

Start

q_0

(a)

Start

q_0

q_1

(b)

Start

q_0 —————ρ————— q_1

(c)

Figure 4-10 Transition diagrams for the regular expressions ε, ϕ, and ρ.

operations of alternation, concatenation, and closure. Figure 4-11 illustrates how two regular expressions, r_1 and r_2, may be represented by an NFA with ε-transitions when one of the operations is applied. In each case, a new starting state S and a new final state Z have been created, both of which are states separate from the finite-state acceptors representing r_1 and r_2. An arc leading into an expression r_1 or r_2 represents a transition to the starting state of the FSA representing that expression, while the arc leading out of the FSA for an expression depicts a transition from the final state of the acceptor to the next state.

The transition diagram for the expression $r_1|r_2$ is given in Fig. 4-11a. As the acceptor must accept one of r_1 and r_2, ε-transitions from the starting state to the FSAs for r_1 and r_2 are drawn. Concatenation, which is illustrated in Fig. 4-11b for the expression r_1r_2, makes an ε-transition from r_1 to r_2 necessary as well as one from the starting state to r_1 and r_2 to the final state. Figure 4-11c depicts the FSA for the expression $\{r_1\}$. The ε-transition from the final state of r_1 to its starting state permits more than one repetition of r_1 by the finite-state acceptor. Zero occurrences of the expression are allowed with the ε-transition from the starting state S to the final state Z.

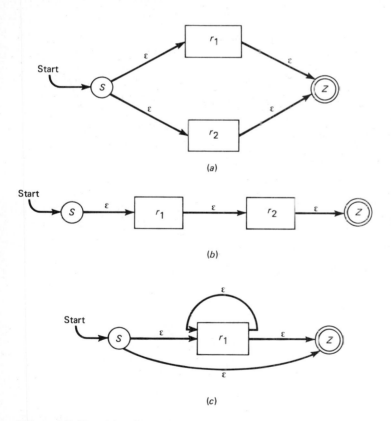

(a)

(b)

(c)

Figure 4-11 Transition diagrams for the expressions $r_1|r_2$, r_1r_2, and $\{r_1\}$.

To demonstrate how the rules for constructing an NFA with ε-transitions from a regular expression may be applied, the regular expression $0\{1|23\}$ is used. Figure 4-12 illustrates the steps involved in creating the acceptor from this expression. By rewriting the expression in a fully parenthesized form, the order of evaluation becomes more evident and the finite-state acceptor can be created in a step-by-step manner starting with the operators to be evaluated first. Hence the expression can be written as $0\{1|(23)\}$. With the terminal symbols of the expression being the set $\{0, 1, 2, 3\}$, the first operation to be performed is

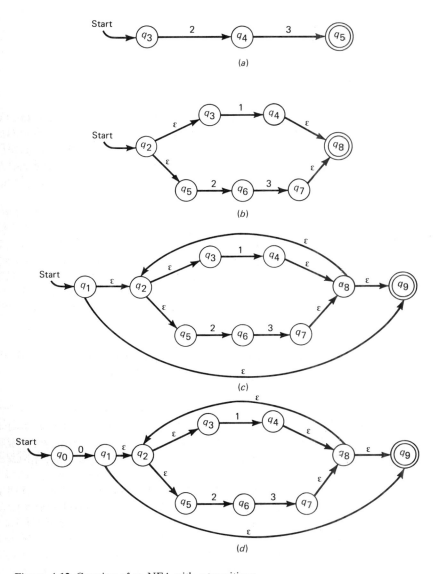

Figure 4-12 Creation of an NFA with ε-transitions.

the concatenation of the two subexpressions 2 and 3. The finite-state acceptor for
the resulting expression 23 is created as shown in Fig. 4-12a. Then the alternation
operator is applied to the two subexpressions 1 and 23, resulting in the finite-state
acceptor of Fig. 4-12b. Figure 4-12c gives the finite-state acceptor for the
expression {1|(23)} once closure has been applied to the preceding expression.
Finally, the zero concatenated with the expression of Fig. 4-12c gives the entire
regular expression, and the finite-state acceptor which is produced is given in Fig.
4-12d. For simplicity, several ε-transitions in Fig. 4-12a were eliminated.

Theorem 4-5 Given a regular expression R, there exists an NFA with
ε-transitions, F, which accepts the language generated by R.

PROOF Only an outline of the proof is given to sketch how an NFA with
ε-transitions is constructed. Details of this proof can be found in Hopcroft
and Ullman (1979), pages 30–32.

The proof is done by induction on each of the three operators found in
regular expressions. In the case of alternation in which the FSAs for the two
subexpressions r_1 and r_2 are $F_1 = (K_1, V_{T_1}, M_1, S_1, Z_1)$ and $F_2 =
(K_2, V_{T_2}, M_2, S_2, Z_2)$, respectively, a new FSA $F = (K, V_T, M, S, Z)$ is defined
as follows: $V_T = V_{T_1} \cup V_{T_2}$, $K = K_1 \cup K_2 \cup \{S, X\}$, where $Z = \{X\}$ and
the sets K_1, K_2, and $\{S, X\}$ are all disjoint. Then the mapping function is
defined as $M = M_1 \cup M_2$ with the following mappings also given:

$$M(S, \varepsilon) = \{S_1, S_2\} \quad \text{and} \quad M(Z_1, \varepsilon) = M(Z_2, \varepsilon) = \{X\}$$

For concatenation, the new FSA is defined as $F = (K, V_T, M, S, Z)$, where K
and V_T are the same as with alternation, and the mapping function is defined
as $M = M_1 \cup M_2$ with the mappings

$$M(S, \varepsilon) = \{S_1\} \quad M(Z_1, \varepsilon) = \{S_2\} \quad \text{and} \quad M(Z_2, \varepsilon) = \{X\}$$

also included with $X \in Z$. Closure requires a new acceptor $F' =
(K', V_T, M', S', Z')$ which is created from the original acceptor $F =
(K, V_T, M, S, Z)$, where $K' = K \cup \{S', X\}$, $Z' = \{X\}$ and M' has the same
mappings as M but with the additions

$$M'(S', \varepsilon) = M'(Z, \varepsilon) = \{S, X\}$$

It is shown by induction that with the application of an operator to the
regular expressions as just described, the newly created finite-state acceptor
accepts the same language as is generated by the expression resulting from
the application of the operator.

Using the regular expression $0\{1|(23)\}$ from the previous example, an FSA
can be derived as $F = (\{q_0, q_1, \ldots, q_9\}, \{0, 1, 2, 3\}, M, q_0, \{q_9\})$ where the
mapping function is defined in Table 4-12. This NFA with ε-transitions is created
by the application of the rules of construction given in the preceding proof to the
expression starting with the most nested operators, as was done when transition
diagrams were used in the previous example.

Table 4-12

State	0	1	2	3	ε
			Input		
q_0	$\{q_1\}$	ϕ	ϕ	ϕ	ϕ
q_1	ϕ	ϕ	ϕ	ϕ	$\{q_2, q_9\}$
q_2	ϕ	ϕ	ϕ	ϕ	$\{q_3, q_5\}$
q_3	ϕ	$\{q_4\}$	ϕ	ϕ	ϕ
q_4	ϕ	ϕ	ϕ	ϕ	$\{q_8\}$
q_5	ϕ	ϕ	$\{q_6\}$	ϕ	ϕ
q_6	ϕ	ϕ	ϕ	$\{q_7\}$	ϕ
q_7	ϕ	ϕ	ϕ	ϕ	$\{q_8\}$
q_8	ϕ	ϕ	ϕ	ϕ	$\{q_2, q_9\}$
q_9	ϕ	ϕ	ϕ	ϕ	ϕ

The combination of the previous and following theorem will establish the equivalence of regular expressions and finite-state acceptors. Because FSAs and regular grammars are also equivalent, it can be seen that regular grammars and regular expressions are equivalent.

Theorem 4-6 Given a deterministic finite-state acceptor which accepts the language L, there exists a regular expression which denotes L.

PROOF As was the case with the previous theorem, only an outline of the proof is given. For details of the proof, see Hopcroft and Ullman (1979), pages 33 and 34.

For the DFA $F = (\{q_1, q_2, \ldots, q_n\}, V_T, M, S, Z)$, R_{ij}^k is defined to be the set of all strings x such that $M(q_i, x) = q_j$ and for any prefix of x, say, y, but not including x or ε, then $M(q_i, y) = q_l$ and $l \le k$. Thus R_{ij}^k is the set of all strings taking the acceptor from state q_i to state q_j without reaching a state numbered greater than k. Then R_{ij}^k can be recursively defined as follows:

$$R_{ij}^k = R_{ik}^{k-1}(R_{kk}^{k-1})^*R_{kj}^{k-1} \cup R_{ij}^{k-1} \qquad \text{for } k \ge 1$$

$$R_{ij}^0 = \begin{cases} \{a|M(q_i, a) = q_j\} & \text{if } i \ne j \\ \{a|M(q_i, a) = q_j\} \cup \{\varepsilon\} & \text{if } i = j \end{cases}$$

It is then shown by induction that for all i, j, and k, a regular expression r_{ij}^k denoting the language R_{ij}^k can be found, starting with R_{ij}^0 as the basis. Finally, the language L accepted by F can be represented as $\bigcup_{q_j \in Z} R_{1j}^n$, where the largest state of F is q_n. Thus the regular expression is given by $r_{1j_1}^n|r_{1j_2}^n| \cdots |r_{1j_m}^n$ where $j_1, j_2, \ldots, j_m$ are final states of F.

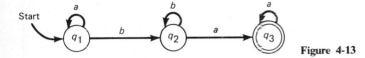

Figure 4-13

The proof of Theorem 4-6 provides the procedure for finding a regular expression which denotes the language accepted by a DFA. Notice that the equation

$$R_{ij}^k = R_{ik}^{k-1}(R_{kk}^{k-1})^* R_{kj}^{k-1} \cup R_{ij}^{k-1}$$

can be represented by the regular-expression equation

$$r_{ij}^k = r_{ik}^{k-1}\{r_{kk}^{k-1}\} r_{kj}^{k-1} | r_{ij}^{k-1}$$

An example should illustrate how this method can be used to create a regular expression. The transition diagram of a DFA which accepts strings of the form $a^m b^n a^p$ where $m \geq 0$ and $n, p \geq 1$ is given in Fig. 4-13. The values of all r_{ij}^k for this DFA are listed in Table 4-13 after they have been simplified. The first column of the table, with $k = 0$, requires that an intermediate state cannot be greater than q_0. As the smallest state is q_1, any expression r_{ij}^0 can only generate a single character or an intermediate state would be required in going from state q_i to state q_j. The expression can also be the empty string if q_i and q_j are the same state. Thus the expression r_{11}^0 can be either the empty-string expression or the expression a, and r_{12}^0 can be the expression b. The expression r_{11}^k, where k is 1, 2, or 3, gives the expression $\{a\}$. Only q_1 can be an intermediate state if q_1 is also to be the end state. The expression for r_{12}^1 is $\{a\}b$ because only q_1 can be an intermediate state. For the expressions r_{12}^2 and r_{12}^3, the expression $\{a\}b\{b\}$ is derived as intermediate states q_1 and q_2 are allowed. The expressions r_{12}^2 and r_{12}^3 are the same, since q_3 cannot be an intermediate state if q_2 is the end state. As the only final state for this DFA is q_3, the regular expression for the DFA is $r_{13}^3 = \{a\}b\{b\}a\{a\}$.

Table 4-13

k	0	1	2	3
r_{11}^k	$\varepsilon \mid a$	$\{a\}$	$\{a\}$	$\{a\}$
r_{12}^k	b	$\{a\}b$	$\{a\}b\{b\}$	$\{a\}b\{b\}$
r_{13}^k	ϕ	ϕ	$\{a\}b\{b\}a$	$\{a\}b\{b\}a\{a\}$
r_{21}^k	ϕ	ϕ	ϕ	ϕ
r_{22}^k	$\varepsilon \mid b$	$\varepsilon \mid b$	$\{b\}$	$\{b\}$
r_{23}^k	a	a	$\{b\}a$	$\{b\}a\{a\}$
r_{31}^k	ϕ	ϕ	ϕ	ϕ
r_{32}^k	ϕ	ϕ	ϕ	ϕ
r_{33}^k	$\varepsilon \mid a$	$\varepsilon \mid a$	$\varepsilon \mid a$	$\{a\}$

To illustrate further how some expressions r_{ij}^k are derived and simplified, the following examples are given:

$$r_{12}^1 = r_{11}^0 \{ r_{11}^0 \} r_{12}^0 | r_{12}^0$$
$$= (\varepsilon | a)\{\varepsilon | a\} b | b$$
$$= (\varepsilon | a)\{ a \} b | b$$
$$= \{ a \} b$$

$$r_{13}^2 = r_{12}^1 \{ r_{22}^1 \} r_{23}^1 | r_{13}^1$$
$$= \{ a \} b \{ \varepsilon | b \} a | \phi$$
$$= \{ a \} b \{ b \} a | \phi$$
$$= \{ a \} b \{ b \} a$$

$$r_{31}^3 = r_{33}^2 \{ r_{33}^2 \} r_{31}^2 | r_{31}^2$$
$$= (\varepsilon | a)\{\varepsilon | a\} \phi | \phi$$
$$= \phi | \phi$$
$$= \phi$$

This section has shown that regular expressions and finite-state acceptors both represent the same class of languages. Methods of converting from one form to the other also were described. The next section uses regular expressions to describe scanners for a scanner generator.

EXERCISES 4-6

1 Convert the regular expression

$$\{ \{ 0 | 1 \} 2 \} | \{ 01 \} | 10$$

to a finite-state acceptor using transition diagrams.

2 Repeat Exercise 1 using the method introduced in the proof of Theorem 4-5.

3 Show that the methods of constructing an FSA from a regular expression using either transition diagrams or the method of Theorem 4-5 are the same.

4 Convert the DFA

$$F = (\{ A, B, C, D \}, \{ 0, 1, 2 \}, M, A, \{ B, D \})$$

with the mapping function given in Table 4-14 to a regular expression.

Table 4-14

State	Input 0	Input 1	Input 2
A	A	A	B
B	B	C	C
C	A	B	D
D	C	C	D

4-7 A SCANNER GENERATOR

The first two sections of this chapter introduced scanners and discussed the tasks which scanners usually perform. The next three sections introduced mathematical models which are useful for programming a scanner in a systematic manner and for creating a scanner using a scanner generator. This section introduces a scanner generator which uses regular expressions as input.

Because the implementation of finite-state acceptors is straightforward, programs have been written which can mechanically generate scanners using a formal method of specifying a finite-state acceptor as input. This subsection introduces one such scanner generator called *Lex*, written by Lesk and Schmidt (1975), which uses regular expressions for specifying a scanner.

Using a set of regular expressions and associated segments of code called *actions* which dictate the tasks associated with each expression, Lex generates a transition table and a program which interprets the tables. An action is executed whenever a token that can be generated by the corresponding regular expression is recognized. Thus, the output from Lex is a program which simulates a finite-state acceptor and performs the additional functions which are associated with the final states of the acceptor. The scanner generated by Lex can be used in conjunction with a parser generator (specifically the program YACC, which was written by Johnson, 1975) for the lexical and syntactic phases of compilation.

The input to Lex, which consists of three parts, has the format

definitions
%%
translation rules
%%
user subprograms

Any section may be empty, but the sections must be separated from each other by a %%.

The definitions section consists of a sequence of statements of the form

name expression

where *name* can be used in any regular expression given later in the Lex input for representing the *regular expression* on the right. *Name* is a valid identifier and is separated from the *expression* by at least one blank. Thus the definition section allows a shorthand notation to be used for, say, the set of digits, within a complex expression. For example, the digits and letters can be represented by

digit 0|1|2|3|4|5|6|7|8|9
letter a|b|c|d|e| $\cdots$ |z|A|B|C|D| $\cdots$ |Z

and an identifier as

iden letter {letter|digit}

We have not been using the format specifications for regular expressions in Lex precisely. This would require a lengthy explanation of the syntax of Lex input and the features which are available in Lex. There are additional regular-expression operators in Lex which, while not making regular expressions more powerful, allow for more convenient methods of specifying tokens. A blank which is normally used to separate an expression from its action must be enclosed in quotes if it is to be included as a character within a regular expression. For the simplicity of this discussion, we use the method of specifying regular expressions which has been used throughout this chapter. The reader should refer to the reference manual by Lesk and Schmidt (1975) for details about Lex.

The translation rules section consists of a sequence of rules of the form

expression action

where each *expression* is a regular expression and *action* is a sequence of code to be executed. Action consists of a piece of code written in the programming language C and is surrounded by braces if more than one C statement is used.

Because the scanner produced by Lex attempts to match one of the set of regular expressions to a sequence of input characters, it can really be considered a deterministic finite-state acceptor of the form

$$r_1|r_2| \cdots |r_n$$

where each r_i is a regular expression found in the translation rules section. An additional feature of Lex over a DFA is that each r_i has an action which is executed if the next input token is matched to that expression.

The scanner matches the longest sequence of input characters to a regular expression. Finally, if two or more regular expressions can produce the token found in the input text for the scanner, a match with the first regular expression occurs. For example, the keyword DO might be recognized in a scanner by the regular expression which specifically matches DO and by the regular expression which matches identifiers. A match with the expression for the keyword DO would occur if it is the first expression listed.

As was mentioned in Sec. 4-2, lookahead can be a useful feature for determining what the next token in the input text is. This feature is available in Lex and is designated by a slash (/) separating two regular expressions. (The character slash is indicated in a regular expression by enclosing it within quotes, i.e., '/'.) The token consists of the input text which is read and can be produced by the regular expression preceding the slash; the input text which follows must be a derivation of the regular expression following the slash in order for a match to occur.

Consider the FORTRAN example from Sec. 4-2 which required lookahead in order to determine if DO10I was just one token or the three tokens DO, 10, and I. If it is three tokens, it is a part of a loop statement which has a comma after the equals sign and an identifier or a constant. The specification for identifying DO as the first token of a loop statement would be

DO/{letter|digit} = {letter|digit},

If this expression fails on the input text, DO is considered as a part of an identifier.

Figure 4-14 illustrates the input to Lex for describing a simple scanner which accepts the same language as the scanner SCAN of Sec. 4-2. The code for the actions is written in C, and the values returned by the actions are the internal representation numbers for the token which can be derived from the corresponding regular expression. The variable token contains the token which was just identified in the input string.

The function keyword returns the internal representation number of the keyword. Zero is returned if the token is not a keyword. The functions *ins_iden*, *ins_cons*, and *ins_lit* perform the symbol-table maintenance routines for identifiers, constants, and string literals, respectively, and each returns the position of the token that was inserted into the table. These subprograms are to be written by the programmer.

For most of the tokens, the scanner just returns the internal representation number. For constants and literals, however, the constant or literal is inserted into the constant table or the literal table, respectively, and the position is stored in the variable called position before returning the representation number. Position is assumed to be a global variable which gives the position where a token was stored in the symbol table to the parser. If the token is matched to the fifteenth regular

```
letter                          A | B | C | D | ••• | Z

digit                           0 | 1 | 2 | 3 | 4 | 5 | 6 | 7 | 8 | 9

%%

<                               return (1);

<=                              return (2);

=                               return (3);

>=                              return (4);

>                               return (5);

<>                              return (6);

"("                             return (7);

")"                             return (8);

+                               return (9);

−                               return (10);

*                               return (11);

"/"                             return (12);

:=                              return (13);

;                               return (14);
```

Figure 4-14 Example input to Lex program.

letter { letter | digit }

```
                                        if (keyword (token) !=0)

                                                return (keyword (token));

                                        else    {

                                                position = ins_iden (token);

                                                return (15);

                                                }
```

digit { digit }

```
                                                {

                                                position = ins_cons (token);

                                                return (16);

                                                }
```

' { letter | digit | "(" | ")" |

    + | − | * | "/" | : | ; |

    " " | > | < | = | (') } '

```
                                                {

                                                position = ins_lit (token);

                                                return (17);

                                                }
```

"/" * { letter | digit | "(" | ")" | + | − | "/" | : | ; |

    " " | > | < | ' | = } { *

    (letter | digit | "(" | ")" | + | − | : | ; | " " | > | < | = | ')

    {letter | digit | "(" | ")" | + | − | "/" | : | ; | " " | > | < |

    = | ' } | * } * "/"   return (0);

%%

code for the procedures keyword, ins_iden, ins_cons, and ins_lit.

Figure 4-14 (*Continued*).

expression, a call to the keyword function determines if the token is a keyword. If it is, the representation number of the keyword is returned; otherwise it is an identifier, and the position where the identifier is stored in the symbol table and its internal representation number are returned.

The scanner returns 0 when a comment has been identified. Because comments are to be ignored, the calling program can call the scanner again to determine the next token in the input stream.

If the input string contains the sequence < = , the < can be matched by the first, second, and sixth regular expressions. Because an equal sign follows, however, the expression < > is rejected, and so is the first one, since the second expression can match an additional character. Thus the scanner returns the value 2.

In this chapter, regular grammars, regular expressions, and finite-state acceptors were introduced. These topics provided an understanding of how scanners are constructed by hand or how a lexical analyzer is specified to a scanner generator. Parsing, the next phase of compilation, uses the internal representation numbers of the tokens identified by the scanner for performing syntactic analysis and is the topic of Chaps. 6 and 7.

EXERCISES 4-7

1 What are the advantages and disadvantages of using a scanner generator such as Lex to coding a scanner by hand?

2 Write a Lex program that will generate a scanner for the language you have designed for your term project.

BIBLIOGRAPHY

Aho, A. V., and J. D. Ullman: *Principles of Compiler Design*, Reading, Mass.: Addison-Wesley, 1977.

Aho, A. V., and J. D. Ullman: *The Theory of Parsing, Translation, and Compiling*, Vol. 1, *Parsing*, Englewood Cliffs, N.J.: Prentice-Hall, 1972.

Barrett, W. A., and J. D. Couch: *Compiler Construction: Theory and Practice*, Chicago: Science Research Associates, Inc., 1979.

Gries, D.: *Compiler Construction for Digital Computers*, New York: John Wiley & Sons, 1971.

Hopcroft, J. E., and J. D. Ullman: *Formal Languages and Their Relation to Automata*, Reading, Mass.: Addison-Wesley, 1969.

Hopcroft, J. E., and J. D. Ullman: *Introduction to Automata Theory, Languages, and Computation*, Reading, Mass.: Addison-Wesley, 1979.

Johnson, S. C.: "Yacc: Yet Another Compiler-Compiler," Computing Services Technical Report No. 32, Bell Laboratories, Murray Hill, N.J., 1975.

Lesk, M. E., and E. Schmidt: "Lex—A Lexical Analyzer Generator," Computing Science Technical Report No. 39, Bell Laboratories, Murray Hill, N. J., 1975.

Lewis, P. M. II, D. J. Rosenkrantz, and R. E. Stearns: *Compiler Design Theory*, Reading, Mass.: Addison-Wesley, 1976.

COMPILE-TIME ERROR HANDLING

Because of the nature of the programming process, a programming language translator is more often confronted with syntactically erroneous programs than with correct ones. Thus the translator must have some strategy for dealing with source programs which are invalid with respect to the rules of the programming language. The response to errors can lie anywhere in the continuum between total collapse of the translator and complete correction of the erroneous program.

This chapter presents a classification of responses to errors with emphasis on what is desirable, what is undesirable, and what is possible with current techniques. Section 5-1 presents an overview of compile-time error handling. Section 5-2 discusses the problems of syntactic error detection in a compiler. Section 5-3 proposes guidelines for the reporting of compiler-detected errors. Sections 5-4 and 5-5 survey error recovery and error repair, respectively.

Sections in Chaps. 6 and 7 present the details of error-handling techniques which are applicable to particular methods of syntax analysis.

5-1 OVERVIEW OF ERROR HANDLING

This section of the chapter classifies the levels of error responses which could conceivably be found in a compiler. We indicate which of these responses are desirable, which are practical, and why. The classification, which is based on Horning (1976), is summarized in Table 5-1.

Table 5-1 Classification of error responses

I. Unacceptable responses
   1. Incorrect responses (error not reported)
      a. Compiler crashes
      b. Compiler loops indefinitely
      c. Compiler continues, producing incorrect object program
   2. Correct (but nearly useless)
      a. Compiler reports first error and then halts
II. Acceptable responses
   1. Possible responses
      a. Compiler reports error and *recovers*, continuing to find later errors if they exist
      b. Compiler reports the error and *repairs* it, continuing the translation and producing a valid object program
   2. Impossible with current techniques
      a. Compiler *corrects* error and produces an object program which is the translation of what the programmer intended to write

---

The lowest level of response to errors is no planned response at all. This type of response might occur in a compiler produced by designers and programmers who never considered the possibility of invalid programs being submitted to the compiler. The compiler might go totally out of control, crashing or going into an unbounded loop. Or it might ignore the error and generate an invalid object program which the user might reasonably believe to be correct. The latter is especially dangerous, because the incorrect translation will show up only when the object program is actually run, perhaps obliterating a portion of a vital data file. Because such a compiler is useless and possibly dangerous, no self-respecting compiler writer allows the release of a compiler which responds to errors in this way. Such behavior can be prevented by careful and consistent design. The same discipline should be applied to compiler writing as to every other software project. Ensuring a correct, bounded, and stable reaction to all possible inputs is a key responsibility of the software engineer.

The next level of error handling is found in compilers constructed by programmers who consider errors in programs to be a rare occurrence. These compilers are capable of detecting and reporting errors—but only at the rate of one per compilation. When an error is detected in the source program, such a compiler reports the error and then halts. The authors of such a compiler may feel morally justified in that the compiler responds correctly to errors. However, the user of a compiler requires a more useful response to errors. The ability to detect one error per compilation is a step upward, but only a small one. The repeated compilations necessary to catch the compile-time detectable errors are a waste of computer time and of programmer time. This time would be better spent in thorough testing of the program to detect its run-time deficiencies.

As indicated in Table 5-1, we classify the aforementioned levels of error handling as unacceptable responses. Our criterion in making this judgment is the safety and convenience of the user, who is, after all, paying for the use of the compiler. We now describe three levels of acceptable error handling, only two of which are currently attainable.

The least ambitious acceptable approach to error handling is *error recovery*. The recovering compiler adjusts its internal data structures and its input stream so that it may continue parsing and checking the program as if nothing has gone wrong. A parser normally checks for the total syntactic validity of a program. The recovering parser localizes the effects of syntactic errors so that it may check the local syntactic validity of other parts of the program. The goal of error recovery is to allow the compiler to continue checking the input for further compile-time detectable errors and to report and recover from these errors as well.

Ideally, a compiler would recover so thoroughly that it would generate exactly one fully descriptive message reporting an error and would not generate further messages due to that error. Such recovery is not a trivial task. Poor error-recovery methods, including the nonmethod of simply ignoring the error, lead to an avalanche of messages produced by one programmer error. Such an avalanche can and must be avoided, since the user begins to ignore messages if they are profuse and inaccurate. The avalanche is avoided by taking care to adjust the state of the parser so that it is ready to accept the remainder of the program if it is valid.

Far more difficult to avoid is the occurrence of multiple messages later in the compilation due to information lost in the original error. For example, if a declaration is erroneous and the compiler fails to locate the attributes of a variable X, then all later occurrences of X may be flagged as erroneous because the attributes of X are incorrect. The adjustment of the parser state just mentioned must include the adjustment of the contents of the various tables maintained by the compiler during compilation. It can become excessively difficult and time-consuming to derive lost information from other parts of the program and fix up these tables. As long as the reason for the extra messages is clear to the user, and as long as these messages are few in number, it is probably not worthwhile to attempt to eliminate all of them.

The next acceptable level of error handling is *error repair*. Error repair is a form of error recovery which modifies the source or internal form of the erroneous program to make it syntactically valid. Other parts of the compiler may assume syntactically valid inputs, and translation may be performed. This requirement on the error recovery makes the compiler larger and more complex but has the advantage that the resulting object program can be executed to discover errors in programming which are undetectable at compile time. The repaired program text may be provided to the user as an error diagnostic—the repair may suggest how the error should be corrected and will certainly make subsequent messages easier to understand. In some environments these capabilities may be highly desirable, while in others they may be quite undesirable. They are most common in student compilers, notably PL/C (Conway and Wilcox, 1973) and SP/k (Barnard 1975). The ability to run programs with repaired errors is most useful on batch-processing systems where the turnaround time may be large and where every run must be as productive as possible. Since even a program with errors is executed, the user derives more information from each submission of the program. In a modern interactive environment, it may be preferable to speed up compilation by not generating an object program if a serious error is found at compile time. Users can correct their syntactic errors, recompile, and get a run of the corrected program. The whole process may take only slightly longer than the time taken by an error-repairing compiler to get a run of the repaired program. Finally, it must be observed that there are some situations in which an erroneous program must not run, i.e., when it might damage irreplaceable programs or data already on the system. One might argue that these vital resources should not be exposed even to a program which compiled successfully but is untested— expendable test versions of the necessary files and programs should be used to check out the new program.

The zenith of error-handling methods is true *error correction*. The term error correction is sometimes used to designate the error-handling method we have called error repair. We believe that this usage is misleading, especially to novice users, and we reserve the term error correction for a type of error repair which, through extrasensory perception or some other means, finds out what the programmer intended to write and substitutes this for the error. In fact, it may be necessary for the error-correcting compiler to know more about the programming language and the problem specifications than the programmer knows, since the programmer may be rather mediocre, and the only good definition of correctness lies in conformity to the program specifications. Clearly this points in the direction of an automatic programmer rather than a compiler. There is little reason for the existence of a high-level language if we have a program which can take problem specifications and generate a correct object language program to solve the problem. The true error-correcting compiler is a dream which will not come true, at least not in the near future.

As we have seen, error recovery and error repair are the only methods of error handling which are both acceptable and possible with present techniques. In the remainder of this chapter we examine the prerequisites of good error handling, namely, effective error detection and reporting, and study the general strategies of error recovery and of error repair.

5-2 ERROR DETECTION

Before we can make any attempt to handle errors, we must be sure that we can detect them. This section discusses how and why we can detect errors, and what kinds of errors can be detected. Some attention is also given to the question of where in the input string an error can be detected and what can be determined about its cause at the time it is detected.

5-2.1 The Nature of Syntax Errors

Recall from Sec. 2-4 the distinction between the syntax and the semantics of a program. The syntax of the program corresponds to its form and determines whether or not it is a legal program according to the rules of some programming language. The semantics of the program is its meaning (the operation it performs) and is invariant during the translation process. The object program has the same semantics as the source program but does not usually have the same syntax. By definition, the compiler can only detect syntactic errors. Even the detection of such errors as the use of a variable before it is initialized may be considered syntactic. They are not errors in the meaning of the program; they are errors which make the program meaningless, simply because any syntactically invalid program is meaningless. Semantic errors manifest themselves only at run time, in terms of deviations from the program specifications. Such errors may someday be detectable by means of program verifiers, relying on the specifications of the program to verify that the program written by the programmer actually does what is required. However, this cannot be done given only the source program and a knowledge of the language in which it is written.

A compiler performs a *syntactic analysis* of the source program in order to discern its structure and in order to check that the program is valid in a given programming language L. Any deviation from the rules of L is termed a *syntactic error*. In most modern compilers, part of the syntactic analysis is performed by a relatively formalized context-free parser (Chaps. 6 and 7), and the remainder (primarily the checking of the attributes of programmer-defined objects in the program) is performed by a somewhat ad hoc mechanism, involving various compile-time tables (discussion in Chaps. 8 and 11). The two stages are necessary because most programming languages cannot be defined by a context-free grammar and because more powerful grammars are rather inconvenient as a basis for a compiler. Therefore, part of the language is expressed as a context-free grammar and the remainder is expressed as a set of context-sensitive restrictions on the context-free grammar. Because of this dichotomy, we speak of *context-free errors* and *context-sensitive errors* which are violations of the syntax specified by the context-free grammar and the context-sensitive restrictions, respectively.

Consider a programming language defined on an alphabet of terminal symbols V_T. If the language L contains all strings in V_T^*, then we can never detect a syntactic error in a program written in the alphabet V_T, since if any symbol of the program is removed or replaced by any other symbol in V_T the result is a valid program in L. We can detect errors only if L is a proper subset of V_T^*. Moreover, error detection becomes more effective as L becomes a smaller subset of V_T^*. The attitude behind some PL/I compilers that any program which could conceivably mean something should be considered valid leads to poor error detection—errors usually do not cause error messages; instead they cause the invocation of special language features not intended by the programmer (see Sec. 3-4.2). It is important that the restrictions on members of V_T^* which define the language L be made in a reasonable and consistent way, both for the sake of the user and so that the compiler writer may easily construct a parser which accepts precisely the language L and not some subtle variation on L.

We may usefully treat the restriction of the language from V_T^* to L as the introduction of redundancy into programs in L. The restriction of the set of valid strings implies an unnecessary increase in the average length of a program. This

increase is due to the requirement that the programmer explicitly state information which can be derived from the rest of the program. Clearly the explicit
restatement of this information is redundant, but it does provide a check against
errors in the program. If two redundant pieces of information are inconsistent, a
syntactic error has been found. Thus error detection is most effective in languages
in which the programmer is required to provide the same information in two or
more ways.

The clearest example of the accuracy of the preceding comments lies in the
type of checking performed in languages with so-called strong-type structures.
The requirement to declare the attributes of all variables is often unnecessary, but
the requirement is made to ease compilation and to increase the effectiveness of
error detection. Given an assignment statement like

    i:= 4

it is possible for the compiler to determine that i should be a variable of integer
type. Thus the declaration

    integer i

would be redundant. However, with the redundant declaration the compiler can
determine that the assignment

    i:= 'this is a string'

is an error, since the assignment indicates that i is a string variable rather than an
integer variable. Possibly the programmer made a typing error or meant to use
another variable name instead of i. In either case the detection of the error by the
compiler frees the programmer from a possibly lengthy attempt to find this error
once the program is being tested. The introduction of typeless variables may have
advantages in very small interactive programming languages intended for writing
short, simple programs. Such departures from ALGOL-like strong typing are
liabilities in languages designed for the implementation of software or large
applications programs (see Sec. 3-5.3). The same comments apply to most other
attempts to reduce redundancy in the hope of lightening the programmer's
burden.

5-2.2 How Errors Are Detected

As mentioned in Sec. 5-2.1, the grammars which define the syntax of programming languages are usually not context-free grammars. They are often specified in
two parts: a rigorous context-free grammar defining a superset of the language,
and a set of context-sensitive restrictions on the context-free syntax. As a
consequence of this, errors are detected in two ways. Errors in the context-free
syntax of the source program are usually easy to detect because of the precise
specification of the context-free syntax. Errors may also be detected by checks on
the context-sensitive syntax of the source program. Errors of this class, including
errors in the types of variables and expressions, are often harder to detect

effectively, because of the vagueness and imprecision of the prose description which defines the context-sensitive syntax.

Context-free errors are most effectively detected by a *syntax-directed* parsing algorithm. This type of parser consists of a general table-driven algorithm and a set of tables which are generated from the context-free grammar of the programming language. Since the parsing algorithm and the table-constructing algorithm are both precisely specified, it can be proven that the parser accepts precisely the language specified by a particular grammar. A context-free error in the source program is detected when the parsing algorithm finds an error entry in the tables. When this happens, the parser calls some recovery or repair routine to handle the error. [These comments apply specifically to the simple-precedence (Sec. 7-3), extended-precedence (Sec. 7-3), LR (Sec. 7-4), and LL (Sec. 6-2) parsing methods described later in the book.]

It is unfortunate, in terms of compiler reliability, that some of the heavily used compilers in existence today use ad hoc methods of syntactic analysis. (By ad hoc we mean any method which is not formalized.) Ad hoc methods are popular because they allow an efficient, direct, and conceptually simple interface between the syntactic analysis and the code generation. The algorithms which generate code for a particular construct may be incorporated into the syntactic analysis for that construct. The ad hoc approach to syntactic analysis consists of writing a special-case program which accepts only strings of the language being analyzed and at the same time generates either object code or some intermediate form which is processed by another pass of the compiler. This statement is simply a loose definition of a syntactic analyzer.

Formalized methods can be proven correct; the correctness of an ad hoc parser depends entirely on the care taken by its designers and programmers to ensure its correctness. The designers of an ad hoc parser must have an extraordinary understanding of the details of the language being implemented and must be extremely thorough in cross-checking their code with the language specifications.

The ad hoc compiler typically consists of a large number of checks of the next input symbol to see that it is legal in the context of the symbols already seen. Thus an error is detected when one of these tests fails unexpectedly. If the compiler has been properly constructed, this failure causes some error-handling mechanism to be invoked, perhaps by means of a procedure call.

The aforementioned shortcomings of ad hoc syntactic-analysis methods should be taken to heart by all prospective compiler writers. No matter how formal their context-free syntactic-analysis methods may be, almost all compilers use ad hoc methods for checking context-sensitive syntax. Such checking includes making sure that variables, constants, labels, and procedure names are defined and have the correct attributes for the context in which they occur. In designing programming languages we attempt to keep the syntax of operations similar for all data types. Because of this, errors in attributes of operands usually have more localized effects than do context-free errors, which often invalidate the structure of a large portion of the source program. Thus it is often easier to recover from context-sensitive errors than from context-free errors.

5-2.3 Where Errors Are Detected

We now briefly turn our attention to the question of where in the input string we can detect an error, and what we can determine about the cause of an error at the time it is detected. Peterson (1972) presents the following incorrect PL/I statement as a demonstration of the fact that the detection of an error may not occur until the parser has proceeded an arbitrary distance beyond the point where the error was actually made:

$$A = B + C + D + E + F + G + H$$
$$\text{THEN } X = X * 2;$$
$$\text{ELSE } X = Y/2;$$

In the example, it is apparent to the eye of a PL/I programmer that the error is a missing IF token. The location of the THEN is the earliest possible point at which the error can be detected in a left-to-right parse. When one's eye reaches the THEN, it is capable of quickly backtracking to discover the actual point of the error.

A parser can be made to backtrack and find the actual error in the preceding example, but in general this process is too time-consuming to be practical. Lyon (1974) gives an algorithm which repairs an invalid program by transforming it into the valid program which is closest to it, in the sense that a minimum number of symbol insertions and deletions is required to do the transformation. The algorithm takes a number of steps proportional to n^3, where n is the number of symbols in the source program. The algorithm is too slow to be suitable for programming-language translation. Barnard (1976) points out that this *minimum-distance* error repair may be preferable to less time-consuming methods but certainly does not ensure a correction of the syntactic error.

Although the THEN token in the preceding example is the earliest point at which a syntactic error can be detected, it is certainly not the latest. Some formal parsing methods, including the precedence parsers of Sec. 7-3, may not detect the syntactic error until several more symbols have been processed. The LL (Sec. 6-2) and LR (Sec. 7-4) parsing methods detect the error when the THEN token is processed. These parsing techniques have the so-called *valid prefix property*, which means that if the parser does not detect an error in the first portion X of a program XY, then there must exist some string of symbols W such that XW is a valid program.

It must be noted that the compiler is not usually able to determine the cause of an error, even if it is detected immediately. The error may be due to a typing mistake, a programmer oversight, or a serious misunderstanding of the programming language. The sooner the error is detected the more likely it is that the compiler can correctly guess the cause and take an appropriate action. This action must always include a precise and complete description of the error. Section 5-3 looks in greater detail at methods and standards for error reporting.

5-3 ERROR REPORTING

In order for effective error detection to be of any value to the users of a compiler, each error, once detected, must be clearly and precisely reported. To those who have never been involved in a large software project, it may not be obvious that error reporting requires special consideration. Small application programs may generate one of a dozen or so messages on the rare occasions when something goes wrong. Such programs can use the standard output routines or PRINT statements of the language in which they are programmed to print out a short message to the user. However, it is the premise of this entire chapter that a compiler's response to errors must be extremely well designed. Where a compiler is used primarily for program development, it may be called upon more often to generate good error messages than to generate good object code.

In the early days of high-level language translators when computing resources were scarce and the usefulness of the highly diagnostic compiler had not yet been demonstrated, it was common for a compiler to print *error codes*, rather than natural-language messages. When confronted with a message like 'SY03', the user would go to a book of explanations provided by the authors of the compiler and would attempt to relate the description found there to the problem at hand. However, this proved inconvenient for users, since they always needed the error book to decipher the compiler's cryptic messages. It also proved difficult to keep the multitude of error books up to date as the compiler was (inevitably) modified. Furthermore, even when the description for 'SY03' was available and accurate, the user was often unable to understand just which objects in the program caused the message and why.

Today it is common for both educational and production compilers to generate natural-language messages. The generation of error codes in lieu of full messages is no longer justifiable, except on the smallest of microcomputers. One approach to generating natural-language messages is to produce error codes in the compiler, save these in a temporary file, and rely on a separate final pass to print the source listing and replace the error codes by the full text of the error messages. This approach is essentially an automation of the error-book method and is probably the minimum acceptable standard of error reporting today. It removes the problems of the inavailability and inaccuracy of the error books, but it does nothing to make the error descriptions more comprehensible.

The error messages already discussed contain no reference to the objects in the source program which are the cause of an error, and they often contain no information about the location of the error other than the number of the line on which it was detected. There are several ways in which we can improve on such error messages. Error messages should specifically mention any information known to the compiler which might be useful to the user in discerning the true cause of an error. Such information may include a visible pointer to the column at which the error was detected, the names and attributes of variables and constants associated with the error, the types involved in type-matching errors, and so on. All this information must be expressed in terms of the source language and must be oriented toward the user. In some cases it may be difficult for the compiler to provide this information, but it is usually easier for the compiler than for the user. The compiler writer should take the necessary pains to ensure that specific messages are printed to describe different errors, rather than relying on the possibly misinformed user to interpret one vague generic message which is used for several different errors. Messages such as "Bad statement syntax" are entirely unacceptable for any compiler which is to be used extensively.

Conway and Wilcox (1973) suggest an additional source of diagnostic information that is useful for compilers which perform effective error repair. They state that "the most effective communication rests not in the specific messages but in a reconstruction of the source statement ...". When their PL/C compiler encounters an erroneous source statement, it states its interpretation of what the programmer intended to write, namely, the repaired form of the source statement. The repaired statement indicates what the error is in terms of how the statement can be made valid, and at the same time gives the user information helpful in the interpretation of later messages. For example, if the compiler reconstructs an invalid declaration in a way other than that intended by the programmer, later messages may be caused by the incorrect declaration. With the PL/C system of error reporting, the programmer can more easily understand the cause of the later errors.

Horning (1976) suggests that error messages should contain the insights about the language which the compiler writer is sure to have acquired during the process of implementation. An error message should contain suggestions about the cause of the error and how it might be fixed. This is the kind of suggestion made immediately by people experienced with a particular language and compiler whenever they see a certain error message. The major problem with this type of information in a syntax-directed compiler is that it is entirely empirical and cannot be generated by any sort of general algorithm. Thus it can be difficult to attach these personalized messages to a general-purpose syntax-directed parsing algorithm.

These elaborate and effective messages are considerably easier to propose than to implement. In the PL/C and PLUTO compilers for PL/I (Conway and Wilcox, 1973; Wagner, 1973; Boulton, 1975) the implementation approach has been the construction of a flexible *message generator* which interprets complex *message patterns*. The goal of this rather elaborate mechanism is to minimize the space consumed by the message patterns while maximizing the flexibility, usefulness, and consistency of the error messages. The approach is a reasonable one, and we now present in some detail the design of a flexible message generator adapted from the message generators of PL/C and PLUTO.

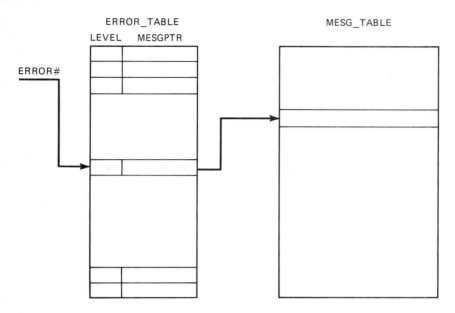

Figure 5-1 Representation of an error-message-generation system.

Figure 5-1 depicts the layout of the two tables which control the generation of error messages. When an error is detected, the message generator is called and is given an ERROR# (error number) to indicate which message should be printed. The ERROR# is used as an index into the ERROR_TABLE. The row of the table selected by the index contains two fields. The LEVEL field indicates the level of severity of the error which caused the message. The MESGPTR field contains the index in MESG_TABLE of the message pattern for the error message.

The first action taken by the message generator is to compare the LEVEL of the message with the global variable MSGLEVEL, which indicates the lowest level of messages which are to be printed. The user is able to control the MSGLEVEL by means of a parameter of the compiler or by means of some construct in the language being compiled. For example, the user may easily suppress all warnings and mild error messages and have only the severe error messages printed. If the LEVEL of the message is less than the MSGLEVEL, the message is not printed, and the message generator returns. If the LEVEL is greater than or equal to the MSGLEVEL, the counts of total error messages and error messages with severity equal to LEVEL are incremented. Finally, the message generator interprets the message pattern indicated by MESGPTR, and prints the error message.

The message pattern consists of a string of bytes in the MESG_TABLE. Each pattern consists of a sequence of *phrases*. Each phrase begins with a letter, specifying what type of phrase it is, and may contain further bytes, depending on its type. The types of phrases are:

L– This letter indicates the literal text phrase and is followed by a byte containing the length of the literal text, and then by the literal text itself.

M– This letter indicates a MESG_TABLE reference and is followed by a byte containing the index in MESG_TABLE of another message pattern to be interpreted before the remainder of the current pattern is interpreted. Thus the scheme is fully recursive, and a stack is necessary in the message generator to keep track of partially interpreted message patterns.

S– Normally phrases are separated by a blank as they are printed, line feeds being added as necessary to prevent running off the edge of the page. The letter 'S' introduces the suffix phrase, which is followed by a single character which is printed immediately after the preceding phrase, with no intervening blank or line feed. This feature may be used to form words such as 'COMPILER' and 'COMPILED' from roots such as 'COMPILE'.

T– This letter introduces the tab phrase and is followed by a byte containing the number of the column where the next phrase is to be printed.

N– The letter 'N' represents the newline phrase, indicating that the next phrase is to be printed on a new output line.

P– The 'P' begins the parameter phrase and is followed by a byte containing the number of the string parameter of the message generator which is to be printed here. The routine which calls the message generator may pass it one or more string arguments containing the output forms of constants, identifiers, attribute names, and other information to be included in the message. A parameter phrase consisting of 'P' followed by the byte-sized integer 2 would indicate that the second of these arguments is to be printed.

E– This letter represents the end phrase and acts as a terminator for the message pattern.

Figure 5-2 shows the layout of the error and message tables for a sample message. The error number passed to the message generator selects an entry in the ERROR_TABLE. That entry contains the MESGPTR value 4. The processing of the message begins with the interpretation of message pattern 4 in the MESG_TABLE. This pattern consists of five phrases, which are separated by blanks in the figure. The first phrase is 'M'0, which causes the interpretation of message pattern 0. Message pattern 0 contains a phrase specifying a piece of literal text nine characters in length, namely, 'IDENTIFIE'. The pattern is terminated by an 'E' phrase. After 'IDENTIFIE' is printed, the message generator resumes the interpretation of message pattern 4. The 'S''R' phrase indicates that the suffix 'R' is to be placed on the preceding word. The 'P'1 phrase indicates that the first of the string parameters of the message generator call is to be printed. The 'M'1 phrase causes the interpretation of message pattern 1, which contains a literal text phrase for the word 'UNDEFINED'. The 'E' phrase signals the end of message pattern 4, and the message generator

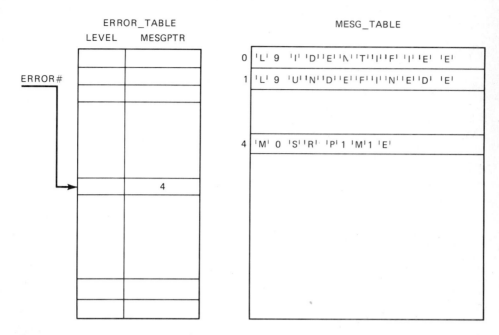

Figure 5-2 An error-message example.

returns to its caller. If the first string parameter had the value 'COUNT', the complete message would be

IDENTIFIER COUNT UNDEFINED

The centralized message generator has several practical advantages. It promotes consistency in the form and content of error messages. Because several messages may have common submessages, the total space consumed by the message text is reduced. Without the central generator, there would be much redundant code associated with printing messages. Because the message-generation strategy is encapsulated in one module, it is easy to change. Furthermore, the centralized generator facilitates the collection of statistics concerning errors and messages, and increases the level of control which may be exercised over the error messages. For example, it becomes possible to count the number of error messages generated for a particular line and suppress further messages for that line if the count grows too large. If a large number of messages have been printed, the message generator may decide to suppress relatively unimportant messages, namely, comments and warnings. All of this is very difficult to do with a diffuse message-generation scheme.

Once a syntactic error has been properly reported, it is necessary to recover from it or repair it so that parsing may continue. Without this crucial step only one error can be detected in each compilation. Error recovery is the key to making a compiler truly useful in the debugging stage of program development.

5-4 ERROR RECOVERY

As shown in Sec. 5-1, a useful compiler must somehow be able to adjust its state after encountering an error so that the compilation may continue in a reasonable way through the remainder of the program. The difficulty in accomplishing this can be seen by comparing a parser to a pyramid delicately balanced on its apex. All goes well as long as there are no surprises for the parser. However, when a syntactic error is encountered in the source text, the pyramid begins to fall off balance. Depending on the parsing method used, the imbalance may be detected immediately or only after the pyramid has fallen into an even more unstable state. Attempting to ignore the error and blindly continue parsing can lead to the total collapse of the parse (and the metaphorical pyramid). The symptom of this is an avalanche of error messages caused by the original error and the increasingly unbalanced parser. The goal of any error-recovery method is to restore the parser to a stable state (rebalance the pyramid) so that the parse can continue in a meaningful way and further syntactic errors can be detected. Error recovery implies no attempt to change the erroneous program into an syntactically valid one.

A large number of different syntactic-analysis methods are presently in use. Therefore, it is difficult to make general comments about the error-recovery process. In the following discussion we develop a model of a syntactic analyzer and discuss error-recovery strategies for this model. More specific and detailed recovery methods for the commonly used syntactic-analysis techniques are discussed in the next two chapters.

Many of the most popular parsing algorithms have the following elements:

1. A pushdown *stack*, used to store the sentential form being constructed by the parser.
2. An *input string* $a_1, a_2, \ldots, a_n$ containing the tokens of the source program.
3. One or more *symbol tables*, used to keep track of the attributes of variables and the identifiers which refer to them. These tables are used by the parser to check the context-sensitive syntax of the program.

In this model a syntactic error is detected when the current input symbol a_i is invalid in the context in which it appears. In a left-to-right analysis the stack and the symbol tables represent the left context of the error and the unprocessed input string $a_{i+1}, a_{i+2}, \ldots, a_n$ contains the right context of the error. Recovery is performed by modifying the stack and tables (left context), or the input string (right context), or both, so that the parser configuration is legal.

5-4.1 Ad Hoc Recovery Mechanisms

The approach taken to error recovery in most high-performance industrial compilers is an informal one. The portion of the compiler which detects an error calls some special-purpose error-recovery routine which is able to handle a particular error or class of errors. The action taken by the routine is decided by compiler writers when they code the routine. In this way compiler writers may anticipate a particular class of syntactic errors and recover from them in whatever way they consider most reasonable and effective.

The ad hoc recovery scheme works well as long as the syntactic errors encountered fall into one of the classes of errors anticipated by the compiler writer. Unfortunately, it is very difficult to anticipate all syntactic errors. Ad hoc recovery methods have a disadvantage in that they tend to react badly to unanticipated situations and may produce avalanches of error messages. This is related to the problem of ensuring that the compiler has a correct, bounded, and stable reaction to errors, as discussed in Sec. 5-1. A further disadvantage of ad hoc error-recovery methods is the large amount of effort which must go into the writing of the error-recovery routines and the careful anticipation of all possible syntactic errors.

It is possible to use ad hoc error-recovery techniques in a syntax-directed or table-driven parser. As mentioned in Sec. 5-2.2, errors are usually detected in table-driven parsers when the indicated parse action in the parsing table is error. To add ad hoc error recovery to such a parser, it is only necessary to change the error actions in the table into calls to hand-coded error-recovery routines. Thus a particular error or group of errors causes a particular routine to be called. This routine then modifies the stack, symbol tables, and/or input string to place the parser into a stable state again. This is roughly the approach used in the PL/C compiler for PL/I (Conway and Wilcox, 1973).

The primary advantage of ad hoc recovery methods is that they allow compiler writers to put their intuitions about common syntactic errors into the error-recovery scheme. Instead of specializing the recovery algorithm, the compiler writer may add this information to the grammar in the form of *error productions*. Error productions are special productions which take effect only when a syntactic error is encountered. The parser and error-recovery system can remain general, while language-specific information is incorporated by means of the error productions. Wirth (1968) uses a table of error productions in his simple-precedence parser for PL360 to select an appropriate error message when an error occurs—the table is searched for a right-hand side which matches the top elements of the stack, and the message attached to this right-hand side is printed. The erroneous phrase matched by the error production is then discarded. Aho and Johnson (1974) use a special *error* token in their LALR(1) grammars to indicate to the parser a way of recovering from a syntactic error. When an error is detected, the parser looks through the input string until it finds some symbol which can legally follow *error* in the grammar. It then adjusts the stack and proceeds as if it had read the token *error* in the input string.

The disadvantages of error productions as a means of recovery are similar to those of other language-dependent methods. Considerable time must be spent inserting error productions and checking that they work correctly. There is always the danger that some error situation will be overlooked and that the parser will react badly in unanticipated situations. Depending on the tabular form used for the grammar, it is possible that the added error productions may make the grammar prohibitively large and impossible to store.

5-4.2 Syntax-Directed Recovery

In view of the possibilities for oversights and mistakes in hand-coding an ad hoc error-recovery mechanism, it appears desirable to have some formalized general approach to generating an error-recovery mechanism. Much research has been devoted to the development of algorithms which operate on the data structures of context-free parsers of various types so as to adjust them to proceed after a context-free syntactic error. This section describes a general approach to syntax-directed error recovery (Rhodes, 1973; Graham and Rhodes, 1975) which is applicable to any bottom-up syntax-directed parser.

An error-recovery strategy can usually make use of only a small part of the context of the error. In the Graham-Rhodes method the error recovery takes place in two phases. The first phase, called the *condensation phase*, attempts to parse the sentential form on the stack and in the unread portion of the input string, so that as much of the context of the error as possible may be used in the second phase of the recovery. First, a *backward move* is attempted. This consists of an attempt to perform reductions on the sentential form on the parser's stack. A reduction consists of the replacement of the right-hand side of some production of the grammar by the left-hand side of that production. When all possible reductions on the top of the stack have been performed, the recovery mechanism attempts a *forward move*, which consists of parsing the portion of the input string immediately following the error. The forward move stops when it encounters a second error in the input string or when it cannot make any more parsing actions without using the context preceding the point of the error. An arbitrary amount of the unread input string may be consumed by the forward move, but since all of this input is parsed and checked for syntactic errors, none of the source text is actually ignored.

To illustrate the backward and forward moves, consider the following productions from an example grammar:

⟨statements⟩::= ⟨statement⟩ ; ⟨statements⟩
             | ⟨statement⟩

and the erroneous ALGOL program segment:

BEGIN A:= B − 2
       B:= A ∗ X;
       Y:= B + 2
END;

In this example, there is a missing semicolon after the statement "A:= B − 2." Let us assume a bottom-up parser without worrying about the details of the parsing strategy. When the missing semicolon is detected, the stack could be

   ... BEGIN ⟨id⟩:= ⟨id⟩ − ⟨integer⟩

with B as the next input token. A backward move would reduce the stack to

...BEGIN ⟨statement⟩

The error point represented by ? is shifted onto the stack, and parsing continues with the forward move until the point

...BEGIN ⟨statement⟩ ? ⟨statements⟩ END

is reached. At this point, a reduction over the error point is required and the stack contents are passed to the second phase. In summary, the backward and forward moves attempt to capture the context surrounding where the error is detected.

The second phase of the error recovery performs a pattern-matching operation on the top elements of the parsing stack in an attempt to find a production in the grammar whose right-hand side is similar to the symbols on the stack. The top part of the stack is then adjusted to match the right-hand side of the production or the beginning of the production. The next input symbol is also considered in the choice of the change made to the stack.

In the previous example, the insertion of a semicolon at the error point permits the reduction of

⟨statement⟩ ? ⟨statements⟩

to

⟨statements⟩.

The correction, however, is not necessarily so simple. Consider the incorrect program segment

A:= B − 2;
A = 2 THEN A:= B ∗ C;

In this program the token "IF" is missing. Assuming that the error is detected when "= " is read, the stack at this point would contain

...⟨statements⟩ ; ⟨id⟩

In this case no backward move is possible. A forward move results in the following stack contents:

...⟨statements⟩ ; ⟨id⟩ ? = ⟨expression⟩

with the next input token of THEN. The forward move can no longer continue, and a reduction over the error point may be necessary. One possibility is to replace "=" by ":="; however, the input token "THEN," in this case, does not follow. Another possibility is to insert the token "IF" before the symbol ⟨id⟩, permitting a reduction to

...statement ; IF expression

This example illustrates that there may be more than one change which seems to permit a recovery from an error. In such instances, a choice can be made based upon the likelihood of which tokens are involved in syntax errors.

The major problem with syntax-directed recovery mechanisms is that they do not reflect the compiler writer's knowledge of possible and plausible errors and their causes. The Graham-Rhodes method mitigates this somewhat by using a weighted minimum-cost criterion in choosing among the several stack changes which might be possible in some recovery situation. Compiler writers use their knowledge of the programming language to set up two vectors, containing the *cost* of deleting or inserting each symbol of the grammar. The cost of making a change represents the undesirability of making the change. The recovery routine attempts to minimize the total cost of all changes it makes to the stack. Thus the compiler writer can tune the recovery system to make it recover better in the most common error situations.

5-4.3 Secondary Error Recovery

Some error-recovery strategies, especially ad hoc strategies, are not always successful in localizing and recovering from an error. Such strategies may be prone to unbounded looping and may have to be limited in order to prevent them from consuming all available time or all of the source text. In such cases, it is necessary to have a secondary recovery scheme to fall back on when the usual system fails. Such a recovery scheme must be guaranteed to recover and must be certain to localize the error condition. The usual methods of performing the secondary recovery are *panic mode* (Graham and Rhodes, 1975) and *unit deletion*.

Panic mode is the process of throwing away source text until any of a number of firm delimiters is found. An example of a firm delimiter is the ';' in PL/I. When such a delimiter is found, the stack is popped to a point where the left context it represents may be followed by the syntactic structure which follows the delimiter. In some simple parsers, panic mode is used as the only form of error recovery. It certainly succeeds in localizing a syntactic error, but it may throw away an arbitrary amount of source text, which is never checked for local validity. When an error is discovered in a PL/I statement, panic mode throws away source symbols until it finds a ';', cleans off the stack so that the parser is ready to accept a statement, and resumes parsing after the semicolon.

Unit deletion refers to the deletion of the whole of a syntactic structure from the source text. Its effects are the same as those of panic mode, but since the whole of the syntactic unit (not just its end) is deleted, unit deletion preserves the syntactic correctness of the source program and is appropriate for error-repairing compilers. It is more difficult to achieve than is panic mode, since the translated form of the whole unit must be saved in the parser so that it may be easily deleted.

It should be noted that some of the formal methods for recovering from errors in syntax-directed parsers are able to recover from any error, and a secondary recovery is unnecessary.

5-4.4 Context-Sensitive Recovery

Sections 5-4.1 and 5-4.2 focused primarily on recovery from context-free errors. Context-free recovery has been more thoroughly studied than context-sensitive recovery because context-free parsing methods have been more adequately formalized. The checking of context-sensitive restrictions is usually done in an ad hoc fashion, and therefore, context-sensitive recovery is also ad hoc. Thus it is rather difficult to formulate a general theory of context-sensitive recovery.

The most efficient form of context-sensitive recovery is often to simply report the error, ignore it, and disable the code-generation portion of the compiler (since the program is no longer syntactically valid, translation may be impossible). Context-sensitive syntax is usually expressed as a set of restrictions on a larger context-free language. The parser is free to accept any member of the context-free language, giving messages and suppressing translation if the program does not fall within the smaller language defined by the context-sensitive restrictions. Context-sensitive errors usually have very local effects, and little need be done to recover from them. If the error involves undefined identifiers, it may be desirable to insert the identifiers into the symbol table, making assumptions about their types based on where they occur. This type of error recovery is discussed in more detail in Chap. 11.

Error recovery is the minimum acceptable response to syntactic errors. The most difficult problem for error recovery arises from the demands of error repair. Section 5-5 discusses error repair as an extension of error recovery, with more ambitious goals and more sophisticated techniques.

5-5 ERROR REPAIR

The advantages of syntactic error repair over error recovery have been discussed in Sec. 5-1. Error repair is a form of error recovery which guarantees the syntactic validity of the intermediate form of the program which is passed to other parts or passes of the compiler. Thus the compiler may perform complete checking and translation of the correct portions of the original program.

Section 5-2.3 mentioned the minimum-distance repair algorithm devised by Lyon (1974) which takes considerable pains in attempting to achieve a good repair, that is, a repair which is often a correction. It must be emphasized that even this expensive algorithm cannot always correct errors. A compiler does not have enough information to determine what is correct, in terms of what the programmer intended, and no present-day compiler is sophisticated enough to make use of this information if it were available.

The general outline of error recovery in Sec. 5-4 allowed modifications to the parse stack, symbol tables, and the unread input string during the process of recovery. When repair is required, modifications to the left context become quite undesirable. The left context represents accumulated information concerning source text which has already been translated and is no longer available. If stack and table modifications are to be performed, the repair system must be able to retract much of the processing already done on the erroneous part of the program. This means added complexity and space for storing parts of the source and its translation.

Fortunately, parsing algorithms which have the valid prefix property (see Sec. 5-2.3) need not tamper with the parse stack in order to recover or repair. LR (Sec. 7-4), LL (Sec. 6-2), and most top-down, no-backup ad hoc parsers have this property and are able to recover or repair by inserting or deleting source text.

5-5.1 Ad Hoc Repair

All the discussion in Sec. 5.4-1 about ad hoc recovery applies to ad hoc repair as well, since error repair is a sophisticated means of error recovery. The methods available for invoking the error-handling routines are unchanged. The error-handling routines must now be coded in such a way as to produce a syntactically valid output for the rest of the compiler. The advantages and disadvantages of the ad hoc repair methods parallel the advantages and disadvantages of ad hoc error recovery.

5-5.2 Syntax-Directed Repair

A syntax-directed repair mechanism is one which is general to a class of languages and which can be generated by a formal algorithm. This section outlines a syntax-directed error-repair strategy for a top-down, no-backup parser (see Sec. 2-4.2). The design is adapted from Holt and Barnard (1976) and uses a cost vector to allow the compiler writer to tune the error repair (see Sec. 5-4.2).

The top-down parser attempts to build a syntax tree describing the source program. It does this by repeatedly replacing the leftmost nonterminal symbol in the tree with the right-hand side of one of its productions. An error is detected when the downward growth of the syntax tree requires a particular terminal symbol to appear in the input string, and that terminal symbol is not present. This parser has the valid prefix property, since it detects a syntactic error when the first erroneous symbol is encountered.

The error-repair strategy is a relatively simple one. When the syntax tree demands that a particular terminal occur in the input string, and the terminal does not occur, the repair algorithm inserts the required terminal into the source text (input string). In some cases the syntax tree may require one of a number of terminal symbols, none of which occurs in the input string. In this case, an insertion-cost vector, which specifies a cost for inserting each symbol of the grammar, is used to determine which of the required terminals should be inserted. The repair algorithm attempts to minimize the cost of the insertion. The input symbol which caused the error is discarded unless the inserted terminal symbol is a special symbol (not an identifier or constant) and the input symbol is not a special symbol.

Notice that the repair action just described need not actually remove the error. If the input symbol is retained, it is possible that it may not validly follow the inserted symbol. In such a case the repair system must perform another insertion. The repair should check for this condition before returning to the parser in order to prevent the parser from reporting the error again. Furthermore, the repair system must contain limits which prevent it from entering an un-bounded sequence of insertions which never correct the error (whether or not this is possible depends on the grammar).

Because this simple repair strategy may fail to repair the syntactic error, Holt and Barnard provide a three-level repair system. If a statement or line boundary is encountered in the syntax tree or in the input string during a repair, a *line-level* repair strategy (akin to the unit deletion of Sec. 5-4.3) is invoked to generate or delete a line of source text. If this strategy also fails, and an end-of-program delimiter is encountered, the highest level of repair takes over and generates the rest of the program or deletes the rest of the input string.

When the inserted terminal symbol is an identifier or a constant, there are several possible choices of identifiers or constants to insert. Based on the information in the symbol table concerning identifier scope and type, it might be possible to insert an identifier which can validly appear in this context. In some cases there may be only one such identifier. If there are several identifiers which can appear at a given point in the source text, the choice must be arbitrary. The choice of a constant to insert is nearly always arbitrary, except where the context restricts the range of values which may appear (in array subscripts, for example). Holt and Barnard (1976) always insert 1 for a numeric constant, "?" for a string constant, and $NIL for an identifier. An arbitrary choice of one of the possible identifiers may sometimes yield a correction of the error; $NIL is never a correction, only a repair. In order to prevent context-sensitive errors due to the attributes of $NIL, there should be a universal type attribute which allows an identifier like $NIL to be an operand of any operator in the language. Care must then be taken by the code generator to produce some sort of reasonable translation for this inserted identifier.

5-5.3 Context-Sensitive Repair

Unlike a simple recovering compiler (Sec. 5-4.3), an error-repairing compiler cannot ignore context-sensitive errors. The intermediate form of the program which is passed to other parts of the compiler must contain operands with correct attributes in every expression. When the attributes of some operand do not match those required by a particular operator, an operand of the required type must be substituted for the invalid operand. The comments of the previous paragraph apply here. A dummy identifier like $NIL with the universal type of attribute may be substituted for the invalid operand. Constants and expressions of incorrect type or value must be replaced by compiler-generated constants and expressions with the correct attributes. The most effective way to do this is usually clear from the characteristics of the error-detection routine itself. Since the context-sensitive restrictions are usually tested in an ad hoc manner, the repair strategy for each case can be tailored to and embedded in the error-detection routine.

5-5.4 Spelling Repair

The alphanumeric identifier plays a very large role in most programming languages. Identifiers are used to denote variables, constants, operators, labels, and data types. Many languages contain a class of special identifiers called *keywords*, which are used as syntactic delimiters. Typing errors and forgetfulness often lead to misspelled identifiers. Thus an identifier or incorrect keyword appears where a particular keyword should be found, or a keyword or undefined identifier appears where a particular variable identifier is intended. In such cases the syntactic error can often be repaired by means of the algorithm described in this section.

Morgan (1970) presents an algorithm which attempts to select a legal identifier which is close to the illegal identifier which occurs in the source program. If the algorithm succeeds, the repair consists of substituting the legal identifier for the illegal one.

Function SPELLING_REPAIR(SUBJECT). Given the incorrect identifier SUBJECT, this function invokes function COMPARE to determine whether two identifiers are similar enough that one could be a misspelling of the other. Local variables are i and j (strings), and I (set of strings).

1. [Generate all possible repairs]
   I ← {i|i is an identifier or keyword, and i
           may properly occur in the current context.
           This last restriction may include checking the
           type and scope of identifiers}
2. [Find a "close" repair]
       Repeat for all j ∈ I
           If COMPARE(SUBJECT, j)
           then Return (j)
3. [Cannot find a close repair; return 0 to indicate failure]
       Return (0)   □

Morgan indicates that "it is inefficient to attempt repair of variable names with fewer than three characters." This applies not only to variable names but to keywords and other identifiers as well.

Morgan's algorithm uses a subalgorithm COMPARE to test whether or not the SUBJECT is in some sense close to the identifier j. The compiler writer may choose any reasonable method for performing this comparison. The algorithm should return true if and only if SUBJECT may be obtained from j by means of some transformations which represent likely spelling mistakes. The particular COMPARE algorithm used by Morgan is based on Damerau (1964). This algorithm returns true if and only if SUBJECT may be obtained from j by one of the following transformations:

1. One symbol changed
2. One symbol deleted
3. One symbol inserted
4. Two adjacent symbols transposed

Damerau and Morgan report that single instances of one of these four transformations account for more than 80 percent of the spelling errors encountered in their computer installations. Based on a COMPARE algorithm which accepts only these transformations, step 1 of Function SPELLING_REPAIR may be modified to reject any identifier i whose length is different from the length of SUBJECT by more than one. In this section no such change has been made to Function SPELLING_REPAIR. The test for length difference is made in step 1 of Function COMPARE.

We now present Damerau's version of the COMPARE algorithm.

Function COMPARE(S, T). This logical function has two string parameters S and T whose order does not matter. The string functions LENGTH and SUB are used to take the length of a string, and to access a substring of a string, respectively. The numeric functions ABS and MIN are used to take the absolute value of a number and to find the smaller of two numbers. Local variables are LS, LT, and j (integers).

1. [Find lengths of S and T, check for difference in lengths]
    LS ← LENGTH(S)
    LT ← LENGTH(T)
    If LS < 3 or LT < 3 or ABS(LS − LT) > 1
    then Return (false)
    EQUAL ← true
2. [Find first position where S and T differ]
    Repeat for j = 1, 2,..., MIN(LS, LT)
      If SUB(S, j, 1) ≠ SUB(T, j, 1)
      then EQUAL ← false
        Exitloop
3. [S and T are equal or differ by an insertion or deletion at end]
    If EQUAL
    then Return (true)
4. [Check for transposition or one-symbol change]
    If LS = LT
    then If j < LS
        then If SUB(S, j + 1, 1) = SUB(T, j, 1) and
            SUB(T, j + 1, 1) = SUB(S, j, 1)
          then j ← j + 1
        If SUB(S, j + 1) = SUB(T, j + 1)
        then Return (true)
        else Return (false)

```
else (Check for insertion or deletion)
    If LS > LT
    then If SUB(T, j) = SUB(S, j + 1)
        then Return (true)
        else Return (false)
    else If SUB(S, j) = SUB(T, j + 1)
        then Return (true)
        else Return (false)                    □
```

The above function works only on single misspelled identifiers. It is possible that an identifier might be misspelled in such a way as to become two identifiers. For example, some symbol in the identifier might be changed to a blank or operator symbol, thus separating the identifier into two parts. Similarly, the first symbol might accidentally be made into a digit, changing the identifier into a number or a number followed by an identifier. Thus Function **SPELLING_REPAIR** does not repair all spelling errors, even within the limited set of transformations just described. However, owing to the layout of the keyboard and to the human mind, spelling errors usually involve changes and insertions of letters, not special characters.

This chapter has presented an introduction to the problems and techniques of compile-time error handling. The detection and reporting of syntactic errors have been treated in depth. The introduction to error recovery and error repair in Secs. 5-4 and 5-5 provides the background needed to understand the discussions of detailed methods of error handling which appear in Chaps. 6, 7, 8, and 11.

CHAPTER EXERCISES

1 Study the error-handling performance of one of the commonly used compilers at your installation. In your report specifically address the following questions:

(*a*) Does the compiler always detect syntax errors?

(*b*) How adequate are the error messages it produces? Are they precise or vague? Is the probable cause of the error clearly indicated in source-language terms? How well do the messages pinpoint the location of the error?

(*c*) How well does the compiler recover from errors? Does one error cause a profusion of messages?

(*d*) Is syntax repair performed? Roughly how often is the repair a correction?

2 Discuss the significance of programming-language design to the detection of incorrect programs at compile time.

3 Figure 5-3 shows the contents of the tables of the message generator described in Sec. 5-3. Given the contents of these tables, indicate precisely the output of the message generator for values of ERROR# from 0 to 4, inclusive. Assume that MSGLEVEL = 2 and that the string parameters are 'COUNTER' and 'SAI'.

4 Estimate the usefulness of the suffix ('S') phrase to the message generator of Sec. 5-3. Based on reasonable estimates of the frequency of identical root words and the average length of phrases, compute the change in the number of bytes needed to store 500 phrases when the suffix phrase is not allowed.

ERROR_TABLE

	LEVEL	MESGPTR
0	2	0
1	3	2
2	1	0
3	2	3
4	2	1
⋮		

MESG_TABLE

0	'L'	2	'H'	'I'	'E'			
1	'T'	4	'M'	3	'N'	'P'	1	'E'
2	'P'	2	'S'	'D'	'M'	0	'E'	
3	'L'	5	'C'	'H'	'E'	'C'	'K'	'E'

Figure 5-3

5 If step 1 of Function SPELLING_REPAIR gives

$$I = \{\,'BASK'\,,'THEN'\,,'THERE'\,,'THAN'\,,'HAND'\,\}$$

as possible repairs for the misspelled identifier 'THANE', which identifier will be chosen as the repair? (Give a trace of step 2 of the algorithm to support your claim.)

6 Sketch a detailed algorithm to perform step 1 of Function SPELLING_REPAIR at a given point in the parsing of some block-structured programming language like ALGOL or PL/I. You may make reasonable assumptions to solve the problem.

7 Explain how you might apply the Graham and Rhodes error-recovery strategy of Sec. 5-4.2 to a top-down parser. If you think this is impossible, explain why.

8 Which of the advantages of error repair over error recovery do you consider most important:
   (*a*) To you personally
   (*b*) To experienced industrial programmers
   (*c*) To novice programming students
Explain why.

BIBLIOGRAPHY

Aho, A. V., and S. C. Johnson: "LR Parsing," *ACM Computing Surveys*, Vol. 6, No. 2, June 1974, pp. 99–124.

Barnard, D. T.: "Automatic Generation of Syntax-Repairing and Paragraphing Parsers," CSRG-52, Computer Systems Research Group Report No. 52, University of Toronto, Toronto, 1975.

Barnard, D. T.: "A Survey of Syntax Error Handling Techniques," Computer Systems Research Group, University of Toronto, 1976.

Boulton, P. I. P.: "The Generation of Diagnostic Messages," *INFOR*, Vol. 13, No. 2, June 1975, pp. 135–146.

Conway, R. W., and T. R. Wilcox: "Design and Implementation of a Diagnostic Compiler for PL/I," *Communications of the ACM*, Vol. 16, No. 3, March 1973, pp. 169–179.

Damerau, F. J.: "A Technique for Computer Detection and Correction of Spelling Errors," *Communications of the ACM*, Vol. 7, No. 3, March 1964, pp. 171–176.

Graham, S. L., and S. P. Rhodes: "Practical Syntactic Error Recovery," *Communications of the ACM*, Vol. 18, No. 11, November 1975, pp. 639–650.

Gries, D.: "Error Recovery and Correction—An Introduction to the Literature," *Compiler Construction: An Advanced Course*, 2d ed., New York: Springer-Verlag, 1976, pp. 628–638.

Holt, R. C., and D. T. Barnard: "Syntax-Directed Error Repair and Paragraphing," Computer Systems Research Group, University of Toronto, 1976.

Horning, J. J.: "What the Compiler Should Tell the User," *Compiler Construction: An Advanced Course*, 2d ed., New York: Springer-Verlag, 1976, pp. 525–548.

Lyon, G.: "Syntax Directed Least-Errors Analysis for Context-Free Languages," *Communications of the ACM*, Vol. 17, No. 1, January 1974, pp. 3–14.

Morgan, H. L.: "Spelling Correction in Systems Programs," *Communications of the ACM*, Vol. 13, No. 2, February 1970, pp. 90–94.

Peterson, T. G.: "Syntax Error Detection, Correction and Recovery in Parsers," Ph.D. Thesis, Stevens Institute of Technology, 1972.

Rhodes, S. P.: "Practical Syntactic Error Recovery for Programming Languages," Ph.D. Thesis, University of California—Berkeley, 1973.

Wagner, R. A.: "Common Phrases and Minimum-Space Text Storage," *Communications of the ACM*, Vol. 16, No. 3, March 1973, pp. 148–152.

Wirth, N.: "PL360, A Programming Language for the 360 Computers," *Journal of the ACM*, Vol. 15, No. 1, January 1968, pp. 37–74.

TOP-DOWN PARSING

In Sec. 2-4.2 the notions of top-down parsing and bottom-up parsing were introduced. Recall that top-down parsing was characterized as a parsing method which, beginning with the goal symbol of the grammar, attempted to produce a string of terminal symbols that was identical to a given source string. This matching process proceeded by successively applying the productions of the grammar to produce substrings from nonterminals. In this chapter we will examine several methods of performing top-down parsing.

The types of grammars that we will be dealing with fall into the class of context-free grammars (see Sec. 2-4). Empty productions will be permitted, with the symbol ε being used throughout to represent the empty string.

This chapter is divided into two major sections. In Sec. 6-1 we will deal with general methods of top-down parsing. In this section brief mention will also be made of methods using partial or limited backup. Section 6-2 will discuss top-down parsing methods without backup.

6-1 GENERAL TOP-DOWN PARSING STRATEGIES

The nature of the top-down parsing technique is characterized by presenting three methods of performing such parses. The first method, called a brute-force method, is presented both informally and formally and is accompanied by a parsing algorithm. The second method, known as recursive descent, is a parsing technique which does not allow backup. The third method is a parsing technique which involves top-down parsing with limited or partial backup. This type of parsing is introduced in the form of a program written in assemblerlike statements. A comparison of this technique with full backup parsing is made. Error-detection and -recovery techniques are discussed briefly.

6-1.1 Brute-Force Approach

A top-down parse moves from the goal symbol to a string of terminal symbols. In the terminology of trees, this is moving from the root of the tree to a set of the leaves in the syntax tree for a program. In using full backup we are willing to attempt to create a syntax tree by following branches until the correct set of terminals is reached. In the worst possible case, that of trying to parse a string which is not in the language, all possible combinations are attempted before the failure to parse is recognized.

Top-down parsing with full backup is a "brute-force" method of parsing. In general terms, this method operates as follows:

1. Given a particular nonterminal that is to be expanded, the first production for this nonterminal is applied.
2. Then, within this newly expanded string, the next (leftmost) nonterminal is selected for expansion and its first production is applied.
3. This process (step 2) of applying productions is repeated for all subsequent nonterminals that are selected until such time as the process cannot or should not be continued. This termination (if it ever occurs) may be due to two causes. First, no more nonterminals may be present, in which case the string has been successfully parsed. Second, it may result from an incorrect expansion which would be indicated by the production of a substring of terminals which does not match the appropriate segment of the source string. In the case of such an incorrect expansion, the process is "backed up" by undoing the most recently applied production. Instead of using the particular expansion that caused the error, the next production of this nonterminal is used as the next expansion, and then the process of production application continues as before.

   If, on the other hand, no further productions are available to replace the production that caused the error, this error-causing expansion is replaced by the nonterminal itself, and the process is backed up again to undo the next most recently applied production. This backing up continues either until we are able to resume normal application of productions to selected nonterminals or until we have backed up to the goal symbol and there are no further productions to be tried. In the latter case, the given string must be unparsable because it is not part of the language determined by this particular grammar.

As an example of this brute-force parsing technique, let us consider the simple grammar

$$S \rightarrow aAd \mid aB \qquad A \rightarrow b \mid c \qquad B \rightarrow ccd \mid ddc$$

where S is the goal or start symbol. Figure 6-1 illustrates the working of this brute-force parsing technique by showing the sequence of syntax trees generated during the parse of the string '$accd$'.

Initially we start with the tree of Fig. 6-1a, which merely contains the goal symbol. We next select the first production for S, thus yielding Fig. 6-1b. At this point we have matched the symbol a in the string to be parsed. We now choose the first production for A and obtain Fig. 6-1c. Note, however, that we have a mismatch between the second symbol c of the input string and the second symbol b in the sentential form abd. At this point in the parse, we must back up. The previous production application for A must be deleted and replaced with its next choice. The result of performing this operation is to transform Fig. 6-1c into Fig. 6-1d with the leftmost two characters of the given input string being matched. When the third symbol c of the input string is compared with the last symbol d of the current sentential form, however, a mismatch again occurs. The previously chosen production for A must be deleted. Since there are no more rules for A which can be selected, we must also delete the production for S and select the next production for S. This sequence of operations yields Fig. 6-1e. The final step involves applying the first rule for B to Fig. 6-1e. This application yields Fig.

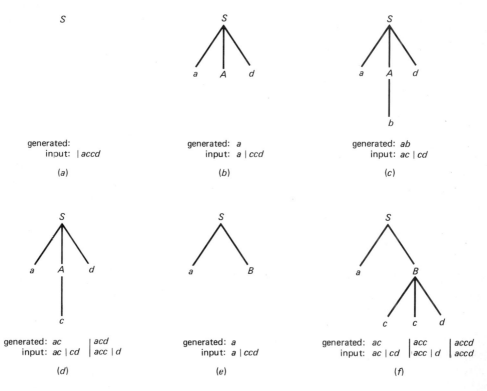

Figure 6-1 Trace of a brute-force top-down parse for string '$accd$'. (*Note*: The symbol | denotes the extent of the scanning process from left to right in the input string.)

6-1f. The remaining input symbols are then matched with the remaining symbols in the sentential form of Fig. 6-1f, thereby resulting in a successful parse.

The top-down parsing method just described will not work on every context-free grammar. We now examine a particular subclass of the context-free grammars which causes this method to fail.

Given a context-free grammar $G = (V_N, V_T, S, \Phi)$, a nonterminal X is said to be *left-recursive* if $X \overset{+}{\Rightarrow} X\alpha$ for some string $\alpha \in V^*$. If a grammar G contains at least one left-recursive nonterminal, G is said to be *left-recursive*.

A grammar which has one or more nonterminals that are left-recursive can be presented with strings to parse that will cause our informal top-down parsing method to enter an infinite loop of production applications. As an example of this phenomenon, consider the grammar

$$S \to aAc \qquad A \to Ab|\varepsilon$$

which generates the language $\{ab^nc|n \geq 0\}$. Figure 6-2 illustrates a trace of this situation for the attempted parse of the string 'abc'.

Of course, this particular infinite loop can be avoided by reversing the order of the productions for A to $A \to \varepsilon|Ab$ or by rewriting the first production for A so that the rule becomes $A \to bA$ (thus eliminating the left recursion). Not all left recursions, however, can be handled in such an easy manner.

The topic of left recursion will be discussed in more detail later in this subsection and in Sec. 6-2.4, where a method will be given that allows us to test whether or not a grammar has any nonterminals that are left-recursive.

We now present a formal characterization of this parsing method due to Aho and Ullman (1972) and an algorithm which implements it. The algorithm makes use of two stacks—one to record the current sentential form established by the series of expansions to date, and the other to record the history of the parse to date (i.e., which productions have been applied and at what point in the parse they were applied).

Letting $A \to \alpha_1|\alpha_2| \ldots |\alpha_n$ be the general form of the rules of the grammar, we specify that the alternative productions can be ordered and that A_i is the index of α_i—the ith alternate of A. The algorithm consists of a set of rules for manipulating the stacks and the input string in such a way that either the parse is constructed or a syntactic error is discovered.

To express these rules, we first define a *configuration* as an ordered 4-tuple

$$(s, i, \alpha, \beta)$$

where s is the state which can be one of q, normal parsing state, b, backtracking state, or t, termination state; where i is the index into the input string $t_1t_2\ldots t_n$, with t_{n+1} being #, an end marker; where $\alpha \in (V_T \cup \{A_i\})^*$ is a stack (top to the right) recording the current history of choices of alternates and input symbols checked; and where $\beta \in (V \cup \{\#\})^*$ is a stack (top to the left) recording the current sentential form, with the top element being the symbol currently being checked.

The initial configuration is $(q, 1, \varepsilon, S\#)$, where S is the goal symbol of the grammar. The algorithm operates by converting this initial configuration into a terminal configuration which yields no further configuration. One configuration

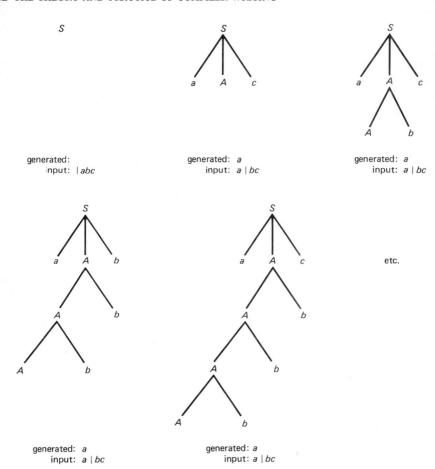

Figure 6-2 Nonterminating sequence of syntax trees generated from a left-recursive grammar in a top-down parse.

gives rise to another according to a particular "yields" relation. We define ⊢ ("yields") as

$$(s, i, \alpha, \beta) \vdash (s', i', \alpha', \beta') \text{ iff } s, s', i, i', \alpha, \alpha', \beta, \text{ and } \beta'$$

fit one of the following patterns:

1. Tree expansion (i.e., apply the first production of a nonterminal)

$$(q, i, \alpha, A\beta) \vdash (q, i, \alpha A_1, \gamma_1\beta) \qquad \text{for } A \rightarrow \gamma_1$$

being a production and γ_1 being the first alternate for A.
2. Input symbol match (i.e., advance the index into the input string)

$$(q, i, \alpha, a\beta) \vdash (q, i + 1, \alpha a, \beta) \qquad \text{for } t_i = a$$

3. Terminate (i.e., a successful parse has been performed)

$$(q, n + 1, \alpha, \#) \vdash (t, n + 1, \alpha, \varepsilon)$$

4. Input symbol mismatch (i.e., a generated substring failed to match the input)

$$(q, i, \alpha, a\beta) \vdash (b, i, \alpha, a\beta) \qquad \text{for all } t_i \neq a$$

5. Backtrack on input (i.e., back up the input string index)

$$(b, i, \alpha a, \beta) \vdash (b, i - 1, \alpha, a\beta) \qquad \text{for all } a \in V_T$$

6. Next alternate (i.e., replace with next production, if it exists, or with the nonterminal)

$$(b, i, \alpha A_j, \gamma_j\beta) \vdash (q, i, \alpha A_{j+1}, \gamma_{j+1}\beta) \text{ if } \gamma_{j+1} \text{ is the } j + 1\text{st alternate of } A.$$
$$\vdash \text{ no entry, if } i = 1, A = S, \text{ and there are only } j \text{ alternates for } A \text{ (there is no parse possible for the string!)}$$
$$\vdash (b, i, \alpha, A\beta) \text{ otherwise; (the alternates for } A \text{ have been exhausted; remove } A_j \text{ and place } A \text{ back in place of } \gamma_j)$$

Configurations yield configurations according to steps 1 to 6 until no further configuration can be produced, at which point the algorithm halts. (We assume here that the problem of left recursion does not arise.) If, upon halting, the final configuration is $(t, n + 1, \alpha, \varepsilon)$, we have produced a left parse of the input (i.e., a parse in which the leftmost nonterminal in a sentential form is the nonterminal that is rewritten). Otherwise the input is not part of the language generated by the grammar. If a left parse is produced, the ordered list of productions used in the parse is $h(x_1), h(x_2), \ldots, h(x_n)$ where $\alpha = x_1 x_2 \ldots x_n$ and h is defined as

$$h(x) = \begin{cases} \varepsilon & \text{if } x \in V_T \cup \{\varepsilon\} \\ k & \text{if } x \text{ is the } i\text{th alternate of } A \text{ and production } k \text{ is } A \rightarrow \gamma_i \end{cases}$$

We now present an algorithm to parse strings according to Aho and Ullman's (1972) top-down method with full backup. We assume that the productions of any grammar used in conjunction with this method have been pretested and all left recursion has been eliminated. To help describe the data structures used in the algorithm, the following grammar for partially parenthesized arithmetic expressions involving addition and multiplication will be used.

$$G_1 = \langle \{E, T, F, E', T'\}, \{+, *, b, (,)\}, E, \Phi \rangle$$

where Φ contains $E \rightarrow TE'$
$$E' \rightarrow +TE'|\varepsilon$$
$$T \rightarrow FT'$$
$$T' \rightarrow *FT'|\varepsilon$$
$$F \rightarrow b|(E)$$

These rules have been rewritten (from their usual form) in order to avoid left recursion. The method of eliminating direct left recursion in this example involves performing the following manipulations:

For the left-recursive nonterminal A whose rule is

$$A \rightarrow A\alpha_1|A\alpha_2| \cdots |A\alpha_n|\beta_1|\beta_2| \ldots |\beta_m$$

where β_i does not begin with A, replace this rule by the rules

$$A \rightarrow \beta_1|\beta_2| \ldots |\beta_m|\beta_1 A'| \ldots |\beta_m A'$$
$$A' \rightarrow \alpha_1|\alpha_2| \ldots |\alpha_n|\alpha_1 A'|\alpha_2 A'| \ldots |\alpha_n A'$$

For example, the familiar set of rules for deriving partially parenthesized arithmetic expressions in $+$ and $*$ is left-recursive in both E and T in the grammar

$$E \rightarrow E + T | T$$
$$T \rightarrow T * F | F$$
$$F \rightarrow (E) | a$$

We can eliminate this left recursion by rewriting the rules as

$$E \rightarrow T | TE'$$
$$E' \rightarrow + T | + TE'$$
$$T \rightarrow F | FT'$$
$$T' \rightarrow * F | * FT'$$
$$F \rightarrow (E) | a$$

Note that in replacing the braces notation of our sample grammar from Chap. 2, we implicitly formulated the productions in a manner very similar to this method of removing direct left recursion.

We store the productions in two arrays: LHS and RHS. Array LHS has elements each of which contains three fields. These fields are NT, containing the string representing a nonterminal symbol, MAX#, containing the number of productions that have this nonterminal as a left-hand side, and FIRST, containing the index into the array of right-hand sides for the first production for this nonterminal. Array LHS can be thought of as these three arrays, NT, MAX#, and FIRST being operated in parallel.

Array RHS is a simple array containing the right-hand sides of all the productions, each right-hand side being stored as a string that fills one entry in RHS. All the productions of a particular nonterminal are stored in successive positions of RHS.

For convenience, we assume that the goal symbol of the grammar is stored as the first entry of array LHS, and that each nonterminal and terminal symbol is a string of length 1. A right side is then just the concatenation of zero or more symbols, each of length 1. In this example, we assume that E' and T' are symbols of length 1.

For our example grammar G_1, the LHS and RHS arrays appear as in Fig. 6-3.

The stacks required for the operation of the algorithm are implemented with an array, HIST, representing the history stack, and a string, SENT, which records the current sentential form. An element of the array HIST contains two fields—SYMB, which contains a stack symbol (either a terminal or a nonterminal symbol) and P#, which contains either the number of the alternate for the

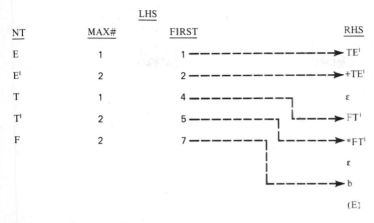

Figure 6-3 Data-structure representation of a grammar.

nonterminal in SYMB or the value zero if SYMB contains a terminal or the empty string. Thus a value of zero in P# marks a stack entry as a terminal symbol, and a value of j in P# (for j > 0) and the nonterminal A in SYMB represent the stack entry A_j. T_HIST points to the top of the history stack, HIST. The stack which represents the current sentential form, the string SENT, has as its top element the first (i.e., leftmost) symbol of SENT.

For example, the configuration $(q, 2, E_1 T_1 F_1 b, T'E'\#)$, which is generated as part of the parse of the input string b, would have its stacks represented as

HIST		SENT
P#	SYMB	
0	ε	T'E'#
1	E	↖ (top of stack)
1	T	
1	F	
T_HIST: → 0	b	

Note that the subscript associated with a nonterminal symbol in a configuration denotes the alternate number of that nonterminal; for example, the subscript in E_1 denotes the first (and only) alternate of E.

Algorithm TD_FULL. Given arrays LHS and RHS which represent the productions of grammar G as described earlier, and stacks represented by the vectors HIST and SENT, this algorithm parses strings to determine if they are part of the language generated by grammar G. The variables NT, MAX#, FIRST, SYMB, and P# are as just described, and T_HIST is the stack-top pointer for stack HIST. The history stack HIST has an initial entry of the empty string (treated as a terminal symbol). The input string, of length n, is in the string variable T. The variable i is the index of T that points to the next symbol of input to be processed. The variable STATE records the state of the parse. It represents either a normal state, a backtracking state, or a termination state. The variables p and s jointly contain the top element of the history stack, and variable t contains the leftmost symbol of the current sentential form. CASE is a local variable which is used to denote the current configuration of the sentential form. For convenience, we assume the availability of a function F, defined as

$$F(x) = \begin{cases} j & \text{if x is the jth nonterminal in array LHS (j > 0)} \\ 0 & \text{otherwise} \end{cases}$$

This algorithm is, in essence, an implementation of the "yields" relation that allows one parse configuration to give way to another.

1. [Initialize]
    n ← LENGTH(T)
    T ← T ∘ '#'
    STATE ← 'q'
    i ← 1
    P#[1] ← 0
    SYMB[1] ← ''
    T_HIST ← 1
    SENT ← NT[1] ∘ '#'
2. [Loop until parse is either successful or unsuccessful]
    Repeat through step 4
3. [Get stack-top elements and determine current configuration]
    p ← P#[T_HIST]
    s ← SYMB[T_HIST]
    t ← SUB(SENT, 1, 1)
    (Determine stack-top elements)
    If STATE = 'q' and i = n + 1 and t = '#'
    then CASE ← 3   (case 3)
    else If STATE = 'q'
        then If F(t) > 0
            then CASE ← 1   (case 1)
            else If t = SUB(T, i, 1)
                then CASE ← 2   (case 2)
                else CASE ← 4   (case 4)
        else If F(s) = 0
            then CASE ← 5   (case 5)
            else If p < MAX#[F(s)]
                then CASE ← 6   (case 6a)
                else If i = 1 and s = NT[1]
                    then Write('UNSUCCESSFUL PARSE')
                        Exit   (case 6b)
                  else CASE ← 7   (case 6c)

4. [Select the correct case]
   Select by (CASE)
   Case '1':
   > (Case 1: $(q, i, \alpha, A\beta) \vdash (q, i, \alpha A_1, \gamma_1\beta)$)
   > T_HIST ← T_HIST + 1
   > P#[T_HIST] ← 1
   > SYMB[T_HIST] ← t
   > SENT ← RHS[FIRST[F(t)]] • SUB(SENT, 2)

   Case '2':
   > (Case 2: $(q, i, \alpha, a\beta) \vdash (q, i + 1, \alpha a, \beta)$)
   > T_HIST ← T_HIST + 1
   > P#[T_HIST] ← 0
   > SYMB[T_HIST] ← t
   > i ← i + 1
   > SENT ← SUB(SENT, 2)

   Case '3':
   > (Case 3: $(q, n + 1, \alpha, \#) \vdash (t, n + 1, \alpha, \varepsilon)$)
   > STATE ← 't'
   > SENT ← ''
   > Write('SUCCESSFUL PARSE')
   > Exit

   Case '4':
   > (Case 4: $(q, i, \alpha, a\beta) \vdash (b, i, \alpha, a\beta)$)
   > STATE ← 'b'

   Case '5':
   > (Case 5: $(b, i, \alpha a, \beta) \vdash (b, i - 1, \alpha, a\beta)$)
   > i ← i − 1
   > T_HIST ← T_HIST − 1
   > SENT ← s ∘ SENT

   Case '6':
   > (Case 6a: $(b, i, \alpha A_j, \gamma_j\beta) \vdash (q, i, \alpha A_{j+1}, \gamma_{j+1}\beta)$)
   > STATE ← 'q'
   > P#[T_HIST] ← p + 1
   > SENT ← RHS[FIRST[F(s) + ɔ] ∘
   >   SUB(SENT, LENGTH(RHS[FIRST[F(s)] + p − 1]) + 1)

   Case '7':
   > (Case 6c: $(b, i, \alpha A_j, \gamma_j\beta) \vdash (b, i, \alpha, A\beta)$)
   > SENT ← s ∘ SUB(SENT, LENGTH(RHS[FIRST[F(s)] + p − 1]) + 1)
   > T_HIST ← T_HIST − 1   □

When this algorithm terminates, if the value of the variable STATE is not the string 't', then the input cannot be parsed. If, on the other hand, the value is 't', then a left parse is produced and the application of function h to the elements of stack HIST (from bottom to top) gives the numbers of the productions in the order in which they are applied in the parse.

For the example expression grammar and the input string $'b'$, a trace of the configurations generated by the algorithm in the course of the parse is

$$(q, 1, \varepsilon, E\#) \vdash (q, 1, E_1, TE'\#) \text{ (Case 1)}$$
$$\vdash (q, 1, E_1 T_1, FT'E'\#) \text{ (Case 1)}$$
$$\vdash (q, 1, E_1 T_1 F_1, bT'E'\#) \text{ (Case 1)}$$
$$\vdash (q, 2, E_1 T_1 F_1 b, T'E'\#) \text{ (Case 2)}$$
$$\vdash (q, 2, E_1 T_1 F_1 b T'_1, * FT'E'\#) \text{ (Case 1)}$$
$$\vdash (b, 2, E_1 T_1 F_1 b T'_1, * FT'E'\#) \text{ (Case 4)}$$
$$\vdash (q, 2, E_1 T_1 F_1 b T'_2, E'\#) \text{ (Case 6a)}$$
$$\vdash (q, 2, E_1 T_1 F_1 b T'_2 E'_1, + TE'\#) \text{ (Case 1)}$$
$$\vdash (b, 2, E_1 T_1 F_1 b T'_2 E'_1, + TE'\#) \text{ (Case 4)}$$
$$\vdash (q, 2, E_1 T_1 F_1 b T'_2 E'_2, \#) \text{ (Case 6a)}$$
$$\vdash (t, 2, E_1 T_1 F_1 b T'_2 E'_2, \varepsilon) \text{ (Case 3)}$$

Assuming that the productions of grammar G as presented earlier numbered 1 to 8 from top to bottom and left to right as they appear on the page, then the application of function H to the history stack $\varepsilon E_1 T_1 F_1 b T'_2 E'_2$ yields the following sequence indicating the productions applied and their order of use in the final parse: 1 4 7 6 3.

By examining the general nature of the operation of the brute-force algorithm, we can see that its basic form is that of a highly recursive set of procedure calls. This view is obvious if we think of each application of a production to expand a nonterminal as an invocation of a procedure which expands the nonterminal.

There are problems associated with methods of top-down parsing with full backup. Because of the many procedure calls or the excessive amount of backtracking required in some cases, they can be exceedingly slow. In some cases, the number of possible paths through all potential syntax trees can become so large that the construction of a parse for certain sentences becomes prohibitively expensive.

Another problem with full backup methods is that error recovery can be very poor. (The reader should refer to Chap. 5 for a discussion of error-recovery techniques.) One does not really find out that the input string is syntactically erroneous until all combinations have been tried, and by that time one cannot tell the first point at which an error was detected and why there is an error because the pointer into the input has been reset.

Another difficulty is that if code has been emitted as the parse has progressed, then every time we have to backtrack, we are forced to erase this code. This requires additional bookkeeping to associate blocks of code with states of the parse so that the required erasing can be performed correctly.

An obvious solution to these difficulties is to minimize the amount of backup performed. How much backup can be eliminated depends, of course, on the grammar, but empirically it has been found that most (if not all!) of the features deemed desirable in a programming language can be described by context-free grammars that can be parsed with no backup or limited backup. We will describe one such method in Sec. 6-2.

We reemphasize that the previous algorithms, due to backup, can be very inefficient. A recursive implementation of a top-down parsing technique which does not allow backup is given in the next subsection.

EXERCISES 6-1.1

1 Consider the grammar whose rules are

$$\langle e \rangle ::= \langle t \rangle + \langle e \rangle | \langle t \rangle$$

$$\langle t \rangle ::= \langle f \rangle * \langle t \rangle | \langle f \rangle$$

$$\langle f \rangle ::= (\langle e \rangle) | i$$

where the starting symbol is $\langle e \rangle$. Using the brute-force approach introduced at the beginning of this subsection, obtain a trace of the parse (see Fig. 6-1) for each of the following strings:

   (a) $i + i$
   (b) $i + i * i$
   (c) $(i + i)$

2 Using the sample grammar given in this section, give a trace of the formal characterization of the brute-force method for the following input strings:

   (a) $b + b$
   (b) $(b * b)$
   (c) $b + * b$

3 Let a grammar have the following rules:

$$\langle s \rangle ::= b \langle b \rangle \langle s \rangle | b$$

$$\langle b \rangle ::= a \langle s \rangle \langle b \rangle | a$$

where $\langle s \rangle$ denotes its starting symbol. Give a trace for the string *babab* of Algorithm TD_FULL if the order of alternates is as shown.

4 Write a computer program that implements Algorithm TD_FULL.

6-1.2 Recursive-Descent Parsers

In this section the brute-force parsing strategy just discussed is restricted so that backup is not allowed. This revised method of parsing, though less general, performs better than the brute-force method. This section also describes an approach to error detection and recovery for this modified parsing technique.

Recursive-descent parsing algorithm.. The top-down parsing method given in the previous section is very general but can be very time-consuming. A more efficient (though less general) method that does not allow backup can be devised. This method of parsing is known as *recursive descent*. It should be noted, however, that this highly recursive technique does not work on *all* context-free grammars. That is, certain grammars require backup in order for successful parsing to occur.

In the recursive-descent method of parsing, a sequence of production applications is realized in a sequence of function calls. In particular, functions are written for each nonterminal. Each function returns a value of *true* or *false* depending on whether or not it recognizes a substring which is an expansion of that nonterminal. The programming mechanism for the handling of recursive function calls provides the stacking capability required, thus freeing the user from having to establish and manipulate a stack explicitly, assuming that the language used supports recursion.

The remainder of this subsection presents an algorithm for the recursive-descent parsing method for the following context-free grammar:

$\langle$factor$\rangle$ ::= ($\langle$expr$\rangle$)|i
$\langle$term$\rangle$ ::= $\langle$factor$\rangle$ * $\langle$term$\rangle$|$\langle$factor$\rangle$
$\langle$expr$\rangle$ ::= $\langle$term$\rangle$ + $\langle$expr$\rangle$|$\langle$term$\rangle$

Note that this grammar contains right-recursive rules. In this way we have avoided the left-recursive problem. Also note that the alternates of $\langle$term$\rangle$ and $\langle$expr$\rangle$ have been ordered in such a way as to check for the longest alternate first. This approach is important when one alternate is a proper head of another alternate, and such is the case for the alternates of both $\langle$term$\rangle$ and $\langle$expr$\rangle$.

A recursive-descent parser for this example grammar contains one recursive function for each nonterminal in the grammar (i.e., $\langle$factor$\rangle$, $\langle$term$\rangle$, and $\langle$expr$\rangle$) which parses phrases for that nonterminal. Each function specifies where to begin a search for a phrase of its associated nonterminal. The function looks for a phrase by comparing the input string beginning at a specified point with the alternates of its associated nonterminal and invoking other functions to recognize the subgoals when required.

The following algorithm and its associated functions parses without any backup the strings of the language described by the example grammar. This is accomplished easily by using one context symbol following the part of the phrase which has already been parsed. The context symbol in question can be either a '+' or a '*'. Note that there are four functions: GET_CHAR, EXPR, FACTOR, and TERM. Also note that each function has no parameters or local variables. These observations are characteristic of recursive-descent parsers.

Algorithm RECDSNT. This algorithm calls four programmer-defined functions: GET_CHAR, EXPR, FACTOR, and TERM. The first one, GET_CHAR, always returns the next character in the input string, INPUT; and assigns it to the global variable NEXT. CHAR is local to GET_CHAR and contains the value to be returned. The latter three functions are all recursive and return either Boolean *true* or *false*. The variable CURSOR is also global to all routines and denotes the present character position in the input string. The variable i is a local index variable. SUB and LENGTH are built-in string-manipulation functions which return a specified substring of a string and the number of characters in a string, respectively.

1. [Initialize]
   Read (INPUT)
2. [Loop through all input strings]
      Repeat while there still remains an input string
         Repeat for i = 1, 2,...,LENGTH(INPUT)
            STRING[i] ← SUB(INPUT, i, 1)
         CURSOR ← 1
         NEXT ← GET_CHAR
         If EXPR
         then If NEXT = '#'
               then Write (INPUT, '□VALID')
               else Write (INPUT, '□INVALID')
         else Write (INPUT, '□INVALID')
         Read (INPUT)
      Exit

Function EXPR

1. [⟨expr⟩::= ⟨term⟩ + ⟨expr⟩|⟨term⟩]
      If not TERM
      then Return(false)
      If NEXT = '+'
      then NEXT ← GET_CHAR
         If NEXT = '#'
         then Return(false)
         If not EXPR
         then Return(false)
         else Return(true)
      else Return(true)

Function TERM

1. [⟨term⟩::= ⟨factor⟩*⟨term⟩|⟨factor⟩]
      If not FACTOR
      then Return(false)
      If NEXT = '*'
      then NEXT ← GET_CHAR
         If NEXT = '#'
         then Return(false)
         If not TERM
         then Return(false)
         else Return(true)
      else Return(true)

Function FACTOR

1. [⟨factor⟩::= (⟨expr⟩)|i]
   If NEXT = '#'
   then Return(false)
   If NEXT = '('
   then NEXT ← GET_CHAR
       If NEXT = '#'
       then Return(false)
       If not EXPR
       then Return(false)
       If NEXT ≠ ')'
       then Return(false)
       else NEXT ← GET_CHAR
           Return(true)
   If NEXT ≠ 'i'
   then Return(false)
   else NEXT ← GET_CHAR
       Return(true)

Function GET_CHAR

1. [Returns the next character from the input string]
   CHAR ← STRING[CURSOR]
   CURSOR ← CURSOR + 1
   Return(CHAR)   □

The following points are made concerning the algorithm:

1. The variable NEXT is global and contains the next symbol of the input string which is being processed. When a function to find a new goal is called, the first symbol to be examined is already in NEXT. Similarly, before returning from a function after a successful match, the symbol following the substring found by the function is put into NEXT.
2. The function GET_CHAR obtains the next input symbol.
3. To begin parsing, the main algorithm invokes the function GET_CHAR, which in turn places the leftmost symbol in the input string in NEXT.

A trace of the parse for the input

$$(i + i) * i\#$$

is given in Fig. 6-4. Note that h denotes the position of the current input symbol.

A final note concerning the parsing algorithm just given concerns the returning of true and false by the recursive functions. These truth values need not be returned. In fact, an explicit call to another routine can be made instead of

Input: $(i + i) * i\#$

h	
1	Perform MAIN
1	Call EXPR
1	Call TERM
1	Call FACTOR
1	check for #. No.
1	check for (. Yes. $h \leftarrow 2$.
2	check for #. No.
2	Call EXPR
2	Call TERM
2	Call FACTOR
2	check for #. No.
2	check for (. No.
2	check for i. Yes. $h \leftarrow 3$.
3	Return true from FACTOR.
3	check for * . No.
3	Return true from TERM.
3	check for +. Yes. $h \leftarrow 4$.
4	check for #. No.
4	Call EXPR
4	Call TERM
4	Call FACTOR
4	check for #. No.
4	check for (. No.
4	check for i. Yes. $h \leftarrow 5$.
5	Return true from FACTOR.
5	check for * . No.
5	Return true from TERM.
5	Return true from EXPR.
5	Return true from EXPR.
5	check for). Yes. $h \leftarrow 6$.
6	Return true from FACTOR.
6	check for * . Yes. $h \leftarrow 7$.
7	check for #. No.
7	Call TERM
7	Call FACTOR
7	check for #. No.
7	check for (. No.
7	check for i. Yes. $h \leftarrow 8$.
8	Return true from FACTOR.
8	check for * . No.
8	Return true from TERM.
8	Return true from TERM.
8	check for +. No.
8	Return true from EXPR.
8	check for #. Yes. $h \leftarrow 9$.
9	Return "VALID" from MAIN.

Figure 6-4 Trace of Algorithm RECDSNT for the string $(i + i) * i\#$.

returning false. The part of the algorithm that returns true can be eliminated. In other words, the recursive functions can be replaced by recursive procedures.

In the previous approach, right recursion was used to avoid the problem of left recursion. Another approach is to use an iterative form of the grammar.

$\langle\text{factor}\rangle ::= (\langle\text{expr}\rangle)|i$
$\langle\text{term}\rangle ::= \langle\text{factor}\rangle\{ * \langle\text{factor}\rangle\}$
$\langle\text{expr}\rangle ::= \langle\text{term}\rangle\{ + \langle\text{term}\rangle\}$

In this case, the constructs $\{ * \langle\text{factor}\rangle\}$ and $\{ + \langle\text{term}\rangle\}$ are implemented by using iteration in the functions of $\langle\text{term}\rangle$ and $\langle\text{factor}\rangle$, respectively. A revised algorithm based on this grammar is left as an exercise.

Thus far we have ignored error detection and error recovery in recursive-descent parsers. We next modify the parser just developed to handle syntax errors.

Error detection in recursive-descent parsers.. The recursive-descent parser presented in the previous subsection has little or no practical value. Any nontrivial grammar parsed in this manner will halt on the first error. A chain of "panic" travels up the stack, and at best, a diagnostic might point to the offending character. Alternately, a single error might put the parser so out of step with the input symbols that it would generate a barrage of near-meaningless error messages. However, a standard method of adding error detection and recovery to recursive-descent parsers has evolved and has been described in detail by Wirth (1976). The language being parsed must have a simple structure and reserved keywords for such a parser to perform sensibly. In general, such parsers either skip or insert symbols upon detecting an error until a reasonable analysis of the source text may be resumed. The following method provides a set of ground rules, which might be modified heursitically.

First, recursive procedures replace recursive functions. As before, each procedure P corresponds to some nonterminal or syntactic class A. However, once called, a procedure does not return any value to the calling procedure but rather insists on finding an instance of a syntactic class.

To illustrate, here is the function **EXPR** rewritten as a procedure.

Procedure EXPR

1. [Expect to find a term]
     Call TERM
2. [Try to obtain an expression]
     If NEXT = '+'
     then NEXT ← GET_CHAR
          (expect to find an expression)
          Call EXPR
3. [Finished]
     Return   □

Next, we must construct the sets of starters, followers, and stoppers for every syntactic class A. The set of *starters* of A is defined as the set of terminals which may legally start an instance of A. The set of *followers* of A is defined as the set of terminals which may follow an instance of A. The set of *stoppers* of A is a set of keywords of the grammar being parsed which may not necessarily follow an instance of A but should not be ignored under any circumstances. The set of stoppers may not be universal to every syntactic class.

Some data structure is necessary to represent these sets. Languages such as PASCAL which provide built-in set constructs greatly simplify this task. At this point, this problem is left to the reader.

Consider the following grammar for a simple block-nested language:

⟨program⟩::= ⟨title⟩ ; ⟨block⟩.
⟨title⟩::= **procedure**⟨procedure-id⟩
⟨block⟩::= **begin**⟨statement-list⟩**end**
⟨statement-list⟩::= ⟨statement⟩ ; ⟨statement-list⟩|⟨statement⟩ ;
⟨statement⟩::= ⟨if-statement⟩|⟨assignment-statement⟩|⟨block⟩
⟨if-statement⟩::= **if**⟨cond⟩⟨statement⟩
⟨assignment-statement⟩::= ⟨identifier⟩:= ⟨expr⟩

To simplify the discussion, we will leave the definition of ⟨cond⟩ up to the reader. We also add the rules:

⟨procedure-id⟩::= p
⟨identifier⟩::= i

We use the iterative definition of ⟨expr⟩ given on page 223.

This constraint artificially makes 'p' and 'i' keywords, which is not usually the case. However, it does not affect the generality of the discussion. When a statement in such a grammar is parsed, a statement not beginning with a keyword is typically assumed to be an assignment statement. This grammar will generate simple programs of the form:

```
procedure p;
begin
    i:= i;
    if⟨cond⟩
    begin
        if⟨cond⟩
            i:= i∗i;
        i:= i;
    end;
end.
```

For the syntactic class ⟨statement⟩, the set of starters consists of the symbols "**begin**," "**if**," and "**i**." The set of followers consists solely of the semicolon symbol. Constructing the set of stoppers is not as simple, but it may be reasonably assumed that it should at least include "**procedure**," "**begin**," "**end**," "**if**," the semicolon, and the period. For the rest of this discussion the set followers will describe the union of the sets of followers and stoppers.

A parsing procedure for some nonterminal *A* is constructed as follows: On entry to p, the current symbol is tested to ensure that it may legally start an instance of *A*. If so, the parsing procedure proceeds as before. But suppose the symbol is illegal. A first impulse might be to report an error and scan symbols until a legitimate starter of *A* is found. However, consider what would happen while parsing a ⟨block⟩ where the word "**begin**" was spelled incorrectly. If the block contained no blocks nested within, the parser working on the syntactic class ⟨block⟩ would scan and therefore ignore all the source inside the block.

A better idea would be to report an error and scan symbols until either a starter or a follower of A is found. Any symbols which have been ignored should be flagged. If the current symbol is a follower, report the appropriate error and return control to the calling program as if an instance of A has been successfully parsed.

Otherwise, procedure p expects to find an instance of A and begins parsing, which may of course include other recursive procedure calls. Upon completion of parsing an instance of A, it is necessary to check that the current symbol is a legitimate follower of A. If not, an error message is printed and input symbols are scanned until a proper follower is found. Control is then returned to the calling program.

In this manner, we create the following very general parsing algorithm for nearly any syntactic class.

Procedure CLASS(STARTERS, FOLLOWERS). This algorithm adds error detection and recovery to the parsing procedures of the type described thus far. CLASS could be any syntactic class—⟨expr⟩, ⟨statement⟩, ⟨block⟩, etc. The function SYM_IN(SYMBOL, SET) performs a search of the set SET and returns the value true if SYMBOL is a member. Otherwise, SYM_IN returns the value false. The procedure SKIP_TO(SET) scans input symbols until a symbol is found which is a member of the set SET. STARTERS is the set of starters of the syntactic class CLASS. FOLLOWERS is the set of followers. STARTERS_OR _FOLLOWERS is the union of the set of starters and the set of followers of CLASS. NEXT is a string which contains the current symbol. We assume the existence of a function GET_SYM which gets the next symbol from the input stream. The dotted lines represent the skeleton for the parsing procedure as it was before error detection and recovery were added.

1. [Is NEXT a valid starter of a syntactic class?]
   If not (SYM_IN(NEXT, STARTERS))
   then Write ('SYMBOL', NEXT, 'MAY NOT START AN INSTANCE
         OF CLASS')
      Call SKIP_TO(STARTERS_OR_FOLLOWERS)
2. [Is NEXT a starter or a follower of the current syntactic class?]
   If (SYM_IN(NEXT, STARTERS))
   then ....
         ....
         ....
      If not (SYM_IN(NEXT, FOLLOWERS))
      then Write ('SYMBOL', NEXT, 'MAY NOT FOLLOW AN
            INSTANCE OF CLASS')
         Call SKIP_TO(FOLLOWERS)
3. [Finished]
   Return   □

For example, the three lines of Procedure **EXPR** presented earlier might replace the dotted lines in the example. As such, this clearly entails a lot of redundant coding. At least two methods exist for eliminating the redundant coding. Welsh and McKeag (1980) make use of the PASCAL construct known as an envelope. In a recent paper, Topcor (1982) describes a parser which can be implemented in languages such as C, PL/1, and PASCAL which allow the passing of procedures as parameters. If PROC is the name of the parsing procedure passed to **CLASS**, then the dotted lines in algorithm **CLASS** are replaced by a call to a bare-bones parsing procedure PROC, which may make recursive calls to **CLASS**, etc.

Still more generalization is possible. The two "Write" statements might be replaced by a procedure ERROR which might be passed several parameters including the value of NEXT, a pointer to a diagnostic, a pointer to the symbol expected, etc., so that more intelligent error reporting might be done.

A strict implementation of this method yields useful results, though certain problems remain. Consider the following trivial program:

```
procedure p;
begin
i := i
end.
```

Assuming a rigorous implementation of this method, the missing semicolon will generate numerous error messages. (Why?) In many instances, it is useful to make a distinction between the stoppers and the followers of a syntactic class to better handle omissions of symbols. Again consider the incorrect assignment statement:

```
p :+ i * (i + i);
```

A difficult problem arises. An identifier "i" has been "misspelled." The assignment operator has also been improperly entered. Both are typical errors encountered using a parser based on this grammar. In a single sentence, we encounter two instances where a strict implementation of this parser would lead to numerous error messages. The decision we must make upon encountering each error is whether or not to persistently parse the current syntactic class or to give up and go on to the next class.

It is trivial to find exceptions to any hard-and-fast rule implemented in the parsing code. The point to remember is that programmers do not make their mistakes algorithmically. It is typical to forget an end statement or a semicolon but not so typical to omit an assignment operator. The parser does not share such prejudices. In practice, many test programs are necessary to test any parser's behavior over as wide as possible a range of human behavior to ensure that detection is complete, reporting is accurate, and recovery is full.

In general a good parser should not collapse on any input sequence. It should be able to detect and mark all incorrect constructs and in particular should recover well from errors that are made frequently.

We have to this point examined parsing strategies which involve no backup or full backup. We next examine a parsing strategy which involves using partial or limited backup.

EXERCISES 6-1.2

1 Expand the recursive-descent parser given in this subsection to include the division and subtraction operators (i.e., / and −).

2 The following grammar describes a string-manipulation expression language.

$\langle$string assign$\rangle$::= I ← $\langle$substr expr$\rangle$
$\langle$substr expr$\rangle$ ::= $\langle$concat expr$\rangle$! $\langle$position$\rangle$: $\langle$position$\rangle$
$\langle$concat expr$\rangle$ ::= S | I | S‖$\langle$concat expr$\rangle$ | I‖$\langle$concat expr$\rangle$
$\langle$position$\rangle$ ::= $\langle$length expr$\rangle$ | $\langle$substr expr$\rangle$? $\langle$substr expr$\rangle$
$\langle$length expr$\rangle$ ::= T | @$\langle$substr expr$\rangle$

Note that ← , !, ‖, ?, @, I (meaning "identifier"), S (meaning "string"), and T (meaning "integer") are all terminals in this grammar. Formulate a recursive-descent parser for this language.

3 Add rules to the grammar on page 225 which define $\langle$expr$\rangle$ and $\langle$cond$\rangle$.

4 (*a*) Implement the grammar on page 225 in algorithmic notation. Consider the sample program on page 227. Illustrate with a trace the number of error messages the single error in the sample program will generate.

(*b*) Using the method described, implement the grammar on page 225 in the language of your choice. Ensure that error reporting is not redundant.

5 Consider the grammar:

$A \rightarrow aB | aC$
$B \rightarrow bB | b$
$C \rightarrow bC | c$

What problem occurs when trying to write a recursive-descent parser for this grammar? Based on this, formulate a general property of grammars which can be parsed by recursive-descent parsers.

6-1.3 Notions of Top-Down Parsing with Limited Backup

Let us assume that we have rules of the form $A \rightarrow \alpha_1 | \alpha_2 | \cdots | \alpha_n$. In the case of full backup parsing we try all alternatives until we ultimately succeed or fail, even if some α_j has been used to derive a string which is a prefix of the input. That is, assume that α_j has been found to derive some prefix but that later in the parse we exhaust all possible alternatives for some other nonterminal. Using parsing with full backup, we then try alternatives $\alpha_{j+1}, \alpha_{j+2}, \ldots, \alpha_n$. In limited backup parsing, however, the parse would fail at this point and terminate. In summary, limited backup parsing will not erase a successful match; instead, it will fail.

This can be explained in more detail as follows: Let $t_1 t_2 \ldots t_n$ be the entire input string and assume we have generated a partial left parse that matches the prefix string $t_1 t_2 \ldots t_{i-1}$. Let A be the next nonterminal to be expanded. A procedure corresponding to A is called, with i being the input index. Now A will succeed at i if A derives a prefix of $t_i t_{i+1} \ldots t_n$; otherwise A will fail at i. So, in expanding A we try α_1. If it fails, we try α_2. If it fails, we try α_3, and so forth. Assume that finally α_j succeeds at i by deriving a string matching $t_i t_{i+1} \ldots t_k$. Full backup parsing could eventually return to position i to discard α_j and try to continue by trying $\alpha_{j+1}, \alpha_{j+2}$, etc., at position i, possibly deriving a prefix $t_i t_{i+1} \ldots t_m$ that is different from $t_i t_{i+1} \ldots t_k$, the string matched by α_j. (This can happen if some later nonterminal fails on all its alternatives.) Partial backup parsing will not discard α_j; it will simply fail. If, ultimately, the matching substring is incorrect in the sense that the entire input cannot be parsed, then A will be treated as if no prefix can be matched. Therefore, once some alternative can be used in deriving some prefix that matches (even if it is a "wrong" prefix), no further alternates will be tried.

Aho and Ullman (1972) present two forms of limited backup parsing. In both cases, the rules of the grammar are considered to be rules that form a program which specifies the particular parsing associated with a grammar. A program looks very much like a grammar that is expressed in a particular normal form.

The rules of these programs have certain intended actions associated with them, and it is in the specifications of these intended actions ("semantics") that the top-down parsing technique has its backup procedures specified and limited. Different intended actions or different normal forms for the rules are used to produce different versions of limited backup parsing. The details of these approaches can be found in Aho and Ullman (1972). One method, however, which behaves like a limited backup is the topic of the next subsection.

6-1.4 Top-Down Parsing with Limited Backup

This section examines a representation of a top-down parsing technique which is more general than the recursive-descent method of Sec. 6-1.2 and less powerful than the brute-force method of Sec. 6-1.1, which had full backup capabilities. In other words, the method which is presented here has a backup capability, but there are some grammars for which the brute-force method succeeds but the method of this subsection fails. An example will be used to show this later.

Knuth (1971) provides a very concise representation of a top-down parsing technique. This representation takes the form of a set of assembler-type statements, each having an opcode and two address fields, AT and AF. Let h be a global index into the input string $t_1 t_2 \ldots t_n$. There are two kinds of opcodes:

1. Terminal symbol; e.g., a

   action: if $t_h = a$,
           then $h \leftarrow h + 1$, and go to AT;
           otherwise go to AF

2. Address of procedure; e.g., $[A]$, a nonterminal symbol in brackets

   action: call the procedure in location A. (The procedure returns
           true or *false* as a value.)
           If *true*, then go to AT; otherwise go to AF.

There are three kinds of address fields:

1. Nonterminal symbol; e.g., A

   meaning: go to the procedure in location A (i.e., a "go to,"
   not a "call")

2. Blank

   meaning: proceed to the next instruction

3. True or false
   true—return to the calling procedure with the value *true*
   false—reset h to the value it had on entry to this procedure;
   return to the calling procedure with the value *false*

In addition, OK is the address in the main program to which control passes when a parse is successful; ERROR is the address to which transfer is made on an unsuccessful parse, either to attempt recovery or simply to emit a message.

For example, given the grammar whose rules are:

$$S \rightarrow E\#$$
$$E \rightarrow TE'$$
$$E' \rightarrow +TE'|\varepsilon$$
$$T \rightarrow FT'$$
$$T' \rightarrow *FT'|\varepsilon$$
$$F \rightarrow b|(E)$$

with S being the goal symbol and $V_T = \{(,), b, +, *, \#\}$, the parsing program could be developed by applying the previous definitions of opcodes and address fields. Such a program is presented in the following discussion. Note that the symbol $\#$ is a special marker symbol which appears only at the end of the given input string.

Empty productions can be handled readily. If we have $X \rightarrow \varepsilon$ as one of the productions, the following subprogram achieves the desired results:

X	$[N]$	True	True
N	a	False	False

where X and N are locations and a is any terminal. The effect is that we automatically return *true* from X but without advancing h, precisely the actions we desire.

There is a standard form into which the rules can be put. This general form is

$$X \rightarrow Y_1|Y_2|\ldots|Y_m|Z_1Z_2\ldots Z_n, \text{ with each } Y_i \text{ and } Z_i \text{ being a}$$
terminal or nonterminal, and $m \geq 0, n \geq 0$.

If $m + n = 0$, then the rule is $X \rightarrow \varepsilon$. A rule which is not in this standard form can always be rewritten so that we have a set of rules that are in this form. Given a rule, $X \rightarrow \alpha_1 | \alpha_2 | \ldots | \alpha_m | Z_1 \ldots Z_n$, we can replace it with

$$X \rightarrow Y_1' | Y_2' | \ldots | Y_m' | Z_1 \ldots Z_n$$
$$Y_1' \rightarrow \alpha_1$$
$$Y_2' \rightarrow \alpha_2$$
$$\vdots$$
$$Y_m' \rightarrow \alpha_m$$

For our example grammar, after adding the new nonterminals E'' and T'' and the productions $E'' \rightarrow + TE'$ and $T'' \rightarrow * FT'$ in order to convert each rule to standard form, Fig. 6-5 can serve as its parsing program.

Let us trace though the action of this program in terms of its calling and checking sequences as it parses the string $(b * b)\#$. Assume an initial call to the procedure associated with the goal symbol of the grammar, and an initial value of 1 for h. Such a trace is given in Fig. 6-6.

Location	Op-code	AT	AF
S	$[E]$		ERROR
	$\#$	OK	ERROR
E	$[T]$		False
	$[E']$	True	False
E'	$[E'']$	True	
	$[N]$	True	True
E''	$+$		False
	$[T]$		False
	$[E']$	True	False
T	$[F]$		False
	$[T']$	True	False
T'	$[T'']$	True	
	$[N]$	True	True
T''	$*$		False
	$[F]$		False
	$[T']$	True	False
F	b	True	
	$($		False
	$[E]$		False
	$)$	True	False
N	b	False	False

Figure 6-5 Parser representation of a sample grammar.

Input $(b * b)$ #

```
 h
 ─
 1    Call S
 1        Call E
 1            Call T
 1                Call F
 1                    check for b.   No.
 1                    check for (.   Yes.   h → 2.
 2                    Call E
 2                        Call T
 2                            Call F
 2                                check for b.   Yes.   h → 3.
 3                                return true from F.
 3                            Call T'
 3                                Call T''
 3                                    check for * .   Yes.   h → 4.
 4                                    Call F
 4                                        check for b.   Yes.   h → 5.
 5                                        Return true from F.
 5                                    Call T'
 5                                        Call T''
 5                                            check for * .   No.
 5                                            Return false from T''.
 5                                        Call N
 5                                            check for b.   No.
 5                                            Return false from N.
 5                                        Return true from T'
 5                                    Return true from T''.
 5                                Return true from T'.
 5                            Return true from T.
 5                            Call E'
 5                                Call E''
 5                                    check for +.   No.
 5                                    Return false from E''.
 5                                Call N
 5                                    check for b.   No.
 5                                    Return false from N.
 5                                Return true from E'.
 5                        Return true from E.
 5                        check for ).   Yes.   h → 6.
 6                    Return true from F.
 6                Call T'
 6                    Call T''
 6                        check for * .   No.
 6                        Return false from T''.
 6                    Call N
 6                        check for b.   No.
 6                        Return false from N.
 6                    Return true from T'.
 6                Return true from T.
 6                Call E'
 6                    Call E''
 6                        check for +.   No.
 6                        Return false from E''.
 6                    Call N
 6                        check for b.   No.
 6                        Return false from N.
 6                    Return true from E'.
 6            Return true from E.
 6        Return to label OK in main program.
```

Figure 6-6 Parse trace of the string $(b * b)$ #.

The problem with this algorithm is that we cannot reconstruct the parse. The *true* returns are actually the steps in the parse, but after parsing is complete, we no longer know this return sequence. A solution, of course, is to emit code whenever we return *true* from a procedure. Alternatively, a list can be constructed of the return sequence.

The syntax tree for this parse is given in Fig. 6-7. By examining it, we see that the order in which productions are applied is precisely the order in which the *true* returns occur in the execution of the parsing program. This order can be shown by listing the nonterminal left-hand sides of the productions applied. This order is *FFT'T''T'TE'EFT'TE'ES*.

In the design of parsing algorithms based on rules similar to those of grammar *G*, or on rules cast into the specified standard form, a certain amount of care must be taken. For example, if we have the rule $X \to a|ab$, the string *ab* will never be recognized as an *X*; the value *true* will always be returned once the *a* has been encountered. Having the rules written in this standard form makes several solutions to this problem possible. One solution is to order the alternatives properly so that the longest is first. In this case, the rule would be rewritten as $X \to ab|a$. Another method is to factor out the common element *a*. The rule could then be written as $X \to a[b]$, and a program to handle this rule would be (after a bit of optimizing):

X	a		False
	b	True	True

This approach has the advantage of saving one backup step.

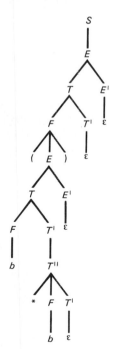

Figure 6-7 Syntax tree for parse of $(b * b)$.

Location	Op-code	AT	AF
S	$[S']$		ERROR
	#	OK	ERROR
S'	$[A]$		False
	$[B]$	True	False
A	$[A']$	True	
	a	True	False
A'	a		False
	a	True	False
B	b	True	
	a		False
	c	True	False

Figure 6-8

As mentioned at the beginning of this subsection, this method does not succeed for all grammars. Consider the grammar

$$S \rightarrow S'\#$$
$$S' \rightarrow AB$$
$$A \rightarrow aa|a$$
$$B \rightarrow b|ac$$

Putting this grammar in standard form yields the following grammar:

$$S \rightarrow S'\#$$
$$S' \rightarrow AB$$
$$A \rightarrow A'|a$$
$$A' \rightarrow aa$$
$$B \rightarrow b|ac$$

A parser program for this grammar is given in Fig. 6-8. For the valid input string *aac*#, the parser program fails in its attempt to construct a parse. We leave it as an exercise for the reader to verify this fact. The brute-force method of Sec. 6-1.1, however, succeeds in parsing the input string *aac*#. We also leave the verification of this point as an exercise.

EXERCISES 6-1.4

1 Write a parser using Knuth's assembler-style notation for a grammar expressing partially parenthesized arithmetic expressions in +, −, *, /, ↑ (exponentiation). The operators + and − are binary operations, left-associative, and of equal precedence (the lowest). The operators * and / are binary operations, left-associative, and of higher precedence than + and −. The operator ↑ is a binary operator, right-associative, and of highest precedence. Design the grammar yourself, and then implement the parser for it.

2 Expand the grammar of Exercise 1 to include the assignment operator, assuming it to be binary but incapable of associating. It has the lowest precedence (lower than + or −).

3 Verify, by tracing the parser program of Fig. 6-3, that the input string $aac\#$ is rejected although it is valid.

4 For the example grammar given at the end of the subsection verify that the brute-force method of Sec. 6-1.1 succeeds for the input string $aac\#$.

6-2 TOP-DOWN PARSING WITH NO BACKUP

In this section top-down parsing with no backup is discussed. The information required during a no-backup parse is first discussed informally and then formally characterized in terms of LL(1) grammars. This class of grammars can be parsed in a deterministic manner by looking at the next input symbol in the input string to be parsed. The discussion will proceed as follows: First the class of simple LL(1) grammars is introduced. This class of grammars is very easily parsed and ε-rules are not allowed. The next step is to permit a more general form of production but still not allow ε-rules to be used. Finally the general class of LL(1) grammars are introduced with ε-rules allowed.

Parsing algorithms are given for each subclass of grammars just discussed. The parsing tables required in these algorithms can be obtained directly from the rules of the grammars. The use of bit matrices (refer to Sec. 2-1.2) can facilitate the generation of such parsing tables.

LL(1) grammars have been used in defining programming languages for some 15 years (Lewis and Stearns, 1968). The parsing algorithm for this class of grammars is efficient. Actually, the performance of this algorithm is a linear function of the input string length. Furthermore, error-detection and -recovery techniques can be easily appended to the parsing algorithm for this class of grammars. Details of such diagnostic techniques will be described in this section.

6-2.1 Notions of Parsing with No Backup

In the situation where no backup is allowed, our problem becomes one of determining which production is to be applied given that we know which nonterminal we are attempting to expand and which head (see Sec. 2-1.3) of the input string has been successfully parsed to this point. We are looking for a left canonical parse (see Sec. 2-4.2), that is, a parse in which the leftmost nonterminal in the current sentential form is always chosen for expansion. (A similar analysis can be made for right canonical parses.)

Another way of stating this requirement is that we must always make the correct choice among alternative productions for a particular nonterminal so that we never undo a particular expansion. Either the parse moves directly from left to right across the input string and concludes successfully or it reaches a point where no production can correctly be applied, in which case the input string is rejected as being invalid.

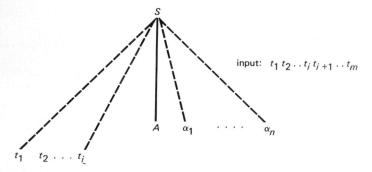

input: $t_1 t_2 \cdots t_i t_{i+1} \cdots t_m$

Figure 6-9

Figure 6-9 illustrates this situation in terms of a generalized syntax diagram. At the point illustrated, the head $t_1 t_2 \ldots t_i$ of the input string $t_1 t_2 \ldots t_m$ has been matched and the nonterminal A is to be expanded. We must now correctly choose which production to use to expand A, the leftmost nonterminal in the current sentential form $t_1 t_2 \ldots t_i A \alpha_1 \ldots \alpha_n$.

A large class of left-parsible grammars, the LL(k) grammars, allow this determination of the correct production to apply. Given the input head (prefix) parsed to this point and the leftmost nonterminal, the correct production can be applied provided that we also know the next few symbols of the unparsed input substring—say, the k symbols $t_{i+1} t_{i+2} \ldots t_{i+k}$. As a simple instance of the nature of the help provided by this lookahead of k symbols, we next turn to a discussion of simple LL(1) grammars.

6-2.2 Simple LL(1) Grammars

In this section we examine a class of grammars which can be parsed by simply looking at the next symbol in the unparsed input string in order to decide which production is to be applied. The parsing method described here is deterministic in the sense that no backup is required. We first describe in an informal manner a parser for this class of grammars. The discussion is followed by an algorithm which will construct a parser from a given grammar in this class.

> **Definition 6-1** A *simple LL*(1) *grammar* is a context-free grammar without ε-rules such that for every $A \in V_N$, the alternates for A each begin with a different terminal symbol. More formally, a context-free grammar is called a *simple LL*(1) *grammar* or an *s-grammar* if all of its rules are of the form
>
> $$A \rightarrow a_1 \alpha_1 | a_2 \alpha_2 | \ldots | a_m \alpha_m, a_i \neq a_j \text{ for } i \neq j \text{ and } a_i \in V_T \text{ for } 1 \leq i \leq m.$$
>
> The language generated by an *s*-grammar is called an *s-language*.

These simple LL(1) grammars were first investigated by Korenjak and Hopcroft (1966).

As an example, consider the grammar whose productions are:

1. $S \rightarrow aS$
2. $S \rightarrow bA$
3. $A \rightarrow d$
4. $A \rightarrow ccA$

Clearly this grammar is a simple LL(1) grammar. It is convenient (and necessary, when ε-rules are introduced in Sec. 6-2.4) to have some end-marker symbol at the end of all input strings to be parsed. We use the symbol # to denote the end of the input string. Because # is not in the terminal vocabulary V_T of the grammar, it is impossible for some malicious person to insert the # in the middle of the input string. Conventionally the grammar is augmented with an extra production

0. $S' \rightarrow S\#$

which facilitates the construction of certain relations and tables later in this chapter.

Let us construct the parse of the string $aabccd\#$ according to the preceding grammar. The leftmost canonical derivation for the sample input string is as follows:

$$S' \underset{L}{\Rightarrow} S\# \underset{L}{\Rightarrow} aS\# \underset{L}{\Rightarrow} aaS\# \underset{L}{\Rightarrow} aabA\# \underset{L}{\Rightarrow} aabccA\# \underset{L}{\Rightarrow} aabccd\#$$

The parse tree for this derivation is given in Fig. 6-10.

We now describe an informal method for constructing, in a top-down manner without backup, the parse tree of Fig. 6-10. This construction process will then be

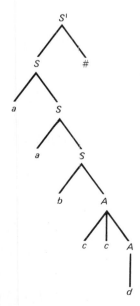

Figure 6-10 Parse tree for the string $aabccd\#$.

formalized. Recall in the brute-force method with full backup (Sec. 6-1.1) that two stacks were used, one for the current sentential form and the other for the history of the parse. In parsing a simple LL(1) grammar, only one stack is required. Its purpose is to record a portion of the current sentential form. If the current sentential form is $t_1 t_2 \ldots t_i A \alpha_1 \ldots \alpha_n$, where the substring $t_1 t_2 \ldots t_i$ denotes the prefix of the given input string which is matched so far, then the portion of the current sentential form which is retained in the stack is the string $A \alpha_1 \ldots \alpha_n$. This string, in the case of a valid input string, will produce the remaining unmatched input symbols. That is, for the input string $t_1 t_2 \ldots t_m$, $A \alpha_1 \alpha_2 \ldots \alpha_n \overset{+}{\underset{L}{\Rightarrow}} t_{i+1} \ldots t_m$. In addition to the stack, an output tape is used to record the production numbers in the order in which they were applied. The symbol # is used as the stack bottom symbol. Initially, the stack is set to the contents

$S\#$

with the leftmost symbol denoting the top symbol in the stack. From this initial configuration, a rule must be selected on the basis of the top stack symbol and the current input character being examined. With a stack symbol of S and the current input symbol a, rule 1 must be chosen if we are to avoid backup. So S is replaced by the right part of rule 1, thus giving a stack contents of

$aS\#$

Now, since the stack symbol is a terminal which matches the current input symbol, the stack is popped and the input cursor is advanced. The current stack contents are

$S\#$

The second symbol a in the original input string then becomes the new current symbol. Rule 1 is again chosen. Note that in each of these two cases the choice is made in a deterministic manner. With this rule application the stack contents change to

$aS\#$

The stack symbol is a, which matches the second input symbol. This condition causes the stack to be popped. The input cursor is then advanced, with b becoming the new current input symbol. The stack contents are

$S\#$

Based on the fact that the stack symbol is S and the current input symbol is b, rule 2 can be chosen in a deterministic manner as the production to apply at this point. The stack symbol is replaced by the right part of this rule, thus yielding a stack contents of

$bA\#$

The stack and the current input symbols now match and the stack is popped and the input cursor is advanced to its next position. The current stack contents are

$A\#$

The stack symbol A and the current input symbol c uniquely specify that rule 4 and not rule 3 must be applied at this point. Therefore, the A on the stack is replaced by ccA, thus giving a new stack contents of

$ccA\#$

This process is continued until the remaining input symbols are processed. A trace of this parse is given in Table 6-1.

We can now, in a more formal manner, formulate a parsing algorithm for the process just described. The heart of this algorithm is a parsing function which is represented in a table. Given the symbol at the top of the stack and the next input symbol, the table yields as a value either the production to apply or else an indication of how to continue or terminate. This table is defined in a manner similar to that given in Sec. 6-1.1 as follows:

$M: \{V \cup \{\#\}\} \times \{V_T \cup \{\#\}\} \rightarrow \{(\beta, i), \ pop, \ accept, \ error\}$
where $\#$ marks the bottom of the stack and the end of the input
string, and where (β, i) is an ordered pair such that β is the
right part of production number i.

In short, if A is the symbol on top of the stack and a is the current input symbol, then $M(A, a)$ is defined as follows:

$$M(A, a) = \begin{cases} pop & \text{if } A = a \text{ for } a \in V_T \\ accept & \text{if } A = \# \text{ and } a = \# \\ (a\alpha, i) & \text{if } A \rightarrow a\alpha \text{ is the } i\text{th production} \\ error & \text{otherwise} \end{cases}$$

Table 6-1 Trace of a top-down parse for the string $aabccd\#$

Unused input string	Stack contents	Output tape
$aabccd\#$	$S\#$	ε
$aabccd\#$	$aS\#$	1
$abccd\#$	$S\#$	1
$abccd\#$	$aS\#$	11
$bccd\#$	$S\#$	11
$bccd\#$	$bA\#$	112
$ccd\#$	$A\#$	112
$ccd\#$	$ccA\#$	1124
$cd\#$	$cA\#$	1124
$d\#$	$A\#$	1124
$d\#$	$d\#$	11243
$\#$	$\#$	11243

The parsing function M for the current example grammar is given in Table 6-2. Note that the column headings of the table are the # end marker and the terminal alphabet of the grammar. The row headings consist of the stack bottom marker # and the vocabulary symbols.

We use the parsing function M to alter configurations as we did in the full backup algorithm of Sec. 6-1.1. Given the general form of a parse configuration, $(az, A\alpha, P)$ where az is the unused input string, $A\alpha$ is the stack with A being the stack top, and P is the output tape contents, we use $M(A, a)$, where a is the current input symbol, to determine the next configuration according to the "yields" relation ($\vdash$) given by

$$
(az, A\alpha, P) \vdash
\begin{cases}
(z, \alpha, P) & \text{if } M(A, a) = pop \\
\text{No entry (terminate)} & \text{if } M(A, a) = accept \\
(az, \beta\alpha, Pi) & \text{if } M(A, a) = (\beta, i) \\
\text{No entry (error stop)} & \text{if } M(A, a) = error
\end{cases}
$$

The initial configuration is $(z, S\#, \varepsilon)$, where z is the entire input string and S is the goal symbol.

As an example, consider the parse of the string $aabccd\#$ according to our current sample grammar. The sequence of configurations in the parse of this string is

$$
\begin{aligned}
(aabccd\#, S\#, \varepsilon) &\vdash (aabccd\#, aS\#, 1) \\
&\vdash (abccd\#, S\#, 1) \\
&\vdash (abccd\#, aS\#, 11) \\
&\vdash (bccd\#, S\#, 11) \\
&\vdash (bccd\#, bA\#, 112) \\
&\vdash (ccd\#, A\#, 112) \\
&\vdash (ccd\#, ccA\#, 1124) \\
&\vdash (cd\#, cA\#, 1124) \\
&\vdash (d\#, A\#, 1124) \\
&\vdash (d\#, d\#, 11243) \\
&\vdash (\#, \#, 11243)
\end{aligned}
$$

terminate with a successful parse.

Table 6-2 Parsing function for a simple LL(1) grammar

Stack symbol	Current input symbol				
	a	b	c	d	#
S	$(aS, 1)$	$(bA, 2)$			
A			$(ccA, 4)$	$(d, 3)$	
a	pop				
b		pop			
c			pop		
d				pop	
#					$accept$

Blank entries are all *error* entries.

Table 6-3

Unused input string	Stack contents	Output tape
aabccd#	S#	ε
abccd#	S#	1
bccd#	S#	11
ccd#	A#	112
cd#	cA#	1124
d#	A#	1124
#	#	11243

An algorithm similar to **Algorithm TD_FULL** of Sec. 6-1.1 can be formulated to parse a simple LL(1) language. This task is left as an exercise.

Before the end of this section, it should be noted that the parsing process, as exemplified by Table 6-1 for the case of simple LL(1) grammars, can be simplified. In particular, since the nonterminal on the stack and the current input symbol uniquely determine which rule is to be used and, furthermore, the leftmost symbol in that rule always matches the current input symbol, only the right part of the rule excluding its leftmost symbol need be stacked. If this is done, a more efficient algorithm results. A trace of the parsing process which uses this approach is given in Table 6-3. It is also left as an exercise to formulate an algorithm which takes advantage of this observation.

In summary, we have introduced a class of grammars which are very easy and efficient to parse. The restrictions placed on the rules of a simple LL(1) grammar, however, are severe. It is highly desirable, for practical reasons, to expand the class of grammars which can be handled by such a straightforward approach. This problem is examined in the next subsection.

EXERCISES 6-2.2

1 For the sample grammar used in this section, give a trace (as in Table 6-1) of the parse for each of the following input strings:
(a) bccd#
(b) abccccd#

2 Formulate a parsing table for the simple LL(1) grammar whose rules are

$$S' \rightarrow S\#$$

$$S \rightarrow aA\,|\,b\,|\,cB\,|\,d$$

$$A \rightarrow aA\,|\,b$$

$$B \rightarrow cB\,|\,d$$

Using this parsing table, give a trace of the parse for each of the following input strings:
(a) aaab#
(b) ccd#

3 Obtain a simple LL(1) grammar for the language $\{ab^na b^{n+1}\,|\,n \geq 0\}$.

4 Obtain a simple LL(1) grammar for an arithmetic expression in ALGOL 60.

5 Formulate a parsing algorithm (similar to Algorithm TD_FULL of Sec. 6-1.1) for simple LL(1) grammars.

6 Based on the suggestions given at the end of this subsection, formulate an improved parsing algorithm for simple LL(1) grammars.

7 Modify the implementation algorithm obtained in Exercise 5 so as to incorporate these improvements.

6-2.3 LL(1) Grammars without ε-Rules

In this section we pursue the discussion of top-down deterministic parsers which require only one lookahead symbol. Our aim is to generalize the simple LL(1) grammars discussed in the previous subsection. This generalization will eliminate some of the restrictions which were imposed on these simple grammars. Specifically, the condition that the leftmost symbol in the right part of a production must be a terminal symbol is removed. One restriction which still remains, however, is that ε-rules are not allowed. This restriction will be removed in the next subsection. Furthermore, it should be noted that LL(1) grammars without ε-rules have the same generative power as s-grammars (see Kurki-Suonio, 1969). That is, given an LL(1) grammar without ε-rules we can obtain an equivalent s-grammar which generates the same language.

Throughout the following discussion, it is assumed that all useless symbols and left-recursive rules have been eliminated from the grammar. We return to the problem of left-recursive grammars later.

Let us attempt to parse, in a deterministic manner which is based on a single lookahead character, the input string $adbbebe\#$ generated by the following grammar:

0. $S' \rightarrow S\#$	4. $A \rightarrow c$
1. $S \rightarrow ABe$	5. $B \rightarrow AS$
2. $A \rightarrow dB$	6. $B \rightarrow b$
3. $A \rightarrow aS$	

The leftmost derivation for the given string is

$$S' \underset{L}{\Rightarrow} S\# \underset{L}{\Rightarrow} ABe\# \underset{L}{\Rightarrow} aSBe\# \underset{L}{\Rightarrow} aABeBe\# \underset{L}{\Rightarrow} adBBeBe\#$$

$$\underset{L}{\Rightarrow} adbBeBe\# \underset{L}{\Rightarrow} adbbeBe\# \underset{L}{\Rightarrow} adbbebe\#$$

and the associated syntax tree is given in Fig. 6-11. Note that this grammar is not in its present form a simple LL(1) grammar. Productions 0, 1, and 5 violate the simple LL(1) condition.

Using the approach taken in the previous subsection, let us now attempt to parse the given string based on a one-character lookahead. As before, the stack is initialized to the contents

$S\#$

with the leftmost symbol denoting the top symbol in the stack. From this initial

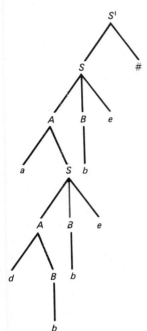

Figure 6-11 Parse tree for the string *adbbebe#*.

configuration, a rule must be selected on the basis of the top stack symbol (S) and the current input character being examined (a). For the simple LL(1) grammar case, we merely had to select the rule whose left part and the leftmost symbol in its right part were the stack symbol and the current input symbol, respectively. In this instance, however, such an approach is inadequate, since the only rule which has S as its left part contains a nonterminal (A) as the leftmost symbol in its right part. If A can eventually leftmost produce the symbol a, then we are assured that by selecting rule 1 we are on the right path and backup beyond this point will never be necessary. More formally, $A \overset{+}{\Rightarrow} a...$ where the notation ... denotes a string (possibly empty) of characters selected from the vocabulary. The replacement of the stack symbol S by the string ABe yields a new stack contents of

$ABe\#$

We now must select a second production based on the knowledge that the stack symbol is A and the current input symbol is a. Three rules are possible: rules 2, 3, and 4. The decision in this case, however, is clear—rule 3 must be selected. This choice results in the following stack contents:

$aSBe\#$

Now that the stack symbol matches the current input symbol, the stack is popped and the input cursor is advanced. As a result of these operations, the new stack symbol and current input symbol become the symbols S and d, respectively, thus yielding a stack contents of

$SBe\#$

At this point in the parse, we observe that the symbol d is leftmost derivable from S; that is, $S \Rightarrow A \cdots \Rightarrow d \ldots$. Consequently, we select rule 1 as the next rule to apply in the parsing process. This choice results in the stack being changed to

$ABeBe\#$

Clearly, A can leftmost produce d. Therefore, we select production 2 as the next rule to apply. Such a selection yields a stack contents of

$dBBeBe\#$

As a result, the stack and current input symbols match. We can now pop the stack and advance the input cursor, thus obtaining the stack contents

$BBeBe\#$

and the new input symbol b.

Two rules for B are possible—rules 5 and 6. Because of the current input symbol, we cannot choose rule 5, since this choice will leftmost produce symbols a, c, or d. Consequently, we must choose rule 6. The new stack contents now become

$bBeBe\#$

The parsing process can be continued until the complete parse is obtained. A trace of this parse is given in Table 6-4.

Table 6-4

Unused input string	Stack	Output tape
$adbbebe\#$	$S\#$	ε
$adbbebe\#$	$ABe\#$	1
$adbbebe\#$	$aSBe\#$	13
$dbbebe\#$	$SBe\#$	13
$dbbebe\#$	$ABeBe\#$	131
$dbbebe\#$	$dBBeBe\#$	1312
$bbebe\#$	$BBeBe\#$	1312
$bbebe\#$	$bBeBe\#$	13126
$bebe\#$	$BeBe\#$	13126
$bebe\#$	$beBe\#$	131266
$ebe\#$	$eBe\#$	131266
$be\#$	$Be\#$	131266
$be\#$	$be\#$	1312666
$e\#$	$e\#$	1312666
$\#$	$\#$	1312666

The sample grammar under consideration seems to be LL(1). Let us now introduce certain notions which will be used to formalize the definition of an LL(1) grammar without ε-rules. In the previous discussion, we introduced the notion of "leftmost derivable." Given some string $\alpha \in V^+$, the set of terminal symbols which are leftmost derivable from α is given by the equation

$$\text{FIRST}(\alpha) = \{ w | \alpha \overset{*}{\Rightarrow} w \dots \text{ and } w \in V_T \}$$

For example, in the current example grammar the set

$$\text{FIRST}(A) = \{ w | A \overset{*}{\Rightarrow} w \dots \text{ and } w \in V_T \} = \{ a, c, d \}$$

and

$$\text{FIRST}(ABe) = \{ w | ABe \overset{*}{\Rightarrow} w \dots \text{ and } w \in V_T \} = \{ a, c, d \}$$

Again referring to our example grammar, we note that there are three rules with a left part of A: the rules $A \rightarrow dB$, $A \rightarrow aS$, and $A \rightarrow c$. The FIRST set of each right part is given by

$$\text{FIRST}(dB) = \{ d \}, \text{FIRST}(aS) = \{ a \}, \text{FIRST}(c) = \{ c \}$$

These FIRST sets are disjoint. There are also two rules with a left part of B whose FIRST sets are also disjoint, namely,

$$\text{FIRST}(AS) = \{ a, c, d \}, \text{FIRST}(b) = \{ b \}$$

We are now in a position to generalize these observations.

Definition 6-2 A grammar without ε-rules is an *LL(1) grammar* if for all rules of the form $A \rightarrow \alpha_1 | \alpha_2 | \dots | \alpha_n$, the sets $\text{FIRST}(\alpha_1)$, $\text{FIRST}(\alpha_2), \dots,$ and $\text{FIRST}(\alpha_n)$ are pairwise disjoint, that is,

$$\text{FIRST}(\alpha_i) \cap \text{FIRST}(\alpha_j) = \phi \text{ for } i \neq j$$

By applying this definition to the sample grammar, we obtain the following:

1. Rules $A \rightarrow dB|aS|c$
   $\text{FIRST}(dB) \cap \text{FIRST}(aS) = \{ d \} \cap \{ a \} = \phi$
   $\text{FIRST}(dB) \cap \text{FIRST}(c) = \{ d \} \cap \{ c \} = \phi$
   $\text{FIRST}(aS) \cap \text{FIRST}(c) = \{ a \} \cap \{ c \} = \phi$
2. Rules $B \rightarrow AS|b$
   $\text{FIRST}(AS) \cap \text{FIRST}(b) = \{ a, c, d \} \cap \{ b \} = \phi$

Therefore, this grammar is LL(1).

Using the approach of Sec. 6-2.2 we can formulate in a formal manner a parsing algorithm for the process just described. The parsing function associated with this parsing algorithm is defined as follows:

$M: \{ V \cup \{ \# \} \} \times \{ V_T \cup \{ \# \} \} \rightarrow \{ (\beta, i), pop, accept, error \}$
   where $\#$ marks the bottom of the stack and the end of the
   input string, and where (β, i) is an ordered pair such
   that β is the right part of production number i.

If A is the top symbol on the stack and a is the current input symbol, then M is defined as follows:

$$M(A, a) = \begin{cases} pop & \text{if } A = a \text{ for } a \in V_T \\ accept & \text{if } A = \# \text{ and } a = \# \\ (\beta, i) & \text{if } a \in \text{FIRST}(\beta) \\ & \text{and } A \to \beta \text{ is the } i\text{th production} \\ error & \text{otherwise} \end{cases}$$

The parsing function of our current grammar is given in Table 6-5.

The parsing function M is used to alter configurations as we did in the simple LL(1) algorithm of Sec. 6-2.1. Given the general form of a parse configuration $(z, A\alpha, P)$, where z is the unused input string, $A\alpha$ is the stack, with A being the stack top, P is the output tape contents, we use $M(A, u)$, where $u = \text{FIRST}(z)$, to determine the next configuration according to the "yields" relation ($\vdash$) given by

1. $(z, A\alpha, P) \vdash (z, \beta\alpha, Pi)$ if $M(A, u) = (\beta, i)$ (i.e., $A \to \beta$ is the ith production)
2. $(z, a\alpha, P) \vdash (z', \alpha, P)$ if $M(a, u) = pop$ and $z = az'$
3. $(\#, \#, P) \vdash$ no entry (terminate)
4. $(z, X\alpha, P) \vdash$ no entry (error stop) if $M(X, u) = error$

The initial configuration is $(z, S\#, \varepsilon)$, where z is the entire input string and S is the goal symbol.

As an example, consider the parse of the string $adbbebe\#$ according to the sample LL(1) grammar given earlier. The sequence of configurations in the parse

Table 6-5 Parsing function (M) for an LL(1) grammar

Stack symbol	Current input symbol					
	a	b	c	d	e	$\#$
S	$(ABe, 1)$		$(ABe, 1)$	$(ABe, 1)$		
A	$(aS, 3)$		$(c, 4)$	$(dB, 2)$		
B	$(AS, 5)$	$(b, 6)$	$(AS, 5)$	$(AS, 5)$		
a	pop					
b		pop				
c			pop			
d				pop		
e					pop	
$\#$						$accept$

Blank entries are all *error* entries.

of this string is as follows:

$$
\begin{aligned}
(adbbebe\#, S\#, \varepsilon) &\vdash (adbbebe\#, ABe\#, 1) \\
&\vdash (adbbebe\#, aSBe\#, 13) \\
&\vdash (dbbebe\#, SBe\#, 13) \\
&\vdash (dbbebe\#, ABeBe\#, 131) \\
&\vdash (dbbebe\#, dBBeBe\#, 1312) \\
&\vdash (bbebe\#, BBeBe\#, 1312) \\
&\vdash (bbebe\#, bBeBe\#, 13126) \\
&\vdash (bebe\#, BeBe\#, 13126) \\
&\vdash (bebe\#, beBe\#, 131266) \\
&\vdash (ebe\#, eBe\#, 131266) \\
&\vdash (be\#, Be\#, 131266) \\
&\vdash (be\#, be\#, 1312666) \\
&\vdash (e\#, e\#, 1312666) \\
&\vdash (\#, \#, 1312666)
\end{aligned}
$$

terminate with a successful parse.

We have defined the FIRST relation, and it is clear that this relation is important in computing the parsing function associated with a particular grammar. Since the mechanical evaluation of FIRST may be cumbersome, we redefine it in terms of another relation over a finite set in the following manner. Let F be a relation over the vocabulary such that

UFX iff there exists a production $U \to X \ldots$.

The transitive closure (see Sec. 2-1.2) of this relation holds between U and $X (UF^+X)$ iff there exists some sequence of rules (at least one) such that

$$U \to A_1 \ldots, A_1 \to A_2 \ldots, \ldots, A_n \to X \ldots$$

It is clear that UF^+X iff $U \overset{+}{\Rightarrow} X \ldots$. This relation is easily computed by using Warshall's algorithm (see Sec. 2-1.2).

Our aim is to compute the FIRST(α) set for $\alpha = x_1 x_2 \ldots x_n$. Now FIRST($\alpha$) = FIRST($x_1$), since we have assumed no ε-rules except the case where $S' \to \varepsilon$ and S' does not occur in the right part of any rule in the grammar. The FIRST sets for terminals are trivial to form. Therefore, in order to compute the FIRST sets, we need only compute those associated with nonterminals. These FIRST sets are given by

For each $A \in V_N$, FIRST(A) = $\{x | x \in V_T$ and $AF^+x\}$

The F, F^+, and FIRST relations for the sample grammar are given in Table 6-6.

In this subsection we have given a definition for LL(1) grammars without ε-rules. Kurki-Suonio (1969) has shown that a grammar belonging to this class of grammars generates an *s-language*. Alternatively, an LL(1) grammar without ε-rules can always be replaced by an equivalent simple LL(1) grammar. The absence of ε-rules results in a rather simple parsing algorithm for this class of

Table 6-6 F and F^+ matrices, and FIRST sets for the sample grammar

	S'	S	A	B	a	b	c	d	e
S'		F			F^+		F^+	F^+	
S			F		F^+		F^+	F^+	
A					F		F	F	
B				F	F^+	F	F^+	F^+	
a									
b									
c									
d									
e									

F entries are marked by F. F^+ entries are marked by F or F^+.   Contributors to a FIRST set are circled. They are the F^+ entries in $V_N \times V_T$ and diagonal elements of $V_T \times V_T$.

grammars. A disadvantage of not allowing ε-rules is that the class of grammars introduced in this section is a proper subset of the class of grammars to be introduced in the following subsection.

EXERCISES 6-2.3

1 Obtain a simple LL(1) grammar which generates the same language as the example grammar used in this subsection.

2 For the LL(1) grammar whose rules are

0. $S' \rightarrow S\#$ 5. $J \rightarrow , EJ$
1. $S \rightarrow LB$ 6. $J \rightarrow)$
2. $B \rightarrow ; S; L$ 7. $E \rightarrow a$
3. $B \rightarrow := L$ 8. $E \rightarrow L$
4. $L \rightarrow (EJ$

give a trace (as in Table 6-4) of the parse for each of the following input strings:
   (a) $(a, a) := (a, a, a, a)\#$
   (b) $((a, a), a) ; (a, a) := (a, a) ; (a, a)\#$

3 Obtain the parsing table (as in Table 6-5) for the grammar given in Exercise 2.

4 Obtain the F and F^+ matrices (as in Table 6-6) for the example grammar of Exercise 2. Also obtain the FIRST sets associated with this grammar.

5 Formulate a parsing algorithm (similar to Algorithm TD_FULL) for the class of LL(1) grammars without ε-rules.

6 The following BNF describes an unsigned number in ALGOL 60:

   $\langle$unsigned integer$\rangle ::= \langle$digit$\rangle \mid \langle$unsigned integer$\rangle\langle$digit$\rangle$
   $\langle$digit$\rangle ::= 0 \mid 1 \mid 2 \mid 3 \mid 4 \mid 5 \mid 6 \mid 7 \mid 8 \mid 9$

   (a) Obtain an LL(1) grammar which generates the same language.
   (b) Obtain the parsing function for the grammar of part a.

7 The following BNF describes a conditional statement:

⟨conditional statement⟩::=⟨if statement⟩|
                      ⟨if statement⟩ *else* ⟨statement⟩
⟨if statement⟩::= ⟨if clause⟩⟨unconditional statement⟩
⟨if clause⟩::= *if* ⟨Boolean expression⟩ *then*
⟨statement⟩::= S
⟨unconditional statement⟩::= U
⟨Boolean expression⟩::= B

where S, U, and B are terminals which represent a statement, unconditional statement, and Boolean expression, respectively.

(*a*) Obtain an LL(1) grammar which generates the same language.
(*b*) Obtain the parsing function for the grammar of part *a*.

6-2.4 LL(1) Grammars with ε-Rules

In this subsection we generalize the LL(1) grammars introduced in the previous subsection to include ε-rules (see Sec. 2-4.3). We will see that such an inclusion defines a larger class of grammars and that the corresponding parsing algorithm is substantially more complex.

Before we proceed with the discussion, however, we must generalize the FIRST sets defined in the previous subsection so that they may contain the empty string. Therefore, the FIRST set of a string α is defined as

$$\text{FIRST}(\alpha) = \left\{ \omega \,|\, \alpha \overset{*}{\Rightarrow} \omega \ldots \quad \text{and} \quad |\omega| \leq 1 \text{ and } \omega \in V_T^* \right\}$$

Note that this definition allows strings of length 0 and 1.

As an example to be used throughout this section, we use the grammar whose rules are:

0. $S' \rightarrow A\#$ 4. $S \rightarrow [eC]$
1. $A \rightarrow iB \leftarrow e$ 5. $S \rightarrow \cdot i$
2. $B \rightarrow SB$ 6. $C \rightarrow eC$
3. $B \rightarrow \varepsilon$ 7. $C \rightarrow \varepsilon$

where $\text{FIRST}(A\#) = \{i\}$, $\text{FIRST}(iB \leftarrow e) = \{i\}$
        $\text{FIRST}(SB) = \{[, \cdot\}$, $\text{FIRST}(\varepsilon) = \{\varepsilon\}$
        $\text{FIRST}([eC]) = \{[\}$, $\text{FIRST}(\cdot i) = \{\cdot\}$
        $\text{FIRST}(eC) = \{e\}$, $\text{FIRST}(\varepsilon) = \{\varepsilon\}$

In constructing this simple grammar, we are careful to avoid the introduction of any left recursion. It is easy to do this because the grammar is very simple. Any discussion of top-down parsing, however, is incomplete if no mention is made of left recursion—the bane of any top-down parse technique—and its elimination. We can check a grammar for having nonterminals that are left-recursive by testing for the following:

If $A \overset{*}{\Rightarrow} A\alpha$, for some α, then A is left-recursive.

A is left-recursive if and only if A can be expanded into a string that begins with A. A rule is said to be direct left-recursive if it is the form $A \rightarrow A\beta$. The relation F^+ introduced at the end of the previous subsection when modified to incorporate empty rules is a convenient method for determining left-recursive nonterminals. This will be done later in this subsection.

We now turn to an informal discussion of a parsing algorithm for handling LL(1) grammars in which ε-rules are permitted. Using the sample grammar introduced at the beginning of this subsection and the top-down parsing approach based on a single lookahead symbol, introduced earlier, we attempt to construct the parse for the input $i[e] \leftarrow e\#$. The leftmost derivation for this string is

$$S' \underset{L}{\Rightarrow} A\# \underset{L}{\Rightarrow} iB \leftarrow e\# \underset{L}{\Rightarrow} iSB \leftarrow e\# \underset{L}{\Rightarrow} i[eC]B \leftarrow e\#$$

$$\underset{L}{\Rightarrow} i[e]B \leftarrow e\# \underset{L}{\Rightarrow} i[e] \leftarrow e\#$$

and the associated syntax tree is given in Fig. 6-12.

As before, the stack is initialized to contain the right-hand side of production 0:

$A\#$

From this initial configuration, a rule must be selected on the basis of the stack symbol A and the current input symbol i. In this instance such a deterministic choice can clearly be made by choosing rule 1. This results in a stack contents of

$iB \leftarrow e\#$

Since the stack top symbol and the current input symbol match at this stage, the stack symbol is discarded and the input cursor is advanced. As a result, the stack

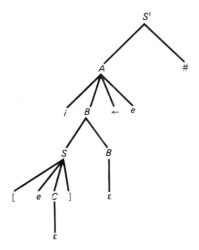

Figure 6-12 Parse tree for the string $i[e] \leftarrow e\#$.

contents are changed to

$B \leftarrow e\#$

and the new current input is [. For the first time we encounter the possibility of selecting an empty rule. Notice that B is a nullable nonterminal (see Sec. 2-4.3); that is, it can generate the empty string. Since in this instance the lookahead symbol is [, we choose rule 2 as the next production to apply. This changes the stack contents to

$SB \leftarrow e\#$

Since the stack symbol is S and the current input symbol is [, it is clear that we must choose rule 4 at this point. This results in a stack contents of

$[eC]B \leftarrow e\#$

The stack can now be popped and the next input symbol scanned. The stack contents become

$eC]B \leftarrow e\#$

Because the stack and the new input symbols match, the stack symbol is discarded and the next input character] is obtained, thus giving a stack contents of

$C]B \leftarrow e\#$

For the second time in this parse we encounter a nullable nonterminal. Note that the input symbol] does not belong to the FIRST sets associated with productions 6 and 7. It seems that we can go no further with our present parsing process. This is indeed the case! We next develop, however, an informal modification and extension to the current parsing algorithm which will permit the parsing of the given string.

At the present position in the parse, it is obvious that rule 6 must not be selected. If we are to continue, rule 7 must be chosen. In order to avoid backup, we must be sure that this is the correct choice. Since for the first time we are faced with the application of an ε-rule, we must develop a strategy for this case which avoids backup. The nonterminal C will be deleted as a direct result of an ε-rule selection. Once this is done, we must have a match between the current input symbol and new stack symbol. Note that this is indeed the case if C is popped from the stack. In short, the symbol] in our sample grammar can *immediately follow* a nullable nonterminal. It is this follow relation that we must now describe.

For a nullable nonterminal A, we define the following sets:

$\text{FOLLOW}(A) = \{w \in V_T | S' \overset{*}{\Rightarrow} \alpha A\gamma$ where $w \in \text{FIRST}(\gamma)$ and S' is the start symbol of the grammar$\}$

In the present case

$\text{FOLLOW}(C) = \{w \in V_T | S' \overset{*}{\Rightarrow} \alpha C\gamma$ and $w \in \text{FIRST}(\gamma)\} = \{]\}$

Also, note that the FIRST sets associated with rules 5 and 7 and the FOLLOW set for nonterminal C are mutually disjoint. Consequently, no confusion can arise in choosing the next production to apply.

After the application of the rule $C \rightarrow \varepsilon$ and the popping of] from the stack, the current stack contents are

$$B \leftarrow e\#$$

Since the current input symbol is $\leftarrow$, it is clear that rule 2 is not the required production. This leaves rule 3 as the only remaining alternative. It was mentioned earlier that B is a nullable nonterminal. The FOLLOW set for this symbol is

$$\text{FOLLOW}(B) = \{\leftarrow\}$$

and this set and the FIRST sets for rules 2 and 3 are mutually disjoint. Consequently, by selecting rule 3 we are certain that no backup will be required later. A trace of the entire parse is given in Table 6-7.

The previous notions are formalized in the following definition.

Definition 6-3 A grammar G is LL(1) if and only if for each pair of rules $A \rightarrow \alpha$, $A \rightarrow \beta$ in Φ, for some nonterminal A,

$$\text{FIRST}(\alpha \circ \text{FOLLOW}(A)) \cap \text{FIRST}(\beta \circ \text{FOLLOW}(A)) = \phi$$

An equivalent but simpler formulation of the LL(1) condition is as follows: For all rules $A \rightarrow \alpha_1|\alpha_2| \ldots |\alpha_n$,

1. $\text{FIRST}(\alpha_i) \cap \text{FIRST}(\alpha_j) = \phi$ for all $i \neq j$
   and, furthermore, if $\alpha_i \overset{*}{\Rightarrow} \varepsilon$, then
2. $\text{FIRST}(\alpha_j) \cap \text{FOLLOW}(A) = \phi$ for all $j \neq i$.

We shall leave it as an exercise to show that the second simpler formulation is equivalent to the first.

Table 6-7 Trace of a parse for the string $i[e] \leftarrow e\#$

$$
\begin{aligned}
(i[e] \leftarrow e\#, A\#, \varepsilon) &\vdash (i[e] \leftarrow e\#, iB \leftarrow e\#, 1) \\
&\vdash ([e] \leftarrow e\#, B \leftarrow e\#, 1) \\
&\vdash ([e] \leftarrow e\#, SB \leftarrow e\#, 12) \\
&\vdash ([e] \leftarrow e\#, [eC]B \leftarrow e\#, 12\varepsilon) \\
&\vdash (e] \leftarrow e\#, eC]B \leftarrow e\#, 124) \\
&\vdash (] \leftarrow e\#, C]B \leftarrow e\#, 124) \\
&\vdash (] \leftarrow e\#,]B \leftarrow e\#, 1247) \\
&\vdash (\leftarrow e\#, B \leftarrow e\#, 1247) \\
&\vdash (\leftarrow e\#, \leftarrow e\#, 12473) \\
&\vdash (e\#, e\#, 12473) \\
&\vdash (\#, \#, 12473) \\
&\quad \text{Terminate with a successful parse}
\end{aligned}
$$

We define first a parsing function which, when given the symbol on top of the stack and the next input symbol, returns as a value either the production to apply or else an indication of how to continue or to terminate. This function is given by

$$M: \{V \cup \{\#\}\} \times \{V_T \cup \{\#\}\} \to \{(\beta, i), \; pop, \; accept, \; error\}$$

where $\#$ marks the bottom of the stack and the end of the input string, and where (β, i) is an ordered pair such that β is the right-hand side of production number i. If A is the symbol on top of the stack and a is the current input symbol, then M is defined as follows:

$$M(A, a) = \begin{cases} pop & \text{if } A = a \text{ for } a \in V_T \\ accept & \text{if } A = \# \text{ and } a = \# \\ (\alpha, i) & \text{if } a \in \text{FIRST}(\alpha) \\ & \text{and } A \to \alpha \text{ is the } i\text{th production} \\ (\alpha, i) & \text{if } a \in \text{FOLLOW}(A) \\ & \text{and } A \to \alpha \text{ is the } i\text{th production and } \varepsilon \text{ is in} \\ & \text{FIRST}(\alpha), \text{ i.e., } A \in V_{N_\varepsilon} \\ error & \text{otherwise} \end{cases}$$

In order to obtain the parsing table for a given LL(1) grammar, we require the FIRST and FOLLOW sets. It is important to note that the presence of ε-rules affects the computation of both FIRST and FOLLOW sets.

Let us investigate the effect of ε-rules on the computation of the FIRST sets. In order to do so, it is convenient to redefine the leftmost relation F of the previous subsection so as to take into consideration the ε-rules in the grammar. The nullable nonterminals (see Sec. 2-4.3) can be computed using Algorithm EMPTY of Chap. 2. As before, we denote the set of nullable nonterminals by V_{N_ε}.

Given a production $X \to Y_1 Y_2 Y_3 \ldots Y_n$ $X \in V_N, Y_i \in V$, we have XFY_1, and if $Y_1 \in V_{N_\varepsilon}$, we also have XFY_2, and if $Y_1, Y_2 \in V_{N_\varepsilon}$, we also have XFY_3, etc. If the sets V_N and V_T contain m and n elements, respectively, these relations can be represented by $(m + n) \times (m + n)$ bit matrices, as was discussed in Sec. 2-1.2. Note that production 0 of the grammar which involves the end-marker symbol $\#$ is to be used in the computations.

We can use Warshall's algorithm to form the transitive closure of F to obtain F^+. The FIRST sets for each nonterminal of the grammar can be obtained directly from the F^+ matrix.

These FIRST sets are given by

For each $A \in V_N$, $\text{FIRST}(A) = \{x \mid x \in V_T \text{ and } AF^+x, \text{ or } x = \varepsilon \text{ and } A \in V_{N_\varepsilon}\}$

As pointed out earlier, this computation can provide a test for left recursion. If for $A \in V_N$, AF^+A holds (i.e., there is a 1 on the main diagonal of F^+ for a nonterminal), then A is a left-recursive nonterminal. $\text{FIRST}(\alpha)$ for $\alpha \in V^+$ and $\alpha = x_1 x_2 \ldots x_n$ contains $\text{FIRST}(x_1)$, and if $x_1 \in V_{N_\varepsilon}$ then also all terminal symbols of $\text{FIRST}(x_2)$, etc. If all $x_i \in V_{N_\varepsilon}$ then $\text{FIRST}(\alpha)$ also contains ε.

Table 6-8 F, F^+, and F^* matrices and FIRST sets for sample grammar

	S'	A	B	S	C	i	$\leftarrow$	e	$[$	$]$	$.$	$\#$
S'	F^*	F				F^+						
A		F^*				F						
B			F^*	F				F^+		F^+		
S				F^*				F		F		
C					F^*			F				
i						F^*						
$\leftarrow$							F^*					
e								F^*				
$[$									F^*			
$]$										F^*		
$.$											F^*	
$\#$												F^*

F entries are marked by F.
F^+ entries are marked by F or F^+.
F^* entries are marked by F or F^+ or F^*.
Contributors to a FIRST set are F^+ entries in $V_N \times V_T$ and diagonal elements of $V_T \times V_T$.

In order to compute the FOLLOW sets, we also require the reflexive transitive closure of F^+, which we denote by F^*. Assuming that there are no left-recursion problems, we proceed to obtain F^* by ORing the bit identity matrix with F^+. This is readily accomplished by setting a 1 on each position of the main diagonal of F^+. The relations F, F^+, F^*, and FIRST for our sample grammar are shown in Table 6-8.

The computation of the FOLLOW sets is simplified by the introduction of the following two relations B and L:

Given a production $X \rightarrow Y_1 Y_2 \ldots Y_n$, $1 \le i < n$, let $Y_i B Y_{i+1}$, and if $Y_{i+1} \in V_{N_\varepsilon}$, we also let $Y_i B Y_{i+2}$, etc.

Given a production $X \rightarrow Y_1 Y_2 \ldots Y_n$, $X \in V_N$, $Y_i \in V$, let $Y_n L X$, and if $Y_n \in V_{N_\varepsilon}$, we also let $Y_{n-1} L X$, and if $Y_n, Y_{n-1} \in V_{N_\varepsilon}$, we let $Y_{n-2} L X$, etc. The transitive and reflexive transitive closures of L can easily be obtained, and these are denoted by L^+ and L^*, respectively. Recall that the FOLLOW sets for each $A \in V_N$ were defined as

FOLLOW$(A) = \{z \mid z \in V_T$ and $S' \overset{*}{\Rightarrow} \alpha A\gamma$ with $z \in$ FIRST$(\gamma)\}$

The follow set for A can be equivalently represented by Fig. 6-13. From the diagram it is clear that AL^*X, XBY, and YF^*z, from which we obtain

FOLLOW$(A) = \{z \mid z \in V_T$ and $A(L^*BF^*)z\}$

Table 6-9 contains the L, L^+, and L^* relations and Table 6-10 exhibits the B and (L^*BF^*) relations along with the FOLLOW sets for the sample grammar. The parsing table can now be generated by using the definition of the M function given earlier. The parsing function obtained in this manner for our sample grammar is given in Table 6-11. Note that for $A \in V_{N_\varepsilon}$ we say that ε is in FIRST(A).

Table 6-9 L, L^+, and L^* matrices for sample grammar

	S'	A	B	S	C	i	←	e	[	]	·	#
S'	L*											
A		L*										
B			L									
S			L	L*								
C				L								
i			L+	L		L*						
←							L*					
e		L		L				L*				
[									L*			
]			L+	L						L*		
·											L*	
#												L*

L entries are marked by L.
L^+ entries are marked by L or L^+.
L^* entries are marked by L or L^+ or L^*.

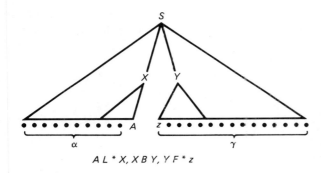

AL*X, XBY, YF*z

Figure 6-13 Tree representation of a FOLLOW set computation in terms of relations.

Table 6-10 B, (L^*BF^*) matrices and FOLLOW sets for sample grammar

	S'	A	B	S	C	i	←	e	[	]	·	#
S'												
A												B
B							B					
S			B	Π			Π		Π	Π		
C									B			
i			B	Π			B		Π	Π		
←								B				
e				B			Π			B		Π
[								B				
]			Π	Π			Π		Π	Π		
·						B						

B entries are marked by B.
L^*BF^* entries are marked by B or Π.
Contributors to a FOLLOW set are L^*BF^* entries in $V_N \times V_T$.

Table 6-11 LL(1) parsing matrix M for sample grammar

Stack symbol	Current input symbol						
	i	←	e	[	]	.	#
A	$(iB \leftarrow e, 1)$						
B		$(\varepsilon, 3)$		$(SB, 2)$		$(SB, 2)$	
S				$([eC], 4)$		$(\cdot i, 5)$	
C			$(eC, 6)$		$(\varepsilon, 7)$		
i	pop						
←		pop					
e			pop				
[				pop			
]					pop		
.						pop	
#							accept

Blank entries are all *error* entries.

We now culminate the previous discussion with the presentation of an algorithm to parse strings according to the top-down approach based on one symbol lookahead. We assume that the productions of any grammar implemented according to this method have been pretested and all left recursion has been eliminated.

Algorithm LL(1)_PARSER. Given the parsing function M for a particular LL(1) grammar G whose V_N and V_T sets contain m and n elements, respectively, this algorithm parses strings to determine whether or not these strings belong to L(G). The input string is stored in the string variable T. The variable p is the index of T that points to the current input symbol. The current sentential form is represented by a string variable, SENT, where t contains the leftmost symbol in the sentential form. Note that SENT is like a stack whose leftmost symbol is the stack top. The variable u contains the current input symbol. For convenience, we assume each terminal and nonterminal symbol is a string of length 1. The list of production numbers for the parse is represented by the string variable PARSE. The starting symbol of the unaugmented grammar is the string variable START. That is, START contains the left-hand side of production number 1.

1. [Initialize]
   T ← T ∘ '#'
   p ← 1
   SENT ← START ∘ '#'
   PARSE ← ' '
2. [Attempt to perform the required parse]
   Repeat while true
   t ← SUB(SENT, 1, 1)
   u ← SUB(T, p, 1)
   If M(t, u) = (β, i)

then SENT ← $\beta \circ$ SUB(SENT, 2)
    PARSE ← PARSE $\circ$ '$\square$' $\circ$ i
else If M(t, u) = pop
    then SENT ← SUB(SENT, 2)
        p ← p + 1
    else If M(t, u) = accept
        then Write('SUCCESSFUL PARSE')
        else Write('UNSUCCESSFUL PARSE')
        Exit   □

Traces of this algorithm for the sample grammar with the strings $i \leftarrow e\#$ and $i \cdot i[e] \leftarrow e\#$ are given in Table 6-12.

This algorithm is very efficient in terms of its operational and storage requirements. In fact, the performance of the LL(1) parser is a linear function of the length of the given input string. For a string of length k the cost is $c_1 k + c_2 k$, where c_1 and c_2 are constants associated with the number of operations and space or storage requirements, respectively.

From the discussion dealing with the construction of the parser, it is clear that an LL(1) grammar must be unambiguous. The proof of this point is left as an exercise.

Another property of a grammar which satisfies the LL(1) condition is that such a grammar cannot contain left-recursive nonterminals. Let us give an informal proof of this fact. If X_0 is a left-recursive nonterminal, then there exists a sequence of production applications $X_{i-1} \Rightarrow X_i \alpha_i$ for $1 \le i \le m$ such that $X_m = X_0$. Clearly, all of the X_i symbols are left-recursive nonterminals. At least

Table 6-12 Traces of two parses using sample grammar

$i \leftarrow e\#$	$i \cdot i[e] \leftarrow e\#$
$(i \leftarrow e\#, A\#, \varepsilon)$	$(i \cdot i[e] \leftarrow e\#, A\#, \varepsilon)$
$(i \leftarrow e\#, iB \leftarrow e\#, 1)$	$(i \cdot i[e] \leftarrow e\#, iB \leftarrow e\#, 1)$
$(\leftarrow e\#, B \leftarrow e\#, 1)$	$(\cdot i[e] \leftarrow e\#, B \leftarrow e\#, 1)$
$(\leftarrow e\#, \leftarrow e\#, 13)$	$(\cdot i[e] \leftarrow e\#, SB \leftarrow e\#, 12)$
$(e\#, e\#, 13)$	$(\cdot i[e] \leftarrow e\#, \cdot iB \leftarrow e\#, 125)$
$(\#, \#, 13)$	$(i[e] \leftarrow e\#, iB \leftarrow e\#, 125)$
accepted	$([e] \leftarrow e\#, B \leftarrow e\#, 125)$
	$([e] \leftarrow e\#, SB \leftarrow e\#, 1252)$
	$([e] \leftarrow e\#, [eC]B \leftarrow e\#, 12524)$
	$(e] \leftarrow e\#, eC]B \leftarrow e\#, 12524)$
	$(] \leftarrow e\#, C]B \leftarrow e\#, 12524)$
	$(] \leftarrow e\#,]B \leftarrow e\#, 125247)$
	$(\leftarrow e\#, B \leftarrow e\#, 125247)$
	$(\leftarrow e\#, \leftarrow e\#, 1252473)$
	$(e\#, e\#, 1252473)$
	$(\#, \#, 1252473)$
	accepted

one of these, however, must have another production if terminal strings are to be produced (the grammar is assumed to be reduced). Let this particular nonterminal be X and let its productions be

$$X \rightarrow \alpha_1 | \alpha_2 | \dots | \alpha_n \qquad (n \geq 2)$$

Now let us further assume without loss of generality that α_1 is the right part of X which leads to the left-recursion problem. Thus we have

$$X \Rightarrow \alpha_1 \overset{*}{\Rightarrow} X\beta \Rightarrow \alpha_2\beta \qquad \text{where } \beta \in V^*$$

Since $\alpha_1 \overset{*}{\Rightarrow} \alpha_2\beta$, it is obvious that the LL(1) condition is not satisfied because the FIRST and/or FOLLOW sets associated with α_1 and α_2 are not disjoint.

The role of ε-rules in LL(1) grammars is important. Recall from Sec. 2-4.3 that context-free grammars with or without ε-rules are equivalent in the sense that both types of grammars generate the same set of languages. This, however, is not the case for LL(1) grammars. In particular, the grammar

$$S \rightarrow aSA \qquad\qquad A \rightarrow bS$$

$$S \rightarrow \varepsilon \qquad\qquad\quad A \rightarrow c$$

is LL(1), but the language it generates is not an s-language. That is, no s-grammar exists which can generate this language. Kurki-Suonio (1969) has shown that the grammar

$$S \rightarrow aABC$$

$$A \rightarrow a \qquad\qquad C \rightarrow b$$

$$A \rightarrow bbD \qquad\quad C \rightarrow \varepsilon$$

$$B \rightarrow a \qquad\qquad D \rightarrow c$$

$$B \rightarrow \varepsilon \qquad\qquad D \rightarrow \varepsilon$$

is LL(1) (as the reader can readily verify) but an equivalent grammar without ε-rules is not LL(1). In fact, the equivalent grammar is LL(2).

One important aspect of top-down parsing, which up to this point has been ignored, concerns error detection and recovery. From our previous discussion, it is obvious that many entries of a typical parsing table are *error* entries. The next subsection examines how these entries can be used in the detection of and recovery from errors in LL(1) parsers.

EXERCISES 6-2.4

1 Given a grammar whose rules are

⟨simple Boolean⟩::=⟨implication⟩
      | ⟨simple Boolean⟩ ≡ ⟨implication⟩
⟨implication⟩::= ⟨Boolean term⟩
      | ⟨implication⟩ ⊃ ⟨Boolean term⟩

⟨Boolean term⟩::= ⟨Boolean factor⟩
                     |⟨Boolean term⟩ ∨ ⟨Boolean factor⟩
⟨Boolean factor⟩::= ⟨Boolean secondary⟩
                     |⟨Boolean factor⟩ ∧ ⟨Boolean secondary⟩
⟨Boolean secondary⟩::= ⟨Boolean primary⟩|−⟨Boolean primary⟩
⟨Boolean primary⟩::= ⟨logical value⟩|i|((⟨simple Boolean⟩))
⟨logical value⟩::= true|false

obtain an equivalent grammar in which all occurrences of left recursion have been eliminated.

2 Determine whether or not the grammar obtained in Exercise 1 is LL(1). If it is not LL(1), explain why. Be specific.

3 Using the formal definition of an LL(1) grammar verify that the following grammar is not LL(1):

$S' \rightarrow S\#$

$S \rightarrow aAa|\varepsilon$

$A \rightarrow abS|c$

4 Verify that the following grammar is LL(1):

$S \rightarrow A\#$

$A \rightarrow Bb|Cd$

$B \rightarrow aB|\varepsilon$

$C \rightarrow cC|\varepsilon$

Give a trace (as in Table 6-7) of the parse for each of the following input strings:

(a) $aab\#$
(b) $ccd\#$

5 For the grammar of Exercise 4 obtain the associated F, F^+, F^*, L, L^+, and L^* matrices. Also, generate the FIRST and FOLLOW sets for this grammar. From this information obtain the parsing function for the given grammar.

6 Show that any LL(1) grammar must be unambiguous.

7 Obtain the LL(1) parsing function associated with the grammar

$S' \rightarrow S\#$

$S \rightarrow aSA|\varepsilon$

$A \rightarrow c|\varepsilon$

8 Verify that the following grammar is LL(1):

$S' \rightarrow S\#$

$S \rightarrow aABC$

$A \rightarrow a|bbD$

$B \rightarrow a|\varepsilon$

$C \rightarrow b|\varepsilon$

$D \rightarrow c|\varepsilon$

Obtain the LL(1) parsing function associated with this grammar.

9 Verify that the following grammar is LL(1):

$S' \rightarrow S\#$

$S \rightarrow AB$

$A \rightarrow a|\varepsilon$

$B \rightarrow b|\varepsilon$

Obtain the LL(1) parsing function for this grammar.

10 Show that Algorithm LL(1)_PARSER performs its task in $c * n$ operations where c is a constant and n is the length of the given input string.

11 Show that the two definitions of an LL(1) grammar given in this subsection are equivalent.

6-2.5 Error Handling for LL(1) Parsers

The LL(1) parser described in the previous section performs a correct parse of any valid input string. Given an erroneous string, however, it parses to the point of the first error, prints 'UNSUCCESSFUL PARSE', and stops. Although this is acceptable behavior for an abstract parser, it is unacceptable in a practical compiler (see Sec. 5-1). This section discusses modifications to the LL(1) parser which allow it to react more intelligently to syntactic errors.

LL(1) parsers detect syntactic errors by means of the *error* entries in their parsing tables. When the symbol A on top of the stack and the input symbol a_k give a table entry $M(A, a_k) = error$, the parser knows that a_k cannot validly follow the already parsed portion of the input, $a_1 a_2 \ldots a_{k-1}$, and a syntactic error is reported.

LL(1) parsers possess the *valid prefix property* discussed in Sec. 5-2.3. This means that if the parser does not detect an error in the first portion $a_1 a_2 \ldots a_{k-1}$ of an input string $a_1 a_2 \ldots a_n$, there must be some string of symbols $a_k a_{k+1} \ldots a_m$ such that $a_1 a_2 \ldots a_m$ is a valid string of the language. Less precisely, we may say that a parser with the valid prefix property detects a syntactic error at the earliest point possible in a single left-to-right scan of the input with no backup. The valid prefix property eliminates the need for inserting or deleting stack symbols in LL(1) error recovery and repair. At any point in the parse the parser has already recognized a valid prefix, that is, the front part of some valid input string. Thus, when input symbol a_k causes an error, the parser can always modify the unparsed input symbols $a_k \ldots a_n$ so that the parse may continue.

The following LL(1) grammar, which generates simple arithmetic expressions, will be used for all examples in this section.

0. $E' \rightarrow E\#$ 3. $A \rightarrow \varepsilon$
1. $E \rightarrow TA$ 4. $T \rightarrow a$
2. $A \rightarrow +TA$ 5. $T \rightarrow (E)$

The LL(1) parsing table for this grammar is shown in Table 6-13.

Table 6-14 gives a trace of the parse of the input string $a)\#$ using the parsing table from Table 6-13. A syntactic error is detected in step 6 of the parse. The error is detected because the entry $M(\#, ')')$ in Table 6-13 is blank (*error*). Notice that the error is detected at the input symbol ')', the first erroneous symbol encountered in the left-to-right parse of the input. This early detection is guaranteed by the valid prefix property mentioned earlier.

Notice that the transition from step 4 to step 5 in Table 6-14 is unnecessary, because the first erroneous symbol is already at the beginning of the unparsed part of the input string. Furthermore, the transition causes the deletion of A from

Table 6-13 LL(1) parsing table for sample grammar

M	a	(	)	+	#
E	$(TA,1)$	$(TA,1)$			
A			$(\varepsilon,3)$	$(+TA,2)$	$(\varepsilon,3)$
T	$(a,4)$	$((E),5)$			
a	pop				
(		pop			
)			pop		
+				pop	
#					accept

Blank table entries represent *error* actions.

the parse stack, reducing the amount of syntactic information available for error recovery. The presence of A on the stack indicates that the parser is ready to accept a string of the form $+ T + T + T...$, that is, zero or more occurrences of the symbols $+ T$, where T represents any string derivable from the nonterminal T in the grammar. If A is prematurely deleted from the stack, this information is lost. We can easily prevent A from being popped from the stack in such a case. Observe that wasted parse actions like the one just described occur only when the stack symbol is a nullable nonterminal, and the erroneous input symbol causes the nonterminal to be expanded to ε (the terminal is in the FOLLOW set of the nonterminal). If we implement the parse stack as a vector with *two* top pointers, we can maintain the nullable nonterminal on the stack, while pretending to pop it. If no error occurs, we let the parser continue, but if an error is detected, we remember that the nonterminal is really still on the stack. Algorithm IMPROVED_LL(1) is a version of the LL(1) parser of the previous section and uses this method to retain nullable nonterminals in the event of an error.

Algorithm IMPROVED_LL(1). Given the parsing table M for a particular LL(1) grammar G, this algorithm parses strings to determine whether or not these strings belong to L(G). The input string is stored in the string variable T. The variable p is the index in T of the current input symbol. The parsing stack is a

Table 6-14 Trace of parse of input string $a)\#$

	INPUT	STACK	PARSE
1	$a)\#$	$E\#$	
2	$a)\#$	$TA\#$	1
3	$a)\#$	$aA\#$	14
4	$)\#$	$A\#$	14
5	$)\#$	$\#$	143
6		Syntactic error detected	

vector S with associated stack top indices TOP and TRUE_TOP. The variable t is used to hold the top symbol of the stack, and the variable u holds the current input symbol. PARSE is the list of production numbers which make up the parse of the input string. The goal symbol of the unaugmented grammar (the left-hand side of production 1) is initially in the variable START.

1. [Initialize]
       T ← T ∘ '#'
       p ← 1
       S[1] ← '#'
       S[2] ← START
       TRUE_TOP ← TOP ← 2
       PARSE ← ' '
2. [Parse]
     Repeat while true
        t ← S[TOP]
        u ← SUB(T, p, 1)
        If $M(t, u) = (\beta, i)$ (apply ith production)
        then TOP ← TOP − 1
            Repeat for $j = \text{LENGTH}(\beta),...,1$
              TOP ← TOP + 1
              S[TOP] ← SUB($\beta, j, 1$)
            If $\beta \neq \varepsilon$
            then TRUE_TOP ← TOP
            PARSE ← PARSE ∘ '□' ∘ i
        else If $M(t, u) = $ pop (input symbol match)
            then TOP ← TRUE_TOP ← TOP − 1
              p ← p + 1
            else If $M(t, u) = $ accept
             then Write('SUCCESSFUL PARSE')
               Exit
             else Call ERROR_HANDLER   □

Now that we have the means to detect syntactic errors and to retain as much contextual information on the stack as is possible, we must devise ways of reporting and recovering from syntactic errors. We present two approaches to error reporting and two approaches to error recovery. In each case the first approach is of the ad hoc type discussed in Chap. 5. The second approach is a more systematic method.

The ad hoc reporting and recovery methods consist of designing an error message and a recovery routine for each of the *error* entries in the parsing table of the LL(1) parser. Table 6-15 shows our sample parsing table with the 28 error entries numbered. The compiler writer must consider the possible input symbols which can cause each error and then formulate a plausible response for each.

Table 6-15 LL(1) parsing table with numbered error entries

M	a	(	)	+	#
E	$(TA,1)$	$(TA,1)$	1	2	3
A	4	5	$(\varepsilon,3)$	$(-TA,2)$	$(\varepsilon,3)$
T	$(A,4)$	$((E),5)$	6	7	8
a	pop	9	10	11	12
(	13	pop	14	15	16
)	17	18	pop	19	20
+	21	22	23	pop	24
#	25	26	27	28	accept

Consider the error entry numbered 1 in Table 6-15. This parsing action is taken when there is a nonterminal E on top of the stack, and the input symbol is ')'. Looking at the grammar, we find that a nonterminal E may arise from either of the expansions:

0. $E' \rightarrow E\#$
5. $T \rightarrow (E)$

Since a ')' appears where an E is required, the author of the erroneous input string must have either:

1. Inserted a ')' at the start of the input, or
2. Omitted the expression between a pair of matched parentheses '( )'.

The error message must indicate these possibilities to the programmer. Such an error message might be as follows:

MISSING EXPRESSION BETWEEN PARENTHESES, OR ')' AT START OF PROGRAM.

To recover from the error, the following algorithm might be invoked:

Algorithm LL_ADHOC1. p is the index into the input string and TOP is an index associated with the top of the stack.

1. [Delete the offending ')']
    p ← p + 1
2. [If a missing expression then pop E and) from stack]
    If TOP > 2
    then TOP ← TOP − 2   □

When the input is ')a + a#', the recovery routine deletes the ')'. When the input is 'a + ( ) + a#', the recovery routine changes the stack and the input string so that the missing expression problem can be ignored.

This error-handling strategy is an instance of the ad hoc approach to error handling. Here we see that the method can recover effectively from errors. We also see that the compiler writer must anticipate all possible errors in order to supply good messages and effective recovery. If the compiler writer makes a mistake or fails to anticipate some syntactic error, the compiler may become unstable and an avalanche of errors may result. There certainly are ample possibilities for mistakes in this ad hoc approach, since a process comparable with the discussion in preceding paragraphs must be performed for each *error* entry in the parsing table. While there are only 28 such entries in our small example, a practical compiler may have thousands of *error* entries in its parsing table.

The preceding discussion of ad hoc methods suggests that systematic techniques may be far simpler than ad hoc techniques. Systematic techniques either avoid the large amount of detail found in the ad hoc approach or else use some automated algorithm to generate the details of the error handler. We now consider systematic approaches to error reporting and error recovery in an LL(1) parser.

Errors in the LL(1) parser consist of a mismatch between some expected construction and the symbol actually occurring in the input string. A possible systematic approach to generating error messages consists of associating a string with each symbol of the grammar and printing error messages of the form:

EXPECTING string associated with symbol on the stack,
BUT FOUND string associated with the input symbol.

The strings to be associated with each symbol of the grammar can be easily generated as follows:

Algorithm COMPUTE_TS. This algorithm computes a table TS of terminal strings to be associated with each symbol of the grammar. The strings associated with the terminal symbols are the terminal symbols themselves. For nonterminals, the FIRST and FOLLOW sets are used to compute a set F consisting of the terminal symbols which can validly appear where the nonterminal is required. The string associated with a nonterminal consists of the names of terminals in its F set concatenated together and separated by the word 'OR'.

1. [Loop through all terminal symbols]
   Repeat for all $x \in V_T \cup \{\#\}$
      $TS(x) \leftarrow x$
2. [Loop through all nonterminals]
   Repeat for all $A \in V_N$
      $F_A \leftarrow FIRST(A)$
      $TS(A) \leftarrow \varepsilon$
      If $\varepsilon \in F_A$
      then $F_A \leftarrow (F_A - \{\varepsilon\}) \cup FOLLOW(A)$
      Repeat for all $x \in F_A$
         $TS(A) \leftarrow TS(A) \circ \text{'}\square OR\square\text{'} \circ x$
      $TS(A) \leftarrow SUB(TS(A), 5)$ □

Table 6-16 gives the TS table for our sample grammar. Compare the message generated by the systematic error reporter for *error* entry number 1 with the ad hoc message designed earlier. The systematic error message for input symbol ')' and stack symbol E is

EXPECTING a OR (,
BUT FOUND)

    The systematic approach to error recovery which we describe here is based on Fischer, Milton, and Quiring (1977), and Fischer and Milton (1977). Gries (1971), Holt and Barnard (1976), and Irons (1963) also present systematic approaches to top-down error recovery; none of these methods are directly applicable to the table-driven LL(1) parser described in Sec. 6-2.4.

    The Fisher, Milton, and Quiring method uses error repair as a means of error recovery. Furthermore, it modifies only the unparsed portion of the input string in making its repair. Since nothing is done to the stack, it is never necessary to withdraw translation actions caused by input symbols already parsed. The error-repair method consists of Algorithm LL_REPAIR, which is called by the ERROR_HANDLER of Algorithm IMPROVED_LL(1). When a syntactic error is detected, the parse stack consists of the symbols $S_t S_{t-1} \ldots S_1$, where each S_i is a terminal symbol, a nonterminal symbol, or the marker symbol $\#$. The input string is $a_1 \ldots a_k \ldots a_{n+1}$ where each a_i is a terminal symbol, except for a_{n+1}, which is the marker symbol $\#$. The symbol a_k has caused the error. In order to repair the syntactic error, Algorithm LL_REPAIR deletes symbols $a_k \ldots a_{j-1}$ so that the next input symbol is a_j (j may be equal to k, i.e., there may be no deletion). Then it inserts symbols preceding a_j so that a_j will be accepted after the inserted symbols have been parsed. This can only be done if for some S_m in the stack, $S_m \overset{*}{\Rightarrow} \ldots a_j \ldots$, that is, S_m generates some terminal string which contains a_j. If this is true, the insertion task is relatively simple. For each stack symbol S_i above S_m on the stack, we insert a terminal string which S_i can generate. Then, if $S_m \overset{*}{\Rightarrow} y a_j \ldots$ for $y \in V_T^*$, the terminal string y (called the

Table 6-16 TS table for sample grammar

Symbol x	$TS(x)$
a	$'a'$
(	$'('$
)	$')'$
+	$'+'$
#	$'\#'$
E	$'a \text{ OR } ('$
A	$'+ \text{ OR }) \text{ OR } \#'$
T	$'a \text{ OR } ('$

prefix of S_m and a_j) is inserted into the input string. If the parser is now restarted, it can match the contents of the input string with the contents of the stack to get a successful parse.

Algorithm LL_PARSE first performs a deletion of symbols from the input string and then performs an insertion of symbols into the input string. In most repair situations, the algorithm must choose from a large number of possible deletion-insertion sequences. The algorithm makes its choice based on a system of weights or "costs." A cost is associated with the deletion of a symbol and with the insertion of a symbol. Algorithm LL_REPAIR selects its repair strategy so that the total cost of the operations it performs is minimized in a local context. Compiler writers choose values for the costs of inserting or deleting each terminal symbol of the grammar. They choose these costs based on their knowledge of the language being parsed. They assign a low insertion cost to symbols likely to be omitted by a programmer, and a low deletion cost to symbols likely to be accidentally inserted by a programmer.

Given that input symbols $a_k \ldots a_{j-1}$ have already been deleted from the input string, the cost of performing the insertion task can be easily calculated. If S_m is the highest symbol in the stack such that $S_m \overset{*}{\Rightarrow} ya_j \ldots$ for $y \in V_T^*$, then the inserted symbols will consist of the least-insertion-cost strings derivable from each of $S_t S_{t-1} \ldots S_{m+1}$ (called the LCS strings for these symbols) and the string y (the prefix of S_m and a_j). The cost of the insertion is the sum of the insertion costs of each symbol in these strings. To ease the calculation of this total cost of insertion, Algorithm LL_REPAIR uses two cost tables. IC is a table containing the insertion costs of terminal symbols (as chosen by the compiler writer) and the insertion costs of nonterminals (the costs of the least-cost strings of terminals derivable from the nonterminals). PC is a table containing the insertion cost of the prefix of a nonterminal A and a terminal a. Thus the total cost of the insertion is

$$IC(S_t) + IC(S_{t-1}) + \cdots + IC(S_{m+1}) + PC(S_m, a_j)$$

The actual string inserted is

$$LCS(S_t) \circ LCS(S_{t-1}) \circ \cdots \circ LCS(S_{m+1}) \circ PREFIX(S_m, a_j)$$

It is useful to set $PC(A, a) = \infty$ if $A \overset{+}{\nRightarrow} \ldots a \ldots$ or $a = \#$. These infinite costs indicate that a prefix does not exist for the symbol pair (A, a).

In order to choose its repair strategy, Algorithm LL_REPAIR computes the total deletion and insertion cost of each possible repair and selects the repair with the lowest cost. The deletion cost of each terminal symbol is in the DC table. Since the deletion cost is strictly increasing as more and more symbols are deleted, it often happens that the best total cost to date is less than or equal to the deletion cost at some point. In such a case, it is unnecessary to look further for a repair with a lower total cost, because the deletion cost will dominate all such repairs.

Table 6-17 Repair tables for sample grammar

IC		DC		LCS	
a	4	*a*	4	*E*	*a*
(	3	(	2	*A*	ε
)	2	)	1	*T*	*a*
+	1	+	3		
E	4				
A	0				
T	4				
#	5				
ε	0				

Prefix table						PC table				
	a	(	)	+			*a*	(	)	−	#
E	ε	ε	(*a*	*a*		*E*	0	0	7	4	∞
A	+	+	+(*a*	ε		*A*	1	1	8	0	∞
T	ε	ε	(*a*	(*a*		*T*	0	0	7	7	∞

Table 6-17 gives the values for all the tables required for our sample grammar. The complete error-repair algorithm is as follows:

Algorithm LL_REPAIR. This algorithm modifies the input string T of Algorithm IMPROVED_LL(1) so that the improved LL(1) parser may continue parsing. LL_REPAIR uses the IC, DC, LCS, PREFIX, and PC tables previously described. It uses the values of variables p and TRUE_TOP from Algorithm IMPROVED _LL(1) and examines the contents of the parse stack S. Local variables C, C_{BEST}, C_{DEL}, and PCT are used to compute costs. E is a variable containing the input symbol being examined. The variables q and i are integer indexes. q_{BEST} is the value of q corresponding to the current optimum.

1. [Initialize costs and select first input symbol]
   $C_{BEST} \leftarrow \infty$
   $C_{DEL} \leftarrow 0$
   q ← p
2. [Choose optimal number of deletions]
   Repeat through step 5 while $C_{DEL} < C_{BEST}$
       C ← 0
       E ← SUB(T, q, 1)
3. [Calculate cost of insertion at this point]
   Repeat for i = TRUE_TOP, TRUE_TOP − 1,...,1
       If S[i] ∈ $V_T \cup \{\#\}$

```
    then If S[i] = E
          then PCT ← 0
          else PCT ← ∞
    else PCT ← PC(S[i], E)
    If PCT < ∞
    then C ← C + PCT
          Exit loop                                    (exits to step 4)
    else C ← C + IC(S[i])
4. [See if it is cheaper to insert here than at previous best point]
    C ← C + C_DEL
    If C < C_BEST
    then C_BEST ← C
    q_BEST ← q
5. [Advance to next input symbol]
    If E = #
    then Exit loop                                     (exits to step 6)
    else q ← q + 1
          C_DEL ← C_DEL + DC(E)
6. [Deletion is now chosen. Perform insertions before pth symbol]
    T ← SUB(T, 1, p − 1) ∘ SUB(T, q_BEST)
    E ← SUB(T, p, 1)
    q ← p
    Repeat for i = TRUE_TOP, TRUE_TOP − 1,...,1
       If S[i] = E
       then Exit loop                                  (exits to step 7)
       If S[i] ∈ V_T ∪ { # }
       then T ← SUB(T, 1, q − 1) ∘ S[i] ∘ SUB(T, q)
             q ← LENGTH(S[i]) + q
       else If PC(S[i], E) = ∞
             then T ← SUB(T, 1, q − 1) ∘ LCS(S[i]) ∘ SUB(T, q)
                   q ← LENGTH(LCS(S[i])) + q
             else T ← SUB(T, 1, q − 1) ∘ PREFIX(S[i], E) ∘ SUB(T, q)
                   q ← LENGTH(PREFIX(S[i], E)) + q
                   Exit loop                           (exits to step 7)
7. [Finished]
    TOP ← TRUE_TOP
    Exit                                                        □
```

We now consider a simple example using our sample grammar. Given the
input string $a + + (a)#$, our IMPROVED_LL(1) parser halts with $TA#$ on its
parse stack and $p = 3$ (the reader is encouraged to verify this). The stack symbol
T and input symbol + lead to an error action. The ERROR_HANDLER
generates an error message and calls LL_REPAIR. LL_REPAIR considers each of
the following possible repairs on the basis of their combined insertion and

deletion costs:

> Deleting no symbols, inserting $(a,$ gives $a + (a + (a)\#$, cost $= 7$
>
> Deleting one symbol, inserting ε, gives $a + (a)\#$, cost $= 3$
>
> Deleting two symbols, inserting ε gives $a + a)\#$, cost $= 5$

Notice that the deletion cost $C_{DEL} = 5$ is now greater than the minimum cost $C_{BEST} = 3$. Since we are seeking to minimize the cost and since C_{DEL} can never decrease, there is no point in considering further deletions. The least-cost repair is to delete the $+$ and insert the empty string. The parser is restarted with $TA\#$ on the stack, input string $T = a + (a)\#$, and $p = 3$. The reader should trace the repair algorithm in detail and observe how the cost minimization is performed.

Another example illustrates the choice of an insertion or deletion based on the insertion and deletion costs chosen by the compiler writer. Given the input string $aa\#$ the parser stops with $A\pm$ on the stack, and $p = 2$. Algorithm **LL_REPAIR** considers the following alternatives:

> Deleting no symbols, inserting $+$, gives $a + a\#$, cost $= 1$
>
> Deleting one symbol, inserting ε, gives $a\#$, cost $= 4$

Since the deletion cost C_{DEL} is now 4 and the minimum cost is 1, no further deletions are considered. Because the cost of deleting or inserting a was set to a high value by the compiler writer, the repair algorithm avoids inserting or deleting a. In a more elaborate grammar the terminal a would be replaced by an identifier or number. Experience indicates that operands are less likely to be accidentally inserted or omitted than are operators.

Algorithms **COMPUTE_COST** and **COMPUTE_PREFIX**, which follow, are used to compute the repair tables necessary for the Fischer, Milton, and Quiring repair method. Algorithm **COMPUTE_COST** calculates the insertion costs of nonterminal symbols of the grammar based on the rule that the cost of a string of symbols is equal to the sum of the costs of the individual symbols in the string. This rule is applied to the right-hand side of each production of the grammar to get the cost of the nonterminal on the left-hand side of the production. When a nonterminal has several right-hand sides, the cost of the nonterminal is set to the cost of the minimum-cost right-hand side. Thus, the entry for a nonterminal in the IC table is the insertion cost of the minimum-cost terminal string derivable from the nonterminal. The LCS table, which contains the minimum-cost strings themselves, is initialized at the same time as the insertion costs are computed.

Initially, only the costs of the terminal symbols are known. Based on these costs, the algorithm computes the costs of nonterminals which have right-hand sides consisting only of terminals. Once the costs of these nonterminals are known, the costs of nonterminals with these nonterminals in their right-hand sides may be computed. This process continues in a "bottom-up" fashion until no changes occur in one complete pass through the grammar. The computation is then complete.

Algorithm COMPUTE_COST. Given the grammar and the insertion costs for the terminals of the language, this algorithm calculates the insertion costs for all nonterminals of a language. It also computes the LCS table values. A logical variable NOCHANGE is used to control the main loop of the algorithm.

1. [Initialize costs]
      Repeat for all $A \in V_N$
          $IC(A) \leftarrow \infty$
2. [Iterate through the grammar]
          NOCHANGE $\leftarrow$ false
      Repeat while not NOCHANGE
      NOCHANGE $\leftarrow$ true
      Repeat for all productions
          Let the production be $A \rightarrow X_1...X_n$
          If $IC(X_1) + IC(X_2) + \cdots + IC(X_n) < IC(A)$
          then $IC(A) \leftarrow IC(X_1) + IC(X_2) + \cdots + IC(X_n)$
              $LCS(A) \leftarrow \varepsilon$
              NOCHANGE $\leftarrow$ false
              Repeat for $i = 1, 2,...,n$
                  If $X_i \in V_N$
                  then $LCS(A) \leftarrow LCS(A) \circ LCS(X_i)$
                  else $LCS(A) \leftarrow LCS(A) \circ X_i$ □

The concept of a prefix was introduced in the discussion preceding Algorithm LL_REPAIR. If a nonterminal A is such that $A \overset{+}{\Rightarrow} ya...$ for $a \in V_T$ and $y \in V_T^*$, then y is called a prefix of the pair (A, a). The PREFIX table computed by Algorithm COMPUTE_PREFIX contains a prefix for each pair consisting of a nonterminal A and a terminal a. In some cases such a prefix may not exist (i.e., $A \overset{+}{\not\Rightarrow} ...a...$). In other cases there may be more than one prefix for a given pair. In such a case, the prefix with the lowest insertion cost is chosen. The PC (prefix cost) table contains the insertion cost of each PREFIX entry. If there is no prefix for (A, a), then $PC(A, a) = \infty$. In addition, $PC(A, \#) = \infty$ for all $A \in V_N$.

Algorithm COMPUTE_PREFIX operates in a "bottom-up" fashion similar to Algorithm COMPUTE_COST. The first iteration through step 3 computes prefixes for pairs (A, a) where $A \rightarrow ya...$ and $y \in V_T^*$. Once this pass is completed, prefixes can be computed for some pairs (B, a) where $B \rightarrow ...A...$ and $A \rightarrow ya...$. This is possible because prefixes have already been computed for the nonterminals A. The process continues, adding one level of derivation with each iteration, until one complete step occurs without changing the table. At this point, the final prefixes have been computed for all pairs of a nonterminal and a terminal. The prefix cost table PC is set to the insertion cost of each prefix as it is computed, and is used to choose the minimum-cost prefix where more than one prefix exists.

Algorithm COMPUTE_PREFIX. This algorithm computes the PREFIX and PC tables used by Algorithm LL_REPAIR. It requires the IC and LCS tables from Algorithm COMPUTE_COST. Temporary variables min, i, j, k, and C are used by the algorithm.

1. [Initialize]
      Repeat for all $A \in V_N$
          Repeat for all $a \in V_T \cup \{\#\}$
             $PC(A, a) \leftarrow \infty$
      NOCHANGE $\leftarrow$ false
2. [Compute tables]
      Repeat through step 3 while not NOCHANGE
          NOCHANGE $\leftarrow$ true
3. [Iterate through the grammar]
      Repeat for all $a \in V_T$
          Repeat for all productions
             Let the production be $A \rightarrow X_1...X_n$
             min $\leftarrow \infty$
             $j \leftarrow C \leftarrow 0$
             Repeat for $i = 1, 2,...,n$
              If $X_i \in V_T \cup \{\#\}$
              then if $X_i = a$
                  then $k \leftarrow 0$
                  else $k \leftarrow \infty$
              else $k \leftarrow PC(X_i, a)$
              If $C + k <$ min
              then min $\leftarrow C + k$
                 $j \leftarrow i$
              $C \leftarrow C + IC(X_i)$
             If min $< PC(A, a)$
             then $PC(A, a) \leftarrow$ min
                 NOCHANGE $\leftarrow$ false
                 PREFIX$(A, a) \leftarrow \varepsilon$
                 Repeat for $i = 1, 2,..., j - 1$
                    If $X_i \in V_T \cup \{\#\}$
                    then PREFIX$(A, a) \leftarrow$ PREFIX$(A, a) \circ X_i$
                    else PREFIX$(A, a) \leftarrow$ PREFIX$(A, a) \circ LCS(X_i)$
                 If $X_j \in V_N$
                 then PREFIX$(A, a) \leftarrow$ PREFIX$(A, a) \circ$ PREFIX(X_j, a) $\square$

    In this section we have presented alternative means of detecting, reporting, and recovering from syntactic errors in table-driven LL(1) parsers. The reporting and recovery methods contain examples of the ad hoc and the systematic approaches to error handling. The papers by Fischer, Milton, and Quiring (1977), and Fischer and Milton (1977) contain recommendations for improvements to the algorithms given in the last part of this section. Further variations of the method can be found in Fischer, Milton, and Quiring (1980).

EXERCISES 6-2.5

1 Design ad hoc error messages and recovery routines for error entries 6, 7, and 8 in Table 6-15. Note the similarities among the messages and recovery routines. Design a message and a recovery routine for another error entry in the table. Note the lack of similarity between two entries in different rows of the table.

2 Discuss the advantages and disadvantages of the ad hoc and systematic error-message-generation schemes described in this section.

3 (*a*) Consider the following LL(1) grammar:

0. $S' \rightarrow S\#$
1. $S \rightarrow \varepsilon$
2. $S \rightarrow aB$
3. $B \rightarrow \varepsilon$
4. $B \rightarrow bC$
5. $C \rightarrow \varepsilon$
6. $C \rightarrow cS$

	IC	DC
a	3	1
b	2	2
c	1	3
ε	0	
$\#$	4	

If the insertion costs of the terminal symbols of the grammar are as given above, compute the IC and LCS tables for the grammar, using Algorithm COMPUTE_COST. Then generate the PREFIX and PC tables using Algorithm COMPUTE_PREFIX.

(*b*) Using the tables generated in part *a*, trace the parse of the following invalid input strings, using Algorithm IMPROVED_LL(1) to parse and Algorithm LL_REPAIR to recover from the syntax errors:

(1) *aac*#
(2) *ababc*#

4 Show that Algorithm LL_REPAIR operates in finite time, i.e., that it cannot enter an "infinite loop." [Hint: Consider the number of symbols in the LL(1) parse stack.]

5 Compare the ad hoc and systematic recovery methods for LL(1) parsers presented in this section. Suggested criteria for comparison are

(*a*) Effectiveness: How often is the repair a correction? Does it allow parsing to continue normally? Does the repair cause further errors?

(*b*) Ease of implementation: How likely is it that you would make a programming error or oversight while implementing this system?

CHAPTER EXERCISES

1 Select some feature of a programming language and write programs that implement three parsers for this feature: one for top-down parsing with full backup, one with no backup, and one with limited backup. Compare the three parsers in terms of speed of operation, ease of implementation, and storage requirements. (Note: Be careful in the selection of the feature you choose to parse or you will be taught an expensive lesson about exponential rates of growth in the full backup case.)

BIBLIOGRAPHY

Aho, A. V., and J. D. Ullman: *The Theory of Parsing, Translation, and Compiling:* Vol. 1, *Parsing*, Vol. 2, *Compiling*, Englewood Cliffs, N.J.: Prentice-Hall, 1972.

Bertrand, M., and M. Griffiths: "Incremental Compilation and Conversational Interpretation," *Annual Review in Automatic Programming*, Vol. 7, New York: Pergamon Press, 1967.

Fischer, C. N., and D. R. Milton: "Modifications to the FMQ LL(1) Error-Corrector," private communication, 1977.

Fischer, C. N., D. R. Milton, and S. B. Quiring: "An Efficient Insertion-Only Error-Corrector for LL(1) Parsers," *Conference Record of the Fourth ACM Symposium on the Principles of Programming Languages*, 1977, pp. 97–103.

Fischer, C. N., D. R. Milton, and S. B. Quiring: "Efficient LL(1) Error Correction and Recovery Using Only Insertions," *ACTA INFORMATICA*, Vol. 13, No. 2, February 1980, pp. 141–154.

Foster, J. M.: "A Syntax Improving Program," *The Computer Journal*, Vol. 11, No. 1, May 1968, pp. 31–34.

Gries, D: *Compiler Construction for Digital Computers*, New York: John Wiley & Sons, 1971.

Griffiths, M: "LL(1) Grammars and Analyses," *Lecture Notes in Computer Science—Compiler Construction*, No. 21, New York: Springer-Verlag, 1974, pp. 57–84.

Holt, R. C., and D. T. Barnard: "Syntax-Directed Error Repair and Paragraphing," Computer Systems Research Group, University of Toronto, 1976.

Irons, E. T.: "An Error-Correcting Parse Algorithm," *Communications of the ACM*, Vol. 6, No. 11, November 1963, pp. 669–673.

Knuth, D. E.: "Top-Down Syntax Analysis," *ACTA INFORMATICA* 1, 1971, pp. 79–110.

Korenjak, A. J., and J. E. Hopcroft: "Simple Deterministic Languages," *Proceedings of the 7th Symposium on Switching and Automata Theory*, *IEEE*, 1966, pp. 36–46.

Kurki-Suonio, R.: "Notes on Top-Down Languages " *BIT*, Vol. 9, 1969, pp. 225–238.

Lewis, P. M. II, and R. E. Stearns: "Syntax-Directed Transduction," *Journal of the ACM*, Vol. 15, No. 3, 1968, pp. 265–288.

Lewis, P. M. II, D. J. Rosenkrantz, and R. E. Stearns: *Compiler Design Theory*, Reading, Mass.: Addison-Wesley, 1976.

Rosenkrantz, D. J., and R. E. Stearns: "Properties of Deterministic Top-Down Grammars," *Information and Control*, Vol. 17, 1970, pp. 226–256.

Topcor, R. W.: "A Note on Error in Recursive Descent Parsers," *SIGPLAN Notices*, Vol. 17, No. 2, February 1982.

Unger, S. H.: "A Global Parser for Context-Free Phrase Structure Grammars," *Communications of the ACM*, Vol. 11, No. 4, 1968, pp. 240–247. A Corrigendum to the Above, *Communications of the ACM*, Vol. 11, No. 6, 1968, p. 427.

Welsh, J., and M. McKeag: *Structured System Programming*, London: Prentice-Hall, 1980.

Wirth, Niklaus: *Algorithms + Data Structures = Programs*, Englewood Cliffs, N.J.: Prentice-Hall, 1976.

# SEVEN

BOTTOM-UP PARSING

A second class of parsing techniques builds a parse tree from the leaves toward its root, i.e., in a bottom-up manner. Several bottom-up parsing techniques with no backup are presented in this chapter. All the parsing techniques except the first are based on formal syntactic notions. Several formal classes of grammars have been created. For a given grammar in a particular class, there corresponds a constructor algorithm that generates parsing tables for that grammar. Each class of grammars has an associated generalized parsing algorithm that uses the automatically generated parsing tables for the given grammar to parse strings in its associated language. Error-detection and -correction techniques for these parsing techniques have, to a significant degree, been automated.

The chapter begins with a description of one of the earliest informal parsing techniques, which is based on Polish notation. Section 7-2 introduces the class of operator precedence grammars. The notions used in parsing operator precedence grammars are extended to define the class of precedence grammars in Sec. 7-3. Section 7-4 gives a detailed description of the classes of SLR(1), LALR(1), and LR(1) grammars and their associated parsers. The chapter concludes with a comparison of the parsing techniques.

All the formal parsing techniques (except for extended-precedence parsing) use one symbol lookahead in order to deterministically parse input strings. Although some techniques can be extended to use more than one symbol of lookahead, the storage requirements of the expanded parsing tables tend to make such extensions too costly. Furthermore most programming language constructs can be parsed with one symbol of lookahead.

7-1 POLISH EXPRESSIONS AND THEIR COMPILATION

In this section we are concerned with the compilation of infix arithmetic expressions. We shall find it to be more efficient to evaluate an infix expression by first converting it to a suffix (or prefix) expression and then evaluating the latter. By using this approach, we can eliminate the repeated scanning of an infix expression in order to obtain its value.

The first subsection introduces the notions of suffix (Polish) notation. The equivalence between infix and suffix expressions is informally described. The second subsection formalizes the previously introduced notions. A general algorithm for converting infix expressions to a suffix form is formulated. The remainder of the section describes syntactic error-detection techniques for suffix (or prefix) expressions.

7-1.1 Polish Notation

In this subsection we introduce the notation for Polish expressions. Although the discussion is confined to expressions, the theory can be expanded to many other language constructs. Such extensions will be discussed in Chap. 10. This notation is also known as Łukasiewiczian notation (after the Polish logician Jan Łukasiewicz). Polish notation offers certain computational advantages over the traditional infix notation. By infix notation we mean that each operator is positioned between its operands, as in the expression $a + b$. Initially, an inductive definition of the set of valid infix expressions is given. The evaluation of infix and suffix expressions is also briefly introduced.

Let us now consider the set of all valid, completely parenthesized arithmetic expressions consisting of single-letter variables, nonnegative integers, and the four operators $+$, $-$, $*$, and $/$. The set of all such valid expressions is contained in the following recursive definition:

1. All single-letter variables and nonnegative integers are valid infix expressions.
2. If α and β are valid infix expressions, then so are $(\alpha + \beta)$, $(\alpha - \beta)$, $(\alpha * \beta)$, and (α / β).
3. The only valid infix expressions are those defined by steps 1 and 2.

Note that in the writing of a valid expression (according to this definition), complete parenthesization must be used. In order to reduce the severity of this restriction, a number of conventions have been developed. Perhaps the most obvious of these is one which permits the dropping of the outermost parentheses. An expression such as $(a + b)*(c + d)$ is considered to be valid, as well as $((a + b)*(c + d))$, the form required by the preceding definition.

Another method of reducing the number of parentheses is to assign an order of precedence to the connectives or operators. Once this assignment is done, further reductions can be made by requiring that for any two operators of equal precedence which appear in a formula, the left one is evaluated first. Such operators are said to be left-associative. Such a convention is commonly used in arithmetic; for example, $2 - 6/3 + 8$ stands for $(2 - (6/3)) + 8$.

Let us first consider the evaluation of unparenthesized arithmetic expressions in which the precedences of the operators $*$ and $/$ are considered to be equal and of higher value than those of $+$ and $-$. An example of such an expression is

$$w - \underbrace{\underbrace{\underbrace{x/y}_{1} \quad + \underbrace{z*5}_{3}}_{2}}_{4}$$

According to the preceding convention, this expression stands for $(w - (x/y)) + (z * 5)$. In evaluating this expression, we must scan it repeatedly from left to right. The numbers associated with the subexpressions indicate the steps of the evaluation. Clearly, this evaluation process is not optimal, since repeated scanning of the expression must be performed.

If an expression contains parentheses, the order of evaluation may be altered by these parentheses. For example, in evaluating the expression $(a + b)*(c + d)$, we first compute $a + b$ and $c + d$ and then perform the indicated multiplication. By the suitable use of parentheses, it is possible to write expressions which make the order of evaluating the subexpressions independent of operator precedence. This independence can be realized by parenthesizing subexpressions in such a manner that, for each operator, there is a pair of parentheses. This pair encloses the operator and its associated operands. The *parenthetical level* of an operator is defined to be the total number of pairs of parentheses that surround it. A pair of parentheses has the same parenthetical level as that of the operator to which it corresponds, that is, of the operator which is immediately enclosed by this pair. Such an expression is known as a *fully parenthesized expression*. For example, in the fully parenthesized expression

$$\underset{\quad 2 \quad \ 3 \quad \ \ 1 \quad \ 2}{((w - (x/y)) + (z*5))}$$

the integers below the operators specify the parenthetical level of each operator. During the evaluation of a fully parenthesized expression, the subexpression which contains the operator with the highest parenthetical level is evaluated first. If two or more operators have the same parenthetical level, they are evaluated from left to right. Once the subexpressions containing operators at the highest parenthetical level have been evaluated, the subexpressions containing the operators at the next highest level are evaluated in the same manner. This process is continued until all the operations have been performed.

Regardless of the extent of parenthesization, repeated scanning of an infix expression in a left-to-right manner is required in order to evaluate it. The repeated scanning of an infix expression can be avoided if it is first converted to an equivalent parenthesis-free *suffix* or *prefix* expression in which the subexpressions have the form

$$\langle \text{operand} \rangle \langle \text{operand} \rangle \langle \text{operator} \rangle \qquad (\text{suffix})$$

or

$$\langle \text{operator} \rangle \langle \text{operand} \rangle \langle \text{operand} \rangle \qquad (\text{prefix})$$

instead of the infix form

$$\langle \text{operand} \rangle \langle \text{operator} \rangle \langle \text{operand} \rangle$$

The prefix and suffix forms of the notation are also called *prefix Polish* and *reverse Polish*, respectively. Examples of expressions in their prefix, infix, and suffix forms are given in Table 7-1.

Note that in the conversion of an infix expression to its Polish equivalent, the variables in each form are all in the same relative positions. Furthermore, both Polish forms are parenthesis-free, and the operators in these forms are rearranged according to the rules of operator precedence.

A fully parenthesized infix expression is easily translated to suffix notation by initially converting the innermost parenthesized subexpression and then proceeding toward the outside of the expression. For example, in the expression

$$(x*((y + z) - 5))$$
$$132$$

the innermost parenthesized subexpression of level 3 is

$$(y + z)$$

and it is converted to $yz +$. This suffix expression becomes the first operand of the operator $-$ at level 2. Consequently, the subexpression $yz + - 5$ of level 2 is converted to the suffix equivalent $yz + 5 -$, and finally at level 1, the term $x * yz + 5 -$ is transformed to the final suffix form $xyz + 5 - *$.

Certain FORTRAN compilers initially convert partially parenthesized expressions to a fully parenthesized form before conversion to a suffix or prefix

Table 7-1 Equivalent expressions

Infix	Suffix (reverse Polish)	Prefix (prefix Polish)
x	x	x
$x - y$	$xy -$	$- xy$
$x - y + z$	$xy - z +$	$+ - xyz$
$(w + x)*(y + z)$	$wx + yz + *$	$* + wx + yz$
$(x + y)/z$	$xy + z/$	$/ + xyz$
$x/y/z$	$xy/z/$	$//xyz$

form is performed. Suffix form is associated with a bottom-up parse while the prefix form is linked to a top-down parse. More will be said about this point in the next subsection. In the remainder of this discussion we concern ourselves with suffix Polish notation. An analogous discussion holds for prefix Polish notation.

Let us now turn to the problem of evaluating a suffix expression. For example, to evaluate the suffix expression $wx + yz + *$ (i.e., $(w + x)*(y + z)$ in infix), we scan this string from left to right until we encounter the operator $+$. The two operands w and x which immediately precede this operator are its operands, and the subexpression $wx +$ is replaced by its value. Let us assume that this value is denoted by α. This reduces the original suffix string to $\alpha yz + *$. Continuing the scanning beyond α, the next operator encountered is $+$, whose operands are y and z, and the evaluation results in a value which we call β. The intermediate string now becomes $\alpha\beta *$. Continuing the scanning beyond β, the next operator is $*$. The operands of this operator are α and β. Performing this multiplication, we obtain the result γ. Note that only a single left-to-right scan was required in our evaluation.

This method of evaluating suffix expressions can be summarized by the following four rules, which are repeatedly applied until all operators have been processed:

1. Find the leftmost operator in the expression.
2. Select the two operands immediately preceding the operator found in step 1.
3. Perform the indicated operation.
4. Replace the operator and its operands with the result.

In this subsection, we have examined the basic notions of Polish notation. We have not, however, indicated how one gets from infix to Polish. We turn to this problem in the next subsection.

7-1.2 Conversion of Infix Expressions to Polish Notation

Initially, we develop an informal algorithm for translating unparenthesized infix expressions to suffix Polish. This informal algorithm is then modified to handle parenthesized expressions. This generalized algorithm is given in our algorithmic notation.

The conversion of an infix expression without parentheses to a suffix Polish expression is a straightforward matter. This conversion is based on the precedence of the operators and requires the use of a stack. The Polish expression is stored in some output string. Recall from the previous subsection that the variables and constants of the expression retain their order throughout the conversion process. The operators, however, are reordered in the output string, depending on their relative precedence, and it is for this reason that a stack is needed.

Consider the precedence values associated with the four arithmetic operators shown in Table 7-2. The precedence values are specified by the precedence function f. Also included in the table is a precedence value for single-letter variables. The special symbol # has the smallest precedence value in the table.

Table 7-2

Symbol	Precedence f
+ , −	1
* , /	2
Variables and nonnegative integers	3
#	0

Initially, the stack is set to the special symbol #. This symbol ensures that the stack is always nonempty. The main portion of the informal algorithm deals with the precedence-value comparison of the current input symbol and the top element of the stack. If the precedence value of this input symbol is greater than that of the symbol on top of the stack, then the current input symbol is pushed onto the stack and the next input symbol is scanned. If, however, the precedence value of the current input symbol is less than or equal to that of the stack top symbol, then we write this top element in the output string, after which we compare the precedence values of the same current input symbol and the new element on the stack. This process continues until all input symbols have been processed. A trace of this informal algorithm for the infix expression $a - b * c + d/5$ is given in Table 7-3.

Note that, because of their high precedence, a variable or a constant is always placed immediately on the stack. When the very next input symbol is encountered, the variable or constant on the stack is written in the output string. Our informal algorithm can be changed so that the precedence value of the current input symbol is tested for a value of 3. If this test is successful, the current input

Table 7-3 Translation of $a - b * c + d/5$ into suffix Polish

Current input symbol	Contents of stack (rightmost symbol is top of stack)	Reverse-Polish expression
	#	
a	#a	
−	# −	a
b	# − b	a
*	# − *	ab
c	# − *c	ab
+	# +	$abc * -$
d	# + d	$abc * -$
/	# +/	$abc * - d$
5	# +/5	$abc * - d$
#	#	$abc * - d5/ +$

symbol is either a variable or a constant and it can be placed in the output string without first being placed on the stack. This is not done, however, for reasons of generality and uniformity which become important as the infix expression becomes more complex than the ones we are now considering.

Also note that a current input symbol with a precedence value greater than that of the stack top will result in the input symbol being placed on the stack. This is natural, since this symbol has priority over other symbols in the stack. This phenomenon reflects the fact that the last operator to be placed on the stack is the first to be written into the output string. Furthermore, for left-associative operators, when the precedence of the current input symbol is equal to that of the symbol in the stack, the leftmost symbol is to be written out first. Therefore, our algorithm will convert $a - b - c$ to $ab - c -$ and not to $abc - -$. The suffix Polish expression $ab - c -$ corresponds to the infix expression $(a - b) - c$, while $abc - -$ is equivalent to $a - (b - c)$.

Let us now turn our attention to the conversion of incompletely parenthesized expressions to suffix Polish. When programmers write an expression containing parentheses, they do not normally write it in a completely parenthesized form. Intuitively, when a left parenthesis is encountered in the infix expression, it should be placed on the stack regardless of its present contents. However, when it is in the stack, it should be removed and discarded only when a right parenthesis is encountered in the infix expression, at which time the right parenthesis is also ignored. A left parenthesis can be forced on the stack by assigning to it a precedence value greater than that of any other operator. Once on the stack, the left parenthesis should have another precedence value (called its stack precedence) which is smaller than that of any other operator. We can get rid of the left parenthesis on the stack by checking for an incoming right parenthesis in the infix expression. The right parenthesis is never inserted on the stack. Actually, we can modify the previous informal algorithm in such a manner that the left and right parentheses can perform the same function as the special symbol '#' used earlier. The original table of precedence values (Table 7-2) can be revised to have both an input- and stack-precedence value for each operator and operand. This revision gets rid of the special symbol '#'. The algorithm also becomes more general, since other operators, such as the relational, logical, unary, and ternary operators, can be added without making the algorithm significantly more complex. Table 7-4 is a revised table which includes parentheses. Each symbol has both input-symbol and stack-symbol precedences, except for a right parenthesis which does not possess a stack precedence since it is never placed on the stack. Table 7-4 also contains the exponentiation operator $\uparrow$. All arithmetic operators except exponentiation have an input precedence which is lower in value than their stack precedence. This preserves the left to right processing of operators of equal precedence in an expression. The exponentiation operator in mathematics is right-associative. The expression $a \uparrow b \uparrow c$ is equivalent to the parenthesized expression $a \uparrow (b \uparrow c)$ and not to the expression $(a \uparrow b) \uparrow c$.

The conversion of an infix expression into reverse Polish operates in much the same way as the previous informal algorithm. A left parenthesis is initially placed

Table 7-4

Symbol	Input-precedence function f	Stack-precedence function g
+ , −	1	2
* , /	3	4
↑	6	5
Variables and constants	7	8
(	9	0
)	0	—

on the stack and a right parenthesis is concatenated onto the end of the infix expression. The algorithm is as follows.

Algorithm REVERSE_POLISH. Given an input string INFIX containing an infix expression which has been padded on the right with ')' and whose symbols have precedence values given by the functions f and g in Table 7-4, a vector S, used as a stack, and a function NEXTCHAR, which when invoked returns the next character of its argument, this algorithm converts the string INFIX to reverse Polish and stores it in a string called POLISH. RIGHT_PAREN is a local variable which is set to true when NEXT is a right parenthesis. TOP is an index into the S stack and points to the top element of the stack. TEMP is a temporary local variable.

1. [Initialize stack]
       TOP ← 1
       S[TOP] ← '('
2. [Initialize output string]
       POLISH ← ''
3. [Scan the infix expression]
       Repeat through step 6 while there are unprocessed symbols in INFIX
4. [Get next input symbol and set flag]
       NEXT ← NEXTCHAR(INFIX)
       RIGHT_PAREN ← false
5. [Emit symbols of higher precedence than NEXT]
       Repeat while f(NEXT) ≤ g(S[TOP])
           TEMP ← S[TOP]
           TOP ← TOP − 1
           If f(NEXT) < g(TEMP)
           then POLISH ← POLISH ∘ TEMP
           else RIGHT_PAREN ← true   (NEXT is a right parenthesis)
              Exit loop   (while f(NEXT) = g(TEMP))

6. [Push **NEXT** on stack?]
   If not **RIGHT_PAREN**
   then **TOP ← TOP + 1**
   S[TOP] ← NEXT

7. [Finished]
   Exit   □

A trace of the stack contents and the output string **POLISH** for the padded infix expression

$$(a + b)*(c + d))$$

is given in Table 7-5.

Note that in this algorithm we have not checked for stack overflow. We have assumed that there is sufficient space in the stack to hold the stacked symbols.

It is possible to extend the precedence functions to handle relational operators, conditional statements, unconditional transfers (go to), subscripted variables, and many other features found in present programming languages. Some exercises at the end of this section will deal with these extensions.

We have been concerned until now with the conversion of an infix expression to reverse Polish. The motivation behind this conversion is that reverse Polish can be converted into object code by linearly scanning the Polish string once.

The problem of converting infix expressions to prefix Polish will not be discussed in this section. A simple algorithm based on the scanning of an infix expression from right to left can be easily formulated. In many cases the entire infix string is not available, but it is obtained one symbol at a time in a left-to-right manner (because this is the way we write programs). Therefore, a practical algorithm for converting infix to prefix must be based on a left-to-right

Table 7-5 Translation of infix expression $(a + b)*(c + d))$ to suffix Polish

Current input symbol	Contents of stack (rightmost symbol is top of stack)	Reverse-Polish expression
	(	
(	((	
a	((a	
+	((+	a
b	((+b	a
)	(	ab +
*	(*	ab +
(	(*(	ab +
c	(*(c	ab +
+	(*(+	ab + c
d	(*(+d	ab + c
)	(*	ab + cd +
)		ab + cd + *

scan of the infix string. To facilitate such an algorithm, however, two stacks instead of the usual one can be used. This is left as an exercise.

In our discussion of the infix-to-suffix conversion process we have ignored the problems of detecting syntactic errors in the infix expressions being converted. We now turn to a discussion of this topic.

7-1.3 Error Detection for Infix Expressions

The preceding subsection describes an algorithm which converts valid infix arithmetic expressions into suffix Polish expressions. This section considers modifications to this algorithm which enable it to detect invalid infix expressions when they are presented to it.

Since we are attempting to detect deviations from the definition of valid infix expressions, we now present a definition similar to that given in Sec. 7-1.1.

1. All single-letter variables and nonnegative integers are valid infix expressions.
2. If α and β are valid infix expressions, then so are $\alpha + \beta$, $\alpha - \beta$, $\alpha * \beta$, α/β, and (α).
3. The only valid infix expressions are those defined by steps 1 and 2.

Note that the definition has been modified to allow incompletely parenthesized infix expressions.

Unparenthesized infix expressions are basically sequences of operators $(+, -, *, /)$ and operands (variables and integers) in which no two operands are adjacent and no two operators are adjacent. Parentheses are inserted into this sequence of symbols subject to the following restrictions:

1. For each left parenthesis in the infix expression there is a right parenthesis appearing later in the expression.
2. The left parenthesis '(' is always followed by an operand or another '('.
3. The right parenthesis ')' is always preceded by an operand or another ')'.

The first restriction can be checked by monitoring the stack level in the infix-to-suffix conversion process. The precedence relationships are such that when a right parenthesis is encountered in the left-to-right scan of the infix expression, all symbols down to and including the first left parenthesis are popped from the stack. Recall that a left parenthesis is initially placed on the stack. If a right parenthesis appears in the infix expression before a matching left parenthesis has appeared, the resulting unstacking operation will completely empty the stack. Unless we have reached the end of the infix expression, this constitutes a syntactic error in the infix expression. In this way an error is detected if there are too many right parentheses in an expression. If there are too few right parentheses in an expression, the final right parenthesis concatenated on the end of the infix expression will fail to empty the stack. Thus we must check that the stack is empty if and only if we have reached the end of the infix expression.

Table 7-6 Valid character pairs for infix expressions

	h		Second symbol			
		α	$+\ -$	$*\ /$	$($	$)$
	α	0	1	1	0	1
First	$+\ -$	1	0	0	1	0
symbol	$*\ /$	1	0	0	1	0
	$($	1	0	0	1	0
	$)$	0	1	1	0	1

α represents a variable or nonnegative integer.

In order to enforce the remaining restrictions on parentheses and the requirement that operands and operators must alternate, we must find a way to reject
certain pairs of characters which cannot appear in valid infix expressions. We do
this by constructing a *character-pair matrix h*, as shown in Table 7-6. This matrix
contains a row and a column for each class of symbols appearing in infix
expressions. If the element of the matrix corresponding to a given pair of symbols
is a 1, the pair of symbols can appear in an infix expression. If the matrix entry is
0, the pair of symbols cannot appear in an infix expression. The entries in the
matrix are chosen in such a way as to prevent adjacent operands and adjacent
operators, as well as to make sure that '(' is followed by an operand or '(' and
that ')' is preceded by an operand or ')'.

We now give the infix-to-suffix conversion algorithm, modified so as to detect
syntactic errors in the infix expression being converted to Polish form. The
algorithm incorporates the stack checking and character-pair checking described
in the preceding paragraphs.

Algorithm IMPROVED_REVERSE_POLISH. Given an input string INFIX containing an infix expression which has been padded on the right with ')', this
algorithm computes the suffix Polish translation of the expression and stores it in
the string POLISH. If INFIX does not contain a well-formed infix expression, the
algorithm prints 'INVALID EXPRESSION' and halts. The values of the precedence functions f and g are given in Table 7-4. The values of the character-pair
matrix h are given in Table 7-6. The function NEXTCHAR returns the next
character of its argument. The vector S, along with the index TOP, is used as a
stack. It is assumed that S is large enough to hold the required number of
symbols. LAST and NEXT contain symbols of the infix expression. TEMP and
RIGHT_PAREN are both local variables.

1. [Initialize]
        TOP ← 1
        NEXT ← S[TOP] ← '('
        POLISH ← ''

2. [Scan the infix expression]
    Repeat through step 5 while there are unprocessed symbols in
    INFIX
3. [Get next input symbol, check character pair, set right-parenthesis flag]
    LAST ← NEXT
    NEXT ← NEXTCHAR(INFIX)
    If h(LAST, NEXT) = 0
    then Write('INVALID SYMBOL PAIR')
        Exit
    RIGHT_PAREN ← false
4. [Emit symbols of higher precedence than NEXT]
    Repeat while f(NEXT) ≤ g(S[TOP])
        TEMP ← S[TOP]
        TOP ← TOP − 1
        If TOP = 0
        then Write('INVALID EXPRESSION')
            Exit
        If f(NEXT) < g(TEMP)
        then POLISH ← POLISH ∘ TEMP
        else RIGHT_PAREN ← true   (NEXT is a right parenthesis)
            Exit loop   (while f(NEXT) = g(TEMP))
5. [Push NEXT onto stack?]
    If not RIGHT_PAREN
    then TOP ← TOP + 1
        S[TOP] ← NEXT
6. [Finished. Check that the stack is empty]
    If TOP = 0
    then Exit
7. [Bad expression]
    Write('INVALID EXPRESSION')
    Exit   ☐

    Algorithm IMPROVED_REVERSE_POLISH will translate valid infix expressions into valid suffix expressions. Furthermore, it will never accept an invalid infix expression as input. Thus the user may have greater confidence in this improved version of the algorithm than in the original.

    In Sec. 7-2 we consider a parsing method which is a logical extension of the infix-to-suffix conversion algorithm. This parsing method can be applied to a class of input languages far more general than infix arithmetic expressions.

EXERCISES 7-1

1 Consider expressions which contain relational operators. In particular, obtain the precedence functions which will handle the relational operators

    <, ≤, =, >, ≠, and ≥

To avoid excessive parenthesization, the relational operators should have a lower priority than the arithmetic operators.

2 As a continuation of Exercise 1, consider extending the expressions so that they contain logical operators. In particular, obtain the precedence functions that will handle the logical operators

> ¬ (not)
> & (and)
> | (or)

which are given in decreasing order of priority. These operators have lower priority than the relational and arithmetic operators.

3 Describe how conditional statements (if . . . then . . . else) can be implemented in the suffix Polish framework. In particular extend the precedence functions obtained in Exercise 2 so as to incorporate conditional statements.

4 Thus far, we have only been concerned with the binary subtraction operator. In mathematics there are three usages of the minus sign: to indicate the binary subtraction operator, the unary minus operator (such as $-x$), and the sign of a constant (such as $x + (-5)$). Obtain a precedence table capable of handling assignment statements containing the unary minus (denoted by θ) and the assignment operator (denoted by ←). (Hint: It is an easy matter to distinguish the different occurrences of minus. A minus symbol will denote a binary operator if it does not occur either at the beginning of an expression or immediately after a left parenthesis. A minus symbol at the beginning of an expression or immediately after a left parenthesis will be a unary operator unless it is followed by a digit or decimal point.)

5 As we mentioned earlier, for certain applications the scanning of the infix expression is restricted to a left-to-right one-character-at-a-time scan. In an infix to prefix conversion, two stacks instead of one (as for infix to suffix conversion) are required: an operator stack and an operand stack (to store temporarily the intermediate operands). Recall that all variables and constants retain their relative order when an infix expression is converted to prefix form. The operators, however, are reordered according to their relative precedence, and the operator stack is used in this reordering. The operand stack is used for temporary storage of intermediate operands so that, when finally the operator which connects them is found to be applicable, it can be placed in front of the concatenated operands. Formulate an algorithm to perform the translation assuming infix expressions consisting of single-letter variables and the four arithmetic operators.

6 Investigate the possibility of obtaining precedence functions for an expression in APL. What difficulties, if any, are there in obtaining these functions?

7-2 OPERATOR PRECEDENCE GRAMMARS

In Sec. 7-1 the technique of establishing precedence relations between symbols was used to convert infix expressions to their suffix Polish equivalents. This conversion was based on the use of the input and stack precedence functions (f and g functions, respectively).

This section describes one of the earliest formal parsing techniques which is based on the notion of operator precedence. This parsing method, which is due to Floyd (1963), involves establishing precedence relations between the operator (terminal) symbols of a grammar. A generalization of this method to involve precedence relations between all symbols (terminal and nonterminal) of a grammar is given in the next section.

7-2.1 Notions and Use of Operator Precedence Relations

In this subsection we generalize the idea of operator precedence which was introduced in the previous section. Through the use of syntax trees, we can obtain an informal understanding of this generalization. Throughout this section, the term "operator" is used to mean a member of the terminal alphabet, V_T.

The parsing method that we present here constructs a parse in essentially a left-to-right manner. The parse thus obtained is not a converse rightmost derivation as described in Sec. 2-4.2. The method, however, is a bottom-up technique which involves no backup.

The generalization of the precedence functions introduced in the previous section results in precedence relations between operator (terminal) symbols only. This means that no relations concerning nonterminal symbols exist. Consequently, the parsing method does not repeatedly locate the handle of each sentential form in the parse. Since the relations are only between operator symbols, the string of symbols reduced at each point in the parse must contain at least one operator symbol.

We now define the class of grammars which is the subject of the discussion in this section.

Definition 7-1 A grammar G is an *operator grammar* if it contains no rules of the form $V \rightarrow \alpha XY\beta$, where $X, Y \in V_N$; that is, the occurrence of consecutive nonterminals in the right part of any rule is forbidden. Also, empty rules are not permitted. We call the language generated by an operator grammar an *operator language*.

The following is an example of an operator grammar in which the start symbol is E:

$$E \rightarrow T|E + T|E - T$$
$$T \rightarrow F|T * F|T/F$$
$$F \rightarrow P|F \uparrow P$$
$$P \rightarrow i|(E)$$

The operator language associated with this grammar is the set of parenthesized arithmetic expressions consisting of variables and the operations of addition, subtraction, multiplication, division, and exponention.

Recall from Sec. 2-4.1 the definition of a phrase associated with a sentential form. A *prime phrase* is a phrase which must contain at least one terminal symbol of the grammar, but no prime phrase other than itself. For example, in the current example grammar, the sentential form

$$P * P/(i + T)$$

contains only the prime phrases $P * P$ and i. All other phrases either are nonterminals or contain one of these prime phrases. At each stage in the parse we want to reduce the leftmost prime phrase. This is why this method of parsing is classified as a essentially left-to-right method.

The previous restriction on grammatical rules in an operator grammar gives rise to important properties concerning its sentential forms. In particular, it can be shown that any sentential form in an operator grammar cannot contain two consecutive nonterminals. The proof of this fact is left as an exercise. (The proof is by induction on the length of the derivation.)

The use of syntax trees can yield the relationships between operator symbols. Each column given in Fig. 7-1 represents a sentential form, a syntax tree for it, the leftmost prime phrase of this sentential form, and the precedence relations that can be derived from the tree after repeated reductions. For example, the leftmost prime phrase of the sentential form $E + i * i$ in Fig. 7-1 is the leftmost i, and the relations $i \gtrdot *$ and $+ \lessdot i$ hold. By the relation $i \gtrdot *$ we mean that i will be reduced before $*$. Similarly, $+ \lessdot i$ denotes that i will be reduced before $+$. When the reduction of i to P is made, i becomes the leftmost prime phrase of the sentential form $E + T * i$ which yields the relations $* \lessdot i$. Continuing in this manner, we can obtain other relations between other pairs of operator symbols. A matrix which displays all the operator precedence relations for the example grammar is given in Table 7-7, where a blank entry indicates that no relationship exists between a pair of operator symbols.

The approach used in Fig. 7-1 yielded some relations for some of the operator symbols in the example grammar; however, it is clear from the table that not all relationships were obtained from the two trees considered. We could examine other syntax trees until all such relations were obtained. We shall show in the next subsection that all these relations can be obtained rather easily.

The obvious question which arises at this point is: How do these relations help us to obtain the parse of a sentence? It turns out that if at most one relation holds between any pair of terminal symbols, the operator precedence relations can be used to determine the leftmost prime phrase of a sentential form. If, however, more than one relation holds between a pair of operator symbols, this approach may not work.

Table 7-7 Operator precedence relations for sample grammar

	(	i	+	−	*	/	↑	)
(	⋖	⋖	⋖	⋖	⋖	⋖	⋖	≐
i			⋗	⋗	⋗	⋗	⋗	⋗
+	⋖	⋖	⋗	⋗	⋖	⋖	⋖	⋗
−	⋖	⋖	⋗	⋗	⋖	⋖	⋖	⋗
*	⋖	⋖	⋗	⋗	⋗	⋗	⋖	⋗
/	⋖	⋖	⋗	⋗	⋗	⋗	⋖	⋗
↑	⋖	⋖	⋗	⋗	⋗	⋗	⋗	⋗
)			⋗	⋗	⋗	⋗	⋗	⋗

Sentential form: $E + i * i$

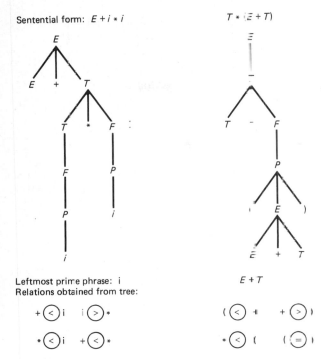

Leftmost prime phrase: i
Relations obtained from tree:

Figure 7-1 Obtaining precedence relations from syntax trees.

Assuming that at most one relation holds between any pair of terminal symbols, there is a straightforward technique for finding the leftmost prime phrase of each sentential form. Let a general sentential form be written as

$$[A_1]c_1[A_2]c_2\ldots[A_n]c_n[A_{n+1}]$$

where $A_i \in V_N$ for $1 \le i \le n+1$ and $c_i \in V_T$ for $1 \le i \le n$. The term $[A_i]$ denotes that the nonterminal A_i can be present or absent in the sentential form. Note, also, that from the previous discussion two adjacent nonterminals cannot occur in the given sentential form. The leftmost prime phrase of this sentential form is the leftmost substring satisfying the conditions

$$c_{i-1} \lessdot c_i \doteq c_{i+1} \doteq \ldots c_{j-1} \doteq c_j \gtrdot c_{j+1}$$

More will be said about this fact in the next subsection. The detection of the leftmost prime phrase $c_i \ldots c_j$ is based on the context symbols c_{i-1} and c_{j+1}, where c_{i-1} denotes the left context and c_{j-1} denotes the right context. In certain instances, we may not have any left and/or right context symbols. In order to prevent this problem, we assume the existence of the special character # such that

$$\# \lessdot c \text{ and } c \gtrdot \# \text{ for all } c \in V_T$$

A given sentential form s is surrounded by instances of the special character, giving the string $\#s\#$. We are now guaranteed the existence of left and right context symbols.

Using the example grammar introduced earlier, let us now, in an informal manner, attempt to construct a syntax tree for the sentence $i*(i + i)$. Padded with $\#$'s on both ends, the sentence is $\#i*(i + i)\#$. Scanning this augmented sentence from left to right and using operator precedence relations, it is seen from Table 7-8 that

$$\# \lessdot i \quad\quad \text{and} \quad\quad i \gtrdot *$$

Therefore, i is the leftmost prime phrase of the initial sentential form. Since the precedence table gives no information about nonterminals per se, we are unable to determine which nonterminal we must reduce the phrase to. Consequently the prime phrase i is replaced by the nonterminal symbol X_1. This substitution yields the new sentential form

$$\#X_1*(i + i)\#$$

By continuing the scan, we obtain the relations

$$(\lessdot i \quad\quad \text{and} \quad\quad i \gtrdot +$$

This indicates that the leftmost i is a prime phrase. We then reduce this phrase to a nonterminal X_2. After this reduction we obtain the revised sentential form

$$\#X_1*(X_2 + i)\#$$

The continuation of the scan yields the relations

$$+ \lessdot i \quad\quad \text{and} \quad\quad i \gtrdot)$$

From these relationships it is clear that i is again a prime phrase. This phrase reduces to the nonterminal X_3, and the resulting sentential form is

$$\#X_1*(X_2 + X_3)\#$$

At this point

$$(\lessdot + \quad\quad \text{and} \quad\quad + \gtrdot)$$

so $X_2 + X_3$ is a prime phrase. A reduction of this phrase to X_4 produces the new sentential form

$$\#X_1*(X_4)\#$$

The relations which now hold are

$$* \lessdot (, \quad\quad (\doteq), \quad\quad \text{and} \quad\quad) \gtrdot \#$$

Consequently, we replace the prime phrase (X_4) by the nonterminal X_5. This substitution results in the sentential form

$$\#X_1*X_5\#$$

Table 7-8 Parse of $i * (i + i)$

Step	Sentential form	Leftmost prime phrase	Reduction
	$\#$ i $*$ $($ i $+$ i $)$ $\#$	i	$X_1 \to i$
2	$\#$ X_1 $*$ $($ i $+$ i $)$ $\#$	i	$X_2 \to i$
3	$\#$ X_1 $*$ $($ X_2 $+$ i $)$ $\#$	i	$X_3 \to i$
4	$\#$ X_1 $*$ $($ X_2 $+$ X_3 $)$ $\#$	$X_2 + X_3$	$X_4 \to X_2 + X_3$
5	$\#$ X_1 $*$ $($ X_4 $)$ $\#$	(X_4)	$X_5 \to (X_4)$
6	$\#$ X_1 $*$ X_5 $\#$	$X_1 * X_5$	$X_6 \to X_1 * X_5$
7	$\#$ X_6 $\#$		

Since

$$\# \lessdot * \qquad \text{and} \qquad * \gtrdot \#$$

a final reduction of the prime phrase $X_1 * X_5$ to X_6 yields the sentential form

$$\# X_6 \#$$

The reader probably has noticed that the parse of the given sentence constructed in the previous manner is not complete. The syntax tree obtained so far is displayed in Fig. 7-2a, with a summary of the parse given in Table 7-8. This tree is merely a skeleton of the complete syntax tree given in Fig. 7-2b.

The absence of certain portions of the complete derivation is obvious when both trees are compared. The omitted portions of the derivations consist of sentential forms where one nonterminal has been reduced to another nonterminal. Since the precedence relations exist only between terminal symbols, it is not surprising that these omissions occur. Clearly, we can complete the derivation by filling in the gaps; namely, we must complete the following:

$$E \overset{*}{\Rightarrow} X_6 \qquad\qquad X_6 \overset{*}{\Rightarrow} X_1 * X_5 \qquad\quad X_1 \overset{*}{\Rightarrow} i$$

$$X_5 \overset{*}{\Rightarrow} (X_4) \qquad\qquad X_4 \overset{*}{\Rightarrow} X_2 + X_3$$

$$X_2 \overset{*}{\Rightarrow} i \qquad\qquad X_3 \overset{*}{\Rightarrow} i$$

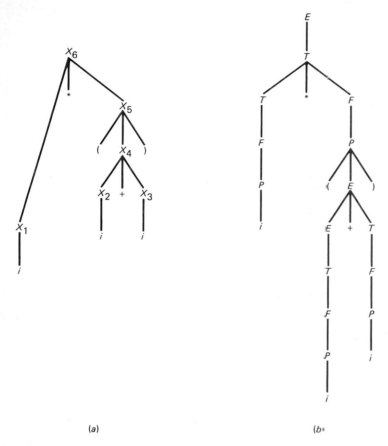

(a)   (b)

Figure 7-2 Parse trees for the sentence $i * (i + i)$.

In this example,

$$E = X_6 \qquad\qquad X_6 = E \Rightarrow T \Rightarrow T * F = X_1 * X_5$$

$$X_1 = T \Rightarrow F \Rightarrow P \Rightarrow i \qquad X_2 = E \Rightarrow T \Rightarrow F \Rightarrow P \Rightarrow i$$

$$X_3 = T \Rightarrow F \Rightarrow P \Rightarrow i \qquad X_4 = E \Rightarrow E + T = X_2 + X_3$$

$$X_5 = F \Rightarrow P \Rightarrow (E) = (X_4)$$

These partial derivations are obtained easily from the rules of the grammar.

The approach taken in this subsection depends exclusively on the precedence table associated with a grammar. The precedence table for our sample grammar was obtained in an ad hoc manner. It would be desirable to be able to generate such a precedence table in a more formal manner. In fact, this goal can be achieved mechanically by examining the rules of the grammar. We turn now to this formalization.

7-2.2 Formal Definition of Operator Precedence Relations

In the previous subsection the operator precedence relations were obtained by examining syntax trees. We now redefine these relations in terms of the productions of the grammar. It is shown that these relations can be computed easily from the grammar.

> **Definition 7-2** The operator precedence relations associated with an operator grammar are defined over its terminal alphabet as follows:
>
> 1. $S_1 \doteq S_2$ iff there exists a production $U \to \alpha S_1 S_2 \beta$ or $U \to \alpha S_1 X S_2 \beta$, where $S_1, S_2 \in V_T$, and $X \in V_N$.
>
> 2. $S_1 \lessdot S_2$ iff there exists a production $U \to \alpha S_1 X \beta$ such that $X \overset{+}{\Rightarrow} S_2 \ldots$ or $X \overset{+}{\Rightarrow} Y S_2 \ldots$, where $S_1, S_2 \in V_T$ and $X, Y \in V_N$.
>
> 3. $S_1 \gtrdot S_2$ iff there exists a production $U \to \alpha X S_2 \beta$ such that $X \overset{+}{\Rightarrow} \ldots S_1$ or $X \overset{+}{\Rightarrow} \ldots S_1 Y$, where $S_1, S_2 \in V_T$, and $X, Y \in V_N$.

The leftmost and rightmost terminal characters which are obtainable from the nonterminals for the example grammar of the previous subsection are given in Table 7-9. Formally, the leftmost and rightmost terminal-character derivations of a nonterminal symbol can be defined as follows:

$$\text{FIRSTOP}(X) = \{ S_1 | X \overset{+}{\Rightarrow} S_1 \ldots \text{ or } X \overset{+}{\Rightarrow} Y S_1 \text{ where } X, Y \in V_N, \text{ and }$$
$$S_1 \in V_T \}$$
$$\text{LASTOP}(X) = \{ S_1 | X \overset{+}{\Rightarrow} \ldots S_1 \text{ or } X \overset{+}{\Rightarrow} \ldots S_1 Y \text{ where } X, Y \in V_N, \text{ and }$$
$$S_1 \in Y_T \}$$

The relation $\doteq$ is obtained easily from the grammar in that there is only one rule which contains two terminal symbols; therefore $(\doteq)$. The relation $\lessdot$ can be evaluated by first considering the symbol pairs $(E, \uparrow P, *F, /F, +T, \text{ and } -T$. The pair $(E$ yields the relations $(\lessdot i, (\lessdot (, (\lessdot \uparrow, (\lessdot *, (\lessdot /, (\lessdot +,$ and $(\lessdot -$. The remaining elements in the $\lessdot$ relation are obtained in an analogous manner. Using a similar approach, the $\gtrdot$ relation can be constructed. In particular, we consider the symbol pairs $E), E-, E+, T*, T/, \text{ and } F\uparrow$. The pair $E)$ yields the elements $i\gtrdot),)\gtrdot), \,\hat{}\,\gtrdot), *\gtrdot), /\gtrdot), +\gtrdot), -\gtrdot)$. The

Table 7-9 Leftmost and rightmost character derivations for sample grammar

Nonterminal symbol	Leftmost terminal character	Rightmost terminal character
P	$i($	$i)$
F	$i(\uparrow$	$i)\uparrow$
T	$i(\uparrow * /$	$i)\uparrow * /$
E	$i(\uparrow * / + -$	$i)\uparrow * / + -$

remaining elements in $\ominus$ are generated by repeating this process on the other symbol pairs.

One or more of these relations may hold between any pair of operator symbols. However, if at most one of the three relations holds between any such pair of symbols, an interesting and useful subset of the operator grammar class results.

> **Definition 7-3** An *operator precedence grammar* is an operator grammar in which at most one of the relations $\doteq$, $\lessdot$, and $\gtrdot$ holds between any pair of operator symbols. We call the language generated by an operator precedence grammar an *operator precedence language*.

The precedence relations associated with our sample grammar indicate that this grammar is an operator precedence grammar.

The computation of the three precedence relations can be facilitated by introducing several intermediate relations which are represented by (Boolean) matrices. Since, however, the next subsection deals with a generalization of operator precedence to all symbols of the grammar, we leave the specification of the precedence relations in terms of simpler intermediate relations until later.

In this subsection we have formalized the notions of precedence relations introduced in the last subsection. If at most one operator relation holds between any pair of operator symbols for a given operator grammar, then this grammar is known as an operator precedence grammar. The next step is to specify an algorithm for the parsing of operator precedence grammars.

7-2.3 Operator Precedence Parsing Algorithm

In Sec. 7-2.1 we informally traced through a sample parse based on the operator relations $\doteq$, $\lessdot$, and $\gtrdot$. Recall that the parse obtained was not a full parse but only a skeleton of the complete parse. This phenomenon was the result of not having any information in the precedence relations about the nonterminals of the grammar. Furthermore, the string reduced at each stage in the skeleton parse was the leftmost prime phrase and not the handle. Also recall that a prime phrase must contain at least one terminal symbol. The purpose of this subsection is to formalize this parsing process into the form of a general algorithm.

The leftmost prime phrase in a sentential form of an operator precedence grammar can be detected by using one symbol on each side of a possible prime phrase. In other words, the leftmost prime phrase is determined by scanning the sentential form from left to right examining successive pairs of terminal symbols until $a \gtrdot b$; in this case a is either the *tail* (last symbol) or the symbol which immediately precedes the tail of the prime phrase, and b is the right context symbol used to find it. Similarly, the *head* (leftmost symbol) of the prime phrase is found by scanning from the tail of the prime phrase from right to left until $a \lessdot b$, where b is now either the head or the symbol which immediately follows the head of the prime phrase and a is the left context symbol. The next theorem, which is stated without proof, is important.

Theorem 7-1 Each sentential form

$$[A_1]c_1[A_2]c_2\ldots[A_n]c_n[A_{n+1}]\quad (A_i \in V_N \text{ for } 1 \le i \le n+1 \text{ and}$$
$$c_i \in V_T \text{ for } 1 \le i \le n)$$

of an operator precedence grammar has a unique leftmost prime phrase which is the leftmost substring

$$[A_i]c_i[A_{i+1}]c_{i+1}\ldots[A_j]c_j[A_{j+1}]$$

that satisfies

$$c_{i-1} \lessdot c_i \doteq c_{i+1} \doteq \cdots \doteq c_j \gtrdot c_{j+1}$$

Note that we are assuming (as we did in Sec. 7-2.1) the presence of a special symbol # such that # $\lessdot$ a and a $\gtrdot$ # for any terminal symbol. This modification permits the detection of a leftmost prime phrase when it contains the leftmost and/or rightmost terminal in the sentential form.

We wish to formulate a parsing algorithm based on this theorem. We assume that the operator precedence matrix and the productions of the grammar are represented in some suitable form.

The algorithm works in the following manner. The symbols of the given input string are scanned from left to right and placed on a stack S. This scanning continues until the relation between the symbol at the top or next to the top of the stack and the current input symbol is $\gtrdot$. Note that, since the relation is between terminal symbols only, we have to ignore the symbol on the top of the stack in the case of a nonterminal. In such a case, however, the next symbol in the stack must be a terminal (since in a sentential form of an operator precedence grammar two consecutive nonterminals cannot occur). At this point, the top element of the stack denotes the tail of the leftmost prime phrase. The head of this prime phrase is determined by comparing successive pairs of adjacent terminal symbols going down the stack until a pair is encountered that is $\lessdot$ related. The symbol which immediately precedes the prime phrase is always a terminal. A pair of terminal symbols separated by a nonterminal symbol is considered to be an adjacent pair. This leftmost prime phrase is reduced (i.e., removed from the stack) to the left part of the applicable production (which is then placed on the stack). The entire process is repeated until the current input symbol is the special symbol #. This parsing approach is incorporated in the following algorithm.

Algorithm OPERATOR_PRECEDENCE. Given an operator precedence grammar, its associated precedence matrix, and a certain input sentence $t = t_1 t_2 \ldots t_n$ which is to be parsed, this algorithm parses this sentence in the manner just described. Let S denote a stack, and let TOP be an index which is used to designate the top element of the stack. The index i is used to locate the leftmost prime phrase on the stack, while k is an index which refers to the current input symbol being scanned. NEXT is a temporary variable which contains the current input symbol. TEMP is a variable which is used in locating the head symbol of a prime phrase.

1. [Initialize]
        S[1] ← '#'
        t ← t ∘ '#'
        TOP ← 1
2. [Scan the first input symbol]
        NEXT ← t_1
        k ← 2
3. [Parse the input string]
        Repeat through step 5 while true
4. [Is stack top an operator?]
        If S[TOP] ∉ V_T ∪ {'#'}
        then i ← TOP
        else i ← TOP − 1
5. [Tail of leftmost prime phrase?]
        If S[i] ⊚> NEXT
        then (Find the head of the leftmost prime phrase)
            TOP ← i + 1
            Repeat while S[TOP − 1] ⊚> NEXT
                TEMP ← S[i]
                i ← i − 1
                If S[i] ∈ V_T ∪ {'#'}
                then i ← i − 1
                If S[i] ⊚< TEMP
                then (Process leftmost prime phrase)
                    TOP ← i + 1
                    S[TOP] ← 'N'
                    (Is the parse complete?)
                    If TOP = 2 and NEXT = '#'
                    then Exit
        else (Push current input symbol onto the stack)
            TOP ← TOP + 1
            S[TOP] ← NEXT
            (Scan next input symbol)
            NEXT ← t_k
            k ← k + 1   □

The first step of the algorithm initializes the stack to contain the special symbol '#'. The input string is also padded with the marker symbol '#'. Step 2 scans the first input symbol and sets the input string index to a value of 2.

Steps 3 to 5 perform the required parse. The third step seems to contain an infinite loop. This loop is exited in step 5 when the stack contains two elements and the current input symbol is '#'. When this occurs, the parse is complete. Step 4 determines whether or not the top element in the stack is an operator. If it is not, the second element in the stack is an operator (since a sentential form cannot contain two consecutive nonterminals). The value of variable i reflects that fact. The purpose of step 5 is to determine the presence of a leftmost prime phrase. The presence of such a phrase results in its reduction. We detect a prime phrase by first determining its tail symbol. The condition S[i]$\ominus$NEXT uses the right context symbol, NEXT (the current input symbol), to make this decision. If at this point in the parse a leftmost prime phrase is not in the stack, then we place the current input symbol on the stack and scan the next input symbol. If, however, the test confirms the presence of the leftmost prime phrase on the stack, we then must find the head symbol of this phrase. Such a search entails the checking of each successive pair of operator symbols in the stack. The desired head symbol is found on encountering the first operator pair that is related by the relation $\ominus$. When this head symbol is detected, the required reduction is performed. This reduction entails the invocation of a semantic routine to handle that particular prime phrase. There is one semantic routine for each distinct prime phrase. We perform the indicated reduction by replacing the prime phrase in the top portion of the stack by some nonterminal symbol which we denote by 'N'. Note that when one reduction occurs, it is possible to have other reductions apply at that point without any new input symbol being scanned. The repeat statement in step 5 handles this particular possibility. A trace of the skeleton parse for the input string $t = (i + i) * i$ of the sample language introduced earlier is given in Table 7-10.

Note that in the previous algorithm no attempt is made to detect and correct errors. These considerations will be discussed in Sec. 7-2.5.

We can represent the operator precedence relations by a precedence matrix P whose element p_{ij} is given as

$$p_{ij} = \begin{cases} 0 & \text{if no relation exists between } a \text{ and } b \\ 1 & \text{if } a \ominus b \\ 2 & \text{if } a \oslash b \\ 3 & \text{if } a \ominus b \end{cases}$$

A 2-bit entry can represent each element of such a matrix. The zero entry in this matrix can be used in the case of error detection and recovery. This possibility is pursued in Sec. 7-2.5.

Operator precedence parsers have been used in several compiler efforts. Operator precedence grammars have been obtained for languages such as ALGOL 60 and ALGOL W. Another approach that has been used is to have an expression in a language recognized by an operator precedence parser submodule which is part of a recursive-descent parser.

Table 7-10 Trace of algorithm OPERATOR_PRECEDENCE for $t = (i + i) * i$

Step	Unexpended input string	Stack contents	Relation	Current input symbol	Leftmost prime phrase
0	$(i + i) * i\#$	$\#$			
1	$i + i) * i\#$	$\#$	$\lessdot$	$($	
2	$+ i) * i\#$	$\#($	$\lessdot$	i	
3	$i) * i\#$	$\#(i$	$\gtrdot$	$+$	i
4	$i) * i\#$	$\#(N$	$\lessdot$	$+$	
5	$) * i\#$	$\#(N +$	$\lessdot$	i	
6	$* i\#$	$\#(N + i$	$\gtrdot$	$)$	i
7	$* i\#$	$\#(N + N$	$\gtrdot$	$)$	$N + N$
8	$* i\#$	$\#(N$	$\doteq$	$)$	
9	$i\#$	$\#(N)$	$\gtrdot$	$*$	(N)
10	$i\#$	$\#N$	$\lessdot$	$*$	
11	$\#$	$\#N *$	$\lessdot$	i	
12	ε	$\#N * i$	$\gtrdot$	$\#$	i
13	ε	$\#N * N$	$\gtrdot$	$\#$	$N * N$
14	ε	$\#N$		$\#$	

For a particular grammar, the size of the precedence matrix varies as the square of the number of operator symbols. In many cases, however, a great reduction in this matrix size can be realized. We explore this possibility in the next subsection.

7-2.4 Precedence Functions in Operator Precedence Parsers

The storage requirements of the precedence matrix require n^2 entries where n is the number of operator symbols in the grammar. It may be desirable to try to reduce this number of entries. For some operator precedence grammars, it is sometimes possible to replace the matrix by two precedence functions. In such cases these precedence functions, which we call f and g, are defined as

If $a \lessdot b$ then $f(a) < g(b)$
If $a \doteq b$ then $f(a) = g(b)$
If $a \gtrdot b$ then $f(a) > g(b)$

where a and b denote operator symbols. The f and g functions can then be used instead of the precedence matrix in Algorithm OPERATOR_PRECEDENCE discussed earlier. Instead of using the relation $a \gtrdot b$ to detect the tail symbol of the leftmost prime phrase on the stack, we use the relation $f(a) > g(b)$. Similarly, instead of using the relation $a \lessdot b$ to detect the head symbol of the leftmost prime phrase, we use the relation $f(a) < g(b)$. The precedence functions require $2n$ entries of storage.

We now present briefly in an informal manner a method for generating the precedence functions if they exist. A detailed discussion of the method is given in Sec. 7-3.4 for obtaining precedence functions for simple precedence grammars. In fact, obtaining precedence functions for operator precedence grammars is a special case of the method presented there.

To describe the method for obtaining the precedence functions, the following simplified grammar is used.

$$E \rightarrow T | E - T$$
$$T \rightarrow F | T/F$$
$$F \rightarrow i | (E)$$

Its precedence matrix is given in Table 7-11. One method of obtaining a pair of precedence functions involves the generation of a directed graph from the precedence matrix. The graph contains $2n$ entries labeled $f(a_1), f(a_2), \ldots,$ $f(a_n), g(a_1), g(a_2), \ldots, g(a_n)$. The following notation is used in the construction of the graph:

$a \gtreqdot b$ is equivalent to $a \doteq b$ or $a \gtrdot b$
$a \lesseqdot b$ is equivalent to $a \doteq b$ or $a \lessdot b$

We define a directed edge from $f(a_i)$ to $g(a_j)$ if $a_i \gtreqdot a_j$. Similarly, define an edge from $g(a_j)$ to $f(a_i)$ if $a_i \lesseqdot a_j$. Assign a number to each node equal to the number of nodes that are reachable from that node, including the node itself. The numbers assigned to $f(a_i)$ and $g(a_i)$ are the numbers assigned to their corresponding nodes.

In the current example, $n = 5$. The graph shown in Fig. 7-3 consists of 10 nodes labeled $f(a_1), f(a_2), \ldots, f(a_5), g(a_1), g(a_2), \ldots, g(a_5)$. Since $i \gtrdot -$, $i \gtrdot /$, and $i \gtrdot)$, there are directed edges $f(a_2)$ to $g(a_3)$, $f(a_2)$ to $g(a_4)$, and $f(a_2)$ to $g(a_5)$, respectively. Also, since $(\lessdot (, (\lessdot i, (\lessdot -, \text{ and } (\lessdot /$, there are directed edges $g(a_1)$ to $f(a_1)$, $g(a_2)$ to $f(a_1)$, $g(a_3)$ to $f(a_1)$, and $g(a_4)$ to $f(a_1)$, respectively. Note that since $(\doteq)$, there are edges from $f(a_1)$ to $g(a_5)$ and $g(a_5)$

Table 7-11

	(	i	$-$	/	)
(	$\lessdot$	$\lessdot$	$\lessdot$	$\lessdot$	$\doteq$
i			$\gtrdot$	$\gtrdot$	$\gtrdot$
$-$	$\lessdot$	$\lessdot$	$\gtrdot$	$\lessdot$	$\gtrdot$
/	$\lessdot$	$\lessdot$	$\gtrdot$	$\gtrdot$	$\gtrdot$
)			$\gtrdot$	$\gtrdot$	$\gtrdot$

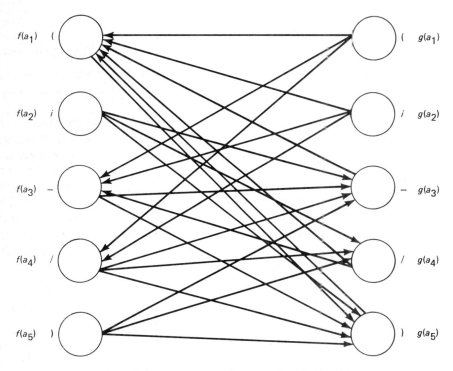

Figure 7-3 Directed graph for operator precedence matrix of Table 7-11.

to $f(a_1)$. The value of $f(a_1)$ [i.e., $f(()$] is 2, since $f(a_1)$ and $g(a_5)$ are both reachable from $f(a_1)$. The same value is assigned to $g())$. $f(a_2)$, that is, $f(i)$, is assigned a value of 6, since 6 nodes are reachable from $f(i)$. The other functional values can be obtained in an analogous manner. The two precedence functions thus obtained are:

	(	i	−	/	)
f	2	6	4	6	6
g	7	7	3	5	2

It can be verified that these functions are valid by comparing them with the precedence matrix. The details of this check are given in Sec. 7-3.4.

So far, syntax errors have not been mentioned. The next subsection examines the detection of errors.

7-2.5 Error Detection in Operator Precedence Parsers

Errors can be detected in operator precedence parsers by making use of the blank entries in the operator precedence matrix. When such a blank entry is referenced in the parsing algorithm, a routine can be invoked that will report the error. The

Table 7-12 Allowable adjacent operator pairs

	(	i	–	/	)
(	x	x			
i			x	x	x
–	x	x			
/	x	x			
)			x	x	x

error message generated depends on the nature of the error. Appropriate and meaningful error messages can be created by a compiler writer who is very familiar with the programming-language syntax. Perhaps the reader should recall at this point the discussion of errors given in Chap. 5.

Errors can also be detected by constructing from the given grammar a table of allowable adjacent operator pairs. In the grammar

$$E \rightarrow T|E - T$$
$$T \rightarrow F|T/F$$
$$F \rightarrow i|(E)$$

adjacent character pairs in the right-hand side of the rules can be used to generate the table. For example, the adjacent character pair $E -$ (from the rule $E \rightarrow E - T$) indicates that the adjacent operator pairs $i -$ and $) -$ are permitted. This follows by noting that the operators i and $)$ are rightmost derivable from E. Similarly, the character pair $(E$ implies that the operator pairs $((\ $ and $(i$ are also allowable adjacent operator pairs since $($ and i are leftmost operator derivable from E. When this process is continued, the set of allowable adjacent operator pairs given in Table 7-12 results. An algorithm to generate such a table is left as an exercise.

It should be noted that since relationships exist only between operator symbols, the phrase structure of the grammar involving nonterminals is essentially ignored. Consequently, nonterminals may not be used to indicate which portions of an input string are in error. Furthermore, since the parser produces only a skeleton parse for an input string, reductions of the form "$A \rightarrow B$" where B is nonterminal do not occur. Therefore, it is possible to accept an input string that is syntactically invalid. A final comment concerns parsers that use precedence functions instead of the operator precedence matrix. Parsers using these functions may take longer to detect an error than if the corresponding precedence matrix had been used. Examples of this possibility are given for simple precedence parsers in the next section.

EXERCISES 7-2

1 Prove that in an operator grammar every sentential form cannot contain two consecutive nonterminals.

2 Given the grammar

$$E \rightarrow T | E - T$$
$$T \rightarrow F | T * F$$
$$F \rightarrow P | \theta P$$
$$P \rightarrow i | (E)$$

Obtain the following:

(a) The phrases and prime phrases of the sentential forms

$$\theta(i - i), i - i * i, i * i - \theta i, T - T * F, P - \theta P$$

(b) Operator precedence matrix
(c) Precedence functions for the grammar, if they exist
(d) The table of allowable adjacent operator pairs
(e) The parse (as in Table 7-10) for the input strings $\theta(i - i)$ and $(i - \theta i)$

3 Given the grammar

$$E \rightarrow I | E \equiv I$$
$$I \rightarrow D | I \supset D$$
$$D \rightarrow C | D \vee C$$
$$C \rightarrow S | C \wedge S$$
$$S \rightarrow P | \neg P$$
$$P \rightarrow t | f | (E)$$

Obtain the following:

(a) Operator precedence matrix
(b) The parse (as in Table 7-10) for the input strings $t \supset f, t \wedge f \vee t, \neg(t \vee f) \equiv t$
(c) Precedence functions for the grammar, if they exist

4 Formulate an algorithm which has as input a given grammar, and produces as output, a table of allowable adjacent operator pairs.

5 Prove that in an operator grammar "if bX occurs in a sentential form ϕ, where b is a terminal and X is a nonterminal, then any phrase of ϕ containing b also contains X."

6 Prove that in an operator grammar no phrase in a sentential form is immediately preceded (or followed) by nonterminal symbols.

7-3 SIMPLE PRECEDENCE GRAMMARS

Wirth and Weber (1966) alleviated some of the shortcomings of operator precedence grammars by generalizing the notion of precedence to all symbols (i.e., terminal and nonterminal) of a grammar. This generalization leads to the definition of simple precedence grammars. Unlike operator precedence parsers which produce only skeleton parses, simple precedence parsers produce complete parses. Also the phrase structure of a simple precedence grammar is captured in a simple precedence matrix because both terminal and nonterminal symbols can be related. Error detection and recovery can be more easily formalized in simple precedence parsers than is possible in operator precedence parsers.

7-3.1 Notions and Use of Precedence Relations

In this section we are again concerned with a left-to-right bottom-up parsing technique which involves no backup. This technique can be viewed as a generalization of the operator precedence parsing strategy. Unlike the operator precedence parser which detects a leftmost prime phrase, however, this method constructs the parse for a sentence by repeatedly finding the handle in each sentential form. As was previously mentioned, once the handle has been found, we must also determine which production to apply, that is, to which nonterminal the handle should be reduced. This parsing method will work for a class of grammars (which is a proper subset of the context-free grammars) called the simple precedence grammars. Since the proposed method proceeds in a left-to-right bottom-up manner, all the sentential forms will represent the converse of a rightmost derivation. In the remainder of the discussion on precedence grammars, all derivations are understood to be the converse of such a rightmost derivation.

Let us now investigate how the handle in the sentential form might be found. Since the parsing method is left to right, we want to scan the sentential form from left to right, looking at only two adjacent symbols at one time so as to be able to determine the rightmost symbol of the handle which is called its tail. Starting at the tail of the handle, and again using only two adjacent symbols, we will then scan from right to left and find the leftmost symbol in the handle which is called its head. We are then faced with the following problem. Given some sentential form

$$\alpha = \ldots S_1 S_2 \ldots$$

where ... denotes a possibly empty string of symbols, four possibilities are obvious: S_1 is the tail of the handle, both S_1 and S_2 are in the handle, S_2 is in the handle but S_1 is not, and neither S_1 nor S_2 is in the handle. This last case is impossible because the grammar is reduced and we are in the process of obtaining the converse of a rightmost derivation.

We would like to develop certain relations from the grammar which would permit us to make such a decision. For any pair of symbols S_1 and S_2 in the vocabulary of the grammar, assume there is a sentential form $\ldots S_1 S_2 \ldots$. At some stage in the reverse of the rightmost derivation, either S_1 or S_2 or both must be in the handle. The following three cases can occur:

1. S_1 is part of the handle (actually its tail) and S_2 is not. This relationship is denoted as $S_1 \gtrdot S_2$, which signifies that S_1 has precedence over S_2 because S_1 must be reduced before S_2. Formally, if $\alpha = \phi_1 \beta \phi_2$ where β is the handle of α and there is a rule $A \rightarrow \beta$, then S_1 is the tail of β.
2. S_1 and S_2 are both contained in the handle. This relationship is specified as $S_1 \doteq S_2$, which means that both symbols have the same precedence and are to be reduced at the same time. This implies that there is a rule of the form $A \rightarrow \ldots S_1 S_2 \ldots$ in the grammar.
3. S_2 is contained in the handle (actually its head) and S_1 is not. We denote such a relationship as $S_1 \lessdot S_2$, which signifies that S_2 has precedence over S_1. The grammar must contain a rule of the form $A \rightarrow S_2 \ldots$.

These three cases can be interpreted pictorially in Fig. 7-4a to c.

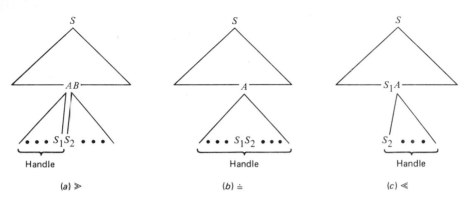

Figure 7-4 Interpretation of precedence relations.

As an example, consider the grammar $G = \langle \{ E, U, T, V, F \}, \{ i, +, *, (,) \},$ $E, \Phi \rangle$, where Φ is the set of productions

$$
\begin{array}{ll}
E \rightarrow U & V \rightarrow F \\
U \rightarrow T & V \rightarrow V * F \\
U \rightarrow U + T & F \rightarrow i \\
T \rightarrow V & F \rightarrow (E)
\end{array}
$$

and i represents a variable name. The language generated by this grammar is the set of parenthesized arithmetic expressions consisting of variables and the operations of addition and multiplication. Each column given in Fig. 7-5 represents a sentential form, a syntax tree for it, the handle of the sentential form, and the precedence relations that can be derived from the tree after repeated reductions. For example, the handle of the sentential for $U + i * i$ in Fig. 7-5 is i, and the relations $i \gtrdot *$ and $+ \lessdot i$ hold. When the reduction $F \rightarrow i$ is made, F is the handle of the sentential form $U + F * i$, which yields the relations $+ \lessdot F$ and $F \gtrdot *$. Continuing in this manner, we can obtain other relations between other pairs of symbols. A matrix which displays all the precedence relations for the example is given in Table 7-13, where a blank entry indicates that no relationship exists between a pair of symbols.

The approach used in Fig. 7-5 has yielded a number of relations for the symbols of the example grammar; however, it can be seen from the table that not all of them were obtained from the two trees considered. We could examine other syntax trees until all such relations were obtained. As was the case in operator precedence grammars these relations can also be obtained rather easily.

If at most one relation holds between any pair of symbols, the precedence relations can be used to determine the handle of a sentential form. If, however, more than one relation holds between a pair of symbols, this approach may not work. In the former case the handle of the sentential for $S_1 S_2 \ldots S_n$ is the leftmost

Sentential form: $U + i * i$ $V * (U + T$ ⌐

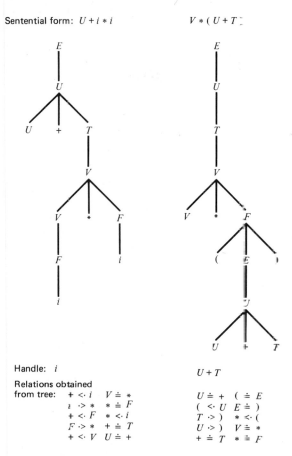

Handle: i $U + T$

Relations obtained
from tree:

$+ <\cdot i$	$V \doteq *$
$i \cdot> *$	$* \doteq F$
$+ <\cdot F$	$* <\cdot i$
$F \cdot> *$	$+ \doteq T$
$+ <\cdot V$	$U \doteq +$

$U \doteq +$	$(\doteq E$
$(<\cdot U$	$E \doteq)$
$T \cdot>)$	$* <\cdot ($
$U \cdot>)$	$V \doteq *$
$+ \doteq T$	$* \doteq F$

Figure 7-5 Obtaining precedence relations from syntax trees.

Table 7-13 Precedence relations for the example grammar

	E	U	T	F	V	$+$	$*$	i	$($	$)$
E										$\doteq$
U						$\doteq$				$\gtrdot$
T						$\gtrdot$				$\gtrdot$
F						$\gtrdot$	$\gtrdot$			$\gtrdot$
V						$\gtrdot$	$\doteq$			$\gtrdot$
$+$		$\doteq$	$\lessdot$	$\lessdot$				$\lessdot$	$\lessdot$	
$*$			$\doteq$					$\lessdot$	$\lessdot$	
i						$\gtrdot$	$\gtrdot$			$\gtrdot$
$($	$\doteq$	$\lessdot$	$\lessdot$	$\lessdot$	$\lessdot$			$\lessdot$	$\lessdot$	
$)$						$\gtrdot$	$\gtrdot$			$\gtrdot$

Table 7-14 Parse for the string $i + i * i$ in the example grammar

Step	Sentential form	Handle	Reduction	Direct derivation obtained
1	# i ⋖ + ⋗ i ⋖ * ⋗ i ⋖ # ⋗	i	$F \rightarrow i$	$\#F + i * i\# \Rightarrow \#i + i * i\#$
2	# F ⋖ + ⋗ i ⋖ * ⋗ i ⋖ # ⋗	F	$V \rightarrow F$	$\#V + i * i\# \Rightarrow \#F + i * i\#$
3	# V ⋖ + ⋗ i ⋖ * ⋗ i ⋖ # ⋗	V	$T \rightarrow V$	$\#T + i * i\# \Rightarrow \#V + i * i\#$
4	# T ⋖ + ⋗ i ⋖ * ⋗ i ⋖ # ⋗	T	$U \rightarrow T$	$\#U + i * i\# \Rightarrow \#T + i * i\#$
5	# U ⋖ + ≐ i ⋖ * ⋗ i ⋖ # ⋗	i	$F \rightarrow i$	$\#U + F * i\# \Rightarrow \#U + i * i\#$
6	# U ⋖ + ≐ F ⋖ * ⋗ i ⋖ # ⋗	F	$V \rightarrow F$	$\#U + V * i\# \Rightarrow \#U + F * i\#$
7	# U ⋖ + ≐ V ⋖ * ≐ i ⋖ # ⋗	i	$F \rightarrow i$	$\#U + V * F\# \Rightarrow \#U + V * i\#$
8	# U ⋖ + ≐ V ⋖ * ≐ F ≐ # ⋗	$V * F$	$V \rightarrow V * F$	$\#U + V\# \Rightarrow \#U + V * F\#$
9	# U ⋖ + ≐ V ⋖ # ⋗	V	$T \rightarrow V$	$\#U + T\# \Rightarrow \#U + V\#$
10	# U ⋖ + ≐ T ≐ # ⋗	$U + T$	$U \rightarrow U + T$	$\#U\# \Rightarrow \#U + T\#$
11	# U ⋖ # ⋗	U	$E \rightarrow U$	$\#E\# \Rightarrow \#U\#$

substring $S_i \ldots S_j$ such that

$$S_{i-1} \lessdot S_i$$
$$S_i \doteq S_{i+1} \doteq S_{i+2} \doteq \cdots \doteq S_j$$
$$S_j \gtrdot S_{j+1}$$

To ensure that this approach will work even when the handle is the first or last symbol in the sentential form, we introduce a special symbol # such that

$$\# \lessdot x \text{ and } x \gtrdot \# \text{ for any } x \text{ in the vocabulary}$$

As an example, Table 7-14 gives a parse for the sentence $i + i * i$. Each step in the table gives the sentential form along with the relations that exist between the symbols according to Table 7-13.

7-3.2 Formal Definition of Precedence Relations

In the previous subsection the precedence relations were defined in terms of syntax trees. We now redefine these relations in terms of the productions of the grammar. It will be shown that these relations can be computed easily from the grammar.

We first define two relations associated with any grammar that will be important when defining precedence relations. For some particular grammar and nonterminal U, the set of head symbols of the strings that can be produced by U will be required. The set of such symbols, head(U) is defined as

$$\text{head}(U) = \left\{ X \mid U \overset{\pm}{\Rightarrow} X\beta \right\}$$

Since the mechanical evaluation of head(U) may be cumbersome, we redefine it in terms of another relation over a finite set in the following manner. Let L be a relation over the vocabulary such that

ULX iff there exists a production $U \rightarrow X\ldots$

The transitive closure (Sec. 2-1.2) of this relation can be obtained

UL^+X iff there exists some sequence of rules (at least one) such that
$U \rightarrow A_1\ldots, \; A_1 \rightarrow A_2\ldots, \; \ldots, \; A_n \rightarrow X\ldots$

It is clear that UL^+X iff $U \overset{\pm}{\Rightarrow} X\ldots$. The reflexive transitive closure L^* can be defined as

UL^*X iff UL^+X or $U = X$

In an analogous manner, the set of tail symbols tail(U) is defined by

$$\text{tail}(U) = \left\{ X \mid U \overset{\pm}{\Rightarrow} \beta X \right\}$$

Another relation R over the vocabulary is defined as

URX iff there exists a production $U \rightarrow \ldots X$

Again R^+ and R^* are defined in an obvious manner. These relations are easily computed using Warshall's algorithm. The two basic relations can now be used to define the precedence relations.

Definition 7-4 The precedence relations for a grammar G are defined over its vocabulary as follows:

1. $S_1 \doteq S_2$ iff there exists a production $U \rightarrow \ldots S_1 S_2 \ldots$ in G.
2. $S_1 \lessdot S_2$ iff there exists a production $U \rightarrow \ldots S_1 A \ldots$ in G such that $AL^+ S_2$ holds.
3. $S_1 \gtrdot S_2$ iff S_2 is a vocabulary symbol and there is production $U \rightarrow \ldots AB \ldots$ such that $AR^+ S_1$ and $BL^* S_2$ hold.

The relations L^+ and R^+ for the example grammar in the previous subsection are given in Table 7-15.

The relation $\doteq$ is easily obtained from the productions of the grammar. The relation $\lessdot$ can be evaluated by first considering the symbol pairs $+T$, $*F$, and $(E$. The pair $+T$ will yield the relations $+ \lessdot V$, $+ \lessdot F$, $+ \lessdot i$, and $+ \lessdot ($. The relations $* \lessdot i$ and $* \lessdot ($ are obtained from the term $*F$. Finally, the pair $(E$ gives the relations $(\lessdot U$, $(\lessdot V$, $(\lessdot F$, $(\lessdot T$, $(\lessdot i$, and $(\lessdot ($. The relation $\gtrdot$ is computed in a similar manner. Using this procedure, Table 7-13 can be easily verified.

Table 7-15

Nonterminal symbol	L^+	R^+
E	$U, T, V, F, i, ($	$U, T, V, F, i,)$
U	$U, T, V, F, i, ($	$T, V, F, i,)$
T	$V, F, i, ($	$V, F, i,)$
V	$V, F, i, ($	$F, i,)$
F	$i, ($	$i,)$

These precedence relations are actually equivalent to those defined in terms of handles in the previous subsection.

Theorem 7-2 $S_1 \doteq S_2$ iff the substring $S_1 S_2$ appears in a handle of some sentential form.

PROOF Let us first assume that $S_1 \doteq S_2$. A syntax tree which has the substring $S_1 S_2$ in its handle must be constructed. By Definition 7-4(1) there exists a production of the form $U \rightarrow \alpha S_1 S_2 \beta$. Since the grammar is assumed to be reduced, we have $S \overset{*}{\underset{R}{\Rightarrow}} \phi_1 U \phi_2$ for some ϕ_1 and ϕ_2, where S is the starting symbol of the grammar. The desired syntax tree can then be constructed as follows:

1. Construct the syntax tree for the sentential form $\phi_1 U \phi_2$.
2. Reduce the tree obtained in step 1 until U becomes part of the handle.
3. Modify the tree obtained in step 2 by extending the tree downward with the application of the production $U \rightarrow \alpha S_1 S_2 \beta$. Since U was in the handle of the previous tree, the handle of the presently constructed tree is $\alpha S_1 S_2 \beta$ and we therefore have the required tree. Conversely, if $S_1 S_2$ is a substring of the handle, then by definition of a handle there must exist a production $U \rightarrow \alpha S_1 S_2 \beta$ and $S_1 \doteq S_2$.

The proofs for the relations $\lessdot$ and $\gtrdot$ are left as exercises.

The formal definitions of the three precedence relations given here are equivalent to those given informally in terms of syntax trees in Sec. 7-3.1. Some insight into these definitions can be obtained by looking at their interpretation from a syntax-tree point of view. A simple precedence grammar is defined as follows:

Definition 7-5 A grammar G is called a *simple precedence grammar* if the following conditions are satisfied:

1. For any pair of symbols in the vocabulary, at most one of the relations $\doteq$, $\lessdot$, and $\gtrdot$ must hold.
2. No two productions can have the same right-hand side.
3. Empty rules are not allowed.

This class of grammars is called simple because only one symbol on each side of a possible handle is used to determine the presence of the handle. In other words, the handle is determined by scanning the sentential form from left to right examining successive pairs of adjacent symbols until $S_1 \gtrdot S_2$; in this case S_1 is the tail of the handle and S_2 is the right context symbol used to find it. Similarly, the head of the handle is found by scanning from right to left until $S_1 \lessdot S_2$, where S_2 is now the head of the handle and S_1 is the left context symbol. So the first condition of the definition tells us how to find the handle while the second condition tells us which production to use.

> **Theorem 7-3** A simple precedence grammar is unambiguous. Furthermore, each sentential form $S_1 S_2 \ldots S_n$ has a unique handle which is the leftmost substring $S_i \ldots S_j$ that satisfies
>
> $$S_{i-1} \lessdot S_i \doteq S_{i+1} \doteq \cdots \doteq S_j \gtrdot S_{j+1}$$

Note that we are assuming the presence of a special symbol $\#$ such that $\# \lessdot x$ and $x \gtrdot \#$ for any symbol in the original vocabulary. This modification will also permit the detection of a handle when it contains the leftmost and/or rightmost symbol in the sentential form.

Once the precedence relations for a simple precedence grammar have been determined, the parsing of a sentence is straightforward. This is one of the simplest classes of grammars that can be used in a practical manner in compiler writing. The relations $\lessdot$ and $\gtrdot$ are easily computed from the basic relations L, R, and $\doteq$. From the definition of the product of relations and the definition for $\lessdot$, we can easily obtain

$$\lessdot = (\doteq) \circ (L^+)$$

where $\circ$ denotes the product operator. Similarly, the relation $\gtrdot$ can be expressed as

$$\gtrdot = (R^+)^T \circ (\doteq) \circ (L^*)$$

where $(R^+)^T$ is the transpose of R^+. These relations can obviously be expressed as bit (Boolean) matrices; the logical capabilities of modern computers make their evaluation easy. Observe that the precedence matrix in the previous discussion has included columns which correspond to the nonterminal symbols of the grammar. The inclusion of these columns facilitates reasonable error recovery. We next turn to the formulation of a parsing algorithm for simple precedence grammars.

7-3.3 Parsing Algorithm for Simple Precedence Grammars

We wish to formulate a general parsing algorithm for any simple precedence grammar. The precedence matrix and the productions of the grammar are represented in some suitable form.

Basically the algorithm works in the following manner. The symbols of the given input string are scanned from left to right and placed on a stack S. This scanning continues until the relation between the symbol at the top of the stack and the next input symbol is $\gtrdot$. At this point the top element of the stack denotes the tail of the handle. The head of the handle is determined by comparing successive pairs of adjacent symbols in the stack until a pair is encountered that is $\lessdot$ related. This handle can then be reduced (i.e., removed from the stack) to the left part of a production (which is placed on the stack) whose right part is that handle. The entire process is repeated until the stack contains the starting symbol for the grammar and the next input symbol is the special symbol #.

Algorithm SP_PARSE. This is the general parsing algorithm for any simple precedence grammar. By using the precedence matrix and the productions for a particular grammar, this algorithm determines whether or not a given input sentence $x_1 x_2 \ldots x_n$ is valid. The algorithm uses parse stack S, whose top entry is indicated by TOP. The current input symbol is stored in INPUT. The local variable i is used to find the head of the handle on the stack, and k gives the position of the current input symbol in the input sentence.

1. [Initialize for parsing]
   TOP ← k ← 1
   S[TOP] ← '#'
   INPUT ← x_k
2. [Determine parse action]
   Repeat while true
       If not S[TOP] $\gtrdot$ INPUT
       then (Push input onto stack)
               TOP ← TOP + 1
               S[TOP] ← INPUT
               k ← k + 1
               INPUT ← x_k
       else (Perform reduction since tail of handle has been found)
               If TOP = 2 and S[TOP] is the start symbol and INPUT = '#'
               then Write('VALID')
                   Exit
               (Find head of handle)
               Repeat while S[i − 1] $\doteq$ S[i]
                   i ← i − 1
               Find a production p whose right-hand side matches
               the stack symbols S[i], S[i + 1], ... , S[TOP]
               If no such production can be found
               then Write('INVALID')
                   Exit
               TOP ← i
               S[TOP] ← the left-hand side of production p   □

Table 7-16

Step	Input string	Stack contents	Relation	Input	Handle
0	$i * i + i\#$	$\#$			
1	$* i + i\#$	$\#$	$\lessdot$	i	
2	$i + i\#$	$\# i$	$\gtrdot$	$*$	$\dot{i}$
3	$i + i\#$	$\# F$	$\gtrdot$	$*$	$\dot{F}$
4	$+ i\#$	$\# V *$	$\lessdot$	i	
5	$i\#$	$\# V * i$	$\gtrdot$	$+$	
6	$i\#$	$\# V * F$	$\gtrdot$	$+$	$V * F$
7	$i\#$	$\# V$	$\gtrdot$	$+$	V
8	$i\#$	$\# T$	$\gtrdot$	$+$	T
9	$\#$	$\# U +$	$\lessdot$	i	
10		$\# U + i$	$\gtrdot$	$\#$	$\dot{i}$
11		$\# U + F$	$\gtrdot$	$\#$	$\dot{F}$
12		$\# U + V$	$\gtrdot$	$\#$	$\dot{V}$
13		$\# U + T$	$>$	$\#$	$U + T$
14		$\# U$	$>$	$\#$	U
15		$\# E$		$\#$	

A trace of this algorithm for the example grammar using the sentence $i * i + i$ and Table 7-13 is given in Table 7-16.

7-3.4 Precedence Functions for Simple Precedence Grammars

The notion of precedence functions was introduced in Sec. 7-2.4. As indicated there, memory restrictions may require a reduction in the amount of space utilized by a precedence matrix, making it necessary to use precedence functions in order to reduce the storage requirements of a compiler. In this subsection, a procedure for generating precedence functions from a precedence matrix is described. A modified version of this procedure is also presented. These methods can easily be extended to operator precedence grammars as well.

If the number of vocabulary symbols $(V_T \cup V_N)$ in a language is n, then the precedence matrix requires n^2 elements. However, the information stored in the matrix can sometimes be *linearized*; that is, two precedence functions can represent the information which is stored in a precedence matrix. For any two symbols A and B of a simple precedence grammar, the precedence functions f and g are defined as

$$\begin{aligned} A \gtrdot B \quad &\text{implies} \quad f(A) > g(B) \\ A \doteq B \quad &\text{implies} \quad f(A) = g(B) \\ A \lessdot B \quad &\text{implies} \quad f(A) < g(B) \end{aligned}$$

Since each function can be stored as a vector of n elements, storage requirements can be reduced from n^2 to $2n$ elements.

Precedence matrices do not always have precedence functions associated with them. For example, the precedence matrix given in Table 7-17 does not have any

Table 7-17 Precedence matrix having no associated precedence functions

$$
\begin{array}{c c}
 & \begin{array}{cc} A & B \end{array} \\
\begin{array}{c} A \\ B \end{array} &
\begin{bmatrix} \doteq & \doteq \\ \lessdot & \doteq \end{bmatrix}
\end{array}
$$

associated precedence functions. Notice, for example, the following relations may be derived from the matrix:

$$ f(B) < g(A),\ g(A) = f(A),\ f(A) = g(B),\ \text{and}\ g(B) = f(B) $$

This results in the contradiction $f(B) < f(B)$. Furthermore, the precedence functions, if they exist, are not necessarily unique. Two pairs of precedence functions for the precedence matrix given in Table 7-18 are

	A	B	C
f	1	6	1
g	6	3	6

	A	B	C
f	1	3	1
g	3	2	3

A theorem given by Bell (1969) describes a simple method for generating a pair of precedence functions from a precedence matrix. The procedure involves representing the precedence matrix as a graph with the vertices representing the elements $f(A_1), f(A_2), \ldots, f(A_n), g(A_1), g(A_2), \ldots, g(A_n)$. The number of nodes reachable from a node representing one of the elements is the value of that element.

In the following theorem, the notation $A \geq B$ is equivalent to $A \doteq B$ or $A \gtrdot B$ and $A \leq B$ is defined to be $A \doteq B$ or $A \lessdot B$.

Theorem 7-4 For a simple precedence grammar with the vocabulary symbols $A_1, A_2, \ldots, A_n$, define a directed graph with $2n$ nodes representing the values of the precedence functions for $f(A_1), f(A_2), \ldots, f(A_n), g(A_1), g(A_2), \ldots, g(A_n)$. Define an edge from $f(A_i)$ to $g(A_j)$ if $A_i \leq A_j$. Similarly, define an edge from $g(A_j)$ to $f(A_i)$ if $A_i \geq A_j$. Assign a number to each node equal to the number of nodes that are reachable from that node (including

Table 7-18 Precedence matrix

$$
\begin{array}{c c}
 & \begin{array}{ccc} A & B & C \end{array} \\
\begin{array}{c} A \\ B \\ C \end{array} &
\begin{bmatrix} & \lessdot & \lessdot \\ \doteq & \gtrdot & \doteq \\ \lessdot & \lessdot & \end{bmatrix}
\end{array}
$$

the node itself). The numbers assigned to $f(A_i)$ and $g(A_i)$ are the numbers assigned to their corresponding nodes. Check that the functions are valid precedence functions by comparing them with the precedence matrix. If they are not valid, no precedence functions exist for this matrix.

PROOF It must be shown that $A_i \doteq A_j$ implies $f(A_i) = g(A_j)$, $A_i \gtrdot A_j$ implies $f(A_i) > g(A_j)$, and $A_i \lessdot A_j$ implies $f(A_i) < g(A_j)$. For the condition of equality, there is an arc from A_i to A_j and from A_j to A_i. Hence any node reachable from one is also reachable from the other.

As the other two conditions are symmetric, only the condition $A_i \lessdot A_j$ implies $f(A_i) < g(A_j)$ will be proven. There is an arc from $g(A_j)$ to $f(A_i)$ because $A_i \lessdot A_j$; so any node accessible from A_i is accessible from A_j; hence $g(A_j) \geq f(A_i)$. It must be shown that strict inequality holds.

Assume that $A_i \lessdot A_j$ but $f(A_i) = g(A_j)$. The nodes $f(A_i)$ and $g(A_j)$ are accessible from one another and there must be the path

$$g_j \to f_i \to g_l \to f_k \to \cdots \to f_m \to g_j$$

This results in the relations

$$A_i \lesseqgtr A_j, A_i \gtreqless A_l, \ldots, A_m \gtreqless A_j$$

which implies that

$$g(A_j) \geq f(A_i) \geq g(A_l) \geq f(A_k) \geq \cdots \geq f(A_m) \geq g(A_j)$$

Unless every relation in this chain is an equality, we have $g(A_j) > g(A_j)$, a contradiction. Thus we have $f(A_i) = g(A_j)$, but since $A_i \lessdot A_j$, the definition of precedence functions has been contradicted. Either no valid precedence functions exist or the original assumption $f(A_i) = g(A_j)$ is false, implying that if precedence functions do exist, then $f(A_i) < g(A_j)$.

In order to illustrate how this theorem is applied, we derive the precedence functions for the grammar $G = (\{A, B\}, \{a, b\}, A, \Phi)$, where Φ is defined as

0. $A \to Ba$
1. $B \to b$
2. $B \to BA$

The precedence matrix for this grammar is given in Table 7-19. Applying the procedure outlined in the previous theorem results in the directed graph given in Fig. 7-6. Summing the number of nodes accessible from each node gives the following precedence-function values:

	A	B	a	b
f	6	3	6	6
g	3	4	3	4

Table 7-19 Precedence matrix for example grammar

	A	B	a	b
A	⋗	⋗	⋗	⋗
B	≐	⋖	≐	⋖
a	⋗	⋗	⋗	⋗
b	⋗	⋗	⋗	⋗

Comparing the precedence matrix with the precedence functions establishes the validity of these functions.

The procedure for constructing precedence functions can easily be implemented on a computer by using an adjacency matrix. An element $A[i, j]$ of an adjacency matrix A is true if a path of length 1 exists from node i to node j; otherwise it is false.

The graph defined in the theorem can be represented by a $2n \times 2n$ adjacency matrix B where its rows and columns, numbered $1, 2 \ldots, 2n$, represent the nodes of the graph $f(A_1), f(A_2), \ldots, f(A_n), g(A_1), g(A_2), \ldots, g(A_n)$. The form of the matrix is given in Table 7-20, where I is the identity matrix, $\geq$ is an $n \times n$ matrix where $\geq [i, j]$ is true if $A_i \geq A_j$, and $\leq^T$ is the transpose of the matrix which has element $\leq [i, j]$ true if $A_i \leq A_j$. The transitive closure of B, B^+ is

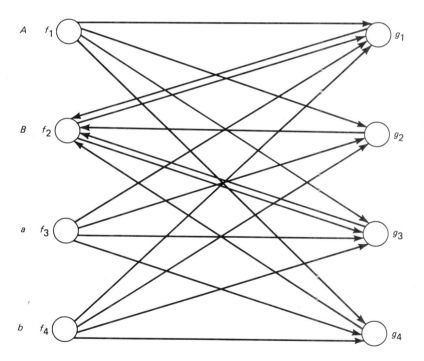

Figure 7-6 Directed graph for precedence matrix of Table 7-21.

Table 7-20 Format of B matrix

$$\begin{bmatrix} I & \geq \\ \leq^T & I \end{bmatrix}$$

derived by using Warshall's algorithm. The result is a path matrix where element $B^+[i, j]$ is true if node j is reachable from node i by some path. The values of the elements $f(A_1)$, $f(A_2)$, and so on, are determined by summing the 1 bits on the rows, with each row representing one of the elements. The number of 1 bits on a row dictates the number of nodes of the graph which are reachable from that node.

Procedure PRECEDENCE_FUNCTION(A, N, F, G). Given the square precedence matrix P of size N, where the value of 0 for element P[i, j] indicates no relation exists between symbols A_i and A_j, 1 indicates that $A_i \lessdot A_j$, 2 indicates that $A_i \doteq A_j$, and 3 indicates that $A_i \gtrdot A_j$, this procedure computes the precedence functions F and G associated with this matrix, and determines the validity of these functions. The adjacency matrix is stored in B while I, J, and K are loop variables.

1. [Initialize the adjacency matrix]
   B ← 0
   Repeat for I = 1, 2,...,N
      B[I, I] ← 1
      Repeat for J = 1, 2,...,N
         If P[I, J] = 2 or P[I, J] = 3
         then B[I, J + N] ← 1
         If P[I, J] = 1 or P[I, J] = 2
         then B[J + N, I] ← 1
   Repeat for I = N + 1, N + 2,...,2*N
      B[I, I] ← 1
2. [Compute the transitive closure of B using Warshall's algorithm]
   Repeat for I = 1, 2,...,2*N
      Repeat for J = 1, 2,...,2*N
         Repeat for K = 1, 2,...,2*N
            B[J, K] ← B[J, K] or (B[J, I] and B[I, K])
3. [Determine the precedence functions]
   F ← G ← 0
   Repeat for I = 1, 2,...,2*N
      Repeat for J = 1, 2,...,2*N
         If B[I, J] and I ≤ N
         then F[I] ← F[I] + 1
         else If B[I, J]
            then G[I − N] ← G[I − N] + 1

Table 7-21 Matrix *B*

$$\begin{bmatrix}
1 & 0 & 0 & 0 & 1 & 1 & 1 & 1 \\
0 & 1 & 0 & 0 & 1 & 0 & 1 & 0 \\
0 & 0 & 1 & 0 & 1 & 1 & 1 & 1 \\
0 & 0 & 0 & 1 & 1 & 1 & 1 & 1 \\
0 & 1 & 0 & 0 & 1 & 0 & 0 & 0 \\
0 & 1 & 0 & 0 & 0 & 1 & 0 & 0 \\
0 & 1 & 0 & 0 & 0 & 0 & 1 & 0 \\
0 & 1 & 0 & 0 & 0 & 0 & 0 & 1
\end{bmatrix}$$

4. [Check for the validity of the precedence functions]
  Repeat for I = 1, 2,...,N
   Repeat for J = 1, 2,...,N
    If (P[I, J] = 1 and F[I] $\geq$ G[J]) or (P[I, J] = 2 and F[I] $\neq$ G[J])
      or (P[I, J] = 3 and F[I] $\leq$ G[J])
    then Write('PRECEDENCE FUNCTIONS ARE NOT VALID')
    Return
  Write('PRECEDENCE FUNCTIONS ARE VALID')
  Return   □

By checking the precedence matrix relations against those between the precedence functions, the algorithm determines the validity of the precedence functions.

  As an example of how the algorithm generates precedence functions from a precedence matrix, we shall use the simple precedence grammar given in the previous example. The precedence matrix for this grammar is given in Table 7-19. Using this matrix as input to the algorithm, the *B* and *B*⁺ matrices which result are given in Tables 7-21 and 7-22, respectively. The precedence functions produced by this algorithm are:

	A	B	a	b
f	6	3	6	6
g	3	4	3	4

These functions are valid.

Table 7-22 Matrix *B* ⁺

$$\begin{bmatrix}
1 & 1 & 0 & 0 & 1 & 1 & 1 & 1 \\
0 & 1 & 0 & 0 & 1 & 0 & 1 & 0 \\
0 & 1 & 1 & 0 & 1 & 1 & 1 & 1 \\
0 & 1 & 0 & 1 & 1 & 1 & 1 & 1 \\
0 & 1 & 0 & 0 & 1 & 0 & 1 & 0 \\
0 & 1 & 0 & 0 & 1 & 1 & 1 & 0 \\
0 & 1 & 0 & 0 & 1 & 0 & 1 & 0 \\
0 & 1 & 0 & 0 & 1 & 0 & 1 & 1
\end{bmatrix}$$

In order to determine whether the precedence functions exist, the precedence functions produced by the algorithm are compared against the precedence matrix. Recall from the example of a precedence matrix which does not have any associated precedence functions that the contradiction $f(B) < f(B)$ was derived. This can occur for a precedence matrix when a cycle exists in the directed graph representing the matrix with at least one of the arcs in the cycle representing either the relation $\gg$ or the relation $\lessdot$. In the example given earlier, the cycle

$$f(B) \rightarrow g(B) \rightarrow f(A) \rightarrow g(A) \rightarrow f(B)$$

exists with the arc $g(A) \rightarrow f(B)$ representing the relation $B \lessdot A$. Martin (1972) presents a modified version of Bell's original algorithm where the existence of the precedence functions is possible only if the directed graph produced has no cycles.

Martin's algorithm proceeds as follows: A directed graph is defined having vertices $f(A_1), f(A_2), \ldots, f(A_n), g(A_1), g(A_2), \ldots, g(A_n)$ and having arcs from $f(A_i)$ to $g(A_j)$ if $A_i \gg A_j$ and from $g(A_j)$ to $f(A_i)$ if $A_i \lessdot A_j$. This can be represented in a computer by the Boolean matrix

$$B_0 = \begin{bmatrix} 0 & \gg \\ \lessdot^T & 0 \end{bmatrix}$$

where the matrix $\gg$ is 1 at $\gg[i, j]$ if $A_i \gg A_j$ and $\lessdot^T[j, i]$ is 1 if $A_i \lessdot A_j$.

The relation $\doteq$ is introduced by defining the matrix

$$C = \begin{bmatrix} I & \doteq \\ \doteq^T & I \end{bmatrix}$$

here the matrix $\doteq[i, j]$ is 1 if $A_i \doteq A_j$ and 0 otherwise. The transitive closure of C, C^+ links all vertices of the directed graph together which are joined by the $\doteq$ relation. Then using Boolean multiplication, the matrix B is defined as $B = C^*B_0$. This matrix indicates all those vertices which are immediately reachable from a given vertex, that is, those nodes which can be reached by traversing one arc only. The identity matrices are included as part of the C matrix to ensure that all those vertices of the original directed graph, which are represented by B_0 and are not immediate successors to other vertices, are not deleted. The transitive closure of B, B^+ dictates all vertices which are reachable from a given vertex. The precedence function's values may then be computed by summing the rows in the same fashion as was done with Bell's method.

Bell's (1969) precedence-function algorithm included the $\doteq$ chains in his B matrix and therefore directly included cycles in the matrix, with the simplest cycles being those on the diagonal. Martin's (1972) algorithm, on the other hand, implicitly includes the $\doteq$ chains with the C^* matrix, having the result that the only cycles being introduced are the ones which prevent the existence of precedence functions. The detection of these cycles, if they exist, can then be done by checking the transitive closure matrix (B^+) for 1's on the principal diagonal; if at least one such bit is found, precedence functions do not exist for the given precedence matrix.

Transcribing the procedure just outlined as an algorithm is left as an exercise. Applying this procedure to the precedence matrix given in Table 7-19 results in the B_0, C, and B^+ matrices of Table 7-23. As no 1's appear on the principal diagonal of B^+, precedence functions exist and are given by

	A	B	a	b
f	5	0	5	5
g	0	1	0	1

Information is lost when precedence matrices are linearized into precedence functions because the information on whether a relation holds between two symbols is lost. If a relation does hold, we can discern what the relation is, but because precedence functions have a value for all elements, it is impossible to tell whether there actually is a relation between two symbols. A syntax error will eventually be detected, however, but this will occur when a reduction of the sentential form stored on the stack is attempted but cannot be done. For example,

Table 7-23

(a) Matrix B_0

$$
\begin{bmatrix}
0 & 0 & 0 & 0 & 1 & 1 & 1 & 1 \\
0 & 0 & 0 & 0 & 0 & 0 & 0 & 0 \\
0 & 0 & 0 & 0 & 1 & 1 & 1 & 1 \\
0 & 0 & 0 & 0 & 1 & 1 & 1 & 1 \\
0 & 0 & 0 & 0 & 0 & 0 & 0 & 0 \\
0 & 1 & 0 & 0 & 0 & 0 & 0 & 0 \\
0 & 0 & 0 & 0 & 0 & 0 & 0 & 0 \\
0 & 1 & 0 & 0 & 0 & 0 & 0 & 0
\end{bmatrix}
$$

(b) Matrix C

$$
\begin{bmatrix}
1 & 0 & 0 & 0 & 0 & 0 & 0 & 0 \\
0 & 1 & 0 & 0 & 1 & 0 & 1 & 0 \\
0 & 0 & 1 & 0 & 0 & 0 & 0 & 0 \\
0 & 0 & 0 & 1 & 0 & 0 & 0 & 0 \\
0 & 1 & 0 & 0 & 1 & 0 & 0 & 0 \\
0 & 0 & 0 & 0 & 0 & 1 & 0 & 0 \\
0 & 1 & 0 & 0 & 0 & 0 & 1 & 0 \\
0 & 0 & 0 & 0 & 0 & 0 & 0 & 1
\end{bmatrix}
$$

(c) Matrix B^+

$$
\begin{bmatrix}
0 & 1 & 0 & 0 & 1 & 1 & 1 & 1 \\
0 & 0 & 0 & 0 & 0 & 0 & 0 & 0 \\
0 & 1 & 0 & 0 & 1 & 1 & 1 & 1 \\
0 & 1 & 0 & 0 & 1 & 1 & 1 & 1 \\
0 & 0 & 0 & 0 & 0 & 0 & 0 & 0 \\
0 & 1 & 0 & 0 & 0 & 0 & 0 & 0 \\
0 & 0 & 0 & 0 & 0 & 0 & 0 & 0 \\
0 & 1 & 0 & 0 & 0 & 0 & 0 & 0
\end{bmatrix}
$$

precedence-function values for the precedence matrix of Table 7-13 are

	E	U	T	F	V	+	*	i	(	)
f	2	4	5	7	6	4	6	7	2	7
g	2	3	4	6	5	4	6	7	7	2

The corresponding grammar is given in Sec. 7-3.1. Table 7-24 illustrates the reduction of the invalid string $i + + i$ using the precedence matrix and the precedence functions. As can be seen the error is detected first using the precedence matrix as two symbols occur which have no relation. A further discussion of error detection and recovery is given in the next subsection.

The method presented in this section also may be applied to operator precedence grammars. The algorithms used are basically the same, with the operation ⊙ replacing ⋖, ⊜ replacing ≐, and ⊙ replacing ⋗. The difference lies in the fact that the precedence relations of a simple precedence grammar can be defined between two nonterminal symbols or between a nonterminal symbol and a terminal symbol, while such relations do not exist for operator precedence grammars. Therefore, only the functional values of the terminal symbols need to be computed, and this can be done in the same fashion as with simple precedence grammars. Therefore no further discussion needs to be given on this topic.

Table 7-24

(a) Parse of $i + + i$ using precedence matrix				(b) Parse of $i + + i$ using precedence functions				
Step	Input string	Relation	Stack contents	Handle	Step	Input string	Relation	Stack contents	Handle
0	$i + + i\#$	⋖	$\#$		0	$i + + i\#$	<	$\#$	
1	$+ + i\#$	⋗	$\#i$	i	1	$+ + i\#$	>	$\#i$	i
2	$+ + i\#$	⋗	$\#F$	F	2	$+ + i\#$	>	$\#F$	F
3	$+ + i\#$	⋗	$\#V$	V	3	$+ + i\#$	>	$\#V$	V
4	$+ + i\#$	⋗	$\#T$	T	4	$+ + i\#$	>	$\#T$	T
5	$+ + i\#$	≐	$\#U$		5	$- + i\#$	=	$\#U$	
6	$+ i\#$	None	$\#U +$		6	$+ i\#$	=	$\#U +$	
					7	$i\#$	<	$\#U + +$	
					8	$\#$	>	$\#U + + i$	i
					9	$\#$	>	$\#U + + F$	F
					10	$\#$	>	$\#U + + V$	V
					11	$\#$	>	$\#U + + T$	None

7-3.5 Error Recovery for Simple Precedence Parsers

The simple precedence parser described in the preceding sections performs a correct parse of any input string which is in the language generated by a particular simple precedence grammar. Furthermore, it refuses to accept any string which is not in the language. Given such a string, the parser stops at the first syntax error and reports that the string is invalid As mentioned in Sec. 5-1, this behavior is unacceptable for a practical compiler. In a compiler, parsing must continue after a syntax error, in order to detect more syntax errors.

The simple precedence parsers described so far can detect errors in two ways. The choice of a parse action is based on the precedence relation between the symbol at the top of the parse stack and the input symbol. This precedence relation may be $\lessdot$, $\doteq$, $\gtrdot$, or ? (error). The ? relation indicates that this pair of symbols (the stack top and input symbols) cannot appear adjacent to one another. Thus, whenever the relation between the stack top and input symbols is ?, a syntax error is detected (a so-called *character-pair error*). Whenever the relation between the stack top and input symbols is $\gtrdot$, a reduction action is indicated and the parser must match the right-hand side of some production in the grammar to the string of stack symbols being reduced. If no matching right-hand side can be found, then a *reduction error* is reported.

In this section we develop a simple precedence parser which has improved error-detection capabilities. However, because the simple precedence parser does not have the valid prefix property discussed in Sec 5-2.3, a syntax error may sometimes go undetected until arbitrarily many symbols have been read beyond the first erroneous symbol. After developing the improved simple precedence parser, we discuss an algorithm which can recover from a syntax error and restart the parser so that the parser can detect further errors. This recovery algorithm was developed by Rhodes (1973) and Graham and Rhodes (1975) (see Sec. 5-4.2). Other simple precedence error-recovery schemes are presented by Wirth (1968) and Leinius (1970). However, the Graham-Rhodes method seems to be superior to these other simple precedence recovery methods.

The improved simple precedence parser uses the character-pair error check and the reduction error check just described. It also contains two additional means of error detection, a *valid prefix* check and a *left stackability* check. The valid prefix check (Rhodes, 1973) consists of checking that the partial handle on top of the parse stack is a prefix of the right-hand side of some production in the grammar. This check is performed whenever a symbol is put onto the stack by a reduction or a shift. The partial handle tested is the string of stack symbols extending from the $\lessdot$ relation nearest the stack top up to the symbol on top of the stack.

The reader might assume that this additional check would take a large amount of time, since the table of production right-hand sides must be searched as each symbol is pushed onto the stack. In fact, the valid prefix check can be combined with the reduction error check and both types of error check can be performed with approximately the same amount of searching as is done by the unmodified simple precedence parser of preceding sections. To do this, the production table is sorted lexically by right-hand sides, and pointers into this table indicate which right-hand sides have prefixes which match the symbols of the partial handle already on the stack. Before a new symbol is stacked, these right-hand sides can be checked to see whether any of them allow the new symbol following the symbols already seen. Notice that each time a $\lessdot$ relation occurs, a new partial handle is begun on the stack. Therefore, a secondary stack must be used to save the pointers into the right-hand side table for the previous partial handle. This treatment of the valid prefix and reduction error checks has not been incorporated into Algorithm **SP_PARSE** (which occurs later in this section) in order to preserve clarity as much as possible. But it should be clear that the method consists of performing an incremental search for matching right-hand sides, rather than searching for a right-hand side whenever a reduction is indicated. The total amount of searching performed is only slightly more than in the unmodified parser.

The left stackability check was originally introduced by Leinius (1970). When the handle is reduced, it is replaced on the stack by the left-hand side of a production whose right-hand side matches the handle. If there is a production $U \rightarrow \beta$ and the stack contains $\alpha A \beta$ before the reduction, then after the reduction the stack will contain $\alpha A U$. Clearly, if further parsing is to be possible, one of $A \lessdot U$, $A \doteq U$, or $A \gtrdot U$ must be true. If $A?U$, a syntax error will eventually be detected. This error can be detected earlier by explicitly checking for the error condition $A?U$ immediately after each reduction.

Another improvement suggested by Leinius has nothing to do with error detection but does significantly speed up the parser. When the tail of the handle is found in the original simple precedence parser, the parser must search down through the stack for a symbol S_i such that $S_{i-1} \lessdot S_i$. The symbol S_i is the head of the handle. Leinius points out that a pointer to such a symbol S_i can be placed on an auxiliary *head stack* when the symbol is shifted onto the parse stack. Then when the tail of the handle is found and a reduction is necessary, the location of the head of the handle is in the top element of the head stack.

In order to neatly join the simple precedence parser and the Graham-Rhodes error-recovery algorithm, we make the parser into a subalgorithm (procedure) **SP_PARSE** which is called by a supervisory algorithm **SP_SUPERVISOR**. Procedure **SP_PARSE** incorporates the modifications which we have been discussing and sets an accept flag to *true* if the input string is parsed without errors. Algorithm **SP_SUPERVISOR** does the necessary initializations for Procedure **SP_PARSE** and calls the recovery procedure **SP_RECOVER** when necessary.

Algorithm SP_SUPERVISOR. This is the supervisory algorithm for the simple precedence parser and recovery system. It contains and initializes the global data structures used throughout the system. These data structures are: S, the parse stack, whose top entry is indicated by **TOP**; H, the head stack, whose top entry is indicated by **HEAD**, the input string $x_1 x_2 ... x_n \#$, with index k and current input symbol INPUT, and a logical variable, ACCEPT. Algorithm SP_SUPERVISOR calls Procedures SP_PARSE and SP_RECOVER.

1. [Initialize for parser]
    ACCEPT ← false
    S[1] ← '#'
    TOP ← k ← 1
    HEAD ← 0
    INPUT ← x_1
2. [Parse-recover cycle]
    Repeat while true
        Call SP_PARSE
        If ACCEPT
        then Write('PROGRAM ACCEPTED')
            Exit
        else Call SP_RECOVER   □

Procedure SP_PARSE. This is a modified and improved simple precedence parser. It is called by Algorithm SP_SUPERVISOR and uses the global data structures defined in that algorithm. A local variable i is also used. Procedure SP_PARSE calls Procedure SP_ERROR to print syntax error messages. Note that the two special symbols '#' and '@' have the following relations with respect to the other vocabulary symbols:

For any $x \in V_N \cup V_T$,
$\# \lessdot x$ and $x \gtrdot \#$
$@ \lessdot x$ and $x \gtrdot @$
As well, $\{\#, @\} \cap \{V_N \cup V_T\} = \phi$.

1. [Determine parse action]
    Repeat through step 5 while true
2. [Character-pair error?]
    If S[TOP] ? INPUT
    then Call SP_ERROR(TOP)
        Return
3. [Shift and save head position]
    If S[TOP] ⋖ INPUT
    then TOP ← TOP + 1
        S[TOP] ← INPUT
        k ← k + 1
        INPUT ← x_k
        HEAD ← HEAD + 1
        H[HEAD] ← TOP

4. [Shift?]
    If S[TOP] $\doteq$ INPUT
    then i ← H[HEAD]
        If the symbols S[i], S[i + 1],...,S[TOP], INPUT
            do not form a prefix of some right-hand
            side of the grammar
        then if the current calling procedure is not SP_RECOVER
            then Call SP_ERROR(i)
        Return
        TOP ← TOP + 1
        S[TOP] ← INPUT
        k ← k + 1
        INPUT ← x_k

5. [Reduction?]
    If S[TOP] $\gg$ INPUT
    then If (TOP = 2) and (S[TOP] is the start symbol)
        and (INPUT = '#')
        then ACCEPT ← true
            Return
        i ← H[HEAD]
        Find a production p whose right-hand side matches
        the stack symbols S[i], S[i + 1],...,S[TOP]
        If no such production can be found
        then If the current calling procedure is not SP_RECOVER
            then Call SP_ERROR(i)
            Return
        (Perform semantic processing for production p)
        TOP ← i
        S[TOP] ← the left-hand side of p
        If (S[TOP − 1] $\gg$ S[TOP]) or (S[TOP − 1] $\doteq$ S[TOP])
        then HEAD ← HEAD − 1
            i ← H[HEAD]
        If (S[TOP − 1] ? S[TOP]) or (S[i], S[i + 1],...,S[TOP] do not
            form a prefix of some right-hand side and S[TOP] is
            not the start symbol)
        then INPUT ← S[TOP]
            k ← k − 1
            TOP ← TOP − 1
            If the current calling procedure is not SP_RECOVER
            then Call SP_ERROR(TOP)
            Return   □

Procedure SP_ERROR(i). This procedure prints a syntax error message for Procedure SP_PARSE. In an actual compiler the error messages generated here should be accompanied by information pinpointing the exact location of the syntax error in the source program. SP_ERROR has one local variable m, and one parameter i, which is the position in the stack of the first unparsible part of the phrase.

1. [Print the partial phrase on top of the stack]
       Repeat for m = i, i + 1,...,TOP − 1
           Write(S[m])
2. [Print the rest of the message]
       Write(S[TOP], 'CANNOT BE FOLLOWED BY', INPUT)
       Return   □

We now present the Graham-Rhodes recovery scheme in the form of Procedure SP_RECOVER, which is called by Algorithm SP_SUPERVISOR. Procedure SP_RECOVER has the task of modifying the parse stack and input stream so that a detected syntax error may be safely bypassed and parsing may continue. When Procedure SP_RECOVER is called, the point at which the syntax error was detected is between the top symbol on the stack and the input symbol in INPUT. We will call this error position $?_1$. The Graham-Rhodes algorithm recovers well from syntax errors because it does not immediately attempt to fix up the stack and input based on a small fixed number of context symbols around $?_1$. Since an error can be detected by the parser an arbitrary number of symbols after the actual programmer error, no fixed amount of context is ever enough for all error cases. In order to get the effect of an unbounded amount of context in the error recovery, Graham and Rhodes have introduced a *condensation phase*, which precedes the *correction phase* of the error recovery.

The condensation phase performs reductions on the stack (the *backward move*) and parses forward in the input (the *forward move*) in order to condense contextual information about the error into as few symbols as possible. The condensation phase consists of two backward moves and a forward move.

The first backward move assumes that the $?_1$ represents a ⋗ relation between the stack top symbol and the input symbol in INPUT. Thus the stack top symbol is the tail of a phrase, and a reduction may be performed if the following three conditions are met:

1. The string of stack symbols to be reduced matches the right-hand side of some production in the grammar.
2. When the symbols at the top of the stack are replaced by the left-hand side of the production, there must be a valid precedence relation (not ?) between the new top symbol of the stack (the left-hand side of the production) and the symbol below it on the stack.
3. After the reduction, the symbols on top of the stack must still form a valid prefix of the right-hand side of some production of the grammar.

After the first backward move has condensed the information on the top of the parse stack, the forward move attempts to gather contextual information by parsing forward in the input. This is done by pushing the special marker '@' onto the stack, pushing the input symbol INPUT onto the stack, and restarting the parser SP_PARSE. The parser will eventually detect another syntax error and return. We call the point of this second error $?_2$.

After the parser returns from its forward move, the second backward move is performed on top of the stack in the same way as the first backward move. The second backward move attempts to condense the information gathered by the forward move.

Once the condensation phase has compressed the contextual information about the syntax error into as few symbols as possible, the correction phase has the task of changing the string of symbols around the error into a phrase that appears to be correct. Rhodes (1973) presents several options which change the complexity and performance of the correction phase. The correction phase described here embodies options which provide simplicity and efficiency without sacrificing good recovery.

The correction phase consists of two parts. The first part computes three *recovery sets*, one set for each of three *correction candidates*. The three correction candidates are the strings of stack symbols between $?_1$ and $?_2$, between the latest $\lessdot$ relation preceding $?_1$ and $?_1$ itself, and between the latest $\lessdot$ relation preceding $?_1$ and $?_2$. The recovery sets are sets of *locally syntactically correct* replacement strings for each of the correction candidates. A replacement string is locally syntactically correct if its left context symbol has a valid precedence relation to its leftmost symbol and its rightmost symbol has a valid precedence relation to its right context symbol.

The second part of the correction phase computes the *cost* of changing each of the correction candidates into each of its possible replacement strings. This cost computation is based on the costs of inserting, deleting, and replacing each terminal symbol of the grammar. The compiler writer supplies four vectors I, D, R, and T. $I(x)$ is the cost of inserting the terminal symbol x, $D(x)$ is the cost of deleting x, and $R(x)$ is the cost of replacing x with the terminal symbol $T(x)$. The R and T vectors are supplied because certain common errors involve accidental substitutions of symbols, for example '=' instead of ':='. After the costs have been computed, the correction candidate and replacement string which together give the lowest cost estimate are used to make the error recovery. The correction candidate is replaced by the replacement string, the extra bottom marker is removed from the stack, and parsing may continue.

Procedure SP_RECOVER. This is a simple precedence error-recovery procedure called by Algorithm SP_SUPERVISOR. This procedure uses the global data structures defined in that algorithm. Three correction candidates, CC_1, CC_2, and CC_3, and three recovery sets, R_1, R_2, and R_3, are used, as well as local variables PREV_LT, TEMP, j, c, and Φ. Also, the variables MIN and JMIN are used in determining the least-cost replacement, PHIMIN. Procedure SP_RECOVER calls Procedure SP_BACKWARD to perform a backward move, and Function SP_COST to compute the cost of a replacement.

1. [First backward move]
   Call SP_BACKWARD
2. [Forward move]
   $?_1 \leftarrow$ TOP + 1
   $S[?_1] \leftarrow$ '@'
   TOP $\leftarrow$ TOP + 2
   S[TOP] $\leftarrow$ INPUT
   HEAD $\leftarrow$ HEAD + 1
   H[HEAD] $\leftarrow$ TOP
   $k \leftarrow k + 1$
   INPUT $\leftarrow x_k$
   Call SP_PARSE
3. [Second backward move]
   Call SP_BACKWARD
   $?_2 \leftarrow$ TOP
4. [First part of correction phase]
   (Get the correct head)
   TEMP $\leftarrow$ HEAD
   Repeat while S[H[TEMP] − 1] = '@'
      TEMP $\leftarrow$ TEMP − 1
      PREV_LT $\leftarrow$ H[TEMP]
   Let the three string correction candidates be:
   CC_1 from $S[?_1]$ to $S[?_2]$
   CC_2 from S[PREV_LT] to $S[?_1]$
   CC_3 from S[PREV_LT] to $S[?_2]$
5. [Compute the three recovery sets]
   Repeat for j = 1, 2, 3
      Let the parse stack contain $\alpha\beta\gamma$ where $\beta = CC_j$
      Let $R_j = \{\Phi|$ the last symbol of α is related to A
         and A is related to the first symbol of γ and
         A $\rightarrow \Phi$ is a production of the grammar}
      If the last symbol of α is related to the first symbol of γ
      then $R_j \leftarrow R_j \cup \{\varepsilon\}$
6. [Compute costs]
   MIN $\leftarrow \infty$
   Repeat for j = 1, 2, 3
      Repeat for each $\Phi \in R_j$
         $c \leftarrow$ SP_COST(CC_j, Φ)
         If c < MIN
         then MIN $\leftarrow$ c
              JMIN $\leftarrow$ j
              PHIMIN $\leftarrow \Phi$
7. [Perform replacement]
   If not (all R_j's = ϕ)
   then j $\leftarrow$ JMIN

Replace CC$_j$ on the parse stack by PHIMIN
Call RESET(CC$_j$, PHIMIN)
If JMIN = 2
then INPUT ← S[TOP]
  k ← k − 1
  TOP ← TOP − 1
else (Update head stack)
  HEAD ← HEAD − 1
  i ← H[HEAD]
Return ☐

Procedure RESET(CC, RS). Given the two parameters CC and RS which hold the correction candidate and the recovery string, respectively, this procedure resets global variable TOP as well as the head stack index, HEAD. TOP will be incremented or decremented correctly depending on whether or not the recovery string adds symbols to the stack or deletes them. For each '@' that is encountered in the correction candidate, HEAD will be decremented by 1. The variables c and r are local and hold the current symbol being looked at from the first and second parameters, respectively.

1. [Initialize r and c]
   r ← First symbol in RS
   c ← First symbol in CC
2. [Loop until end of correction string found]
   Repeat while c ≠ ' '
     If r = c
     then r ← Next symbol of RS
       c ← Next symbol of CC
     else HEAD ← HEAD − 1
       c ← Next symbol of CC
       If c = ' ' and r ≠ ' '
       then r ← Next symbol of RS
       else If r ≠ c and r ≠ ' '
         then r ← Next symbol of RS
         else TOP ← TOP − 1
       Repeat while r ≠ c and r ≠ ' '
         TOP ← TOP + 1
         r ← Next symbol of RS
   Return ☐

As an example of this error-detection and -recovery technique, consider the following simple grammar:

⟨rec def⟩   ::=   *record*⟨comp list⟩*end record*;
⟨comp list⟩ ::=   ⟨obj decls⟩
                  |*null*;

$$\langle\text{obj decls}\rangle \quad ::= \quad \text{id} : range\langle\text{delim}\rangle;$$
$$|\text{id} : range\langle\text{delim}\rangle ; \langle\text{obj decls}\rangle$$
$$\langle\text{delim}\rangle \quad ::= \quad \langle\text{cons}\rangle .. \langle\text{cons}\rangle$$
$$\langle\text{cons}\rangle \quad ::= \quad \text{id}$$
$$|\text{expr}$$
$$V_N = \{\langle\text{rec def}\rangle, \langle\text{comp list}\rangle, \langle\text{obj decls}\rangle, \langle\text{delim}\rangle, \langle\text{cons}\rangle\}$$
$$V_T = \{ record, end, null, range, ;, :, .., \text{id}, \text{expr}\}$$

This sample grammar, which is taken from the programming language Ada, gives the syntax for a simplified version of a record definition. It is not intended to be a complete definition of a record description in Ada, since only simple integer objects are allowed. It should be noted that the terminal symbol 'expr' denotes any (possibly parenthesized) integer arithmetic expression involving numbers and/or arithmetic operators. Integer variables are denoted by the terminal 'id'. The precedence matrix for the example grammar is given in Table 7-25.

The following example is used to demonstrate the simple precedence parsing and error-recovery scheme as shown by Algorithm SP_SUPERVISOR and its associated subalgorithms

> *record*
> $\quad\quad\quad\quad$ num : (min + 1) .. MAX ;
> *end record* ; #

The variables 'num' and 'MAX' are read as identifiers (id) while '(min + 1)' represents an integer expression denoted by 'expr'. In this example the keyword *range* is missing after the colon. Given the costs of certain insertions and deletions, the recovery method will detect the error and, furthermore, will be able to insert the keyword into its proper place in order to continue parsing to the end of the input string.

In connection with the following discussion, the reader is referred to the table showing the various stacks and variable values.

Step 1 shows the initializations which are done by calling Algorithm SP_SUPERVISOR. The parser, Procedure SP_PARSE, is then called, and parsing proceeds correctly until the position in step 4 in Table 7-26 is reached. An error relation (?) between ':' and 'expr' has been encountered which causes Procedure SP_ ERROR to generate the message

$\quad$: CANNOT BE FOLLOWED BY expr.

Control is passed back to the supervisor, and since ACCEPT is still false, the recovery procedure, SP_RECOVER, is invoked.

The first backward move is attempted and fails, as nothing can be reduced prior to the point of error.

A forward move is done by pushing an error delimiter (@) and the current input symbol on the stack and then calling the parser once more. Before calling Procedure SP_PARSE, we have the position shown in step 5. When processing a

Table 7-25 Simple precedence parsing table in record-description example

	⟨rec def⟩	⟨comp list⟩	⟨obj decls⟩	⟨delim⟩	⟨cons⟩	record	end	null	range	;	:	::	id	expr
⟨rec def⟩														
⟨comp list⟩							≐			⋖				
⟨obj decls⟩			⋖				⋗			⋗				
⟨delim⟩										≐				
⟨cons⟩					⋖			⋗		≐		≐	⋖	
record	≐												⋖	
end						⋖				⋗				
null										⋗				
range				⋖	⋖					≐			⋖	⋖
;			≐	⋖			⋗						⋖	⋖
:									≐					
::											⋗		⋗	⋗
id							⋗			⋖	⋗	⋗	⋖	⋖
expr										⋖		⋗	⋖	⋖

All blank entries denote an error (?) relation.

Table 7-26 Simple trace in record-description example illustrating error recovery

Step	TOP	k	HEAD	INPUT	i	$?_1$	$?_2$	H	S	PR
1	1	1	0	record					#	⋖
2	2	2	1	id				2	#record	⋖
3	3	3	2	:	3			23	#record id	≐
4	4	4	2	expr	3			23	#record id :	?
5	6	5	3	..	3	5		236	#record id : @ expr	⋗
6	6	5	3	..	6	5		236	#record id : @⟨cons⟩	≐
7	7	6	3	id	6	5		236	#record id : @⟨cons⟩..	⋖
8	8	7	4	;	6	5		2368	#record id : @⟨cons⟩..id	⋗
9	8	7	3	;	6	5		236	#record id : @⟨cons⟩..⟨cons⟩	⋗
10	6	7	3	;	6	5		236	#record id : @⟨delim⟩	≐
11	5	6	3	⟨delim⟩	6	5	5	236	#record id : @	⋖
12	6	7	3	;	6			236	#record id : @⟨delim⟩	≐
13	8	8	4	end	3	7	8	2368	#record id : @⟨delim⟩@ ;	⋗
14	8	8	4	end	8	7	8	2368	#record id : range⟨delim⟩ ;	⋗
15	7	8	2	end	3			23	#record id : range⟨delim⟩ ;	⋗
16	3	8	2	end	3			23	#record⟨obj decls⟩	⋗
17	3	8	1	end	2			2	#record⟨comp list⟩	≐
18	4	9	1	record	2			2	#record⟨comp list⟩ end	≐
19	5	10	1	;	2			2	#record⟨comp list⟩ end record	≐
20	6	11	1	#	2			2	#record⟨comp list⟩ end record ;	⋗
21	2	11	1	#	2			2	#⟨rec def⟩	⋗

Terminate with a successful parse.

forward move, it is assumed that the new symbol on top of the stack is the head of some simple phrase. In this case, the assumption is true; so the parser can move ahead in the input string with no errors until step 10. At this step, ⟨cons⟩ .. ⟨cons⟩ has just been reduced to ⟨delim⟩. Now a check is done to make sure that all symbols from the previous phrase head to the new top symbol form a valid prefix. The check fails because of the previous error, and the current position is now as in step 11.

Returning to the recovery procedure, the second backward move cannot be done; so the three correction candidates with their corresponding α's and γ's are chosen as

$$CC_1 = @ \qquad \alpha_1 = \ldots : \qquad \gamma_1 = ⟨delim⟩ \ldots$$
$$CC_2 = id : @ \qquad \alpha_2 = \ldots record \qquad \gamma_2 = ⟨delim⟩ \ldots$$
$$CC_3 = CC_2 \qquad \alpha_3 = \ldots record \qquad \gamma_3 = ⟨delim⟩ \ldots$$

The R_j's are all equal to the empty set, and thus HEAD is decremented by 1 and control is passed back to the supervisor. The error delimiter is left on the stack and the parser is called again as if no previous interruption had occurred. In this case, upon comparing @ and ⟨delim⟩, a ⋖ relation is found and all variables are updated as in the normal case. Following this we again run into an invalid prefix problem. The nonterminal ⟨delim⟩ is actually ≐ to ';', but because of the previous error $\langle$delim$\rangle$ is assumed to be the head of a simple phrase and consequently $\langle$delim$\rangle$ followed by ';' is not a valid prefix of any right-hand side.

No more can be done in the parsing algorithm at this stage; so we return to the supervisor, which invokes the recovery procedure just as if it was the first error being encountered. The backward-move attempt fails once more, and the stacks now contain the values as in step 13. Neither a forward move nor a second backward move is possible at this time, and three new correction candidates are chosen:

$$CC_1 = @; \qquad \alpha_1 = \ldots \langle\text{delim}\rangle \qquad \gamma_1 = end\ldots$$
$$CC_2 = \text{id} : @\langle\text{delim}\rangle@ \qquad \alpha_2 = \ldots record \qquad \gamma_2 = ;\ldots$$
$$CC_3 = \text{id} : @\langle\text{delim}\rangle@; \qquad \alpha_3 = \ldots record \qquad \gamma_3 = end\ldots$$

This time,

$$R_1 = \phi$$
$$R_2 = \varepsilon$$
$$R_3 = \{$$

    1. id : $range\langle$delim$\rangle$;
    2. $\langle$obj decls$\rangle$
    3. *null*;
    4. id : $range\langle$delim$\rangle$; $\langle$obj decls$\rangle$
    }

Presumably the first listed choice from R_3 will be the least-cost replacement, **PHIMIN**, and thus CC_3 will be replaced on the parse stack by

    id : $range\langle$delim$\rangle$;

RESET is now invoked with step 14 values. For each of the two error symbols (@'s) found in CC_3, **HEAD** is decremented by 1. The first one is replaced by the missing keyword *range*, which causes no change to **TOP**, but the second is replaced by the empty string, and therefore **TOP** is decremented by 1 before going back to the parser for the last time with the position as in step 15.

There are no more errors, and the corrections made are indeed the right ones; so the parse will terminate successfully.

Rhodes (1973) states that "Some sort of fail-safe device must be incorporated into the system in order to guarantee that the recovery system terminates, i.e., that it does not get into an infinite loop of trying various corrections to the same error." In his implementation of the system, Rhodes specifies that if no new input symbols have been read after two attempts at recovering from an error, the recovery has failed. In this case Rhodes resorts to panic mode (Sec. 5-4.3) to recover from the error.

Graham and Rhodes implemented their error-recovery method in a parser for a subset of **ALGOL** and in a **PASCAL** parser. Their error-recovery results were compared with those obtained in the PL/C and Zurich PASCHAL compilers.

While these comparisons are somewhat subjective, their method compared quite favorably, with the diagnostics of the latter tending to be more intelligible and fewer errors being left undetected.

In closing we point out that the Graham-Rhodes recovery method can easily be modified to work with any precedence parsing method. In particular, the Graham-Rhodes technique is appropriate for recovery in the extended precedence and mixed-strategy precedence parsers described in the following section.

7-3.6 Notions of Extended Precedence

This subsection first examines a few example grammars that fail to be of the type simple precedence. One approach that can be used is to rewrite the given grammar into an equivalent grammar which is simple precedence. This approach, however, may not work if the language described by the original grammar requires more than a pair of context symbols in order to parse sentences from that language. A possible drawback in rewriting a grammar in order to make it simple precedence is that the original structure of the language may be severely altered. A second approach in dealing with simple precedence conflicts in the relations table is to extend the context used to more than two symbols in an attempt to uniquely determine the handle at each parse step. This second approach may often prove to be successful. However, the space required to store the extended relations can be large. Certain steps can be taken to reduce such large space requirements. Some practical steps in trying to economize on storage space are outlined.

Consider, as a first example, a grammar having the following set of productions:

$$E \rightarrow T \mid E + T$$
$$T \rightarrow P \mid T * P$$
$$P \rightarrow F \mid F \uparrow P$$
$$F \rightarrow i \mid (E)$$

where the symbol $\uparrow$ denotes the exponentiation operator. The precedence matrix for this grammar is given in Table 7-27. Note that for the symbol pair $+$ and T, we have both $+ \doteq T$ and $+ \lessdot T$. There is a local ambiguity here. When an attempt is made to find the head symbol of the handle by examining only two adjacent symbols, T could be that symbol, or both the symbols $+$ and T could be in the same handle. More than two symbols are required in order to make the correct decision. The same problem exists for the symbol pair $($ and E. Consequently, the grammar is not a simple precedence grammar. Note that, in this example, there is no difficulty in always determining the tail symbol of a handle.

As a second example, consider the grammar whose productions are

$$X \rightarrow Y \mid X; a$$
$$Y \rightarrow b \mid b; Y$$

where X and Y are nonterminal symbols. The precedence matrix of this grammar

Table 7-27 Example grammar which is not simple precedence

	E	T	P	F	+	*	↑	i	(	)
E					≐					≐
T					⋗	≐				⋗
P					⋗	⋗				⋗
F					⋗	⋗	≐			⋗
+		≐ ⋖		⋖	⋖				⋖	⋖
*			≐	⋖					⋖	⋖
↑			≐	⋖					⋖	⋖
i					⋗	⋗	⋗			⋗
(	≐ ⋖		⋖	⋖	⋖				⋖	⋖
)					⋗	⋗	⋗			⋗

is given in Table 7-28. There is a local ambiguity in determining whether b is the tail symbol of the handle or both symbols b and ; are in the same handle. Again, more than two symbols are required in order to make the right decision.

Wirth and Weber (1966) proposed an extension to their simple precedence relations. Such an extension involved using more than two symbols in making parsing decisions. For example, ternary relations involving three symbols of a grammar could be defined instead of just binary relations (as was the case for simple precedence grammars). The decision in determining the head and tail of a handle can involve looking at three symbols instead of two. The price to be paid for this extension, however, is the larger storage requirements for a three-dimensional array representation of ternary relations. Storage requirements therefore increase from $O(n^2)$ to $O(n^3)$, where n denotes the vocabulary size.

Using an extended-precedence approach in the example grammar for arithmetic expressions given earlier, the local ambiguity involving the two symbols $+$ and T could be resolved by using a third symbol (or rewriting the grammar, see exercises). For example, the symbol triplets $-T\#$, $+T$), and $+T+$ indicate that T is not the head of the handle (i.e., $+ \doteq T\#$, $+ \doteq T$), and $+ \doteq T+$) while the triplet $+T*$ does (i.e., $+ \lessdot T*$). Similarly, the triplet $(E+$ indicates that E is the head symbol of the handle (i.e., $(\lessdot E+$) while the triplet (E) indicates the opposite (i.e., $(\doteq E)$).

Table 7-28

	X	Y	a	b	;
X					≐
Y					⋗
a					⋗
b					≐ ⋗
;		≐	≐	⋖	

The use of a third symbol in the decision process can also resolve the local ambiguity in the second example grammar given earlier. The triplet $b; b$ indicates that b is not the tail symbol of the handle ($b \doteq ; b$) while the triple $b; a$ indicates it is (i.e., $b \gtrdot ; a$).

As mentioned earlier, the storage requirements for a three-dimensional matrix can be substantial. Typically, many entries in such a matrix are empty in the sense that many triplets cannot occur. A sparse matrix representation of a three-dimensional matrix can be used. In such a representation, only those entries that indicate one of three possible relations are stored. Unfortunately, for certain programming languages the storage requirements may still be large. Furthermore, the processing of a sparse array usually requires a search in order to access its elements. Typically, there are few local ambiguities that occur when only two symbols of context (i.e., a simple precedence matrix) are used. One possible approach is to use the simple precedence matrix for making the parsing decisions that are unambiguous. However, for those cases where more than one precedence relation holds between a pair of symbols (i.e., there is a local ambiguity), additional context involving three symbols can be used. McKeeman (1966) proposed such an extension to Wirth and Weber's simple precedence parsing method. Note that in this parsing method two decisions must be made in finding the handle that must be reduced at each parsing step. McKeeman proposed a split in the simple precedence matrix into two separate tables. One table can be used to determine the tail of the handle and the other for finding the head of that handle. The local ambiguities can be resolved, if possible, by using extra context (i.e., three symbols instead of two).

McKeeman's strategy is to use the topmost two symbols in the stack and the incoming input symbol in order to resolve local ambiguities associated with the tail of a handle. Similarly, the first two symbols of a handle (if there are two) and the symbol immediately preceding the handle in the stack were used in resolving local ambiguities involving the head symbol of the handle. Of course, there are instances where local ambiguities are not resolvable using three symbols of context. In such instances additional symbols are required.

Note that the tail of a handle is indicated by a relation of $\gtrdot$ between the topmost symbol of the stack and the incoming input symbol. In searching for the tail of the handle, it is irrelevant if both the relations $\doteq$ and $\lessdot$ hold. A local ambiguity exists if either relation $\lessdot$ or relation $\doteq$ holds and the relation $\gtrdot$ also holds. Similarly, the head of a handle is indicated by the $\lessdot$ relation. In the search for the head of a handle, it is irrelevant if both the relations $\doteq$ and $\gtrdot$ hold. A local ambiguity arises when either relation $\doteq$ or relation $\gtrdot$ holds and relation $\lessdot$ also holds. These observations lead to the definition of an extended-precedence grammar.

Definition 7-6 Let the stack contents be represented by the symbols

$$S_1 S_2 \ldots S_{j-1} S_j S_{j-1} \ldots S_{i-1} S_i$$

in which the substring $S_j \ldots S_i$ represents a potential handle and the input is

T. Then an $(1, 2)$ $(2, 1)$ *extended-precedence grammar* satisfies the following conditions:

1. In searching for the tail of a handle, both the relations $S_{i-1}S_i \gtrdot T$ and $S_{i-1}S_i \leqslant T$ must not hold where the relation $\leqslant$ denotes the relation $\lessdot$ or the relation $\doteq$.

2. In searching for the head of a handle, both the relations $S_{j-1} \geqslant S_jS_{j+1}$ and $S_{j-1} \lessdot S_jS_{j+1}$ must not hold where the relation $\geqslant$ denotes the relation $\gtrdot$ or the relation $\doteq$; .

3. All productions have unique right-hand sides.

We now outline a parsing strategy for the class of $(1, 2)$ $(2, 1)$ extended-precedence grammars. First, the determination of the tail of a handle requires a table TAILT, whose entries are defined as follows:

$$\text{TAILT}[S_i, T] = \begin{cases} \gtrdot & \text{if } S_i \gtrdot T \\ \leqslant & \text{if } S_i \lessdot T \text{ or } S_i \doteq T \\ @ & \text{if } (S_i \gtrdot T) \text{ and } ((S_i \lessdot T) \text{ or } (S_i \doteq T)) \end{cases}$$

Note that since the symbol T denotes a lookahead terminal symbol in the input string, the number of columns in the table TAILT is given by the size of the terminal alphabet (V_T). Also, if there are local ambiguities based on a context of two symbols, we need a single-valued ternary function FT, whose values are given as follows:

$$FT(S_{i-1}, S_i, T) = \begin{cases} \text{true} & \text{if } S_i \text{ is the tail of the handle in the context} \\ & S_{i-1}S_iT \\ \text{false} & \text{if } S_i \text{ is not the tail of the handle in the} \\ & \text{context } S_{i-1}S_iT \end{cases}$$

Second, the detection of the head of a handle requires a second table, HEADT, whose entries are defined as follows:

$$\text{HEADT}[S_{j-1}, S_j] = \begin{cases} \lessdot & \text{if } S_{j-1} \lessdot S_j \\ \geqslant & \text{if } S_{j-1} \gtrdot S_j \text{ or } S_{j-1} \doteq S_j \\ @ & \text{if } (S_{j-1} \lessdot S_j) \text{ and } ((S_{j-1} \gtrdot S_j) \text{ or} \\ & (S_{j-1} \doteq S_j)) \end{cases}$$

The resolution of any local ambiguity in finding the head of a handle again requires a single-valued ternary function FH with the following binary values:

$$FH(S_{j-1}, S_j, S_{j+1}) = \begin{cases} \text{true} & \text{if } S_j \text{ is the head of the handle in the context} \\ & S_{j-1}S_jS_{j+1} \\ \text{false} & \text{if } S_j \text{ is not the head in the context} \\ & S_{j-1}S_jS_{j+1} \end{cases}$$

Table 7-29 Function and tables required for an extended-precedence grammar

	E	T	P	F	+	*	↑	i	(	)
					TAILT					
E					⋖					⋖
T					⋗	⋖				⋗
P					⋗	⋗				⋗
F					⋗	⋗	⋖			⋗
+		⋖	⋖	⋖				⋖	⋖	
*			⋖	⋖				⋖	⋖	
↑			⋖	⋖				⋖	⋖	
i					⋗	⋗	⋗			⋗
(	⋖	⋖	⋖	⋖				⋖	⋖	
)					⋗	⋗	⋗			⋗

	E	T	P	F	+	*	↑	i	(	)
					HEADT					
E					⋗					⋗
T					⋗	⋗				⋗
P					⋗	⋗				⋗
F					⋗	⋗	⋗			⋗
+		@*	⋖	⋖				⋖	⋖	
*		⋗	⋖					⋖	⋖	
↑		⋗	⋗					⋖	⋖	
i					⋗	⋗	⋗			⋗
(	@*		⋖	⋖				⋖	⋖	
)					⋗	⋗	⋗			⋗

@* denotes a local ambiguity.
Function of triplets for detecting head of handle:

$FH(+, T, *) =$ true $\qquad FH(+, T, \#) =$ false
$FH(\#, E, +) =$ true $\qquad FH(+, T, +) =$ false
$FH((, E, +) =$ true $\qquad FH(+, T,)) =$ false
$\qquad\qquad\qquad\qquad FH((, E,)) =$ false

Table 7-29 contains the two tables, TAILT and HEADT, and the ternary function FH for the first example grammar introduced earlier. Note that since there is no problem in finding the tail of a handle, the function FT is not required.

An algorithm which is based on the previous approach to parsing $(1, 2)$ $(2, 1)$ extended-precedence grammars follows.

Algorithm EXTENDED_PRECEDENCE. Given the two tables TAILT and HEADT, and the two ternary functions FT and FH which were described earlier, this algorithm determines whether the given input string $x_1 x_2 \ldots x_n$ is valid. This algorithm uses a parse stack represented by a vector S, whose top entry is indicated by TOP. The current input symbol is stored in INPUT. The variable j is used in the search to find the head of a handle on the stack, and k gives the position of the current input symbol. TE and HE represent the current entries of the tables TAILT and HEADT, respectively, which are used to make the parse decision. R contains the third symbol of context, which may be used in determining the head of the handle. PUSH is a procedure for pushing elements onto the stack.

1. [Initialize]
  TOP ← 0
  Call PUSH(S, TOP, '#')
  Call PUSH(S, TOP, '#')
  k ← 1
  INPUT ← x_k
2. [Perform the parse]
  Repeat step 3 while true
3. [Determine parse action]
  TE ← TAILT[S[TOP], INPUT] (entry in tail table)
  If TE is blank
  then Write('INVALID INPUT')
    Exit
  If (TE = ≤) or ((TE = @) and not FT(S[TOP − 1], S[TOP], INPUT))
  then If TOP = 3 and INPUT = '#' and S[TOP] is the start symbol
    then Write('VALID INPUT')
      Exit
    else (Push input symbol onto stack)
      Call PUSH(S, TOP, INPUT)
      (Scan next input symbol)
      k ← k + 1
      INPUT ← x_k
  else If (TE = ≥) or ((TE = @) and FT(S[TOP − 1], S[TOP], INPUT))
    then j ← TOP
      Repeat while true
        HE ← HEADT[S_{j-1}, S_j]
        If j = TOP
        then R ← INPUT
        else R ← S_{j+1}
        If (HE = ≥) or ((HE = @) and not FH(S_{j-1}, S_j, R))
        then j ← j − 1 (keep looking for head)
        else If (HE = <) or ((HE = @) and FH(S_{j-1}, S_j, R))
          then Process the handle $S_j S_{j+1} \dots S_{TOP}$
            TOP ← j
            S[TOP] ← A (Assuming A is left part of rule)
            Exitloop
          else Write('INVALID INPUT')
            Exit   □

The first step of the algorithm initializes the stack to two marker symbols ('#') instead of the usual one, as was the case in the simple precedence parser given in the previous section. The need for two marker symbols may arise when three symbols are used to determine the parse action. This step also obtains the first input symbol.

Step 2 contains a potentially infinite loop. An exit from this loop, however, occurs in step 3.

The third step, although lengthy, is straightforward. A check is first made on the tail entry to determine whether it is a blank. Such a blank value indicates an error. A matrix entry of $\lessdot$ indicates the tail of the handle has not been found. The same indication is given when there is a local ambiguity and the ternary value of the tail function is false. In any case, a check is made for the acceptance of the input string before proceeding to push the current input symbol on the stack and scan the next input symbol. If the tail symbol of the handle is found, we search the stack for the head symbol. The decision logic here is very similar to that used in locating the tail symbol, except that we make use of the head table and ternary head function instead of the corresponding tail information. Note, however, that if there is a local ambiguity and the handle is a single symbol, the current input symbol becomes the third (i.e., rightmost) context symbol. The left part of the applicable rule replaces its right part (handle) on the stack. If no rule is found to apply, an error occurs. Such a failure would be reported in the statement "Process the handle...".

The previous algorithm requires storage space for two tables and possibly two ternary functions. This storage requirement, however, can be reduced. McKeeman et al. (1970) proposed a *mixed-strategy precedence* parsing algorithm which reduces the storage requirement of the algorithm given earlier. Their approach to determining the tail symbol of a handle is essentially the same as that taken in the algorithm just presented. The difference in their approach occurs in the determination of the head symbol of a handle. An outline of their approach for a $(1, 2)$ $(2, 1)$ extended-precedence grammar follows.

The table, HEADT, which was used earlier to find the head symbol of a handle, is discarded. The determination of the head symbol and, consequently, the handle can be obtained in another way. The production to be applied at this point in the parsing process requires that the tail symbol of its right part match the top symbol of the stack. Therefore, keeping the productions of the grammar lexically sorted by tail symbol will substantially narrow the search for the correct production. The simplest case that can arise is when there is only one production whose right-part tail matches the top symbol of the stack. In this case we have found the only rule which applies. Another more complex situation has the right part of one production be a suffix part of the right-hand side of another production. For example, the two productions $T \rightarrow P$ and $T \rightarrow T * P$ have such an overlap. In many instances, it is possible to resolve the selection of the appropriate production by merely choosing the one with the longest right part. To incorporate this second possibility, the productions with the same tail symbol in their right parts can be further sorted by length on these right parts. That is, the productions are sorted in order of decreasing length of their right parts. Candidate productions whose right parts all contain more than one symbol can be chosen on the basis of longest length. Not all grammars, however, can be handled by such simple heuristics.

If a candidate production has a right part of only one symbol that matches the tail symbol of the longer right part of some other production, a set of triplets may have to be consulted in order to determine the correct parse action.

Another desirable feature of a parser is to allow productions with identical right parts. This case is also handled by the mixed-strategy parsing approach. We shall not, however, go into any further details of this approach.

The next section deals with a powerful and general bottom-up method for parsing grammars. This method is more general than that used in the precedence parsers that we have presented. This new parsing approach is also more difficult to explain and understand.

EXERCISES 7-3

1 Let a grammar G be defined by

$\langle$string$\rangle ::= \langle$head$\rangle$'
$\langle$head$\rangle ::= '|\langle$head$\rangle c|\langle$head$\rangle\langle$string$\rangle$

Using only syntax trees, obtain as many of the precedence relations as possible.

2 Using the formal definition of precedence relations, obtain the precedence matrix for Exercise 1.

3 Using the grammar of Exercise 1 and the precedence matrix of Exercise 2, obtain a parse (as in Table 7-14) for each of the following sentences:

  (a) 'c'
  (b) 'c'c"
  (c) 'c'cc"

4 Prove the following theorem:

$S_1 \lessdot S_2$ if and only if there exists a canonical sentential form $\alpha S_1 S_2 \beta$ in which S_2 is the head of the handle.

5 Prove the following theorem:

$S_1 \gtrdot S_2$ if and only if there exists a canonical sentential form $\alpha S_1 S_2 \beta$ in which S_1 is the tail of the handle.

6 Given the grammar

$\langle$list$\rangle ::= \langle$paren$\rangle\langle$sublist$\rangle)|\langle$paren$\rangle)$
$\langle$paren$\rangle ::= ($
$\langle$sublist$\rangle ::= aa|a\langle$list$\rangle|\langle$list$\rangle a\langle$list$\rangle\langle$list$\rangle$

obtain a precedence matrix for this grammar.

7 Obtain precedence functions for the grammar of Exercise 6.

8 Implement Martin's modifications to Bell's original precedence-function-generation procedure as an algorithm. Be sure to include a revised procedure for determining the validity of the resulting precedence functions by taking advantage of the fact that the directed graph is acyclic if the precedence functions exist.

9 Generate the precedence functions f and g for the precedence matrix given in Table 7-30 using both Bell's original formulation and Martin's later modifications. Does it matter whether the precedence matrix represents a simple precedence grammar or an operator precedence grammar?

Table 7-30

$$
\begin{bmatrix}
\lessdot & \gtrdot & & \\
\doteq & \gtrdot & & \\
& & \lessdot & \lessdot \\
& & \doteq & \lessdot
\end{bmatrix}
$$

10 Prove that $\lessdot = (\doteq) \circ (L^+)$.

11 Prove that $\gtrdot = (R^+)^T \circ (\doteq) \circ (L^*)$.

12 Is the following grammar a simple precedence grammar?

$$
\begin{aligned}
S &\rightarrow E \\
E &\rightarrow T \mid E + T \\
T &\rightarrow F \mid T * F \\
F &\rightarrow i \mid (E)
\end{aligned}
$$

If not, rewrite the given grammar so that its revised equivalent is simple precedence.

13 Exercises 10 and 11 express the simple precedence relations $\lessdot$ and $\gtrdot$ in terms of simpler relations. Express the operator precedence relations $\overset{\circ}{=}$, $\overset{\circ}{<}$, and $\overset{\circ}{>}$ in terms of simpler relations.

14 Is the following grammar a simple precedence grammar? If not, why not?

$$
\begin{aligned}
E &\rightarrow a & B &\rightarrow R \\
E &\rightarrow b & B &\rightarrow (B) \\
E &\rightarrow (E + E) & R &\rightarrow E = E
\end{aligned}
$$

15 Trace Algorithm SP_SUPERVISOR (as was done in Table 7-26) for the input string

> *record*
>> *: range x .. y;*
> *end record;* #

16 For the arithmetic expression grammar (see Table 7-29) given in the section, trace Algorithm EXTENDED_PRECEDENCE for the following input strings:

$$
\begin{aligned}
& i + i * i \\
& i * (i + i)
\end{aligned}
$$

17 For the grammar whose precedence matrix is given in Table 7-28, obtain the tables TAILT and HEADT. Also obtain the ternary function FH.

18 Revise Algorithm EXTENDED_PRECEDENCE so that it will handle the mixed-strategy approach to determining which production should be applied in the parsing process. Do not handle the case where productions can have the same right parts.

19 Using the algorithm obtained in Exercise 18, construct the required set of context triplets for the example grammar whose precedence matrix is given in Table 7-27.

20 Consider the following grammar:

$$
\begin{aligned}
S &\rightarrow A; A \\
A &\rightarrow [S] \\
A &\rightarrow [i] \\
A &\rightarrow i \\
V_N &= \{S, A\}, \ V_T = \{;, [,], i\}
\end{aligned}
$$

Is this a simple precedence grammar? If not, why not? If not, construct the required matrices for the detection of the head and tail symbols of a handle as outlined in McKeeman's extended-precedence method. Define the ternary function required for each matrix. Is the grammar an extended-precedence grammar?

21 Repeat Exercise 20, using the following grammar:

$$X \rightarrow Y$$
$$X \rightarrow [Y]$$
$$Y \rightarrow [i]$$
$$Y \rightarrow i$$
$$V_N = \{X, Y\}, \ V_T = \{i, [,]\}$$

7-4 *LR* GRAMMARS

This section deals with the construction of deterministic parsers for a class of grammars called $LR(k)$ grammars. This class of grammars is essentially the set of all unambiguous context-free grammars and properly contains other previously encountered classes of grammars such as $LL(k)$ and precedence grammars. An $LR(k)$ parser scans a given input string from left to right and constructs, as was done in a simple precedence parser, the reverse of a rightmost derivation for that string. An $LR(k)$ parser makes all parsing decisions based on the contents of a parse stack and the next k lookahead symbols in an input string. Besides being efficient and general, an $LR(k)$ parser also possesses the "valid prefix property" (see Sec. 5-2.3). Recall that a parser having this property can detect an error in the input string at the earliest possible time. These parsers, however, are more complicated than some of the other kinds of parsers encountered thus far. $LR(k)$ parsers are tedious to construct. For more than one symbol of lookahead (i.e., $k > 1$), the LR approach tends to be too expensive. Consequently, this section concentrates on the development of parsers that use at most one lookahead symbol. An $LR(0)$ parser does not require any lookahead symbols in order to deterministically parse a language. Because of this simplicity, and the fact that an unsuccessful attempt at its construction can be the starting point or first step in constructing other more general parsers, we discuss $LR(0)$ parsers in detail. Other parsers based on one symbol of lookahead follow in order of increasing strength: $SLR(1)$, $LALR(1)$, and $LR(1)$. We next present some storage and optimization considerations in building these parsers. The section concludes with a discussion of the aspects of error detection and recovery in LR parsers.

7-4.1 Concepts and Terminology

An LR parser constructs the reverse of a rightmost derivation for a given input string. Consider a grammar G whose starting symbol is S. For an input string x, its rightmost derivation is given by

$$S \underset{R}{\Rightarrow} \alpha_1 \underset{R}{\Rightarrow} \alpha_2 \underset{R}{\Rightarrow} \cdots \underset{R}{\Rightarrow} \alpha_{m-1} \underset{R}{\Rightarrow} \alpha_m = x$$

where the rightmost nonterminal in each α_i, for $1 \leq i < m$, is the one selected to be rewritten (see Sec. 2-4.2). A representative step in this derivation would have the form

$$\phi Bt \Rightarrow \phi \beta t$$

where $\alpha_i = \phi Bt$ and $B \rightarrow \beta$ is the production that has been applied. Observe that, since we are concerned with a rightmost derivation, t must be a string of terminal symbols.

A grammar is said to be $LR(k)$ if, for any given input string, at each step of any derivation the handle β can be detected by examining the string $\phi \beta$ and scanning at most the first k symbols of the unexpended input string t.

We now define a term which is central to the discussion of LR parsers. A *viable prefix* of a sentential form $\phi \beta t$, where β denotes the handle, is any prefix or head string of $\phi \beta$. That is, if $\phi \beta = u_1 u_2 \ldots u_r$, a string $u_1 u_2 \ldots u_i$, where $1 \le i \le r$, is a viable prefix of the sentential form $\phi \beta t$. Note that a viable prefix cannot contain symbols to the right of the handle (i.e., symbols in t).

As an example, consider the grammar with the following productions:

$$S \rightarrow E\#$$
$$E \rightarrow T | E + T | E - T$$
$$T \rightarrow i | (E)$$

The production $S \rightarrow E\#$ is a padding production which ensures that S is the left part of only one production. This production is useful in determining when to halt in a parsing algorithm. Consider the sentential form $E - (i + i)\#$ in the following rightmost derivation step:

$$E - (T + i)\# \Rightarrow E - (i + i)\#$$

Using the previous notation, $B = T$, $\phi \beta = E - (i$, and the handle $\beta = i$. The strings E, $E -$, $E - ($, and $E - (i$ are all viable prefixes of $E - (i + i)\#$.

Knuth (1965), in his important paper dealing with $LR(k)$ grammars, showed that the set of all viable prefixes of all rightmost derivations associated with a particular grammar can be recognized by a finite-state machine (see Chap. 4). This machine becomes the finite-control part of a parser called an LR parser. Observe that, in general, a useful grammar has an infinite number of associated viable prefixes. An important aspect in obtaining an LR parser is to construct (automatically) the finite-state machine directly from the productions of the grammar. The question that arises is: How can we accomplish this from an infinite number of viable prefixes? We will return to this question in the next subsection.

In the remainder of this subsection we assume that a finite control for a parser already exists. The set of all viable prefixes associated with a grammar is partitioned among the states in the finite-state machine that recognize these viable prefixes. Unless otherwise stated, we concentrate on LR parsers that need at most one symbol lookahead in the input string, that is, $LR(0)$ and $LR(1)$ parsers. The remaining pages of this subsection outline how an LR parser works.

An LR parser, like most other types of parsers, is a pushdown machine that has, as input, a given string; a stack, and a finite-control mechanism. This mechanism is a finite-state machine with, in general, many states. Figure 7-7 contains a finite control for the example grammar given earlier. This machine contains 12 states, with state 0 as its initial or start state. Two types of states are present: read states and apply or reduce states. A *read state* causes a transition from one state to another to occur on reading a terminal or nonterminal symbol. States 0, 1, 4, 6, 7, and 10 are all read states. A *reduce* or *apply state* recognizes the handle part of a viable prefix associated with the current sentential form. The result of being in such a reduce state is to reduce the detected handle to a nonterminal symbol. As mentioned earlier, a state can be associated with an infinite number of viable prefixes. For example, in Fig. 7-7 state 4 can be reached from state 0 with the viable prefixes: $($, $E - ($, $E + ($, $E + (($, $E + ((($, etc. Similarly, any viable prefix whose tail symbol is i will reach state 3. Similar observations can be made about other states in the finite-state machine. Note that the machine in Fig. 7-7 is deterministic.

An $LR(0)$ parser maintains a stack of symbol pairs. The first element in each pair is a symbol of the vocabulary. The second element in the pair denotes the state entered on scanning a vocabulary symbol. The stack initially contains state 0, the start state of the finite control associated with the parser. When the parser is in a read state, it stacks the current symbol being scanned and performs the indicated transition based on the symbol read. This subsequently entered state is also stacked. When the parser enters an apply or reduce state which is associated with a production $B \rightarrow \beta$, it pops the top $2 * |\beta|$ symbols off the stack. If the goal symbol is reached at this point (i.e., $B = S$) the parser accepts the given input string and halts. Otherwise, the state which appears at the top of the stack after the reduction and the left part of the rule that applies determine the next transition state. We then stack both B and this next state. Note that since the

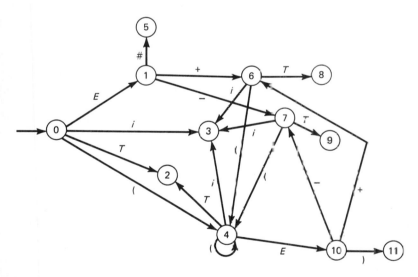

Figure 7-7 Parser for an $LR(0)$ grammar.

finite control associated with the parser is deterministic, the grammar symbols need not be stacked. We do so only to make the discussion more understandable. Also observe that on reaching a reduce or apply state, the entire handle is known at that point. Unlike precedence parsers, there is no need to enter the stack to find the head symbol of the handle.

A trace of the informal parsing strategy for the given input string, $i - (i + i)\#$, appears in Table 7-31. Initially, the stack contains state 0 and the current input symbol is i. The finite control causes a transition from read state 0 to state 3 on reading an i. The symbol pair, i and state 3, is stacked at this point. Since state 3 is a reduce state and the production $T \rightarrow i$ applies, the symbol pair at the top of the stack is discarded. This deletion operation brings state 0 to the top of the stack. Based on state 0 and the nonterminal T, the next transition is to state 2. We now stack the symbol pair, T and state 2. The stack content becomes

$$0\ T2$$

Observe that one step in the reverse of the rightmost derivation has been obtained. That is,

$$T - (i + i)\# \underset{R}{\Rightarrow} i - (i + i)\#$$

Continuing the trace, we are now in state 2, which is another reduce state. At this time, production $E \rightarrow T$ applies. Consequently, the top symbol pair in the stack, T and state 2, is discarded. State 0 again appears at the top of the stack. This state and E causes a transition to state 1. Therefore the symbol pair, E and state

Table 7-31 Trace of $LR(0)$ parser for the string $i - (i + i)\#$

Step	Stack contents	Input string	Viable prefix	Handle
0	0	$i - (i + i)\#$		
1	0 $i3$	$-(i + i)\#$	i	i
2	0 $T2$	$-(i + i)\#$	T	T
3	0 $E1$	$-(i + i)\#$	E	
4	0 $E1 - 7$	$(i + i)\#$	$E -$	
5	0 $E1 - 7 (4$	$i + i)\#$	$E - ($	
6	0 $E1 - 7 (4\ i3$	$+i)\#$	$E - (i$	i
7	0 $E1 - 7 (4\ T2$	$+i)\#$	$E - (T$	T
8	0 $E1 - 7 (4\ E10$	$+i)\#$	$E - (E$	
9	0 $E1 - 7 (4\ E10 + 6$	$i)\#$	$E - (E +$	
10	0 $E1 - 7 (4\ E10 + 6\ i3$	$)\#$	$E - (E + i$	i
11	0 $E1 - 7 (4\ E10 + 6\ T8$	$)\#$	$E - (E + T$	$E + T$
12	0 $E1 - 7 (4\ E10$	$)\#$	$E - (E$	
13	0 $E1 - 7 (4\ E10)11$	$\#$	$E - (E)$	(E)
14	0 $E1 - 7\ T9$	$\#$	$E - T$	$E - T$
15	0 $E1$	$\#$	E	
16	0 $E1 \#5$		$E\#$	$E\#$
17	0	*accept*		

1, is pushed on the stack, thus giving the following stack contents:

> 0 $E1$

The next step in the reverse of the rightmost derivation is complete. That is,

$$E - (i + i)\# \underset{R}{\Rightarrow} T - (i + i)\#$$

The next transition is from state 1 to state 7 because the current input symbol is $-$. The minus sign and state 7 is the next symbol pair to be stacked. The stack content becomes

> 0 $E1$ -7

The new current input symbol is (. Based on this symbol, a state transition occurs from state 7 to state 4 with symbol pair (and state 7 being pushed on the stack, giving a new stack content of

> 0 $E1$ -7 (4

The next input symbol is now i. A transition from state 4 to state 3 occurs on i. The pushing of the new symbol pair, i and state 3, on the stack yields

> 0 $E1$ -7 (4 $i3$

Since state 3 is a reduce state, the rule $T \rightarrow i$ applies. The top symbol pair on the stack is discarded. A transition from state 4 to state 2 then occurs on T. The new symbol pair, T and state 2, is pushed on the stack, with its contents now becoming

> 0 $E1$ -7 (4 $T2$

The new step in the parse that has been obtained is

$$E - (T + i)\# \underset{R}{\Rightarrow} E - (i + i)\#$$

The remaining steps of the trace can be obtained in an analogous manner. On reaching state 5, an apply state, the starting symbol of the grammar (S) is recognized after performing the indicated reduction. At this point the parser accepts the given input string and halts.

Note that LR parsers use a somewhat different approach to parsing than do precedence parsers. Both types of parsers detect the tail of a handle by looking at the top entry of the parse stack and the current input symbol. Precedence parsers, with the use of precedence relations, must search the stack for the head of the handle. LR parsers, however, make that decision based on the top entry of the stack and the current input symbol. The parse stack in an LR parser is more complex than the corresponding parse stack in a precedence parser. The top entry of the stack in any LR parser essentially summarizes all the information about the parse up to that point in the parsing process.

The existence of the finite control for the $LR(0)$ parser just discussed was assumed. The next subsection deals with the construction of such a finite control from a given grammar.

EXERCISES 7-4.1

1 Consider the grammar with the following rules:

$$S \rightarrow E\#$$
$$E \rightarrow T | E + T$$
$$T \rightarrow P | P \uparrow T$$
$$P \rightarrow F | P * F$$
$$F \rightarrow i | (E)$$

(a) What are the sets of viable prefixes in a rightmost derivation step for the following sentential forms:

    (1) $E + i * i\#$
    (2) $E + P \uparrow (i + i)\#$

(b) Construct the reverse of the rightmost derivation for the following input strings:

    (1) $i + i * i\#$
    (2) $i + i \uparrow (i + i)\#$

2 For the example grammar in this subsection, give a parse (as in Table 7-31) for the following input strings:

    (a) $i + i - i\#$
    (b) $(i + i) - i\#$

7-4.2 $LR(0)$ Parsers

This subsection describes how to construct, from the productions of a given $LR(0)$ grammar, a parser for that grammar. Although few useful grammars are $LR(0)$, the construction of $LR(0)$ parsers can be the basis of construction for more complicated parsers such as the class of $SLR(1)$ parsers. $LR(0)$ parsers require no lookahead from the unexpended input string in order to make all parsing decisions.

Recall from the last subsection that the finite control associated with an $LR(0)$ parser consisted of a finite number of states. Each state was associated with the set of viable prefixes that was recognized by that state. Since the number of viable prefixes associated with a particular state is often infinite, it is difficult to use the sets of viable prefixes to construct the finite control of a parser. Although the notion of a viable prefix is intuitively useful in talking about an LR parser, it is of little direct use in obtaining the parser itself. In order to determine the states of the finite control for a parser, we want to associate each state with a finite set. Such a finite set can be defined by using the notion of a viable prefix.

Although an LR parser recognizes viable prefixes, its principal goal is to output the sequence of productions that was used in constructing the reverse rightmost derivation for a given input string. From this point of view, the parser wants to detect handles. In order to detect a handle (the right part of a production), however, a parser must first recognize certain parts or prefixes of that handle. This observation and the previous comment on infinite sets of viable prefixes lead us to the following definition.

Definition 7-7 An *item* or a *configuration* of a given grammar G is a marked production of the form

$$[A \to \alpha_1.\alpha_2]$$

where $A \to \alpha_1\alpha_2$ is a production of G and the period or dot denotes the mark.

The brackets help distinguish an item from its associated production. In general, there are several items or configurations associated with the same production. For example, the production $E \to E - T$ has the following four associated items:

$$[E \to .E - T]$$
$$[E \to E. - T]$$
$$[E \to E - .T]$$
$$[E \to E - T.]$$

In order to construct the finite control of an LR parser, we want to associate items with viable prefixes. Therefore, an item $[A \to \alpha_1.\alpha_2]$ is *valid* for some viable prefix $\phi\alpha_1$ if and only if there exists some rightmost derivation

$$S \overset{*}{\underset{R}{\Rightarrow}} \phi A t \underset{R}{\Rightarrow} \phi\alpha_1\alpha_2 t$$

in which t is a string of terminal symbols. In general, there may be many valid items for a viable prefix. For example, in the $LR(0)$ grammar of the previous subsection which contained the productions

$$S \to E\#$$
$$E \to T|E + T|E - T$$
$$T \to i|(E)$$

the items $[E \to E - .T]$, $[T \to .i]$, and $[T \to .(E)]$ are all valid for the viable prefix $E - $. The rightmost derivation

$$S \Rightarrow E\#$$
$$\Rightarrow E - .T$$

shows that the item $[E \to E - .T]$ is valid for $E - $. In this case, by using the previous definition of valid item, we have $\phi = \varepsilon$, $\alpha_1 = E - $, $\alpha_2 = T$, and $t = \varepsilon$. Similarly, the rightmost derivation

$$S \Rightarrow E\#$$
$$\Rightarrow E - .T$$
$$\Rightarrow E - .i$$

shows that $[T \rightarrow .i]$ is also valid. In this case, $\phi = E -$, $\alpha_1 = \varepsilon$, $\alpha_2 = i$, and $t = \varepsilon$. Finally, the rightmost derivation

$$S \Rightarrow E\#$$
$$\Rightarrow E - .T$$
$$\Rightarrow E - .(E)$$

demonstrates that the item $[T \rightarrow .(E)]$ is valid. These observations can also be verified by examining the finite control of the parser given in Fig. 7-7. Since a grammar has a finite number of productions, it follows that the number of valid items associated with a viable prefix will also be finite.

We want to associate a finite set of valid items with each state in a parser's finite-control mechanism. Since each viable prefix has a finite number of valid items, it follows that a potentially infinite set of viable prefixes (representing one state of the parser) will also have only a finite number of associated valid items. Consequently, if we can obtain the finite set of valid items associated with a state of the parser, the finite-state control of the parser can be derived. This is the approach that we will follow. The machine of Fig. 7-7 will be constructed using the notion of a valid item.

We now, in an informal manner, proceed to construct the sets of items associated with an $LR(0)$ parser. To get the construction process started, the item $[S \rightarrow .\alpha]$ is associated with the start state of the finite-state control, where S denotes the distinguished symbol of the grammar. The item $[S \rightarrow .\alpha]$ reflects the fact that the parser has not recognized any (nonempty) viable prefixes. For the current example, state 0 is associated with the item $[S \rightarrow .E\#]$.

A *closure* or *completion* operation is required on the initial item in the item set. To obtain the *closure* of an item $[A \rightarrow \alpha_1.X\alpha_2]$ where X is a nonterminal, we include in the item set all items of the form $[X \rightarrow .\lambda]$. In the example, the closure of the item $[S \rightarrow .E\#]$ first generates the items $[E \rightarrow .T]$, $[E \rightarrow .E + T]$, and $[E \rightarrow .E - T]$. Note that using the previous notation, $A = S$, $\alpha_1 = \varepsilon$, $X = E$, and $\alpha_2 = \#$. Applying the closure operation to the item $[E \rightarrow .T]$ yields two more items: $[T \rightarrow .i]$ and $[T \rightarrow .(E)]$. Repeating the closure operation on any of the items obtained so far does not produce any new items. The initial item set C_0 associated with the start state of the parser is

$$[S \rightarrow .E\#]$$
$$[E \rightarrow .T]$$
$$[E \rightarrow .E + T]$$
$$[E \rightarrow .E - T]$$
$$[T \rightarrow .i]$$
$$[T \rightarrow .(E)]$$

Intuitively, the parser in state 0 expects to encounter a string derivable from $E\#$. Strings derivable from E are those which are derivable from either T, $E + T$, or $E - T$. The strings derivable from T will begin with either an i or a $($. The first item in C_0 is the *basis* item. The remaining items in C_0 are the result of performing the closure or completion operation.

Thus far, the machine does not recognize symbols in a viable prefix. To have a machine recognize symbols, we need to define a new operation called a *read* or *successor* operation. Let an item of the form $[A \rightarrow \alpha . X\beta]$ be associated with some state U, where X denotes any symbol in the grammar vocabulary. A *read* or *successor* operation associates the item $[A \rightarrow \alpha X.\beta]$ with some state V in the machine. The read operation defines a transition from state U to state V on scanning the symbol X. Recall from the previous subsection that transitions in the finite control of an *LR* parser occur when an input symbol is scanned or the parser is in a reduce state. The read operation is instrumental in the creation of new states in the construction process.

In the current example, a read operation on the nonterminal E results in the creation of three new items associated with a new state, say, state 1. These items, which form the basis set of the current state, are the following:

$$[S \rightarrow E.\#]$$
$$[E \rightarrow E.+ T]$$
$$[E \rightarrow E.- T]$$

The completion or closure of these items yields no new items, since in each case a terminal symbol follows the dot. Let C_1 denote the new item set.

Similarly, a read operation or transition from state 0 to state 2 on nonterminal T yields a basis item $[E \rightarrow T.]$. The closure of this item also yields no new items. We call the item set C_2. A similar situation occurs when performing a transition from state 0 to state 3 on the terminal i, thus yielding the item $[T \rightarrow i.]$. C_3 denotes this new item set. A fourth (and final) transition from state 0 to state 4 occurs on reading a left parenthesis. The basis set of state 4 is the item $[T \rightarrow (.E)]$. The closure operation on this set, however, generates the following new items:

$$[E \rightarrow .T]$$
$$[E \rightarrow .E + T]$$
$$[E \rightarrow .E - T]$$
$$[T \rightarrow .i]$$
$$[T \rightarrow .(E)]$$

The six items form the item set C_4. The portion of the machine constructed thus far is illustrated in Fig. 7-8.

Intuitively, state 1 has recognized an E and the next symbol expected is $\#$, $+$, or $-$. State 3 recognizes a handle (i) and is a reduce state. Similarly, state 2 is a reduce state which recognizes a handle (T). Finally, state 4 reflects the fact that a left parenthesis was scanned. The next symbols to be encountered are those derivable from an expression (E). The symbols derivable from an expression are those derivable from a term (T).

Continuing the machine-generation process, we can perform a transition from state 1 to state 5 on reading the symbol $\#$. The item set for state 5 is $C_5 = \{[S \rightarrow E\#.]\}$ and denotes another reduce state. Generating a new basis set of items through a read operation and then performing a completion operation on

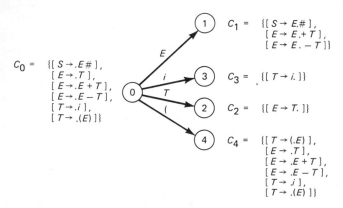

$C_0 = \{[S \to .E\#],$
$\quad [E \to .T],$
$\quad [E \to .E + T],$
$\quad [E \to .E - T],$
$\quad [T \to .i],$
$\quad [T \to .(E)]\}$

$C_1 = \{[S \to E.\#],$
$\quad [E \to E.+ T],$
$\quad [E \to E.-T]\}$

$C_3 = \{[T \to i.]\}$

$C_2 = \{[E \to T.]\}$

$C_4 = \{[T \to (.E)],$
$\quad [E \to .T],$
$\quad [E \to .E + T],$
$\quad [E \to .E - T],$
$\quad [T \to .i],$
$\quad [T \to .(E)]\}$

Figure 7-8 Partial construction of an $LR(0)$ machine.

that set yields another collection of items associated with some perhaps new state. Observe at this point that it is possible to generate a basis set of items which has already been associated with a previously generated state. If such a "duplicate" state occurs, it is simply ignored. The process of creating a new state by performing a read (or transition) operation and subsequent completions of the basis items must terminate. Since each set of items is finite, the machine must have a finite number of states. Continuing the state-generation process just described for the current grammar yields the machine given earlier in Fig. 7-7. The sets of items associated with each state of the machine are summarized in Table 7-32.

Before giving an algorithm for constructing the finite control of an $LR(0)$ parser, we summarize the operations required for its construction. We want to

Table 7-32 The items sets for an $LR(0)$ parser

State 0:	$C_0 = \{[S \to .E\#],$	State 5:	$C_5 = \{[S \to E\#.]\}$
	$\quad [E \to .T],$	State 6:	$C_6 = \{[E \to E + .T],$
	$\quad [E \to .E + T],$		$\quad [E \to .i],$
	$\quad [E \to .E - T],$		$\quad [T \to .(E)]\}$
	$\quad [E \to .i],$	State 7:	$C_7 = \{[E \to E - .T],$
	$\quad [E \to .(E)]\}$		$\quad [T \to .i],$
State 1:	$C_1 = \{[S \to E.\#],$		$\quad [T \to .(E)]\}$
	$\quad [E \to E.+ T],$	State 8:	$C_8 = \{[E \to E + T.]\}$
	$\quad [E \to E.-T]\}$	State 9:	$C_9 = \{[E \to E - T.]\}$
State 2:	$C_2 = \{[E \to T.]\}$	State 10:	$C_{10} = \{[T \to (E.)],$
State 3:	$C_3 = \{[T \to i.]\}$		$\quad [E \to E.+ T],$
State 4:	$C_4 = \{[T \to (.E)],$		$\quad [E \to E.-T]\}$
	$\quad [E \to .T],$	State 11:	$C_{11} = \{[T \to (E).]\}$
	$\quad [E \to .E + T],$		
	$\quad [E \to .E - T],$		
	$\quad [T \to .i],$		
	$\quad [T \to .(E)]\}$		

generate the item sets associated with each state of the parser. The three following rules are used to construct the finite-state control of the parser:

1. *Start operation*: Let $S \rightarrow \delta$ be a rule in grammar G where S denotes the starting symbol of the grammar. Then the item $[S \rightarrow .\delta]$ is associated with the start state. This operation gets the construction process started. The *start* state, in general, will eventually contain several items.
2. *The closure (or completion) operation*: If $[A \rightarrow \alpha. X\beta]$ is an item associated with a state U, where X is a nonterminal symbol, then each item of the form $[X \rightarrow .\lambda]$ must also be associated with state U. This operation is applied repeatedly until no more items are associated with that state.
3. *The read (or successor) operation*: Let X be a vocabulary symbol in an item $[A \rightarrow \alpha. X\beta]$ associated with some state U. Then the item $[A \rightarrow \alpha X.\beta]$ is associated with a transition to state V on reading symbol X. Note that U and V can be the same state (see state 4 in Fig. 7-7).

These operations are used in the following algorithm, which generates the finite control for an $LR(0)$ parser.

Algorithm LR(0)_MACHINE. Given a grammar G, with starting symbol S, this algorithm generates the finite control of the $LR(0)$ parser for the given grammar. The machine contains the following sets of items:

$$C = \{C_0, C_1, \ldots, C_m\}$$

where C_0 is the *initial* or *start* item set. The states of the $LR(0)$ parser are

$$\{0, 1, \ldots, m\}$$

where each state j is constructed or obtained from the item set C_j. The algorithm generates the collection of items C.

1. [Generate the starting item set]
    (a) Assign the starting item set a subscript (say, 0) and then place the item $[S \rightarrow .\delta]$ in the set C_0.
    (b) Perform the completion operation on the item, i.e., look for a nonterminal symbol X which follows the dot ".", and include the items of the form $[X \rightarrow .\delta]$ in the set where $X \rightarrow \delta$ is a production in G. The completion operation is also performed on all new items derived.
    (c) Call the set of items obtained in parts a and b the set C_0.
2. [Generate the sets of items C]
    Repeat through step 4 until no more distinct item sets occur.
3. [Perform a read operation on an item]
    (a) Perform a read operation on an item (initially, in set C_0). Start a new state set, say, C_j.

(b) If this item set is already there, ignore it. At any rate, obtain a new basis item set or exit.

4. [Perform the completion of the new state set]
   Perform the completion operation on the basis set of items for C_j. □

The algorithm generates the item sets from which a machine, such as that given in Fig. 7-7, can be derived. As mentioned earlier, there are two kinds of states in an $LR(0)$ machine, *read* states and *reduce* (or apply) states. A *reduce* state is associated with a *completed item*, i.e., one in which the dot is at the right end of the item. Such a state indicates that a handle has been detected. An $LR(0)$ parser with a finite control can be described by a pair of tables, one table to indicate the action taken by the parser such as *accept*, *reduce*, *push*, and *invalid*, and the other to indicate the transition from one state to another. We return to the specifics of these tables later.

An $LR(0)$ grammar (see exercises) is clearly not sufficiently powerful to express the constructs contained in current programming languages. These languages require at least one symbol lookahead in order to be parsed deterministically. The generation of an $LR(0)$ machine, however, can be a starting point for obtaining an LR parser based on one symbol of lookahead. We develop such a simple class of parsers in the next subsection.

EXERCISES 7-4.2

1 Given the grammar with the productions

$$S \rightarrow E\#$$
$$E \rightarrow E - T \mid T$$
$$T \rightarrow F \mid F \uparrow T$$
$$F \rightarrow i \mid (E)$$

obtain the set of valid items for the following viable prefixes:

(a) $F \uparrow$
(b) $E - ($
(c) $E - T$

2 Given the grammar having the rules

$$S \rightarrow E\#$$
$$E \rightarrow wX \mid xY$$
$$X \rightarrow yX \mid z$$
$$Y \rightarrow yY \mid z$$

obtain the $LR(0)$ machine (as in Fig. 7-7 and Table 7-32) for this grammar.

3 Using the machine of Exercise 2, give parses, such as that given in Table 7-31, for the following input strings:

(a) $wyyz\#$
(b) $xyyyz\#$

4 Repeat Exercise 2 for the grammar with the following rules:

$$S \rightarrow E\#$$
$$E \rightarrow X \mid Y$$
$$X \rightarrow aX \mid b$$
$$Y \rightarrow aY \mid c$$

5 Is the grammar of Exercise 1 $LR(0)$? If not, why not?

7-4.3 $SLR(1)$ Parsers

This subsection formulates a parsing algorithm for the simplest class of LR grammars, which are based on a lookahead of one symbol, known as the class of $SLR(1)$ grammars. The parser for an $SLR(1)$ grammar can be obtained from the $LR(0)$ machine for that grammar and other easily obtained information (derivable from the machine). Certain $LR(1)$ grammars, however, are not $SLR(1)$. The subsection concludes with an example of such a grammar.

Consider the example grammar which contains the following productions:

0. $S \rightarrow E\#$ 4. $T \rightarrow F$
1. $E \rightarrow E - T$ 5. $F \rightarrow (E)$
2. $E \rightarrow T$ 6. $F \rightarrow i$
3. $T \rightarrow F \uparrow T$

Note that production 0 serves the purpose of a padding production in an augmented grammar. Using the $LR(0)$ construction method of the previous subsection, we can obtain the collection of item sets for this grammar. These sets are given in Table 7-33, and the corresponding finite-state control is shown in Fig. 7-9. Each item set is given in two parts. The first part gives the items in the basis set (due to a read operation). The second part gives the completion or closure of the basis set.

Observe that the example grammar is not $LR(0)$. This fact is evident by examining the item set associated with state 3. This set contains two items, one of which is a completed item. Recall that such an item indicates an apply or reduce state (i.e., F should be reduced to T). The other is a partially completed item which indicates that an F has been matched and that $\uparrow$ and T still remain to be scanned. A state whose associated item set contains one completed item and at least one more item (complete or partial) is said to be an *incdequate state*. Such a state indicates a local ambiguity at that point in the parsing process. The symbol F can be taken as a handle, or we can continue pushing elements on the stack until the handle $F \uparrow T$ is obtained. If the finite control of an LR parser contains no inadequate states, the grammar is $LR(0)$.

The local ambiguity can often be resolved based on a simple computation. For example, in the current situation, we have an inadequate state containing the items

$$[T \rightarrow F.]$$
$$[T \rightarrow F. \uparrow T]$$

Table 7-33 The $LR(0)$ item sets for an $SLR(1)$ grammar

State	Basis set		Closure set
0	$[S \rightarrow .E\#]$		$[E \rightarrow .E - T]$
			$[E \rightarrow .T]$
			$[T \rightarrow .F \uparrow T]$
			$[T \rightarrow .F]$
			$[F \rightarrow .i]$
			$[F \rightarrow .(E)]$
1	$[S \rightarrow E.\#]$		empty
	$[E \rightarrow E. - T]$		
2	$[E \rightarrow T.]$		empty
3	$[T \rightarrow F.\uparrow T]$	inadequate	empty
	$[T \rightarrow F.]$	state	
4	$[F \rightarrow i.]$		empty
5	$[F \rightarrow (.E)]$		$[E \rightarrow .E - T]$
			$[E \rightarrow .T]$
			$[T \rightarrow .F \uparrow T]$
			$[T \rightarrow .F]$
			$[F \rightarrow .(E)]$
			$[F \rightarrow .i]$
6	$[S \rightarrow E\#.]$		empty
7	$[E \rightarrow E - .T]$		$[T \rightarrow .F \uparrow T]$
			$[T \rightarrow .F]$
			$[F \rightarrow .(E)]$
			$[F \rightarrow .i]$
8	$[E \rightarrow E - T.]$		empty
9	$[F \rightarrow (E.)]$		empty
	$[E \rightarrow E. - T]$		
10	$[F \rightarrow (E).]$		empty
11	$[T \rightarrow F \uparrow .T]$		$[T \rightarrow .F \uparrow T]$
			$[T \rightarrow .F]$
			$[F \rightarrow .i]$
			$[F \rightarrow .(E)]$
12	$[T \rightarrow F \uparrow T.]$		empty

By examining the $LR(0)$ machine, we may be able to resolve the local ambiguity. If we choose to reduce the handle F to T, then several symbols, in general, will follow T. If this set of symbols is disjoint from the symbol that follows F when a reduction is not made, the situation is resolved. In the present case, T can be followed by any symbol in the set $\{\#, -,)\}$. Since this set is disjoint from $\{\uparrow\}$, the local ambiguity is resolved by examining one lookahead symbol. When this simple method of inadequate state resolution works, the grammar is said to be an $SLR(1)$ *grammar*. $SLR(1)$ grammars are due to DeRemer (1971). Recall from Chap. 6 the introduction of a FOLLOW set computation. This same computation can be used here to mechanically compute the desired sets of symbols. The computation of these sets, however, is independent of what state we are presently at in the parser. We return to this point at the end of the subsection.

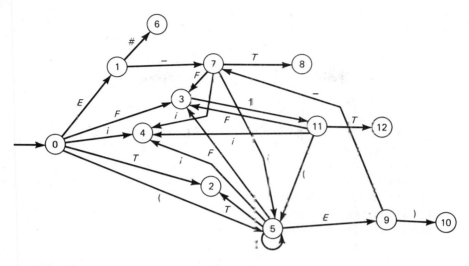

Figure 7-9 $LR(0)$ finite control for an SLR(1) grammar.

An *SLR*(1) parser can be represented by a pair of functions, F and G, which specify the finite control for a deterministic pushdown machine as follows:

Function F: The *action function* maps a state and a current symbol into the following actions:

(a) Shift—abbreviated S,

(b) Reduce k—where k is the production number abbreviated rk,

(c) Accept—abbreviated A, and

(d) Error—denoted by a blank entry.

Therefore, F: state $\times$ current input $\rightarrow$ {Reduce k, Shift, Accept, Error}

Function G: The *next-state* or *goto* function maps a state and a vocabulary symbol of V into the following entries:

(a) a state, and

(b) Error—denoted by a blank entry.

Therefore, G: state $\times$ vocabulary symbol $\rightarrow$ {state number, Error}

The following algorithm constructs a parser for an *SLR*(1) grammar.

Algorithm SLR(1)_CONSTRUCTOR. Given an $LR(0)$ machine represented by the collection of sets of items

$$C = \{C_0, C_1,...,C_m\}$$

where C_0 is the *initial* or *start* item set and the states of the parser

$$\{0, 1,...,m\}$$

where each state j is constructed or obtained from the item set C_j, this algorithm computes the **F** and **G** functions.

1. [Construct the required functions]
   Repeat through step 3 for each state i in the state set
2. [Compute the action function entries]
   (a) If $[A \rightarrow \alpha.x\beta] \in C_i$ where
   $x \in V_T \cup \{\varepsilon\}$ and there is a transition from C_i to C_j
   on terminal symbol x
   then $F(i, x) \leftarrow$ Shift
   (b) If $[A \rightarrow \lambda.] \in C_i$ where $A \rightarrow \lambda$ is the jth production
   then $F(i, x) \leftarrow$ Reduce j for all $x \in$ FOLLOW(A)
   (c) If $[S \rightarrow \alpha.] \in C_i$
   then $F(i, \varepsilon) \leftarrow$ Accept
   (d) All undefined entries are error entries (i.e., blank).
3. [Compute the next state entries]
   (a) If there is a transition from item set C_i to C_j
   on vocabulary symbol X
   then $G(i, X) \leftarrow j$
   (b) All undefined entries are error entries (i.e., blank)
   (c) The start state of the parser is state 0. □

The algorithm is simple. The computation of the F entries in step 2 can lead to multiple entries, that is, an F(i, x) entry can both be a Shift or a Reduce k or two or more reduce actions. Such a multiple entry signals a local ambiguity which is unresolvable within the *SLR* framework. The given grammar is therefore not *SLR*(1). Consequently, in such a situation, no *SLR*(1) parser exists for this grammar. The F and G functions for the example grammar appear in Table 7-34. These functions are obtained directly from Table 7-33 (or equivalently from Fig.

Table 7-34 Parsing tables for an *SLR*(1) parser

	Action function F							Next state or goto function G									
State	i	−	↑	(	)	#	ε	S	E	T	F	i	−	↑	(	)	#
0	S			S					1	2	3	4			5		
1		S				S							7				6
2		r2			r2	r2											
3		r4	S		r4	r4								11			
4		r6	r6		r6	r6											
5	S			S					9	2	3	4			5		
6							A										
7	S			S						8	3	4			5		
8		r1			r1	r1											
9		S			S								7			10	
10		r5	r5		r5	r5											
11	S			S						12	3	4			5		
12		r3			r3	r3											

7-9) and the FOLLOW set computations which are

FOLLOW(F) = $\{\uparrow, -,), \# \}$
FOLLOW(E) = FOLLOW(T) = $\{-,), \# \}$

For example, the items $[F \to .i]$ and $[F \to .(E)]$ associated with state 0 cause the generation of shift entries. When the current input symbol is i or (, a shift entry is entered in the first row of the action table under the columns labeled i and (. All other entries in this row are error entries. From state 0, transitions can occur to states 1, 2, 3, 4, and 5. The latter entries appear in the first row of the next state table, G, under the appropriately labeled columns. Since $[E \to T.]$ is a completed item associated with state 2, the entry $r2$ (apply production 2) is entered under the columns labeled $-$,), and $\#$ (because FOLLOW(E) = $\{-,), \# \}$). Consider the state 3 entries of the action table. Since this state is inadequate, the action table entries can be of the reduce or shift form. The item $[T \to F.\uparrow T]$ generates a shift entry under the column labeled $\uparrow$. The completed item $[T \to F.]$ accounts for the three "reduce 3" entries because FOLLOW(T) = $\{-,), \# \}$. The remaining entries can be obtained in a similar manner. The production $S \to E\#$ is essentially a production which "augments' the grammar such that it is the only rule which has S as a left part. Upon recognizing S, the parsing process halts. In the current example we shift the marker symbol ($\#$) on the stack while parsing. Another approach could be used, in which, upon encountering the nonterminal E and $\#$ as the current input symbol, the given input string would be accepted.

The F and G functions derived from an $SLR(1)$ grammar can be used in the following general parser, which handles any $SLR(1)$ grammar.

Procedure SLR_PARSER(Φ, F, G, x). Given the action and next state transition table represented by the functions F and G as discussed earlier, an input string x, and the set of numbered productions Φ for the given grammar, this procedure outputs a parse for the given input string or reports failure, if the input string is invalid. The following are used in the procedure:

STACK—a stack which contains state numbers
NEXTCHAR—a function which returns the next character or symbol in the input string
CURRENT—the current input symbol
TOPV(STACK)—a function which returns the top state of the parse stack
PUSH—a procedure which pushes a state on the stack
POP—a procedure which pops the top state from the stack
LHS—vector which contains the left-hand side symbols of the productions
SIZE—vector which contains the number of symbols in the right-hand side of each production
T, J—local variables

1. [Initialize the stack to the initial or start state]
    Call PUSH(STACK, 0) (push the start state on the stack)

2. [Scan the first input symbol or token]
    CURRENT ← NEXTCHAR
3. [Construct the required parse, if possible]
    Repeat step 4 while true
4. [Perform indicated action]
        If F(TOPV(STACK), CURRENT) = 'S'
        then (perform a shift operation)
            T ← G(TOPV(STACK), CURRENT)
            Call PUSH(STACK, T) (push current state on stack)
            CURRENT ← NEXTCHAR (Scan next token)
        else If F(TOPV(STACK), CURRENT) = Reduce k
            then (a reduction using production k is indicated)
                Write (k) (Output the production in the reduction)
                Repeat J = 1, 2,...,SIZE(k)
                    Call POP(STACK)
                T ← G(TOPV(STACK), LHS(k))
                Call PUSH(STACK, T) (push state on stack)
            else If F(TOPV(STACK), CURRENT) = 'A'
                then write('VALID STRING')
                else write('INVALID STRING')
                Return   □

Table 7-35 Sample trace of *SLR*(1) parser for the string $i \uparrow (i - i) \#$

Step	Stack contents	Input string	Action	Output
0	0	$i \uparrow (i - i)\#$		
1	0 4	$\uparrow (i - i)\#$	S4	
2	0 3	$\uparrow (i - i)\#$	R6	6
3	0 3 11	$(i - i)\#$	S11	
4	0 3 11 5	$i - i)\#$	S5	
5	0 3 11 5 4	$-i)\#$	S4	
6	0 3 11 5 3	$-i)\#$	R6	6
7	0 3 11 5 2	$-i)\#$	R4	4
8	0 3 11 5 9	$-i)\#$	R2	2
9	0 3 11 5 9 7	$i)\#$	S7	
10	0 3 11 5 9 7 4	$)\#$	S4	
11	0 3 11 5 9 7 3	$)\#$	R6	6
12	0 3 11 5 9 7 8	$)\#$	R4	4
13	0 3 11 5 9	$)\#$	R1	1
14	0 3 11 5 9 10	$\#$	S10	
15	0 3 11 3	$\#$	R5	5
16	0 3 11 12	$\#$	R4	4
17	0 2	$\#$	R3	3
18	0 1	$\#$	R2	2
19	0 1 6	ε	S6	
20	0 1 6		A	

This algorithm is straightforward. The stack contains only states and not the vocabulary symbols of the grammar. Recall that it is not necessary to actually push these symbols onto the stack. When the action table entry contains a "shift," a state corresponding to a transition on the current input symbol is pushed on the stack. When a reduction occurs, the state symbols corresponding to the symbols of the handle are popped from the stack. The left part of the rule which applies and the new top state in the stack determine which state should be pushed on the stack. A trace of the parse for the string $i\uparrow(i-i)\#$ is given in Table 7-35. The terms "Sj" and "Ri" in the action column denote the pushing of state j onto the stack and an application of production i, respectively. The output column of the table gives the production number which applies in a particular step of the parsing process.

The generation of the action table (F) can lead to multiple entries indicating that the grammar is not $SLR(1)$. In such a case the simple method introduced in this section for generating a parser fails. Consider another example grammar that contains the productions

$$S \rightarrow G\#$$
$$G \rightarrow E = E | f$$
$$E \rightarrow T | E + T$$
$$T \rightarrow f | T * f$$

where the terminal symbol "f" denotes a factor in an arithmetic expression. The items sets for the $LR(0)$ machine appear in Table 7-36. A transition diagram for the $LR(0)$ machine is given in Figure 7-10.

Note that there are several inadequate states: states 2, 4, 9, and 10. Is this grammar $SLR(1)$? Consider state 2, which contains the following two completed items:

$$[G \rightarrow f.]$$
$$[T \rightarrow f.]$$

Using the FOLLOW set computations in an attempt to resolve the local ambiguity yields

$$\text{FOLLOW}(G) = \{\#\}$$
$$\text{FOLLOW}(T) = \{\#, +, =, *\}$$

Since these sets are not disjoint, the grammar is not $SLR(1)$.

Consider the transition that takes place in the machine if we apply production $G \rightarrow f$. With G, we have a transition to state 1 that yields a lookahead of $\#$. Now consider the transitions which take place when we apply production $T \rightarrow f$. On T a transition to state 4 occurs with a lookahead of $*$. At this point the production $E \rightarrow T$ applies and a subsequent transition on E brings us to state 3 with a lookahead of $+$ and $=$. Therefore, the lookahead sets for the offending productions are

$$G \rightarrow f \quad \{\#\}$$
$$T \rightarrow f \quad \{+, =, *\}$$

Table 7-36 Item sets for a grammar which is not $SLR(1)$

State	Basis set	Closure set
0	$[S \rightarrow .G\#]$	$[G \rightarrow .f]$
		$[G \rightarrow .E = E]$
		$[E \rightarrow .T]$
		$[E \rightarrow .E + T]$
		$[T \rightarrow .f]$
		$[T \rightarrow .T * f]$
1	$[S \rightarrow G.\#]$	
2	$[G \rightarrow f.]$	
	$[T \rightarrow f.]$	
3	$[G \rightarrow E. = E]$	
	$[E \rightarrow E. + T]$	
4	$[E \rightarrow T.]$	
	$[T \rightarrow T. * f]$	
5	$[S \rightarrow G\#.]$	
6	$[E \rightarrow E + .T]$	$[T \rightarrow .f]$
		$[T \rightarrow .T * f]$
7	$[T \rightarrow f.]$	
8	$[G \rightarrow E = .E]$	$[E \rightarrow .T]$
		$[E \rightarrow .E + T]$
		$[T \rightarrow .f]$
		$[T \rightarrow .T * f]$
9	$[E \rightarrow E. + T]$	
	$[G \rightarrow E = E.]$	
10	$[E \rightarrow E + T.]$	
	$[T \rightarrow T. * f]$	
11	$[T \rightarrow T * .f]$	
12	$[T \rightarrow T * f.]$	

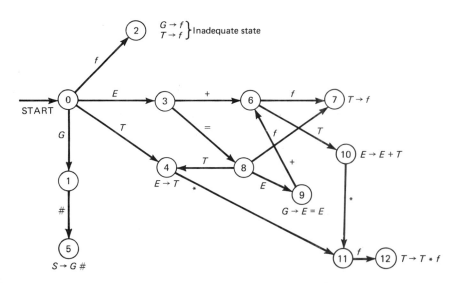

Figure 7-10 $LR(0)$ machine for a grammar that is not $SLR(1)$.

The inadequate state 2 is resolved with one symbol lookahead. The $SLR(1)$ method of resolving inadequate states depends on computing the FOLLOW sets independently of where we are in the transition diagram. If we follow the sequence of transitions, as was just done, some lookahead symbols that are obtained through the FOLLOW set computations do not in reality occur. The FOLLOW sets are then "larger" than the set of actual lookahead symbols. The next subsection introduces a method of generating parsers for grammars that can be parsed with one lookahead symbol but are not $SLR(1)$.

EXERCISES 7-4.3

1 Given a grammar with the following productions:

$$S \rightarrow E\#$$
$$E \rightarrow T | E + T$$
$$T \rightarrow P | T * P$$
$$P \rightarrow F | F \uparrow P$$
$$F \rightarrow i | (E)$$

(*a*) Construct the $LR(0)$ machine for this grammar.
(*b*) Show that the grammar is $SLR(1)$.
(*c*) Construct the $SLR(1)$ parsing table for this grammar.
(*d*) Give a trace of the parse for each of the following input strings:
(1) $i + i \uparrow (i * i) \#$
(2) $(i * i) \uparrow (i + i) \#$

2 Given the grammar with the following rules:

$$G \rightarrow I\#$$
$$I \rightarrow I \supset T | T$$
$$T \rightarrow T \vee F | F$$
$$F \rightarrow F \wedge S | S$$
$$S \rightarrow \neg P | P$$
$$P \rightarrow (E) | t | f$$

Repeat Exercise 1 for the following input strings:

$$\neg t \vee f \#$$
$$(t \supset f) \vee (f \wedge t) \#$$

3 For the grammar with the following productions:

$$S \rightarrow P\#$$
$$P \rightarrow C | B$$
$$B \rightarrow H; T$$
$$H \rightarrow bd | H; d$$
$$T \rightarrow se | s; T$$
$$C \rightarrow bT$$

(*a*) Show that the grammar is $SLR(1)$.
(*b*) Design an $SLR(1)$ parser.

4 Given the grammar with the following rules:

$$S \to E\#$$
$$E \to T \,|\, E \,;\, T$$
$$T \to \varepsilon \,|\, Ta$$

(*a*) Compute the FOLLOW sets of the nonterminals.
(*b*) Is the grammar $SLR(1)$? If so construct its $SLR(1)$ parser.

5 Show that the following grammar is not $SLR(1)$:

$$S \to E\#$$
$$E \to bEa \,|\, aEb \,|\, ba$$

6 Show that the following grammar is not $SLR(1)$:

$$S \to XYa\#$$
$$X \to a \,|\, Yb$$
$$Y \to \varepsilon \,|\, c$$

7-4.4 Canonical $LR(1)$ Parsers

The previous subsection gave an example of a grammar that was not $SLR(1)$. The method of resolving inadequate states in the $SLR(1)$ method is to obtain lookahead information through FOLLOW set computations. Recall that the sets of lookahead symbols obtained by the FOLLOW set computations yield supersets of the sets of lookahead that actually can occur. This subsection presents a general method for computing lookahead information that can be used to resolve inadequate states. This method, which is the most general parsing method for $LR(1)$ grammars, computes the lookahead information as part of generating the finite-state control for the parser. The lookahead information generated by this new method is appended to the items in the item sets generated earlier. Specifically, we expand an item to contain two components instead of one. The first component is identical to the item used in the previous subsection. The second component is a lookahead string of one terminal symbol. Based on lookahead information, it is possible to split a state into several states when necessary.

Definition 7-8 An $LR(1)$ *item* is a two-component element of the form

$$[A \to \alpha.\beta, u]$$

where the first component is a marked production, $A \to \alpha.\beta$, called the *core* of the item, and u is a lookahead character that belongs to the set $V_T \cup \{\varepsilon\}$. An $LR(1)$ item $[A \to \alpha.\beta, u]$ is said to be *valid* for viable prefix λ if there exists a rightmost derivation

$$S \overset{*}{\underset{R}{\Rightarrow}} \phi At \underset{R}{\Rightarrow} \phi \alpha \beta t$$

where $\lambda = \phi\alpha$ is the viable prefix and u is the first symbol of t, or ε if $t = \varepsilon$.

Consider the example grammar that contains the productions

0. $G \rightarrow S$ 4. $E \rightarrow E + T$
1. $S \rightarrow E = E$ 5. $T \rightarrow f$
2. $S \rightarrow f$ 6. $T \rightarrow T * f$
3. $E \rightarrow T$

with $V_T = \{ f, +, *, = \}$. The following is a rightmost derivation in the grammar

$$G \overset{*}{\underset{R}{\Rightarrow}} E = T + f \underset{R}{\Rightarrow} E = T * f + f$$

with item $[T \rightarrow T. * f, +]$ being valid for the viable prefix $E = T$. According to the previous definition, we have $A = T$, $\alpha = T$, $\beta = * f$, $t = +f$, and $u = +$. Another rightmost derivation is

$$G \overset{*}{\underset{R}{\Rightarrow}} E = T * f \underset{R}{\Rightarrow} E = T * f * f$$

with a valid item of $[T \rightarrow T. * f, *]$ for the viable prefix $E = T$. For notational convenience we reunite the items $[T \rightarrow T. * f, +]$ and $[T \rightarrow T. * f, *]$ as the composite item $[T \rightarrow T. * f, + : *]$. Note that the two original items have the same core (or first component). In general the items $[A \rightarrow \alpha.\beta, a_1]$, $[A \rightarrow \alpha.\beta, a_2]$, $\ldots, [A \rightarrow \alpha.\beta, a_m]$ can be rewritten as the item $[A \rightarrow \alpha.\beta, a_1 : a_2 : \ldots : a_m]$.

A finite-state control for an $LR(1)$ parser can be generated in a manner similar to that used for an $LR(0)$ parser. The main difference is that in an $LR(1)$ parser the lookahead symbols of the items must also be determined. The approach taken is to use successive read and closure (or completion) operations to generate the item sets associated with the states of the finite-state machine. The read operation is the same as that used in the generation of an $LR(0)$ machine. The closure operation for generating $LR(1)$ item sets, however, is more complex than its $LR(0)$ machine counterpart, since lookahead information must also be generated.

Let us take a closer look at the closure operation for generating $LR(1)$ items. For an $LR(1)$ item $[A \rightarrow \alpha. X\beta, u]$, where X denotes a nonterminal and $X \rightarrow \delta$ is a production, there exists a rightmost derivation

$$G \overset{*}{\underset{R}{\Rightarrow}} \phi Auw \underset{R}{\Rightarrow} \phi\alpha X\beta uw$$

The item $[X \rightarrow .\delta, v]$ is valid for the viable prefix $\phi\alpha$ with $v \in \text{FIRST}(\beta uw)$. Note that if $\beta \overset{*}{\Rightarrow} \varepsilon$, then $v = u$; otherwise, $v \in \text{FIRST}(\beta)$. Consider the closure of item $[E \rightarrow .T, =]$ in the example grammar. Since $T \rightarrow f$, the item $[T \rightarrow .f, =]$ also belongs to the item set. Note that in this case $\beta = \varepsilon$. Similarly, $[T \rightarrow .T * f, =]$ is a member of the item set. The completion of the item $[T \rightarrow .T * f, =]$ yields two new items—$[T \rightarrow .f, *]$ and $[T \rightarrow .T * f, *]$. Observe that in these last two cases $\beta = * f$ and, therefore, the lookahead symbol is $*$.

The generation of the $LR(1)$ item sets is realized by the following algorithm.

Algorithm LR(1)_ITEM_CONSTRUCTION. Given a grammar $G = (V_T, V_N, S, \Phi)$, this algorithm constructs the sets of $LR(1)$ items for that grammar.

1. [Generate the set of items for the start state]
   - (a) (generate the basis set for the start state)
     - If $S \rightarrow \alpha \in \Phi$
     - then add $[S \rightarrow .\alpha, \varepsilon]$ to the initial state set
   - (b) (perform the closure of the basis item(s) obtained in part a)
     - Repeat until no more items can be added to the initial state
       - If $[A \rightarrow .X\alpha, u]$ is in the initial state and $X \rightarrow \lambda \in \Phi$
       - then add all the items, if they are not already there,
         - of the form $[X \rightarrow .\lambda, v]$ to the initial state
         - where $v \in$ FIRST(αu).
2. [Generate the remaining item sets of the grammar]
   - Repeat through step 4 until no additional new states can be created or completed
3. [Start a new state by performing a read operation]
   - For each item $[A \rightarrow \alpha.X\beta, c]$ in some state U
     - Include the item $[A \rightarrow \alpha X.\beta, c]$ in some new state
       - V (i.e., we perform a transition from state U to state V on symbol X)
     - If the basis set of items in this new state already exists in the form of some other state V
     - then merge these two states
4. [Generate the closure of the new state]
   - Repeat until no more items can be added to state V
     - For each item of the form $[A \rightarrow \alpha.X\beta, c]$ in state V and every production $X \rightarrow \lambda \in \Phi$
       - Add all the items of the form $[X \rightarrow .\lambda, d]$ to state V where $d \in$ FIRST(βc)
5. [Finished]
   - Exit   □

Using the previous example grammar as input, we now use this algorithm to generate the $LR(1)$ sets of items. Initially, we associate the basis item $[G \rightarrow .S, \varepsilon]$ with state 0. On performing the completion operation on this item, we obtain the two items $[S \rightarrow .E = E, \varepsilon]$ and $[S \rightarrow .f, \varepsilon]$. Using the notation in step 1b of the algorithm on the first of these items, we have $A = G$, $X = S$, $\alpha = \varepsilon$, $u = \varepsilon$, $\lambda = E = E$, and $v =$ FIRST$(\varepsilon) = \varepsilon$. Applying the completion operation to the item $[S \rightarrow .f, \varepsilon]$ yields no new items, since f is a terminal. The completion of item $[S \rightarrow .E = E, \varepsilon]$, however, yields several new items. Since $E \rightarrow T$ and $E \rightarrow E + T$ are productions of the grammar and the mark immediately precedes the non-terminal E, the items $[E \rightarrow .T, =]$ and $[E \rightarrow .E + T, =]$ are valid. According to the notation used in the algorithm, $A = S$, $X = E$, $\alpha = = E$, $u = \varepsilon$, $\lambda = T$, and

$v = $ FIRST($= E$) for the first item. FIRST($= E$) yields a lookahead character of $=$.

The closure of item $[E \to .T, =]$ generates items $[T \to .f, =]$ and $[T \to .T * f, =]$ because $T \to f$ and $T \to T * f$ are productions of the grammar. The second of these items, $[T \to .T * f, =]$, further generates the new items $[T \to .f, *]$ and $[T \to .T * f, *]$. At this point no new items are possible. The item $[E \to .E + T, =]$ generates several new items, some of which have previously been encountered. The closure operation on the initial item $[G \to S, \varepsilon]$ is shown in Fig. 7-11.

The initial set of $LR(1)$ items (C_0) resulting from the first step of the algorithm is

state 0: $*[G \to .S, \varepsilon]$
$[S \to .E = E, \varepsilon]$
$[S \to .f, \varepsilon]$
$[E \to .T, = : +]$
$[T \to .f, = : + : *]$
$[T \to .T * f, = : + : *]$
$[E \to .E + T, = : +]$

where the item marked by $*$ denotes a basis item.

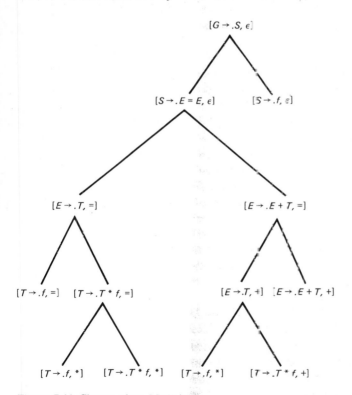

Figure 7-11 Closure of an $LR(1)$ item.

Steps 3 and 4 of the algorithm can now be used to generate new states (and associated item sets). Four possible transitions are possible from state 0. The first transition is to state 1 on the symbol E. Two items in state 0 are associated with this transition: $[S \rightarrow .E = E, \varepsilon]$ and $[E \rightarrow .E + T, = : +]$. The basis items of state 1 are $[S \rightarrow E. = E, \varepsilon]$ and $[E \rightarrow E. + T, = : +]$. The completion of these basis items yields no new items. The second transition from state 0 is to state 2 on symbol T. The items $[E \rightarrow .T, = : +]$ and $[T \rightarrow .T * f, = : + : *]$ from state 0 are involved in this transition. Therefore, the basis items for state 2 are $[E \rightarrow T., = : +]$ and $[T \rightarrow T. * f, = : + : *]$. Again the closures of these items are empty. The third transition is from state 0 to state 3 on the symbol f. The two items $[S \rightarrow .f, \varepsilon]$ and $[T \rightarrow .f, = : + : *]$ from state 0 yield the basis items $[S \rightarrow f., \varepsilon]$ and $[T \rightarrow f., = : + : *]$ for state 3. Since these are completed items, no new items occur because of closure. Observe that this state is inadequate, but resolvable. If the current input symbol is ε, the production $S \rightarrow f$ applies. On the other hand, if the input symbol is $=$, $+$, or $*$, then the rule $T \rightarrow f$ applies. Recall that the SLR method failed to resolve this inadequate state. The fourth and last transition is from state 0 to state 17 on the symbol S. The item $[G \rightarrow S., \varepsilon]$ is the only item associated with state 17. When we reach this state, the parser will halt and accept the input string.

New states can be started from states 1 and 2. There are two possible transitions from state 1: to state 4 on $=$ and to state 5 on $+$. Similarly, there is one transition from state 2 to state 11 on $*$. By executing steps 3 and 4 repeatedly, the set of states for the finite control of the $LR(1)$ parser will converge. The states of the control with their associated $LR(1)$ item sets are shown in Table 7-37. Observe that some states have the same first component (core) as other states but different lookahead sets. States 8 and 9 are such a pair of states. In an $LR(0)$ machine without lookahead these two states would have been merged into one state. We return to this point in the next subsection. The finite-state diagram of the control for the $LR(1)$ parser is given in Fig. 7-12.

The following algorithm generates a parser for the collection of $LR(1)$ item sets.

Algorithm LR(1)_CONSTRUCTOR. Given the $LR(1)$ sets of items for a grammar G of the form

$$C = \{C_0, C_1, ..., C_m\}$$

where C_0 is the *initial* or *start* set and states of the parser

$$\{0, 1, ..., m\}$$

where each state j is constructed from the item set C_j, this algorithm computes the F and G functions for the parser as follows:

1. [Construct the required functions for the parser]
   Repeat through step 3 for each state i in the state set

Table 7-37 $LR(1)$ item sets for an example grammar

State	$LR(1)$ item	Next state or reduce
0	$*[G \to .S, \varepsilon]$	17
	$[S \to .E = E, \varepsilon]$	1
	$[S \to .f, \varepsilon]$	3
	$[E \to .T, = :+]$	2
	$[T \to .f, = :+:*]$	3
	$[T \to .T*f, = :+:*]$	2
	$[E \to .E + T, = :+]$	1
1	$*[S \to E. = E, \varepsilon]$	4
	$*[E \to E.+ T, = :+]$	5
2	$*[E \to T., = :+]$	Reduce 3
	$*[T \to T.*f, = :+:*]$	11
3	$*[S \to f., \varepsilon]$	Reduce 2
	$*[T \to f., = :+:*]$	Reduce 5
4	$*[S \to E = .E, \varepsilon]$	6
	$[E \to .T, \varepsilon: +]$	7
	$[T \to .f, \varepsilon: +:*]$	8
	$[T \to .T*f, \varepsilon: +:*]$	7
	$[E \to .E + T, \varepsilon: +]$	6
5	$*[E \to E + .T, = :+]$	10
	$[T \to .f, = :+:*]$	9
	$[T \to .T*f, = :+:*]$	10
6	$*[S \to E = E., \varepsilon]$	Reduce 1
	$*[E \to E.+ T, \varepsilon: +]$	13
7	$*[E \to T., \varepsilon: +]$	Reduce 3
	$*[T \to T.*f, \varepsilon: +:*]$	15
8	$*[T \to f., \varepsilon: +:*]$	Reduce 5
9	$*[T \to f., = :+:*]$	Reduce 5
10	$*[E \to E + T., = :+]$	Reduce 4
	$*[T \to T.*f, = :+:*]$	11
11	$*[T \to T*.f, = :+:*]$	12
12	$*[T \to T*f., = :+:*]$	Reduce 6
13	$*[E \to E + .T, \varepsilon: +]$	14
	$[T \to .f, \varepsilon: +:*]$	3
	$[T \to .T*f, \varepsilon: +:*]$	14
14	$*[E \to E + T., \varepsilon: +]$	Reduce 4
	$*[T \to T.*f, \varepsilon: +:*]$	15
15	$*[T \to T*.f, \varepsilon: +:*]$	16
16	$*[T \to T*f., \varepsilon: +:*]$	Reduce 6
17	$*[G \to S., \varepsilon]$	Accept

2. [Compute the F(action) entries]
   (a) If item $[A \to \alpha.u\beta, v] \in C_i$ where $u \in V_T \cup \{\varepsilon\}$ and there is a transition from state i to state j on u then F(i, u) ← Shift
   (b) If item $[A \to \alpha., u] \in C_i$ where $A \to \alpha$ is the jth production then F(i, u) ← Reduce j
   (c) If item $[G \to \alpha., \varepsilon] \in C_i$ then F(i, ε) ← Accept
   (d) All undefined entries are error entries (i.e., blank)

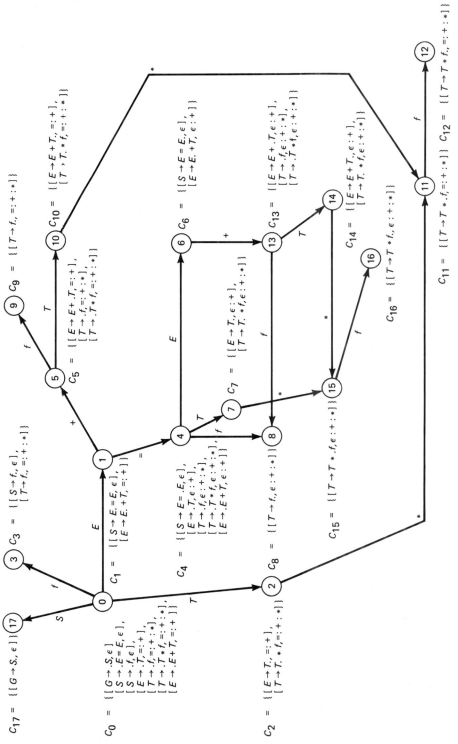

Figure 7-12 Finite control for an *LR*(1) parser.

Table 7-38 Parsing functions for an $LR(1)$ parser

State	Action function, F					Next state or goto function, G						
	f	$=$	$+$	$*$	ε	S	E	T	f	$=$	$+$	$*$
0	S					17	1	2	3			
1		S	S							4	5	
2		$R3$	$R3$	S								11
3		$R5$	$R5$	$R5$	$R2$							
4	S						6	7	8			
5	S							10	9			
6			S		$R1$						13	
7			$R3$	S	$R3$							15
8			$R5$	$R5$	$R5$							
9		$R5$	$R5$	$R5$								
10		$R4$	$R4$	S								11
11	S								12			
12		$R6$	$R6$	$R6$								
13	S							14	8			
14			$R4$	S	$R4$							15
15	S								16			
16			$R6$	$R6$	$R6$							
17					A							

3. [Compute the G entries]
   (a) If there is a transition from state i to state j on symbol A
        then G(i, A) ← j
   (b) All undefined entries are error
   (c) The start state of the parser is state 0   □

The parsing functions generated by this algorithm can be used by a parser similar to the one discussed in the previous subsection for *SLR* grammars. The parser for $LR(1)$ grammars is often called a canonical $LR(1)$ parser. If the F function is multiple-valued, i.e., there is more than one action that can apply at a particular point in the parsing process, then the grammar is not $LR(1)$. For the example grammar, the F and G functions appear in Table 7-38. The trace of a parse for the input string $f = f * f + f$ is given in Table 7-39.

Observe that the finite-state control of an $LR(1)$ parser contains many more states than that of a corresponding $LR(0)$ parser. It is frequently possible to reduce the number of states in the former by merging certain states. The next subsection examines this possibility.

EXERCISES 7-4.4

1 Given a grammar with the following productions:

$S \to E$ $T \to F \mid T * F$
$E \to T \mid E - T$ $F \to i \mid (E)$

Table 7-39 Sample trace of $LR(1)$ parser for the string $f = f * f + f$

Step	Stack contents	Input string	Action	Output
0	0	$f = f * f + f$		
1	0 3	$= f * f + f$	S3	
2	0 2	$= f * f + f$	R5	5
3	0 1	$= f * f + f$	R3	3
4	0 1 4	$f * f + f$	S4	
5	0 1 4 8	$* f + f$	S8	
6	0 1 4 7	$* f + f$	R5	5
7	0 1 4 7 15	$f + f$	S15	
8	0 1 4 7 15 16	$+ f$	S16	
9	0 1 4 7	$+ f$	R6	6
10	0 1 4 6	$+ f$	R3	3
11	0 1 4 6 13	f	S13	
12	0 1 4 6 13 8	ε	S8	
13	0 1 4 6 13 14	ε	R5	5
14	0 1 4 6	ε	R4	4
15	0 17	ε	R1	1
16	0 17	ε	Accept	

(a) Generate the sets of $LR(1)$ items.
(b) Obtain the parsing functions (tables) for this grammar.
(c) Give a trace as in Table 7-39 of the parse for each of the following input strings:
   (1) $(i - i) * i$
   (2) $i - i * i$

2 Given a grammar with the following rules:

0. $S \to A\#$	3. $B \to cCe$
1. $A \to bB$	4. $C \to dA$
2. $B \to cC$	5. $A \to a$

(a) Generate the sets of $LR(1)$ items.
(b) Is the grammar $SLR(1)$?
(c) Is the grammar $LR(1)$? If not, why not?

7-4.5 $LALR(1)$ Parsers

In this subsection we present a parsing technique known as $LALR(1)$ parsing. This method of parsing is similar to but more powerful than the $SLR(1)$ method because it uses lookahead information which can be obtained, for example, from the $LR(1)$ construction process given in the previous subsection. Although an $LALR(1)$ parser is not as powerful as an $LR(1)$ parser, the former offers the important advantage of requiring much less space for its parsing tables than the latter. The $LALR(1)$ parsing tables can be obtained directly from the sets of $LR(1)$ items obtained previously.

Table 7-40 *LALR*(1) item sets for an example grammar

State	LALR(1) item	Next state or reduce
[0]	$*[G \to .S, \varepsilon]$	[11]
	$[S \to .E = E, \varepsilon]$	[1]
	$[S \to .f, \varepsilon]$	[3]
	$[E \to .T, = :+]$	[2]
	$[T \to .f, = :+:*]$	[3]
	$[T \to .T * f, = :+:*]$	[2]
	$[E \to .E + T, = :+]$	[1]
[1]	$*[S \to E. = E, \varepsilon]$	[4]
	$*[E \to E. + T, = :+]$	[5]
[2]	$*[E \to T., \varepsilon: = :+]$	Reduce 3
	$[T \to T. * f, \varepsilon: = :+:*]$	[9]
[3]	$*[S \to f., \varepsilon]$	Reduce 2
	$*[T \to f., = :+:*]$	Reduce 5
[4]	$*[S \to E = .E, \varepsilon]$	[6]
	$[E \to .T, \varepsilon: +]$	[2]
	$[T \to .f, \varepsilon: +:*]$	[7]
	$[T \to .T * f, \varepsilon: +:*]$	[2]
	$[E \to .E + T, \varepsilon: +]$	[6]
[5]	$*[E \to E + .T, \varepsilon: = :+]$	[8]
	$[T \to .f, \varepsilon: = :+:*]$	[7]
	$[T \to .T * f, \varepsilon: = :+:*]$	[8]
[6]	$*[S \to E = E., \varepsilon]$	Reduce 1
	$*[E \to E. + T, \varepsilon: +]$	[5]
[7]	$*[T \to f., \varepsilon: = :+:*]$	Reduce 5
[8]	$*[E \to E + T., \varepsilon: = :+]$	Reduce 4
	$*[T \to T. * f, \varepsilon: = :+:*]$	[9]
[9]	$*[T \to T *. f, \varepsilon: = :+:*]$	[10]
[10]	$*[T \to T * f., \varepsilon: = :+:*]$	Reduce 6
[11]	$*[G \to S., \varepsilon]$	Accept

Consider the $LR(1)$ sets of items given in Table 7-37. The item sets associated with, say, states 8 and 9 are very similar. In fact, the first components (or cores) of these two items are identical. The only difference is in their second components, that is, the lookahead sets. The sets of $LR(1)$ items for states 8 and 9 can be merged into one set yielding the item

$$[T \to f., \varepsilon: = :+:*]$$

where the lookahead symbols of both item sets have been combined into one set of symbols. Similarly, states 5 and 13 can be merged into one state. For convenience, we present C_5 and C_{13} again as follows:

$$C_5 = \{[E \to E + .T, = :+],$$
$$[T \to .f, = :+:*],$$
$$[T \to .T * f, = :+:*]\}$$
$$C_{13} = \{[E \to E + .T, \varepsilon: +],$$
$$[T \to .f, \varepsilon: +:*],$$
$$[T \to .T * f, \varepsilon: +:*]\}$$

Note that the cores of the corresponding items in the two sets are the same. Therefore, the two sets can be combined into the following set:

$$\{[E \rightarrow E + .T, \varepsilon: = :+],$$
$$[T \rightarrow .f, \varepsilon: = :+:*],$$
$$[T \rightarrow .T * f, \varepsilon: = :+:*]\}$$

Continuing this process, each pair of sets of items for states 2 and 7, 12 and 16, 10 and 14, and 11 and 15, can also be merged into one state. The resulting finite-state control is the same (in their first component) as that obtained by the $LR(0)$ construction process. The only difference is that the items derived from the $LR(1)$ sets of items have a second lookahead component.

An $LALR(1)$ parser obtained by the previous merging process behaves in a manner very similar to that of its $LR(1)$ counterpart. In some instances, however, an $LALR(1)$ parser may perform a *reduce* action instead of signaling an error that would be detected by the corresponding $LR(1)$ parser. Such an error will eventually be detected by the $LALR(1)$ parser before any further input symbols are shifted onto the parse stack. More will be said about this point shortly.

Using the example grammar of the previous subsection, we will now construct its $LALR(1)$ parsing tables from the $LR(1)$ sets of items. The item sets in the $LALR(1)$ machine are derived by the merging of the $LR(1)$ sets of items as follows:

$$0 \rightarrow [0]$$
$$1 \rightarrow [1]$$
$$2, 7 \rightarrow [2]$$
$$3 \rightarrow [3]$$
$$4 \rightarrow [4]$$
$$5, 13 \rightarrow [5]$$
$$6 \rightarrow [6]$$
$$8, 9 \rightarrow [7]$$
$$10, 14 \rightarrow [8]$$
$$11, 15 \rightarrow [9]$$
$$12, 16 \rightarrow [10]$$
$$17 \rightarrow [11]$$

where the symbol $[i]$ denotes state i in the $LALR(1)$ machine. The collections of items for the finite control of the $LALR(1)$ parser appear in Table 7-40.

Consider some of the next-state transition entries in this table. In particular, let us examine state [2], which was obtained by merging states 2 and 7 in the original $LR(1)$ machine. In that machine there is a transition from state 0 to state 2 on the symbol T; also, there is a transition from state 4 to state 7 on the symbol T. These two transitions in the $LALR(1)$ machine will be denoted as follows:

from state [0] to state [2] on T
from state [4] to state [2] on T

Similarly, there are transitions from state 2 to state 11 and from state 7 to state 15 on the symbol $*$ in the original machine. Since states 11 and 15 in the $LR(1)$ item

sets have been merged into state [9] in the $LALR(1)$ machine, the two aforementioned transitions can be merged into one transition from state [2] to state [9] on
the symbol * in the $LALR(1)$ machine. As another example, consider the states 8
and 9 in the $LR(1)$ machine which have been merged into the state [7] in the
$LALR(1)$ machine. In the original machine there are transitions on the symbol f
from state 5 to state 9, state 4 to state 8 and state 13 to state 8. Since original
states 5 and 13 have been merged into state [5], there are transitions from state [5]
to state [7] and from state [4] to state [7] on the symbol f in the $LALR(1)$
machine. It is apparent from this discussion that the next-state transitions depend
only on the core of an item set and, consequently, the next-state transitions of
merged sets can also be merged. The remaining next-state entries of Table 7-40
can be obtained in a similar fashion.

The parsing functions for the $LALR(1)$ parser are derived by using Table
7-40 as input to Algorithm LR(1)_CONSTRUCTOR of the previous subsection.
The application of this algorithm to the current item table yields the parsing
functions given in Table 7-41. Since these functions are not multiple-valued, the
given grammar is $LALR(1)$. It is instructive for the reader to compare Tables 7-38
and 7-41 at this point and note their similarities.

The previous approach to obtaining parsing functions for an $LALR(1)$
grammar is summarized in the following high-level algorithm.

1. Obtain the sets of LR(1) items

$$C = \{C_0, C_1, \ldots, C_m\}$$

2. Merge all the sets of LR(1) items that have the same core. Let this new
   collection of items be denoted by

$$M = \{M_0, M_1, \ldots, M_n\}$$

   where $n \le m$.

Table 7-41 Parsing functions for an $LALR(1)$ grammar

State	Action function, F					Next state or goto function, G						
	f	$=$	$+$	$*$	ε	S	E	T	f	$=$	$+$	$*$
[0]	S					[11]	[1]	[2]	[3]			
[1]		S	S							[4]	[5]	
[2]		$R3$	$R3$	S	$R3$							[9]
[3]		$R5$	$R5$	$R5$	$R2$							
[4]	S						[6]	[2]	[7]			
[5]	S							[8]	[7]			
[6]			S		$R1$						[5]	
[7]		$R5$	$R5$	$R5$	$R5$							
[8]		$R4$	$R4$	S	$R4$							[9]
[9]	S								[10]			
[10]		$R5$	$R6$	$R6$	$R6$							
[11]					A							

3. The next-state transition table for the merged machine is obtained in the following manner: Let M_p be the new item set obtained from the merging of the original LR(1) item sets, say,

$$M_p = C_{j_1} \cup C_{j_2} \cup \cdots \cup C_{j_k}$$

where $1 \le j_1 \le m, 1 \le j_2 \le m, \ldots, 1 \le j_k \le m$. Recall that each item set $C_{j_c}, 1 \le c \le k$ has the same core. The next-state transition entry from item set M_p to some other item set M_q on a symbol X can be obtained from the next-state transition entries of the LR(1) machine.

4. The item sets and next-state transition information of the merged machine is used as input to Algorithm LR(1)_CONSTRUCTOR to derive the parsing functions F and G. If these functions are single-valued, the grammar is LALR(1); otherwise it is not.   □

Given an $LR(1)$ grammar with its associated collection of $LR(1)$ item sets, let us examine under what circumstances the previously described merging process can yield multiple-valued entries in the parsing tables, that is, an $LR(1)$ grammar is not $LALR(1)$. Parsing conflicts (or local ambiguities) can be of either the shift-reduce or the reduce-reduce varieties. A shift-reduce conflict depends solely on the core of an $LR(1)$ item and not on its lookahead part. Consequently, shift-reduce conflicts cannot arise in an $LALR(1)$ parser that is derived from the collection of $LR(1)$ items of an $LR(1)$ grammar. Reduce-reduce conflicts, however, can arise in the state-merging process which is followed in attempting to

Table 7-42 Error detection in an (a) $LR(1)$ parser and (b) $LALR(1)$ parser

(a) $LR(1)$ parser

Step	Stack contents	Input string	Action	Output
0	0	$f + f$		
1	0 3	$+ f$	$S3$	
2	0 2	$+ f$	$R5$	5
3	0 1	$+ f$	$R3$	3
4	0 1 5	f	$S5$	
5	0 1 5 9	ε	$S9$	
6	error			

(b) $LALR(1)$ parser

0	[0]	$f + f$		
1	[0] [3]	$+ f$	$S[3]$	
2	[0] [2]	$+ f$	$R5$	5
3	[0] [1]	$+ f$	$R3$	3
4	[0] [1] [5]	f	$S[5]$	
5	[0] [1] [5] [7]	ε	$S[7]$	
6	[0] [1] [5] [8]	ε	$R5$	5
7	[0] [1]	ε	$R4$	4
8	error			

obtain an $LALR(1)$ parser. An example of such a phenomenon is left to the exercises.

Earlier in this subsection, mention was made that an $LALR(1)$ parser may not detect an input error as quickly as its corresponding $LR(1)$ parser. Table 7-42 contains two traces in an attempt to parse the invalid string $f + f$. The first trace given is that of of an $LR(1)$ parser (with the parsing tables of Table 7-38). Observe that two reductions occur before an error is detected in the input string. The second trace represents an attempt by the $LALR(1)$ parser to parse the given input string. Note that four reductions are performed here. The last two reductions ($T \rightarrow f$ and $E \rightarrow E + T$) were not generated by the $LR(1)$ parser. In general, $LALR(1)$ parsers may perform more reductions than $LR(1)$ parsers before detecting errors.

The approach used in this subsection for generating an $LALR(1)$ parser from the collection of $LR(1)$ items has one major drawback. It requires the initial storage of a large collection of items. Another approach is to start with the $LR(0)$ collection of items and generate the necessary lookahead information required by the $LALR(1)$ parser. The next subsection examines this approach.

EXERCISES 7-4.5

1 Given the grammar with the following rules:

$\langle$block$\rangle ::=$ **begin**$\langle$decs$\rangle$; $\langle$stmts$\rangle$**end** ;
$\langle$decs$\rangle ::= d | \langle$decs$\rangle$; d
$\langle$stmts$\rangle ::= s | \langle$stmts$\rangle$; s

generate:
(*a*) The $LR(1)$ collection of items
(*b*) The $LALR(1)$ parsing tables
(*c*) If the grammar is $LALR(1)$ then give a parse for the input string

begin d; d; s; s; s **end**

2 Prove that shift-reduce conflicts cannot occur in an $LALR(1)$ parser that is derived from the collection of $LR(1)$ items of an $LR(1)$ grammar.

3 Given the grammar whose rules are:

$S \rightarrow wAz | xBz | wBy | xAy$
$A \rightarrow \gamma$
$B \rightarrow \gamma$

construct:
(*a*) The $LR(1)$ sets of items
(*b*) Obtain the $LALR(1)$ parser from the results of *a*
(*c*) What conflicts, if any, arise in *b*

7-4.6 Efficient Generation of Lookahead Sets for $LALR(1)$ Parsers

This subsection formulates an algorithm for generating lookahead information for $LALR(1)$ parsers. The lookahead sets are to be derived directly from the $LR(0)$ machine associated with a given grammar.

Recall from Sec. 7-4.3 that inadequate states in $SLR(1)$ grammars can be resolved with information succeeding each inadequate state, that is, right context which is derived from FOLLOW set computations. The resolution of inadequate states in $LALR(1)$ parsers, however, requires in general information both preceding and following each inadequate state, that is, both left and right context.

There have been several efforts to generate the lookahead sets for an $LR(1)$ parser from the $LR(0)$ machine of its associated grammar. Some of these efforts, however, have not generated the lookahead information for the set of $LALR(1)$ grammars. For example, Lalonde (1971) and Barrett and Couch (1979) give algorithms for the generation of lookahead information for the set of $SLALR(1)$. This set of grammars is a superset of the class of $SLR(1)$ grammars but a proper subset of the $LALR(1)$ grammars. Anderson et al. (1973) have also formulated an algorithm for generating lookahead sets.

Aho and Ullman (1977) give an algorithm for generating the required lookahead information for an $LALR(1)$ grammar from its $LR(0)$ machine. Their algorithm is essentially the one used in the compiler-compiler system YACC (Johnson, 1974).

The method that we outline in this subsection is due to DeRemer and Pennello (1979, 1982). Their method appears to be the most efficient way of generating $LALR(1)$ lookahead information.

Each inadequate state in the $LR(0)$ machine associated with a given grammar requires lookahead information for its resolution. Recall that there is at least one shift-reduce or reduce-reduce conflict in an inadequate state. The lookahead set for an inadequate state q, where a reduction involving the application of a rule $A \rightarrow \alpha$ may apply, is defined as

$$LA(q, A \rightarrow \alpha) = \left\{ a \in V_T | S \underset{R}{\overset{+}{\Rightarrow}} \delta A a w \text{ and } \delta\alpha \text{ accesses } q \right\}$$

where "$\delta\alpha$ accesses q" means that starting from the start state of the machine the scanning of the string $\delta\alpha$ will result in a sequence of state transitions, the last of which is state q. The approach to computing the lookahead sets is to express them in terms of intermediate relations.

This subsection first introduces notation which facilitates the formulation of an efficient algorithm for computing lookahead sets. We then formulate several relations which give the underlying structure of the lookahead sets. Finally, an algorithm for computing lookahead sets is given. The details of the method are given in DeRemer and Pennello (1982).

A transition from state p to state q on symbol X, denoted by (p, X), is shown as $p \overset{X}{\rightarrow} q$, where $G(p, X) = q$, or by $p \overset{X}{\rightarrow}$ if q is not important.

Given an $LR(0)$ machine, we define

$$\text{Reduce}(q, a) = \left\{ A \rightarrow \alpha | [A \rightarrow \alpha.] \in C_q \right\}$$

where C_q is the set of items associated with state q and $a \in V_T$. Recall state q in an $LR(0)$ parser is inadequate if and only if there exists an $a \in V_T$ such that

$G(q, a)$ is defined and Reduce $(q, a) \neq \phi$ (a shift reduce conflict) or Reduce (q, a) contains more than one rule (a reduce-reduce conflict), or both.

In an $LALR(1)$ parser the previous definition can be reformulated as

$$\text{Reduce } (q, a) = \{ A \rightarrow \alpha | a \in LA(q, A \rightarrow \alpha) \}$$

In order to compute the lookahead sets, it is useful to concentrate on nonterminal transitions and define their FOLLOW sets.

$$\text{FOLLOW}(p, A) = \{ a \in V_T | S \overset{+}{\underset{R}{\Rightarrow}} \delta A a w \text{ and } \delta \text{ accesses state } p \}$$

Intuitively, a FOLLOW set specifies the terminals that can immediately follow the nonterminal A in a sentential form where prefix δ accesses state p. It turns out that a lookahead set is the union of associated FOLLOW sets. It can be shown that

$$LA(q, A \rightarrow \alpha) = \bigcup \{ \text{FOLLOW}(p, A) | (p, A) \text{ is a nonterminal transition}$$
$$\text{and } p - \cdot \overset{\alpha}{\cdots} \rightarrow q \}$$

where $p - \cdot \overset{\alpha}{\cdots} \rightarrow q$ denotes a sequence of single transitions $p \rightarrow r_0 \rightarrow \cdots \rightarrow r_n \rightarrow q$. In words, the lookahead set for the rule $A \rightarrow \alpha$ in state q is the set union of the FOLLOW sets for the transitions on A from some state p, which on "reading" α, will terminate in state q. Alternatively, when the rule $A \rightarrow \alpha$ is applied in state q and $|\alpha|$ states are popped off the parse stack, a state p appears on top of the stack which reads A with a lookahead symbol of a. Figure 7-13 exhibits this situation. When in state q with the next input symbol a that belongs to any of the follow sets FOLLOW(p_i, A) for $1 \leq i \leq m$, the parser will apply rule $A \rightarrow \alpha$. States p_1 through p_m serve to remember left context. The following relation is useful in capturing the nonterminal transitions (p_i, A):

$$(q, A \rightarrow \alpha)\text{LOOKBACK}(p, A) \text{ if and only if } p - \cdot \overset{\alpha}{\cdots} \rightarrow q$$

Therefore,

$$LA(q, A \rightarrow \alpha) = \bigcup \{ \text{FOLLOW}(p, A) | (q, A \rightarrow \alpha)\text{LOOKBACK}(p, A) \}$$

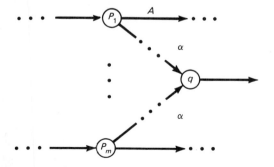

Figure 7-13 Look-ahead set in terms of FOLLOW sets.

Throughout the discussion, we will exhibit various relations for the grammar whose rules are:

$$S \rightarrow G\#$$
$$G \rightarrow E = E | f$$
$$E \rightarrow T | E + T$$
$$T \rightarrow f | T * f$$

The $LR(0)$ machine for this grammar was given in Fig. 7-10. The set of nonterminal transitions for this machine is

$$\{(0, E), (0, G), (0, T), (6, T), (8, T), (8, E)\}$$

The relation LOOKBACK consists of the following ordered pairs:

$$\{((2, G \rightarrow f), (0, G)), ((2, T \rightarrow f), (0, T)),$$
$$((4, E \rightarrow T), (0, E)), ((4, E \rightarrow T), (8, E))$$
$$((7, T \rightarrow f), (6, T)), ((7, T \rightarrow f), (8, T)),$$
$$((9, G \rightarrow E = E), (0, G)),$$
$$((10, E \rightarrow E + T), (0, E)), ((10, E \rightarrow E + T), (8, E)),$$
$$((12, T \rightarrow T * f), (0, T)), ((12, T \rightarrow T * f), (6, T))\}$$

The FOLLOW sets are interrelated. More specifically, it can be shown that

$$\text{FOLLOW}(p', B) \subseteq \text{FOLLOW}(p, A) \text{ if}$$
$$B \rightarrow \lambda A\theta, \theta \overset{*}{\underset{R}{\Rightarrow}} \varepsilon \text{ and } p' - \cdot^{\lambda} \cdot \rightarrow p$$

Pictorially, the situation is depicted in Fig. 7-14. For a given string δ which accesses state p', the string $\delta\lambda$ accesses state p. Furthermore, in a proper right context, $\delta\lambda A$ is first reduced to $\delta\lambda A\theta$ since $\theta \overset{*}{\underset{R}{\Rightarrow}} \varepsilon$ and then to δB. The inclusion relation states that those symbols that can follow B in state p' can also follow A

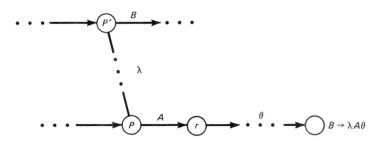

Figure 7-14 Interrelationships among FOLLOW sets.

in state p. This inclusion can be more easily specified by defining a new relation on nonterminal transitions.

(p, A) INCLUDES (p', B) if and only if

$$B \rightarrow \lambda A \theta, \; \theta \overset{*}{\underset{R}{\Rightarrow}} \varepsilon \text{ and } p'— \cdot \overset{\lambda}{\cdot} \; \rightarrow p$$

Therefore, FOLLOW$(p', B) \subseteq$ FOLLOW(p, A) if (p, A) INCLUDES (p', B). Note that λ in the current discussion can be the empty string.

Returning to our example, the INCLUDES relation is the following set of ordered pairs:

$$\{((8, E), (0, G)), ((6, T), (0, E)), ((6, T), (8, E)) ((0, T), (0, E)), ((8, T), (8, E))\}$$

The first ordered pair is due to the rule $G \rightarrow E = E$. The rule $E \rightarrow E + T$ accounts for the generation of the next two ordered pairs. The production $E \rightarrow T$ is responsible for the last two ordered pairs (λ is empty in this case).

We next define Read(p, A) to be the set of terminal symbols that can be read before phrases that contain A can be reduced. The following diagram illustrates this situation:

$$p \overset{A}{\rightarrow} q_0— \; \cdot \overset{\theta}{\cdot} \cdot \; \rightarrow q_m \overset{a}{\rightarrow}$$

Observe that because of nullable nonterminals there can be several reductions before the next input symbol is read. If there are no empty productions, the case becomes

$$p \overset{A}{\rightarrow} q_0 \overset{a}{\rightarrow}$$

and Read(p, A) are the symbols that can be directly read. The following theorem specifies how the FOLLOW sets are computed:

$$\text{FOLLOW}(p, A) = \text{Read}(p, A) \cup \cup \{\text{FOLLOW}(p', B)|(p, A) \text{ INCLUDES } (p', B)\}$$

The set Read(p, A) is computed in the following manner:

$$\text{Read}(p, A) = DR(p, A) \cup \cup \{\text{Read}(t, C)|(p, A) \text{ READS } (t, C)\}$$

where DR and READS are defined as

$$DR(p, A) = \{a \in V_T | p \overset{A}{\rightarrow} t \overset{a}{\rightarrow}\}$$

$$(p, A) \text{ READS } (t, C) \text{ if and only if } p \overset{A}{\rightarrow} t \overset{C}{\rightarrow} \text{ and } C \overset{*}{\Rightarrow} \varepsilon$$

The DR function specifies those symbols that can be directly read from the successor state t of the transition from p to t on A. Symbols can be indirectly read when nullable nonterminals can follow the nonterminal A. For example, in

Fig. 7-15 we have

$$(p, A) \text{ READS } (q_0, B_1)$$
$$(q_0, B_1) \text{ READS } (q_1, B_2)$$
$$\vdots$$
$$(q_{m-2}, B_{m-1}) \text{ READS } (q_{m-1}, B_m)$$

Therefore, $DR(q_{m-1}, B_m) \subseteq \text{Read}(p, A)$ and $a \in \text{Read}(p, A)$.

Returning to the current example, the function DR is obtained easily from the $LR(0)$ machine as follows:

$$DR(0, E) = \{+, =\} \qquad DR(8, T) = \{*\}$$
$$DR(0, T) = \{*\} \qquad DR(8, E) = \{+\}$$
$$DR(0, G) = \{\#\} \qquad DR(6, T) = \{*\}$$

Since the example grammar does not contain any empty productions, the READS relation is empty. Consequently,

$$\text{Read}(p, A) = DR(p, A)$$

The FOLLOW set computations for our example can now be performed.

$$\text{FOLLOW}(0, G) = \text{Read}(0, G) = \{\#\}$$
$$\text{FOLLOW}(0, E) = \text{Read}(0, E) = \{+, =\}$$
$$\text{FOLLOW}(0, T) = \text{Read}(0, T) \cup \text{FOLLOW}(0, E) = \{*\} \cup \{+, =\}$$
$$= \{*, +, =\}$$
$$\text{FOLLOW}(8, E) = \text{Read}(8, E) \cup \text{FOLLOW}(0, G) = \{+\} \cup \{\#\} = \{+, \#\}$$
$$\text{FOLLOW}(6, T) = \text{Read}(6, T) \cup \text{FOLLOW}(8, E) \cup \text{FOLLOW}(0, E)$$
$$= \{*\} \cup \{+, \#\} \cup \{+, =\} = \{*, +, =, \#\}$$
$$\text{FOLLOW}(8, T) = \text{Read}(8, T) \cup \text{FOLLOW}(8, E) = \{*\} \cup \{+, \#\}$$
$$= \{*, +, \#\}$$

Using the LOOKBACK relation, the LA sets can be finally computed. These computations are as follows:

$$LA(2, G \rightarrow f) = \text{FOLLOW}(0, G) = \{\#\}$$
$$LA(2, T \rightarrow f) = \text{FOLLOW}(0, T) = \{*, +, =\}$$
$$LA(4, E \rightarrow T) = \text{FOLLOW}(0, E) \cup \text{FOLLOW}(8, E) = \{+, =\} \cup \{+, \#\}$$
$$= \{+, =, \#\}$$
$$LA(7, T \rightarrow f) = \text{FOLLOW}(6, T) \cup \text{FOLLOW}(8, T) = \{*, +, =, \#\} \cup$$
$$\{*, +, \#\} = \{*, +, =, \#\}$$
$$LA(9, G \rightarrow E = E) = \text{FOLLOW}(0, G) = \{\#\}$$

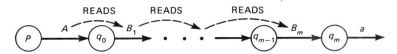

Figure 7-15 Structural representation of the READS relation.

$$LA(10, E \rightarrow E + T) = \text{FOLLOW}(0, E) \cup \text{FOLLOW}(8, E) = \{+, =\} \cup$$
$$\{+, \#\} = \{+, =, \#\}$$
$$LA(12, T \rightarrow T * f) = \text{FOLLOW}(0, T) \cup \text{FOLLOW}(6, T)$$
$$= \{*, +, =\} \cup \{*, +, =, \#\}$$
$$= \{*, +, =, \#\}$$

Recall that state 2 in the machine of Fig. 7-10 is inadequate. However, since the lookahead sets for the two rules giving rise to a reduce-reduce conflict are disjoint, the inadequate state is resolved.

In summary, the computations are:

$$LA(q, A \rightarrow \alpha) = \cup\{\text{FOLLOW}(p, A) | (q, A \rightarrow \alpha)\text{LOOKBACK}(p, A)\}$$
$$\text{FOLLOW}(p, A) = \text{Read}(p, A) \cup \cup\{\text{FOLLOW}(p', B) | (p, A) \text{ INCLUDES}$$
$$(p', B)\}$$
$$\text{Read}(p, A) = DR(p, A) \cup \cup\{\text{Read}(t, C) | (p, A) \text{ READS } (t, C)\}$$

Using relations we have:

$a \in LA(q, A \rightarrow \alpha)$ if and only if
$(q, A \rightarrow \alpha)$ LOOKBACK (p, A) INCLUDES* (p', B) READS* (t, C)
DIRECTLY_READS a

where INCLUDES* and READS* represent the reflexive transitive closures of the INCLUDES and READS relations, respectively, and

(t, C) DIRECTLY_READS a if and only if $a \in DR(t, C)$

A general algorithm for computing the lookahead sets contains the following steps.

1. Compute the set of nullable nonterminals.
2. Obtain the DR relation from the $LR(0)$ machine.
3. Compute the READS relation from the $LR(0)$ machine.
4. Obtain the Read sets.
5. Compute the INCLUDES and LOOKBACK relations.
6. Obtain the FOLLOW sets.
7. Generate the LA sets by taking the union of the FOLLOW sets.
8. Check to see that all inadequate states are resolved; if so, an $LALR(1)$ parser can be obtained.

DeRemer and Pennello (1982) have formulated an efficient algorithm for computing the Read and FOLLOW sets in steps 4 and 6 of the previous algorithm, respectively. Their algorithm has an input a set X, a relation R, and a set-valued function F'; and it produces as output the set-valued function F as follows:

$$F(x) = F'(x) \cup \cup\{F(y) | xRy\}$$

The relation R induces a directed graph $G = (X, R)$, where X and R denote the set of nodes (or vertices) and edge set in the graph, respectively. $F(x)$ is efficiently computed by traversing the graph G in an appropriate manner. The following algorithm computes the strongly connected components of the graph and generates the set-valued function F.

Procedure DIGRAPH(X, R, F′ F). Given X, R, and F′ as just described, this procedure generates the set-valued function F. STACK is a stack that contains elements of X and is initially empty. N is a vector of integers which is indexed by elements of X with each of the elements initialized to zero.

1. [Initialize]
   N ← 0
   STACK ← ϕ (set stack to empty)
2. [Compute the functions F]
   Repeat for each x ∈ X
       If N(x) = 0
           then Call TRAVERSE(x)
3. [Finished]
   Return   □

Procedure TRAVERSE(x). Given a vertex of a graph, this procedure computes the function F. Stack routines PUSH and POP are assumed. TOPV is a function that returns the top element of the stack. The function MIN returns the smallest of its two arguments. DEPTH is a function which returns the number of items on the stack. STACK, N, X, and R are global and are as previously described. The variables d, ELEMENT, and y are local variables.

1. [Initialize]
   Call PUSH(STACK, x)
   d ← DEPTH(STACK)
   N[x] ← d
   F(x) ← F′(x)
2. [Complete the closure process]
   Repeat for each y ∈ X such that xRy
           If N[y] = 0
               then Call Traverse(y) (recursive call)
               N[x] ← MIN(N[x], N[y])
               F(x) ← F(x) ∪ F(y)
   If N[x] = d
   then N[TOPV(STACK] ← Infinity (a very large number)
           F(TOPV(STACK)) ← F(x)
           ELEMENT ← POP(STACK)
           Repeat while ELEMENT ≠ x
                   N(TOPV(STACK)) ← Infinity
                   F(TOPV(STACK) ← F(x)
                   ELEMENT ← POP(STACK)
   Return   □

As mentioned earlier, this algorithm is invoked twice in computing lookahead sets. In computing Read sets (step 4 of the general algorithm) X is the set of nonterminal transitions, F' is DR, and R is the READS relation. The output F is Read. In the second invocation of Procedure DIGRAPH, X is again the set of nonterminal transition, F' is Read, and R is the relation INCLUDES. The procedure in this case generates the set-valued function FOLLOW. Procedure DIGRAPH can also check for cycles (due to nontrivial strongly connected components). If such a component is detected, the grammar may not be $LALR(1)$.

DeRemer and Pennello have performed a comparison of their lookahead generation technique with that of YACC. The result of this comparison indicates that their method is significantly more efficient than YACC's.

EXERCISES 7-4.6

1 Given the grammar with the following rules:

$S \rightarrow aAd\#$ $S \rightarrow bAc$
$S \rightarrow aec$ $A \rightarrow e$

obtain

(a) the $LR(0)$ machine
(b) the $LALR(1)$ lookahead sets for the inadequate states of the $LR(0)$ machine.

2 Repeat Exercise 1 for the grammar with the following rules:

$S \rightarrow A\#$
$B \rightarrow \varepsilon$
$C \rightarrow \varepsilon$
$A \rightarrow BCA$
$A \rightarrow a$

3 Repeat Exercise 1 for the grammar with the following rules:

$S \rightarrow A\#$
$A \rightarrow bB$
$B \rightarrow cC$
$B \rightarrow cCe$
$C \rightarrow dA$
$A \rightarrow a$

Is the grammar $LALR(1)$?

7-4.7 Representation and Optimization of LR Parsers

Thus far in this chapter we have represented the F and G functions by two-dimensional matrices. Such representations are very efficient from a table-lookup standpoint. Since parsers for typical programming languages contain hundreds of states, the space requirements for storing the matrices can be very considerable. It has been shown (Purdom 1974) that the number of states in a parser can be accurately estimated by the following formula:

Number of states $= xC + y$

where $x = 0.5949 \pm 0.0048$, $y = 0.02 \pm 0.45$, and C is the sum of all tokens in the right parts of all rules in the grammar plus the number of productions. Furthermore, the matrices tend to be sparse in the sense that many of their entries are blank (i.e., denote an error).

Two general approaches are used to reduce the size of the parsing tables. The first approach is to attempt to represent sparse matrices by suitable encodings. Several sparse-matrix encodings are possible. The second approach is to apply various transformations to the parsing tables. Some of these transformations can substantially reduce the number of states in the tables. The traditional state-minimization techniques that have been applied to finite-state machines cannot be applied to the parsing tables. This section examines both approaches with the aim of reducing space requirements for a parser.

There is a trade-off between the space taken by the parse tables on the one hand and the time taken to parse a given input string on the other. The matrix representation of the tables is expensive in storage requirements but fast in parsing time. A sparse-matrix (say, list) representation yields smaller tables, but usually at the expense of slower parsing times. In the past the designers of LR parsers have often chosen to reduce space requirements at the direct expense of compilation time. This choice is understandable in view of the large size requirements of early parsers and the high cost of main memory. Over the last decade, however, the cost of main memory has decreased substantially.

An important consideration in attempting to reduce the size of a parser is to preserve the same error-detection capabilities of an unreduced parser.

In this section we first examine sparse-matrix encodings and then present several space-saving transformations on the parsing tables.

Sparse-matrix representations. First, it is possible to combine the corresponding "terminal" columns of the F and G functions into "composite" columns. Such a reduction is based on the observation that if s is a state and a is a terminal symbol, the parsing-action entry in F is a shift operation if and only if the corresponding entry in G is not blank (Anderson et al., 1973; Aho and Ullman, 1973). For example, in Table 7-41, $F(0, f) = $ Shift and $G(0, f) = 3$. These two entries can be combined into a single ordered pair of the form

Shift 3

which indicates a shift and stack operation. All the next-state transition entries on terminals can be similarly represented as part of the F function, leaving the G table with only "nonterminal" columns. Using this approach, Table 7-41 can be represented as Table 7-43. The shift and reduce entries in the new representation can be encoded as positive and negative integers, respectively.

The blank entries in the next-state transition matrix are never used because errors are detected by the parsing-action table. The G table tends to be very sparse. Each column corresponding to a nonterminal symbol can be represented by a list. For example, the list for the column headed by T in Table 7-42 can be

Table 7-43 Encoded parsing tables for an $LALR(1)$ grammar

State	f	$=$	$+$	$*$	ε	S	E	T
0	$S3$					11	1	2
1		$S4$	$S5$					
2		$R3$	$R3$	$S9$	$R3$			
3		$R5$	$R5$	$R5$	$R2$			
4	$S7$						6	2
5	$S7$							8
6			$S5$		$R1$			
7		$R5$	$R5$	$R5$	$R5$			
8		$R4$	$R4$	$S9$	$R4$			
9	$S10$							
10		$R6$	$R6$	$R6$	$R6$			
11					A			

represented as follows:

$T:$ 　 0: 2
　　　4: 2
　　　5: 8

where the list is identified by a nonterminal label and the first entry of an ordered pair is the row state number and the second the next-state transition value.

The remaining nonterminal columns are represented as

$S:$ 　 0: 11
$E:$ 　 0: 1
　　　4: 6

The parse-action table can also be encoded in a similar manner but by rows instead of columns. It is convenient to introduce a default action, which specifies which entry applied when all others fail to match the current input symbol. The list representation of the first row of the action table becomes

0: 　 f: S3
Default: *error*

As another example, the representation of the row labeled by state 2 becomes:

2: 　 f: *error*
　　　 $*$: S9
Default: R3

It is usually desirable to select as a default the most frequently occurring entry in the list. This selection reduces the size of the list. The default entry is always at the end of the list. The default approach can also be applied to representing the columns in the function G. The default list for the T column becomes

> T: 5: 8
> Default: 2

We can save more space in yet another way. Consider a state (i.e., a row) that contains only error and reduce entries. We can replace all the error entries with one of the reduce entries in that row. With this new representation, the parser may make more reductions than was the case with the original tables. In both cases, however, the error will be detected before the next input symbol is shifted. For example, the representation of the row associated with state 3 is

> 3: ε: $R2$
> Default: $R5$

In general, any shift and accept entries should precede reduce entries in the list. The most frequently occurring reduce entry can be made a default action and all error entries can be ignored. The default action in a state that contains only shift entries is error.

Another way of compacting the parsing table is to take advantage of overlap between rows in the action table (F). For example, the two following rows:

	'a'	'b'	'c'	'd'
row p	e1	e2	e3	e4
row q			e3	e4

indicate that the actions in row q are a suffix of those in row p. Row q can now be deleted by adding a label to part of row p as follows:

> p: a: e1
> b: e2
> q: c: e3
> d: e4

We next examine several transformations that optimize LR parsers.

Optimization transformations. Many transformations are possible that either reduce the space requirements of the parsing tables or decrease parsing time. Here we examine some of the most effective transformations. Some of the transformations depend on certain properties of the tables, while others take advantage of particular representations of these tables.

The subsection focuses on the following transformations:

1. $LR(0)$ row elimination
2. Single-production elimination
3. Compatible state merger

These transformations all preserve the immediate error-detection property of LR parsers.

LR(0) row elimination Table 7-43 contains rows that have the $LR(0)$ property. A row which has this property need not inspect the current input symbol in order to determine which action should be performed. For example, rows 7 and 10 have the $LR(0)$ property. In each case a single reduce action is indicated. If we do not consult the current input symbol before performing a reduction, no significant delay in error detection will occur, since the left part of the rule which applies determines the next state. At some subsequent step the input symbol must be examined. We can eliminate rows that have a single reduce action by creating a new form of entry in the table that originally caused a transition to an $LR(0)$ state. We denote this new form of entry a ' shift-reduce" entry. As an example, row 7 can be detected by changing the entries for the parsing-action part of the table in the present example to the following:

4:     f: SR5
5:     f: SR5

where the entry *SR*5 denotes a shift and reduce by production number 5 action.

Single-production elimination Many programming-language grammars contain productions of the form $A \to B$, where $A, B \in V_N$. In many instances these productions, called *single productions*, have no associated semantics. Therefore, the actions that recognize productions whose right-hand sides consist of single nonterminals are not necessary.

Productions of this form occur in most programming languages to define various kinds of expressions having a hierarchy (precedence levels) of operators. For example, the following grammar for arithmetic expressions contains such rules:

$E \to E + T | T$
$T \to T * F | F$
$F \to (E) | i$

The two single productions are $E \to T$ and $T \to F$. In the parsing of the input string '$i + i$', the reductions $F \to i$, $T \to F$, and $E \to T$ must be performed on the first i. These reductions must be followed by the reductions $F \to i$ and $T \to F$ on the second i. At this point the reduction $E \to E + T$ can be performed. It is desirable to eliminate single productions having no semantic significance for two reasons. The parser resulting from this type of transformation is faster and in many cases more space-efficient.

Consider as an example the incomplete parsing tables given in Table 7-44 in which the only reductions of the single production $A \to B$, specified by the entries R_i, occur in the row denoted by state p. Furthermore, assume that there is only one entry in the next-state transition table (G) which refers to state p. This entry appears in the column labeled by the nonterminal B. Observe that the only way to reach state p is by the transition

1:     B: p

Table 7-44 Example of a single-production elimination for the ith production $A \rightarrow B$

| | Action table, F | | | | | | Next-state transition, G | | | | | |
							A	$B\dots$				
0												
1							q	$\not p q$				
p			R_i		R_i							

Assume that after the parser performs the reduction $A \rightarrow B$ in state p, it then consults the only next-state entry

    A: 1: q

and then transfers to state q. The single reduction can be eliminated by changing the entry under column B from state p to state q. In this way we skip over the reduction and enter state q immediately. Since it was assumed that there was only one entry in the G table which referred to state p, this state becomes inaccessible. Therefore, row p can now be deleted from the tables. As a result, it is sometimes possible to merge nonterminal columns such as columns A and B in the example table.

The previous example illustrates a simple case that can arise. In general, there may be several states which indicate that reductions involving the same single productions are to be performed. Some methods (Anderson et al., 1973) can eliminate all single-production reductions from the tables, but sometimes at a cost of increasing the number of states because of state splitting in the parsing tables. Other methods (Aho and Ullman, 1973) eliminate most (but not all) of the single productions without increasing the size of the tables. Another method (Pager, 1973) eliminates all single productions and decreases the size of the tables. This method, however, is very complex. Yet another method (Lalonde, 1976) directly eliminates single productions at the initial table-construction phase.

Merging compatible states A straightforward optimization involves merging states with identical parsing actions. For example, rows 4 and 5 in Table 7-42 contain the same parsing action, the action "$S7$". These two rows can be represented as

    4, 5: f: S7
    Default: *error*

where the default action denotes an error entry. Recall that states 4 and 5 were already deleted because both were $LR(0)$ states. In general, there may be several non-$LR(0)$ state rows which may be merged.

The preceding application of compatibility is very narrow, as both action rows must be identical. The notion of compatibility is as follows:

> Two action rows are compatible if either their corresponding entries are identical, or one of them is an error entry.

Error detection is adversely affected by such a general definition.

Another approach (Aho and Ullman, 1972) to merging rows in the tables is to introduce the notion of *don't care* entries in the tables. Some error entries in the parse-action entry (F) can never be referenced in parsing both valid and erroneous input strings. These don't care entries can be overlaid as required to achieve compactness without significantly affecting error detection. The definition of compatibility used by Aho and Ullman is the following:

> Two rows are compatible if either their corresponding entries are identical or one of them is a don't care entry.

Pager (see Pager, 1973) has proposed a method which permits otherwise incompatible states to be merged on their compatible subsets.

Most compatibility methods are complex. The methods, however, reduce storage requirements by at least a factor of 2.

7-4.8 Error Detection and Recovery in *LR* Parsers

Acceptable error recovery, which often involves some error repair, has been difficult to incorporate within LR, SLR, and $LALR$ parsers. This section outlines some of the approaches to error detection and recovery, concentrating on recent efforts in implementing error-repair strategies based upon the context surrounding the error point in a source program.

We first describe some of the earlier methods of error recovery which have been used. The discussion mentions some advantages and disadvantages of these methods, providing the motivation for other error-recovery implementations.

We next identify some of the difficulties in applying the Graham-Rhodes method of error recovery to LR parsers. We then present several approaches to error recovery that have been based on the Graham-Rhodes approach.

Early methods of error recovery. To be usable, a parser requires some method which it can use to recover from errors. This section examines three methods of error recovery which are applicable to LR parsers. While some of these methods have been used in parsers, they are not considered to provide satisfactory error recovery today. Recall from Chap. 5 that *error recovery* refers to an attempt to manipulate the stack configuration of the parser and the input stream so that parsing may continue. *Error repair*, a more stringent form of error recovery, involves changing the erroneous input sequence to one that is syntactically correct so that parsing may continue. Error-repair procedures tend to provide better diagnostics, giving the programmer hints as to how the parser recovered from the error and, hopefully, giving some hints on how to fix the error for a later run.

Error-recovery and -repair methods can be considered unsatisfactory for a number of reasons. Some methods react badly to unanticipated situations; some require a large programming effort and careful anticipation of possible syntactic errors. Because of increasing software-development costs, it has become advantageous to use parser generators to generate a parser. A few recovery methods cannot be included within a parser generator, requiring the parser writer to provide a significant portion of the coding effort. Finally some error-recovery methods are overly simplistic, throwing away stack and input contents until it appears that parsing may continue. They do not take advantage of available information which would lead to better error diagnostics and recovery.

One of the earliest methods of error recovery is referred to as *panic mode*. Panic mode has been popular because it is very simple to implement. Furthermore, the method is compatible with automatic parser generation and can be easily included in parsers generated by parser generators.

When an error is detected by a parser that uses panic mode for error recovery, the parser throws away input symbols and stack symbols until an input symbol and state on top of the stack permit parsing to continue. The usual approach to implementing panic mode involves defining a set of *synchronizing symbols*. These symbols are terminal symbols of the language that constitute *firm delimiters*. Usually, firm delimiters end statements or structured constructs and only minimally constrain the strings which may follow. PL/I examples of synchronizing symbols are the semicolon and the keyword end. For most languages, the set of synchronizing symbols can be determined easily (Graham, 1975).

Panic mode proceeds as follows: Input tokens are thrown away until a synchronizing symbol is read. Then elements are popped off the parsing stack until a state that permits a move based on the synchronizing symbol ends up on top of the stack. Control is passed back to the parser once a parsing move can be performed. Some improvements to this approach make use of predictions as to what symbols may follow the one on the stack and throw away input symbols until one is found or insert symbols into the input stream until parsing can continue.

As an example of panic-mode error recovery, consider the following program statement:

$$a := b + c\,d(6) * e;$$

There is a missing operator between the variables "c" and "d". After the terminal symbol for the variable "c" has been pushed onto the stack, an error is detected when the variable name "d" is read. This error-recovery method throws away source tokens until a token which would permit a move is read. Hence the tokens for "d", "(", "6", and ")" are discarded and parsing resumes with the multiplication operator that follows the character ")".

Table 7-45 Action table augmented with error routines

State						
				Action table (F)		
	i	$+$	$*$	$($	$)$	$\#$
0	s	$e1$	$e1$	s	$e2$	$e1$
1	$e3$	s	$e6$	$e6$	$e2$	a
2	$e3$	$r2$	s	$e6$	$r2$	$r2$
3	$e5$	$r4$	$r4$	$e5$	$r4$	$r4$
4	s	$e1$	$e1$	s	$e2$	$e1$
5	$e5$	$r6$	$r6$	$e5$	$r6$	$r6$
6	s	$e1$	$e1$	s	$e2$	$e1$
7	s	$e1$	$e1$	s	$e2$	$e1$
8	$e3$	s	$e6$	$e5$	s	$e4$
9	$e5$	$r1$	s	$e5$	$r1$	$r1$
10	$e5$	$r3$	$r3$	$e5$	$r3$	$r3$
11	$e5$	$r5$	$r5$	$e5$	$r5$	$r5$

The advantage of using panic mode is that this form of error recovery is fast and requires little code. However, because input symbols are thrown away, not all errors in a program may be detected, possibly necessitating several runs to detect all the errors. Finally, little information is provided to the user concerning the nature of the error.

A more ad hoc method of error recovery has been used in table-driven parsers, including *LR* parsers. Whenever an error entry in the action table would normally occur, the name of an error-recovery routine is designated. The error routines, which must be hand-coded, manipulate the input stream and the stack based upon the nature of the error (as indicated by which location is being accessed in the parse table).

Table 7-45 contains an example of an action table which is augmented with the names of error routines. These names begin with *e* and end with a digit. The error routine whose name is the one returned by the action table is called when an error occurs. For example, the error routine *e1* handles the case of a missing operand, generating a suitable error message and inserting an operand into the input stream. Likewise, *e2* might generate a message stating that the parentheses are unbalanced and would delete the extra right parenthesis.

The advantage of using error routines is that compiler writers are allowed to use their intuitions about the likely causes of syntax errors, and error recovery and meaningful diagnostic error messages can be provided. Because the size of *LR* parsing tables tends to be large for most programming languages, it is not feasible for these error routines to be implemented by hand. As this approach requires human insight to indicate the likely cause of an error, it is impossible to generate the error routines automatically. Also unanticipated errors can cause the error-recovery process to collapse and cause the parser to become unstable.

Another approach which does provide automatic error recovery is used in YACC (yet another compiler-compiler), an *LALR* parser generator (Johnson,

1975). The user identifies "major" nonterminals that the parser uses as a basis for error recovery. The idea is similar to that of panic mode, where synchronizing symbols also provide a basis for recovering from erroneous input. Examples of major nonterminals include ⟨program⟩, ⟨block⟩, and ⟨statement⟩. The user adds to the grammar an error production of the form

$$A \rightarrow error\ \alpha$$

where A is a major nonterminal and α is an often empty string of terminal and nonterminal symbols.

When an error is detected by the parser, the error routine pops the stack until it finds an element whose state is associated with the production $A \rightarrow error\ \alpha$ and then shifts the special token *error* onto the stack as though *error* had been read as input. Then, the parser attempts to resume parsing by discarding input symbols until a valid input symbol is read. For example, a grammar might have the productions

⟨program⟩ → ⟨stmts⟩**end**;
⟨stmts⟩ →   ⟨stmt⟩ ; ⟨stmts⟩
        |ε
⟨stmt⟩ →   *error*
       | ⋅ ⋅ ⋅

where ⟨stmt⟩ represents assignment statements, flow of control statements, and so forth. If an error is detected while a string of tokens which would reduce to ⟨stmt⟩ is being parsed, the parser first pops elements off the stack until a state which would permit the error token associated with the production

⟨stmt⟩ → *error*

to be shifted onto the stack is found. As *error* reduces to ⟨stmt⟩, input tokens are then discarded until a semicolon appears in the input text. At this point, parsing resumes.

The programmer can take advantage of intuitions concerning the likely causes of errors when including error productions in a grammar; if these error productions are improperly specified, the worst case for error recovery behaves like panic mode. Furthermore, YACC has demonstrated that this method can be implemented in parser generators. While this method permits automatic error recovery, its failings include the poor handling of unanticipated errors. Also, if no state on the stack is associated with an error production, the parser dies after popping the contents of the entire stack.

The error-recovery methods discussed here are not considered totally satisfactory. We next describe a better method of error recovery, which is based on the Graham and Rhodes method introduced earlier (see Sec. 7-3.5) for simple precedence parsers.

Application of the Graham-Rhodes method to *LR* parsers. Recall that the Graham-Rhodes method uses a two-phase approach. The first phase, or *con-*

densation phase, condenses the surrounding context by first trying to continue reducing the sentential form on the stack and then trying to continue to parse the unread portion of the input string without referring to what has been previously parsed before the error point. The second phase is the *correction phase*, which analyzes the context in which the error occurs and provides diagnostic information and a repair.

The condensation phase can further be subdivided into two parts. The first part tries to make further reductions on the stack preceding the point at which the error was detected. This is referred to as a *backward move*. The backward move endeavors to replace right-hand sides of some productions by their left-hand sides. Reductions continue until no more can be performed.

A *forward move* is then tried. In this case, parsing beyond the point of error detection is performed. The parser must be started up without any left context; in some cases, this is relatively simple (such as in simple precedence parsing). Parsing continues until one of two possibilities arise. In one possibility a second error occurs. One solution to resolving the second error is to recursively invoke the error-recovery scheme on the error in order to correct it; another solution tries to redo the parse using a different parsing sequence. The second possibility, which is the most likely according to Graham and Rhodes, occurs when a reduction that includes elements on the parsing stack that are below the point where the error was detected is required. The stack configuration is then passed to the correction phase.

The backward and forward moves attempt to summarize the surrounding context where the error is detected. The forward move provides an unbounded form of lookahead; while it consumes input, none of the input is ignored.

The correction phase attempts to exploit the information provided by the condensation phase in order to correct the error by considering changes to sequences of symbols rather than isolated changes to single symbols. The correction phase attempts to find a change to the stack so that the stack matches the right-hand side of some production in the grammar. Then a reduction over the error point is performed and the correction phase returns a valid correct stack configuration to the parser.

To determine which correction should be chosen, deletion and insertion costs can be associated with the terminal and nonterminal symbols of the language based on the likelihood that such a symbol might have been inserted or omitted from the language. Also, a substitution cost can be used which is based on the possibility that one symbol was accidentally used in place of another one. This cost is typically less than the sum of the deletion and insertion costs. An example where this is useful is by associating a low replacement cost of "=" for ":=" as the equality relation might often be used in place of the assignment operator.

The correction phase attempts to find all possible repairs and returns the one which is associated with the minimum cost.

The costs for the symbols can be based on certain heuristics. For example, brackets (i.e., **do, end**, '(', and ')') and the nonterminals generating them (i.e., ⟨blockbody⟩) should have relatively high deletion costs. Graham and Rhodes hold that the cost functions can be determiend mechanically, but they do not give details as to how this is done (Graham and Rhodes, 1975).

If no correction can be found or it exceeds a maximum threshold value, the correction phase returns a failure. At this point, more global-context error recovery may be needed, but work on this is only in the initial stages (Pai and Keiburtz, 1980). One of the error-recovery methods discussed previously might be invoked only as a last resort.

The Graham-Rhodes method has provided the basis upon which some *LR* error-repair methods have been implemented. However, it is difficult to directly apply the method to *LR* parsers for a number of reasons which we discuss next. The remainder of the discussion presents error-recovery methods which try to circumvent these difficulties. In particular, we describe the methods by Mickanus and Modry and Pennello and DeRemer, which are applicable to *LR*, *SLR*, and *LALR* parsers.

Problems of implementing the Graham-Rhodes method Several authors have reported difficulties with the direct application of the Graham-Rhodes method to *LR*, *SLR*, and *LALR* parsers. This presentation tries to outline the problems which have been encountered and why these problems occur.

The total amount of context information concerning the contents of the stack which is relevant to continue parsing is given by the state which the parser is in, that is, the topmost state of the stack. By referencing this state and the current input symbol (assuming a single lookahead symbol parser), it is a simple matter to determine what the next move is. When an error occurs, it is difficult to perform reductions on the stack for the backward move because the parser can no longer determine which reductions are permissible. This is because lookahead *LR* parsers require the state on top of the stack and the current input token to determine the next move. As the input token cannot follow in the source string given the state on top of the stack, the action table indicates an error rather than indicating what reductions can be performed on the stack.

Recall that only *LR* and *LL* parsers always detect an error at the earliest opportunity. While *SLR* and *LALR* parsers never shift an erroneous symbol onto the stack, they may perform some reductions before detecting the error. Because the symbol is not a valid one given the preceding source string, some undesirable reductions may have been performed. The error-recovery strategy must take this into account. Handling both the backward move and the possibility of incorrect reductions is usually performed in the correction phase because they are more easily dealt with when repairs to a source program are being considered. The forward move is usually still done in the condensation phase. Incorrect reductions in the backward move are best considered when forward context is available and possible repairs are being weighed.

Another problem with applying the Graham-Rhodes method to *LR* parsers involves the forward move. In order to determine what the next state to be pushed onto the stack is, reference is made to the left context, using the current state on the top of the stack. With an error, no such reference can be made. To start the forward move, the next input symbol is shifted onto the stack, but the state to be associated with this symbol is difficult to determine. It cannot be the starting state, as this restricts the next valid input symbol to be only one of those which may begin the language. The usual approach is to push all the states which may be associated with this token onto the stack and then begin the forward move. Two different approaches to performing this type of forward move are discussed in the next two methods.

The error-recovery method of Mickanus and Modry Mickanus and Modry describe an error-recovery method (Modry, 1976; Mickanus and Modry, 1978) which is based quite closely on the Graham-Rhodes method and consists of a condensation phase and a correction phase. Because of the problems with implementing the backward move in *LR* parsers, it has not been included within the condensation phase.

We first present an overview of the error-recovery method. A somewhat detailed algorithm follows this overview.

In the following discussion the parsing stack is assumed to contain both state symbols and vocabulary symbols. Recall that the stack need not contain vocabulary symbols. Their inclusion, however, facilitates the explanations to follow.

Recall that an *LR* parser proceeds from one configuration to another by performing shift and reduce operations. Each of the operations alters the state on the parse stack. A *configuration* is composed of the parse stack concatenated with the unexpended input string. In the following discussion the configurations given do not usually include all the state symbols. While these state symbols would normally be stored in the stack, they are not included in order to improve the readability of the presentation and because the names of the states are frequently not important in the discussion.

An error is detected in an *LR* parser when the top state in the parse stack and the current input symbol indicates an error entry in the action table. At this point in the parsing process, no shift or reduce operation applies. An *error configuration* which consists of the current stack contents and the unexpended input string is passed to the error-recovery method. This method will either fail or produce a repair configuration that will permit the resumption of normal parsing.

In the forward move which constitutes the condensation phase, parsing from the error point continues until one of the following situations arises:

1. An attempt is made to perform a reduction over the error point.
2. A second syntax error occurs.

In general, there are many ways of condensing an error configuration. We must consider each possibility. An attempt to perform a reduction over the error point indicates that the configuration at that point is a *correction candidate*. This correction candidate can now be passed to the correction phase of the error-recovery method. If we encounter a second syntax error, however, this indicates that either there are actually two errors in the vicinity or the present condensation attempt fails. If all condensation attempts fail, however, the error-recovery method is invoked recursively to try to repair the second error. A holding candidate is used as input in this case.

The correction phase attempts to produce a repair configuration based on the application of the following operations:

1. Inserting a terminal symbol.
2. Reversing the parse, that is, changing the current configuration to a former configuration.
3. Deleting a terminal symbol (and its associated state) from the top of the stack. If the state on top of the stack is associated with a nonterminal symbol, the parse must be reversed until a terminal symbol (and its associated state) appears at the top of the stack.
4. Assigning a cost of each insertion and stack deletion. The total cost of the current attempted repair is also accumulated.
5. Abandoning the current attempted repair when its cost exceeds a preset threshold value and choosing some other alternative.

The correction candidate that is passed to the correction phase consists of a sequence of states which begins with the start state and leads up to the error point. A second sequence of states that is produced by the condensation phase starts from the other side of the error point. We represent this situation by

$$0 \ldots q ? p \ldots$$

where "?" denotes the error point. The simplest case is to connect these two sequences of states by inserting a terminal symbol, that is, performing a transition from state q to state p on a terminal symbol, say, x. If the gap between the two states cannot be bridged by a terminal insertion, an attempt is made to back up the error point. Such a move means that some parser actions may have been incorrect prior to the error point. Performing successive backups of the parse stack frees previously processed input symbols that can be used to extend the condensation-phase sequence. After each backup step, an attempt is made to connect the two sequences by inserting a terminal symbol. If at any time the sequence of condensation-phase states cannot be extended backward to incorporate a freed symbol, then that symbol is deleted. The backup process fails if the parse retreats to the start state or too many symbols are deleted.

The details of the condensation phase just described are presented in the following subalgorithm.

Function CONDENSE (CONFIG). Given a set of parser configurations, CONFIG, this function performs a forward move on each configuration. CONDENSE returns to the calling algorithm the repair with the least cost or a null configuration (i.e., ε) if no correction can be found. It tries all possible moves as described in the text, calling the function REPAIR on each forward move. REPAIR returns the cost of the repair it finds and, through its argument, returns the repaired stack configuration. The function LR_PARSE parses the configuration, performing the forward move, and returning '*error*' if another error is detected or '*reduce*' if a reduction over the error point is required. The function FIRST returns the first symbol from the string passed to it. SAVE_STACK and SAVE_INPUT store the state and remaining unexpended input for the minimum-cost repair found, respectively. FOUND_REPAIR is a logical variable which indicates whether a repair has been found. MIN contains the cost of the repair having the least cost while MAX gives the maximum permissible repair cost. The variable HOLD_CONFIG contains the set of holding candidates while the variable HOLD_INPUT saves the original unexpended input string. NEW_S contains the stack configuration upon which a repair is attempted. '?' is a special token stored on the stack which indicates the point at which the error was detected. P is the set of states which may shift on the first element of the input string after the error point. Q is the set of parser states and the variable q stores parser states. The function SHIFT returns the set of terminal symbols which permit shift moves for the state passed to it. C is a parser configuration from the set CONFIG. The algorithm assumes that the configuration CONFIG is of the form (S, I), where S is the stack and I is the unexpended input string. The stack is treated as a string for notational convenience.

1. [Initialize]
      MIN ← MAX   (maximum permissible repair cost)
      HOLD_CONFIG ← ϕ (the empty set)
      HOLD_INPUT ← I
      FOUND_REPAIR ← false
2. [Try to parse each configuration]
      Repeat through step 6 for each C ∈ CONFIG   (assume C = (S, I))
3. [Compute the set of states which may shift on the first element of the input string]
      P ← {q ∈ Q|FIRST(I) ∈ SHIFT(q)}
4. [Try to parse each case]
      I ← HOLD_INPUT
      Repeat for each q ∈ P
         NEW_S ← S ∘ ? ∘ q   (initial stack configuration)
         If LR_PARSE(NEW_S, I) = '*error*'
         then HOLD_CONFIG ← HOLD_CONFIG ∪ {(NEW_S, I)}(holding
                                        candidate)
         else If REPAIR(NEW_S) ≤ MIN   (found a repair)
            then SAVE_STACK ← NEW_S
                SAVE_INPUT ← I
                FOUND_REPAIR ← true
5. [Return the minimum-cost correction]
      If FOUND_REPAIR
      then C ← (SAVE_STACK, SAVE_INPUT)
         Return(C)

6. [No corrections, recursively try to repair the second error]
   If HOLD_CONFIG = ϕ
      then Return(ε) (no second error was found, return a null configuration)
   else CONFIG ← {CONDENSE(HOLD_CONFIG)}
      If CONFIG = ϕ
      then Return(ε)   (no repair was found)
                                                                              □

When an error is detected by the parser, it calls the function CONDENSE to perform the forward move. This function receives (via the parameter CONFIG) a parser configuration set. Initially, only one configuration is received from the first (i.e., main) invocation. After a forward move, CONDENSE calls another function, REPAIR, to find a repair for the error. Because several different repairs might be possible, CONDENSE returns the configuration with the minimum repair cost based on the costs of deleting and inserting symbols.

As it is difficult to determine what state the forward move should begin in, the algorithm computes every state which will shift the first character of the unexpended portion of the input onto the stack in step 3. For notational convenience the set SHIFT(q) is defined to be the set of symbols which permit shift moves where $q \in Q$. These sets can be determined directly from the action table. For each of these states, step 4 calls a function LR_PARSE to parse the resulting stack configuration. In this step, the stack is initialized to permit a forward move. Note that the stack is treated as a string for notational convenience. The character "?" denotes the point in the stack where the error was detected. The function LR_PARSE returns to the calling function CONDENSE whenever another error occurs or a reduction over the error point is attempted. In the second case, the function REPAIR is called to find a repair and the repair cost. If this cost is the minimum one found so far, the configuration is saved.

In the case that LR_PARSE returns because another parsing error occurs, the stack configuration is saved as a *holding candidate*. If no repair can be found for those forward moves which lead to a reduction over the error point, CONDENSE is recursively called to try to correct the second error using the holding candidates. The loop at step 2 handles each holding candidate which was stored in the set of holding candidates. When CONDENSE is initially called by the parser, it is passed only one configuration; recursive invocations may pass several holding-candidate configurations.

Recall that in the correction phase, the stack consists of a sequence of states and symbols up to the error point and another sequence afterward. The correction phase tries to link the two together, first by inserting a terminal symbol. If that fails, the error point is backed up as it is assumed that the error might have occurred earlier in the stack. For example, consider the erroneous program segment

$a := a + b;$
$i = 2 * a$
then call compute(a);

In this program the token "if" is missing. An LR parser will not detect the error until the " = " is read. At this point the stack would be

$\quad \ldots \langle \text{stmts} \rangle ; \langle \text{var} \rangle .$

A forward move results in the configuration

$\quad \ldots \langle \text{stmts} \rangle ; \langle \text{var} \rangle ? = \langle \text{expression} \rangle$

with the "then" as the next input symbol. The forward move can no longer continue, and a reduction over the error point may be necessary. One possibility is to insert ":"; however, the "then" seen in the input stream does not follow. Another possibility is to back up the parser. After the backup the insertion is tried again. However, if no backup can be made, the topmost symbol on the stack is deleted and if it is a nonterminal symbol, this is done by backing up the parse to the point just before the reduction to that symbol is made. In this case, the algorithm assumes that the error might have occurred in some part of the source program which had been reduced to that nonterminal symbol. When a backup of the error point is performed, it is impossible to tell from the stack what the previous state and input symbol are. Hence there are several possible states that are called *rightstates*.

The following subalgorithm performs the correction phase:

Function REPAIR(S). Given a stack configuration, S, of the form $\alpha'b'Xb?a\beta$ where $\alpha' \in (Q \circ V_T \cup V_N)^*$, b', b, and $a \in Q$, $\beta \in (V_T \cup V_N \circ Q)^*$, $X \in V_T \cup V_N$, and Q is the set of parser states, this algorithm tries to repair the stack configuration. For clarity, it is assumed that the stack is in the above form whenever the loop of statement 2 is reexecuted. P and P' are sets of rightstates. The variables a, b, b', b'', r, r', and $r'' \in Q$ are states on the stack S while δ and δ' are terminal symbols on the stack. y is a terminal symbol. The variable COST gives the cost of the repair; MAX contains the maximum permissible repair cost. The vectors INSERT and DELETE give the insertion and deletion costs for inserting and deleting terminal symbols. A(b) and D(b) are the sets of ancestors and descendents of $b \in Q$, respectively. The table G represents the goto table for the parser. The statement Recheck is used in the algorithm to cause a jump to the beginning of the innermost loop in which it is nested. If the condition of the loop evaluates to true, the loop is executed again. Note that P contains initially only one state, but as backup occurs, P is expanded to contain several states.

1. [Initialize the cost of the repair and the set of rightstates]
   COST ← 0
   P ← {a}   (from the stack configuration $\alpha'b'Xb?a\beta$)
2. [Continue until a repair is found]
   Repeat through step 5 while true

3. [Try to find an insertion repair]
     Repeat for each $y \in V_T$
        Repeat for each $\tau \in D(b)$
           If $G[r, y] \in A(P)$
           then $S \rightarrow \alpha' \circ b' \circ X \circ b \circ y \circ G[r, y] \circ \beta$
              Return (COST + INSERT[y])   (insertion repair)

4. [Attempt a backup]
       $P' \leftarrow \{a \in Q | G[a, y] \in A(P)$ and $y \in V_T\}$ (new set of rightstates)
       If $P' \neq \phi$
       then $S \leftarrow \alpha' \circ b' \circ ? \circ P' \circ X \circ a \circ \beta$
       $P \leftarrow P'$
       Recheck

5. [No backups are possible over X, delete it]
     If $X \in V_T$ (terminal symbol)
     then COST $\leftarrow$ COST + DELETE[X]
        If COST > MAX
        then Return (COST)   (no repair found)
        If $D(b') \cup P \neq \phi$ (deletion repair)
        then $S \leftarrow \alpha' \circ b \circ ? \circ P \circ \beta$
           Return (COST)
        else $S \leftarrow \alpha' \circ b \circ ? \circ P \circ \beta$
           Recheck   (try to find a substitution for X)
     else Reparse stack from $\alpha' b' \delta r$ getting $\alpha\, b' \delta' r' y_m r''$
           (where $\delta r \overset{*}{\rightarrow} \delta' r' y_m r'' \rightarrow Xq$)
     $S \leftarrow \alpha' \circ b' \circ \delta' \circ r' \circ y_m \circ r'' \circ ? \circ P \circ \beta$ □

In step 3 of the algorithm the problem of inserting a symbol y involves more than just finding a $y \in V_T$ such that $G(b, y) = a$ (assuming that the stack is of the form $\alpha' b' Xb?a\beta$ as described in the function's preamble). Some reductions might be necessary on $\alpha' b' Xb$ before y can be shifted onto the stack. This problem can be resolved by examining not only the state b but also the states which are reachable from state b after a reduction. Thus the *descendent states* of the state must be considered. $D(b)$ is defined to be those states r, such that if the parser is in state b, some reduction permits the parser to change to state r. By definition, $b \in D(b)$. Similarly, when y is pushed onto the stack, some reductions involving y might be needed on the stack so that the parser ends up in state a. $A(a)$ is defined to be the set of *ancestor states* r such that if the parser is in state r, some reduction permits the parser to change to state a. By definition, $a \in A(a)$. This means that we are looking for a $y \in V_T$ such that for some $r \in D(b)$, $G(r, y) \in A(a)$.

If no repair can be found, it is possible that the error might have occurred earlier in the source program. Hence a backward move on the stack is needed which undoes the most previous shift or reduction on the stack. Step 4 computes the set of rightstates which are the possible states that might have been on the stack. Initially, a is the only member of the set.

If a backup cannot be performed, the symbol on top of the stack is deleted in step 5. If this symbol is a *terminal*, deletion is simple. Furthermore, if a descendent state of the state on top of the stack after it is popped is also in the set of rightstates, a repair has been found. If not, execution returns to step 3 to see if a replacement for the deleted symbol can be found. On the other hand, if the symbol to be deleted is a *nonterminal*, the stack is reparsed from a previous configuration until the point just before the reduction to be made is reached. This allows the error-recovery method to determine if the error occurred at a point which had previously been reduced. To perform this parse, it is necessary for the parser to save the input program and previous stack configurations. Mickanus and Modry do not report on how much input is to be saved or what parser configurations are to be saved.

If the correction phase fails, Mickanus and Modry assume that it was spurious and have their parser delete the input token at the point the error was detected. It is possible that some other error-recovery method, such as panic mode, could be used at this point.

In order to illustrate this error-recovery method, consider the program segment

begin
    a:= 2
    b:= 3;
    c:= 5;
end;

There is a missing semicolon after the second statement. The stack configuration at the point where the error is detected is

    ... **begin**⟨var⟩:= ⟨integer⟩

For simplicity, assume that there is only one initial state which can be used to start up the forward move that does not end because of a second error. Hence there is only one forward move to be considered initially.

After the forward move, the function CONDENSE would produce the stack configuration

    ... **begin**⟨var⟩:= ⟨integer⟩ ? ⟨stmts⟩

where the third and fourth statements of the program segment are reduced to ⟨stmts⟩. The token **end** is the current input token. The forward move terminates at this point because of a reduction over the error point due to the production

    ⟨stmts⟩ → ⟨stmt⟩ ; ⟨stmts⟩

The function REPAIR is then called to find a repair to the error. First, an insertion is attempted. An insertion of a semicolon succeeds because a descendent of the top state on the stack before the error point is one which would become on top of the stack if "var:= ⟨integer⟩ ;" is reduced, and this descendent state is an ancestor of the state associated with ⟨stmts⟩.

If no insertion of a terminal symbol is possible, a backup of the error point on the stack is tried. The resulting stack configuration becomes

...**begin**⟨var⟩:= ? ⟨integer⟩⟨stmts⟩

The set of rightstates associated with ⟨integer⟩ is also stored on the stack; these states are all the possible ones that can be associated with ⟨integer⟩ given the set of descendent states for ⟨stmts⟩. Then a repair is tried again. If no backup was possible, step 5 of the function would have deleted ⟨integer⟩.

Once all the possible repair candidates have been determined and no repair cost is below the maximum permissible value, repairs on the holding candidates are tried. These candidates would be passed to a recursive invocation of CONDENSE in step 6. If a repair is found, an attempt is made on the repaired forward move to correct the first error.

Mickanus and Modry report that finding a symbol for insertion can be simplified by adding states to the *LR* parser. Their method can easily be included within a parser generator. They do indicate, however, that the resulting table can be significantly larger.

This error-recovery method appears to be quite effective. The method requires that, in general, the parse be backed up. This can cause some semantic problems. It may be too difficult and time-consuming to alter the semantic actions on performing such a backup operation. A second problem with the method is that a repaired configuration may not be a rightmost cannonical sentential form (see Mickanus and Modry, 1978).

An error-recovery method by Pennello and DeRemer Another error-recovery method which is based upon the Graham-Rhodes method is put forward by Pennello and DeRemer (1978). Their method attempts to take advantage of a property of *LR* grammars in order to reduce the number of reparses. Like the method of the previous subsection, their method also avoids the backward move in the condensation phase.

The forward-move algorithm is based upon the observation that many symbols which occur in a language are followed by the same set of strings so that the parser can continue parsing in the same fashion. For example, in many languages a semicolon is used as statement terminator and a statement usually follows a semicolon. As another example, consider the following productions from the PASCAL grammar (Wirth and Jensen, 1974):

⟨for stmt⟩ → ⟨control var⟩:= ⟨for list⟩**do**⟨stmt⟩
⟨with stmt⟩ → **with**⟨record var list⟩**do**⟨stmt⟩
⟨while stmt⟩ → **while**⟨expression⟩**do**⟨stmt⟩

In each case, the symbol **do** is followed by ⟨stmt⟩. Hence, no matter in which of these statement types an error occurs just before the **do**, a statement is expected to follow the **do**.

The forward-move algorithm, which is to be given shortly, operates in a manner similar to that of Mickanus and Modry except that it stacks all the initial states as a set and continues parsing using all these states at the same time. Parsing continues until another error occurs, a reduction requiring left context is needed (i.e., over the error point), or more than one move is indicated. The important idea behind this approach is that once such a parse is done, the input which has been parsed does not need to be parsed again because the same sets of moves would be made in all cases. Consider the statements

while $(i < 7)$ **do** $i := i + 1$

and

with managers **do** $i := i + 1$

from the PASCAL grammar example given earlier. In either case if an error occurs before the token **do**, the statement "$i := i + 1$" will reduce to $\langle\text{stmt}\rangle$.

The main idea behind the forward-move algorithm is to continue parsing the input string just past the error point using a particular kind of parser called an *error parser*. The approach is to obtain all possible parses of the remainder of the input past the error point. These parses, however, must manipulate the stack in the same manner at each parse step. The forward-move algorithm behaves like an *LR* parser. The error parser pushes sets of states rather than simple states (as is the case in an ordinary *LR* parser) onto the parse stack. These sets of states enable us to keep track of parallel parses. At each step in the error parser, each state in the top state set of the stack is examined along with the next input symbol. If each state in the top state set indicates a shift (or an error), then the stack is pushed. In this case the set of all states obtained from making a transition from each state in the top state set on the next input symbol is pushed on the stack. If, however, the indicated move for each state in the top state set is a reduce (or an error) action and context to the left of the error point is not required, then a reduce operation is performed. In such a case state sets are popped from the stack and a new state set (depending on the reduction) is pushed on the stack. The process stops because of either another error, the lack of input tokens, more than one move being permitted, or more context to the left of the error point being required.

The following subalgorithm implements the forward-move strategy just described.

Function FORWARD_MOVE(I). This function performs the forward move to generate the configuration C as described earlier using the unread input string I. The input is assumed to be delimited by the end-of-file marker '#'. The variables r, t, and t' are states of Q, and P is a set of states from the set of parser states Q. S is the stack of the parser. K is the set of states on top of a stack configuration U_i. MOVES gives a set of parser moves given by the action table for some input symbol and set of states. The variable i is an index variable. The function REST deletes the first symbol from the string passed to it and returns the result. The function TOPV returns the topmost set of states on the top of the stack. The functions FIRST and SHIFT are the same as in previous algorithms. PUSH and POP are procedures for pushing and popping the stack, respectively.

1. [Initialize stack]
   Call PUSH(S, Q) (let Q be denoted by ?)
2. [Compute the sets of states which may shift on the first symbol of the input]
   $P \leftarrow \{r \in Q | FIRST(I) \in SHIFT(r)\}$
   Call PUSH(S, P)
   $I \leftarrow REST(I)$
3. [Perform the forward move]
   Repeat through step 7 while I ≠ '#'
4. [Initialize]
   $h \leftarrow FIRST(I)$
   $K \leftarrow TOPV(S)$
5. [Determine the moves to make]
   $MOVES \leftarrow \bigcup_{t \in K} F(t, h)$
6. [Finished this configuration if more than one possible move]
   If |MOVES| > 1
   then Exitloop
7. [Perform the parsing action]
   If MOVES = { *shift* }   (shift move)
   then P ← {t'|G(t, h) = t' and t ∈ K}
         Call PUSH(S, P)
         I ← REST(I)
   else If MOVES = { *reduce n* }   (assume production n is A → α)
         then If |S| > |α|
               then For each symbol in α
                     Call POP(S)
                     P ← {t'|G(t, A) = t' and t ∈ TOPV(S)}
                     Call PUSH(S, P)
               else Exitloop   (reduction over the error point)
         else Exitloop   (*accept* or *error* move)
8. [Finished]
   Let C be the configuration returned
   Return(C)   □

   The first step of the algorithm initializes the stack to the set of parser states Q (denoted by ? in a trace which follows shortly). Step 2 next computes the state set, which may shift the first symbol in the remaining input. The third step contains a loop to process, potentially, all of the remaining input tokens. Step 4 obtains the next input token and the top state set on the stack. Step 5 determines the set of possible moves that the parser can make at this point. The next step exits from the loop if more than one move is possible. Step 7 performs, if possible, the indicated action. If the move is a shift operation, the set of destination states is pushed on the stack. On the other hand, a reduce move involves popping the appropriate number of state sets from the stack, provided the reduction does not involve the error point (?). The algorithm exits the loop if there are not enough state sets on the stack or if the indicated move is either an error or accept move. The last step of the algorithm returns the stack configuration.

As an example, consider the application of the previous algorithm to the grammar whose rules are the following:

0. $S \rightarrow E\#$	4. $T \rightarrow F$
1. $E \rightarrow E - T$	5. $F \rightarrow (E)$
2. $E \rightarrow T$	6. $F \rightarrow i$
3. $T \rightarrow F \uparrow T$	

The parsing tables for this grammar are given in Table 7-46. Consider the erroneous input string $i(i - i)\#$. On detecting a missing operator, the parser halts with the stack containing state 0 at its bottom and state 2 on its top. Table 7-47 contains a trace of the forward-move algorithm on the remaining string $(i - i)\#$. Observe that the parser halts with a top state set of $\{4, 8, 11\}$. In applying the last reduction in the table (i e., $T \rightarrow F$), we pop the state set $\{3\}$ from the stack. This causes the state set ? to become the new top state set. Based on the state set ? and the nonterminal T, there are four transitions possible:

$$G(0, T) = 4, \; G(5, T) = 4, \; G(6, T) = 8, \; G(10, T) = 11$$

Consequently, we stack the state set $\{4, 8, 11\}$. Step 5 of the algorithm then computes the set MOVES as follows:

$$\begin{aligned}
\text{MOVES} &= F(4, \#) \cup F(8, \#) \cup F(11, \#) \\
&= \{r1, r2, r3\} \\
&= \{E \rightarrow E - T, E \rightarrow T, T \rightarrow F \uparrow T\}
\end{aligned}$$

Table 7-46 Parsing tables for sample grammar

State	Action function, F						Next state or goto function, G							
	i	$-$	$\uparrow$	$($	$)$	$\#$	S	E	T	F	i	$-$	$\uparrow$	$($	$)$
0	S			S			1	4	3	2				5	
1		S				A						6			
2		$r6$	$r6$		$r6$	$r6$									
3		$r4$	S		$r4$	$r4$							10		
4		$r2$			$r2$	$r2$									
5	S			S			7	4	3	2				5	
6	S			S				8	3	2				5	
7		S			S							6			9
8		$r1$			$r1$	$r1$									
9		$r5$	$r5$		$r5$	$r5$									
10	S			S					11	3	2				5
11		$r3$			$r3$	$r3$									

Table 7-47 Trace of an error parser for the input string $i(i - i)\#$

Step	Stack contents	Rest of input	Action taken
1	?	$(i - i)\#$	
2	? {5}	$i - i)\#$	Shift {5}
3	? {5} {2}	$- i)\#$	Shift {2}
4	? {5} {3}	$- i)\#$	$F \rightarrow i$
5	? {5} {4}	$- i)\#$	$T \rightarrow F$
6	? {5} {7}	$- i)\#$	$E \rightarrow T$
7	? {5} {7} {6}	$i)\#$	Shift {6}
8	? {5} {7} {6} {2}	$)\#$	Shift {2}
9	? {5} {7} {6} {3}	$)\#$	$F \rightarrow i$
10	? {5} {7} {6} {8}	$)\#$	$T \rightarrow F$
11	? {5} {7}	$)\#$	$E \rightarrow E - T$
12	? {5} {7} {9}	$\#$	Shift {9}
13	? {3}	$\#$	$F \rightarrow (E)$
14	? {4, 8, 11}	$\#$	$T \rightarrow F$

Since there are three possible moves (i.e., reductions), the algorithm stops. The reduction $T \rightarrow F \uparrow T$ holds only if $F \uparrow$ immediately precedes T on the stack. $E \rightarrow E - T$ is the proper reduction only if $E -$ immediately precedes T. Similarly, $E \rightarrow T$ applies only if nothing or a left parenthesis immediately precedes T. Since there is no left context on the stack, parsing cannot continue in a deterministic manner. This example, however, indicates three possible guesses at the reduction.

Recall that the parse stack in an LR parser represents, at any given point in the parsing process, a viable prefix of a sentential form. A string is *viable fragment* of the remainder of an input sentence $z = xy$ where $x, y \in V_T^*$ if and only if

1. $U \overset{*}{\Rightarrow} x$
2. If α is a viable prefix of a sentential form $S \overset{*}{\Rightarrow} \alpha U y \overset{*}{\Rightarrow} \alpha x y$

In other words, during the parsing of any sentence whose suffix is xy, x must reduce to the valid fragment U. The forward-move algorithm produces a viable fragment. In the previous example (see Table 7-47) $xy = (i - i)\#$. $T = U$, $x = (i - i)$, and $y = \#$.

The significance of a derived viable fragment to an error-recovery method is the following: Assume that the parser detects an error in the given input such that α represents the parse stack and the string xy is a suffix of the given input sentence. If the repair algorithm generates several α' as possible replacements for α, we could reparse x for each replacement. Because of the notion of a derived viable fragment, we need reduce x to U only once. That is, x is reduced to U no matter what lies to the left of string xy. Pennello (1977) presents a theorem and proof of this assertion.

Once an error is detected, the forward-move algorithm can be invoked to consume all of the input; once another error is found, a reduction is required, or more than one move is possible, the forward move is performed again, resulting in another stack configuration. This leads to the set of stack configurations (derived viable fragments) $U_1, U_2, \ldots, U_n$ once the entire source program has been read. The following algorithm generates the desired set of derived valid fragments. The algorithm returns the resulting set of viable fragments once all of the input has been read.

Function T_FORWARD_MOVE(I). This function generates the set of configurations $U_1, U_2, \ldots, U_n$ as described earlier using the unread input string I. C denotes the collection of viable fragments.

1. [Initialize]
      $C \leftarrow \phi$ (the empty set)
      $j \leftarrow 1$
2. [Generate the set of derived viable fragments]
      Repeat while $I \neq$ '$\neq$'
         $U_j \leftarrow$ FORWARD_MOVE(I)
         $C \leftarrow C \cup U_j$
         $j \leftarrow j + 1$
3. Finished
      Return(C)   □

The above approach generates state sets dynamically by referring to the parser states. We can, however, precompute these state sets and their associated transitions. The approach is similar to that taken in converting a nondeterministic machine to its deterministic equivalent (see Chap. 4). The details of this approach are not pursued further.

The correction phase attempts to find insertions, deletions, or substitutions which would repair the error. The algorithm which tries to find a repair follows. To simplify the error-repair process, the forward-move algorithm is applied to the input following the input character at which the error was detected. This method handles the case that this character might be erroneous much sooner than does the method of Mickanus and Modry. The method used by Pennello and DeRemer tries a deletion of the input token before considering other possible approaches to finding a repair. This is unlike the method of Mickanus and Modry, which deletes the input token only if no repair can be found by the error-recovery procedures.

Function ERROR_RECOVERY(C). Given the erroneous parser configuration C, this function attempts to find a repair for this configuration; if none can be found, it returns the stack configuration FAIL, which indicates that no repair could be found. The parser configuration C is also represented by (S, I), where S is the stack and I is the unexpended input string. C' (which includes the stack S' and input string I') is a parser configuration. The variable h stores the first token of the input string which is not used in the foward move. FMC and FMC' are sets storing the forward-move configurations returned by the function T_FORWARD

_MOVE. The function TRY(S, T, C, CONFIG) attempts to "join" the stack configuration S to the set of configurations C using one of the terminal symbols in the set T. The resulting configuration is returned in CONFIG. The function also returns a logical value which indicates whether the stack and set of configurations can be joined. The function ATTACH returns a logical value indicating whether the terminal symbol passed to it as its first argument can be attached to the set of configurations also passed. The resulting set of configurations is returned through the second argument. The function ACCESSING_SYMBOL returns the input symbol which led to the top state on the stack. The functions FIRST and REST are the same as in previous algorithms.

1. [Initialize, save the input and stack configuration]
   h ← FIRST(I)
   C' ← C   (also initializes S' to S)
2. [Perform the forward move]
   FMC ← FMC' ← T_FORWARD_MOVE(REST(I))
3. [Try to repair the error]
   Repeat through step 7 while C' ≠ φ
4. [Try a deletion of symbol h]
   If TRY (S', {ε}, FMC, CONFIG)
   then Return (CONFIG)
5. [Try a replacement]
   If TRY (S', V_T, FMC, CONFIG)
   then Return (CONFIG)
6. [Try an insertion]
   If not ATTACH(h, FMC)
                           (try to attach h to the set of configurations FMC)
   then Exitloop
   If TRY (S', V_T, FMC, CONFIG)
   then Return (CONFIG)
7. [Back up the stack (h has been attached to FMC)]
   h ← ACCESSING_SYMBOL(TOP(S'))
   Delete the topmost state and symbol from stack S'
8. [Failure]
   Return(FAIL)   □

The function ERROR_RECOVERY first attempts to delete the input character. The function TRY, which is called tries to "join" the stack S' with the set of forward-move configurations FMC which were returned by the forward-move algorithm using one in the set of characters passed to it as its second argument. The "join" can be performed in a manner similar to the way Mickanus and Modry did it and is not described in this subsection. TRY does attempt to join as many configurations together as possible. For example, once S' and configuration U_1 are joined, reductions might be possible on the result which then permit the result to be joined with U_2. This is repeated until no more joins are possible.

If a deletion fails a substitution for the character h is attempted by passing the set of terminal symbols to TRY instead of an empty string. If a repair is found, the repaired configuration is returned to the parser.

The next repair attempt, which is performed in step 6, tries to find an insertion before the character h. The function ATTACH is used to join h with U_1 and, possibly, the other configurations. TRY is then called to see if a terminal symbol can be inserted before h. If the insertion attempt succeeds, the repaired configuration is returned.

If none of the repair methods succeed, the algorithm tries to back up the stack. It cannot if h could not be attached to the forward-move configurations. Step 8 reports a failure and returns in this case. Step 7 performs the backup, attempting to undo reductions on the stack which should not have been done. The current approach used by Pennello and DeRemer is to back up the stack to the point where the previous input symbol was shifted onto the stack. The function ACCESSING_SYMBOL returns this symbol and resets the stack. Pennello and DeRemer (1978) state that this approach is only in the formative stage, and they are still considering other approaches.

In the program segment

```
do;
    ctr:= ctr + 1;
    save_val next;
    for i:= 1 to 8 do;
    save(i):= ctr * i;
    save(ctr):= 0;
end;
```

a syntax error occurs in the third statement where the assignment operator has been omitted. The forward-move algorithm begins by generating stack configurations with the semicolon following the variable "next". Depending upon the grammar for the language, stack configurations would likely be formed as follows: The semicolon cannot be reduced and is in the first configuration. It is the only symbol in the first configuration, as there may be more than one possible move beginning with the variable "save_val". However, the **for** loop and the statement "save(ctr):= 0" which follows are reduced to "⟨stmt⟩⟨stmt⟩". The token **end** cannot follow the second statement without the context, which indicates that there is a preceding **do**. Hence the three resulting stack configurations would be ";", "⟨stmt⟩⟨stmt⟩", and **end**.

In order to repair the error, the error-recovery function first tries to delete the variable "next" and to join together the stack with the stack configuration U_1. As this attempted repair will not work, a replacement for the terminal symbol for "next" is then tried. First of all, the terminal symbol for "next" is joined with the stack configuration U_1, resulting in the configuration "⟨var⟩ ;". Then an insertion of a terminal symbol which permits the stack and the configuration U_1 to be joined is tried. In this case, inserting the assignment operator succeeds. However, if no insertion is found, the stack is backed up and another try at repairing the error is done.

When an insertion was being tried in the preceding example, if the terminal symbol for "next" could not be joined with the first stack configuration, the error-recovery procedure would have failed.

Like the previous method described earlier, if the present method fails to find a repair, another method is required to repair the error. However, Pennello and DeRemer state that which approach to use is not clear and the algorithm given merely returns, reporting a failure. A method such as panic mode might then be used.

In order to implement their method, Pennello and DeRemer indicate that the parser tables can be expanded to include states which represent the sets of states used for error repair. These states can be computed mechanically and do not generate an overly large number of states. They also give further algorithms for their implementation method (Pennello and DeRemer, 1978).

Pennello and DeRemer report that their error-recovery method has about 70 percent of the error diagnoses rated as either good or excellent, 12 percent rated poor, and 18 percent unrepaired. Their measures include spurious errors which are not considered by other authors. Such errors are usually not repaired. Pennello and DeRemer report that their error-recovery method requires an increase in the number of parser states by 20 to 30 percent.

Other *LR* error-recovery methods. Other methods of error recovery for *LR* parsers have been designed. This section briefly discusses two approaches. These methods are not as rigorous as the previously described methods in attempting to repair an error.

One approach, discussed by Graham, Haley, and Joy (1979) tries to provide good error diagnostics without attempting to provide the best, if any, repair. They use a two-phase approach. The first phase tries to find a repair by inserting a terminal symbol or by deleting or substituting the input token at the point where the error occurred. Error recovery is simple and does not try to perform or undo any necessary reductions on the stack like the method of Mickanus and Modry.

If no repair can be found, error recovery switches to a second phase which operates in a manner similar to the way error recovery in YACC is done. For this method, the grammar is augmented with error productions. The stack is popped and input is ignored in order to resume parsing.

Druseikis and Ripley (1976) describe an approach to error recovery for an *SLR*(1) parser. Their method performs simple, fast recovery without any repair. A forward move is made, but there is no attempt to integrate the information provided by the forward move into the correct prefix. Pennello and DeRemer's method described in the previous subsection is a generalization of Druseikis and Ripley's method. The former method works for all types of *LR*(1) parsers.

7-5 COMPARISON OF PARSING METHODS

Throughout the last two chapters we have presented several parsing methods. Each method is usually associated with a class of grammars. All parsing methods, except those discussed in Sec. 6-1, have linear parse times. That is, the time taken to parse a given input string is proportional to the number of tokens in that string. This section briefly compares most of the parsing techniques introduced earlier. The criteria of comparison include the following:

1. Generality
2. Ease of writing a grammar
3. Ease of debugging a grammar
4. Error detection
5. Space requirements
6. Time requirements
7. Ease of application of semantics

Each criterion will now be discussed in turn.

Generality. An $LR(1)$ parser generator is the most general type of parse. Figure 7-16 gives the inclusion tree for the classes of formal grammars (and associated parsers) discussed so far. Although $LR(1)$ grammars are shown as a subset of the $LR(k)$ class, Knuth has shown that any $LR(k)$ grammar can be written as an equivalent $LR(1)$ grammar. There is no great difference between the classes of $LR(1)$ and $LALR(1)$ grammars or $SLR(1)$ grammars. It has been shown (Thompson, 1977) that the $LL(1)$ grammars are a subset of the $LALR(1)$ class, with the

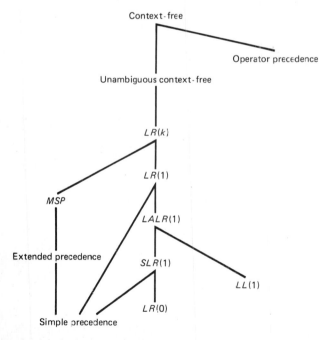

Figure 7-16 Grammar class inclusion tree.

former being a significantly smaller class than the latter. The simple precedence class of grammars is also a small subset of the $SLR(1)$ class. Since operator precedence gramars can be ambiguous, this class does not form a subset of the LR classes of grammars.

Ease of writing. To get a given grammar into a simple precedence form can require significant changes to the original grammar. These changes can affect the structure of the original language constructs and the application of semantics. Furthermore, empty productions are not allowed. The rewriting of a given grammar to be $LL(1)$ is often awkward and difficult because of the problem of left recursion. The rewriting of a grammar to be $SLR(1)$, $LALR(1)$, or $LR(1)$ is usually easier to achieve without substantially changing the original grammar. An $LL(1)$ grammar may often contain more productions than an $LR(1)$ grammar for the same language.

Ease of debugging. Because of the complexity of the construction process to obtain an LR parser, it may be nontrivial (especially for a novice) to eliminate local ambiguities from the given grammar so that it becomes an LR grammar. It is somewhat easier to debug the precedence and $LL(1)$ grammars. The relations in these methods can, if necessary, be generated by hand.

Error detection. Operator precedence parsers can, in fact, accept erroneous strings. $LR(1)$ and $LL(1)$ parsers possess the valid prefix property. Errors in both types of parsers can be detected at the earliest possible point without pushing the next character onto the stack. The action table contains useful information for producing suitable error messages and attempting error recovery.

Space requirements. All of the parsers can be represented by tables. The simple precedence and operator precedence parsers have tables whose size depends on the number of vocabulary ($V_T \cup V_N$) and terminal symbols, respectively. The size of $LL(1)$ parsing tables is generally more efficient than that of precedence parsers. $LALR(1)$ and $SLR(1)$ parsers, however, are more space-efficient than the precedence parsers.

Typically, an $LL(1)$ grammar will contain more productions than an $LALR(1)$ grammar for the same language. The elimination of left recursion in $LL(1)$ grammars frequently requires additional nonterminal symbols. These extra nonterminal symbols adversely affect the size of the $LL(1)$ parsing tables. From our experience, however, it appears that the space requirements of $LL(1)$ and $LALR(1)$ parsers are comparable.

Several comparative studies of space requirements have been done. An early study by Lalonde (Lalonde, 1971) compares the table sizes (in bytes) of $LALR(1)$, MSP, and SP (Wirth and Weber, 1966) parsers for four programming languages.

Part of his results follow:

Grammar	Number of productions	MSP	SP	LALR
XPL	109	3274	*	1250
EULER	120	3922	4321	1606
EULER-11	100	3017	3204	1276
ALGOL 60	173	> 6800†	> 6100*	2821

*Not an SP grammar.
† Not an MSP grammar.

Observe that the *LALR* space requirements are substantially less than those for *SP* and *MSP* parsers. Furthermore, as to be expected, the space requirements for both *SP* and *MSP* parsers are comparable.

Another study (Anderson et al., 1973) compared *SLR*(1), *SP*, and *MSP* space requirements for the languages ALGOL W and XPL. The ALGOL W compiler, which was developed at Stanford, contains a simple precedence parser which completely eliminates (due to Susan Graham) single productions. Some of their space-requirements results are as follows:

Grammar	Number of productions	SLR(1)PC	SLR(1)C	SPC	MSP
XPL	108	1182	—	—	2962
ALGOL W	190	2434	5523	6730	—

SLR(1)*PC* and *SLR*(1)*C* denote the parsers with partial and complete single-production elimination, respectively. *SPC* denotes the simple precedence parser with complete single-production elimination. The *MSP* parser did not eliminate single production.

Note that the space requirements for the *SLR*(1) parser with partial single-production elimination are substantially less than those of a simple precedence parser with full elimination. Observe, however, that the space requirements of the *SLR*(1) parser with full elimination are not as impressive. Recall that there are now techniques for eliminating single productions that do not increase the original size of the *SLR*(1) tables.

Recall that a matrix form of the parsing tables is usually preferred from a fast-lookup standpoint. One approach that has been taken (Joliat, 1972) is to retain the matrix form. This form, however, is factored into several special-purpose matrices. Although this approach has somewhat increased the storage requirements of the parser very fast time performance has been observed. More will be said about the timing results of the approach shortly.

Time requirements. Comparing different parsing techniques with respect to timing requirements depends on many factors. Some of these factors depend on a particular parsing technique. Other factors depend on the particular hardware system (such as the size of main memory and disk-access speed) and software-system environment (e.g., the efficiency of an operating system).

A timing comparison for several programs has been reported by Lalonde for *MSP* and *LALR* parsers. The comparison is summarized in the following table:

Program	Size		Number of reductions	*MSP*	*LALR*
	Lines	Tokens			
Compactify	77	439	1,262	0.84	0.52
LCS	3,322	17,369	58,707	28.86	15.88
XCOM	4,241	24,390	66,108	45.35	25.11
SIMPAC	5,577	24,990	92,245	46.11	25.38
DIAL	6,405	32,136	116,803	58.24	32.65
DOSYS	7,291	29,334	81,581	55.58	30.49

In this comparison the *LALR* parser significantly outperforms the *MSP* parser. Apparently, looking for a handle on top of a stack in the *MSP* parser by comparing a substring on top of the stack with a table of sorted right parts of productions takes longer than searching a list represented matrix in the *LALR* method.

Another study (Anderson et al., 1973) has compared the time requirements of an *SLR*(1) parser and the simple precedence (Wirth and Weber) parser used in the ALGOL W compiler. The results obtained for five different programs are as follows:

Program	Parsing method				
	SLR(1)	*SP*	*SLR*(1)*PC*	*SLR*(1)*C*	*SPC*
Program 1	0.43	0.41	0.35	0.28	0.27
Program 2	1.12	1.09	0.94	0.76	0.75
Program 3	1.64	1.59	1.39	1.09	1.10
Program 4	2.40	2.32	2.02	1.61	1.60
Program 5	4.07	3.92	3.42	2.76	2.75

SPC and *SP* denote a simple precedence parser with and without single-production elimination, respectively. *SLR*(1)*C*, *SLR*(1)*PC*, and *SLR*(1) denote an *SLR*(1) parser with complete, partial, and no single-production elimination.

Note that the performances of the *SLR*(1) and simple precedence parsers with single-production elimination are very nearly the same. These results are not consistent with the study by Lalonde. The simple precedence parser in the ALGOL W compiler has used a hashing function to determine the number of symbols to be replaced on the parse stack while performing a reduction. This strategy has apparently nullified the advantage that an *SLR*(1) parser has in knowing in advance what production is to be applied (i.e., without searching the stack). Recall the *MSP* parser must search a list of productions in order to determine which production applies at each reduction. Also note that single-production elimination has resulted in an increase in parser speed of 50 percent over parsers without elimination.

Anderson et al. achieved this speedup in parsing partly by taking advantage of special hardware instructions for performing list searching. This advantage would have been significantly reduced had the list-searching part of the parser been programmed in a higher-level language. Joliat (1973) achieved the same parser speed without taking advantage of specialized hardware features.

Semantic application. Semantic actions are easily incorporated in both $LL(1)$ and LR parsing action tables. More will be said about this topic in Chap. 11 when attributed grammar translation will be discussed. In bottom-up parsers we usually only associate semantic actions with reduction actions, which thereby results in a cleaner separation of syntax and semantics. Because $LL(1)$ and LR parsers allow empty productions, these null productions can be used in a beneficial manner both in applying semantic actions and in error detection and recovery. Recall that empty productions are not allowed in precedence grammars.

We have examined the performance and merits of several parsing techniques. In practice, however, the choice of parsing methods used by a compiler writer may well be dictated by what is available on the local computer system. Provided that a reliable parser generator is available and it does not use too many systems resources, the compiler writer may well be indifferent to the actual parsing method used. If, however, there is more than one parser generator available on a given system, factors such as class of grammars accepted, ease of debugging a grammar, space requirements, and parsing speed may become important issues. With the high costs of programmers, good error detection, reporting, and recovery techniques are becoming much more important than in the past. A compiler that possesses good qualities with respect to assisting a programmer to debug programs more quickly is definitely preferred. Several years ago, interest in having good error diagnostics as an aid to debugging programs was of concern primarily in academic institutions. Today, because of high programming costs, all institutions are concerned with increasing programmer productivity in any way possible.

A compiler writer who does not have access to a parser generator can with a relatively small effort write an $LL(1)$ parser generator. In fact, the $LL(1)$ parsing table for an average-sized grammar can be constructed by hand. A straightforward way of getting the job done is to use a recursive-descent parser.

BIBLIOGRAPHY

Aho, A. V., and J. D. Ullman: *The Theory of Parsing, Translation, and Compiling*, Vol. 1, *Parsing*, Englewood Cliffs, N.J.: Prentice-Hall, 1972.

Aho, A. V., and J. D. Ullman: "Optimization of LR(k) Parsers," *Journal of Computer and Systems Sciences*, Vol. 6, 1972, pp. 573–602.

Aho, A. V., and J. D. Ullman: *The Theory of Parsing, Translation, and Compilation*, Vol. 2, *Compilation*, Englewood Cliffs, N.J.: Prentice-Hall, 1973.

Aho, A. V., and J. D. Ullman: "A Technique for Speeding Up LR(k) Parsers," *SIAM Journal of Computing*, Vol. 2, No. 2, June 1973.

Aho, A. V., and J. D. Ullman: *Principles of Compiler Design*, Reading, Mass.: Addison-Wesley, 1977.

Aho, A. V., and S. C. Johnson: "LR Parsing," *Computing Surveys of the ACM*, Vol. 6, No. 2, June 1974, pp. 99–124.

Anderson, T., J. Eve, and J. J. Horning: "Efficient LR(1) Parsers," *Acta Informatica*, Vol. 2, 1973, pp. 12–39.

Barrett, W. A., and J. D. Couch: *Compiler Construction: Theory and Practice*, Chicago: Science Research Associates, Inc., 1979.

Bell, J. R.: "A New Method for Determining Linear Precedence Functions for Precedence Grammars," *Communications of the ACM*, Vol. 12, No. 10, Oct. 1969, pp. 567–569.

Berrtsch, E.: "The Storage Requirement in Precedence Parsing," *Communications of the ACM*, Vol. 20, No. 3, March 1977, pp. 192–194.

Burke, M., and G. A. Fisher: "A Practical Method for Syntactic Error Diagnosis and Recovery," *Proceedings of the SIGPLAN Symposium on Compiler Construction*, Boston, Mass., June 1982, pp. 67–78.

DeRemer, F. L.: "Practical Translators for LR(k) Languages," Ph.D. Thesis, MIT, Cambridge, Mass., August 1969.

DeRemer, F. L.: "Simple LR(k) Grammars," *Communications of the ACM*, Vol. 14, No. 7, July 1971.

DeRemer, F. L., and T. J. Pennello: "Efficient Computation of LALR(1) Look-Ahead Sets," *Proceedings of the SIGPLAN Symposium on Compiler Construction*, Denver, Colo., Aug. 6–10, 1979, pp. 176–187.

DeRemer, F. L., and T. J. Pennello: "Efficient Computation of LALR(1) Look-Ahead Sets," *ACM Transactions on Programming Languages and Systems*, Vol. 4, No. 4, Oct. 1982, pp. 615–649.

Druseikis, F. C., and G. D. Ripley: "Error Recovery for Simple LR(k) Parsers," *Proceedings of the Annual Conference of the ACM*, Houston, Texas, Oct. 1976, pp. 20–22.

Duong, C., H. J. Hoffmann, and D. Muth: "An Improvement to Martin's Algorithm for Computation of Linear Precedence Functions," *Communications of the ACM*, Vol. 19, No. 10, Oct. 1976, pp. 576–577.

Feldman, J., and D. Gries: "Translator Writing Systems," *Communications of the ACM*, Vol. 10, No. 2, July 1963, pp. 77–113.

Floyd, R. W.: "Syntactic Analysis and Operator Precedence," *Journal of the ACM*, Vol. 10, No. 3, 1963, pp. 313–316.

Graham, S. L., C. B. Haley, and W. N. Joy: "Practical LR Error Recovery," *Proceedings of the SIGPLAN Symposium on Compiler Construction*, Denver, Colo., Aug. 6–10, 1979, pp. 168–175.

Graham, S. L., and S. P. Rhodes: "Practical Syntactic Error Recovery," *Communications of the ACM*, Vol. 18, No. 11, Nov. 1975, pp. 639–650.

Gries, D.: *Compiler Construction for Digital Computers*, New York: John Wiley & Sons, 1971.

Horning, J. J.: "LR Grammars and Analyzers," in F. L. Bauer (ed.), *Compiler Construction: An Advanced Course*, Berlin: Springer-Verlag, 1974, pp. 85–108.

Horning, J. J., and W. R. Lalonde,: "Empirical Comparison of LR(k) and Precedence Parsers," Technical Report CSRG-1, University of Toronto, 1971.

Johnson, S. C.: *YACC—Yet Another Compiler-Compiler*, Murray Hill, N.J.: Bell Laboratories, 1977.

Joliat, M. L.: "On the Reduced Matrix Representation of LR(k) Parser Tables," Ph.D. Thesis, University of Toronto, Computer Systems Research Group, Technical Report CSRG-28, Oct. 1973.

Korenjak, A. J.: "A Practical Method for Constructing LR(k) Processors," *Communications of the ACM*, Vol. 12, No. 11, Nov. 1969, pp. 613–623.

Knuth, D. E.: "On the Translation of Languages from Left to Right," *Information and Control*, Vol. 8, Oct. 1965, pp. 607–639.

Lalonde, W. R.: "An Efficient LALR Parser Generator," Technical Report CSRG-2, University of Toronto, 1971.

Lalonde, W. R.: "On Directly Constructing LA(k LR(m) Parsers without Chain Productions," *ACM Symposium on the Principles of Programming Languages*, Jan. 1976.

Leinius, R. P.: "Error Detection and Recovery for Syntax Directed Compiler Systems," Ph.D. Thesis, University of Wisconsin at Madison, 1970.

Martin, D. F.: "Boolean Matrix Method for the Detection of Simple Precedence Grammars," *Communications of the ACM*, Vol. 11, No. 10 Oct. 1968, pp. 685–687.

Martin, D. F.: "A Boolean Matrix Method for the Computation of Linear Precedence Functions," *Communications of the ACM*, Vol. 15, No. 6, June 1972, pp. 448–454.

Mauney, J., and C. N. Fischer: "A Forward Move Algorithm for LL and LR Parsers," *Proceedings of the SIGPLAN Symposium on Compiler Construction*, Boston, Mass., June 1982, pp. 79–87.

McKeeman, W. M.: "An Approach to Computer Language Design," Ph.D. Thesis, Stanford University, 1966.

McKeeman, W. M., J. J. Horning, and D. B. Wortman: *A Compiler Generator*, Englewood Cliffs, N.J.: Prentice-Hall, 1970.

Mickanus, M. D., and J. A. Modry: "Automatic Error Recovery for LR Parsers," *Communications of the ACM*, Vol. 21, No. 6, June 1978, pp. 465–495.

Modry, J. A.: "Syntactic Error Recovery for LR Parsers," M.S. Thesis, University of Illinois, 1976.

Pager, D.: "On Eliminating Unit Productions from LR(k) Parsers," Department of Information and Computer Sciences, University of Hawaii, 1975.

Pai, A. B., and R. B. Keiburtz: "Global Context Recovery: A New Strategy for Syntactic Error Recovery by Table-Driven Parsers," *ACM Transactions of Programming Languages and Systems*, Vol. 2, No. 1, Jan. 1980, pp. 16–41.

Pennello, T. J.: "Error Recovery for LR Parsers," M.Sc. Thesis, Dept. of Information Sciences, University of California at Santa Cruz, Calif., June 1977.

Pennello, T. J., and F. DeRemer: "A Forward Move Algorithm for LR Error Recovery," *Conference Record of the Fifth Annual ACM Symposium of Principles of Programming Languages*, Tucson, Ariz., Jan. 23–25, 1978, pp. 241–254.

Purdom, P. W.: "The Size of LALR(1) Parsers," *BIT*, Vol. 14, No. 3, July 1974, pp. 326–337.

Rhodes, S. P.: "Practical Syntactic Recovery for Programming Languages," Ph.D. Thesis, University of California at Berkeley, 1973.

Thompson, D. H.: "The Design and Implementation of an Advanced LALR Parse Table Constructor," University of Toronto, Computer Systems Research Group, Technical Report CSRG-79, April 1977.

Wirth, N.: "PL360, A Programming Language for the 360 Computers," *Journal of the ACM*, Vol. 15, No. 1, Jan. 1968.

Wirth, N., and K. Jensen: *PASCAL User Manual and Report*, New York: Springer-Verlag, 1974.

Wirth, N., and H. Weber: "EULER: A Generalization of ALGOL and Its Formal Definition: Part 1," *Communications of the ACM*, Vol. 9, No. 1, 1966 pp. 13–23.

EIGHT

SYMBOL-TABLE-HANDLING TECHNIQUES

Symbol tables (also called identifier tables and name tables) assist two important functions in the translation process: in checking for semantic (i.e., context-sensitive) correctness and aiding in the proper generation of code. Both of these functions are achieved by inserting into, and retrieving from the symbol table, attributes of the variables used in the source program. These attributes, such as the name, type, object-time address, and dimension of a variable, are usually found explicitly in declarations or more implicitly through the context in which the variable name appears in the program. In this chapter we do not describe how declarations, per se, are handled but describe the routines for organizing, creating, and searching symbol tables. It is these routines which are invoked when declarations are handled at compile time. Declaration handling will be discussed in Chap. 11.

Table-handling techniques for both block-structured and non-block-structured languages are described in this chapter.

8-1 PERSPECTIVE AND MOTIVATION

In Chap. 4, we described how the scanner identified different lexical classes for the constants, identifiers, reserved words, and operators of a language. Recall that identifiers were detected by first searching for a lexical unit, as isolated by the

418

scanner, in a reserved-word table. If the lexical unit was found, its index value in the table was output by the scanner. This index value is used in subsequent parts of the compilation process to identify the reserved word that was isolated. If the lexical unit was not found in the table, it was assumed to be an identifier, and a token indicating this was output from the scanner.

Our discussion in this chapter continues from Chap. 4 in the sense that we describe how the attributes of a variable are associated with a particular variable name (i.e., identifier) using a symbol table. It must be noted that a symbol table is generally a volatile table because entries are being added continually to and, in some cases, deleted from the table. While some of the techniques to be discussed in this chapter, such as the binary search and hashing, can be applied to both static and volatile tables, maintaining a volatile symbol table is more difficult than maintaining a static table such as the reserved-word table.

The importance of a symbol table is best realized when we consider that every occurrence of an identifier in a source program requires some symbol-table interaction. Because of this continual interaction, symbol-table access may consume a major portion of the processor time during compilation. A study, cited by McKeeman (1974), indicated that for an efficient translator of a PL/I-like language XPL one-fourth of the translation time was devoted to interrogating the symbol table when a linear search method was employed. When the symbol-table access method was changed to a more efficient hash-table technique, the majority of the time previously expended in table accessing was saved. Hence we are motivated to study in some detail methods for efficient symbol-table handling.

This chapter describes a number of symbol-table organizations for both nested and nonnested languages. Techniques involving ordered tables, tree-structured tables, and hash tables are presented. Routines for inserting and looking up table elements are discussed for each organization. These insertion and lookup routines are invoked when declarations are handled at compile time—precisely how and when they are invoked will not be considered in this chapter but will be examined in Chap. 11 in the section dealing with declaration handling.

8-2 WHEN TO CONSTRUCT AND INTERACT WITH THE SYMBOL TABLE

The point in the translation process at which the symbol-table handling routines are invoked depends primarily on the number and the nature of the passes in the compiler. The following discussion is somewhat simplistic but nevertheless illustrates the reasons for this dependency.

In a multipass compiler, such as the one depicted in Fig. 8-1, the symbol table is created during the lexical-analysis (scanning) pass. Index entries for variables in the symbol table form part of the token string produced by the scanner. For example, in Fig. 8-1 when X and Y occupy symbol-table positions 1 and 2, respectively, a token string such as $i1 := i2 + i1$ is created. The syntactic-analysis pass receives the token string, checks for syntactic correctness, and generates a

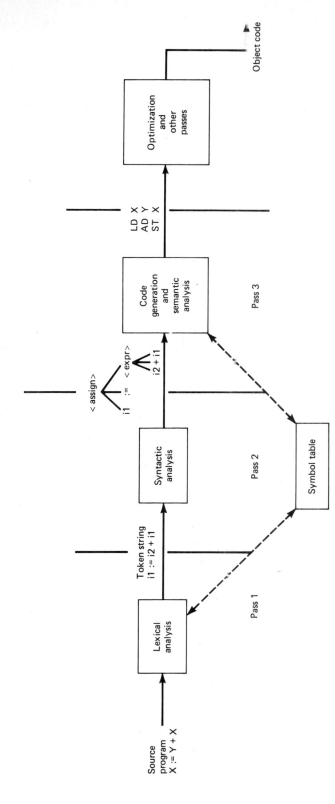

Figure 8-1 Multipass compiler configuration.

parse tree or some encoded form of the parse tree. This encoded form is then analyzed for semantic correctness (i.e., context-dependent correctness) and is used in the code-generation phase to generate a series of object-code instructions. The leaves of the parse tree contain indices into the symbol table. Note that no table-handling routines are used during the syntactic-analysis phase. It is not until the semantic-checking and code-generation phases that many of the attributes associated with a variable can be assigned values in the symbol table. For example, in a language with explicit declarations, the type of a variable can be assigned only when it is recognized that a declaration statement is being compiled. It is in the code-generation phase that the full context of the declaration (i.e., both the identifier name and its type) is known through the sequence of parsing actions performed by the syntactic analyzer.

Attempts can be made to assign attributes to the symbol table at other points in the translation process, most notably in the lexical-analysis phase. Such an approach, however, necessitates that some syntactic and semantic (i.e., context-sensitive) analysis for declarations be placed in the scanner. This strategy tends to produce a fragmented compiler in the sense that the functions of lexical analysis, syntactic analysis, and semantic analysis are intermixed in several modules of the compiler. It is generally conceded that the intermixing of functions produces an unstructured compiler and is not conducive to good software-engineering practices (McKeeman, 1973).

A second approach to symbol-table handling is illustrated in Fig. 8-2. The lexical-analysis, syntactic-analysis, and code-generation phases are completed in one pass. As a result, it is possible in the code-generation phase to recognize that a declaration statement is being processed before the entire source statement is scanned. This helps immensely, since the attributes of a variable, as dictated by the declaration statement, can be placed in the table as they are identified during

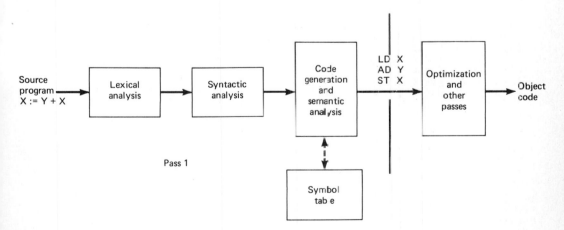

Figure 8-2 Combined-pass compiler configuration.

code generation. Therefore, in the second approach, the only module which needs to interact with the symbol table is the code generator.

An exception to this rule occurs when certain context-dependent information is required during compilation to assist in parsing activities. For example, in many programming languages it is convenient to recognize, with a table lookup in the scanner, the type of a particular identifier. With this information the scanner can pass on to the parser a more meaningful token such as "real identifier" or "integer identifier" rather than just "identifier." This strategy has two benefits. It reduces the complexity of the grammar for the parser (certain conflicts generated by using the general syntactic construct "identifier" can be resolved), and it allows a more systematic approach to error detection and recovery for context-sensitive types of errors.

In summary, it is suggested that in multipass compilers variable names should be inserted into the symbol table during lexical analysis and the other attributes of the variable should be assigned during code generation. If the lexical-analysis, syntactic-analysis, and code-generation phases are combined in one pass, all symbol-table interaction can be confined to the code-generation phase.

8-3 SYMBOL-TABLE CONTENTS

A symbol table is most often conceptualized as a series of rows, each row containing a list of attribute values that are associated with a particular variable. Figure 8-3 illustrates this conceptualization. The kinds of attributes appearing in a symbol table are dependent to some degree on the nature of the programming language for which the compiler is written. For example, a language may be typeless, and therefore the type attribute need not appear in the table. Similarly, the organization of the symbol table will vary depending on memory and access-time constraints. This point is exemplified throughout this chapter.

	Variable Name	Address	Type	Dimension	Line Declared	Lines Referenced	Pointer
1	COMPANY#	0	2	1	2	9, 14, 25	7
2	X3	4	1	0	3	12, 14	0
3	FORM1	8	3	2	4	36, 37, 38	6
4	B	48	1	0	5	10, 11, 13, 23	1
5	ANS	52	1	0	5	11, 23, 25	4
6	M	56	6	0	6	17, 21	2
7	FIRST	64	1	0	7	28, 29, 30, 38	3

Figure 8-3 Typical view of a symbol table.

The following list of attributes are not necessary for all compilers; however, each should be considered for a particular compiler implementation.

1. Variable name
2. Object time address
3. Type
4. Dimension or number of parameters for a procedure
5. Source line number at which the variable is declared
6. Source line numbers at which the variable is referenced
7. Link field for listing in alphabetical order

In the remainder of this section, each of the attributes is considered with respect to when it should be included and what problems arise in representing these attributes in a table.

A variable's name must always reside in the symbol table, since it is the means by which a particular variable is identified for semantic analysis and code generation. A major problem in symbol-table organization can be the variability in the length of identifier names. For languages such as BASIC with its one- and two-character names and FORTRAN with names up to six characters in length, this problem is minimal and can usually be handled by storing the complete identifier (padded to the right with blanks if necessary) in a fixed-size maximum-length field. However, as pointed out in Chap. 3, such severe restrictions on variable names are unwarranted.

While there are many ways of handling the storage of variable names, two popular approaches will be outlined—one which facilitates quick table access and another which supports the efficient storage of variable names. To provide quick access, it is best to insist on a predefined, yet sufficiently large, maximum variable name length. A length of sixteen or greater is very likely adequate. The complete identifier can then be stored, left-justified, in a fixed-length field in the symbol table. With this straightforward approach, table access is fast but the storage of short variable names is inefficient.

A second approach is to place a string descriptor in the variable-name field of the table. The descriptor contains position and length subfields, as shown in Fig. 8-4. The pointer subfield indicates the position of the first character of the variable name in a general string area, and the length subfield describes the number of characters in the variable name. A table access must always go through the descriptor to the string area for variable-name matching. Therefore, this approach results in slow table access, but the savings in storage can be considerable.

In the compilation process, an object-code address must be associated with every variable in a program. This address dictates the relative location for values of a variable at run time. The object-code address is entered in the symbol table when a variable is declared (or first encountered). This address is recalled from the table when the variable is referenced in the source program. The address is

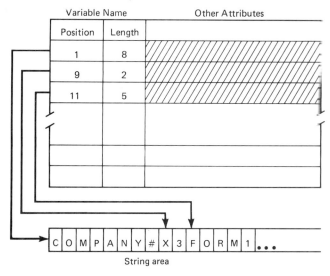

Figure 8-4 Using a string descriptor to represent a variable name.

then used in an object instruction that accesses (loads or stores) the value of that variable. For a language without dynamic storage-allocation requirements, such as FORTRAN, the object-code address is assigned in a sequential order starting at 1 and proceeding to m, where m is the maximum size of the data area allotted to a program. For block-structured languages, a 2-tuple address containing a block-level (BL) field and an occurrence number (ON) field is commonly adopted (see Randell and Russell, 1964). At run time the block-level value helps to locate the base of the data area allocated to the block in which the variable is declared. The occurrence number indicates the offset into the data area at which the value of the variable is stored. For now, it is not important to understand these object-code addressing schemes thoroughly—they will be elaborated upon in Chap. 9. This brief discussion should, however, aid in the understanding of why it is important that the object-code address should be included as a symbol-table attribute.

The type attribute is stored in the symbol table when compiling languages having either implicit or explicit data types. Of course, for typeless languages such as BLISS (Wulf et al., 1971), this attribute is excluded. FORTRAN provides an example of what is meant by implicit data typing. Variables which are not declared to be a particular type are assigned default types implicitly (variables with names starting with I, J, K, L, M, or N are integers; all other variables are real). The type of the variable, whether it be assigned implicitly or explicitly, is most important for semantic checking. If a variable, say S, is declared to be of type string, then the expression "S * 3.14" should be detected as erroneous (or at least a warning should be posted), since in most languages it is semantically inconsistent to multiply a string by a number. Numerous other examples of semantic-type checking will be discussed in Chap. 11. The type of a variable is also used as an indication of the amount of memory that must be allocated to a variable at run time. For example, if the type of a variable is integer, then a single word may be allocated in the data area; whereas, if the type is real, a double word may be required. Typically, the type of a variable is stored in the symbol table in an encoded form; that is, real is encoded as 1, integer is encoded as 2, etc.

The number-of-dimensions attribute and the number-of-parameters attribute are both important for semantic checking. In array references, the number of dimensions should agree with the number specified in the declaration of the array, and this agreement must be validated during semantic analysis. The number of dimensions is also used as a parameter in a generalized formula for calculating the address of a particular array element. In Chap. 9, we describe precisely how this is accomplished. The number of parameters in a procedure call must also agree with the number used in the procedure heading or declaration. In fact, in symbol-table construction it is convenient to view the number of parameters for a procedure as its number of dimensions and thus combine these two attributes into one. In addition to being convenient, this approach is also consistent, since the type of semantic checking for both attributes is similar.

In the example figures given in this chapter simple variables (i.e., scalars) are considered to be of dimension 0, vectors of dimension 1, matrices of dimension 2, etc.

A very important programming aid that can be provided by a compiler is a cross-reference listing. This listing contains many of the attributes we have discussed already, plus the source line number at which a variable is declared (if explicitly declared) or first referenced (if implicitly declared) and the source line numbers of all other references to the variable. Figure 8-5 illustrates a typical cross-reference listing. Note that problems arise when trying to represent a list of all source line-number references. Generally some form of linked representation into an area separate from the table is adopted to handle this problem.

Name	Type	Dimension	Declared at	Reference
ANS	Real	0	5	11, 23, 25
B	Real	0	5	10, 11, 13, 23
COMPANY#	Int	1	2	9, 14, 25
FIRST	Real	0	7	28, 29, 30, 38
FORM1	Char	2	4	36, 37, 38
M	Proc	0	6	17, 21
X3	Real	0	3	12, 14

Figure 8-5 Example of a cross-reference listing.

The final attribute, which we call the link field, is included simply to facilitate the production of a cross-reference listing that is ordered alphabetically by variable name. If a cross-reference listing is not to be included as one of the compiler aids, the link field as well as the source line-number attributes can be omitted from the symbol table.

Let us now look in more detail at the operations performed on a symbol table.

8-4 OPERATIONS ON SYMBOL TABLES

The two operations that are most commonly performed on symbol tables are *insertion* and *lookup* (also referred to as *retrieval*). The nature of each of these operations differs slightly depending on whether or not the language being compiled has explicit declarations.

For languages in which explicit declaration of all variables is mandatory, the two operations are invoked at clearly defined points in the compilation. It is obvious that an insertion operation is required when processing a declaration, since a declaration is intended to be an initial description of a variable's attributes in the program. If the symbol table is ordered, say, alphabetically by variable name (such symbol-table organizations will be described in the next section), then an insertion operation may also involve a lookup to find the locations at which the variable's attributes are to be placed. In such a situation an insertion is at least as expensive as a retrieval. If the symbol table is not ordered, the insertion operation is greatly simplified, since an initial lookup phase may be avoided; but the retrieval is expensive, since we may have to examine the entire table.

Retrieval operations are performed for all references to variables which do not involve declaration statements. The retrieved information (i.e., the type, object-code address, number of dimensions, etc.) is used for semantic checking and code generation as indicated in the previous section. Retrieval operations for variables which have not been previously declared are detected at this stage and appropriate error messages or warnings can be emitted. Some recovery from such semantic errors can be achieved by posting a warning message and incorporating the nondeclared variable in the symbol table. The attributes associated with such variables would have to be deduced, as much as possible, through the context in which the variable is referenced.

When a programming language permits implicit declarations of variables, the operations of insertion and retrieval are closely linked. If declarations are not explicit and mandatory, any variable reference must be treated as an initial reference, since there is no way of knowing a priori if the variable's attributes have been entered in the symbol table. Hence any variable reference generates a lookup operation followed by an insertion if the variable's name is not found in the symbol table. All attributes associated with an implicitly declared variable must be deduced from the variable's role in the program.

For block-structured languages, two additional operations, which we denote as *set* and *reset*, are required for symbol-table interaction. The set operation is invoked when the beginning of a block is recognized during compilation. The complementary operation, the reset operation, is applied when the end of a block is encountered. The nature of and the need for these operations can be illustrated by examining the program segment in Fig. 3-6.

In this figure, the variable X is declared in more than one block; in each of these blocks, X assumes different attributes. In a nested language, it is necessary to ensure that each instance of a variable name is associated with a set of unique table locations for storing the variable's attributes. To handle this problem adequately, two types of adjustments—as realized in the set and reset operations —are required in the symbol table.

Upon block entry, the set operation establishes a new subtable (within the symbol table) in which the attributes for the variables declared in the new block can be stored. Exactly how this new subtable is established is dependent upon the

```
BBLOCK;

        REAL X, Y; STRING NAME;
        •
        •
        •
      M1:   PBLOCK (INTEGER IND);

            INTEGER X;
            •
            •
            •
            CALL M2(IND + 1);
            •
            •
            •
      END M1;


      M2:   PBLOCK (INTEGER J);
            •
            •
            •
            BBLOCK;

                ARRAY INTEGER F(J); LOGICAL TEST1;

                •
                •
                •
            END;
      END M2;
        •
        •
        •
        CALL M1 (X / Y);
        •
        •
        •
END;
```

Figure 8-6 Program segment from a block-structured language.

symbol-table organization. A number of different techniques for subtable creation will be discussed in Sec. 8-6.

Because a new subtable is established for each block, the duplicate variable-name problem can be resolved in the following manner. Assume a table-lookup operation is performed for a variable X and the subtables that are currently active are numbered $1, 2, \ldots, n$ according to the order in which they were created (i.e., subtable 1 was the first to be created, subtable n was the last to be created). If the search begins at subtable n and proceeds to subtable 1, then the desired variable, that is, the latest occurrence of X, is located first. In this manner, any ambiguity associated with duplicate names is resolved. Note that duplicate occurrences of a variable name in the same block are not allowed.

Upon block exit, the reset operation removes the subtable entries for the variables of the completed block. The removal of these entries reflects the fact that the variables in the terminated block can no longer be referenced. Again, the different methods for removing table entries are dependent on the symbol-table organization and hence are discussed in Sec. 8-6.

Now that the types of operations on a symbol table have been described, we are in a position to consider a number of different symbol-table organizations. In particular, an examination will be undertaken of how efficiently the symbol-table operations can be performed for each organization.

8-5 SYMBOL-TABLE ORGANIZATIONS FOR NON-BLOCK-STRUCTURED LANGUAGES

In this section, a number of symbol-table organizations are described for non-block-structured languages. By a non-block-structured language we mean a language in which each separately compiled unit is a single module that has no submodules. All variables declared in a module are known throughout the module.

Many of the organizations discussed in this section can be applied to block-structured languages also. These organizations along with some additional symbol-table methods for nested languages will be described in Sec. 8-6.

The organizations presented in this section proceed from the conceptually simple organizations, which generally are storage-efficient, to the more complex organizations, which provide fast table access. The primary measure which is used to determine the complexity of a symbol-table operation is the *average length of search*. This measure is the average number of comparisons required to retrieve a symbol-table record in a particular table organization. The collection of attributes stored in the table for a given variable will be called a *symbol-table record*. The name of the variable for which an insertion or lookup operation is to be performed will be referred to as the *search argument*.

8-5.1 Unordered Symbol Tables

The simplest method of organizing a symbol table is to add the attribute entries to the table in the order in which the variables are declared. Of course, if variables are declared implicitly, attributes are added according to the order in which variables are encountered during compilation.

Let us first examine the insertion and lookup operations for languages with explicit declarations. In an insertion operation no comparisons are required (other than checking for symbol-table overflow), since the attributes for a newly defined variable are simply added at the current end of the table. This procedure is somewhat idealistic, however, because it ignores the problem of duplicate variable-name declarations. To check for this type of error, a complete table search must precede the insertion operation. The lookup operation requires, on the average, a search length of $(n + 1)/2$, assuming that there are n records in the table. This result can be derived easily by noting that the first record in the table is accessible in one comparison, the second record is accessible in two comparisons, and so on. Therefore, the expected length of search is

$$\frac{1}{n} \sum_{i=1}^{n} i = \frac{1}{n}((n + 1) * (n)/2) = (n + 1)/2$$

Of course, if the element is not found, an error has occurred and a recovery strategy, such as one of those discussed in the previous section, is necessary.

For a language with implicit declarations, an insertion operation must always be preceded by a lookup operation. In fact, it is the absence of a variable as determined by the lookup operation that indicates the variable's attributes must be inserted in the symbol table. If this process requires a lookup followed by an insertion (in the case of a first occurrence of a variable), then n comparisons plus an insertion are necessary. If only a lookup is needed (in the case in which the variable was previously referenced), then an average of $(n + 1)/2$ comparisons are used to locate the appropriate set of variable attributes. Therefore, if the ratio of first variable references to total variable references is denoted as ρ, the lookup and insertion process requires, on the average,

$$\rho n + (1 - \rho) * (n + 1)/2$$

comparisons.

An unordered table organization should be used only if the expected size of the symbol table is small, since the average time for lookup and insertion is directly proportional to the table size. In the subsections to follow we will look at some organizations which reduce the search time substantially.

8-5.2 Ordered Symbol Tables

In this and the following two subsections, we describe symbol-table organizations in which the table position of a variable's set of attributes is based on the variable's name. In such circumstances, an insertion must be accompanied by a lookup procedure which determines where in the symbol table the variable's attributes should be placed. The actual insertion of a new set of attributes may generate some additional overhead primarily because other sets of attributes may have to be moved in order to achieve the insertion. These notions will be illustrated often in the remaining discussion in this section.

An ordered symbol table is illustrated in Fig. 8-7. Note that the table is lexically ordered on the variable names. While a number of table-lookup strategies can be applied to such a table organization, we will examine the two most popular search techniques: the linear search and the binary search.

In the previous subsection we discussed the linear search with respect to an unordered symbol-table organization. The question that must be addressed is whether ordering the table is beneficial when using the linear-search technique. The lookup operation still requires an average search length of $(n + 1)/2$ if the search argument is in the table. An analysis deriving this result is identical to that given in the previous subsection for unordered tables. Note, however, that if the search argument is not in an ordered table, its absence can be detected without having to search the complete table. Upon encountering the first argument in the table which is lexically greater than the search argument, it is decidable that the search argument is not in the table. Therefore, the average length of search required to determine if an argument is in an ordered table or not is $(n + 1)/2$ (again, assuming the same analysis given previously).

Using an ordered table organization avoids the necessity of a complete table search. An additional complexity, however, is introduced when performing the insertion operation. For example, if the variable COUNT is inserted in the table which is stored sequentially as shown in Fig. 8-7, then the elements lexically larger than COUNT must be moved down in the table to make room for the insertion of the set of attributes for COUNT. Therefore, using a linear-search technique on an ordered table, an insertion operation requires $n - c$ comparisons followed by c moves (i.e., a total of n basic operations). The movement of a table record can be eliminated by using a singly linked list form of table representation which facilitates a single-step insertion. This approach, however, requires that an additional link field be attached to each table record.

From the previous analysis, we can conclude that ordering the symbol table affords few appreciable advantages over the unordered organization if a linear

Variable Name	Type	Dimension	Other Attributes
ANS	1	0	
B	1	0	
COMPANY#	2	1	
FIRST	1	0	
FORM1	3	2	
M	6	0	
X3	1	0	

Figure 8-7 An ordered symbol table.

search is used. In fact the one major advantage is that the ordered symbol table can be used in the direct generation of a cross-reference listing, whereas an unordered table would have to be sorted before printing such a listing.

It can be shown that the most efficient way to search an ordered table using only comparisons is the *binary search* (see Knuth, 1973). In this search strategy we begin by comparing a search argument, say X, with the middle element of the table. This comparison either locates the desired element or dictates which half of the table should be searched next. If the desired element is not located, the appropriate half of the table is selected as a new subtable upon which the halving or bisection procedure is repeated. The middle element of the new subtable is compared with the search element as before, and this process is continued until the desired table element is found. For example, a search for the variable named FORM1 in the table given in Fig. 8-7 produces the following sequence of probes: FIRST, M, and finally FORM1.

The following algorithm formally describes the binary search method.

Function BINARY_SEARCH(SARG). Given a table of global records $R_1, R_2, \ldots, R_n$ whose variable names as denoted by $NAME_i$ are in increasing order, this function searches the structure for a given search argument SARG. The local variables B and E denote the lower and upper limits of the search interval, respectively. If any $NAME_i$ matches SARG, the index i is returned. If no match is found, the negation of the latest value of i is returned.

1. [Initialize]
        B ← 1
        E ← n
2. [Perform search]
        Repeat through step 4 while B ≤ E
3. [Obtain index of midpoint]
        i ← ⌊(B + E)/2⌋
4. [Compare]
        If SARG < $NAME_i$
        then E ← i − 1
        else If SARG > $NAME_i$
                then B ← i + 1
                else Return(i)
5. [Unsuccessful search]
        Write('ELEMENT NOT FOUND')
        Return(−i)   □

The size of the set of table records that are potentially accessible in a particular iteration (i.e., step 2 in Function BINARY_SEARCH) grows as the square of the iteration. That is, in the first pass one record is compared, in the second pass two records are potential candidates for comparison, in the third pass four records are potential candidates, and in general, in the nth pass 2^{n-1} records are potential candidates. From this analysis, it is easy to establish that the maximum length of search using a binary search is $\lfloor \log_2 n \rfloor + 1$ for a table of size n. Therefore, in the example table given in Fig. 8-7, the maximum length of search is $\lfloor \log_2 7 \rfloor + 1$ or 3.

The average length of search is given in the following expression:

$$\frac{1}{n}\left(1*1 + 2*2 + 4*3 + \cdots + 2^{\lfloor \log_2 n \rfloor} * (\lfloor \log_2 n \rfloor + 1)\right)$$

$$= \frac{1}{n} \sum_{i=1}^{\lfloor \log_2 n \rfloor + 1} 2^{i-1} * i \tag{1}$$

The term $2^{i-1} * i$ is the product of the number of elements with a search length of i (namely, 2^{i-1} elements) and the search length i. It can be shown that the average search length, as given in (1), approximates to $\lfloor \log_2 n \rfloor - 1$ (see Knuth, 1973) for a reasonable size of n.

From this analysis, it is clear that the binary search performs as well as or better than the linear search for any size of table. However, because of the complexities of the binary-search strategy, additional overhead is necessary. Updating the lower and upper indices (namely, B and E in Function BINARY_SEARCH) is an example of such overhead.

In implementing a symbol-table handler, this overhead must be taken into consideration. Unfortunately this overhead is somewhat machine-dependent, and therefore some performance experimentation should be completed before this search technique is adopted. Table 8-1 illustrates the results from two such experiments. In both experiments every element of the table was searched for 10,000 times. The results in Table 8-1a are for PL/I programs running on an IBM 370/158 under OS/VS2 and the results in Table 8-1b are for C programs running on a PDP-11/40 using Bell Laboratories' UNIX operating system.

For the PL/I programs the crossover point is approximately 22, while for the C programs the crossover point is about 12. From this we may conclude that if

Table 8-1 Linear-search and binary-search statistics

(a) PL/I			(b) C		
Table size	Running time, seconds		Table size	Running time, seconds	
n	Linear	Binary	n	Linear	Binary
7	10.34	12.79	7	8.5	9.5
15	27.53	30.33	15	26.8	24.3
31	87.49	70.25	31	89.3	57.7

the average number of table elements per program module is less than 10, a linear-search strategy should be considered; whereas, if the average number of elements is greater than 25, a binary-search strategy provides better performance.

While a binary search may improve the table-lookup operation, the problem of inserting an element into an ordered table persists. Recall that in Function BINARY_SEARCH a negative index is returned if the search element is not found. The absolute value of this index generally points to the lexically largest variable name which is less than the search argument. (Some exceptions to this rule occur, for example, when the search argument is less than any element in the table, in which case a -1 is returned.) Therefore Function BINARY_SEARCH yields the position at which the new record should be inserted. Unfortunately, on the average $(n + 1)/2$ moves are still required to insert the record.

8-5.3 Tree-Structured Symbol Tables

The time to perform a table-insertion operation can be reduced from that of an ordered table by using a tree-structured type of storage organization. In this type of organization an attempt is made to reflect the search structure of the binary search in the structural links of a binary-search tree.

A binary tree-structured symbol table that contains the same records as the table in Fig. 8-7 is illustrated in Fig. 8-8a. Note that two new fields are present in a record structure. These two link fields will be called the left pointer and right pointer fields. Access to the tree is gained through the *root node* (i.e., the top node of the tree). A search proceeds down the structural links of the tree until the desired node is found or a NULL link field (denoted by /) is encountered. In the latter case, the search is unsuccessful, since a match between the search argument and the names in the table is not achieved.

The tree representation given in Fig. 8-8a shows only the logical relationship between table records in the tree. Because link fields define only the logical relationships between the table records, we are free to store the records in a contiguous area and in any order, provided the correct structural relationships between nodes are preserved. Figure 8-8b depicts the more familiar representation for a table (i.e., a representation in which table records are physically adjacent). In the figure, the pointer-field value of zero represents a NULL structural link. In this representation the root node is always located at the first record location in the table.

In a binary-tree organization, a new record is inserted as a *leaf node* (i.e., a node with NULL in both link fields) in a tree. This insertion is completed so as to preserve a lexical ordering of table records as dictated by the structural links of the tree. To describe the notion of lexical ordering more clearly, the concepts of a left and right subtree must be introduced.

The left subtree of a node X is defined to be that part of the tree containing all those nodes reachable from the left branch of X. For example, the set of nodes for the variables B, ANS, and COMPANY# plus the interconnecting structural

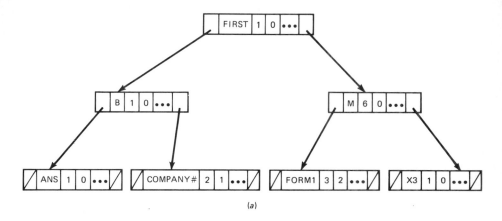

(a)

Table Position	Name Field	Type	Dimension	Other Attributes	Left Pointer	Right Pointer
1	FIRST	1	0		2	5
2	B	1	0		3	4
3	ANS	1	0		0	0
4	COMPANY #	2	1		0	0
5	M	6	0		6	7
6	FORM1	3	2		0	0
7	X3	1	0		0	0

(b)

Figure 8-8 Binary-tree organization of a symbol table showing (a) the logical relationships and (b) a physical representation.

links form the left subtree of the node for the variable FIRST in Fig. 8-8. The right subtree has an obvious complementary meaning.

Therefore, in a binary-tree organization, the tree is ordered such that every node in its left subtree precedes lexicographically the root node of the tree. Similarly, every node in its right subtree follows lexicographically the root node of the tree. This ordering holds for all subtrees in a tree as well. For example, if a record for the variable COUNT is inserted in the tree given in Fig. 8-8a, it is treated as a leaf node and is placed to the right of the record for the variable COMPANY #. The insertion is shown in Fig. 8-9.

It is important to realize that because of this insertion strategy the organization of the tree structure is dependent upon the order of insertion. To illustrate

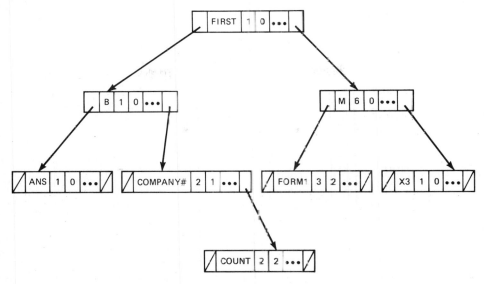

Figure 8-9 The insertion of a record for the variable name COUNT.

this point, let us examine Fig. 8-8*a*. This tree structure is created if, for example, the records are inserted in the order

> FIRST, B, ANS, COMPANY#, M, FORM1, and X3

or

> FIRST, B, M, ANS, COMPANY#, FORM1, and X3

However, if the insertion order is, for example,

> FORM1, B, COMPANY#, ANS, M, X3, and FIRST

a different tree is created. Figure 8-10 shows the stages in the development of the tree assuming the latter insertion order.

Because records are inserted so as to preserve a particular ordering, an insertion operation must always include the same tree-search procedure required for a lookup operation. This combined search procedure is described in Function **BIN_TREE**, which follows. In the algorithm we distinguish between the insertion and lookup operations by a logical parameter **INSERT**. If **INSERT** is *true*, an insertion operation is requested; if it is *false*, a lookup operation is implied. For both operations, **SARG** is a parameter containing the search argument, i.e., the name of the variable being inserted or searched for. **DATA** is a parameter containing additional attribute information for an insertion operation.

If the operation is an insertion and it is successful, the location of the new node is returned. If it is unsuccessful, a negated pointer value is returned which

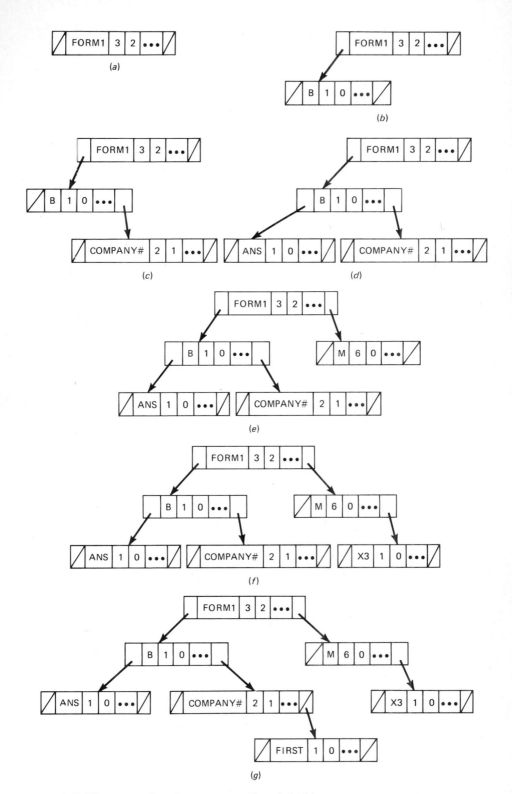

Figure 8-10 The construction of a tree-structured symbol table.

indicates the position of a previously inserted record with the same name as the search argument.

For a table-lookup operation, a successful search returns the location of the record with a name field that matches the search argument. If the search is unsuccessful (i.e., the variable has not been previously declared), then a negated pointer value is returned, indicating the last node examined during the search. This value can be used to insert a new node as part of an error-recovery procedure.

Function BIN_TREE(INSERT, SARG, DATA, ROOT). Given the parameters INSERT, SARG, and DATA as described previously, as well as ROOT, which is a variable containing the location of the root node in the tree, this function performs the requested operation on the tree-structured symbol table. The global record node, NODE, has a name field called NAME, the attribute fields of a record node are denoted by ATTR, and the left pointer and right pointer fields in a record node are identified by LPTR and RPTR, respectively. T and P are temporary pointer variables. If the requested operation is performed successfully, the address of any newly created node is returned; otherwise, the negation of the latest value of T is returned.

1. [Initialize search variable T]
    T ← ROOT
2. [Loop until requested operation is complete]
    Repeat step 3 while true
3. [Compare the search argument and the name field of the record]
    If SARG < NAME(T)
    then If LPTR(T) ≠ NULL
            then T ← LPTR(T)
            else If INSERT
                then (create a new left leaf node and insert)
                    P ⇐ NODE
                    NAME(P) ← SARG
                    ATTR(P) ← DATA
                    LPTR(P) ← RPTR(P) ← NULL
                    LPTR(T) ← P
                    Return(P)
                else Return(− T)   (lookup unsuccessful)
    else If SARG > NAME(T)
        then If RPTR(T) ≠ NULL
                then T ← RPTR(T)
                else If INSERT
                    then (create a new right leaf node and insert)
                        P ⇐ NODE
                        NAME(P) ← SARG
                        ATTR(P) ← DATA

$$LPTR(P) \leftarrow RPTR(P) \leftarrow NULL$$
$$RPTR(T) \leftarrow P$$
Return(P)
    else Return(− T)   (lookup unsuccessful)
else (a match)
    If INSERT
    then Return(− T)
    else Return(T)   □

The algorithm should be easy to understand based on the previous discussion. Basically a search proceeds down the tree structure via a series of comparisons which are performed iteratively in step 3 of the algorithm. If a match occurs, then either a negated pointer value is returned, indicating an error in the insertion operation, or the position of the record with the name equal to the search

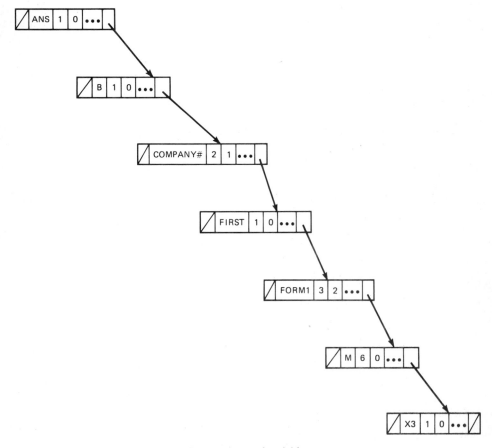

Figure 8-11 The ordered insertion of a sample set of variables.

argument is returned for a lookup operation. If a match is not found, that is, a NULL link field is encountered in step 3, then either a negated pointer value is returned for the lookup operation or a new record is created and appended to the tree in an insertion operation.

A major problem exists with the binary tree organization just described. Since insertion always takes place at the leaves of the tree, a search tree can become very unbalanced. For example, it is a common practice when writing large programs to declare the variables in a module in lexicographic order. If this practice is applied to a module containing the variables in Fig. 8-8, a tree as depicted in Fig. 8-11 will be created. It is obvious that in this situation the binary tree structure has degenerated to an ordered linked list with an average search length of $(n + 1)/2$. Hibbard (1962) showed that for randomly generated trees an average search length of $1.4 \log_2 n$ is expected.

The ideal search tree is, of course, one in which all maximum-length search paths are of equal or nearly equal length and thus elongated search paths such as the one shown in Fig. 8-11 are avoided. This ideal situation is realized in a tree-structured organization called an *optimally balanced binary tree*. In such a structure the distances (i.e., path length) from the root node to any two incomplete nodes of the tree differ by at most 1. By an *incomplete node*, we mean a node in which at least one of its link fields has a NULL value. Note that our definition of an optimally balanced tree is somewhat restrictive in the sense that all nodes are considered to have the same probability of access. For a more general definition, see Knuth (1973).

The search trees in Figs. 8-8 and 8-9 are both optimally balanced. Unfortunately, it is difficult to keep a tree structure optimally balanced when records are continually inserted into the structure. Consider the optimally balanced tree given in Fig. 8-12. The insertion of a record for the variable ANS constitutes almost a complete reorganization (i.e., a change in every link field) of the tree structure to arrive at an optimally balanced tree such as that in Fig. 8-8.

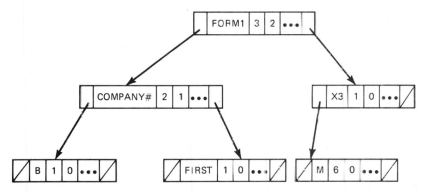

Figure 8-12 Example of optimal balanced tree where the insertion of ANS requires a complete reorganization.

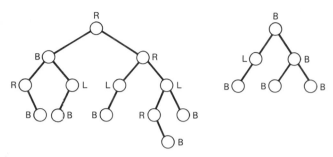

Figure 8-13 Examples of AVL trees.

Therefore, to attain an optimally balanced tree may require at least the examination of every node in the tree. Such an examination takes on the order of n basic operations.

By reducing the balancing criteria from optimally balanced to almost optimally balanced as defined by Adel'son-Vel'skii and Landis (1962), we are able to locate, to insert, or to delete an item in the order of $\log_2 n$ basic operations. An *AVL tree* (named after the original authors) is a binary-search tree in which each node of the tree is in one of three states:

1. A node is *left-heavy* if the longest path in its left subtree is one longer than the longest path of its right subtree.
2. A node is *balanced* if the longest paths in both of its subtrees are equal.
3. A node is *right-heavy* if the longest path in its right subtree is one longer than the longest path in its left subtree.

If each node in the tree is in one of the three previous states, the tree is said to be balanced; otherwise it is unbalanced. Each node in the tree structure contains a balance indicator field which indicates the current state of node. Figure 8-13 illustrates two balanced trees with the state, left (L), balanced (B), or right (R), marked on each node. Figure 8-14 represents examples of unbalanced trees.

Let us now examine the symbol-table operations of insertion and lookup as they apply to AVL trees. Again a lexicographic ordering is assumed in the relationships between record nodes of the tree-symbol table and, therefore, node insertion must be preceded by a search procedure to locate where the node should

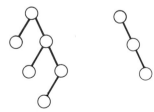

Figure 8-14 Examples of unbalanced trees.

reside. A placement of the node using the strategy in Function BIN_TREE can cause the AVL tree to become unbalanced. Upon detection of an unbalanced tree, a rebalancing strategy must be applied. We next concentrate on how to detect an unbalanced tree and how to rebalance such a tree.

In the following discussion, it is assumed that a new node is inserted at the leaf level (as either a left or a right subtree of some incomplete node). The only nodes which can have their balance indicator changed by such an insertion are those which lie on a path between the root of the tree and the newly inserted leaf. The possible changes which can occur to a node on this path are as follows:

1. The node was either left- or right-heavy and has now become balanced.
2. The node was balanced and has now become left- or right-heavy.
3. The node was heavy and the new node has been inserted in the heavy subtree, thus creating an unbalanced subtree. Such a node is said to be a *critical node*.

If condition 1 applies to a current node, then the balance indicators of all ancestor nodes of this node remain unchanged, since the longest path in the subtree (of which the current node is its root) remains unchanged. When condition 2 applies to a current node, the balance indicators of the ancestors of this node will change. If condition 3 applies to a current node, the tree has become unbalanced and this node has become critical. Figure 8-15 contains examples of the three cases which can arise. The dotted branch and node denote the new element which is being inserted.

Let us now address the problem of rebalancing a tree when a critical node is encountered. There are two broad cases which can arise, each of which can be further subdivided into two similar subcases. A general representation of case 1, which is often called *single rotation*, is given in Fig. 8-16. The rectangles labeled T_1, T_2, and T_3 represent subtrees and the node labeled NEW denotes the node being inserted. The expression at the bottom of each rectangle denotes the maximum path length in that subtree *after* insertion. With the insertion of node NEW in Fig. 8-16a the node X becomes critical since the maximum path lengths for the left subtree and the right subtree are $n + 2$ and n respectively. To rebalance, we simply rotate the positions of X and Y as shown to arrive at a balanced tree. A specific example of the second subcase for single rotation (i.e., X is critically unbalanced to the right) is exemplified in Fig. 8-17. The PATH and DIRECTION vectors are explained in the Function AVL_TREE which follows.

The second case, called *double rotation*, is illustrated in Fig. 8-18. It is much like the first, except that node Y becomes heavy in an opposite direction to that in which X was heavy. It is necessary to move node Z up the tree in such a way as to reduce the maximum path length of the left subtree of X. In effect, two interchanges are required: one between Y and Z, and then one between Z and X. Again, a specific example of the second subcase (i.e., X is critically unbalanced to the right) is shown in Fig. 8-19.

We now consider the formulation of Function AVL_TREE for the insertion and lookup of a search argument SARG. The record structure (NODE) for the

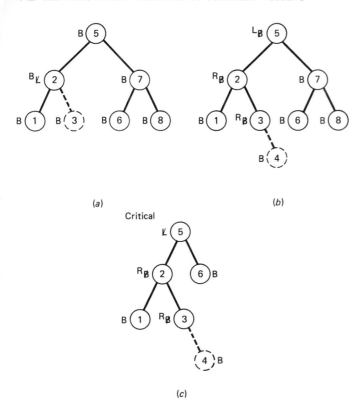

(a)   (b)

(c)

Figure 8-15 Examples of insertions into a balanced tree. (*a*) Condition 1. (*b*) Condition 2. (*c*) Condition 3.

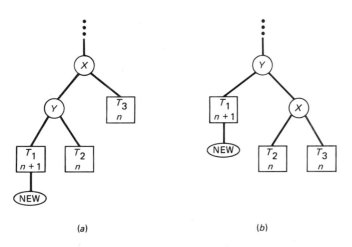

(a)   (b)

Figure 8-16 Rebalancing using a single rotation.

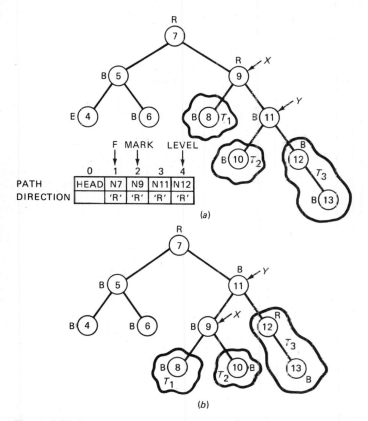

	F	MARK	LEVEL	
	↓	↓	↓	
0	1	2	3	4
PATH	HEAD	N7	N9	N11	N12
DIRECTION		'R'	'R'	'R'	'R'

(a)

(b)

Figure 8-17 Example of single rotation. (a) Before balancing. (b) After balancing.

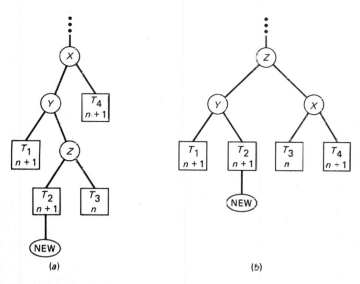

(a)

(b)

Figure 8-18 Rebalancing using a double rotation.

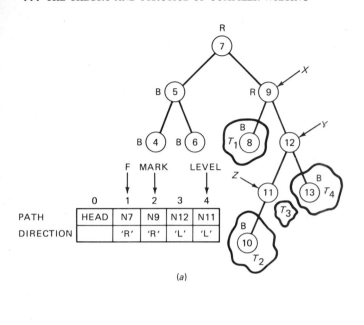

	0	1	2	3	4
PATH	HEAD	N7	N9	N12	N11
DIRECTION		'R'	'R'	'L'	'L'

(a)

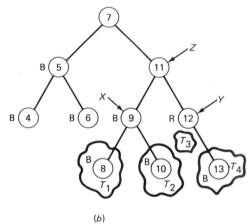

(b)

Figure 8-19 Example of double rotation. (*a*) Before balancing. (*b*) After balancing.

tree consists of a left pointer field (LPTR), a name field (NAME), a set of attribute fields (ATTR), a balance indicator (BI), and a right pointer field (RPTR). The balance indicator can have values of 'L' (left-heavy), 'R' (right-heavy), or 'B' (balanced). The root node is pointed to by the left pointer of a special node called the list head. The list-head node is important in the following algorithm because it ensures that the algorithm is general enough to handle rotations involving the root node of the tree. The list head is accessible through the pointer variable HEAD, and its balance indicator BI always has a value of 'L'. The logical variable INSERT and the variables SARG and DATA assume the same roles as in Function BIN_TREE.

Function AVL_TREE(INSERT, SARG, DATA, HEAD). Given a tree representation as just discussed and the parameters INSERT, SARG, DATA, and HEAD, this function performs the table lookup and insertion operations on an AVL tree. The array PATH is used to store the addresses of the nodes between the list head and the point in the tree where the insertion is made. The corresponding vector DIRECTION is used to store the direction of each branch in this path. The values of 'L' and 'R' are used to denote a left and right branch, respectively. The variable MARK denotes the index of an array element in PATH which contains the address of the critical node (X). F points to the parent of the critical node before rebalancing takes place. The variables X, Y, and Z are pointer variables whose functions have been previously described. LEVEL is an index variable. NEW is the address of the new node created, and this address is returned if the requested operation is successful. Otherwise, either NULL or the negation of the address of T is returned. T is a temporary pointer used in traversing the tree from the root to where the node is to be being inserted.

1. [Is the table empty?]
    If LPTR(HEAD) = HEAD   (tree is empty)
    then If INSERT
        then NEW $\Leftarrow$ NODE
            LPTR(NEW) $\leftarrow$ RPTR(NEW) $\leftarrow$ NULL
            BI(NEW) $\leftarrow$ 'B'
            NAME(NEW) $\leftarrow$ SARG
            ATTR(NEW) $\leftarrow$ DATA
            LPTR(HEAD) $\leftarrow$ NEW
            Return(NEW)
        else Return(NULL)   (table is empty)
2. [Initialize]
    LEVEL $\leftarrow$ 0
    PATH[LEVEL] $\leftarrow$ HEAD
    T $\leftarrow$ LPTR(HEAD)
3. [Set up loop]
    Repeat step 4 while true
4. [Compare and insert, if required]
    If SARG < NAME(T)
    then If LPTR(T) $\neq$ NULL
        then LEVEL $\leftarrow$ LEVEL + 1
            PATH[LEVEL] $\leftarrow$ T
            DIRECTION[LEVEL] $\leftarrow$ 'L'
            T $\leftarrow$ LPTR(T)
        else If INSERT
            then NEW $\Leftarrow$ NODE
                LPTR(NEW) $\leftarrow$ RPTR(NEW) $\leftarrow$ NULL
                BI(NEW) $\leftarrow$ 'B'
                NAME(NEW) $\leftarrow$ SARG
                ATTR(NEW) $\leftarrow$ DATA

```
                    LPTR(T) ← NEW
                    LEVEL ← LEVEL + 1
                    PATH[LEVEL] ← T
                    DIRECTION[LEVEL] ← 'L'
                    Exit loop
              else Return( − T)              (record not found in a lookup)
        else If SARG > NAME(T)
              then If RPTR(T) ≠ NULL
                    then LEVEL ← LEVEL + 1
                         PATH[LEVEL] ← T
                         DIRECTION[LEVEL] ← 'R'
                         T ← RPTR(T)
                    else If INSERT
                         then NEW ⇐ NODE
                              LPTR(NEW) ← RPTR(NEW) ← NULL
                              BI(NEW) ← 'B'
                              NAME(NEW) ← SARG
                              ATTR(NEW) ← DATA
                              RPTR(T) ← NEW
                              LEVEL ← LEVEL + 1
                              PATH[LEVEL] ← T
                              DIRECTION[LEVEL] ← 'R'
                              Exit loop
                         else Return( − T)
              else (a match)
                    If INSERT
                    then Write('DUPLICATE DECLARATION ERROR')
                         Return( − T)
                    else Return(T)
5. [Search for an unbalanced node]
        MARK ← LEVEL
        i ← LEVEL
        P ← PATH[i]
        Repeat while BI(P) = 'B'
            MARK ← i ← i − 1
            P ← PATH[i]
6. [Adjust balance indicators]
        Repeat for i = MARK + 1, MARK + 2 ,...., LEVEL
            If SARG < NAME(PATH[i])
            then BI(PATH[i]) ← 'L'
            else BI(PATH[i]) ← 'R'
7. [Is there a critical node?]
        If MARK = 0
        then Return(NEW)
        D ← DIRECTION[MARK]
        X ← PATH[MARK]
```

Y ← PATH[MARK + 1]
IF BI(X) ≠ D
then BI(X) ← 'B' (The node X was heavy and now becomes balanced)
    Return(NEW)

8. [Rebalancing: single rotation]
    If BI(Y) = D
    then If D = 'L'   (left-heavy, see Fig. 8-16)
            then LPTR(X) ← RPTR(Y)
                 RPTR(Y) ← X
            else RPTR(X) ← LPTR(Y)   (right-heavy, see Fig. 8-17)
                 LPTR(Y) ← X
         BI(X) ← BI(Y) ← 'B'
         F ← PATH[MARK − 1]
         If X = LPTR(F)
         then LPTR(F) ← Y
         else RPTR(F) ← Y
         Return(NEW)

9. [Rebalancing: double rotation]
    (a) (Change structural links)
    If D = 'L'   (left-heavy, see Fig. 8-18)
    then Z ← RPTR(Y)
         RPTR(Y) ← LPTR(Z)
         LPTR(Z) ← Y
         LPTR(X) ← RPTR(Z)
         RPTR(Z) ← X
    else Z ← LPTR(Y)   (right-heavy, see Fig. 8-19)
         LPTR(Y) ← RPTR(Z)
         RPTR(Z) ← Y
         RPTR(X) ← LPTR(Z)
         LPTR(Z) ← X
    F ← PATH[MARK − 1]
    If X = LPTR(F)
    then LPTR(F) ← Z
    else RPTR(F) ← Z
    (b) (Change balance indicators)
    If BI(Z) = D
    then BI(Y) ← BI(Z) ← 'B'
         If D = 'L'
         then BI(X) ← 'R'
         else BI(X) ← 'L'
    else If BI(Z) = 'B'
         then BI(X) ← BI(Y) ← BI(Z) ← 'B'
         else BI(X) ← BI(Z) ← 'B'
              BI(Y) ← D
    Return(NEW)   □

Steps 1 through 4 are closely patterned after Function BIN_TREE. If an insertion operation is performed, step 4 attaches the new node to the existing tree. In addition, it stores into vectors PATH and DIRECTION the address of the nodes on the path between the root node and the leaf being inserted, and direction of the path at each node, respectively. If a NULL link field is encountered in step 4 during a lookup operation, a negated pointer value of the current node T is returned, thereby signaling an error condition. Step 5 of the algorithm searches for an unbalanced node which is closest to the new node just inserted. In step 6 the balance indicators of the nodes between the unbalanced node found in the previous step and the new node are adjusted. Step 7 determines whether or not there is a critical node. If there is, control proceeds either to step 8 (single-rotation) or step 9 (double-rotation). When no critical node is found, the balance indicator of the unbalanced node found in step 5 is adjusted. The last two steps of the algorithm correspond to case 1 and case 2 in the previous discussion, and rebalancing of the tree is performed in each case. The reader should trace through the algorithm for the examples given in Figs. 8-17 and 8-19.

Let us look more closely at the performance of Function AVL_TREE. It can be shown that the maximum path length m in an AVL tree of n nodes is $1.5 \log_2(n + 1)$ (see Stone, 1972). Knuth (1973) shows with the aid of some empirical evidence that the expected search time is $\log_2(n + 1) + a$ constant. Therefore, for a reasonable size n, the AVL tree organization is almost as good as an optimally balanced tree organization.

A number of other suboptimal search-tree organizations have been proposed, and a survey of these methods can be found in Knuth (1973) and Nievergelt (1974). Two of the more popular organizations are the weight-balanced (WB) tree (Knuth, 1973; Baer, 1975) and the bounded-balance (BB) tree (Nievergelt and Reingold, 1973). In a weight-balanced tree certain access frequencies are assumed to be known for the table elements. In particular let $\beta_1, \ldots, \beta_n$ denote the access frequencies of the variables $X_1, X_2, \ldots, X_n$ where $X_i < X_j$ if $i < j$, and $\alpha_0, \alpha_1, \ldots, \alpha_n$ denote the frequencies with which search arguments would lie between the variable names (i.e., α_i is the frequency with which a search argument S satisfies $X_i < S < X_{i+1}$). Then the average length of search for both successful and unsuccessful searches is

$$\sum_{i=1}^{n} \beta_i l_i + \sum_{i=0}^{n} \alpha_i l_i \tag{2}$$

where l_i is the level of a node or the level at which it is discovered that the search argument is not in the table. An optimal weight-balanced tree is one in which expression (2) is minimized.

Two major problems exist with weight-balanced trees. The most obvious is that the sets of frequencies $\beta_1, \ldots, \beta_n$ and $\alpha_0, \alpha_1, \ldots, \alpha_n$ are never really known a priori during the compilation process. Second, the time to construct such trees is on the order of n^3 basic operations.

BB trees are based on a height-balancing principle as are AVL trees. The difference is that the balancing parameter attempts to provide a compromise between short search time and infrequent rebalancing in the following sense. A tree T is of bounded balance α, or is $BB[\alpha]$, if and only if, for each subtree T' of T, the fraction of nodes in the left subtree of T' lies between α and $1 - \alpha$. Therefore, in a tree of bounded balance $1/4$, one subtree of a node may be up to 3 times the size of the other. The rebalancing of a bounded-balanced tree has been shown to be slightly less time-consuming than for AVL trees.

Baer and Schwab (1977) have conducted a comparative study of these different search-tree organizations. The results of their study showed that "the AVL tree construction is the most efficient when the operations on trees are limited to insertion and queries." Some of the other search-tree organizations may provide better performance for large directories in file-processing applications; however, the AVL tree appears to be the best search-tree organization for a symbol table.

Before we conclude our discussion of binary tree-structured symbol tables, we should mention some other tree-oriented organizations. In particular, a forest of six trees has been used in the FORTRAN H compiler (IBM). A separate tree is constructed for identifiers of lengths 1 through 6. The FORTRAN H compiler also uses tree-structured tables for constants and statement numbers.

Severance (1974) has suggested that in situations in which a large number of variables appear in a symbol table, a special m-ary type of tree structure called a *trie* be used in conjunction with a binary tree. The basic idea is to use a trie node with 26 link fields (one for each letter in the alphabet) at the first level and to use a binary tree structure at lower levels of the structure. Figure 8-20 exhibits an example of this type of organization.

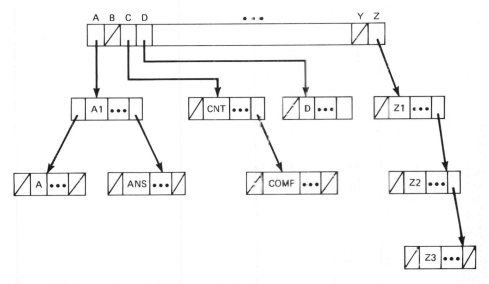

Figure 8-20 A tree-tree symbol table organization.

8-5.4 Hash Symbol Tables

The best search methods for the symbol-table organizations we have discussed so far have had an average length of search requiring on the order of $\log_2 n$ comparisons. In this section we investigate an organization in which the search time is essentially independent of the number of records in the table (i.e., the search time is constant for any n). We begin our discussion by introducing some basic terminology and describing the notion of a hashing function. Next, a number of hashing-function strategies are surveyed and the problem of collision resolution is addressed. Finally, a comparison of hash-table organizations and the other table organizations discussed in the section is presented. A large portion of the discussion in this section is taken from Tremblay and Sorenson (1984).

To describe adequately the concept of a hash symbol table, some new terminology must be introduced. First, the notions of name space and address space must be described. The *name space* (also called *identifier space* or *key space*) is the set K of unique variable names that can appear in a program. For example, in FORTRAN, the name space is the set of one to six character identifiers each of which begins with a letter and consists of letters and digits. Some programming languages do not have any restriction on the length of variable names. Of course, in a particular implementation of a compiler some maximum length must be assumed, and therefore the name space is always finite.

The *address space* (or *table space*) A is the set of record locations $\{1, 2, \ldots, m\}$ in a table. An important measure of space utilization is the *load factor*, which is defined as the ratio of the number of records to the number of record locations in a table. Therefore, if n records currently reside in a table, the load factor α is n/m.

Formally, a *hashing function* (or *key-to-address transformation*) is defined as a mapping $H: K \rightarrow A$. That is, a hashing function H takes as its argument a variable name and produces a table address (i.e., location) at which the set of attributes for that variable are stored. The function generates this address by performing some simple arithmetic or logical operations on the name or some part of the name.

Before we describe a number of hashing functions, we should introduce the notion of preconditioning as it relates to the name space K. Each element of K usually contains characters which are numeric, alphabetic, or special (i.e., punctuation or operator types of characters). The individual characters of a name are not particularly amenable to arithmetical or logical operation. The process of transforming a variable's name to a form which can be easily manipulated by a hashing function is often called *preconditioning*. To illustrate this process, let us consider the problem of preconditioning the name AD#1. One alternative is to encode the letters as the numbers $11, 12, \ldots, 36$ and the set of special characters (e.g., #, +, −, *, /, ...) as $37, 38, 39, \ldots$. Using this scheme, AD#1 can be encoded as 11143701.

Preconditioning can be handled most efficiently by using the numerically coded internal representation (e.g., ASCII or EBCDIC) of each character in the name. On an ASCII machine, AD#1 can be encoded as 1000001 1000100 0100011 0110001 in binary, or 137,433,521. Expressed in EBCDIC, AD#1 is C1C47BF1 in hexadecimal, or 3,250,879,473. The last two preconditioned results generate very large numbers that may not be conveniently represented in a given machine (especially a 16-bit word microcomputer). Note also that our example variable name is only four characters in length. The solution to this size problem is to disregard certain digits of the preconditioned result. In fact some of the hashing functions to be described perform various types of size-reduction transformations to generate a table address. It is common practice to use one hashing function to map names to an intermediate preconditioned key space and then a second hashing function to map the values in that space to a final table location.

Let us now examine a number of hashing functions that are applicable to symbol-table handling. For notational convenience, we use the term *key* throughout the discussion to mean a preconditioned numeric representation of a variable name.

The most widely accepted hashing function is the *division method*, which is defined as

$$H(x) = (x \bmod m) + 1$$

for divisor m. In mapping keys to addresses, the division method preserves, to a certain extent, the uniformity that exists in a key set. Keys which are closely bunched together or clustered are mapped to unique addresses. For example, keys $2000, 2001, \ldots,$ and 2017 would be mapped to addresses $82, 83, \ldots,$ and 99 if the divisor for the division method is 101. Unfortunately, this preservation of uniformity is a disadvantage if two or more clusters of keys are mapped to the same addresses. For example, if another cluster of keys is $3310, 3311, 3313, 3314, \ldots, 3323,$ and 3324, then those keys are mapped to addresses $79, 80, 82, 83, \ldots, 92,$ and 93 by divisor 101, and there are many collisions with keys from the cluster starting at 2000. The reason for this is that keys in the two clusters are congruent modulo 101.

In general, if many keys are congruent modulo d, and m is not relatively prime to d, then using m as a divisor can result in poor performance of the division method. This is shown in the preceding example, where $m = d = 101$. As another example, if all the keys in a table are congruent modulo 5 and the divisor is 65, the keys are mapped to only 13 different positions. Since it is uncommon for a number of keys to be congruent modulo m, where m is a large prime number, a prime divisor should be used, although research has shown that odd divisors without factors less than 20 are also satisfactory. In particular, divisors which are even numbers are to be avoided, since even and odd keys would be mapped to odd and even addresses, respectively (assuming that the address space is $\{1, 2, \ldots, m\}$). This would be a problem in a table containing predominantly even or predominantly odd keys.

A second hashing function that performs reasonably well is the *midsquare hashing method*. In this method, a key is multiplied by itself and an address is obtained by truncating bits or digits at both ends of the product until the number of bits or digits left is equal to the desired address length. The same positions must be used for all products. As an example, consider a six-digit key, 113586. Squaring the key gives 12901779396. If a four-digit address is required, positions 5 to 8 could be chosen, giving address 1779. The midsquare method has been criticized by Buchholz (1963), but it has given good results when applied to some key sets (see Lum et al., 1971).

For the *folding method*, a key is partitioned into a number of parts, each of which has the same length as the required address with the possible exception of the last part. The parts are then added together, ignoring the final carry, to form an address. If the keys are in binary form, the exclusive-or operation may be substituted for addition. There are variations of this technique which can best be illustrated by an example involving the key 187249653. In the fold-shifting method, 187, 249, and 653 are added to yield 89. In the fold-boundary method, the digits of the outermost partitions are reversed, so that 781, 249, and 356 are added, yielding 386. Folding is a hashing function which is useful for compressing multiword keys so that other hashing functions can be used.

Another hashing technique which we will refer to as a *length-dependent method* is used commonly in symbol-table handling. In this approach, the length of the variable name is used in conjunction with some subpart of the name to produce either a table address directly or, more commonly, an intermediate key which is used, for example, with the division method to produce a final table address. McKeeman (1974) experimented with six different length-dependent functions. The function that produced the best results summed the internal binary representation of the first and last characters and the length of the variable name shifted left four binary places (or equivalently the length multiplied by 16). Therefore, ID#1 becomes $201 + 241 + (4 \times 16) = 506$ assuming an EBCDIC representation. If we treat 506 as an intermediate key and apply the division method with a divisor of 29, the resulting address is 14.

Thus far we have described how to perform variable name to address transformations using hashing functions, but we have neglected an important aspect relevant to this process, the problem of colliding records. A hashing function is a many-to-one mapping. That is, the name space K is in general much larger than the address space A onto which K is mapped. For example, a FORTRAN program has a name space of $26 + 26 \times 36 + 26 \times 36^2 + \cdots + 26 \times 36^5 \simeq 1.6 \times 10^9$. Typically this space is mapped to the address space of a symbol table containing a few hundred record locations. Obviously in this mapping two names can be transformed into the same address. For example, AD#1 and ALL1 are both mapped to the same location 14 using the length-dependent transformation discussed earlier. Of course, two records cannot occupy the same location, and therefore some method must be used to resolve the collisions that can result. A major part of the remainder of this subsection is devoted to the topic of collision resolution.

Open addressing. To minimize the number of collisions, a hashing function should map the variable names in a program to the address space as uniformly as possible. The question of which hashing techniques provide the best such mapping has been addressed in two empirical studies by Buchholz (1963) and Lum et al. (1971). In the Lum study, the division, folding, and midsquare methods, along with some computationally complex methods such as digital analysis, radix transformation, and algebraic coding were compared using a variety of key sets. We purposely have not discussed some of the more computationally complex methods. They involve considerable preanalysis of the set of variable names in a program or a lot of arithmetic operations. In some of these methods the time to perform an address transformation becomes significant when compared with the small search time needed to resolve a collision. Therefore, in such instances, one does better to use a less sophisticated method that may generate more collisions. It is interesting to note, however, that in both of the studies cited earlier one of the simplest methods, the division method, provided the overall best performance.

There are basically two collision-resolution techniques: *open addressing* and *chaining*. Algorithms will be presented for both techniques, and certain variations of the basic methods are mentioned. Whenever possible, we will use the same notation as used previously and introduce new notation only when necessary.

With open addressing, if a variable name x is mapped to a storage location d, and this location is already occupied, then other locations in the table are scanned until a free record location is found for the new record. It is possible that the free record location contains a record that was previously deleted. When a record with name field NAME$_i$ is deleted, NAME$_i$ is set to a special value called DEL, which is not equal to the value of any variable name (e.g., a field of all nines). The locations are scanned according to a sequence which can be defined in many ways. The simplest technique for handling collisions is to use the following sequence:

$$d, d + 1, ..., m - 1, m, 1, 2, ..., d - 1$$

A free record location is always found if at least one is available; otherwise, the search halts after scanning m locations. When a record is looked up, the same sequence of locations is scanned until that record is located, or until an empty (never used) record position is found. In the latter case, the required record is not in the table and the search fails. This method of collision resolution is called *linear probing*.

The following algorithm performs the table-lookup and insertion operations for a hashed symbol table using linear probing with the sequence $d, d + 1, ..., m - 1, m, 1, 2, ..., d - 1$. The record to be inserted or located is identified by a search argument SARG; any attributes to be inserted are contained in a subrecord called DATA, and the type of operation to be performed is indicated by the logical parameter INSERT as described previously in this section. It is assumed that if a record location has never contained a record, the corresponding name field has a special value called DUMMY.

Function OPENLP(INSERT, SARG, DATA). Given the parameters INSERT, SARG, and DATA, this function performs the table-lookup and insertion operations on a hashed symbol table using a linear-probe collision-resolution technique. The ith record location in the table holds a name field NAME$_i$ and a subrecord ATTR$_i$ which can contain the other attributes for a variable. The hashing function H is used to calculate an initial address. If the requested operation is successful, the index of the NAME being inserted or searched for is returned; otherwise a negative value is returned. DUMMY and DEL have predefined values which denote the NAME fields of a record not in use and a record marked for deletion, respectively.

1. [Calculate address]
      $i \leftarrow d \leftarrow$ H(SARG)
2. [Loop until lookup complete or error found]
      Repeat through step 4
3. [Perform operation if location is found]
      If SARG $=$ NAME$_i$
      then If INSERT
          then Return($-i$ **)**   (error in insertion)
          else Return(i)
      If NAME$_i$ $=$ DUMMY **or** NAME$_i$ $=$ DEL
      then If INSERT
          then NAME$_i$ $\leftarrow$ SARG
              ATTR$_i$ $\leftarrow$ DATA
              Return(i)
          else If NAME$_i$ $=$ DUMMY
              then Return($-i$ **)**   (error in lookup)
4. [Increment and test index]
      $i \leftarrow i + 1$
      If $i > m$
      then $i \leftarrow 1$
      If $i = d$
      then Write('OVERFLOW')
          Return(0)   □

In step 1 of the function an initial address is calculated—any of the hashing functions discussed previously can be used. Step 3 scans a position i, and if the NAME field and the search argument match, the table location is returned in the case of a lookup operation. For an insertion, the negated index is returned, indicating a duplicate variable-name error. If position i is empty or contains a deleted record, the new record is placed into this location during an insertion operation. If the location is empty and a lookup operation is performed, a negated index is returned, indicating the search argument is not present in the table. Step 4 increments the index i and resets i to 1 if necessary. If i becomes equal to d, its initial value, either no record locations are available or the lookup operation fails. In either case, an unsuccessful operation is indicated by returning an index value of 0.

Let us look at an example involving open addressing. We assume a hashing function which performs the following mapping:

the name NODE is mapped into 1
the name STORAGE is mapped into 2
the names AN and ADD are mapped into 3
the names FUNCTION, B, BRAND, and PARAMETER are mapped into 9

Assuming that the insertions are performed in the following order:

NODE, STORAGE, AN, ADD, FUNCTION, B, BRAND, and PARAMETER

Figure 8-21 represents the resulting structure with $m = 11$. The first three keys are each placed in a single probe, but then ADD must go into position 4 instead of 3, which is already occupied. FUNCTION is placed in position 9 in one probe, but B and BRAND take two and three probes, respectively. Finally, PARAMETER ends up in position 5 after eight probes, since positions 9, 10, 11, 1, 2, 3, and 4 are all occupied. A lookup is completed successfully when the record with its name equal to SARG is found, or unsuccessfully if an empty record location is encountered. Since steps 1 and 3 apply equally to insertions and lookups, the number of probes for the lookup operations are identical to those just given for the insertion operations for this example.

Each time that step 2 of Function OPENLP is executed for either insertion or lookup, one comparison is required. For a table of n records, if all records are stored or retrieved, the number of times that step 2 is executed divided by n is the average length of search (ALOS). Knuth (1973) gives a probabilistic model for analyzing collision-resolution techniques and develops formulas for the expected average length of a successful search (E[ALOS]) in the case of open addressing. The model assumes that each key has probability $1/m$ of being mapped to each

	NAME	ATTR	Number of Probes
A_1	NODE	/////////	1
A_2	STORAGE	/////////	1
A_3	AN	/////////	1
A_4	ADD	/////////	2
A_5	PARAMETER	/////////	8
A_6	Empty		
A_7	Empty		
A_8	Empty		
A_9	FUNCTION	/////////	1
A_{10}	B	/////////	2
A_{11}	BRAND	/////////	3

Figure 8-21 Collision resolution by using open addressing.

of the m addresses in the table. Therefore, there are m^n ways of mapping keys to the address space.

E[ALOS] is dependent on the load factor. If $\alpha = n/m$ is the load factor for n and m as defined previously, then Knuth derives the following formulas:

$$E[ALOS] \simeq \begin{cases} \dfrac{1}{2}\left(1 + \dfrac{1}{1 - \alpha}\right) & \text{for a successful search} \\[3mm] \dfrac{1}{2}\left(1 + \dfrac{1}{(1 - \alpha)^2}\right) & \text{for an unsuccessful search} \end{cases}$$

Table 8-2 gives representative values for these formulas with a number of different load factors. E[ALOS] increases with increasing load factor, since a greater number of collisions is probable as more records are being stored in the table. Note that for $\alpha < 0.80$, the results are quite good as compared with the search strategies discussed previously. The number of comparisons is proportional to the load factor. This result, however, is based on the key set being uniformly mapped onto the address space.

The linear-probing method of collision resolution has a number of shortcomings. The first is related to how deletions are performed. The approach that is used consists of having a special table entry for the name field with a value of DEL, which denoted the deletion of that entry. This strategy enables us to search the table properly. For example, assume that the record whose key is FUNCTION in Fig. 8-21 is marked for deletion by assigning the value of DEL to A_9. Then, if it is desired to retrieve the record with a key value of BRAND, our previous algorithm will still work. The reader may wonder: Why bother to use a special value such as DEL to denote deleted entries? Why not just assign a negative value to the entry which is to be deleted? The reason is that if this were done in the previous example, the algorithm would find an empty position in position 9, decide that BRAND is not in the table, and proceed to insert it once more.

Table 8-2 E[ALOS] for linear probing

Load factor	Number of probes	
α	Successful	Unsuccessful
0.10	1.056	1.118
0.20	1.125	1.281
0.30	1.214	1.520
0.40	1.333	1.889
0.50	1.500	2.500
0.60	1.750	3.625
0.70	2.167	6.060
0.80	3.000	13.000
0.90	5.500	50.500
0.95	10.500	200.500

This solution to the handling of deletions is tolerable if few deletions are made as is the normal situation when interacting with a symbol table. For the case of many deletions, however, the table will contain numerous entries that are marked for deletion, and this may result in extensive search times.

Another shortcoming of the linear-probing method is due to *clustering* effects which tend to become severe when the table becomes nearly full. This phenomenon can be explained by considering a trace of Fig. 8-21 that would show the state of the table after each insertion. Such a trace is given in Fig. 8-22. When the first insertion is made, the probability of a new element being inserted in a particular position is clearly $1/11$. For the second insertion, however, the probability that position 2 becomes occupied is twice as likely as any remaining available position; namely, the entry is placed in position 2 if the variable name is mapped into either 1 or 2. Continuing in this manner, on the fifth insertion the probability that the new entry is placed in position 5 is five times as likely as its being placed in any remaining unoccupied position. Thus the trend is for long sequences of occupied positions to become longer. Such a phenomenon is called *primary clustering*.

The primary-clustering problem can be reduced if a different probing method is used. A method which accomplishes this is called *random probing*. This technique generates a random sequence of positions rather than an ordered sequence, as was the case in the linear-probing method. The random sequence generated must contain every integer between 1 and m exactly once. The table is considered to be full when the first duplicate number is encountered. An example of a random-number generator which generates such a cyclic permutation of numbers consists of the statement

$$y \leftarrow (y + c) \bmod m$$

where y is the initial number of the sequence (the generator) and c and m are relatively prime; i.e., their greatest common divisor is 1. For example, assuming that $m = 11$ and $c = 7$, this statement starting with an initial value of 3 will generate the sequence 10, 6, 2, 9, 5, 1, 8, 4, 0, 7, and 3. Thus, adding 1 to each element transforms the sequence to a number in the desired interval $[1, 11]$.

Although random probing improves the problem of primary clustering, clustering can still occur. This situation arises when two keys are hashed into the same value. In such a case, the same sequence or path will be generated for both keys by the random-probe method just discussed. This phenomenon is called *secondary clustering*.

This clustering phenomenon can be alleviated by *double hashing* (also called *rehashing*), a method first described by de Balbine (1968). In this technique, the increment value c is computed by using a second hashing function H_2 which is independent of the initial hashing function H_1 and which generates a value that is relatively prime to the table size. (If the probability that a name is mapped to the same address is on the order of $1/m^2$ when applied to two hashing functions, these functions are said to be independent.) The function $H_2(k)$ is used to compute the value for c as given earlier in the cyclic-permutation formula [i.e.,

Contents of table after insertion

After inserting record								
NODE	NODE							
STORAGE	NODE	STORAGE						
AN	NODE	STORAGE	AN					
ADD	NODE	STORAGE	AN	ADD				
FUNCTION	NODE	STORAGE	AN	ADD		FUNCTION		
B	NODE	STORAGE	AN	ADD		FUNCTION	B	
BRAND	NODE	STORAGE	AN	ADD		FUNCTION	B	BRAND
PARAMETER	NODE	STORAGE	AN	ADD	PARAMETER	FUNCTION	B	BRAND

Figure 8-22 Trace of insertions using open addressing.

$(y + c) \bmod m]$ for random probing. Knuth (1973) suggests selecting m to be prime (when using the division method), and setting $H_1(k) = 1 + k \bmod m$ and $H_2(k) = 1 + (k \bmod(m - 2))$, where k is the key and m is the table size. This works particularly well if m and $m - 2$ are "twin primes" such as 1021 and 1019. A key of 125 generates the following sequence of probes for H_1 and H_2 as just given and assuming m is 13 (H_1 and H_2 will have values of 9 and 5, respectively):

$$9, 1, 6, 11, 3, 8, 0, 5, 10, 2, 7, 12, 4$$

The average length of search for a double-hashing technique where H_1 and H_2 are independent is given by the following pair of formulas

$$E[ALOS] \simeq \begin{cases} -\dfrac{1}{\alpha} \ln(1 - \alpha) & \text{for a successful search} \\ \dfrac{1}{1 - \alpha} & \text{for an unsuccessful search} \end{cases}$$

Table 8-3 gives a summary of representative values for a double-hashing method. Its performance is certainly better than that obtained for linear probing.

There are three main difficulties with the open-addressing method discussed thus far. First, when trying to locate an open location for record insertion, there is, in many instances, the necessity to examine records that do not have the same initial hash value (i.e., lists of colliding records for different hash values become intermixed). Second, a table-overflow situation cannot be satisfactorily handled using open addressing. If an overflow occurs, the entire table must be reorganized. The overflow problem cannot be ignored in symbol tables for compilers because the table-space requirements can vary significantly depending on the size of the source program. The third problem is the difficulty of physically deleting records —although, as mentioned previously, the deletion of individual records rarely occurs in symbol-table handling. Let us turn to a chained-allocation organization to alleviate some of these problems.

Table 8-3 E[ALOS] for random probing with double hashing

Load factor	Number of probes	
α	Successful	Unsuccessful
0.10	1.054	1.111
0.20	1.116	1.250
0.30	1.189	1.429
0.40	1.277	1.667
0.50	1.386	2.000
0.60	1.527	2.500
0.70	1.720	3.333
0.80	2.012	5.000
0.90	2.558	10.000
0.95	3.153	20.000

Separate chaining. Chaining can be used in a variety of ways to handle overflow records; however, we will concentrate only on the most popular method called *separate chaining*. This method involves the chaining of colliding records into a special *overflow area* which is separate from the *prime area* (i.e., the area of the table into which records are hashed initially). A separate chain (i.e., linked list) is kept for each set of colliding records, and consequently a pointer field must accompany each record in a primary or an overflow location. Figure 8-23 shows a separate chaining representation of the variables used earlier in this subsection assuming a prime area of 11 locations and the same order of declarations. Note that the insertions in a list of colliding records are made in alphabetical order of the variable names. This is a technique suggested by Amble and Knuth (1974), and it has been shown to reduce the lookup time for unsuccessful searches. Since an unsuccessful search determines that a variable should be declared implicitly, this strategy is commonly adopted.

In the following algorithm, named CHAINSL (meaning chaining with separate lists), the three fields in both a prime area record and an overflow record are designated as NAME, ATTR, and LINK. NAME and ATTR have identical roles as in previous algorithms, and LINK contains the address of the next node in the list of colliding records for a given primary location. The end of a list is signified by placing a NULL value in the link field of the last record in the list. The prime and overflow areas of the symbol table can be implemented as two separate tables, or they can be considered as subtables within a single symbol table.

Function CHAINSL(INSERT, SARG, DATA). Given the parameters INSERT, SARG, and DATA as described previously, this algorithm performs the table

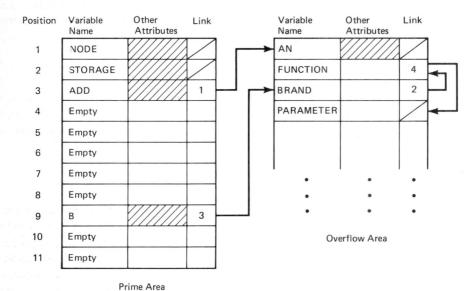

Figure 8-23 Collision resolution with separate chaining.

lookup and insertion operations on a hashed symbol table using the separate chaining collision-resolution technique. The ith record location in the prime area of the table holds a name field $NAME_i$, a subrecord $ATTR_i$ which contains the other attributes for a variable, and a link field $LINK_i$. In a similar fashion, the index j is used to denote the current overflow record that is being examined. The index p contains the previous value of j, and k is used as a temporary index variable. The hashing function H is used to calculate an initial address. If the requested operation is successful, the index of the NAME being inserted or searched for is returned; otherwise a negative value is returned. DUMMY has a predefined value which denotes the NAME field of a record not in use.

1. [Apply hashing function]
    i ← H(SARG)
2. [Examine the primary area location]
    If SARG = $NAME_i$
    then If INSERT
        then Return(−i)   (error in insertion)
        else Return(i)
    If SARG < $NAME_i$
    then If INSERT
        then obtain a free overflow record location from a list
            of available locations and assign its index to j
            $NAME_j$ ← $NAME_i$
            $ATTR_j$ ← $ATTR_i$
            $LINK_j$ ← $LINK_i$
            $NAME_i$ ← SARG
            $ATTR_i$ ← DATA
            $LINK_i$ ← j
            Return(i)
        else Return(−i)   (error in lookup)
    If $NAME_i$ = DUMMY
    then If INSERT
        then $NAME_i$ ← SARG
            $ATTR_i$ ← DATA
            $LINK_i$ ← NULL
            Return(i)
        else Return(−i)   (error in lookup)
3. [Look for record in overflow area]
    p ← j ← i
    Repeat while $LINK_j$ ≠ NULL
        j ← $LINK_j$
        If $NAME_j$ = SARG
        then If INSERT
            then Return(−j)   (error in insertion)
            else Return(j)

If SARG < NAME$_j$
then If INSERT
 then obtain an overflow location and assign its index to k
  LINK$_p$ ← k
  NAME$_k$ ← SARG
  ATTR$_k$ ← DATA
  LINK$_k$ ← j
  Return(k)
 else Return(−j)   (error in lookup)
p ← j

4. [Record not located]
 If INSERT
 then obtain an overflow location and assign its index to k
  LINK$_j$ ← k
  NAME$_k$ ← SARG
  ATTR$_k$ ← DATA
  LINK$_k$ ← NULL
  Return(k)
 else Return(−j) (error in lookup)   □

  The algorithm performs the insertion and lookup operations by first examining the prime area location, as determined by the hashing function, and then the overflow area if necessary. Note that for explicit declarations the algorithm can be improved by having insertions performed at the front of a list of unordered overflow records. This approach allows for fast insertion; however, it does not guarantee that duplicate declarations will be detected.

  It should be observed that the special deletion marker DEL is not considered in Function CHAINSL. On the rare occasions when a deletion may be necessary (e.g., recovering from a error in a declaration), it is assumed that the erroneous record is physically deleted. A deletion operation can be performed easily when a chaining type of collision resolution is used.

  Knuth shows that an expected average length of search for separate chaining is given as follows:

$$E[ALOS] \simeq \begin{cases} 1 + \dfrac{\alpha}{2} & \text{for a successful search} \\ \alpha + e^{-\alpha} & \text{for an unsuccessful search} \end{cases}$$

Representative values for this method are given in Table 8-4. It is desirable to make the load factor as small as possible, which can be achieved by making m large. Although additional storage is required to store the links using this resolution technique, its performance and versatility make chaining superior to open addressing for most symbol-table applications. The open-addressing scheme is easier to implement, and because of its efficient utilization of storage, it should be considered when implementing a compiler on a small machine.

Table 8-4 E[ALOS] with separate chaining

| Load factor | Number of probes | |
α	Successful	Unsuccessful
0.10	1.050	1.005
0.20	1.100	1.019
0.30	1.150	1.041
0.40	1.200	1.070
0.50	1.250	1.107
0.60	1.300	1.149
0.70	1.350	1.197
0.80	1.400	1.249
0.90	1.450	1.307
0.95	1.475	1.337

Before this subsection is concluded, a few remarks are necessary concerning the representation of a symbol table when using a hashing scheme. First, we should observe that the address space A into which a set of variable names is mapped is assumed always to be of some fixed size m. In general, the larger the size of A relative to the number n of table records stored, the better the hashing function performs (i.e., the smaller the load factor α the better the performance). This is verified in Tables 8-2 to 8-4. To avoid making the symbol table extremely large and hence expensive storagewise, an intermediate table—often called the *hash table*—is created. Figure 8-24 illustrates how a hash table is used in conjunction with the symbol table assuming the same variables, hashing function,

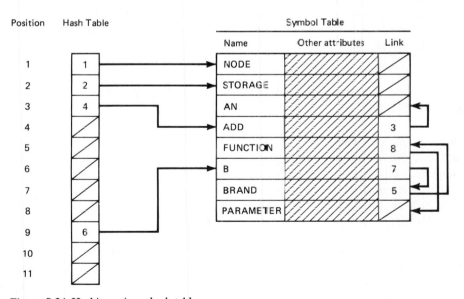

Figure 8-24 Hashing using a hash table.

and collision-resolution technique as in Fig. 8-23. In this method all of the table records can be thought of as residing in an overflow area and the prime area (i.e., the hash table) contains only link fields. Therefore, the symbol table, which contains large records, is packed densely and the hash table, which contains records with only a link field, can be made large while still requiring little space overall. It is a relatively straightforward process to adapt a hash table to an open-addressing strategy. In the section to follow, a hash table is of particular importance and is used extensively when discussing symbol tables for block-structured languages.

We conclude this section with a synopsis of the table organizations discussed. If it is known that only a few variables (i.e., 10 or fewer) are going to appear in a program, an unordered table should be considered. Such situations are rare, however. Adopting a binary-search strategy for an ordered table can improve the lookup operation if more than 25 records occur. Also, ordering the table facilitates making a cross-reference listing. If insertion activity is high, a tree-structured table can provide a better performance overall—mainly because of the ease with which insertions can be handled. Tree-structured tables are particularly good if certain properties of a language are present (e.g., six or fewer character names as in FORTRAN). The best method to use if memory is not at a premium is hashing. An average length of search of between one and three accesses is relatively easy to achieve. The main disadvantage with a hash symbol table is that since the records are not ordered either physically or logically by variable name, such an organization is not conducive to building a cross-reference listing.

It is common practice, when designing a compiler, to include a parameter which allows the user to estimate the size of the symbol-table requirements for a program. A possible strategy is to have the compiler select an appropriate symbol-table organization depending upon the table size requested.

Let us now turn to an examination of symbol-table handling for block-structured programming languages.

8-6 SYMBOL-TABLE ORGANIZATIONS FOR BLOCK-STRUCTURED LANGUAGES

In this section we concentrate on the problems of symbol-table handling when compiling block-structured languages. By a block-structured language we mean a language in which a module can contain nested submodules and each submodule can have its own set of locally declared variables. A variable declared within a module A is accessible throughout that module unless the same variable name is redefined within a submodule of A. The redefinition of a variable holds throughout the scope (i.e., physical limits) of the submodule.

In the first subsection, the concepts related to variable declaration in block-structured languages are examined in more detail with the aid of an example. In the remaining subsections, we describe how many of the symbol-table organizations and search strategies described for non-block-structured languages can be adapted to a block-structured language situation. In particular stack symbol tables, stack-implemented tree-structured tables, and stack-implemented hash symbol tables will be considered.

8-6.1 Block-Structured Language Concepts

In Sec. 8-4, the two additional symbol-table operations, set and reset, were introduced for block-structured languages. In this subsection, we examine in more detail the functions and the processing requirements of these operations. We will do so with the aid of the example program segment as given in Fig. 8-6 and reproduced in Fig. 8-25 with some block numbers added. First, it should be noted that in the program segment a BBLOCK is interpreted to be a BEGIN-like block (i.e., execution flows into and out of the block in a sequential manner) and a PBLOCK is a procedure-like block (i.e., execution of the block is invoked by a call and flow of control returns to the point of the call when execution of the block is terminated).

```
1 │ BBLOCK;

          REAL X, Y; STRING NAME;
          •
          •
          •
     2 │ M1:   PBLOCK (INTEGER IND);

              INTEGER X;
              •
              •
              •
              CALL M2(IND + 1);
              •
              •
         END M1;


     3 │ M2:   PBLOCK (INTEGER J);
              •
              •
          4 │ BBLOCK;

                  ARRAY INTEGER F(J); LOGICAL TEST1;

                  •
                  •
                  •
              END;
         END M2;
          •
          •
          •
          CALL M1 (X / Y);
          •
          •
          •
   END;
```

Figure 8-25 A program segment from a nested language.

While at execution time these two types of blocks behave quite differently, during compilation both types of blocks demand similar types of processing as embodied in the set and reset operations. When a block is entered at compilation time a subtable for all newly declared variables is established by the set operation. As we shall see when discussing various table organizations, the establishment of a new subtable does not necessarily imply the procurement of additional symbol-table space. The attributes for the newly declared variables must be entered in the symbol table with the understanding that they will be deleted when the end of the block is reached during compilation. The actual deletion of the table entries for a block is handled by the reset operation. On completion of a reset operation at the end of the compilation of a block, the active part of the symbol table must contain the same elements as were present before this latest block was entered. For example, in Fig. 8-25, before block number 2 is entered and immediately after it is concluded only the attributes for the variables X, Y, NAME, and M1 should be in the active part of the symbol table. Table 8-5 traces the contents of the symbol table as they would be *prior* to the invocations of the various set and reset operations that take place while compiling the program segment in Fig. 8-25. Initially both the active and inactive segments of the symbol table are empty. Prior to the beginning of the second block, records for M1, NAME, Y, and X are located in the active portion of the symbol table. The records for X and IND are added during the compilation of block 2. The reset operation, executed at the end of block 2, places X and IND into the inactive portion of the symbol table, since these variables cannot be accessed outside the bounds of block 2. This process of introducing records for new variables into the active area and moving records for inaccessible variables into the inactive area continues until the compilation of all blocks is completed and all the symbol-table records are considered inactive.

In our sample block-structured language program, procedure (i.e., PBLOCK) declarations occur when the name of the procedure is first encountered. Because of this, the symbol-table record for M2 is added after block 2 has been compiled. Note, however, that a reference to M2 takes place in block 1, and therefore a

Table 8-5 A trace showing the effects of the set and reset operations

| Operation | Symbol-table contents (variable name only) | |
	Active	Inactive
Set BLK1	empty	empty
Set BLK2	M1, NAME, Y, X	empty
Reset BLK2	X, IND, M1, NAME, Y, X	empty
Set BLK3	M2, M1, NAME, Y, X	X, IND
Set BLK4	J, M2, M1, NAME, Y, X	X, IND
Reset BLK4	TEST1, F, J, M2, M1, NAME, Y, X	X, IND
Reset BLK3	J, M2, M1, NAME, Y, X	TEST1, F, X, IND
Reset BLK1	M2, M1, NAME, Y, X	J, TEST1, F, X, IND
End of compilation	empty	M2, M1, NAME, Y, X, J, TEST1, F, X, IND

problem exists with respect to the ordering of declarations. This problem will be ignored in this chapter but will be discussed in detail in Chap. 11 when declaration handling is considered. For now, a procedure declaration will be handled in the same manner as any other declaration.

A close examination of the symbol-table activity as given in Table 8-5 should lead to the realization that the set and reset operations behave like the pop and push operations for a stack. This is not coincidental but is a direct consequence of the nested characteristics of the program being compiled. The table organizations discussed in this subsection must take this type of activity into account.

Another property of block-structured languages that must be considered in designing a symbol table is the duplicate use of names. For example, any reference to X in block 2 of Fig. 8-25 is to the integer variable X, even though the set of attributes for both variables named X are active in block 2. Therefore, the search strategy in the lookup operations must be such as to always locate the latest instance of a variable name first.

Having listed some fundamental requirements for the set and reset operations, let us examine various symbol-table organizations for block-structured languages.

8-6.2 Stack Symbol Tables

The conceptually simplest symbol-table organization for a block-structured language is the *stack symbol table*. In this organization the records containing the variables' attributes are simply stacked as the declarations are encountered. Upon reaching the end of a block, all records for variables declared in the block are removed since these variables cannot be referenced outside the block. Figure 8-26a and b illustrates the contents of a stack symbol table for the program given

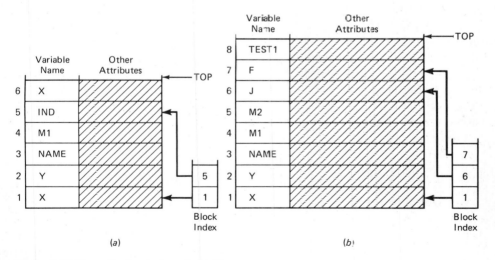

Figure 8-26 Example of a stack symbol table.

in Fig. 8-25 just prior to completing the compilation of blocks 2 and 4, respectively. The role of the *block index*, the structure adjacent to the symbol table, will be explained when the set and reset operations are discussed.

The insertion operation is very simple in a stack symbol table. New records are added at the top location in the stack. Declarations involving duplicate names can exist in block-structured languages, but they cannot occur in the same block. Therefore, to detect duplicate-name errors prior to an insertion, we need only examine, using a linear search, the records for variables declared in the latest block to be compiled.

The lookup operation involves a linear search of the table from the top to the bottom. The search must be conducted in this order to guarantee that the latest occurrence of a variable with a particular name is located first. Hence the topmost variable X (i.e., the integer variable X) would be found first in Fig. 8-26a. Notice that because sets of symbol-table records are discarded as blocks are terminated, the average length of search for a stack symbol table may be less than for the corresponding unordered symbol table. This is true because an unordered symbol table generally contains, throughout the compilation of a program module, all the records for the active variables in a non-block-structured program. This lower expected length of search is a characteristic that holds for the other organizations we discuss in this section.

The set operation for a stack symbol table generates a new block index entry at the top of the block index structure. This entry is assigned the value of the current top of the symbol stack and therefore establishes a pointer to the first record location for a record in the block just entered.

The reset operation effectively removes all the records in the stack symbol table for the block just compiled. This is accomplished by setting TOP, the index pointing at the first open record location at the top of the symbol table, to the value of the top element in the block index. For example, when block 2 is terminated, the reset operation assigns the value 5 to TOP (refer to Fig. 8-26a). Note that the reset operation may also physically move deleted records to an inactive area. This should be done if the entire symbol table is to be used later to form a cross-reference listing or to aid in run-time error diagnostics.

The similarity of the stack symbol table and the unordered symbol table should be obvious. Unfortunately the stack symbol table also suffers from the same poor performance characteristics. Only in instances where the symbol table remains small throughout the compilation of a program should a stack organization be used.

8-6.3 Stack-Implemented Tree-Structured Symbol Tables

It was argued in Sec. 8-5.3 that the time to perform the table insertion and lookup operations on large tables can be reduced by using a tree-structured type of storage organization. This same argument holds when considering symbol-table organization for block-structured languages. In this subsection it is not our intent to describe in detail a tree-structured organization, since this was accomplished in

Sec. 8-5.3. Instead, we wish only to examine how this type of organization can be applied successfully to the compilation of a nested language.

Two possible approaches to organizing a symbol table using a tree-structured organization immediately come to mind. The first approach involves a single tree organization and therefore is essentially the same as that described in Sec. 8-5.3. The major difference that arises when the compilation of block-structured languages is considered is the fact that records for a block must be removed from the table when the compilation of the block is completed. As a result, the problem of deleting table records must be addressed. Since the records for all blocks are merged in one tree, a number of steps are necessary in order to delete a record:

1. Locate the position of the record in the tree.
2. Remove the record from the tree by altering the structural links so as to bypass the record.
3. Rebalance the tree if the deletion of the record has left the tree unbalanced.

In Sec. 8-5.3 it was pointed out that steps 1 and 3 require on the order of $\log_2 n$ operations. Since this three-step procedure must be repeated for each record to be deleted, it is easy to appreciate that the single-tree approach is not particularly well suited to the compilation of a nested language. So that its difficulty can be truly appreciated, the problem of deleting records from a tree is given as an exercise at the end of this chapter.

A second organization which we will call a forest of trees is amenable to the problem of deleting records. In this organization each block is allocated its own tree-structured table. When the compilation of a block is finished, the entire table associated with that block is released.

Figure 8-27a and b illustrates this type of organization using the program segment in Fig. 8-25. We have again displayed the contents of the symbol table just prior to the completion of the compilation of blocks 2 and 4.

In this organization the elements of the block index point to the root nodes of each of the trees in the table. The left pointer (LPTR) and right pointer (RPTR) fields indicate the structural links in each of the AVL tree structures. Note that in the process of compiling block 3 a procedure declaration for M2 is encountered. The attributes for M2 are stored in a record in block 1, since M2 is accessible from within block 1. The insertion of M2 requires that the tree structure for block 1 be rebalanced (using a double rotation), and the result of this rebalancing is shown in Fig. 8-27b.

It should be observed that the symbol table is maintained as a stack. When a block is entered during compilation, the value of TOP is assigned as a new, topmost entry in the block index. As declarations are encountered, records are inserted on the top of the symbol table. The tree for a particular block can be balanced as records are inserted, or a balancing procedure may be invoked just once after all records for a block have been placed on the stack.

A lookup operation must follow a particular search strategy in order to guarantee that the latest occurrence of a variable name is located. The search

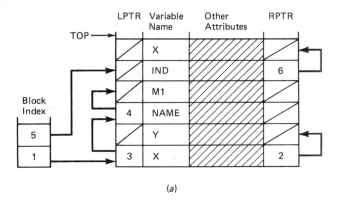

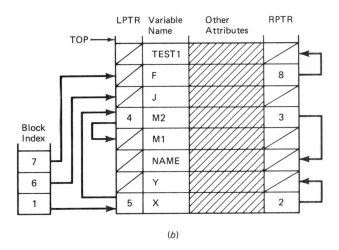

Figure 8-27 Example of a stack-implemented, tree-structured symbol table.

must begin at the tree structure for the last block to be entered (i.e., begin with tree pointed to by the topmost block index element) and proceed down the block index to the tree for the first block entered (i.e., end with the tree pointed to by the bottommost block index element).

When the compilation of a block is finished, the reset operation logically deletes the associated tree structure by setting TOP to the value of the topmost element in the block index and then removing this element from the block index. If the entire symbol table is to be kept for the duration of the compilation process, the records in the compiled block should be moved to an inactive area. An alternative to moving the records is simply not to readjust the index TOP during the reset operation and thereby continue to add records to previously unused symbol-table locations.

Our criterion for deciding when to use a tree-structured symbol table remains unchanged from the previous section; namely, it should be used for a reasonably large number of entries when memory space is at a premium.

8-6.4 Stack-Implemented Hash-Structured Symbol Tables

Initially, it may appear that it is difficult to apply a hashing scheme to a symbol table for a block-structured language. Because hashing is, in general, a non-order-preserving transformation and because block-structured languages require that the variables in a block be grouped in some manner, it would seem that a hashing methodology and a symbol-table organization for block-structured languages are incompatible. However, with the use of an intermediate hash table, as discussed in Sec. 8-5.4, hashing can be used in a relatively straightforward manner.

In the discussion in this subsection, we consider a hashing technique which uses chaining to resolve collisions in the hash table. As mentioned in Sec. 8-5.4, open addressing can also be used for collision resolution; however, it offers few clear advantages over chaining.

We again rely on an illustrated example to explain the symbol-table organization. Figure 8-28 depicts a symbol-table organization for the program segment in Fig. 8-25, assuming a hashing function which performs the following transformations:

the names X and M1 are mapped to 1
the name NAME is mapped to 3
the names IND and J are mapped to 5
the name TEST1 is mapped to 6
the names F and Y are mapped to 8
the name M2 is mapped to 11

An intermediate hash table of size 11 is used in the example.

Figure 8-28a shows the symbol-table organization just prior to the completion of the compilation of block 2. Again, new records are inserted at the top of the symbol table and the block indices point to the first records in each of the blocks that are currently active. Of particular interest in this example is the manner in which the duplicate use of the name X is handled. Before the second declaration of X occurs in block 2, the record for the variable M1 is chained to the record for X (as declared in block 1) and the location of M1 is stored in the first entry in the hash table. When the second declaration for X is encountered, it is inserted at the head of the list of records which have hash values of 1. By inserting new records at the head of a list of colliding records, we are guaranteed of locating the latest occurrence of a variable name when performing a lookup operation. The one problem that does persist, however, is the determination of duplicate names declared illegally in the same block. This can be handled in the insertion operation by continually checking each element in a collision chain to see if (1) there is a match in names, and (2) the location of the matched name is

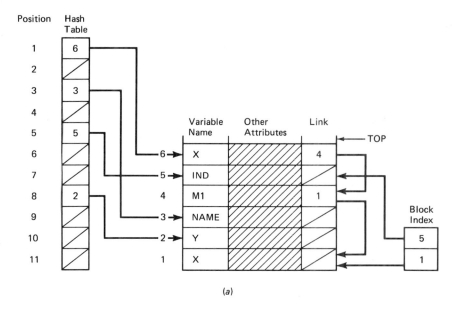

(a)

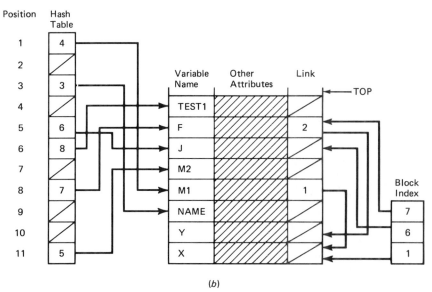

(b)

Figure 8-28 Example of a stack-implemented hash symbol table.

greater than or equal to the block index value associated with the block being compiled. If both of these conditions hold, an illegal declaration has occurred.

Figure 8-28*b* depicts the symbol-table organization just prior to the completion of the compilation of block 4. It is important to note that the variables X and IND as declared in block 2 have been removed from the top of the symbol table. Because a deleted record (in particular the record for the integer variable X) may belong to a chain of colliding records, the link fields in the hash table must be adjusted so as to remove the record from the chain. Generally this process can be completed very quickly, since any record to be deleted is at the head of a collision chain.

The insert and lookup operations for stack-implemented hash symbol tables are essentially the same as the corresponding operations discussed in Sec. 8-5.4 except for the peculiarities introduced when duplicate names are allowed. The expected length of search may be slightly less than for the hash symbol table for non-block-structured languages because local variables are deleted as blocks are compiled in a block-structured language.

The set operation again involves a simple update to the block index. When a new block is recognized during compilation, the block index is set to the value of TOP, the index pointing to the top location in the symbol table.

The reset operation is, as usual, much more complicated. When a block has been compiled, its associated records must be removed, either logically or physically, from the active part of the symbol table. The logical deletion of a record requires that the variable name be hashed to generate a hash-table location and that the collision chain associated with the hash-table location be altered so as to remove the record. If it is desirable to move the records to an inactive area, this can be easily accomplished, since the records for a block are grouped at the top of the symbol table. Algorithms for the insert, lookup, set, and reset operations on stack-implemented hash symbol tables are left as exercises at the end of the chapter.

It is best to conclude this section and the chapter with some remarks summarizing the organizations we have examined and with a restatement of the purpose (or function) of a symbol table in a compiler. It has been shown in both analytical and empirical studies that a hashing type of organization is generally the best symbol-table organization to use. If it is known a priori that the table will contain few records, a linearly organized table (i.e., a stack or ordered symbol table) should be adopted. If memory constraints exist and it is desirable to have the symbol table ordered by variable name, a tree-structured table should be considered.

In this chapter we have mainly considered what attributes should go into the symbol table and how the table can be best organized to facilitate fast table access. These are important topics which should now be well understood. However, the primary functions of a symbol table, that is, assisting in the processes of checking for semantic correctness and generating correct object code, have been largely ignored in the discussion. Hence we have likely frustrated the reader by discussing a tool in some detail but have not indicated how the tool should be applied. A major part of Chap. 11 describes the type of symbol-table interactions that take place in the semantic (i.e., context-dependent) analysis and code-generation phases of the compiler. With this understanding, let us proceed to a discussion of the organization and management of run-time storage for compiled programs.

CHAPTER EXERCISES

1 Suggest any other variable attributes that should be included in a symbol-table record in addition to those given in Sec. 8-3.

2 Does the "object-code address" attribute make sense when forming a symbol-table record for a procedure? If so, what is its role?

3 Discuss the validity of the statement, "Considering symbol-table interaction only, it is more efficient to compile languages with implicit declarations than languages with explicit declarations."

4 The declaration of a record structure such as those available in PL/I or COBOL is quite complex. Suggest a scheme for handling PL/I structures and illustrate the table record or records that would be created for the structure

```
DECLARE 1 SYM_TBL(100),
            2 NAME CHAR(30),
            2 ADDR,
                3 BL FIXED,
                3 ON FIXED,
            2 TYPE FIXED,
            2 DIM FIXED;
```

using the scheme you developed.

5 Figure 8-29 illustrates a program segment from a non-block-structured language. Draw a diagram of the ordered symbol table that would result when compiling the program segment.

6 Draw a diagram of a tree-structured (AVL tree) symbol table that would result when compiling the program segment in Fig. 8-29.

```
BLOCK

REAL X, Y, Z1, Z2, Z3;

INTEGER I, J, K, LAST1;

STRING LIST_OF_NAMES;

LOGICAL ENTRY_ON, EXIT_OFF;

ARRAY REAL VAL (20);

ARRAY INTEGER MIN_VAL_IND (20);

    •

    •

    •

    •

END OF BLOCK;
```

Figure 8-29 Example segment from non-block-structured language.

7 Draw a diagram of a hash symbol table that would result when compiling the program segment in Fig. 8-29. Use the hashing function described in the discussion of length-dependent hashing functions, assume a table size of 13 locations, and use a chaining resolution technique with an intermediate hash table.

8 Answer Exercise 7 using a double-hashing technique to resolve collisions.

9 Figure 8-30 illustrates a program segment from a block-structured language. Draw diagrams of the stack symbol table (both active and inactive parts) just prior to the completion of the compilation of blocks 3 and 4.

10 Answer Exercise 9 for a stack-implemented tree-structured symbol table.

11 Formulate a deletion algorithm which deletes a record from a stack-implemented tree-structured symbol table. The symbol table is assumed to be organized as a single AVL tree.

12 Give algorithms for the insertion, lookup, set, and reset operations for a stack-implemented tree-structured symbol table in which a forest of AVL trees is created for the active blocks during compilation.

13 Answer Exercise 9 for a stack-implemented hash symbol table. Use the hashing function described in the discussion of length-dependent hashing functions, assume a table size of 13 locations, and use a chaining resolution technique with an intermediate hash table.

1

```
┌ ─
│ BBLOCK;
│
│      REAL Z; INTEGER Y;
│
│    2
│    ┌ ─
│    │ SUB_1:  PBLOCK (INTEGER J);
│    │
│    │             •
│    │             •
│    │             •
│    │
│    │   3 ┌ ─
│    │     │ BBLOCK;
│    │     │
│    │     │        ARRAY STRING S(J + 2); LOGICAL FLAG; INTEGER Y;
│    │     │   •
│    │     │   •
│    │     │   •
│    │     │ END;
│    │     └ ─
│    │   4 ┌ ─
│    │     │ SUB_2: PBLOCK (REAL W);
│    │     │
│    │     │        REAL J; LOGICAL TEST1, TEST2, TEST3;
│    │     │
│    │     │           •
│    │     │           •
│    │     │           •
│    │     │ END SUB_2;
│    │     └ ─
│    │ END SUB_1;
│    └ ─
│ END;
└ ─
```

Figure 8-30 Example segment from block-structured language.

14 Formulate algorithms for the insertion, lookup, set, and reset operations for a stack-implemented hash symbol table as described in this chapter. A chaining technique should be used for collision resolution.

15 As part of a term project and keeping in mind the discussion in this chapter, implement an appropriate symbol-table organization and the associated operations of insertion, lookup, and set and reset (if applicable) for your language.

BIBLIOGRAPHY

Adel'son-Vel'skii, G. M., and E. M. Landis: "An Algorithm for the Organization of Information," *Doklady Akademii Nauk SSSR, Mathemat.*, Vol. 14, No. 2, 1962, pp. 263–266.

Amble, O., and D. E. Knuth: "Ordered Hash Tables," *The Computer Journal*, Vol. 17, No. 2, 1974, pp. 135–142.

Baer, J. L.: "Weight-Balanced Trees," *Proceedings of AFIPS 1975 NCC*, Vol. 44, Montvale, N.J.: AFIPS Press, pp. 467–472.

Baer, J. L., and B. Schwab: "A Comparison of Tree-Balancing Algorithms," *Communications of the ACM*, Vol. 20, No. 5, May 1977, pp. 322–330.

Buchholz, W.: "File Organization and Addressing," *IBM Systems Journal*, Vol. 2, June 1963, pp. 86–110.

de Balbine, G.: Ph.D. Thesis, California Institute of Technology, 1968.

Hibbard, T.: "Some Combinatorial Properties of Certain Trees, with Applications to Searching and Sorting," *Journal of the ACM*, Vol. 9, No. 1, Jan. 1962, pp. 13–28.

IBM: *FORTRAN (H) Compiler, Program Logic Manual*, Form Y28-6642.

Knuth, D. E.: *Sorting and Searching, The Art of Programming*, Vol. 3, Reading, Mass.: Addison-Wesley, 1973.

Lum, V. Y., P. S. T. Yuen, and M. Dodd: "Key-to-Address Transformation Techniques: A Fundamental Performance Study on Large Existing Formatted Files," *Communications of the ACM*, Vol. 14, No. 4, 1971, pp. 228–239.

McKeeman, W. M.: "Compiler Structure," University of Toronto, Computer Systems Research Group (CSRG) Report No. 23, Jan. 1973.

McKeeman, W. M.: Symbol Table Access, from "Compiler Construction: an Advanced Course," Goos and Hartmanis (eds.), *Lecture Notes in Computer Science*, New York: Springer-Verlag, 1974, pp. 253–301.

Nievergelt, J.: "Binary Search Trees and File Organization," *Computing Surveys*, Vol. 6, No. 3, Sept. 1974, pp. 195–207.

Nievergelt, J., and E. M. Reingold: "Binary Search Trees of Bounded Balance," *SIAM Journal of Computing*, Vol. 2, No. 1, March 1973, pp. 33–43.

Randell, B., and L. J. Russell: *ALGOL 60 Implementation*, London: Academic Press, 1964.

Severance, D. G.: "Identifier Search Mechanisms: A Survey and Generalized Model," *Computing Surveys*, Vol. 6, No. 3, Sept. 1974, pp. 175–194.

Stone, H. S.: *Introduction to Computer Organization and Data Structures*, New York: McGraw-Hill, 1972.

Tremblay, J. P., and P. G. Sorenson: *Introduction to Data Structures with Applications*, 2d ed., New York: McGraw-Hill, 1984.

Wulf, W. A., D. B. Russell, and A. N. Habermann: "BLISS: A Language for Systems Programming," *Communications of the ACM*, Vol. 14, No. 12, Dec. 1971, pp. 780–790.

RUN-TIME STORAGE ORGANIZATION AND MANAGEMENT

Thus far we have concentrated on those parts of the compiler that are responsible for recognizing the syntactic correctness of a program. In the remainder of the text, the synthesis part of the compilation process is highlighted. Before we can begin to consider the generation of code for the constituent parts of a program (as recognized in the analysis phase), a clear understanding must be obtained of how the information in an executing program is to be stored and accessed. This chapter is intended to provide this understanding. In particular, this chapter provides a description of the static, dynamic, explicit, and implicit storage-allocation strategies that are most often adopted when compiling programs for the wide variety of languages that exist currently. The first section describes a rather simple storage-allocation strategy that is sufficient to handle statically defined data structures. Next dynamic storage allocation, which is commonly provided in block-oriented languages such as ALGOL, is discussed. Finally, the problems of managing a heap storage facility, which is frequently used in conjunction with explicit and implicit execution-time storage requests, are addressed.

9-1 STATIC STORAGE ALLOCATION

In a static storage-allocation strategy, it is necessary to be able to decide at compile time exactly where each data object will reside at run time. In order to make such a decision, at least two criteria must be met:

1. The size of each object must be known at compile time.
2. Only one occurrence of each object is allowable at a given moment during program execution.

Because of the first criterion, variable-length strings are disallowed, since their length cannot be established at compile time. Similarly dynamic arrays are disallowed, since their bounds are not known at compile time and hence the size of the data object is unknown.

Because of the second criterion, nested procedures are not possible in a static storage-allocation scheme. This is the case because it is not known at compile time which or how many nested procedures, and hence their local variables, will be active at execution time.

At compile time it is also impossible to determine how many times a recursive procedure is going to be invoked. Each invocation of a recursive procedure necessitates the creation of a new occurrence of each data object for that procedure. Therefore, by implication, the second criterion is violated and recursion cannot be accommodated in a static storage-allocation strategy.

It must be noted that FORTRAN does not provide variable-length strings, dynamic arrays, nested procedures, or recursive procedures. In fact FORTRAN typifies those languages in which a static storage-allocation policy is sufficient to handle the storage requirements of the data objects in a program.

A static storage-allocation strategy is very simple to implement. During an initial pass of the source text, a symbol-table entry is created for each variable and the set of attributes, as discussed in Chap. 8, is filled in. Included in these attributes is the object address. Because the precise amount of space required by each variable is known at compile time, the object address for a variable can be assigned according to the following simple scheme. The first variable is assigned some address A near the beginning of an allocated data area, the second variable is assigned address $A + n_1$ assuming the first variable requires n_1 storage units (e.g., bytes), the third variable is assigned address $A + n_1 + n_2$ assuming the second variable requires n_2 storage units, and so on. Figure 9-1 illustrates part of a symbol table that would be created for the given FORTRAN program segment assuming integer values require four storage units and real values require eight.

The data area that is required to hold the values of the program variables at run time can be allocated at compile time if desired. Generally this is unnecessary, since the data area can be established by a system utility (usually called the loader) prior to the beginning of program execution.

An object address can be either an absolute or a relative address. If the compiler is written for a single-job-at-a-time environment, the object address assigned is often an absolute address. The initial address A is set such that the program and data area reside in a section of memory separate from the resident parts of the operating system. If the compiler resides in a multiprogramming environment, the object address assigned is a relative address, that is, an address that is relative to the base or initial address of the data area that is allocated to a program. With a relative-addressing scheme, a program and its data area may reside at a different set of memory locations each time the program is executed. The loader accomplishes this relocation by reserving a set of memory locations for the program and setting a base register to the address of the first location in the data area.

```
REAL MAXPRN, RATE
INTEGER IND1, IND2
REAL PRIN (100), YRINT (5,100), TOTINT
    •
    •
    •           (a)
```

Name	Type	Dimension		Address
MAXPRN	R	0		26⊄
RATE	R	0		272
IND1	I	0		28C
IND2	I	0		28⊄
PRIN	R	1		28E
YRINT	R	2		108E
TOTINT	R	0		508E

Starting relative address in data area

(b)

Figure 9-1 (*a*) FORTRAN program segment. (*b*) Associated symbol table.

A typical data area for a module of a program in which a static storage-allocation strategy is sufficient (e.g., a FORTRAN subroutine) is given in Fig. 9-2. We have adopted the notation of Gries (1971) and have divided the data area into three sections, one for the implicit parameters, one for the actual parameters, and one for the program variables. An implicit parameter is primarily used for communication with the calling module. Typically such a parameter is the return address to the calling procedure, or the return value of a functional procedure, when it is not convenient to return this value in a register. An actual parameter contains the value or address of the value of an argument that is designated in a call to the module. More will be said about parameter-passing schemes in Chap. 11. Finally, the program variables' section contains the storage space for the

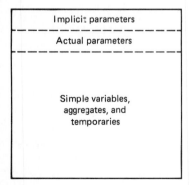

Implicit parameters

Actual parameters

Simple variables, aggregates, and temporaries

Figure 9-2 A typical data area for a static storage allocation strategy.

simple variables, aggregates (i.e., arrays and records), compiler-generated temporary variables, etc.

A call to a procedure consists of the following steps:

1. Bring forward the values or evaluate the addresses of the actual parameters (i.e., arguments from the calling procedure) and store them in a list in the calling procedure's data area.
2. Place the address of the parameter list in a register.
3. Branch to the procedure.

Prior to the execution of the procedure both the implicit and explicit parameters must be moved into the special locations that have been previously reserved in the data area. When returning to the calling procedure, the implicit parameters are loaded into registers and a jump back to the calling procedure occurs as dictated by the return address.

Let us turn our attention to the more complex dynamic storage-allocation strategy.

EXERCISES 9-1

1 Variable-length strings, dynamic arrays, nested procedures, and recursive procedures were cited as examples of language constructs that cannot be handled with a static storage-allocation strategy. Name two other language constructs that cannot be handled with static storage.

2 Name two commonly used programming languages, excluding FORTRAN, in which a static storage-allocation strategy is sufficient for run-time storage management.

3 Since for some programming languages, storage requirements can be determined at compile time, it may be possible to augment the symbol table of variables so that values of variables can be stored in the symbol table during program execution. Discuss the advantages and disadvantages of adopting this strategy. If this strategy is adopted, are there any new, major implementation problems that arise in static storage allocation?

9-2 DYNAMIC STORAGE ALLOCATION

In a dynamic storage-allocation strategy, the data area requirements for a program are not known entirely at compilation time. In particular, the two criteria that were given in the previous section as necessary for static storage allocation do not apply for a dynamic storage-allocation scheme. The size and number of each object need not be known at compile time; however, they must be known at run time when a block is entered. Similarly more than one occurrence of a data object is allowed, provided that each new occurrence is initiated at run time when a block is entered.

As is indicated by the previous discussion, a dynamic storage-allocation strategy is very much a block-oriented strategy and hence is used in block-structured languages such as ALGOL and PL/I. Because of the nested properties of the blocks, a dynamic storage-allocation strategy can be modeled fairly simply using a stacklike data area commonly called the *run-time stack*. Each block within the program can be viewed as having its own data area. When the block is invoked at run time, space for its data area is requested from the entire data area allotted to the program (i.e., from the run-time stack). This space is reserved until the entire block has been executed, at which time it is released (i.e., popped from the run-time stack). Note that between the invocation of a block and its eventual termination, several other blocks may be invoked through procedural calls or "BEGIN" block entries. The data areas for these blocks are simply pushed onto and popped off the stack in the fashion just described. Whenever execution returns to a block from which a call is initiated, the contents of the run-time stack should be the same as they were immediately prior to the call.

The action of this dynamic storage-allocation model can best be illustrated by an example. Figure 9-3, a reproduction of Fig. 8-25, illustrates a skeleton of a program segment from a nested language. Figure 9-4 provides a trace of the contents of the run-time stack as this module is executed.

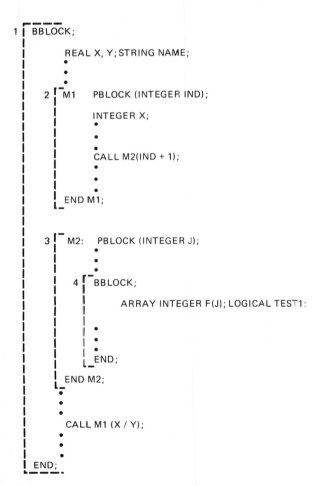

```
1 │ BBLOCK;
  │
  │        REAL X, Y; STRING NAME;
  │        •
  │        •
  │  2 │ M1     PBLOCK (INTEGER IND);
  │    │
  │    │        INTEGER X;
  │    │        •
  │    │        •
  │    │        CALL M2(IND + 1);
  │    │        •
  │    │        •
  │    │ END M1;
  │
  │  3 │ M2:    PBLOCK (INTEGER J);
  │    │        •
  │    │        •
  │    │  4 │ BBLOCK;
  │    │    │
  │    │    │        ARRAY INTEGER F(J); LOGICAL TEST1:
  │    │    │        •
  │    │    │        •
  │    │    │ END;
  │    │ END M2;
  │        •
  │        •
  │        CALL M1 (X / Y);
  │        •
  │        •
  │ END;
```

Figure 9-3 A program segment from a nested language.

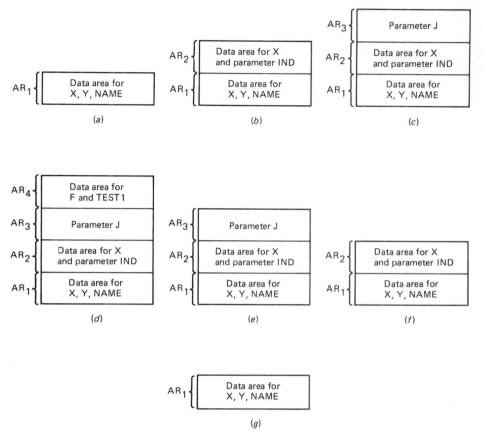

Figure 9-4 Trace of the run-time stack.

A number of important points are exemplified in the trace of Fig. 9-4. First, it is clear that the run-time stack does behave as a stack. When a block, say block i, is entered, a special data area is created on top of the run-time stack. This data area is commonly called an *activation record*, and it contains, among other things, the memory space necessary to hold the values of the variables local to that block. When execution of the ith block is ended (i.e., a block exit occurs), the corresponding activation record, denoted as AR_i, is removed from the top of the run-time stack, since the variables defined in the ith block cannot be accessed outside of the block.

9-2.1 Activation Records

A brief scenario clarifying the trace of Fig. 9-4 follows. This scenario is intended to illustrate the role of an activation record in the execution of a program that uses dynamic storage allocation.

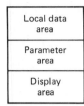

Figure 9-5 Layout of a typical activation record.

The program module is entered and an activation record for the first BBLOCK is created on the run-time stack as shown in Fig. 9-4a. Within the BBLOCK, a call is made to the PBLOCK named M1. An activation record for M1, designated as AR_2, is then stacked as shown in Fig. 9-4b. During the execution of M1, the PBLOCK named M2 is invoked, and this causes the stacking of the activation record AR_3, as illustrated in Fig. 9-4c. Assuming the BBLOCK within M2 is entered, a new activation record AR_4 is stacked as depicted in Fig. 9-4d.

Upon completion of the BBLOCK numbered 4 in Fig. 9-3, activation record AR_4 is popped from the run-time stack, since the variables for that block are no longer accessible. As the run-time activity progresses and execution is terminated for the remaining blocks, the other activation records AR_3, AR_2, and AR_1 are unstacked in the same manner as AR_4.

In addition to providing space for the storage of local variables, an activation record contains a *parameter area* and a *display area*. This is illustrated in Fig. 9-5, which depicts the layout of a typical activation record. In the next two subsections, each of these two areas is examined in detail.

9-2.2 Parameter Area

The parameter area holds both implicit and explicit parameters. *Implicit parameters* may include a return address, a pointer to the base of the previous activation record, and a return value. The *return address* is the address corresponding to the point in the program at which execution commences upon completion of the execution of the current block. A return address is not required for BEGIN-type blocks; however, space is sometimes allotted to standardize the form of the parameter area. The *previous-activation-base pointer* contains the base location of the activation record for the block from which control, say through a procedure call, was just transferred. This information must be maintained to ensure that the eventual return of control to the invoking procedure results in the restoration of the run-time environment as it was before the call was made. Finally, the *return value* for a functional procedure is sometimes included in the implicit parameter area. There are, however, other possibly better ways of handling return values, and these will be outlined in Sec. 11-6. In the remaining discussion in this section, a return value will not be included as an implicit parameter.

The set of *explicit parameters* (sometimes called the arguments of a procedure call) forms the other component of the parameter area. A variety of parameter-passing schemes exist, and some of these will be discussed in Sec. 11-6. In the detailed example given later in this subsection, a call-by-value parameter-passing scheme will be assumed. In such a scheme the values of the arguments (sometimes called actual parameters) are assigned to the formal parameters. The formal parameters are those parameters that are defined locally in the called procedure. Because the formal parameter values are identical to the values of the arguments, the formal parameters are usually considered to be situated in the parameter area in a call-by-value scheme.

9-2.3 Display Area

The final area that may be present in an activation record is the display area. This area contains the information necessary to access variables that are global to the block that is currently being executed. It is composed of a series of pointers, each pointer pointing to the base of an activation record of a block that is global to the block currently being executed. Referring to the program segment in Fig. 9-3, for example, it can be seen that when the block labeled 4 is executed, the variables declared in blocks 1 and 3 are accessible on a global basis. Therefore, the display area created when block 4 is activated should contain two pointer entries: one pointing at the base of the activation record for block 1 and the other pointing at the base of the activation record for block 3.

As mentioned in Sec. 8-3, a 2-tuple addressing scheme containing a block-level (BL) component and occurrence-number (ON) component is commonly adopted for block-structured languages. For example, in the procedure block M1 in Fig. 9-3, the variables IND and X would be assigned tuple addresses of $(2, 0)$, and $(2, 1)$, respectively. The block level of 2 is assigned because M1 is nested to depth 2. The occurrence numbers are assigned to the variables in order starting from 0 (hence in the example the values 0 and 1 are assigned).

The tuple address is used in conjunction with the display area to locate the value of a variable in the run-time stack. If the variable being referenced is a local variable, the location of the variable can be found at ON locations after the location of the first explicit parameter in the activation record. If the variable being referenced is a global variable, its BL component must be less than the block level of the block being executed currently. If this is the case, the base of the activation record which contains the location of the global variable can be referenced indirectly through the appropriate pointer in the display area of the current activation record. For example, if the variable X declared in the outermost block in Fig. 9-3 is referenced inside of the block numbered 4, its block level (i.e., 1) will be less than the current block level (i.e., 3). Its location can be found by referring to the BL $= 1$ or first element of the display area and using this activation-base-pointer value plus the occurrence number of 0 to locate the variable X in the activation record for the outermost block.

A trace of the run-time stack during part of the execution of the program segment in Fig. 9-3 is given in Fig. 9-6. In this trace, the display and the implicit parameters (i.e., the return address and previous-activation-base pointer) are

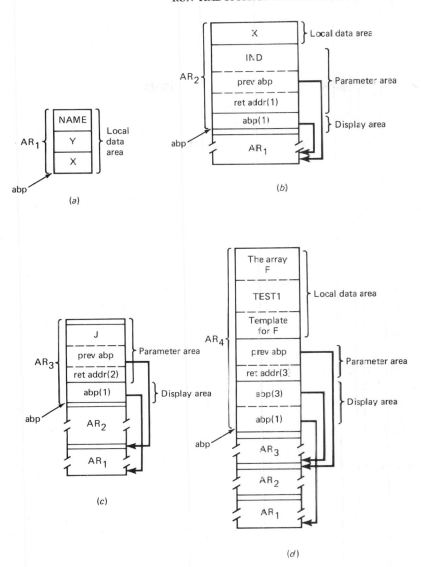

Figure 9-6 Detailed trace of the run-time stack.

shown. The trace proceeds only far enough to show the state of the run-time stack when execution begins on the BBLOCK numbered 4.

Execution begins with the BBLOCK numbered 1. Note that the activation record for this block does not contain a display, since there are no variables global to this block, or a parameter area, since this block was not invoked from another block. In practice there may in fact be a parameter area which contains a return address to some part of the operating system. Also, external parameters may be passed to the program through the parameter area.

When the procedure block M1 is invoked, a single-element display is constructed as depicted in Fig. 9-6b. The pointer abp(1), which is called an activation-base pointer, points to the base of the latest activation record for the block numbered 1. This display element facilitates the referencing of the global variables X, Y, or NAME. The return address, designated as "ret addr(1)," denotes the address to which control returns after M1 has been executed. The previous activation-base pointer (prev abp) is stacked in the parameter area along with the value that is assigned to the formal parameter IND.

Note that when the procedure block M2 is called, a single-element display is again created as shown in Fig. 9-6c. It is identical to the previous display, as it should be, since the variables that are global to procedure block M2 are the same as those for procedure block M1, namely, those found in the block numbered 1. A more formal set of rules for how to construct a display will be given immediately after a discussion of the trace.

When the basic block numbered 4 is entered in the procedure block M2, the display that is created contains pointers to the base of the activation record for each of the blocks number 1 and 3. Therefore, the variables X, Y, NAME, and J, which are all variables global to the basic block numbered, are accessible through the two-element display.

After the basic block numbered 4 has been executed, control is returned to the procedure block M2. At this time, the activation record for the basic block must be logically removed from the run-time stack so as to create a run-time environment identical to what existed prior to the execution of the basic block. To achieve this recreated environment, the activation-base pointer is reset to the value of the "prev abp" so that the activation-base pointer ("abp") will be pointing at the base of the activation record AR_3 for the procedure block M2. This process of resetting the activation-base pointer must take place each time the execution of a block is terminated and control returns to a block that was previously active.

The rules for constructing a display area can be summarized as follows. If a block at level j is entered (e.g., called) from a block at level i, then

1. If $j = i + 1$ (i.e., entering a BEGIN-type of block or calling a procedure block that is declared locally to the current block), then recopy the display for the block at level i and append to this a pointer pointing to the base of the activation record for the block at level i (see Fig. 9-7a).
2. If $j \le i$ (i.e., calling a procedure block that is declared globally to the current block), then the first $j - 1$ entries from the display area in the activation record for the block at level i form the display area for the block at level j (see Fig. 9-7b).

It should be noted that a display area need not be created for every activation record. If memory is a constraint, it may be better to have only a single display, namely, a display for the current block, created at any one time. Upon exiting a

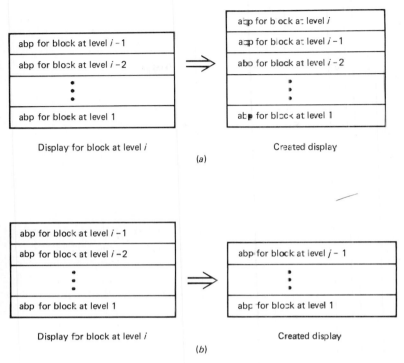

Figure 9-7 Illustration of two rules for constructing a display.

block, a history stack must then be used to help recreate the display the way it was prior to the execution of a block. This recreation process is particularly a problem when a return is made to a block at level j from a block at level i when j is less than or equal to i (i.e., case b given earlier). A discussion of this approach can be found in McKeeman et al. (1970).

A third and very storage-efficient approach to the creation of a display area for a given block is to store in the activation record a pointer to the base of the activation record for the block that most closely surrounds the given block in the program. In this way, references to global variables can be resolved by descending a chain of activation-base pointers until the appropriate activation record is located. Although this method is storage-efficient, it is not time-efficient because we must travel along a number of pointers to get to the appropriate activation record.

9-2.4 Run-Time Address Calculation

We are now in a position to formalize a procedure for run-time address calculation in our dynamic storage-allocation model. Given a variable with a tuple address of (BL, ON) that is accessible in a block at level LEV, the address ADDR of the variable is found as follows:

> if BL = LEV
> then ADDR ← adp + (BL − 1) + nip + ON
> else if BL < LEV
>   then ADDR ← $display$[BL] + (BL − 1) + nip + ON
>   else write ("addressing error: illegal block level")

where abp means the current activation-base pointer value
        $display$[BL] means the BL element of the display area in the current activation record
        nip means the number of implicit parameters, which has been two in the model presented in this section.

Notice that the expression (BL − 1) + nip accounts for the size of the display (i.e., a block at level BL must have a display of size BL − 1) plus the number of implicit parameters. Since both of these values are known at compile time, some compilers begin their ON assignment at (BL − 1) + nip. This scheme reduces the complexity of the address calculation at run time to abp + ON for local variables and $display$ [BL] + ON for global variables.

9-2.5 Handling Recursive Procedures

Before we conclude our discussion of dynamic storage allocation, it is important to point out that for recursive block-structured languages more than one activation record may be associated with a block at any one time. This property can be illustrated through the ALGOL program in Fig. 9-8, which contains a recursive FACTORIAL procedure. A trace of the run-time stack during execution is depicted in Fig. 9-9. The recursive procedure is assumed to be called initially with a value of 4 for M.

    With each invocation of the FACTORIAL procedure, a new activation record (and hence a new copy of the formal parameter N) is placed on top of the run-time stack. A return address is also associated with each activation record. A return address with a value of FACT indicates that the return from that particular

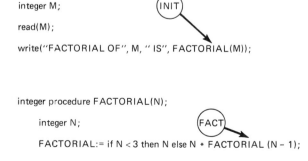

```
integer M;                        (INIT)

read(M);

write("FACTORIAL OF", M, " IS", FACTORIAL(M));



integer procedure FACTORIAL(N);

    integer N;                    (FACT)

    FACTORIAL:= if N < 3 then N else N * FACTORIAL (N - 1);
```

Figure 9-8 Recursive FACTORIAL procedure.

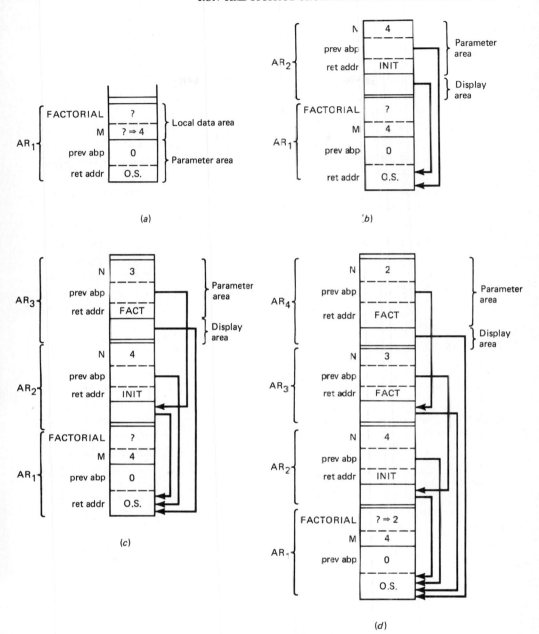

Figure 9-9 Trace of the run-time stack for the FACTORIAL procedure up to the basis condition.

activation of FACTORIAL is to the point of invocation within the FACTORIAL procedure as indicated in Fig. 9-8. A return address with the value of INIT designates that the return should be to the point at which the FACTORIAL procedure was initially invoked. Finally, a return address with the value of "O.S." indicates that a return to the operating system takes place when the entire program has terminated execution.

The trace in Fig. 9-9 begins with the stacking of the activation record for the outer block. Note that space is left for the return value of the FACTORIAL functional procedure, which is declared local to the outermost block. The activation record for the first invocation of the FACTORIAL procedure is shown in Fig. 9-9b. Subsequent invocations of the recursive procedure are represented by the stacking of activation records as shown in Fig. 9-9c and d.

The trace proceeds until the basis condition (i.e., N < 3) is met. At this point the current value of N is returned (i.e., assigned to the storage location for

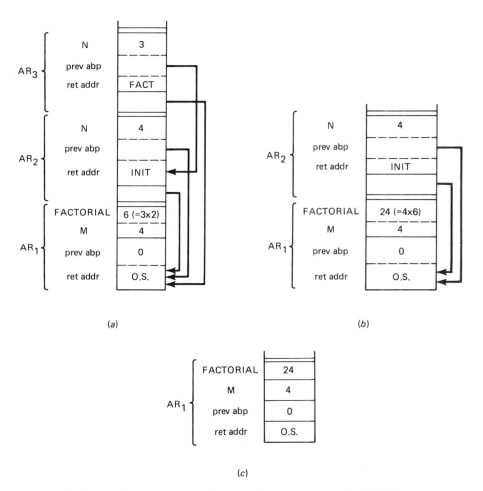

Figure 9-10 The remainder of the trace of the run-time stack for the FACTORIAL procedure.

FACTORIAL). The flow of control is then returned to the address indicated as FACT and the expression $N * FACTORIAL(N - 1)$ is evaluated. The result of this expression (i.e., $3 * 2 = 6$) is subsequently returned, and the process of unstacking the activation records and returning values for FACTORIAL continues as shown in Fig. 9-10. Finally, flow of control returns to the outer block through the return address INIT, and the value of FACTORIAL (i.e., 24) is printed.

From the FACTORIAL example, it is most important to understand that the value of N referenced during execution is located in the latest activation record to be allocated to FACTORIAL. This referencing is guaranteed because the calculation of the run-time address is always computed with respect to the current activation-base-pointer value.

It should be evident from the discussion of dynamic storage allocation that referencing a variable can involve a relatively complex run-time address calculation. This complexity suggests that languages with dynamic storage allocation should be used only for those applications involving rather dynamic storage demands at run time. In general, many applications, such as the traditional data-processing applications, do not require a very dynamic run-time environment, and therefore a language like COBOL, which has no dynamic storage allocation, is often used. It should be pointed out, however, that some machines, such as the Burroughs 6700, do support dynamic storage allocation with machine-level instructions. The apparent overhead in dynamic storage addressing is significantly reduced in these machines.

Let us turn our attention to a third type of storage allocation that is often required in programming languages.

EXERCISES 9-2

1 Why is the dynamic-storage-allocation strategy particularly amenable to the run-time storage requirements of block-structured languages?

2 Consider the following ALGOL-like program:

```
BEGIN
    INTEGER I;
    REAL X, Y;
    READ (I, X, Y);
    EXAMPLEPROC (I, X, Y);
    :
    :
    PROCEDURE EXAMPLEPROC (INTEGER J, REAL X, Y)
    BEGIN
①  ⟶  STRING S(8);
        :
        BEGIN;
②  ⟶  REAL R(J, J);
            :
        END
    END
END
```

Draw pictures of the contents of the run-time stack at points ① and ② as they would be during the execution of the previous program. The pictures should be similar to those given in Fig. 9-6.

3 Consider the following ALGOL-like program for recursively computing the greatest common divisor (GCD):

```
BEGIN
   INTEGER M, N;
   READ (M, N);
   GCD (M, N);
   INTEGER PROCEDURE GCD (INTEGER M, N)
   BEGIN
      IF N > M
      THEN RETURN (GCD(N, M));
      ELSE IF N = 0
            THEN RETURN (M);
            ELSE RETURN (GCD(N, REM(M, N)));
   END
END
```

Given input values of 40 and 12 for M and N, respectively, provide a trace of the run-time stack during the execution of the GCD program. Your trace should be as detailed as the trace given in Fig. 9-9.

4 Suppose that the activation-base pointers of the activation records for the outer block, the procedure **EXAMPLEPROC**, and the inner block are 5, 12, and 26, respectively, when point ② is reached during the execution of the program in Exercise 2. Provide a detailed run-time address calculation for the variables R(1,1), I, and Y at point ② during the execution of the program in Exercise 2.

5 Give an example of when a run-time address can be calculated without the display and when a display must be used in a run-time address calculation.

9-3 HEAP STORAGE ALLOCATION

From the discussion thus far, we established that for the case of static storage specific storage requirements must be known at compile time. For the case of dynamic storage allocation, storage requirements had to be known at a precise point during execution, namely, at block entry. These allocation strategies are not sufficient to handle the storage requirements of some data structures that may appear in a programming language. Variable-length strings in SNOBOL 4 and lists in LISP 1.5 are two examples of data structures with storage requirements that are not known at compile time or at block-entry time—in fact, their storage requirements are known only at the time a new value is assigned or a new instance of the structure is created.

Requests for storage for these types of data structures are handled through a heap storage-allocation strategy. The strategy involves the reserving of a large contiguous block of memory commonly called the *heap*. As requests for additional storage are received, a run-time storage manager allocates space from the heap. Similarly as space is no longer required for a data structure, the manager attempts, where possible, to release the storage so that it can be reused at a later date.

Two types of heap storage requests can occur: implicit and explicit requests. We begin our discussion by giving examples of both.

9-3.1 Implicit Storage Requests

As an example of an implicit storage request, consider the following SNOBOL 4 program segment:

```
READIN     LINE = INPUT          :F(OUT)
           TEXT = TEXT LINE      :(READIN)
OUT        OUTPUT = TEXT
END
```

The first statement reads in a line (or buffer full) of input and assigns it to the string LINE. If there is no more input, a transfer is made to the statement labeled OUT, the value of the variable TEXT is printed, and the program terminates. If there is input, the second statement is executed. The execution of this statement causes the value of LINE to be concatenated to the current value of TEXT, the result to be assigned to TEXT, and control to be unconditionally passed to the first statement. In this manner, the string TEXT is built up to contain all the characters present in the input file. Since the input file can vary in size, the total storage requirements for TEXT cannot possibly be known until the final input character is read.

Note that in the SNOBOL program there is no command that explicitly requests additional storage to handle the requirements for the variable-length string TEXT. Rather, it is assumed that a storage manager exists which acquires additional storage as the string increases in size.

There are also instances in which storage for a string can be released. For example, suppose a SNOBOL 4 program exists which builds up a string to a significant length in a fashion similar to the previous program segment. The string that is constructed is then used in some fashion, the string variable is reinitialized to the empty string (i.e., TEXT = ''), and the process of constructing a new string is reinitiated. At the point in which the variable is reinitialized to the empty string, it should be clear that the space occupied by the previous string value can be released in order that it may be reused in the construction of a new string. The releasing of heap storage in this instance occurs implicitly.

9-3.2 Explicit Storage Requests

Some programming languages, such as PL/I and PASCAL, allow the programmer to have explicit control over the creation or destruction of instances of a data structure. The PL/I procedure in Fig. 9-11 illustrates how a linked list of stocks and their quotations can be maintained in order by stock name. The procedure begins with the allocation of a record named STOCK. The variable STOCK is assumed to be global to the procedure and declared to have a BASED storage attribute as follows:

> DECLARE 1 STOCK BASED(P),
> 2 NAME CHARACTER(20),
> 2 QUOTE FIXED (6, 2),
> 2 LINK POINTER;

The ALLOCATE statement signifies to the heap manager that enough storage must be found to hold the contents of a new copy of the STOCK record. The pointer P is assigned an address pointing to the first storage location for the new copy of STOCK. The NAME and QUOTE fields of the record are filled in

```
STOCK_LIST_UPDATE:  PROCEDURE (FIRST);
        DECLARE (FIRST, TEMP, PREV) POINTER;

        ON ENDFILE (STOCKFILE) STOP;

        ALLOCATE STOCK;
        GET LIST (P -> NAME, P -> QUOTE);

        IF FIRST = NULL /* IS LIST EMPTY?*/
        THEN DO;
                FIRST = P;
                P -> LINK = NULL;
                RETURN;
        END;

        If P -> NAME < FIRST -> NAME    /* PLACE AT START OF LIST?*/
        THEN DO;
                P -> LINK = FIRST;
                FIRST = P;
                RETURN;
        END;

        PREV, TEMP = FIRST;
        DO WHILE (TEMP ¬= NULL);   /* INSERT IN MIDDLE OF LIST?*/
                IF P -> NAME = TEMP -> NAME   /* UPDATE OF A QUOTE?*/
                THEN DO;
                        TEMP -> QUOTE = P -> QUOTE;
                        FREE P -> STOCK;
                        RETURN;
                END;

                If P -> NAME < TEMP -> NAME    /*INSERT NEW STOCK?*/
                THEN DO;
                        PREV -> LINK = P;
                        P -> LINK = TEMP;
                        RETURN;
                END;

                /*OTHERWISE CONTINUE SEARCH */
                PREV = TEMP;
                TEMP = TEMP -> LINK;
        END;   /*FOR DO WHILE (TEMP ¬= NULL) */

        /* P NAME GREATER THAN ALL NAMES IN LIST */
        PREV -> LINK = P;
        P -> LINK = NULL;
END STOCK_LIST_UPDATE:
```

Figure 9-11 PL/I procedure illustrating explicit allocation and freeing of heap storage.

via an input statement. Then the record is either inserted into a linked list of STOCK records if that stock has not been placed in the list previously, or a previous STOCK record is updated with a new QUOTE value. If a previous record does exist, the newly created duplicate record should be destroyed, and this is accomplished with the FREE statement. In effect, the FREE statement tells the heap manager to release the storage allocated to the STOCK record, thus enabling this storage to be reused at a later point in the program.

Because the storage requirements can be dependent upon the size and nature of the input file as illustrated in the stock-quotation example, explicit data-structure creation and destruction cannot be handled at compile time or at block-entry time. As was the case with implicit storage requests, the indeterminancy until run time of storage requirements necessitates that a sophisticated heap storage manager be created as part of the run-time environment to handle this type of dynamic data-structure activity. Let us now turn to discussion of heap storage-management techniques.

9-3.3 Management of Fixed-Length Blocks

The simplest type of heap storage management is that involving storage requests which are always for a fixed number of storage locations. Such a situation might arise in a language like LISP, which is devoted to the manipulation of list structures whose BLOCKS are all of a single type and size. In this case, the total available heap storage can be subdivided into a series of blocks, each of the correct size. These blocks can be linked by LINK fields in the first word of each block to form a one-way linear list which will be called an *availability list*. A request for a storage block is then handled by a routine such as Function GET_BLOCK.

Function GET_BLOCK(HEAD). Given HEAD, the pointer to the first block on the linked list of available storage blocks, GET_BLOCK returns the address, P, of an available block.

1. [Overflow?]
   If HEAD = NULL
   then Exit to error routine
2. [Allocate block]
   P ← HEAD
   HEAD ← LINK(P)
   Return (P)   □

In step 1, if we are out of storage (HEAD = NULL), then we can only terminate the program or attempt to recover some storage by a garbage-collection technique which will be discussed later in this chapter. Recoverable storage is available from instances of data structures that are no longer used (i.e., referenced) by the program.

The return of a block to the availability list in heap storage is equally trivial. Simply attach the freed block as the new first block in the availability list. The question of when a block is returned will be discussed later in this chapter. It should be noted, however, that all that is needed to return a block is P, the block address, and HEAD, the pointer to the first block on the availability list.

9-3.4 Management of Variable-Length Blocks

The situation becomes more complicated if the storage requests can be for blocks of varying sizes, as is common with variable-length strings or when the allocation of data structures of varying sizes is being explicitly controlled. We can no longer treat the available heap storage as a linked list of blocks of the correct size, for there is no correct size. Instead, our linked list can contain blocks of various sizes, each being a potential candidate for allocation or for subdivision into two blocks of smaller size—one subblock for immediate allocation and one for retention on the available list.

With variable-sized blocks, the problem of fragmentation is encountered. This is a problem which did not appear in the case of fixed-size requests. Two types of memory fragmentation can arise: external fragmentation and internal fragmentation. These are explained as follows.

If a large number of storage blocks are requested and later returned to heap storage, the linked list of available blocks can be reasonably lengthy (especially if returned contiguous blocks are not fused into one). This means that the average size of an available block becomes small and that there are probably very few blocks which are large. If a request for a large block is received, it may have to be refused because there is no single block on the availability list that is big enough even though the total amount of available storage may be much greater than the requested amount. This phenomenon of decomposing the total available storage into a large number of relatively small blocks is called *external fragmentation*.

We can attempt to inhibit external fragmentation somewhat by occasionally allocating a block that is larger than the requested size (i.e., by refusing to split a block into pieces, one of which might be quite small). If we do this, it could happen that a request for heap storage must be refused because of the lack of blocks of the required size. This can take place even though the amount of storage that is "wasted" (i.e., allocated but unused) is more than sufficient to satisfy the request. This phenomenon of partitioning the total unused storage into available blocks and allocating these blocks with some portion of the blocks remaining unused and unavailable is called *internal fragmentation*.

Any algorithm for heap storage management in a context where variable-sized blocks will be used must seek, in some way or another, to minimize the inefficiencies due to fragmentation. Fragmentation is the major factor in making these algorithms more complicated than those for fixed-size blocks. In addition, because the sizes of blocks cannot be known in advance, each block generally uses a SIZE field to record its current size as well as a LINK field to maintain the linked structure of the availability list. For convenience it is assumed that these fields are in the first word of each block or can be accessed directly once the address of the first word of the block is provided.

First-fit heap storage-management strategy. Assume the availability list has a list head of the form given in Fig. 9-12, with AVAIL being the address of this list head, LINK(AVAIL) being a pointer to the first block on the free list, and SIZE(AVAIL) being set to 0. Then one method for servicing a request for a block of size *n* can be formulated as follows.

Function ALLOCATE_FIRST (AVAIL, MIN, n). Given AVAIL, the address of the list head in heap storage and n, the size of block requested, this function returns P, the address of a block of length $\geq$ n, with SIZE(P) set to the actual length of the block. The variable MIN records the amount of heap storage that is willing to be wasted in order to reduce external fragmentation. That is, no block of size MIN or smaller will be formed by splitting a particular block. k is a local variable which contains the difference between the size of a block and the requested block size. Q is also a local variable and points to the block previous to P in the linked list of available blocks.

1. [Initialize]
   Q ← AVAIL
   P ← LINK(Q)
2. [Find block large enough for request]
   Repeat while P ≠ NULL
       If SIZE(P) ≥ n
       then k ← SIZE(P) − n
           If k ≤ MIN
           then LINK(Q) ← LINK(P)
           else SIZE(P) ← k
               P ← P + k
               SIZE(P) ← n
           Return(P)
       else Q ← P
           P ← LINK(Q)
3. [No suitable block]
   Exit to error routine   □

This function assumes that arithmetic can be performed on addresses. If it is desired to eliminate internal fragmentation completely, simply set MIN to

AVAIL ⟶	SIZE	LINK

Figure 9-12

0—though the utility of a block of size 1 is not very clear, especially since this single location (and perhaps, more!) is taken up by the SIZE and LINK fields.

The function just given is commonly called a *first-fit algorithm* because the block that is allocated is the first block (or a part) that is found to be larger than the requested amount. One might suspect that a *best-fit algorithm* might be preferable, but, in fact, this is not necessarily the case. The best-fit method does not use the first suitable block found but instead continues searching the list until the smallest suitable block has been found. This tends to save the larger blocks for times when they are needed to service large requests. However, the best-fit method does have the unfortunate tendency to produce a larger number of very small free blocks, and these are often unusable by almost all requests. Furthermore, the best-fit method requires a search of the entire availability list containing, say, N blocks, while the average length of search for the first-fit method would be $N/2$ or less, depending on the requested size.

The choice of methods, in any case, must be made in the context of some knowledge about the types of requests that will be encountered. Given a particular set of circumstances, the best-fit method might give better performance than the first-fit method, offsetting the potentially longer search time. It is interesting to note, however, that during the same series of simulations of storage-usage patterns performed in order to compare various management strategies, Knuth (1973) discovered that the first-fit method outperformed the best-fit method in all cases examined.

To this point, nothing has been said about any ordering imposed on the list of free blocks. This can have a significant effect on performance. If blocks on the availability list are ordered by size, the search time of the best-fit method can be reduced. An ascending-order sort has the effect of converting first fit to best fit. Descending order reduces the first fit's search time to one because the first block found would be the largest. However, this can potentially convert first-fit into a method known as "worst-fit," in which the largest block is always used regardless of the size of the request. It may also cause unnecessary generation of many small blocks.

There is another ordering that might be imposed, however. This is to have the blocks on the availability list ordered by address (increasing, let us assume). This type of ordering does not necessarily improve search times for blocks of particular sizes, because there is no relation between block address and block size. However, it does make it possible to reduce external fragmentation, and it would tend to reduce all search times because the availability list can be shorter. Blocks sorted by address can be checked upon release, and if two consecutive blocks on the list are found to be contiguous, they are fused to form one larger block. This technique tends to keep block sizes larger and hence to keep the number of blocks smaller. More will be said on this fusing of blocks when algorithms are formulated for the release of allocated blocks. There is a lot of evidence, though, to suggest that, in the absence of special offsetting conditions, first-fit applied to an availability list ordered by address is a good method to adopt.

Another addition that can be made to the first-fit algorithm that can reduce its search time quite noticeably is also described by Knuth. The modification lies in starting a search for a suitable block at the point where the previous search terminated rather than always with the first block. This tends to distribute smaller blocks evenly over the entire list, rather than having them concentrated near the front of the list. Knuth (1973) has shown through a series of simulations that this modification reduces the average length of search for the first-fit method to $N/3$ as opposed to $N/2$. Function ALLOCATE_FIRST_M is the first-fit algorithm modified to make use of this varying search start point.

Function ALLOCATE_FIRST_M (AVAIL, MIN, n, M). Given AVAIL, n, and MIN as before, and M, a pointer to the last examined available block on the previous invocation of this routine, the function returns P, the address of a suitable block, and defines a new value for M. Prior to the first call to this routine, M is assumed to have been initialized to AVAIL. TIME is a flag associated with the traversal of the list. This flag is set to 1 when the end of the list is encountered. k is a local variable which contains the difference between the size of a block and the requested block size. Q is a local variable as well and points to the block previous to P in the linked list of available nodes.

1. [Initialize]
   Q ← M
   P ← LINK(Q)
   TIME ← 0
2. [Find large enough block]
   Repeat while TIME = 0 or Q ≠ M
   If P = NULL
   then Q ← AVAIL
   P ← LINK(Q)
   TIME ← 1
   else If SIZE(P) ≥ n
   then k ← SIZE(P) − n
   If k ≤ MIN
   then LINK(Q) ← LINK(P)
   M ← Q
   else SIZE(P) ← k
   M ← P
   P ← P + k
   SIZE(P) ← n
   Return(P)
   else Q ← P
   P ← LINK(Q)
3. [No suitable block]
   Exit to error routine □

Let us now consider the release of an allocated block of storage and its return to the free list. We still ignore the question of when and how the decision is made to free a block of storage and simply assume that a block of storage, starting at address RB, is now considered to be unused and a candidate for reallocation. It is also assumed that a size field, SIZE(RB), is located in the first word of the block and contains the actual size of the block being freed.

The simplest solution is to insert every freed block as a new first block on an unordered free list. This does, indeed, require a minimum of processing, but it has a serious drawback. After the heap storage manager has been operating for a while, the availability list is very likely to contain a large number of small blocks. The search time for the allocation routine will become longer and longer and there will be an ever-increasing risk of being unable to meet certain requests because all the blocks are simply too small. The problem is, of course, that in this simple freeing method no mechanism is running in opposition to the splitting mechanism in the allocation routine. In other words, big blocks are never recreated.

The obvious solution is to form one block out of two contiguous free blocks. If every newly released block is checked for contiguity with its predecessor and successor blocks on the availability list and merged with them whenever contiguity occurs, the availability list will always contain the smallest number of blocks. Each block is as large as possible given the current segments that are allocated. In order for this to work, however, the availability list must be kept in order by block address, and this then requires a search of the availability list in order to determine the position for insertion of a newly freed block.

The following algorithm can be used to insert a block on the availability list, merging it as necessary with contiguous neighbors. Since we have available a second pointer into the availability list—the variable search start point—we can make use of it as a starting point rather than AVAIL on some occasions. It can be shown that this reduces the average length of search from $N/2$ to $N/3$. The algorithm incorporates this modification.

Procedure FREE_BLOCK (AVAIL, RB, M). Given AVAIL, the address of the list head, M, the variable starting point for searching in the allocation routine, and RB, the address of the block to be inserted, this procedure inserts block RB into the availability list and merges contiguous blocks whenever possible. The algorithm assumes that AVAIL is less than the address of any block. This is guaranteed if the list head (with SIZE(AVAIL) set to 0) is the first word of the entire section of memory available for allocation. It is also assumed that the value NULL can be compared with valid addresses using any of the relational operators, with only $\neq$ yielding a *true* result. Q is a pointer which denotes the predecessor of the node being freed.

1. [Initialize to either beginning or variable search point]
   If RB > M
   then Q ← M
   else Q ← AVAIL
   P ← LINK(Q)

2. [Find predecessor and successor in sorted list]
      Repeat while P ≠ NULL and RB > P
        Q ← P
        P ← LINK(Q)
3. [Collapse with successor, P?]
      If P = NULL or RB + SIZE(RB) ≠ P
      then LINK(RB) ← P
      else LINK(RB) ← LINK(P)
          SIZE(RB) ← SIZE(RB) + SIZE(P)
          If M = P then M ← RB
4. [Collapse with predecessor, Q?]
      If Q = AVAIL or Q + SIZE(Q) ≠ RB
      then LINK(Q) ← RB
      else LINK(Q) ← LINK(RB)
          SIZE(Q) ← SIZE(Q) + SIZE(RB)
          If M = RB then M ← Q
      Return   □

To summarize, we now have a heap storage-allocation method with an average search time that can be very short, and we have a heap storage-freeing method with an average search time of about $N/3$. Our release technique tends to reduce external fragmentation because it maintains block sizes as large as possible. The degree of internal fragmentation is under our control through the variable MIN, though there is a trade-off between internal fragmentation and both external fragmentation and search times. Yet looking at these two heap storage-management mechanisms in terms of search times, we can see that the dealloca-tion routine is a potential bottleneck because of the $N/3$ average length of search. It is appropriate, therefore, to consider a deallocation routine which does not require this length of searching time. The "boundary-tag" method of Knuth is the strategy chosen.

Boundary-tag heap storage-management strategy. In the storage-release procedure just given, it is the search through the blocks in the sorted list which allows the determination of the predecessor and successor blocks. Having these, it is simple to determine if they and the released block are contiguous. Without the search, all that one can do is examine the two words that are the immediate predecessor and successor of the released block. But unless they are specially marked with flags, there is no immediate way of telling whether or not the predecessor and successor blocks are on the availability list. Consequently, in the boundary-tag method the first and last words of blocks are made to contain a flag field which indicates whether or not the block is allocated. It is also useful to have the last word of a block also contain a size field. From the last word of a block, the address of the first word can be determined directly. And finally, since searching is being avoided, the availability list is maintained as a doubly linked list. The price paid for eliminating searching is therefore more storage taken up for control fields.

This may not be worthwhile if, depending on the frequency and the nature of the deallocations, the availability list tends to be fairly short or the average block size is small. In other cases, it may be a very useful way of speeding up the deallocation of storage. The details can be found in Knuth's book.

The storage representation of the blocks is of the form given in Fig. 9-13a and b when the blocks are on the availability list and allocated, respectively. If the block starting at address P is free, the FLAG and FL fields are set to 0; otherwise these fields are set to a positive value for a block which is allocated. The fields SIZE and SZ contain the length of block P. SUC(P) and PRED(P) are pointers to the successor and predecessor, respectively, of block P on the availability list. A list head is also assumed of the form given in Fig. 9-13c, with AVAIL being its address. The list head is considered to be the successor and the predecessor of the last and first blocks on the availability list. For convenience, we assume that the list head is outside the segment of storage that is to be managed and that the first and last words of this segment have the correct flags set to show that these two words have been allocated. We now proceed to formulate a deallocation algorithm based on this representation.

Procedure FREE_BOUNDARY_TAG (RB, M). Given the block structure just described, this procedure inserts a block with address RB onto the availability list, merging it with contiguous blocks as necessary. It also redefines M, the variable search start point, if required. It is assumed that having the address of the first word of the block is sufficient to access immediately the FLAG, SIZE, SUC, and PRED fields, and that the address of the last word of the block gives direct access to the SZ and FL fields. The algorithm itself basically performs an insertion into a two-way linked list. Q is a local variable which points to various blocks during the

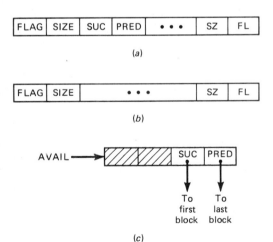

(a)

(b)

(c)

Figure 9-13 Boundary-tag block structure. (a) Free block. (b) Allocated block. (c) List head block.

process of merging.

1. [Remove predecessor Q and merge?]
    If FL(RB − 1) = 0
    then Q ← RB − SZ(RB − 1)
        PRED(SUC(Q)) ← PRED(Q)
        SUC(PRED(Q)) ← SUC(Q)
        SIZE(Q) ← SIZE(Q) + SIZE(RB)
        RB ← Q
2. [Remove successor Q and merge?]
    If FLAG(RB + SIZE(RB)) = 0
    then Q ← RB + SIZE(RB)
        PRED(SUC(Q)) ← PRED(Q)
        SUC(PRED(Q)) ← SUC(Q)
        SIZE(RB) ← SIZE(Q) + SIZE(RB)
        If M = Q
        then M ← RB
3. [Add locations between RB and Q inclusive as new first block]
    Q ← RB + SIZE(RB) − 1
    FLAG(RB) ← FL(Q) ← 0
    SZ(Q) ← SIZE(RB)
    SUC(RB) ← SUC(AVAIL)
    SUC(AVAIL) ← RB
    PRED(RB) ← AVAIL
    PRED(SUC(RB)) ← RB
    Return   □

In performing the deallocation, four possible cases arise in Procedure
FREE_BOUNDARY_TAG, and these are exhibited in Fig. 9-14. In the first case,
as shown in Fig. 9-14a, the freed block pointed to by RB is of size B and has no
immediate neighbors that are already marked as free. That is, both the block with
a size field of A and the block with the size field of C are already allocated and
hence their flag fields are marked with a 1. In this case, neither step 1 or 2 of the
algorithm is applied, and with the application of step 3 the freed block is simply
placed at the front of the availability list as depicted in the right-hand side of Fig.
9-14a.

The second case is shown in Fig. 9-14b. The neighbor block of size A is
shown to be on the availability list. In this case, step 1 of the algorithm collapses
the block pointed to by RB and its neighbor of size A to a new block of size
$A + B$. Note that in collapsing the blocks the block of size A is removed from the
availability list. Step 2 is not applied in this case and step 3 simply inserts the new
collapsed block at the front of the availability list.

The third case shows the situation in which the freed block is collapsed with a
neighbor that succeeds it in heap storage. The condition in step 1 is not met;

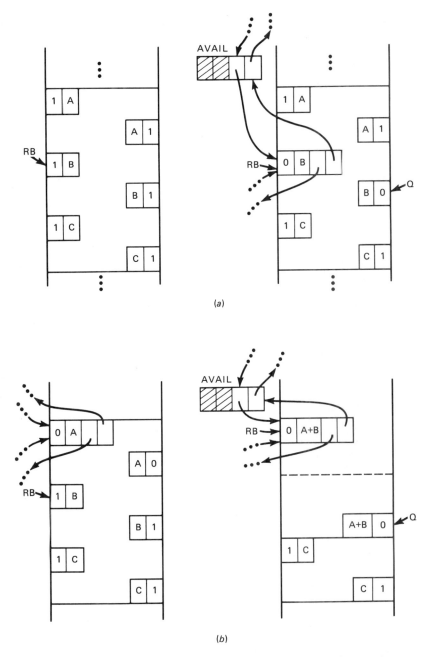

Figure 9-14 An illustration of the four cases of block deallocation in the boundary-tag method.

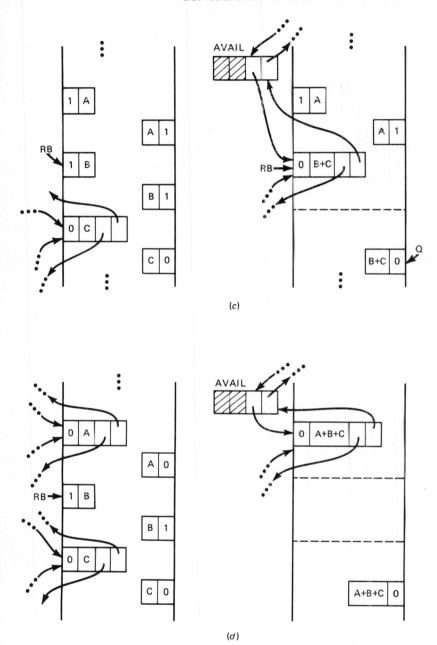

(c)

(d)

however, the condition in step 2 is true. The freed block is collapsed with the block of length C, and the block of length C is removed from the free list. The final step places the collapsed block at the head of the availability list.

The fourth case combines the effects of cases 2 and 3 discussed previously. Both neighbor blocks are collapsed in steps 1 and 2, and the large collapsed block is again inserted as the first block in the availability list.

Buddy-system heap storage-management strategy. Up to this point the sizes of blocks have either been fixed or completely arbitrary (though larger than some minimum value). Another technique used in heap storage management is to restrict the sizes of blocks to some fixed set of sizes. All the blocks of each size can be linked together with the intent of speeding up the search for a block of suitable size. For a request for a block of size n, the number m, the smallest of the fixed sizes equal to or larger than n, is determined, and a block of size m is allocated. If no block of size m is available, a larger block is split into two subblocks (known as "buddies"), each also of fixed size, and this process is repeated until a block of size m is produced.

Besides the improvement in search time, there is another advantage in using this technique. The collapsing of two smaller blocks into one larger block is relatively easy, since only the two buddies formed by splitting a larger block may be combined to form this larger block once again Because the sizes are fixed relative to one another, the address of the buddy of a block is relatively easily determined.

There are, however, some potential disadvantages associated with this technique. Internal fragmentation will be increased generally, because of the allocation of blocks which may be somewhat larger than the requested size. As well, there can be an increased amount of external fragmentation due to the fact that two blocks may be contiguous and yet not merged because they are not buddies. Generally, though, this technique of storage management has proved to be quite efficient with performance comparable with the previous methods discussed.

The usual approach in implementing this method of storage management is to specify the fixed sizes, $F_0, F_1, \ldots, F_{\text{MAX}}$, for blocks according to some pattern such as the recurrence relation

$$\begin{cases} F_n = F_{n-1} + F_{n-k} & k \le n \le \text{MAX} \\ F_0 = a, F_1 = b, \ldots, F_{k-1} = c \end{cases}$$

where $a, b, \ldots, c$ are minimum block sizes that are used, and where $k = 1$ or 2 or 3 or.... For example, if k is 1 and F_0 is 1, the block sizes, which are $1, 2, 4, 8, 16, \ldots$, are the successive powers of 2 and the method is called the "binary buddy system." If $k = 2$ with $F_0 = F_1 = 1$, the sizes are just the successive members of the Fibonacci sequence $1, 1, 2, 3, 5, 8, 13, \ldots$. In all likelihood, though, the F_0, F_1, etc., terms are not defined to be such small values. Blocks of size 1 are not of much use, especially if they must also carry control information so that the allocation and release mechanisms will work.

The feature that makes this system work is that the merges must correspond exactly to the splits. By this we mean that the only two blocks that can be merged are precisely the two that were formed by splitting. Furthermore, before each block can be reformed, each of its subblocks must be reformed from their subblocks. Consequently, the storage block pattern formed by the sequence of splits has the form of a binary tree. The problem that is faced is the recording of the position of a particular block within this tree structure. A rather elegant solution has been provided by Hinds (1975) in a storage-management application.

His solution consists of a coding for each block in such a way that the splitting sequence which produced that block can be reconstructed. Looking at the recurrence relation $F_n = F_{n-1} + F_{n-k}$, if we specify that the F_{n-1} term corresponds to the block that forms the left branch of a split (assumed to be at the lower address) and the F_{n-k} term is the right branch, then all that must be recorded for each block is the size of the block, the number of splits it took to form the block, and whether it is a left block or a right block. Since one left block and one right block are formed in each split, we need only record the count of left blocks. In fact, this allows us to code the left-or-right factor together with the split count in one coded field. The left block has the relative split count (a number greater than 0) while the right block has a code of 0. The code for the parent block is thus determined in relation to the left block. The formulas to use are the following:

initially, $\quad \text{CODE}_{\text{MAX}} = 0 \quad$ where F_{MAX} is the entire segment considered to be a right block

splitting, $\quad \text{CODE}_{\text{LEFT}} = \text{CODE}_{\text{PARENT}} + 1$
$\quad\quad\quad\quad\quad \text{CODE}_{\text{RIGHT}} = 0$

merging, $\quad \text{CODE}_{\text{PARENT}} = \text{CODE}_{\text{LEFT}} - 1$

As an example, consider a storage block of 144 cells and the recurrence relation

$$F_n = F_{n-1} + F_{n-2} \quad\quad 2 \le n \le 6$$

$$F_0 = 8, F_1 = 13$$

The entire tree of possible splits is given in Fig. 9-15, where the vertex value is the block size and the superscript is the code value as computed by the previous formulas.

Consider the tree cross section which is the set of potential blocks of size 13. A block of size 13 with code of 0 is the right block formed by splitting a block of size 34. The left or right nature of this size 34 block is determined by the left buddy for the block of size 13. If its left buddy (of size 21) has a code of 1, the size 34 block is a right block for some larger block of size 89, while if the left buddy has a code greater than 1, the block of size 34 is a left block of some still larger block. A block of size 13 with a code value greater than 0 is the left block of a split block of size 21. The numeric value of the code for a left block of size 13 is the number of splits of some higher right block that had to be made to get this

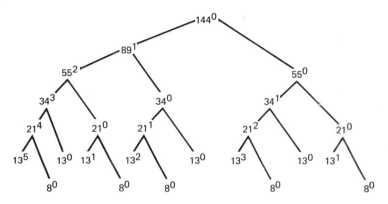

Figure 9-15 Storage-management tree.

left block of size 13. Or, in other words, the value of the code for a left block is the number of merges that this left block must undergo to become the first 13 locations of some larger block which is finally a right block.

For the algorithms to be presented, it will be assumed that blocks are of the structure given in Fig. 9-16a and b, which correspond to free and allocated blocks, respectively. FREE(P) is 0 or greater than 0 depending on whether block P is free or not, SIZE(P) contains the value i for block P of size F_i, and SUC(P) and PRED(P) are the forward and backward pointers to other free blocks of size F_i in a doubly linked list of all the free blocks of size F_i. The list head with address AVAIL[i] for this list is given in Fig. 9-16c. CODE(P) for block P is the code giving the left- or right-handedness of block P and the relative split count, if P is a left block. In addition to the array of list heads AVAIL[0:MAX], we also have the array F[0:MAX] which records the block sizes F_i, $0 \le i \le$ MAX, as determined by the recurrence relation. It is assumed that F_0 has a value large enough to allow the storage of all the control fields.

The following are two subalgorithms which take care of the insertion and deletion of blocks into and from the above linked lists.

Procedure INSERT(P, i). Given the arrays and block structures as previously described and parameters i and P (address of a block of size F_i), this procedure inserts P into the list headed by AVAIL[i].

1. [Insert at the front of the list]
       FREE(P) ← 0
       SIZE(P) ← i
       SUC(P) ← SUC(AVAIL[i])
       SUC(AVAIL[i]) ← P
       PRED(P) ← AVAIL[i]
       PRED(SUC(P)) ← P
       Return   □

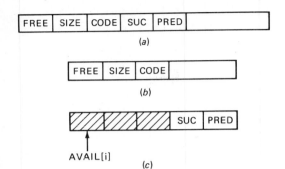

Figure 9-16 Buddy-system block structure. (*a*) Free block. (*b*) Allocated block. (*c*) List head block.

Procedure DELETE(P). Given the arrays and block structures as previously described and parameter P (the address of a block), this procedure deletes block P from the list in which it appears.

1. [Delete block P by unlinking it]
   SUC(PRED(P)) ← SUC(P)
   PRED(SUC(P)) ← PRED(P)
   Return   □

   The following algorithms service the requests for storage blocks and the deallocation of blocks in heap storage. Both presume that the value of k has been fixed so as to determine which recurrence relation is being used.

Function ALLOCATE_BUDDY (n). Given the arrays and block structures as previously described, this function receives a request for a block of size n and returns the pointer P set to the address of a block of size F_i which is the smallest size larger than or equal to n. It is assumed that the value of k has been fixed so as to determine which recurrence relation is being used. Local variables include i and j (integers) and Q (pointer).

1. [Determine size code]
   If n > F[MAX]
   then Exit to error routine
   else i ← 0
   Repeat while n > F[i]
       i ← i + 1
2. [Find first available block]
   j ← i
   Repeat while SUC(AVAIL[j]) = AVAIL[j]
       j ← j + 1
       If j > MAX
       then Exit to error routine
   P ← SUC(AVAIL[j])
   Call DELETE(P)

3. [Split as required until correct size is reached]
 Repeat while j > i and j ≥ k
  Q ← P + F[j − 1]
  CODE(P) ← CODE(P) + 1
  CODE(Q) ← 0
  If i > j − k
  then Call INSERT(Q, j − k)
   j ← SIZE(P) ← j − 1
  else Call INSERT(P, j − 1)
   j ← SIZE(Q) ← j − k
   P ← Q
4. [Allocate block P of size F_i]
 FREE(P) ← 1
 Return(P)   □

Procedure FREE_BUDDY (P). Given a block beginning at address P as well as the block structure and arrays described previously, this procedure inserts P (or the mergers of it with appropriate buddies) onto the proper free list. It is assumed that the value of k has been fixed so as to determine which recurrence relation is being used. Q is a local pointer variable.

1. [Perform all possible merges]
 Repeat step 2 while SIZE(P) < MAX
2. [P is a left block?]
 If CODE(P) > 0
 then Q ← P + F[SIZE(P)]
  If FREE(Q) > 0 or SIZE(Q) ≠ SIZE(P) − k + 1
  then Call INSERT(P, SIZE(P))
   Return
  else CODE(P) ← CODE(P) − 1
   SIZE(P) ← SIZE(P) + 1
   Call DELETE(Q)
 else (P is a right block)
  Q ← P − F[SIZE(P) + k − 1]
  If FREE(Q) > 0 or SIZE(Q) ≠ SIZE(P) + k − 1
  then Call INSERT(P, SIZE(P))
   Return
  else CODE(Q) ← CODE(Q) − 1
   SIZE(Q) ← SIZE(Q) + 1
   Call DELETE(Q)
   P ← Q
3. [We get here only if P is the maximal block]
 Call INSERT(P, MAX)
 Return   □

It should be noted that when $k = 1$ (when the strategy is the binary buddy system) the addresses of buddies differ from each other by amounts that are integral powers of 2. Since all addresses are in binary representation in a computer, the address calculation given above can be replaced by a method that makes use of this fact, thus possibly speeding up these algorithms.

With regard to the performance of these algorithms, Knuth's simulations showed that the buddy system performed quite well, comparable with his boundary-tag method, and, in fact, the buddy system has proven itself in practice. Statistical analysis has been performed on the Fibonacci system, and the results show it to be superior to the binary buddy system. The advantage of the Fibonacci buddy system is that the average amount of wasted storage is less than for the binary buddy system. A wider range of block sizes is available in the Fibonacci system because, for a given integer, there are at least as many Fibonacci numbers as there are integral powers of 2. Hence more block sizes are available and, therefore, it is more likely that a fit between the requested amount and the allocated amount is possible. One can conclude, however, that both storage-allocation methods are suitable candidates for a storage-management system.

Thus far in the section we have surveyed a number of heap storage-allocation strategies. Yet to be fully considered, however, is the question of when and how a decision to free storage is made.

The question of when to free static and dynamic storage is easily answered. As we have seen earlier in this chapter, static storage is freed when the execution of a program is completed and dynamic storage is released upon termination of a block.

With explicitly controlled heap storage-allocation strategies (such as that adopted using PL/I's ALLOCATE and FREE statements on based storage), the explicit use of free statements should dictate exactly when storage can be released. However, the blind adoption of such a strategy can lead to disastrous results through the creation of dangling references. Consider, for example, the following sequence of PL/I instructions:

```
ALLOCATE (NODE);        /*NODE is a based storage variable */
SET P;

  .
  .
  .

Q = P;                  /*Q is a pointer variable */
FREE (P − > NODE);
```

First, a copy of NODE is created. The address of this created variable is copied into the base-pointer variable P. Next, the pointer variable Q is set to point to the copy of NODE allocated previously. Finally, the copy of NODE is released, the base pointer P is set to NULL but the value of Q remains unchanged and pointing to a released block of storage. Obviously some difficult-to-detect errors can arise when programmers are given such a direct control over the relinquishing of heap storage.

To circumvent this problem, and to protect programmers from themselves, most language implementors reserve the task of heap storage release for the heap manager, even if the language provides a free command that the programmer can use. The problem that then arises is one of determining when storage can actually be freed. Two main methods can be used, and these are described in the next two subsections.

9-3.5 Free-as-You-Go Storage Release

The first method is to free each block of heap storage as soon as it becomes unused. This prevents the accumulation of garbage blocks but can require more run-time checking. This method is generally implemented by means of reference counters—counters which record how many pointers to this block are still in existence. When a block is first allocated, its reference counter is set to 1. Each time another link is made pointing to this block, the reference counter is incremented; each time a link to it is broken, the reference counter is decremented. When the count reaches 0, the block is inaccessible and hence unusable. At this point it is returned to the free list. Notice that this technique completely eliminates the dangling-reference problem. The block is returned after there are no references to it in the program.

There are certain drawbacks in using this method, however. First, if the blocks that are allocated form a circular structure, their reference counts will always remain set to at least 1, and none of the blocks will ever be freed, even if all pointers from outside the circular structure to blocks in the circular list are destroyed. We then have a circle of blocks, each of which is inaccessible from the program, and yet all the blocks will remain allocated—as permanent garbage. There are solutions for this, of course. One is simply to prohibit circular or recursive structures. In a number of applications, however, a circular structure is the most natural and reasonable one to use. Another solution is to flag circular structures as such, thereby signifying that they are to receive special treatment from the point of view of storage release. A third solution is to require that circular structures always use a special list head whose reference counter counts only references from outside the circle, and that all access to blocks in the circular structure are made through this list head. This is then a prohibition against direct accessing of any block in the circle. When a list head goes to 0, the header block and all blocks in the circle can be freed.

Another drawback to the reference-counter method is the overhead involved in maintaining the reference counts. This is a more serious objection because it can increase the execution time of the program significantly. Every processing operation will have to be checked for effects on the reference counts, and these must be updated as necessary. For example, the simple statement $P = \text{PRED}(Q)$ can generate code to do the following assuming that P and Q are known (perhaps by declarations) to be pointer variables:

1. Access block P and decrement its reference count. Let this new reference count be t.

2. Test t for zero. If so, free block P.
3. Evaluate PRED (Q). Let the result be the address r.
4. Access block r and increment its reference count.
5. Assign the value r to the variable P.

Examination of even the simpler algorithms that may be used in the context where heap storage allocation and release are reasonable should indicate that the cost of this counter maintenance can easily become excessive.

9-3.6 Garbage Collection

The second method of determining when to free storage is *garbage collection*. This method makes use of a special routine which is invoked whenever the available storage is almost exhausted, whenever a particular request cannot be met, or, perhaps, whenever the amount of available storage has decreased beyond a certain predefined point. Normal program execution is interrupted while this routine frees garbage blocks and is resumed when the garbage collector has finished its work. The garbage-collection algorithm generally has two phases. The first phase consists of tracing all the access paths from all the program and system variables through the allocated blocks. Each block accessed in this way is marked. The second phase consists of moving through the entire segment of memory, resetting the marks of the marked blocks, and returning to the free list every allocated block that has not been marked.

This method prevents the generation of dangling references, because if there is any path of references leading to a block, the block is marked and is not freed in the second phase. Because the garbage collector must trace paths of pointers from block to block, however, it is essential that, every time the garbage collector is invoked, all list and block structures are in a stable state with pointers pointing where they should. Otherwise the garbage collector will not be able to make the proper tracing of all the reference paths, and either some garbage will remain uncollected or, more seriously, blocks still in use will be freed. Since the garbage collector can be invoked by the system at almost any point in program execution, it is required that the use of pointers be disciplined. There are certain algorithms, however, which, during their operation, temporarily distort structures—e.g., having pointers pointing up a tree instead of downward to branches. If the garbage collector is invoked while the program is executing one of these algorithms, it is quite possible that the garbage collector will meet such a distorted tree. The marking phase can then no longer mark the correct blocks, and the situation when normal execution resumes can be horrendous.

A solution to this is, of course, to use pointers responsibly, avoiding the kind of algorithm that momentarily distorts structures. Certain applications, however, could well need that type of algorithm; it may be the only way to do the required task. In this case, the algorithm should begin by disabling the garbage collector so that it cannot be invoked while the algorithm is executing. If the algorithm should ever request storage and have the request refused, however, a stalemate has developed. There is not necessarily any ready solution to this problem other than to terminate the job and rerun with more storage initially allocated to the job.

One of the drawbacks to the garbage-collection technique is that its costs increase as the amount of free storage decreases, and yet it is at this point that one would hope for efficient and cheap release of storage. When you have little free storage left, you expect the garbage collector to be called more often, and you want its use to cost as little as possible. The reason for the inverse relationship is, of course, that when there is little free storage, there is a lot of allocated storage and hence the marking process has to trace through many blocks. Because of this factor, and also perhaps to avoid the stalemate situation mentioned earlier, garbage-collection methods are sometimes implemented so that the collector is invoked well before memory becomes completely allocated. For example, whenever the amount of free storage drops below half the total amount, the collector can be invoked intermittently. Also, to eliminate the intolerably repetitive calls to the collector that can result when memory is almost full, some systems consider the memory to be full whenever the garbage collector fails to restore the amount of free storage to a certain level. Such a condition causes the system to terminate when the next unsatisfiable request is encountered.

We now look at some of the algorithms that have been developed for garbage collection. We concentrate on the marking phase because the actual freeing phase, the sequential stepping through memory-freeing unmarked blocks, is relatively simple. For fixed-size blocks of size n, with P being the address of the block with the lowest address in the total memory segment, the address of all the r blocks that were formed out of the total memory segment is given by $P + i*n$, $0 \le i < r$. For variable-sized blocks, with P and Q being the addresses of the first and last words of the total memory segment, the addresses of all the blocks are given by the sequence of P values formed by

$$P_1(= P), \; P_2(= P_1 + \text{SIZE}(P_1)), \ldots, P_m(= P_{m-1} + \text{SIZE}(P_{m-1}))$$

where $P_m + \text{SIZE}(P_m) = Q + 1$.

In the marking phase, the garbage collector must mark all blocks that are accessible by any path of references that begins with a program or system variable. Consequently, the collection algorithm must have access to a list of all the variables that currently contain references into the heap storage area. To access such a list either the address of each block must be maintained at run time, say, in the symbol table, or all pointers to allocated blocks in the heap must be readily available, say, in some contiguous area in storage at run time. Once a variable has been found that points to a block of allocated storage, that block must be marked along with all the other blocks that are accessed by pointers within the first block, and all blocks are accessed from these blocks, etc. Once all of the blocks accessible from this variable have been marked, the next variable is processed in the same way. When all the variables have been processed, the total memory segment is stepped through and unmarked blocks are freed.

For the convenience of the marking algorithm, we assume that blocks which contain pointers to other blocks, thus forming a list-type structure, have these pointers located so that they are readily accessible given the block address. They can be located in the first words of the block following the block control fields.

FREE	SIZE	SAVE	MARK
LINK			
LINK			

⋮	⋮	

Figure 9-17 Block structure for garbage collection.

Therefore, we assume that block P, when allocated, has a structure of the form given in Fig. 9-17.

FREE(P) contains a value equal to 1 + the number of LINK fields, SIZE(P) is the size of block P (or the coding for the size of block P as in the binary buddy or Fibonacci allocation system), SAVE(P) is a field to be used in the marking process by which a temporary distortion of the list structure needed for traversal can be eventually undone, MARK(P) is a field initially set to *false* which is set *true* to denote that block P has been marked, and the LINK(P) fields are pointers to other blocks. Note that there need not be any such LINK fields. Observe that the LINK fields can be accessed by the addresses Q, for $P < Q < P + FREE(P)$. The allocation technique or release method may well require additional control fields. In such cases, simply assume that the correct fields are present.

The marking algorithm that will be presented is based on one proposed by Schorr and Waite (1967). Basic to the algorithm is the strategy of following each access path until it terminates. In particular, this implies that a path is followed until there are no more LINK fields to process or until a block is examined which is already marked because it is also on some other previously marked path. As this forward path is followed, the LINK fields which we traverse are set to point to the block from which we came. This temporary distortion of the structure is, however, the factor that enables the one-way path to be retraced. The SAVE field is used to record which of the several LINK fields in a block is currently reversed. When this path is retraced, as we enter a block on the return journey, we reset the altered LINK field to its correct value and then process all the other LINK fields of that block as if they initiated subpaths. That is, we follow one to its end, reversing LINK fields, and then trace it backward, resetting LINK fields and following still further subpaths. It therefore follows that the logical structure of this algorithm involves a considerable degree of "nesting" of path fragments within path fragments. If it were not for the storage shortage, this would make an ideal candidate for a recursive treatment. The actual algorithm follows.

Procedure LINK_MARK (P). Given P, the address of a block which is directly accessible and blocks with the structure described earlier, this procedure marks block P and all blocks accessible from P. The pointers P and Q refer to the current block under process and the previous block, respectively. Local variables include t (contains the LINK field which is currently reversed) and TEMP (pointer).

1. [Initialize]
    Q ← NULL

2. [Repeat while there are blocks to mark]
      Repeat through step 4 while not MARK(P) or Q ≠ NULL
3. [Mark a block?]
      If not MARK(P)
      then MARK(P) ← true
            SAVE(P) ← 0
      else (go backward one step)
            t ← SAVE(Q)
            TEMP ← LINK(Q + t)
            LINK(Q + t) ← P
            P ← Q
            Q ← TEMP
4. [Initiate a forward traversal?]
      t ← SAVE(P) + 1
      If t < FREE(P)   (reverse a link)
      then SAVE(P) ← t
            TEMP ← LINK(P + t)
            LINK(P + t) ← Q
            Q ← P
            P ← TEMP
5. [Finished marking beginning at P]
      Return   □

Figure 9-18 illustrates a trace of Procedure LINK_MARK for nodes N_1, N_2, N_3, and N_4. A snapshot of the state of each node is given when step 2 of the algorithm is executed. Notice that initially the MARK field of all nodes is false (i.e., "f") and at the completion of the trace all accessible nodes are marked true (i.e., "t").

The marking procedure in Procedure LINK_MARK can be altered so as to use a stack to keep track of what nodes have been marked rather than temporarily adjusting the link fields. The stack approach simplifies the algorithm; however, extra space is required for the stack. We leave the development of the stack-oriented algorithm as an exercise for the reader at the end of this section.

9-3.7 Compaction

As a final topic, we briefly discuss compaction as a technique for reclaiming heap storage. Compaction works by actually moving blocks of data, etc., from one location in memory to another so as to collect all the free blocks into one large block. The allocation problem then becomes completely simplified. Allocation now consists of merely moving a pointer which points to the top of this successively shortening block of storage. Once this single block gets too small again, the compaction mechanism is again invoked to reclaim the unused storage that may now exist among allocated blocks.

There is generally no storage-release mechanism. Instead, a marking algorithm is used to mark blocks that are still in use. Then, instead of freeing each unmarked block by calling a release mechanism to put it on a free list, the

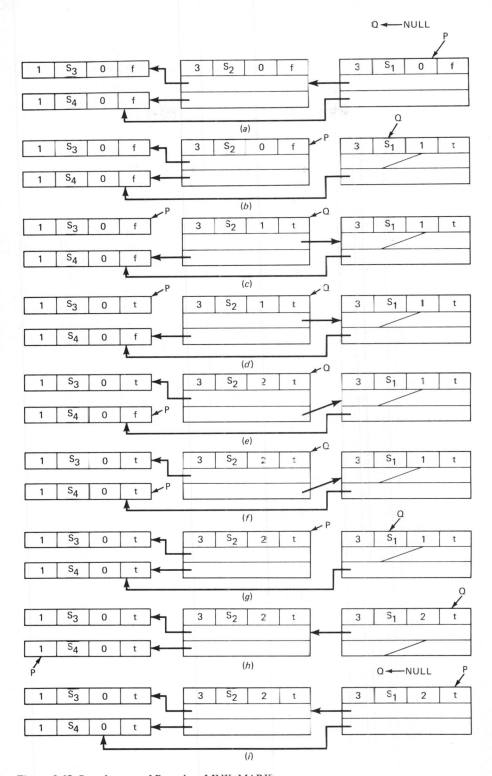

Figure 9-18 Sample trace of Procedure LINK_MARK.

compactor simply collects all unmarked blocks into one large block at one end of the memory segment, for heap storage. The only real problem in this method is the redefining of pointers. This is solved by making extra passes through memory. After blocks are marked, the entire heap memory is stepped through and the new address for each marked block is determined. This new address is stored in the block itself. Then another pass over heap memory is made. On this pass, pointers that point to marked blocks are reset to point to where the marked blocks will be after compaction. This is why the new address is stored right in the block—it is easily obtainable. After all pointers have been reset, the marked blocks are moved to their new locations. An example of a compaction algorithm is the following.

Procedure COMPACT (START, STOP). Given blocks of the structure as described for garbage collection, this procedure performs a compaction of unused heap storage into one large block whose starting address is TOP and which extends from TOP to STOP, the highest address in the entire memory segment for heap storage. It is assumed that START is the address of the first word of the memory segment. The SAVE field in the marked blocks is used by the compaction routine to record the new address of each block. LOC is a pointer to various memory locations. k and t are local variables which are used during the moving of marked blocks to their new locations.

1. [Mark blocks]
    Invoke garbage collection marking routine to mark blocks
2. [Compute new addresses for marked blocks]
        LOC ← TOP ← START
        Repeat while LOC ≤ STOP
            If MARK(LOC)
            then SAVE(LOC) ← TOP
                    TOP ← TOP + SIZE(LOC)
            LOC ← LOC + SIZE(LOC)
3. [Redefine variable references for program and system pointer variables]
        Repeat for each variable
            P ← location of variable
            variable ← SAVE(P)
4. [Define new values for pointers in marked blocks]
        LOC ← START
        Repeat while LOC ≤ STOP
            If MARK(LOC)
            then P ← LOC + 1
                    Repeat while P < LOC + FREE(LOC)
                        LINK(P) ← SAVE(LINK(P))
                        P ← P + 1
5. [Move the marked blocks]
        LOC ← TOP ← START
        Repeat while LOC ≤ STOP
            If MARK(LOC)

then t ← SIZE(LOC)
    k ← 0
    Repeat while k < t
        Copy contents of LOC + k into location TOP + k
        k ← k + 1
    MARK(TOP) ← false
    TOP ← TOP + t
    LOC ← LOC + t
else LOC ← LOC + SIZE(LOC)
6. [Finished]
    Return   □

It should be noted that this compaction routine is a relatively costly process in terms of execution time because of its three passes through heap memory. However, the increased speed of allocation might well make it a reasonable option in certain circumstances. Many implementations of SNOBOL use this compaction algorithm (or a variant); so presumably, it cannot be too inefficient.

A formal trace of Procedure **COMPACT** is not given; however, an exercise involving a trace appears at the end of this section.

Our discussion of storage allocation and management is now completed. A number of algorithms have been presented which are typical of those that are commonly used in a translator and its run-time support system. In practice, several of these techniques are combined in one translator. It should be realized, however, that the operating environment of the language translator strongly determines which methods should be used especially when considering heap storage techniques. Parameters such as request frequency, size-of-request distribution, usage (e.g., batch or on-line), and even the charging policy of a particular computer center may affect the decision as to what techniques should be adopted.

EXERCISES 9-3

1 Provide two examples of language constructs that can invoke implicit heap storage requests.

2 Let us assume that we have available a heap storage area of 652 words and that size and link fields each require one word of storage for their representation. Suppose that in an application program requests for three types of data blocks A, B, and C are made. The blocks are of size 15, 24, and 40 for A, B, and C, respectively. The following sequence of commands is a scenario of the storage requests made during the execution of the application program:

REQUEST B
REQUEST C
REQUEST B
REQUEST A
RELEASE B(1)
REQUEST A
RELEASE C(1)
REQUEST A
REQUEST B
RELEASE A(2)

The parenthesized numbers after a release command determine which copy of a block is released. Therefore, RELEASE B(1) means release the first copy of B that was requested.

You are to provide a trace of how heap storage would be managed using a first-fit storage-management policy. Your trace should provide a snapshot of how heap storage is allocated just prior to and just after each release command.

3 Answer Exercise 2, but instead assume the boundary-tag storage-management strategy is to be used. Assume flag fields require one word of storage for their representation.

4 Given the fixed sizes of $F_0 = 7$, $F_1 = 17$, $F_2 = 37$, and $k = 3$, draw a storage-management tree for the Fibonacci buddy system assuming a heap storage of size 203.

5 Answer Exercise 2, assuming a Fibonacci buddy storage-management strategy with fixed sizes of $F_0 = 13$, $F_1 = 23$, and $k = 2$.

6 Give a procedure called STACK_MARK for the stack-oriented version of Procedure LINK_MARK. Provide a trace for Procedure STACK_MARK using the same example set of data blocks as given in Fig. 9-18.

7 Suppose the following list of data blocks have been marked as being used by a garbage-collection routine for the heap storage of size 652:

Block	Starting location	Size	References
A	1	45	D
B	92	48	—
C	246	102	A, B, E
D	543	36	—
E	579	73	—

Draw a memory map of heap storage after Procedure COMPACT has been applied to the previous set of usable blocks. Can the compacted heap storage area handle a request for a block of size 258?

BIBLIOGRAPHY

Gries, D. E.: *Compiler Construction for Digital Computers*, New York: John Wiley & Sons, 1971.

Hinds, J. A.: "An Algorithm for Locating Adjacent Storage Blocks in the Buddy System," *Communications of the ACM*, Vol. 18, No. 4, 1975, pp. 221–225.

Hirschberg, D. S.: "A Class of Dynamic Memory Allocation Algorithms," *Communications of the ACM*, Vol. 16, No. 10, 1973, pp. 615–618.

Knuth, D. E.: *The Art of Computer Programming*, Vol. 1, *Fundamental Algorithms*, 2d ed., Reading, Mass.: Addison-Wesley, 1973.

McKeeman, W. M., J. J. Horning, and D. B. Wortman: *A Compiler Generator*, Englewood Cliffs, N.J.: Prentice-Hall, 1970.

Pratt, T. W.: *Programming Languages: Design and Implementation*, Englewood Cliffs, N.J.: Prentice-Hall, 1975.

Randell, B., and L. J. Russell: *Algol 60 Implementation*, London: Academic Press, 1964.

Schorr, H., and W. H. Waite: "An Efficient Machine-Independent Procedure for Garbage Collection in Various List Structures," *Communications of the ACM*, Vol. 10, No. 8, 1967, pp. 501–506.

Shen, K. K., and J. L. Peterson: "A Weighted Buddy Method for Dynamic Storage Allocation," *Communications of the ACM*, Vol. 17, No. 10, 1974, pp. 558–562.

Tremblay, J. P., and P. G. Sorenson: *An Introduction to Data Structures with Applications*, 2d ed., New York: McGraw-Hill, 1984.

INTERMEDIATE FORMS
OF SOURCE PROGRAMS

An *intermediate source form* is an internal form of a program created by the compiler while translating the program from a high-level language to assembly-level or machine-level code. There are a number of advantages to using intermediate source forms. An intermediate source form represents a more attractive form of target code than does assembly or machine code. For example, machine idiosyncrasies, such as requiring certain operands to be in even- or odd-numbered registers, can be ignored. Also, bookkeeping tasks, such as keeping track of operand stacks, can be avoided.

Certain optimization strategies can be more easily performed on intermediate source forms than on either the original program or the assembly-level or machine-level code. For example, optimizations which depend on flow analysis, such as register allocation (see Sec. 13-2), are facilitated by the use of an intermediate source form.

An intermediate source form is useful when both a checkout "compiler" and an optimizing compiler are produced for the same programming language. Intermediate code is produced for both compilers. An intermediate-code interpreter is written for the checkout version. This interpreter can be used to produce meaningful run-time error diagnostics and traces that are difficult to produce when executing object modules. The optimizing compiler performs optimizations on the intermediate source form and produces an object module.

Compilers which produce a machine-independent intermediate source form are more portable than those which do not. The intermediate source form can be run on a machine by writing a corresponding macro in the assembly language of the machine for each instruction of the intermediate source language. This advantage is especially true of threaded code and pseudo machine code.

The major disadvantage of using an intermediate language is that code produced can be less efficient than producing machine-level code directly. Obviously the reason why this is argued is that an intermediate language necessitates another level of translation (i.e., from the intermediate source form to the machine-level code). However, the types of optimization that can be performed because an intermediate language is used can more than offset the apparent inefficiency of a two-step translation. This aspect will become clearer in Chaps. 12 and 13 when we discuss optimization.

In this chapter, we discuss five types of intermediate source forms: Polish notation, n-tuple notation, abstract syntax trees, threaded code, and pseudo or abstract machine code. We devote one section to each of these types.

10-1 POLISH NOTATION

Suffix or reverse Polish notation was one of the earliest intermediate source forms developed and remains among the most popular. It has been used in some FORTRAN compilers as an intermediate form for arithmetic expressions. It has also been used in some interpreters, such as Hewlett Packard's interpreter for BASIC. We introduced suffix Polish notation as a method of specifying arithmetic expressions unambiguously without recourse to parentheses. In this section, we demonstrate how Polish notation can be used as an intermediate source form not only for arithmetic expressions but also for other language constructs.

In Sec. 7-1.2, we presented Algorithm REVERSE_POLISH for converting infix expressions into their suffix Polish equivalents. This algorithm works well for expressions such as A + B which have binary operators but does not handle expressions such as −A which have unary operators. Unary operators can be handled by making allowance for the type of the operator when removing operands from the stack, or by converting unary operations into binary ones. For example, −A could be represented as 0 − A and then handled as a binary operation.

An algorithm to translate the Polish intermediate source form of an arithmetic expression into a simple machine language can easily be written. Algorithm ASSEMBLY_CODE, which is presented later in Sec. 13-2, is an example of such an algorithm.

When Polish notation is extended to include nonarithmetic language constructs, the more powerful notation which results is often called *extended reverse Polish notation* (henceforth referred to as *extended Polish*). For example, operators can be added to handle the assignment operation, conditional branching, and subscripted variables. To illustrate this, let us examine how Polish notation can be extended to include conditional branching.

Consider an if statement with the following format:

If⟨expr⟩then⟨stmt$_1$⟩else⟨stmt$_2$⟩

This statement cannot be represented in Polish as

⟨expr⟩⟨stmt$_1$⟩⟨stmt$_2$⟩If

because both ⟨stmt$_1$⟩ and ⟨stmt$_2$⟩ would be evaluated before being placed on the stack. Since the purpose of the if statement is to perform only one of $\langle stmt_1 \rangle$ and $\langle stmt_2 \rangle$, a different representation must be adopted. Writing the statement as

$$\langle expr \rangle \langle label_1 \rangle BZ \langle stmt_1 \rangle \langle label_2 \rangle BR \langle stmt_2 \rangle$$

solves this problem by introducing the more primitive constructs of BZ and BR. BZ is a binary operator that causes a branch to $\langle label_1 \rangle$, which is the first symbol of $\langle stmt_2 \rangle$, if $\langle expr \rangle$ evaluates to zero (*false*). BR is a unary operator that causes a branch to $\langle label_2 \rangle$, which is the symbol immediately following the last symbol of $\langle stmt_2 \rangle$. Both branching operators clear the stack of their operands but do not add any result to the top of the stack.

As a second example of extending Polish notation to nonarithmetic operators, let us look at how subscripted variables, which indicate array references, are handled. In extended Polish, the string

10 5 7 MY_ARRAY ARRAY_REF

can be evaluated to determine the address of array element MY_ARRAY[7, 5, 10]. ARRAY_REF is the array-reference operator. It determines the number of dimensions of the array, in this case MY_ARRAY, and pops this many operands off the evaluation stack. The address of the array element is then calculated using these operands, and information about array bounds is obtained from the symbol table.

Some compiler writers have used prefix Polish notation as an intermediate form of source code. Chapter 14 will describe a system that uses this form of notation.

A Polish string is not very convenient for optimization purposes. It is therefore desirable to transform a Polish string to other more suitable forms. The next two sections describe these forms.

We have presented a small number of examples of how Polish notation can be extended to nonarithmetic operations. The exercises aid the reader in examining how some other language constructs can also be represented in extended Polish.

10-2 *N*-TUPLE NOTATION

N-tuple notation is an intermediate source form in which each instruction consists of n fields. Usually, the first field specifies an operator and the remaining $n - 1$ fields can be used as operands. This standardized format of n-tuple notation allows for easy translation into code for register machines because the operands are often specified as the result of some previous operation. In this section, we examine the two most popular forms of n-tuple notation, triples and quadruples, which are the source forms corresponding to values for n of 3 and 4, respectively.

Triple notation is a type of n-tuple notation in which each instruction has three fields. Consider the arithmetic expression $Y + Z$. The three parts of this binary operation are the operator $(+)$ and the two operands (Y and Z). Triple notation is ideal for representing a binary operation by using the following format:

$$\langle \text{operator} \rangle, \langle \text{operand}_1 \rangle, \langle \text{operand}_2 \rangle$$

The expression $W * X + (Y + Z)$ is represented in triple notation as follows:

1. $*$, W, X
2. $+$, Y, Z
3. $+$, (1), (2)

Each triple is numbered, and the result of a previous triple is specified by its number in parentheses. Thus the (1) and (2) which appear in triple 3 specify that the results of triple 1 and triple 2 are to be used as operands.

The conditional statement

If $X > Y$
then $Z \leftarrow X$
else $Z \leftarrow Y + 1$

can be represented in triple notation as follows:

1. $-$, X, Y
2. BMZ, (1), 5
3. $\leftarrow$, Z, X
4. BR, , (7)
5. $+$, Y, 1
6. $\leftarrow$, Z, (5)
7. :

The BMZ and BR operators specify branch on minus or zero and unconditional branch, respectively. The second field of these instructions gives the value, if any, to be tested for the condition, and the third field gives the number of the triple which is the destination of the branch.

Performing code optimization (see Chaps. 12 and 13) on triples can be difficult. As will be shown later, code optimization often involves the movement of code, but triples cannot be moved without changing all references to affected triples. For example, if triple 4 is moved after triple 7, triples 4, 5, 6, and 7 must all be renumbered. Of course, all references to these triples must also be adjusted. As a result, simple triples are not a particularly good intermediate source form when optimization is to be performed.

Indirect triples can be used instead of triples. A separate table which gives the order of execution for the triples is used. When optimization is performed, the order of the entries in this table is changed; the actual triples are left alone. If two triples are identical, one can be deleted from the triple table. This optimization must be performed carefully, however, since only one temporary variable is ordinarily associated with each triple. The following example statements

$$A \leftarrow B + C * D/E$$
$$F \leftarrow C * D$$

can be represented by indirect triples as follows:

Operations	Triples
1. (1)	(1) $*, C, D$
2. (2)	(2) $/, (1), E$
3. (3)	(3) $+, B, (2)$
4. (4)	(4) $\leftarrow, A, (3)$
5. (1)	(5) $\leftarrow, F, (1)$
6. (5)	

Quadruple notation is another type of *n*-tuple notation in which each instruction has four fields of the form:

$$\langle operator \rangle, \langle operand_1 \rangle, \langle operand_2 \rangle, \langle result \rangle$$

where $\langle operand_1 \rangle$ and $\langle operand_2 \rangle$ denote the first and second operand, respectively, and $\langle result \rangle$ specifies the result of the operation. The result is usually a temporary variable. Such a variable may be assigned to either a register or main memory location later on by the compiler. For example, the expression $(A + B)*(C + D) - E$ can be represented by the following sequence of quadruples:

$$+, A, B, T_1$$
$$+, C, D, T_2$$
$$*, T_1, T_2, T_3$$
$$-, T_3, E, T_4$$

where T_1, T_2, T_3, and T_4 are temporary variables.

Quadruples facilitate the performance of several program optimizations. One drawback of using quadruples is that the allocation of temporary names must be managed. Such a management strategy will reuse some temporaries.

Quadruples will be used extensively in the optimization chapters (i.e., Chaps. 12 and 13).

10-3 ABSTRACT SYNTAX TREES

A parse tree is another popular intermediate form of source code. Because a tree structure can be easily restructured, it is a suitable intermediate form for optimization compilers. A parse tree can be stripped of unnecessary information to produce a more efficient representation of the source program. Such a trans-

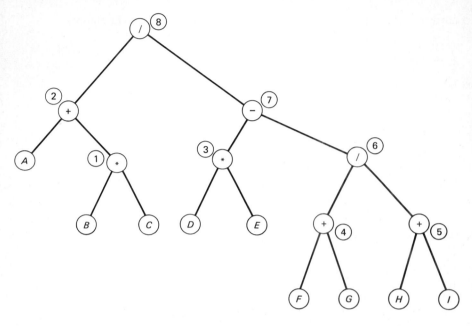

Figure 10-1 Example of an abstract syntax tree.

formed parse tree is sometimes called an *abstract syntax tree*. In this type of tree each nonleaf and leaf node represents an operator and variable name, respectively. For example, the expression

$$(A + B * C)/(D * E - (F + G)/(H + I))$$

can be represented by the abstract syntax tree in Fig. 10-1. In the tree structure, the circled numbers indicate the order in which the tree nodes are created by a bottom-up parser. Observe that each nonleaf node has a left and right direct descendent which is either a variable name (leaf) or a nonleaf node.

The traversal of an abstract syntax tree can yield the Polish notation forms introduced earlier. The preorder and postorder traversals of the tree given in Fig. 10-1, for example, yield the prefix and suffix Polish form of the given expression, respectively:

$$/ + A * BC - * DE/ + FG + HI$$
$$ABC * + DE * FG + HI + / - /$$

These Polish strings are linear representations of the syntax tree.

Also the triples that represent an expression can be viewed as a direct representation of a syntax tree. The following set of triples correspond to the tree given in Fig. 10-1:

(1) $*$, B, C
(2) $+$, A, (1)
(3) $*$, D, E
(4) $+$, F, G
(5) $+$, H, I
(6) $/$, (4), (5)
(7) $-$, (3), (6)
(8) $/$, (2), (7)

with the last triple being associated with the root node of the tree. Note that each triple represents a subtree. The operator in a triple corresponds to the root of a subtree. Each operand is either a variable name (a leaf) or a triple number (a sub-subtree). With this interpretation, the circled numbers in Fig. 10-1 directly correspond to the triple numbers.

Variants of abstract syntax trees have been used as an intermediate form of source code in several compilers. In Chap. 14 we examine one form of abstract syntax tree called TCOL which is used in a compiler-compiler system.

10-4 THREADED CODE

This section describes an intermediate form of source code which is amenable to machine-independent implementation. Threaded code is included because of its semi-interpreted nature. We first introduce the notion of direct threaded code and then present indirect threaded code. The ideas in both approaches are illustrated using PDP-11 code.

Direct threaded code (Bell, 1973) concerns generating code that consists of a linear list of addresses for routines which are to be executed. Some routines are program-specific and deal with operand access; these must be generated by the compiler. Other routines are standard library routines. Figure 10-2 illustrates the model for a direct-threaded-code system.

Indirect threaded code (Dewar, 1975) introduces a level of indirection to the model given in Fig. 10-2. Instead of having a linear list of addresses of routines, indirect threaded code has a linear list of addresses of words which in turn contain the addresses of the routines to be executed. The model which incorporates this level of indirection is exhibited in Fig. 10-3.

The comparison of the two threaded-code models indicates that the indirect-threaded-code model involves only the manipulation of addresses and not the generation of code. Indirect threaded code often can be generated in an essentially machine-independent manner. On the other hand, direct threaded code contains operand access routines. Machine independence in this case is more difficult to achieve.

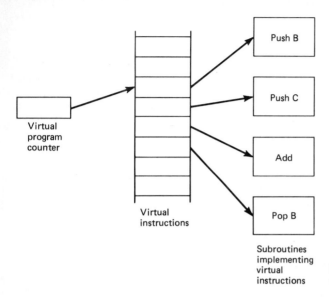

Figure 10-2 A model for direct threaded code.

Both threaded-code models will be exhibited using PDP-11 code. The PDP-11 (see Sec. 13-3.1) has eight (16-bit) general registers: R0–R5, SP, and PC. The registers R0–R5 are of a general-purpose nature. SP serves as a hardware stack pointer where (SP)+ is an addressing mode which pops the stack, $-$(SP) is an addressing mode which pushes the stack, and PC is a hardware program counter.

In the direct-threaded-code model (see Fig. 10-2) the virtual program counter is denoted by register R4. Each routine which implements a virtual instruction

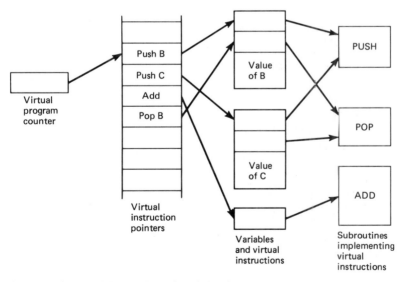

Figure 10-3 A model for indirect threaded code.

passes control to the next operation by means of the following instruction:

JMP @(R4)+

which indicates a jump to the routine whose address is contained in the virtual instruction. The address of the virtual instruction is contained in R4. At the same time, R4 is incremented to point to the next virtual instruction.

The virtual-instruction list for the direct-threaded-code evaluation of the statement B ← B + C is

PUSHB	;	operation to push B on the stack
PUSHC	;	operation to push C on the stack
ADD	;	add two top stack elements, popping
	;	the original top one (i.e., C)
POPB	;	operation to store top stack element in B

The routines implementing the virtual instructions are as follows:

PUSHB:	MOV #B + 4, R0	; get address of B
	BR DOPUSH	
PUSHC:	MOV #C + 4, R0	; get address of C
DOPUSH:	MOV −(R0), −(SP)	; push addressed
	MOV −(R0), −(SP)	; variable on stack
	JMP @(R4)+	; do next virtual instruction
ADD:	ADD (SP)+, 2(SP)	; add high-order portions
	ADD (SP)+, 2(SP)	; add low-order portions
	ADC (SP)	; propagate the carry
	JMP @(R4)+	; do next virtual instruction
POPB:	MOV #B, R0	; get address of B
	BR DOPOP	
DOPOP:	MOV (SP)+, (R0)+	; pop addressed
	MOV (SP)+, (R0)+	; variable from stack
	JMP @(R4)+	; do next virtual instruction

The code for the storage of variables is the following:

B:	0	; high-order part
	0	; low-order part
C:	0	; high-order part
	0	; low-order part

In the indirect-threaded-code model (see Fig. 10-3) the virtual program counter is also register R4. The register, however, contains the address of an address of an address of a routine implementing a virtual instruction. Each routine which executes a virtual instruction passes control to the next virtual instruction by the instruction pair:

MOV (R4)+, R0
JMP (R0)

which places the address of the address of the current virtual instruction in R0 while incrementing R4. The address in R0 is then used to invoke the next virtual instruction.

The virtual-instruction list for the indirect-threaded-code evaluation of the statement B ← B + C is

B + 4	; address of B's push address
C + 4	; address of C's push address
ADDPTR	; address of ADD's address
B + 6	; address of B's pop address

The routines implementing the virtual instructions are as follows:

```
PUSH:   MOV −(R0), −(SP)
        MOV −(R0), −(SP)
        MOV (R4)+, R0
        JMP (R0)
ADD:    ADD (SP)+, 2(SP)
        ADD (SP)+, 2(SP)
        ADC (SP)
        MOV (R4)+, R0
        JMP (R0)
POP:    SUB #6, R0
        MOV (SP)+, (R0)+
        MOV (SP)+, (R0)
        MOV (R4)+, R0
        JMP (R0)
```

The code for the storage of variables is the following:

```
B:                0         ; high-order part
                  0         ; low-order part
                  PUSH      ; push routine address
                  POP       ; pop routine address
C:                0         ; high-order part
                  0         ; low-order part
                  PUSH      ; push routine address
                  POP       ; pop routine address
ADDPTR:           ADD       ; address of ADD routine
```

Note that because of the peculiarities of addressing on the PDP-11 the values of variables have been placed at the beginning of a block as indicated in Fig. 10-3.

The concept of threaded code has general applicability to code generation for several languages. In particular, a machine-independent version of SPITBOL (Dewar, 1971), which is based on the technique of indirect threaded code, has been developed.

10-5 ABSTRACT MACHINE CODE

Current emphasis in compiler design includes producing compilers that are both portable and adaptable. One approach that has been used to achieve portability and adaptability in compilers is to produce, as a form of intermediate source code, code for an abstract machine. The instruction set for this machine should closely model the constructs of the source languages that are to be compiled. This section begins by examining the notions of portability and adaptability. We also present the concept of an abstract machine. The section also contains a description of an abstract machine that has been created to facilitate the portability of PASCAL programs. A brief description of the intermediate form of source code (P-code) produced for this machine is given.

10-5.1 Portability and Abstract Machine

A program is said to be *portable* if it can be moved to another machine with relative ease. That is, the effort to move the program is substantially less than the initial effort to write it. On the other hand, a program is *adaptable* if it can be readily customized to meet several user and system requirements.

Suppose that we want to move a given compiler from, say, machine X to a different machine Y. To realize such a move, we must rewrite the code-generation routines of the existing compiler to produce code for machine Y. The rewriting task is much easier to accomplish if the original compiler has been divided into two parts with a well-defined interface. The first part (or front end) deals with the source language and the second (or back end) with the target machine. For a well-defined interface only the target-machine part need be changed. One form of interface is a symbolic program in an intermediate assembly system.

The flow of information between the two parts of a compiler takes the form of language constructs in one direction (front end to back end), and target-machine information in the other direction (back end to front end). The interface can be realized by using an abstract machine. The source-language constructs can be mapped into pseudo operations on this abstract machine. The abstract machine is designed for the particular source language, for example, a PASCAL machine.

The abstract machine is modeled on the basis of the operations and modes that are primitive in the source language (e.g., PASCAL). The first part of the compiler translates every primitive operation and primitive mode in a source program into abstract-machine instructions. The primitive operations of the abstract machine correspond to the simplest and most direct operations constituting a source program. Also, the primitive data modes of the abstract machine can be the simplest types in the language (e.g., INTEGER and CHAR in PASCAL), or more complex modes (e.g., structured types in PASCAL). A pair, consisting of a primitive mode and a primitive operation, describes an instruction on the abstract machine.

The abstract-machine architecture has an environment in which the modes and operations interact to model the language. The designer of an abstract machine can concentrate on a structure which facilitates the operations in the given source language. The designer must also, however, take into consideration the efficient implementation of the abstract machine cn an actual computer.

One important advantage of using an abstract machine is the clean separation of the front end and back end of the compiler. This separation, in theory at least, means that moving a compiler to a new machine will require a new back end to the compiler with little, if any, change to its front end.

Suppose that it is required to implement m distinct languages on n different machines. Without using some form of intermediate source code, such as an abstract machine, $m * n$ different compilers would have to be written, that is, one for each language/machine combination. In an abstract-machine approach, however, only m front ends and n back ends are required. A compiler for a certain programming language and target machine can then be generated by selecting the appropriate front end and back end. Using this approach, $m * n$ different compilers can be generated from $m + n$ components.

Today, it is quite feasible for a given programming language such as PASCAL to produce efficient object code for several different target machines. A more difficult problem is to have an abstract machine from which efficient object code can be produced for several programming languages. The difficulty is to have one abstract machine that efficiently models all of these programming languages. Since various programming language such as FORTRAN, LISP, BASIC, and PASCAL are so different, it is almost impossible to find an appropriate abstract machine. The pseudocode produced can often become real machine code for computers in which the pseudo machine code can be micropro- grammed into the instruction set.

We have introduced the notion of an abstract machine in compiler writing in this section. The next section gives a description of an abstract machine for the PASCAL language.

10-5.2 The P-Code Abstract Machine for PASCAL

The *Pascal-P* compiler (Nori et al., 1981) is a portable compiler for essentially "standard PASCAL." The compiler produces object code (P-code) for an abstract machine. This section briefly describes this abstract machine.

The abstract machine called a *P-machine* is a simple machine-independent stack computer. The Pascal-P language is easily transported, at low cost, to a variety of real machines.

The hypothetical stack machine has five registers and a memory. The registers are

1. PC—the program counter
2. NP—the *new* pointer
3. SP—the *stack* pointer
4. MP—the *mark* pointer
5. EP—the *extremestack* pointer

The last four pointers are associated with the management of storage in memory.

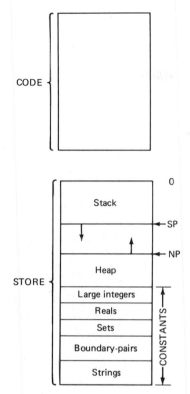

Figure 10-4 Memory layout of stack computer.

The memory, which can be viewed as a linear array of words, is divided into two main parts. The first part of memory, CODE, contains the machine instructions. The second part of memory, STORE, contains the data (i.e., noninstructions) part of a program. The layout of the computer's memory is illustrated in Fig. 10-4. Observe that PC refers to the location of an instruction in CODE. On the other hand, the pointers EP, MP, NP, and SP refer to positions in STORE.

STORE contains two parts; the first part represents the various constants of a given program while the second part is dedicated to the other data requirements of the executing program.

The stack, whose top element is denoted by SP, contains all directly addressable data according to the data declarations in the program. The heap, with associated top element NP, consists of the data that have been created as a result of direct programmer control (i.e., **new** statements). The heap is similar to a second stack structure.

The stack consists of a sequence of *data segments*. Each data segment is associated with the activation of a procedure or a function.

Each data segment contains the following sequence of items:

1. A *mark stack* part
2. A (possibly empty) parameter section for the routine associated with the data segment

3. A *local-data* section for any local variables
4. Temporary elements that are required by the processing statements

The mark stack part has the following fields:

1. Value field for a function (present but not used in a procedure)
2. Static link
3. Dynamic link
4. Maximum stack size value
5. Return address

Observe that the static and dynamic links refer to STORE and the return address denotes a position in CODE.

The basic modes of PASCAL (e.g., INTEGER, REAL) are supported on the stack computer. The machine has several classes of instructions, for example, arithmetic (for integers and real), logical, and relational. Each instruction has an opcode and possibly two parameters. The second parameter denotes an address. Many of the instructions in the instruction repertoire are closely related to the PASCAL language. For example, there is an instruction for set, set intersection, set union, and set membership to support the operations on sets in PASCAL.

The Pascal-P compiler has been transported to several real machines. In fact, an implementation kit has been prepared to assist systems people to move the compiler.

P-code has been extended to U-code (Perkins and Sites, 1979) to facilitate certain kinds of code optimization. Although P-code is a good language for specifying a variety of optimization techniques, it appears that it is incomplete for performing good optimization.

CHAPTER EXERCISES

1 Convert the following statement

$$A \leftarrow (B + C) \uparrow E + (B + C) * F$$

into triple, indirect triple, and quadruple form.

2 Formulate a quadruple formulation for the following statements:

(a) $A[1] := B$
(b) $B := A[1]$

3 Design a quadruple formulation of a procedure/function call with parameters of the following form:

$$\text{NAME}(A, B, C, \ldots, Z)$$

where each parameter can be a constant, variable name, or arithmetic expression.

4 Obtain an algorithm that detects and deletes useless indirect triples from a given set. Assume that the triples are as described by the tables OPERATIONS and TRIPLES in the text.

5 Formulate a quadruple formulation of a case statement in PASCAL.

BIBLIOGRAPHY

Bell, J. R.: "Threaded Code," *Communications of the ACM*, Vol. 16, No. 6, June 1973, pp. 370–372.

Dewar, R. B. K.: "SPITBOL: SNOBOL 4," Doc. S4D23, Illinois Institute of Technology, Chicago, Ill., February 1971.

Dewar, R. B. K.: "Indirect Threaded Code," *Communications of the ACM*, Vol. 18, No. 6, June 1975, pp. 330–331.

Gries, D.: *Compiler Construction for Digital Computers*, New York: John Wiley & Sons, 1971.

Nori, K. V., U. Ammann, K. Jenson, H. H. Nageli, and C. Jacobi: "Pascal-P Implementation Notes," in *Pascal—The Language and Its Implementation*, D. W Barron, ed., New York: John Wiley & Sons, 1981.

Perkins, D. R., and R. L. Sites: "Machine-Independent Pascal Code Optimization," *Proceedings of the SIGPLAN Symposium on Compiler Construction*, Denver, Colo., August 1979, pp. 201–207.

Poole, P. C.: "Portable and Adaptable Compiler," in G. Goos and J. Hartmanis, *Lecture Notes in Compiler Science*, 2d ed., New York: Springer-Verlag, 1976, pp. 427–497.

# ELEVEN

SEMANTIC ANALYSIS AND CODE GENERATION

Thus far we have been mainly concerned with the process of recognizing whether or not strings of symbols are correct statements in a programming language. With the aid of the material presented in Chaps. 9 and 10, we can now discuss how to further refine the recognition process through the use of semantic analysis and introduce techniques for generating object code for a variety of constructs that are commonly found in high-level procedure-oriented programming languages.

The methods we discuss for performing semantic analysis and code generation assume a common strategy for processing source-language statements. The technique is based on the idea that the type of semantic analysis performed and the nature of the code produced is specified (i.e., determined) for each production of the grammar. Hence, as the production rules for a language are applied, the parser can simply invoke the appropriate semantic-analysis and code-generation routine and correct object code can be generated in a systematic fashion. This type of compiling is often called "syntax-directed" because the production rules of the grammar are used to direct the type of processing that is to be performed on the source-language statements.

Four types of syntax-directed processing are presented in this chapter. In particular, the implicit stacking of local variables in the recursive routines for a recursive-descent parser is introduced as a method for syntax-directed processing in Sec. 11-2. The use of semantic stacks that are synchronized with the activities of the parse stack is described for bottom-up parsing strategies in Sec. 11-3. The introduction of action symbols in a source grammar to produce a translation grammar that is processed by an LL parser is presented as yet another syntax-directed technique in Sec. 11-4. Attribute translation is introduced as a final syntax-directed method in Sec. 11-5.

The remainder of the chapter, Sec. 11-6, provides many examples of the type of semantic analysis and code generation that occurs for a variety of language constructs such as declarations, assignment statements, control statements, and procedure calls.

Prior to a detailed discussion of semantic-analysis and code-generation techniques, it is beneficial to begin with an explanation of what is meant by semantic analysis.

11-1 WHAT IS MEANT BY SEMANTIC ANALYSIS

In our discussion of syntactic analysis in Chaps. 6 and 7, it was pointed out that context-free grammars are not sufficiently powerful to describe a number of programming-language constructs. It was suggested that the context-dependent aspects of a programming language would be taken care of during the semantic-analysis and code-generation phase. To exemplify how context-dependent features are handled, let us consider the following series of programming-language statements:

```
BEGIN
    INTEGER I;
        .
        .
        .
END
    .
    .
    .
    J:= I*K;
```

If I is not also declared outside the scope of the BEGIN block, then the statement "J:= I*K;" is an illegal statement. The illegality of I in this statement is dependent upon the declarations in the block-structured program. To illustrate this point, assume that a legal instance of variable I is to be replaced in a bottom-up parse by (or generated in a top-down parse from) the nonterminal VAR meaning legally defined variable. A snapshot of the sentential form prior to this replacement might be

α INT I β I

where α and β are strings of symbols (terminals and/or nonterminals) making up the partial parse and INT I represents a previous and still active declaration of I. After the replacement, the sentential form would be

α INT I β VAR

implying that the production VAR::= I is applicable independent of the context of an INT I symbol pair. To ensure that such a symbol pair is present when the reduction is made, the production rule VAR::= I must have additional symbols on its left- (and right-) hand side to capture the context in which I is a legal instance of a variable. In particular, a production rule necessary to represent this context-dependent transformation might be

INT I β VAR::= INT I β I

Notice that INT I is retained in the right-hand side of the production because it may be necessary in the determination of other legal references to I appearing in the same scope in the program. INT I should be replaced when the definition of the block in which it appears is terminated. Therefore, for example, a portion of the sentential form, namely,

α BEGIN β INT I γ END

is replaced by α when the end of the BEGIN block containing the declaration of I is encountered, that is, when the following production is applied:

BEGIN β INT I γ END::= ε

An obvious question that should be asked at this point is "Why not construct a context-dependent grammar for a language that will represent these types of nested dependency properties?" This can be done, but based on the previous discussion, it is easy to appreciate that the formulation of a set of context-dependent rules is not an easy task. Moreover, a context-sensitive parser is very complex and executes very slowly (Woods, 1970).

The common solution to handling the problem of context dependencies is to augment the activities of a (context-free) parser with special *semantic actions*. These actions record the additional context-dependent information in the symbol table, in semantic stacks, or in parameters and local variables for the routines that generate the semantics, that is, the object code for a source program. For instance, the previous example involving the enforcement of scope rules can be handled by making use of a stack symbol table similar to those discussed in Chap. 8.

To illustrate how this might be accomplished, let us suppose that integer declarations are handled when the following production is applied:

⟨decl statement⟩::= INT ⟨identifier⟩;

In Chap. 8, a description was given of how the symbolic name for ⟨identifier⟩ can be recognized by the scanner and placed in the symbol table either during lexical analysis or at code-generation time. Once placed in the symbol table, the name remains there as long as the block in which it is declared is visible during compilation. Therefore, when an expression involving an identifier, say I, is encountered, for example,

X = Y * I;

then the correctness of the use of I is determined by examining the symbol table either at the time the identifier is recognized by the scanner or at the time of code generation.

In the remaining discussion in this chapter, other semantic-analysis techniques involving the use of semantic stacks, parameters, and local variables will be used to illustrate how certain context dependencies can be handled for a variety of parsing strategies. To clarify the discussion of these techniques, a self-bracketing form of if statement is used as a common example throughout.

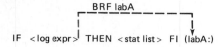

Figure 11-1 Execution flow for if statement.

This construct is defined by the following grammar:

⟨if statement⟩::= IF ⟨log expr⟩ THEN ⟨stat list⟩ FI
               |IF ⟨log expr⟩ THEN ⟨stat list⟩ ELSE ⟨stat list⟩ FI
⟨stat⟩::= ⟨basic stat⟩|⟨if statement⟩
⟨stat list⟩::= ⟨stat⟩|⟨stat list⟩ ⟨stat⟩

The grammar may have to be altered depending on the type of parsing that is being performed, as will be illustrated later in this chapter.

In processing the if statement, we will be concentrating on the problem of generating the branch instructions that are required for the proper flow of execution through the if construct. The branch instructions that are required for the two forms of the if statement are illustrated in Fig. 11-1.

In the discussion, it is assumed that ⟨log expr⟩ places a logical value (i.e., *true* or *false*) on an operand stack or in a "register" of a hypothetical machine. The hypothetical machine instruction "BRF labA" transfers control to labA if the result of the ⟨log expr⟩ is *false*; otherwise control passes to the next pseudo machine instruction in the sequence of generated hypothetical machine instructions. BR instruction is simply an unconditional branch instruction for the hypothetical machine.

It should also be realized that our code-generation problem is complicated by the fact that the statement may be nested to many levels. As an example, consider the program segment in Fig. 11-2.

To handle this type of nesting, it is necessary to stack branch labels temporarily while other branch labels corresponding to deeper-nested if statements are processed. For example, the location of lab3 cannot be determined until labels 4, 5, and 6 are processed. That is, when compiling the nested if construct, it will be necessary to hold temporarily the fact that lab3 has not been bound to a hypothetical machine location until all intermediate if statements are processed.

Having introduced some basic notions relating to semantic analysis, let us now turn to an examination of four types of code-generation and semantic-analysis strategies.

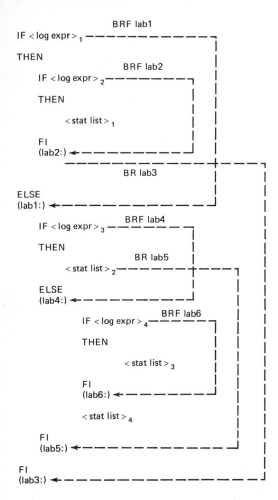

Figure 11-2 Example of a nested if construct.

11-2 IMPLICIT STACKING IN RECURSIVE-DESCENT COMPILATION

The discussion in the previous section briefly indicated why it is necessary to capture and store temporarily certain information in order to produce correct code during compilation. The first syntax-directed method that will be examined uses local variables and parameter passing to store the required information. Let us look in detail at how the if statement can be compiled using a recursive-descent parser with no backup. Figure 11-3 illustrates program excerpts from such a compiler, written in PL/I. In particular, procedures for handling the processing of statement lists (Fig. 11-3a) and if statements (Fig. 11-3b) are illustrated. In addition, a procedure that performs simple error recovery is shown in Fig. 11-3c.

The STATLIST procedure handles the processing of a statement list in an iterative fashion in the sense that statements are processed one at a time until an

```
COMPILE:  PROCEDURE OPTIONS(MAIN);
    DECLARE CODE(20000) CHAR(15),
              (SCRUBPT, LOCNCNTR) FIXED BIN(31),
              NEXTSYM CHAR(10);
    CALL STATLIST;
    IF NEXTSYM ¬= 'EOF' THEN CALL ERROR (1 ");
    /* <STATLIST> ::= <STAT> | <STATLIST><STAT> */
    STATLIST:  PROCEDURE RECURSIVE;
        DO WHILE ('1'B/* UNTIL EOF CONDITION */);
            CALL SCAN(NEXTSYM);
            SCRUBPT = LOCNCNTR:
            IF NEXTSYM = 'IF'
            THEN CALL IF_STAT;
            ELSE IF •••
                       •
                       •
                       •
                       /* THE REMAINING STATEMENT TYPES */
                       •
                       •
                       •
            ELSE DO;
                CALL UNSCAN;
                RETURN;
            END;
        END; /* FOR DO WHILE */
    END STATLIST;
    /* OTHER PROCEDURES (I.E. IF_STAT, LEXPR SCAN,
       ERRCR, EMIT, GENLAB, SETLAB, ETC.) ARE PLACED HERE */
END COMPILE;
```

Figure 11-3a

```
/* <if statement> ::= IF <log expr> THEN <stat list> FI
            | IF <log expr> THEN <stat list> ELSE <stat list> FI */
IF_STAT: PROCEDURE RECURSIVE;

      DECLARE (BRLAB, FLSLAB) CHAR(7);

      /* NEXTSYM IS CURRENTLY 'IF' */

      CALL LEXPR;

      FLSLAB = GENLAB;

      CALL EMIT('BRF', FLSLAB);

      CALL SCAN(NEXTSYM);

      IF NEXTSYM ¬= 'THEN'

      THEN DO;

            CALL ERROR(2, ';');

            RETURN;

      END;

      CALL STAT_LIST;

      CALL SCAN(NEXTSYM);

      IF NEXTSYM = 'ELSE'

      THEN DO;

            BRLAB = GENLAB;

            CALL EMIT('BR', BRLAB);

            CALL SETLAB(FLSLAB);

            CALL STATLIST;

            CALL SCAN(NEXTSYM);

            IF NEXTSYM ¬= 'FI'

            THEN DO;

                  CALL ERROR(3, ';');

                  RETURN;

            END;

            CALL SETLAB(BRLAB);

            RETURN;

      END;

      IF NEXTSYM ¬= 'FI'

      THEN DO;

            CALL ERROR(4, ';');

            RETURN;

      END;

      CALL SETLAB(FLSLAB);

END IF_STAT;
```

Figure 11-3b

```
ERROR: PROCEDURE(NUMB, SCRUBSYM);

      DECLARE NUMB FIXED, SCRUBSYM CHAR(1) VARYING;

      DECLARE ERRMSG(100) CHAR(60) INITIAL(

            '***ERROR — UNEXPECTED END OF FILE',

            '***ERROR — MISSING "THEN" IN IF STATEMENT',

            '***ERROR — MISSING "FI" FOLLOWING "ELSE" IN IF STATEMENT',

            '***ERROR — MISSING "FI" FOLLOWING "THEN" IN IF STATEMENT',

                  •
                  •
                  •

            '***ERROR — UNEXPECTED END OF FILE'):

      PUT SKIP EDIT(ERRMSG(NUMB))(A(60));

      IF SCRUBSYM = '' /* EMPTY */

      THEN RETURN;

      DO WHILE(NEXTSYM ¬= SCRUBSYM),

            CALL SCAN(NEXTSYM);

      END;

      CALL SCAN(NEXTSYM);

      LOCNCNTR = SCRUBPT — 1;

END ERROR;
```

Figure 11-3c

'EOF' (meaning "end of file" for the source program) occurs. Note that if a statement type is not recognized in Procedure STATLIST in Fig. 11-3a, then an UNSCAN routine must be called at the end of the DO WHILE loop to "undo" the effects of the extra call to the SCAN routine that takes place at the beginning of the DO WHILE loop. The variables SCRUBPT and LOCNCNTR are indexes into the CODE array, which is an array that contains the hypothetical machine instructions generated by the COMPILE program. LOCNCNTR indicates the position in CODE at which the next generated hypothetical machine instruction is to be placed. SCRUBPT marks the position in CODE of the first instruction from the set of instructions for the statement currently being compiled. The SCRUBPT index is particularly important for error recovery. If a statement has a syntax error, the ERROR procedure is invoked, an appropriate error message is produced, and then LOCNCNTR is reset to SCRUBPT, which effectively removes the incomplete set of hypothetical machine instructions produced thus far during the compilation of the erroneous statement.

Within the procedure STATLIST, the NEXTSYM is recognized by calling the scanner and then used as a basis for determining the type of statement currently being compiled. If NEXTSYM is 'IF', then the procedure IF_STAT, which handles if statements, is invoked.

The full details of IF_STAT are exhibited in Fig. 11-3b. The use of the local variables FLSLAB (meaning "false label") and BRLAB (meaning "branch label") is of particular concern in this section. FLSLAB is used to store the label, as produced by the GENLAB function, to which a generated BRF instruction will transfer at execution time if the result of the logical expression is *false* for the if statement. Similarly, BRLAB records the label, again produced by GENLAB, to which the generated BR instruction will transfer after execution completes for the then part of an if statement that has an else part. These types of branches were depicted earlier in Figs. 11-1 and 11-2.

It is crucial to realize the FLSLAB and BRLAB are reserved for the labels generated for the *same* if statement. Hence, if another if statement is part of the ⟨stat list⟩ of a then or else part of a given if statement, the FLSLAB and BRLAB for the embedded if statement will be assigned (i.e., allocated) when the IF_STAT procedure is reinvoked to handle the embedded if statement. To illustrate clearly how the information identifying the *false* and unconditional branch labels are generated and kept track of, a trace of the if statement example, as given in Fig. 11-2, is provided in Fig. 11-4.

The trace illustrates the series of calls that would be made to the various procedures by the compiler as the entire if statement is compiled. Indentations in the trace indicate that a deeper (i.e., more nested) call of the IF_STAT or STATLIST procedure has occurred. A return from one of these procedures is exhibited with the complementary "exdentation." By carefully following the trace, the reader will obtain a true appreciation of how semantic information can be handled in recursive-descent parsing.

Before we conclude our discussion of code-generation and semantic-analysis techniques in recursive-descent compilation, it is important to note that parameter passing is an important vehicle for transferring semantic information *between* procedures invoked during compilation. To exemplify this fact, consider the following grammar describing a simplified assignment statement for a language that has integer and string types. In the grammar description, the double quotes enclosing the concatenation operator || are required to ensure that these strokes are not confused with the alternation stroke used in the metalanguage.

⟨assign stat⟩::= ⟨variable⟩:= ⟨expression⟩;
⟨expression⟩::= ⟨string expr⟩|⟨arith expr⟩
⟨string expr⟩::=⟨string⟩
        |⟨variable⟩
        |⟨string⟩ "||" ⟨string expr⟩
        |⟨variable⟩ "||" ⟨string expr⟩
⟨arith expr⟩::= ⟨number⟩
        |⟨variable⟩
        |⟨number⟩ ⟨op⟩ ⟨arith expr⟩
        |⟨variable⟩ ⟨op⟩ ⟨arith expr⟩
⟨variable⟩::= ⟨ident⟩|⟨ident⟩ (⟨array subscripts⟩)

Execution Trace	Code Generated
SCAN 'IF'	
CALL IF_STAT	
CALL LEXPR	Code for $<$ log expr $>_1$
FLSLAB ← GENLAB ('LAB1')	
EMIT 'BRF LAB1'	BRF LAB1
SCAN 'THEN'	
CALL STATLIST	
SCAN 'IF'	
CALL IF_STAT	
CALL LEXPR	Code for $<$ log expr $>_2$
FLSLAB ← GENLAB ('LAB2')	
EMIT 'BRF LAB2'	BRF LAB2
SCAN 'THEN'	
CALL STATLIST	Code for $<$ stat list $>_1$

•
                 •
                 •	

SCAN 'FI'	
SETLAB FLSLAB	LAB2:
RETURN(FROM IF_STAT)	
RETURN(FROM STATLIST)	
SCAN 'ELSE'	
BRLAB ← GENLAB ('LAB3')	
EMIT 'BR LAB3'	BR LAB3
SETLAB FLSLAB	LAB1:
CALL STATLIST	
SCAN 'IF'	
CALL IF_STAT	
CALL LEXPR	Code for $<$ log expr $>_3$
FLSLAB ← GENLAB('LAB4')	
EMIT 'BRF LAB4'	BRF LAB4
SCAN 'THEN'	
CALL STATLIST	Code for $<$ stat list $>_2$
SCAN 'ELSE'	
BRLAB ← GENLAB('LAB5')	
EMIT 'BR LAB5'	BR LAB5

Figure 11-4 Trace of compilation of IF construct.

Execution Trace	Code Generated
SETLAB FLSLAB	LAB4:
CALL STATLIST	
SCAN 'IF'	
CALL IF_STAT	
CALL LEXPR	Code for $<$ log expr $>_4$
FLSLAB ← GENLAB('LAB6')	
EMIT 'BRF LAB6'	BRF LAB6
SCAN 'THEN'	
CALL STATLIST	Code for $<$ stat list $>_3$
SCAN 'FI'	
SETLAB FLSLAB	LAB6:
RETURN(FROM IF_STAT)	
CALL STATLIST	Code for $<$ stat list $>_4$
RETURN(FROM STATLIST)	
SCAN 'FI'	
SETLAB BRLAB	LAB5:
RETURN(FROM IF_STAT)	
RETURN(FROM STATLIST)	
SCAN 'FI'	
SETLAB BRLAB	LAB3:
RETURN(FROM IF_STAT)	

Figure 11-4 (*Continued*)

It is assumed that in this language certain types of conversions (really coercions) are allowed. For example,

X:= X || Y;

where Y, a variable of type numeric, is allowed since at run time the value of Y will be converted to a string and then concatenated with X. Similarly,

X:= X + Y;

where Y is a string variable, is allowed if the value for Y at run time is a numeric string of an appropriate length. To produce these conversions at run time, it is necessary for the compiler to generate code that produces a branch to a run-time routine that performs the appropriate conversions. In order to decide if and when to generate the branch instruction, it is necessary for the type of variable to be

```
/* <STRING EXPR> ::= <STRING> | <VARIABLE> |
                  | <STRING> "||" <STRING EXPR>

                  | <VARIABLE> "||" <STRING EXPR>
STR_EXPR: PROCEDURE (TYPE) FIXED RECURSIVE;

    DECLARE TYPE FIXED;

    CALL SCAN(NEXTSYM);

    IF NEXTSYM = '@STRING' /* MEANING STRING CONSTANT */

    THEN DO;

        /* PRODUCE CODE TO HANDLE A STRING CONSTANT */

           •
           •
           •

    END;

    ELSE DO;

        IF VARIABLE(TYPE) = 1 /* 1 MEANS TYPE NUMERIC */

        THEN DO;

            /* GENERATE BRANCH TO CONVERSION ROUTINE */

               •
               •
               •

        END;

    END;

    CALL SCAN(NEXTSYM);

    IF NEXTSYM ¬= '||'

    THEN RETURN(2); /* 2 MEANS TYPE STRING */

    ELSE

        /* REMAINDER OF STR_EXPR */

           •
           •
           •

END STR_EXPR;

/* <VARIABLE> ::= <IDENT> | <IDENT> (<SUBSCR>) */

VARIABLE: PROCEDURE(TYPE) FIXED RECURSIVE;

    DECLARE TYPE FIXED;
    /* NAME OF <INDENT> IS IN NEXTSYM */

    CALL TABLELOOKUP(NEXTSYM, TYPE, POSITION);

    /* TABLELOOKUP RETURNS TYPE OF NEXTSYM */

       •
       •
       •

    /* REMAINDER OF <VARIABLE> PROCEDURE */

    RETURN(TYPE);

END VARIABLE;
```

Figure 11-5 Procedures for ⟨string expr⟩ and ⟨variable⟩.

known at compile time by the procedures associated with the ⟨string expr⟩ and ⟨arith expr⟩ language constructs. This type information can be passed to these procedures by returning a parameter called TYPE from the procedure for ⟨variable⟩. Then, when the return from the procedure ⟨variable⟩ takes place, the type information can be used in the ⟨string expr⟩ and ⟨arith expr⟩ procedures.

Skeletons of the procedures for ⟨string expr⟩ and ⟨variable⟩ are shown in Fig. 11-5, to illustrate more clearly this method of information passing. Only the initial call of the procedure VARIABLE is shown in the skeleton of procedure STR_EXPR. In the procedure VARIABLE, a procedure for symbol-table lookup is invoked and the type of the identifier is found. Upon return from VARIABLE, the type of the variable is passed to STR_EXPR, which uses this information to aid in code generation.

It should be noted, furthermore, that for the example grammar the type information should be passed on to the procedure for handling ⟨expression⟩ and in turn further on to the procedure for ⟨assign stat⟩. This is necessary to ensure that type differences between the left- and right-hand sides of an assignment statement can be detected at compile time so that the appropriate branch-to-conversion-routine instruction can be generated, if necessary.

We have completed our discussion of how semantic actions can be added to a recursive-descent parser to affect code generation and semantic analysis. Let us now turn our attention to bottom-up compilation.

11-3 SEMANTIC STACKS IN BOTTOM-UP COMPILATION

We begin our discussion by reviewing the general parsing strategy of a bottom-up parser as introduced in Chap. 7. Basically, a bottom-up parser proceeds by successively matching a right-hand side of the set of production rules with the string of symbols representing the partial parse at a given point in time. The matched symbols in the partial parse string are then replaced by the left-hand side of the matched production. Or, more formally, a production of the form

$$A \rightarrow \alpha$$

is applied if the parser recognizes in the input string the substring w which has a derivation of the form

$$A \Rightarrow \alpha \overset{*}{\Rightarrow} w$$

In a bottom-up parser, it is possible to take some semantic action when the production is reduced, and clearly the nature of the action to be taken depends on the production that is being reduced.

It is perhaps easiest to illustrate how and when semantic actions can be applied in a bottom-up parse by considering once again the if statement example. It is advisable to recall the set of productions describing the if language construct that were given in Sec. 11-1. We begin by pointing out a main problem related to

Reduction
Step

IF X < Y THEN X := Y ELSE X := Y + 1 FI   1

$\overset{*}{\Rightarrow}$ IF < log expr > THEN X := Y ELSE X := Y + 1 FI   2

$\overset{*}{\Rightarrow}$ IF < log expr > THEN < stat list >₁ ELSE X := Y − 1 FI   3

$\overset{*}{\Rightarrow}$ IF < log expr > THEN < stat list >₁ ELSE < stat list >₂ FI   4

$\overset{*}{\Rightarrow}$ < if statement >   5

Figure 11-6 Reduction steps for the parse of 'IF X < Y THEN X := Y ELSE X := Y + 1 FI'.

when semantic actions can be applied in a bottom-up parse. To illustrate the problem, let us show the series of reductions that would take place for the following source statement (the branch instructions that must be produced are illustrated also).

$$\text{BRF lab1}$$
$$\text{IF X < Y } | \text{THEN X:= Y ELSE} \downarrow \text{X:= Y − 1 FI} \uparrow$$
$$\text{BR lab2}$$

     Assuming the grammar for if statements is expanded to describe more completely assignment statements and logical expressions, a trace of the reductions for the previous if statement is given in Fig. 11-6. Note that between reduction step 1, when the ⟨log expr⟩ is recognized and code for the logical expression is produced, and reduction step 2, when ⟨stat⟩ is recognized and code for the first assignment statement is produced, it is necessary to generate the BRF instruction. Based on the given grammar and the types of reductions that take place, the only opportunity to generate the BRF instruction is either as the last reduction step when the parser reduces X < Y to ⟨log expr⟩ or the first reduction step when the parser reduces X:= Y to a statement. For the given grammar, it would be acceptable to generate a BRF instruction at either of these two steps; however, for a grammar of a more complete language, either strategy would be unacceptable. For example, if ⟨log expr⟩ is used in many language constructs (e.g., in other control statements such as DO UNTIL or in Boolean variable assignments), it would be erroneous to generate a BRF instruction as the last semantic action for a logical expression. Similarly, it would be erroneous to always generate a BRF instruction as the first semantic action of every statement list.

     Let us examine a common way of solving this problem. The method involves the *stratification* of the grammar to create additional reduction points to allow for the proper generation of code. In the example just discussed, this can be accomplished by stratifying the grammar as follows (note that for simplicity ⟨stat list⟩ has been restricted to assignment and if statements):

Production
no.

1	⟨if stat⟩::= ⟨if head⟩ ⟨then part⟩
2	|⟨if head⟩ ⟨then-else part⟩
3	⟨if head⟩::= IF ⟨log expr⟩
4	⟨then part⟩::= THEN ⟨stat list⟩ FI
5	⟨then-else part⟩::= ⟨then head⟩ ⟨stat list⟩ FI
6	⟨then head⟩::= THEN ⟨stat list⟩ ELSE
7	⟨stat⟩::= ⟨assign stat⟩
8	|⟨if stat⟩
9	⟨stat list⟩::= ⟨stat⟩
10	|⟨stat list⟩ ⟨stat⟩
11	⟨assign stat⟩::= ...
12	⟨log expr⟩::= ...

From a brief examination of the new grammar, it should be clear that the BRF instruction can be emitted when production 3 is reduced and the BR instruction, if necessary, can be emitted when production 6 is reduced.

This fact is verified in the skeleton version of a code generator written in PL/I as given in Fig. 11-7. This version is typical of code generators for bottom-up parsers in the sense that the production number of the production being reduced is passed as a parameter to a code generator via a call within the parser. The separation of the code generator from the parser offers the tremendous advantage that the parser can be implemented, tested, and then essentially forgotten while the code-generating procedure is being created and then debugged. This form of separation does not exist, for example, when the semantic action routines for a code generator in a recursive-descent compiler are implemented.

Another aspect typical of bottom-up code generators is the large "caselike" construct of which they are constituted. In the PL/I program CODEGEN, the case construct is simulated using the multibranched GO TO on a labeled array PROD. (Note that in more recent versions of the PL/I compiler this form of GO TO can be substituted for by a SELECT statement.) Only semantic actions for the first six productions are shown in Fig. 11-7. These six productions make use of essentially the same routines as those used in parts of the recursive-descent compiler given in Sec. 11-2, namely, EMIT and SETLAB. Note that the branch labels for the BRF and BR instructions are stored in the SEM_STACK (meaning "semantic stack"), which is a stack that grows and shrinks in conjunction with the parse stack. In fact, both stacks are referenced using the same index SP (meaning "stack pointer").

To illustrate how the CODEGEN procedure can be used to generate code, a trace of the compilation of the if statement in Fig. 11-8 is given in Fig. 11-9. In the trace, it is easy to see how semantic actions, such as storing a forward branch

```
CODEGEN: PROCEDURE(PR#);

   DECLARE PR# FIXED, /* PRODUCTION NUMBER */

          PROD(100) LABEL, /* ASSUMING A TOTAL OF 100 PRODUCTIONS */

          (BRFLAB, BRLAB) FIXED;

GO TO PROD(PR#);

PROD(1): /* <IF STAT> ::= <IF HEAD> <THEN PART> */

   CALL SETLAB(SEM_STACK(SP));

   RETURN;

PROD(2): /* <IF STAT> ::= <IF HEAD> <THEN_ELSE PART> */

   RETURN;

PROD(3): /* <IF HEAD> ::= IF <LOG EXPR> */

   BRFLAB = GENLAB;

   CALL EMIT('BRF', BRFLAB);

   SEM_STACK(SP) = BRFLAB;

   RETURN;

PROD(4): /* <THEN PART> ::= THEN <STAT LIST> FI */

   RETURN;

PROD(5): /* <THEN_ELSE PART> ::= <THEN HEAD> <STAT LIST> FI */

   CALL SETLAB(SEM_STACK(SP));

   RETURN;

PROD(6): /* <THEN HEAD> ::= THEN <STAT LIST> ELSE */

   BRLAB = GENLAB;

   CALL EMIT('BR', BRLAB);

   SEM_STACK(SP) = BRLAB;

   CALL SETLAB (SEM_STACK (SP−1));

   RETURN;

   •
   •
   •

/* REMAINING PRODUCTIONS */

   •
   •
   •

END CODEGEN;
```

Figure 11-7 Skeleton of a code generator for a bottom-up parser.

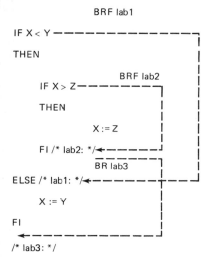

Figure 11-8 Sample if construct.

label until it can be properly placed in the generated code, are associated with certain nonterminals in the parse (e.g., the BRF label is associated with ⟨if head⟩ and the BR label is associated with the ⟨then head⟩). In this manner, the code generation is clearly syntax-directed. Note particularly how nested if statements can be handled with the aid of the semantic stack. For each outstanding (i.e., not fully completed) if statement structure, there will be an ⟨if head⟩ or possibly a ⟨then head⟩ that is on the stack.

An obvious question that arises when considering semantic actions in a bottom-up parse is how to pass information between action routines. In the recursive-descent compiler described in the previous section, we were able to pass such information with the use of formal parameters (see the example involving conversions for arithmetic and string expressions as described in the previous section). In the general bottom-up approach, this type of information can again be conveniently passed by using the semantic stack. Consider the following example, which involves the checking of a simple assignment statement for conversions, if required:

⟨assign stat⟩::= ⟨variable⟩:= ⟨expression⟩;

When this production is reduced, the parse and semantic stacks will contain the information shown in Fig. 11-10. Note that the parser would have previously replaced the left-hand side of the reduced production on the parse stack. A semantic action routine to handle the assignment statement is illustrated in Fig. 11-11. In the action routine, it is assumed that only character string and numeric types are present in the programming language.

This concludes our discussion of basic techniques for code generation and semantic analysis in bottom-up compilation, however, some extended techniques involving attributed grammars in bottom-up compilation will be briefly described in Sec. 11-4.

Production No.	Reduction	Parse Stack	Semantic Stack	Code Produced
..., 12	$X < Y \overset{*}{\Rightarrow} <\text{log expr}>_1$	$<\text{log expr}>_1$ / IF		code for $<\text{log expr}>_1$
3	IF $<\text{log expr}>_1 \Rightarrow <\text{if head}>_1$	$<\text{if head}>_1$	lab1	BRF lab1
..., 12	$X < Z \overset{*}{\Rightarrow} <\text{log expr}>_2$	$<\text{log expr}>_2$ / IF / THEN / $<\text{if head}>_1$	lab1	code for $<\text{log expr}>_2$
3	IF $<\text{log expr}>_2 \Rightarrow <\text{if head}>_2$	$<\text{if head}>_2$ / THEN / $<\text{if head}>_1$	lab2 / / lab1	BRF lab2
..., 11	$X := Z \overset{*}{\Rightarrow} <\text{assign stat}>_1$	$<\text{assign stat}>_1$ / THEN / $<\text{if head}>_2$ / THEN / $<\text{if head}>_1$	lab2 / / lab1	code for $<\text{assign stat}>_2$
7, 9	$<\text{assign stat}>_1 \overset{*}{\Rightarrow} <\text{stat list}>$			
4	THEN $<\text{stat list}>$ FI $\Rightarrow <\text{then part}>$	$<\text{then part}>$ / $<\text{if head}>$ / THEN / $<\text{if head}>$	lab2 / / lab1	
1	$<\text{if head}>_2 <\text{then part}> \Rightarrow <\text{if stat}>$	$<\text{if stat}>$ / THEN / $<\text{if head}>_1$	ab1	SETLAB(lab2)
8, 9	$<\text{if stat}> \overset{*}{\Rightarrow} <\text{stat list}>$			
6	THEN $<\text{stat list}>$ ELSE $\Rightarrow <\text{then head}>$	$<\text{then head}>$ / $<\text{if head}>_1$	lab3 / lab1	BR lab3 / SETLAB(lab1)

Figure 11-9 Trace of bottom-up parse illustrating the use of a semantic stack.

Production No.	Reduction	Parse Stack	Semantic Stack	Code Produced

...11	$X := Y \overset{*}{\Rightarrow} <\text{assign stat}>_2$	\<stat list\>		code for
7, 9	$\overset{*}{\Rightarrow} <\text{stat list}>$	\<then head\>	lab3	\<assign stat\>$_2$
		\<if head\>$_1$		
5	\<then head\> \<stat list\> FI			
	$\Rightarrow <\text{then-else part}>$	\<then-else part\>		SETLAB(lab3)
		\<if head\>$_1$		
2	\<if head\>$_1$ \<then-else part\>			
	$\Rightarrow <\text{if stat}>$	\<if stat\>		

Figure 11-9 (*Continued*)

11-4 ACTION SYMBOLS IN TOP-DOWN COMPILATION

In this section, action symbols are introduced as aids in the production of semantic actions during the code-generation and semantic-analysis phases of top-down compilation. The action symbols are placed at key locations in the *source grammar* (also sometimes called the *input grammar*) to provide cues that indicate when particular semantic activities should take place. A source grammar together with the action symbols is often referred to as a *translation grammar*.

The introduction of action symbols in the source grammar is particularly appropriate for a top-down parsing strategy such as is used in LL(1) parsing, because very few changes must be made to the parsing algorithm and its associated tables. Recall from Chap. 6 that the top-down parsing strategy involves the continual expansion of the leftmost nonterminal, starting with the distinguished symbol, say A, to produce the source string, say, s. That is,

$$A \overset{*}{\Rightarrow} \alpha\beta\ldots\gamma \overset{*}{\Rightarrow} s$$

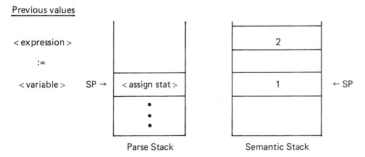

Figure 11-10 Illustration of the parse and semantic stacks for an assignment statement.

PROD(/* < ASSIGN STAT > ::= < VARIABLE > := < EXPRESSION >; */):

    IF SEM_STACK(SP) ⌐= SEM_STACK(SP+2)

       /* DO TYPES MATCH? */

    THEN IF SEM_STACK(SP) = 1 /* NUMERIC TYPE */

        THEN CALL EMIT(CONVN);

           /* CONVN MEANS CONVERT TO NUMERIC */

        ELSE CALL EMIT(CONVC);

           /* CONVC MEANS CONVERT TO CHARACTER */

    IF SEM_STACK(SP) = 1

    THEN CALL EMIT(STRN); /* STORE NUMERIC */

    ELSE CALL EMIT(STRC); /* STORE CHARACTER STRING */

       /* IT IS ASSUMED THAT THE ADDRESS OF

          < VARIABLE > HAS BEEN PREVIOUSLY PLACED ON THE STACK */

    RETURN

Figure 11-11 Semantic action routine for handling conversions for assignment statements.

Do case of action#;

    a1: /* IF < log expr > a_1 THEN < stat list > */

        brflab ← genlab

        Call emit('BRF', brflab)

        sem_stack [s] ← brflab

        s ← s + 1

    a2: /* ELSE a_2 < stat list > ... */

        brlab ← genlab

        Call emit('BR', brlab)

        Call setlab(sem_stack [s - 1])

        sem_stack [s - 1] ← brlab

    a3: /* ... < stat list > FI a_3 */

        s ← s - 1

        Call setlab(sem_stack [s])

    a4: /* FI a_4 */

        s ← s - 1

        Call setlab(sem_stack [s]);

End case;

Figure 11-12 Algorithmic description of action routines.

where $\alpha\beta$ and γ can be terminals or nonterminals. The introduction of an action symbol, say a, into the grammar can result in its appearance in the partial parse string. That is,

$$A \overset{*}{\Rightarrow} \alpha\beta\ldots a\ldots\gamma \overset{*}{\Rightarrow} s$$

Eventually the nonterminals to the left of a are expanded to match terminal symbols of the source string. When the parser encounters the a, the parser calls the code generator, which, in turn, invokes the appropriate action routine to effect the desired actions.

The introduction of action symbols also affects the parse tables that are generated by a parser generator in the sense that the indices for the terminal and nonterminal symbols in the grammar specification are altered. If the first two productions in a language description are, for example,

⟨program⟩::= ⟨statement⟩ EOF
⟨statement⟩::= ⟨assign stat⟩| ...

then the assigned table indices might be ⟨program⟩ = 1, ⟨statement⟩ = 2, EOF = 3, ⟨assign stat⟩ = 4, etc. The introduction of the action symbol a_1 as follows:

⟨program⟩::= ⟨statement⟩ a_1 EOF
⟨statement⟩::= ⟨assign stat⟩| ...

would alter the indices for EOF and ⟨assign stat⟩ to 4 and 5, respectively, and the index value of 3 would be assigned to a_1. It is relatively easy to write a program to change the old index values in a parse table to the newly assigned index values.

To illustrate how translation grammars operate, let us return again to our example grammar for the if statement. Recall that the code which must be generated to provide correct branch logic is illustrated in Fig. 11-1. From this figure, it is easy to see that in the if-then-else construct some semantic actions must be performed after ⟨log expr⟩, after the ⟨stat list⟩ in the then part, after the ELSE, and after FI. For the if-then construct, semantic actions are required after the ⟨log expr⟩ and after the FI.

A grammar augmented with action symbols to handle the branch semantics for the if statement is now given. The grammar excludes a description of ⟨stat list⟩.

⟨if statement⟩::= ⟨if head⟩ ⟨if tail⟩
⟨if head⟩::= IF ⟨log expr⟩ a_1 THEN ⟨stat list⟩
⟨if tail⟩::= ELSE a_2 ⟨stat list⟩ FI a_3|FI a_4

Semantic routines for these action symbols are shown in algorithmiclike notation in Fig. 11-12. These routines are assumed to have the same behavior as the procedures with the same names that were described in Secs. 11-2 and 11-3. Notice that action routines a_3 and a_4 are identical and can be collapsed into a single case.

A trace illustrating the semantic routines for the "program" given in Fig. 11-8 is provided in Fig. 11-13. To gain a clear understanding of how the action

Parse String	Unprocessed Source String	Generated Code
< program >		
$\overset{*}{\Rightarrow}$ < if head > < if tail >	IF X < Y THEN . . .	
⇒ IF < log expr > a₁	IF X < Y THEN . . .	
THEN < stat list > < if tail >		
•		
•		
•		
/* process IF and < log expr > */	IF X < Y THEN . .	code for 'X < Y'
•		
•		
•		
$\overset{*}{\Rightarrow}$ a₁ THEN < stat list > < if tail >	THEN IF X > Z THEN . . .	
⇒ < stat list > < if tail >	IF X > Z THEN X := Z . . .	BRF lab1
$\overset{*}{\Rightarrow}$ < if head > < if tail > < if tail >	IF X > Z THEN X := Z . . .	
⇒ IF < log expr > a₁ THEN	IF X > Z THEN X := Z . . .	
< stat list > < if tail > < if tail >		
•		
•		
•		
/* process IF and < log expr > */	IF X > Z THEN X := Z . . .	code for 'X > Z'
$\overset{*}{\Rightarrow}$ a₁ THEN < stat list >	THEN X := Z FI ELSE . . .	
< if tail > < if tail >		
⇒ < stat list > < if tail > < if tail >	X := Z FI ELSE . . .	BRF lab2
•		
•		
•		
/* process < stat list > */	FI ELSE X := Y FI	code for 'X := Z'
•		
•		
•		
$\overset{*}{\Rightarrow}$ < if tail > < if tail >	FI ELSE X := Y FI	
⇒ FI a₄ < if tail >	FI ELSE X := Y F	
⇒ < if tail >	ELSE X := Y FI	lab2:
⇒ ELSE a₂ < stat list > FI a₃	X := Y FI	
⇒ < stat list > FI a₃	X := Y FI	BR lab3
•		lab1:
•		
•		
/* process < stat list > */	FI	code for 'X := Y'
•		
•		
•		
$\overset{*}{\Rightarrow}$ FI a₃	FI	
⇒ —	—	lab3:

Figure 11-13 Trace of top-down compilation involving action symbols.

routines can be used in code generation and semantic analysis, the reader is once again encouraged to follow the details of the trace.

The passing of information between nonnested language constructs can also be accommodated by using the semantic stack. To illustrate how, we can return to our familiar example of type conversion between the left-hand and right-hand sides of an assignment statement. The relationship between the left-hand side and the right-hand side is nonnested, because (based on the grammar description given at the end of Sec. 11-2) one assignment statement is completely defined before the definition of another assignment statement begins. We have seen that this is not true for a nested construct such as an if statement.

Consider the following set of augmented productions that are involved in the definition of an assignment statement:

$$\langle \text{assign stat} \rangle ::= \langle \text{variable} \rangle := a_1 \langle \text{expression} \rangle \ a_2$$
$$\langle \text{expression} \rangle ::= \langle \text{string expr} \rangle | \langle \text{arith expr} \rangle$$
$$\langle \text{string expr} \rangle ::= \langle \text{variable} \rangle | \dots$$
$$\langle \text{arith expr} \rangle ::= \langle \text{variable} \rangle | \dots$$
$$\langle \text{variable} \rangle ::= \langle \text{ident} \rangle a_3 | \dots$$

Figure 11-14 contains the algorithmiclike notation for the action routines corresponding to action symbols a_1, a_2, and a_3. It is assumed that only character string and integer types are available in the language.

Action routine a_1 sets a Boolean variable value_mode indicating that the left-hand side of an assignment has been processed and that code for the "value" of variables on the right-hand side must now be generated. Action routine a_2 compares the type of the left- and right-hand sides by examining the top two locations in the semantic stack. If the types differ, the appropriate hypothetical machine conversion instruction is emitted. The value of the right-hand side is then stored at the address of the variable on the left-hand side. Finally, action routine a_3 records the address and type of a variable, if it is on the left-hand side of an assignment (i.e., reference node), or records the type and generates a "LOAD" instruction if the variable appears on the right-hand side.

From our discussion of type conversion, it should be apparent that there is very little relationship between the parse stack and semantic stack; that is, one stack grows and shrinks somewhat independently of the other. By the nature of the top-down parsing strategy, information about the previous parse steps is not explicitly retained in the parse stack as the leftmost nonterminal is expanded to match (possibly after several other expansions) terminal symbols in the input string. On the other hand, the role of the semantic stack is one of keeping semantic information about previous activities in the compilation. It becomes, therefore, an impossible task to directly associate the activities of the top-down parser, as encapsulated in the parse stack, with semantic activities affecting the semantic stack. This independence makes the problem of semantic stack management much more difficult than it is for bottom-up parsing where, as we saw in Sec. 11-3, the semantic stack can be synchronized with the parse stack.

In the next section, we will introduce a technique that eliminates the semantic-stack-management problem by eliminating the need for a semantic

```
Do case of action#;

a₁:    /* < assign stat> ::= <variable> := a₁ <expression> a₂ */
       /* Turn value mode on*/
       value_mode ← on

a₂:    /* <assign stat> ::= <variable> := a₁ <expression> a₂ */
       If sem_stack[sp] ≠ sem_stack[sp-1]
       then /* types of <variable> and <expression> don't match */
            if sem_stack[sp-1] = 1 /* numeric type */
            then call emit('CONVN') /* convert expression to numeric */
            else call emit('CONVC') /* convert expression to character string */
       address ← sem_stack[sp-2]
       call emit('STOR', addr) /* store the value of expression at
                                   the address of variable */

       sp ← sp - 3
       value_mode ← off

a₃:    /* <variable> ::= <ident> a₃ | ... */
       Call tablelookup (nextsym, type, position);
       If not value_mode /* i.e., reference node */
       then sp ← sp + 1
            sem_stack[sp] ← addr[position]
            sp ← sp + 1
            sem_stack[sp] ← type
       else sp ← sp + 1
            sem_stack[sp] ← type
            call emit('LOAD', addr[position])
            /* load value of the variable */

●
●
●

End case;
```

Figure 11-14

stack. This is accomplished by adding parameters to the nonterminal, terminal, and action symbols of the grammar. These parameters take on the role associated with the elements of the semantic stack; however, the management problem is virtually eliminated because a unique identifier name (i.e., the parameter's name) can be associated with each piece of semantic information rather than a relative location on a semantic stack. Let us examine this idea more closely.

11-5 ATTRIBUTED TRANSLATION

Attributed translation grammars are translation grammars whose symbols (both vocabulary and action) are augmented with attributes and rules describing how the attributes are used for generating semantic actions. Therefore, attributed translation grammars extend the notion of a translation grammar by employing attributes as an explicit means of communication between various semantic action routines rather than through more implicit means such as a semantic stack.

In this section, we begin by defining formally what is meant by attributed translation. Next, an attributed translation grammar is exemplified using the if-then-else construct adopted throughout the chapter. Finally, attributed translation techniques are discussed in the context of bottom-up parsing.

11-5.1 Attributed Translation Grammar

In the previous section we introduced translation grammars and described the role of action symbols in these grammars. The terminology utilized in that section is altered in this section in the sense that an action symbol is denoted by an identifier that is prefixed by the '@' character. The remaining terminology is introduced in the following definitions.

An *attributed translation grammar* (ATG) is a translation grammar with the following additional specifications:

1. Each symbol has an associated finite set of attributes.
2. Each nonterminal and action symbol attribute is classified as being either *inherited* or *synthesized*.
3. An initial value is specified for each inherited attribute in the starting (i.e., distinguished) symbol and each synthesized attribute in an input symbol.
4. Given a production, the value of an inherited attribute on the right-hand side is computed as a function of the other attributes in the production.
5. Given a production, the value of a synthesized attribute on the left-hand side is computed as a function of other attributes in the production.
6. Given an action symbol, the value of a synthesized attribute is computed as a function of other attributes of the action symbol.

An *inherited attribute* is an attribute whose value is directly derived by assignments from other attributes in the productions of the grammar.

A *synthesized attribute* is an attribute whose value is usually derived based on some function that uses inherited attributes as parameters.

In the case of synthesized attributes of terminal symbols, the value assigned to the synthesized attribute is derived from strings of the source language as isolated by the scanner.

To exemplify these two types of attributes, consider the example productions in Fig. 11-15, which describes an arithmetic expression language interpreter.

In the example, all inherited attributes are prefixed with the downward arrow ($\downarrow$) and all synthesized attributes are prefixed with the upward arrow ($\uparrow$). The attributes in a list of attributes are separated by commas. The *evaluation rules* or functions that describe how the synthesized attributes are derived appear to the right of the production rules. Only one action symbol, "@print", appears in this example of an attributed translation grammar. The action associated with this symbol is simply to print the calculated result of the interpreted source string.

				Evaluation Rule
1.	\<expression\>	::=	\<expr\>↑v @print↓w;	w←v
2.	\<expr\>↑v	::=	\<term\>↑x \<terms\>↓y↑z	y←x; v←z
3.	\<terms\>↓s↑t	::=	ε { meaning empty}	t←s
4.			| + \<term\>↑a \<terms\>↓b↑c	b←s+a; t←c
5.			| − \<term\>↑a \<terms\>↓b↑c	b←s− a; t←c
6.	\<term\>↑v	::=	\<factor\>↑x \<factors\>↓y↑z	y←x; v←z
7.	\<factors\>↓s↑t	::=	ε { meaning empty}	t←s
8.			| * \<factor\>↑a \<factors\>↓b↑c	b←s∗a; t←c
9.			| / \<factor\>↑a \<factors\>↓b↑c	b←s/a; t←c
10.	\<factor\>↑v	::=	NUMBER↑w	v←w
11.			| (\<expr\>↑w)	v←w

Figure 11-15 Sample ATG grammar.

Let us follow the trace of how the source string "6 + 7;" would be processed using the attribute translation grammar (henceforth ATG) in Fig. 11-15. The trace is given in Fig. 11-16. In the trace, the part of the parse string that has been most recently altered is depicted in italics.

The parse begins by expanding the goal symbol ⟨expression⟩ using production 1. The leftmost nonterminal (i.e., ⟨expr⟩↑v) is then expanded using production 2. Note that the right-hand side of an expanded production is enclosed by brackets [ ] and the associated attributes of the left-hand side are placed immediately outside these brackets. These attributes are eventually used as attribute values and are synthesized based on the results of the successful application of productions later in the parse.

The first synthesizing of an attribute occurs in step 4 when the terminal symbol NUMBER is matched with 6, the first character in the source string. The value of 6 is assigned to the synthesized attribute w. In the trace, the generated parse string is viewed as a parse stack that is pushed and popped from the left end. This stack is popped only after all of the inherited attributes have inherited (i..e, have been assigned) their proper values from synthesized attributes whose values have been synthesized previously. Thus, in step 6, for example, the phrase "[[[NUMBER↑6]↑6" can be removed from the parse stack after the inherited attribute y in the phrase "⟨factors⟩↓y↑z..." has had its proper value of 6 assigned.

It should be noted that in step 10, the production number 4 is applied (as opposed to 3 or 5) based on a lookahead symbol of "+", as would be required in an LL(1) grammar. The remaining steps of the trace, although tedious, should be quite straightforward except for possibly step 18. Here, the inherited attribute z of the previously expanded right-hand side "⟨term⟩↑x ⟨terms⟩↓y↑z" in step 2 assumes the role of t. The value for c (i.e., 13) has previously been generated as

STEP

1. {applying production1}
   < expression > → < expr >↑v @print↓w;

2. {applying production 2}
   ⇒ [< *term* >↑x < *terms* >↓y↑z] ↑v @print↓w;

3. {applying production 6}
   ⇒ [[< *factor* >↑x < *factors* >↓y↑z] ↑v < terms >↓y↑z] ↑v @print↓w;

4. {appling production 10 and synthesizing w←6}
   ⇒ [[[*NUMBER*↑6] ↑v < factors >↓y↑z] ↑v < terms >↓y↑z] ↑v @print↓w;

5. {applying v ← w in production 10}
   ⇒ [[[NUMBER↑6] ↑*6* < factors >↓y↑z] ↑v < terms>↓y↑z] ↑v @print↓w;

6. {popping parse stack and applying y ← x in production 6}
   ⇒ < factors >↓*6*↑z] ↑v < terms >↓y↑z] ↑v @print↓w;

7. {applying production 7 and t ← s}
   ⇒ < factors >↓6↑*6*] ↑v < terms >↓y↑z] ↑v @print↓w;

8. {popping parse stack and applying v ← z, in production 6}
   ⇒ ↑*6*< terms >↓y↑z] ↑v @print↓w;

9. {applying y ← x in production 2}
   ⇒ < terms >↓*6*↑z] ↑v @print↓w;

10. {applying production 4 based on lookahead symbol of + in source string}
    ⇒ [+< *term* >↑*a* < *terms* >↓*b*↑*c*] ↓6↑z] ↑v @print↓w;

11. {popping parse stack and applying production 6}
    ⇒ [< *factor* >↑x < *factors* >↓y↑z] ↑v < terms >↓*b*↑c] ↓6↑z] ↑v @print↓w;

12. {applying production 10 and synthesizing w ← 7}
    ⇒ [[*NUMBER*↑7] ↑v < factors >↓y↑z] ↑v < terms >↓b↑c] ↓6↑z] ↑v @print↓w;

13. {applying v ← w in production 10}
    ⇒ [[NUMBER↑7] ↑*7* < factors >↓y↑z] ↑v < terms >↓b↑c] ↓6↑z] ↑v @print↓w;

14. {popping parse stack and applying y ← x in production 6}
    ⇒ < factors >↓*7*↑z] ↑v < terms >↓b↑c] ↓6↑z] ↑v @print↓w;

15. {applying production 7 and t ← s}
    ⇒ < factors >↓7↑*7*] ↑*7* < terms >↓b↑c] ↓6↑z] ↑v @print↓w;

16. {popping parse stack and applying b ← s + a in production 4}
    ⇒ < terms >↓*13*↑c] ↓6↑z] ↑v @print↓w;

17. {applying production 3 and t ← s}
    ⇒ < terms >↓13↑*13*] ↓6↑z] ↑v @print↓w;

18. {popping parse stock and applying t ← c in production 4 where z takes on the role of t}
    ⇒ ↑*13*] ↑v @print↓w;

19. {popping parse stack and applying v ← z in production 6}
    ⇒ ↑*13* @print↓w;

20. {popping parse stack and applying w ← v in production 1}
    ⇒@print↓*13*;

21. {print 13, match ";" and terminate}
    ⇒*empty parse stack*

Figure 11-16 Trace of ATG parse for the simple expression '6 + 7'.

part of the expansion of the right-hand side "$- \langle\text{term}\rangle \uparrow a \langle\text{terms}\rangle \downarrow b \uparrow c$" in step 10. The work associated with keeping track of which attributes must take on the role of other attributes in the assignment of inherited attribute values must be handled in the LL(1) ATG parser. This activity complicates the parser unnecessarily, and in the next section we will show how to remove this problem.

11-5.2 L-Attributed Translation Grammar

It is important to realize that although each attribute in a grammar has an evaluation rule, there is no guarantee that the evaluation can take place. A rule can be used only after values have been obtained for its arguments, and a circular dependence of one attribute on another can sometimes occur. There are algorithms which detect such circularity (Knuth, 1968; Bochman, 1976). In particular, Bochman's algorithm evaluates the attributes in a minimal number of passes from left to right. Often, however, one wishes to restrict the number of passes to exactly one. The L-attributed translation grammar (from now on L-ATG) is designed to accomplish this.

There exist several equivalent characterizations of L-ATGs. The following characterization (Lewis, 1976) assumes specifications 1, 2, and 3 of an ATG given earlier in the section, plus the following modified specifications of the original ATG characterization:

4'. Given a production, the value of an inherited attribute of a right-hand-side symbol is computed as a function of inherited attributes of the left-hand side and arbitrary attributes of symbols which appear to the left of the given symbol.

5'. Given a production, the value of a synthesized attribute on the left-hand side is computed as a function of inherited attributes of the left-hand side and arbitrary attributes on the right-hand side.

6'. Given an action symbol, the value of a synthesized attribute is computed as a function of inherited attributes of the action symbol.

By closely inspecting the sample ATG given in Fig. 11-15, the reader can verify that there are no circulate dependencies in the grammar and that it is indeed an L-ATG.

To remove the problems arising with associating attribute names between production rules, we introduce one further alteration to our original ATG definition. An L-ATG is defined to be in *simple assignment form* if it satisfies:

4''. Given a production, the value of an inherited attribute of a right-hand-side symbol is a constant, the value of an inherited attribute of the left-hand side, or the value of a synthesized attribute of a symbol which appears to the left of the given symbol.

5''. Given a production, the value of a synthesized attribute on the left-hand side is a constant, the value of an inherited attribute of the left-hand side or the value of a synthesized attribute of a symbol on the right-hand side.

1. < expression >   ::= < expr >↑v @print↓w;   w←v

2. < expr >↑v   ::= < term >↑x < terms >↓y↑z   y←x, v←z

3. < terms >↓s↑t   ::= ε   t←s

4. | + < term >↑a @add↓b, c↑d < terms >↓e↑f   b←s, c←a, e←d, t←f

5. | - < term >↑a @minus↓b, c↑d < terms >↓e↑f   b←s, c←a, e←d, t←f

6. < term >↑v   ::= < factor >↑x < factors >↓y↑z   y←x, v←z

7. < factors >↓s↑t   ::= ε   t←s

8. | * < factor >↑a @mult↓b, c↑d < factors >↓e↑f   b←s, c←a, e←d, t←f

9. | / < factor >↑a @div↓b, c↑d < factors >↓e↑f   b←s, c←a, e←d, t←f

10. < factor >↑v   ::= NUMBER↑w   v←w

11. | (< expr >↑w)   v←w

Figure 11-17 Expression L-ATG in simple assignment form.

Given an L-ATG, an "equivalent" L-ATG in simple assignment form can be constructed by adding action symbols. The grammars are equivalent in the sense they they generate the same input parts and use the same functions to evaluate the attributes.

The ATG in the example of Fig. 11-15 is not in simple assignment form. The grammar given in Fig. 11-17 is an equivalent grammar in simple assignment form. Note that the essential difference between the two grammars is that the evaluation rules given in Fig. 11-15 have been replaced by action symbols in the simple assignment form L-ATG of Fig. 11-17. These action symbols signal to the parser that a corresponding action routine should be invoked that uses the inherited attributes as input parameters and produces values for the given synthesized attributes. For example, the action symbol @add indicates that the parser should invoke an "add" code-generation routine that takes as input parameters the inherited attributes b and c and generates an output parameter that corresponds to the synthesized attribute d (i.e., routine "add" evaluates d ← b + c).

It is possible to alter the explicit assignment form given in Fig. 11-17 to an implicit assignment form by introducing the notion of an *attribute variable*. Specifically, by renaming an attribute that occurs on the left-hand side of an assignment by the name of the attribute or constant appearing on the right-hand side, it is possible to remove the assignments associated with attributes in a simple assignment form of production. Therefore, production 4 in Fig. 11-17 can be written as

$$\langle terms \rangle \downarrow s \uparrow f ::= + \langle term \rangle \uparrow a \; @add \downarrow s, a \uparrow d \; \langle terms \rangle \downarrow d \uparrow f$$

Because the attributes in a production no longer have a unique name, they are called *attribute variables*. The rules governing these implicit assignments are as follows:

1. In a production, an inherited attribute, say, a, on the right-hand side receives its value from the rightmost inherited or synthesized attribute with the same

name that is to the left of a. For example, in the attribute variable, simple assignment form just given for production 4, the inherited attribute s on the right-hand side receives its value from the inherited attribute s on the left-hand side of the production. The inherited attribute d receives its value from the synthesized attribute d associated with the @add action symbol.

2. In a production, an inherited attribute, say, a, on the left-hand side inherits its value from the application of a production during the parsing process which involves the left-hand side. Therefore, the inherited attribute s on the left-hand side of the example production 4 just given would receive its value from the application of productions 2, 4, or 5, each of which contains ⟨terms⟩ on its right-hand side.

3. In a production, a synthesized attribute, say, a, on the right-hand side receives its value from either the application of an action routine directly or the synthesizing of information produced from the application of action routines invoked at a later stage in the parsing process. For example, the synthesized attribute d on the right-hand side of production 4 receives its information from the invocation of the @add action routine. The synthesized attribute f on the right-hand side receives its value when ⟨terms⟩↓e↑f eventually matches the empty string and f receives the value of e as shown in production 3.

4. In a production, a synthesized attribute, say, a, on the left-hand side receives its value from the rightmost synthesized attribute with the same name that is on the right-hand side of a production. Therefore, the synthesized attribute f on the left-hand side receives its value from the synthesized attribute f on the right-hand side in the altered form of production 4 given earlier.

Figure 11-18 illustrates the simple assignment form grammar of Fig. 11-17 with attribute variables. Note that a new action routine @echo is introduced for the productions with empty right-hand sides. This is done to ensure that the synthesized attribute f will be assigned the value inherited thus far in the parse

1. <expression>   ::= <expr>↑v @print↓v;

2. <expr>↑z   ::= <term>↑x <terms>↓x↑z

3. <terms>↓s↑f   ::= @echo↓s↑f

4. | + <term>↑a @add↓s, a↑d <terms>↓d↑f

5. | - <term>↑a @minus↓s, a↑d <terms>↓d^f

6. <term>↑z   ::= <factor>↑x <factors>↓x↑z

7. <factors>↓s↑f   ::= @echo↓s↑f

8. | * <factor>↑a @mult↓s, a↑d <factors>↓d↑f

9. | / <factor>↑a @div↓s, a↑d <factors>↓d↑f

10. <factor>↑w   ::= NUMBER↑w

11. | (<expr>↑w)

Figure 11-18 Expression L-ATG in simple assignment form using attribute variables.

{apply production 1}
< expression > ⇒ < expr >↑v @print↓v;

{apply production 2 to <expr>↑v where z takes on the role of v}
⇒ < term >↑x < terms >↓x↑z @print↓v;

{apply production 6 to < term >↑x where z takes on the role of x }
⇒ < factor >↑x < factors >↓x↑z < terms >↓x↑z @print↓v;

{apply production 10 to < factor >↑x }
⇒ NUMBER↑x < factors >↓x↑z < terms >↓x↑z @print↓v;

{NUMBER↑x yields 6 based on the first input from the expression "6+7*8;" .
    Substitution for the inherited attribute ↓x is made }
⇒ < factors >↓6↑z < terms >↓x↑z @print↓v;

{apply production 7 based on look ahead symbol of "+"}
⇒ @echo↓6↑z < terms >↓x↑z @print↓v;

{ activate @echo action routine to yield value of 6 for synthesized attribute ↑z
    then substitute for ↓x}
⇒ < terms >↓6↑z @print↓v;

{apply prodution 4 to < terms >↓6↑z based on a look ahead symbol "+" where f
    takes on the role of z}
⇒ + < term >↑a @add↓6, a↑d < term >↓d↑f @print↓v;

{ pop the symbol "+" based on match with input symbol }
⇒ < term >↑a @add↓6, a↑d < term >↓d↑f @print↓v;

{ apply production 6 to < term >↑a where z takes on the role of a }
⇒ < factor >↑x < factors >↓x↑z @add↓6, a↑d < terms >↓d↑f @print↓v;

{apply production 10 to < factor >↑x }
⇒ NUMBER↑x < factors >↓x↑z @add↓6, a↑d < terms >↓d↑f @print↓v;

{NUMBER↑x yields 7 based on the remaining input string "7*8;" . Substitution for
    the inherited attribute ↓x is made. }
⇒ < factors >↓7↑z @add↓6, a↑d < terms >↓d↑f @print↓v;

{ apply production 8 to < factors >↓7↑z where f takes on the role of z }
⇒ * < factor >↑a @mult↓7, a↑d < factors >↓d↑f @add↓6, a↑d < terms >↓d↑f @print↓v;

{ pop the symbol "*" based on match with input symbol }
⇒ < factor >↑a @mult↓7, a↑d < factors >↓d↑f @add↓6, a↑d < terms >↓d↑f @print↓v;

{apply production 10 to < factor >↑a }
⇒ NUMBER↑x @mult↓7, a↑d < factors >↓d↑f @add↓6, a↑d < terms >↓d↑f @print↓v;

{NUMBER↑x yield 8 based on the current input string "8;" . Substitution for the
    inherited attributed ↓x is made}
⇒ @mult↓7, 8↑d < factors >↓d↑f @add↓6, a↑d < terms >↓d↑f @print↓v;

{ activate @mult action routine to yield the value 56 for the synthesized attribute
    ↑d. Then substitute for ↓d }
⇒ < factors >↓56↑f @add↓6, a↑d < terms >↓d↑f @print↓v;

{apply production 7 based on look ahead of ";"}
⇒ @echo↓56↑f @add↓6, a↑d < terms >↓d↑f @print↓v;

{ activate @echo action routine to yield value of 56 from synthesized attribute ↑f.
    Then substitute for ↓a }
⇒ @add↓6, 56↑d < terms >↓d↑f @print↓v;

{ activate @add action routine to yield the value 62 for the synthesized attribute ↑d.
    Then substitute for ↑d }
⇒ < terms >↓62↑f @print↓v;

{apply production 3 to < terms >↓62↑f based on look ahead of ";"}
⇒ @echo↓62↑f @print↓v;

{activate @echo action routine to yield value of 62 from synthesized attribute ↑f.
    Substitute for ↓v }
⇒ @print↓62;

{ activate @print action routine to finally print the value of the expression 62 }

Figure 11-19 Trace of interpretation of "6 + 7*8".

```
@print(x)
    {printf ("%d\n", x)};

@add(x, y)
    {return(x+y)}

@minus(x, y)
    {return(x-y)}

@mult(x, y)
    {return(x*y) }

@div(x, y)
    {if y ≠ 0 then return (x/y) else return (0)}

@echo(x)
    {return(x)}
```

Figure 11-20 Typical action routines for expression interpreter.

when an empty right-hand side is generated. To appreciate how a parser would invoke the action routines necessary to interpret an expression such as "$6 + 7*8$;" consider the trace given in Fig. 11-19. The code for the action routines written in a language-independent form is given in Fig. 11-20. Observe that inherited attributes correspond to parameters of a routine, and synthesized attributes to expressions in the return statment.

It should be noted that in the trace given in Fig. 11-19 the associations between inherited attributes are indicated with an arc below a parse string. In most parser implementations these arcs are represented with pointers in the parse stack and the actual names of the attributes need not be stored in the parse stack. Clearly, however, space must be left for the pointers associated with chains of inherited attributes and the values that will be synthesized at a later stage in the parse for the synthesized attributes.

```
<if stat>        ::= <if head >↑y <if tail >↓y

<if head >↑y     ::= IF <log expr> @brf↑y THEN <stat list>

<if tail >↓y     ::= FI @labprod↓y | ELSE @br↑z @labprod↓y <stat list> FI @labprod↓z

@brf( )    /*no inherited attributes*/
    {dcl labx string;

    labx ← genlab;
    call emit ('BRF', labx);
    return (labx)}

@br( )    /*no inherited attributes*/
    {dcl labz string;

    labz ← genlab;
    call emit('BR', labz);
    return (labz)}

@labprod(y)
    {dcl y string
    call setlab(y)}
```

Figure 11-21 Attribute translation scheme for the example if statement.

1. $<$ if stat $>$ ::= $<$ then form $>$

2. $|<$ then - else form $>$

3. $<$ if head $>\uparrow$x ::= IF $<$ log expr $>$ @brf$\uparrow$x

4. $<$ then part $>$ ::= THEN $<$ stat list $>$ FI

5. $<$ then form $>$ ::= $<$ if head $>\uparrow$x $<$ then part $>$ @labprod$\downarrow$x

6. $<$ then head $>$::= THEN $<$ stat list $>$ ELSE

7. $<$ then-else part $>\uparrow$y ::= $<$ if head $>\uparrow$x $<$ then head $>$ @br$\uparrow$y @labprod$_\smile$x

8. $<$ then-else form $>$ ::= $<$ then-else part $>\uparrow$y $<$ stat list $>$ FI @labprod$\downarrow$y

Figure 11-22 An attribute grammar augmented for bottom-up parsing.

Let us illustrate how the if statement that we have used throughout this chapter could be handled using an attributed translation scheme. Figure 11-21 shows the augmented attributed translation form of a grammar for the if statement along with the three associated action routines.

It is also possible to augment a grammar stratified for bottom-up parsing with attributes and action routines in a manner similar to that just described for LL parsing. Figure 11-22 illustrates such an augmented grammar for our now familiar "if statement" example. Note that the action routines appear only on the extreme right of a production. This restricted form of grammar augmentation is necessary because parser activity—in particular, production reduction—takes place only after the entire right-hand side is recognized. In the third production of the example grammar, the parameter x is synthesized from the @brf routine and passed via the syntactic unit ⟨if head⟩ to either the ⟨then form⟩ or the ⟨then-else part⟩ form. In these productions the label-producing actions are invoked with the appropriate parameters.

Again, we leave as an exercise the trace of the parse and derivation of the correct semantics for the grammar in Fig 11-22.

11-6 EXAMPLE LANGUAGE CONSTRUCTS

In this large section, semantics associated with a number of language constructs typically found in procedural language are examined. An attributed translation form of specification will be used in outlining the nature of the semantic actions and in identifying when these actions should be placed in the grammar description.

11-6.1 Declarations

The declaration is perhaps one of the most controversial language constructs found in a high-level programming language. Some languages have been defined without declaration statements (e.g., APL, SNOBOL, and LISP), others require them only rarely (e.g., BASIC and FORTRAN), and others insist upon their inclusion for all entities used in a program (e.g., PASCAL and Ada). The declaration associates identifiers with a program entity before that entity is used in the program. By using defaults for assigning names (e.g., in FORTRAN names beginning with I, J, K, L, M, or N are assumed to be of type integer) or by relying on implicit contextual definitions of types (e.g., in SNOBOL, TEXT = 'STRING A' implies TEXT is a character string), it is possible to avoid the use of declarations.

This avoidance of the declaration is not always desirable, however, especially when a primary goal of the software developer is to produce reliable software. In "reliable" programming languages the declaration serves as an explicit statement of the programmer's intended use of the defined entity in the program. If the programmer strays from this declared intention during the development of the program, the compiler should be able to detect this failing and notify the user during compilation. As a consequence, more reliable programs should be produced. With the increasing emphasis on reliable software, most "modern-day" programming languages are very declaration-oriented.

From a code-generation and semantic-analysis perspective, it is evident that the primary task of the compiler when handling declarations is twofold:

1. To isolate each declared entity and enter its name in the symbol table
2. To fill in as much as possible the other properties about the entity that are kept in the symbol table, as outlined in Chap. 8

It is these two aspects that we concentrate on in this subsection.

Once an entity is declared, the compiler must use the stored information in the symbol table:

1. To verify that future references to the declared entity are appropriate (i.e., semantic analysis is applied)
2. To use the properties of the declared entity such as its type and assigned object code address to aid in the production of correct target code for a given source program

It is the latter two aspects that we concentrate on in the other subsections of this section on language constructs.

In this subsection some of the more common declarations are discussed, namely, declarations of constants, variables (simple, array, and record), and procedures. However, before we discuss these declaration types, it is appropriate to deviate slightly and make a brief comment concerning the syntactic form of the declaration statements.

There are two major philosophies regarding the allowed form of declarations: one insists that each entity be declared in a separate declaration statement (e.g., Ada), and the other allows declarations to be grouped in one definition (e.g.,

PL/I or FORTRAN). Adoption of the latter philosophy can present some difficulty for the compiler writer, especially if names are grouped prior to the type specification as in PL/I. For example, consider the PL/I declaration

DECLARE (X, Y(N), YTOTAL) FLOAT;

where X and YTOTAL are simple variables and Y(N) denotes an array. To process this declaration statement in a left-to-right parse, the compiler must reserve a series of locations in the symbol table (one per defined entity) prior to knowing the type of the entities. Once the type is discovered, some entries (e.g., object code address and type) must be filled in the symbol table for all entities in the declaration list.

To illustrate how this problem could be handled, consider the following attributed translation grammar:

⟨declaration⟩::= DECLARE @dcl_on↑x (⟨entity list⟩) ⟨type⟩↑t @fix_up↓x,t
⟨entity list⟩::=⟨entity name⟩↑n @name_defn↓n
        |⟨entity name⟩↑n, @name_defn↓n ⟨entity list⟩
⟨type⟩↑t::= FIXED↑t
        |FLOAT↑t
        |CHAR↑t

The action routine @dcl_on is invoked immediately upon commencing the compilation of a declaration statement and an attribute x containing the location of the next open location in the symbol table is synthesized. Next the entity list elements are compiled and each entity name as synthesized in the attribute n is placed in the symbol table by the action routine @name_defn. The types of the entities are uncovered and assigned to the attribute t. This attribute is finally inherited in the action routine @fix_up of the first production. The @fix_up routine fills in the symbol table of all entries beginning at location x until the current location with the type information t and appropriate object code addresses.

It should be obvious that if only one declared variable is allowed per declaration statement or if the type and dimension of the variables precede the names in a declaration statement that allows grouping, then "backfilling" the symbol table becomes unnecessary.

This brief example shows the type of discussion that will be adopted in the remainder of this section. We first discuss the issues and problems concerning a particular language construct and then describe using a small attributed translation specification how these problems can be handled. Let us now examine each of the different declaration types.

Constant type. To a relatively novice programmer it may seem somewhat paradoxical to have the ability to declare a constant—a constant is constant (i.e., nonchanging), so why declare it? While it is true that constants cannot be modified during a particular execution of a program, it is an important asset to be able to define a constant such as symbsize (meaning size of symbol table) once and use it several times in the program. Making a change to a constant only involves changing the declaration. This one change will then be reflected wherever the declared constant is used; for example, a change to symbsize can have the effect of changing the size of the symbol table and altering all the checks that are made for symbol-table overflow in a compiler.

In most programming languages with constant declarations, a constant can only be declared once in any separably compilable module. The constants are viewed as defined at the global level and are therefore stored in the global (sometimes called the "constant") part of the symbol table (see Chap. 8).

To illustrate some of the semantic actions associated with constant declarations, consider the following example grammar:

$\langle$const del$\rangle$::=*constant* $\langle$type$\rangle\uparrow$t $\langle$entity$\rangle\uparrow$n:= $\langle$const expr$\rangle\uparrow$c,s
            @insert$\downarrow$t,n,c,s;
$\langle$type$\rangle\uparrow$t::=*real*$\uparrow$t
       |*integer*$\uparrow$t
       |*string*$\uparrow$t
$\langle$const expr$\rangle\uparrow$c,s::= $\langle$integ const$\rangle\uparrow$c,s
          |$\langle$real const$\rangle\uparrow$c,s
          |$\langle$string const$\rangle\uparrow$c,s

An example statement from this grammar is

constant integer SYMBSIZE:= 1024;

When this statement is compiled, first the type is identified and assigned to the attribute t, then the name of the constant is identified and assigned to the attribute n, and finally the constant expression is synthesized and placed in c and the type of the expression is assigned to s. The action routine @insert is responsible for the following:

1. Checking to see if the declared type t and the constant expression type s match. If they do not, generate an error message.
2. Placing the name n along with the type t and expression c in the symbol table.

The details of how step 2 is executed will depend on the symbol-table organization that is chosen as outlined in Chap. 8.

Variable declarations. By far the most common type of declaration involves the definition of program variables. In our discussion we will consider the declaration of three broad classes of variables: the simple variable, the array variable, and the record variable.

Simple variables The *simple variable* represents a place holder for a single data entity that is usually declared to be of a specific type in a program, for example, integer, real, character, logical, string. Based on the type of the declared variable it is often possible to determine the amount of memory that must be reserved for the variable at run time. Certainly this is true for real, integer, logical, and fixed-length character string variables. More dynamic primitive data types such as variable-length character strings or special subtypes or class data types require some special attention that will be described after examining some typical semantic actions that apply to the more standard, static-sized primitive data types.

Consider the following attributed translation specification for a simple variable declaration:

$\langle$svar dcl$\rangle$::= $\langle$type$\rangle\uparrow$t,i $\langle$entity$\rangle\uparrow$n @svardef$\downarrow$ $\ulcorner$,i,n @allocsv$\downarrow$ i;
$\langle$type$\rangle\uparrow$t,i::=*real* $\uparrow$t,i
         |*integer* $\uparrow$t,i
         |*character* $\uparrow$t ($\langle$number$\rangle\uparrow$i)
         |*logical* $\uparrow$t,i

Some example declarations that obey this specification are

real X;
integer J;
character(20) S;

In the following discussion of declaration semantics, it is assumed that a large data space exists that is addressed through the index *codeptr*. This data space can either be thought of as existing at compile time (static storage allocation) or be allocated dynamically when the compiled module is invoked at execution time. Algorithmic descriptions for the two action routines included in the previous grammar are as follows:

Procedure svardef (t,i,n). Given the type t and size i of a simple variable with name n, this procedure inserts n into the symbol table along with the attributes i and t. j is used as a temporary variable.

        j $\leftarrow$ tableinsert (n,t,i,)
        if j = 0
        then call errmsg (duplident, statmtno)
        else if j = -1
            then call errmsg (tblovflow, statno)
                abort/*compiler*/
end svardef

Procedure allocsv(i). Given the amount of space i required by the simple variable, the codeptr index is updated accordingly.

        codeptr $\leftarrow$ codeptr + i
end allocsv

In Procedure *svardef* (simple variable definition), an attempt is made to insert the variable n into the symbol table with the function *tableinsert*. If the name n already exists in the table, a value of zero is returned and an appropriate error message is generated using Procedure *errmsg*. A returned value of -1 indicates the symbol table is filled, and the compiler is aborted at that point since further compilation would be likely to cause a cascade of semantic errors.

The second procedure, *allocsv* (allocate space for simple variable), simply reserves the space required for the variable as indicated in the attribute i. Note that this attribute would be synthesized in the lexical analyzer, and clearly its value is dependent on the type t.

We conclude our discussion of simple variables by briefly describing the problems of handling subtype and class type declarations. A subtype specification usually involves a more refined specification of a given type. For example, it may be desirable to define a variable for the days of the month as follows:

subtype DAYSOFMONTH *integer* 1..31;

In this example, DAYSOFMONTH is defined as a subtype of the type integer. Obviously it is illegal to assign DAYSOFMONTH any value other than an integer between 1 and 31, inclusive. In order to implement subtypes efficiently, it is often the case that a special compiler-generated procedure is produced at declaration time. This routine is invoked at run time each time a new value is assigned to a subtype variable. Some further discussion concerning these special compiler-generated procedures takes place when semantics for the assignment statement are described in Sec. 11-6.5.

In a similar manner compiler-generated routines can be used to implement class types (sometimes called "sets") such as the following:

class COLOR *is* 'RED', 'BLUE', 'GREEN', 'YELLOW', 'ORANGE';

As before, a routine can be generated at the time the class type declaration is compiled to ensure that only legal values are stored for a given class.

It should also be mentioned that special techniques to encode class types efficiently are often used. For example, a simple encoding for the COLOR class type just defined might associate the integers 1 through 5 with the five colors defined in the class.

Hashing techniques can also be used to associate class values with the indices of a hash table which serve as the coding set for the class values.

The final topic that should be discussed related to simple variable declarations is dealing with variable-length types such as variable-length strings. Variable-length strings are data entities that vary in length at execution time. To solve the storage-allocation problem for such entities, a heap-storage technique is used to manage string space. References to strings in this string space are typically via descriptors which are fixed-length storage segments that contain the current length of the variable-length string and a pointer to the first character in the character string. As a result of using the descriptor technique, the only space that must be allocated by the compiler for a variable-length string at declaration time is the length of a descriptor. The descriptor technique outlined for variable-length strings can be adopted for any variable-length data entity. The storage for the entity itself resides in a heap-storage area, and the descriptor contains an address to that area.

Array Variables An array is a data entity containing elements all of the same type that share a common name. A subscript list is appended to the name to reference an element of an array uniquely or, in some languages, to reference a subarray.

The size of an array may be known at compile time, that is, static (as is the case for FORTRAN IV), or they may be established dynamically at run time when the procedure or module in which the array is declared is loaded for execution. When an array declaration is handled at compile-time, a *template* (i.e., a fixed-length description of the array) is built so that array elements can be dereferenced during execution. For static arrays, the template is built at compile time. For dynamic arrays, space is allocated for the template at compile time and the template itself is constructed at run time.

Before describing the contents of a template, let us examine how an array is typically stored in memory. As an example, consider the following array declaration:

$$array\ B(N, -2:1)integer;$$

If the value of N is set at 3 when the data space for B is allocated, the storage representation for B is illustrated in Fig. 11-23. This representation linearizes the two-dimension array in row-major order; that is, the elements are stored in adjacent memory locations row after row beginning at row 1. Row major order is the order that is usually adopted for most languages. The FORTRAN IV language is an exception to this rule, as array elements are stored in column-major order.

Let us now examine the contents of a template. Let n be the number of dimensions of an array, $L(i)$ the lower bound of dimension i, and $U(i)$ the upper bound of dimension i. The integer array B is of dimension $n = 2$, with $L(1) = 1$ (by default), $U(1) = N$, $L(2) = -2$, and $U(2) = 1$. The values n, $L(i)$, and $U(i)$ are stored in the template to detect a subscript out of range or the wrong number of subscripts. These values are, in fact, sufficient to calculate the address of any

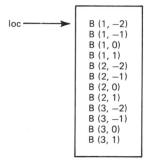

Figure 11-23 Storage representation of the example array B.

array element relative to the base location of the data space allocated to the array.

Let *loc* be the base location of the allocated data space. The absolute address of an array element with subscripts represented as $V(1), V(2), \ldots, V(n)$ can be computed as follows:

$$\text{Absolute address} = loc + \sum_{i=1}^{n} [V(i) - L(i)] P(i)$$

where

$$P(n) = 1$$

and

$$P(i) = \prod_{j=i+1}^{n} [U(j) - L(j) + 1] \qquad \text{for } 1 \le i < n$$

If we let

$$RC = - \sum_{i=1}^{n} L(i)P(i)$$

then

$$\text{Absolute address} = loc + RC + \sum_{i=1}^{n} V(i)P(i)$$

RC represents the *relative constant* part of the address calculation for the absolute address of an array element. This part of the array addressing function is known for all array references once the upper and lower bounds of each dimension of the array are known. For example, in array B, defined earlier, if $N = 3$ for some invocation of the procedure in which B is defined, then

$$P(1) = [U(2) - L(2) + 1] = 1 - (-2) + 1 = 4$$
$$P(2) = 1$$

and therefore

$$RC = - \sum_{i=1}^{n} L(i)P(i)$$
$$= -[1 \times 4 + (-2) \times 1] = -2$$

The absolute address of the array element $B(2, 1)$ would be

$$loc - 2 + \sum_{i=1}^{n} V(i)P(i) = loc - 2 + (2 \times 4 + 1 \times 1) = loc + 7$$

as can be verified by examining Fig. 11-23.

Figure 11-24a depicts the general form of a template, and Fig. 11-24b shows the template for the example B array assuming $N = 3$.

To illustrate some of the semantics associated with array declarations, consider the following attributed translation specification which syntactically agrees

(a)   (b)   **Figure 11-24** A template. (*a*) General form. (*b*) For the array B.

with the example array declaration given earlier:

$\langle$array del$\rangle$::=*array* @init$\uparrow$i $\langle$entity$\rangle$$\uparrow$n (($\langle$sublist$\rangle$$\downarrow$i$\uparrow$j)
                    $\langle$type$\rangle$$\uparrow$t @symbinsert$\downarrow$j,n,t
$\langle$sublist$\rangle$$\downarrow$i$\uparrow$j::=$\langle$subscript$\rangle$ @dimen#$\downarrow$i$\uparrow$j
                    |$\langle$subscript$\rangle$, $\langle$sublist$\rangle$$\downarrow$i$\uparrow$j @dimen#$\downarrow$i$\uparrow$j
$\langle$subscript$\rangle$::= $\langle$integer expr$\rangle$ @bounds
                    |$\langle$integer expr$\rangle$: @lowerbnd $\langle$integer expr$\rangle$ @upperbnd

In this grammar the init action routine is responsible for reserving two slots in the data space to be allocated for an array template (i.e., for n and RC) and initializing i, an attribute that holds a count of the dimension of the array, to zero. The @dimen# routine simply inherits i and synthesizes j as $i + 1$ to reflect the fact that one more dimension has been encountered in a $\langle$subscript$\rangle$ specification.

The @bounds routine merely generates a store command that would take the value of the associated $\langle$integer expr$\rangle$, which typically would be on top of an operation stack or in a specified register, and assign it to $U(i)$ in the data space allocated for the array's template. Also it would assign l, the default lower bound to $L(i)$ and then calculate $P(i)$. Note that the recurrence relation $P(i) = [U(i + 1) - L(i + 1) + 1] \times P(i + 1)$ can be used to reduce the horrendous calculations associated with $P(i)$.

In a similar fashion @lowerbnd emits code to store the $\langle$integer expr$\rangle$ for $L(i)$ in the template and @upperbnd generates code to calculate $P(i)$ and then code to store $P(i)$ and the $\langle$integer expr$\rangle$ for $U(i)$ in the template. Finally, the action routine @symbinsert inserts the array name, n, its type t, and dimension j at an appropriate location in the symbol table. It also produces code that, at run time, would invoke a compiler-generated routine that calculates RC for the given template and stores this calculated value along with n in the template area.

Record variables A record variable is used to reference a data entity composed of several other named data entities that can usually be a mixture of simple, array, and other record variables. As an example consider the following declaration of a record variable:

> *record* BUFFER *is*
>   *integer* LENGTH;
>   *subtype* CURSOR *integer* 1..LENGTH;
>   *array* STORAGE *is integer* (1..LENGTH);
> *end* BUFFER;

The semantic actions associated with handling a record variable declaration are primarily the composite of those actions required to handle the constituents of the declaration. That is, the semantics associated with the declaration of the record variable BUFFER are tantamount to the combination of the semantics for the declaration LENGTH, CURSOR, and STORAGE. The only additional actions involve the storage of the record name in the symbol table along with its type specification, i.e., type *record*. Because records can be nested (i.e., records can be defined within records), it is also necessary to indicate, usually in the dimension field of the symbol table entry, the level of nesting of the record. It is important and most efficient to choose a symbol table organization that allows the constituents of the record to be stored contiguously in the table. In particular, this aids in the dereferencing of fully qualified record names such as BUFFER. CURSOR from our example.

Thus far we have been discussing variable declarations assuming either static or dynamic storage allocation. In many languages, for example, PL/I, PASCAL, and Ada, programmer-controlled data entities are usually provided. A form of heap storage management is used to support explicit requests for new copies of a particular record. To illustrate, consider the following redefinition of the BUFFER record as a controlled data structure:

> *record* BUFFER *controlled by* P *is*
>   *integer* LENGTH;
>   *subtype* CURSOR *integer* 1..LENGTH;
>   *array* STORAGE *is integer* (1..LENGTH);
> *end* BUFFER;

To allocate a copy of the BUFFER record, a program statement such as

> *allocate* BUFFER:

is executed. Automatically enough space for a copy of BUFFER should be allocated in a heap storage area and the control pointer variable P would be set to the address of the latest copy of BUFFER. The space required for a copy may not be known until run time if the record contains any variable-sized parts. As in the case of the implementation of subtypes and classes, it may be most efficient to calculate the size of a dynamically varying record variable by making use of a compiler-generated internal procedure. This procedure would be invoked each time a copy of the controlled record is requested. The calculated size would then be supplied to the heap-storage manager, who would then find the required space from heap storage.

Procedure declarations. Most programming languages do not require an explicit declaration statement for a procedure that is separate from the specification of the procedure body. Languages that do include such a statement are often nested languages for which a single-pass compiler is to be written. The declaration becomes necessary in order to produce correct code for a procedure call that appears prior to the procedure definition in the program as illustrated in the following skeletal program:

> *module* MAIN;
> :
> :
> *call* PROCA(X, Y, S);
> :
> :
> *procedure* PROCA(*in: real* X, Y, *out: string* S);
> :
> :
> *end* PROCA;
> *end* MAIN;

In order to generate correct code for the call statement, it is necessary that the types, order, and number of the parameters for PROCA be known at that time. Of course, this information is not available until the module itself is defined. If a statement such as

> *entry module* PROCA(*in: real* X, Y; *out: string* S)

is inserted prior to the call statement, the required parameter-related information would exist in the symbol table at the time the call statement is completed.

A second very good reason for using procedure declarations is to permit the hiding of procedure or module specifications through the use of program libraries and separately compiled modules. Ada is an excellent example of a language that supports these notions. The basic idea is to separate the declaration part of a module specification from the body. The contents of the declarative part need only be visible to a program segment that wishes to make use of the module, and the details of the module's specification (i.e., the body) are hidden away in a program library. Various levels of permission can be imposed by the program library manager to restrict those who should not have access to the module body. Clearly, for this scheme to work it is necessary that the symbol tables associated with each separately compilable module be under the control of the program library manager. The importance of the role of a program library manager in modern languages will be discussed further when we discuss compiler aids.

11-6.2 Expressions

Most procedural languages are very rich in expressions, especially if they are general-purpose languages such as PL/I or Ada. In this section we will review some of the basic problems associated with the generation of code and semantic analysis for expressions of different types. The main goal in synthesizing an expression is to generate the code that produces the correct value for the expression. To this end the primary strategy is first to load the operands of the expression on top of an operation stack or in a register and then to execute the operation associated with the expression, leaving the result on the operation stack or in a register. Consider the following attributed translation grammar description of an integer expression:

```
 1 ⟨expression⟩ ::= ⟨expr⟩
 2 ⟨expr⟩        ::= ⟨term⟩ ⟨terms⟩
 3 ⟨terms⟩       ::= ε
 4                   | + ⟨term⟩ @add ⟨terms⟩
 5                   | − ⟨term⟩ @subt ⟨terms⟩
 6 ⟨term⟩        ::= ⟨factor⟩ ⟨factors⟩
 7 ⟨factors⟩     ::= ε
 8                   | * ⟨factor⟩ @mult ⟨factors⟩
 9                   | / ⟨factor⟩ @div ⟨factors⟩
10 ⟨factor⟩      ::= ⟨variable⟩ ↑n @lookup ↓n↑j @push ↓j
11                   | ⟨integer⟩ ↑i @pushi ↓i
12                   | (⟨expr⟩)
```

The following action routines illustrate the type of semantic actions associated with compiling the integer expressions just defined:

```
Procedure add                    Procedure push(j)
     call emit ('ADD')                integer j
end add                               call emitl('LOAD', symbtbl.objaddr(j))
                                 end push
Procedure lookup(n)
     string n; integer j
     j ← symblookup(n)
     if j < 1
     then { ...error conditions... }
     else return (j)
end lookup

Procedure pushi(i) {push integer}
     integer i
     call emitl('LOADI',i)
end pushi
```

In the specialized notation for action routines used in the remainder of this section, each action routine is written as a procedure. Values for the parameters of the procedure are obtained from the inherited attributes. Values are returned to the synthesized attributes by one or more expressions listed in the return statement of the procedure.

In the previous action routines we have assumed a stack machine model as a target machine. Therefore, when the *add* routine is called, all that needs to be generated is an ADD instruction with no operands, since it is assumed that the two operands are previously loaded on top of the operation stack.

The *lookup* routine is used to locate the index of the variable in the symbol table and assign it to the synthesized attribute j. The *push* routine inherits this attribute and uses it to generate a LOAD instruction with the previously assigned object address as the single operand.

The *pushi* routine is invoked when an integer constant appears in the expression. A LOADI (load immediate) instruction is emitted. It loads the integer constant on the operation stack when executed at run time.

A trace of the top-down parse of the expression X + Y ∗ 3 is now given. In the trace, the syntactic units that are being expanded or matched to source tokens are italicized:

$$\langle \text{expression} \rangle \Rightarrow \langle expr \rangle \qquad \text{by prod 1}$$
$$\Rightarrow \langle term \rangle \langle \text{terms} \rangle \qquad \text{by prod 2}$$
$$\Rightarrow \langle factor \rangle \langle \text{factors} \rangle \langle \text{terms} \rangle \qquad \text{by prod 6}$$
$$\Rightarrow \langle variable \rangle \uparrow n \; @\text{lookup} \downarrow n \uparrow j \; @\text{push} \downarrow j \; \langle \text{factors} \rangle \; \langle \text{terms} \rangle$$
$$\text{by prod 10}$$

At this point the following activities occur:

The parse matches the variable X
n ← 'X'
The action routine lookup(n) with n ← 'X' is invoked
A value for j is returned
The action routine push(j) is invoked
The instruction "LOAD, ⟨ll,on⟩" is generated where "⟨ll,on⟩" represents the object address assigned to X
The parse at this point would be

$$\Rightarrow \langle factors \rangle \langle \text{terms} \rangle$$
$$\Rightarrow \langle terms \rangle \qquad \text{by prod 7}$$
$$\Rightarrow + \langle term \rangle \; @\text{add} \; \langle \text{terms} \rangle \qquad \text{by prod 4}$$
$$\Rightarrow \langle term \rangle \; @\text{add} \; \langle \text{terms} \rangle \qquad \text{match "} + \text{"}$$
$$\Rightarrow \langle factor \rangle \langle \text{factors} \rangle \; @\text{add} \; \langle \text{terms} \rangle \qquad \text{by prod 6}$$
$$\Rightarrow \langle variable \rangle \uparrow n \; @\text{lookup} \downarrow n \uparrow j \; @\text{push} \downarrow j \; \langle \text{factors} \rangle \; @\text{add} \; \langle \text{terms} \rangle$$
$$\text{by prod 10}$$

Y is matched, and the same set of activities as when X was matched previously takes place. The instruction "LOAD, ⟨ll,on⟩" is emitted to load Y. The sentential form is reduced to:

⇒ ⟨*factors*⟩ @add ⟨terms⟩
⇒ * ⟨factor⟩ @mult ⟨factors⟩ @add ⟨terms⟩   by prod 8
⇒ ⟨*factor*⟩ @mult ⟨factors⟩ @add ⟨terms⟩   match " * "
⇒ ⟨*integer*⟩↑i @pushi↓i @mult ⟨factors⟩ @add ⟨terms⟩   by prod 11

At this point the following activities occur:

The parse matches the integer 3 contained in the source string
The action routine pushi is invoked
The instruction "LOADI,3" is generated
The sentential form at this point would then be

⇒ @*mult*⟨factors⟩ @add ⟨terms⟩

Next the action routine @mult is invoked and the stack machine instruction "MULT" is generated. The sentential form is then reduced to:

⇒ ⟨*factors*⟩ @add ⟨terms⟩
⇒ @*add*⟨terms⟩   by prod 7

Next the action routine @add is invoked and the stack machine instruction "ADD" is generated. The sentential form is then reduced to:

⇒ ⟨*terms*⟩
⇒ ε   by prod 3

Since the entire source expression has now been parsed, the compilation process can stop. The code produced by these actions is:

LOAD, ⟨ll,on⟩ {for X}
LOAD, ⟨ll,on⟩ {for Y}
LOADI,3
MULT
ADD

which is correct.

The previous discussion of expressions was purposely kept simple so that some of the basic issues could be clearly explained.

Suppose we want to augment the expression grammar to include a mixture of real and integer expressions. The grammar would have to undergo some serious alterations, as indicated in the description given in Fig. 11-25.

The most major change is the insertion of attributes to perform some semantic analysis related to type checking and operand control. For example, the *add* routine is altered to the following procedural description:

< expression > ::= < expr >↑t

  < expr >↑t ::= < term >↑s < terms >↓s↑t

< terms >↓s↑u ::= @echo↓s↑u

       | + < term >↑t @add↓t, s↑v < terms >↓v↑u

       | − < term >↑t @sub↓t, s↑v < terms >↓v↑u

  < term >↑u ::= < factor >↑s < factors >↓s↑u

< factors >↓s↑u ::= @echo↓s↑u

       | * < factor >↑t @mult↓t, s↑v < factors >↓v↑u

       | / < factor >↑t @div↓t, s↑v < factors >↓v↑u

  < factor >↑t ::= < variable >↑i @type↓i↑t

       | < integer >↑i @pushi↓i↑t

       | < real >↑r @pushi↓r↑t

< variable >↑j ::= < identifier >↑n @lookup↓n↑j @push↓j

       | < identifier >↑n @lookup↓n↑j (@template↓j↑k < sublist >↓k, j)

< sublist >↓k, j ::= < subscript >↑t @offset↓k, t↑i < subscripts >↓i, j

< subscripts >↓k, j ::= @checkdim↓k, j

       | , < subscript >↑t @offset↓k, t↑i < subscripts >↓i, j

< subscript >↑t ::= < expr >↑t

Figure 11-25 Extended attributed grammar for expressions.

Procedure add(t,s)
     string t,s
     if t = 'real' and s = 'integer'
     then call emit (CONVIR,$top − 1)
          call emit ('ADD')
          return ('real')
     if t = 'integer' and s = 'real'
     then call emit (CONVIR,$top)
          call emit ('ADD')
          return ('real')
     call emit ('ADD')
     return (t)
  end add

In the *add* procedure the input attributes (i.e., the parameters) contain the types of the operands for the addition expression. These are checked to make certain both operands are of the same type. If they differ, the procedure ensures, through the generation of a CONVIR (convert integer to real) target machine instruction, that the operand either on top of the operand stack (i.e., $top) or second from the top is correctly converted. The 'ADD' instruction is then emitted, and finally the type of the expression is returned as a synthesized attribute.

The *lookup* and *push* action routines have roles identical or very similar to that described earlier. The type action routine simply synthesizes the type of a variable based on the index i to the symbol table. Other procedures are as follows:

```
Procedure template(j)
      integer j
      call emit1 ('TEMPLATE', symbtbl.objaddr(j))
      k ← 0 {initialize subscript counts}
      return(k)
end template


Procedure offset(k,t)
      integer k, string t
      k ← k + 1
      if type ≠ 'integer'
      then errmsg('EXPECTING INTEGER EXPRESSION AS ARRAY
                  SUBSCRIPT', statno)
      else emit1('OFFSET', k)
      return(k)
end offset


Procedure checkdim(k, j)
      integer k, j
      if k ≠ symbtbl.dim(j)
      then call errmsg('NUMBER OF DIMENSIONS DO NOT MATCH
                  DECLARATION', stateno)
      else call emit(ARREF)
          call emit(DEREF)
end checkdim
```

The procedure *template* emits a target machine instruction that loads the *address* of the template for the array variable on top of the operand stack. The subscript counter is then initialized to zero.

The *offset* procedure ensures that each subscript is of type integer and then emits an OFFSET instruction. This instruction, when executed at run time, accomplishes the following:

1. Checks to ensure that the value for the kth subscript, which should be on top of the operand stack, is in the range of the declared subscript values for the kth dimension of the variable array.

2. Computes a portion of the variable part of the array addressing function using the following recurrence function:

$$VP(0) = 0$$
$$VP(k) = VP(k - 1) + V(k) * P(k) \qquad 1 \le k \le n$$

This function is derived from the variable part calculation, $\sum_{k=1}^{n} V(k) * P(k)$, given earlier in the discussion of array variable declarations. Figure 11-26 illustrates the contents of the operand stack during the calculation of the offsets for the array element B(2,1) assuming the array B is declared as

array $B(N, -2 : 1)$ integer;

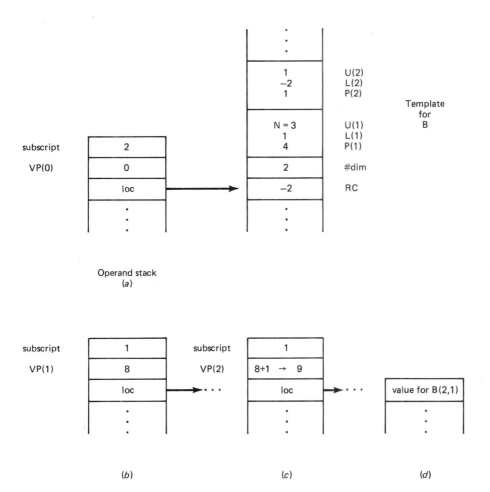

Operand stack
(a)

(b)   (c)   (d)

Figure 11-26 Illustration of the contents of the operand stack during the execution of the OFFSET instruction.

which is the same example used earlier in the discussion of array variables. In Fig. 11-26*a* the operand stack contains the value of the first dimension for B(2,1) namely, 2, the initial value of VP = 0, which is set by the template instruction, and the address of the template in data space. Figure 11-26*b* and *c* illustrates the contents of the operand stack after the first and second OFFSET instructions are executed. Note that all of these compiled instructions are executed at run time and not compile time.

The procedure *checkdim* is invoked at compile time after all of the subscripts for an array have been compiled. At this point, a check is made to ensure that the number of subscripts agrees with the declared number of dimensions for the array. If it does, the target code instructions ARREF and DEREF are emitted. ARREF simply computes at run time the value of the address of the specified array element. For the example B(2,1), ARREF would add loc + VP(2) + RC or loc + 7, where RC is found in the template at the address designated as loc. The target code instruction DEREF simply replaces the address of the array element on the top of the operand stack by the value of that array element as shown in Fig. 11-26*d*.

The final type of expression compilation that will be discussed is the compilation of relational expressions with the logical connective operators "and" (&) "or" (|), and "not" (~). The primary purpose for including this discussion is to illustrate how relational expression evaluation can be optimized during semantic analysis and code generation.

To illustrate in a general way what we mean by logical expression evaluation let us consider the following example:

$$(X = Y \& Y = Z)|Z < X$$

First it should be noted that if X is not equal to Y there is no need to evaluate the logical expression Y = Z because regardless of whether the second relational expression is *true* or *false*, the entire parenthesized expression will be *false*. Similarly, if the entire expression (X = Y & Y = Z) is *true*, then it is not necessary to evaluate Z < X. A sufficient flow of computation for this expression is illustrated in Fig. 11-27.

One might wonder if it is worthwhile to generate this fairly intricate flow of computation for expressions involving so few operands. Table 11-1 illustrates, for all possible truth values assigned to the relational expression, that the number of

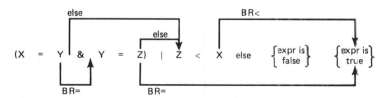

Figure 11-27 Flow of computation for example logical expression.

Table 11-1 Number of evaluations for logical expression computation

X = Y	Y = Z	Z < X	Number of expression evaluations
T	T	T	2
T	T	F	2
T	F	T	3
T	F	F	3
F	T	T	2
F	T	F	2
F	F	T	2
F	F	F	2

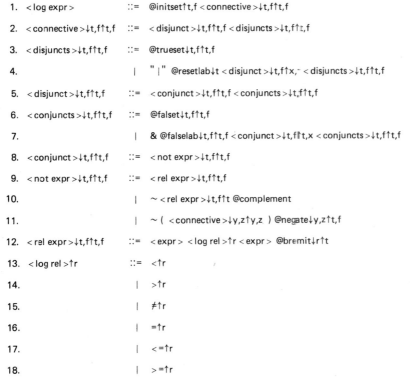

1. < log expr >   ::= @initset↑t,f < connective >↓t,f↑t,f

2. < connective >↓t,f↑t,f   ::= < disjunct >↓t,f↑t,f < disjuncts >↓t,f↑t,f

3. < disjuncts >↓t,f↑t,f   ::= @trueset↓t,f↑t,f

4. | " | " @resetlab↓t < disjunct >↓t,f↑x,⁻ < disjuncts >↓t,f↑t,f

5. < disjunct >↓t,f↑t,f   ::= < conjunct >↓t,f↑t,f < conjuncts >↓t,f↑t,f

6. < conjuncts >↓t,f↑t,f   ::= @false↓t,f↑t,f

7. | & @falselab↓t,f↑t,f < conjunct >↓t,f↑t,x < conjuncts >↓t,f↑t,f

8. < conjunct >↓t,f↑t,f   ::= < not expr >↓t,f↑t,f

9. < not expr >↓t,f↑t,f   ::= < rel expr >↓t,f↑t,f

10. | ~ < rel expr >↓t,f↑t @complement

11. | ~ (< connective >↓y,z↑y,z) @negate↓y,z↑t,f

12. < rel expr >↓t,f↑t,f   ::= < expr > < log rel >↑r < expr > @bremit↓r↑t

13. < log rel >↑r   ::= <↑r

14. | >↑r

15. | ≠↑r

16. | =↑r

17. | <=↑r

18. | >=↑r

Figure 11-28 An attributed grammar for logical expressions.

relational expression evaluations is usually less than 3, the number of relational expressions involved in the logical expression. Clearly, it is worthwhile in this and most examples to consider the logical flow of a logical expression's computation.

Another reason to consider optimizing logical flow is that some programmers expect it to be considered. Let us examine the following PL/I if statement:

IF N¬= 0 & X/N < 1
THEN ...

In this statement, the programmer may have specifically put in the relational expression N¬= 0 as a logical guard against division by zero in the second expression X/N < 1. If N = 0, the application of optimized logical flow would avoid the computation of X/N < 1 and the division by zero, whereas, if both logical expressions are always computed regardless of the value of the first expression, an overflow interrupt will occur at run time. In fact, the first PL/I compilers that were written did not include optimized logical flow in their logical expression evaluation.

An attributed grammar that optimizes logical expression in terms of computation flow is given in Fig. 11-28. To illustrate how a logical expression is processed using this attributed translation grammar, let us consider the expression ~ (X = Y|X < Y & Y > Z). A skeletal trace is given in Fig. 11-29; a full trace is quite long and involved. The reader is invited to complete the full trace to gain a full appreciation of how the action routines work.

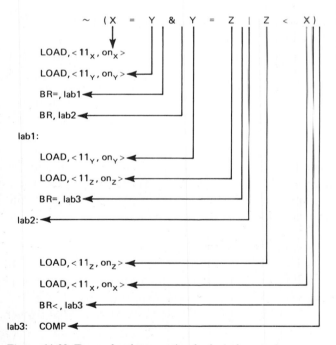

Figure 11-29 Trace of code generation for logical expression.

The action routine *initset* is activated first in the parse. It simply sets the synthesized attributes t and f to a special address "set". The importance of "setting" these attributes will be described shortly. The second action routine given in the grammar that is invoked during the parse is *bremit*. A procedural specification of the routine is as follows:

```
Procedure bremit (r)
        string r, address lab
        call labelprod (lab)
        do case of r
           ' < ': call emit1 ('BR < ', lab)
           ' > ': call emit1 ('BR > ', lab)
           ' ≠ ': call emit1 ('BR ≠ ', lab)
           ' = ': call emit1 ('BR = ', lab)
           ' <= ': call emit1 ('BR <= ', lab)
           ' >= ': call emit1 ('BR >= ', lab)
        end case
        return (lab)
    end bremit
```

The main purpose of this routine is to generate a conditional branch instruction for the current relational expression. The conditional branch instructions are assumed to be pseudo stack machine instructions. When "executed," they do the following:

1. Compare the top two operands on the operand stack (i.e., X and Y in the relational expression $'X = Y'$).
2. If the prescribed relation is *true*, the branch is taken to the label address that is the operand of the branch instruction; otherwise pseudo machine control passes to the next instruction in sequence.
3. The top two operands (i.e., X and Y in $'X = Y'$) are removed from the operand stack and replaced by a single operand which is a 1 if the branch condition is *true* and a 0 otherwise.

Therefore, if the second from the top operand on the operand stack is 4 and the top operand is 5, then the execution of a "BR <, lab" instruction would cause a transfer to the instruction at pseudo machine address "lab", the removal of the operands 4 and 5 from the stack, and then the placement of a 1 on top of the stack.

The label that is generated for the branch instruction becomes part of what we will call the "true chain" of logical flow. This label may initiate a true chain or form part of a true chain that is typically associated with a series of disjunctive (|) clauses. For example, in the expression given in Fig. 11-30, a series of 'BR =' instructions are emitted and chained together with 'lab' in an optimized logical expression.

Figure 11-30

True chains are terminated either at the end of a set of disjunctions (i.e., in the action routine *trueset* of production 3) or when a conjunction is encountered (i.e., in action routine *falselab* in production 7).

False chains also exist. One is initiated when a conjunction is recognized (i.e., in action routine *falselab* in production 7) and is terminated at the conclusion of a set of conjunctions (i.e., in action routine *falset* in production 6). The expression in Fig. 11-31 illustrates how a false chain might arise. In this case, the false chain is a set of unconditional branch instructions generated in the *falselab* action routine. A procedural specification for *falselab* follows:

```
Procedure falselab(t,f)
        address t, f
        if f = 'set' {'set' is a special address}
        then call labprod(f)
        call emit1('BR ',f)
        call setlab(t) {emit true chain label}
        t ← 'set'    {set true chain}
        return (t,f)
end falselab
```

Initially, a check is made to see if a new false chain must be initiated. If f has the special address 'set', a false chain does not currently exist and one must be initiated by producing a new internal label (i.e., by invoking *labprod* procedure). After the 'BR' instruction that is part of the false chain is generated, the current true chain is terminated by generating the true chain label and then resetting the true label t to 'set'.

It is no accident that all of the syntactic units and action routines have two inherited and two synthesized attributes. The attribute t represents the current true chain label and f represents the current false chain label. These chains are terminated with the *trueset* and *falset* routines which perform the following

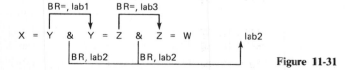

Figure 11-31

semantic activities:

Procedure trueset(t, f)   **Procedure** falset(t, f)
    address t, f   address t, f
    call setlab(t)   call setlab(f)
    t ← 'set'   f ← 'set'
    return(t, f)   return(t ,f)
end trueset   **end** falset

To ensure that new labels are not needlessly generated for the true chain, an action routine *resetlab* is used to reset the label of the last BR⟨cond⟩ produced in *bremit* to the label t that was originally generated for the true chain of the latest ⟨connective⟩. This has the effect of incorporating the BR⟨cond⟩ for the latest ⟨disjoint⟩ on a single true chain.

The final action routine to be described is *negate*. *Negate* is responsible for producing the actions necessary to generate the logical complement of a connective (production 11) that is currently being compiled. A procedural specification for *negate* is as follows:

Procedure negate (x,y)
    address x,y,t,f
    t ← y {set true chain to existing false chain}
    f ← x {set false chain to existing true chain}
    call emit ('COMP')
    return (t,f)
end negate

To generate the logical complement it is necessary to first switch the false chain to true chain and vice versa and then generate a COMP instruction. This instruction simply replaces the existing logical value (i.e., 0 or 1) on top of the operand stack by its complement.

The *complement* action routine, found in production 10, simply emits a COMP instruction. It is unnecessary to exchange the false and true chains in this case because a false or true chain cannot build up in the complementation of a relational expression.

It should be observed that the attributed grammar for logical expressions ignores type checking of operands in relational expressions. This could be easily added using the techniques discussed earlier for arithmetic (i.e., real and integer) expressions. Indeed, the techniques discussed in this subsection could be applied more generally to other expressions not discussed, such as string expressions. Let us now examine the type of semantic actions that are typical of assignment statements.

11-6.3 Assignment Statements

As noted in Chap. 3, the inclusion of the assignment statement in a programming language has not been without controversy—during the early 1970s when the virtues of expression languages were being expounded it was felt that the use of assignment statements in programming could be drastically reduced, if not eliminated. The current interest in functional languages also promises to deemphasize the role of the assignment statement. It may be argued that the assignment statement supports the specification of "how to do" rather than "what to do" programming. Regardless of this controversy, it is almost certain that assignment statements will play a major role in programming at least for some time in the future.

The unique aspect about the assignment statement from a semantic-analysis point of view is that a reference to a variable's *location* rather than its *value* is required. To illustrate, consider the following source statement:

$$X := Y + X;$$

A set of pseudo stack machine instructions that realize this statement is

LOAD, $(\langle ll_X, on_X \rangle)$ {load the address of the location at which the value of X is stored}

LOAD, $\langle ll_Y, on_Y \rangle$ {load the value of Y}

LOAD, $\langle ll_X, on_X \rangle$ {load the value of X}

ADD   {add the top two operands on the stack and replace with summation}

STORIN   {store the value on top of the stack at the address that is stored at the second from the top position}

The first LOAD instruction places the ⟨lexic level, order number⟩ tuple address for X on top of the operand stack. The values for X and Y are then loaded and added. Finally, a STORIN (i.e., store indirect) instruction is emitted. When executed, it stores the value on top of the operand stack at the address location stored at the second from the top position.

The ability to have access to the address of a variable is not generally required in most high-level programming languages except to handle assignments, pass-by-reference parameter parsing, and input statement argument lists. Sometimes these constructs are called "L-expressions" (meaning left-hand-side expressions) because they yield references as opposed to values. Most languages do not adopt a special notation to distinguish between yielding a value of a variable versus a reference to a variable; rather they rely on semantic analysis for determining the context in which a reference should be yielded. Because references to a variable are required extensively in system development, languages such as C which are designed for system development often incorporate explicit syntactic constructs to yield variable references. For example, in C it is possible to make the assignment

$$X = \&Y$$

in which X is assigned the address of Y. Here, the & operator yields a reference to its operand.

The following attribute translation grammar of an assignment statement contains three semantic action routines:

$\langle$assignstat$\rangle$::=@setL↑L $\langle$variable$\rangle$↓L↑t:= @resetL↑L $\langle$expr$\rangle$↑s
@storin↓t,s;

The setL routine is used to set the attribute L (indicating an L-expression) because the syntactic unit $\langle$variable$\rangle$ must yield a reference. Its specification follows:

Procedure setL
    return(*true*)
end setL

In a similar fashion, *resetL* simply sets the logical attribute L to *false*, indicating that the expression on the right-hand side of the assignment is to yield a value.

The final action routine, *storin*, has the following skeletal procedural specification:

Procedure storin(t,s)
    string t,s
    if t ≠ s
    then ... {check types and issue appropriate conversion instruction or
            instructions to convert the expression value to the type
            of the variable}
    call emit('STORIN')
end deref

In our discussion of assignments we have not considered in detail the case in which the assignment variable is an array element or possibly an entire array. In the discussion of array variables described earlier, a description was given of how the addressing function of an array is calculated before a value is yielded. Clearly, this same process should be followed in order to generate the sequence of instructions to produce an array element reference. If an assignment is allowable to an entire array, the obvious method of locating the first element of the array and then incrementing an internal counter to yield references to all elements should be applied.

11-6.4 Control Statements

Our discussion of control statements will be broad in scope, including both selection and looping constructs. Because most of our discussion involving the various semantic-analysis and code-generation strategies in Secs. 11-1 through 11-5 involved the if statement, it will not be described again. Rather we will examine a generalized case-selection construct. Our investigation of looping constructs will include a repeat-while construct and a counted for loop construct.

Case-selection statement. A case-selection statement is a multiway branch construct intended to provide a case-by-case decomposition of a logical condition arising in a program. As such it is a generalization of the if statement. An example of one possible form of a case statement is as follows:

> do case of rate * gross_sal:
>   > 22000: surcharge ← .8;
>   > = 16000: surcharge ← .6;
>   > = 10000: surcharge ← .4;
>   else: surcharge ← 0
>   print ("no surcharge");
> end case

    A general schemata of the logical flow of a case construct is illustrated in Fig. 11-32. Note that ⟨cond⟩ represents one of the standard relational operators and ⟨stat list⟩ is a list of statements possibly including another case statement. The construct ⟨ ~ cond⟩ means complement of condition. Therefore, if ⟨cond⟩ is >, then ⟨ ~ cond⟩ is <= .

    An attributed translation grammar for the case construct is given in Fig. 11-33. In production 2, the action routine *doubload* is responsible for loading a second copy of ⟨expr⟩ on the operand stack, since a value of ⟨expr⟩ will always be destroyed in the branch instruction emitted by the *brcomp* routine in produc-

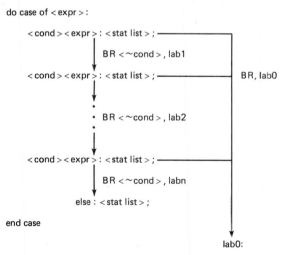

do case of < expr > :

    < cond > < expr > : < stat list > ;

        BR < ~cond > , lab1

    < cond > < expr > : < stat list > ;   BR, lab0

        • BR < ~cond > , lab2

    < cond > < expr > : < stat list > ;

        BR < ~cond > , labn

      else : < stat list > ;

end case

                lab0:

Figure 11-32 Logical flow of a case construct.

tion 6. Procedural specifications of these two routines are as follows:

> **Procedure** doubload
>> address lab
>> call emit1('LOAD', $top) {load another copy of the current stack top}
>> call labprod(lab)
>> return(lab)   {produce lab for BR, lab instruction}
> end doubload

> **Procedure** brcomp(r)
>> string r, address lab
>> call labprod(lab)
>> do case of r   {produce complementary branches}
>>> '<': call emit1 ('BR > =', lab)
>>> '>': call emit1 ('BR < =', lab)
>>> '≠': call emit1 ('BR =', lab)
>>> '=': call emit1 ('BR ≠', lab)
>>> '> =': call emit1 ('BR <', lab)
>>> '< =': call emit1 ('BR >', lab)
>> end case
>> call emit ('POP')   {pop logical value from stack}
>> call emit1 ('LOAD', $top)   {reload "do-case-of" ⟨expr⟩}
> end brcomp

Note that in *brcomp* it is necessary to remove the logical value stored on top of the stack prior to the execution of the statement list in a ⟨cond stat⟩ construct and to reload the original case expression.

The *labemit* routine in productions 1 and 6 simply generates the label specified in the inherited attribute. The label that is generated in production 1 is for the general BR instruction that concludes each case. It is set at the end of the entire case statement. The label that is produced in production 6 is for the conditional branches generated in each ⟨cond stat⟩.

1.   < case stat > ::= < case head >↑x < case body >↓x < case tail > @labemit↓x

2.   < case head >↑x ::= do case of < expr > : @doubload↑x

3.   < case body >↓x ::= < cond stats >↓x

4.   < cond stats >↓x ::= ε

5. | < cond stat >↓x↑y < cond stats >↓y

6. < cond stat >↓x↑y ::= < rel cond >↑r : @brcomp↓r↑f < statlist > ; @reload↓x↑y @labemit↓f

7.   < case tail > ::= else: < statlist > ; end case

Figure 11-33 Attributed translation grammar for case construct.

The *reload* routine first removes the logical value created from the conditional branch and then generates the common branch instruction that is taken after the ⟨stat list⟩ for each case (i.e., each ⟨cond stat⟩). The semantics in the *reload* routine are as follows:

> **Procedure** reload (x)
>> addr x
>> call emit ('POP')
>>> {remove logical value of *true* associated with BR⟨ ~ cond⟩, lab}
>> call emit1 ('BR', x)
>> return (x)
> end reload

As an additional example of a control type of statement, let us now examine a repeat-while construct.

Repeat-while statement. The following example illustrates a repeat-while construct that we will examine:

> repeat while test(j) ≠ ';':
>> if j < length
>> then j ← j + 1
> end repeat

A general schemata for the repeat-while construct is shown in Fig. 11-34. An examination of the logical flow in the construct indicates four semantic actions, as captured in the following attributed translation specification:

1 ⟨repeat while⟩::= ⟨repeat head⟩↑f,r⟨stat list⟩ @retbranch↓r ⟨repeat end⟩
   @labemit↓f
2 ⟨repeat head⟩↑f,r::= repeat while @labgen↑r ⟨log expr⟩ @falsebranch↑f:
3 ⟨repeat end⟩::= end repeat

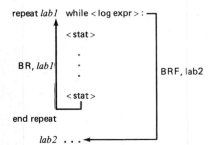

Figure 11-34 Logical flow for repeat-while construct.

The *labgen* routine simply sets the return label in production 2 as follows:

Procedure labgen
        address r
        call labprod(r)
        call setlab(r)
        return(r)
    end labgen

The *falsebranch* routine generates the branch-on false instruction which is taken if the ⟨log expr⟩ in production 2 is *false*. A procedural specification follows:

Procedure falsebranch
        address f
        call labprod(f)
        call emit1('BRF',f)
        return(f)
    end falsegen

The *retbranch* routine simply generates the unconditional return branch that forms the loop. The *labemit* routine (described in Sec. 11-6.2) sets the label produced for the branch-on-false instruction.

The final control structure we will examine is a counted for loop.

For loop statement. The for loop can be thought of as a more structured form of repeat-while loop. Built into the for loop is a loop variable that is incremented and tested with each reexecution of a loop body. An example illustrating the general form of a counted loop follows:

for i← 1 to n by 2 do
    ⟨stat⟩
      ⋮ {loop body}
    ⟨stat⟩
end for

Figure 11-35 provides a schematic view of the code that must be generated to realize the semantics of the for loop. The arcs in the figure illustrate the connection between the syntactic units of the construct and the code that is generated. The semantic routines for realizing the generation of this code can be inserted in an attribute translation grammar as shown in the following specification:

⟨for loop⟩ ::= ⟨for head⟩ ↑ a,f,r ⟨rest of loop⟩ ↓ a,f,r
⟨for head⟩ ↑ a,f,r ::= for ⟨id⟩ ↑ a ← ⟨expr⟩ @initload ↑ s to @labgen ↑ r ⟨expr⟩
                    by @loadid ↓ a ⟨expr⟩ @compare ↓ a,s ↑ f
⟨rest of loop⟩ ↓ a,f,r ::= do ⟨stat list⟩ end for @retbranch ↓ r @labemit ↓ f

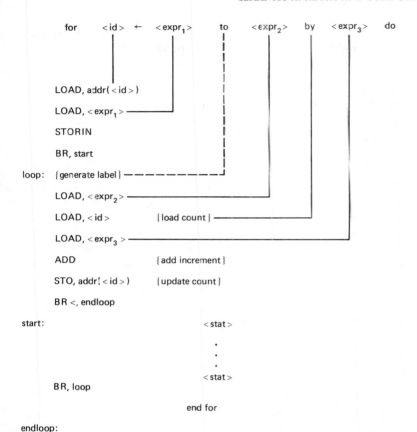

for   < id >   ←   < expr$_1$ >   to   < expr$_2$ >   by   < expr$_3$ >   do

LOAD, addr(< id >)

LOAD, < expr$_1$ > ─────┘

STORIN

BR, start

loop: {generate label } ─ ─ ─ ─ ─ ─ ─ ─┘

LOAD, < expr$_2$ > ─────

LOAD, < id >   {load count } ─────

LOAD, < expr$_3$ > ─────

ADD   { add increment }

STO, addr(< id >)   { update count }

BR <, endloop

start: < stat >

.
.
.

                        < stat >

BR, loop

                 end for

endloop:

Figure 11-35 Schematic view illustrating the code that should be generated for a for loop.

In the specification we have assumed that the code for each ⟨expr⟩ (as represented by LOAD, ⟨expr⟩ in Fig. 11-35) is generated correctly during the expansion of ⟨expr⟩ as was described in Sec. 11-6.2. The action routine *initload* simply emits instructions to store the initial value for the loop variable, i.e., STORIN instruction, and to branch pass the test for the loop variable. The proposed semantics are for a for loop in which the loop variable is not tested against its limit the first time the loop is executed. The reader is invited to write action routines that allow for this initial test. You will find the semantics are somewhat messy and complicated.

The *labgen, retbranch*, and *labemit* have identical semantics as that described in the previous discussion of the repeat-while construct. The *labgen* routine in production 2 generates the label that is returned to at the end of the loop as illustrated in Fig. 11-35. The *retbranch* routine in production 3 generates the unconditional branch instruction that causes control to return to the "loop" label generated by the *labgen* routine. Finally, the *labemit* emits the "endloop" label that is generated as part of the conditional branch BR > during the *compare* routine which is now given:

>   **Procedure** compare(a,s)
>   address a,f,s
>   call emit('ADD')
>   call emit1('STO', a) {STO is nondestructive}
>   call labprod(f)
>   call emit1('BR >', f)
>   call setlab(s)
>   return(f)
>   end compare

The remaining action routine, *loadid* in production 2, is responsible for loading the value of the count variable (i.e., ⟨id⟩) in preparation of its comparison with the limit expression ⟨expr₃⟩. A semantic specification is as follows:

>   **Procedure** loadid(a)
>   address a
>   call emit1('LOAD', a) {load count}
>   end loadid

It should be observed that all of the control language constructs described in this section are recursively defined, not only syntactically but semantically. Of course, this is one of the real advantages of attaching semantic actions to a syntactic description that is recursive in nature—the necessity of having to manage semantic stacks disappears.

Let us now examine the semantics associated with procedure calls.

11-6.5 Procedure Calls and Returns

Procedure calls and returns also affect the flow of control in a program; nevertheless, we have chosen to discuss procedure semantics in a separate section because these semantics differ significantly from those we discussed in the last subsection. We begin by concentrating on the semantics of procedure calls.

Procedure calls. The major activities associated with a procedure call include:

1. Ensuring that the procedure has been defined and that this definition agrees with the type of the procedure (i.e., pure or functional procedure), and that the number and type of arguments agree with the formal parameter specification in the procedure definition.
2. Loading the arguments.
3. Loading the return address.
4. Transferring to the procedure body.

An example call format that will be used in our discussion is the following:

call process_symb(symb, cursor, replacestr);

A set of pseudo code instructions that could be produced to realize this call statement might be:

```
        LOAD,⟨addr of symb⟩
        LOAD,⟨addr of cursor⟩
        LOAD,⟨addr of replacestr⟩
        JSR,⟨addr of process_symb⟩
⟨retaddr⟩: . . .
```

We assume in the code that is produced that a call-by-value parameter passing scheme is used. The first three instructions simply load the arguments of the procedure call onto the operand stack. If an argument is a more general expression, then clearly the code to realize the expression would be generated in place of a simple LOAD instruction. In either case, the value of the argument would be loaded.

Next, a "Jump-to-Subroutine" instruction is emitted. This instruction jumps to the address that begins the body of the called procedure (in this case, process_symb) and stores the return address (which is the address following the JSR instruction) on top of the operand stack.

The body of the called procedure for this example might have the following form:

procedure process_symb(string:symbol, int:cur, string:repl);

$$\vdots$$

end process_symb;

At the beginning of the procedure body, the following instruction set would have to be generated to store the return address and the values of the formal parameters:

```
ALLOCATE,4 + x          {x is space for fixed-length items}
STO,⟨actrec loc 1⟩      {store return address}
STO,⟨actrec loc 4⟩      {store replacestr}
STO,⟨actrec loc 3⟩      {store cursor}
STO,⟨actrec loc 2⟩      {store symb}
```

A special ALLOCATE instruction is generated first. It is responsible for allocating a new activation record on top of the run-time stack as was described in Chap. 9. Enough space is allocated initially to hold the return address, the three formal parameters, and "x" amount of space of the other fixed-length data items that are declared locally in the procedure. The return address and the values for the formal parameters are loaded next. Notice that the argument values of the calling procedure are stored in the activation record (abbreviated actrec) in the same order as their corresponding parameters in the parameter list, even though they are placed on the stack in reverse order. The proper association between the loaded values on the operand stack and the stored location of the formal parameters in the run-time stack must be handled at the time the definition of the procedure is compiled.

An attributed translation specification for a procedure call is as follows:

```
1 ⟨proc call⟩ ::= ⟨call head⟩↑i,z ⟨arguments⟩↓i,z @genjsr↓i
2 ⟨call head⟩↑i,z ::= call ⟨id⟩↑n @lookupproc↓n↑i,z
3 ⟨arguments⟩↓i,z ::=@chklength↓i,z
4                    |( ⟨arg list⟩↓i,z )
5 ⟨arg list⟩↓i,z ::= ⟨expr⟩↑t @chktype↓t,i,z↑z ⟨exprs⟩↓i,z
6 ⟨exprs⟩↓i,z ::= @chklength↓i,z
7                |, ⟨expr⟩↑t @chktype↓t,i,z↑z⟨exprs⟩↓i,z
```

The action routine *lookupproc* in production 2 takes as input the name of the called procedure (assigned to the attribute n as synthesized from ⟨id⟩), looks up its location in the symbol table, and returns the symbol table location i and the number of formal parameters z that are defined for the procedure. These values are inherited in the *chktype* routine in productions 5 and 7. The procedural specifications for *lookupproc* and *chktype* are as follows:

Procedure lookupproc(n)
    string n; integer i,z
    i ← lookup(n) {search symbol table}
    if i < 1
    then call error ('Procedure' ∘ n ∘
                  'not previously defined', statno)
        call errorrecovery(panic)
          return (i ← 0; z ← 0)
    else return (i; z ← symbtbl.dim[i])
             {z is the number of formal parameters}
  end lookupproc

Procedure chktype(t,i,z)
    string t; integer i,z
    if z < 1
    then call error('Number of arguments is greater' ∘
           'than the number of formal parameters' ∘
           'for procedure' ∘ symbtbl.name[i], statno)
        return(z)
    if t ≠ symbtbl.type[i]
    then call error('Type mismatch between argument' ∘
           'and formal parameter for' ∘
           symbtbl.name[i], statno)
    z ← z − 1 {decrease number of formal parameters
             remaining to be considered}
    return(z)
  end chktype

Observe that in the *lookupproc* routine, if the called procedure has not been previously defined, an error is emitted and the error recovery procedure is invoked. It is assumed, in this case, that the error recovery involves a panic mode recovery in which the entire call statement (i.e., what has been parsed to this point in the statement and the remainder of the call statement in the input source form) would be removed, thus enabling the parser to continue at the succeeding source statement. In this situation, the excising of the entire call statement is warranted because if parsing is allowed to continue, a cascade of semantic errors would result from the repeated invocation of the *chktype* action routine. This cascading would occur because the number and type of each formal parameter would not be defined.

The final action routine, *genjsr*, simply generates a JSR instruction whose branch location can be found in the symbol table (i.e., at symbtbl.addr[i]).

An attributed translation specification for a procedure definition statement is as follows:

```
1 ⟨proc defn⟩::= ⟨proc defn head⟩ @initcnt↑j
                   ⟨parameters⟩↓j↑k @emitstores↓k
2 ⟨proc defn head⟩::= procedure↑t ⟨id⟩↑n @tblinsert↓t,n
3 ⟨parameters⟩↓j↑k::= @echo↓j↑k
4                     |(⟨parm list⟩↓j↑k)
5 ⟨parm list⟩↓j↑l::= ⟨type⟩↑t : ⟨id⟩↑n @tblinsert↓t,n
                     @upcnt↓j↑k ⟨parms⟩↓k↑l
6 ⟨parms⟩↓j↑l::= @echo↓j↑l
7              |;⟨type⟩↑t : ⟨id⟩↑n @tblinsert↓t,n
                @upcnt↓j↑k ⟨parms⟩↓k↑l
```

When a procedure definition is compiled, information about the procedure and its formal parameters are stored in the symbol table. The insertion of this information begins with the action routine *tblinsert* as specified in productions 2, 5, and 6 in the previous grammar. A procedural description of *tblinsert* is as follows:

```
Procedure tblinsert(t,n)
    string t,n; integer hloc
    if lookup(n) > 0 {name is already in symbol table?}
    then call error('Redefinition of '∘ n ∘' is illegal',
              statno)
    else {enter new name in symbol table}
        hloc ← hashfctn(n) {find open location in hash table}
        hashtbl[hloc] ← s
        symbtbl.name[s] ← n
        symbtbl.type[s] ← t
        s ← s + 1 {increment global symbtbl index s}
    end tblinsert
```

In the routine *tblinsert*, a check is made to ensure that the name identifier being inserted is not already in the table. If it is not, it is inserted, its type is inserted, and the index to the symbol table (i.e., s) is incremented in preparation for the next insertion. Note that we have assumed that both s and symbtbl are global to this action routine.

It is necessary to maintain a count of the number of formal parameters in the procedure definition to ensure that the number of formal parameters and the number of arguments in a procedure call match. The count also indicates the proper number of STO instructions to be emitted for storing parameter values. Therefore, two action routines, one to initialize the count and one to update the count, are specified in productions 1, and 5 and 7, respectively. Their simple procedural descriptions are as follows:

Procedure initcnt   **Procedure** upcnt(j)
    return(0)   integer j
    end initcnt   return(j + 1)
                    end upcnt

Finally, the procedure *emitstores* is responsible for generating the object code necessary to allocate a new activation record, store the return address, and store the values for the formal parameters.

```
Procedure emitstores(k)
    integer k
    call emit1('ALLOCATE',k + 1)
    call emit1('STO',⟨ll,1⟩) {store return address}
    for i ← k + 1 downto 2 {store parameter values}
        call emit1('STO',⟨ll,i⟩)
    endfor
end emitstores
```

The ALLOCATE instruction creates a new activation record that is large enough to hold only the return address and formal parameters. Clearly, after all local variables are defined and their fixed-space requirements are known, the argument for the ALLOCATE instruction will have to be modified with a "fix-up" to handle the additional space required. These types of fix-ups are often necessary for a compiler in which code is generated in a single pass. In the generation of the store instructions, a lexic-level, order-number addressing scheme is assumed.

In our discussion of the procedure call statement, we have only described how pass-by-value parameter passing is handled. The other popular method of parameter passing, pass-by-reference, can be implemented in a manner very similar to that described for pass-by-value. Instead of loading the value of an argument, a reference (i.e., address) to an argument is passed. This address is then associated with the formal parameter such that any change to the value of the formal parameter inside the called procedure will automatically change the value of the argument outside the procedure. In the instance when the call argument is not a variable (e.g., a computed expression), a dummy location is set aside for the argument and a reference to this location is passed to the called procedure and associated with the corresponding formal parameter. Clearly, changes to a formal parameter for a dummy argument will not have any effect outside the called procedure.

The implementation of two other less-popular parameter passing techniques, pass-by-result and pass-by-name (referenced in Chap. 3), will not be described. These are much more complicated to implement and their specification will be left as an interesting exercise for the reader.

Return statements and procedure termination. The main semantic activities associated with procedure terminations, whether by explicit return statement or "falling off the end" of a procedure body, are as follows:

1. If the procedure is a functional procedure, emit instructions to store the value to be returned on the operand stack or at a previously allocated location in the run-time stack that is associated with the function (as was described in Chap. 9).
2. Emit an instruction to load the return address on top of the operand stack.
3. Emit a DEALLOCATE instruction to remove the activation record for the called procedure.
4. Emit an unconditional branch instruction to return to the calling procedure at the instruction following the point of invocation.

The placement of action routines in an attributed grammar specification for either a return statement or procedure termination statement (e.g. an end statement) is quite straightforward and is therefore omitted from our discussion.

11-6.6 Input and Output Statements

Traditionally, I/O statements are the most difficult to define from a semantic point of view, primarily because they depend so heavily on both the target machine's architecture and the operating system. This is why some language definitions are very vague about I/O specification, or even omit them altogether, as was the case in the specification of ALGOL 60. Nevertheless, in this subsection an effort is made to introduce some of the important factors or techniques that must be considered when generating semantics for input and output. We begin with an examination of input statements.

Input statements. In general, input is handled by either accepting a stream of character data or a set of previously stored records. Stream character data input is usually produced by a standard input device which today is typically a video display terminal. Record-at-a-time input is most often associated with external storage media such as a magnetic disk device.

Normally, in a multiuser system, input in the form of stream character data is first read into a special system-supplied buffer to assist in distributing the system demand among the users. It is then brought into the program area and converted as required to match the format specification that is given in the input statement or implied by the type of each input variable. As an illustration, consider the following input statement:

input name%c12, %x1, mark%d2, %x2, addr%c18;

where the % is used to delineate the input variable and the format associated with input data assigned to that variable. In this C language type of format specification, %cn means the next n elements from the data stream are to be treated as characters, %dn means the next n elements are digits, and %xn means the next n elements are to be ignored.

If the input stream contains the following data:

Johns,ƀK.M.ƀƀ87ƀƀ84ƀForestƀDriveƀƀƀ . . .

and the previous input statement is executed, the input variables name, mark, and addr will be assigned, respectively, the following values:

'Johns,ƀK.M.ƀ', 87 and '84ƀForestƀDriveƀƀƀ'

The following attributed translation specification illustrates what type of semantic actions might typically be required to handle input statements similar to the example just given.

```
1 ⟨input stat⟩::= input @setL↑L ⟨input list⟩ @resetL↑L
2 ⟨input list⟩::= ⟨input item⟩ ⟨input items⟩
3 ⟨input items⟩::=ε
4                |⟨var⟩↑t % ⟨format⟩↑r @inputitem↓t,r
                    ⟨input items⟩
5                |% x ⟨numb⟩↑n @movecur↓n ⟨input items⟩
6 ⟨input item⟩::= ⟨var⟩↑t % ⟨format⟩↑r @inputitem↓t,r
7                |% x ⟨numb⟩↑n @movecur↓n
8 ⟨format⟩↑r::= c↑r ⟨numb⟩↑n @genload↓n
9                |d↑r ⟨numb⟩↑n @genload↓n
```

The action routines *setL* and *resetL* in production 1 are used to indicate to the action routines invoked when compiling ⟨var⟩ that a reference to the input variable as opposed to the value of the variable is to be generated. *SetL* and *resetL* were described in Sec. 11-6.3. The *genload* routine (productions 8 and 9) simply emits a load immediate instruction that places the length of the input field, as assigned to the attribute n, on the operand stack. Notice that if an ⟨expr⟩ rather than ⟨numb⟩ is allowed in the format statement, the resulting semantics would be significantly more complicated. In particular, the *resetL* action routine would have to immediately precede the specification of each format statement because it is the value of the ⟨expr⟩ and not a reference that must be yielded. The *setL* routine would then be placed immediately after the ⟨format⟩ specification.

The *movecur* routine, used in productions 5 and 7, emits instructions to update a cursor associated with an input buffer by the number of characters specified in the x format field. This cursor is assumed to be stored at location $IN.

A procedural specification of *movecur* follows:

```
Procedure movecur(n)
    integer n
    call emit1('LOADI',n)
    call emit1('LOAD',$IN) {load input cursor value}
    call emit('ADD')
    call emit1('STO',$IN) {store updated cursor}
end movecur
```

The *inputitem* routine is responsible for generating code that assigns a portion of the input stream to the next input variable according to the format specifications given for that input variable. It first determines if the type of the input variable matches the format specification—if it does not an error is generated. Next, if the type of the input variable is numeric, it is necessary to convert the specified portion of the input character stream to an internal numeric format. Once the conversion (if necessary) is done, the resulting value is stored at the address associated with the input variable. Finally, the input buffer cursor, $IN, is updated. The procedural specification for *inputitem* follows:

```
Procedure inputitem(t,r)
    string t,r
    if (t = 'string' & r ≠ 'c') or (t = 'int' & r ≠ 'd')
    then call error ('Mismatch in type of input variable'
                  ∘ 'and format specification', statno)
        call errorrecovery(local)
        return
    call emit1('LOAD',$IN) {load input buffer cursor}
    if t = 'string'
    then call emit('INPC') {create string descriptor}
    else call emit('CONVCI') {convert to integer}
    call emit1('STO',@$TOP-3) {store at addr of input var}
    call emit('POP') {remove value from stack top}
    call emit('ADD') {add $IN and width of format specification}
    call emit1('STO',$IN) {update input buffer cursor}
    call emit('POP')
    call emit('POP')
end inputitem
```

An explanation of some of the details of *inputitem* is necessary. First, in the event of a type and format mismatch error, the error recovery procedure is invoked with an argument of local. This implies that the recovery mechanism should try to recover by removing portions of the stack and source string associated only with the current input variable and its format specification. Panic mode recovery would "scrub" the whole input statement. Local mode recovery would remove only the offending input item and would continue to compile the remainder of the input statement in the hope of detecting all errors, not just the first error.

The pseudo machine instruction INPC does a number of things. It takes the character string as specified by its location (as stored on top of the operand stack) and its length (as stored second from the top of the operand stack) and copies this string into string space. It then forms a string descriptor for the string in string space and places this descriptor on top of the operand stack.

The pseudo machine instruction CONVCI converts the character representation of the numeric field located in the input stream to an integer representation. This field is defined by the position and length information stored in the top two positions of the operand stack. The resulting integer is stored on top of the operand stack.

The instruction "'STO',@$TOP − 3" stores the value (either string descriptor or integer) at the address of the input variable which at run-time should be found at the third location from the top of the operand stack. The remainder of the *inputitem* procedure should be fairly obvious.

From our discussion thus far it should be noticable that handling I/O semantics is not clean. It becomes much more messy when we begin to consider other data types (e.g., floating-point or fixed-point numbers). However, it is hoped we have given some appreciation of the problems. In particular, it should be clear that several assembly-level routines or pseudo code instructions are necessary to handle all the conversions that are required to take the input data and convert it to its proper internal form. Conversion from character representation to internal form is necessary for input and conversion from internal form to character representation is needed for output.

The major difference between record at a time input and stream input as just described is twofold. First, records are usually stored in their internal form. They are not converted to an external character representation that is associated with standard input or output devices such as a terminal or printer. The second major difference is that only one input variable is specified in an input statement, and it is usually a record (or structure) variable. An example of a record-oriented input statement is as follows:

    read studentrec;

where studentrec might be defined as

    record studentrec:
      integer(6) stid,
      record name:
        string(12) sname,
        string(1) init,
        string(15) surname
      endrec;
      string(4) college,
      integer(2) year,
      real(3,1) average
    endrec;

The process of reading a record generally involves bringing a set of records from a file into an input buffer area that is supplied by the operating system. From the input buffer, an individual record is then moved to the program area and its contents are assigned to the individual fields of the record structure as declared in the program. At this point the program can process the record as necessary.

Output statements. The semantics associated with output statements involve, for the most part, a reverse process to that outlined for input statements. For stream-oriented output, the internal form of the variables or expressions in the output statement must be converted to the machine's standard external character representation (usually ASCII or EBCDIC) and then concatenated together as a line of character data to be output. The presence of literal text in the format specification also makes an output statement somewhat unique from an input statement.

Writing record-oriented data is also very much the reverse process to reading a record. When writing a record, information in the record is first placed in a system-supplied output buffer. If the file is created sequentially, the record is kept in the buffer until enough other records of the same type are written to fill the buffer. At this point the full buffer is written to the file in external memory. If a record is written to a direct (sometimes called random) file, the contents of the output buffer are written immediately to the file in external memory.

11-6.7 Compiler Aids

Here we examine some of the semantic activities that must be provided when implementing various aids in support of the processes of compilation and program execution. The aids that we consider are facilities for debugging, program tracing, and system development support. These aspects of compilation are sometimes referred to as pragma.

It is common for most languages to provide a facility to assist the programmer in debugging his or her program. Usually, this facility allows the programmer to specify certain variables (we refer to them as debug variables) whose values are to be output automatically during specified stages of execution. Typically, the value for a debug variable is only output when the value of the variable is altered.

There are primarily two ways of specifying debug variables: by using executable comments or separate in-line statements. The following examples illustrate the two approaches:

/ *# #x,y turns on debugging for x and y in this comment */
    ⋮

/* ~ ~x,y turns off debugging for x and y in this comment */

and

    debug on x, y;
       ⋮

    debug off x, y;

The disadvantage of using the executable comment approach is that it requires each comment to be parsed to determine if a pragma is contained in its midst. A second parser for comments must be created. The in-line approach allows the debug statement to be part of the language and hence only a single parser is required.

    The semantic actions for supporting debugging are fairly simple. They involve updating the symbol table to identify (usually with a flag field) when a variable is selected to be a debug variable. Each time the compiler determines that the value of a debug variable is to be altered, extra code is generated that outputs this new value along with the source statement number in which the value is changed. When the debugging for a variable is turned off, the special flag field in the symbol table for the variable is set to false. Notice that debugging aids are rather static aids in the sense that they apply only to the compile-time structure of the program and not to the execution sequence of the program. A potentially more powerful compiler aid, variable tracing, does depend on the dynamic behaviour of the program at run time.

    An example of a trace specification might be as follows:

    trace on x, y;
       ⋮

    trace off x, y;

Its syntax is very similar to that of the in-line debugging specification given earlier. The semantic action differs appreciably, however. When a variable is marked for tracing at compile time, all occasions in which that variable is altered must be recorded. On a separate pass of the compiler, code must be generated that will output the altered value of the trace variable if at run time the trace is on. Clearly, the overhead associated with tracing is appreciably greater than that for debugging both at compile time and run time.

    Notice that, relatively speaking, tracing is not a major additional overhead in an interpretive environment. An interpreter can quite easily check, at the time a variable's value is altered, whether the variable is a trace variable. An indication of whether a variable is currently being traced can easily be kept in the symbol table that typically is maintained by the interpreter at execution time.

    The final compiler aid that we examine briefly is the system development support environment. In such environments the compiler is only one component, albeit a very important one. Central to a system development support environment is a database that contains descriptions and definitions of the various modules and program variables of the system being developed. This database supports the easy recompilation and linkage of separately compilable modules. In essence, most of the semantic activity associated with such environments involves the database actions needed to maintain the extended symbol table, which is really a sophisticated data dictionary.

System development support environments promise to be increasingly more important in the future. The Ada support environment (see in Chap. 3), is an excellent example.

CHAPTER EXERCISES

1 Develop a grammar for an arithmetic expression. Then develop three compilers: one using recursive descent, another using bottom-up parsing with simple precedence or LALR(1), and another using top-down parsing with LL(1) for your expression language. Compare and contrast the compilers you developed.

2 List the advantages of attributed translation. List any disadvantages you feel exist.

3 Develop an attributed translation specification for a DO-WHILE construct in which an EXIT statement can be placed inside the loop that will allow unconditional exiting from the loop to the statement immediately following the loop body. Give a procedural specification of all action routines used in the attributed translation grammar.

4 Develop an attributed translation specification for a functional procedure with pass-by-reference parameter passing. Be sure to give procedural specifications of all action routines.

5 Develop an attributed translation specification for a procedure call with either pass-by-result or pass-by-name parameter passing.

6 Develop an attributed translation specification for the compilation of a record declaration. Choose any syntactic variant of a record you wish.

7 Develop an attributed translation specification for a stream-oriented output statement. Be sure to describe the details of any pseudo instructions or assembly-level macros used to implement "x-to-character" conversions.

BIBLIOGRAPHY

Bochman, G. V.: "Semantic Evaluation from Left to Right," *Communications of the ACM*, Vol. 19, No. 2, 1976, pp. 55–62.

Gries, D.: *Compiler Construction for Digital Computers*, Toronto: John Wiley & Sons, 1971.

Knuth, D. E.: "Semantics of Context-Free Languages," *Math Systems Theory*, Vol. 2, No. 2, June 1968, pp. 127–145.

Lewis, P. M. II, D. J. Rosenkrantz, and R. E. Stearns: *Compiler Design Theory*, Reading, Mass.: Addison-Wesley, 1976.

Woods, W. A.: "Context Sensitive Parsing," *Communications of the ACM*, Vol. 13, No. 7, 1970, pp. 437–445.

TWELVE

CODE OPTIMIZATION

This chapter presents a number of machine-independent optimization strategies —that is, strategies that can be applied to language constructs irrespective of what target machine the generated code is to be executed upon. Examples of machine-independent optimization strategies that will be described in Sec. 12-2 through 12-5 are folding, redundant-subexpression elimination, and various optimizations within loops. Initially, these optimizations are presented as they would apply within a program block. Program flow analysis is introduced in Sec. 12-6 as a method of achieving more global forms of optimization.

12-1 INTRODUCTION

It is well known that the price-performance ratio for computers has dropped dramatically since the inception of the first computers and most particularly in the last 5 years. It may therefore be argued that it is not worth expending a significant effort to produce good code, that is, code that executes rapidly and/or takes up very little space. History has shown, however, that the complexity of the applications and systems developed on computers has grown to match the rapidly decreased price-performance curve and that even on very powerful machines it is not cost-effective to be executing poor code.

Optimization is the strategy of examining intermediate code as produced by or during the code-generation phase with the aim of producing code that runs very efficiently. With the recent popularity of personal microcomputers, the production of code that uses very little space has also been a goal for some optimizers; nevertheless, the main emphasis has traditionally been and will be in this chapter on the generation of very fast executing code.

Some optimization strategies can be applied independent of a particular target machine, while others such as register-allocation strategies can be adapted only to a specific machine architecture. These machine-dependent optimizations will be examined in Chap. 13.

To begin the discussion of machine-independent optimization as it applies in a local context, it is necessary to introduce what is meant by a basic block.

12-2 BASIC BLOCKS

In the next three sections a number of the more common optimizing techniques are introduced. Initially, the discussion is concerned only with "local optimizations," that is, optimizations that can be implemented on a local basis within a program source text so that no information dealing with program flow is utilized. Program flow information is required for the more extensive optimizations that are referred to as global optimizations, a topic discussed in Sec. 12-6.

It is possible to restrict an optimizer's range of application to single program statements and perform strictly intrastatement optimization. However, this is

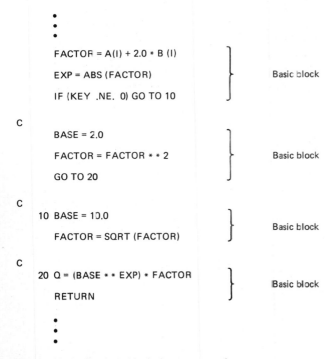

```
      •
      •
      •
      FACTOR = A(I) + 2.0 * B (I)
      EXP = ABS (FACTOR)              Basic block
      IF (KEY .NE. 0) GO TO 10

C
      BASE = 2.0
      FACTOR = FACTOR * * 2           Basic block
      GO TO 20

C
   10 BASE = 10.0
                                      Basic block
      FACTOR = SQRT (FACTOR)

C
   20 Q = (BASE * * EXP) * FACTOR
                                      Basic block
      RETURN
      •
      •
      •
```

Figure 12-1 The basic blocks in a program fragment.

often felt to be too restrictive, since many quite easily handled optimizations are missed. It is more common to focus the optimization process on a somewhat more extensive local text. The customary choice for a local context is the basic block.

The *basic block* is a program fragment that has only one entry point and whose transfer mechanism between statements is that of proceeding to the next statement. An alternate definition (Gries, 1971) states that a basic block is a sequence of program statements organized in such a way that all transfers to the block are to the first statement in the block. Also, if any statement in the block is executed, all statements in the block are executed. Figure 12-1 illustrates the decomposition of a part of a FORTRAN program into its constituent basic blocks.

Using the basic block, rather than the single statement, as the primary region that an optimizer concentrates on provides more information upon which to base optimizing decisions. This generally leads to the generation of better-quality code.

12-3 FOLDING

The first optimization technique that we discuss is folding with constant propagation. From the outset, it must be noted that this technique is of a somewhat different nature than the other techniques which follow in this chapter. Although folding is still oriented to the basic blocks that are the components of the source program, this method can in some instances be applied over the entire program without requiring a separate phase of optimization analysis.

Folding is the replacement of expressions that can be evaluated at compile time by their computed values. That is, if the values of all the operands of an expression are known to the compiler at compile time, the expression can be replaced by its computed value.

For example, the statement

$$A = 2 + 3 + A + C$$

could be replaced under these conditions by the statement

$$A = 5 + A + C$$

where the value "5" has replaced the expression "2 + 3."

Constant propagation is simply folding applied in such a way that values known at compile time to be associated with variables are used to replace certain uses of these variables in the translated program text. Thus the program fragment written (perhaps to enhance clarity) as

$$PI = 3.141592$$
$$D\_TO\_R = PI/180.0$$

can be rewritten as

    PI = 3.141592
    D_TO_R = 3.141592/180.0

Furthermore, another application of folding eventually yields

    PI = 3.141592
    D_TO_R = 0.0174644

Note that each occurrence of PI or D_TO_R can be replaced by its associated value in all subsequent statements up to a statement at which the variable is redefined. In Sec. 12-4 we examine other optimization procedures which will allow us to delete the assignment statements that initially define the two variables.

From the previous example, it is easy to see that folding allows a programmer to assign meaningful names to constants without introducing inefficiencies.

It was mentioned earlier that folding can be applied to the entire program in a way that does not require an additional pass in the analysis phase. In fact, it is commonly performed during the production of intermediate-language code. During this phase, each of these operands can be examined to determine whether or not it is a constant or a value which is currently defined for such an operand. Appropriate replacements are then made easily as the intermediate code is produced.

It should be noted that extensive use of the algebraic laws of commutativity and associativity may be required in order to uncover some of the foldable subexpressions. For example, the expression

    5 + A + B + 7

would require that its operands and operators be examined in the light of these laws in order to discover that the expression can really be represented as

    12 + A + B

Note, however, that the sequence

    A = 1
    B = 2
    C = 5 + A + B + 7

would give rise to no problems. The operands of

    5 + A + B + 7

can simply be summed as the grammatical reductions are made. Because of constant propagation, the variables A and B already have values which can be substituted as the entire expression is folded.

Folding is commonly thought of as a local optimization technique mainly because it can easily be performed with respect to the basic block currently being parsed. Certainly, a folding operation can take place involving a variable that is common to a set of contiguous blocks in a program. The detection of such situations is not easily incorporated as part of the basic parsing step, however. Only after a global flow analysis is performed can it be decided which values can still be folded when a particular block is entered. Unfortunately, global flow analysis is a complex activity, as will be illustrated in Sec. 12-6. Therefore, during the initial code-generation phase it is often assumed that all variables which are candidates for folding become nonfoldable upon the completion of the initial compilation of a block.

As an example of the type of error that can occur if this restriction to basic blocks is not followed, consider the program segment

$$I = 0$$
$$10 \quad I = I + 1$$
$$\vdots$$
$$\text{IF (I.LT.10) GO TO 10}$$

If this segment is blindly subjected to folding, without observing boundaries between basic blocks, the segment becomes

$$I = 0$$
$$10 \quad I = 1$$
$$\vdots$$
$$\text{IF (1.LT.10) GO TO 10}$$

Instead of a nice, simple loop which would execute ten times, the program has now a loop which never terminates.

The technique of folding is usually applied only to unsubscripted variables. The reason for this is that it is sometimes impossible to determine whether or not two array references refer to the same element. As an example, consider the following program fragment:

$$\vdots$$
$$A(I) = 0.0$$
$$\vdots$$
$$B = 2.0 * A(J)$$
$$\vdots$$

If at compile time the value of I is known (say, 3) but J is unknown, then the assumption that the value 0.0 is associated with A(3) does not provide any assistance in the compile-time evaluation of the expression $2.0 * A(J)$. The variable A(J) can be referring to the third element of the array (assuming that indexing starts at 1), but it can also be referring to some other element. In the absence of any information about the value of J, no folding can be done for $2.0 * A(J)$, and the association of the value 0.0 with A(3) has been of no help.

It may be construed from the previous discussion that an array can be handled properly if each element of the array is treated as a simple variable (i.e., a variable containing a single value). This is not the case, however, as is shown in the following example:

$$\vdots$$

$$A(J) = 0$$

$$\vdots$$

Assume that at compile time the value of J is unknown. The assignment of a value 0 to A(J) is an association; however, it is an association with an unknown element of A. Any previous associations of values with elements of A must now be disregarded by necessity, since this new association can potentially invalidate any of the old associations.

Folding can be implemented during the initial code-generation phase by making use of additional fields in the symbol-table entries for unsubscripted variables. These fields would contain the following:

1. A flag indicating whether or not an association with a constant value currently exists for this variable.
2. The constant that is currently associated with the variable, if such a constant exists.

For the purpose of clarity in the following discussion, the internal form into which the program is being translated during the initial code-generation process is considered to be in the form of tree structure as described in Chap. 10. During the folding process, certain nodes in this tree will have values attached to them. These values are the constant values (or evaluated expressions) that have been determined at compile time and are being propagated through the basic block.

Folding can be accomplished by intercepting parse tokens as they are being presented for reduction according to the rules of grammar in a bottom-up parse. These tokens are examined to determine whether or not folding can be performed. If it can, the appropriate modifications are made to the tree structure being formed or to the symbol-table entries associated with simple variables. For top-down parsing, folding can take place at the time the appropriate production rules are applied for foldable expressions. Tree modification can occur when the associated semantic routines are invoked.

If the token being parsed represents a simple variable, the symbol-table entry for that variable must be examined. If a constant value is currently associated with the variable, the leaf node generated for that variable in the tree has this constant value associated with it.

When the tokens representing an assignment operation have all been collected by the parser and are finally released for reduction according to some grammatical rule of the form

$$\langle assignment \rangle ::= \langle var \rangle = \langle expr \rangle$$

the $\langle expr \rangle$ operand of the assignment operation has already been parsed. If the node generated to represent this expression has a constant associated with it, and if the variable being assigned to is a simple variable, then the symbol-table entry for that variable must be modified. The value of the constant must be stored and the flag must be set to indicate that there is a constant currently established.

On the other hand, if there is no compile-time known value associated with the expression, the symbol-table entry for the variable (assuming it is a simple variable) must have the flag cleared. The assignment operation in this case is associating an unknown value with the variable.

When the tokens representing the evaluation of an expression are released for reduction by grammatical rules of the form

$$\langle \text{term} \rangle ::= \langle \text{term} \rangle + \langle \text{factor} \rangle$$

the two operands (or one operand, in the case of a unary operation) have already been parsed and their tree nodes generated. If all the operand nodes have values associated with them, these values are used to compute the result of the operation. The subtrees representing the operands are pruned from the tree; they have served their purpose of specifying the computations to be performed. The root node in the tree which represents the operation performed on the operands is replaced by a leaf node. The constant value of the replaced expression associated with this leaf node is the constant value computed for the expression.

On the other hand, if any one or more of the operands does not have a value associated with it, no constant propagation can be accomplished. In this case, the parser simply generates the root node representing the operation symbol. No value is associated with this node.

It is in the situation where one or more operands do not have constant values associated with them that the rules of associativity and commutativity may profitably be applied in order to propagate constants as much as possible. This would involve transformations applied to the subtrees of the operation node. For example, the tree fragment of Fig. 12-2a which represents the expression $(2 * I) * 3$ (where the value of I is not known) cannot be evaluated any further. Since multiplication is associative, however, this expression is equivalent to $2 * (I * 3)$, and by the commutativity rule the latter expression is equivalent to $2 * (3 * I)$. By applying the associativity rule once again, the expression $(2 * 3) * I$ can be formed. Thus appropriate use of the commutativity and associativity rules can transform the tree fragment of Fig. 12-2a into that of Fig. 12-2b. The latter form of the expression is suitable for additional folding to yield the final tree form as shown in Fig. 12-2c.

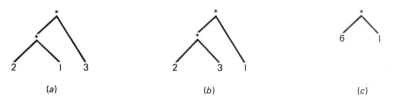

(a)   (b)   (c)

Figure 12-2 Effect of associativity and commutativity rules on constant propagation.

The steps involved in implementing folding as an optimization technique can be presented in the form of the following informal algorithm.

Algorithm FOLD. Given the reduced form of an assignment operation of the form A = EX, arithmetic or logical expressions of the form EX1 op EX2, or the parse of a simple variable represented as A, this algorithm implements the technique of folding just discussed. For convenience, the existence of a number of auxiliary subalgorithms is assumed. In the following discussion a special value NULL, which cannot be considered as a foldable value, is assumed to exist. The subalgorithms are:

1. LOOKUP(A, k) which searches the symbol table for the simple variable A and returns in k either the constant or the value NULL.
2. CLEAR(A) which clears the symbol flag entry for the variable A and SET(A, k) sets the symbol flag entry and stores the constant value k in the symbol-table entry for A.
3. CHECK(N, k) which examines node N and returns in k either the constant value associated with that node or the value NULL.
4. DELETE(N) which deletes node N (and any subtrees) from the tree structure.
5. CREATE (node-type, k, operand-list) which creates either a leaf node (referred to as leaf-A), in which case the operand-list is NULL, or a root node of the proper type with the items in the operand-list considered to be subtrees. The value of k (either NULL or a constant value associated with the node) is attached to the newly created node.

In addition, the appropriate routines to perform transformations based on associative and commutative operations are assumed to exist.

1. [Reduction of a simple variable]
   If the variable A is being parsed
   then If variable A is a simple variable
       then Call LOOKUP(A, k)
           Call CREATE(leaf-A, k, NULL)
           Exit
       else return to the parsing routine for regular processing
2. [Reduction of an assignment operation]
   If the form A = EX is being reduced
   then If variable A is a simple variable
       then Call CHECK(EX, k)
           If k is NULL
           then Call CLEAR(A)
           else Call SET(A, k)
           Call CREATE(root = , k, A, EX)
           Exit
       else return to the parsing routine for regular processing

3. [Reduction of an arithmetic or logical expression]
    If the form EX1 op EX2 is being reduced
    then Call CHECK(EX1, k1)   (a unary op is
          Call CHECK(EX2, k2)   handled in comparable
          If k1 and k2 are both not NULL   fashion)
          then k3 ← k1 op k2
               Call DELETE(EX1),
               Call DELETE(EX2)
               Call CREATE(leaf-constant, k3, NULL)
          else Call CREATE(root-op, NULL, EX1, EX2)
               apply associativity and commutativity to the newly
               created node for EX1 op EX2 to force folding if it can
               be performed
    Exit
    else return to the parsing routine for regular processing   □

This algorithm is intended to outline the special processing required to implement folding. Accordingly, when the conditions under which folding is to be done are not met, this algorithm immediately returns control to the parsing routine so that the regular processing can be performed. This would include parse stack operations to effect the reductions, node generation for the parse tree, etc.

On the other hand, if the conditions for folding are met, the appropriate node structure for the parse tree is generated under control of this folding algorithm. Consequently, when this algorithm finally returns control to the parsing routine, additional root-node generation for the parse tree is not required. The Exit and **return** phrases are used in the algorithm to differentiate between these two situations.

The application of these folding steps during the reductions associated with the parse of a string permits a simplified internal tree form to be constructed. For example, the program fragment (within a basic block):

$$\vdots$$

$$I = 1$$
$$J = 2*I + 1$$
$$A(2*I + J) = 0$$

$$\vdots$$

can be parsed, with folding operations applied, to yield the internal tree of Fig. 12-3. In the figure, the artificial semicolon simply serves to express statement association, as per the grammatical rule:

⟨statement list⟩::= ⟨statement⟩|⟨statement list⟩ ; ⟨statement⟩

The intermediate sequence of tree forms generated during this parsing and folding process are shown in Fig. 12-4, with the current symbol-table associations shown below the trees. Note that, in order to shorten this sequence of tree forms,

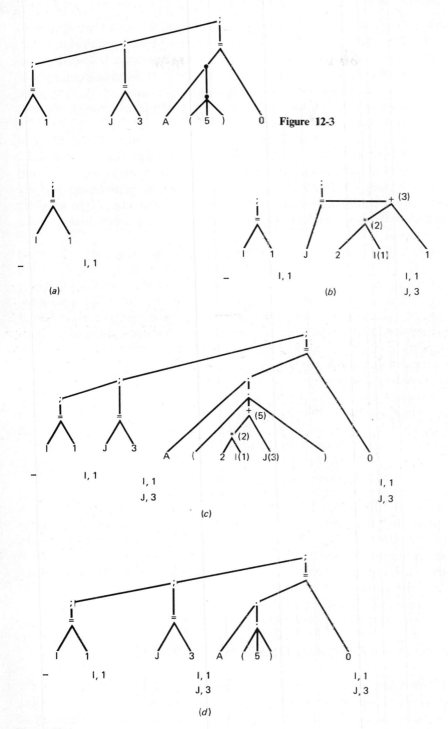

Figure 12-3

(a)

(b)

(c)

(d)

Figure 12-4

not all the intermediate steps of pruning operand subtrees have been illustrated within individual statements. Rather only their aggregate effects are shown.

Several cautionary notes should be kept in mind with respect to folding. First, the application of associativity and commutativity rules to floating-point expressions should not be done. Because of the finite precision of floating-point operations, these laws are not universally valid. For example, assuming a machine with only two decimal digits of precision, $(11 + 2.8) + 0.3 \neq 11 + (2.8 + 0.3)$, because $(11 + 2.8) + 0.3$ yields $(13) + 0.3$ which is 13, while $11 + (2.8 + 0.3)$ yields $11 + (3.1)$ which is 14. Computers have more than two digits of precision, but with suitable choices of operands, counterexamples to the associativity and commutativity rules for floating-point expressions can be constructed for any precision. Consequently, the use of associativity or a combination of associativity and commutativity can introduce additional round-off error when folding floating-point values.

Second, folding should not introduce into the program any additional errors at compile time. For example, folding expressions such as $3/0$ or $SQRT(-3.0)$ would result in an error and the immediate abortion of the compilation. These types of errors should be recognized in the folding process, and such expressions should not be evaluated. It might well be that a particular run-time execution of the program would never cause these errors to be generated. The folding optimizer should therefore produce a warning message so that the people responsible for this program can decide whether or not to eliminate the dangerous situation.

The preceding discussion has all been concerned with folding applied to the initial translation (during parsing) of the source program into an internal tree-structured form—a form which explicitly shows the computations to be performed and which is very suitable to optimizations. Folding can also be applied when generating other types of intermediate-language code. The basic strategy remains the same, namely, that of massaging the code as it is generated so as to remove unnecessary instructions and to eliminate storage references from operands and replace them with propagated constants.

Folding can also be applied in later phases of optimization. For example, it can be used after the movement of expressions and statements on the basis of global-control flow analysis. In such cases, the current internal form of the program (as modified by other optimizations) is again processed with the object of folding and propagating any new constant values available. The latter use of folding will be commented on when appropriate as part of the discussions of various other techniques of optimization.

12-4 REDUNDANT-SUBEXPRESSION ELIMINATION

Another operation which is commonly applied to yield improved code is the elimination of redundant expressions. By means of this technique, an expression, once computed, is reused rather than recomputed. This will reduce the number of operations that must be performed when the program is eventually executed.

In terms of the tree structure representing the translated source program, what this means is that only one copy of each distinct node is retained rather than the several copies of the same node as would be the case if expression redundancy were permitted. All instances involving this particular expression are represented by references to the one node that computes the expression. This policy of node sharing, however, converts the tree structure into a directed acyclic graph (DAG), a somewhat more complex data structure than a tree.

As is the case with folding, the elimination of redundancy is an operation that can be carried out at the local level and also at a global level using program-flow information. In this section the discussion will be confined to redundancy elimination at the local level.

To aid in redundancy elimination, the operands of expressions may be rearranged in a standard form. Often the law of commutativity is applied to order the operands so the recognition of identical expressions is simpler. This ordering is typically constants first, then scalar variables alphabetically, then array variables alphabetically, and then subexpression operands. The law of associativity can also be used, if circumstances are suitable, to group a series of operands together as the operands of an n-ary associative operator. The program segment

$$X = C + 3 + A + 5$$
$$Y = 2 + A + 4 + C$$

can be rearranged to give

$$X = 3 + 5 + A + C$$
$$Y = 2 + 4 + A + C$$

which allows the constants to be folded and the recognition that the second occurrence of $A + C$ is redundant.

The use of a bit flag can also permit the rearrangement of the operands of certain noncommutative operators. For example, $B - A$ or B/A can be treated as $A - B$ and A/B as long as the bit flag is set, denoting that the operands are reversed relative to their intended order and that an additional inverting operation is required to generate the original intended value.

Subtraction can also be handled in terms of the unary minus, since $B - A$ is the same as $B + \theta A$ (using θ to denote unary minus), which could then be treated as $\theta A + B$. In a similar fashion, a unary reciprocation operation can be used to express the expression B/A. Using this approach, B/A becomes $B * \lambda A$ (with λ representing the unary reciprocation operator) or equivalently $\lambda A * B$.

This type of operand permutation can be applied as an aid to folding and common subexpression recognition. The use of the law of associativity, however, requires that a number of subexpressions be examined while carrying out the search for a sequence of the same associative operator. This means that if folding and common subexpression recognition are to make use of associative and commutative permutations, then most of the optimizing transformations cannot simply take place with the parsing of a single operation (e.g., $+$, $-$) and its associated operands. Instead, the optimizing transformation must be delayed until the entire expression has been parsed.

This, however, is not a major difficulty. It simply means that the internal tree structure is left untouched by optimizing techniques (except for replacement of simple variables by constant values currently associated with them) until the complete expression is recognized and reduced. Once such a reduction takes place, the tree representation of the expression is subjected to the permutation of operands so that a standard order, as just described, can take place. Folding and constant propagation are then applied as described previously. At the point at which folding has been completed and the possibly modified tree structure has been formed, redundant subexpressions can be eliminated.

Because the elimination of redundant expressions is being performed within a basic block (which can contain assignments altering the value of variables appearing later as operands in the block), it is not sufficient merely to recognize syntactically identical expressions. Changes to the values of operands between earlier and later operations in the block must also be taken into account.

For example, in the program segment

$$\vdots$$

$$P = B + I$$
$$Q = A + B$$
$$A = Q**2 + 2$$
$$C(1) = A + B + P$$

$$\vdots$$

the second appearance of the expression $A + B$ is not redundant. Between the first and second appearances of $A + B$, there has been an assignment to one of the operands, namely, A of this subexpression. The second occurrence of $A + B$ must be associated with a new computation of the value of $A + B$ because of the altered value of A.

As an example illustrating the effect of redundant-expression elimination, consider the following program segment:

$$\vdots$$

$$J = 2*D + 3;$$
$$D = D*2;$$
$$J = J + D;$$

$$\vdots$$

The parse-tree structure formed by this sequence of statements is given in Fig. 12-5a. Sequence numbers have been attached to the nonleaf nodes in the tree; these numbers simply give the position of the nodes in a postorder traversal of the tree. A directed acyclic graph (or DAG) representation of this tree is depicted in Fig. 12-5b. In this representation, a reference to a previously computed expression or variable is depicted as an arc to a given node provided that this previous value has not been altered since its last reference. For example, the

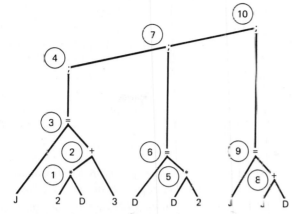

Figure 12-5a An example parse tree of a sequence of expressions.

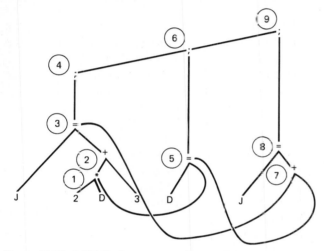

Figure 12-5b A DAG of a sequence of expressions.

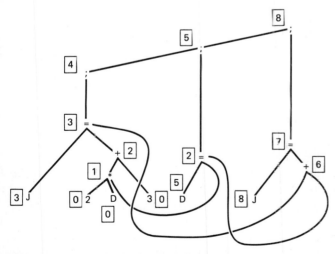

Figure 12-5c Index-number assignment for the DAG of a sequence of expressions.

assigned value for the variable J in the first statement of the example is connected via an arc to the reference for J in the third statement. Note that the expression $2*D$, assigned the sequence number ①, is referred to next in assignment statement sequence number ⑤ and a dependency arc between the two statements is created. Clearly, it is assumed that commutativity is applied in this case. Such a dependency arc can be drawn provided that none of the variables involved in the expression are altered from one instance of the expression to the next within a block.

In order to express the dependencies of the one expression on another and on changes of operand values, *index numbers* are associated with the variables in the expressions and also with the nodes that express an operation to be performed. An index number serves to indicate the active range of a computed value of a variable.

As the redundant-subexpression-elimination algorithm proceeds, it converts the nodes of the tree representing a basic block into the nodes of a directed acyclic graph (DAG) representing the block. It does this by making use of the index numbers associated with the variables and with the nodes generated for the DAG. In order to explain how the index numbers are computed, some preliminary discussion of node *sequence numbers* is required.

The internal nodes in the tree structure can be assumed to have sequence numbers associated with them. These sequence numbers are simply the position numbers in a sequence of nodes that is derived by a postorder traversal of the tree (see Tremblay and Sorenson, 1984). These tree nodes are processed by the redundancy-elimination algorithm to form a DAG. Some of the tree nodes are found to be redundant, while others are retained in the DAG structure. The sequence numbers of the nodes accepted into the DAG structure are simply the numbers indicating the order in which the DAG nodes are formed. Because the tree nodes are processed by the algorithm in their postorder sequence (i.e., by their tree sequence numbers), the sequence number of a DAG node is less than or equal to the sequence number of the corresponding tree node. Until the first redundant tree node has been encountered, DAG-node sequence numbers are the same as their corresponding tree-node sequence numbers. After the first redundant tree node has been found, a DAG-node sequence number is less than its corresponding tree-node sequence number. This is illustrated in Fig. 12-5*b*, in which the first redundant node has a sequence number of 5.

Index numbers are assigned to variables and to nodes in the DAG according to the following rules:

1. The index number of a variable is the sequence number of the DAG node which last assigned a value to the variable, or zero if no assignment has yet been made to the variable in the current basic block.
2. The index number of an internal node is 1 + the largest index number of its operands.

The process of assigning index numbers takes place as the original tree structure is reduced to a DAG during the application of the common subexpression-elimination algorithm to be described shortly. Using the rules just discussed, the index numbers for our example set of statements would be assigned as shown in boxes in Fig. 12-5c.

Two aspects about this definition of index numbers should be elaborated upon. First, the definition of the index number of a variable holds for both simple variables and array variables. When any element of an array is assigned a value, the index number of the array variable is set equal to the sequence number of the DAG node corresponding to the assignment operation. Second, the definition of the index number of a node associated with an expression is interpreted to be extended to subscripted variable operands as well as simple variables or other subexpressions. In the case of an operand that is a subscripted variable, the index numbers of both the subscript expression and the array variable are considered, along with the index numbers of the other operands, in determining the largest index number associated with the node operands.

In the following small example the second array variable referenced is not a redundant common subexpression because one of its subscript variables, J, has been altered between references. This can be detected because the index numbers of the second subscript will not match in the two subexpressions:

$$X = A(I + 1, J);$$
$$J = I;$$
$$Y = A(I + 1, J);$$

Note that the definition of the index number of a node is such that the expression represented by the node is forced to be dependent (as it should be!) on the prior evaluation of its operands. Note also that it is the definition of the index number of a variable that encodes the fact that the current value of a variable has been altered. This coding can be used to ensure that all nodes referencing the variable will always result in the access of the most current value for that variable.

The algorithm to implement redundant-expression elimination operates in the following manner. A node from the tree structure is selected and its index number is computed according to the previous definition for index numbers. This node is then matched against the existing DAG nodes. If there is an identical DAG node, with the same index number as that computed for the tree node, then the tree node is redundant. On the other hand, if there is no matching DAG node, or if a matching DAG node does exist but does not have the same index number, then the tree node is not redundant and a new DAG node must be generated to represent it.

The algorithm processes tree nodes, one by one, forming new DAG nodes for the nonredundant tree nodes. Because the tree nodes are selected in order of their postorder traversal, all the operands of a node will be processed before the node itself is processed. Hence each operand that is a node itself will already be associated with some DAG node that computes the same expression as the operand.

As tree nodes are processed to form DAG nodes, an index number is created for each DAG node according to the two rules described earlier in this section.

In order to implement the redundant-subexpression-elimination algorithm, a number of subsidiary algorithms must be developed. The first of these algorithms determines the index number of an operand and replaces the operand, if it is a reference to a tree node, by a reference to a DAG node.

Algorithm OPERAND_INDEX(A, i). Given an operand A which represents either a constant, a simple variable, a subscripted variable, or an expression (i.e., a reference to a node in the tree structure), this algorithm computes i, the index number of A, recursively. The auxiliary functions assumed to be available are:

1. LOOKUP(A, i) which returns i, the index number of variable A (either a simple variable or an array variable) by searching the symbol-table entry for variable A;
2. RETRIEVE(A, i, j) which returns i, the index number for the expression node A which has a sequence number of j in the DAG being constructed.

1. [A is a constant]
       If operand A is a constant
       then i ← 0
           Return
2. [A is a simple variable]
       If operand A is a simple variable
       then Call LOOKUP(A, i)
           Return
3. [A is a subscripted variable]
       If operand A is a subscripted variable of the form $B[n_1, n_2, ..., n_t]$
       then Call LOOKUP(B, i1)
           Repeat for k = 1, 2, ..., t
               Call OPERAND_INDEX(n_k, i2)
               i1 ← MAX(i1, i2)
           Return
4. [A is an expression]
       Call RETRIEVE(A, i, j)
       Return   ☐

Steps 1 and 2 handle the cases where A denotes a constant and a simple variable, respectively. In both of these cases A remains unchanged. The third step corresponds to the subscripted variable case. A is altered if the subscript is an expression. Finally, step 4 is executed if A denotes an expression. Assuming A is a node with a sequence number j in the tree structure, this step returns the index number for A as it appears in the DAG that is being constructed.

Other auxiliary algorithms that are required are:

1. ASSIGN(A, i) which establishes the value i as the index number for variable A in the symbol-table entry for A;
2. CREATE(j, i, op, operand-list) which creates a DAG node with sequence number j and index number i—the DAG node represents the application of the operation op to the operands in the operand-list;
3. MARK(A, j) which attaches to tree node A a reference to the DAG node with sequence number j;
4. CHECK(A, j, k, i) which tests A, the current node under examination, for formal identity against the DAG nodes 1, 2,..., j − 1 and returns in k either the sequence number of a matching node with the matched node's index number in i or the value zero if no match is found (with i also set to zero).

The algorithm to implement the elimination of redundant subexpressions is expressed as follows:

Algorithm REDUNDANT. Given a tree T representing a basic block, this algorithm produces a directed acyclic graph D to represent the same block and then replaces tree T by DAG D. The auxiliary algorithms previously indicated are used to implement various subtasks of this algorithm.

1. [Associativity and commutativity permutations]
   Apply the laws of associativity and commutativity to the nodes of T to permit as many folding-operation simplifications to be performed as possible and to reorder the operands of the various subtrees of T into a standard order
   Let the resulting tree be T′
2. [Form tree sequence numbers]
   Perform a postorder traversal of tree T′, numbering the internal (nonleaf) nodes of T′ as they are visited during traversal with sequence numbers 1, 2,..., p
3. [Process T′ to form D]
   j ← 1
   Initialize variable index numbers in symbol-table entries to 0
   Repeat through step 5 for the nodes of tree T′ with sequence number
   t = 1, 2,..., p
4. [Copy node and compute index number for node]
   Let N be a node from tree T′ with sequence number t
   Form a copy of N, say, N′, having the form ⟨op⟩⟨operand-list⟩
   i ← 0
   Repeat for each operand A in the operand-list of N′
       Call OPERAND_INDEX(A, k)
       i ← MAX(i, k)
   i ← i + 1

5. [Test N′ against the j − 1 DAG nodes and process accordingly]
    Call CHECK(N′, j, k, s)
    If k > 0 and s = i
    then Call MARK(N, k)
    else Call CREATE(j, i, op, operand-list)
        Call MARK(N, j)
        If node N′ is an assignment to an operand variable A
          (either simple or array)
        then call ASSIGN(A, j)
        j ← j + 1
6. [Replace the tree by the DAG]
    Attach the DAG D consisting of the j − 1 nodes created during the looping through step 5 to the previous y constructed DAG struc-ture. The new DAG D replaces tree T′ that was formed in step 1 as a replacement for original tree T   □

Upon exiting Algorithm **REDUNDANT**, the tree T which was initially formed to represent the current basic block has been converted into a DAG D. This DAG D is attached to the previous DAGs, thus forming one DAG representing all basic blocks processed to date (including the current block just finished).

To illustrate the elimination of redundant expressions, the parse-tree struc-ture given in Fig. 12-5 will be processed according to the algorithm previously outlined. The result of this processing is a new set of nodes with new sequence numbers forming a directed acyclic graph rather than a tree.

The progress of the processing is illustrated in Table 12-1. In the column "Node Being Processed" the sequence numbers are those leftmost sequence numbers of the original tree nodes. Nodes serving as operands are referred to by their sequence number. In all the other columns of the table, any use of sequence numbers is in terms of the new sequence numbers (i.e., the index numbers) being formed as the nonredundant nodes of the DAG are generated.

Note particularly the flexibility that is provided by the index numbers attached to the variables. When processing tree nodes ③ and ⑥ assignments are made to variables J and D, respectively. These variables then receive as new index numbers the sequence numbers of the nonredundant nodes that make these assignments (nodes ③ and ⑤, respectively, as depicted in Fig. 5-12c). (Thus, in further uses of these variables as operands, there is available to the code-genera-tion routines the required information specifying where the current values for the variables are to be found.) The index number of the variable specifies the node which last assigned the current value to the variable. The code-generation routines can use this information to acquire this current value from the register used for the assignment (if it is still present in the register) and thus, in certain cases, eliminate unnecessary load operations.

Additionally, the use of index numbers for variables can prevent unnecessary store operations. In the example just given, variable J is assigned a value by nonredundant DAG nodes ③ and ⑧. But since this program fragment is part of a basic block, only the value assigned by node ⑧ is associated with J when the

Table 12-1 A trace of the redundant-expression elimination algorithm for the construction of a DAG

	Index numbers				Result		
						Variables' index no.	
Node being processed	Left operand	Right operand	Match with previous node	DAG node	Computed DAG-node index	J	D
① 2*D	0	0	—	① 2*D	1	0	0
② ①+3	1	0	—	② ①−3	2	0	0
③ J=②	0	2	—	③ J=②	3	3	0
④ ;③	—	3	—	④ ;③	4	3	0
⑤ D*2	0	0	①	ref. ①	1	3	0
⑥ D=⑤	0	1	—	⑤ D=①	2	3	5
⑦ ④;⑥	4	2	—	⑥ ④;⑤	5	3	5
⑧ J+D	3	5	—	⑦ ③+⑤	6	3	5
⑨ J=⑧	3	6	—	⑧ J=⑦	7	8	5
⑩ ⑦;⑨	5	7	—	⑨ ⑥;⑧	8	8	5

block is exited. Accordingly, the store operation of node ③ is not necessary, and the code-generation routine can safely omit this store operation.

The resulting graph formed by the nonredundant nodes is given in Fig. 12-5. The sequence numbers attached to the nonleaf nodes are the numbers indicating the sequence in which these nonredundant nodes were generated, as illustrated in Table 12-1.

Normally, most programmers attempt to avoid excessive redundant expressions. No one deliberately tries to program inefficiently except perhaps to provide code that is more self-documenting. However, certain language structures, by the nature of their implementation, can introduce inefficiencies of this sort that are beyond the control of the programmer.

The prime example of such a language feature is array subscripting. It is likely that redundant subexpression elimination is of greatest value insofar as it optimizes such array references.

Arrays are stored in a linear form (i.e., as a vector of storage elements) while a source language permits a reference to array elements in terms of n subscripts (e.g., A[2, 1, 4] where n is 3). The problem arises in the mapping of the n-dimensional array reference in the source code onto the 1-dimensional storage structure used for the array.

The mapping function used to translate array references in the source code to references to the linear storage structure varies with the language. The semantic specifications of the language generally include a description of the intended linear storage structure. For example, FORTRAN specifies that arrays are stored in column major order (a sequential storing of the array that selects elements in such a manner that the leftmost subscript varies the fastest). PL/I, ALGOL, and most other languages, in fact, specify row-major order in which the rightmost subscript varies fastest. For example, the column-major mapping function for a 3-element by 4-element array A can be depicted as

Addr($A[i, j]$) = Addr($A[(j - 1)*3 + i]$) or Addr($A[3j + i - 3]$)
(in the source code)   (in the linear storage structure for A)

The indexing for both dimensions of the array is assumed to begin at 1. Using the same array A with indexing beginning at 1 again, the comparable row-major mapping function would be

Addr($A[i, j]$) = Addr($A[(i - 1)*4 + j]$) or Addr($A[4i + j - 4]$)

Similar mapping functions exist for all n-dimensional arrays ($n \geq 2$) and for all combinations of subscript upper and lower bounds. These mapping functions were discussed in Chap. 11.

Let us illustrate an example of a redundant expression that would not explicitly appear in the program yet can be eliminated through optimization by a compiler. Consider the simple segment of code that interchanges elements of two adjacent rows of a two-dimensional array X. Let us assume that X is 3 by 4 and is stored in column-major order such as in FORTRAN. The code can be written as

TEMP = X(I, J)
X(I, J) = X(I + 1, J)
X(I + 1, J) = TEMP

Assuming that, as a part of the translation process, the code to implement the mapping function is automatically inserted into the tree, then the nodes that might be formed after folding can be listed in a simplified form in their postorder traversal order as shown in Table 12-2.

There is a considerable amount of redundant computation in this list of nodes, but the programmer cannot normally reduce it by altering the source code. After eliminating redundant computations as in the previous example, the nodes remaining are those shown in Table 12-3. By operation count, the optimizing process has eliminated 3 multiplications and 5 additions/subtractions. In itself,

Table 12-2 Postorder traversal representation of unoptimized parse tree

①: 3 * J	⑦: ⑥ + I	⑬: ⑤ ; ⑫
②: ① + I	⑧: ⑦ − 3	⑭: 3 * J
③: ② − 3	⑨: 3 * J	⑮: ⑭ + I
④: TEMP = X[③]	⑩: ⑨ + I	⑯: ⑮ − 2
⑤: ; ④	⑪: ⑩ − 2	⑰: X[⑯] = TEMP
⑥: 3 * J	⑫: X[⑧] = X[⑪]	⑱: ⑬ ; ⑰

Table 12-3 Postorder traversal representation of optimized parse tree

(1) : 3 ∗ J	(6) : (2) − 2
(2) : (1) + I	(7) : X[(3)] = X[(6)]
(3) : (2) − 3	(8) : (5) ; (7)
(4) : TEMP = X[(3)]	(9) : X[(6)] = TEMP
(5) : ; (4)	(10) : (8) ; (9)

this may not be much of a saving, but it is quite significant if the statements are deeply nested inside many loop structures.

Note that in this example, both the law of associativity and unary minus identities were used as part of the folding optimization to generate tree nodes (11) and (16) in Table 12-2. Using the development of node (11) as an example, the mapping function 3j + i − 3 together with the parse tokens for X(I + 1, J) would actually generate the sequence of nodes

$$(9) : 3 ∗ J \quad (9)' : I + 1 \quad (10) : (9) + (9)' \quad (11) : (10) − 3$$

corresponding to the tree structure for ((3∗J) + (I + 1)) − 3 as shown in Fig. 12-6a. But by associativity, the expression ((3∗J) + (I + 1)) − 3 can be rewritten (((3∗J) + I) + 1) − 3. The latter expression can be rewritten, through the use of associativity together with the unary minus θ, as ((3∗J) + I) + (1 + θ3) (see Fig. 12-6b). Folding now can take place to yield ((3∗J) + I) + θ2. Replacing the addition of a unary minus by a subtraction yields nodes (9), (10), and (11) as listed in Table 12-2.

12-5 OPTIMIZATION WITHIN ITERATIVE LOOPS

The optimization techniques discussed thus far in the chapter have been applied to individual basic blocks. In this section we extend the discussion to include groups of basic blocks. The simple iterative loop which causes the repetitive

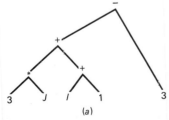

(a)

Figure 12-6a Tree structure for ((3 ∗ J) + (I + 1)) − 3.

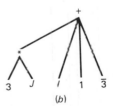

(b)

Figure 12-6b Tree structure for +[(3 ∗ J), I, 1, 03].

execution of one or more basic blocks becomes the prime area in which optimization will be considered. As with folding and redundant-expression elimination, we will not now describe how the loop-optimization techniques can be applied during global optimization.

In Sec. 12-5.1, the technique of *loop unrolling* will be discussed. In Sec. 12-5.2, *frequency reduction* is considered, and the final iterative-loop optimization technique, *strength reduction*, is examined in Sec. 12-5.3.

To begin our discussion of loop optimization, it is necessary to specify what is meant by a simple iterative loop. The simple iterative loops that will be considered are those which are clearly identifiable through language syntax. Most high-level programming languages provide a construct that permits the specification of a loop which is to be executed a chosen number of times. Figure 12-7 illustrates three iterative loops expressed in FORTRAN, ALGOL, and PL/I. Certainly, iterative loops can be expressed in a less obvious manner (e.g., using a labeled conditional statement and go to statements). We will not attempt to apply any optimization techniques to these types of loops, since they can be very difficult to detect.

In the discussion to follow the value that is initially assigned to the iterative-loop variable will be called the *initial value*, the value with which the loop variable's value is compared will be called the *terminal value*, and the value indicating the amount by which the loop variable is adjusted in each iteration will be called the *change value*.

It must be noted that the semantics of a simple iterative construct can vary from one language to another. For example, a FORTRAN IV DO-loop is always executed at least once, while ALGOL and PL/I loops can be executed zero or more times. In addition, there may be differing restrictions on the loop control parameters (e.g., only positive increments, only integer expressions) all of which must be considered when applying a loop optimization technique in a compiler

```
DO    10    I = 1, 25, 2

        <FORTRAN statements>

10   CONTINUE
```
                               (a)
```
FOR   I := 1 STEP 2 UNTIL 25 DO

BEGIN

        <ALGOL statements>

END;
```
                               (b)
```
DO    I = 1 TO 25 BY 2;

        <PL/I statements>

END;
```
                               (c)

Figure 12-7 Examples of (*a*) FORTRAN, (*b*) ALGOL, and (*c*) PL/I iterative loops.

for a given language. Also in some languages it is illegal to alter the loop variable inside the loop body, while in other languages such adjustments are legal. Throughout the discussion in this section we will assume that assignments to loop variables are illegal.

Iterative loops can be analyzed during the process of optimization by subdividing them into a number of distinct parts. These are:

1. An initialization part, in which the loop variable is assigned its initial value. This component constitutes a basic block that is executed once prior to beginning the execution of the statements in the loop body.
2. An adjustment part, in which the loop variable is incremented (or decremented) by a specified amount. The component can be viewed as the last basic block forming the iterative loop.
3. The test, in which the loop variable is tested to determine whether or not the termination condition has been met. The location of this component varies with the semantic interpretation of the loop. A loop that can be executed zero times performs the test prior to an execution of the iterated statements, whereas a loop that must be executed at least once has the test after an execution of the loop.
4. The loop body, which consists of one or more basic blocks formed from the statements that are to be executed repeatedly. Note that the adjustment and test components of the loop structure can be considered to be found in basic blocks along with other statements in the loop body.

Figure 12-8 illustrates how a FORTRAN DO-loop that computes $A_i = \sum_{n=1}^{i-1} n$, $1 \le i \le 25$, can be decomposed into the component parts just described. In the

```
NSUM = 0

DO 10 I = 1,25

    A(I) = NSUM

    NSUM = NSUM + I

10 CONTINUE
```

(a)

```
    NSUM = 0

    I = 1                           ← Initialization

9   A(I) = NSUM                     Iterated statements

    NSUM = NSUM + I                 of the DO-loop

    I = I + 1                       ← Adjustment

    IF (I.LE.25) GO TO 9           ← Test
```

(b)

Figure 12-8 (a) A FORTRAN program with a simple iterative loop. (b) Its decomposed form.

decomposition, the CONTINUE statement is deleted since it is only used to help clearly mark the end of the loop. Note also that the initialization is placed outside the loop body and the incrementation component is combined with the iterated statements in a common basic block.

The loop body can contain several basic blocks, as is illustrated in Fig. 12-9. In this case the CONTINUE statement serves as more than a marker for the end

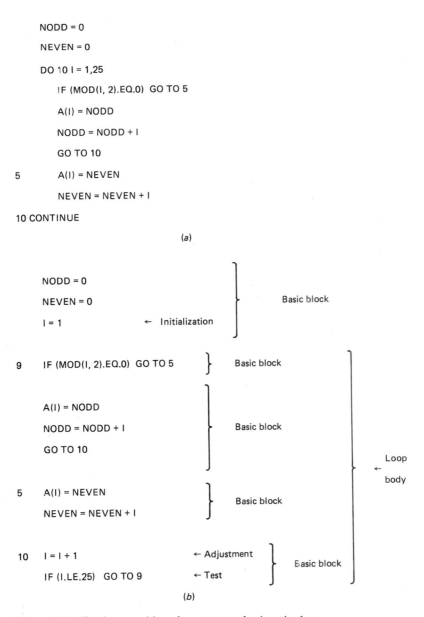

Figure 12-9 The decomposition of a more complex iterative loop.

of the loop; it is also a control transfer point within the loop. Of course, more complex loop structures can be created and often do arise in programs. As we will see, the more complex the loop structure the more difficult is the optimization analysis.

Now that the notion of a simple iterative loop has been outlined, the various iterative loop-optimization techniques can be presented.

12-5.1 Loop Unrolling

Loop unrolling is an optimization technique in which the code constituting the loop body (excluding the adjustment and test) is reproduced a number of times (that is determinable at compile time) rather than just once. Basically, loop unrolling is an optimization process that trades space (i.e., object code size) for time. By increasing the amount of code through the generation of many copies of the loop body, the loop overhead due to calculations required to modify and test the loop variable can be reduced.

For example, consider the following simple initialization loop in PL/I.

DO I = 1 TO 30;
  A(J + I) = 0.0;
END;

An equivalent decomposed form for this loop structure is given in Fig. 12-10. This example loop can be transformed into the sequence

A(J + 1) = 0.0;
A(J + 2) = 0.0;
 ⋮
 ⋮
A(J + 30) = 0.0;

in which case the loop structure has completely disappeared. Note that if the assignment statement in the loop body was simply A(I) = 0.0, the unrolled loop

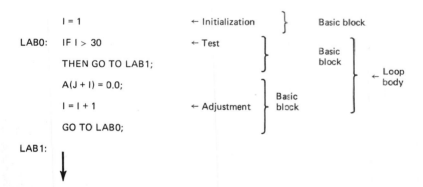

Figure 12-10 Decomposed form of initialization loop.

would be transformed into

A(1) = 0.0;
A(2) = 0.0;
$$\vdots$$
A(30) = 0.0;

assuming folding is performed.

It is important to see that the loop's limit value, initial value, and adjustment value must be known at compile time in order to perform loop unrolling. If the iteration statement in the previous example had been either

            DO I = 1 TO 30 BY K;

or

            DO I = K TO 30;

or

            DO I = 1 TO N;

where K and N are unknown at compile time, then loop unrolling would not be possible.

To perform loop unrolling, the following steps must be undertaken:

1. The loop structure must be recognized and the loop's initial, terminal, and change values must be determined at compile time.
2. A decision must be made as to whether the space versus time trade-off is acceptable. If it is not, continue compiling the loop as a loop structure.
3. If the space versus time trade-off is acceptable, reproduce the loop body the required number of times. In reproducing this code, care must be taken to ensure that the loop variable is folded properly for each reproduction.

Step 1 of the previous procedure can be easily handled through the recognition capabilities of the parser and the capture of the loop's initial, terminal, and change values in a semantic stack or attributed translation attributes. Step 2 is not so straightforward, as it requires a new type of analysis. To illustrate this, let us assume that the loop body of the initialization loop described previously in this subsection contained 40 source statements instead of just one. Loop unrolling would cause the generation of $40 \times 30 = 1200$ source statements in this case. Note that the time saving in this case is identical to the time saving for the case in which the loop body is but a single statement form. In both cases two "statements," the incrementation and the test, are not executed for each pass through the loop at run time. Therefore, the total net time saving is $2 \times 30 = 60$ statements. Hence we have in the original example a saving of 60 executed statements at a cost of 29 additional compile-time-generated statements, whereas in the extended 40-statement example, we have a saving of 60 executed statements at a cost of $40 \times 29 = 1160$ additional compile-time-generated statements. It is obvious that in the latter case the space versus time trade-off may not be very attractive. As a general rule, the less expensive main memory resources are and the more expensive processing time is, the more attractive loop unrolling becomes. It is a very attractive optimization technique on many of today's large virtual memory computers, but it should be used rarely when constructing compilers for microcomputers.

Some comments are necessary concerning step 3 of the general loop-unrolling procedure. If some of the other loop-optimization techniques such as frequency and strength reductions are to be applied during the optimization phase, it is best to generate loop-oriented code in a high-level intermediate language during an initial code-generation phase for all iterative loop constructs Then, in a pass separate from the parse, a scan of the intermediate language code will allow the other forms of optimization to be applied and then the loop can be unrolled. This strategy will avoid the reproduction of code for loop-invariant statements many times during the unrolling process. Obviously, if loop unrolling is the only iterative loop optimization to be performed, it can be applied during the initial code-generation phase.

As a final comment concerning loop unrolling, it should be pointed out that during step 2 of a general loop-unrolling procedure partial loop unrolling can be considered as yet another alternative when making a space versus time decision. For example, the initialization loop presented earlier in this section can be partially unrolled to a form equivalent to

```
DO      I = 1 TO 30 BY 3;
        A(I) = 0.0;
        A(I + 1) = 0.0;
        A(I + 2) = 0.0;
END;
```

This partial unrolling would result in a saving of 20 tests at run time but would increase the amount of code by two additional source statements both of which involve array referencing. Clearly the introduction of partial unrolling significantly increases the complexity of the space versus time decision that occurs in step 2.

Let us turn our discussion to some other loop-optimization techniques.

12-5.2 Frequency Reduction

Frequency reduction is, as its name implies, an optimization technique that moves certain computations from program regions where they are very frequently executed to regions where they are less frequently executed. Specifically with respect to loop structures, frequency reduction is implemented by moving certain invariant operations out of the loop body and placing them in a block just prior to the start of the loop. It is for this reason that frequency reduction is also commonly called *invariant operation elimination*.

As an example consider the loop

```
DO    I = 1 TO 5000;
      D = I * SIN(A)/SIN(B);
      .
      .
      / * rest of loop * /
      .
      .
END;
```

A considerable amount of inefficiency can be removed if the computation, SIN(A)/SIN(B), can be moved out of the loop as follows:

```
T = SIN(A)/SIN(B);
DO I = 1 TO 5000;
      D = I * T;
      .
      .
      / * rest of loop * /
      .
      .
END;
```

This frequency reduction in the execution of SIN(A)/SIN(B) can only take place if both A and B are *loop invariant*; i.e., their values do not change in the loop.

It is important to note that rearranging code to achieve frequency reduction does not introduce additional errors at run time. In the previous example, an overflow will still occur whenever the value of B is zero whether the SIN(A)/SIN(B) is removed from the loop or not.

It can be argued with justification that the tremendous savings in computation time (approximately 10,000 invocations of the sine function) accrued in the earlier example should rarely occur if a programmer is following good programming practices. However, if the invariant operation is embedded in a large loop structure in a program that has undergone several evolutionary stages, it may not be obvious that the expression can be successfully removed from the loop. In addition some programmers believe that leaving the computation "in-line" may make the source program much more readable.

A less obvious source of invariant operations that is out of the control of the source-language programmer can result through the use of array references. For example, consider the following PL/I program segment:

```
DO WHILE (J < N & A(I, J)¬= 0);
      A(I, J) = A(I, J) + A(I, J + 1);
      J = J + 1;
END;
```

LOOPSTART:

    IF J < N THEN

      { T1 = CONSPART(A(I,J)) + I ∗ d_2 + J

      IF A[T1] ¬ = 0 THEN

         { T2 = CONSPART(A(I,J)) + I ∗ d_2 + J;

         T3 = CONSPART(A(I,J)) + I ∗ d_2 + J;

         T4 = CONSPART(A(I,J)) + I ∗ d_2 + J + 1;

         A[T2] = A[T3] + A[T4];

         J = J + 1;

         GO TO LOOPSTART; }

    }

Figure 12-11 Unoptimized decomposed loop with invariant operations.

It is desirable to decompose this loop into a lower-level form which illustrates how the array references would be mapped using a linear storage-addressing function. The addressing function for $A(I, J)$ can be expressed as

$$\text{ADDR}(A(I, J)) = \text{BASE\_LOC} + (I - l_1) \ast d_2 + J - l_2$$
$$= (\text{BASE\_LOC} - l_1 \ast d_2 - l_2) + (I \ast d_2 + J)$$

where $\text{CONSPART}(A(I, J)) = \text{BASE\_LOC} - l_1 \ast d_2 - l_2,$

           $\text{VARPART}(A(I, J)) = I \ast d_2 + J,$

and l_i and u_i are respectively the lower bounds and upper bounds for dimension i and $d_i = u_i - l_i + 1$.

The decomposed loop is shown in Fig. 12-11. Note that common subexpressions have not been recognized and the loop is in a very unoptimized form. By recognizing that the expression

$$\text{CONSPART}(A(I, J)) + I \ast d_2$$

is loop-invariant as well as a common subexpression, the program segment can be expressed in an optimized form as shown in Fig. 12-12. If J was initialized to 1

T1 = CONSPART(A(I,J)) + I ∗ d_2

LOOPSTART: IF J < N THEN

         { T2 = T1 + J;

         IF A[T2] ¬ = 0 THEN

            { T3 = T2 + 1;

            A[T2] = A[T2] + A[T3];

            J = J + 1;

            GO TO LOOPSTART; }

         }

Figure 12-12 Optimized decomposed loop with invariant operations.

before entering the loop, then the optimized form has a potential savings of approximately

$$4*(N-1)*\text{cost of computing }(\text{CONSPART}(A(I,J)) + I*d_2)$$
$$+ 3*(N-1)*\text{additions of } J \text{ in the calculation of}$$
$$T2, T3, T4 \text{ in the unoptimized form}$$

In terms of arithmetic operations these savings are:

$7N - 7$ additions and $4N - 4$ multiplications

Therefore, for $N > 1$, the optimized form performs better. In addition, it must be noted that the optimized form produces some storage savings and reduces the number of temporaires required.

For most of the discussion in the remainder of this section, only arithmetic and logical operations will be considered for frecuency reduction. Frequency reduction related to string operations is possible but is relatively hard to detect.

Before beginning to describe how to perform frequency reduction, we must identify exactly what types of operations can or cannot be reduced in this manner. As a general and obvious rule, it would seem that any operation with operands which do not change their values throughout the loop can be moved outside the loop. The operation $I*d_2$ in the previous example illustrates such a loop-invariant operation. Unfortunately this rule is not entirely true. The notable exception involves output types of statements as exemplified by the following PL/I program segment:

```
DO I = 1 TO N;
    PUT SKIP LIST ('INITIALIZATION MODULE');
    A(I) = 0;
END;
```

If the PUT statement is moved outside the loop, the transformed program will obviously perform differently.

It is perhaps easier to catalog the set of operations that are not candidates for frequency reduction rather than those that are candidates. Three types of operations which will be considered loop-variant are:

1. Assignments
2. Function and procedure calls using call-by-reference parameter passing
3. Output statements and the parameters in read (i.e., input) statements

Note that for library functions (e.g., the exponential function, the remainder function, trigonometric functions) a call-by-value type of parameter-passing scheme is almost always adopted, and therefore library function calls are candidates for loop reduction.

The following PL/I program segment helps illustrate the notion of a loop-variant operation:

```
DO I = 1 TO N;
    GET LIST(Z);
    CALL ROUTINE_A(X);
    A(I) = X + Z;
END;
```

In this example, the input, call, and assignment operations are variant in accordance with the discussion earlier. Note that the expression $X + Z$ is also variant because one of the operands (in this case potentially both operands) is loop-variant. Therefore, no operations can be removed from the example loop.

One might question why assignment operations have been tagged as operations that are always loop-variant in nature—obviously this is not always the case, as is demonstrated by the following simple example.

```
DO I = 1 TO 12;
    X(I) = Y + I;
    Z = Y;
END;
```

Clearly, the assignment $Z = Y$ can be brought outside the loop without changing the computational effects of the program segment. Notice, however, if the loop was of the form:

```
DO I = 1 TO N;
    X(I) = Y + I;
    Z = Y;
END;
```

then bringing $Z = Y$ outside the loop can result in an erroneous program. If N has a value of 0 or less, the body of the PL/I loop is never executed. In this case the execution of $Z = Y$ outside the loop would incorrectly alter the value of Z. From this example, it can be observed that any loop construct in which the loop test is at the beginning of the loop (e.g., PL/I's DO WHILE statement and PASCAL's WHILE statement) presents problems in terms of frequency reduction because it is generally not recognizable at compile time whether or not an assignment in the loop body will be executed.

In some loop constructs, such as FORTRAN's iterative DO and PASCAL's REPEAT UNTIL, loop tests are not performed until the end of the loop. Under what conditions are assignments moved outside the loop for these constructs? Consider the PASCAL program segment in Fig. 12-13a. On the first pass of the loop body, it is easy to see that the assignment $B := D$ can be removed since the right-hand-side D is loop-invariant. If this statement is pulled out of the loop, it can be observed in Fig. 12-13b that the assignment $C := B$ is now loop-invariant and can be removed from the loop. Also notice that the relative order of the two assignments has been changed from what it was inside the loop. Clearly this

```
REPEAT                          B  :=  D;                         B  :=  D;

    C  :=  B;                   REPEAT                            C  :=  B;

    B  :=  D;                       C  :=  B;                     REPEAT

    ( * REST OF LOOP BODY * )       ( * REST OF LOOP BODY * )         ( * REST OF LOOP BODY * )

UNTIL  X  <  0;                 UNTIL X < 0;                      UNTIL X < 0;



    (a)                             (b)                               (c)
```

Figure 12-13 Example illustrating problems with removing assignments from loops.

change can alter the results of the program. This example is simply intended to point out that the relative order of assignment statements must be maintained when performing code motion involving assignments. Keeping track of the relative order of assignments is a nontrivial task—so much so as to discourage the movement of assignment statements. The exercises at the end of this chapter illustrate further some problems with trying to apply frequency reduction to assignments.

Let us now turn to the problem of specifying how frequency reduction can be performed. Basically it requires a two-step process. Initially we will present an informal specification and then give a more formal algorithmic specification.

The first step in optimizing a loop by frequency reduction is to formulate a list of all variables whose values are changed within the loop. Hence a scan is made of the basic blocks constituting the loop body and a list is made of all variables (simple and array) that are assigned to or are in a read statement, or that are arguments to a procedure that are not call by value.

The second step identifies the expressions in which the operands are loop-invariant. This step involves a scan of the intermediate code (i.e., the internal DAG structure) that represents the loop body. Note that the decision as to whether an expression is invariant can be made as it is encountered during the pass, since this decision is based solely on whether the operands of the expression are invariant. It should also be evident that this pass can be performed on an internal form which already has been optimized with respect to folding and common subexpression elimination.

The algorithm that follows immediately can be used to process a list of triples (an internal form described in Chap. 10) for a loop body by marking those computations that are loop invariant. As such, the algorithm handles only the second step described previously. It is assumed that a list named CHANGED is available which contains all the variables in a loop body whose values are changed either by assignment, by a read operation, or by being an argument of a procedure (i.e., the first step described previously has been completed). Furthermore, assume that OPERATIONS is a list of the operations acceptable for frequency reduction. The list would contain at least the arithmetic and logical expressions, plus any library function calls.

Algorithm LOOP_INVARIANT. Given a list of n triples constituting a DAG that represents the body of a loop, along with the lists CHANGED and OPERATIONS as described previously, this algorithm marks each triple either invariant or variant. TEST is a temporary logical variable.

1. [Process the n triples in sequence]
   Repeat through step 3 for i = 1, 2,...,n.
2. [Analyze a triple]
   Let OP be the operation associated with triple [i]
      and OP1 and OP2 the left and right operands respectively.
   If OP is not in OPERATIONS
   then TEST ← false
   else TEST ← true
      Repeat for OPERAND = OP1, OP2
         If OPERAND is a variable
         then If OPERAND is in CHANGED
            then TEST ← false
         else (OPERAND is a reference to another triple)
            If OPERAND is marked variant
            then TEST ← false
3. [Mark the triple]
   If TEST is true
   then mark triple [i] as invariant
   else mark triple [i] as variant   □

When completed, all triples in the list have been marked. While step 2 has been written for binary operations only, the modifications for unary or n-ary operations are obvious. Note that in step 2 an operand which references a triple outside the loop body (e.g., a triple found in the loop-initialization block) should be treated as loop-invariant for the algorithm to work properly.

Once the loop-invariant computations have been identified by Algorithm LOOP_INVARIANT, the final step in frequency-reduction optimization is to move the invariant computations out of the loop. This step is accomplished by moving the triples marked as invariant out of the list of triples for the loop body and placing them, and maintaining their relative order, into the list of triples associated with the loop initialization. As part of a cleanup procedure, all references to the moved triples must be modified.

As a simple example to illustrate the algorithm, consider the FORTRAN program segment in Fig. 12-14. A decomposed form of this loop is shown in Fig. 12-15. The list of translated triples [1] to [13] in infix form are shown to the left of the program in Fig. 12-15, and the basic blocks are indicated to the right of the program.

```
      N = 0
      DO 10  I = J, K
          IF (I.LT.10)  GO TO 5
          N = J + K + I
5         N = N + I
10    CONTINUE
```

Figure 12-14

From an examination of the loop body (i.e., the triples [3] to [13]), it can be seen that CHANGED contains the variables I and N. We will assume the OPERATIONS contains just the arithmetic and logical operations. The execution of Algorithm LOOP_INVARIANT would mark triple [5] as invariant and all other triples as variant. Accordingly, only the computation $J + K$ can be moved out of the loop, which will result in the list of triples shown in Fig. 12-16.

Whenever a compiler modifies a source program (or some intermediate representation of the program), care must be taken to ensure that the modification does not introduce any errors that were not in the original program. For example, if logical expressions are not considered as candidates for frequency reduction, which they usually are not, then the arithmetic expression A/B in the FORTRAN statement

IF (B.NE.0) C = A/B + I

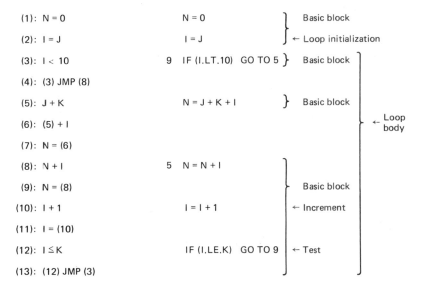

Figure 12-15

```
(1):      N = 0

(1.1):    J + K          ← Triple moved out of loop body

(2):      I = J

(3):      I < 10

(4):      (3) JMP (8)

(6):      (1.1) + I      ← Reference to moved triplet

(7):      N = (6)

(8):      N + I

(9):      N = (8)

(10):     I + 1

(11):     I = (10)

(12):     I ≤ K

(13):     (12) JMP (3)
```

Figure 12-16

would be moved out of the loop assuming both A and B are loop-invariant. Ironically, the IF statement was put in to prevent division by zero, but by moving it out of the loop a potential error has been introduced.

A possible solution to this problem is not to permit the movement of computations involving operations such as division, or special library routines such as those for the trigonometric functions to be moved if their execution is dependent upon conditional statements. Obviously the detection of such conditions requires some flow analysis—a topic to be examined further in Sec. 12-6.

Other problems that potentially arise when considering frequency reduction can be attributable to the side effects that take place when a variable's value is redefined outside the context of the loop being considered. For example, in FORTRAN, a variable, say, A may at first appear to be loop-invariant. However, if a call inside the loop is made to a subroutine that changes the value of a variable which is "EQUIVALENT" to A, A is in fact not loop-invariant. A similar side effect can take place in a nested language such as PL/I. Once more a variable, A, may appear to be loop-invariant inside a loop under consideration. However, if a call is made from inside the loop to a procedure for which A is a global variable, then any potential change to the value of A within this procedure necessitates that A not be considered loop-invariant. Again, some flow analysis is necessary to detect these types of situations.

We conclude this subsection by reiterating that, while most of the examples in this subsection have been numerical in nature, frequency reduction can be applied in a straightforward manner to nonnumerical operations such as those operations associated with strings, lists, or other more complex data structures.

```
          DO I = A TO N BY K;

             Z(I) = 3 * I;

          END;

             (a)


          I = A;
LAB0:     IF I > N THEN GO TO LAB1;

          Z(I) = 3 * I;

          I = I + K;

          GO TO LAB0:

LAB1:     • • • •
             (b)
```

Figure 12-17 (*a*) A PL/I example program used to illustrate strength reduction. (*b*) Its equivalent decomposed form.

12-5.3 Strength Reduction

Strength reduction is an optimization technique which consists of the replacement of one type of operation by another operation that takes less time to execute. For example, on most computers a multiplication takes more time to execute than does an addition. This is especially true on many of today's minicomputers. A time savings is achieved if certain multiplications can be replaced by additions, especially if the replacement takes place inside a loop where the time saving is achieved each time and loop body is executed As an example of strength reduction involving the replacement of a multiplication by addition, consider the program in Fig. 12-17a and its decomposed form in Fig. 12-17b.

An equivalent form in which the multiplication $3 * I$ has been replaced by an addition $T1 + T2$ in the loop body and two multiplications, $3 * I$ and $3 * K$, in the loop-initialization section is illustrated in Fig. 12-18. Assuming the loop is executed a total of M times, a saving of M multiplications is accrued at a cost of two multiplications and M additions. For most machines, M would have to be at

```
          I = A;

          T1 = 3 * I;

          T2 = 3 * K;

LAB0:     IF I > N THEN GO TO LAB1;

          Z(I) = T1;

          I = I + K;

          T1 = T1 + T2;

          GO TO LAB0:

LAB1:     • • • •
```

Figure 12-18 An illustration of strength reduction.

least 10 before any major savings are accomplished. And, as a general rule, strength reduction is a technique which is practical only if applied inside a loop structure.

Traditionally, the replacement of multiplications by additions has been the classical example of strength reduction. In this section, we expend most of our efforts in describing this classical case.

Other cases in which strength reduction can be applied have been noted, however. One obvious form of strength reduction is possible by replacing a call to an exponentiation routine when evaluating X^2 by a less expensive multiplication and thus evaluating $X * X$. The multiplication or division of positive fixed-point numbers by a power of 2 (e.g., $J * 4$ and $K/16$) can be implemented more efficiently through shift operations (i.e., shift_left$(J, 2)$ and shift_right$(K, 4)$). With respect to string-handling operations, it is definitely more efficient, for example, to implement

N = LENGTH(B||C),

as

N = LENGTH(B) + LENGTH(C)

in PL/I. In other words, an addition and a LENGTH operation have replaced a concatenation operation. All these examples occur relatively infrequently and in some instances are language-dependent. Major savings are achieved only if these transformations occur in a part of the program that is executed very frequently. We will now focus our attention on describing how strength reduction can be applied to certain types of multiplications inside a loop. This traditional form of strength reduction can be applied relatively frequently in programs for numerical applications.

In attempting to identify when strength reduction can be applied to multiplication operations, it is necessary to locate expressions in which one operand is an induction variable and the other is loop-invariant. The expression $3 * I$ in Fig. 12-17 is clearly an example of such an expression. It should be noted that an induction variable does not have to be the loop variable—any variable in the loop that is defined in terms of itself can be considered an induction variable. For example, if the statement $L = L + 4$ was inserted inside the loop in the program for Fig. 12-17a, then L would also be considered an induction variable for this loop. An example of strength reduction involving an induction variable which is not a loop variable will be given later in this section.

It should also be pointed out that a loop variable may not be an induction variable if it is allowable to change the value of the loop variable inside the loop. Some languages, such as ALGOL W, do not allow loop variables to be altered other than via the normal loop alteration. Whether or not a language allows this type of alteration, it is a poor programming technique and should rarely occur in programs.

The major significance of induction variables is that the difference between their successively assigned values in the loop is predictable. As a result an expression involving an induction variable can be formed by adding (or in some cases subtracting) an appropriate quantity to the old value of the induction variable rather than using a more expensive multiplication operation.

By referring to Fig. 12-18, some insight can be gained into how strength reduction can be accomplished. The induction variable I appears as an operand in the expression $3 * I$. The difference between two successive values of the expression during the execution of the loop is

$$3 * (I + K) - 3 * I = 3 * I + 3 * K - 3 * I = 3 * K$$

given that there is a loop variable increment of K. Accordingly, a new induction variable can be introduced into the loop to record the sequence of values of the expression $3 * I$ by successively incrementing its current value by the amount $3 * K$ each time I is incremented by K. Then the computation $3 * I$ may be deleted from the loop, and thus the multiplication in the loop is replaced, in effect, by an addition.

Let us examine the steps required to implement the strength reduction for a multiplication operation in a loop. We will refer to Fig. 12-19 throughout the discussion. The first step involves a scan that identifies the induction variables of the loop. In general, this can be easily accomplished; however, for some intermediate forms, more than one instruction may be involved in the inductive definition. For example, if triples are used, an inductive statement of the form $A = A \pm K$ ($\pm$ means plus or minus) could appear typically as (m): $A \pm K$ followed by $(m + 1)$: $A = (m)$. Note that the loop-differential variable, in this case K, must be a loop-invariant operand. This loop-invariancy property is known if frequency reduction is performed before strength reduction. The list of induction variables that is formed would usually contain at least one variable, the loop index, in an iterative loop. In the example in Fig. 12-19, I should be recognized as an induction variable.

The second step is to search the intermediate code for multiplications involving an induction variable and a loop-invariant operand. If one is found, say (n): $A * C$, and an equivalent triple (i.e., either (i): $A * C$ or (j): $C * A$) has not

DO WHILE (I < N);		(1):	I < N
		(2):	(1) BRF (8)
		(3):	I + 4
I = I + 4;	← Induction variable	(4):	I = (3)
		(5):	(4) * J
X(I) = I * J;		(6):	X (4) = (5
END;		(7):	BR(1)
		(8):	
(a)		(b)	

Figure 12-19 (*a*) An example program for illustrating the steps in applying strength reduction. (*b*) Its equivalent form expressed in triple notation.

been located previously, then the triple can be subjected to strength reduction. Note that if common subexpression elimination has been performed prior to strength reduction, checking for duplicate expressions is unnecessary.

Once a multiplication operation that can be reduced in strength is located, the multiplication can be replaced by an addition or subtraction which accounts for the difference between the values the assigned variable has during successive executions of the loop body. This procedure is evident through a close examination of Fig. 12-19. In the program, the operation $I * J$ is replaced by $T1$, where $T1$ is an induction temporary that is defined by adding the loop-differential value $T2$ to the previous value of $T1$. Both $T1$ and $T2$ are initialized through assignments that are placed just prior to the set of instructions that compose the loop body. This replacement procedure is illustrated in Fig. 12-20.

It is important to note that the new induction temporary must be introduced *immediately after* the definition of the induction variable, and *not immediately after* the location at which the removal of the multiplication takes place. This placement strategy is also illustrated in the example in Fig. 12-18, where the update of the temporary variable $T1$ occurs after the incrementation of the loop variable I. If an induction variable is involved in more than one multiplication that can be reduced in strength, then two new temporaries are set up for each strength reduction and all of the induction temporaries are updated immediately after the redefinition of the associated induction variable.

	(0.1):	J * I
T1 = J * I;	(0.2):	T1 = (0.1)
	(0.3):	J * 4
T2 = J * 4;	(0.4):	T2 = (0.3)
DO WHILE (I < N);	(1):	I < N
I = I + 4; ← Induction variable	(2):	(1) BFF (8)
	(3):	I + 4
	(4):	I = (3)
T1 = T1 + T2; ← Induction temporary	(4.1):	T1 + T2
	(4.2):	T1 = (4.1)
X(I) = T1;	(6):	X (4) = (4.2)
	(7):	BR (1)
END;	(8):	
(a)		(b)

Figure 12-20 (*a*) An expanded form of the DO-WHILE loop with strength reduction applied. (*b*) Its equivalent form expressed in triple notation.

After performing the appropriate replacements as described previously, it is necessary to ensure that all references to the reduced multiplication operation (e.g., triple(5) in Fig. 12-19b) are changed to refer to the value of the induction temporary (e.g., triple (4.2) in Fig. 12-20b).

A more concise description of the steps outlined in the previous discussion follows:

1. Scan the loop body compiling a list of induction variables.
2. Scan the loop body searching for multiplications that can be reduced in strength. For a given multiplication, say, $L = I * J$, that qualifies for strength reduction:

   Replace the multiplication by a temporary induction variable, TI, i.e., $L = I * J$ becomes $L = TI$.

   Place assignments which initialize the temporary induction variable TI and the loop differential TJ just prior to the set of instructions that comprise the loop body. Therefore, given an induction variable of I, a loop-invariant multiplicand J, and the loop increment/decrement for I of D, the assignments

   $$TI = J * I$$
   $$TJ = J * D$$

   should be located prior to the loop body.

   Place the inductive definition for TI immediately after the inductive definition for the induction variable, i.e., in this case, the variable I.
3. Alter all references to the results of the multiplication operation so that they now refer to the value of the temporary induction variable TI.

After the strength reduction for a multiplication associated with a induction variable has been applied, it may be possible to eliminate the induction variable itself. In particular, if the only reference to the induction variable, excluding the inductive definition of the variable and the loop test, is in the multiplication that is reduced in strength, the inductive variable can be eliminated. For example, in Fig. 12-19a, we assume if the program statement

$$X(I) = I * J;$$

is replaced by

$$X = I * J;$$

i.e., the other reference to I does not exist, then the induction variable I can be eliminated from the loop as shown in Fig. 12-21. Note that it is necessary to replace the variable N in the loop test by the temporary variable $T3$ that is equal to the product of N and J. Since the original test was $I < N$, an equivalent new test involving $T1$ must be $T1 < N * J$ or $T1 < T3$, because the value of $T1$ is equal to $I * J$ during the execution of the loop.

```
T1 = J * I;

T2 = J * 4;

T3 = N * J

DO WHILE (T1 < T3);

    T1 = T1 + T2;

    X = T1;

END;
```

Figure 12-21 An example of a reduced program illustrating the removal of an induction variable.

An examination of the program in Fig. 12-21 reveals that the temporary $T1$ is now redundant and can be replaced by the variable X. Obviously the detection and removal of induction variables and temporaries involves an amount of work on the part of the compiler. Consequently, these types of extended optimization techniques are implemented only in compilers that have a single purpose of producing highly optimized code.

12-5.4 Combining Loop-Optimization Techniques

We conclude our discussion on loop optimization by considering the optimization of a program segment that involves the optimization techniques discussed previously. The example program segment, found in Fig. 12-22, performs a transpose operation on a matrix A. An expanded version of this program with the loop in a decomposed form is shown in Fig. 12-23.

The first step in optimization is to perform folding and to remove redundant expressions—these can actually be accomplished as the source code is being translated to an intermediate language form.

The second step is to detect loop-invariant operations and to move these operations outside the loop. Figure 12-24 depicts how the redundant operations that are associated with array-element computations are eliminated. Then, frequency reduction can be applied to the expressions conspart(A) + $I * d_2$ and conspart(A) + I in the inner loop by moving these invariant operations to the body of the outer loop and assigning their computed values to the new tem-

```
DO I = 1 TO 10;

    DO J = 1 TO 10;

        TEMP = A(I, J);

        A(I, J) = A(J, I);

        A(J, I) = TEMP;

    END;

END;
```

Figure 12-22 A program segment for performing a matrix operation.

```
        I = 1;

LAB1:   IF  I ≤ 10 THEN DO;

            J = 1;

        LAB2:   IF  J ≤ 10 THEN DO;

                    T1 = conspart(A) + I * d₂ + J;

                    TEMP = A[T1] ;

                    T2 = conspart(A) + I * d₂ + J;

                    T3 = conspart(A) + J * d₂ + I;

                    A[T2] = A[T3] ;

                    T4 = conspart(A) + J * d₂ + I;

                    A[T4] = TEMP;

                    J = J + 1;

                    GO TO LAB2;

                END;

                I = I + 1;

                GO TO LAB1;

            END;
```

Figure 12-23 An expanded form of the matrix operation program.

```
        I = 1;

LAB1:   IF  I ≤ 10 THEN DO;

            J = 1;

            T5 = conspart(A) + I * d₂;

            T6 = conspart(A) + I;

        LAB2:   IF  J ≤ 10 THEN DO;

                    T1 = T5 + J;

                    TEMP = A[T1] ;

                    T3 = T6 + J * d₂

                    A[T1] = A[T3] ;

                    A[T3] = TEMP;

                    J = J + 1;

                    GO TO LAB2;

                END;

                I = I + 1;

                GO TO LAB1;

            END;
```

Figure 12-24 The matrix-operation program with redundant expressions removed and frequency reduction applied.

```
        I = 1;
        T7 = I  *  d₂;
        T8 = 1  *  d₂;
LAB1:   IF  I ≤ 10 THEN DO;
            J = 1;
            T5 = conspart(A) + T7;
            T6 = conspart(A) + I;
            T9 = J  *  d₂;
           T10 = 1  *  d₂;
            LAB2:  IF  J ≤ 10 THEN DO;
                    T1 = T5 + J;
                    TEMP = A[T1];
                    T3 = T6 + T9;
                    A[T1] = A[T3];
                    A[T3] = TEMP;
                    J = J + 1;
                    T9 = T9 + T10;
                    GO TO LAB2;
                END;
                I = I + 1;
                T7 = T7 + T8;
                GO TO LAB1;
        END;
```

Figure 12-25 The matrix-operation program after the application of strength reduction.

poraries $T5$ and $T6$. Note that because of redundant-expression elimination the temporaries $T2$ and $T4$ are no longer needed.

Figure 12-25 illustrates the application of strength reduction on the induction variables I and J. In the outer loop, a new temporary $T7$ replaces the evaluation of $I * d_2$ and $T8$ contains the loop-differential value associated with the strength reduction. Similarly, in the inner loop, $T9$ replaces the evaluation of $J * d_2$ and $T10$ holds the loop-differential value. Note that the incrementation of a temporary takes place immediately after the incrementation of the corresponding induction variable (i.e., $T7$ is incremented immediately after I). It should also be observed that folding has not been applied to the program segment in Fig. 12-25. This type of optimization could, for example, reduce the complexity of the calculations for $T7$, $T8$, $T9$, and $T10$.

```
       I = 1;
       T7 = d₂;
LAB1:  IF  I ≤ 10 THEN DO;
           J = 1;
           T5 = conspart(A) + T7;
           T6 = conspart(A) + I;


           T1 = T5 + 1;
           TEMP = A[T1];
           T3 = T6 + d₂;
           A[T1] = A[T3];
           A[T3] = TEMP;
           T1 = T5 + 2;
           TEMP = A[T1];
           T3 = T6 + (2 * d₂)
           A[T1] = A[T3];
           A[T3] = TEMP;
              .
              .
              .
           T1 = T5 + 10;
           TEMP = A[T1];
           T3 = T6 + (10 * d₂);
           A[T1] = A[T3];
           A[T3] = TEMP;


           I = I + 1;
           T7 = T7 + d₂
           GO TO LAB1;
       END;
```

Figure 12-26 The matrix operation program with loop unrolling.

In Fig. 12-26, folding has been applied and the inner loop (i.e., the loop with loop index J) has been unrolled. The outer loop can also be unrolled; however, the space requirements associated with such a process would, for most applications, overshadow the savings in processing time.

By comparing the original program in Fig. 12-22 with the final optimized form in Fig. 12-26 a true appreciation can be gained of what can be accomplished through optimization. In the next section we introduce some additional optimization techniques that can be applied with the aid of global flow analysis.

12-6 GLOBAL OPTIMIZATION THROUGH FLOWGRAPH ANALYSIS

Designers of optimizing compilers have found that flowgraph analysis is necessary before global optimizations on a program can be performed. Informally, a flowgraph can be thought of as a directed graph which shows possible paths of program execution. In this section, techniques for building and analyzing flowgraphs are presented. Then methods are suggested for using information obtained from flow analysis to perform several program optimizations.

Flowgraph analysis yields information useful to both programmers and optimizing compilers. The programmer can be told about unreachable (or dead) code, unused parameters to procedures, and variables which are used before being given an initial value. On the basis of this information, he or she can make changes to the program before compiling it again. Although we occasionally mention how such user-oriented information can be obtained, we center our discussion on compiler-oriented information which flowgraph analysis can yield.

Information about a program's flowgraph can be used by an optimizing compiler to improve the code produced for the program. The efficiency of program execution can be increased by constant propagation, by eliminating useless code, and by allocating registers more effectively. Such optimizations are worthwhile only if the object program produced by the compiler is reexecuted so frequently that the cumulative run-time savings more than offset the additional cost of compilation. For example, the component programs of a computer's operating system are executed often enough to justify a large expenditure of effort at compile time to enhance efficiency. In this section, we present flowgraph analysis as a method of gathering information which can then be used by an optimizing compiler to improve code.

12-6.1 Flowgraph Construction

Before flowgraph analysis can be performed on a program, the flowgraph for the program must be obtained. In this section, we define the term *flowgraph*. We explain how a flowgraph is constructed using an informal example. Finally, we present and discuss the time complexity of an algorithm for constructing flowgraphs.

In general, a computer program consists of a main program module and zero or more procedural modules. Since we are interested in flowgraph analysis for its contribution to compilation, we restrict our attention to modules compiled together. We make worst-case assumptions about the effects of separately compiled modules on the portion of the program being compiled.

Some languages encourage the use of many small, often parameterless procedures. In such languages, the procedure call is little more than a flow of control statement. The flowgraphs used for such languages are complicated by the many call statements. In other languages, procedures tend to be well-defined independent modules. For such languages, the usual approach is to build a *call graph*, which shows the flow of control among the procedures, and then to build and analyze the flowgraphs of each procedure separately. In this section, we focus on the flowgraph for a single procedure. The reader is referred to Allen (1974) and Strong et al. (1975) for a discussion of the methods necessary to perform flow analysis on a call graph.

We use the following definition of a flowgraph, which is based on that of Hecht (1977). A *flowgraph G* is a triple (N, E, i) where (N, E) is a directed graph with set of nodes N and set of edges E, and where $i \in N$ is the *initial node* such that there is a path from i to j for all $j \in N$. We represent the number of nodes in N by n, and the number of edges in E by r.

For some languages, such as BLISS, which exclude arbitrary branching instructions (GOTO statements), the program itself can be used as a flowgraph by performing recursive descent on it. (See Wulf et al., 1975.) Good optimizing compilers for such languages make full use of the control structures used in the programs when analyzing the flow of control; however, most programs are written in languages whose flow of control instructions is not sufficiently structured to allow the program structure to be mapped directly to a flowgraph. For these languages, a separate flowgraph is constructed by the compiler for each procedure.

Let us now look at an example of how a flowgraph is constructed for a procedure. Consider the functional procedure in Fig. 12-27 for finding the factorial of a nonnegative integer.

Typically, a flowgraph for a program written in a language which is less than completely structured is built from some intermediate source form of the program. Quadruples and indirect triples are appropriate choices for intermediate

Function FACTORIAL(X).

1.   FACT ← 1

2.   Repeat for i = 2 to X

          FACT ← FACT * i

3.   Return (FACT)

Figure 12-27 A simple functional procedure to compute factorials.

Revised function FACTORIAL(X).

1.   FACT ← 1

2.   ← 2

3.   f i > X then go to step 7

4.   FACT ← FACT * i

5.   i ← i + 1

6.   Go to step 3

7.   FACTORIAL ← FACT

8.   Go to "point in calling program"

Figure 12-28 FACTORIAL functional procedure with explicit branching shown.

source forms as outlined in Chap. 10. These intermediate source forms are useful because they use explicit branching instructions for all flow of control. Also, in such representations flow of control structures which allow three or more choices are rewritten as binary choices. For example, each case statement is replaced by a series of if statements. A computed GOTO statement, such as is present in FORTRAN, could be easily rewritten as several conditional GOTOs.

For our purpose, it is sufficient to rewrite FACTORIAL with all control structures replaced by explicit branching instructions. The revised functional procedure is presented in Fig. 12-28.

The first step in building a flowgraph is determining the basic blocks in the procedure. Examining the revised functional procedure, we find that there are four basic blocks. In Fig. 12-29, we present a version of FACTORIAL with each of the basic blocks enclosed in rectangles. The arrows show possible transfers of control between the basic blocks.

A flowgraph is constructed by treating each basic block as a node, and each possible transfer of control as a directed edge. The flowgraph for FACTORIAL is shown in Fig. 12-30.

Before presenting the algorithm for constructing flowgraphs, we look briefly at the data structures necessary to represent a flowgraph. The original statements

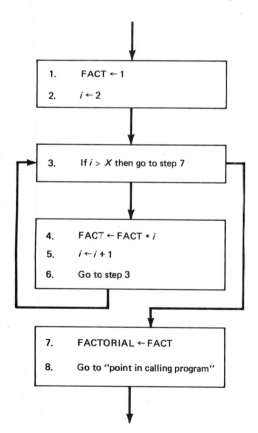

Figure 12-29 Basic blocks in FACTORIAL.

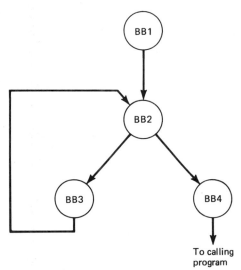

To calling program   **Figure 12-30** Flowgraph for FACTORIAL.

of the program are labeled $S_1, S_2, S_3,...,S_k$. To represent basic block j, we need only the number of the first statement in the block (**FIRST**$_j$) and the number of statements in the block (**NBR_STMTS**$_j$). This information could be saved in two vectors. A list of the successors of block j (**SUC**$_j$) is also required to represent a flowgraph. Since we have assumed that no multiway branching instructions are present, a basic block can have at most two successors. Therefore, instead of having a linked list of successor nodes, we could use a 2 by **NBR_BLOCKS** two-dimensional array. A list of the predecessors of each block is required by some algorithms. Since a block can have any number of predecessors, we use a linked list **PRED**$_j$ to represent the predecessors of block j. As an example, a representation of the flowgraph of **FACTORIAL** is shown in Fig. 12-31.

The following is an algorithm for constructing the flowgraph of a given procedure.

Algorithm CONSTRUCT_FLOWGRAPH. Given a procedure **P** consisting of statements $S_1, S_2,...,S_k$, this algorithm constructs a flowgraph **G = (BLOCK, SUC, INITIAL_BLOCK)** corresponding to **P. BLOCK** is a vector whose

FIRST	NBR_STMTS	SUC		PRED
1	2	2		•
3	1	3	4	1 → 3
4	3	2		2
7	2	MAIN		2

Figure 12-31 Representation of the flowgraph for FACTORIAL.

elements are the sets of statements in a given block. SUC is a vector whose elements are the sets of successor blocks for the blocks. INITIAL_BLOCK contains the initial block of the flowgraph. FIRST is a set containing the first statements of the basic blocks. In step 2, b indicates which block is being created, and FLAG is a logical variable which is true as long as more statements remain to be added to BLOCK$_b$. A stack called UNADDED is used to hold block numbers while the flowgraph is being constructed. PUSH and POP subalgorithms are used with this stack. The MARK vector is used to record which basic blocks have already had their successors found.

1. [Determine the first statements of all basic blocks.]
   FIRST ← S$_1$
   Repeat for j = 2, 3,...,k
       If S$_j$ is a goto statement with destination S$_d$
       then FIRST ← FIRST ∪ S$_d$
       If S$_{j-1}$ is a conditional goto statement
       then FIRST ← FIRST ∪ S$_j$
2. [Find the basic block corresponding to each FIRST statement]
   b ← 0
   Repeat for all statements S$_f$ ∈ FIRST
       b ← b + 1
       BLOCK$_b$ ← S$_f$
       FLAG ← true
       (Examine instructions in sequence after FIRST until block end is found)
       Repeat for j = f + 1, f + 2,...,k while FLAG
           If S$_j$ ∈ FIRST
           then FLAG ← false
           else BLOCK$_b$ ← BLOCK$_b$ ∪ S$_j$
               If S$_j$ is a goto or halt instruction
               then FLAG ← false
3. [Construct the flowgraph]
   SUC ← φ   (φ denotes the empty set)
   MARK ← false (set all elements of MARK to false)
   INITIAL_BLOCK ← the basic block which contains S$_1$
   Call PUSH (UNADDED, INITIAL_BLOCK)
   Repeat while blocks remain on the UNADDED stack
       CUR_BLOCK ← POP (UNADDED)
       MARK$_{CUR\_BLOCK}$ ← true
       Find the last statement S$_{LAST}$ of CUR_BLOCK
       If S$_{LAST}$ is a goto statement with destination S$_d$
       then DEST_BLOCK ← block with FIRST statement S$_d$
           SUC$_{CUR\_BLOCK}$ ← SUC$_{CUR\_BLOCK}$ ∪ DEST_BLOCK
           If MARK$_{DEST\_BLOCK}$ = false
           then Call PUSH (UNADDED, NEXT_BLOCK)
       If S$_{LAST}$ is neither an unconditional goto nor a halt instruction

   then NEXT_BLOCK ← block with FIRST statement S_{LAST+1}
   $SUC_{CUR\_BLOCK} ← SUC_{CUR\_BLOCK} \cup$ NEXT_BLOCK
   If $MARK_{NEXT\_BLOCK}$ = false
   then Call PUSH (UNADDED, NEXT_BLOCK)

4. [Finished]
  Exit   □

Step 1 of the algorithm identifies as first statements of basic blocks the following three types of statements: the first statement of the procedure, any statement following a conditional goto statement, and any statement which is the destination of a goto statement. The second step of the algorithm finds the basic block associated with each of the first statements by examining in sequence the statements which follow until an unconditional goto statement (indicating the last statement of this basic block) or the first statement of another block is found. The third step constructs the flowgraph by beginning at the block containing the first statement of the procedure and adding all reachable blocks. Once the successors have been computed for each block, the predecessor lists could also be produced.

  Algorithm CONSTRUCT_FLOWGRAPH runs in linear time. The first step executes in $O(k)$ time, where k is the number of elementary statements in the procedure. Similarly, the second step is $O(k)$ since each statement can only be added to one block. The third step is $O(r)$ where r is the number of edges in the flowgraph. Since we have assumed that each basic block has no more than 2 successors, $r \leq 2n$, where n is the number of basic blocks. Therefore, the whole algorithm is $O(k) + O(k) + O(2n) = O(k) + O(n)$, which is linear.

  The algorithm could be used to identify unreachable code by the addition of two more steps. After step 2 has been executed, all statements which are not in some block are unreachable. The following step involving the set difference of the S and BLOCK sets could be added after step 2 to collect the dead statements in DEAD_STMTS:

$$DEAD\_STMTS ← \bigcup_{m=1}^{k} S_m - \bigcup_{m=1}^{b} BLOCK_m$$

After statement 3, a step could be added to place all the statements in blocks which are not in the flowgraph (i.e., blocks whose MARK fields are not set true) in DEAD_STMTS. As mentioned, information about unreachable code is useful to the programmer. For the rest of this section, we assume (without loss of generality) that no unreachable code is present in the programs we discuss.

  Now that it has been shown how flowgraphs can be obtained for programs, an examination of how such flowgraphs are analyzed is undertaken.

12-6.2 Flowgraph Analysis

Useful information is obtained from a flowgraph by examining the way in which information about variables or expressions is propagated through the graph. In this section, several graph problems whose solutions are useful to optimizers are discussed. Then the types of algorithms which can be used to solve these problems are discussed and several example algorithms are given.

Flowgraph-analysis problems. Four problems which are typically solved during flowgraph analysis are available expressions, reaching definitions, live variables, and very busy expressions. Cocke (1970) and Ullman (1973) discuss available expressions, Allen (1970) discusses reaching definitions, Kennedy (1975) discusses live variables, and Lowry and Medlock (1969) discuss very busy expressions. Each of these problems can be written as a pair of set equations (called information-flow equations). Aho and Ullman (1977) and Hecht (1977) formulate the four problems using a common set notation and by doing so show clearly the similarities and differences among the problems.

When discussing the flow of information in a flowgraph, we refer to *points* in programs. If statement S_j follows S_i in program execution, the information available immediately after the execution of S_i but before the execution of S_j is described as being available at the *point p* between statements S_i and S_j. We also refer to the points between basic blocks.

An expression is *available* at point p of a program if along every path from the initial node of the graph to point p, the expression is evaluated, and the operands of the expression are not changed in value after the last evaluation on the path. The *available-expressions problem* consists of determining which expressions are available at the beginning of each basic block. When deriving available expressions, four sets are used with each node (basic block) i:

AE_TOP$_i$ the expressions available at the point preceding basic block i
AE_KILL$_i$ the expressions which are killed in the basic block by having one or more of their operands changed
AE_GEN$_i$ the available expressions which are evaluated in basic block i without subsequently having one of their operands changed in value in that block
AE_BOT$_i$ the expressions available just after the end of basic block i

Consider the segment of a flowgraph shown in Fig. 12-32. Let us first look at basic block number 4 (BB4). No expressions are available at the top of this block, i.e, AE_TOP$_4 = \phi$. Two expressions ($A + B$ and $E + F$) are generated in the block, i.e., AE_GEN$_4 = \{A + B, E + F\}$. The expression $C + D$ is created in BB4 but does not reach the end of the block because the value of C is changed. Thus $C + D$ is not included in AE_GEN$_4$. AE_KILL$_4 = \{C + D, Y + Z\}$ since C and Y are assigned values within the block. The first set equation for the available expressions of node i is

$$AE\_BOT_i = (AE\_TOP_i - AE\_KILL_i) \cup AE\_GEN_i$$

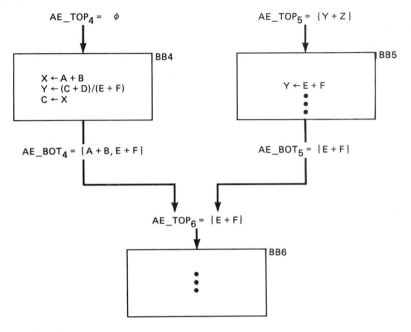

Figure 12-32 Flowgraph segment with available expressions shown.

Therefore,

$$AE\_BOT_4 = (\phi - \{C + D, Y + Z\}) \cup \{A + B, E + F\}$$
$$= \{A + B, E + F\}$$

Similarly,

$$AE\_BOT_5 = (AE\_TOP_5 - AE\_KILL_5) \cup AE\_GEN_5$$
$$= (\{Y + Z\} - \{Y + Z\}) \cup \{E + F\}$$
$$= \{E + F\}$$

Let us assume that BB4 and BB5 are the only predecessors of BB6. Recall that for an expression to be available at the top of BB6 it must be available along all paths leading to that point. Therefore,

$$AE\_TOP_6 = AE\_BOT_4 \cap AE\_BOT_5$$
$$= \{A + B, E + F\} \cap \{E + F\}$$
$$= \{E + F\}$$

For example, if we needed expression A + B in BB6, we could not assume it was available because control might have reached BB6 through BB5. In general,

$$AE\_TOP_i = \bigcap_{\substack{p \text{ is a} \\ \text{predecessor} \\ \text{of } i}} AE\_BOT_p$$

Let us now look at reaching definitions. A variable V is said to be *defined* at point p if it receives a value at p, i.e., if a value is read into V or if V is used as the object of an assignment statement. A definition of a variable V made at point p is said to *reach* point q if there exists a path from p to q along which V is not redefined. The *reaching-definitions problem* is as follows: for each block, list for each variable all definitions of that variable which reach the beginning of the block. The four sets RD_TOP, RD_BOT, RD_GEN, and RD_KILL correspond to AE_TOP, AE_BOT, AE_GEN, and AE_KILL of the available-expressions problem. The information-flow equations for reaching definitions are as follows:

$$RD\_BOT_i = (RD\_TOP_i - RD\_KILL_i) \cup RD\_GEN_i$$
$$RD\_TOP_i = \bigcup_{\substack{p \text{ is a} \\ \text{predecessor} \\ \text{of } i}} RD\_BOT_p$$

Note that the union operation is used in the equation giving RD_TOP_i since a definition reaches a block if it reaches the bottom of any of its predecessors.

In Fig. 12-33, we present a flowgraph fragment illustrating reaching definitions. We use the notation $d_1.d_2$ to represent statement d_2 of block d_1. For example, as part of RD_TOP_4, two definitions for A, one in statement 47 of block 1 and the other in statement 23 of block 2, reach the top of block 4, and thus RD_TOP_4 includes $\{1.47, 2.23\}$. Since no new definition of A occurs in block 4, these same definitions are present in RD_BOT_4. There is only one definition of B in statement 17 of block 4; and hence B in RD_BOT_4 contains 4.17. Thus, for $RD\_KILL_4 = \{2.25\}$ and $RD\_GEN_4 = \{4.17\}$, we compute RD_BOT_4 for B definitions as follows:

$$
\begin{aligned}
RD\_BOT_4 &= (RD\_TOP_4 - RD\_KILL_4) \cup RD\_GEN_4 \\
&= (\{2.25\} - \{2.25\}) \cup \{4.17\} \\
&= \phi \cup \{4.17\} \\
&= \{4.17\}
\end{aligned}
$$

The definitions present at the top of block 6 are those present at the bottom of block 4 or block 5. Therefore, for A,

$$
\begin{aligned}
RD\_TOP_6 &= RD\_BOT_4 \cup RD\_BOT_5 \\
&= \{1.47, 2.23)\} \cup \{5.20\} \\
&= \{1.47, 2.23, 5.20\}
\end{aligned}
$$

A variable is *alive* at point p if its current value is required along some path in the flowgraph beginning at point p. The *live-variables problem* consists of determining which variables are alive at the bottom of each basic block. This problem is a *backward-flow problem* since we can only decide if a variable is alive by looking to see if its current value is used later in the program. LV_DEF_i is the set of variables which are given values in block i before being used in that block. LV_USE_i is the set of variables which are used in block i before being given a

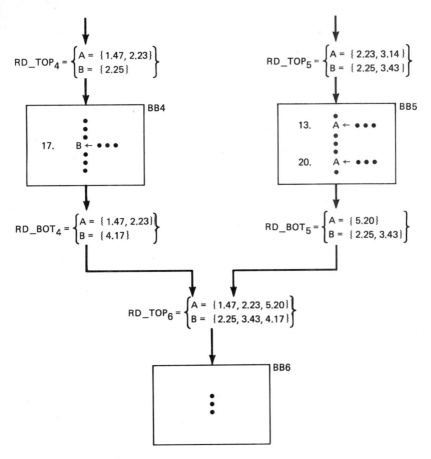

Figure 12-33 Flowgraph fragment showing reaching definitions.

value in that block.

The information-flow equations are as follows:

$$LV\_TOP_i = (LV\_BOT_i - LV\_DEF_i) \cup LV\_USE_i$$
$$LV\_BOT_i = \bigcup_{\substack{s \text{ is a} \\ \text{successor} \\ \text{of } i}} LV\_TOP_s$$

The union operator is used in the equation giving LV_BOT_i because a variable is alive at the end of a block if it is alive in any one of its successors.

Consider the flowgraph fragment shown in Fig. 12-34. We assume that variables B, D, E, and F are alive at the bottom of block 5, i.e., $LV\_BOT_5 = \{B, D, E, F\}$. In block 5, A, B, and C are used, and E and F are defined. We

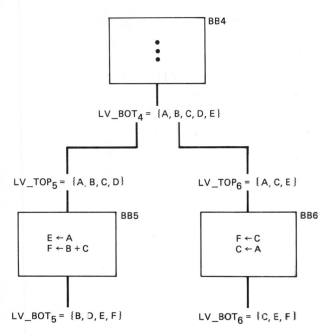

Figure 12-34 Flowgraph fragment showing live variables.

determine which values are alive at the top of block 5 as follows:

$$LV\_TOP_5 = (LV\_BOT_5 - LV\_DEF_5) \cup LV\_USE_5$$
$$= (\{B, D, E, F\} - \{E, F\}) \cup \{A, B, C\}$$
$$= \{B, D\} \cup \{A, B, C\}$$
$$= \{A, B, C, D\}$$

All variables which are alive at the top of either block 5 or block 6 are alive at the bottom of block 4. Therefore,

$$LV\_BOT_4 = LV\_TOP_5 \cup LV\_TOP_6$$
$$= \{A, B, C, D\} \cup \{A, C, E\}$$
$$= \{A, B, C, D, E\}$$

An expression is said to be *very busy* at point p if the value of the expression is required before the value of any of its terms along every path beginning at p. Typically, we might restrict ourselves to simple binary expressions of the form X op Y. The *very-busy-expression problem* consists of determining which expressions are very busy at the end of each block. Since an expression can only be very busy at the end of a block if it is very busy at the beginning of all of that block's successors, the very-busy-expression problem is a backward-flow problem.

In Fig. 12-35, we present an example of the very busy expressions in a portion of a flowgraph. VBE_DEF_i is the set of expressions X op Y (which are not necessarily in block i) such that either X or Y is defined in block i before the first (if any) occurrence of X op Y. For example, in BB5 of the flowgraph shown in Fig. 12-35, assume that $VBE\_BOT_5 = \{Y + Z\}$. Therefore,

$$VBE\_DEF_5 = \{C + D, Y + Z\}$$

because C is given a new value in block 5 before C + D occurs, and both Y and Z are given new values. The assignments to C and Z define the limits to which the very busy expressions C + D and Y + Z, respectively, can be propagated upward. Intuitively, VBE_DEF corresponds to a "KILL" on the upward flow of a very busy expression.

VBE_USE_i is the set of expressions X op Y computed in block i for which there are no prior definitions of X or Y in that block. Therefore,

$$VBE\_USE_5 = \{A + B, E + F\}$$
$$VBE\_USE_6 = \{A + B\}$$

in the example.

The information-flow equations for this backward-flow problem are as follows:

$$VBE\_TOP_i = (VBE\_BOT_i - VBE\_DEF_i) \cup VBE\_USE_i$$
$$AE\_BOT_i = \bigcap_{\substack{s \text{ is a} \\ \text{successor} \\ \text{of } i}} AE\_TOP_s$$

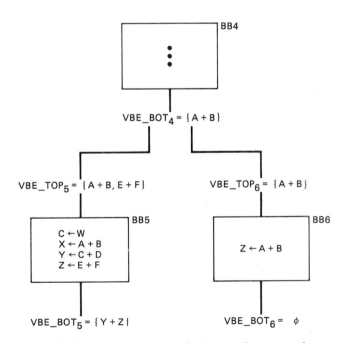

Figure 12-35 Flowgraph fragment showing very busy expressions.

Using the equation giving VBE_TOP$_i$, we compute VBE_TOP$_5$ as follows:

$$\text{VBE\_TOP}_5 = (\{Y + Z\} - \{C + D, Y + Z\}) \cup \{A + B, E - F\}$$
$$= \{\phi\} \cup \{A + B, E + F\}$$
$$= \{A + B, E + F\}$$

Following Aho and Ullman (1977) and Hecht (1977), we can classify the four problems in two different ways: by direction of flow and by the type of joining operator used. Both available expressions and reaching definitions are forward-flow problems: the information available at the top of a basic block depends on the information available at the bottom of its predecessors. The live-variables problem and the very-busy-expressions problems are backward-flow problems: the information available at the bottom of a basic block depends on the information available at the top of its successors. To compute available expressions or very busy expressions, a set intersection operation is used. That is, an expression is available at the beginning of block i only if it is available at the end of *all* its predecessors and an expression is very busy at the bottom of block i only if it is very busy at the top of *all* the successors of i. Reaching definitions and live variables are computed using the set union operation. A definition reaches the top of block i if it reaches the bottom of *any* of its predecessors, and a variable is alive at the bottom of block i if it is alive at the top of *any* of its successors.

Now that we have described several of the most important flow-analysis problems, we can examine some of the algorithms used to solve these problems.

Flow-analysis algorithms. Algorithms used for flowgraph analysis can be divided roughly into two groups, those based on the loop structure of the graph and those using iterative methods. Algorithms which take advantage of the loop structure are generally faster than those using iterative methods but require that the flowgraph be reducible. Typically, any program not having a branch into the middle of a loop is reducible. Examinations of real programs have shown that almost all (even FORTRAN programs!) are reducible (see Knuth 1971; Aho and Ullman, 1977). All programs in languages which exclude arbitrary branching (such as BLISS; see Wulf, 1971) have reducible flowgraphs. Therefore, reducibility is not an unfulfillable requirement. In this section, we describe several iterative algorithms and also explain how the loop structure of a program can be determined as the first step toward more efficient loop-based algorithms.

Iterative algorithms for analyzing flowgraphs The three types of iterative algorithms are worklist, round-robin, and node listing. Worklist algorithms are distinguished by the presence of a *worklist*, a list containing "work to be done." This worklist is initialized, perhaps with a single item, at the beginning of the algorithm. As the algorithm executes, new items are added to the worklist. When one task has been completed, the next task is taken from the front of the worklist. One can think of the worklist as containing information whose effect has not yet been completely propagated throughout the graph. The algorithm halts when a task has been completed and no tasks remain in the worklist. The order in which a worklist algorithm visits the nodes depends on the order of the tasks in the worklist.

The following is a worklist algorithm (based on that of Hecht, 1977) for computing available expressions. There are **NBR_EXPR** expressions in the procedure, and the algorithm assumes that they have been found and placed in **EXPR**. Typically, the expressions might be determined by finding all the different expressions appearing in the quadruples. In order to detect expressions which are equivalent under commutativity, the operands of commutative operators might be reordered with constants first and variables following in alphabetical order. AE _TOP_TABLE is a two-dimensional array with rows corresponding to basic blocks and columns corresponding to the expressions that are used. If AE_TOP _TABLE[i, j] is 0, then expression j is not available at the top of basic block i. The expressions are processed one at a time. Originally, an expression $EXPR_j$ is considered unavailable in block i if it is killed in one of block i's immediate predecessors; otherwise, it is considered available. In such a case, block i is placed in the worklist. Then the unavailabilty of the expression at a node is propagated forward to all that node's successors where it was previously available, and these successors are placed in the worklist. When no blocks are available in the worklist for processing, the algorithm goes on to the next expression.

Algorithm AE_WORKLIST. This algorithm solves the available-expressions problem using a worklist. A queue, WORKLIST_Q, is used to hold blocks awaiting processing. The expressions are stored in a set **EXPR**. There are assumed to be NBR_EXPR expressions and n basic blocks in the flowgraph being examined. AE_TOP_TABLE is a two-dimensional array and AE_GEN and AE_KILL are sets, all as previously described.

1. [Initialize worklist]
    WORKLIST_Q ← φ
2. [Process each expression]
    Repeat through step 4 for j = 1, 2,...,NBR_EXPR
3. [Initialize worklist by examining each basic block]
    Repeat for i = 1, 2,...,n
        If i = 1 or $EXPR_j \in (AE\_KILL_k - AE\_GEN_k)$ for some predecessor k of block i
        then AE_TOP_TABLE[i, j] ← 0
            Add i to end of WORKLIST_Q
        else AE_TOP_TABLE[i, j] ← 1
4. [Process blocks from worklist until it becomes empty]
    Repeat while WORKLIST_Q ≠ φ
        Remove the first element from the WORKLIST_Q and place it in i.
        If $EXPR_j \notin AE\_GEN_i$
        then Repeat for each successor k of i
                If AE_TOP_TABLE[k, j] = 1
                then AE_TOP_TABLE[k, j] ← 0
                    Add k to end of WORKLIST_Q

5. [Finished]
   Exit

☐

Let us consider the operation of Algorithm AE_WORKLIST on the fourth expression, I + J, in the program flowgraph shown in Fig. 12-36. Step 3 sets the fourth column of the AE_TOP_TABLE to $(C, 1, 1, 1)$, and adds block 1 to the worklist. In step 4, block 1 is removed from the worklist and since I + J is not in AE_GEN$_1$, the successors of block are examined. AE_TOP_TABLE[2, 4] and AE_TOP_TABLE[3, 4] are set to 0 and blocks 2 and 3 are added to the worklist. Since I + J is in AE_GEN$_2$ and AE_GEN$_3$, blocks 2 and 3 are removed without having their successors examined. The algorithm finds that I + J is available only at the top of block 4.

The second type of iterative algorithm is the round-robin type. A round-robin algorithm repeatedly visits the nodes in some order, such as $1, 2, 3, \ldots, n$. The algorithm begins with an initial estimate of the condition of the flowgraph. For example, an available-expressions algorithm might begin with the assumption that all expressions are available at the top of each block. Then the algorithm processes the nodes in a round-robin order propagating information. The algorithm continues to make visits in a round-robin manner until no change takes place in a complete pass.

The following is a round-robin algorithm (based on that of Aho and Ullman, 1977) for computing available expressions. The algorithm originally assumes that all expressions are available at the top of each block, and all expressions not

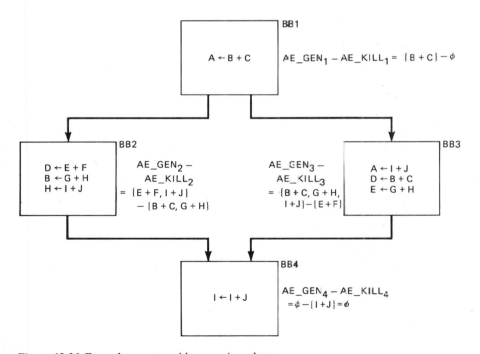

Figure 12-36 Example program with expressions shown.

killed in the block are available at the bottom of that block. Then round-robin visiting is performed on the nodes. Each time a node is visited, the set of expressions which reach the bottoms of all its predecessors is determined. If this set is different from (and if different, it will always be a subset of) the previously calculated AE_TOP, it replaces the old set. The algorithm continues to visit the nodes in a round-robin fashion until no changes take place in one visiting of all nodes.

Algorithm AE_ROUND_ROBIN. This algorithm solves the available-expressions problem using a round-robin approach. The blocks are visited in the order $1, 2, \ldots, n, 1, 2 \ldots$ etc. AE_TOP, AE_BOT, AE_GEN, AE_KILL, and EXPR are sets as previously described. FLAG is a logical variable which is true as long as information is being propagated through the flowgraph. NEW_TOP is a temporary set variable used to hold the newly computed AE_TOP set.

1. [Initialize to an appropriate solution]
   AE_TOP$_1$ ← ϕ
   AE_BOT$_1$ ← AE_GEN$_1$
   Repeat for i = 2, 3,....,n
      AE_TOP$_i$ ← EXPR
      AE_BOT$_i$ ← EXPR − AE_KILL$_i$
2. [Perform round-robin visiting until information flow stabilizes]
   FLAG ← true
   Repeat while FLAG
      FLAG ← false
      Repeat for i = 2, 3,....,n
         NEW_TOP ← $\bigcap\limits_{\substack{p \text{ is a} \\ \text{predecessor} \\ \text{of } i}}$ AE_BOT$_p$

         If NEW_TOP ≠ AE_TOP$_i$
         then AE_TOP$_i$ ← NEW_TOP
            AE_BOT$_i$ ← (AE_TOP$_i$ − AE_KILL$_i$) $\cup$ AE_GEN$_i$
            FLAG ← true
3. [Finished]
   Exit   □

For example, if Algorithm AE_ROUND_ROBIN is used to determine the available expressions for the flowgraph shown in Fig. 12-36, the same results are obtained as were obtained using Algorithm AE_WORKLIST. Step 1 performs the following initializations:

AE_TOP$_1$ = ϕ
AE_BOT$_1$ = {B + C}
AE_TOP$_2$ = AE_TOP$_3$ = AE_TOP$_4$ = {B + C, E + F, G + H, I + J}
AE_BOT$_2$ = {E + F, I + J}
AE_BOT$_3$ = {B + C, G + H, I + J}
AE_BOT$_4$ = {B + C, E + F, G + H}

In step 2, block 2 is examined first. AE_TOP_2 is set to $\{B + C\}$ and AE_BOT_3 is recomputed, but remains as $\{E + F, I + J\}$. When block 3 is examined, AE_TOP_3 is set to $\{B + C\}$ and AE_BOT_3 remains unchanged. Finally, AE_TOP_4 is computed as the intersection of the AE_BOTs of its predecessors, blocks 2 and 3; the new value is $\{E + F, I + J\} \cap \{B + C, G + H, I + J\} = \{I + J\}$. AE_BOT_4 is accordingly updated to ϕ since $I + J$ is killed by the assignment to I, and FLAG is set to *true*. Since FLAG is *true*, blocks 2, 3, and 4 are reexamined but no further changes take place. In round-robin algorithms, an extra pass to show that no further changes are taking place is required.

The third form of iterative algorithm, which we only briefly introduce, is the node-listing algorithm. The first step is to obtain a list giving the order in which the nodes should be visited. A node list will usually contain frequent repetitions of some nodes. Then information is propagated to all nodes by processing the nodes in the order given in the list. By using such an approach, two problems with the round-robin algorithm can be avoided. An extra pass to see that no changes have taken place is not necessary, and visits are avoided to nodes unaffected by the information currently being propagated.

Let us consider the problem of obtaining a node list. One order which could be used is the order in which nodes are added to the worklist in a worklist algorithm (i.e., 1, 4, and finally 2 and 3 in the example in Fig. 12-36). The difference is that in a node-listing algorithm the whole list is known before information propagation is begun, while in a worklist algorithm, the last part of the list is generated during the execution of the algorithm. If the number of nodes visited was no fewer with the node-listing approach than with the worklist algorithm, the worklist approach would clearly be superior since it avoids the cost of storing a long list. But a good node-listing algorithm can produce a list shorter than its worklist counterpart. For example, to solve the available-expressions problem, a listing including every acyclic path (that is, every path which can be traversed without returning to any node along that path) as a separate subsequence is sufficient to guarantee information propagation throughout the graph. Aho and Ullman (1975) give an algorithm suitable for the available-expressions problem which is of $O(n \log n)$ which finds a node listing of length $O(n \log n)$. The reader is referred to Kennedy (1975), Aho and Ullman (1975), and Hecht (1977) for more complete details and examples of node-listing algorithms.

The worklist and round-robin types of iterative algorithms are more widely used than the node-listing type. These algorithms are easy to program and can be used for all types of information-flow analysis problems. They do not require that the flowgraph be reducible. Of the two algorithms, the worklist algorithm is more appealing because only those nodes which are directly affected by information propagation are visited; in the round-robin algorithm, all nodes are repeatedly visited, whether affected or not. Both these algorithms can be expensive: even if each basic block is limited to two successors, the worst-case time complexity of these algorithms is $O(n^2)$ (Hecht, 1977). Also, these algorithms do not yield any information about the loop structure of the flowgraph, should such information be desired by the optimizing compiler or programmer. In spite of these disadvantages, these two types of iterative algorithms are frequently used in compilers to avoid performing an analysis of the program's loops. In the next subsection, we discuss algorithms which make use of information about loops.

Analyzing information flow in program loops The path of execution of a procedure depends on the loops which are present in the procedure. As a result, nodes within a loop often have common properties. For example, an expression available at one node of the loop may be available at all other nodes in the loop as well. Since information propagation depends on the loops present in the flowgraph, effective information-flow analysis algorithms depend on first finding the loops.

Up to this point, we have not defined precisely what constitutes a loop in a program. We want our definition of a loop to agree with our conception of a loop in a program. A loop is a group of statements which can be repeatedly executed together. In structured programs, a loop has a single entry point and a single exit. Finally, nesting of loops is allowed.

Two concepts from graph theory, the cycle and the strongly connected component, are not suitable choices for our definition of a loop. Consider the example FIDDLE shown in Fig. 12-37a and b and its corresponding flowgraph as shown in Fig. 12-38. A *cycle* is any path which starts and ends at the same node. In the flowgraph shown, $\{1, 2, 6, 1\}$ is a cycle, but these nodes do not form a program loop since node 2 corresponds to an if statement whose then part is node 3, which is not in the cycle. A *strongly connected component* is a maximal strongly connected subgraph. For example, the strongly connected components in the flowgraph are $\{1, 2, 3, 4, 5, 6, 7, 8, 9\}$ and $\{10\}$. Strongly connected components do not allow for the possibility of loops within loops. Neither of these terms from graph theory is appropriate for the definition of a loop.

Two other terms, *interval* and *strongly connected region*, have been proposed

Algorithm FIDDLE.

1. Repeat thru step 6 while X > A

2. If X > B

    then Repeat while X > C

          If X > D

          then X ← X − 1

3. Repeat thru step 6 while X > E

4. Repeat thru step 5 while X > F

5. X ← 2 * X

6. F ← F − 2

7. ...

Figure 12-37a Example algorithm.

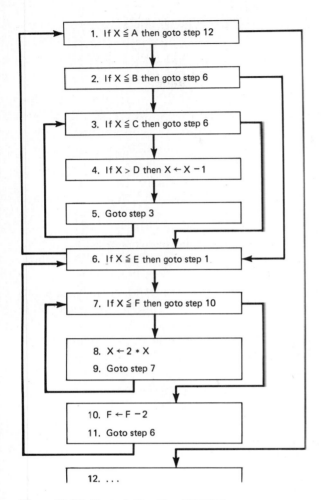

Figure 12-37b Revised Algorithm FIDDLE.

by other authors. Cocke (1970) and Allen (1970) describe interval analysis. Strongly connected regions were first described by Allen (1969).

An interval is defined as follows (Hecht, 1977): An *interval with header h*, denoted $I(h)$, in a flowgraph $G = (N, E, i)$ is a set of nodes in G obtained using the following algorithm:

$I(h) \leftarrow \{h\}$

Repeat while there exists a node m in G such that $m \notin I(h)$ and $m \neq i$ and all edges entering m come from nodes in $I(h)$

$I(h) \leftarrow I(h) \cup \{m\}$

The intervals in the flowgraph given in Fig. 12-38 are as follows:

$I(1) = \{1, 2, 10\}$
$I(2) = \{2\}$
$I(3) = \{3, 4, 5\}$
$I(4) = \{4, 5\}$
$I(5) = \{5\}$
$I(6) = \{6\}$
$I(7) = \{7, 8, 9\}$
$I(8) = \{8\}$
$I(9) = \{9\}$
$I(10) = \{10\}$

For example, consider obtaining the interval with header 3, that is, $I(3)$. First, $I(3)$ is initialized to $\{3\}$. Then node 4 is identified as a node not in $I(3)$ whose predecessors are all in $I(3)$, and is added to $I(3)$. Similarly, node 5's only predecessor, node 4, is now in $I(3)$, and thus $I(3)$ becomes $\{3, 4, 5\}$. Node 6 can not be added to the interval because one of that node's predecessors, node 2, is not in $I(3)$.

The definition can be restricted so that a partition is generated. If all intervals which are proper subsets of other intervals are eliminated, the following partition

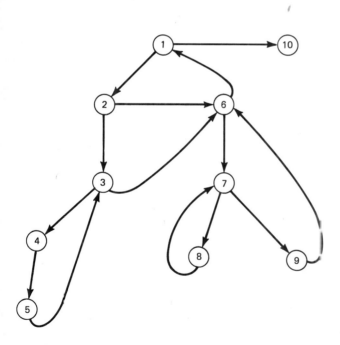

Figure 12-38 Flowgraph containing loops.

is generated:

$$I(1) = \{1, 2, 10\}$$
$$I(3) = \{3, 4, 5\}$$
$$I(6) = \{6\}$$
$$I(7) = \{7, 8, 9\}$$

Intervals do not correspond directly to program loops, since parts of the program which are not in any program loop are included as separate intervals. The intervals can be organized into a hierarchy similar to the nesting of loops. The techniques used to analyze flowgraphs broken into intervals are called interval-analysis techniques. The reader is referred to Hecht (1977) for a more detailed discussion of these techniques.

A *strongly connected region* (or *region*) R in a flowgraph $G = (N, E, i)$ is a subgraph of G with the following three properties:

1. There is a path completely within R from any node in R to any other node in R.
2. Any path from a node outside R to a node in R must go through a single node in R called the *entry node*.
3. If the initial node i of G is in R, then i is the entry node for R.

This definition is similar to the definition of *loop* given by Aho and Ullman (1977). The third condition is included so that if the entry point to the procedure is in a region, it is at an entry node for that region. The regions in the flowgraph given in Fig. 12-38 are $\{3, 4, 5\}$, $\{7, 8\}$, $\{6, 7, 8, 9\}$, and $\{1, 2, 3, 4, 5, 6, 7, 8, 9\}$. Since edges enter both at 6 and 7, $\{6, 7, 9\}$ is not a region. The reader can verify that our definition of region corresponds well to the concept of a program loop by examining the algorithm given in Fig. 12-37. The flowgraph shown in Fig. 12-38 is based on this algorithm.

In order to determine the regions, we must first obtain a reducible flowgraph for the procedure. Node n is said to *dominate* node m if every path from the initial node to m passes through n. For example, in the flowgraph shown in Fig. 12-38, node 2 dominates all nodes except nodes 1 and 10 because there is no path from node 1 to any of these nodes which does not pass through node 2. Node 3 does not dominate node 6 because the path $(1, 2, 6)$ reaches 6 without passing through node 3.

In an edge $(n:m)$, also designated as $n \rightarrow m$, n is the *tail* of the edge and m is the *head* of the edge. Using these terms, we define a reducible flowgraph as follows: a flowgraph G is *reducible* if the edges can be partitioned into *forward* edges and *back* edges. The forward edges make up a graph that is without cycles and in which each node can be reached from the initial node of G. An edge is a back edge if its head dominates its tail.

For example, in the flowgraph shown in Fig. 12-38, edges such as $3 \rightarrow 4$, $4 \rightarrow 5$, and $3 \rightarrow 6$ are forward edges, while $5 \rightarrow 3$ is a back edge because node 3 dominates node 5. The flowgraph shown is reducible since except for back edges $5 \to 3$, $8 \to 7$, $9 \to 6$, and $6 \to 1$, all other edges make up a graph that is without cycles and that includes all nodes.

Not all flowgraphs are reducible. For example, if the flowgraph includes a subgraph such as that shown in Fig. 12-39, the flowgraph is said to be irreducible. By splitting nodes (that is, by creating two copies of them), such an irreducible flowgraph can be converted into an "equivalent" reducible flowgraph. But the best-known algorithms for producing reducible flowgraphs from irreducible flowgraphs by performing node splitting are NP-Complete (see Hecht, 1977). Fortunately, most real programs require very little, if any, node splitting.

The following algorithm determines the regions of a procedure for which the reducible flowgraph is available. The algorithm first obtains a node listing by calling upon the recursive procedure DEPTH, which is given later. The ordering used is *depth-first order*, which is the reverse of the order in which nodes are last visited when a preorder traversal is performed. The procedure DEPTH also constructs a *depth-first spanning tree*, which is the tree that is constructed when the flowgraph is visited in depth-first order. In step 3 of Algorithm FIND _REGIONS, the back edges are identified as those edges whose heads precede their tails in the depth-first ordered node list. Then the region corresponding to each back edge is found by taking the head node and all other nodes which can reach the tail of the back edge without passing through the head. The head node is the entry node for the region.

Algorithm FIND_REGIONS. Given the reducible flowgraph G = (BLOCK, SUC, INITIAL_BLOCK) of a procedure, this algorithm finds the regions in G. BLOCK, SUC, and INITIAL_BLOCK are as in Algorithm CONSTRUCT_FLOW-GRAPH given earlier in Sec. 12-6.1. The procedure DEPTH uses the global vector MARK and the global variable CTR. DFST is a global set variable used to contain the depth-first spanning tree built by DEPTH. NODE_POSITION gives the position of the node in a one-pass processing order. REGION is a vector of sets containing the regions; r is used as an index to this vector. TEMP is a temporary variable used to hold nodes while their predecessors are being examined. STACK is the stack of nodes whose predecessors must be examined for possible inclusion in the current region. PUSH and POP subalgorithms are assumed for use with this stack. n is the number of nodes.

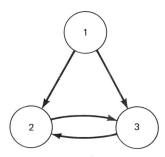

Figure 12-39 Irreducible portion of a flowgraph.

1. [Initialize global variables for depth-first search procedure]
   > MARK ← false
   > DFST ← ϕ (ϕ denotes the empty set)
   > CTR ← n
   > r ← 0
2. [Obtain NODE_POSITION and DFST using the depth-first search procedure]
   > Call DEPTH (INITIAL_BLOCK)
3. [Find the region associated with each back edge]
   > Repeat for all edges t → h in G where
   > > NODE_POSITION[t] ≥ NODE_POSITION[h]
   > > r ← r + 1
   > > STACK ← ϕ
   > > REGION$_r$ ← BLOCK$_h$
   > > If t ∉ REGION$_r$
   > > then REGION$_r$ ← REGION$_r$ ∪ BLOCK$_t$
   > > > Call PUSH(STACK, t)
   > > Repeat while blocks remain on STACK
   > > > TEMP ← POP (STACK)
   > > > Repeat for each p ∈ PRED[TEMP]
   > > > > If p ∉ REGION$_r$
   > > > > then REGION$_r$ ← REGION$_r$ ∪ BLOCK$_p$
   > > > > > Call PUSH(STACK, p)
4. [Finished]
   > Exit   □

Procedure DEPTH (i). This recursive procedure builds a depth-first spanning tree for a graph starting from node i. The set DFST contains the depth-first spanning tree. The vector NODE_POSITION gives the position of the node in the depth-first ordering. CTR counts from n, the number of nodes, down to 1, and is used to ensure that nodes are placed in NODE_POSITION in the reverse of the order in which they are last visited. All variables are global to the procedure.

1. [Mark current node as visited]
   > MARK[i] ← true
2. [Examine successors of current node]
   > Repeat for each j ∈ SUC[i]
   > > If not MARK[j]
   > > then DFST ← DFST ∪ (i, j)
   > > > Call DEPTH (j)
3. [Determine position of current node in depth-first ordered list]
   > NODE_POSITION[i] ← CTR
   > CTR ← CTR − 1
4. [Finished]
   > Return   □

Let us consider how the algorithm would find the regions in the flowgraph shown in Fig. 12-38. The initial call to DEPTH with i = 1 causes MARK[1] to be set to *true*. Then a successor of node 1, in this case one of nodes 2 and 10, is chosen. If node 2 is chosen, edge (1, 2) is added to DFST and a recursive call to DEPTH with i = 2 is made. If it is assumed that in all cases the successors are examined in left-to-right order, the nodes are visited in the following order:

1, 2, 3, 4, 5, 4, 3, 6, 7, 8, 7, 9, 7, 6, 3, 2, 1, 10, 1

Choosing an order based on the last visit to each node as given in a right-to-left scan of the previous sequence, we derive the sequence:

5, 4, 8, 9, 7, 6, 3, 2, 10, 1

Reversing this order gives the following depth-first order:

1, 10, 2, 3, 6, 7, 9, 8, 4, 5

Finally, we can derive the positions of the nodes in the list as follows:

Node number	1	2	3	4	5	6	7	8	9	10
NODE_POSITION	1	3	4	9	10	5	6	8	7	2

In step 3, for a forward edge such as $1 \rightarrow 2$, NODE_POSITION[1] = 1 is less than NODE_POSITION[2] = 3, but for a back edge, such as $5 \rightarrow 3$, NODE_POSITION[5] = 10 is greater than or equal to NODE_POSITION[3] = 4. The region corresponding to back edge $5 \rightarrow 3$ is found by first placing the head, node 3, in the region, then adding node 5, and then adding node 5's predecessor, node 4. The regions $\{3, 4, 5\}$, $\{7, 8\}$, $\{6, 7, 8, 9\}$, and $\{1, 2, 3, 4, 5, 6, 7, 8, 9\}$ are found corresponding, respectively, to back edges $5 \rightarrow 3$, $8 \rightarrow 7$, $9 \rightarrow 6$, and $6 \rightarrow 1$.

Now that the techniques of flowgraph analysis have been reviewed, we can proceed to a discussion in the next section of how the information obtained can be used in performing program optimizations.

12-6.3 Applications to Program Optimization

Our justification for performing flowgraph analysis is its usefulness to an optimizing compiler. In this section, we discuss one way in which information obtained from flowgraph analysis is used in program optimization. In particular, constant propagation is examined.

Let us first consider how the solution to the reaching-definitions problem can be of use to a compiler. Once the reaching definitions are known, a *ud-chain* can be readily constructed, which is a list giving all the possible definitions of variable *V* for every use of *V* in block *B*. If a use of *V* occurs in *B* after the definition of *V*, then the ud-chain for this use of *V* is the most recent definition of *V*. If no definition of V appears in B before a use, then the ud-chain consists of all the definitions which reach the top of B.

The most important use of ud-chains is in constant propagation. For example, if it is found that the only possible definition for a variable V is a constant, then the use of V can be replaced by a use of the constant. This constant may perhaps be combined with other constants for further simplification. If all uses of V can be replaced, then V becomes unnecessary.

The following algorithm shows how ud-chains can be incorporated in a constant propagation.

Algorithm CONSTANT_PROPAGATION. This algorithm folds constants by finding operands which have only one definition, a constant. Each such operand is replaced by the appropriate constant. OPND contains the current operand. UD_CHAIN contains a list of all possible definitions for the current use of OPND. The set RD_TOP is as previously described. LENGTH is a function giving the number of elements in the ud-chain.

1. [Examine all blocks]
    Repeat through step 6 for each block B in the procedure
2. [Examine all statements in the current block]
    Repeat through step 6 for each statement S in block B
3. [Examine all operands in the current statement]
    Repeat through step 5 for each operand OPND in S
4. [Compute ud-chain]
    If OPND has been defined in B
    then UD_CHAIN ← statement containing most recent definition in B
    else UD_CHAIN ← all definitions of OPND in RD_TOP$_B$
5. [Replace operand with appropriate constant]
    If LENGTH(UD_CHAIN) = 1 and that definition is a constant c
    then Replace OPND by c in S
6. [Combine constants]
    Rewrite S combining as many constants as possible
7. [Finished]
    Exit   ☐

The algorithm makes one pass through the procedure. In steps 4 and 5, each operand whose value is known to be a constant is replaced with the appropriate constant, and in step 6, an effort is made to combine all the constants in a statement. If in step 6 the right-hand side of the statement is reduced to a single constant, then a new constant definition has been created. Depending on the order in which the blocks are examined, this new constant might possibly have been used in place of some operand which has already been examined. The problem of making full use of new constants created by the algorithm can be handled in two different ways. The whole algorithm could be repeated over and over again until no new constant right-hand sides are generated. (In compilers, such an algorithm is usually limited to 1, 2, or at most 3 iterations.) On the other hand, we might note that if a single definition for a use of a variable exists, this definition must be in a block which dominates the block in which the use occurs. If the blocks are visited in an order that ensures that when a block is visited all blocks which dominate it have already been visited, then the problem of operands later being found to be constant never occurs. The order in which blocks are first visited in a depth-first search of the flowgraph is such an order. Of these two approaches, the use of an ordered list of blocks is preferable to repeated iteration, especially if the depth-first spanning tree is already available.

In this section we presented an algorithm which uses information gathered by flowgraph analysis to perform code optimizations. In the next section, we consider some of the problems which arise in implementing such optimizations.

12-6.4 Implementation and Further Considerations

There are a number of factors to consider before implementing flowgraph analysis in an optimizing compiler. First, we must consider the type of language for which the compiler is being written. The methods of optimization discussed in this section are mainly concerned with operations on variables and expressions. The optimizations are more applicable to languages involving numeric calculations than to those concerned with input and output. For example, consider the languages FORTRAN and COBOL. Since FORTRAN programs frequently contain many numerical calculations, many of the optimization techniques discussed have been used in FORTRAN compilers (see Lowry and Medlock, 1969, for example). On the other hand, COBOL programs, which are often primarily concerned with file handling, are not as amenable to these optimizations.

The methods discussed in this section assume that a single constant flowgraph can be constructed for each procedure. However, some languages allow statements which change the flowgraph during program execution. For example, in COBOL, the *alter* verb can change the destination of goto statements during execution. A COBOL compiler which allowed the alter verb could not use the flowgraph analysis techniques discussed in this section.

A reducible flowgraph corresponding to the program should be obtained if region-based optimizations are to be performed. Since sometimes reducible flowgraphs are difficult to obtain, a way of disabling region-based optimizations should exist. The compiler may disable them automatically if any or if too much node splitting is required. Also, programmers should have the option of deciding that these optimizations are not worthwhile for a program.

If the language does not permit arbitrary branches (goto's), the flowgraph is guaranteed to be reducible. Since program regions or intervals can be determined much more readily for such languages, optimizations depending on knowing the regions or intervals are more likely to be included.

Finally, the use of the object modules produced by the compiler should be considered. If the modules are executed once and then discarded, much optimization is rarely worthwhile. The more frequently the object module will be executed, the more optimizations can be justified. The time complexity of the iterative algorithms discussed is $O(n^2)$; their region-based counterparts execute in $O(n \log n)$ time. Therefore, if a lot of optimization is to be performed, a reasonable strategy is to first obtain a reducible flowgraph, then determine the program regions, and then analyze and optimize the program.

We have presented a survey of some methods of flowgraph analysis and suggested how they might be applied to the optimization of programs. A program can be represented as a flowgraph whose nodes are the basic blocks of the program. Information about variables and expressions can be derived from this flowgraph by flowgraph analysis. Any flowgraph can be analyzed using iterative algorithms, and reducible flowgraphs can be analyzed more efficiently using algorithms which take advantage of the loop structure of the program. The amount the resulting object module will be used determines the number and complexity of optimization techniques which should be applied to the program.

We have concentrated on fairly large, independent procedures. One interesting area of research involves an investigation of how small procedures with few parameters can be incorporated as flow of control instructions rather than procedure calls. Typically, procedure calls are treated as having the worst possible effects. This assumption could perhaps be reduced for many programs. Pointers and arrays lead to similar problems for the optimizing compiler because their exact effect cannot be determined at compile time. At the present time, the optimizing parts of many compilers are frequently disabled to prevent them from changing the meaning of the program they are optimizing. Reliability can be improved by more rigorous methods of optimization using flowgraph analysis.

Another interesting research possibility concerns languages whose structure lends to efficient flowgraph analysis without sacrificing user convenience. Both BLISS and SIMPL-T (see Hecht, 1977) have reducible flowgraphs for all programs since the GOTO statement is not included in these languages. One method of limiting the number of exits from program loops is to include a special exit node in the programming language. Knowing that the flowgraph is reducible allows the immediate application of techniques such as interval analysis. Two efficient algorithms currently known for performing flowgraph analysis are those presented in Ullman (1973) and Graham and Wegman (1975). These algorithms solve some information-flow problems for reducible flowgraphs in $O(n)$ time for programs whose loops have a limited number of exits.

CHAPTER EXERCISES

1 The following ALGOL W program has been compiled into a quadruple internal form. The compilation has not been optimized and the code may contain bad properties such as unfolded arithmetics, redundant expressions, dead assignments, invariant operations, operations without strength reduction (assume it costs much more to multiply than to add) and others. Optimize the code generated and point out all the bad properties you remove

ALGOL W program	Generated quadruples
IF A(1) < 0	1. (:= ,1,,T1)
	2. (:= ,A[T1],,T2)
	3. (:= ,0,,T3)
	4. (B < ,7,T2,T3)
	5. (:= ,0,,T4)
	6. (BR,,,8)
	7. (:= ,1,,T4)
&J > 0	8. (:= ,J,,T5)
	9. (:= ,0,,T6)
	10. (B > ,13,T5,T6)
	11. := ,0,,T4)
	12. (BR,,,14)
	13. (:= ,1,,T4)
THEN	14. (B,T4,15,17)
L:= 1	15. (:= ,1,,L)
	16. (BR,,,18)
ELSE L:= 2;	17. (:= ,2,,L)
J:= 2;	18. (:= ,2,,J)
FOR K:= 1	19. (:= ,1,,K)
	20. (BR,,,23)/*miss increment initially*/
STEP 2	21. (+,K,2,K)
UNTIL J DO BEGIN	22. (B > ,30,K,J)/*GO TO END_OF_FOR*/
A(K + 1):= A(K) + A(K + 1);	23. (+,K,1,T5)
	24. (+,A[K],A[T5],T6)
	25. (+,K,1,T7)
	26. (:= ,T6,,A[T7])
I:= J;	27. (:= ,I,,J)
L:= K*I	28. (*,K,I,L)
END	29. (BR,,,21)/*GO TO TEST*/

2 Assume we are given the following PL/I procedure:

```
CORREL: PROCEDURE(A,N);
    DECLARE A(*,*) FLOAT,
            N FIXED;
    DO I = 1 TO N;
        DO J = 1 TO 10;
            K = I*N;
            A(I,J) = (A(I,J) − A(I,J + 1))/(J + K);
        END;
    END;
END CORREL;
```

Translate this procedure into a triple notation similar to that given in Sec. 12-5. Then apply as many optimizations as you can (i.e., constant folding, common subexpression eliminations, loop unrolling, frequency reduction, strength reduction) assuming memory is free of charge, processing time is expensive, and multiplications are very expensive relative to additions.

3 Consider the problem of moving loop invariant assignment statements outside of a loop. It was pointed out earlier in Sec. 12-5.2 that this type of frequency reduction can inadvertently cause changes to a program because assignment statements may be executed "out of order" when they are moved outside a loop. Develop a strategy and then formulate an algorithm that will successfully handle the frequency reduction of assignment statements.

BIBLIOGRAPHY

Aho, A. V., and Ullman, J. D.: *The Theory of Parsing, Translation, and Compiling*, Vol. 2, *Compiling*, Englewood Cliffs, N.J.: Prentice-Hall, 1973.

Aho, A. V., and J. D. Ullman: "Listings for Reducible Flow Graphs," *7th ACM Symposium on Theory of Computing*, 1975, pp. 177–185.

Aho, A. V., and J. D. Ullman: *Principles of Compiler Design*, Reading, Mass.: Addison-Wesley, 1977.

Allen, F. E.: "Program Optimization," *Annual Review of Automatic Programming*, Vol. 5, pp. 239–307.

Allen, F. E.: "Control Flow Analysis," *SIGPLAN Notices*, Vol. 5, No. 7, 1970, pp. 1–19.

Allen, F. E.: "Interprocedural Data Flow Analysis," *Proceedings IFIP Congress*, Vol. 74, Amsterdam, North-Holland, 1974, pp. 398–402.

Allen, F. E., and J. Cocke: "A Program Data Flow Analysis Procedure," *Communications of the ACM*, Vol. 1, No. 3, 1976, pp. 137–147.

Beatty, J. C.: "A Global Register Assignment Algorithm," in R. Rustin, *Design and Optimization of Compilers*, Englewood Cliffs, N.J.: Prentice-Hall, 1972 pp 65–68.

Belady, L. A.: "A Study of Replacement Algorithms for a Virtual Storage Computer," *IBM Systems Journal*, Vol. 5, No. 2, 1966, pp. 78–101.

Cocke, J.: "Global Common Subexpression Elimination " *SIGPLAN Notices*, Vol. 5, No. 7, 1970, pp. 20–24.

Cocke, J., and J. P. Schwartz: "Programming Languages and Their Compilers," Preliminary Version, Courant Institute of Mathematical Sciences, New York, 1974.

Gries, D.: *Compiler Construction for Digital Computers*, New York: John Wiley & Sons, 1971.

Graham, S. L., and M. Wegman: "A Fast and Usually Linear Algorithm for Global Flow Analysis," *2d ACM Symposium on Principles of Programming Languages*, 1975, pp. 22–34.

Hecht, M.S.: *Flow Analysis of Computer Programs*, New York: Elsevier North-Holland, 1977.

Hopgood, F. R. A.: *Compiling Techniques*, Aylesbury, Great Britain: Macdonald, 1969.

Kennedy, K.: "Node Listings Applied to Data Flow Analysis," *2d ACM Symposium on Principles of Programming Languages*, 1975, pp. 10–21.

Knuth, D. E.: "An Empirical Study of FORTRAN Programs," *Software Practice and Experience*, Vol. 1, No. 12, 1971, pp. 105–134.

Lowry, E., and C. W. Medlock: "Object Code Optimization," *Communications of the ACM*, Vol. 12, No. 1, 1969, pp. 13–22.

Strong, H. R., A. Maggiolo-Schettini, and B. A. Rosen: "Recursion Structure Simplification," *SIAM Journal of Computing*, Vol. 4, No. 3, 1975, pp. 307–320.

Tremblay, J. P., and P. G. Sorenson: *An Introduction to Data Structures with Applications*, 2d ed., New York: McGraw-Hill, 1984.

Ullman, J. D.: "Fast Algorithms for the Elimination of Common Subexpressions," *Acta Informatica*, Vol. 2, No. 3, 1973, pp. 191–213.

Wulf, W. A., R. K. Johnson, C. B. Weinstock, S. O. Hobbs, and C. M. Geschke: "The Design of an Optimizing Compiler," Carnegie-Mellon University, Pittsburgh, Pa., 1973. (Since published as W. A. Wulf, et al.: *The Design of an Optimizing Compiler*, New York: Elsevier North-Holland, 1975.)

Wulf, W. A., Russell, and A. N. Habermann: "BLISS: A Language for Systems Programming," *Communications of the ACN*, Vol. 14, no. 12, pp. 780–790.

THIRTEEN

MACHINE-DEPENDENT OPTIMIZATION

Ultimately, the object program of a compiler must run on a real computer. In this chapter, we examine those parts of the compiling process which depend greatly on the nature of the machine for which the code is intended. First, we describe some well-known optimization techniques that apply to certain machines (e.g., the PDP-11 family) or to classes of machines (e.g., multiregister machines). Then in Sec. 13-2, we examine techniques of register allocation for both single- and multiregister machines. Finally, in Sec. 13-3, we discuss the problems of generating real code (either assembly-language or machine-language code).

13-1 INTRODUCTION TO MACHINE-DEPENDENT OPTIMIZATION

As we mentioned in the previous chapter, not all optimization techniques are machine-independent. When code is modified to make it more efficient on a particular machine, a *machine-dependent optimization* is being performed. Machine-dependent optimization uses information about the limits and special features of the target machine to produce code which is shorter or which executes more quickly on the machine. Clearly, in a general book on compiling, we cannot go into the details of machine-dependent optimization for specific machines. Instead, we review the most important techniques of machine-dependent optimization, and present a variety of examples illustrating the application of these techniques.

The code produced by the compiler should take advantage of the special features of the target machine. For example, consider code intended for machines of the PDP-11 family. These computers have autoincrement and autodecrement modes for instructions. When an instruction is given in the autoincrement mode, the contents of the register are incremented after being used. The register is incremented by one for byte instructions and by two for word instructions. The use of instructions in these modes reduces the code necessary for pushing and popping stacks. The PDP-11 computers also have machine-level instructions to increment (INC), or to decrement (DEC), by one, values stored in memory. Whenever possible, the INC and DEC operations should be used instead of creating a constant with value 1 and adding or subtracting this constant from the value stored in memory.

The PDP-11 machines have left- and right-shift operations. Shifting the bits one position to the left is equivalent to multiplying by 2. Since shifting is faster than multiplication or division, more efficient code is generated if multiplication and division by multiples of 2 are implemented with shift operations.

If two instructions do not depend on one another, they may be executed in parallel. Consider an expression such as $A * B + Y * Z$. The two factors $A * B$ and $Y * Z$ can be evaluated at the same time. If the target machine allows parallel processing of two multiplications, the compiler should generate code to take advantage of this capability. Also, compilers generating code for pipelined vector machines should take advantage of these machines' ability to perform vector operations in parallel.

When different instructions are available to perform a task, the most efficient should be chosen. For instance, on the IBM 370 and 30XX computers, a number of move instructions exist. When more than 256 characters are to be moved, the MVCL (move character long) instruction should be used; otherwise, the MVC (move character) instruction should be employed. The compiler should always make the best use of the instruction set.

Some machines have immediate instructions. Immediate instructions are those instructions which have a value included as part of the instruction. For example, the IBM 370, the MVI (move immediate) instruction can be used when only a single byte needs to be moved. Similarly the PDP-11 immediate mode allows fast access of constant operands by placing the desired constant in the word of memory just after the instruction.

Often appreciably better code is generated if the addressing features provided by the computer are considered. The indexing and indirect-addressing capabilities of the machine should be used effectively. For an indexed instruction, the contents of a specified register, called the *index register*, are added to the given address to obtain the address of the operand.

Indirect addressing is provided by many machines to shorten access time. When indirect addressing is used, the address of the true operand is given as the operand of the instruction. The distinction between direct and indirect addressing is illustrated in the following example. Consider a PDP-11 machine with register 0 (r0) containing the value 15, register 1 (r1) containing 2575, and memory location

2575 containing 1. An ADD instruction without indirect addressing is as follows:

ADD r1, r0

This instruction adds the contents of r1 to those of r0 and leaves the result in r0; therefore, after execution r0 would contain 2590 (the sum of 2575 + 15). Indirect addressing is specified by the symbol @ in PDP-11 assembly language. An instruction similar to that just given, but using indirect addressing, is as follows:

ADD @r1, r0

This instruction uses the value of r1 (2575) as the address of the operand. Thus, it adds the contents of memory location 2575 to the contents of r0; therefore, after execution r0 would contain 16 (the sum of 1 and 15).

Indirect addressing can be used, for example, to access values in stored tables by simply incrementing an address pointing to the table each time a new table element is required. It is a very important machine feature when index registers are not available or are in short supply.

In this section, we have suggested some of the types of machine-dependent optimizations which can be performed. So far, we have made no mention of the most important machine-dependent optimization, reorganizing code to make efficient use of the target machine's registers. In the following section, we examine several register-allocation techniques.

13-2 REGISTER-ALLOCATION OPTIMIZATION

In this section, we present a general discussion of register-allocation techniques. *Register allocation* refers to the choosing of which values are kept in registers during program execution. Values stored in registers can be accessed more quickly than values stored in other types of memory. Since computers have only a limited number of registers, the efficient use of these registers is important in producing good code. First we discuss how the register of a single-register machine can be used effectively. We then generalize our discussion to the more complex case of multiregister machines.

13-2.1 Register Allocation in Single-Register Machines

Register allocation is simplest on single-register machines. Such machines represent the simplest case of both multiregister and stack machines. A discussion of the register-allocation problem for single-register machines illustrates techniques used in simple computers, such as hand calculators, and provides a good introduction to the more general case of multiregister machines.

Since a single-register machine has only one register, the problem of choosing which values are stored in which register does not exist. All calculations must be performed in the single register, which is often called the *accumulator*. Operations should be performed in the order which reduces the number of load and store operations required. The accumulator should be continually allocated to different variables in a manner which minimizes the total number of instructions in the code produced.

Let us first look at a simplified example which shows how the single register can be used efficiently. For this example, we assume that the target computer is a single-accumulator machine with main memory that is sequentially organized into words. The following instructions are among those available in the assembly language.

LOD X   Loads the value of variable X in the accumulator and leaves the contents of X unchanged.

STO X   Stores the contents of the accumulator in a word of memory denoted by X. The accumulator contents remain unchanged.

ADD X   Adds the value of variable X to the value of the accumulator.

SUB X   The value of variable X is subtracted from the value of the accumulator.

MUL X   The value of variable X is multiplied by the value of the accumulator.

DIV X   The value of the accumulator is divided by the value of variable X.

All four arithmetic operations place the result of their computations in the accumulator; these operations do not alter the contents of X.

Code for the machine is generated in a straightforward manner. The compiler uses reverse Polish as an intermediate form (see Secs. 7-1 and 10-1). Suppose that code for the binary arithmetic operators is generated according to the following simple algorithm:

1. Load first operand into the accumulator
2. Apply operator using second operand, leaving result in the accumulator.
3. Store result into a temporary variable.

For example, the expression $X + Y$, which is represented in reverse Polish as $XY + $, would result in the generation of the following instructions:

    LOD X
    ADD Y
    STO T_i

Whenever code for an arithmetic operator is generated, the third instruction is of the form STO T_i, where T_i represents the address of a location (word) in memory that is to contain the value of the intermediate result. By incrementing i by 1 each time a new temporary variable is required, a sequence of unique names, $T_1, T_2, T_3, \ldots$, is generated.

Code for the assignment operator ' $\leftarrow$ ' is generated according to the following simple algorithm:

1. Load the value of the right part of the assignment statement into the accumulator.
2. Store this result into the specified variable.

We now present Algorithm ASSEMBLY_CODE which generates assembly-language instructions for the single-register computer just described.

Algorithm ASSEMBLY_CODE (POLISH). Given a string POLISH consisting of N symbols representing a reverse Polish expression equivalent to some well-formed assignment statement, this algorithm translates the string POLISH into assembly-language instructions. The Polish expression contains the four basic arithmetic operators, the assignment operator, and single-letter variables. The algorithm uses a stack STACK with an index TOP. CURRENT contains the current input character. The integer variable i is associated with the generation of temporary storage locations. The string variable OPCODE contains the operation code that corresponds to the current operation being processed. The subalgorithms PUSH and POP perform the pushing and popping of symbols on and from the stack, respectively.

1. [Initialize]
     TOP ← i ← 0
2. [Process all N symbols]
     Repeat through step 4 for J = 1, 2,...,N
3. [Obtain current input symbol]
     CURRENT ← SUB(POLISH, J, 1)
4. [Determine the type of CURRENT]
     If 'A' ≤ CURRENT and CURRENT ≤ 'Z'
     then Call PUSH(STACK, TOP, CURRENT)   (push variable on stack)
     else If CURRENT = ' ← '   (assignment operator)
        then If TOP ≠ 2
             then Write ('INVALID ASSIGNMENT STATEMENT')
                  Exit
             Write ('LOD□', POP(STACK, TOP))
             Write('STO□', POP(STACK, TOP))
        else Select case (CURRENT)   (process current operator)
             Case '+':
                  OPCODE ← 'ADD□'
             Case '−':
                  OPCODE ← 'SUB□'
             Case '*':
                  OPCODE ← 'MUL□'
             Case '/':
                  OPCODE ← 'DIV□'
             If TOP < 2
             then Write ('INVALID ASSIGNMENT STATEMENT')
                  Exit
             RIGHT ← POP(STACK, TOP)   (unstack two operands)
             LEFT ← POP(STACK, TOP)

Write ('LOD□', LEFT)   (output load instruction)
Write(OPCODE, RIGHT)   (output arithmetic instruction)
i ← i + 1
TEMP ← 'T'∘i   (create a new temporary name)
Write ('STO□', TEMP)
                                        (output store instruction for temporary)
            Call PUSH(STACK, TOP, TEMP)   (stack intermediate result)
5. [Check that all operands have been used]
        If TOP ≠ 0
        then Write ('INVALID ASSIGNMENT STATEMENT')
        Exit   □

The algorithm performs a linear scan on the string POLISH, stacking operands as it progresses. When an operator is encountered, two symbols are removed from the stack, the indicated operation is output, and the intermediate result is placed on the stack. Since all operators are binary, an error message is printed if the stack does not contain at least two operands when an operator is encountered. If operands remain on the stack when the algorithm is about to terminate, the expression is not a valid assignment statement.

Consider an assignment statement such as $X \leftarrow A + (B*C + D)$, which is represented in reverse Polish as $XABC*D + + \leftarrow$. Algorithm ASSEMBLY _CODE would produce the following code for this input:

LOD B
MUL C
STO T1
LOD T1
ADD D
STO T2
LOD A
ADD T2
STO T3
LOD T3
STO X

There are obvious inefficiencies in this code. Sequences of code such as

STO T_i
LOD T_i

are useless, since T_i is never really needed. Also, no advantage is taken of the commutativity of the addition and multiplication operators. Consider the sequence

STO T2
LOD A
ADD T2

Since $T2*A$ has the same value as $A*T2$, we could rewrite this sequence as

    STO T2
    LOD T2
    ADD A

This rewriting exposes a useless store/load pair, which can then be removed. After making improvements to avoid useless store/load pairs and to take advantage of commutativity, the code for $XABC*D + + \leftarrow$ can be improved as follows:

    LOD B
    MUL C
    ADD D
    ADD A
    STO X

The redundant pairs of store and load instructions and the unnecessary temporary storing and subsequent reloading of a right operand can be eliminated by the following technique. Instead of always storing a partial result in temporary storage, the generation of a STO instruction can be delayed until it is absolutely necessary. An intermediate result marker, '@', can be placed on the stack instead of always generating a store instruction. This marker represents the contents of the accumulator; as long as this marker is in one of the top two positions of the stack, store instructions can be avoided for commutative operators. These changes result in an algorithm which makes better use of the accumulator; whenever possible, the current value in the accumulator is used immediately, rather than stored and then later loaded.

Algorithm **ASSEMBLY_CODE** makes no effort to economize the number of temporary locations required to store intermediate results. Indeed, if m arithmetic operations are performed, m temporary variables are created. For example, even if unnecessary store/load instructions were not eliminated, the sixth instruction of

    LOD B
    MUL C
    STO T1
    LOD T1
    ADD D
    STO T2

could be replaced by

    STO T1

since the previous temporary value is no longer needed.

The number of temporary variables required can be greatly reduced by a few additions to the algorithm. Each time an arithmetic operator is processed, the names of two operands are popped off the stack into **RIGHT** and **LEFT**. After generating instructions for the operator, a test should be performed on the contents of RIGHT and LEFT. For each operand stored in RIGHT and LEFT which corresponds to a created variable T_i, the temporary-variable counter i should be decremented by 1. Temporary variables are also created to store the value of the accumulator when this value is later needed as the right operand of a noncommutative operator. Immediately after this value has been used, the temporary storage which it was allocated can be released.

Changes to Algorithm ASSEMBLY_CODE to make use of commutativity, to eliminate store/load pairs of instructions, and to reduce the numbers of temporary variables required are incorporated in the following algorithm.

Algorithm IMPROVED_ASSEMBLY_CODE (POLISH). In this modified version of Algorithm ASSEMBLY_CODE the variables of ASSEMBLY_CODE have been retained. COMMUT is a flag which is set to *true* when the current operation is a commutative one. A special marker, '@', is placed on the stack to indicate the contents of the accumulator. Only when this value must be removed from the accumulator to allow another calculation to be performed is the store instruction issued.

1. [Initialize]
        TOP ← i ← 0
2. [Process all N symbols]
        Repeat through step 4 for J = 1, 2,...,N
3. [Obtain current input symbol]
        CURRENT ← SUB(POLISH, J, 1)
4. [Determine the type of CURRENT]
        If 'A' ≤ CURRENT and CURRENT ≤ 'Z'
        then Call PUSH(STACK, TOP, CURRENT)   (push variable on stack)
           If TOP > 2
           then If STACK[TOP − 2] = '@'
              then i ← i + 1
              TEMP ← 'T' ∘ i
              STACK[TOP − 2] ← TEMP
              Write('STO□', TEMP)
                     (store temporary more than 2 deep)
      else If CURRENT = '←'   (assignment operator)
        then If TOP ≠ 2
           then Write('INVALID ASSIGNMENT STATEMENT')
           Exit
           RESULT ← POP(STACK, TOP)
           If RESULT ≠ '@'
           then Write('LOD□', RESULT)
           Write('STO□', POP(STACK, TOP))
      else If CURRENT = '+' or CURRENT = '*'
                     (commutative operator)

```
                then COMMUT ← true
                    If CURRENT = '+'
                    then OPCODE ← 'ADD□'
                    else OPCODE ← 'MUL□'
                else If CURRENT = '−' or CURRENT = '/'
                                            (noncommutative operator)
                    then COMMUT ← false
                        If CURRENT = '−'
                        then OPCODE ← 'SUB□'
                        else OPCODE ← 'DIV□'
                If TOP < 2
                then WRITE('INVALID ASSIGNMENT STATEMENT')
                    Exit
                RIGHT ← POP(S, TOP)                (unstack two operands)
                LEFT ← POP(S, TOP)
                If RIGHT = '@'
                then If COMMUT
                    then Write(OPCODE ∘ LEFT)
                    else i ← i + 1
                        TEMP ← 'T' ∘ i    (create a new temporary name)
                        Write('STO□', ∘ TEMP)
                        Write('LOD□', ∘ LEFT)
                        Write(OPCODE, ∘ TEMP)
                        i ← i − 1
                else If LEFT ≠ '@'
                        then Write('LOD□', ∘ LEFT)
                        Write(OPCODE, ∘ RIGHT)
                If RIGHT is a temporary variable
                then i ← i − 1
                If LEFT is a temporary variable
                then i ← i − 1
                Call PUSH(STACK, TOP, '@')        (place marker on stack)
    5. [Check that all operands have been used]
            If TOP ≠ 0
            then Write('INVALID ASSIGNMENT STATEMENT')
            Exit                                              □
```

Algorithm IMPROVED_ASSEMBLY_CODE acts in a manner similar to the unimproved version. However, near the beginning of step 4, a check is made to determine whether the marker @ is in the third position from the top of the stack. If there are two values above the marker, the accumulator will be needed for another calculation before its present contents can be used. Therefore, the contents of the accumulator are stored in a temporary variable.

While generating code, the algorithm takes advantage of commutativity. The LEFT and RIGHT operands are examined after being popped off the stack. If RIGHT is '@', less code is necessary for a commutative operator than for a noncommutative one. A commutative operator can be applied using the left operand, but a noncommutative one can only be applied after storing the right operand and loading the left operand. If RIGHT is not '@', the left operand is loaded, if necessary, and then the operator is applied using the right operand.

In Table 13-1, we present a trace of Algorithm IMPROVED_ASSEMBLY _CODE for the input string 'ZAB + C + DE + /FG − * ← '. After the first two ' + ' symbols are encountered, instructions to add A and B and then C are generated. A STO instruction to store the result of this calculation in temporary variable T_1 is generated only when two other operands, D and E, have been encountered. Note that when the right operand is '@', three instructions are generated for the noncommutative operation of division, but only one instruction is generated for the commutative operation of multiplication. Also note that after the contents of temporary storage locations T_1 and T_2 have been used in the division operation, these locations are available for reuse.

Algorithm IMPROVED_ASSEMBLY_CODE does not generate optimal code. For example, if D + E had been computed before A + B + C, one store and one

Table 13-1 Sample code generated by Algorithm IMPROVED_ASSEMBLY_CODE for the reverse Polish string 'ZAB + C + DE + / FG − * ← '

Current input character	Contents of stack (rightmost symbol is top of stack)	Left operand	Right operand	Code generated
Z	Z			
A	ZA			
B	ZAB			
+	Z@	A	B	LOD A
				ADD B
C	Z@C			
+	Z@	@	C	ADD C
D	Z@D			
E	ZT_1 DE			STO T_1
+	ZT_1 @	D	E	LOD D
				ADD E
/	Z@	T_1	@	STO T_2
				LOD T_1
				DIV T_2
F	Z@F			
G	ZT_1 FG			STO T_1
−	ZT_1 @	F	G	LOD F
				SUB G
*	Z@	T_1	@	MUL T_1
←		Z	@	STO Z

load instruction could have been avoided. Since the algorithm generates code for each operator as it is encountered, such a savings could not be detected. Although we have not presented an algorithm which generates optimal code for assignment statements, we have shown how an algorithm can be modified to generate better code for a specific type of machine, the one-register machine. In the following subsection we generalize our discussion of register allocation to the multiregister machine.

13-2.2 Register Allocation in Multiregister Machines

In this subsection, we generalize our discussion of register allocation to multiregister machines. First the terms *register allocation* and *register assignment* are explained. An algorithm which determines the minimum number of registers necessary to evaluate an arithmetic expression is presented. The Belady (1966) algorithm is suggested for register allocation within a single basic block. Then register allocation for a complete program is discussed. Finally some less optimal, but faster techniques of register allocation are mentioned.

In a multiregister machine, the register-allocation process involves two steps: register allocation and register assignment. A variable is *allocated* a register when the decision is made to keep its value in some register during program execution; a variable is *assigned* a register when a specific register is chosen for the variable. For example, suppose that the loop-counter variable, CTR, is frequently used. CTR is allocated a register when the decision is reached that the variable is important enough to be kept in a register. CTR is assigned a register when register 4 is chosen for the variable.

Register assignment is an important part of the register-allocation process. If some of a machine's registers have restricted uses, such as two of the PDP-11's six floating-point registers, register assignment must take into account these limitations. Also, a variable allocated a register in consecutive blocks should be assigned the same register in these blocks, to avoid unnecessarily transferring the value between registers. For example, suppose that in a two-register machine X and Y are allocated registers in block 1, and Y and Z are allocated registers in block 2. If Y is assigned register 1 in block 1, it should be assigned the same register in block 2.

Let us look at how an expression can be evaluated using a minimum number of registers. For the purpose of this discussion, we assume that expressions are represented as trees. Each node of an expression tree is of the form shown in Fig. 13-1.

Consider an expression of the form $\langle expr_1 \rangle$ $\langle binary\ operator \rangle$ $\langle expr_2 \rangle$ which is represented as a tree as shown in Fig. 13-2. Assume that n_1 registers are necessary to evaluate $expr_1$ and n_2 to evaluate $expr_2$. Before the complete

LPTR	SYMBOL	REGS_REQ	RPTR

Figure 13-1 Expression-tree node.

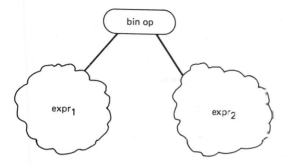

Figure 13-2 Expression tree for $\langle expr_1 \rangle$ $\langle bin\ op \rangle$ $\langle expr_2 \rangle$.

expression can be evaluated, both $expr_1$ and $expr_2$ must be evaluated. Suppose $expr_1$ is evaluated first, using n_1 registers. Since the result of this evaluation must be saved in a register, a total of $n_2 + 1$ registers are in use while $expr_2$ is being evaluated. Therefore, the evaluation of the complete expression requires $\max(n_1, n_2 + 1)$ registers. Similarly, if $expr_2$ is evaluated first, $\max(n_2, n_1 + 1)$ registers are needed. Clearly, if $n_1 < n_2$, evaluating $expr_2$ first requires fewer registers, and if $n_2 < n_1$, evaluating $expr_1$ requires fewer.

We now present Algorithm REG_COUNT which determines how many registers are necessary to evaluate an expression. This algorithm also indicates the order of evaluation for the minimum number of registers by negating the register count for operators which should have their right operand evaluated before their left operand. Throughout, it is assumed that all variables used as operands must be in registers.

Procedure REG_COUNT (ROOT). Given ROOT, the root of an expression tree, this algorithm determines how many registers are necessary to evaluate the expression. A postorder traversal of the tree is performed, placing the number of registers required in the REGS_REQ field of each node. LEFT and RIGHT hold the register counts for the left and right subtrees of the current operator node. If the right subexpression should be evaluated before the left, the value in REGS_REQ is negated. Thus, the absolute value of the REGS_REQ field of ROOT gives the number of registers necessary to evaluate the expression.

1. [Operand?]
        If NODE(ROOT) is a leaf
        then REGS_REQ(ROOT) ← 1
             Return
2. [Count registers needed to evaluate subexpressions]
        Call REG_COUNT(LPTR(ROOT))
        LEFT ← ABS(REGS_REQ(LPTR(ROOT)))
        Call REG_COUNT(RPTR(ROOT))
        RIGHT ← ABS(REGS_REQ(RPTR(ROOT)))

3. [Determine count for current operator node]
   If LEFT < RIGHT
   then REGS_REQ(ROOT) ← −RIGHT
   else If LEFT > RIGHT
           then REGS_REQ(ROOT) ← LEFT
           else REGS_REQ(ROOT) ← LEFT + 1
4. [Finished]
   Return   □

Given an expression tree representing the Arithmetic expression A * (B * C + D/((E − F) * G)), Procedure REG_COUNT sets the REGS_REQ fields to the values indicated by the numbers beside the nodes in the expression tree shown in Fig. 13-3.

When applied to the expression tree, a code-generation algorithm is able to determine the total number of registers required by taking the absolute value of the REGS_REQ field of the root, and the evaluation order by checking whether the REGS_REQ field of each operator node is negative or positive. Although Procedure REG_COUNT assumes all operators are binary, it can be generalized to handle nonbinary operators. Note, however, that the algorithm does not handle common subexpressions well; no effort is made to retain useful subtotals to avoid recomputing subexpressions.

The approach we have just described does minimize the number of registers necessary to evaluate an expression. However, no mention has been made of what should be done if the number of registers necessary is greater than the number

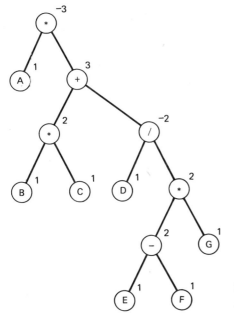

Figure 13-3 REGS_REQ values for A * (B * C + D/((E − F) * G)).

available. The true register allocation involves deciding which register must be stored when a register shortage occurs.

Nakata (1967) suggests two rules for deciding which register to store while evaluating arithmetic expressions:

1. When the value of some register must be stored, a partial result which is the left-hand operand of either "$-$" or "$/$" should not be stored if any other partial result could be chosen instead.
2. When the value of a register must be stored, the value which is not required for the longest time should be stored.

The first of these rules relates to the handling of noncommutative operators. In our discussion of the final example given in Sec. 13-1, we mentioned that shorter code could have been produced if the left operand was already in the accumulator when the noncommutative division operator was to be performed. Nakata's first rule says that for n-register machines which allow one operand to be in memory, the left operands of noncommutative operators should be kept in registers. When instructions for negation and inverse divide are available on a machine, this first rule becomes irrelevant.

As Nakata recognized, the second of his two rules is the more important. Redziejowski (1969) reformulated this second rule in terms of graph theory, and proved that this approach yields the minimum number of registers for commutative operators. Actually, Nakata's second rule represents an application to register allocation of an earlier algorithm given by Belady (1966) for page replacement in a two-level storage system. Ironically, it happens that the Belady algorithm is not achievable in page replacement because future page requirements are not known. It is, however, realizable in register allocation because information about register requirements for a complete sequence of code can be obtained before any register allocation is performed.

In a simple form, the Belady algorithm consists of performing the following steps whenever a variable V_i requires a register:

> If all registers have not been allocated
> then allocate an unused one to V_i
> else If any value contained in a register is no longer required
>   then allocate this register to V_i
>   else choose the register allocated to the variable, say V_j, whose next use is
>   farthest away
>   store the value of variable V_j if it has been changed
>   allocate the register to V_i

Let us now see how the Belady algorithm is used. Suppose that enough flow analysis has been performed to determine the NEXT_USE for a variable each time it is used (see Sec. 12-6). The NEXT_USE of a variable is 0 if the value of the variable is never needed again, either because the variable next appears on the left-hand side of an assignment statement, or because it never appears in the

Table 13-2 NEXT_USE information for a sample program

Program statement	Variable name	NEXT_USE
1	C	3
	B	2
2	A	−1
	B	0
3	D	4
	C	5
4	B	−1
	D	0
5	E	−1
	C	0

program again. For the purpose of this example, the NEXT_USE of a variable is −1 if the variable is not used again in the current basic block.

Consider a basic block consisting of the following statements:

1. C ← C * B
2. A ← A + B
3. D ← D * C
4. B ← D
5. E ← C

The NEXT_USE information for this basic block is shown in Table 13-2.

A variable is considered to be *live* when its current value is still required. In other words, if the value of a variable V is used at or after program statement i, then V is *live* at step i. Figure 13-4 shows the times when the variables of the sample program are live. It is assumed that variables A, B, C, and D are live at block entry, and that A, B, and E are live at block exit.

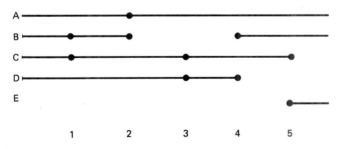

Figure 13-4 Graph showing live variables in each step of the sample program.

Table 13-3 Register allocation for the sample program

After program statement	Register 0	Register 1	Register 2
1	B	C	—
2	B	C	A
3	D	C	A
4	D	C	B
5	E	C	B

The number of lines intersected by a vertical line at any point gives the number of live variables at that point. For our purpose, we assume that all variables used as operands must be in registers; we ignore instructions which allow one or both operands to be in main memory, such as the RS and SS instructions in IBM 360 and 370 assembly language. Therefore, if the number of live variables exceeds the number of registers, variables are allocated in the manner shown in Table 13-3.

Register allocation is easily performed for program statements 1 and 2. For statement 3, the variable D requires a register. Since the value of B is no longer needed, register 0 is reallocated to D. In statement 4, B again requires a register, but on this occasion, no register has an unneeded value. An examination of the NEXT_USE values of A, C, and D shows that variable A is not needed again in this block. Therefore, register 2 is reallocated from A to B.

The Belady algorithm performs register allocation in an optimal manner as long as the values of variables are not altered while they are in registers. In reality, however, such alterations do take place. The cost of removing a variable from a register is higher if the variable has been changed than if it has not, since in the first case an additional instruction to store the variable's new value must be generated.

The algorithm can be improved to allow for different costs of removing variables by analyzing the problem using graph theory. A graph of all possible states through which the registers can pass is constructed. The cost of each transition between the states is placed on the corresponding edge of the graph. The least-cost path leading from the initial register configuration to the end of the last statement of the basic block gives the optimal sequence of register allocations.

Let us now look at a technique which was developed by Horowitz, Karp, Miller, and Winograd (1966) for pruning the graph of register transitions to allow the least-cost path to be determined more quickly. In the following discussion, we let V_j^* denote the contents of a register which contains a new unstored value for V_j. The previously mentioned authors proved that the least-cost path for the complete graph exists in the minimal-change subgraph. A *minimal-change subgraph* is constructed by beginning with the initial register configuration and adding only those edges $N_1 N_2$ which meet the following requirements for node N_1

associated with statement i and node N_2 associated with statement $i + 1$:

1. The configurations for N_1 and N_2 are identical.
2. If a variable V_j which is needed at statement $i + 1$ is already in a register at statement i, then this copy of V_j is used. If V_j is modified in statement $i + 1$, the register contents are afterward denoted by V_j^*.
3. If a variable V_j which is needed at statement $i + 1$ is not in a register at statement i, then one variable is removed from a register and replaced by V_j.

Horowitz, Karp, Miller, and Winograd (1966) also suggest several rules for pruning the minimal-change subgraph still further. Let $W(N_1)$ be the minimum cost of reaching node N_1 and let $W(N_1, N_2)$ be the cost of changing configuration N_1 into configuration N_2. Some of the rules are as follows:

1. If more than one edge enters node N, all entering edges can be deleted except the one on that path which has the least cost for reaching node N.
2. If no edges leave a node, the node and all edges entering it can be deleted.
3. If N_1 and N_2 are nodes of statement i and $W(N_1) + W(N_1, N_2) \leq W(N_2)$, then N_2 can be eliminated.

Other rules to still further reduce the graph size by looking ahead at the code sequence can also be formulated. The reader is referred to Horowitz, Karp, Miller, and Winograd (1966) for the detailed formulation of several such rules.

So far in this subsection, we have considered register allocation within a single basic block. Applying the Belady algorithm directly to a complete program would be difficult because the NEXT_USE values for some variables depend on which of a basic block's possible successor blocks is executed next. One simple strategy for allocating registers for a complete program is to perform the following steps for each basic block of the program:

1. Make a backward pass over the basic block to determine the NEXT_USE of each variable. Assume that the values of all variabless are useful at the end of the block; i.e., set the last NEXT_USE of all variable to -1;
2. Generate code for the basic block using the Belady algorithm to perform register allocation;
3. Store the contents of all registers in main memory.

Some improvements to this approach are called for. Variables which are used in two consecutive blocks should not be stored at the end of the first block, only to be reloaded at the beginning of the next. At the very least, even if all registers are stored at the end of a block, information about the contents of the register should be kept to prevent loading the same values again. Values which have not been changed or which are never needed again should not be stored at the end of the block. If a backward pass through the program flowgraph does not find any program execution path on which a value is used, then the value is never needed again in the program.

Finally, some use should be made of the unused registers when fewer than n variables occur in the block. To make effective use of these unused registers, and to provide a systematic solution to some of the other problems just discussed, register allocation should be given a wider scope than the basic block.

Register allocation can be made more effective by identifying variables which are frequently used in program regions. A *region* of a program consists of a number of strongly interconnected basic blocks. An example of a program region is a loop consisting of several basic blocks. Typically, several variables are frequently used in all the basic blocks of a region. An effective register-allocation approach should maintain these more important variables in registers whenever possible. For example, when the number of variables required for a basic block is less than the total number of registers available, important region variables should be kept in the extra registers.

Before register allocation can be performed on a regional basis, certain information must be known. The scope of each region must be determined. The number of times each variable is used in each block prior to any change in its value must be known. Also whether or not a variable has received a new value in a block which is needed in some successor block must be determined for each variable for each block. All this information can be obtained from flow analysis.

Beginning with the innermost region in a program, the choice must be made of which variables should be allocated registers for the region. By assuming that each block of a region is executed an equal number of times, an approximation to the best choices for register allocation can be determined using Algorithm COMPUTE_SAVINGS.

Algorithm COMPUTE_SAVINGS. This algorithm finds the n variables in region R which are the best choices for being allocated registers. The savings which result from choosing to allocate a register to variable V_i are calculated and stored in SAVINGS$_i$.

1. Repeat through step 5 for each variable V_i in region R
2. SAVINGS$_i$ ← 0
3. Repeat through step 5 for each block B_j in region R
4. SAVINGS$_i$ ← SAVINGS$_i$ + number of times V_i is used in B_j before its value is changed
5. If V_i is live on exit from B_j then SAVINGS$_i$ ← SAVINGS$_i$ + cost of storing V_i
6. Choose the n variables which have the highest SAVINGS values and allocate them registers
7. Exit

The variables which are chosen to be allocated registers for the region are always preferred to other variables when a tie for NEXT_USE occurs. Since these variables are known to be the most used in the region, they are assigned certain registers and kept in these registers whenever possible. This approach is applied to successively larger program regions, until register allocation has been performed for the whole program.

Some other approaches to register allocation result in less than optimal allocation but are much faster than the approach we have outlined. For example, the Belady algorithm does result in optimal register allocation within a basic block but requires graph construction and analysis. A simpler approach is to choose the n variables most frequently used in the block and assign registers to them. When other variables must be placed in registers, some of the chosen variables are temporarily removed and then replaced. A modified version of this approach was implemented in the FORTRAN H compiler (Lowry and Medlock, 1969). In this approach, the three most frequently used variables within an inner loop (or basic block) are identified and assigned registers for the duration of the loop. Also, it is often true that certain registers are restricted to certain uses, such as holding base addresses or return addresses. The use of regional and global register-allocation strategies becomes more important when less than optimal strategies are used at the basic block level.

13-3 MACHINE ARCHITECTURE AND THE GENERATION OF REAL CODE

In Chap. 10 the notion of an intermediate machine-independent instruction set was introduced. The primary motivation for introducing this notation was two-fold:

1. To provide an intermediate form upon which optimization strategies such as those discussed in Chap. 12 and Sec. 13-2 could be applied.
2. To allow for the production of machine-independent code that could later be "targeted" to a particular machine by writing an intermediate to target machine-code translater (e.g., similar to that illustrated in Sec. 13-2 for the translation of postfix to simple register machine code).

The general form of an intermediate to target machine-code translator is often implemented as a large case construct in which a separate routine is developed to translate each intermediate-level instruction into a series of target (or real) machine-code instructions. Usually, the target code is in the form of macro assembler-level instructions.

A second and probably more preferable form of translator involves a table-driven strategy. A hashing function is generally applied to an intermediate instruction to obtain a hash-table address as shown in Fig. 13-5. The hash table contains a pointer to an area of memory containing the set of macro assember instructions for a particular machine (e.g., PDP-11 code is used in Fig. 13-5). The hash table can be augmented on the right to contain pointers to several sets of

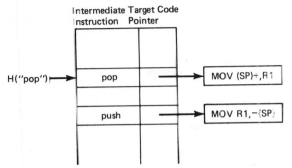

Figure 13-5 Example of table for intermediate to target machine code.

target code for several different machines and thereby provide a generalized translator.

The primary purpose of this section is to illustrate how some of the more common language constructs can be realized with sets of instructions from three of the more popular machine architectures: the PDP-11, VAX-11, and Motorola MC68000. Each architecture is described in a separate subsection and is reviewed in terms of its instruction set organization, data types, and flow of control instructions including branching, procedure invocation, and return. A familiarity with concepts in machine organization and assembler language is assumed throughout this section. A number of small examples are provided illustrating how common language constructs such as the for loop, procedure invocation, and parameter passing are realized in the different machines.

13-3.1 The PDP-11

The Digital PDP-11 family of computers was introduced in 1970 as general-purpose 16-bit minicomputers. Like many other machines of its day, the PDP-11 computer has one instruction set, instead of sets of special memory reference instructions, operation instructions, and I/O instructions. With the addition of floating-point numbers and arithmetic, a full instruction set is constituted. It is a register machine that contains six general-purpose registers and two special-purpose registers. There are eight addressing modes all of which can be used with any register, even the special registers, to form effective addresses. Push and pop operations can be applied to all the registers, thus making extensive stack facilities available.

Memory. Since the PDP-11 uses 16-bit addresses, it can address 64 K of memory. The basic memory unit is the 8-bit byte. A word is 16 bits and consists of a pair of adjacent bytes. The lower-order byte always has an even address, and its address is also the address of the word.

Registers. There are eight 16-bit registers, R0–R7. The registers R0–R5 are general-purposes registers. The other two registers have special purposes. R7 is the program counter (PC) and R6 is the stack pointer (SP), as it points to the top of the user stack. These special registers can also be used as general-purpose registers.

Data types. The data types supported by the PDP-11 are limited. The most basic machine supports only simple word and byte operations. With the common extended instruction set option (EIS), double-precision register operations are provided. PDP-11s with the floating-point instruction set (FIS) have operations for floating-point numbers stored with double precision.

Instructions. The PDP-11 has one and two operand instructions, along with some special instructions. The machine-language format of each type is shown in Fig. 13-6. For the one- and two-operand instructions, the operation code denotes the operation to be performed and the address fields give the addressing modes that are used. Since some addressing modes require a word immediately after the instruction, a two-address instruction may use one, two, or three words of memory.

Single - Operand Group

Operation code	Address field

15   6 5   0

Double - Operand Group

Operation code	Address field	Address field

15   12 11   6 5   0

Branch

Operation code	Offset

Condition Code Operators

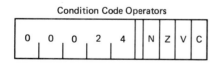

Subroutine Return

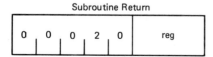

Figure 13-6 Major instruction formats of PDP-11.

Table 13-4 PDP-11 primitive addressing modes

Name	Assembler symbol	Description
Register	Rn	Rr is the operand.
Register deferred	@Rn or (Rn)	Rr points to the operand.
Indexed	X(Rn)	Rr + X points to the operand. X is an offset.
Indexed deferred	@X(Rn)	Rn + X points to a memory location, which in turn points to the operand.
Autoincrement	(Rn) +	Rn points to the operand. After the operand is obtained, Rn is incremented by 1 cr 2, depending on whether a byte or word instruction is being executed.
Autoincrement deferred	@(Rn) +	Rn points to the operand indirectly. After the operand is accessed, Rn is incremented by 2.
Autodecrement	−(Rn)	Rn is decremented by 1 or 2. Then Rn points to the operand.
Autodecrement deferred	@−(Rn)	Rn is decremented by 2. Then Rn indirectly points to the operand.

Addressing modes. A variety of addressing modes are supported by this machine. The eight primitive addressing modes are shown in Table 13-4. Any addressing mode that uses a register can use any register including the PC and SP.

The following are a couple of simple instructions.

```
MOV     @R0, 1000(R1)
MOV     R0, (R1) +
```

The first instruction moves the contents of the word pointed to by R0 into the word located at the address 1000 (octal) plus the contents of R1. The second moves in the contents of R0 to the word pointed to by R1; then R1 is incremented by 2.

Two important instructions involving the stack are

```
MOV     R1, −(SP)
MOV     (SP)+, R1
```

The stack is assumed to grow toward the lower positions of memory and the SP points to the top word of the stack. The first instruction causes the SP to be decremented by 2 so it points to the previous word and stores the contents of R1 there. In other words it pushes the contents of R1 on the stack. The second instruction pops the stack into R1. Since autoincrement and autodecrement can be used with any register, any register can be conveniently used as a stack pointer.

Some methods of addressing that are primitive on many machines are not on the PDP-11. For immediate, absolute, relative and relative deferred addressing, one uses addressing on the PC. These nonprimitive modes are shown in Table 13-5.

Table 13-5 PDP-11 program counter addressing

Name	Assembler symbol	Description
Immediate	#n	Operand is n. Actual instruction is autoincrement on R7, the PC, with n stored in a word following the instruction.
Absolute	@#n	Operand is contents of memory location n. This is an absolute address; it is constant no matter where the instruction is executed. Actual instruction is autoincrement deferred on R7, with n stored after the instruction.
Relative	name	Operand is the contents of the memory location corresponding to name. Relative addressing is used to allow position-independent code. It actually means indexing on R7, with the offset stored after the instruction. The offset is the difference between the address corresponding to name and the address of the word after the instruction.
Relative deferred	@name	The operand is the contents of the memory location pointed to by the contents of the memory position corresponding to name. Actually indexed deferred addressing on R7, with the offset to the memory location corresponding to name following the instruction.

The following instructions are a simple example.

```
DATA:     .WORD     400, 2000        ;.WORD X1, X2, . . . , Xn is an as-
                                     ;sembler directive
                                     ;which reserves n words and ini-
                                     ;tializes them
                                     ;to X1, X2, . . . , Xn respectively.
          MOV       #5, @DATA
```

This instruction is equivalent to:

```
DATA:     .WORD     400, 2000
          MOV       (R7)+, @ − 12(R7)
          .WORD     5
```

In either case the instruction results in 5 being moved into word 400 (octal).

Branches. Most branches are dependent on the program status register (PS). Execution of most instructions cause the condition codes, the last four bits of the PS called N, Z, V, and C, to be assigned values. The values assigned depend on the instruction and the operands. The meaning of the bits is shown in Table 13-6. The PDP-11 has instructions to specifically set and clear the condition codes, the most important of which are CMP (compare), CMPB (compare byte), TST (test), and TSTB (test byte). The compare instructions compare two operands and set the condition codes depending on the result of the first minus the second. The test instructions have a single operand and act like compare instructions with their second operand being zero. Neither compare nor test instructions change their operands, just the condition codes.

A wide variety of branch instructions are available. The machine-language format of the branch instruction is shown in Fig. 13-6. Except for the unconditional branch, BR, they function by checking the condition codes. If the condition codes are properly set, the instruction causes a branch to a location given by the sum of two times the offset plus the contents of the PC. Because the space for the offset is only 8 bits long, a branch can only be to a position between -127 and $+128$ words away from the branch instruction. Since offsets are used, the operand must be either a label or an actual offset.

The following PDP-11 macro assembler code is for a restricted PASCAL for loop:

```
        for var: = const1 to const2 do statement
        MOV     CONST1, I    ;I is the loop variable.
UP:     CMP     I, CONST2
        BGT     END          ;(Branch on greater than)
                             ;If I is greater than CONST2 we are
                             ;finished

        Code for statement.
        INC     I            ;(Increment)
        BR      UP
END:
```

To allow further branches, the JMP instruction can be used. JMP gives an unconditional branch to an effective address given by any addressing mode except register, as registers cannot be branched to.

Table 13-6 PDP-11 condition codes

Bit	Value	Meaning
N	0	Nonnegative result
	1	Negative result
Z	0	Nonzero result
	1	Zero result
C	0	No carry out of $n-1$ bit of result
	1	Carry out of $n-1$ bit
V	0	No overflow
	1	Overflow

Procedures. The PDP-11 has a few features that simplify the use of procedures. The instructions JSR, jump to subroutine, and RTS, return from subroutine, allow control to be passed to the procedure and then back again when the procedure is finished. These instructions use the stack to keep track of either the return address or some register whose contents are saved on the stack and later restored. A full description of the instructions is given in Table 13-7.

However, there is no standardized way to pass parameters on the PDP-11. One way is to have the parameters stored after the JSR instruction.

```
            JSR        R5, SUB
PARM1:      .WORD      0
PARM2:      .WORD      0
```

They can be accessed in the procedure by using autoincrement on the return address, which also changes the return address so it points after the parameters.

```
SUB:     MOV      (R5)+, PAR1      ;R5 contains return address
         MOV      (R5)+, PAR2
           .
           .
         RTS      R5
```

The method used by DEC FORTRAN is to use a register to point to a list. To allow pass by reference, a list of pointers to the parameters is formed. For a call with three parameters, A, B and C the following would be used:

```
MOV      #3, LIST          ;Number of parameters.
MOV      #A, LIST + 2      ;#A gives the address of the parameter A
                           ;instead of value of the parameter
MOV      #B, LIST + 4
MOV      #C, LIST + 6
MOV      #LIST, R5
JSR      PC, SUB
```

Table 13-7 PDP-11 procedure instructions

Instruction	Operation	Description
JSR Rn, dst	Push(Rn) Rn ← PC PC ← dst	The old contents of Rn are pushed on the stack so they are not lost. The old contents of the PC are placed in Rn so we know where to return. Control is transferred to dst. If Rn is the PC, then the contents of the PC are saved on the stack.
RTS Rn	PC ← Rn Rn ← Pop	Control is returned to the instruction after the procedure call. The contents of Rn are restored.

In the called procedure the following instruction moves the *value* of the first parameter into R2:

MOV   @2(R5), R2

For the language C, the parameters are pushed on the stack. This results in pass by value. In the calling procedure we first push the parameters in reverse order and then jump to the procedure. This leaves the parameters and the return address on the stack.

MOV   C, −(SP)
MOV   B, −(SP)
MOV   A, −(SP)
JSR   PC, SUB

In the procedure we save the content of the registers R5 through R2 on the stack and allocate storage for local variables. R5 is changed to point to its saved value on the stack. The parameters can be referenced with indexing on R5. Fig. 13-7 shows the stack contents at this point. When leaving the procedure, we restore the saved registers, temporarily saving where R5 points on the stack. The SP is changed to point to two more than where R5 used to, so that the return address is on top of the stack. An RTS is then invoked, and the calling routine cleans up the parameters on the stack. Returned values are in R0 or R0 and R1 if they are stored in double precision.

SUB: JSR   R5, CSV   ;CSV saves the registers R5-R2 and
                                  ;changes R5 to point to its old
                                  ;value on the stack. It also pushes
                                  ;a blank word on the stack.

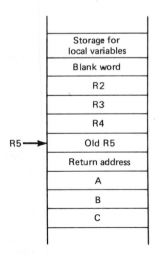

Figure 13-7 Contents of stack before restoring registers in C procedure.

Allocate storage on the
stack for local variables.
⋮

MOV   4(R5), PAR1   ;Moves A into PAR1
⋮

JMP   CRET   ;CRET restores R5-R2, changes SP to
                                   ;point to the return address and
                                   ;then returns to the calling
                                   ;procedure

In conclusion, the PDP-11 machine has a simple architecture when compared with more modern computers. It lacks many of the high-level features found in newer machines; thus complicated code must be generated for some high-level language features. However, the simplicity and uniformity of its instruction set and addressing modes at times make it easier to decide what code must be generated for a given construct.

13-3.2 The VAX-11

The Digital VAX-11 family of general-purpose 32-bit minicomputers was introduced to extend the capabilities of and to have a high degree of compatibility with the PDP-11. The amount of virtual addressing space is much greater than in the PDP-11. In fact, VAX stands for Virtual Address eXtension. There are new data types, but they are in general consistent with those from the PDP-11. New instructions, also compatible, give the VAX-11 much more power. Although the VAX-11 was designed to extend the PDP-11 capabilities, it is in essence an entirely new system.

Memory. The VAX-11 forms addresses with 32 bits, which allows the machine to recognize 4 billion addresses. Although the main memory is not this large, such a large virtual memory makes memory management simpler.

    The basic addressable unit is the 8-bit byte. Adjacent bytes can be grouped as 16-bit words, 32-bit longwords, 64-bit quadwords, and 128-bit octawords. These units must be contiguous in memory, and the address of the lowest-order byte must be divisible by the number of bytes in the unit. The address of the lowest-order byte of a word must be divisible by 2, a longword by 4, etc. The address of any these units is the address of the lowest-order byte.

Registers. There are sixteen 32-bit registers, R0–R15. The registers R0–R11 are general-purpose registers. R12, the argument pointer (AP), and R13, the frame pointer (FP), are used in calling procedures. R14 and R15 are the SP and PC, respectively. As with the PDP-11, all may be used as general-purpose registers.

Data types. The instruction set supports many data types. Integers represented by unsigned and two's-complement numbers may be stored as bytes, words, longwords, quadwords, and octawords. Floating-point numbers can be of 32-bit (F-floating), 64-bit (D-floating and G-floating), and 128-bit (H-floating) sizes. Characters are stored using the ASCII character set and in one byte. Characters can be taken together as strings, as the VAX-11 has instructions for the manipulation of character strings. Numbers can be represented as a series of decimal digits in two different ways; decimal strings, which have one decimal digit per byte and packed decimal strings, which have two decimal digits per byte. Variable bit fields are 0 to 32 contiguous bits and may cross byte boundaries. Queues formed as circular, doubly linked lists are supported by the VAX-11. The links can be of two types: absolute, which give the absolute address of the entry pointed to, and self-relative, which give the displacement to the entry.

Instructions. The VAX-11 has variable-length instructions. The general format is shown in Fig. 13-8. Each instruction has an opcode, which specifies the instruction to be performed, and zero to six operand specifiers, which give the information needed to find the operands. Operand specifers may be one to nine bytes long. The number and type of operand specifiers depend on the opcode.

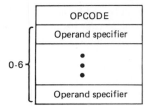

Figure **13-8** Major instruction formats of VAX-11.

Table 13-8 VAX-11 add instructions

Mnemonic	Instruction
ADDB2	Add byte 2 operand.
ADDB3	Add byte 3 operand.
ADDD2	Add D-floating 2 operand.
ADDD3	Add D-floating 3 operand.
ADDF2	Add F-floating 2 operand.
ADDF3	Add F-floating 2 operand.
ADDG2	Add G-floating 2 operand.
ADDG3	Add G-floating 3 operand.
ADDH2	Add H-floating 2 operand.
ADDH3	Add H-floating 3 operand.
ADDL2	Add longword 2 operand.
ADDL3	Add longword 3 operand.
ADDP4	Add packed 4 operand.
ADDP6	Add packed 6 operand.
ADDW2	Add word 2 operand.
ADDW3	Add word 3 operand.

Table 13-9 VAX-11 addressing modes

Name	Assembler symbol	Description
		General register addressing
Register	Rn	Rn is the operand.
Register deferred	(Rn)	Rn points to the operand.
Autoincrement	(Rn)+	Rn points to the operand. After the operand address is determined, Rn is incremented by the size of the operand in bytes.
Autoincrement deferred	@(Rn)+	Rn points to the operand indirectly. After the operand address is determined, Rn is incremented appropriately.
Autodecrement	−(Rn)	Rn is decremented by the size of the operand in bytes. Then Rn points to the operand.
Autodecrement deferred	@ − (Rn)	Rn is decremented appropriately; then it points indirectly to the operand.
Short literal	#literal	The operand is the literal. This is an efficient way of specifying integer constants from 0 to 63 (decimal).
Displacement	D(Rn)	The displacement, D, plus the contents of Rn is the address of the operand. This is equivalent to index mode in the PDP-11.
Displacement deferred	@D(Rn)	The displacement, D, plus the contents of Rn is the address of the pointer to the operand.
Index	base[Rx]	The address of the operand is the sum of the effective address of the array base and the contents of Rx multiplied by the size of the array elements. Index mode is used in accessing arrays. The various forms of index mode addressing are given in Table 13-10.
		PC addressing
Immediate	#constant	Operand is the constant. The constant follows the address mode. Same as autoincrement on the PC.
Absolute	@#address	Operand is at absolute address location. Location follows the address mode. Same as autoincrement deferred on the PC.
Relative	address	Operand is at specified address. Address is calculated by adding the value of the PC to the offset, which follows the address mode. Same as displacement mode using the PC.
Relative deferred	@address	The effective address of the pointer to the operand is calculated the same as in relative addressing. Same as displacement deferred using the PC.

The instructions have some degree of orthogonality. The operation, data type, and addressing mode are all at least somewhat independent. For example, the add instruction can be used on most of the data types (see Table 13-8), and with any addressing mode. Two-operand addition means the operands are added and the result stored in the second operand; three means the first two are added and the result is stored in the third operand.

Addressing modes. The VAX-11 has a wide variety of addressing modes, many of which are the same as for the PDP-11. The addressing modes are shown in Table 13-9. Register modes can, in general, be applied to all registers except the PC, as its contents are sometimes unpredictable.

An example of index-mode addressing as outlined in Tables 13-9 and 13-10 follows. Clearly, VAX-11 indexing is not the same as PDP-11 indexing.

```
ARRAY:    .LONG    10
          .LONG    400
          ⋮

          MOVL     ARRAY(#0), R0    ;R0 now contains 10
          MOVL     ARRAY(#1), R1    ;R1 now contains 400
```

Table 13-10 VAX-11 index modes

Name	Assembler symbol	Description
Register deferred indexed	(Rn)[Rx]	The adjusting address is the contents of Rx times the size in bytes of the operand. This is added to the contents of Rn to give the address of the operand.
Autoincrement indexed	(Rn) + [Rx]	Same as register deferred indexed except Rn is incremented by the size in bytes of the operand after the operand address is calculated.
Autodecrement indexed	− (Rn)[Rx]	Rn is decremented appropriately before the operand address is calculated.
Displacement indexed	D(Rn)[Rx]	The base address is the displacement D plus the contents of Rn. This is added to the appropriately multiplied contents of Rx to give the address of the operand.
Displacement deferred indexed	@D(Rn)[Rx]	The displacement D plus the contents of Rn gives the address of the pointer to the base address. This is added to the multiplied contents of Rx to give the address of the operand.
Autoincrement deferred	@(Rn) + [Rx]	The contents of Rn is the address of the pointer to the base address. This is added to the multiplied contents of Rx to give the address of the operand. Then Rn is incremented by 4.

Branches and other control structures. Branches check the condition codes, just as in a PDP-11. The condition codes are the last four bits of the processor status word (PSW), which is the low-order word of the processor status longword register (PSL). Test and compare can be used on bytes, words, longwords, floating, and double floating to set the condition codes. Branch instructions add their byte or word displacement to the PC if the condition codes are set appropriately.

The jump instruction (JMP), which results in an unconditional change in control, does not use a displacement. Instead any legal addressing mode is allowed, provided the effective address is inside the user's program.

The VAX-11 has a case statement. Its general form is shown below.

$$\text{CASE SELECTOR, BASE, LIMIT}$$

TABLE: displacement_0

                   displacement_1

                   $\vdots$

                   $\text{displacement}_{n-1}$

OUTOFBOUNDS:

                   $\vdots$

BASE is subtracted from SELECTOR, both of which are integers, to give the displacement to be added to the PC. If the result is larger than LIMIT, the PC is set to 2 times the sum of LIMIT plus 1. Therefore, in the skeletal example just given, if the result is larger than LIMIT, the PC is set to OUTOFBOUNDS.

The VAX-11 has higher-level structures for looping than just simple branches. The instructions subtract 1 and branch (SOB) and add 1 and branch (AOB) implement a normal for loop where the index or loop variable changes by one each time. The add compare and branch (ACB) is a more general structure. It allows the index to be changed by a specified value. The instructions are given in Table 13-11. The following is the VAX-11 macro code for the restricted PASCAL for loop given in the PDP-11 section.

```
          for var: = const1 to const2 do statement
          CMPL    CONST1, CONST2
          BGTR    END
          MOVL    CONST1, I              ;I is the loop variable.
UP:
          Code for statement
          AOBLEQ CONST2, I, UP
END:
```

Procedures. The VAX-11 has many features that support procedures. There are two different ways of transferring control to procedures. The instruction CALLG, the more general form, is more powerful in handling arguments, while CALLS, subroutine call, is simpler and faster. Arguments are pointed to by the AP,

Table 13-11 VAX-11 loop instructions

Instruction	Description
SOBGEQ INDEX, LOOP SOBGTR INDEX, LOOP	In both instructions the INDEX is decremented by 1. For SOBGEQ, if the INDEX is greater than or equal to 0, the branch is taken. For SOBGTR, if it is greater than or equal to 1 the branch is taken.
AOBLEQ LIMIT, INDEX, LOOP AOBLSS LIMIT, INDEX, LOOP	In both instructions the INDEX is incremented by 1. The INDEX is compared with the LIMIT. On AOBLEQ the branch to LOOP is taken if it is less than or equal to the LIMIT. On AOBLSS the branch is taken if it is less than the LIMIT.
ACB LIMIT, INCR, INDEX, LOOP	The operands can be of type byte, word, longword, F-floating, G-floating, and H-floating. INCR is added to INDEX. INDEX is compared to LIMIT. If INDEX is now positive and the comparison less than or equal to LIMIT, or if INDEX is negative and the comparison greater than or equal to LIMIT, the branch to LOOP is taken.

argument pointer, and can be accessed via offsets from the AP. Registers are automatically saved on calling a procedure. The FP, frame pointer, points to local storage on the stack. The instruction RET restores the stack and saved registers and returns control to the instruction following the call.

The arguments to a procedure are passed in an argument list, that is, an array of longwords with the first byte containing the number of arguments. Fig. 13-9 shows the format. The argument list can be located in static memory or it can be pushed on the stack. The CALLG instruction uses the address of the argument list which can be anywhere in memory. The CALLS instruction uses the argument list pushed on the stack, where the arguments are pushed in reverse order. The stack grows toward lower positions in memory. When CALLS is used, the execution of RET cleans the parameter list off the stack. The following case

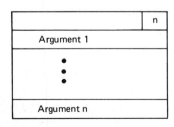

Figure 13-9 Format for VAX-11 argument list.

demonstrates the two calling instructions.

```
ARLIST:    .LONG    3              ;Three parameters.
           .LONG    400            ;First argument.
           .LONG    40             ;Second.
           .LONG    200            ;Third.
             .
             .
             .
           CALLG    ARLIST, PROC   ;Call procedure PROC
                                   ;with argument list ARLIST.
             .
             .
             .
           PUSHL    #200           ;Push arguments on the stack
                                   ;in reverse order
           PUSHL    #40
           PUSHL    #400
           CALLS    #2, PROC
```

Inside the procedure, both call instructions load the AP with the address of the argument list. Thus the procedure can access the arguments as offsets from the AP. The first word of the procedure is a save mask. The registers corresponding to the bits set in the mask are saved on the stack. The RET instruction will restore the registers.

The following is an example procedure.

```
PROC:    .WORD    M⟨R2, R3, R4, R5⟩    ;Save registers R2-R5.
           .
           .
           .
         MOVL     4(AP), R2            ;Gets the first argument.
           .
           .
           .
         RET
```

In conclusion, the VAX-11 has many high-level features that simplify the translation of high-level language constructs into assembler code. Although not illustrated here, it has some particularly powerful capabilities for handling character strings and converting between different data types.

13-3.3 The MC68000

Motorola's MC68000 family of general-purpose 16-bit microprocessors was designed to expand on the capabilities of the old 8-bit microprocessors. The MC68000 machine has a much larger and complete instruction set. It has more registers and can address much more memory.

Memory. The MC68000 uses 32-bit addresses. However, it has only a 24-bit address bus; so it can address 16 megabytes of memory. Memory is organized into 8-bit bytes, 16-bit words, and 32-bit longwords. The basic memory unit is the 8-bit byte. Words are two bytes of contiguous memory where the lower-order byte has an even address. The address of the lower-order even byte is the address of the word. Longwords are four bytes, and again their address is the address of a lower-order even byte.

Registers. There are sixteen 32-bit registers, divided into two types. The registers D0–D7 are data registers and A0–A7 are address registers. As would be expected, data registers are for holding data and address registers are used for holding addresses. Address register A7 is the SP or system stack pointer. Operations on an address register do not change the condition codes, as the programmer does not want the value of an address to affect the program control.

Data types. The data types of the MC68000 are simple. The five basic data types are bits, 4-bit BCD (binary coded decimal) digits, 8-bit bytes, 16-bit words, and 32-bit long words.

Instructions. The general format for instructions is shown in Fig. 13-10. Instructions are from one to five words in length, depending on the instruction and the number and type of addressing modes. The operation word specifies the operation to be performed. The remaining words are extension words to the addressing modes being used, which give some further information necessary to find the effective address of the operands.

The arithmetic and logical instructions are reasonably orthogonal. Instructions of these types are similar in the way they function, the way they set the condition codes, what data types they can use, and the way they access operands. Two operand arithmetic instructions must have a register as one operand.

Addressing modes. The MC68000 has a wide variety of addressing modes, as shown in Table 13-12. Data registers use data-register modes and address registers use address-register modes. These addressing modes are all similar to addressing modes of the VAX-11 and the PDP-11.

The following code uses some of the addressing modes.

ARRAY	DC.L	10	Declare constant 10, pointed to by ARRAY.
	DC.L	20	
	DC.L	30	
	DC.L	40	

Operation word
Immediate operation $\left(\begin{array}{c}\text{0-2}\\\text{words}\end{array}\right)$
Source effective address extension $\left(\begin{array}{c}\text{0-2}\\\text{words}\end{array}\right)$
Destination effective address extension $\left(\begin{array}{c}\text{0-2}\\\text{words}\end{array}\right)$

Figure 13-10 General instruction format of MC68000.

Table 13-12 MC68000 addressing modes

Name	Assembler syntax	Description
Data register direct	Dn	Dn is the operand.
Address register direct	An	An is the operand.
Address register indirect	(An)	An points to the operand.
Address register indirect with postincrement	(An) +	An points to the operand. After the operand address is obtained, An is incremented by 1, 2, or 4, depending whether the size of the operand is a byte, word, or long word.
Address register indirect with predecrement	−(An)	Before the operand address is obtained, An is decremented appropriately. Then An points to the operand.
Address register indirect with displacement	d(An)	There is a word of extension, which holds the displacement. The address of the operand is the sum of the contents of An and the displacement.
Address register indirect with index	d(An, Ri)	There is a word of extension. The displacement in the low-order eight bits of the extension word, and the register Ri, taken as either a word or longword, is indicated by the high-order five bits. The address of the operand is the sum of the displacement, the contents of Ri, and the contents of An.
Absolute short address	address.W	There is one word of extension. The address of the operand is in the extension word.
Absolute long address	address.L	The address of the operand is the two words of extension. The high-order part of the address is in the first extension word, the low-order in the second.
Program counter with displacement	d(PC)	There is one word of extension. The address of the operand is the sum of the contents of the PC and the displacement in the extension word.
Program counter with index	d(PC, Ri)	The address of the operand is the sum of the contents of the PC, the displacement in the lower-order eight bits of the extension word, and the contents of Ri, which can be taken as a word or longword.
Immediate data	#constant	There are one or two words of extension, depending on the size of the operand. The operand is the word or words of extension.

MOVE.L	#0, D0	D0 now contains 0.
LEA	ARRAY, A0	Load effective address of ARRAY into A0.
MOVE.L	(A0) + , D1	D1 now contains 10, the contents of the first long word of the array. A0 now points to the second long word of the array.

MOVE.L   0(A0), D1   D1 now contains 20, the contents of the second long word of the array.

MOVE.L   4(A0, D0), D1   D1 now contains 40, the contents of the fourth long word of the array.

Branches and other control structures. The condition codes are the low-order five bits of the status register. In addition to the N (negative), Z (zero), V (overflow), and C (carry) bits there is the X (extend), which is used instead of carry for multiple-precision arithmetic. There is an add with extend bit (ADDX) instead of add with carry. The normal instructions exist to set the condition codes, such as test and compare.

The MC68000 has a wide variety of branch instructions, denoted Bcc, where cc is one of 14 different conditions. If the condition codes are set properly, the branch instruction results in a byte or word signed displacement being added to the contents of the PC. The JMP instruction allows unconditional branching using any addressing modes whose effective address is part of memory.

There is a higher-level instruction for looping. Decrement counter and branch conditionally (DBcc) results in the next instruction being executed. This could mean, for example, that the loop is ended, if its condition is *true* with respect to the condition codes. Otherwise its counter, a data register, is decremented by 1. If the counter is now -1, the loop is also ended; otherwise the branch occurs. Therefore, DBcc can simulate a loop that can end either with a given condition or after a number of iterations.

The following assembler code is for a restricted PASCAL for loop:

```
for var: = const1 to const2 do statement
        MOVE.W      CONST1, D0      D0 is the loop variable.
UP      CMP.W       CONST2, D0
        BGT         END             If D0 is greater than
                                    CONST2 we are finished.

        Code for statement.
        ADDQ.W      #1, D0          Increment.
        BR          UP
END
```

Procedures. There are a few instructions that support procedures. Transferring control to procedures can be done in two ways. Branch to subroutine (BSR) uses a displacement and jump to subroutine (JSR) uses an absolute address. Both instructions save the return address on the stack. Return from subroutine (RTS) pops the return address from the stack and restores the PC.

Two special instructions aid procedures in allocating space on the stack for local variables. One address register can be designated as the frame pointer (FP), which points to the area on the stack allocated for local variables. The LINK instruction, which is used at the beginning of a procedure, has two operands: the address register designated as the FP and the amount of space that is to be reserved for the local variables. It starts by saving the FP on the stack, so that the

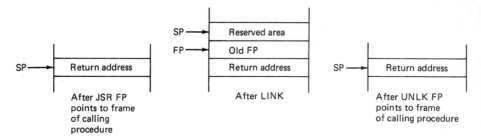

Figure 13-11 Stack contents during procedure invocation.

FP of the calling procedure is not destroyed. Then the FP is made equal to the SP, since this is the bottom of the saved area for local variables. Finally, the SP is changed by the given displacement; this displacement must be negative to reserve a fresh area on the stack. UNLK, which is used at the end of the procedure, reverses this process, restoring the return address to the top of the stack and the FP to its old value.

The following is an example procedure call and procedure. The contents of the stack are shown at various stages in Fig. 13-11.

```
          ⋮
          JSR      SUB
          ⋮

SUB       LINK     A0, # − 4            A0 is the FP. Reserve one long
                                        word.

          ⋮

          MOVEQ.L#10, − 4(A0)           Stores 10 in reserved long word.

          ⋮

          UNLK     A0
          RTS
```

In conclusion, the MC68000's high-level instructions ease the translation from high-level language. In particular, the orthogonality of the instruction set makes code generation quite simple.

CHAPTER EXERCISES

1 Consider the following PL/I expression:

$$Z = 5 - (A + INDEX(S,I,J)) * (X/Y(I,J))$$

(*a*) Generate quadruples for this expression that minimize the number of temporaries (and hence registers as well). Assume that a function call requires that the parameters be loaded into registers before a "branch to subroutine" is invoked.

(*b*) How does the appearance of a common subexpression affect your general decision strategy as to the order in which quadruples should be emitted in the completion of an expression?

2 Suppose we are given a target machine in which all arithmetic operations must be applied when the operands are in registers (i.e., ADD RI,RJ; SUB RI,RJ; MULT RI,RJ; and DIV RI,RJ). The result of an operation is left in the second register specified in the instruction. That is, the result of ADD R1,R2 is left in R2. To move values to and from main storage there exist load and store instructions. They are of the following form:

LOAD X,R1   moves the value of X into register R1

and

STORE R1,X   moves the value in R1 to location X

Generate target machine code for the following source statements:

    C:= (A + B)*C;
    D:= C/A;
    B:= D*(B + A);
    A:= C;

assuming the target machine has only three registers available to hold temporary results. The code should be optimized with respect to register allocation.

3 Assume a target machine exists with only two registers available to hold temporary results. Show an optimal register assignment for the quadruples given in Exercise 1 of Chap. 12 (*a*) before machine-independent optimizations are applied and (*b*) after machine-independent optimizations are applied.

4 Assume we are generating register machine code for an expression of the form:

⟨subexpression1⟩ ⟨op⟩ ⟨subexpression2⟩

where ⟨subexpression1⟩ requires at most *n* registers and ⟨subexpression2⟩ requires at most *m* registers. Then a general rule relating to the order of evaluating the expression is that ⟨subexpression1⟩ should be evaluated before ⟨subexpression2⟩ if $n \geq m$, otherwise ⟨subexpression2⟩ should be evaluated first. Give two reasons why this rule cannot always be applied to give an optimal register assignment.

BIBLIOGRAPHY

Belady, L. A.: "A Study of Replacement Algorithms for a Virtual Storage Computer," *IBM Systems Journal*, Vol. 5, No. 2, 1966, pp. 78–101.

Horowitz, L. P., R. M. Karp, R. M. Miller, and S. Winograd: "Index Register Allocation," *Journal of the ACM*, Vol. 13, No. 1, 1966, pp. 43–61.

Levey, H. M., and R. H. Eckhouse, Jr.: *Computer Programming and Architecture: The VAX-11*, Bedford, Mass.: Digital Press, 1980.

Lowry, E., and C. W. Medlock: "Object Code Optimization," *Communications of the ACM*, Vol. 12, No. 1, 1969, pp. 13–22.

MacEwen, G. H.: *Introduction to Computer Systems: Using the PDP-11 and PASCAL*, New York: McGraw-Hill, 1980.

MC68000 16-bit Microprocessor User's Manual, Englewood Cliffs, N.J.: Prentice-Hall, 1982.

Nakata, I.: "On Compiling Algorithms for Arithmetic Expressions," *Communications of the ACM*, Vol. 10, No. 8, 1967, pp. 492–494.

PDP 11/20/15/r20 Processor Handbook, Digital Equipment Corporation, Maynard, Mass., 1971.

Redziejowski, R. R.: "On Arithmetic Expressions and Trees," *Communications of the ACM*, Vol. 12, No. 2, 1969, pp. 81–84.

Ritchie, D. M., S. C. Johnson, M. E. Lesk, and B. W. Kernighan: "The UNIX Time Sharing System: The C Programming Language," *Bell System Technical Journal* Vol. 57, 1978, pp. 1991–2019.

Starnes, T. W.: "Design Philosophy behind Motorola's MC68000," *BYTE*, April 1983, pp. 70–92, May 1983, pp. 342–367, June 1983, pp. 339–349.

FOURTEEN

COMPILER-COMPILERS

From the previous chapters it should be obvious that the writing of a compiler for a major language is not a simple task. Many new languages such as Ada, BLISS, C, FORTRAN 77, and PASCAL have emerged during the 1970s. In addition, many specialized languages have appeared. Furthermore, VLSI technology has produced many interesting machine architectures. Consequently, the need for tools to assist the compiler writer has grown greatly. The first set of available tools dealt with the lexical and parsing phases of a compiler. These tools were widely available by the late 1970s. Tools to support the back end of a compiler, however, have only recently begun to appear. The reason for this, in part, is the difficulties in formalizing the code-generation and optimization phases of a compiler.

Throughout this book, we have been mainly concerned with the theory and design of compilers. These concepts can be applied to the development of compiler-compilers; i.e., translators that generate a compiler from an input specification of the compiler. The basic philosophy of a compiler-compiler is discussed in Sec. 14-1. The second section examines two compiler-compiler systems which are essentially parser generators. Given a specification for a language, both systems generate a parser for that language. The third section examines four systems that deal with the back end of a compiler.

This chapter attempts to give a brief overview of compiler-compiler systems. It is not meant to survey or compare various systems. A recent survey of systems that deal with the code-generation phase of a compiler appears in Ganapathi et al. (1982).

14-1 INTRODUCTION TO COMPILER-COMPILERS

With the increasing costs of software development, it has become desirable to generate software tools that aid in the production of new programs. Much research has been devoted to programs called translator writing systems. Translator writing systems include programs which aid the user in writing translators, that is, compilers, assemblers, and interpreters. In this section, we present an introduction to translator writing systems that aid in producing a compiler or some portion of a compiler. These programs are often termed *compiler generators* or *compiler-compilers*.

In the late 1950s an attempt was made to define a language UNCOL (universal computer-oriented language) (Sammet, 1969) which would serve as an intermediate language that would permit a "compiler" for every language to be made available on every different machine To meet this goal, normally M * N compilers and translators would be needed for M machines and N languages. It was proposed that one need only write a translator which would translate a program written in some language into UNCOL. Then only one UNCOL compiler would be required for each machine. Thus, only M + N compilers would be needed. This system failed, however, because of the difficulty of being able to represent all languages, computer architectures, and instruction sets in a single language.

A compiler-compiler is a specialized program that generates a compiler and, as such, is only one form of a translator writing system. UNCOL, while not a compiler-compiler, was designed with a philosophy similar to that of compiler-compiler designers—making the availability of programming languages on computers less costly. Input usually consists of a formalized description of the language and either a formalized description of the machine or hand-coded semantic routines which perform the synthesis phase of compilation. The handwritten code is included for a particular phase if the compiler-compiler does not generate that phase of compilation. We will refer to such systems as parser generators. The compiler produced by such a system can then be used to generate code for programs written in the programming language that was defined for the compiler-compiler. An overview of the generation of a compiler using a compiler-compiler is illustrated in Fig. 14-1.

An idealized compiler-compiler uses the specifications of a programming language and a target machine and generates a compiler that translates statements for that language into target-machine code. In reality, however, most "compiler-compilers" perform only some phase of compilation, such as scanning, parsing, or code generation. Such a separation allows the compiler-compiler designer to concentrate on one aspect of compilation at a time. A generator for one phase (i.e., a scanner generator) permits the programmer to include or invoke other generators for the other phases of compilation. For example, a scanner that has been generated by a generator can be used to pass tokens of a program to a parser that has been generated by a parser generator. The parser can then generate a parse tree, triples, or quadruples from which a code generator produces code.

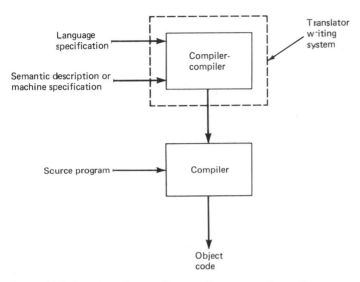

Figure 14-1 Overview of a compiler-compiler–generated compiler.

The major portion of the research on compiler generation, until recently, has been involved with the scanning and parsing phases, with the greatest emphasis on the parsing phase. This research emphasis has occurred because the description of language lexicon and syntax can be done using regular expressions or grammars, something which is more difficult to do in the other phases of compilation. Research has led to the design of several parsing algorithms, such as the LL(1), LR(1), and precedence parsing algorithms described in Chaps. 6 and 7. Furthermore, the derivation of the parsing tables required by these algorithms from grammars has been specified in mathematical terms and can be programmed quite easily.

The previous paragraph has alluded to the design philosophy of most scanner and parser generators. The generator uses a syntactic or lexical description of a language to generate the tables for a parsing or lexical algorithm. The algorithm is implemented as a skeleton compiler which requires a set of tables to parse or scan a language. These sets of tables are supplied by the scanner or parser generator. Some method of associating semantic routines with the rules of the grammar is usually provided as well, allowing the compiler writer to include code for the other phases of the compiler.

Lex, which was discussed in Chap. 4, is an example of a scanner generator. The tokens of a language are described using regular expressions. An action or program fragment may be associated with each expression and used to return the identified tokens to a parser and perform other functions, such as conversions to numeric data.

YACC, an LALR(1) parser generator (Johnson, 1975), is discussed in the next section. It generates a set of parse tables from an LALR grammar. Actions may be included with the rules of the grammar. When a rule is reduced, the corresponding action is executed.

Another parser generator is the ANALYZER program that generates the tables for a mixed-strategy precedence parsing algorithm of degree $(2, 1; 1, 2)$. The program is written by McKeeman et al. (1970). A discussion of mixed-strategy precedence parsing was given in Sec. 7-3.6. Recall that this parsing strategy uses simple precedence parsing; however, whenever a terminal symbol pair occurs for which no unique relationship holds, it uses a ternary precedence function to continue parsing.

The interesting aspect of this system is that XPL is the language in which the XPL compiler XCOM and the program ANALYZER are written. A procedure SKELETON is the basic parser used in the XCOM compiler—using the tables generated by ANALYZER instead, a new parser is created. Additional XPL code must be included by the compiler writer for the synthesis phases of the compiler.

The procedure SCAN, which is the XCOM scanner, may be used as the scanner after some of the code has been rewritten to incorporate the unique aspects of the lexical structure of the new language.

The compiler-writing system provides a high-level language, XPL, in which the semantic routines are to be coded. It is a dialect of PL/I but contains additional features, including system-defined procedures, that are not available in PL/I but assist in writing a compiler.

Some recent projects have involved promising research into code-optimization and -generation systems. The PQCC system (Leverett et al., 1980), which is examined in more detail in Sec. 14-3.1, is such a system. By using language and machine descriptions, PQCC generates the tables necessary for a skeleton compiler PQC to perform code optimization and generation. A second system (Graham and Glanville, 1978), which initially dealt with code generation, has been extended to perform several types of code optimizations. Both systems generate code by pattern matching. The PQCC system takes a heuristic approach to pattern matching while the Graham and Glanville approach is to use an LR-based algorithm to pattern match. The success of both systems is partially due to their applicability over a wider range of machines than has been achieved before.

Extensible compiler-compilers are those compiler-compilers which are easily defined in terms of themselves. New statements may be defined using the language of the extendible compiler-compiler, and these statements then become included within that language. Thus, a programming language for which a compiler is desired may be added to the extendible compiler-compiler's language and statements written in the defined language may be compiled. The language accepted by an extensible compiler-compiler is the union of the languages the compiler writer defined and that which was in the compiler-compiler's original vocabulary. In order for such a system to be a compiler-compiler, it must be possible to limit the language accepted by the compiler-compiler to only that subset which was defined by the compiler writer.

An example of an early extensible compiler-compiler is the Brooker-Morris compiler-compiler (BMCC). A more detailed discussion of BMCC can be found in an article by Rosen (1964).

BMCC allows the compiler writer to define a language using a form of a grammar. Such a grammar is typically separated into two classes: phrases and formats. The phrase classes are used to define the lexical structure of the language and some of its syntax. The format class is defined in terms of phrases, but it defines the statements of the language. Each member of the format class has a format routine associated with it that performs the semantic processing and code generation required.

A set of built-in format routines and their associated format classes is provided by BMCC. The format routines are required because they define some low-level semantic processing required by the user and define the machine code that is to be generated. These sets of format classes and routines are extended by compiler writers when they define new format classes and routines. New format routines are defined using calls to the system-defined format routines.

The language accepted by the compiler generated by BMCC is restricted to that which was defined by the compiler writer because the system has no predefined phrase classes. Hence, the only format classes recognized by the compiler are those which the user defined using phrases and the only format routines which can be called are those explicitly called by the format routines associated with the user-defined format classes.

Before we conclude this section, it should be noted that the notational formalization of language syntax and lexicon as grammars (or regular expressions) and the mathematical formalization of the parsing and scanning procedures has resulted in a large number of parser and scanner generators being written. Many of these were designed as research tools concerning different methods of parsing. Much more difficulty has arisen in attempts at formalizing the specifications required for code generation and code optimization.

The next two sections discuss several compiler-compilers. Some of these systems are essentially parser generators which deal with the front end (i.e., lexical and parsing phases) of a compiler. Other systems deal primarily with a compiler's back end (i.e., code-optimization and -generation phases).

There are several major compiler-compiler projects that will not be discussed in this chapter. These include the MUG 2 project at the University of Munich (Ganzinger et al., 1977), the ECS project at IBM Yorktown Heights (Allen et al., 1977), and the HLP project at the University of Helsinki (Raiha et al., 1978). With these two sections, we attempt to further promote an appreciation of the design and use of compiler-compilers.

14-2 EXAMPLES OF PARSER GENERATORS

This section describes two parser generators. The first system generates from an input grammar an extended LALR(1) parser and the second an extended LL(1) parser. Many parser generators have been written in the last decade. The two systems that we discuss here, however, are representative.

14-2.1 YACC: A LALR(1) Parser Generator

The phase of compilation which has received the most attention concerning automation is that of parsing. This section describes one parser generator which has been developed: YACC (yet another compiler-compiler), a parser generator written by Johnson (1975).

As has been demonstrated earlier in this book, parsing algorithms can be written which will parse more than one particular language; a parser for a new language can be created by changing the parse tables. This is the design philosophy of YACC. YACC generates the tables necessary for its LALR(1) syntax analyzer to parse the language defined by the grammar. The theory of LALR(1) and LR(1) parsing was introduced in Sec. 7-4 and will not receive any further attention in this section. Rather, this section discusses those features available in YACC which assist the user in developing a parser.

YACC is a program which, using a grammar and the actions associated with the rules of the grammar, generates the tables required by the basic syntax analyzer to parse the language described by the grammar. YACC's parser works in conjunction with a scanner and its creation and use within a compiler system is illustrated in Fig. 14-2. The scanner required by the parser reads the input source and returns tokens to the parser. The tokens are the terminal symbols of the grammar. Values can also be returned along with the token by assigning the value to the global variable. The scanner can be coded by hand or created using a scanner generator such as Lex, which was described in Sec. 4-7.

Values may be associated with the symbols of a grammar and passed up the parse tree. For each rule of the grammar, a section of code can be given in which the user may specify semantic-analysis and code-generation actions, possibly making use of the values associated with the symbols in the right-hand side of the rule. A value for the left-hand side of the rule can also be defined. Facilities for error recovery are also available in YACC. These were briefly mentioned in Chap. 7.

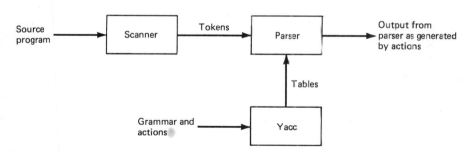

Figure 14-2 YACC system as it relates to a compiler.

YACC is limited by the power of LALR(1) parsing and may fail to generate tables for the parser if the specified grammar is not LALR(1). It will accept many ambiguous grammars, providing the user with methods of resolving the ambiguous conflicts or, without such specifications, using defaults instead.

The input to YACC has a format similar to that of Lex with an optional definitions section preceding the section containing the grammar. An optional user subprograms section follows the grammar section. The sections are all separated by %% as is done with Lex. An example of input to YACC is illustrated in Fig. 14-3. The grammar is used in an interpreter which allows the user to predefine the values of some variables before the execution of a program by using a table of variable names and values. These variables, with their corresponding values, are then stored in the symbol table.

During the generation of pseudocode, certain parts of the expression can be evaluated in the actions associated with the productions if the values of the operands are known. The procedure *push* generates code to load the value of an identifier. In the case of subexpressions which can be evaluated at compile time, *remove* is used to delete the code which loads the values of its operands. The subprocedure *con_table* pushes a constant value which has been computed into the symbol table.

The grammar section of YACC consists of a grammar which specifies the syntax of some language using a BNF-like format similar to that introduced in Sec. 2-2. As can be seen in Fig. 14-3, the rules having the same left-hand side are separated by a vertical stroke (|) and the entire assemblage is ended with a semicolon. Actions, if given, normally precede the vertical stroke or semicolon. The left-hand symbol of the first rule in the grammar is, by default, the starting symbol. Empty rules are denoted by rules having no symbols on the right-hand side. An example is the rule:

empty: ;

The terminal symbols returned by the scanner can be either the actual characters read from the input text that are to be matched with character strings given in the set of productions or token values which can represent a series of characters such as a reserved word. Tokens must be declared in the *definitions* section with an optional value which represents the numeric representation of this token that is returned by the scanner. In Fig. 14-3 IDENTIFIER is a token which has the value 200. Each token must have a unique nonnegative value. If characters are to be returned by the scanner, tokens values should be greater than the representation value of any character; in this case, IDENTIFIER is given the value 200. The reason for this is that characters and tokens are both represented numerically and it is impossible for the parser to differentiate between tokens and characters which are represented by the same value.

Once all the input has been read by the scanner, the parser is notified by receiving the value zero from the scanner. If the tokens seen by the parser before the zero can be derived from the starting symbol, the input is accepted by the parser.

```
% {

        / * symbol table * /

        extern int  value [], known [] ;

        extern char name [] ;

        extern int  sym_size;

% }

% token IDENTIFIER 200

%%

start:      expr ;

expr:       expr '+' term    = { if ($1 >= 0 && $3 >= 0 &&

                                    known [$1]  && krown [$3]) {

                                       $$ = cons_table (value[$1] +

                                           value[$3] );

                                       remove (2);

                                       push ($$);

                                    }

                                    else { printf ("ADD\n");

                                       $$ = -1;

                                    }

                                 } |

            term             = { $$ = $1; } ;

term:       term '*' factor  = { if ($1 >= 0 && $3 >= 0 &&

                                    known [$1] && known[$3]) {

                                       $$ = cons_table (value[$1] *

                                           value[$3] );

                                       remove (2);

                                       push ($$);

                                    }

                                    else { printf ("MUL\n");

                                       $$ = -1;

                                    }

                                 } |

            factor           = { $$ = $1; } ;

factor:     '(' expr ')'     = { $$ = $2; } |

            IDENTIFIER       = { push ($1);

                                 $$ = $1;

                                 } ;
```

Figure 14-3 Example of YACC grammar and actions.

A segment of code may be associated with each grammar rule in YACC. Once the parser can reduce the right-hand side of some rule, the semantic routine corresponding to this rule is invoked. The compiler writer can use this code to perform semantic processing, code generation, and so forth. The code is included directly in the grammar by following the rule with " = { *code* }" where *code* is the segment of code to be executed. (The equal sign is actually optional.) The code can be written in either C or RATFOR. As can be seen in the example illustrated in Fig. 14-3, the code normally precedes the vertical stroke or semicolon.

Variables used in the code are declared in the *definitions* section and have the format

%{ *declaration* %}

where *declaration* is a set of C or RATFOR declarations. Pseudovariables may be used to associate values with the symbols in the right-hand side of a rule. The variables $1 and $2 give the values of the first and second symbols, respectively. A nonterminal symbol receives its values when a value is assigned to the pseudovariable $$ for the rule which has that symbol on the left-hand side. Terminal symbols receive their values when the scanner assigns a value to the external variable *yylval*.

If the compiler writer desires actions to be performed in the middle of a rule, this can be achieved by breaking the rule into two rules or inserting a nonterminal symbol which, in another rule, matches the empty. Also this can be accomplished by inserting an action in the middle of the rule, as in

x: y{ *f*();}*z* string.

Code can easily be included where necessary.

In the previous example, the actions generate code to compute the value of a subexpression wherever possible. It is assumed that the scanner returns the position where a variable is stored in the symbol table. By passing the positions where the operands (or their values) are stored in the symbol table to the parse tree, the operands can be accessed to determine if their values are known.

YACC calls the scanner, a functional procedure named *yylex*, whenever the next input item is required. This routine can be either coded by hand or generated by a scanner generator. Lex, the lexical analyzer generator introduced in Sec. 4-7, was designed so that it can be used in conjunction with YACC for generating the scanner and parser.

Figure 14-4a gives a programmer-written scanner which can be used by the parser specified in Fig. 14-3. The scanner is a very simple one designed to illustrate how the parser and scanner interact. The scanner assumes that identifiers consist of only one character. Function *insert_table* is not included in the figure. This function places the identifier in the symbol table if it is a new one. The function returns the storage position of the identifier in the symbol table. This value, by assigning it to *yylval*, allows the parser to determine whether the value of the identifier is known.

End of input is indicated by returning the value zero to the parser. In the scanner given in Fig. 14-4a, the value zero is returned by the scanner when the end of input is reached. Because zero is returned by *getchar* when the end of input is reached in C, it is not necessary to check for this value in this example. It is included to emphasize that zero must be returned to the parser after the entire input stream has been read. This special check may occur in scanners which return only numeric values for tokens rather than characters. Notice that the constant IDENTIFIER is defined in the scanner to have the same value as the token IDENTIFIER so that the token returned by the scanner can be identified by the parser.

In order for a parser generator to be useful it must have some method of error recovery. Some simple facilities are available in YACC to perform error recovery and give the user a limited amount of control on how error recovery is to proceed. If the user has not specified some relevant directives concerning error recovery at a point where an error is detected, the parser will print an error message and parsing will terminate.

Error recovery for LALR(1) parsers is discussed in Sec. 7-4 8. We now discuss how error recovery can be specified by the user. Given that an error occurs, the point at which these algorithms are to be invoked is determined by the occurrence of the special token "error" in the grammar. When an error occurs, the parser attempts to find a production that the parser might have been in at the point where the error token could most recently have been returned from the scanner. Parsing continues at this production, with the token that had caused the error being the next input token. If no rule exists, parsing terminates; otherwise, the

```
#define END_OF_INPUT  0

#define IDENTIFIER      200

yylex ( ) {

        extern int  yylval;

        extern int  value [], known [];

        extern char name [];

        extern int  sym_size;

        char c;

        c = getchar ( );

        if (c == END_OF_INPUT) return (0);

        if (c >= 'a' && c <= 'z' || c >= 'A' && c <= 'Z') {

            yylval = insert_table (c);

            return (IDENTIFIER);

        }

        return (c);

}
```

(a)

Figure 14-4a Example of lexical analyzer for use with the parser generated by YACC.

```
% {

        / * symbol table * /

        extern int   value [] , known [] ;

        extern char name [] ;

        extern int   sym_size;

% }

% token IDENTIFIER 200

% token POWER        201

% left   '+'

% left   '*'

% right  POWER

%%

start:    expr ;

expr:    expr '+' expr        = { if ($1 >= 0 && $3 >= 0 &&

                                      known [$1]  && known [$3] ) {

                                          $$ = cons_table (value[$1]  +

                                                  value[$3] );

                                          remove (2);

                                          push ($$);

                                      }

                                  else { printf ("ADD\n");

                                          $$ = -1;

                                      }

                              } |

         expr '*' expr        = { if ($1 >= 0 && $3 >= 0 &&

                                      known [$1]  && known [$3] ) {

                                          $$ = cons_table (value[$1]  *

                                                  value[$3] );

                                          remove (2);

                                          push ($$);

                                      }

                                  else { printf ("MUL\n");

                                          $$ = -1;

                                      }

                              } |
```

```
expr POWER expr    = { if ($1 >= 0 && $3 >= 0 &&
                           known [$1] && known [$3]) {
                             $$ = cons_table (conv_int (pow
                                     (value[$1], value[$3])));
                             remove (2);
                             push ($$);
                           }
                         else { printf ("POW\n");
                             $$ = -1;
                           }
                        } |
'(' expr ')'       = { $$ = $2; } |
IDENTIFIER         = { push ($1);
                       $$ = $1;
                     } |
error ;
                        (b)
```

Figure 14-4b Example of input to YACC.

parser behaves as if it sees "error" as an input token and tries to continue parsing with the rule containing the error token.

The parser enters an error state and remains in this state until three tokens have been parsed successfully, beginning with the token at which the error occurred. If a token is seen in the error state and it cannot be parsed, it is deleted. Error messages are not printed for errors occurring in the error state in order to prevent a cascade of error messages from being printed before the parser has recovered from the error state.

The use of the error token is illustrated in Fig. 14-4b; it permits error recovery to occur when a syntax error occurs by ignoring tokens until a new expression may be started.

The user must place the "error" token in the best locations for error recovery. Actions can also be associated with rules containing the error token and used to recover from the effects of syntax errors.

The grammar used in this example generates (possibly parenthesized) expressions consisting of the operations of addition, multiplication, and exponentiation. The actions associated with the rules of the grammar generate code to compute the value of the expression for an interpreter as was the case in Fig. 14-3. The disambiguating features for LALR grammars, also illustrated in this example, will be described shortly.

Two other error-recovery features of YACC may prove useful and appear in the action routines. The statement *yyerrok*, which is included as a statement for an action, is replaced by a segment of code which causes the parser to exit from the error state immediately, whether or not three tokens have been successfully parsed. It is useful with interactive applications, such as using a parser generated by YACC, to process the on-line commands of a text-editing system.

The other feature is the statement *yyclearin*. When an error is detected, the parser goes to the rule which contains the error token and attempts to continue parsing with the token which caused the error. Sometimes it is inconvenient to resume parsing with this token and *yyclearin* tells the parser to resume parsing with the token returned by the next call to the scanner.

In addition to error recovery, YACC provides methods and defaults by which the parsing of ambiguous grammars can be resolved. For example, the rule

  term: term'*' term;

results in an ambiguous grammar as the expression "term * term * term" can be parsed with left association {(term * term) * term} or right association {term * (term * term)}. In such cases, YACC uses right association when parsing unless the user specifies otherwise. Another type of ambiguity occurs when a sentential form is reducible by one or more rules. This ambiguity is resolved by *reducing*, with the first rule listed in the BNF grammar.

The compiler writer is warned if either type of ambiguity occurs. If it is desirable, an ambiguity can be corrected by either rewriting the grammar or specifying the associativities and precedences of the rules. This specification is designated by the associativity and precedence of the last token of that rule. Left associativity is defined in the section using

  %left $token_1 token_2 \ldots token_n$

Right associativity is indicated in a similar manner, by using %*right* instead. In the example illustrated in Fig. 14-4b, the rules containing the operators addition and multiplication are defined to be parsed using left association and the rule containing exponentiation using right association.

Precedence is specified by the ordering of the associativity definitions. Tokens listed on the same line have equal precedence; tokens given in one line have lower precedence than those listed in a line succeeding it. Tokens for which associativity does not apply but precedence must be indicated can be included in the ordering just described using the keyword %*nonassoc* instead of %*left* or %*right*. In Fig. 14-4b, addition has the lowest precedence. Exponentiation, because of the ordering of the rules, has the highest precedence.

It should be noted that as a matter of style the tokens represented by an identifier name should be defined using %*token* whether or not they appear later in the *definitions* section. This occurs when a token also has its precedence and associativity specified. Furthermore, any ambiguities not resolved using the precedence and associativity definitions are still reported by YACC.

YACC was designed with the goal of automating the production of a compiler. Used in conjunction with a scanner generator, the front end of a compiler can be generated from formalized descriptions. YACC still requires the compiler writer to code the semantic routines and the code-generation and code-optimization phases of a compiler. In the next section, a parser-generator system that is based on LL(1) parsing theory is presented.

14-2.2 An Attributed LL(1) Parser Generator

This subsection describes an attributed LL(1) parser generator which incorporates recent developments in attribute parsing and error correction. The discussion of the system will be somewhat brief. The reader can find a more detailed treatment of the system in Berg et al. (1984).

With the recent availability of powerful microcomputers, many system development tools, hitherto only available on mainframe computers, are now being implemented on personal computers or personal workstations. In many cases, the capabilities of these tools must be restricted somewhat because of size considerations resulting from a lack of main or auxiliary memory or operating system functionality. On the other hand, personal computers can be used to create a very intimate workstation environment supporting full screen editors and interactive interfaces using graphics support.

The development of VATS, the Visible Attributed Translation System, has followed the scenario just described. The original version, called ATS, was designed and implemented as an LL(1) parser generator. Its first implementation was in the C language on a PDP-11 running the UNIX operating system. It was later augmented with an attributed translation system and an error recovery mechanism. This version of ATS currently runs on a VAX-11 computer under UNIX. Ports to the Zilog ZEUS, a DECSystem 2060, the Perkin-Elmer 3200 series, and SUN-2 machines are currently under way.

In the last year, the ATS system has been ported to a personal microcomputer running PC-DOS. More important, it has been augmented with a visible tracing aid which assists the compiler writer with the task of debugging a translator specification. This visibility module displays the current state of the parser at each step, showing parsing reductions, semantic actions, and error recovery actions dynamically as they occur. As a result, a very helpful tool has evolved which can be used to develop simple compilers for microcomputers. Its uses also include providing students with an effective compiler development tool for use when studying compiler construction techniques.

Recall from Sec. 6-2 that LL(1) parsing is a deterministic top-down method of constructing a parse tree. The notions of attributed translation were also introduced in Sec. 11-5. The system uses an error-correction approach that is very similar to the method described in Sec. 6-2.

Recall from Sec. 11-5 that an attributed grammar is a context-free grammar whose symbols are augmented with attributes and rules describing how these attributes are to be used. Each production in the grammar can be associated with several evaluation rules. Such a rule specifies the computation of an attribute value as a function of the other attribute values (associated with symbols appearing in the same production). There are two types of attributes: inherited and synthesized attributes which can be used to convey context into and out of a subtree in a derivation.

A top-down parsing strategy, such as the LL(1) parsing approach, is well suited to attribute processing, since it constructs the desired parse tree in a left-to-right depth-first manner. Recall from Sec. 6-2 that a parsing decision is made on the basis of the nonterminal on top of the parse stack and the current input symbol. The attributed parsing approach is to also use the evaluated attributes of the stack and input symbols in making parsing decisions. The parsing algorithm requires that attribute values be available at the proper time. The synthesized attribute values of the current input symbol are always available. The attribute values of the nonterminal on top of the stack, however, may pose a problem. The synthesized attribute values of this nonterminal, which are evaluated in terms of the attributes of the right part of an associated production, are simply not available (because of the top-down parsing strategy). The inherited attribute values are available only for L-attributed grammars (see Sec. 11-5.2).

We first introduce the form of the specification of an attributed translator supported by ATS. We next present the visible parser, describe the process of specifying an attributed translator, and discuss the dynamic *window on the compiler* tracing capability. Finally, we list some interesting extensions to VATS.

Form of input to VATS. Recall that the explicit assignments in an L-ATG grammar can be made implicit by renaming the attributes occurring on the right-hand side of an assignment with the name of the attribute occurring in the left-hand side of the assignment. Since the attributes in a production no longer have a unique name, they are called *attribute variables*. An example of an L-ATG in simple assignment form with implicit assignments through attribute variables follows:

```
expression:      expr⟩x @print⟨x;
expr⟩v:          term⟩x terms⟨x⟩v;
terms⟨x⟩v:       @echo⟨x⟩v
     |           PLUS term⟩y @add⟨x, y⟩z terms⟨z⟩v
     |           MINUS term⟩y @minus⟨x, y⟩z terms⟨z⟩v;
term⟩v:          factor⟩x factors⟨x⟩v;
factors⟨x⟩v:     @echo⟨x⟩v
     |           MULT factor⟩y @mult⟨x, y⟩z factors⟨z⟩v
     |           DIV factor⟩y @div⟨x, y⟩z factors⟨z⟩v;
factor⟩v:        NUMBER⟩v
     |           LP expr⟩v RP;
```

Each symbol of a translation grammar to be processed by VATS is denoted by an identifier of arbitrary length. Action symbols are denoted by an identifier which begins with the character '@'; other symbols are denoted by identifiers which begin with a letter. The first character of an identifier can be followed by zero or more letters, digits, or underscores ('_'). Upper- and lowercase letters are treated as distinct. A production of the grammar consists of an identifier (the left-hand side), followed by a colon (':'), followed by zero or more identifiers (the right-hand side), terminated by a semicolon (';'). For example

    terms: PLUS term @add terms; $this is a production

By convention, the names of input symbols are capitalized to make them stand out in the grammar. All text beginning with '$' to the end of the line designates a comment and has no meaning in the grammar. Alternate right-hand sides may be separated by the vertical bar ('|'). In the simple calculator example above, the symbols PLUS, MINUS, MULT, DIV, NUMBER, LP, and RP are terminal or input symbols. The symbols @print, @add, @minus, @mult, @div, and @echo are action symbols.

Attributes are denoted by lowercase letters which follow a symbol using the following rules: Inherited attributes are preceded by a '⟨' and are separated by commas; synthesized attributes are preceded by a '⟩' and are separated by commas. For example

    zap⟨a, b, c⟩x, y

denotes a symbol with inherited attributes $\{a, b, c\}$ and synthesized attributes $\{x, y\}$. Note that an additional action symbol '@echo' is used when an assignment is made based on an empty production.

The visible parser. The major motivation for the creation of a *visible* parser is to provide a *window on the compiler* for tutorial and debugging purposes. That is, the visible parser dynamically shows the state of the parser at every step, allowing the compiler writer to more clearly understand how the parser processes the grammar. The same benefit is accorded a student who is studying parsing algorithms and applying them in the construction of a real compiler. The ability to view the parsing process is especially important in an attributed parsing system because the compiler writer must know the sequence in which semantic action routines are invoked.

The visible parser in VATS shows the following components of the parser to the user:

1. The input source line with the most recently scanned token marked by a token cursor,
2. A parser message area which provides a narrative description of the actions of the parser,
3. A recovery message area which describes the actions taken by the syntax error recovery algorithm, and
4. A display of the primary parse stack, containing terminal input, nonterminal, and action symbols.

A *user translator source* is a complete specification of a translator. It is comprised of an LL(1) ATG, a main procedure, a scanner, and action routines. Figure 14-5 illustrates the entire user translator source for the simple calculator example. We now describe the components of the user translator source and how they are used to generate a translator.

Recall that an LL(1) ATG is an ATG which, when stripped of the attributes and action symbols, is an LL(1) grammar. The notation introduced earlier is used to represent LL(1) ATGs in the user translator source. A percent sign (%) is used to signal the end of the LL(1) ATG and the beginning of the main procedure.

The user-supplied main procedure must contain a call to the ATS parser *llparse( )*. Control is not returned from the parser until the scanner returns the end-of-parse symbol.

The user-supplied scanner must be named *llscan( )*. It is called by *llparse( )* to return a token representing the next input symbol and produce its synthesized attributes, if any. The token to be returned must be an identifier denoting an

```
$ The grammar for the desk calculator language:

program:      expr > x @print < x RETURN program;

expr > v:     term > x terms < x > v;

terms < x > v:  @echo < x > v
       |        PLUS term > y @add < x,y > z terms < z > v
       |        MINUS term > y @minus < x,y > z terms < z > v;

term > v:     factor > x factors < x > v;

factors < x > v: @echo < x > v
       |        MULT factor > y @mult < x,y > z factors < z > v
       |        DIV factor > y @div < x,y > z factors < z > v;

factor > v:    NUMBER > v
       |       LP expr > v RP;
%
        /* The subroutines of the desk calculator: */

int     peek   -1;

main ()        /* Main program — just calls the parser. */
{
        llparse ();
}
llscan ()       /* Lexical scanner routine */
{
        register int c;
        int z;

        c = peek;
        if (c >= 0)
                peek = -1;
        else
                c = getchar ();

        while (1) {
                switch (c) {
                case 0:
                        return (lleof);
                case '\n':
                        return (RETURN);
                case '\t':
                case ' ':
                        break;
```

```
          case '+':
                  return (PLUS);
          case '-':
                  return (MINUS);
          case '*':
                  return (MULT);
          case '/':
                  return (DIV);
          case '(':
                  return (LP);
          case ')':
                  return (RP);
          default:
                  if (c < '0' || c > '9') {
                          printf ("unknown char '%c'\n", c);
                          break;

                  }

                  z = c - '0';
                  while ((c = getchar ()) > = '0' && c <= '9')
                          z = 10 * z + c - '0';

                  peek = c;
                  llsyn (z);
                  return (NUMBER);
          }
          c = getchar ();
     }
}

          /* Semantic action routines follow: */

_print ()
{
     printf ("%d\n", llinh ());
}
_add ()
{
     llsyn (llinh () + llinh ());
}
_minus ()
{
     int x, y;
     x = llinh ();
     y = llinh ();
     llsyn (x - y);
}
_mult ()
{
     llsyn (llinh () * llinh ());
}


_div ()
{
     int x, y;
     x = llinh ();
     y = llinh ();
     if (y)
             llsyn (x / y);
     else
             llsyn (0);
}
_echo ()
{
     llsyn (llinh ());
}
```

Figure 14-5 Example of input to VATS.

input symbol used in the LL(1) ATG of the user translator source. The scanner generates the synthesized attributes by calling the *llsyn( )* procedure with the value of the attribute as a parameter. The ith call to the *llsyn( )* procedure produces the ith synthesized attribute. After the last synthesized attribute has been produced, the input symbol token must be returned.

For each action symbol of the form @X in the LL(1) ATG, there must be an action routine of the form _X( ) defined in the user translator source. The action routine receives the inherited attributes by calling the *llinh( )* procedure. The ith call to the *llinh( )* procedure obtains the value of the ith inherited attribute. The action routine generates the synthesized attributes by calling the *llsyn( )* procedure with the value of the attribute as a parameter. The ith call to the *llsyn( )* procedure produces the ith synthesized attribute.

For example, if @mult$\langle x, y \rangle z$ is an attributed action symbol, then an action routine which specifies the multiplication of x and y to produce z is as follows:

```
_mult( )
{
        int x, y, z;
        x = llinh( );
        y = llinh( );
        z = x * y;
        llsyn (z);

}
```

The user translator source cannot be directly compiled because the ATG has no meaning in the system source language. Therefore, the *ATS generator* is used to convert the user translator source to the *ATS translator source*. In particular, the ATG is translated into a set of parsing tables. The ATS translator source is compiled with the *ATS parser source* to yield the *user translator*. The user translator is a program which performs the translation specified by the user translator source.

The operation of the visible parser during the operation of the simple desk calculator is now discussed. The input string being parsed is assumed to be:

$6 + 7 * 8$

The initial configuration of the parser is displayed as follows. The input source string is displayed in the scanner input region. The token cursor is located just in front of the first input token. The parser's stack initially contains the starting symbol of the grammar, *program*, followed by the end-of-parse symbol, *lleof*. Since no input tokens have been read, nothing is displayed in the current input token window. Further, since no parser actions have occurred, nothing is displayed in the parser message area. The recovery context message area is visible just below the parser message area. For the purposes of this discussion, it will not contain any messages.

Given these initial conditions, the operation of the parser begins when an input token, *NUMBER*, is obtained from the scanner. The name of the current token is displayed on the screen and the input string cursor is moved so that it is located directly beneath the token just scanned. The parser expands the start symbol, *program*, which was on top of the stack with the right-hand side of the first production of the grammar. After this expansion, the stack contains the symbols *expr*, *_print*, *RETURN*, *program*, and *lleof*. Notice that productions are pushed on the stack so that the leftmost symbol of the right-hand side of the production is on the top of the stack. The altered contents of the parse stack are displayed on the screen and a message describing the parse action is displayed in the parser message area of the screen.

Several more production applications occur in a fashion similar to that just described. Each time, the production to be applied is identified by the parse table and each time, the effects of the production application are displayed on the screen. The application of productions continues as long as the top of stack symbol is a nonterminal. However, this process eventually terminates when a terminal symbol remains on the top of the stack. At this stage, the stack contents are *NUMBER*, *factors*, *terms*, *_print*, *RETURN*, *program*, and *lleof*. The parser action in this situation is to match the terminal symbol *NUMBER* on the top of the stack with the then current input token, pop the stack, and obtain the next input token, *PLUS*. All of this activity is recorded on the screen. The current input token is changed to *PLUS* and the input cursor is advanced so that it is located just beneath the plus sign in the input string. The parser message area displays a message indicating that a symbol was popped from the stack and the displayed stack contents are changed accordingly.

The next parser action involves the application of a production which replaces the top of stack symbol *factors* with a production right hand side containing only an action routine. At this point, the stack contains the following: *_echo*, *terms*, *_print*, *RETURN*, *program*, and *lleof*. Since the top of the stack is an action symbol, the parser executes the action routine and removes its token from the stack.

Extensions. A number of extensions and enhancements to VATS are under development, including:

1. Adding global attributes.
2. Automating the generation of error recovery tables.
3. Providing a capability whereby the observer of the parse can single step the parsing algorithm.
4. Displaying the flow of attribute values during the parse.
5. Providing special action routines to modify the parse stack to support backtracking and the parsing of ambiguous grammars.
6. Scrolling the displayed parse stack to overcome the screen size limitations.

VATS has evolved considerably since it was originally written.* Its predecessor, ATS, has been used extensively by students taking a class in compiler writing

---

*For information on VATS software, contact the Computer Facilities Manager, Department of Computational Science, 86 Commerce Building, University of Saskatchewan, Saskatoon, Sask, Canada S7N 0W0.

given by the Department of Computational Science at the University of Saskatchewan. It was also used in writing the PICASSO (Sorenson and Wald, 1977), PANEL (Bocking, 1983), and PICDRAW (Wald and Sorenson, 1979) systems, and a data base query language (Wald, 1984). It will be used in the next generation of the SPSL/SPSA system (Sorenson et al., 1981).

This section has concentrated on generators for the front end of a compiler. Formal syntactic methods have been around for many years. The automated generation of the back end of a compiler, however, is a much more difficult and current problem. The next section examines several systems for the code-generation and -optimization phases of a compiler.

14-3 MACHINE-INDEPENDENT CODE GENERATION

This section introduces machine-independent code generation. *Machine-independent code generation* describes the separation of information dependent on the target machine from the machine-independent algorithms. The algorithms use machine specifications provided by the compiler implementor to generate optimized code for the target machine.

There have been two approaches to the automatic production of code generators. The earliest methods used *procedural languages* having built-in functions to deal with many of the common details found in different computers. McKeeman, Horning, and Wortman's (1970) XCOM compiler generator is an example. XPL is a compiler writing language derived from PL/I that contains a number of additional procedures that the compiler writer uses to implement a new compiler. Examples include the function "ARITHEMIT" that emits code for arithmetic infix operators and the function "BRANCH_BD" that emits branch instructions.

The success with the procedural-language approach has been limited, especially with automating the generation of the synthesis phase. For the most part, the synthesis phase still has to be hand-coded. Some people feel that the lack of progress in automating the synthesis phase of compilation is primarily due to inadequate formalization of machines and the code-generation process, rather than fundamental difficulties in automating the process (Cattell, 1978). The lack of success has led to a second approach.

The second approach to automated code-generator production is referred to as the *descriptive-language* approach. A code generator is developed from a structural and behavioral machine description. It appears that the descriptive approach is more desirable than the procedural approach. The remainder of this section examines the descriptive-language approach to automating the production of the code-generation and -optimization phases of a compiler.

Table-driven code-generation approaches have received much attention recently. A code-generator generator receives, as input, the machine and language descriptions and *constructs* tables that code-generation and -optimization algorithms use. This is the same approach used in YACC. Just as YACC's parsing algorithm is language-independent, it is necessary to make the code-generation and -optimization algorithms machine-independent.

The practicality of the table-driven code-generation approach has been demonstrated by the portable C compiler (Johnson, 1978). The portable C compiler tabularizes the information necessary to describe the target machine. Currently, there is no automated means to generate these tables for the C compiler.

The first two code-generation systems discussed in this section are table-driven. The first system uses heuristic strategies for generating target code. The second system uses a context-free grammar to describe the capabilities of the intermediate form of the source program. Also, the generation of code is done by a syntax-directed translation scheme (an LR parser). The input to the code generator is a set of templates that associate each intermediate form operator to target-machine instructions. The syntax-directed approach is attractive, since the operation of the code generator can be proven to be correct. The third system uses a knowledge base in order to automatically generate code. The fourth and final system for code generation is based on the representation of the target machine by a finite-state machine. Most systems discussed in this section assume that the original source program has been converted to a suitable intermediate form by the front end of the compiler.

Before proceeding to the discussion of the various systems, recall from Chaps. 11, 12, and 13 some of the problems associated with code generation:

1. Common subexpression evaluation
2. Evaluation order of operands and expressions
3. Register allocation
4. Storage allocation, binding, and management
5. Emission of code for procedure invocations and returns
6. Instruction selections
7. Machine-dependent optimizations

Some of the systems address most of these problems while others do not.

14-3.1 The Production-Quality Compiler-Compiler System

A current effort that deals with automating the code-generation and -optimization phases of a compiler is the production-quality compiler-compiler (PQCC) system. This section gives a brief description of this project. We first present an overview of the project. We next formalize a machine-description approach for specifying various machine architectures. We then describe the phases of the compiler-compiler system and their organization.

Introduction. The production-quality compiler-compiler project currently under development by Wulf (Leverett et al., 1980) at Carnegie-Mellon University, is a system which generates those parts of a compiler that produce and optimize object code for some language and target computer. This section gives an overview of the design of PQCC and how it is used in the production of a compiler—especially in the code-generation and -optimization phases.

As was mentioned in the first section of this chapter, little success has been achieved in producing a truly automated compiler-compiler which includes both code generation and code optimization. This is especially the case when good optimization and retargetability (i.e., the capability of generating compilers for many different computers) is desired. Cattell (1980) attributes part of the problem to the failure of making the formalizations of language and machine descriptions and the code generator general enough. PQCC allows for both the specification of details of the language and the target computer system and therefore is designed to be general enough to permit the production of compilers for a wide variety of machines.

In a similar fashion to YACC, PQCC accepts as input a formalized description of a language and target machine and generates the tables by which a skeleton code-generator and -optimizer program named PQC generates code. PQC and the tables embody the back end of a compiler. Figure 14-6 illustrates how the PQCC system relates to PQC, and how PQC is included within a compiler.

In order to keep the size of the PQCC project manageable, PQCC excludes languages which support complex data abstractions: this includes the string, list, and array processing languages of SNOBOL, LISP, and APL, respectively. Interpreters are often used to execute programs in such languages. Furthermore, the target machines for PQCC have one-, two-, and three-address instructions and are general register machines. This includes many machines such as the PDP-8, PDP-11, S/370, Cray-1, and VAX. Stack machines, on the other hand, have not been included. Even with the above restrictions, the optimized code produced by PQCC is estimated to be comparable to that of the BLISS-11 compiler (see Wulf et al., 1975), making the system useful for a wide variety of applications.

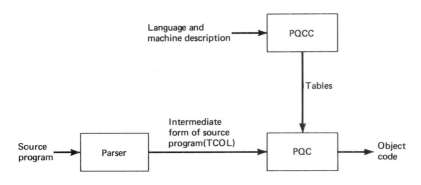

Figure 14-6 PQCC system.

The PQCC project studies the code-optimization and code-generation phases of a compiler. Because parsing and lexical analysis have been studied in depth by others, PQCC does not perform any lexical or syntactic analysis. A parser, which is supplied by the user, provides an intermediate form of the source program in TCOL—a tree representation. With such an approach, a parser such as YACC can be used to perform syntax analysis and generate a TCOL representation of the source program.

An important early step in the productions of automatic code generators is to specify the class of target machines to be used. The following subsection discusses this crucial step.

The formalization of instruction-set processors and TCOL. To permit the code-generation and -optimization algorithms to be machine-independent, it is necessary to define a machine model that permits a complete and unambiguous description of the computer and its instruction set. The model must make some implicit assumptions about the structure of computers in general. The details of the machine for which a compiler is being developed can be indicated by a machine-description language.

Siewiorek et al. (1982) provide a computer model that is the basis for the models used by several researchers. Siewiorek et al. present a multilevel model of a computer. The highest level in their model is the *processor-memory switch* (PMS) level. This level describes the entire machine and its peripherals in their most aggregate behavior. The level immediately beneath this is the program level, which describes the memories and sets of operations. It is this level that provides a model of computers necessary for code generation. Lower levels describe the hardware details underlying the design of the computer.

The components of the program level include a set of *memories* and a set of *operations*. The memories hold data structures while the operators take the contents of the memories as input and produce new data structures which are again stored in memories. Operations are described by *instructions*. A *control structure* specifies the order in which the instructions are to be executed. The model is suitable for a wide variety of machines, including many IBM, DEC, and HP models.

Siewiorek et al. (1982) provide a procedural *instruction-set processor* (ISP) language for describing instruction sets. It is used to describe the instruction formats, the registers, and the semantics of each instruction (i.e., input/output mapping). An ISP description specifies data types, instructions, operations, and processors. The data-type component of the ISP description is used to define the permissible types of data that may be stored (e.g., real, integer, character). Instructions are data types; instruction expressions describe the transformations instructions may perform such as the movement and transformation of data. Transformations are defined by operations. The ISP definition of a processor indicates the sequencing of instructions to be executed, the definition of memories, and address calculations.

The machine model used in the PQCC system is based on the ISP model. Some changes to the model were required because the machine descriptions in PQCC are in machine-processable form. Other changes were necessary in order to achieve certain desired results. For example, it is assumed that a machine has a single processor which executes instructions from a primary memory.

The machine formalization must, on one hand, be sufficiently restrictive so that code can be produced by an efficient algorithm, and on the other hand, permit the specifications of several typical computer architectures.

A machine is assumed to consist of an *instruction-set processor* that repeatedly fetches an instruction from a primary memory and modifies the contents of a processor state (a set of locations) according to that instruction.

An instruction-set processor can be defined in terms of five main types of components: storage bases, operand addressing, machine operations, data types, and instruction fields and formats.

A *storage base* is an array of one or more words, each word containing a fixed number of bits. Each storage base has a *length* (the number of words in the array), a *width* (the bit size of a word), and a *type* which specifies how the storage base can be used. The type may be temporary (for storing condition codes), general-purpose (for storing values), and reserved (for storing special items such as a stack pointer). Furthermore, two storage bases are singled out as special: primary memory and program counter which are of type general-purpose and reserved, respectively.

Operand addressing deals with the locations available on a machine and how they become accessed as operands in various instructions. An *address mode* refers to a type of addressing on a machine. For example, indirect through a memory location, indexed by a register, and an accumulator are examples of address modes. Each operand of an instruction has an associated set of access modes, called an *operand class*, which may be valid depending on context. For example, a subtract instruction might require a general-purpose register for its first (necessary) operand and an immediate value or a memory location for its second operand. Each access mode is an operand class containing a time/space cost and a field value specification. While access modes and operand classes are not essential components of the machine model, their presence facilitates code generation and reduces the number of instructions that must be described. For example, if each operand of a two-operand instruction has n access modes independently, the instruction could be specified as n^2 instructions which each refer to only a specific pair of access modes. Some machines have instructions which permit a dozen different access modes of their operands.

Machine operations represent the actual instructions available on the machine. Each instruction may require the following items: time/space cost, formatting information, and input/output assertions which describe the action of the instruction. An *output assertion* specifies a processor state location and its associated value resulting from the execution of the instruction. This specification is a function of the process state before the instruction is executed. An *input assertion* is paired with each output assertion. The former specifies a conditional function of the processor state locations before the instruction is executed. If an input assertion is satisfied, its corresponding output assertion holds (i.e., a new value is obtained for a location). As an example, the following two assertions

$$R \leftarrow R + 1$$
$$\text{If } R + 1 = 0 \quad \text{then} \quad PC \leftarrow PC + 1$$

could describe an increment and skip on zero (ISZ) instruction for a PDP-8 computer. The assertions are not ordered; that is, they are nonprocedural. The PQCC systems represents the assertions as tree patterns which correspond to the action the instruction performs. The advantage of such a representation is that tree patterns for assertions can be matched against the source program trees in the code-generation process.

A computer usually has several *data types*. The domain (e.g., integer, real) of each data type must be given. Also required is a data-type encoding/decoding function. Each instruction that represents an arithmetic or logical operator has assertions that describe the data types which it manipulates.

Construction fields and formats specify the binary representation of instructions as to opcode, operand address, etc.

The machine-description language used in the PQCC system is nonprocedural. Furthermore, the language is structured for expository purposes, permitting it to be easily read by humans. A program in this language gives a mapping from the machine operation to the intermediate representations language, TCOL, whose form is now examined.

A TCOL tree is not the same as a parse tree; rather it reflects abstract syntax. For example, control constructs are represented as tree nodes rather than a series of tests and jumps. As a result, the optimization of loops is simpler than if the program is in the form of quadruples, triples, or a parse tree. TCOL also permits the specification of semantic rules within the tree, such as the type checking of variables and range checking of subscripts.

Other less significant reasons are given for using TCOL. For example, it is difficult to generate good, optimized code for two-address machines from quadruples, and for three-address machines from triples. It is also believed that TCOL is more psychologically appealing, as trees tend to be easier to comprehend than triples and quadruples.

Figure 14-7a and b provides two examples of TCOL trees for the statements $a \leftarrow i$ and $i \leftarrow i * 2$ where a is a real variable and i is an integer variable. These examples illustrate the inclusion of dereferencing and type conversions in TCOL trees. All implicit operations, such as type conversion, dereferencing, and the dynamic checking of types and subscript ranges must be included in the trees. The TCOL tree of Fig. 14-7c illustrates a "WHILE" loop. The loop control structure is represented by a single node. The subtree *e1* describes the Boolean expression of the loop and the subtree *s1* represents the body of the loop.

Input (and output) of the source program as a TCOL tree is done using linear graph notation (LGN). We shall not delve into the syntax details of LGN in this

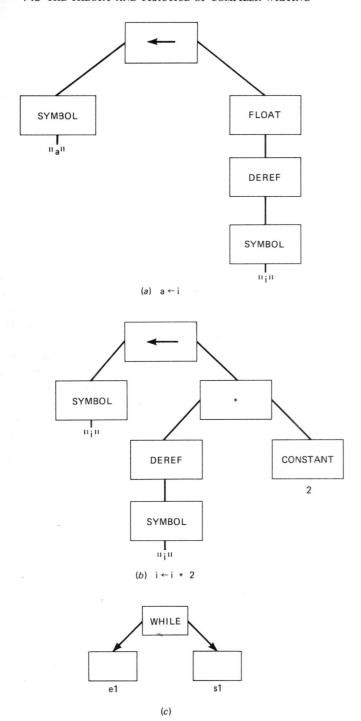

Figure 14-7 Examples of TCOL trees.

book. This information can be found in the Carnegie-Mellon Technical Report by Leverett et al. (1979).

The PQCC skeleton compiler takes a representation of the program in the form of a TCOL tree. From this tree, it generates code by using tables which specify the conversion of TCOL instructions to machine-code instructions. As a consequence, it is necessary for the compiler writer to describe the relationship between the operations or instructions of the machine language and the set of TCOL operations. From this description, PQCC generates the tables for the compiler by reversing the mapping of machine instruction to language operation. Thus, templates which give nodes or possible subtrees of some TCOL intermediate forms are related to code sequences to be generated.

The next subsection examines the structure and phases of the PQCC system in more detail.

The code-generation process: its phases and organization. Figure 14-6 is a very high-level block diagram on the PQCC system. This subsection gives more details of the system.

PQCC contains several separate phases, each phase performing some aspect of code optimization or code generation. The phases are executed serially in the compiler as shown in Fig. 14-8.

The separation of PQCC into phases permits work on each phase to be done independently, allowing the entire system to be written and debugged in smaller,

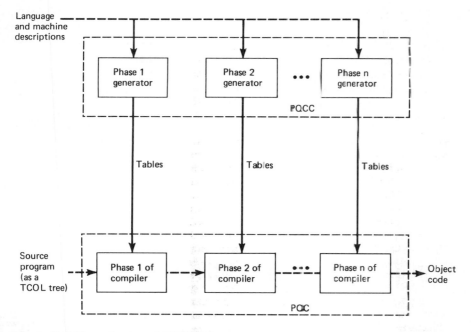

Figure 14-8 Phase structure of PQCC system.

manageable pieces. TCOL is used throughout as the interface medium between successive phases. The phase division incorporates the problem of ordering optimizations, however. This occurs whenever a multiphase optimizing compiler or compiler-compiler is being written. Often, one phase of optimization aids or hinders another phase and vice versa. PQCC attempts to handle this as effectively as possible. For example, one phase handles flow optimizations, yet other phases perform, to a limited extent, some flow analysis as well.

Brief descriptions of the phases of PQCC are now given in the order in which they are executed. Details on how the optimizations and code-generation methods are implemented have already been discussed in other chapters (Chaps. 11, 12, and 13) in the book. Optimizations are passed from one phase to the next by changing or appending the TCOL tree with only the first phase having the original TCOL tree as its input. Recall from Chaps. 12 and 13 that some code optimizations are independent of the target machine and others are not. PQCC attempts to parametrize the code-optimization techniques such that the optimization algorithms are usable on a host of machines with only the tables being changed. The PQCC system is based on the BLISS-11 optimization compiler. The major phases in that compiler structure are given in Fig. 14-9. These phases are also found in the PQCC system. Description of each phase, except for the lexical and parsing phase (LEXSYM), is now given.

The FLOWAN phase, which is entirely machine-independent, constructs a graph whose nodes represent the basic blocks of the source program. Then some flow analysis is performed, including the elimination of redundant expressions and changing the order of executable code. For example, this phase performs frequency reduction, where code whose generated values are static within a loop is moved out of the loop.

The next group of phases, collectively named DELAY, performs source-to-source transformations of the program tree and adds semantic information to the tree. For example, constant folding transforms the tree by trying to reduce the number of operations which use constant values that are known at compile time. Many of these phases are target-machine-dependent.

One of the DELAY phases, the context-determination phase, adds semantic information to the TCOL tree concerning how the nodes of the tree are to be used as operands. For example, Boolean values which are used as conditions for loop

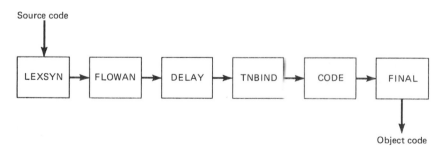

Figure 14-9 Simplified compiler structure.

constructs do not need to be saved. Another context, an address context, includes expressions which are to be deferenced or assigned.

The optimizations of complementary operator propagation, targeting, and evaluation-order determination are performed in another phase. In complementary operator propagation, the number of unary negation operators are reduced if possible. Targeting uses commutativity of operators to avoid loading and storing operands. Evaluation-order determination may change the order in which operands are to be evaluated.

Another DELAY phase determines the best method of performing address computations on the target machine. Indexing, if available, may be preferable to computing the address explicitly. Other DELAY phases use the associative and distributive laws to the best advantage, as well as other transformations if possible.

After the DELAY phases are completed, register allocation is performed in the TNBIND phase. This phase is divided into two smaller subphases. The first subphase determines the entities such as variables and temporary results of expressions, which must be allocated storage and the span over which the entity's value is to be stored. The second subphase performs packing where storage for the entities is allocated such that no conflicts for storage in registers, accumulators, or temporary storage locations in primary memory occur.

The second to last phase generates the code for the source program whose intermediate form is an optimized TCOL program tree. Observe that the machine description described earlier does not indicate how to generate code for that machine. Essentially, what is given is a mapping from machine operations to TCOL operations. The code-generation problem, however, is to invert this mapping, that is, produce machine instructions from TCOL operations. TCOL templates, which were mentioned earlier, are generated by PQCC for this phase and consists of a TCOL subtree pattern and code sequence. Code generation is performed by attempting to match one of the templates with a subtree of the program tree. A successful match causes the code sequence for this template to be emitted.

Note that for efficiency reasons, the database of templates (also called tree productions) should not be generated at code-generation time. These templates should be generated by the compiler-compiler system, that is, by a code-generator generator. Figure 14-10 illustrates the relationship between a code-generator generator and a code generator. The code-generator generator is provided with a machine description that describes the machine instructions. From this, an intermediate-form instruction to machine-instruction mapping is extracted and tabularized. The code-generation and -optimization algorithms use the tables (i.e., templates) to produce optimized machine code or assembly code.

Each code-selection template contains a *subtree pattern* and an associated code sequence. Figure 14-11 gives a template for the addition of a value "e1" to the value "a1" with the result stored in "a1"'s location. If the code generator finds a match between a subtree of a program tree and a template tree, the code part of that template is output. If no match can be found, a set of *tree axioms* can be applied to manipulate the program subtree to determine whether the subtree is

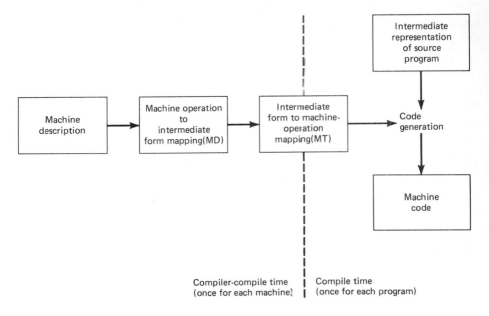

Compiler-compile time | Compile time
(once for each machine) | (once for each program)

Figure 14-10 Automated code-generator generation.

equivalent to a template tree. For example, a tree which adds the constant 0 to another operand is equivalent to a tree consisting of just the operand.

This goal-directed searching process can almost all be done prior to compile time by the code-generator generator (GEN). Tree axioms are rules for transforming trees into equivalent trees. There are several classes of axioms. We now present examples of axioms from some of these classes. The advantage of using axioms in the searching process is their relative machine independence.

These axioms include the single Boolean axioms such as

not not E ≡ E
E1 and E2 ≡ E2 and E1
E1 and E2 ≡ not ((not E1) or (not E2))

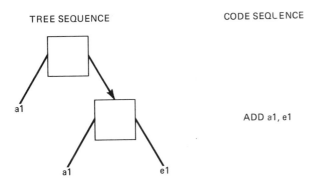

TREE SEQUENCE CODE SEQUENCE

ADD a1, e1

Figure 14-11 A TCOL template.

which indicate the double-complement rule, the commutativity rule, and DeMorgan's law. In addition there are arithmetic axioms such as

$$E + 0 \equiv E$$
$$-(-E) \equiv E$$
$$E1 * E2 \equiv E2 * E1$$

whose meanings are obvious. There are also relational axioms such as

$$\text{not } (E1 \geq E2) \equiv (E1 < E2).$$

In addition there are new kinds of axioms like the fetch/store decomposition axioms which have the form

$$E1(E2) \equiv S \leftarrow E2; E1(S)$$
$$S1 \leftarrow E \equiv S2 \leftarrow E; S1 \leftarrow S2$$

The first axiom indicates that a storage location can hold an intermediate result. The second axiom, called store-decomposition, is a special case of the first. Yet other axioms deal with the flow of control as in the following:

$$\text{goto } E \equiv PC \leftarrow E$$
$$\text{if } E \text{ then } S \equiv \text{if (not } E) \text{ then goto } L; S; L:$$

where the first axiom defines the program counter and the second specifies how to implement an if statement with an unconditional jump. A complete list of axioms can be found in Cattell (1980).

The only axiom which is applied at compile time is fetch-decomposition. All other rules are applied at compiler compile time by the code-generator generator, GEN.

GEN uses heuristic search techniques and goal-oriented searches in generating templates that will be used to generate code at code-generation time. The search for these templates can be improved by classifying the axioms to include the following classes:

1. *Transformation axioms* that deal with arithmetic and Boolean equivalence. These transformations are used in conjunction with means-end analysis in the searching process.
2. *Decomposition axioms* that are usually concerned with control constructs which can be decomposed into simpler constructs. This approach leads to a search which proceeds recursively on a sequence of subgoals.

The search does not guarantee an optimal solution. In some cases, however, the code sequences may be optimum. There may be cases where the search may fail. An example of such a failure may be due to a missing axiom. In the machines that were tested, however, the set of some 50 axioms was adequate. Another failure can occur if the depth of the recursive searching process exceeds a preset limit before finding the feasible code sequence. Preliminary results indicate that this factor was not significant.

We now describe the process that selects the templates which constitute the MT table in Fig. 14-10. Recall that these templates are used by the code generator at compile time. The set of templates is created according to several rules. These rules include the following:

1. For each TCOL operator there is one template. The simplicity of the subtree pattern guarantees its applicability when the operator appears. An example of such a template is given in Fig. 14-11. Observe that, because of different contexts, it may be desirable to generate more than one template.
2. There is one template for every possible data move. For an assignment of the form $A \leftarrow B$ where there are n distinct access nodes, n^2 templates are required in order to generate code to move one data item from one type of storage to another.
3. Templates must be included to handle control constructs (or operators) such as the if-the-else and while-do constructs.
4. There are rules for generating templates that discover "clever" code sequences. Also, templates are generated to deal with multiple input/output assertions.

The code generator uses the set of patterns generated by GEN to generate code for a source program represented by a TCOL parse tree. Specifically, the set of all patterns that could apply to the given parse tree is selected and from these is selected the lowest-cost target construction sequence that applies. There may be instances where the leaves of the parse tree do not match the leaves of the pattern. The fetch/store decomposition rules can be used to deal with such a situation. An example of such a mismatch is encountering an expression instead of a simple storage unit.

Recall that many of the tasks performed by a conventional code generator have already been done. One such task is register allocation. The actual storage locations used are of concern to the code generator because they partially determine which templates match.

The database of patterns is indexed by context (i.e., address, flow, real, void). Within each context, the patterns are ordered by the primary operator of the pattern tree. There is further ordering by a cost metric (involving such factors as cost of instruction, cost of access modes, cost of register spill, cost of fetch decomposition for operands that do not match the pattern and the number of nodes in the tree matched by the pattern).

The code generator produces code in *reverse execution order*. Ordinarily, a code generator performs a postorder traversal of the tree in generating code. The approach in PQCC is to take advantage of instruction set and addressing modes of the machine. This is achieved by starting at the tree's root node and usually selecting the pattern that spans the largest set of nodes in that tree. This process involving the application of fetch/store decompositions can be applied recursively to the nodes of the tree, thereby resulting in the use of a minimum of patterns to match the tree. Corresponding to this set of patterns is the lowest-cost target code sequence. Without an exhaustive search this process does not guarantee that the lowest-cost sequence is found. The technique used, however, does produce near optimum code. The output from the code-generation phase is in the form of a doubly linked list of instructions and labels.

The last phase, or FINAL phase, of PQCC outputs the actual code after performing some optimizations that were not evident at the TCOL tree level. These optimizations may arise from the side effects of instructions, such as the setting of conditions. Thus, instructions whose sole purpose is to set condition codes may be subsumed by other instructions. Other optimizations are evident because the TCOL tree nodes have been broken down into individual instructions where one node may generate several instructions. PQCC does not perform loading and relocation of this code. To make the code executable, a "back-end" to the compiler must be used, as is the case for the scanner and parser used in the "front-end" of the compiler.

Preliminary results are encouraging. The machine representation method was general enough to represent several architectures such as the IBM-360, PDP-10, and Intel 8080. The method of heuristic search used found optimum code sequences for the machines listed.

The code-generator speed was quite impressive even if a table-driven pattern-matching approach was used. For example, some 2000 instructions per second were generated from a TCOL tree for a PDP-10 machine. The code-generator generator was also fast when compared to other formal methods. Its speed did not seem to be greatly affected by the number of axioms and the size of target-machine instruction repertoire. The machine-description effort was also impressive. The time required to write and debug a typical machine description, such as the PDP-11, was one person-week.

The success of the project is partially due to the formalization of the machine and language descriptions. Through the use of optimization and code-generation algorithms which are retargetable (in the sense that by modifying the parameters of the algorithms, optimized code can be generated for different target machines), a versatile code-generation system can be realized.

The database of patterns used in the code-generation process can be organized in a different manner than was described in this subsection. The next subsection describes another table-driven code generator that takes such an approach.

14-3.2 The Table-Driven Generator of Graham and Glanville

This subsection examines another table-driven code-generation system. The approach taken in this system is similar to that taken in the PQCC system with code being generated by a pattern-matching algorithm. The Graham and Glanville approach, however, uses an LR-based algorithm to pattern match instead of the heuristic approach taken in the previous subsection.

We first give an overview of the method. We next describe the target-machine description language used in specifying the intermediate representation language to machine-description mapping. Finally, results and extensions to the basic model are discussed.

Introduction. Graham and Glanville have implemented a table-driven code generator and a code-table constructor that generates tables describing target machines for the code generator (Graham, 1980; Glanville, 1977). The code generator produces code from a tabular description of the functional properties of the target machine. The code-table constructor accepts a machine description of a target machine and generates the tables necessary for the code generator. Reliability, ease of use, and flexibility are the advantages sought by Graham and Glanville with their code generator.

They make several assumptions about the environment in which their code generator is run. The compiler implementor supplies the analysis phase of the compiler. This phase must generate an intermediate form of the source program (IR) usable by the code generator. Storage allocation, binding, and optimizing procedures also must be supplied by the compiler writer.

Figure 14-12 illustrates the organization of the Glanville and Graham approach. The intermediate form of the source language is a sequence of Polish-prefix expressions. The target-machine description is specified by the productions of a context-free grammar. The left part of each production denotes the destination of the result from the computation. The right part contains the prefix expression (and associated semantics) in the intermediate representation language along with its equivalent assembly-language format. The table constructor uses the context-free description of the target machine to generate the tables used by the code generator. The pattern-matching process used in the code generator is based on LR(1) parsing theory. Prefix expressions in the IR form of the source program are recognized (parsed), and the corresponding target machine instructions are then emitted. This approach to code generation is very similar to the method used in table-driven syntax analysis given in Sec. 7-4 and has many of the same advantages such as modularity, correctness, and ease of use.

The parsing tables generated by the table-construction algorithm usually have many inadequate states (see Sec. 7-4). These ambiguities indicate shift-reduce and reduce-reduce conflicts in the corresponding parser. These ambiguities must be resolved at code-generation time. Since the code-generation algorithm is based on LR parsing theory, its speed is very fast, i.e., proportional to the length of the IR source program.

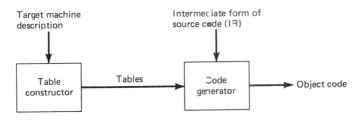

Figure 14-12 The Graham and Glanville systems.

We next give more details on the intermediate representation of the source program.

The target-machine description. The intermediate representation of source programs used (called the internal representation (IR)) is a low-level prefix notation. An IR program representing a source program is a sequence of prefix expressions. An IR program breaks all high-level constructs into a series of test and jumps, permitting IR expressions to be evaluated without their contexts. Hence the assignment

D:= E

would be represented in IR as

:= + d r↑ + e r

where "r" is the base address register, the locations of the variables "D" and "E" are "d" and "e", respectively, "+" is the additive operator, "↑" is a unary operator giving the value of the location that is its operand, and ":= " is the assignment operator. As with TCOL, an IR program must provide all operations necessary for dereferencing and coercions.

The target-machine description is written in target-machine description language (TMDL). The code-table constructor uses a TMDL program to construct the tables for the code generator.

One section of a TMDL program describes the registers on the target computer. Registers are divided into two groups: allocated and dedicated. The allocated set of registers are available for any use; the dedicated set of registers serve specific purposes. For example, registers 0 to 5 on the PDP-11 are allocatable registers, while registers 6 and 7, which are the stack pointer and program counter registers, respectively, are dedicated.

Another TMDL section describes the symbols that are used in the grammar. Nonterminals define classes of registers or ordered pairs of classes. The terminals classify symbols as constants, unary operators, or binary operators. It is this section that defines the particular IR format being generated by the analysis phase of the compiler.

The final section describes the IR-operation to machine-instruction mapping. For example, the instruction description

r.1 ::= (+ r.1 r.2)   "add r.1 r.2"

describes the code to be generated when an IR instruction is encountered. In this example, the generated code adds the contents of a second register to the contents of the first and saves the result in the first register. The numbers following the registers are semantic attributes that indicate which registers must be the same and which may differ. For this example, the result of the operation is to be saved in the location of the first operand (i.e., "r.1"). The left part of an instruction description may not be significant. For example some instructions are executed because of their side effects. An assignment (store) instruction is such an example. In such a case a special value, such as lambda, is used as the left part.

Observe that the IR form of a source language is a sequence of Polish-prefix expressions whose symbols are the same syntax symbols that are used in the target-language description. In an IR program, however, semantic qualifications actually contain specific information.

The TMDL description of a computer differs from its PQCC counterpart. In the PQCC system, a compiler writer describes the instructions and their semantics. PQCC uses this description to construct a TCOL-operation to machine-instruction mapping. With TMDL, the implementor directly describes an IR-instruction to machine-instruction mapping by giving the code to be generated for each IR instruction. Furthermore, the IR operator set is not fixed as in the case with TCOL. Rather, the IR operator set has a one-to-one correspondence with the target machine's set of instructions. Each IR operator has a corresponding machine instruction. The TMDL has the problem that intermediate-form operators may not have corresponding machine instructions. For example, AND is a common logical operator in many languages but the PDP-11 has no corresponding machine instruction. When such situations are identified, they must be handled as special cases.

The code-generation process. Given the tables generated from the TMDL program, the code generator produces code from the IR description of a program. The code-generation algorithm performs a depth-first, left-to-right traversal of the IR description. The code-generation algorithm is essentially an LR parsing algorithm that examines subtrees of the IR description. It attempts to match these subtrees with the set of IR instructions given in the TMDL description for the target machine. Once a match is found, the associated code is produced. While Graham and Glanville require that register decisions have been previously made by other parts of the compiler, the code generator makes the actual register allocations. For the TMDL example given earlier, the code generator may define "r.1" and "r.2" to be the registers "r2" and "r5", respectively, if code is being generated for the PDP-11. This separation makes register-allocation optimizations difficult because the registers should be allocated before code generation.

Although the code-generation algorithm is similar to an LR parsing algorithm, there are some important differences. The target-machine description is usually ambiguous. One reason for such ambiguity is that many operators access their operands in several ways. An important issue in the code-generation process is the approach used in resolving such ambiguities. Another difference is in performing a reduce action. Performing such an action in the code-generation process is more difficult than in syntax analysis. In general, the selection of target code is made from several possible instructions on the basis of syntactic and semantic information. Also, special attention must be given to reducing productions whose left part is denoted by lambda. Finally, the semantic information associated with a rule is kept on the code-generation stack. An LR parser generator creates the code-generator tables from the target-machine description. As a result of the ambiguity problem just discussed, there typically are many inadequate states resulting in both shift-reduce and reduce-reduce conflicts. The table constructor must deal with these ambiguities. Shift-reduce conflicts are resolved by performing shift actions. This approach usually results in the use of more powerful instructions. Reduce-reduce conflicts are resolved by choosing the longest rule. If all candidate rules have the same length, the selection is made based on semantics. The approach to resolving ambiguities is therefore based on selecting the largest possible pattern. The same approach to pattern matching was taken in the PQCC system.

An important aspect of the current approach to code generation is the correctness considerations of the method. We now examine these considerations.

Assuming that the target machine description is correct, the following errors may occur at code-generation time:

1. The emitted code could be in the wrong order.
2. The code generator may loop because of the ambiguity of the target-machine description.
3. The code generator may enter an error state which is called *syntactic blocking*.
4. All instructions that correspond to a particular syntactic pattern are semantically constrained; that is, the semantic qualifications of the matched instruction pattern are not compatible with those on the stack. Such a situation is called *semantic blocking*.

We now deal with each of these error possibilities. The table constructor will either avoid these errors or give an error message at code-generator generation time.

The code generated will always be in the correct order provided that the IR form of the source program is a valid sequence of prefix expressions.

Loops can occur only when the code generator performs a sequence of chain reductions such as $X \rightarrow Y \rightarrow Z \rightarrow X$ corresponding to register-to-register moves. Each loop can be detected and broken by changing the resolution of a reduce-reduce conflict. The approach is to use a state-splitting process in the table constructor.

Assuming that the sequence of prefix expressions in the IR form in the input is valid, the code-generation algorithm will not syntactically block if the operators and operands of the IR are from the same set as those in the target-machine description, and have the same meaning in both. If the condition holds, the code generator is said to be *uniform*. A test for uniformity can be incorporated in the table constructor. In essence a check is made if there is some input for which the pattern matcher will attempt an error action. A situation of nonuniformity appears to be rare when complete machine descriptions of real machines are given. Nonuniformity occurrences usually imply an incomplete machine description, with some aspects of the machine having been omitted.

A semantic blocking situation indicates that the code generator cannot select an instruction. Semantic blocking can be avoided by constructing a default action alternative, usually resulting in the generation of more than one instruction. This alternative sequence of instructions contains no semantic restrictions and computes the desired expression. The table constructor generates the required default instruction lists. Each list is obtained by simulating the action of the code generator using as input the right part of the semantically constrained instruction. The quality of the default instruction lists can affect the quality of the generated code. The best default list may not be found by the table constructor.

Results and extensions. Several code-generation experiments have been based on the Graham and Glanville method. Graham and Glanville (1978) implemented a code generator and table constructor in PASCAL. Target-machine descriptions were formulated for a variety of architectures including the PDP-11 and IBM-370. The PDP-11 code generator produced code that was comparable to that produced by the C compiler. Graham et al. (1982) replaced the back end of the UNIX portable C compiler (Johnson, 1978) on a VAX-11. Because of the richness of the instruction set on this machine, a *factored* machine-description grammar was used. In such a grammar additional nonterminals group together symbols having a common function (such as classes of operator symbols) in the grammar. The code produced by their code generator appears to have been as good as or better than that produced by the portable C compiler.

Other implementations of the Graham and Glanville model include the efforts of Bird (1982), Landwehr et al. (1982), and Ganapathi (1980). Bird has implemented a code generator for a PASCAL production compiler on an Amdahl 470. Landwehr et al. produced code generators for PASCAL on a Siemens 7.000 and Motorola MC 68000. Ganapathi has produced code generators for machines such as the VAX-11, PDP-11, and Intel 8086/8087. Again the target-code quality was of comparable quality to handwritten efforts.

The basic Graham and Glanville model has several shortcomings that include the following:

1. Because of the low-level nature of the IR, assumptions must be made about the addressing structure of the target machine. Also, there must be a one-to-one correspondence between machine instructions and the IR operators.
2. The machine-description language TMDL is not independent of the language which is to be compiled. The IR operator set may have to be redefined if a compiler is being written for a different language. This requires that the TMDL machine description be rewritten. Similarly, the IR may have to be redefined if a compiler for another target machine is desired because of the different instruction set of the machine. Changes to the target machine may imply changing the analysis phase, while changes to the language may require changes to the synthesis phase.
3. Graham and Glanville have ignored the problem of machine-dependent optimizations. To retarget the compiler, the machine-dependent optimization algorithms have to be rewritten. If the IR must be redefined, the machine-independent optimization algorithms may also require revision.

4. The quality of target code produced is affected by the exact IR form generated by the front end of the compiler and the completeness of the target-machine description.

Several extensions have been made to the basic model. For example, Bird (1982) has proposed extensions that were necessary for generating code for a production compiler. These included enhancements to the machine-description language to handle machine idioms (such as the use of even/odd register pairs on the IBM 360 for performing certain arithmetic operations) by semantic action, addressing, register allocation, common subexpression evaluation, and the typing of operands.

Significant extensions to the basic model were proposed by Ganapathi (1980). These extensions included the use of attributed grammars to describe the target machine, attributed parsing in the code-generation process, storage binding, machine-dependent optimizations, and code-generator structure and modularization.

14-3.3 Other Code-Generation Systems

The previous subsections have described two automated machine-independent code-generation systems using the descriptive-language approach. This subsection gives the reader a better appreciation of this approach by briefly introducing two other systems. The first system is based on Fraser's knowledge-based approach and the second approach, due to Donegan, uses a finite-state machine model.

Fraser's knowledge-based code-generator generator. Fraser (1977) designed a knowledge-based code-generator generator called XGEN. He attempted to formalize many of the ad hoc rules employed by programmers writing assembly-language programs. The code generator has a knowledge of how programmers program, using the rules they use when programming on a particular machine. For example, a loop can be implemented using a subtract-index-and-test instruction if one is available or a conditional jump can be programmed using skip jumps.

XGEN is designed to generate good local code for ALGOL-like languages such as PL/I and PASCAL. The XGEN system does not include machine-independent optimizations or global register allocation, but it does incorporate many machine-dependent optimizations and local register-allocation algorithms.

Fraser uses an assembler generator implemented by Wick (1975) to generate a suitable machine description for XGEN. Wick's assembler generator accepts an ISP form of description that is somewhat different from Bell and Newell's original ISP definition and generates a syntactically simpler ISP machine description (along with an assembler for the machine). Some human input along with the ISP description is required by Wick's assembler generator to deal with the mnemonics and syntax of some of the ISP descriptions. XGEN assumes idiomatic operators

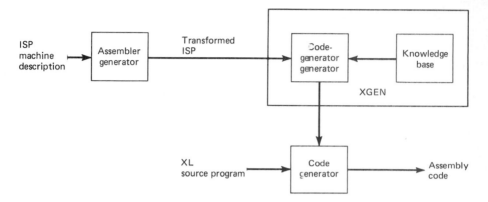

Figure 14-13 The XGEN system.

in ISP: operators are not expressed as bit manipulations but expressed with mathematical operators. Thus, ' + ' is used to represent the addition operator.

The XGEN system is illustrated in Fig. 14-13. An ISP description is modified by Wick's assembler generator. The modified ISP description is used by XGEN as the specification of the target machine. Using the knowledge base of ad hoc programming rules, a code generator is produced. The code generator compiles an intermediate form for representing source programs, XL, and generates assembly code.

The intermediate form of source code understood by XGEN is XL, a language of tuples suited to describing local behavior. A tuple can have only one operator but can have an arbitrary number of operands. XL allows the operators to be high-level enough such that additional context can be given with the tuple, simplifying optimization and permitting the generation of "large" instructions such as a subtract-index-and-test instruction for a loop. For example, a "for" loop tuple would contain start, stop, and step values and the index variable. XL operators are still as low-level as possible without interfering with the goal of portable, efficient programs. XL operations include moves, jumps, loops, calls, and returns.

XL permits only the declaration of static variables. Dynamic allocations must be implemented using primitives such as stack operations.

XGEN accepts XL statements for which code is to be generated. XGEN recursively breaks XL tuples into more primitive operations until corresponding machine instructions are found. Fraser's implementation uses problem-reduction techniques from the artificial intelligence field. This approach to code generation is best illustrated by a simple example. To access the value of an indexed array location, say "x[a]", the subscripting operation must be defined as a simpler set of operations. Hence, accessing the value is decomposed into the operations of adding the value of the index variable "a" to the base value of the array "x". The resulting value is then used to access the value of the "a"th location of the element "x".

The ad hoc rules that XGEN uses to generate code come from a knowledge base of machine architectures. Fraser observes that most current computer architectures are similar and the number of rules in the knowledge base is manageable. He presents evidence that the amount of time to introduce XGEN to the rules for new machines decreases rapidly with each new machine. A description of the model he uses for his knowledge base, can be found in Fraser, 1977.

The intermediate representation of source programs used by XGEN is a linear notation that has high-level operators. These operators help to circumvent some of the problems found when context is lost using low-level operators. Fraser's reliance on a linear notation is probably due to its easy representation in LISP, the language in which XGEN is implemented. However, the loss of the two-dimensional flow structure of languages makes optimizations requiring flow analysis more difficult.

The finite-state machine approach of Donegan. Donegan et al. (1979) describe the code-generator generator language (CGGL), a machine-description language based on modeling a computer as a finite-state machine.

The CGGL compiler uses a machine description to generate a code generator that is written in PASCAL. The compiler implementor must supply procedures to input the intermediate code and format the machine code for the code generator.

Donegan (1973) models a computer as a finite-state machine, and the code generator is constructed as such. The code generator enters various states as it attempts to generate code from a parse tree. The code emitted is based upon the state the code generator is in. Code generation is complete when the code generator enters a final state.

A machine is described in terms of conditions, transitions, operations, variables, conflicts, procedures, and code-generation statements. (Donegan does not describe the format of the machine description supplied by the compiler writer to the CGGL compiler.) *Variables* are used to associate semantic information with the parse tree. *Conflicts* describe operators having the same operands. For example, if an operator has one operand in an accumulator, a conflict would indicate that the other operand cannot be put into an accumulator. *Operations* specify the states of the code generator and the code to be generated for this state. PASCAL *procedures* generate the code. *Conditions* describe the states that keep track of the statuses of the operands. *Transitions* describe the state changes associated with the conditions.

Donegan's model is noted for its simplicity. It aids with human understanding and mechanization. Representing a machine as a finite-state model may be an oversimplification of a computer. For example, the model has trouble dealing with machines having more than one register because an excessive number of states is required for each possible register condition. Furthermore, the finite-state machine model is unsuitable for machine-dependent optimizations. Nevertheless, the finite-state model just discussed provides an interesting contrast to previous machine models.

The compiler writing field has progressed substantially in the last 15 years. Good lexical analyzers and parsers can now be automatically produced for many programming languages. More work, however, on good error-handling strategies remains to be done. The automatic generation of the remaining phases of a compiler have recently been attempted with some success. Some of these efforts look quite promising. More work has to be done in the formalization of these phases. With the arrival of VLSI technology, the question that often arises concerns what machine should be built to implement a given language. Compiler-compilers will play an important role in answering this question.

BIBLIOGRAPHY

Aho, A. V.: "Translator Writing Systems: Where Do They Now Stand," *IEEE Computer*, Vol. 13, No. 8, August 1980, pp. 9–14.

Allen, F. E., et al.: "The Experimental Compiling Systems Project," RC 6718, IBM T. J. Watson Research Center, Yorktown Heights, N.Y., September 1977.

Berg, A., D. A. Bocking, D. R. Peachey, P. G. Sorenson, J. P. Tremblay, and J. A. Wald: "VATS-The Visible Attributed Translation System," Technical Report 84-19, Department of Computational Science, University of Saskatchewan, 1984.

Bird, P. L.: "An Implementation of a Code Generator Specification Language for Table Driven Code Generators," *Proceedings of the SIGPLAN Symposium on Compiler Construction*, Boston, Mass., June 1982, pp. 44–50.

Bocking, D. A.: "An Approach to Designing Distributed Computer Applications," M.Sc. Thesis, Department of Computational Science, University of Saskatchewan, 1983

Cattell, R. G. G.: "A Survey and Critique of Some Models of Code Generation," Technical Report, Carnegie-Mellon University, Pittsburgh, Pa., November 1977.

Cattell, R. G. G.: "Formalization and Automatic Derivation of Code Generators," Ph.D. Dissertation, Technical Report, Department of Computer Science, Carnegie-Mellon University, Pittsburgh, Pa., April 1978.

Cattell, R. G. G.: "Automatic Derivation of Code Generators from Machine Descriptions," *ACM Transactions on Programming Languages and Systems* Vol. 2, No. 2, April 1980.

Cattell, R. G. G., J. M. Newcomer, and B. W. Leverett, "Code Generation in a Machine-Independent Compiler," *Proceedings of the SIGPLAN Symposium on Compiler Construction*, Denver, Colo., August 1979, pp. 65–75.

Donegan, M. K.: "An Approach to the Automatic Generation of Code Generators," Ph.D. Thesis, Computer Science and Engineering, Rice University, 1973.

Donegan, M. K., R. E. Noonan, and S. Feycock: "A Generator Generator Language," *Proceedings of the SIGPLAN Symposium on Compiler Construction*, Denver, Colo., August 1979, pp. 58–64.

Fraser, C. W.: "A Knowledge Based Code Generator Generator," *Proceedings of the Symposium on Artificial Intelligence and Programming Languages*, August 1977, pp. 126–129.

Fraser, C. W.: "Automatic Generation of Code Generators," Ph.D. dissertation, Computer Science Department, Yale University, New Haven, Conn., 1977.

Ganapathi, M.: "Retargetable Code Generation and Optimization Using Attribute Grammars," Ph.D. Thesis, Computer Science Department, University of Wisconsin at Madison, 1980.

Ganapathi, M., and C. N. Fischer: "Bibliography on Automated Retargetable Code Generation," *ACM SIGPLAN Notice*, Vol. 16, No. 10, October 1981, pp. 9–12.

Ganapathi, M., and C. N. Fischer: "Description-Driven Code Generation Using Attribute Grammars," *Proceeding of the Annual ACM Symposium on Principles of Programming Languages*, Albuquerque, N.M., January 1983.

Ganapathi, M., C. N. Fischer, and J. L. Hennessy: "Retargetable Compiler Code Generation," *ACM Computing Surveys*, Vol. 14, No. 4, December 1982, pp. 573–592.

Ganzinger, H., K. Ripken, and R. Wilheim: "Automatic Derivation of Optimizing Compilers," *Information Processing 77, IFIP Congress Series*, Vol. 7. B. Gilchrist (ed.), Amsterdam: North-Holland, 1977.

Glanville, R. S.: "A Machine Independent Algorithm for Code Generation and Its Use in Retargetable Compilers," Ph.D. Thesis, Departments of Electrical Engineering and Computer Science, University of California, Berkeley, December 1977.

Graham, S. L.: "Table-Driven Code Generation," *IEEE Computer*, Vol. 13, No. 8, August 1980, pp. 25–34.

Graham, S. L., and R. S. Glanville: *Fifth ACM Symposium on Principles of Programming Languages, SIGPLAN-SIGACT*, January 1978, pp. 23–240.

Graham, S. L., R. R. Henry, and R. A. Schulman: "An Experiment in Table Driven Code Generation," *Proceedings of the SIGPLAN Symposium on Compiler Construction*, Boston, Mass., June 1982, pp. 32–42.

Gries, D.: *Compiler Construction for Digital Computers*, New York: John Wiley & Sons, 1971.

Hopgood, F. R. A.: *Compiling Techniques*, London: MacDonald, and New York: American Elsevier, 1969.

Johnson, S. C.: "Yacc: Yet Another Compiler-Compiler," Computing Services Technical Report No. 32, Bell Laboratories, Murray Hill, N.J., 1975.

Johnson, S. C.: "A Portable Compiler: Theory and Practice," *Fifth ACM Symposium on Principles of Programming Languages, SIGPLAN-SIGACT*, January 1978, pp. 97–104.

Johnson, S. C., and D. M. Ritchie: "Portability of C Programs and the UNIX System," *Bell System Technical Journal*, Vol. 57, No. 6, July–August 1978, pp. 2021.

Johnson, S. C., and M. E. Lesk: "Language Development Tools," *Bell System Technical Journal*, Vol. 57, No. 6, July–August 1978.

Landwehr, R., H. S. Jansohn, and G. Goos: "Experience with an Automatic Code Generator Generator," *Proceeding of the SIGPLAN Symposium on Compiler Construction*, Boston, Mass., June 1982, pp. 56–66.

Lesk, M. E., and E. Schmidt: "Lex—A Lexical Analyzer Generator," Computing Services Technical Report No. 39, Bell Laboratories, Murray Hill, N.J., 1975.

Leverett, B. W., R. G. G. Cattell, S. O. Hobbs, J. M. Newcomer, A. H. Reiner, B. R. Schatz, and W. A. Wulf: "An Overview of the Production Quality Compiler-Compiler Projects," Technical Report CMU-CS-79-105, Carnegie-Mellon University, Pittsburgh, Pa., 1979.

Leverett, B. W., R. G. G. Cattell, S. O. Hobbs, J. M. Newcomer, A. H. Reiner, B. R. Schatz, and W. A. Wulf: "An Overview of the Production Quality Compiler-Compiler Projects," *IEEE Computer*, Vol. 13, No. 8, August 1980, pp. 38–49.

McKeeman, W. M., J. J. Horning, and D. B. Wortman: *A Compiler Generator*, Englewood Cliffs, N.J.: Prentice-Hall, 1970.

Raiha, K. J., M. Saarinen, E. Soisanlon-Soininen, and M. Tienari: "The Compiler Writing System HLP," Report A-1978-2, Department of Computer Science, University of Helsinki, Finland, 1978.

Rosen, S., "A Compiler-Building System Developed by Brooker and Morris," *Communications of the ACM*, Vol. 7, No. 7, 1964.

Sammet, J. E., *Programming Languages: History and Fundamentals*, Englewood Cliffs, N.J.: Prentice-Hall, 1969.

Siewiorek, D. P., G. C. Bell, and A. Newell: *Computer Structures: Principles and Examples*, New York: McGraw-Hill, 1982.

Sorenson, P. G., J. P. Tremblay, and A. W. Friesen: "SPSL/SPSA: A Minicomputer Database System for Structured Systems Analysis and Design," *Joint Proceedings of the SIGMINI and SIGMOD Workshop on Small Database Systems, SIGSMALL Newsletter*, Vol. 17, No. 2, October, 1981, pp 109–118

Sorenson, P. G. and J. A. Wald: "PICASSO—An Aid to an End User Facility," *ACM 1977 SIGMOD Proceedings*, pp. 30–39.

Wald, J. A.: Problems in Query Inference, Ph.D. Thesis in progress, Department of Computational Science, University of Saskatchewan, 1984.

Wald, J. A. and P. G. Sorenson: "PICDRAW—An Interactive Form Design Facility," Tech. Report 79-3 Department of Computational Science, University of Saskatchewan, 1979.

Wick, J. D.: "Automatic Generation of Assemblers," Ph.D. Thesis, Yale University, Conn., December 1975.

Wulf, W. A., R. K. Johnson, C. B. Weinstock, S. O. Hobbs, and C. M. Geschke: *The Design of an Optimizing Compiler*, New York: Elsevier-North Holland, 1975.

ALGORITHMIC NOTATION

In this appendix we present a full description of the algorithmic notation used in this book. The algorithmic notation is best described with the aid of examples. Consider the following algorithm which determines the largest algebraic element of a vector:

Algorithm GREATEST. This algorithm finds the largest algebraic element of vector A which contains N elements and places the result in MAX. I is used to subscript A.

1. [Is the vector empty?]
   If $N < 1$
   then Write ('EMPTY VECTOR')
        Exit
2. [Initialize]
   MAX ← A[1] (We assume initially that A[1] is the greatest element)
   I ← 2
3. [Examine all elements of vector]
   Repeat through step 5 while $I \leq N$
4. [Change MAX if it is smaller than the next element]
   If $MAX < A[I]$
   then MAX ← A[I]
5. [Prepare to examine next element in vector]
   I ← I + 1
6. [Finished]
   Exit   □

The execution of an algorithm begins at step 1 and continues from there in sequential order unless the result of a condition tested or an unconditional transfer ('Go to', 'Exitloop', or 'Exit') specifies otherwise. In the sample algorithm, step 1 is executed first. If vector A is empty, the algorithm terminates; otherwise, step 2 is performed. In this step MAX is initialized to the value of A[1] and the subscript variable, I, is assigned the value 2. Step 3 leads to the termination of this algorithm if we have already tested the last element of A; otherwise, step 4 is performed. In this step, the value of MAX is compared with the value of the next element of the vector. If MAX is less than the next element, then MAX is assigned this new value. If the test fails, no reassignment takes place. The completion of step 4 is followed by step 5. where the subscript value is incremented; control then returns to the testing step, step 3.

A-1 FORMAT CONVENTIONS

The following subsections summarize the basic format conventions used in the formulation of algorithms.

A-1.1 Name of Algorithm

Every algorithm is given an identifying name (GREATEST in the sample algorithm) written in capital letters.

A-1.2 Introductory Comment

The algorithm name is followed by a brief description of the tasks the algorithm performs and any assumptions that have been made. The description gives the names and types of the variables used in the algorithm.

A-1.3 Steps

The actual algorithm is made up of a sequence of numbered steps, each beginning with a phrase enclosed in square brackets which gives an abbreviated description of that step. Following this phrase is an ordered sequence of statements which describe actions to be executed or tasks to be performed. The statements in each step are executed in a left-to-right order.

A-1.4 Comments

An algorithm step may terminate with a comment enclosed in round parentheses intended to help the reader better understand that step. Comments specify no action and are included only for clarity.

A-2 STATEMENTS AND CONTROL STRUCTURES

The following subsections summarize the types of statements and control structures available in the algorithmic notation.

A-2.1 Assignment Statement

The assignment statement is indicated by placing an arrow ($\leftarrow$) between the right-hand side of the statement and the variable receiving the value. In step 2 of the sample algorithm, MAX $\leftarrow$ A[1] is taken to mean that the value of the vector element A[1] is to replace the contents of the variable MAX. Note that in this notation, the symbol " $=$ " is used as a relational operator and never as an assignment operator. In step 5, I is incremented by I $\leftarrow$ I $+$ 1. An exchange of the values of two variables (accomplished by the sequence of statements TEMP $\leftarrow$ A, A $\leftarrow$ B, B $\leftarrow$ TEMP) is written as A $\leftrightarrow$ B. Finally, many variables can be set to the same value by using a multiple assignment; for example, I $\leftarrow$ 0, J $\leftarrow$ 0, K $\leftarrow$ 0 could be written as I $\leftarrow$ J $\leftarrow$ K $\leftarrow$ 0.

A-2.2 If Statement

The if statement has one of the following two forms:

1. If *condition*
     then _____

        _____
        $\vdots$
        _____

2. If *condition*
     then _____

        _____
        $\vdots$
        _____
     else _____

        _____
        $\vdots$
        _____

Following the "then" is an ordered sequence of statements which are all to be executed if the condition is *true*. These statements are referred to as the then clause. After execution of the then clause, control passes to the first statement after the if statement. The range of the then clause is indicated by indentation. If the tested condition is *false*, then either the next statement (type *1*) or the ordered sequence of statements following the "else" (type *2*) is executed. In the latter case, control goes to the next statement when the else-clause has been completed. Of course, any unconditional transfer ('Go to', 'Exitloop', or 'Exit') in either the then or else clause must immediately be followed. If statements can be nested within other if-statements, but for the sake of clarity, excessive nesting of if statements should be avoided.

A-2.3 Case Statement

The case statement is used when a choice from among several mutually exclusive alternatives must be made on the basis of the value of an expression. The following segment of an algorithm contains an example of the case statement.

$$\vdots$$

4. [Process string beginning with either digit or letter]
      Select case (SUB(STRING, 1, 1))
           Case 'A' thru 'Z':
              Call WORD_OUT(STR NG)
           Case '1' thru '9':
              Call DIGIT_OUT(STRING)
              DIGIT_CTR ← DIGIT_CTR + 1
           Case '□' or ',' or ';' or '.' or '?':
              (no action taken)
           Default:
              Write('ERROR_INVALID STRING')
              Return
5. [Continue processing]

$$\vdots$$

In general, the case statement has the form:

    Select case (*expression*)
        Case *value 1*:
        Case *value 2*:

$$\vdots$$

        Case *value N*:
        Default:

First, the expression is evaluated [in the example, Select case (SUB(STRING, 1, 1)) takes the first character of a string], and its value is compared to that of all the cases. A branch is then made to the appropriate case. If the value of the expression does not match that of any case, then a branch is made to the default case if there is one or to the next step if there is not.

A-2.4 Repeat Statement

For easy control of iteration (looping), a repeat statement has been provided. This statement has one of the following forms:

1. Repeat for INDEX = *sequence*
2. Repeat while *logical expression*
3. Repeat for INDEX = *sequence* while *logical expression*

Type 1 is used when a step is to be repeated for a counted number of times. INDEX is simply some variable used as a loop counter, and *sequence* is some representation of the sequence of values that INDEX will successively take. The starting value, the final value, and the increment size must be indicated in some way by the representation chosen; Repeat for $I = 1, 2, \ldots, 25$, Repeat for TOP $= N + K, N + K - 1, \ldots, 0$, and Repeat for $K = 9, 11, \ldots, 2*MAX + 1$ are various examples of valid repeat statements. Once all statements in the range of the repeat statement have been executed, the index assumes the next value in the sequence, and the statements in the range are executed in order once again. We assume testing of an index for completion takes place prior to the execution of any statement; thus, a repeat statement may result in the loop being executed zero times. As an example, Repeat for $I = -1, -2, \ldots, 10$ and Repeat for $K = 5, 6, \ldots, -17$ would not cause any statements to be executed; instead, the repeat statements would be treated as having completed their execution. Type 2 is used to repeat a step until a given logical expression is *false*. The evaluation and testing of the logical expression is performed at the beginning of the loop, and semantically the statement is similar to the while-clause of PL/I. As a special case of type 2, we may write "Repeat while true." Since *true* is a valid logical expression, this is, in effect, an infinite loop. This possibility is rarely used but may be considered when we wish to exit a program, or just a loop, from within a loop. Consider the following segment:

.
.
.

5. [Loop to read data while there remains input]
        Repeat while true
            Read(ARRAY[I])
            If there is no more data
            then Exitloop
            else $I \leftarrow I + 1$

.
.
.

Type 3 is merely a combination of types 1 and 2 and is used to repeat a step for a sequence whose values are taken successively by INDEX until a logical expression is *false*. For each of the above types, the loop may extend over more than one step, in which case the repeat statement has the form "Repeat through step N...."

As soon as a repeat statement has finished its execution, control is transferred to the first statement outside the range of the repeat statement. If, however, an "Exitloop" statement is encountered during the execution of a repeat statement, control is transferred to the first step following the loop and the repeat statement is considered to have finished its execution. Here is another example of a repeat statement:

$$\vdots$$

6. [Initialize counter]
       COUNT ← 0
7. [Processing loop]
       Repeat through step 9 for I = 1, 2,...,N
8. [Get number]
       Read(A[I])
9. [Count if negative]
       If A[I] < 0
       then COUNT ← COUNT + 1
10. [Output result]
       Write(COUNT)

If N has the value 5 and the first numbers in the data stream are 7, 4, − 3, − 2, 6, − 17, 8, ..., then steps 8 and 9 would be executed five times and the number 2 would be printed in step 10 because there are two negative numbers among the first five. Control is *not* passed to step 10 after step 9 has been executed; instead, it is returned to the repeat statement where I is incremented, and steps 8 and 9 are allowed to execute once again if I is not greater than N.

A-2.5 Go To and Exitloop Statements

These two statements are rather extraordinary and are seldom used. The go to statement causes unconditional transfer of control to the step referenced. Thus, "Go to step N" will cause transfer of control to step N regardless of whether the statements of a loop or of a then or else clause have been completed. The exitloop statement is similar to the go to statement, but the range to which it can transfer control is limited. As the name implies, exitloop causes an immediate, unconditional exit from a loop. Note that an exitloop statement applies to only one level; thus, if one loop is nested within another, an exitloop from the inner loop will transfer control back to the outer loop. In general, go to and exitloop statements should be avoided since they lead to unstructured algorithms and, ultimately, to bad programming practice.

A-2.6 Exit Statement

The exit statement is used to terminate an algorithm. It is usually the last step:

$$\vdots$$

7. [Finished]
       Exit

However, there are often situations in which one may wish termination in midstream:

$$\vdots$$

4. [Check to see if processing can continue]
     If *condition*
     then Exit

$$\vdots$$

In any case, "Exit" causes immediate termination of an algorithm.

A-2.7 Variable Names

A variable is an entity that possesses a value, and its name is chosen to reflect the meaning of the value it holds (in the sample algorithm, MAX holds the largest algebraic element of a vector). For our purposes, a variable name always begins with a letter followed by characters which may be chosen from a set of possible characters including letters, numeric digits, and some special characters. Blanks are not permitted within a name, and all letters are capitalized. The following are examples of valid variable names:

BLACK_BOX
X_SQUARED
ZEKE

The most useful of the special characters is "_" (called the *break character*), which may be used as a separator in names made up of several words; POT_OF_TEA is easier to read than POTOFTEA. The following are examples of invalid variable names:

4PLAY	Does not begin with a letter
A-Z	'-' is not one of the special characters allowed; otherwise, one could not differentiate this from the symbol for subtraction
TWO WORDS	Blanks are not allowed

A-3 DATA STRUCTURES

The following subsections summarize some of the nonprimitive data structures available in the algorithmic language.

A-3.1 Arrays

Array elements are denoted by ARRAY[DIM1, DIM2, ..., DIMN], where ARRAY is the name of the array and DIM1 through DIMN are its subscripts. Array subscripts are always enclosed in square brackets.

A-3.2 Dynamic Storage

The algorithmic notation facilitates the allocation of dynamic storage. One may define a block of storage to be made up of certain fields; for example, a block may have pointer (PTR, LINK, etc.) fields, information (INFO, DATA, etc.) fields, etc. The block is given an identifying name such as NODE. Schematically, a block of storage may look like one of the following:

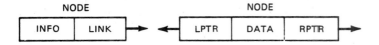

Definition of storage is informal, simply being described in the preamble to an algorithm.

The allocation symbol for dynamic storage is the heavy arrow ($\Leftarrow$), indicating that a pointer variable is to be given the address of an available block of storage (for example, X $\Leftarrow$ NODE). Referencing a field of a given block is done by naming the field and following this by the pointer variable name enclosed in round parentheses; INFO(X) $\leftarrow$ 'JUB JUB BIRD' sets the information field of node X to the given string. Finally, the freeing of a block of storage which is no longer needed is done by the restore statement; Restore(X) restores the block pointed to by X to the available storage area.

A-4 ARITHMETIC OPERATIONS AND EXPRESSIONS

The algorithmic notation includes the standard binary and unary operators, and, of course, these are given the standard mathematical order of precedence. Table A-1 should make this clear.

Arithmetic expressions may contain variables which have been assigned numeric values and are evaluated the same way as in mathematics. Thus, we may write GRADE $\leftarrow$ 0.20 * LAB_WORK + 0.30 * MIDTERM + 0.50 * FINAL. In

Table A-1 Arithmetic Operators and Precedence

	Operation	Symbol	Order of evaluation
1.	Parentheses	( )	Inner to outer
2.	Exponentiation	$\uparrow$	Right to left
	Unary plus, minus	+, −	
3.	Multiplication	*	Left to right
	Division	/	
4.	Addition	+	Left to right
	Subtraction	−	

the notation we assume two types of numeric values, real and integer. As this implies, a real variable can hold any value, whereas an integer variable can only hold integer values with any fraction being truncated. As an example, if R is of type real and I of type integer, R ← 3 / 4 will assign a value of .75 to R while I ← 3 / 4 will assign a value of 0 to I.

A-5 STRINGS AND STRING OPERATIONS

The algorithmic notation facilitates the processing of nonnumeric information. A character string is just that, a string of capitalized characters enclosed in single quotation marks ('THIS IS A VALID STRING'). For clarity, a blank is often denoted by a box; '□□' is a string containing two blanks. The null, or empty, string is denoted by two adjacent quotation marks, ''. Note that this is not the same as '□' which is a string containing a single blank.

The simplest string operation is that of concatenation denoted by ' ∘ '; for example, 'FRUMIOUS' ∘ '□' ∘ 'BANDERSNATCH' is equivalent to 'FRUMIOUS□BANDERSNATCH'. Just as variables may hold numeric constants or values of arithmetic expressions, so they may represent character strings, thus, we may write G ← 'GRYPHON'. Other string manipulations include functions such as LENGTH, INDEX, and SUB, which are patterned after PL/I's LENGTH, INDEX, and SUBSTR functions, respectively. The SUB function, however, is more general and is as follows:

SUB(SUBJECT, i, j) or SUB(SUBJECT, i) returns as a value the substring of SUBJECT that is specified by the parameters i and j, or i and an assumed value of j. The parameter i indicates the starting cursor position of the substring, while j specifies the length of the required substring. If j is not provided, j is assumed to be equal to k − i + 1, where k is equal to the length of the argument SUBJECT. To complete a definition of SUB, some additional cases must be handled.

1 If j ≤ 0 (regardless of i), then the null string is returned.
2 If i ≤ 0 (regardless of j), then the null string is returned.
3 If i > k (regardless of j), then the null string is returned.
4 If i + j > k + 1, then j is assumed to be k − i + 1.

Consider the following examples for the function SUB. SUB('ABCDE', 2) and SUB('ABCDE', 2, 7); both return 'BCDE', SUB('ABCD', 3, 2) returns 'CD', and SUB('ABCDE', 0, 3) and SUB('ABCDE', 6) both return ''.

A-6 RELATIONS AND RELATIONAL OPERATORS

In this book the relational operators ($<$, $>$, $\leq$, $\geq$, $=$, $\neq$) are written the same way as, and have the same meaning as, their mathematical counterparts. Relations between variables and expressions will be considered valid if the variables have been assigned some value. A relation evaluates to a logical expression, that is, it has one of two possible values, *true* or *false*. Numerical relations are clear. Relations between strings are possible and depend on a collating sequence such as '□ & # ... ABC ... Z01 ... 9'. According to this sequence, special characters are lexically less than letters which, in turn, are lexically less than digits. Of course, relations between data types are not possible. In the following examples, Z has the value 10 and MT has the value 'MOCK TURTLE':

1. $Z \leq 9 / 3 + 2$
2. $Z \neq Z + 5$
3. MT < 'MOCK TURTLE SOUP'

Relations 1, 2, and 3 have the values *false*, *true*, and *true*, respectively.

A-7 LOGICAL OPERATIONS AND EXPRESSIONS

The algorithmic notation also includes the standard logical operators. These are:

Operator	Notation
negation	not
logical and	and
logical or	or

which are given in decreasing order of their precedence. These may be used to connect relations to form compound relations whose only values are *true* and *false*. In order that logical expressions be clear, we assume that operator precedence is as follows:

Precedence	Operator
1	Parentheses
2	Arithmetic
3	Relational
4	Logical

Consider the following, assuming that ONE is a variable whose value is 1:

1. (ONE < 2) and (ONE < 0)
2. (ONE < 2) or (ONE < 0)
3. not(ONE < 2)

Expressions 1, 2, and 3 have the values *false*, *true*, and *false*, respectively.

Just as we have numeric and character variables, so we have logical variables (for example, FLAG ← *true*). Logical expressions are most often used as conditions in repeat and if statements. In a repeat statement one might have:

3. [Loop on pass]
      Repeat through step 6 while NUM ≠ MAX and not ERROR_FLAG

In an if statement one might have:

If X ≤ 100
then X ← X↑2

A-8 INPUT AND OUTPUT

In the algorithmic notation, input is obtained and placed in a variable by the statement "Read(variable name)." Output has the form "Write(literal or variable name)" with literals enclosed in quotation marks. For example, we may output the value of X by writing Write(X) if X is any variable, or we may output messages by writing Write('STACK UNDERFLOW'). Input and output are not limited to single variables; Read(X, Y, Z) is certainly valid and causes three consecutive pieces of data to be read into X Y, and Z, respectively. In fact, we may extend input and output to arrays; for example:

$$\vdots$$

10. [Output data]
      Repeat for I = 1, 2, . . . , N
         Write(A[I])

$$\vdots$$

Lastly, end of file may be used as the terminating condition of a repeat statement (e.g., Repeat while there is input data).

A-9 SUBALGORITHMS

A subalgorithm is an independent component of an algorithm and for this reason is defined separately from the main algorithm. The purpose of a subalgorithm is to perform some computation, when required, under control of the main algorithm. This computation may be performed on zero or more parameters passed by the calling routine. The format used is the same as for algorithms except that a return statement replaces an exit statement and a list of parameters follows the subalgorithm's name. Note that subalgorithms may invoke each other and that a subalgorithm may also invoke itself recursively. Consider the following recursive function:

Function FACTORIAL(N). This function computes N! recursively. N is assumed to be a nonnegative integer.

  1. [Apply recursive definition]
      If N = 0
      then Return(1)
      else Return(N * FACTORIAL(N − 1))   □

In the algorithmic notation there are two types of subalgorithms: functions and procedures.

A-9.1 Functions

A function is used when one wants a single value returned to the calling routine. Transfer of control and returning of the value are accomplished by "Return(value)". A function begins as follows: Function NAME (PARM1, PARM2, ..., PARMN). The following example function should make clear the format of functions:

Function AVERAGE(VAL1, VAL2, VAL3). The purpose of this function is to compute the average of three values. We assume all variables to be real. AV is a local variable of type real used to return the computed value.

  1. [Compute average]
      AV ← (VAL1 + VAL2 + VAL3) / 3.0
  2. [Return result]
      Return(AV)   □

A function is invoked as an implicit part of an expression; for example, E ← AVERAGE(X, Y, Z) results in the returned value being put into E.

A-9.2 Procedures

A procedure is similar to a function but there is no value returned explicitly. A procedure is also invoked differently. Where there are parameters, a procedure returns its results through the parameters. Here is an example of a typical procedure:

Procedure DIVIDE(DIVIDEND, DIVISOR, QUOTIENT, REMAINDER). This procedure divides the DIVIDEND by the DIVISOR giving the QUOTIENT and REMAINDER. Assume all numbers to be integer.

  1. [Perform integer division]
      QUOTIENT ← DIVIDEND / DIVISOR

2. [Determine remainder]
    REMAINDER ← DIVIDEND − QUOTIENT ∗ DIVISOR
3. [Return to point of call]
    Return □

Note that no value is returned explicitly but that the quotient and remainder are returned through two of the parameters. A procedure is invoked by means of a call statement: for example, "CALL DIVIDE(DDEND, DIV, Q, R)".

A-9.3 Parameters

In all subalgorithms there is a one-to-one positional correspondence between the arguments of the invocation and the subalgorithm parameters. With the AVERAGE function we just described there is a one-to-one correspondence between the parameters VAL1, VAL2, and VAL3 and the arguments X, Y, and Z of the invocation E ← AVERAGE(X, Y, Z). All parameters are assumed to be "call by reference" unless otherwise specified; therefore, if parameters are to be "call by value", this should be stated in the preamble, as should all other assumptions. Lastly, as mentioned before, there may not be any parameters. In this case, all variables are assumed to be global. Of course, there may be global variables as well as parameters.

Adel'son-Vel'skii, G. M., 440, 476
Aho, A. V., 11, 67, 181, 196, 206, 212–213, 229,
    273, 376, 384, 388–389, 415–416, 661, 667,
    669, 671, 675, 683, 764
Alexander, W. G., 73, 91, 97, 104, 106, 108, 135
Allen, F. E., 656, 661, 673, 683, 726, 764
Amble, O., 460, 476
Ammann, V., 535
Anderson, T., 384, 388, 413–416

Baer, J. L., 448–449, 476
Bar-Hillel, Y., 67
Barnard, D. T., 67, 117, 135, 184, 201–202,
    206–207, 265, 273
Barrett, W. A., 11, 181, 376, 416
Beatty, J. C., 683
Belady, L. A., 683, 697, 721
Bell, J. R., 312, 317, 416, 527, 535, 765
Berard, E. V., 135
Berg, A., 735, 764
Bertrand, M., 273
Bird, P. L., 760–761, 764
Bobrow, D. G., 112, 135
Bochman, G. V., 563, 609
Bocking, D. A., 742, 764
Booch, G., 135
Boulton, P. I. P., 191, 206
Brender, R. F., 135
Brinch Hansen, P., 111, 135
Buchholz, W., 452–453, 476
Burke, M., 416

Calingaert, P., 11
Carlson, W. E., 135
Cattell, R. G. G., 742, 744, 764–765
Chomsky, N., 37, 40, 42, 67
Clark, B. L., 94, 104, 112, 120, 135
Cocke, J., 12, 661, 673, 683

Conway, R. W., 184, 191, 196, 206
Couch, J. D., 11, 181, 376, 416

Dahl, O. J., 87, 94, 99, 117, 135
Damerau, F. J., 203, 204, 207
Davis, M., 40, 67
deBalbine, G., 457, 476
DeRemer, F., 80, 114, 135, 376, 381, 383, 402,
    407, 409–410, 416–417
Dewar, R. B. K., 527, 530, 535
Dijkstra, E. W., 87, 94, 99, 117, 135
Dodd, M., 476
Donegan, M. K., 763–764
Druffel, L. E., 135
Druseikis, F. C., 410, 416
Duong, C., 416

Eckhouse, R. H., Jr., 721
Elson, M., 70, 135
Eve, T. J., 416

Fadin, C., 69, 136
Feldman, J., 416
Feycock, S., 764
Fisher, C. N., 265, 271–273, 416
Fisher, G. A., 416
Floyd, R. W., 286, 416
Foster, J. M., 273
Fraser, C. W., 761, 763–764
Friesen, A. W., 765

Ganapathi, M., 722, 760–761, 764–765
Gannon, J. D., 74, 92, 104, 109, 135
Ganzinger, H., 726, 765
Gehani, N., 135
Geller, D. P., 106, 137

Geschke, C. M., 683, 766
Ginsberg, S., 67
Glanville, R. S., 725, 756, 760, 765
Goos, G., 765
Graham, S. L., 197, 199, 207, 320, 324, 331,
  390–395, 410, 413, 416, 681–683, 725, 756,
  760, 765
Gries, D., 12, 67, 135, 181, 207, 265, 273, 416,
  479, 497, 520, 535, 609, 612, 683, 765
Griffiths, M., 273

Habermann, A. N., 476, 683
Haley, C. B., 410, 416
Harrison, M. A., 67
Hecht, M. S., 656, 661, 667–668, 671, 673,
  675–676, 681–683
Hehner, E. C. R., 94, 118, 135
Heliard, J. C., 79, 136
Hennessy, J. L., 765
Henry, R. R., 765
Hilbard, T., 439, 476
Hinds, J. A., 507, 520
Hirshberg, D. S., 520
Hoare, C. A. R., 74, 77, 81, 87, 88, 91, 94, 96, 99,
  108, 112, 135
Hobbs, S. O., 683, 765–766
Hoffmann, H. J., 416
Holt, R. C., 201, 202, 207, 265, 273
Hopcroft, J. E., 40, 67, 173–174, 181, 236, 273
Hopgood, F. R. A., 683, 765
Horning, J. J., 75, 79, 94, 100, 112, 136, 182, 191,
  207, 416, 417, 520, 742, 765
Horowitz, L. P., 699–700, 721
Hughes, J. K., 78, 136

Ichbiah, J. D., 79, 121, 136
Ingerman, P. Z., 80, 136
Irons, E. T., 265, 273

Jacobi, C., 535
Jansohn, H. S., 765
Jenson, K., 82, 94, 117, 136, 402, 417, 535
Johnson, R. K., 766
Johnson, S. C., 177, 181, 196, 206, 376, 391, 416,
  683, 721, 724, 727, 743, 760, 765
Joliot, M. L., 413, 415, 416
Joy, W. N., 410, 416

Karp, R. M., 699–700, 721
Keilburtz, R. B., 417
Kennedy, K., 661, 671, 683

Kernighan, B. W., 71, 74, 80, 136, 721
Knuth, D. E., 12, 80, 107, 111, 136, 229, 273, 342,
  416, 439, 448, 455, 459–460, 462, 476,
  498–499, 501–502, 511, 520, 563, 609, 667,
  683
Korenjak, A. J., 236, 273, 416
Kurki-Suonio, R., 242, 247, 258, 273

Lalonde, W. R., 376, 388, 412, 414, 416–417
Lampson, B. W., 75, 112, 136
Landis, E. M., 440, 476
Landwehr, R. H., 760, 765
Leavitt, R., 136
Ledgard, H., 136
Leinius, R. P., 320–321, 416
Lesk, M. E., 177–178, 181, 721, 765
Leverett, B. W., 725, 743, 764
Levey, H. M., 721
Lewis, P. M., II, 12, 67, 181, 235, 273, 563, 609
Lindsey, C., 90, 117, 136
London, R. L., 75, 112, 136
Lowry, E., 661, 680, 683, 702, 721
Lum, V. Y., 452–453, 476
Lyon, G., 200, 207

MacEwen, G. H., 721
McKeag, M., 227, 273
McKeeman, W. M., 80, 136, 334, 338, 417, 419,
  421, 452, 476, 487, 520
Maggiolo-Schettini, A., 683
Manohar, R. P., 13, 67
Martin, D. F., 317, 416
Martin, E. W., 136
Martin, J., 70, 136
Medlock, C. W., 661, 680, 683, 702, 721
Mickanus, M. D., 395, 401–403, 407–408, 410,
  417
Miller, R. M., 699–700, 721
Milton, D. R., 265, 271–273
Mitchell, J. G., 75, 112, 136
Modry, J. A., 395, 401–403, 407–408, 410, 417
Morgan, H. L., 203, 204, 207
Muth, D., 416

Nageli, H. H., 535
Nakata, I., 697, 721
Nassi, I. R., 135
Nelson, R. J., 67
Newcomer, J. M., 764–765
Newell, A., 765
Nicholls, J. E., 70, 136
Nievergelt, J., 448, 476

Noonan, R. E., 764
Nori, K. V., 532, 535

Pager, D., 388–389, 417
Pai, A. B., 417
Peachey, D. R., 764
Pederson, T. G., 207
Pennello, T. J., 376, 381, 383, 402, 406–407,
    409–410, 416–417
Perkins, D. R., 534–535
Peterson, J. L., 520
Plauger, P. J., 71, 74, 136
Plum, T. W. S., 106, 137
Pollack, B. W., 12
Poole, P. C., 535
Popek, G. L., 75, 112, 136
Pratt, T. W., 70, 136, 520
Prenner, C. J., 112, 136
Purdon, P. W., 383, 417
Pyle, I. C., 136

Quiring, S. B., 265, 271–273

Raiha, K. J., 726, 765
Randell, B., 424, 476, 520
Raphael, B., 112, 135
Redime, S. T., Jr., 135
Redziejowski, R. R., 697, 721
Reiner, A. H., 765
Reingold, E. M., 448, 476
Rhodes, S. P., 197, 199, 207, 320, 324, 331,
    390–395, 416–417
Riddle, W. E., 135
Ripken, K., 765
Ripley, G. D., 410, 416
Rissen, J. P., 79, 136
Ritchie, D. M., 80, 103, 112, 136, 721, 765
Rogoway, H. P., 69, 136
Rosen, B. A., 683
Rosen, S., 12, 726, 765
Rosenkrantz, D. J., 12, 67, 80, 136, 181, 273, 609
Russell, D. B., 476, 520, 683
Russell, L. J., 424, 476

Saarinen, M., 765
Salomaa, A., 67
Sammet, J. E., 69, 136, 732, 765
Schatz, B. R., 765
Schmidt, E., 177–178, 181, 765
Schorr, H., 515, 520
Schulman, R. A., 765

Schwab, B., 449, 476
Schwartz, J. P., 12, 683
Severance, D. G., 449, 476
Shaw, M., 79, 100, 136
Shen, K. K., 520
Siewiorek, D. P., 745, 765
Sites, R. L., 534–535
Soisanlon-Soininen, E., 765
Sorenson, P. G., 12, 450, 476, 520, 624, 683, 742,
    764–766
Spitze, J. M., 112, 136
Starnes, T. W., 721
Stearns, R. E., 12, 67, 80, 135, 181, 235, 273, 609
Stenning, V., 132, 137
Stone, H. S., 448, 476
Strong, H. R., 656, 683

Tennent, R. D., 94, 102, 137
Thompson, D. H., 417
Tienari, M., 765
Topcor, R. W., 227, 273
Tremblay, J. P., 12, 13, 67, 450, 476, 520, 624,
    683, 764–765

Ullman, J. D., 11, 40, 67, 173–174, 181, 212–213,
    229, 273, 376, 384, 388–389, 415–416, 661,
    667, 669, 671, 675, 681–683
Unger, S. H., 273

van der Meulen, S. G., 90, 117, 136
van Wijngaarden, A., 42, 67, 90, 93, 104, 114, 117,
    137

Wagner, R. A., 191, 207
Waite, W. H., 515, 520
Wald, J. A., 742, 764–766
Weber, H., 80, 302, 333, 412, 414, 417
Wegbreit, B., 112, 136
Wegman, M., 681–683
Wegner, P., 137
Weinberg, G., 71, 75, 106, 137
Weingarten, F. W., 67
Weinstock, C. B., 683, 766
Welsh, J., 227, 273
Wick, J. D., 761, 766
Wickmann, B. A., 130, 137
Wilcox, T. R., 184, 191, 196, 206
Wilheim, R., 765
Winograd, S., 699–700, 721
Wirth, N., 67, 76, 80, 82, 84, 94–95, 104, 117,
    135–137, 196, 207, 224, 273, 302, 320, 333,
    402, 412, 414, 417

Wolfe, M. I., 132, 137
Woods, W. A., 609
Wortman, D. B., 417, 520, 742, 765
Wulf, W. A., 81, 110, 112, 137, 424, 476, 656, 667, 683, 743–744, 765–766

Yuen, P. S. T., 476

Zilles, S., 79, 100, 136

SUBJECT INDEX

Absolute address, 478
Absolute complement, 16
Abstract machine code, 531–534
Abstract syntax tree (*see* Parse tree)
Acceptance by a finite-state automation, 156, 159
Acceptance action, 352, 355
Accepting state (*see* Final state)
Acceptor, 31
Accumulator, 686
Action function, 355
Action symbol, 554
Activation-based pointer, 486
Activation record, 482
Active nonterminal, 58
Actual parameter, 479
Ad hoc error recovery, 195–197, 391
Ad hoc error repair, 201
Ada, 97, 99, 120–132, 328, 569, 577–579, 609, 722
Adaptable program, 531
Address space, 450
Addressing mode, 704–706, 712–713, 717–719, 746
ALGOL 60, 2, 5, 36, 66, 73, 76, 78, 80, 91, 98, 101, 103, 109–110, 115, 297, 331, 477, 480, 488, 603, 630, 632
ALGOL 68, 71, 75–78, 84–86, 90–91, 93, 97, 100–101, 113–114, 117, 121
ALGOL W, 647
Algorithm:
  ACTIVE, 58
  AE_ROUND_ROBIN, 670
  AE_WORKLIST, 668–669
  ASSEMBLY_CODE, 668–689
  COMPUTE_PREFIX, 271
  COMPUTE_SAVINGS, 701
  COMPUTE_TS, 264
  CONSTANT_PROPAGATION, 679
  CONSTRUCT_FLOWGRAPH, 658–660
  ε-RULE_FREE, 62

Algorithm (*Cont.*):
  EXTENDED_PRECEDENCE, 336–337
  FIND_REGIONS, 676–677
  FOLD, 617–618
  GREATEST, 767
  IMPROVED_ASSEMBLY_CODE, 691–692
  IMPROVED_LL(1), 261–262
  IMPROVED_REVERSE_POLISH, 284–285
  LL(1)_PARSER, 256–257
  LL_REPAIR, 267–258
  LOOP_INVARIANT, 643
  LR(0)_MACHINE, 351–352
  LR(1)_CONSTRUCTOR, 366–369
  LR(1)_ITEM_CONSTRUCTION, 364
  OPERAND_INDEX, 626
  OPERATOR_PRECEDENCE, 295–296
  REACHABLE, 59
  RECDSCT, 220–221
  REDUNDANT, 627–628
  REGULAR_EXPRESSION, 154–155
  REVERSE_POLISH, 281–282
  SLR(1)_CONSTRUCTOR, 355–356
  SP_PARSE, 310
  SP_SUPERVISOR, 321–322
  TD_FULL, 215–218
Algorithmic notation:
  arithmetic expressions, 774–775
  arithmetic operations, 774–775
  array, 773
  assignment statement, 769
  case statement, 770
  comment, 768
  concatenation, 775
  dynamic storage, 774
  exchange statement, 769
  exit statement, 772
  function, 778
  go to statement, 772
  if statement, 769
  INDEX, 775

Algorithmic notation (*Cont.*):
  input, 777
  LENGTH, 775
  logical expression, 776–777
  logical operations, 776–777
  name of, 768
  node-structure terminology, 774
  output, 777
  parameter, 779
  procedure, 778–779
  relation, 776
  relational operator, 776
  repeat statement, 770–772
  steps, 768
  string, 775
  string operations, 775
  SUB, 775
  variable name, 773
Allocated variable, 694
ALOS (*see* Average length of search)
Alphabet, 35
Alternation, 151, 297
Ambiguous grammar, 48
Amdahl 470, 760
ANALYZER, 725
Ancestor state, 400
Antisymmetric relation, 20
APL, 5, 72–74, 78, 80, 92, 95, 569, 744
Apply state (*see* Reduce state)
APSE, 122, 131–132
Arithmetic expression, 92–93, 275–285, 579–585
Array, 98, 574–576, 581–585, 630, 639–640
Array template, 574
ASCII, 88, 450–451, 607
Assembler, 4
Assembler code, 9, 528–530, 702–720
Assembly language, 2
Assignment statement, 89, 591–592
Associativity, 613, 621
ATG (*see* Attributed translation grammar)
Attribute, 560
Attribute value, 422
Attribute variable, 564, 736
Attributed translation, 559–468
Attributed translation grammar (ATG), 560
Augmented grammar, 353
Autoincrement mode, 685, 705, 712–713
Available expression, 661
Available-expression problem, 661
Available list, 495
Average length of search (ALOS), 428, 455
AVL tree (*see* Balanced Binary tree)

Back edge, 675

Back flow, 663
Backtracking [*see* Backup (in parsing)]
Backup (in parsing), 56, 209, 219
Backus-Naur form (BNF), 36, 117
Backward-flow problem, 663
Backward move, 324, 393
Balanced binary tree, 440
Balanced node, 440
Balanced parenthesis, 276
Base register, 478, 757
BASIC, 5, 84, 103, 423, 522, 532, 569
Basic block, 612
Basis (of a set of items), 348
Basis item, 348
BB (bounded-balance) binary tree, 448
BCD (binary coded decimal), 717
Binary relation, 19
Binary search, 431
Binary tree, 433–449
BLISS, 424, 656, 667, 681, 722
BLISS-11 compiler, 744
Block, 465
Block (of a partition), 21
Block index, 468
Block level, 484
Block record (*see* Activation record)
Block-structured language, 464–467
Block-structured symbol table, 464–474
BMCC (Brooker-Morris compiler-compiler),
  726
BNF (*see* Backus-Naur form)
Boolean expression, 105
Bottom-up parser, 52
Bounded-balance (BB) binary tree, 448
Burroughs 6700, 491

C, 80, 92, 103, 115, 178, 432, 591, 604, 722, 730,
  735
Call by name, 80, 109
Call by reference, 109, 602
Call by value, 109, 484, 599, 602
Call graph, 656
Canonical collection of items, 362–366
Canonical derivation, 53–54
Canonical LR(1) parser, 362–369
Cartesian product, 17
Case construct, 105–107, 593–595
CGGL (code-generator generator language),
  763
Character-pair error, 320
Character-pair matrix, 284
Character set (*see* Alphabet)
Character string, 29–30, 97
Character type, 97

Closure, 25, 151
Closure (of items), 348
Closure operation, 351
Clustering, 457
COBOL, 3–4, 51, 66, 72, 83, 99, 102, 113, 115, 474, 491, 680
COGO, 2
Code generation constructs:
  array variable, 574–576
  assignment statement, 591–592
  case-selection statement, 593–595
  constant type declaration, 570–571
  expression, 579–590
  for loop statement, 596–598
  input statement, 603–607
  output statement, 607
  procedure call, 598–603
  procedure declaration, 578
  procedure return, 603
  record variable, 577–578
  repeat-while statement, 595–596
  simple variable, 571–574
Code generation procedure:
  add, 579, 582
  allocsv, 572
  brcomp, 594
  bremit, 588
  checkdim, 583
  chktype, 600
  compare, 598
  doubload, 594
  emitstores, 602
  falsebranch, 596
  falselab, 589
  falset, 590
  initcnt, 602
  inputitem, 605
  labgen, 596
  loadid, 598
  lookup, 579
  lookupproc, 600
  movecur, 605
  negate, 590
  offset, 583
  push, 579
  pushi, 580
  reload, 595
  setL, 592
  storein, 592
  svardef, 572
  tblinsert, 601
  template, 583
  trueset, 590
  upcnt, 602
Code generation template, 749, 751, 754

Code-generator generator, 742–764
Code optimization, 9, 610–721
Code optimizer, 9
Coercion, 76, 546, 757
Collision resolution:
  chaining, 453
  linear probing, 453
  open addressing, 453
  random probing, 457
  separate chaining, 460
Column-major form, 574–576, 629–630
Comment, 7, 91, 113, 144
COMMON, 76
Common subexpression (*see* Redundant-subexpression eliminator)
Commutativity, 613, 621, 693
Comparison of parsing methods:
  ease of debugging, 412
  ease of writing, 412
  error detection, 412
  generality, 411–412
  semantic application, 415
  space requirements, 412–413
  time requirements, 414–415
Compile time, 4
Compiler, 4
Compiler aid, 607–609
Compiler-compiler, 11, 723
Compiler structure, 113–114, 130
Completed item, 352
Completion [*see* Closure (of items)]
Composite relation, 22
Compound type, 98–99
Compression of parsing tables, 383–389
Concatenation, 29–30, 151
Condensation phase, 197–198, 324, 393
Condition code, 706–707, 714, 719–720, 755
Configuration, 212, 240, 246, 347
Configuration (in error recovery), 395
Constant declaration, 94, 570–571
Constant folding, 612–620
Constant propagation, 612
Context-dependent restriction, 537–538
Context-free error, 186
Context-free grammar, 38
  [*See also* Extended-precedence grammar; LALR(1) grammar; LL(1) grammar; LR(0) grammar; LR(1) grammar; Operator grammar; Operator precedence grammar; Simple precedence grammar; SLR(1) grammar]
Context-free syntax, 42
Context-sensitive error, 186
Context-sensitive error recovery, 200
Context-sensitive error repair, 202–203
Context-sensitive grammar, 38

Context-sensitive restriction, 42–43, 186, 421
Control structure, 102–113, 592–603, 655–681
Converse (of a relation), 26
Core (of an item), 362
Coroutine, 112
Correction candidate, 325, 395
Correction phase, 324, 393, 407
Cover, 21
Cray-1, 744
Critical node, 441
Cross-reference listing, 425
CSMP, 2
Cycle, 672

DAG (directed acyclic graph), 621
DAG node, 622
Data abstraction, 100
Data segment, 533
Data structure (*see* Array; Record structure)
Data structure (in language design), 93–102
Data type, 76, 94–99, 422–423
Debugging, 607–608
DEC 2060, 735
Declaration, 93–102, 418–421, 568–578
Declaration of constants, 94
Decomposition axiom, 753
Deference, 76, 585, 757
Deletion cost, 266, 325, 393–394, 399
Depth-first order, 676
Depth-first search, 680
Depth-first spanning tree, 676
Derivation, 35–36
Descent state, 400
Descriptive-language approach, 742
Detection of errors, 75–78, 185–190, 234,
    283–285, 300–301
Deterministic finite automaton (DFA), 142–150,
    156–157, 162
DFA (*see* Deterministic finite automaton)
Diagnostic (*see* Error message)
Difference (of sets), 16
Direct derivative, 35
Directed acyclic graph (DAG), 621
Directed graph, 21
DIRECTLY__READS, 381
Disjoint (sets), 16
Disjoint collection, 16
Display area, 483
Domain (of a relation), 19
Dominant node, 675
Don't care entry, 389
Double hashing, 457
Double rotation, 441
DR relation, 379–380

Dynamic storage allocation, 101, 480–492, 720

ε-closure 163–165
ε-production (*see* ε-rule)
ε-rule, 57
ε-transition, 162–165
EBCDIC, 88, 450–452, 607
ECS project, 726
Element (of a set), 14
Empty set, 15
Entry node, 675
Enumeration type, 95–96
Environment, 131–134, 608–609
Equivalence:
    of finite automata, 160–162
    of finite automata and regular expressions,
        170–176
    of finite automata and regular grammars,
        166–169
    of regular grammars and regular expressions,
        154–155
Equivalence relation, 21
Error action, 352, 355
Error code, 190
Error configuration, 395
Error correction, 185
Error detection, 75–78, 185–190, 234, 283–285,
    300–301
Error entry, 260–265
Error handling:
    infix expressions, 283–285
    LL(1) parsers, 260–272
    LR parsers, 389–410
    operator precedence parsers, 300–301
    recursive-descent parsers, 224–225
    simple precedence parsers, 320–332
Error message, 190–194
Error parser, 403
Error production, 196, 392
Error recovery, 11, 184, 195–200, 218, 224,
    320–322, 389
Error repair, 184, 200–205, 389
Error reporting, 190–194
Error token, 392, 733
Escape construct, 111
EUCLID, 75, 112
Evaluation rule, 560
Exception handling, 111–112
Existential quanitfier, 15
Explicit parameter, 483
Explicit storage request, 493–495
Expression (*see* Arithmetic expression; Logical
    expression)
Expression structure (in language design), 92–93

Expression tree, 694–695
  (*See also* Parse tree)
Extended BNF, 64–66, 117
Extended-precedence grammar, 335
Extended-precedence parser, 332–339
External fragmentation, 496

Factoring of grammars, 760
False chain, 589
Final state, 142
Finite automata (*see* Deterministic finite automaton;
    Nondeterministic finite automaton)
Finite-state acceptor (*see* Deterministic finite
    automaton)
Finite-state diagram, 142
Firm delimiter, 390
FIRST, 245, 247, 249
FIRSTOP, 293
Fixed-length block, 495–496
Flowgraph, 656
Flowgraph analysis, 655–681
Flowgraph construction, 655–660
Flowgraph node, 656
Folding, 612
FOLLOW set, 251, 354, 359, 361, 377–383
For statement, 108–109, 596–598
Forest of trees, 469
Formal parameter, 484
Format statement, 114–116, 603
FORTRAN, 2–4, 10, 34, 50, 66, 71, 73, 76–77,
    81–83, 85, 89, 101–103, 113, 115, 141, 150,
    178, 277, 423–424, 449, 450, 452, 464,
    478–480, 522, 532, 569–570, 574, 612,
    629–630, 632–633, 641, 643–645, 657, 667,
    680, 708
FORTRAN 77, 69, 722
FORTRAN H, 702
FORTRAN IV (*see* FORTRAN)
Forward edge, 675
Forward move, 197–198, 324, 393, 403
Fragmentation, 496
Frequency reduction, 637
FSA (*see* Deterministic finite automaton)
Fully decidable decision, 40
Fully parenthesized expression, 276
Function:
  ALLOCATE_BUDDY, 509–510
  ALLOCATE_FIRST, 497
  ALLOCATE_FIRST_M, 499
  AVERAGE, 778
  AVL_TREE, 445–447
  BINARY_SEARCH, 431
  BIN_TREE, 437–438
  CHAINSL, 460–462
  COMPARE, 203–205

Function (*Cont.*):
  CONDENSE, 396–398
  ERROR_RECOVERY, 407–408
  EXPR, 221
  FACTOR, 222
  FACTORIAL, 778
  FORWARD_MOVE, 403–404
  GET_BLOCK, 495
  GET_CHAR, 222
  OPENLP, 453–454
  REPAIR, 399–400
  SPELLING_REPAIR, 203
  TERM, 221
  T_FORWARD_MOVE, 407

Garbage collection, 513–517
GAUSS, 5
Generic program structure, 126–127
Global common subexpression (*see* Redundant-
    subexpression elimination)
Global data-flow analysis (*see* Flowgraph analysis)
Global variable, 484
GOTO, 112–113
Goto function (*see* Next-state function)
Graham-Rhodes error recovery method, 197–199,
    389–395
Grammar, 7, 31, 35
  ambiguous, 48
  augmented, 353
  context-free, 38
  context-sensitive, 38
  extended-precedence, 335
  LALR(1), 139, 196, 374, 383, 727
  LL(1), 188–189, 201, 235–273
  LR(0), 346
  LR(1), 139, 362
  operator, 287
  operator precedence, 294
  reduced, 57, 60
  regular, 39, 151–155
  simple precedence, 308
  SLR(1), 354
  unambiguous, 48, 309
  unrestricted, 38
Graph (of a relation), 21

Handle, 44, 56, 346
Hash-structured symbol table, 450–464
Hash table, 450, 463
Hashing function, 450
  division method, 451
  folding method, 452
  length-dependent method, 452
  midsquare method, 451

Head (of an edge), 675
Head (of a handle), 303
Head (of string), 30
Head stack, 321
Headset (of a nonterminal), 307
Heap, 492
Heap storage, 100–101
Heap storage allocation, 492–519
High-level language, 2
HLP project, 726
Holding candidate, 398
Human communications, 74–75

IBM 360, 699, 755, 761
IBM 370, 685, 699, 760
IBM 370/158, 432
IBM 709, 82, 85
Identifier, 91, 140, 203–205, 418, 568–578
Identifier space, 450
If statement, 103–105, 538–546, 548–554,
    556–558, 567–568
Immediate address mode, 706, 712, 718
Implicit parameter, 483
Inadequate state, 353
INCLUDES relation, 379
Incomplete node, 439
Incomplete parenthesized expression, 280
Index, 5
Index number, 624
Index register, 685
Index set, 15
Indirect triple, 524–525, 656
Induction variable, 647–651
Infix expression, 275
Inherently ambiguous language, 48
Inherited attribute, 560
Initial node, 656
Input assertion, 746
Input buffer, 603
Input grammar, 554
Input/output (I/O) structure, 114–116
Insertion cost, 266, 325, 393–394, 399
Instruction-set processor (ISP), 745
Intel 8080, 755, 760
Intermediate source form, 521
    abstract machine code, 531–534
    direct threaded code, 527–530
    indirect threaded code, 527, 529–530
    indirect triple, 524–525, 656
    IR notation, 756
    n-tuple, 523
    P-code, 531–534
    parse tree, 17, 31, 45, 47, 525–534
    Polish notation, 275–286, 522–525

Intermediate source form (*Cont.*):
    quadruples, 8, 525, 656
    TCOL, 745, 747–749
    threaded code, 527–530
    triple, 523–524, 527, 644–645, 648–649
        (*See also* Indirect triple)
    U-code, 534
    XL notation, 762
Internal fragmentation, 496
Internal representation number, 6, 140
Interpreter, 4
Intersection (of sets), 16
Interval, 673
Invariant operation elimination, 637–646
IR notation, 756
Irreflexive relation, 20
ISP (*see* Instruction-set processor)
Item, 347
Item set, 348
Iterative for loop, 107–108, 596–598

KAPSE, 132
Key, 451
Key space, 450
Key-to-address transformation (*see* Hashing
    function)
Keyword, 90, 203
Knowledge-based code generator (*see* XGEN)

L-ATG (*see* L-attributed translation grammar)
L-attributed translation grammar (L-ATG), 563, 736
LALR(1) grammar, 139, 196, 374, 383, 727
LALR(1) parser, 370–383
Language, 1–4, 36
Language abstraction, 79
Language declarations, 93, 102
Language efficiency, 81–82, 129
Language generalization and specification, 86
Language maintainability, 129–130
Language minimality, 87
Language modularity, 129–130
Language orthogonality, 85–86
Language simplicity, 84, 130–131
Language uniformity, 84
LASTOP, 293
Leaf node, 433
Left-associative operator, 276, 280, 734
Left canonical derivation, 53
Left-heavy node, 440
Left recursion, 211, 213, 249
Left-stackability check, 320
Leftmost derivation (*see* Left canonical derivation)
Leftmost prime phrase, 289, 295

Leftmost terminal character, 293
Lex, 177–181, 724, 730
Lexical analysis (*see* Lexical analyzer)
Lexical analyzer, 6, 138, 418–422
Line-level error repair, 202
Linear graph notation, 428, 747
Linear search, 428–429
Linear storage-addressing function, 639
LIS, 79
LISP, 5, 92, 99, 495, 532, 744, 763
LISP 1.5, 492, 569
List, 460–464, 495–506
Live variable, 663, 698
Live-variables problem, 663
LL(1) grammar, 188–189, 201, 235–273
    simple, 236
    with ε-rule, 252
    without ε-rule, 252
LL(1) parser, 188–189, 201
LL(k) grammar, 236
Load factor, 450
Local ambiguity, 332
Local optimization, 611–621
Locally syntactically correct set, 325
Logical expression, 585–590
Lookahead LR [*see* LALR(1) parser]
Lookahead set generation, 362–366, 375–383
LOOKBACK relation, 377–378
Loop, 107–109, 595–598, 631–632, 672–678
Loop construct, 107–109
Loop-invariant computation, 638
Loop optimization, 631–655, 672–678
Loop unrolling, 635
LR parser, 341–410, 756
LR(0) grammar, 346
LR(0) parser, 346–352
LR(1) grammar, 139, 362
LR(1) item, 362
LR(1) parser, 362–370
Łukasiewiczian notation (*see* Polish notation)

Machine dependence, 83–84, 129
Machine-dependent optimization, 10, 684
Machine-independent code generation, 742
Machine-independent optimization, 10, 610
Machine-level language, 2
Macroinstruction, 4
Major nonterminal, 392
MAPSE, 132
Memory unit, 478, 703, 710, 716–717, 745–746
Message generator, 191
Meta compiler (*see* Compiler-compiler)
Metalanguage, 32
Microstructure (in language design), 88–92

Minimal-change subgraph, 699
Minimum-distance error repair, 189
Mixed-strategy precedence (MSP) parser, 338
Module, 113
Motorola 68000, 703, 716–720, 760
MSP parsing, (*see* Mixed-strategy precedence parser)
MUG 2 project, 726
Multiregister optimization, 694–702
Mutually disjoint (sets), 16

Name (*see* Identifier)
Name space, 450
Next-state function, 355
NFA (*see* Nondeterministic finite automaton)
Node:
    balanced, 440
    critical, 441
    DAG, 622
    entry, 675
    flowgraph, 656
    initial, 656
    leaf, 433
    left-heavy, 440
    right-heavy, 440
    root, 433
Node-listing algorithm, 671
Nonassociative operator, 734
Non-block-structured language, 428
Nondeterministic finite automaton (NFA), 157–166
Nonterminal symbol, 35
NP-Complete algorithm, 676
Null set (*see* Empty set)
Nullable nonterminal, 61–63, 251, 253–254
Number-of-dimensions attribute, 425
Number-of-parameters attribute, 425

Object-code address, 423–424
Object language, 4
Object program, 4
Occurrence number, 424, 484
Op-code, 704, 711–713, 717
Operand class, 746
    (*See also* Addressing mode)
Operator grammar, 287
Operator language, 287
Operator precedence functions, 298–300, 319
Operator precedence grammar, 294
Operator precedence language, 294
Operator precedence parser, 294–298
Operator precedence relations, 293
Optimal weight-balanced tree, 448

Optimally balanced binary tree, 439
Optimization of LR parsers, 386–389
Optimizing compilers, 82
Ordered pair, 16
Output assertion, 746
Overflow area, 460
Overload name, 124
OWN variable, 101

P-code, 531–534
P-machine, 532–533
Package, 122–129
Padding production, 353
PANEL, 742
Panic mode, 199, 331, 390
Parameter (*see* Actual parameter; Call by name;
    Call by reference; Call by value; Formal
    parameter)
Parameter area, 483
Parameter passing, 109–110, 708–709, 714–716
Parenthetical level, 276
Parse tree, 17, 31, 45, 47, 525–534
Parser, 7, 18
    (*See also* Bottom-up parser; Extended-
    precedence parser; LALR(1) parser; LL(1) par-
    ser; LR(0) parser; LR(1) parser; Mixed-strat-
    egy precedence parser; Operator precedence
    parser; Recursive-descent parser; Simple prec-
    edence parser; SLR(1) parser; Top-down par-
    ser)
Parser generator, 235–272, 286–410, 727–742
Parsing function, 239–240, 245–246, 253–256,
    260–261, 280–281, 355–357, 366–370,
    373–374, 383–389
Parsing methods, comparison of, 412–415
Parsing table (*see* Parsing function)
Partition, 21
PASCAL, 2, 4, 34, 76, 82–83, 92, 94, 97–99, 102,
    108–109, 117–118, 121–122, 402, 493,
    531–534, 569, 577, 641, 707, 714, 719, 722,
    760–761, 763
Pascal machine, 532
Pascal-P compiler, 532
Pascal-P language, 532
Pass, 10, 419, 422
Pass by name (*see* Call by name)
PC-DOS, 735
PDP-8, 744, 747
PDP-10, 755
PDP-11, 432, 528–530, 684–686, 703–710, 735,
    744, 755, 757–758, 760
Perkin-Elmer 3200, 735
Phase, 10

Phrase, 43, 192
PICASSO, 742
PICDRAW, 742
PL/I, 2, 7, 10, 51, 71, 75, 77–78, 80, 83–86, 88,
    90–91, 97, 101, 103, 112–113, 115, 120–121,
    143, 150, 189, 191, 196, 199, 390, 432, 474,
    480, 493, 511, 540, 550, 570, 577, 579, 587,
    630, 632, 635, 638, 640–641, 645, 647, 725,
    742, 761, 775
PL/360, 196
PL/C, 10, 184, 191, 196, 331
PLUTO, 191
Pointer, 77–78, 705
Polish expression, 275–277, 522–523, 526
Polish notation, 275–286, 522–525
Portability, 129, 531–532, 723
    (*See also* Machine dependence)
Portable C compiler, 743, 760
Portable program, 531
Postfix notation, 275–286, 522–523
Postfix translation, 275–286, 522–523, 686–694
Postorder traversal, 622
Postorder traversal (of trees), 526
Power set, 15
PQCC system (*see* Production-quality compiler-
    compiler system)
Pragmat, 113, 129, 602
Pragmatics (in a language design), 116–120
Precedence of operators, 92–93, 275–282
Precedence function, 278, 298–300, 311–319
Precedence relation, 302–303, 307
Preconditioned name, 450
Predecessor block, 500–503
Predicate, 14
Prefix (of a string), 30
Prefix expression, 275–277
Prefix notation, 277, 282–283, 523–526, 756
Preorder traversal (of trees), 526
Prevention of errors, 75–78
Previous-activation-base pointer, 483
Primary clustering, 457
Prime area, 460
Prime phrase, 287
Problem-oriented language, 2
Procedure:
    CLASS, 226
    COMPACT, 518–519
    DELETE, 509
    DEPTH, 677–678
    DIGRAPH, 382
    DIVIDE, 778–779
    EMPTY, 161
    EXPR, 224
    FREE_BLOCK, 500–501

Procedure (*Cont.*):
FREE__BOUNDARY__TAG, 502–503
FREE__BUDDY, 510
INSERT, 508
LINK__MARK, 515–517
PRECEDENCE__FUNCTION, 315–316
REG__COUNT, 695–696
RESET, 327
SCAN, 146–149
SLR__PARSER, 357–358
SP__ERROR, 323–324
SP__PARSE, 322–323
SP__RECOVER, 325–327
TRAVERSE, 382
WARSHALL, 25
Procedure parameter, 108–109, 477–487, 598–603
Processor-memory switch, 745
Produce relation, 36
Production, 31–32, 35
Production-quality compiler-compiler (PQCC) system, 725, 743–755
Program point, 661
Program region, 701
Programming language (*see* Ada; ALGOL 60; ALGOL 68; ALGOL W; APL; BASIC; BLISS; C; COGO; CSMP; EUCLID; FORTRAN; GAUSS; LIS; LISP; PASCAL; PL/I; PL/360; PLUTO; PSL; RATFOR; SEQUEL; SMALLTALK-80; SNOBOL; SP/k)
Programming language design goals, 74–87
Programming language effectiveness, 78–80
Proper head (of a string), 30
Proper prefix (of a string), 30
Proper subset, 15
Proper suffix (of a string), 30
Proper tail (of a string), 30
Pseudo operation, 531–532
PSL, 2

Quadruple, 8, 525, 656

Range (of a relation), 19
Range checking, 96
RATFOR, 71, 730
Reach point, 663
Reachable symbol, 59
Reaching definitions, 663
Read operation, 349, 351, 379
Read state, 343, 352
READS relation, 379–380
Record in symbol table, 442–426
Record structure, 98
Recovery set, 325

Recursion:
in grammars (*see* Left recursion)
in programs, 219, 478, 488–491
Recursive data type, 99
Recursive-descent compilation, 540–548
Recursive-descent parser, 219–228
Recursive procedure handling, 488–491
Recursively enumerable language, 40
Reduce action, 355
Reduce-reduce conflict, 356, 359, 374
Reduce relation, 377
Reduce state, 343, 352
Reduced grammar, 57, 60
Reducible flowgraph, 675
Reduction, 55, 197–198
[*See also* LALR(1) parser; LR(0) parser; LR(1) parser; Operator precedence parser; Simple precedence parser; SLR(1) parser]
Reduction error, 320
Reduction state (in language design), 116
Redundancy (in programming language), 76
Redundant-subexpression elimination, 620–631
Reflexive relation, 20
Register allocation, 686, 694
Register-allocation optimization, 686–702
Register assignment, 694
Register mode, 705, 712, 718
Register pair, 761
Regular expression, 151–155, 170–181
Regular grammar, 39, 151–155
Rehashing (*see* Double hashing)
Relation matrix, 20
Relational expression, 585–587
Relative address, 478
Relative complement (of sets), 16
Relative constant, 575
Reliability, 75–78, 80, 183
Relocatable program, 478
Rendezvous, 127
Replacement rule (*see* Production)
Representation of LR parsers, 383–386
Reserved word, 90–91, 150
Retention allocation, 101
Return address, 483
Return value, 483
Reverse execution order, 754
Reverse Polish (*see* Suffix expression)
Rewriting rule (*see* Production)
Right-associative operator, 276, 280, 734
Right canonical derivation, 54
Right-heavy node, 440
Rightmost derivation (*see* Right canonical derivation)
Rightmost terminal character, 293

Rightstate, 399
Root (of a syntax tree), 45
Root node, 433
Round-robin algorithm, 669–672
Row-major form, 574–576, 630
Rule of syntax (*see* Production)
Run time, 4
Run-time address, 487–488
Run-time organization, 11
Run-time stack, 481
Run-time support, 101, 495

S-grammar [*see* Simple LL(1) grammar]
S-language, 236, 258
Scanner (*see* Lexical analyzer)
Scanner design, 141–150
Scanner generator, 177–181
Scope, 101–102
Search argument, 428
Search tree, 433–449
Secondary clustering, 457
Secondary error recovery, 199
Semantic action, 538
Semantic analysis, 537–538
Semantic analyzer, 8
Semantic blocking, 759
Semantic error, 186
Semantic routine, 8
Semantic stack, 548–554, 558
Semantics, 8
Semidecidable problem, 40
Sentence, 31
Sentential form, 36
Separate compilation, 114
SEQUEL, 2
Sequence number, 622–624
Set, 14
Sets of items construction, 348–352, 363–369
Shared node, 621
Shift action, 355
Shift-reduce conflict, 356, 374, 376
Shift-reduce parser [*see* LALR(1) parser; LR(0) parser; LR(1) parser; Operator precedence parser; Simple precedence parser; SLR(1) parser]
Side effect, 109
Siemens 7.000, 760
SIMPL-T, 681
Simple assignment form, 563
Simple iterative loop, 632
Simple LL(1) grammar, 236–241, 242, 258
Simple LR [*see* SLR(1) parser]
Simple phrase, 44
Simple precedence grammar, 308
Simple precedence parser, 309–311

Simple precedence relation (*see* Precedence relation)
Single production, 291, 301, 387–388
Single-register machine, 686
Single rotation, 441
Sling, 21
SLR(1) grammar, 354
SLR(1) parser, 353–361
SMALLTALK-80, 5
SNOBOL, 4, 11, 66, 95, 97, 99, 492–493, 569, 744
Software tools (*see* Code-generator generator; Compiler-compiler; Parser generator; Scanner generator)
Source grammar, 554
Source language, 4
Source program, 4
Sources of ideas (in programming language design), 72–74
SP/k, 184
Spelling error repair, 203–205
SPITBOL, 530
SPSL/SPSA, 742
Stack allocation (*see* Dynamic storage allocation)
Stack symbol table, 467–474
STARS, 122, 132–134
Start operation, 351
Start state, 142, 156
Start symbol, 156
State, 142
State of transition diagram, 142, 156
Static allocation, 101
Static storage allocation, 101, 477–480
Storage allocation, 477
Storage base, 746
Storage-decomposition axiom, 753
Storage management, 11
    best-fit algorithm, 498
    boundary-tag algorithm, 500–506
    buddy-system algorithm, 506–512
    compaction algorithm, 517–519
    first-fit algorithm, 497–501
    garbage-collection algorithm, 513–517
Stratification, 549
Strength reduction, 646
String, 29–30
Strong type structure, 187
Strong typing, 76
Strongly connected component, 672
Strongly connected region, 675
Stub, 128
Subrange, 96
Subroutine (*see* Procedure)
Subscript (*see* Array)
Subtree pattern, 751